ANCIENT ROME

In this second edition, *Ancient Rome* presents an extensive range of material, from the early Republic to the death of Augustus, with two new chapters on the Second Triumvirate and The Age of Augustus. Dillon and Garland have also included more extensive late Republican and Augustan sources on social developments, as well as further information on the Golden Age of Roman literature.

Providing comprehensive coverage of all important documents pertaining to the Roman Republic and the Augustan age, *Ancient Rome* includes:

- source material on political and military developments in the Roman Republic and Augustan age (509 BC–AD 14)
- detailed chapters on social phenomena, such as Roman religion, slavery and freedmen, women and the family, and the public face of Rome
- clear, precise translations of documents taken not only from historical sources but also from inscriptions, laws and decrees, epitaphs, graffiti, public speeches, poetry, private letters and drama
- concise up-to-date bibliographies and commentaries for each document and chapter
- a definitive collection of source material on the Roman Republic and early empire.

Students of ancient Rome and classical studies will find this new edition of the sourcebook, and the companion textbook *The Ancient Romans*, invaluable at all levels of study.

Matthew Dillon is Associate Professor of Ancient History, School of Humanities, University of New England, Australia. His main research interests are ancient Greek history and religion. With Lynda Garland, he is the author of *Ancient Greece: Social and Historical Documents from Archaic Times to the Death of Alexander*, Third Edition (Routledge, 2010) and *The Ancient Greeks* (Routledge, 2012).

Lynda Garland is a Professor of Medieval History, University of New England, Australia. Her main research interests are in the areas of Byzantine Studies, the crusades and ancient history.

Routledge Sourcebooks for the Ancient World

ANCIENT ROME

Social and Historical Documents
from the Early Republic to the
Death of Augustus

Second edition

Matthew Dillon

and

Lynda Garland

Routledge
Taylor & Francis Group

LONDON AND NEW YORK

First published 2005
This second edition published 2015
by Routledge
2 Park Square, Milton Park, Abingdon, Oxon OX14 4RN

and by Routledge
711 Third Avenue, New York, NY 10017

Routledge is an imprint of the Taylor & Francis Group, an informa business

© 2005, 2015 M. Dillon and L. Garland

British Library Cataloguing-in-Publication Data
A catalogue record for this book is available from the British Library

Library of Congress Cataloging-in-Publication Data
A catalog record for this book has been requested

ISBN: 978-0-415-72698-6 (hbk)
ISBN: 978-0-415-72699-3 (pbk)
ISBN: 978-1-315-70924-6 (ebk)

Typeset in Times New Roman
by Swales & Willis Ltd, Exeter, Devon, UK

Contents

CONTENTS

CONTENTS

CONTENTS

CONTENTS

CONTENTS

Preface to the Second Edition

This second edition of *Ancient Rome: Social and Historical Documents from the Early Republic to the Death of Augustus* owes its existence to all those readers who found the first edition of use and who commented on its strengths and omissions. We have been prompted by these comments to produce a second edition rather than reprinting the original *Ancient Rome*, and are especially pleased that a number of scholars have found these translated documents useful resources for their publications.

This second edition of *Ancient Rome* has been expanded in its historical range down to the death of Augustus in AD 14 and so has a new title: *Ancient Rome: Social and Historical Documents from the Early Republic to the Death of Augustus*. Over the last ten years since the publication of the first edition, the authors have become convinced that it was necessary to give a fuller historical treatment of Roman history so that users of the book could follow what was happening in Rome during the Second Triumvirate and the principate of Augustus. This also means that the social history chapters in this volume have been expanded to include documents from this half-century down to AD 14, giving a wider and more detailed indication of what Roman society was like during this period.

In addition we feel that there is need for a textbook, to appear in conjunction with this second edition, which will give the full background to the texts translated in *Ancient Rome*. This textbook, *The Ancient Romans: History and Culture from the Early Republic to the Death of Augustus*, has the same chapter titles as *Ancient Rome* and will provide students with the necessary background knowledge and detailed information for an understanding of each historical period and social aspects of the Roman world. In this, it will parallel our textbook *The Ancient Greeks: History and Culture from Archaic Times to the Death of Alexander the Great* (2012), which accompanies the sourcebook *Ancient Greece: Social and Historical Documents from Archaic Times to the Death of Alexander the Great (c. 800–323 BC)* (2010). *The Ancient Romans* will also include a wide range of maps, illustrations and photographs, as well as chronological tables and family trees.

Due to the additional material in this second edition, many of the extensive comments accompanying individual documents have been reduced in scope and size in *Ancient Rome* itself. What we aim to give here is enough commentary on each document to make it comprehensible, with the overall background to be provided in the textbook. Our teaching from *Ancient Greece* and *Ancient Rome* over the last twenty years has also taught us that less is often more, and, while we have tried to give the necessary context for each document, we have tried not to 'overload' students with information in this sourcebook.

We give especial thanks to all our students over the last twenty years, not just at the University of New England but to all those who have used this book in the United States, the UK, Ireland and Germany, as well as in Australia and New Zealand. We would like to thank Routledge most sincerely for the invitation to write a second edition.

As far as a dedication is concerned, we would like to offer this book, once again, with all our thanks and best wishes, to our students in all areas of Ancient History, past, present and future, as well as to *liberis nostris dilectissimis*, who are now at universities of their own, with assurances not only that this book on which we have been working for 'hundreds of years' has finally been completed but also that we have yet another in progress. A further dedication, therefore, is to *collega nostro optimo maxximo*, who will be collaborating with us on this new sourcebook and textbook, which will cover the imperial period from Tiberius to Constantine.

Armidale, Australia
October 2014

Glossary

Aedile: one of four lesser magistrates (two curule, two plebeian) elected in the comitia tributa. Their main duties concerned the infrastructure of the city of Rome as well as the organisation of public games (the ludi Romani and Megalensia by the curule aediles, the ludi Ceriales and Plebeii by the plebeian aediles). The aedileship was not an essential rung in the cursus honorum.

Ager publicus: land under Roman public ownership, generally confiscated during wars in Italy. It was leased out by the censors to occupiers for a minimal rent.

Ambitio: 'Walking around', or candidature for office. There was no pejorative meaning attached.

Ambitus: the act of acquiring support during candidature for office through illegal means, such as bribery.

Amicitia: an informal political alliance (literally 'friendship') in which amici ('friends') provided mutually beneficial services.

Apparitor: an official attendant to a magistrate.

As: the smallest bronze coin. Ten asses equalled a denarius, two and a half equalled a sesterce.

Assembly: see comitia.

Atrium: the main reception room of a Roman house, containing a rectangular opening in the roof below which was a pool (the impluvium).

Auctoritas: the ability to influence people and events through one's status (i.e., as a magistrate) or one's personal reputation.

Augur: a member of the priestly college of augures, concerned with divination. Augurs took the auspices prior to the undertaking of military campaigns and before public meetings. From 300 BC five of the nine augurs were plebeians.

Auspicium: the right to take auspices (to consult the will of the gods) before elections and other public business. Auspicium was possessed by both senior magistrates (greater auspices) and junior magistrates (lesser auspices).

Basilica: a large building for public use, which might contain law-courts, shops, banking institutions and offices.

Boni: the 'good' or 'honest' men, a term which by the first century BC had come to mean the conservative element in government; see optimates.

Bulla: a locket worn by freeborn boys prior to assuming the toga of manhood.

GLOSSARY

Campus Martius: the 'Field of Mars'; this lay outside the pomerium and was the assembly point for armies awaiting their commander's triumph, a training-ground, and the site of the comitia centuriata. The lustratio, the closing ceremony of the census, was performed there by the censors.

Capite censi: the 'head count', Roman citizens too poor to belong to one of the five economic classes in the comitia centuriata and, before the reforms of Marius, below the minimum property qualification for army service.

Censor: the most senior of Roman magistrates, though without imperium; in the later Republic two were elected every five years for a period of 18 months. Their duties included conducting a census of all citizens, letting out contracts for public works, and scrutinising the membership of the senate and equestrian class.

Census: a census was conducted every five years by the censors to update the list of Roman citizens, their family, and their property qualification.

Clientela: clientship or patronage. Clients were free men (including freedmen) who received the protection of a patron (often in legal matters), in return supporting him in political life and enhancing his prestige.

Cognomen (plural: cognomina): the final name of a Roman citizen, denoting the branch of the gens to which he belonged; cognomina were generally assigned on the basis of some defect – Cicero (wart), Brutus (stupid) – or were formally granted to commemorate a great military victory (Numidicus, Africanus, Dalmaticus). In aristocratic families more than one cognomen could be hereditary (e.g., the Cornelii *Scipiones Nasicae*). Adoptive sons took their adoptive father's name but could add an additional cognomen from their original nomen, such as Publius Cornelius Scipio who also took the name Aemilianus, because he was the son of L. Aemilius Paullus.

Collegia: societies, such as the priestly colleges, the collegium of the tribunes of the plebs, or work-related organisations.

Comitia: an assembly, or formal gathering of the Roman people.

Comitia centuriata: a political assembly (initially a military assembly) in which the people were organised by classes on an economic basis, favouring the wealthy. It met on the Campus Martius, elected consuls, praetors and censors, heard treason trials, declared war and peace, and passed laws.

Comitia curiata: the earliest assembly, whose functions were gradually subsumed by the comitia centuriata. By the late Republic it primarily ratified the appointment of priests, adoptions and wills.

Comitia tributa: a political assembly organised on the basis of the 35 tribes (four urban, the others rural), which elected curule aediles, quaestors and military tribunes, and passed laws. It met initially in the comitium (to the north-east of the forum) and then in the forum itself.

Concilium plebis: a plebeian assembly, which elected tribunes of the plebs and plebeian aediles, enacted plebiscites, and held non-capital trials.

Consularis: an ex-consul. Consulars had great prestige in the senate.

Consuls: the two senior magistrates, with imperium and auspicium. The consuls' primary duties were military and their imperium was senior to that of any other magistrate (except that of a dictator) or provincial governor.

Consul suffectus: a substitute consul (suffect-consul) who took over the office for part of the year in the event that a consul died in office or was removed.

GLOSSARY

Contio (plural: contiones): a public meeting of an informal nature, which could be called by a tribune of the plebs or another magistrate, used for preliminary discussion of laws or other business.

Curia (hostilia): the senate house in the forum Romanum (or the senatorial body in a municipality). Curia also meant a tenth of each of the three earliest tribes in the time of the kings and was the unit on which the comitia curiata was based.

Cursus honorum: the 'road of honour' or career path. It was necessary to serve as quaestor and praetor before running for the consulship, and the lex Villia annalis in 180 BC (updated by Sulla) prescribed set intervals between each magistracy and minimum ages for candidature.

Curule chair: the sella curulis, originally Etruscan, a backless stool made of ivory, reserved for consuls, praetors and curule aediles as a sign of rank.

Dedicitii: peoples who had unconditionally surrendered to Rome by making a deditio in fidem (surrendering to Rome's good faith).

Denarius: a silver coin, usually the largest denomination in the Republic; 10 asses made a denarius (or four sesterces) and 6,250 denarii a silver talent. A denarius was roughy equivalent to the Greek drachma.

Dictator: an extraordinary magistrate who, before Sulla, held power for a fixed period of time (six months or less) either to command an army or to hold elections. The dictator was preceded by 24 lictors and existing magistrates were subordinate to him. He appointed a master of horse (magister equitum) as his second-in-command.

Dignitas: a man's personal standing based on his achievements and reputation.

Drachma: a Greek coin roughly equivalent to the Roman denarius.

Duumvir, duoviri: chief magistrate or magistrates in Italian towns or Roman colonies.

Emancipation: the act of freeing a son or daughter from dependence (patria potestas); the emancipated person became legally independent (sui iuris) of the father.

Equites (sing.: eques): the equites, or equestrian order, were originally the cavalry and later the business class.

Fasces: a bundle of birch rods tied with leather thongs, carried by 12 lictors before the consuls (on alternate months); praetors were allowed six lictors. The fasces, which outside of Rome included an axe, symbolised the power of the kings and then the magistrates to punish citizens.

Fasti: the calendar listing festivals of the gods and days on which assemblies and business could or could not be held. Fasti consulares listed magistrates, fasti triumphales triumphs.

Flamen (plural: flamines): a member of the college of pontifices, a priest in charge of the worship of a particular deity, such as the flamen dialis (the priest of Jupiter).

Forum Romanum: a forum was an open-air meeting place. The main forum in Rome was the forum Romanum, the chief public square, where the comitia tributa was held (from 145 BC), the senate-house was sited, and most public business, such as law-suits, took place.

Gens (plural: gentes): a clan whose members shared the same nomen or family name, such as Cornelius, Julius, Licinius or Pompeius, and who could trace their descent back to a common ancestor. Groups within a gens could be distinguished by different cognomina: members of the gens Cornelius, for example, could be distinguished by cogomina such as (Cornelius) Cinna, Dolabella, Lentulus, Scipio and Sulla.

Haruspices (sing.: haruspex): diviners or soothsayers, members of the Etruscan aristocracy, concerned particularly with examining the entrails of animals after sacrifice.

Hospitium: ritualised friendship, often hereditary, maintained particularly between Romans and non-Romans in Italy and elsewhere.

Ides: the thirteenth day of every month, except March, May, July and October, when they fell on the fifteenth.

Imagines (sing.: imago): masks of ancestors kept in the atrium and carried in funeral processions. The rank of censor, consul, praetor or aedile conferred the right to keep such imagines.

Imperator: a commander-in-chief or general, especially one who had won a great victory and been hailed by his troops.

Imperium: supreme power, including command in war and the execution of law, possessed by senior magistrates for their year of office (or longer if prorogued). Imperium was symbolised by the fasces, carried by the lictors. Imperium pro praetore: the imperium possessed by a propraetor, prorogued after his year in office as praetor; imperium pro consule: the imperium possessed by a proconsul.

Interrex (plural: interreges): literally 'between the kings', a patrician member of the senate with full imperium appointed to conduct business for five days in cases where the consuls had been killed and elections had not yet been held.

Iugera (sing.: iugerum): a unit of land measurement, roughly equivalent to 5/8 of an acre or 1/4 of a hectare.

Kalends: the first day of the month.

Latifundia: estates in Sicily and Italy consisting of large areas of farming land, usually worked by slaves.

Lectisternium: a public ceremony in which a meal was offered to deities, the gods being represented by images laid on couches.

Legate: a senior member of a general's military staff who was of senatorial rank.

Lex (plural: leges): a law passed by one of the assemblies of the Roman people.

Lictors: Roman citizens who accompanied senior magistrates with imperium and carried the fasces.

Ludi: games put on at the state's expense and organised by the aediles, who often contributed to the expense to win popularity with the electorate.

Lustrum: the five-year period during which the censors technically served (though they were actually in office only for 18 months) and the purification ceremony (lustrum) with which one of the censors, chosen by lot, concluded the five-yearly census of the Roman people.

Magister equitum: the master of the horse, a dictator's second-in-command.

Manumission: the act of freeing a slave. Freed slaves (freedmen) automatically became citizens.

Manus: literally 'hand', the authority which a husband could possess over his wife if she was married 'in manu' (i.e., came into his authority); in this case she entered her husband's family. For women to be married 'in manu' was uncommon by the end of the Republic.

GLOSSARY

Municipium: a township in Italy, or in the provinces, with its own magistrates and own citizen rights.

Nobilis (plural: nobiles): literally 'known men', members of the families which formed the political elite of Rome, which came to mean that one of the family's ancestors had held the consulship. The nobiles tended to dominate, though not exclusively, the higher magistrates.

Nomen: family name of a citizen, such as Cornelius, Julius or Tullius, denoting the gens to which he belonged. Daughters were called by the feminine form of the nomen: i.e., Cornelia, Julia, Tullia.

Nomenclator: a slave whose job was to remember the names of his master's associates, clients and voters.

Nones: the fifth day of every month, except March, May, July and October, when it was the seventh.

Novus homo (plural: novi homines): literally a 'new man', or non-nobilis, none of whose ancestors had held the consulship (such as Marius or Cicero) or perhaps even reached senatorial rank.

Nundina (plural: nundinae): a market-day; markets were held eight days apart; three market-days (at least 17 days) had to pass before a bill which had been presented could be put to the vote.

Optimates: literally 'the best', another term for the boni or conservative element in government, contrasted in the first century BC with the populares.

Paterfamilias: the male head of the family, with potestas over all household members who had not been emancipated.

Patria potestas: literally 'power of the father', the power of the head of the family over all descendants (unless emancipated).

Patricians: the first Roman aristocracy which originated under the monarchy, hence a privileged group of senatorial families.

Peculium: property that a father or master allowed a son or a slave to hold as his own.

Plebeians: non-patricians, members of the plebs, the mass of Roman citizens, who had their own officials (tribunes of the plebs and plebeian aediles).

Pomerium: the religious boundary of Rome.

Pontiff (plural: pontifices): one of a college of priests who advised on sacred ceremonial. Their number was increased to eight in 300 BC and to 15 by Sulla. The pontifex maximus was the chief of these.

Populares (sing.: popularis): literally 'supporters of the people', politicians who proposed popular measures, generally bypassing the senate in doing so and going directly to the people.

Praenomen: a Roman man's first name. Only some 18 personal names were in use in the Republic, such as Gaius, Lucius, Marcus, Publius.

Praetor: a senior magistrate, with imperium and auspicium; praetors were initially the senior magistrates, and after the appointment of consuls a praetor could perform consular duties in the consuls' absence. They were generally in charge of the administration of law in Rome. From c. 244 BC there were two praetors, the praetor urbanus (for Rome) and a praetor peregrinus (for foreigners and non-citizens). Their number was increased to eight under Sulla.

GLOSSARY

Princeps: 'first' or 'chief', a title used from the time of Augustus to denote the emperor.

Princeps senatus: the 'leader of the senate'; a patrician ex-consular or ex-censor who had the right to speak first on any motion in the senate. The position was for life.

Privatus: a private citizen, with no military rank.

Promagistrate: a magistrate (a proconsul or propraetor) whose command was prorogued (continued) into the following year.

Prorogation: the extension of a magistrate's imperium beyond the end of his year of office.

Publicani: tax-collectors, businessmen who bid for the right to collect taxes in the provinces.

Quaestio (plural: quaestiones): a tribunal of inquiry or a standing court (quaestio perpetua: introduced in 149 BC).

Quaestor: a junior magistrate with fiscal responsibilities. Sulla raised their number to 20, set their minimum age qualification at 30 years and gave them automatic entry to the senate.

Quindecimviri sacris faciundis: the 15 keepers of the Sibylline Books (earlier the duumviri, two men, and then the decemviri, ten men).

Quirites: Roman citizens who were civilians; the usual term by which citizens are addressed by orators.

Repetundae: literally '(money) to be recovered', or extortion by officials in authority, especially Roman governors in provinces.

Respublica: the state or government, originally res publica, 'the thing which unites the people', 'public affairs'.

Rostra: the 'beaks' (prows from captured ships) in the forum from which the assembly was addressed.

Senate: a group of 100 unelected patricians under the monarchy, which became 300 in the Republic, who acted as an advisory body to the magistrates. Their number was raised to 600 by Sulla and then to 900 by Julius Caesar.

Senatus consultum (plural: senatus consulta): a senatorial decree which went to one of the comitia for ratification; the 'senatus consultum ultimum' (SCU) was a suspension of the constitution and declaration of a state of emergency.

Sesterces (sing.: sesterce): Roman coins, each worth two and a half asses or a quarter of a denarius.

SPQR: the senate and people of Rome (senatus populusque Romanus).

Suffect consuls: see consuls.

Sui iuris: legally independent.

Suovetaurilia: the sacrifice of a pig, sheep and ox.

Toga: the formal dress of a male Roman citizen made of undyed wool; the toga praetexta, which had a purple border along one edge, was worn by officials and children. Candidates for office wore a whitened toga, the toga candida. People in mourning wore the toga pulla, made of dark wool.

Tribune of the plebs: ten plebeian officials created c. 494 to convene popular assemblies and represent the interests of the people. They took up office on 10 December.

Triumvirate: the 'rule of three', government by three men, as in the Second Triumvirate (Mark Antony, Octavian and Lepidus).

How to Use and Cite *Ancient Rome*

Students frequently ask the authors about **the setting out of the documents** which are contained in *Ancient Rome*. This is best explained by taking the example given below. Here doc. **15.24** is simply the document number of the extract in *Ancient Rome*: document number **24** in chapter **15**. This has nothing to do with the ancient source itself. The document is taken from Dio, *Roman History*, in which **Dio** is the name of the author and **56.3.3–5** refers to the passage in Dio's work, the *Roman History*, from which the extract has been taken: from book 56, chapter 3, paragraphs 3 to 5. This is followed by a short title: **Augustus on married life**. This is not a title given by Dio. Rather, it is a description given by Dillon and Garland to the document to give the reader an idea of what the extract is about. Under the actual heading comes a comment by Dillon and Garland: once again this is not the ancient source itself but a brief introduction to the passage that is intended to help elucidate its main features. In a larger font size, under this comment, comes the ancient source itself.

For example:

15.24 Dio *Roman History* 56.3.3–5: Augustus on married life

Augustus is talking here in AD 9 to the unmarried members of the equites, who had persistently sought the repeal of his marriage legislation, in an attempt to encourage them to marry and bring up children. Apart from Julia, banished for adultery in 2 BC, Augustus himself had no other child and none by Livia. For acknowledging an infant, see doc. 1.34.

3 What could be better than a wife who is decorous, a home-body, manager of the household, rearer of your children, who gives you joy when you are well, and cares for you when you are sick, who shares your successes, and comforts your ill-fortune, who restrains the wild nature of youth, and softens the harsh austerity of old age? **4** How can it not be delightful to pick up and acknowledge a baby born from you both and to feed and educate it, a mirror of your body and of your soul, so that as it grows another self comes into being? **5** How can it not be the greatest of blessings, that when you depart this life you leave behind your own successor and heir both to the family and property, born of yourself, so that while the corporeal human body passes away, we live on in our successor, so that the family does not fall into the hands of strangers and be as obliterated as totally as in warfare?

Another question which is often asked is **how to give a traditional footnote or in-text reference** to a document in *Ancient Rome*. Once again, taking the above example, we would suggest:

Dio, *Roman History* 56.3.3–5, in Dillon, M. & Garland, L. *Ancient Rome: Social and Historical Documents from the Early Republic to the Death of Augustus*, London, 2015, doc. 15.24, p. 000.

An abbreviated form of this could be:

Dio 56.3.3–5, in Dillon & Garland, *Ancient Rome*, doc. 15.24, p. 000.

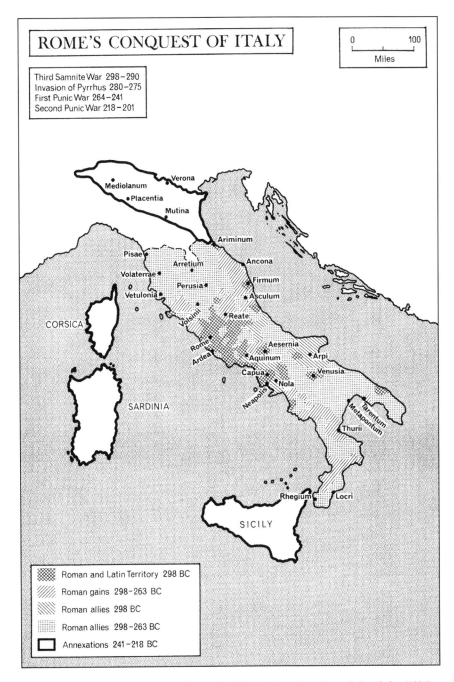

ROME'S CONQUEST OF ITALY

Third Samnite War 298–290
Invasion of Pyrrhus 280–275
First Punic War 264–241
Second Punic War 218–201

0   100
Miles

Verona
Mediolanum
Placentia
Mutina
Ariminum
Pisae
Arretium
Ancona
Volaterrae
Perusia
Firmum
Vetulonia
Asculum
CORSICA
Volsinii
Reate
Rome
Aesernia
Ardea
Aquinum
Arpi
Capua
Venusia
Nola
Neapolis
SARDINIA
Tarentum
Metapontum
Thurii
Rhegium
Locri
SICILY

Roman and Latin Territory 298 BC
Roman gains 298–263 BC
Roman allies 298 BC
Roman allies 298–263 BC
Annexations 241–218 BC

From *The Routledge Atlas of Classical History* by Michael Grant. Map 48, p. 48. Routledge (1994).

BRITANNIA

LWR. GERMANY (17 BC)

FREE GERMANY

Temporarily conquered from 15 BC but abandoned after ambushing of Varus by Arminius in AD 9

Colonia Agrippinensis

Rhine

BELGICA

Moguntiacum

LOWER PANNONIA

LUGDUNENSIS

UPR. GERMANY (17 BC)

Danube

RHAETIA (15 BC)

NORICUM (15 BC)

UPPER PANNONIA

Lugdunum

P

Aquileia

AQUITANIA

NARBONENSIS

C

M

I T A L Y

Adriatic Sea

Nemausus

Rome

TARRACONENSIS

Tarraco

LUSITANIA (c. 27 BC)

Naulochus

Corduba

SICILY

BAETICA

Carthage

Gades

Naval victory ov Sextus Pompeiu 36 BC

M A U R E T A N I A

A F R I C A

Imperial frontier as in AD 14

Provincial frontiers

ASIA   Senatorial provinces

ALPINE PROVINCES (15 - 14 BC)
M: Maritime, C: Cottian, P: Pennine

The hatched areas represent the more important dependent ('client') states, whose monarchs enjoyed internal autonomy but had to support Rome's foreign policy and help defend the imperial frontiers.

Principal client states

From *The Routledge Atlas of Classical History* by Michael Grant. Map 57, pp. 74–75. Routledge (1994).

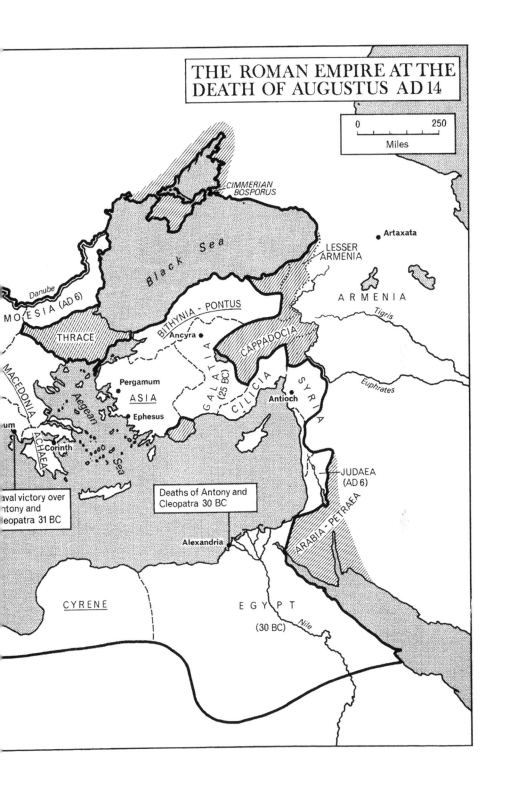

THE ROMAN EMPIRE AT THE DEATH OF AUGUSTUS AD 14

0   250

Miles

CIMMERIAN BOSPORUS

• Artaxata

Black Sea

LESSER ARMENIA

Danube

A R M E N I A

M O E S I A (AD 6)

BITHYNIA - PONTUS

Tigris

THRACE

Ancyra •

CAPPADOCIA

MACEDONIA

G A L A T I A (25 BC)

C I L I C I A

Euphrates

Pergamum

ASIA

S Y R I A

Antioch •

Aegean Sea

Ephesus

•um

ACHAEA

• Corinth

JUDAEA (AD 6)

aval victory over
ntony and
eopatra 31 BC

Deaths of Antony and
Cleopatra 30 BC

ARABIA - PETRAEA

Alexandria

CYRENE

E G Y P T

(30 BC)

Nile

1

Early Republican Rome: 507–264 BC

The city of Rome, halfway down the western coast of Italy and some 15 kilometres inland, started its history as a few primitive huts on adjacent hills; the earliest archaeological remains belong to the foundations of dwellings on the Palatine dating to the middle of the eighth century BC. The city would eventually be built over and around the famous seven hills: the Aventine, Caelian, Capitoline, Esquiline, Palatine, Quirinal and Viminal. Tradition and myth gave the city a founder, Romulus, but nearly everything about him is probably fictitious. For the Romans, he was the first of seven kings, before the Republic came into being in 509 BC with the overthrow of the last king, the Etruscan Tarquinius Superbus 'the Proud'. Livy and Dionysius record much about these seven kings, who ruled over some 250 years, but the pre-regal and regal history of Rome is more or less lost except for the archaeological record. There was a tendency to ascribe Roman institutions and customs to these kings, as well as developments in the physical structure of the city (docs 1.1–2, 1.5, 2.3), though the idea of monarchy was hated throughout the Republic (doc. 1.10, 13.55).

By the sixth and fifth centuries BC, Rome was part of the wider Mediterranean world: Herodotus knows of Agylla, 30 kilometres from Rome (Hdt. 1.167), and calls the defeat of Tarentum by the Iapygians in 473 BC the worst ever suffered by the Greeks (7.170), while Aristotle referred to the sack of Rome by the Gauls in the fourth century BC (Plutarch *Camillus* 22). The inscription of Sostratus found at Gravisca, the port of Etrurian Tarquinia, dated to c. 500 BC ('I am of Aeginetan Apollo. Sostratus . . . '; *LSAG*² p. 439), is evidence for Greeks trading on the Etruscan coast in the late sixth century, and this Sostratus is mentioned by Herodotus (4.152) as the archetypal profiteer: he may have been bringing Attic vases to Etruria. Athenian black-figure pottery dated to c. 570–560 BC has been found in the Roman forum, near the 'Black Stone' (lapis niger), on which there is an inscription in undecipherable Latin.

The standard abbreviation for the government of Rome was *SPQR*: 'senatus populusque Romanus' (the senate and people of Rome), and the state was known as res publica, literally 'public affairs', sometimes written as one word, respublica. The roles of the senate and people were seen as equally significant in the government of the city. As regards officials, Roman political life was highly competitive and underpinned by the principle of collegiality. From the expulsion of the kings, the tenure of magistracies was strictly annual, and supreme power was shared between two consuls (initially called praetors). It was the elected magistrates who convened the senate and assemblies, administered the law and finances, and commanded the armies and provinces. By the first century BC, the senior magistrates were the consuls, the supreme commanders of the army (docs 1.11–13) and the praetors, who were in charge of the administration of the law and, like the consuls, able to lead an army and convene the centuriate assembly. These senior magistrates possessed the powers of imperium (military command) and auspicium (the right to take auspices: see docs 3.45–50). Junior magistrates consisted of the quaestors (whose duties were primarily financial) and the aediles (two curule and two plebeian), who were in charge of the infrastructure of Rome as a city and the holding of games. In times of crisis in early Rome a single dictator could be appointed for a limited period of time, usually six months (doc. 1.14), and two censors with an 18-month term of office were regularly elected to deal with the census (the registration of citizens) and carry out other duties (docs 1.15–17).

The senate was essentially an advisory body to the magistrates, as it had been to the kings, and before Sulla consisted of some 300 members (though in early Rome there were considerably fewer); the number was then raised by Sulla to 600 and by Julius Caesar to 900. The senate's numbers were kept up by the enrolment of elected magistrates, and hence as a body of ex-officials it possessed great influence over magistrates and people. However, the senate could not decide on war or peace, since it was the people, as the comitia tributa, 'tribal assembly' (in the comitium or forum), who voted for legislation and, as the comitia centuriata, 'centuriate assembly' (on the Campus Martius), for war or peace (doc. 1.59, cf. 1.20).

The people (the populus Romanus) had the constitutional rights of direct voting on legislation, electing magistrates, and making decisions on trials in the popular assembly (docs 1.20–21). Duties included military service (for those with the requisite economic status), paying the poll tax (up to 168 BC) and serving as jurors. Ten tribunes, who were also magistrates elected annually, represented the rights of the people and prevented them from exploitation (docs 1.23–24). Technically, therefore, the populus Romanus was sovereign, but of course only adult citizen males were members of assemblies (though these included freedmen). Polybius, writing in the mid-second century BC, saw the Roman constitution as a 'mixed' one and believed that the system of checks and balances between magistrates, senate and people was one of the factors in its successful working (doc. 1.59).

The forum was the centre of political life in Rome, as well as containing shops and businesses, while trials, gladiatorial and theatrical shows and the funeral orations of prominent citizens took place there. Political life revolved around the assemblies (held both in the forum and on the Campus Martius, the 'Field of Mars') and the senate house (the curia) in the forum, while important temples fronted onto the forum, where the residences of the pontifex maximus and Vestals were sited (docs 1.5–8).

Early Rome was dominated by two long-standing areas of conflict: the struggle between patricians and plebeians, the 'Conflict of the Orders', which lasted from

494 to 287 BC (docs 1.25–58), and Rome's drive to become the dominant state in Italy (docs 1.27–28, 61–74). The plebeians, those who were not patricians (members of specific clans originally with responsibility for religious rites), increasingly gained access to magistracies and the priesthoods (docs 1.48–56) and by 300 BC the wealthy plebeian families had joined Rome's political elite. As part of this conflict, the XII Tables were codified supposedly in response to popular agitation over the patricians' control of the law (docs 1.32–43, 45). Within Italy, Rome was engaged in continuous wars with its Italic neighbours from its foundation. The Etruscan city of Veii, some 15 kilometres north of Rome, was finally taken in 396 BC (doc. 1.61); Latium, the area inhabited by the Latins, was conquered by 300 BC (docs 1.27, 63–65); and the Samnites, though fierce enemies of Rome from 343 to 290 BC (and again in the Social War, 91–89 BC), were effectively neutralised, along with the Greek cities of southern Italy, by 272 BC: Rome's dominance over Italy was now complete.

Ancient sources: family history and heroic tales had a long oral tradition in early Rome. However, there was also documentary evidence from the earliest period of the Republic in the *Fasti* (the list of consuls for each year), and historians use, as their chronological framework, lists of the consuls, triumphs, military campaigns, alliances, colonies, public works, natural disasters and other such archival material. Cicero (*de orat.* 2.52) suggests that there was an official chronicle called the *Annales Maximi* kept by the pontifex maximus which listed all important events in a certain year and continued from the earliest times down to c. 120 BC (P. Mucius Scaevola). In addition state documents were kept in the temple of Saturn on the Capitol and pontifical colleges kept their own records.

Fragments of the *XII Tables*, the law-code compiled in 451/0 BC, survive from quotations in later writers; while the XII Tables might have regulated existing legal practices (rather than reforming them), they are a very valuable source for law and society in the mid-fifth century and were later seen as the basis of all Roman law.

Antiquarians: antiquarianism of language or customs became a popular study in the first century BC. M. Terentius Varro (116–27 BC) is said to have written 490 books (or more). Six of his 25 books *De lingua latina* (*On the Latin Language*) are extant; his *Antiquities* are lost, but his work was highly significant as a source for later writers: Pliny the Elder, for example, in his 37 books of *Natural History*, relied on his account. Another noted antiquarian was Dionysius of Halicarnassus, who is a very valuable source for the constitution and customs of early Rome. A Greek historian, he lived in Rome in the time of Augustus as a teacher of rhetoric and published his 20 books of *Roman Antiquities* (down to the beginning of the first Punic War) 22 years after Augustus' assumption of power. The first 11 books (to 441 BC) survive. As an outsider, Dionysius describes much in Roman society which is otherwise not mentioned, but he is concerned with showing Rome as essentially a Greek city and emphasising its intrinsic virtues, and his work is full of lengthy rhetorical speeches. Gellius' *Attic Nights* (Gellius was born c. AD 125) is a series of short notes which he put together for his children and contains useful citations from earlier works now lost. Macrobius used him extensively: his

3

Saturnalia is in the form of a series of dialogues which took place before and during the Saturnalia of perhaps AD 383 and contains nostalgic reminiscences of Rome's pagan past.

The main historian of early Rome is Titus Livius (59 BC–AD 17). His *Ad urbe condita* (*From the Foundation of the City*) consisted of 142 books from Rome's origins to 9 BC. Only books 1–10 and 21–45 survive (with some fragments); books 11–20 are lost, and this leaves a gap in the history for the period 293–264 BC. The *Epitome* of Livy (early third century AD) gives summaries of books 37–40 and 48–55, and the *Periochae* (fourth century AD) summaries of all books except 136 and 137. Livy used literary sources almost exclusively, seldom bothering to consult archival records. In books 31–145 he mainly followed Polybius' account with a few additions from later writers such as Valerius Antias and Claudius Quadrigarius; he tended, though not exclusively, to follow one author for various sections of his work. Livy sees a grave moral decline in his own time, compared with the virtues that enabled Rome to defeat Hannibal, and his aim in his writing is ostensibly a moral one (preface 10). From 318 BC, Livy can be supplemented by Diodorus (down to 302) and the *Fasti*. Polybius (c. 200–c. 118), in Rome from 167 until 146, was a close companion of Scipio Aemilianus and wrote a history of Rome's speedy rise to power from the end of the First Punic War down to 167. His summary of Rome's constitution, supposedly at the time of the Second Punic War, is central to any discussion of Rome's early government (doc. 1.59).

GEOGRAPHY AND LOCATION

Despite Cicero's eulogy of Rome's location (doc. 1.4), the site grew from small beginnings, and Strabo sees the Romans as having later made the best of its disadvantages (doc. 1.2). The Tiber, Italy's major river, begins in the Apennines, Italy's mountain 'backbone', and flows 400 kilometres to the sea. It was navigable by sea-going vessels from its mouth to Rome (doc. 1.1), and the city increasingly relied upon it for supplies.

Rome had an inaugurated boundary, the pomerium, consecrated by religion (docs 1.3, 3.17). There was a wall, ascribed to the sixth king, Servius Tullius (doc. 1.2), but actually dating to the fourth century BC, 11 kilometres in circumference, embracing all the hills except the Palatine, which had its own defences; the Servian Wall enclosed about 400 hectares, but Rome quickly outgrew this, and by the late Republican period the city sprawled significantly outside the wall, a testimony to Roman power and military confidence.

1.1 Dionysius of Halicarnassus *Roman Antiquities* 3.44.1–4: The Tiber

At 1.37.1–5 Dionysius praises the natural advantages of Italy in bearing crops and timber and in raising cattle, as well as its climate. Tradition had it that Ancus Marcius (the fourth king of Rome: 640–617 BC) developed a trading post at the mouth of the Tiber at Ostia. There was no harbour as such there in the Republican period and, as Dionysius notes, sea-going vessels went through the mouth of the Tiber at Ostia and were assisted on their way to Rome.

1 The River Tiber, descending from the Apennine Mountains and flowing close to Rome, discharges itself on harbourless and continuous shores which the Tyrrhenian Sea has made, but it gave slight advantages to Rome, not worth mentioning, because of the lack of a trading post (emporion) at its outlet, where goods brought by sea and down river from the interior could be received and exchanged with the merchants. However, as it was adequate for river boats of good size as far as its source, and as far as Rome itself for large sea-going merchant ships, Ancus Marcius decided to construct a sea-port at its outlet, making use of the river's mouth itself as a harbour. 2 For the Tiber broadens considerably when it unites with the sea and forms great bays, such as those of the greatest seaports; and, what anyone might marvel at, its mouth is not blocked by sandbanks heaped up by the sea, as happens to many of even the largest rivers . . . and it discharges itself through its one genuine mouth, repelling the ocean's breakers, despite the violence of the prevailing westerly wind. 3 As a result oared ships of any size and merchant ships of up to 3,000 measures (bushels) enter through the mouth of the river and are brought to Rome by rowing or by being dragged with towing-lines, while the larger ones ride at anchor off the mouth, where they are unloaded and loaded by river boats. 4 On the elbow of land between the river and the sea the king built a city, which he named 'Ostia' from its position, or as we should say 'thyra' or door, thus making Rome not only an inland city but a seaport, and gave it a taste of good things from across the seas.

1.2 Strabo *Geography* 5.3.7: The city of Rome

Compare the eulogistic picture of Rome's situation given by Cicero (doc. 1.4). Titus Tatius was the Sabine king who attacked Rome after the 'rape of the Sabine women' and who afterwards formed a joint community with Romulus. 'Servius' wall' in fact dates to after the conquest of Veii (perhaps to 378 BC).

In the interior, the first city above Ostia is Rome, and this is the only city which lies on the Tiber; concerning this city of Rome, I have already stated (5.3.2) that it was founded out of necessity, not choice, and I must add that those who later established certain additional districts could not, as masters, choose what was better, but had, like slaves, to fall into line with what was already there. The first founders walled the Capitol and Palatine and the Quirinal hill, which was so easy for outsiders to climb that Titus Tatius took it at his first attempt, in his attack when he came to avenge the insult of the abducted girls. Ancus Marcius added in Mount Caelium and Mount Aventine and the plain in between them, which were separated from each other and from the parts already walled, as a matter of necessity; for it was not a good idea to leave hills which were naturally strong outside the walls for those who wanted strongholds against the city, and he was not able to fill out the whole circle round to the Quirinal. Servius (Tullius) noticed the omission and filled it out, adding the Esquiline and the Viminal hills. It is easy, too, for outsiders to attack these, and therefore they dug a deep ditch, putting the earth on the inside, and extended the bank of earth about six stades on the inner side of the ditch, and placed on it a wall and towers from the Colline Gate to the Esquiline; below the centre of the mound there is a third gate, with the same name as the Viminal hill. This is what, then, the fortifications of the city are like, though it needs another set of fortifications. In my view the first founders had the same point of view both for themselves and their successors, that Romans ought to depend for their security and other welfare not on fortifications but on arms and innate courage, believing that walls should not defend men, but men walls. So in the beginning, as the large and fertile country around them belonged to other people, and the site of the city was so open to attack, there was no good luck in their situation demanding congratulations; but when the land became their own, through their bravery and toil, there was a clear inrush of good things which surpassed any advantages of situation; it is because of this that, although the city has increased to such an extent, it has adequate supplies both of food and of wood and stones for building work, which goes on continuously because of collapses and fires and sales, these last being never-ending . . . To cater for this, the quantity of mines and timber and rivers for transport provide an amazing supply of materials, first the Anio which flows from Alba, the Latin city near the Marsi, through the plain below Alba to its junction with the Tiber, then the Nar and Teneas which flow through Ombrica to the same river, the Tiber, and the Clanis too, which runs through Etruria and the territory of Clusium.

1.3 Gellius *Attic Nights* 13.14.1–2: The pomerium

The actual inhabited area of Rome extended well beyond the pomerium, which was a religious boundary, the consecrated space within which the auspices connected with the city were taken (cf. docs 3.17, 3.40). Military imperium could not be exercised within the pomerium, and a general could only enter the pomerium if – and on the day or days – he was celebrating his triumph.

1 'Pomerium' has been defined by the augurs of the Roman people who wrote the books *On the Auspices* in the following terms: 'The pomerium is the space inside what has been designated as the rural district around the circuit of the whole city outside the walls, marked by fixed boundary-lines and forming the limit of the city auspices.' **2** The most ancient pomerium, which was established by Romulus, ended at the foot of the Palatine hill. But that pomerium was extended a number of times, as the Republic grew, and enclosed many high hills.

1.4 Cicero *Republic* 2.10–11: Cicero on the site of Rome

Cicero here presents Scipio Aemilianus arguing that Romulus showed foresight in not founding Rome on the coast, because of the dangers of attack, and the moral degeneration suffered by maritime cities such as Corinth and Carthage.

10 So how could Romulus have employed more divine wisdom in his making use of the advantages provided by the sea and in avoiding its disadvantages than by positioning his city on the bank of a broad river which flows constantly and unvaryingly down to the sea? This allows the city both to import from the sea what it needs and to export what it has in superfluity, and can also be used to convey items essential for life and civilisation not only from the sea but also from inland – which suggests to me that Romulus must even in his day have foreseen that this city would one day be the centre and homeland of a vast empire, for hardly any city sited anywhere else in Italy could more easily have acquired the far-reaching sovereignty we currently possess.

11 As regards the city's own natural defences, is there anyone so blind that he does not have them clearly visualised and engraved on his mind? It was the wisdom first of Romulus and then of the kings who followed him which defined the line and course of its wall, so positioned on steep and precipitous hills that the only approach, lying between the Esquiline and the Quirinal hills, was surrounded by an immense defensive rampart and a huge ditch, and the citadel was so well defended by its precipitous situation and the rock which looks as if it has been cut away on all sides that even in those awful times when the Gauls arrived (390 BC) it remained unharmed and impregnable. Furthermore, he selected a site which enjoys plentiful springs and is healthy, despite the pestilential nature of the area, for there are hills which not only get the benefit of the breezes but provide shade for the valleys.

THE FORUM

A forum (plural: fora) was the open area of a Roman town or city, around which clustered shops and which served as a market area. It was used for all forms of collective activity – trials, contiones (meetings; singular: contio), funeral orations, business, theatrical performances and gladiatorial shows. The forum as such was a religious, political, administrative, judicial and mercantile centre. At Rome, the main forum was the Forum Romanum; other fora were the Forum Boarium and Forum Holitorium (for both, see below). The forum was a crucial public space in Republican Rome. The popular assemblies met here from 145 BC, while judicial proceedings were conducted in the nearby comitium. The curia hostilia, senate house, stood adjacent to the comitium.

1.5 Dionysius of Halicarnassus *Roman Antiquities* 3.67.4: The institution of the forum

Tarquinius Priscus was the fifth king of Rome, 616–579 BC, who reputedly undertook drainage work in the forum, while the seventh king, Tarquinius Superbus, canalised the Cloaca Maxima stream which ran through it. Shops (tabernae) lined the Sacred Way (Sacra Via) which ran through the forum; these were the 'old shops' of Plautus Curc. 480 (doc. 1.6), as opposed to the new ones constructed in the northern forum at the front of the basilica Aemilia.

Tarquinius Priscus also adorned the forum, in which court cases are held, the assemblies meet and other political business is transacted, surrounding it with shops and colonnades.

1.6 Plautus *Curculio* 467–84: The forum, as it really was

Plautus' lively description of the Forum Romanum in the early second century BC reveals it as the centre of political and social life. For prostitution (male and female), see docs 7.57–65. The temple of Venus Cloacina was a small shrine devoted to the deity (assimilated to Venus) of the stream which ran through the forum. In line 470, 'perjurer' refers to the law courts and litigants.

> I will show you where you can easily find every type of person,
> So no one will have to work too hard if he wants to meet anyone
> Vicious or virtuous, worthy or worthless.
> 470   If he wants to meet a perjurer, he should go to the assembly (comitium);
> If a liar and braggart, to the temple of Venus Cloacina,
> While for rich, married spendthrifts, try the basilica.
> There too he'll find prostitutes past their prime and men who look for a bargain,
> While members of dining-clubs can be found at the fish-market.
> In the lower forum men of good repute and riches stroll around,
> In the middle forum near the canal you'll find the fellows who are just for show;
> Above the lake there's the bold, talkative, spiteful types,
> Who presumptuously slander other people for no reason
> And who could have plenty of home-truths said about themselves.
> 480   Under the old shops are those who lend and borrow at interest.
> Behind Castor's temple are those whom it would be unwise to trust too quickly.
> In the Tuscan quarter are the men who sell themselves,
> Who either turn over or give others the chance to do so.
> But there's a noise at the door: I must guard my tongue!

1.7 Lucilius *Satires* 1145–51: Life in the forum

Lucilius (180–102/1 BC) is here satirising life in the forum. From 145 BC the people met in the forum for the passing of laws. The law-courts were also in the forum and trials took place, in public view, in the open air.

> 1145   But now from morning to night, whether holiday or working-day,
> The entire people and senators in exactly the same way
> All strut about in the forum and never leave it;
> And they all give themselves to one and the same passion and skill –
> To be able to cheat within the letter of the law, to fight craftily,
> 1150   To strive through the use of flattery, to pretend they're 'honest fellows', and
> To set ambushes, as if they were all the enemies of all men.

1.8 Cicero *On His Return from Exile* 6: Rome's political centre

Cicero's picture might be overdrawn but he does point to the forum (Romanum) as the centre of political life in Rome.

And so from this time on, citizens, you gave no responses to allies, or even kings; the juries gave no verdicts, the people gave no votes, this senate approved no measures; you looked upon a forum that was dumb, a senate house without a tongue, a state that was silent and enfeebled.

SENATE AND MAGISTRACIES

Down to the mid-second century, holding the consulate twice in the space of ten years was forbidden and the Genucian laws in 342 (doc. 1.50) had supposedly laid down that there had to be a ten-year interval between consulships. In 81, Sulla raised the minimum age limits in the year of election from 36 to 42 (for consuls), from 33 to 39 (for praetors) and from 27 to 30 (for quaestors). Sulla also raised the number of magistrates elected every year: praetors from six to eight and quaestors from 12 to 20 (earlier two, in 447, four in 421, and eight in 267). There was a rigid cursus honorum ('race of honour', or career path) for Roman magistrates from the early second century: the praetorship could be held only by an ex-quaestor and the consulship by an ex-praetor. As the number of consuls remained fixed at two per year, there was clearly a 'pyramid' effect, leading to intense rivalry for the consulship. From the time of Sulla the quaestorship involved automatic membership of the senate (before that most, but not all, quaestors would have become senators), and among the senators the most influential after the current consuls were the consulares (or ex-consuls). The presiding magistrate consulted members of the senate according to their seniority: the consulares first, among whom was a princeps senatus (chief of the senate) appointed by the censors when in office.

1.9 Ennius *Annals* 467: The importance of traditions

One of the most important concepts for the Romans was that of mos maiorum ('the custom of (our) ancestors'), the maintenance of the traditions and behaviour that had made Rome great. This line may have been spoken by Titus Manlius Torquatus (cos. 340 BC) before his execution of his son in 337: cf. doc. 7.15.

On manners and men of olden times stands the Roman state.

1.10 Ennius *Tragedies* FF402–3: The dangers of kingship

The first king of Rome was believed to have been Romulus, its founder. The tradition that the last of the seven kings, Tarquinius Superbus, was deposed by a group of aristocrats is generally accepted. The concept of kingship was viewed with horror during the Republic, and Julius Caesar avoided accepting the title 'rex': see docs 8.14–15, 13.55.

To a king no association, no promise, is sacred.

1.11 Livy *History of Rome* 2.1.8–10: The first consuls, 509 BC

The first senior magistrates were initially called not consuls, but praetors. Consuls were originally military figures and possessed supreme power (imperium) in the field. The fasces (a bundle of rods tied with red thongs and containing an axe, though not within the city) formed a symbol of the consul's power and were carried by the 12 lictors before each consul on alternate months, signalling their precedence over the other for that period. The fasces formed part of the Etruscan regalia that, apart from the embroidered robe and crown, were retained by the consuls.

8 The first consuls (Lucius Junius Brutus and Lucius Tarquinius Collatinus, Lucretia's husband) possessed all the rights and insignia of the kings, but care was taken in one respect, that twice the terror should not be inspired by their both having the fasces. Brutus, with his colleague's consent, was the first to have them, and he was no less zealous as a guard of liberty than he had been as its champion. **9** First of all, while the people were still covetous of their new freedom, in case, in the future, they should be swayed by the entreaties or presents of would-be kings, he made them swear an oath that they would never permit anyone to be king in Rome. **10** Next, in order that the numbers in the senate might give greater authority to that order, he made up the number of senators, which had been diminished by the king's murders, to the total of 300 by choosing the leading men of equestrian rank.

1.12 Cicero *On Duties* 1.124: The magistracies

Cicero dedicated this work to his son Marcus; it was completed in November 44 BC. Due to the frequent absence of the consuls from Rome, the senate and lesser magistrates handled most day-to-day business and decisions.

It is especially the duty of a magistrate to bear in mind that he is the representative of the state and that he must uphold its dignity and honour, preserve its laws, apportion to all their constitutional rights, and remember that all this has been granted to him as a sacred trust . . .

1.13 Varro *On the Latin Language* 5.80–82, 87: The early magistracies

The secession here is that of 494 BC (doc. 1.25). Tribunus (tribune) is actually derived from tribus, man of the tribe. Varro wrote his work on the Latin language between 47 and 45 BC; Lucius Accius was born in 170 BC at Pisaurum and wrote a number of tragedies.

80 The consul was given this name because he had to consult the people and senate, unless it comes rather from the etymology which Accius uses in his *Brutus*: 'He who counsels rightly, let him be called consul.'

The praetor was so called because he should 'go before' (*praeire*) the law and the army; from which Lucilius says, 'So the role of the praetors is to go in front and before'.

81 The censor was so named as the one at whose *censio*, rating – that is, his assessment – the people should be rated; the aedile as the one to look after sacred and private *aedes*, buildings; the quaestors from *quaerere*, seek, as they have to seek into public moneys and wrongdoing, which the *triumviri capitales* now look into: from this name later on those who give judgement on the investigations were named *quaesitores*, investigators; the *tribuni militum*, military tribunes, because in the olden days three were sent to the army by the three tribes of Ramnes, Luceres and Tities; the *tribuni plebis*, tribunes of the plebs, because tribunes of the plebs were first created from the tribunes of the soldiers in the secession to Crustumerium with the role of defending the *plebs*, populace.

82 The dictator was so called because he was named by the consul as one to whose *dictum*, order, all should listen; the *magister equitum*, master of the horse, because he has supreme power over the cavalry and reserves, just as the dictator has supreme power over the people, from which he is also called 'master' of the people. The remainder, because they are subordinate to these *magistri*, masters, are called *magistratus*, magistrates, derived in the same way as *albatus*, clothed in white, is derived from *albus*, white. . . .

87 The *imperator*, commander, is named from the *imperium*, authority, of the people, as the one who subdued the enemies who had attacked it; the *legati*, legates, those who were officially *lecti*, chosen, whose aid or advice magistrates should use when away from Rome, or who should be messengers of the senate or people; the *exercitus*, army, because it is improved by *exercitando*, training; the *legio*, legion, because the soldiers *leguntur*, are gathered, in a levy.

1.14 Dionysius of Halicarnassus *Roman Antiquities* 5.73.1–2: The dictatorship

Dictators were extraordinary magistrates, who were appointed to lead the army or hold elections. The maximum time-limit for a dictatorship was six months, and the dictator appointed as his second-in-command a master of horse (magister equitum); a dictator was preceded by 24 lictors. Titus Larcius Flavus was the first dictator in 501 or 498; Spurius Cassius was his master of horse.

1 Larcius was the first man to be appointed sole ruler in Rome with absolute authority in war, peace, and all other matters. They call this person a dictator, either from his power of giving whatever orders he wishes and of laying down justice and right for the other citizens as he thinks best (for the Romans call commands and decrees regarding right and wrong edicts, '*edicta*') or, as some record, from the form of election which was then brought in, since he was not to receive the magistracy from the people, according to ancestral custom, but was appointed by one man . . . **2** For the immensity of the power which the dictator holds is not at all indicated by his title; for the dictatorship is actually an elective tyranny.

1.15 Livy *History of Rome* 4.8.2–5: The censorship, 443 BC

Censors were senior magistrates, but without imperium. Two were elected for a period of 18 months every four, later five years; censors wore distinctive purple togas. Censors' initial duties will have been to register citizens for military duty and taxation, and, before Sulla, censors were responsible for admitting members to the senate. Enrolment in the census was necessary for voting privileges in the comitia centuriata.

2 In this same year the censorship was inaugurated, an institution which started in a small way but which later grew so immensely as to be responsible for regulating the morals and lifestyle of the Romans: the distribution of honour and dishonour to the senators and centuries of the equites was under the control of this magistracy along with jurisdiction over public and private places, while the revenues of the Roman people were entirely subject to its judgement. **3** The reason behind the institution was that the people had not been rated for a number of years and the census could not be postponed, but the consuls had no time for this duty, with wars against so many peoples hanging over them. **4** The matter was referred to the senate, on the grounds that so laborious a task, and one beneath the consuls' dignity, needed its own special magistrates, who should have a staff of clerks, the task of supervising the records, and the charge of regulating the form of the census. **5** Although it was a small matter, the senators were pleased to accept the suggestion, so that there might be more patrician magistrates in the government.

1.16 Cicero *On the Laws* 3.7: The censorship in Cicero's ideal state

Cicero here gives the censors their traditional duties; the prevention of celibacy was a concern of censors such as Metellus Macedonicus in 131 and Metellus Numidicus in 102.

Censors shall complete a register of the people, their ages, offspring, households and property; they shall be in charge of the city's temples, streets, aqueducts, treasury and revenues; they shall divide the people into tribes and other divisions by wealth, age and rank; they shall enrol the youth into the cavalry and infantry; they shall forbid celibates; they shall regulate the behaviour of the people; they shall ensure no reprobate remains in the senate; they shall be two in number and hold a five-year magistracy – the other magistrates shall have an annual term. The position of censor shall never be vacant.

1.17 Plutarch *Life of Cato the Elder* 16.1–3: Cato as censor

Cf. Livy 39.40–41. Cato was elected censor for 184 BC with L. Valerius Flaccus. Both had a programme of arresting moral decline, and Cato expelled numerous senators and equites (including L. Quinctius Flamininus and a senator who had kissed his wife in daylight: docs 7.20, 58).

1 Ten years after his consulship, Cato stood for the censorship. This magistracy was at the peak, as it were, of every office and was, in a way, the culmination of a political career, as it had numerous powers including that of the examination of character and lifestyle. **2** They thought that neither marriage, nor procreation of children, nor daily life, nor entertainment of guests should be as each man should desire and choose, without investigation and examination, but rather, considering that these revealed the character of a man more than public and political actions, they appointed as guard, moderator and chastiser, so that no one for the sake of pleasure should turn aside and deviate from his native and customary lifestyle, one of the so-called patricians and one of the plebeians. **3** They named these 'censors', and they had the authority to demote an eques and expel from the senate anyone who lived in an unbridled and irregular fashion. They also reviewed property assessments and organised citizens in lists according to class and age, while the office also had other great powers.

1.18 Cicero *On the Laws* 3.6–9, 12: The ideal constitution

One of Cicero's last works, written before the Second Triumvirate. He believed in the value of a mixed constitution, with its checks and balances, and in strong censors to maintain and define the law (doc. 3.16).

6 Edicts shall be just, and citizens shall obey them attentively and without argument; the magistrate shall use coercion towards the disobedient and criminal citizen by means of a fine, imprisonment or flogging, unless an equal or higher authority, or the people, forbids it: to these the citizen shall have right of appeal (provocatio). When the magistrate has passed judgement and proposed a penalty, the decision as to the fine or punishment will be decided by a trial before the people. There shall be no right of appeal from orders given by a commander, and whoever is in command, while he is waging war, his orders will be authoritative and unalterable. There shall be minor magistrates with partial authority in specific roles. In the army they shall command those under their authority and be their tribunes; in the city they shall be the guardians of the public money (quaestores); they shall oversee the imprisonment of criminals; they shall carry out capital punishment (triumviri capitales); they shall officially coin bronze, silver and gold (triumviri aere argento auro flando feriundo); they shall judge law-suits (decemviri litibus iudicandis); and they shall execute the decrees of the senate. **7** There shall be aediles, who will be curators of the city, grain supply and customary games, and this shall be the first step in the advancement to higher magistracies. . . .

8 The arbitrator of justice, who shall decide or direct civil law-suits, shall be the praetor; he shall be the guardian of civil law; there shall be as many of these, with equal powers, as the senate shall decree or the people command. There shall be two magistrates with royal powers, and these by leading, judging and consulting shall be called praetors, judges and consuls; in war they shall hold the highest authority and be subject to no one; the safety of the people shall be their highest law. **9** No one shall hold the same magistracy, except after an interval of ten years; they shall observe the age limits prescribed by laws defining the ages for office. But when a serious war or civil discord should arise, one man shall hold, for no more than six months, if the senate should so decree, the authority of the two consuls; appointed under favourable auspices, he shall be master of the people (dictator). He shall have a colleague in charge of the cavalry (magister equitum), with rank equal to that of the arbitrator of justice . . . The ten officials whom the plebs shall elect to protect them from violence (vis auxilii) shall be their tribunes; whatever they prohibit or put to the people shall be unalterable; their persons shall be inviolable and they shall not leave the plebs without tribunes . . .

12 Quintus: How succinctly, brother, your description of all the magistrates has been placed before us – but they are almost those of our constitution, though you have suggested some slight innovations!

Marcus: Your comment is absolutely correct, Quintus . . . Since our ancestors devised the wisest and most balanced government, I thought no innovation – or at least very little – should be introduced into the laws.

THE ASSEMBLIES AND TRIBUNATE

Of the various assemblies, the oldest was the comitia curiata (consisting of divisions, curiae, of the three original tribes: docs 1.19, 21); the last known law passed in this assembly dated to 390 BC. By the first century BC this comitia met only for certain religious or legal matters, such as adoptions. The comitia centuriata was traditionally instituted by Servius Tullius and was based on field units in the army (the 193 centuriae, 'centuries', organized by property qualifications), though by the late Republic it had become primarily an electoral body. Higher magistrates (with imperium), the consuls and praetors, were elected here; the others (the magistrates without imperium) in the comitia tributa. The comitia tributa was based on the division of people into tribes (also ascribed to Servius Tullius). There were four urban tribes, while by 241 BC the rural tribes had gradually increased to 31, a total of 35. The normal way of legislating was through the comitia tributa, which comprised the whole citizen body under the direction of a curule magistrate; it voted by majority, i.e., there were 35 votes, one for each tribe voting *en bloc*, and every citizen voted on an equal basis. A further tribal assembly, the concilium plebis (supposedly established after the secessio of 494), was summoned by a tribune and open only to plebeians.

While it was the assemblies that passed laws, elected magistrates, and (early in the Republic) heard major trials and declared wars, their powers were often limited by patronage, political manipulation and bribery. In addition, there were no opportunities for debate – Roman democracy was non-participatory and assemblies had to be presided over by magistrates.

1.19 Varro *On the Latin Language* 5.55–6: The earliest tribes

Ennius *Annals* 112–13. The terms for the three tribes were non-Latin, hence Ennius' etymologies, according to Varro, are incorrect. These three tribes were divided into curiae, ten for each tribe, which formed the basis for Rome's early military organisation and earliest assembly (the comitia curiata), which went back to the regal period. Nothing is known of Volnius.

55 Roman territory (*ager*) was at first divided into three (*tris*) parts, from which came the term tribe, used of the Titienses, Ramnes and Luceres. They were named, as Ennius says, the Titienses from Tatius, the Ramnenses from Romulus, and the Luceres, according to Junius, from Lucumo; but all these words are Etruscan, as Volnius says, who wrote tragedies in Etruscan.

56 From this, four parts of the city were also used as the names of tribes, from the places – the Suburan, the Palatine, the Esquiline, the Colline (the four urban tribes); a fifth because it was 'under the walls of Rome', the Romilian (the first of the rural tribes); so also the other thirty for those reasons I wrote about in my *Book of the Tribes*.

1.20 Dionysius of Halicarnassus 4.20.1–5: The comitia centuriata

Cf. Livy 1.42–3. Servius Tullius was thought to have organised this assembly to ensure that the votes of the poor (i.e., the proletarii, who were confined to just one century) would be minimised. Dionysius makes it clear that this early system later became 'more democratic' (4.21.3). The original system was clearly timocratic, with the voting controlled by the rich, as the senators, equites and first property class comprised 98 of the 193 centuries. Dionysius and Livy essentially agree on the property qualifications: 100,000 asses for the first class, 75,000 for the second, 50,000 for the third, 25,000 for the fourth, and 11,000 (or 12,500) for the fifth. The proletarii (the greater proportion of the citizens) who had a census rating of less than 1,500 asses were all included in a single century, while those without any property (and hence no right to vote) were the 'capite censi' (literally: counted by head).

1 Having in this way placed on the rich the burden of danger and expense, he noticed that they were unhappy and relieved their dissatisfaction and mollified their anger in another way by giving them an advantage, through which they would become masters of the state, and excluding the poor from public affairs; and he achieved this without the plebeians noticing. This advantage concerned the assemblies, in which the most important matters were ratified by the people. 2 I have already mentioned earlier (2.14.3) that by the ancient laws the people was sovereign over the three most important and essential matters: they elected the magistrates both for the city and the army, ratified and repealed laws, and decided on matters of war and peace. Voting with regard to discussion and decision-making on these matters was carried out by curiae; and those who had the least property possessed an equal vote to those who had the most; but as there were few who were wealthy, as one might expect, when it came to voting the poor prevailed because of their far superior numbers. 3 Tullius saw this and transferred this voting power to the rich. For, whenever he thought it right to have magistrates elected or a law to be determined or war to be declared, he assembled the people by centuries rather than curiae. The first centuries he called on to give their vote were those with the highest property assessment, which consisted of the 18 centuries of equites and the 80 of infantry. 4 As these consisted of three more than all the rest put together, if they were of one mind they prevailed over the others and the decision was made; if they were not all of the same opinion, then he called on the 22 centuries of the second class. If the votes were still indecisive, he called on those of the third class; and fourthly those of the fourth class; and he kept doing this until 97 centuries voted alike. 5 If this had not happened after the fifth class was called, but the opinions of the 192 centuries were divided equally, then he called on the last century, which consisted of the mass of citizens who were poor and for that reason exempted from all military service and taxation; whichever side this century sided with, that side won. But this was rare and almost impossible. Most

issues were determined by calling on the first class and rarely got down as far as the fourth, and so the fifth and last class was superfluous.

1.21 Gellius *Attic Nights* 15.27.5: The three popular assemblies

Laelius was a jurist in the time of Hadrian who wrote on the work of Q. Mucius Scaevola (cos. 95 BC) on civil law.

It is also written in the same book (of Laelius Felix, *To Quintus Mucius*) that, 'Whenever voting is carried on according to people's families, it is called a "curiate" assembly (comitia curiata), when by property and age a "centuriate" assembly (comitia centuriata), and when by regions and localities a "tribal" assembly (comitia tributa); moreover, it is against sacred law for a centuriate assembly to be held within the pomerium, because the army must be assembled outside the city, and it is unlawful for it to be assembled within the city. As a result, it was usual to hold the centuriate assembly on the Campus Martius (Field of Mars) and for the army to be summoned there for the purpose of protection while the people was occupied with casting votes.'

1.22 Polybius *Histories* 6.14.6–8: The assembly's judicial function

Crimes against the people were dealt with in assemblies with the case brought by a magistrate. In this way it was possible for the people to censor corrupt or incompetent magistrates after their term of office. The right to citizenship had to be discussed at the comitia centuriata, and men tried on capital charges had the right of appeal to this comitia because the whole people had to be involved in a capital charge. Generally, those likely to be convicted of a capital charge went into exile; context of this passage: doc. 1.58.

6 It is the people, then, who frequently judge cases where the offence is punishable by a fine, and particularly when the accused have held the most distinguished offices; they alone can try a capital charge. **7** Regarding this they have a practice which is praiseworthy and should be mentioned. Custom allows those on trial for their lives, when they are being condemned, to depart openly, voluntarily sentencing themselves to exile, even if only one of the tribes which pronounce the verdict has not yet voted. **8** Such exiles find refuge in the territories of Naples, Praeneste, Tibur and other towns with whom treaties are in place.

1.23 Dionysius of Halicarnassus 8.87.6–8: The tribunes

The setting for this passage is 485 BC (cf. Livy 2.42), with the tribune Maenius attempting to prevent a further military levy; the consuls therefore enrolled troops outside the city. The first tribunes were apparently military tribunes who acted as spokespersons for the plebs in the 'First Secession' in 494 (doc. 1.25, cf. 1.13). The original number of tribunes is given as two, four or five. Their role was the protection of the plebeians (the ius auxilii); they were elected by the plebeian assembly and possessed inviolability (i.e., they were sacrosanct). Shortly after their inception they possessed the right to veto the act of any magistrate, other tribune, law or senatorial decree.

6 The tribune who opposed the levy was no longer able to do anything. For those who possess tribunician power have no authority over anything outside the city; their jurisdiction is circumscribed by the city walls, and it is not lawful for them even to pass a night away from the city, except on a single occasion, when all the magistrates of the state ascend the Alban mount and make a common sacrifice to Jupiter on behalf of the Latin people. **7** This custom, of the tribunes possessing no authority over anything outside the city, continues to our own day; and indeed the motivating reason, among many others, of the civil war among the Romans which took place in my day and was greater than any war before it, which seemed of great importance and reason enough to divide the state, was this – that some of the tribunes, complaining that they had been forcibly driven out of the city by the general (Pompey) who was then in control of affairs in Italy, in order that they might no longer have any authority, fled to the general in command of the armies in Gaul (Caesar), as they had nowhere to turn to. **8** And the latter, making use of this pretext that he was coming with right and justice to the assistance of the sacrosanct magistracy of the people, deprived of its authority contrary to the oaths of their ancestors, himself entered the city in arms and restored the men to their magistracy.

1.24 Dionysius of Halicarnassus 9.1.4–5: Manipulation of tribunician power

Spurius Icilius, a tribune, opposed all legislation in 481 BC until a redistribution of land took place.

4 As the senate was at a loss and had no idea what to do, Appius Claudius proposed that they should consider how the other tribunes might be brought to disagree with Icilius, pointing out that, when a tribune opposes and obstructs the senate's decrees, since he is sacrosanct and legally has the authority to do this, there is no other method of putting an end to his power, unless another of those of equal rank who possess the same power opposes him and orders the measures which the other is obstructing. **5** And he advised all consuls who succeeded him in this office to do this and to consider how they might always have some of the tribunes on their side as their friends, saying that the only way of destroying the power of their college was for them to fight among themselves.

THE BEGINNINGS OF THE 'CONFLICT OF THE ORDERS'

The traditional dates of the 'Conflict of the Orders', the struggle between patricians and plebeians, are from 494 to 287 BC. In the fourth century the plebeians increasingly challenged the patrician control of the magistracies; patricians also had total control over the religious sphere: only a patrician could hold a major priesthood. The term 'patrician' is probably connected with 'patres' (fathers). From 367 plebeians were eligible for the consulship, and from 342 one of each pair of consuls supposedly had to be a plebeian; the first plebeian dictator was appointed in 356; the first plebeian censor in 351. In 300, plebeians were admitted to the major priestly colleges.

1.25 Livy *History of Rome* 2.31.7–33.3: The 'first secession', 494 BC

Cf. Dion. Hal. 6.83–86. In this secession of the plebs in 494, caused by the burden of debts, the plebeians withdrew outside the pomerium of the city and refused their military service; they created their own assembly and officials. To deal with this emergency, Manius Valerius was appointed dictator. The tribunes were granted initially the ius auxilii (to protect plebeians against the magistrates) and then the ius intercessionis (veto) against senate, assemblies and magistrates (but not a dictator). There were further secessions in 449 and 287.

31.7 Although a threefold success (over the Sabines, Volsci and Aequi) had been won in the war, regarding the outcome of domestic matters both senators and plebeians were as anxious as ever, so great was the influence and cleverness with which the moneylenders had put things in train so as to frustrate not only the plebs but even the dictator himself. **8** For after the return of the consul (Titus) Vetusius, the first business which Valerius brought to the senate was on behalf of the victorious people, when he demanded that the senate should declare their policy about those bound over for debt. **9** When his proposal was rejected, he made the following statement: 'You do not approve of my being the instigator of harmony; you will very soon, I assure you, wish that the Roman plebs had spokespersons (patrons) like myself. For my part, I will neither disappoint my fellow citizens any further, nor will I be an ineffectual dictator. **10** Internal discord and foreign war have made this magistracy necessary for the state: peace has been made abroad but hindered at home; I prefer to meet the revolt as a private citizen rather than as dictator.' With these words he left the senate house and resigned his dictatorship. **11** It was clear to the people that the reason for his resignation was his indignation on their account. Accordingly, just as if he had fulfilled his promise, since it was not his fault that it had not been kept, they escorted him as he left for home with demonstrations of gratitude and praise.

32.1 The senators then began to be anxious that, if the army were disbanded, there would again be secret gatherings and conspiracies. As a result, although the levy had been ordered by the dictator, they considered the men still bound by their oath because they had been sworn in by the consuls and, on the grounds that the Aequi had recommenced hostilities, instructed that the legions be led out of the city. **2** This brought matters to a head. Initially, it is said, there was talk of murdering the consuls, to release them from their oath; but when they were told that they could not be released from a sacred obligation by a crime, on the advice of one Sicinius, and without orders from the consuls, they withdrew to the Sacred Mount, across the River Anio, 3 miles from the city. **3** This version is more generally accepted than that related by Piso, in which their withdrawal was made to the Aventine. **4** There, without any leader, they fortified their camp with a rampart and ditch and remained there peacefully for several days, taking only what they needed for subsistence and neither receiving nor provoking hostility. **5** There was great panic at Rome, with all business ground to a halt due to the fear felt by everyone. The plebs, abandoned by their defenders, were afraid of violence by the senators; the senators were afraid of the plebeians who remained in the city, unsure whether they would rather see them stay or go. **6** Moreover, for how long would the mob which had seceded stay quiet? And what would happen if some foreign war should arise in the meantime? **7** Clearly there was no hope except in harmony between the citizens; by fair means or foul the state's harmony must be restored. **8** They therefore decided to send someone to speak to the people, Agrippa Menenius (Lanatus, cos. 503), a man of eloquence and dear to the plebs because he was one of them. Being admitted to the camp, he is said, in that time's antiquated and rough mode of speech, to have related the following tale: **9** 'At the time when all the parts of a man did not agree among themselves, as they do now, but each of them had its own will and voice, all the other parts were indignant that they should have the trouble and hard work and toil of providing everything for the stomach, while the stomach remained peacefully in their midst with nothing to do but enjoy the delights they gave it; **10** as a result they conspired together that the hands should not take any food to the mouth, nor should the mouth accept what it was given, nor the teeth chew up what they received. But, while in their anger they wanted to tame the stomach by hunger, the individual parts and the whole body were reduced to total weakness . . . ' **12** Drawing a comparison from this to demonstrate how similar was the internal conflict within the body to the plebs' anger against the senators, he won the men over to his viewpoint. **33.1** They then began to work towards harmony, and an agreement was reached on condition that the plebs were to have magistrates, who would be sacrosanct, and who should have the right to protect the plebs against the consuls, while no patrician was to be allowed to take on this magistracy. **2** So two tribunes of the plebs were created, Gaius Licinius and Lucius Albinus. These appointed three other colleagues, among whom was Sicinius, the instigator of the revolt; there is less agreement about who the other two were. **3** There are those who say that only two tribunes were created on the Sacred Mount and that the law of their inviolability was passed there.

1.26 Dionysius of Halicarnassus 6.89.1–3: The inviolability of the tribunate

Tribunes were sacrosanct: physical violence could not be employed against them. They customarily entered office on 10 December; for fetials, see doc. 3.14.

1 On the next day, Brutus and his fellows returned, after making the compact with the senate through the arbiters whom the Romans call 'fetials'. The people divided themselves into the phratries of the time, or whatever one wishes to name the divisions which they call 'curiae', and appointed the following as their annual magistrates: Lucius Junius Brutus and Gaius Sicinnius Bellutus, whom they had had as their leaders up to then, and as well as these Gaius and Publius Licinius and Gaius Visellius Ruga. **2** These five were the first men to take on the tribunician power on the fourth day before the Ides of December (December 10), as has been the custom until our own time . . . Brutus called an assembly and advised the plebeians to make this magistracy sacred and inviolable, confirming its security by both a law and an oath. **3** Everyone approved of this, and a law was drawn up by Brutus and his colleagues as follows: 'Let no one compel a tribune to do anything against his will, as if he were an ordinary citizen, let no one whip him, or command another to whip him, or kill him or command another to kill him. And if anyone should commit any of these prohibited acts, let him be accursed and his goods consecrated to Ceres, and whoever should kill any person who has committed such acts, let him be innocent of murder.'

ROME AND ITS ITALIAN NEIGHBOURS

The Latins inhabited ancient Latium, which was conquered by Rome by 300 BC. Rome is shown as dominant over Latium in the treaty between Rome and Carthage in 509 (doc. 4.1). Rebellion by the Latins led to a struggle which ended with the Latin defeat at the battle of Lake Regillus (499 or 496).

1.27 Dionysius of Halicarnassus 6.95.1–3: The 'treaty of Cassius', 493 BC

Following the 'first secession' of the plebeians, Spurius Cassius Vecellinus signed a treaty in 493 and established a defensive military alliance between Rome and the Latin cities.

1 At the same time a new treaty of peace and friendship was made on oath with all the Latin cities, since they had not tried to stir up trouble during the revolt, had been openly pleased at the people's return (from secession), and had appeared to be prompt in coming to the assistance of the Romans against the rebels. **2** The provisions of the treaty were as follows: 'Let there be peace between the Romans and all the Latin cities as long as heaven and earth remain in the same position; let them neither make war on each other, nor call in enemies from elsewhere, nor grant safe passage to those who make war, but let them assist the other, when attacked, with all their might, and let each have an equal share of the spoils and booty taken in their joint wars; let suits relating to private contracts be judged within ten days and in the place where the contract was made. And let it not be permitted to add anything to or take anything from this treaty except with the consent of both the Romans and all the Latins.' **3** This was the treaty which the Romans and the Latins made with each other, and which was confirmed by their oaths over sacrificial victims.

1.28 Dionysius of Halicarnassus 9.59.3–5: Treaty of alliance with the Aequi, 467 BC

According to Livy (6.12) the Aequi's numbers were small, but they had taken over part of the Alban Mount, perhaps in 484 BC, and were not driven back until 431, though Cincinnatus supposedly crushed them in 458 (cf. docs 2.13–14). They were defeated and Romanised at the end of the fourth century. Fabius is Q. Fabius Vibulanus.

3 The Aequi sent ambassadors to Fabius to negotiate a reconciliation and friendship even before they were forced to do so by the destruction of their army or capture of their towns. **4** The consul exacted from them two months' supplies for his army, two tunics for each man, six months' pay, and anything else urgently needed, and concluded a truce with them till they could go to Rome and obtain peace terms from the senate. However, when the senate learnt of this, it gave Fabius full powers to make peace with the Aequi on whatever terms he should prefer. **5** After this, as a result of the consul's arbitration, the two people made an alliance, on these conditions: that the Aequi should be subject to the Romans while still possessing their cities and territories; and that they should not have to send anything to the Romans except troops, when ordered, to be maintained at their own expense.

THE ORIGINS OF THE TWELVE TABLES

In 451 BC, supposedly as a result of popular agitation over the control of the law by patricians and priests, normal magistracies were suspended and ten patricians with consular powers (a decemvirate: board of ten men) were appointed to draw up legal statutes in writing. After this decemvirate had codified ten tables, a second decemvirate (said to have been half patrician, half plebeian) was appointed for 450 and compiled two more tables, including a ban on marriages between patricians and plebeians; they attempted to remain in power for 449 but were deposed and normal government resumed.

1.29 Dionysius of Halicarnassus 10.1.1–4: Dissatisfaction within Rome

1 Publius Volumnius and Servius Sulpicius Camerinus were elected as consuls at Rome (461 BC). They led out no army either to inflict punishment on those who had injured the Romans or their allies or to protect their possessions; they paid attention to evils within Rome, to prevent the people uniting against the senate and committing some horrendous deed. **2** For they were being roused up again by the tribunes and told that the best political institution for free men was equal rights, and they wanted private and public business to be administered according to laws. For there was not as yet among the Romans equality either of laws or of rights, nor had all their rules of justice been put in writing; but, initially, their kings had laid down judgements for those who asked for it, and whatever they decreed was law . . . **4** A few decisions were kept in sacred books and had the force of laws, but only the patricians were aware of these because they spent their time in the city, while the majority of people were either merchants or farmers and came to the capital to the markets at intervals of many days, and were still unacquainted with them.

1.30 Livy *History of Rome* 3.32.5–7: The creation of the decemvirate

5 The next consuls were Gaius Menenius and Publius Sestius Capitolinus. In this year again (452 BC) there was no foreign war; disturbances, however, sprang up at home. **6** The legates had now returned with the Athenian laws. For that reason the tribunes demanded more insistently that a start should finally be made towards the codification of laws. It was decided to create decemvirs, subject to no appeal, and for there to be no other magistrates for that year. **7** Whether plebeians should be members of the decemvirate was a matter of dispute for some time; finally they gave in to the patricians, with the proviso that the Icilian law about the Aventine (i.e., the law establishing the tribunate: 2.33.1) and the other sacred laws should not be abolished.

1.31 Dionysius of Halicarnassus 10.55.4–5, 56.6–7: The 'codification' of the law

55.4 The motion carried was that of the consuls-designate and was put forward by Appius Claudius, who was the first to be called on: that ten of the most distinguished senators be elected; that these should govern for a year from the day of their appointment, having the same authority over everything to do with Rome as the consuls, and, before them, the kings had possessed; that all the other magistracies be abolished while the decemvirs were in charge of government; **5** that these men select out of ancestral customs and the Greek laws which the envoys brought back those best and appropriate for the Romans' city and codify them in the form of laws; that what was decided by the decemvirs, if the senate approved and the people ratified it, should be valid for all time, and all magistrates in the future should decide private contracts and administer public affairs in accordance with these laws. . . .

56.6 When they were satisfied with what they had drawn up, they first assembled the senate and, when no new objection was made to the laws, had them pass a preliminary decree about them. They then summoned the people to the centuriate assembly (comitia centuriata) and, once the pontiffs, augurs and other priests present had conducted the rites according to custom, distributed the votes to the centuries. **7** When the people too had ratified the laws, they had them inscribed on bronze tablets and placed them in sequence in the forum, selecting the most conspicuous spot.

THE XII TABLES

Crawford *Statutes* no. 40. The primary areas of concern in the XII Tables are family law, marriage and divorce; assault and injuries against person or property; inheritance and ownership; debt, slavery and nexum (debt-slavery). While in the Republic the laws were learnt by heart by schoolchildren, they became increasingly obsolete.

1.32 Table 1: Rules for a trial

In a trial, the action began with the defendant being summoned to appear before the magistrate, by force if necessary. **1.1–3**: the rights and duties of the plaintiff against a defendant; **1.13–15**: penalties for 'iniuria', bodily harm or damage to property and theft. The XII Tables laid down monetary penalties for physical assault.

1.1 If he (anyone) summons him (the defendant) to court, he shall go. If he does not go, he (the plaintiff) shall call a witness; then he shall take him. **2** If he (the defendant) delays or drags his feet, he (the plaintiff) shall lay hand on him. **3** If there is sickness or age, he (the plaintiff) shall provide a yoked beast of burden; if he does not wish to, he should not prepare a carriage. **7** If they do not agree, they are to present their case in the comitium or forum before midday. They are to finish bringing action together, both being present . . .

13 If he has maimed a part (of a body), unless he settles it with him, there is to be retaliation in kind. **14** If he has broken a bone of a free man, 300 (asses), if of a slave 150 are to be the penalty. **15** If he do (other) injury ?to another? (i.e., not as serious as the injury above), 25 (asses) are to be the penalty. **16** If he has felled a productive tree, 25 (asses) are to be the penalty. **17** If he committed theft by night and he killed him, he shall have been lawfully killed. **19** If the theft is manifest, if he does not settle, he (the magistrate) shall flog him and hand him over. If a slave, he is to flog him and throw him from the (Tarpeian) rock. If underage, he is to flog him and the thief is to repair the damage.

1.33 Table 3.1–4, 3.6: Debt law

Those judged liable for an unpaid debt had 30 days in which to find the money. (The 30 days' delay might have applied to all kinds of cases, not just debt.) They were then summoned to the praetor's court. There was a chance of compromising, presumably by the debtors choosing to become nexi ('bondsmen'; sing.: nexus) and paying off their debt by working for their creditor. If no compromise was reached after the third market-day on which their debt was announced, they suffered capital punishment or were sold into slavery 'across the Tiber', i.e., in Etruscan territory (3.5). Debt-slavery, or nexum, was obviously an important issue in the mid-fifth century; cf. doc. 1.53.

3.1 In respect of an admitted sum (of debt) and judgement, 30 days (period of grace) shall be allowed. **2** After that there shall be laying on of a hand. **3** He (the plaintiff) shall bring him into court. Unless he does what has been judged, or someone acts as his protector in court, he (the plaintiff) shall take him with him. He is to bind him with rope or shackles for the feet. He shall bind him with not more than 15 pounds, or less if he wishes. **4** If he (the defendant) wishes, he is to live on his own. If he does not live on his own, he who shall have him bound shall give him a pound of spelt for each day; if he wishes he is to give more. 5 On three successive market-days, he shall produce him in the comitium. **6** Unless he settles, on the third market-day they (the creditors) shall cut (?his property?) into pieces. If they should have cut more or less, it shall be without penalty. **7** If he (the plaintiff) wishes, he is to sell him abroad, beyond the Tiber.

1.34 Table 4: Family law

Fathers had the right to accept newborn children into the household ('to pick them up') or to expose them. It appears here that a father could sell his son into slavery, and, if freed by the buyer, the son was returned to his father's control (patria potestas); the son could be sold into nexum a maximum of three times.

4.1 If he is born deformed, and he does not pick him up, it is without liability.
4.2 If a father sells his son three times, the son shall be free from his father.

1.35 Table 5: Women and lunatics

Plutarch *Numa* 10.3 ascribes the Vestals' freedom from tutelage to Numa; Vestals could also make wills. Paternal kinsmen (agnates) or clansmen (gentiles) administered the property of a madman or spendthrift.

5.1 A Vestal Virgin is to be free of guardianship (tutela).
5.7 If there be a madman ?or spendthrift?, power in respect of him and his familia (estate) is to belong to his agnates and gentiles.

1.36 Table 5: Inheritance

These clauses concern intestate succession (i.e., where the deceased had not made a will). Blood relations of both sexes would normally inherit if the head of a family died intestate, and a wife in her husband's control (in manu: 'in his hand') would rank equally with his sons and daughters; cf. doc. 7.1.

5.4 If he dies intestate and has no heir of his own (suus heres), the nearest agnate shall have possession of the estate (familia) ?and goods?
5.5 If there is no agnate, the clansmen (gentiles) shall have the estate and goods.

1.37 Table 5.8, 8.10: Freedmen and patrons

Guardianship of freedmen belonged to their patron (the ex-owner), like the right of inheritance if the freedman died intestate or without an heir. Presumably otherwise freedmen had the right of making wills and clearly they could own property.

5.8 If a freedman (dies intestate) . . . from that familia . . . to that familia.
8.10 If a patron shall have wronged his client, he must be forfeited (sacer).

1.38 Tables 6 and 7: Property and possession of land

The term res mancipi included land, slaves and some farm animals; mancipatio was a formal act of conveyance, requiring five witnesses and a formal weighing out of bronze; cf. doc. 7.4. Other items, res nec mancipi, were transferred by physical delivery (traditio). Usucapio was the right of ownership after a period of use, for example of a parcel of land. Usucapio of movable things could be completed in a year, but for an estate and buildings it took two years. **6.5**: Guardianship of a woman could be transferred by usucapio, and a woman who remained married for a year was transferred by the year's ownership (usus) into the estate of her husband; to avoid coming into her husband's control, a woman had to be absent for three nights a year; cf. doc. 7.10.

6.1 When he shall perform nexum (bond) and mancipium (formal purchase), as he has proclaimed by word of mouth, so shall it be legal. **1b** (Ulpian *Tit.* 2.4)

A person who has been made a free man under this condition, that he should give 10,000 pieces to the heir, even if he has been legally transferred by the heir, shall achieve his liberty by giving the money to the purchaser; and the Law of the Twelve Tables lays this down. **3** For a piece of land, right of possession (auctoritas) (is to be) two years for other things it is to be one year. **4** Against a foreigner right of possession is to be perpetual. **5** If she is absent three nights in a year . . . **6** He is not to detach from its joint a beam from a house or a vineyard . . . **7.9** If a tree overhangs someone's land, he is to cut it back more than 15 feet.

1.39 Table 8: Animal damage

8.2 If a quadruped cause loss, unless he repair it he is to give it up for the damage.

1.40 Table 8: Slander, libel and witchcraft

8.1: Cic. *Rep.* 4.12: the Tables laid down a capital penalty for anyone who 'sang or composed a song, such as caused dishonour or disgrace to another person'; singing or chanting against someone might imply witchcraft (cf. doc. 3.69).

8.1 Whoever casts an evil spell . . . or whoever sings or composes a spell . . .
8.4 Whoever has bewitched crops . . . or has enticed someone else's harvest . . .

1.41 Table 8: Capital crimes: damaging crops, perjury and arson

Damage to crops, perjury and arson were all capital offences. **8.5**: the penalty for secretly cutting crops at night was execution, with the offender's property confiscated to Ceres. **8.6**: anyone who deliberately burnt a building or a heap of corn placed next to a house was to be bound, flogged and put to death by fire; if it was an accident, he was to repair the damage. **8.13**: the penalty for unintentional homicide.

8.5 If he has grazed or cut a crop by night, he is to be hanged for Ceres. If he is underage, he (the magistrate) is to flog (him) and he is to settle for double penalty.
6 If he shall have burnt a building or a heap of corn placed near ?a house?, bound and beaten (he is to be killed) by fire. If by chance . . . , he is to repair the damage.
12 If he shall have given false evidence, he (the magistrate) shall throw (him) from the (Tarpeian) rock.
13 If a weapon has escaped his hand rather than that he has thrown it, a ram is to be offered as a substitute.

1.42 Table 8: Moneylending and interest

Thieves paid double the amount they stole. Lending money at interest was a long-standing problem for the city. The XII Tables were the first to establish that no one should charge interest of more than one-twelfth, i.e., 1 per cent a month.

8.18 Our ancestors followed this (principle) and laid it down in their laws that a thief is condemned for double, the usurer for quadruple (the amount).

1.43 Table 10: Sacred law

No burial or cremation was allowed in the city because of the danger of fire and pollution (cf. doc. 3.78); there were also sumptuary regulations about burials, concerning expenses and mourners. **10.7**: garlands to honour games winners or valour were allowed at funerals; **10.8**: explains that gold on the corpse is forbidden, except for gold dental work.

10.1 He is not to bury or burn a dead man in the city. **2** He is not to do more than this; he is not to smooth the pyre with a trowel. **3** . . . three shawls, a small purple tunic . . . ten flute-players . . . **4** Women are not to tear their cheeks or hold a wake on account of the funeral. **5** He is not to collect the bones of a dead man to hold a funeral later (i.e., part of the dead body is not to be preserved for another ceremony). **7** Whoever wins a crown himself or his family, or it be given to him for courage, and it is placed on him or his parent when dead, it is to be without liability. **8** . . . nor is he to add gold, but whoever has teeth joined with gold, and if he should bury or burn it with him, it is without liability.

THE SUPPLEMENTARY TABLES

1.44 Dionysius of Halicarnassus 10.58.1–4, 60.5–6: The second decemvirate, 450 BC

Appius is Appius Claudius Crassinus Inregillensis Sabinus (cos. 471), head of the commission. The fall of the decemvirate and the second secession was supposedly caused by Appius' attempted seduction of the beautiful young girl Verginia: the decemvirs thereupon committed suicide or went into exile.

58.1 Following a lengthy debate (in the senate), the view of those who preferred electing a decemvirate again to govern the state prevailed. For not only was their codification of laws clearly unfinished, in as much as it had been compiled in a short period, but in the case of the laws which had already been ratified a magistracy with absolute powers seemed essential so that, whether willingly or unwillingly, people should observe them. The main reason, however, which led them to choose the decemvirate was the disbanding of the tribunes, which they all desired more than anything . . .

3 On this occasion Appius, who was the leading member of the decemvirate, was greatly praised by everyone, and the whole mob of plebeians wanted to keep him in office, as they considered that no one else would govern better . . . **4** So he was again chosen in the centuriate assembly as a law-giver, for the second time; chosen along with him were Quintus Fabius, surnamed Vibulanus, who had been three times consul and was a man without reproach up to that time and possessed of every good quality. From among the other patricians, whom Appius favoured, Marcus Cornelius, Marcus Sergius, Lucius Minucius, Titus Antonius and Manius

Rabuleius were elected, men of no particular distinction; and, from among the plebeians, Quintus Poetelius, Caeso Duilius and Spurius Oppius. For these too were admitted by Appius as colleagues to flatter the plebeians, and he stated that since there was one magistracy governing everyone it was fair that the people should have some share in it . . .

60.5 Appius and his colleagues had the other laws inscribed on two tablets and added them to those published before. Among these new laws was this one, that it was not legal for the patricians to intermarry with the plebeians – a law, in my view, made simply to prevent the two orders from uniting in harmony once mingled by intermarriages and family connections. **6** And when the time for the election of magistrates came round, the decemvirs said goodbye to both the ancestral customs and the newly written laws, and remained in the same magistracy without putting it to the vote by either senate or people.

1.45 Tables 11–12: A ban on intermarriage

In the supplementary laws of 449 BC, intermarriage (connubium) between patricians and plebeians was disallowed, which was clearly an innovation. This was repealed shortly afterwards, in 445, by the *lex Canuleia*. If a slave committed a crime, the action lay against his master; should a slave be injured, his master was compensated (cf. doc. 1.32).

11.1 There is not to be connubium with the plebs.
12.2 If a slave commit theft or cause damage, he is to be given for the damage.

THE CONFLICT OF THE ORDERS CONTINUES

One of the most important issues in the Conflict of the Orders was the opening up to plebeians of the important magistracies, especially the consulship, as well as the priesthoods. Legislation concerning the consulship was passed (supposedly) in 367 BC (doc. 1.48) and in 342 (when both consulships were open to plebeians: doc. 1.50); despite Livy, the first consular college of two plebeians was in 172, and pairs of patrician consuls are recorded in 355, 354, 353, 351, 349 and 343.

1.46 Livy *History of Rome* 3.55.1–7, 13–15: The Valerio–Horatian laws, 449 BC

Cf. Dion. Hal. 11.45. The Valerio–Horatian laws were supposedly passed in response to dissatisfaction felt with the second decemvirate. The law imposing plebiscites on the whole people was in fact the *lex Hortensia* of 287 BC: these laws may have validated plebiscites which had senatorial sanction.

1 They then, through an interrex, elected Lucius Valerius and Marcus Horatius as consuls (499 BC), who at once took up their magistracies. Their consulship favoured the people's cause without wronging the patricians in any way, although it still managed to offend them; **2** for whatever protected the liberty of the plebs was seen as detracting from their own powers. **3** First of all, since it was still an open question whether patricians were legally bound by plebiscites, they passed a law in the comitia centuriata that whatever the people should lay down in the tribal assembly should be binding on the people; this law furnished the tribunes' proposals (rogationes) with a very sharp weapon indeed. **4** Secondly, they not only restored a consular law about the appeal (provocatio), the unique safeguard of liberty which had been overturned by the power of the decemvirate, but even protected it for the future by enacting a new inviolable law, **5** that no one should appoint any magistrate without appeal; if anyone should do so, he might be put to death without violating law or religion, and this homicide would not be a capital crime. **6** And now they had fortified the plebs sufficiently through the right of appeal, on the one hand, and the tribunician help, on the other, they also revived for the benefit of the tribunes themselves the consideration of their sacrosanct status, a matter that had come to be almost forgotten, by bringing back certain rites which had lapsed for a considerable period; **7** and they made them inviolate both on the grounds of religion and also by a law, which ordained that, should any person harm the tribunes of the plebs, (plebeian) aediles or decemviral judges, his head would be forfeit to Jupiter and his household possessions be put up for sale at the temple of Ceres, Liber and Libera . . . **13** These were the consular laws. The same consuls also inaugurated the practice whereby senatorial decrees were handed over to the aediles of the plebs at the temple of Ceres, for previously these were often suppressed or falsified at the discretion of the consuls. **14** A tribune of the plebs, Marcus Duillius, then proposed to the plebs, and they decreed, that anyone who left the plebs without tribunes, and anyone who appointed a magistrate without appeal, should be scourged and beheaded. **15** None of these measures were opposed by the patricians (though they were not in favour of them), because as yet no one in particular was being targeted.

1.47 Livy *History of Rome* 4.1.1–3, 6.1–11: The Canuleian Laws, 445 BC

Cf. Dion. Hal. 11.53. Gaius Canuleius was tribune of the plebs in 445; his law repealed that of the second decemvirate which banned patrician–plebeian marriages. This is the first recorded tribunician veto of a decree of the senate. A contio was an official, non-voting assembly of the people, summoned by a magistrate or priest.

1.1 Marcus Genucius and Gaius Curtius succeeded these (Titus Quinctius Capitolinus and Agrippa Furius) as consuls. It was a troubled year both at home and abroad. For, when it began, Gaius Canuleius, a tribune of the plebs, put forward a proposal concerning the intermarriage of patricians and plebeians, **2** which the patricians considered would contaminate their blood and mix up the proper classification of the gentes (clans), while a suggestion initially put forward hesitantly by the tribunes, that it should be permissible for one of the consuls to be a plebeian, later went so far that nine tribunes put forward a proposal **3** that the people should have the power to elect consuls of their choice, whether from the plebs or the patricians . . . **6.1** When the consuls had joined the meeting (contio) and formal speeches had been succeeded by bickering, the tribune asked why a plebeian should not be chosen as consul. **2** Curtius replied, perhaps truthfully, yet for the present not very profitably, 'Because no plebeian has the auspices, and that was the reason why the decemvirs prohibited intermarriage, in case the auspices be disturbed by the ill-defined status of the offspring of such intermarriage.' **3** At this the plebs blazed up with extreme indignation, at the suggestion that they were not allowed to take auspices, as if they were detestable to the immortal gods; nor did the controversy end – for the plebs had found a zealous promoter in the tribune and rivalled him themselves in perseverance – until the patricians were finally overcome and allowed the law about intermarriage to be carried, **4** because they thought that the tribunes would either entirely abandon their struggle for plebeian consuls or put it aside until after the war, and that, in the meantime, the plebs would be satisfied with the right to intermarry and be prepared for the levy . . . **6** Since the consuls were unable to achieve anything through the senate while the tribunes interposed their veto, they privately held councils of their leading men. It was obvious that they would have to give in to being defeated by either the enemy or their own citizens. **7** Of all the consulars, Valerius and Horatius were the only ones who did not take part in these councils. Gaius Claudius' view was that they should arm the consuls against the tribunes; the Quinctii, both Cincinnatus and Capitolinus, were averse both to bloodshed and to harming those whom they had accepted as being sacrosanct in the treaty they had struck with the plebs. **8** The outcome of these deliberations was that they allowed military tribunes with consular powers to be elected indiscriminately from among the patricians and plebs but made no alteration in the consular elections; with this, both tribunes and plebs were satisfied. **9** An election was called to elect three tribunes with consular powers . . . **11** The result of this election demonstrated how differently people behave when struggling for liberty and status and when discord is put aside and their judgement unbiased; for the people elected all the (consular) tribunes from patricians, satisfied that the plebeians had been allowed to stand for election.

1.48 Livy *History of Rome* 6.35.1–5: The Licinio–Sextian laws, 367 BC

L. Sextius Sextinus Lateranus (cos. 366) and C. Licinius Stolo (cos. 364 or 361), as tribunes in 367 (they had reputedly been in office since 376), are recorded as having passed a package of laws in the interests of the plebeians, many of whom had been reduced to debt-slavery: interest paid on a debt should be deducted from the principal; at least one of the consuls was to be chosen from the plebs; and individual holdings of ager publicus (state land) should be limited to 500 iugera (a standard smallholding was 7 iugera).

1 A chance for innovation was provided by the immense weight of debt, an evil which the plebs had no hope of lifting except by positioning their representatives in the highest magistracies: their view was that they had to get ready to plan for this; **2** with effort and toil the plebeians had got to the stage where, if they continued their struggles, they could reach the top and rival the patricians in honours as much as in merit. **3** For the moment, it was agreed that they should have tribunes of the plebs, through which office they might be able to open up a way to the other magistracies. **4** Gaius Licinius and Lucius Sextius were elected and proposed all their laws to the detriment of the patricians and for the advantage of the plebs – one concerning debt, that what had been paid back as interest should be deducted from the original, while the remainder should be paid back in equal instalments over three years. **5** Another limited the possession of land, forbidding anyone from holding more than 500 iugera. A third abolished the election of military tribunes and provided that one of the consuls, at least, should be elected from the plebs.

1.49 Livy *History of Rome* 6.42.9–14: The first plebeian consul

Sextius and Licinius had been tribunes ten times: the plebeian Sextius was elected consul for 366 BC as a 'new man'. According to Livy (7.1.4), the patricians purposely deferred all business to avoid anything being achieved by a plebeian consul. When in 362 the first plebeian consul to lead an army under his own auspices, Genucius, was ambushed and killed by the Hernici, the patricians took this as a sign of divine displeasure. The Gauls were driven off by M. Furius Camillus; for the Great Games, see doc. 2.70.

9 Camillus had hardly put an end to the war when he was faced by even more violent conflict at home, and after immense struggles the dictator and senate were beaten, the tribunes' proposals were adopted, and consular elections were held, against the wishes of the nobles, in which Lucius Sextius was made the first plebeian consul. **10** Not even this put an end to the disputes. The patricians refused to ratify the election, which almost brought about a secession of the plebs and threatened other terrible manifestations of civil strife, **11** when finally through the dictator the unrest was allayed by compromise: the nobles gave way to the plebs on the question of the plebeian consul, and the plebs conceded to the nobles that one praetor should be elected from the patricians to administer justice in the city. **12** So, after long rivalry, the orders were finally reconciled. The senate decided that this was a fitting occasion, and appropriate if ever any occasion was, to honour the immortal gods by a celebration of the Great Games, and an extra day was added to the normal three. **13** When the people's aediles refused this additional burden, the young patricians cried out that they would willingly take it on in honour of the gods. **14** They were thanked by the entire people, and the senate decreed that the dictator should propose the election of two aediles (later the curule aediles) from the patricians and that the senate should ratify all the elections of that year.

1.50 Livy *History of Rome* 7.42.1–3, 7: The leges Genuciae, 342 BC

This legislation, which included further concessions from the patricians, reputedly followed an army mutiny in 342 BC. The first year in which both consuls were plebeian was actually 172; possibly Lucius Genucius legislated as tribune that one of the consuls had to be plebeian.

1 In addition to these events, I find in certain writers that Lucius Genucius, a tribune of the plebs, brought a proposal before the plebs that lending money at interest should not be permitted; **2** also that in other plebiscites it was laid down that no one should hold the same magistracy twice within ten years, nor two magistracies in the same year, and that it should be permissible for both consuls to be chosen from the plebs. If all these concessions were made to the plebs, it seems that the revolt had considerable impact. **3** It is recorded in other annals that Valerius (M. Valerius Maximus Corvus) was not made dictator, but that the whole affair was managed through the consuls, and that it was not before they came to Rome but at Rome itself that the enormous number of conspirators were frightened into taking up arms; . . . . **7** On no single point do ancient historians agree except on their having been a revolt and that it was settled.

1.51 Livy *History of Rome* 8.12.14–17: A radical dictator, 339 BC

Quintus Publilius Philo was consul in 339, 327, 320 and 315 BC; first plebeian praetor in 336 (doc. 1.52); censor in 332; and dictator in 339. The proposal that plebiscites should be binding on the whole people duplicates the *lex Hortensia* of 287 and should probably not be accepted.

14 The dictatorship of Publilius was a popular one, both for his accusatory speeches against the senators and because he brought in three laws extremely favourable to the plebs and damaging to the nobility: **15** one, that plebiscites were to be binding on all the Quirites (Roman citizens); a second, that the senate should ratify measures proposed at the comitia centuriata before the beginning of voting; **16** and a third, that at least one censor should be chosen from the plebs, since they had already gone so far as to allow both to be plebeian. **17** The senators considered that the mischief done at home in that year by the consuls and dictator outweighed the increase in empire which resulted from their victory and management of campaigns away from home.

1.52 Livy *History of Rome* 8.15.9: The first plebeian praetor, 336 BC

Quintus Publilius Philo, as a plebeian, was opposed by the consul, C. Sulpicius Longus (cos. 337), but not by the senate.

In the same year Quintus Publilius Philo was made praetor, the first plebeian to be so, though Sulpicius the consul opposed his election and refused to receive votes for him. The senate, however, since it had failed in achieving this for the highest magistracies, was less stubborn with regard to the praetorship.

1.53 Livy *History of Rome* 8.28.1–2, 5–8: No imprisonment for debt, 326 BC

The date of this is disputed, but it probably belongs to 326 BC. This treatment of a young man inflamed the people, and the consuls brought a proposal to the people that none should be confined in shackles or in the stocks except those guilty of some crime. From now on, by law, only a debtor's goods could be seized, not his person.

1 In that year it was as if the liberty of the Roman plebs had a fresh start, for men were no longer to be imprisoned for debt; this change in the law was brought about by the equally outrageous lust and inhumanity of a single moneylender. **2** This was Lucius Papirius, whose mind, when Gaius Publilius gave himself up to him as a debt-bondsman (nexus) for his father's debt, was inflamed to lust and outrage by his youth and beauty, though they might well have roused his compassion . . . **5** Lacerated with whip-marks, the youth rushed into the street, crying out against the moneylender's lust and inhumanity, **6** at which an immense mob of people, infuriated by compassion for his youth and anger at his treatment, as well as by consideration for their own status and that of their children, flocked into the forum and from there *en masse* into the senate house; **7** the consuls were compelled by this unexpected uproar to convene the senate, and the mob threw themselves at the feet of each of the senators as they entered the senate house, pointing to the youth's scourged back. **8** On that day, due to the unbridled wrongdoing of one man, the oppressive shackles of credit were overthrown, and the consuls were instructed to put a motion before the people that no one should be confined in shackles or fetters, apart from those who had been guilty of some offence and were awaiting punishment.

1.54 Livy *History of Rome* 9.33.3–6, 34.26: Appius Claudius as censor

Appius Claudius Caecus (the 'Blind') was censor in 312 BC (cos. 307 and 296; praetor 295). He commissioned, as censor, the construction of the Appian Way and Appia aqueduct (docs 2.4, 6). In 300 he opposed the inclusion of plebeians in the major priestly colleges. In this episode he refuses to resign after his 18 months as censor.

33.3 For many years now there had been no struggles between the patrician magistrates and the tribunes, when a dispute arose from that family which appeared destined to contend with the tribunes and plebs. **4** The censor, Appius Claudius, when the 18 months laid down by the Aemilian law as the term of the censorship had expired, and although his colleague Gaius Plautius had retired, could by no means be made to step down. **5** It was Publius Sempronius, a tribune of the plebs, who started proceedings to limit the censorship to its legal period, an action no less just than popular and as welcome to every aristocrat as to the common people. **6** He repeatedly quoted the Aemilian law and praised its promoter, the dictator Mamercus Aemilius (434 BC: Livy 4.24.5–6), for restricting the censorship, which had until then been held for five years and was proving itself tyrannical on account of the long period its authority lasted, to a limit of a year and a half . . . **34.26** After making all these accusations, he ordered the censor to be seized and led off to prison. Six tribunes approved their colleague's action, while three protected Appius on his appeal, and he continued as sole censor despite his extreme unpopularity with all classes.

1.55 Livy *History of Rome* 9.46.1–15: A novus homo in 304 BC

This passage demonstrates the possibility of social mobility in late fourth-century Rome and the general intransigence of nobles towards outsiders (see docs 2.45–46; 7.74). A paid bureaucrat (in this case an apparitor: a high-ranking salaried official attendant on magistrates) could not become a magistrate himself unless he resigned his post. The night watch (tresviri capitals) was not regularly instituted until c. 290–287.

1 In the same year Gnaeus Flavius, son of Gnaeus, a government clerk, who had been born in humble circumstances (his father being a freedman) but who was still a shrewd and eloquent man, was curule aedile. **2** I find in certain annals that, when he was in attendance upon the aediles and saw that the tribes would elect him aedile had not his candidature been unacceptable because he was acting as recorder, he put away his writing-tablet and swore that he would keep no record; **3** however, Licinius Macer alleges that he had ceased being a clerk some time before this, having already been a tribune and a triumvir, once on a commission in charge of the night watch and once in the foundation of a colony. **4** In any case, there is no argument about the obstinacy with which he battled with the nobles who despised his lowly birth; **5** he published the civil law, which had been put away in the secret archives of the pontiffs, and posted up the official calendar (the fasti) on white notice-boards around the forum for people to know when they could bring a legal action; **6** he dedicated a temple of Concord in the precinct of Vulcan, to the great resentment of the nobles; and Cornelius Barbatus, the pontifex maximus, was forced by the unanimous wish of the people to dictate the formula (of dedication) to him, although he insisted that by ancestral custom no one except a consul or imperator could dedicate a temple. **7** As a result, in accordance with a resolution of the senate, a measure was passed by the people that no one could dedicate a temple or altar without the authorisation of the senate or of a majority of the tribunes of the plebs. **8** I will relate an incident, not memorable in itself, except as evidence of the way the plebs asserted their liberty against the arrogance of the nobles. **9** Flavius had come to visit a colleague who was sick, and the young nobles who were sitting by the bed were united in their resolution not to rise to greet him, so he ordered his curule chair to be brought in and from his official seat gazed at his enemies, who were overpowered with jealous resentment. . . .

12 So great was the indignation over the election of Flavius that many of the nobles put aside their gold rings and military decorations. **13** From that time the citizens were divided into two parties – the honest men, who supported and upheld right principles, had one point of view, and the rabble (factio) of the forum another, **14** until Quintus Fabius (Maximus Rullianus) and Publius Decius (Mus) became censors (304 BC) and Fabius, partly for the sake of harmony, partly so that the elections might not fall into the hands of the base-born element, separated out all the forum mob and threw it into four tribes, which he called the urban tribes. **15** It is said that this was so gratefully received that by this regulation of the orders he gained the surname of Maximus, which all his many victories had been insufficient to win him.

1.56 Livy *History of Rome* 10.6.3–11: Priesthoods open to plebeians, 300 BC

Quintus Ogulnius Gallus (cos. 269), as tribune in 300, carried a law that positions in the two major priestly colleges should be shared between patricians and plebeians. From this point, four of the eight pontiffs and five of the nine augurs were plebeians. The first plebeian pontifex maximus was in c. 254.

3 However, so that the tranquillity (caused by the sending out of colonies) might not be universal, dissension was stirred up among the leading citizens, patricians and plebeians, by the tribunes of the plebs Quintus and Gnaeus Ogulnius, **4** who had taken every opportunity of criticising the senators to the plebs and, when all their other attempts had been frustrated, brought forward a course of action by which they would arouse not just the lowest of the plebeians but their very leaders – **5** those who had won consulships and triumphs, and who had lacked no official positions except the priesthoods, which were not yet open to everyone. **6** They therefore proposed that, since there were at that time four augurs and four pontiffs, and it was desired to increase the number of priests, four pontiffs and five augurs should be added to them, all taken from the plebs . . . **9** But since these were to be chosen from the plebs, the senators were as upset by the proposal as they had been when they saw the consulship thrown open. **10** They pretended that it was more the gods' concern than their own: that the gods would see to it that their rites were not polluted; for their part, they hoped only that no calamity should come upon the state. **11** But they put up little resistance, being now accustomed to being worsted in conflicts of this kind.

1.57 Livy *Periochae* 11: The final secession, 287 BC

Quintus Hortensius, a plebeian, was made dictator to solve the problem of the plebs' final secession to the Janiculum, caused by a debt crisis in 287.

The plebeians, after serious and lengthy dissension, seceded to the Janiculum Hill on account of their debts. They were brought back from there by the dictator Q. Hortensius, who died during his magistracy.

1.58 Gellius *Attic Nights* 15.27.4: The Hortensian law, 287 BC

From this point, plebiscites in the tribal assembly had the force of law.

In the same book of Laelius Felix (*To Quintus Mucius*), it is written: . . . 'Tribunes, however, do not summon the patricians or consult them on any question. And so, measures which are passed on the proposals of tribunes of the plebs are not properly called "laws" but "plebiscites", and these decrees were not binding on patricians until Quintus Hortensius as dictator brought in a law that whatever the plebs decided upon should be binding on all Quirites.'

POLYBIUS ON THE ROMAN CONSTITUTION

Polybius sees Rome as a mixed constitution, blending monarchy, aristocracy and democracy. He has frequently been criticised for his attempt to analyse Roman institutions on the model of Greek ones and for misunderstanding the political situation at Rome. He is here describing political institutions at their most perfect – supposedly, the time of the Second Punic War – though inevitably his depiction is coloured by the practices of his own time: 'From the crossing of Xerxes into Greece . . . and for 30 years after that event it (the constitution) was continually modified detail by detail, being at its best and most perfect at the time of the Hannibalic war . . . ' (6.11.1).

1.59 Polybius *Histories* 6.12.1–16.5: The Roman Constitution

(i) The consuls

12.1 The consuls, before leading out the legions, remain in Rome and have supreme authority over all public affairs. **2** All the other magistrates are subordinate to them and bound to obey them except the tribunes, and they present foreign embassies to the senate. **3** In addition to these duties, they refer urgent matters to the senate for discussion and carry out all the administrative details of the senate's decrees. **4** Also, as far as concerns all affairs of state administered by the people, it is their duty to supervise these and summon assemblies, bring forward measures, and preside over the execution of the people's decrees. **5** As regards preparation for war, and management of operations in the field generally, their authority is almost absolute. **6** They are permitted to make whatever demands on the allies they think appropriate, appoint military tribunes, and levy soldiers and select the most suitable. **7** In addition, they have the power to punish anyone they wish under their command while in the field; **8** and they have the authority to spend whatever amount they decide on from the public funds, being accompanied by a quaestor who readily carries out all their instructions. **9** So one could reasonably say, looking just at this part (of the constitution), that it is purely a monarchy or kingship.

(ii) The senate

13.1 To pass on to the senate, first of all it has control of the treasury and regulates all revenue and expenditure. **2** For the quaestors are not allowed to disburse payments on any given projects without a decree of the senate, with the exception of payments made to the consuls; **3** the senate even controls the item of expenditure which is far more important and greater than all the others, that which the censors expend every five years on the restoration and construction of public works, and it makes a grant to the censors for this purpose. **4** Similarly, any crimes committed in Italy which require public investigation, such as treason, conspiracy, poisoning and assassination, are under the jurisdiction of the senate. **5** Furthermore, if any private person or community in Italy requires arbitration or censure or help or protection, the senate deals with all these matters. **6** Again, if any embassy has to be sent outside Italy to settle differences, or offer advice, or indeed impose demands, or receive submission, or declare war, this is also the responsibility of the senate. **7** Similarly, when embassies arrive in Rome, all the details of how they should be received and what answer should be given them are handled by the senate and are in no way the concern of the people. **8** As a result, to anyone residing in Rome in the absence of the consuls, the constitution appears totally aristocratic; **9** this is the belief of many of the Greeks and also of the kings, as the senate handles almost all the business which concerns them.

(iii) The people

14.1 After this one might reasonably inquire what part in the constitution is left for the people? . . . **3** Nevertheless, there is a role left for the people too, and a very important one. **4** For the people alone in the state have the power to award honours and punishments (the control of elections and the law-courts), which alone hold together kingdoms and states and all human society generally . . . **6** The people, then, frequently judge cases where the offence is punishable by a fine, and particularly when the accused have held the most distinguished offices; the people alone can try a capital charge . . . **9** Furthermore it is the people who bestow offices on those who deserve them – the noblest reward for virtue in a state. **10** The people have the power to approve or reject laws, and, most important of all, they deliberate on matters of peace and war. **11** Again, in the case of alliances and the cessation of hostilities and treaties, it is the people who ratify each of these or the reverse. **12** So again one might reasonably say that the people have the greatest role in government and that the constitution is a democratic one.

(iv) The senate as a check on the consuls

15.2 The consul, when he sets out with his army, possessed of the powers mentioned earlier, seems to possess absolute authority with regard to completing the task before him, **3** but in fact he needs the support of both the people and the senate, and without these he is unable to bring his operations to a conclusion. **4** For it is clear that the legions need constant supplies, and without the consent of the senate neither corn, nor clothing, nor pay can be provided, **5** so that a commander's plans are unworkable if the senate chooses to be negligent or obstructive. **6** It also rests with the senate as to whether a general's plans and designs can be carried to completion, since it has the authority to send out another general, when the former's term of office has expired, or to continue him in his command. **7** Moreover, the senate has the power to celebrate generals' successes with pomp and magnify them or to obscure and belittle them; **8** for the processions they call triumphs, in which the spectacle of what the generals have achieved is brought before the citizens, cannot be properly organised, and in some cases not even held at all, unless the senate agrees and grants the necessary funds.

(v) The people as a check on the senate

16.1 The senate, again, though it has such great power, is obliged in the first place to pay attention to the people in public affairs and to respect its wishes, **2** while it is unable to carry out inquiries into the most serious and important crimes against the state, such as involve the death penalty, or take steps to exact punishment for them, unless the people ratifies the decree. **3** It is the same with regard to matters which concern the senate itself. For if anyone introduces a law, intended either to deprive the senate of some of its traditional authority or to abolish the senators' precedence and other distinctions or even to reduce their private property, in all these cases the people has the power to pass or reject them. **4** And, most important of all, if a single tribune interposes a veto, the senate is not only unable to reach a final decision on any matter but may not even meet or sit in council. **5** The tribunes are always obliged to carry out the people's decrees and especially to respect its wishes – for all these reasons the senate is afraid of the masses and takes notice of the people.

1.60 Sallust *The Catilinarian Conspiracy* 29.1–3: The 'senatus consultum ultimum'

The term 'senatus consultum ultimum' ('final decree of the senate') is a modern one, following Caesar *BC* 1.5 (doc. 13.24), where he describes the senate's resolution to suspend the constitution as 'that extreme and ultimate decree'. A declaration of emergency, the decree instructed the consuls to take measures to ensure 'that the state suffer no harm'. It was first passed in 121 BC (docs 8.32–33). Cicero here, as consul in 63, has heard of Catiline's plot to murder him.

1 Cicero reported the matter, which had already been the subject of popular gossip, to the senate. **2** Thereupon, in accordance with its usual practice in dangerous crises, the senate decreed that 'the consuls should take measures that the state suffer no harm'. **3** The power thus conferred by the senate on a magistrate by Roman custom is supreme: they may raise an army, wage war, apply force by any means to allies and citizens, and exercise supreme command and jurisdiction at home and in the field; otherwise the consul has none of these privileges unless the people decrees it.

ROME'S STRUGGLE FOR ITALY

1.61 Livy *History of Rome* 5.21.10–13, 22.1, 8, 23.3: Veii, 396 BC

Veii, an Etruscan city 15 kilometres north of Rome, was captured in 396 after a long-drawn-out siege (supposedly lasting ten years) by the dictator M. Furius Camillus; Rome had been engaged in intermittent conflict with Veii since the first Veientine War (483–474 BC).

21.10 The mine, which was now filled with selected soldiers, suddenly discharged armed men into the temple of Juno, which was on Veii's citadel, of whom some attacked the enemies who had their backs to them on the walls, some tore down the bars on the gates, others set fires to stop the women and slaves throwing down rocks and tiles from the roofs. **11** Everywhere was filled with shouting – the varying cries of those who threatened and those who trembled, mixed with the lamentation of women and children. **12** In a moment the armed men were everywhere cast from the walls and the doors were thrown open, while some of the attackers rushed in *en masse*, others climbed the walls, and the city was overrun with enemies; fighting was everywhere; **13** then, after great slaughter, the fighting slowed and the dictator ordered heralds to declare that the unarmed would be spared . . . **22.1** On the next day the dictator sold the free inhabitants into slavery . . . **8** Such was the fall of Veii, the wealthiest city of the Etruscan people, which demonstrated its strength even in its final calamity, since after a siege of ten continuous summers and winters, in which it had inflicted far more disasters than it had received, when finally even fate turned against it, it was captured by siege-engines and not by force . . . **23.3** The senate decreed four days of supplications, a greater number of days than in any previous war.

1.62 Livy *History of Rome* 5.48.6–9: The Gallic sack of Rome

Traditionally dated to 390 BC, the Gallic sack of Rome took place c. 386 BC after the Romans were defeated at the River Allia. The Gauls were said to have been driven back from the Capitol by M. Manlius Capitolinus, who had been warned of their attack by Juno's sacred geese.

6 Meanwhile the army on the Capitol was exhausted from picket and guard duty, and, though they overcame all human evils, nature would not permit them to get the better of one, which was starvation. Day after day they looked to see if any help from the dictator was on its way, **7** but finally not only food but hope, too, began to fail them, and when they went out on picket duty their bodies were nearly too weak to wear their armour, so they declared that they had either to surrender or ransom themselves on whatever terms they could, for the Gauls were throwing out clear hints that it would not take a very great price to persuade them to abandon the siege. **8** The senate then met and gave the military tribunes the task of negotiating terms. The matter was arranged at a conference between Quintus Sulpicius, the tribune, and Brennus, chieftain of the Gauls, with 1,000 pounds of gold as the price of a nation that was soon to rule the world. **9** This was an intense dishonour in itself, but a further insult was added: the weights brought by the Gauls were too heavy and, when the tribune objected, the insolent Gaul added his sword to the weight, with the words which Romans could not bear to hear, 'Woe to the conquered!' ('Vae victis!')

ROME AND THE LATINS

Following the establishment of the Republic, the Latins revolted and formed an alliance (the 'Latin league'). Towards the end of the fifth century, Rome began its conquest of southern Latium and southern Etruria with Vcii in 396 BC. In 341 the Latins revolted after their request for a consulship and half the places in the senate was refused. They were defeated and their territory was settled by Rome.

1.63 Livy *History of Rome* 8.6.15–16: Brothers in blood, 340 BC

Livy comments at 8.8.2 that this conflict resembled a civil war – so little did the Latins differ from the Romans in anything but courage. The Romans are here concerned about making war against the Latins because of their social and cultural links.

15 Their anxiety was exacerbated by the fact that they had to make war against the Latins, who were similar to themselves in language, customs, type of arms and, above all, military institutions; soldiers had mixed with soldiers, centurions with centurions, tribunes with tribunes as equals and colleagues in the same garrisons, and often in the same maniples. **16** To prevent the men falling into some misjudgement because of this, the consuls proclaimed that no one was to leave his position to fight the enemy.

1.64 Livy *History of Rome* 8.11.11–16: Defeat of the Latins, 340 BC

Both of the consuls, T. Manlius Torquatus and P. Decius Mus, had a dream that a devotio (ritual dedication to the gods of the underworld) was required for victory. They agreed that, whichever flank gave way, the consul commanding it would devote himself. Decius Mus did so (doc. 3.18) and the Latins were defeated. The silver denarius was not struck until 211.

11 The consul Torquatus met this force at Trifanum, a place between Sinuessa and Minternae. Without waiting to choose sites for their camps, both sides piled up their baggage and fought the battle that ended the war; **12** for the enemy suffered such great losses that, when the consul led his victorious army to plunder their lands, the Latins all surrendered, and their surrender was followed by the Campanians. **13** Latium and Capua were deprived of their territory. The Latin territory, with the addition of that belonging to Privernum, and the Falernian territory as well (which had belonged to the Campanian people) as far as the River Volturnus, was divided up among the Roman people. **14** The allocation was 2 iugera for each man in Latium supplemented by three-quarters of a iugerum from the land of Privernum or 3 iugera in Falernian territory with another quarter being added because of the distance involved. **15** The Laurentians and Campanian equites were exempted from the punishment of the Latins because they had not revolted. It was ordered that the treaty with the Laurentians be renewed, and it has been renewed every year from that time on the tenth day after the Latin festival. **16** Roman citizenship was granted to the Campanian equites, and in commemoration of this a bronze tablet was put up in the temple of Castor at Rome. In addition, the Campanian people – there were 1,600 of them – were ordered to pay per head an annual sum of 450 denarii.

1.65 Livy *History of Rome* 8.14.1–12: Settlement with the Latins, 338 BC

L. Furius Camillus and C. Maenius, as consuls in 338, put down Latium, which was still discontented; Camillus has here been urging the senate to decide on a settlement. Camillus was awarded a triumph; Maenius dedicated the 'beaks' (rostra) of the ships he captured at Antium under the speakers' platform in the forum, henceforth called the Rostra.

1 The leading senators praised the motion of the consul (Camillus) on the policy to be followed but said that, as the Latins were not all in the same position, his advice could best be carried out by the consuls' bringing forward proposals concerning the different peoples by name, so that a decision could be made on the merits of each. **2** Accordingly motions and decrees were taken on them individually. The city of Lanuvium was granted citizenship and their shrines restored to them, on condition that the temple and grove of Juno Sospita should be held in common by the townsfolk of Lanuvium and the Roman people. **3** The Aricini, Nomentani and Pedani were received as citizens on the same terms as the Lanuvini. **4** The Tusculans kept the citizenship they already had, and the charge of revolt was laid not to the detriment of the community but against a few leaders. **5** The Veliterni, long-time Roman citizens, were severely penalised for having rebelled so many times: not only were their walls pulled down, but their senate was deported and ordered to live on the far side of the Tiber, **6** on the understanding that, if any of them were caught on the near side, his ransom should be no less than 1,000 pounds of bronze, nor should his captor release him from bondage until the money had been paid. **7** Colonists were sent to the senators' lands, and once they were enrolled Velitrae regained its former appearance of being well populated. **8** A new colony was sent to Antium too, on the understanding that the Antiates, if they wished, should be permitted to enrol themselves as colonists; their warships were taken from them and their people were forbidden the sea and they were granted citizenship. **9** The Tiburtes and Praenestians were deprived of their territory, not only because of the latest charge of rebellion brought against them together with the other Latins but also because they had once, in disgust at Roman rule, joined forces with the Gauls, a savage race. **10** The rest of the Latin peoples were deprived of their rights of intermarriage (connubium) and mutual trade (commercium) and of holding councils with each other. To show honour to their equites, because they had chosen not to revolt with the Latins, the Campanians were granted citizenship without the vote (*civitas sine suffragio*), as were the Fundani and Formiani, because they had always allowed a safe and peaceful passage through their territories. **11** It was resolved to give the people of Cumae and Suessula the same rights and terms as Capua. **12** Some of the ships from Antium were laid up in the dockyards at Rome, others were burnt, and it was resolved to use their prows (rostra) to adorn a platform constructed in the forum, and this sacred place was named the Rostra, or beaks.

THE SAMNITE WARS AND PYRRHUS

Samnium is situated in the central southern Apennines. Following the 'Latin War', the Romans began incursions into central Italy and came into conflict with the Samnites. They fought three Samnite wars in all: the First (343–341 BC) gave Rome control over northern Campania; the Second (326–321, 316–304) hindered Samnite expansion into Apulia, Lucania and southern Campania; and, despite defeat in the Third (298–290), the Samnites aided both Pyrrhus and Hannibal, and at the beginning of the first century BC were one of Rome's most intractable enemies in the Social War (docs 10.10–11, 27–28). In an attempt to keep their independence, Tarentum and other Greek cities of southern Italy invited Pyrrhus of Epirus to lead their defence in 280 (doc. 1.74); his defeat in 275 and the fall of Tarentum in 272 marked Rome's total dominance over the rest of Italy.

1.66 Livy *History of Rome* 8.23.1–7: The Second Samnite War (326–304 BC)

In 327 the Greek city of Palaepolis, not far from Naples, engaged in hostilities against Campania and Falerii. The senate decided for war against Palaepolis under one consul, Q. Publilius Philo (docs 1.51–52), while the other, L. Cornelius Lentulus, was given command against the Samnites. Fregellae was established as a Latin colony in 328.

1 The senate was informed by both consuls that there was minimal hope of peace with the Samnites: Publilius reported that 2,000 soldiers from Nola and 4,000 Samnites had been taken into Palaepolis, rather under pressure from the Nolani than of the Greeks' own choice; **2** Cornelius that a levy had been called by the magistrates and that all Samnium was up in arms, while the neighbouring towns of Privernum, Fundi and Formiae were being openly invited to join them. **3** It was decided, for these reasons, to send legates to the Samnites before declaring war, and a defiant response was returned by the Samnites. **4** For their part, they accused the Romans of wrongdoing, while doing their best to clear themselves of the charges brought against them: **5** they stated that they were not assisting the Greeks with any public advice or support, nor had they invited Fundi or Formiae to join them; they were quite confident in their own forces, if they chose to fight. **6** However, they were unable to disguise the fact that the Samnite nation was angry that Fregellae, which they had captured from the Volsci and destroyed, should have been restored by the Roman people, and that they should have planted a colony in Samnite territory, which the colonists called Fregellae; **7** that was an insult and injury which, if those responsible for it did not undo it themselves, they would combat with all the force in their power.

1.67 Livy *History of Rome* 9.7.6–12: The Caudine Forks, 321 BC

In 321 the Roman army was trapped in a narrow defile by the Samnite leader C. Pontius, upon which it surrendered and the army was made to pass under the yoke. The Romans were shocked not so much at the defeat as at the surrender. The defeat was avenged in the following year, when Pontius was himself sent under the yoke at Luceria by the consul Lucius Papirius Cursor; cf. doc. 5.3.

6 By this time Rome had also heard of its dishonourable defeat. The first report was that the army had been trapped; then came news which was even more melancholy on account of the shameful peace than on account of the danger they faced.

7 At the report of a blockade they had started holding a levy; they then, on hearing of so disgraceful a surrender, disbanded their preparations to send assistance, and at once, without any authorisation from the state, the whole people adopted every type of mourning. **8** The shops around the forum were closed, all public business in the forum was automatically suspended even before a public announcement; **9** tunics with broad purple stripes and golden rings were put away; and the citizenry was almost more depressed than the army itself – they were not only infuriated at the generals and those who had made and guaranteed the peace, but even detested the innocent soldiers and were unwilling to allow them into the city or their homes. **10** But the arrival of the army, which roused pity even in angry men, softened this general agitation. For they entered the city not like men returning home safely from a hopeless situation but late in the day, with the appearance and bearing of captives, **11** with each man concealing himself in his own home, and on the next and subsequent days not one of them was prepared to look into the forum or out into the streets. **12** The consuls shut themselves up at home and transacted no public business, apart from the fact that a senatorial decree ordered them to name a dictator to preside over the elections. . . .

1.68 Livy *History of Rome* 10.1.1–2: More colonies, 303 BC

The Hernici and Aequi were conquered in 306–304, while their neighbours signed treaties of alliance with Rome. The colonies at Alba and Sora clearly had the strategic aim of consolidating this region: inhabitants were granted Latin rights, sharing the rights of intermarriage and trade with Romans: any who settled in Rome were granted citizenship.

1 In the consulship of Lucius Genucius and Servius Cornelius there was almost a complete rest from foreign wars. Colonies were sent out to Sora and Alba. 6,000 settlers were enrolled for Alba in the Aequian region: **2** Sora had belonged to Volscian territory, but the Samnites had occupied it; 4,000 men were sent there.

1.69 *ILS* 1: Epitaph of a conqueror of Italy

Lucius Cornelius Scipio Barbatus ('Long-beard') was consul in 298 BC and censor perhaps in 280. He was probably the founder of the tomb of the Scipiones, on the Appian Way. The date of his epitaph has been disputed, but it now appears to have been written shortly after his death, perhaps c. 250. In 298 the Romans were campaigning annually in Etruria and Umbria, while war against the Samnites recommenced in 298. The victory over the Lucanians was in 298; Livy mentions only Barbatus' successes in Etruria (Livy 10.11–12; cf. 10.14, 11.26).

> Lucius Cornelius Scipio, son of Gnaeus.
> Lucius Cornelius Scipio Barbatus,
> Offspring of his father Gnaeus, a man brave and wise,
> Whose looks well matched his courage,

Was consul, censor and aedile among you.
He took Taurasia and Cisauna from Samnium,
Totally subdued the Lucanian land and brought back hostages.

1.70 Livy *History of Rome* 10.28.12–18: The devotio of Decius Mus, 295 BC

The Third Samnite War broke out in 298 BC, and in 296 a joint attack on Rome by Samnites, Etruscans, Umbrians and Gauls was planned. Q. Fabius Maximus Rullianus and P. Decius Mus (junior) were appointed consuls for 295, and they pursued the Samnites and Gauls over the Apennines. In 295 Decius sacrificed himself against the Gauls and Samnites as his father had done in 340 (docs 1.64, 3.18), thus saving the battle.

12 Then, as he was powerless to stop their flight, he called on the name of his father Publius Decius: **13** 'Why do I delay longer', he cried, 'to fulfil our house's destiny? Our family was granted the privilege of being sacrificed to avert our country's dangers. It is now my turn to offer up the legions of the enemy as victims to Earth and the gods of the underworld (di manes).' **14** With these words he ordered Marcus Livius, the pontifex, whom he had already told as he went into battle not to leave his side, to dictate the words with which he could devote himself and the legions of the enemy on behalf of the Roman people, the Quirites. **15** He was then devoted with the same form of prayer and the same dress as when his father Publius Decius had ordered himself to be devoted at Veseris in the Latin war. **16** Following the ritual prayers, he added that he was driving before him fear and rout, slaughter and bloodshed, **17** and the anger of the celestial and underworld gods, and would pollute with a deadly curse the standards, spears and arms of the enemy, while the same place would mark his own destruction and that of the Gauls and Samnites **18** – after uttering these curses upon himself and the enemy, he galloped his horse into the Gallic battle-lines, where he saw them thickest, and threw himself on the enemy's weapons to meet his death.

1.71 Livy *History of Rome* 10.31.10–15: The Samnite wars continue

The year is 295 BC, after the victory at Sentinum. The Samnites were again overwhelmingly defeated at Aquilonia in 293.

10 There are still more Samnite wars to come, though we have been dealing with them continuously through four volumes over a period of 46 years, from the consulship of Marcus Valerius and Aulus Cornelius (343 BC), who were the first to bear arms in Samnium. **11** Without at this point going through the disasters suffered by both peoples over so many years and the hardships endured, by which nevertheless those brave hearts refused to be conquered, **12** in the past year the Samnites had fought in the territory of Sentinum, among the Paeligni, at Tifernum, in the Stellate plains, now by themselves, now with the addition of troops from other peoples, and had been cut to pieces by four armies under four

Roman commanders; **13** they had lost their people's most distinguished general; they saw their allies in war, the Etruscans, Umbrians and Gauls, in the same plight as their own; **14** nor were they able to carry on, either with their own resources or outside support; but they would not abstain from war – so far were they from being tired of freedom, even though their defence of it had been unsuccessful, preferring to be defeated rather than not to try for victory. **15** Who then could begrudge the time spent on the reading and writing of wars when these did not weary those who fought them?

1.72 Livy *History of Rome* 10.38.2–4, 10–13: The 'linen legion', 293 BC

Livy's descriptions of Samnite weaponry conflict with the archaeological evidence, and at 9.40.3 (308 BC) Livy mentions that the Samnite soldiers wore linen (rather than enrolling under it).

2 The Samnites held a levy throughout all Samnium under a new law, **3** which stated that any man of military age who did not respond to the generals' proclamation or who left the army without orders would forfeit his life to Jupiter. **4** The entire army was then instructed to meet at Aquilonia. Some 40,000 soldiers, Samnium's fighting force, assembled . . . **10** Each man was then forced to swear an oath following a certain grim formula, invoking a curse on himself, his household and his family if he did not go into battle where his generals led or if he fled from the battle-line himself or saw someone else fleeing and did not immediately cut him down. **11** At first, there were some who refused to swear, and they were beheaded in front of the altars; lying there among the piles of sacrificial victims, they acted as a warning to others not to refuse to comply. **12** When the leading Samnites had bound themselves by this curse, ten of them were named by the general, and each was told to choose a man until their number had reached 16,000. This was called the 'linen legion', from the covering of the enclosure in which the nobles were sworn in; these were given distinguished armour and crested helmets to make them stand out among the others. **13** A little more than 20,000 men formed another force which was inferior to the linen legion in neither physical appearance, nor martial reputation, nor equipment. This was the number of men, their fighting force, which encamped at Aquilonia.

1.73 Pliny *Natural History* 34.43: Colossal art from Samnite spoils

Sp. Carvilius Maximus was consul in 293 BC and was awarded a triumph both for his victories against the Samnites in 293 and for his defeat of Tarentum and the other Greek cities in 272. For Jupiter Latiaris and the Feriae Latinae, see doc. 3.9.

Italy also used frequently to make colossal statues . . . When the Samnites were defeated after fighting under an inviolable oath (in 293 BC), Spurius Carvilius made the Jupiter, which stands in the Capitol, out of their breastplates, greaves and helmets. Its size is so great that it can be seen from the temple of Jupiter Latiaris (10 miles away on the Alban mount). Out of the left-over filings, he made a statue of himself, which stands at the feet of Jupiter's statue.

1.74 Livy *Periochae* 12–14: Pyrrhus of Epirus

Pyrrhus of Epirus (319–272 BC) was approached by Tarentum for help against Rome, which had begun interfering in the affairs of the Greek cities of southern Italy in 285. Pyrrhus' aims included the conquest of Sicily and Carthage, as well as Italy, and his involvement gave rise to a simultaneous revolt of Samnites, Lucanians and Bruttians. He defeated the Romans at Heraclea in 280 and, after an abortive march on Rome, again at Ausculum in 279. In 278 he fought the Carthaginians (Rome's allies: Polyb. 3.25.1–5) in Sicily, returning to Italy in 276. After a defeat at Beneventum, he went back to Epirus.

12 A Roman fleet was seized by the Tarentines, the duumvir who commanded it was killed, and the envoys sent to them by the senate to complain about these injuries were driven away. On this account, war was declared against them. The Samnites revolted. Several battles were successfully fought against them and the Lucanians, Brittii (Bruttians) and Etruscans by numerous generals. Pyrrhus, the Epirote king, came to Italy to aid the Tarentines. A Campanian legion led by Decius Vibellius sent to protect the people of Rhegium slaughtered the inhabitants and seized Rhegium. **13** The consul Valerius Laevinus (cos. 280) fought an unsuccessful battle against Pyrrhus, as the soldiers were extremely terrified by the unaccustomed sight of elephants . . . Cineas was sent by Pyrrhus to the senate as an envoy to request that the king be received into the city for the sake of arranging peace terms. It was resolved that this be referred to a more well-attended meeting of the senate, and Appius Claudius (Caecus), who because of problems with his eyesight had for some time abstained from public business, entered the senate and won it over to his opinion that this be refused Pyrrhus . . . There was a second battle against Pyrrhus of which the result was indecisive . . . **14** Pyrrhus crossed over to Sicily . . . The consul Curius Dentatus (cos. 290, 275, 274) held a levy and was the first to sell the goods of anyone who did not answer when summoned; he also defeated Pyrrhus, who had returned from Sicily to Italy and drove him out of Italy . . . A Carthaginian fleet came to the aid of the Tarentines, which was a violation of the treaty by them. The book also deals with successful wars against the Lucanians, Bruttians and Samnites and the death of King Pyrrhus.

1.75 Plutarch *Life of Pyrrhus* 19.5–7: Romans as the 'hydra'

A Roman army under Laevinus (cos. 280 BC) was defeated by Pyrrhus at Heraclea. Pyrrhus then sent Cineas as an envoy to discuss peace terms, but the blind Appius Claudius Caecus persuaded the Romans not to surrender and to make peace with Pyrrhus only after he had left Italy.

5 When Appius had made this speech, the senators were possessed with enthusiasm for prosecuting the war, and they sent back Cineas with the response that, when Pyrrhus had left Italy, then, if he wished, the Romans would discuss the question of friendship and alliance, but as long as he remained there in arms they would continue the war with all their strength, even if he were to meet in battle and vanquish 10,000 men of Laevinus' stamp. **6** It is also said that Cineas, while conducting this mission, made it at the same time his business zealously to observe their lifestyle and learn about their excellence of their government. He also met their nobles and conversed with them, and among the many things he told Pyrrhus was his statement that the senate appeared to him a council of many kings, **7** and that, with regard to the populace, he was afraid that they might find it a Lernaean hydra to fight against – since the consul had already collected twice as many soldiers as faced them before, and there were many times the same number of Romans still able to take up arms.

2

The Public Face of Rome

Even from the time of the kings, the city of Rome and especially its public works impressed visitors: as Strabo comments (doc. 2.1), the Romans concentrated on utilitarian projects rather than on aspects of beautification, and Rome was noted for its aqueducts and sewers (docs 2.1–4), while its road-building (docs 2.5–8) was rivalled by no other ancient empire. Thus Rome signalled its territorial domination and control of the resources of the land through which the roads travelled, as well as aiding transport and movement throughout an increasing empire. The amenities of the city, too, whose inhabitants may have approached near to a million in the first century BC, were continually updated and designed to improve conditions for the growing urban population.

The Romans in general, and particularly the senatorial class, prided themselves on the traditions of austerity, frugality and common sense that they had inherited from their earliest ancestors: heroes of renowned military campaigns such as Cincinnatus and Curius Dentatus in early Rome were remembered for their pride in being simple farmers (docs 2.12–13), and this image was revived by Cato the Elder who, though a 'new man' in the early second century BC, took pride in his parsimony and lack of interest in the expensive items which were introducing Romans of the mid-second century to luxury, gluttony and epicureanism (docs 2.14–17). Cato's instructions for the practical and profitable running of a country estate provide unrivalled details of the procedures and practices involved at this period on a small slave-run property (docs 2.15–16, cf. 6.32–34), while his prescriptions for the medicinal use of cabbage show that no item in the household was too trivial to escape his attention (doc. 2.17). Seneca the Younger similarly pays homage to the moral standards of olden days when he contrasts the baths thought appropriate for his own use by the great Scipio Africanus, conqueror of the Carthaginians, with those constructed in Seneca's own time (doc. 2.20).

Cato's adherence to traditional values was not, however, shared by the majority of the Roman upper classes, particularly as immense wealth and resources became available with the second-century BC conquests of the eastern and western Mediterranean. Marcus Licinius Crassus in the first century BC may have been unusual in considering the term 'wealthy' to comprise the ability to keep a legion (some 4,200 men) on one's income, and he was also unusual in the way in which the bulk of his money had been acquired (from 'fire-sale' tactics: docs 6.3, 2.21). More common was the acquisition of wealth through conquest and administration of a province, and the lifestyle of L. Licinius Lucullus shows to what degree of dilettantism this might lead (doc. 2.22); even official pontifical (priestly) banquets could have a menu that defies imagination, while by the late Republic delicacies such as peafowl and lampreys for consumption at banquets could be bred by aristocrats and command immense sums of money (docs 2.23–24).

Underpinning this lifestyle was a highly competitive, militaristic society, in which the ultimate goal was to attain the consulship, along with a provincial command which might lead to a triumph. It was seen as essential to live up to the virtues and achievements of one's ancestors and to acquire gloria (reputation) which would enhance the family's status and increase the number of imagines – masks of noble ancestors – in the house's vestibule (docs 2.25–28): the funeral oration for L. Caecilius Metellus demonstrates the achievements and status most sought after by a consular in the third century BC (doc. 2.29). These aims changed little, and desire for public office and political influence won by one's merits was a major virtue according to Cicero, who criticises his brother Quintus for possibly, by his conduct as governor of Asia, detracting from the family gloria won by Cicero himself in his consulship (docs 2.30–31).

The ultimate achievement was the celebration of a military triumph in Rome, which gave the triumphator the chance to display his captives, booty and dedicated soldiery (docs 2.32–35), and Cicero tried hard, but unsuccessfully, to persuade his political friends to award him a triumph for his governorship of Cilicia, which would have been the pinnacle of his career (docs 2.44, 13.20). As a result of this competitive culture, candidature for office was keenly contested: with only two consuls and a number of lesser magistrates per year, only a lucky few could hope to win the consulship. Largesse and bribery of the electorate were thus endemic to the process of canvassing, which could be an extremely costly business and which was expected to involve all one's friends and connections (docs 2.36–42). The electorate tended to prefer candidates of known ancestry, and even wealthy non-nobles, those without a consul in their ancestry, found it as outsiders difficult, though not of course impossible, to achieve the consulship: Cato the censor, Marius and Cicero were some of the exceptions, and such men were known as novi homines ('new men'; sing.: novus homo). Sallust sees such men as generally resented by the nobility, and Cicero prides himself on the personal merits that have won him the prestigious position of consul (docs 2.44–45). New men were particularly disadvantaged by their lack of political friends (amici) and clients (clientes) to help them in their candidature and canvassing. As Roman politics lacked formal political parties, unofficial political friendships (amicitiae) were invaluable in bringing together, even if only temporarily, men with common aims who could further each other's goals; Cicero gives numerous examples of how the system worked in practice (docs 2.47–50). New men in the political arena had to create their own amicitiae and were also disadvantaged by their lack of clients, who were often inherited within the family and could number several thousands: a politician's retinue of clients (his clientela) demonstrated his importance and prestige and was a significant aid in canvassing for office (docs 2.38, 54–59). Generals and governors could also include entire provinces and foreign communities among their clientela (docs 2.60–62).

Even for well-known military figures, undertaking important prosecutions or defences in the law-courts was a way of winning clients and popularity generally. It was considered honourable to prosecute family enemies, though gratitude was won especially through a successful defence (docs 2.63–65). The ability to speak well in public was essential in Rome, not merely on the political stage but also in the courts, and the training could be long and arduous (docs 2.66–68, 69). Included among the notably impressive speakers in the late Republic were the Gracchi (docs 8.3, 26–27) and Julius Caesar (doc. 2.68), as well, of course, as Cicero, whose career was built on his skill in forensic oratory (doc. 2.67). It was naturally an important factor in success as a politician to have popular support, which could be gained by high birth, military achievements and oratorical ability but also be attained by entertainment of the populace. The putting on of costly games was a common way for aediles to court the attention of the people with a view to their election later to the higher magistracies (docs 2.76–77), and gladiatorial shows, theatrical performances, wild-beast fights, and public banquets and other hand-outs were often aimed at canvassing support for current or potential candidates for office (docs 2.73–75, 78–79). Such expenditure, of course, made it even more desirable to achieve high office and the chance of the governorship of a profitable province afterwards to enable candidates to recoup their electioneering expenses.

Ancient sources: the evidence for the public face of Rome is scattered among the literary sources; the geographer Strabo, who wrote his vast work in the reigns of Augustus and Tiberius, and the antiquarian Dionysius of Halicarnassus in the early first century AD provide useful information on Rome's infrastructure and buildings, as does the work of Frontinus *On Aqueducts* (consul in 72 or 73, 98 and 100 and superintendent of aqueducts under Nerva in AD 97). Livy and Dionysius are the main sources for details of the history of early Rome, such as temples and dedications. Inscriptions also testify to specific contracts for public works such as roads and to traffic regulations in Rome (docs 2.7–8, cf. 10–11). Cato the Elder is the principal witness to the details of farming villa-estates in the mid-second century (docs 2.15–17) and to the accompanying traditional values. Cicero's 58 speeches and huge collection of letters to his friends, Atticus, and his brother Quintus are of course the main evidence for political concepts such as amicitia, gloria, clientela and the novus homo, as well as for electioneering practices such as the prevalence of bribery and the importance of oratorical training, while aristocratic values are also evidenced by epitaphs of *nobiles* (such as docs 2.25–26). The *Lives* of Plutarch, especially *Pompey, Lucullus, Crassus* and *Cato the Elder*, provide useful anecdotal information on the contrast between the supposed frugality of older times and the luxurious and wealthy lifestyle of first-century *nobiles* and the enormous power which such wealth and clientela gave them.

THE INFRASTRUCTURE OF THE CITY

The main architectural features of Rome in the Republic were its aqueducts (doc. 2.4), its sewers (docs 2.1–3), the buildings in the forum (such as the prison: doc. 12.22) and Jupiter's temple. As Rome's power grew, many new buildings, mainly temples, were constructed, often in fulfilment of vows made in war or at the introduction of new cults (docs 3.57–64). Plans of the city survive, but from the imperial period, and much of what can be seen in Rome today dates from the building projects of the emperors, such as Augustus: cf. docs 15.1, 15.81. These projects, however, had Republican antecedents, not just in Pompey's works (docs 2.73–74) and Caesar's (docs 13.56) but in the various buildings constructed in the forum and Campus Martius areas from the third century BC onwards.

2.1 Strabo *Geography* 5.3.8: Engineering projects

Strabo, who admired the physical infrastructure of the city of Rome, is describing Rome in the past. Houses were not individually connected to the sewers, the main purpose of which was to drain rainwater and the Cloaca stream; cf. doc. 15.40.

The Greeks had the reputation for making good choices in their foundation of cities, because they aimed for beauty, defensibility, harbours and fertile soil, while the Romans were especially farsighted in matters to which the Greeks paid little attention, such as the construction of roads and aqueducts, and of sewers which could wash out the city's filth into the Tiber; and they have constructed roads throughout the country, adding the levelling of hills and the filling in of valleys, so that their wagons can carry boat-loads; and the sewers, vaulted with tightly fitting stones, have enough room in some places for wagons loaded with hay to pass through. And such quantities of water are brought into the city by aqueducts that actual rivers flow through the city and the sewers, and almost every house has cisterns, service pipes and plentiful fountains . . . In short, the ancient Romans paid little attention to the beauty of Rome because they were occupied with other, greater and more necessary, matters.

2.2 Dionysius of Halicarnassus *Roman Antiquities* 3.67.5: Plumbing!

Livy and Dionysius follow a tradition that the fifth and seventh kings of Rome, the Tarquins, played a major part in the provision of public works. Tarquinius Priscus was credited with the adornment of the forum, as well as the walls of the city, the sewers, the Circus Maximus and the temple of Jupiter, Juno and Minerva on the Capitoline Hill. Other sources give the second Tarquin the credit for the same works. Acilius wrote a history of Rome in Greek in the second century BC.

Tarquinius (Priscus) also began the digging of the sewers, through which all the water which flows off from the roads is diverted into the Tiber, thus constructing marvellous works which defy description. Indeed I would rate as the three most magnificent constructions of Rome, from which the greatness of her empire can particularly be seen, as the aqueducts, the paved roads, and the construction of the sewers. I say this not only with regard to the usefulness of the work, about which I shall speak in its proper place, but also to the size of the cost involved, which one can judge from a single example if one takes Gaius Acilius as his authority, who says that once, when the sewers had been neglected and no longer carried the water, the censors let out their cleaning and repair at the cost of a thousand talents.

2.3 Cicero *In Defence of Sestius* 77: Blocked sewers

Publius Sestius (tr. pl. 57) was prosecuted for using armed force during his tribunate and was successfully defended by Cicero, who is here referring to the bloodshed caused by the proposal of his own recall in January 57, which was hotly opposed by Clodius. Appius Claudius Pulcher, then praetor, lent his brother Clodius a troop of gladiators intended for funeral games. The sewers and the Tiber had been used for the disposal of the bodies of both the Gracchi and their supporters.

Surely you remember, jurors, how the Tiber was then filled with the bodies of citizens, how the sewers were blocked, how the blood was wiped from the forum with sponges, so that everyone thought that such an immense band and magnificent display was the work not of a private citizen or plebeian, but of a patrician and praetor.

2.4 Frontinus *On Aqueducts* 1.5: Rome's water supply

Four aqueducts were constructed for Rome in the Republican period: the aqua Appia (312 BC), Anio Vetus (272 BC), the aqua Marcia (144 BC) and the aqua Tepula (125 BC). In the city, water was diverted into settling tanks and then distributed to public fountains. The Appia was 16.5 kilometres in length and brought 75,700 cubic metres of water per day to the city. For Agrippa and Augustus' aqueducts, see docs 15.1, 15.52.

In the consulship of Marcus Valerius Maximus and Publius Decius Mus (312 BC), the thirtieth year after the start of the Samnite War, the Appian aqueduct was brought into the city by Appius Claudius Crassus, the censor, who was later given the surname Caecus ('the blind'); he was also responsible for the construction of the Appian Way from the Capena gate up to the city of Capua . . . The Appia draws water from the Lucullan estate on the Praenestine Way, between the seventh and eighth milestones, on a by-road, 780 paces to the left. From its intake to the Salinae, which is at the Trigemina gate, the length of the channel is 11,190 paces; of this, 11,130 paces run underground, while 60 paces are supported above ground by substructures and, near the Capena gate, by arches.

COMMUNICATIONS AND PUBLIC WORKS

The first major road in Italy, the Via Appia, was constructed in 312 BC. In the third century BC, roads radiated out from Rome through central Italy, and by the end of the second century major Roman roads linked the north, south, east and west of Italy with the capital. Besides the Via Appia, other major roads were the Via Flaminia (220 BC), running north from Rome to the east coast, the Via Egnatia (c. 130), which ran from the Adriatic to Byzantium and provided Rome with its main route to the east, and the Via Aurelia (241, extended in 109), which ran up the Italian north-west coast.

2.5 Procopius *History of the Wars* 5.14.6–11: The Appian Way

The Via Appia built (but not paved) by Appius Claudius Caecus as censor in 312 BC extended some 210 kilometres from Rome to Capua, providing the Romans with their main route to southern Italy. Appius also built the Aqua Appia (doc. 2.5). Procopius is describing Belisarius' reconquest of Italy in the sixth century AD.

6 Belisarius led his army by the Latin Way, leaving on their left the Appian Way, which the Romans' consul Appius built 900 years earlier and to which he gave his name. The Appian Way is five days' journey for an active man, for it extends from Rome to Capua. **7** The breadth of the road is such that two wagons going in opposite directions can pass each other, and it is one of the sights most worth seeing anywhere. **8** Appius quarried all the stone, which is millstone and naturally hard, from another place far away and brought it there, for it is not found anywhere in this region. **9** He worked the stones smooth and level, cut them square, and bound them to each other without putting gravel or anything else between them. **10** They were fixed together so securely, with the joints so tight, that they give the appearance, when you look at them, of not being fitted together but of having grown together. **11** And although so long a period has passed, and so many wagons and all kinds of animals have travelled over it each day, the stones have not separated at all at the joints, nor have any of them been worn out or become thinner – in fact they have not even lost any of their finish. Such, then, is the Appian Way.

2.6 Plutarch *Life of Gaius Gracchus* 7.1–4: Communications within Italy

See docs 8.28–29 for Gaius' other public works during his tribunates.

1 Gaius devoted particular attention to the construction of roads, bearing in mind practical considerations as well as those relating to grace and beauty. His roads ran straight across the country without deviations, the surface consisting partly of dressed stone and partly of tight-packed sand. **2** Depressions were filled up, watercourses or ravines which crossed the road were bridged, and both sides of the road were of equal and corresponding height, so that the whole work presented a symmetrical and beautiful appearance. **3** In addition to this, he measured every road in miles (the mile is a little less than 8 stades) and positioned stone pillars to mark the distances. **4** He set up other stones, too, at shorter intervals on both sides of the road, so that horsemen should be able to mount from these without assistance.

2.7 *ILS* 5799: Contract for repairs to the Via Caecilia

A tablet of stone, dating to approximately 90–80 BC, found in a wall at Rome, records a public document dealing with repairs to the (unidentified) Via Caecilia; 1,000 paces equals a Roman mile.

. . . Works . . . on the Via Caecilia let out at contract . . . out of . . . thousand sesterces. At the thirty-fifth milestone a bridge over the river, the sum assigned, at the cost to the people of **5** . . . sesterces; Quintus Pamphilus, contractor, and workmen, with Titus Vibius Temudinus, city quaestor, as overseer of roads; the road must be laid in gravel from the 78th milestone and paved through the Apennines for a distance of 20,000 paces, the sum assigned, at the **10** cost to the people of 150,000 sesterces. Lucius Rufilius, freedman of Lucius and Lucius, . . . contractor, with Titus Vibius, quaestor, as overseer of roads; the road must be laid from the 98th milestone to the 11 . . . milestone . . . turn-off to Interamnium up to the 120th milestone; the sum assigned, at the cost to the people of 600,000(?) sesterces . . .

15 Titus Sepunius O . . . , son of Titus, contractor, with Titus Vibius Temudinus, city quaestor, as overseer of roads . . . fallen down arch . . . the sum assigned, at a cost to the people of . . . sesterces . . . ; . . . contractor, **20** with Titus Vibius, city quaestor, as overseer of roads . . .

2.8 *ILS* 6085, 53–67: The *lex Julia Municipalis*

This is an extract from Julius Caesar's town-planning law of 44 BC; included here are the sections which deal with roads, clearly an attempt to solve Rome's daytime traffic and waste disposal problems. For this law, see also doc. 13.59.

53 Where a building adjoins an alleyway, the owner shall keep this alleyway properly paved along the entire face of the building with durable, whole stones to the satisfaction of the aedile in charge of roads in that district in accordance with this law . . .

56 Regarding the roads which are or shall be within the city of Rome or where there is continuous habitation, no one after the first day of January next shall in the daytime lead or drive a wagon on them after sunrise or before the tenth hour of the day, except for the purposes of transporting materials for the construction of the sacred temples of the immortal gods, or for the carrying out of public works, or for removing from the city materials from those places which are being demolished by public contract. For those cases it shall be permitted by this law for specified people to drive or lead wagons for the reasons specified.

62 On those days on which the Vestal Virgins, the rex sacrorum, and the flamines have to ride on wagons in the city for the sake of the public sacrifices of the Roman people, or wagons have to be led in a triumphal procession on the day when someone celebrates a triumph, or wagons are needed for games publicly celebrated in Rome or within one mile of the city or for the procession for the games in the Circus Maximus, it is not the intention of this law to prevent the use of wagons in the city for these reasons and on those days.

66 It is not the intention of this law to prevent whatever ox wagons or donkey wagons have been driven into the city at night from leaving the city of Rome or within one mile of the city, empty or carrying excrement, between sunrise and the tenth hour of the day.

68 Regarding public places and public porticoes which are or shall be within the city of Rome or within one mile of the city of Rome, which are by law under the charge of aediles or of those magistrates who supervise the cleaning of roads and public places within the city of Rome or within one mile of the city of Rome, no one shall have anything built or erected in such places or porticoes, nor shall anyone acquire possession of any of these areas or porticoes, nor shall anyone have any part of them enclosed or shut off to prevent the people from access to and use of such places and porticoes, except for those people to whom permission has been granted by laws, plebiscites and senatorial decrees.

2.9 Livy *History of Rome* 9.43.25: The temple of Safety

Salus was deified 'safety', or the welfare of the state. The terms which ended the Second Samnite War (307/6 BC) were that the Samnites should provide grain for three months and a year's pay and tunic for each Roman soldier. Vowed in 311, the temple, on the Quirinal, was dedicated in 302.

In the same year, the contract for the temple of Safety was let out by the censor Gaius Junius Bubulcus, which he had vowed, while consul, during the Samnite war. He and his colleague Marcus Valerius Maximus built roads throughout the countryside at the public expense.

2.10 *ILS* 5348: Public amenities at Aletrium, c. 100 BC

On the front of a temple at Aletrium, 70 kilometres south-east of Rome. Varus spent a fortune on the town, as he restructured Aletrium on the lines of towns in the Greek East.

Lucius Betilienus Varus, son of Lucius, on the advice of the senate (of Aletrium), superintended the construction of the following works: all the streets **5** in the town, the colonnade leading to the citadel, a playing-field, a clock (horologium), a meat-market, the stuccoing of the basilica, the seats, the bathing pool; **10** he made a reservoir by the gate, with an aqueduct some 340 feet long bringing water to the town and citadel, and arches and sound water-pipes. On account of all this, they made him censor for the second time, and the senate ordered his son exempt from military service, **15** and the people gave him a statue and the title Censorinus (because he had been censor).

2.11 *ILS* 5706: Amenities at Pompeii

This inscription dates to c. 90–80 BC; the decurions are the members of the local senate.

Gaius Ulius, son of Gaius, and Publius Aninius, son of Gaius, Board of Two for pronouncing justice, let out a contract by decree of the decurions for the construction of a Spartan sweating-room and rub-down room and for repairs to porticoes and a wrestling-school **5** out of the money which they were required by law to expend on games or a memorial. They superintended and approved the completed work.

THE IDEOLOGY OF THE ROMAN SENATORIAL CLASS

Romans of the first century BC saw their ancestors as hard-working and frugal. Much of this perception is idealised by contrast with contemporary standards of living; there is evidence, however, that before the conquests of the second-century BC many of the senatorial class were farmers on a small scale. Lower down the social scale, the centurion Spurius Ligustinus in 171 had inherited one iugerum, less than an acre, of land, his wife was undowered, and he had to support eight children on this and his army service (doc. 5.9).

2.12 Cicero *On Old Age* 16.55–56: The mythology of the 'farmer-general'

From 218 BC (the *lex Claudia*) senators were forbidden to engage in large-scale trade and from then on they were mainly landowners. Cato the Elder is here praising the fact that senators of olden times lived and worked on their farms unless called on for public service. Of course this bears no relation to the reality of landowning aristocrats in the later Republic. Dentatus defeated the Samnites in 290 BC and Pyrrhus in 276. Cincinnatus was dictator in 458.

55 I could relate at length all the various charms of country life, but I realise I have already spoken too much . . . Well, it was in this sort of life that Manius Curius Dentatus spent his remaining years after his triumphs over the Samnites, the Sabines and Pyrrhus; and whenever I look at his farm, which is not far from mine, I cannot admire enough the frugality of the man and the spirit of his generation. **56** When the Samnites brought Curius a great weight of gold, as he sat before the fire, he refused it; for he said that he thought the glory was not in possessing the gold but in ruling those who had it. . . . In those times senators, that is, *senes* (elders), lived on farms – if it is true that Lucius Quinctius Cincinnatus was ploughing his fields when he was told that he had been appointed dictator . . . Marcus Curius Dentatus and other elders were summoned from their farms to serve in the senate, which is why the messengers who were sent to summon them were called travellers (*viatores*). Surely then the old age of men such as these, who took pleasure in cultivating the soil, was not unhappy? Indeed, in my opinion, I think that nothing could be happier than a farmer's life, not only because of the service he performs, since agriculture benefits the whole human race, but also because of the pleasure, which I have mentioned earlier, and the plenty and abundance of all things which contribute to the sustenance of men and even to the worship of the gods.

2.13 Dionysius of Halicarnassus *Roman Antiquities* 10.17.4–6: Cincinnatus, 458 BC

Suffect (substitute) consul in 460, Lucius Quinctius Cincinnatus was appointed dictator in 458 when a Roman army was besieged by the Aequi on Mount Algidus. Within 15 days, he raised an army, defeated the Aequi and returned to his plough.

4 It happened that at that moment Quinctius was ploughing some ground for sowing, and was himself following the lean oxen that were breaking up the fallow, without a tunic and wearing a small loin-cloth and a cap on his head. When he saw a crowd of people coming into the field, he halted his plough and for some time was uncertain who they were or what they wanted with him; then, when one ran up to him and told him to make himself look more decent, he went into the cottage, dressed, and came out to meet them. **5** The men who were there to escort him all greeted him not by his name but as consul, dressed him in the purple-bordered robe, placing in front of him the axes and other insignia of his magistracy, and asked him to follow them to the city. He paused for a moment and shed tears, only saying: 'So my field will be unsown this year, and we shall be in danger of not having enough food to support us.' Then he kissed his wife and, instructing her to look after things at home, went off to the city. **6** I am led to narrate these details for no other reason than to make clear to everyone what type of men the leaders of Rome were at that time, that they worked with their own hands, led self-disciplined lives, did not complain about honourable poverty, and, far from pursuing positions of royal power, actually refused them when offered.

2.14 Plutarch *Life of Cato the Elder* 3.1–2, 4.4–6:
The old-style Roman

Marcus Porcius Cato, Cato the Elder, was consul in 195 and censor in 184. He was noted for his parsimony and adherence to traditional Roman values. He was against all unnecessary expenditure; for his views on the treatment of slaves, see docs 6.35–38.

3.1 There was a certain man of high birth and great influence at Rome, who was skilled at perceiving excellence in its early stages and well disposed to cultivate it and bring it into repute, Valerius Flaccus. **2** He had a farm adjoining that of Cato and, learning from Cato's servants of the way he farmed his own land and of his lifestyle, was amazed to hear them relate how Cato, early in the morning, walked to the market-place and pleaded the cases of all who wanted his aid and then returned to his farm, where, clad in a sleeveless tunic in the winter, and stripped in summer, he worked with his servants, then sat down with them to eat the same bread and drink the same wine. . . .
    4.4 He tells us that he never wore clothing worth more than 100 drachmas; that, even when he was praetor or consul, he drank the same wine as his slaves and that, as for fish and meat, he would buy for his dinner 30 asses worth from the market, and even this for the city's sake to strengthen his body for military service; **5** that he once inherited an embroidered Babylonian mantle, but sold it at once; that not a single one of his cottages was plastered; that he never paid more than 1,500 drachmas for a slave, as he wanted not the delicate or handsome types but tough workmen like grooms and herdsmen . . . **6** In general, he said, he thought nothing cheap that one could do without, but that what a person did not need, even if it cost one cent (an as), was expensive; also that he acquired lands where crops were raised and cattle herded, not those where lawns were sprinkled and paths swept.

2.15 Cato *On Farming* 11.1–5: Running a vineyard

The *De agri cultura* (*On Farming*) of c. 160 BC is the only work of Cato which survives complete. In it Cato gives detailed advice to landowners of moderately sized slave-run estates producing wine and olive oil (the 'villa system' or estates of some 25 to 75 hectares). A culleus holds 20 amphorae; an amphora some 26 litres or one cubic foot of dry goods.

1 This is the equipment necessary for a vineyard of 100 iugera: an overseer, a house-keeper, 10 labourers, 1 oxherd, 1 donkey-driver, 1 willow-worker, 1 swineherd – a total of 16 persons; 2 oxen, 2 cart-donkeys, 1 donkey for the mill; 3 complete presses, jars to hold five harvests of a total of 800 cullei, 20 jars for holding grape-pulp, **2** 20 for grain, and the tops and covers for each jar, 6 pots made of broom, 4 amphorae of broom, 2 funnels, 3 wicker-work strainers, 3 strainers to remove the flower, 10 vessels for the unfermented juice; 2 carts, 2 ploughs, 1 wagon-yoke, 1 yoke for carrying wine (probably a manuscript error for ox harnesses), 1 donkey yoke, 1 bronze disk, 1 grinding-stone; a bronze vessel holding a culleus, 1 cover for a bronze vessel, 3 iron hooks, 1 cooking-pot holding a culleus, **3** 2 water pots, 1 watering-pot, 1 basin, 1 small pot, 1 slop-basin, 1 water bucket, 1 little dish, 1 ladle, 1 candlestick, 1 chamber-pot, 4 beds, 1 bench, 2 tables, 1 stone table, 1 clothes chest, 1 cupboard, 6 long benches, 1 well-wheel, 1 iron-tipped corn-measure, 1 half-measure, 1 wash-tub, 1 soaking-tub, 1 vat for lupines, 10 large jars; **4** ox-harnesses, donkey-harnesses, 3 rugs, 3 utensils, 3 strainers for wine-lees, 3 donkey-mills, 1 hand-mill; tools: 5 reed knives, 6 vine-dresser's knives, 3 pruning-hooks, 5 axes, 4 wedges, 2 ploughshares, 10 forks, 6 spades, 4 shovels, 2 four-toothed rakes, 4 manure-hampers, 1 manure-basket, 40 grape-harvesting hooks, 10 bill-hooks for cutting broom, 2 braziers, 2 pairs of fire-tongs, 1 fire-shovel; **5** 20 small Amerine baskets, 40 planting baskets or trays, 40 wooden spades, 2 treading vats, 4 mattresses, 4 coverlets, 6 cushions, 6 bed-covers, 3 towels, 6 patchwork cloaks for slaves.

2.16 Cato *On Farming* 135.1–3: Retail goods

Cato was born at Tusculum, and his advice in this work is directed especially to farmers in Latium and Campania.

1 At Rome buy tunics, togas, coats, patchwork cloaks and boots; caps, iron tools, knives, spades, mattocks, axes, harness, bits, and small chains at Cales and Minturnae; spades at Venafrum; carts at Suessa and in Lucania; vats and tubs at Trebla, Alba and at Rome; **2** and tiles at Venafrum. Roman ploughs will be good for fertile soil, Campanian for blackish earth. Roman yokes will be the best. Detachable ploughshares will be the best. Olive-crushers at Pompeii, Nola and at the wall of Rufrium; locks and bolts at Rome; buckets, oil-urns, water-pitchers, wine-urns, and other bronze vessels at Capua and Nola; Campanian strainers will be found useful; **3** pulley-ropes and all goods made of broom at Capua; Roman strainers at Suessa and Casinum, but the best will be at Rome. Who makes press-ropes? Lucius Tunnius at Casinum, Gaius Mennius, son of Lucius, at Venafrum.

2.17 Cato *On Farming* 156.1: The uses of cabbage

Cato also gives recipes for cleaning out the digestive tract, cures for colic, strangury, head-aches and ulcers, and poultices (a cabbage poultice helps to heal a dislocation). The urine of those who eat cabbage can be used to bath babies and cure weak eyes.

On cabbage and how it promotes digestion. It is the cabbage which surpasses all other vegetables. It may be eaten either cooked or raw. If you eat it raw, dip it in vinegar. It promotes digestion marvellously, makes a good laxative, and the urine is good for everything (i.e., medicinally). If you want to drink a good deal and dine freely at a dinner party, before dinner eat as much raw cabbage, seasoned with vinegar, as you wish, and similarly after dinner eat some five leaves; it will make you feel as though you had not dined and you can drink as much as you want.

2.18 Cicero *Letters to his Friends* 16.21.7: A Roman farmer

In 44 BC, in a letter to his father's freedman Tiro, who had bought a farm, Marcus Cicero junior jokes about his becoming a proper countryman, even to keeping the stones from dessert to sow them later. For Tiro, see docs 6.51–52.

You're a land-owner! You'll have to drop all citified refinements – you've become a country Roman! How I picture you before my eyes right now, and a very pleasant sight it is! For I seem to see you buying country gear, talking to your bailiff, and saving up in your hem the fruit-stones from dessert.

2.19 Plutarch *Life of Cato the Elder* 21.5–7: Cato's mercantile activities

Though Cic. *Off.* 2.89 says Cato compared moneylending to murder, Cato engaged in it himself – though only at low risk; compare the moneylending activities of Marcus Junius Brutus (doc. 5.72).

5 When he applied himself more seriously to making money, he considered agriculture more as an amusement than profitable, and he invested his capital in safe and certain ventures, buying ponds, hot springs, places given over to fullers, pitch works, land with natural pastures and woods – from which he acquired a great deal of money and which could not, as he used to say, 'be ruined by Jupiter'. **6** He also engaged in the most criticised type of moneylending, namely on ships, in the following way. He required the borrowers to form a large partnership; when there were 50 partners and as many ships, he acquired one share in this company himself through his freedman Quintio, who worked with the borrowers and sailed with them. **7** So the entire risk was not his, only a small part of it, and his profits were large.

2.20 Seneca the Younger *Letters* 86.1, 4–6, 11–12: Scipio Africanus' baths

Seneca (died AD 65) paid a visit to the villa at Liternum (north of Cumae) which had belonged to P. Cornelius Scipio Africanus, the victor over Hannibal. In describing the villa's baths he contrasts modern luxury with antique austerity.

1 I am writing this letter to you while staying at the villa of Scipio Africanus himself . . . **4** I have looked at the house, which is built of squared stone . . . and at the narrow little bath, dark in keeping with ancient custom (for our ancestors thought that a bath should not be hot unless dark too). It was, therefore, a great delight to me to compare Scipio's habits with our own. **5** In this recess, the 'terror of Carthage', to whom Rome is indebted for having been captured only once (i.e., by the Gauls), used to bathe a body exhausted by farm work. For Scipio kept himself busy with hard work and even cultivated the land himself, as was the custom with the Romans of old. He stood under this mean roof, and this paltry floor bore his weight. **6** But who is there today who could bear to bathe like this? Everyone thinks himself poor and worthless unless his walls sparkle with large and costly decorations, unless marbles from Alexandria are set off by Numidian mosaics, unless their borders are covered on all sides with elaborate designs and multi-coloured like paintings, unless the vaulted roof is covered with glass, unless Thasian marble, once a rare sight even in a temple, lines our swimming pools . . . **11** Of what uncouthness some people nowadays condemn Scipio, because he did not let daylight into his caldarium through wide windows, because he did not cook himself in a sunlit room and hang around before boiling in his bath. 'Wretched man!' they say. 'He didn't know how to live well. He did not bathe in unfiltered water – it was often dirty and after heavy rain was almost muddy!' But it didn't bother Scipio much if he had to bathe like that; he came to the baths to wash off sweat, not unguents. **12** And what do you suppose some people will comment? 'I don't envy Scipio; whoever had to bathe like that was really living in exile!' Actually, if you only knew, he didn't bathe every day. Those who have recorded the ancient customs say that they washed just their arms and legs every day, since those parts of the body gathered dirt from work, and washed the rest only once a week. Someone will say at this point, 'They must have been filthy chaps! Can you imagine how they smelled?' But they smelled of the army, hard work and manliness!

CONSPICUOUS CONSUMPTION IN ROME

Despite the ideals of frugality, simplicity and adherence to traditional values, there was increasing dependence on luxury goods and magnificent lifestyles from the mid-second century BC: see also docs 5.54–66. Cicero's friend Atticus may not have been a typical equestrian, but some idea of inherited wealth in the first century BC can be seen from the fact that he inherited 2 million sesterces from his father and a further 10 million from his uncle who adopted him (doc. 12.26).

2.21 Plutarch *Life of Crassus* 2.1–7: A very wealthy Roman

Crassus played the major part in defeating the slave rebellion of Spartacus and was consul in 70 and 55 (both times with Pompey). He became enormously wealthy during Sulla's proscriptions (docs 11.19–25).

1 The Romans say that this one vice, avarice, overshadowed Crassus' many virtues; it seems that this one became stronger in him than all other vices and obscured the rest. **2** The greatest proofs of his avarice are considered to be the way he made his money and the immensity of his wealth. **3** For, to begin with, he possessed no more than 300 talents, but during his consulship he dedicated a tenth to Hercules and provided a feast for all the people, as well as giving every Roman from his own purse enough grain to live on for three months, and yet, when he made a calculation of his assets before his Parthian expedition, he found he was worth 7,100 talents. **4** Most of this money, if the truth, though scandalous, be told, he collected through fire and war, making his greatest profits from public misfortunes. For, when Sulla took over Rome and sold the property of the men he had proscribed, considering it and calling it spoils of war, he wanted to share the guilt with as many of the most influential men as possible, while Crassus refused neither to take nor to buy it from him. **5** In addition, when he saw what familiar and normal disasters at Rome fires were, and the collapse of buildings because of their weight and contiguity, he started buying slaves who were architects and builders. When he had more than 500 of these, he used to purchase houses that were on fire and ones next to those on fire, since because of their fear and uncertainty the owners would sell at a low price, and, as a result, the greater part of Rome came into his possession. . . . **7** And although he owned numerous silver mines and very valuable land with labourers on it, yet one might consider all this to be nothing in comparison with the value of his slaves, of whom he owned large numbers and who were highly qualified – readers, secretaries, silversmiths, stewards, waiters . . .

2.22 Plutarch *Life of Lucullus* 39.2–5, 42.1–2: Lucullus and luxury

L. Licinius Lucullus was one of Sulla's supporters and the only officer who backed his march on Rome in 88 BC. Consul in 74, he was given the command against Mithridates, which Pompey took over through the *lex Manilia* in 66. After attempts to frustrate ratification of Pompey's eastern settlements (docs 12.36, 44), he retired from politics to live in luxury.

39.2 I must assign to frivolity the extravagant buildings and covered walks and baths, and, still more, his paintings and statues and his devotion to these arts, which he collected at enormous expense, pouring lavishly into these the immense and splendid wealth which he had amassed during his commands – and even now, when luxurious living has increased to such an extent, the gardens of Lucullus are numbered among the most extravagant of the imperial gardens. **3** As for his constructions on the seashore and near Naples, where he suspended hills over immense tunnels and circled his residences with rings of sea and streams for fish-breeding and built dwellings surrounded by sea, Tubero the Stoic on seeing them called him 'Xerxes in a toga'. **4** He also had country residences near Tusculum with belvederes commanding the view and complexes of open dining-rooms and walkways, where Pompey once criticised Lucullus for having organised his country residence in the best possible way for summer but having made it uninhabitable in winter. **5** Lucullus just laughed at him and said, 'Do you suppose then that I have less sense than cranes and storks and fail to change abodes according to the seasons?' . . . **42.1** He collected many well-written books, his use of which reflected better on him than the way he acquired them, and his libraries were thrown open to everyone, as well as the colonnades around them and rooms for study, which were always open without restriction to the Greeks, who frequented them as if they were a lodging place of the Muses and spent the day there with each other, gladly escaping from their other occupations. **2** Lucullus often also spent time there with them, walking in the colonnades with their scholars and assisting their statesmen in whatever they wanted; and in general his house was a home and town hall (prytaneion) for any Greeks who came to Rome.

2.23 Macrobius *Saturnalia* 3.13.10–12: A pontifical banquet

Q. Caecilius Metellus Pius was the son of Metellus Numidicus (see docs 9.6–9, 28). He was pontifex maximus and Sulla's colleague as consul in 80 BC. Here L. Cornelius Lentulus Niger is being installed as flamen of Mars (flamen Martialis) c. 69 BC; four of the six Vestals were present. Feasts were a traditional part of the ritual of priestly colleges.

10 You must understand that extravagance was found among the most respectable dignitaries, for I would like to put before you the details of a very early pontifical banquet which is recorded in the fourth *Register* of the famous pontifex maximus Metellus, in the following words: **11** 'On the ninth day before the Kalends of September, the day on which Lentulus was installed as flamen of Mars, the house was decorated, the dining-room furnished with ivory couches, and the pontiffs reclined on two of the dining-couches: Quintus Catulus, Marcus Aemilius Lepidus, Decimus Silvanus, Gaius Caesar, . . . the chief priest (rex sacrorum), Publius Scaevola, Sextus . . . Quintus Cornelius, Publius Volumnius, Publius Albinovanus and Lucius Julius Caesar, the augur who installed Lentulus. On the third dining-couch were Popilia, Perpennia, Licinia and Arruntia, the Vestal virgins, and Lentulus' wife Publicia the flaminica and Sempronia his mother-in-law. **12** 'This was the dinner: for the first course, sea urchins, raw oysters, as many as they wanted, giant mussels, cockles, thrushes on asparagus, fattened hens, a dish of oysters and mussels, shell-fish (both black and white); then came a course of cockles, shell-fish, sea-nettles, fig-peckers, haunches of goat and boar, fattened fowls in pastry, fig-peckers, murex and purple fish. For the main course, sow's udders, half-heads of boar, a dish of fish, a dish of sow's udders, ducks, boiled teal, hares, roast fattened fowls, creamed wheat and Picentine rolls.'

2.24 Varro *On Farming* 3.6.1, 6, 15.1–2, 17.2–3: Peafowl, dormice and lampreys

Murena (cos. 87 BC and flamen dialis) is here speaking with the augur Appius Claudius and other colleagues. Hirrus is the son-in-law of one of the speakers, Cossinius; Hortensius, one of Cicero's rivals in the courts, was consul in 69.

6.1 (Lucius Cornelius) Merula said, 'As to peafowl, it is within our memory that flocks of them began to be kept and sold at high prices. Marcus Aufidius Lurco is said to pull in more than 60,000 sesterces a year from them (here follows detailed advice on how to keep them) . . . **6** It is said that Quintus Hortensius (cos. 69) was the first to serve these on the occasion of his inauguration as aedile, which was lauded rather by the dilettanti than by men of strict virtue. As many quickly followed his example, they raised the price to such an extent that their eggs now sell for 5 denarii each, the birds themselves easily for 50, and a flock of 100 easily brings in 40,000 sesterces – indeed, Abuccius used to say that if you wanted three chicks for every hen you could get as much as 60,000 . . . '

15.1 The accommodation for dormice is built on a different design (than that for snails), the ground being surrounded not by water but by a wall; this is entirely covered on the inside by smooth stone or plaster, so that they cannot climb out. Inside it there should be small nut-bearing trees. When these do not bear fruit, acorns and chestnuts should be thrown inside the wall for them to fill up on. **2** They should have rather roomy holes made for them in which they can have their young; there should be little water as they don't use a great deal of it and prefer a dry spot. They are fattened up in large jars, which a lot of people even keep inside their villas, and which potters fashion in a very different shape from other jars, as they make channels along the sides and a hollow in which to put the food. In a jar like this people place acorns, walnuts or chestnuts. When a cover is placed over them the dormice grow fat in the dark . . .

17.2 There are two types of fish-ponds, fresh and salt, the one is open to ordinary people and not without profit, where the Nymphs provide water for our farm-house fish; the sea-water ponds of our nobles, however, for which Neptune has to provide the water and the fish, concern the eye more than the purse, and drain the owner's pocket rather than fill it. In the first place, they are constructed at great expense, secondly they are stocked at great expense, and thirdly they are maintained at great expense. **3** (Gaius Lucilius) Hirrus used to receive 12,000 sesterces from the buildings around his fish-ponds, but he spent all that income on the food he gave his fish. No wonder – I remember that, on one occasion, he lent Caesar 2,000 lampreys by weight and that, on account of the great number of fish, his villa sold for 4,000,000 sesterces.

GLORIA

Aristocratic Rome was a highly competitive culture. It was important to be seen to live up to one's ancestors' achievements and fulfil family expectations, ideally by achieving the highest political office, the consulship. This gave a man, and his family, dignitas (prestige), gloria (renown) and auctoritas (influence and authoritative position). The successful consular candidate would then hope for a province where he could show his abilities, recoup his electioneering expenses and, with luck, achieve a military triumph, the highest and most conspicuous honour. Roman values were those of a warrior culture based on a cult of victory, and aristocratic competition and ambition provided the necessary officers of state on an annual basis. Attitudes towards aristocratic virtues can be seen in epitaphs, especially those of the Scipiones (docs 2.25–26), which stress the magistracies they have held (or could have held) and their military victories.

2.25 *ILS* 4: Epitaph for Publius Cornelius Scipio

This inscription is probably the epitaph of a son of Scipio Africanus who died c. 170 BC, presented here as young to emphasise the reason for his lack of public office – he was in fact an invalid for most of his life; as flamen dialis he could not have a military career (doc. 3.21) and he became an augur in 180.

> You who have worn the distinguished cap of the flamen dialis,
> Death caused all your qualities to be short-lived –
> Your honour and reputation and courage, your glory and talents,
> Through which, if you had been permitted to enjoy a long life,
> You would easily have surpassed by your deeds the glory of your ancestors.
> For which reason, Scipio, Earth joyfully receives you in her embrace,
> Publius Cornelius, child of Publius.

2.26 *ILS* 6: A noble Roman

This Scipio was praetor in 139 (the name Hispanus implies service in Spain). This epitaph dates to c. 135. Scipio died at about 40 years of age, before he could stand for the consulship. The Board of Ten for making sacrifices was the college of priests who preserved the Sibylline books: docs 3.38–39.

> Gnaeus Cornelius Scipio Hispanus, son of Gnaeus, praetor, curule aedile, quaestor, twice military tribune, member of the Board of Ten for judging lawsuits, member of the Board of Ten for making sacrifices.

> By my conduct I augmented the virtues of my family,
> I had a family, I emulated the deeds of my father.
> I upheld the praise of my ancestors, so that they are glad
> I was created of their line; my magistracies have ennobled my lineage.

2.27 Sallust *Jugurthine War* 4.5–6: Ancestral masks

Wax masks of ancestors (imagines) were carried in the funeral processions of nobles and, according to Polybius, were kept in a prominent place in the house at other times (doc. 3.77). Sallust is here presumably referring to the brothers Q. Fabius Maximus Aemilianus and P. Cornelius Scipio Aemilianus, the sons of L. Aemilius Paullus.

5 I have often heard that Quintus Maximus, Publius Scipio, and other distinguished men of our country were accustomed to declare that, whenever they looked on the masks of their ancestors, their hearts were set aflame in the pursuit of virtue. **6** Of course, they did not mean that the wax or the effigy had any such power over them, but that it is the memory of great achievements that kindles a flame in the breasts of eminent men that cannot be extinguished until their own excellence (virtus) has come to rival the reputation (fama) and glory (gloria) of their forefathers.

2.28 Livy *History of Rome* 8.40.3–5: Family pride falsifies historical records

Livy is here discussing the events of 322 BC and the dictatorship of Aulus Cornelius Cossus (cos. 343, 332 BC).

3 It is not easy to choose between the facts and the authorities. **4** The record has been falsified, I think, by funeral eulogies and lying inscriptions on portrait busts, each family trying to appropriate to itself by deception and falsification the fame of successes and dignities, **5** and this practice has led to confusion both in the achievements of individuals and in the public records of events.

2.29 Pliny *Natural History* 7.139–40: A consular's greatest aims

Lucius Caecilius Metellus, consul in 251 and 247 BC, magister equitum in 249, pontifex maximus from 243, and dictator in charge of holding elections in 224, had been a general in the First Punic War, winning a major victory over the Carthaginians at Panormus in Sicily in 250, which included the capture of numerous elephants. His funeral speech was delivered by his son Quintus in 221 BC.

139 Quintus Metellus, in the oration which he gave at the final eulogy of his father the pontiff Lucius Metellus, twice consul, dictator, Master of the Horse, and land-commissioner, who was the first to lead elephants in his triumph from the First Punic War, left it in writing that his father had achieved the ten greatest and most glorious objects in the pursuit of which wise men pass their lives: **140** for he had aimed at being a first-class warrior, an outstanding orator, a brave and courageous general, at taking charge of events of the highest importance, enjoying the greatest honour, possessing exceptional wisdom, being considered the chief of all the senators, acquiring great wealth in a respectable way, leaving many children, and being the most distinguished person in the state; and stated that these had befallen his father and none other since the foundation of Rome.

2.30 Cicero *On Duties* 1.72–73: The importance of ambition

On Duties (*De officiis*) was written for Cicero's son Marcus in 44 BC. Quintus supposedly wrote a guidebook on how to stand for the consulship (doc. 2.38). Despite a rather 'wild youth', Marcus junior did become consul, in 30 BC, and then proconsul of Asia.

72 Those to whom nature has given the qualities necessary for engaging in public affairs should cast aside all hesitation, strive for election to magistracies, and take part in government; for there is no other way that the state can be governed or greatness of mind be displayed. Those in charge of government, no less than philosophers, and perhaps even more so, need to possess that greatness of spirit and contempt for human affairs which I so often mention, together with peace of mind and freedom from care, if they are to avoid worry and live with dignity and consistency. **73** This is easier for philosophers, as, their lives being less subject to the blows of fortune, their wants are fewer and, if any misfortune occurs, their fall is not so heavy. It is, therefore, not without reason that stronger emotions are aroused in those who engage in public life than in those who live quietly, as well as greater efforts to succeed; all the more, then, is their need to possess greatness of spirit and freedom from troubles.

Whoever enters government should take care to consider not only the honour involved but also whether he has the capacity to succeed; at the same time, he should ensure that he does not despair prematurely through cowardice nor be over-confident through ambition. In all such enterprises, before undertaking them, careful preparation is essential.

2.31 Cicero *Letters to his Brother Quintus* 1.1.43–44: Family prestige

This letter was written in 60 BC, when Quintus was propraetor of Asia: he had been praetor in 62 and governed Asia from 61 to 58. Cicero is here presenting his own consulship of 63 BC as a benchmark for the rest of the family.

43 At the same time, bear in mind that we are not now working towards a glory we do not yet possess and which we hope for, but are striving for a glory already won, which, indeed, it was not so much our aim to win in the past as it is now to defend in the present. And if anything I possess could be disassociated from you, I would desire nothing greater than the status I have already won. But now, indeed, the circumstances are such that, unless all your deeds and words over there accord with my achievements, I think that, great as have been my labours and achievements – all of which you have shared – they have gained me nothing at all. If, however, you have helped me more than anyone to acquire a splendid name, you will certainly work harder than others to ensure that I retain it. You should take into account the opinions and judgements not only of the men of today but of those to come in the future; and their judgement will be the more accurate, being free from detraction and malice. **44** Finally, you also ought to recollect that you are not seeking glory for yourself alone; even if that were the case you would not be unmindful of it, especially as you have always wished to immortalise the memory of your name with the most splendid memorials, but that you have to share it with me and hand it on to our children.

THE ROMAN TRIUMPH

The celebration of a triumph was the ultimate goal for the Roman senatorial class. Victorious generals processed into Rome via the triumphal gate to the temple of Jupiter Capitolinus. The triumphator was carried on a four-horse chariot preceded by his lictors, accompanied by his army, captives, spoils, freed prisoners of war, and the senate and magistrates. A prerequisite for the triumph was to have killed 5,000 of the enemy. A general could be awarded an oratio, or lesser triumph, for more minor victories; triumphs could not be celebrated over Roman citizens.

2.32 Dionysius of Halicarnassus *Roman Antiquities* 5.47.1–3, 8.67.9: The triumph and ovatio

Postumius and Menenius were consuls in 503 BC. Postumius was given the lesser triumph because he had previously been defeated and lost a large number of his men. Lucius Siccius Dentatus was a plebeian general of the mid-fifth century BC. Licinius Macer was tribune in 73 and praetor in 68.

5.47.1 After achieving a brilliant victory, they returned home. **2** They were both honoured with triumphs by the senate, Menenius with the greater and more honourable type, entering the city in a royal chariot, and Postumius with the lesser and inferior type which they call ouastes (ovation), altering the name which is Greek to this meaningless form. For it was originally called euastes, from what actually took place, from what I conjecture and find recorded in many native histories, **3** and the senate, as Licinius (Macer) relates, introduced this type of triumph for the first time on this occasion. It differs from the other, firstly in that the general who celebrates the triumph called the ovation enters the city on foot, followed by his army, and not in a chariot like the other; and secondly because he does not wear the embroidered robe decorated with gold, with which the other is adorned, nor does he have the golden crown, but is dressed in a white toga bordered with purple, the native dress of the consuls and praetors, and wears a crown of laurel; he is also inferior to the other in not holding a sceptre, though everything else is the same.

8.67.9 Since Siccius seemed to have freed the state from the greater fear by his destruction of the insolent army of the Volscians and slaughter of their general, they voted him the greater triumph; he therefore drove into the city with the spoils, the prisoners, and the army that had fought under him, riding in a chariot drawn by horses with golden bridles and dressed in the royal robes, as is the custom in the greater triumphs. To Aquilius they granted the lesser triumph, which they call an ovation . . .

2.33 Livy *History of Rome* 10.46.2–6: A triumph over Samnites

Livy describes the triumph of Lucius Papirius Cursor, consul in 293 BC, over the Samnites, whom he defeated at Aquilonia. For crowns as military decorations, see doc. 5.7.

2 On his arrival at Rome Papirius was unanimously granted a triumph. He celebrated his triumph while still in office, in a style which was splendid for those times. **3** Infantry and cavalry marched or rode past adorned with their decorations; many civic crowns and crowns won by the first to climb a rampart or wall were to be seen; **4** the spoils won from the Samnites were examined and compared in splendour and beauty with those his father had won, which were well known from being often used to decorate public places; a number of noble prisoners, distinguished for their own and their fathers' deeds, were led in the procession. **5** 2,533,000 pounds of heavy bronze were carried past; this bronze was said to have been acquired from the sale of prisoners; there were 1,830 pounds of silver which had been taken from the cities. All the bronze and silver was put in the treasury, with none of the booty being given to the soldiers; **6** the bad feeling to which this gave rise among the people was augmented by the collection of a war-tax to pay the soldiers, since, if he had forgone the glory of placing the captured money in the treasury, the soldiers could have been given a donative out of the booty, as well as providing for their pay.

2.34 Plutarch *Life of Lucullus* 37.3–6: Lucullus' triumph

Lucullus' triumph in 66 BC was blocked by his political opponents, and he was accused of deliberately prolonging the war against Mithridates and appropriating money. His triumph was finally celebrated in 63.

3 Lucullus exerted himself strongly against this, and the foremost and most influential men mingled with the tribes and, after much entreaty and hard work, eventually persuaded the people to allow him a triumph, but not, like some, a triumph which was astonishing and tumultuous from the length of the procession and the multitude of objects carried in it. Instead, he adorned the circus of Flaminius with the arms of the enemy, of which there was an immense number, and with the royal war-engines; and this was a great spectacle in itself which was hardly despicable. **4** Some of the mail-clad horsemen and ten of the scythe-bearing chariots took part in the procession, as well as 60 of the king's friends and generals, and 110 bronze-beaked war-ships were also carried in it, with a golden statue of Mithridates himself, 6 feet high, a shield decorated with jewels, 20 litters of silver vessels and 32 litters of gold cups, armour and coins. **5** These were carried by men; and there were eight mules carrying golden couches, 56 with ingots of silver and 107 more with somewhat less than 2,700,000 pieces of silver coin. **6** There were also records on tablets of the money already paid by him to Pompey for the war against the pirates and to the public treasurers, and of the fact, too, that each of his soldiers had received 950 drachmas. Moreover, Lucullus gave a splendid feast to the city and the surrounding villages, which are called Vici.

2.35 Suetonius *Life of the Deified Julius* 37.1–39.4: Caesar's triumphs

Caesar celebrated triumphs over Gaul, Egypt, Pontus, Africa and Spain. The Gallic, Egyptian, Pontic and African triumphs were celebrated between 20 September and 1 October 46, the Spanish one after the victory over the Pompeians at Munda in October 45 BC.

37.1 With the wars over, Caesar celebrated five triumphs, four in the same month after defeating Scipio, with a few days' interval between them, and a fifth after overcoming Pompey's sons. The first and most splendid of his triumphs was the Gallic, after this came the Alexandrian, the Pontic, the African and, lastly, the Spanish, each different in its splendour and staging. **2** On the day of his Gallic triumph, as he rode through the Velabrum, he was nearly thrown from his chariot when the axle broke, and he ascended to the Capital between forty elephants, in two lines on his right and left, carrying torches. In the Pontic triumph, among the procession's litters, one carried a sign of three words: 'I came, I saw, I conquered!' This referred not to the events of the war, like the others, but to the swiftness of the victory. **38.1** Every infantryman in Caesar's veteran legions received as booty 24,000 sesterces, in addition to the 2,000 sesterces paid them at the beginning of the civil war. He also gave them all a farm, but not grouped together so as not to evict the possessors. To the 10 modii of grain and 10 pounds of oil given to every individual of the people, he added the 300 sesterces, which he had promised at first and now raised to 400, because of the delay. **2** He also remitted a year's rent at Rome to those who paid up to 2,000 sesterces, though in Italy not above 500 sesterces. He added a banquet and distribution of meat, and two dinners following his Spanish victory; for he considered that the first had not been sufficiently splendid, and five days later served a second more magnificent one.

39.1 He put on spectacles of various kinds: a gladiatorial contest, plays for all districts of Rome with actors in all languages, chariot-races in the circus, athletic competitions and a naval battle. At the contest in the forum, Furius Leptinus, of praetorian family, fought Quintus Calpenus, a former senator and lawyer. The sons of leaders of Asia and Bithynia danced the Pyrrhic sword dance. **2** In the plays, Decimus Laberius, a Roman eques, staged his own farce and, after being given 500,000 sesterces and his gold ring (the badge of equestrian rank), walked across from the stage through the orchestra to the equites' 14 rows of seats. At the circus the track was lengthened at either end, and on the race-course, around which a trench had been dug, young aristocrats drove four-horse and two-horse chariots or rode pairs of horses, jumping from one to another. Two troops of older and younger boys performed the Troy game. **3** Wild-beast hunts were put on five days in a row and ended with a battle between two forces comprised of 500 infantry, 20 elephants and 30 cavalry . . . The athletes competed over a three-day period in a temporary stadium built on the Campus Martius.

4 In the naval battle, on a lake dug in the Lesser Codeta, Tyrian and Egyptian fleets, with ships with two, three or four banks of oars and a great number of combatants, engaged each other. Such huge numbers of spectators flocked to these shows from all directions that many visitors had to sleep in tents pitched along the streets or roads, and large numbers were crushed to death by the crowd, among them two senators.

CANDIDATURE FOR OFFICE

The term for canvassing for office was petitio (literally, seeking or asking); ambitio was the pursuit of office, from ambire (to go around), implying the solicitation of votes; from the term ambitio comes ambitus (initially the acting of canvassing, but later meaning electoral malpractice or bribery), which was endemic to the Roman electoral system, since, due to the workings of the cursus honorum, there was intense competition for the consulship in most years. Candidates for office were of course supposed to engage in legitimate expenses in order to entertain or materially benefit sections of the electorate, particularly fellow tribesmen and clients, and the giving of games earlier in one's career, specifically as aedile, was a good electioneering ploy for the future: cf. Caesar's games as aedile (doc. 2.76). Canvassers in Rome wore a specially whitened toga (the toga candidata: hence the term 'candidate').

2.36 Plutarch *Roman Questions* 49: The toga without the tunic

Candidates for office went about in the forum dressed in a toga but without a tunic, to emphasise their humility or to display their wounds. Cato the Younger did this, presumably to show his adherence to traditional customs and values.

Why was it the custom for those canvassing for a magistracy to do this in a toga but without a tunic, as Cato has recorded? Was it so they did not carry money in its folds and hand out bribes? Or was it, rather, because they used to judge those worthy of office not by their family, wealth or reputation, but by their wounds and scars? So, to ensure that these were visible to anyone who met them, they used to go down to canvass without tunics. Or were they trying to curry popular favour through thus humiliating themselves by their lack of clothes, as they do by hand-shaking, appeals and subservience?

2.37 Valerius Maximus 7.5.2: How a Scipio can lose an election

Publius Cornelius Scipio Nasica Serapio was praetor in 118 and consul in 111. Despite his stellar lineage as the son of the Nasica (cos. 138 BC) who had Tiberius Gracchus killed and great-grandson of Africanus, his ill-timed joke was enough to persuade the voters not to elect him aedile. Valerius has here confused this Nasica with the one who in 204 received the image of the Magna Mater when it arrived at Ostia (doc. 3.61).

Publius Scipio Nasica, a shining light of togate power, who as consul declared war on Jugurtha, who received in the most pious hands the Idaean mother, as she migrated from her Phrygian seat to our altars and hearths, who quelled numerous virulent uprisings by the weight of his auctoritas, in whom as their princeps the senate prided itself for so many years, when standing as a youth for the curule aedileship firmly grasped, as candidates do, someone's hand which had been toughened by farm labour and asked him as a joke whether he was accustomed to walk on his hands. The remark was picked up by those standing nearby and spread to the populace, thus causing Scipio's rejection: for all the rural tribes considered that this was a reflection on their poverty and unleashed their anger against his insolent raillery. So by restraining the minds of young aristocrats from rudeness, our state made them great and valuable citizens, and added to magistracies the weight of authority by not letting them assume they were sure of election.

2.38 [Q. Cicero] *A Short Guide to Electioneering* 2–3, 16–18, 34–38, 41–43, 50–53

This handbook on how to run for the consulship was supposedly written by Quintus for Marcus' campaign in 64, but it may be a later rhetorical exercise by someone well versed in Cicero's works and life.

2 Consider what city this is, what you are trying for, who you are. Nearly every day as you go down to the forum, you must keep repeating to yourself: 'I am a "novus homo", I am seeking the consulship, this is Rome.' You will compensate for your status as a 'new man' mainly through your reputation as a speaker. This has always granted great prestige; someone thought worthy of defending ex-consuls cannot be considered unworthy of the consulship. So, since you have this reputation to start with and you are what you are because of it, come prepared to speak as if in each law-suit it is your talents and abilities that are being judged. **3** Make sure that those aids in this regard, which I know you have in reserve, are ready and available, and often remind yourself of what Demetrius wrote about Demosthenes' hard work and practice. Next, see that people know about both the number of your friends and the type of people they are; for not many 'new men' have had as many as you have – all the publicani, almost all of the order of equites, many townships entirely your own, many men of all kinds of rank that you have defended, several guilds, as well as large numbers of young men drawn to you by the study of oratory, and a crowd of friends in daily and assiduous attendance.

16 Canvassing for magistracies is divided into persistent hard work towards two objects, of which one is ensuring the support of friends and the other obtaining the goodwill of the people. The efforts of friends should be procured by services and obligations, long intimacy, good humour and natural charm. But this term 'friends' has a broader meaning in canvassing than in the rest of life: for anyone who shows you some goodwill, who cultivates your acquaintance, who frequents your house, should be counted among the number of your 'friends'. It is, however, very valuable to be on pleasant and agreeable terms with those who are friends on more genuine grounds, such as kinship, relationship by marriage, membership of a sodality, or some other tie. **17** Next, all those intimate with you and many in your family circle must be brought to feel as much affection for you as possible and wish you every success, so too your fellow tribesmen, neighbours, clients, then your freedmen, and finally even your slaves – for nearly all the talk that shapes your public reputation comes from members of your own household. **18** Then you must set up friends of every sort – for show, men illustrious in rank or name (who, even if they do not actively work at canvassing, bring a candidate some prestige); for maintaining your legal rights, magistrates (particularly the consuls, then the tribunes of the plebs); for getting the support of the centuries, men of outstanding influence. Make a great effort above all to gain and retain the backing of those who have or hope to have from you control of a tribe, century or other advantage: for today men of ambition have worked out with every effort and exertion how to get what they want from their fellow tribesmen. Work by any means possible to get these men as genuine and wholehearted supporters of your candidature.

34 Now that I have mentioned attendance, you must ensure that you have it daily, from all types, ranks and ages, for the numbers themselves will indicate the strength of the support you will have at the actual election. There are three different kinds: first those who come to greet you at your house, next those who escort you when you leave home, and thirdly attendants generally. **35** The callers are more undiscriminating and, as is usual nowadays, call on a number of people. You must make even this minuscule service of theirs seem to be very gratifying to you. Show that you notice who comes to your house (mention it to their friends, who will repeat it to them, and say it often to them yourself); it often happens that men who visit numerous candidates, when they see that one takes special notice of this service, often attach themselves to him and abandon the rest, gradually becoming his supporters rather than shared and single-minded partisans rather than frauds . . . **36** As for the escorts, a more important service than that of the callers, make it quite clear that they are more gratifying to you, and as far as possible go down to the forum at fixed times – a crowd of escorts there daily makes a great impact and conveys great prestige. **37** The third group is the body of people who attend you constantly. To those who do this voluntarily, make sure that they realise that you are eternally indebted to them for this great service. To those who owe you this, openly demand this duty from those of them not too old or too busy, that they must regularly attend you themselves, and that those who are not able to do so in person must co-opt their relatives for this duty. I desire you very strongly and think it very pertinent to the occasion that you should always have a large gathering with you. **38** Furthermore, it will bring you great credit and the highest prestige if you have with you those whom you have defended and who have been rescued and set free in law-suits by you. Demand this openly from them, that, since it is through your doing, unpaid, that they have kept their property, their reputation, or their life and all their fortunes, and since there will never be another time for them to express their gratitude, they should repay you by this service. . . .

41 Since enough has been said of establishing friendships, I must now talk about the other part of the canvassing, which relates to dealing with the people. This requires the ability to address people by their names, ingratiation, constant attendance, generosity, publicity, outward show and promise in public life. **42** First of all show that ability of yours, that you know people, so that it stands out, and work on it so that it improves daily – nothing in my view appears more popular and gratifying. Then, something you lack naturally, resolve to adopt the appearance of it so well that it seems to be natural: you do not lack the affability appropriate to a pleasant and agreeable man, but what you desperately need is the ability to ingratiate yourself, which (even if it is a fault and shortcoming in other aspects of life) is indispensable when canvassing: when used to corrupt someone it is hateful, when used to strengthen friendship it is not so blameable, but it is indispensable for a candidate for office, whose face and appearance and conversation must be adapted and geared to the feelings and wishes of everyone he meets. **43** As for attendance, that needs no clarification – the word itself explains what it is. It is extremely important for you not to leave town, yet the gains you obtain from this attendance are not just that you are in Rome and in the forum, but canvassing uninterruptedly, calling on the same people often and, as far as possible, not allowing anyone to be in a position to say that they had not been canvassed by you, and canvassed enthusiastically and assiduously . . . .

50 The next point to be talked about is publicity, which you have to follow up as strongly as possible. All that I have already said earlier in this treatise involves wide publicity – your reputation in oratory, the efforts on your behalf of the publicani and order of equites, the goodwill of the nobles, the crowd of young men around you, the attendance of those who have been defended by you, the throng from Italian towns who have obviously come to Rome because of you. To ensure that they will say, and believe, that you know people well and are considerate and generous, appeal to them courteously and canvass continuously and assiduously and, to ensure that your house is full long before dawn with a multitude made up from all classes, give satisfaction to everyone in what you say, and to many in what you actually do, and see to it (in so far as it can be achieved by hard work, talent and diligence) that the people, instead of hearing of your reputation at second-hand from these persons, is of its own accord your enthusiastic supporter.

51 You have already won the support of the city mob and that of their political manipulators by promoting the career of Pompey, accepting the case of Manilius and defending Cornelius; we have to inspire backing which no one has ever possessed, as well as the goodwill of the most prestigious persons. You also have to make sure that everyone knows that Gnaeus Pompey gives you his strongest support and that your successful candidature would fit his plans exceptionally well. **52** And finally make sure that your whole canvass makes a great show, so magnificent, so impressive, so popular that it has the utmost splendour and prestige, and also, if it can be done in some way, there should be scandalous comments, fitting their lifestyles, about the criminal actions, lust and bribery of your rivals. **53** And also during your canvass it must be seen that great hopes and honourable views for the state hinge on you – but in your canvassing you must not deal with politics either in the senate or in popular meetings. Just keep this in mind: the senate should think that you, judging by your career, will be a future defender of its authority, the Roman knights and men of worth and property, from your past life, that you are committed to repose and peace and quiet, and the mob, since you have been a popularis at least in your speeches in political meetings and the courts, that you are devoted to their interests.

2.39 Cicero *In Defence of Murena* 77: Liberality or bribery?

Cicero's *Pro Murena* defends a consul-elect for 62 BC against the charge of bribery, arguing that the populace had been won over by Murena's splendid games as praetor in 65, as well as by his 'traditional' feasts and shows during his campaign in 63.

And so the Roman plebs should not be prevented from enjoying games, or gladiatorial contests, or banquets – all these our ancestors established – nor should candidates be restrained from showing that generosity which means liberality rather than bribery.

2.40 *CIL* I² 1641c, 1644a&c, 1656a&g, 1645a, 1665: Electioneering notices

These notices supporting candidates for election were painted, in red, on walls at Pompeii around the time of Sulla: the 'colonists' were Sulla's veterans. The shorthand must have been readily comprehensible to the passers-by: 1641c reads, 'L. Aqutium d. v. v. b. o. v. c.' – that is, 'duovirum, virum bonum, oro vos, coloni': 'as a member of the Board of Two, a fine man, I urge you, colonists (to elect him)'.

1641c	Lucius Aqutius – a fine chap! Colonists, I appeal to you (to elect him) member of the Board of Two!
1644a	Numerius Barcha – a fine chap! I appeal to you (to elect him) member of the Board of Two! So may Venus of Pompeii, holy, blessed (goddess) be kind to you.
1644c	Numerius Veius Barcha – may you rot!
1656a	Marcus Marius – I appeal to you to elect him aedile!

1656g Marcus Marius – a fine chap, I appeal to you, colonists!

1645c Quintus Caecilius – a generous man – for quaestor, I appeal to you!

1665 Quinctius. Anyone who votes against him should go and sit next
to a donkey!

2.41 Plutarch *Life of Aemilius Paullus* 38.2–7: Scipio Aemilianus and his supporters

Plutarch stresses here the popular nature of Scipio's support and the ways in which he promoted his image as popularis (cf. docs 5.51–53).

2 It was particular and noteworthy of Aemilius (Paullus) that, though he was
encouraged and honoured by the people to an exceptional degree, he remained
one of the aristocratic faction and neither said nor did anything to win the favour
of the multitude, but always aligned himself in politics with the leading and most
influential men. **3** And Appius later made this a point of criticism against Scipio
Africanus, when these two, the most powerful in the city, were candidates for
the censorship (142 BC), one having the senate and nobles in his support – this
was the traditional position of the Appii – while the other, though great on his
own account, always built on the immense favour and affection of the people.
4 So when Appius saw Scipio hastening into the forum accompanied by men of
no family and ex-slaves, who hung around the forum and were able to collect a
mob and force through all measures by canvassing and shouting, he cried loudly,
5 'Paullus Aemilius, groan beneath the earth, when you learn that it is Aemilius
the crier and Licinius Philonicus who are ushering your son to the censorship.'
6 But Scipio had the people's goodwill because he supported them on most issues,
while Aemilius, though one of the aristocratic faction, was no less loved by the
multitude than the one who was thought the greatest supporter of the populace and
who sought their favour in all his dealings with them. **7** They demonstrated this
by granting him along with all his other honours the censorship (164 BC), which
is of all magistracies the most sacred and of great influence in terms of both other
matters and the examination into people's lives.

2.42 Cicero *On the Laws* 3.34–36: The secret ballot

In the second half of the second century BC, a number of laws introduced the secret ballot
into Roman assemblies. Open voting had allowed the aristocracy considerable power over
the assemblies, and Quintus Cicero argues here that the reform has destroyed the influence
of the optimates.

34 Quintus: Who does not realise that the balloting laws have stripped the nobility
of all its power and influence? The people never wanted it when they were free,
but insisted on it when they were downtrodden by the dominance and ascendancy
of the leading senators. That is why there were more serious condemnations of
people in power by the oral method than by voting tablets. Accordingly powerful leaders should have been deprived of the people's immoderate eagerness for

voting for them even in the case of bad measures, but the people should not have been given a hidey-hole where they could use the ballot to conceal an ill-advised vote and keep the aristocracy ignorant of what they really felt. Consequently no 'good' man has ever proposed or supported such a motion. **35** Indeed, there are four balloting laws extant: the first concerns the election of magistrates – that's the Gabinian law, proposed by a man of unknown and humble background (Aulus Gabinius, tr. 139). The Cassian law followed this two years later, dealing with trials before the people, proposed by Lucius Cassius (tr. 137), a nobleman, but (I say without prejudice to his family) one at odds with the 'honest men' and who used popular measures to win popular adulation. The third law, that of Carbo (*lex Papiria*, C. Papirius Carbo, tr. 131), deals with the approval or rejection of laws, and he was a subversive and irresponsible citizen, who could not even gain his safety from the 'boni' when he returned to their party. **36** Oral voting seems to have remained only in one case, which even Cassius had omitted, that of treason. Gaius Coelius (*lex Coelia*, C. Coelius Calidus, tr. 107) arranged for the ballot for this type of trial as well, though he regretted, as long as he lived, that he had so harmed the state in order to overcome Gaius Popilius.

2.43 Cicero *In Defence of Plancius* 64–67: Cicero's quaestorship

Gn. Plancius was elected as aedile for 54 BC but was prosecuted by Laterensis, an unsuccessful candidate, for illegal methods such as employing the support of associations (sodalicia). In Sicily, Cicero had been quaestor at Lilybaeum, not Syracuse. Cassius (not *the* Cassius) is one of the prosecution team.

64 I have no fear, jurors, of appearing to flatter myself in some way if I say a little about my own quaestorship. While it was successful enough, I consider that my later conduct in the highest magistracies has led to my not seeking any great distinction from the praise I received for the quaestorship – although I have no fear that anyone would dare assert that any other holder of the quaestorship in Sicily received more gratitude or renown. I can indeed state absolutely as the truth that, at that time, I considered that men at Rome were speaking of nothing other than my quaestorship. I had dispatched an immense quantity of grain at a time of the highest prices; I appeared to everyone to be courteous to businessmen, fair to merchants, openhanded to the citizens, restrained in my demands on the allies, and most conscientious in all my responsibilities. In fact the Sicilians considered bestowing on me unprecedented honours. **65** Consequently I left there with the expectation that the Roman people would spontaneously endow me with every distinction. However, it turned out that, as I returned from the province, I arrived at Puteoli to make my journey from there during those days when the greatest numbers of distinguished visitors congregated there, and I nearly fell over, jurors, when someone asked me on what day I had left Rome and whether there was any news. When I responded to him that I was returning from my province, he said, 'Why of course! You are coming from Africa, am I right?' I replied rather coldly, for I was more than a little offended, 'No, from Sicily.' At which point another fellow – one of those apparent know-alls – put in, 'What? Don't you know that our friend here has been quaestor at Syracuse?' What else can I say? I put aside my disgruntlement, and made myself just one of the chaps who had come for the waters.

66 This episode, jurors, I rather consider to have been of more value to me than if everyone had been lauding my achievements – for once I had realised that, if the Roman people have ears which are slow on the uptake, their eyes are sharp and keen-sighted, I stopped thinking about what people were going to hear about me, and from thenceforth behaved in such a way that they should see me in person every day; I lived in the public eye; I haunted the forum; neither my doorkeeper nor sleep prevented anyone gaining an audience with me. And what should I tell you of the times when I was fully occupied, I who had no leisure time that was ever leisured? Those speeches, Cassius, which you inform us it is your practice to read whenever you were at leisure – I wrote them during festivals and holidays, and so have never had the chance to know what leisure was! Indeed I have always thought that an awe-inspiring and splendid standpoint of Marcus Cato which he wrote at the beginning of his *Origines* – that men of eminence and greatness should consider their times of leisure as of no importance than those of business. And so, if I possess any reputation – and I have no idea how great that might be – it has been acquired at Rome and been sought in the forum, while my private intentions have also been justified by public events, and as a result I have had to transact at home even the most important of state business – and it is in the city that work to preserve the city has had to take place. **67** And so the same way forward, Cassius, is available to Laterensis as well as virtue's same path to eminence – perhaps easier for him than for me, as I have risen to this position on my own initiative and through my own efforts (with no ancestors and dependent on no one but myself), while his outstanding qualities will be enhanced by the recommendation of his forefathers.

THE NOVUS HOMO

In Rome's competitive society, it was a struggle even for those of consular families (the nobiles or optimates) to reach the consulship; for those without such a background, the task was far more difficult, though not impossible. Political power was generally in the hands of the optimates, who stayed in power partly through their financial resources and partly through their ability to attract voters by using their clients and friends and the Romans' respect for family and lineage. The term novus homo ('new man') is vague but could include both the first in a family to enter the senate and gain a magistracy and a senator whose ancestors had never reached the consulship.

2.44 Sallust *The Catilinarian Conspiracy* 23.5–6: The jealousy of the nobles

Sallust states that it was the information that Catiline planned a conspiracy that gave rise to a general desire to give Cicero the consulship – implying that his success was due to that factor: cf. docs 9.6, 12.13–23.

5 It was this in particular that gave rise to general enthusiasm for bestowing the consulship on Marcus Tullius Cicero. **6** For, before this, most of the nobility were inflamed with jealousy and considered the consulship to be contaminated if a new man, however distinguished, acquired it. But at the approach of danger, jealousy and pride came to be of secondary importance.

2.45 Cicero *On the Agrarian Law* 2.1–4: Cicero as novus homo

This was Cicero's first speech as consul to the people, made against the Rullan agricultural legislation (cf. doc. 12.13). Incoming consuls held a public meeting (contio) in which they traditionally thanked the citizens for electing them. Cicero makes great play of the fact that he is a novus homo, without consular lineage (the last 'new man' being C. Coelius Caldus in 94 BC), and that he was elected in 'his year', suo anno (the minimum age: 42 in the year of election for consuls: doc. 11.30).

1 It is a custom, Romans, instituted by our ancestors, that those who by your favour have acquired the right to images of their family should, in their first oration before the people, combine thanks for your favour with praise of their own ancestors. In such speeches, some men are sometimes found to be worthy of their ancestors' rank, though the majority manage to make clear only that the debt owed to their ancestors is so great that something is still left over to be paid to their descendants. I myself, Romans, have no possibility of speaking of my ancestors before you, not that they were not such as you see us to be, begotten from their family and raised in their teaching, but because they lacked the people's praise and the light of the honour you granted. . . . **3** I am the first new man after a very long interval – nearly more remote than our times can remember – that you have made consul, and that rank, which the nobility kept secured by guards and entrenched in every way, you have broken open and shown that for the future it should be open to merit, with me taking the lead. And not only did you elect me consul, which is a glorious honour in itself, but you did it in such a way in which few nobles have ever been made consuls in this city, and no new man before me.

For indeed, if you would be kind enough to consult your memory in regard to new men, you will find that those who were made consuls without rejection became so only after lengthy labour and at a favourable opportunity, becoming candidates many years after they had been praetors, and somewhat later than their age and the laws allowed, while those who became candidates in their own year (*suo anno*) were not elected without rejection; and that I am the only one of all the new men whom we can remember who became a candidate for the consulship in the first year it was permitted and was made consul in my first candidacy, so that this honour granted by you, which I stood for as soon as I was allowed, does not appear to have been snatched on the occasion of the candidacy of an unsuitable person, nor to have been urgently requested with frequent petitions, but to have been obtained by merit. **4** It is a glorious honour, as I have just mentioned, Romans, that I was the first of the new men on whom, after so many years, you have bestowed this honour, that it was at my first candidacy, and that it was in my 'own year', and yet nothing can be more glorious or distinguished than the fact that at the comitia at which I was elected you did not hand in voting-tablets – their secrecy being the guarantee of freedom – but showed with unanimous voice your goodwill and attachment to me. Thus, it was not the last sorting of the votes but your first rush to vote (i.e., he soon had a majority), not the individual voices of the heralds but the unanimous voice of the Roman people which declared me consul.

AMICITIA

Political friends were amici (sing.: amicus), as opposed to personal friends, who were familiares (see docs 2.48–53). There were no political parties in Rome, and such amicitiae (friendships or political alliances) were unofficial, fluid and often changing, though regulated by ties of obligation and honour; political amici could also be inherited within a family. The features of such relationships were mutual assistance, a common political approach, and friendship through mutual respect, the key being an interchange of services. What friends called an 'amicitia' could be titled a 'factio' (faction) by political opponents. The opposite of amici were inimici (personal or political enemies), exemplified by Caesar's relationship with Bibulus and Cato the Younger.

2.46 Livy *History of Rome* 6.20.1–3: Family support in a crisis

M. Manlius Capitolinus, consul in 392 BC and hero of the Gallic attack in 390, was supposedly brought to trial by his enemies for his courting of the populace (through a programme of cancellation of debts) and possible insurrectionist tendencies; he was executed in 385 (or 384). Not only family members but also friends and clients were expected to show their support in emergencies. The mourning toga, the toga pulla, was made of dark wool.

1 Manlius was committed for trial. The first effect of this was that the people were greatly disturbed, **2** especially when they saw the defendant dressed in mourning and unattended by any of the senators, or indeed by any of his relatives and connections, and not even by his brothers Aulus and Titus Manlius, for it had never happened before that day that a person's closest connections had not gone into mourning when he was threatened by such a crisis. **3** They recalled that, when Appius Claudius was imprisoned, his enemy Gaius Claudius and the entire Claudian family had gone into mourning, and they considered that there was a plot to put down the people's friend because he had been the first to abandon the patricians for the plebs.

2.47 Cicero *On Friendship* 10.33–34: The short-lived nature of friendship

Cicero's *De amicitia* was probably written in 44 BC; it was set in 129 after the death of Scipio Aemilianus; Gaius Laelius, Scipio's close friend and consul in 140, is here talking to his sons-in-law about his relationship with Scipio.

33 Then listen, worthy gentlemen, to the points about friendship most often discussed between Scipio and myself (Laelius). He, indeed, used to say that nothing was more difficult than for a friendship to last to the final day of life: for it often used to happen either that it might not be mutually advantageous or that the parties did not share the same political views; he used to say, too, that men's characters frequently change, sometimes by adverse circumstances, at other times by the increasing burdens of old age. And then he would cite an example of this by analogy with adolescence, that boys' greatest attachments are often laid aside with the toga praetexta; **34** but if they continue to the mid-teens they are sometimes broken off by rivalry, either over a marriage or some other advantage, in which both parties cannot be equally successful. If they should continue to be friends for a longer period, the friendship is often destroyed should a struggle for magisterial office take place; since, while for the majority of people there is no greater ruin to friendship than monetary greed, for the most worthy men it is the rivalry for official rank and glory from which have frequently arisen the greatest enmities between most devoted friends.

2.48 Cicero *In Defence of Murena* 7–10: Amicitia and its demands

In 63 BC Cicero defended L. Licinius Murena, who had been elected consul for 62 but was prosecuted for bribery by Servius Sulpicius Rufus, a loser in the same election and another friend of Cicero's, for whom Cicero had canvassed.

7 I admit, Servius Sulpicius, that in your canvass for the consulship I owed you all my energy and my support in view of our close relationship, and I think that I discharged my duty. When you were canvassing for the consulship, there was nothing additional on my part which could have been demanded either of a friend or of a supporter or of a consul. That time is past. The situation has changed. My view and conviction is this, that to prevent Murena's election I owed you as much as you dared ask me, but to prevent his acquittal I owe you nothing . . . **8** My friendship with Murena, jurors, is both great and of long duration and will accordingly not be destroyed by Servius Sulpicius in his prosecution of Murena on capital charges, simply because it was overcome in a contest for election with this same man. Even if this were not the case, either the public standing of this man or the greatness of the rank he has attained would have branded me with the worst reputation for pride and cruelty had I refused to take on the perilous case of a man so distinguished by his own honours and those of the Roman people . . . **10** I, jurors, would think myself despicable if I failed a friend, cruel if I failed a man in distress, arrogant if I failed a consul.

2.49 Cicero *Letters to his Friends* 15.10: Cicero asks for support

This letter was written at Tarsus in Asia Minor, at the end of 51 BC, to C. Claudius Marcellus, consul-elect for 50, asking him to support a supplicatio for Cicero's governorship of Cilicia; for Cato's reply to a similar request, see doc. 13.19. The first sentence suggests that Marcellus' consulship will be a good opportunity for him to show the devotion his family feels to Cicero.

Marcus Cicero, Imperator, to Gaius Marcellus, son of Gaius, consul, greetings.
 1 Since it has happened, as I so greatly desired, that the devotion of all the Marcelli, and Marcellini too (for the goodwill always shown me by your family and those of your name is remarkable) – since, therefore, it has happened that the

devotion of you all can be put into practice by your consulship, because in this consulship my achievements and the praise and honour relating to them especially coincide, I am asking you – and it can be most easily done, for I am sure that the senate will not reject it – to see to it that the decree of the senate, after my dispatch has been read, be as complimentary as possible.

2 If I had been less closely associated with you than with all your family, I would commission those by whom you know I am especially regarded to present my case to you. Your father's services to me have been most splendid; no one can be said to be more supportive of my well-being or my honour. There is no man, I believe, who is unaware of how highly your cousin (M. Claudius Marcellus, cos. 51) values and has always valued me. In short, your whole family has always honoured me with the greatest favours of every kind. And, indeed, you have yielded to none of your family in your regard for me. Accordingly, may I ask especially that you desire me to win every possible honour through your doing, and that in the matter of my being decreed a supplicatio, and in everything else, you consider my reputation as sufficiently committed into your hands?

2.50 Cicero *Letters to his Friends* 13.3: Cicero recommends a friend

This is a typical letter of recommendation written by Cicero to Memmius in 50 BC. Gaius Memmius was in Athens in exile after a charge of electioneering bribery in 54; he was praetor in 58 and propraetor in Bithynia in 57; nothing is known of Fufius.

Aulus Fufius, one of my most intimate friends, treats me with the greatest deference and devotion; a man of learning and great refinement, he is extremely worthy of your friendship. I would be glad if you would behave towards him as you promised when we met. That would be more pleasing to me than anything else could be. Moreover, you will bind the man himself to you for perpetuity by the strongest sense of obligation and regard.

2.51 Ennius *Annals* 210–27: Ennius on Servilius Geminus

Gell. 12.4.4. Ennius is probably referring to Gn. Servilius Geminus (cos. 217), who was killed at the battle of Cannae in 216 (or to his father, P. Servilius Geminus, a hero of the time of the First Punic War). Geminus is portrayed as a noble and affable friend, and Ennius may here be presenting his own view of his relationship with aristocrats such as the Scipiones.

210   Saying this he called to one with whom, willingly and gladly
       His table, conversation, and personal affairs
       He often courteously shared, when tired out
       He had spent a great part of the day managing matters of utmost importance,
       Through counsel given in the wide forum and sacred senate;
215   One to whom, without anxiety, he would boldly speak
       Matters great and small and jests, and would burst forth and utter words
       Good and bad, if he so wished, and place them in safe-keeping;

Who could share many pleasures and joys, both secretly and openly,
Whose nature no thought could persuade to do a wrong deed
220 Lightly or with evil intent; a learned, loyal,
Pleasant, eloquent man, content with his own, happy,
Shrewd, who spoke the right things at the right time, affable,
A man of few words, tenacious of many old ways created by that antiquity
Which is now buried, and of manners both old and new,
225 Holding to the ways of many of our elders, and the laws of gods and men,
Able, with discretion, both to speak and to keep silent.
This man, among the battles, Servilius thus addressed.

2.52 Caesar *Gallic War* 1.53.5–6: Caesar's pleasure in a friend's rescue

This passage is a notable exception to Caesar's generally objective tone in his narrative. The incident occurred in 58 BC, with the expulsion of Aristovistus, king of the Suebi, from Gaul; for Procillus, cf. Caes. *BG* 1.47.4.

5 In the flight, Gaius Valerius Procillus was being dragged along by his guards bound with three chains, when he fell in with Caesar himself, who was pursuing the enemy with the cavalry. **6** This, indeed, delighted Caesar no less than the victory itself, for he saw the worthiest man in the whole province of Gaul, and his own personal friend and host, snatched from the hands of the enemy and restored to himself, nor did Fortune lessen any of the pleasure and rejoicing by Procillus' misfortune.

2.53 Catullus 9: Catullus on the return of his friends

Veranius is not known, but he has clearly returned from Spain and is mentioned in poems 12, 28 and 47 in company with Fabullus; they may have served together in Spain and then in Macedonia under L. Calpurnius Piso Caesoninus (cos. 58).

Veranius, out of all of my friends
Superior in my view to three hundred thousand,
Have you come home to your household gods
And affectionate brothers and elderly mother?
You have come. O what joyful news!
I shall look upon you safe and sound and I shall hear you
Speaking of the places, history and tribes of the Hiberians,
In your accustomed way, and drawing your neck close to me
I shall kiss your beloved mouth and eyes.
Of all the world's most blessed men,
Who is more happy or blessed than I?

CLIENTELA AND PATROCINIUM

Early clientela ('patronage') was characterised by strict mutual obligations, supported by law; see XII Tables 8.10 (doc. 1.37), where a sacred obligation on the side of both patron and client is involved. By the later Republic, patronage and clientship played a large part in public and private life, with a patron–client relationship seen between generals and soldiers, founders and colonists, and conquerors and dependent foreign communities, as well as, naturally, between the large numbers of freedmen and their previous owners (duties for such freedmen were laid down and enforceable in law). The prestige, or dignitas, of nobles was publicly demonstrated by the number of their clients. The duties of a client included the customary early-morning salutatio (greetings) at the residence of the patron, after which clients could follow the patron into the forum and elsewhere. A client might also be expected to canvass and vote for their patron, or in his interests, and in return the patron would give the client legal advice and representation in court.

2.54 Dionysius of Halicarnassus *Roman Antiquities* 2.9.1–3: Class divisions

Clearly the situation described by Dionysius was not applicable in the late Republic, and he has idealised the institution, placing its origins anachronistically back in the regal period and stressing the goodwill and affections felt by both parties.

1 After Romulus had distinguished the more powerful members of society from the less powerful, he then set up laws and established what things were to be done by each of the two groups. The patricians were to serve as priests, magistrates and judges and were to aid him in the management of public business, devoting themselves to the city's affairs, while the plebeians were excused from these official duties because they were inexperienced in them and without leisure, because of their lack of means: they were to farm and breed cattle and practise trades that bring in a livelihood, so that they would not be seditious, as happens in other cities when either those in power maltreat the humble or the common people and the poor are jealous of their superiors. **2** He gave the plebeians into the guardianship of the patricians, allowing each plebeian to choose the patron he wanted . . . **3** Romulus beautified the arrangement with an attractive title, calling this protection of the poor and humble 'patronage' (clientela), and laid down friendly duties for both, making their relationship a kindly one suited to fellow citizens.

2.55 Dionysius of Halicarnassus *Roman Antiquities* 2.10.1–11.2: Rules for patrons

Dionysius considers clientela as one of the most important Roman institutions and as directly responsible for political stability. In his estimate of 630 years of harmony (down to 121 BC), he omits the murder of Tiberius Gracchus in 133.

10.1 The customs which Romulus then laid down concerning patronage, and which continued for a long time in use among the Romans, were as follows: it was the duty of patricians to explain to their clients the laws, of which they had no knowledge, and to take care of them in the same way whether they were present or absent, doing everything for them that fathers do for sons, with regard both to money and to contracts relating to money; to bring legal cases on behalf of clients who were wronged in any way to do with contracts, and to support them against those bringing charges against them; in short, to provide all the peace, both in private and in state affairs, which they particularly needed. **2** It was the duty of clients to assist their patrons with raising dowries when their daughters were getting married, if the fathers lacked money, and to pay ransoms to enemies, if any of them or their children were taken prisoner; to pay out of their own funds their patrons' losses in private legal cases or fines that they owed to the state, doing this not as loans but as a debt of gratitude; and to share with them the costs incurred in standing for magistracies and privileges and other public expenditures, just as if they were their relations. **3** For both alike, it was impious and unlawful to bring charges against the other in law-suits, or act as a hostile witness, or vote in opposition, or be numbered among the other's enemies. If anyone was convicted of having done any of these things, he was guilty of treason by the law which Romulus had sanctioned, and it was lawful for anyone who wished to put him to death as a victim dedicated to infernal Jupiter – for it was a Roman custom to dedicate the bodies of those persons whom they wished to kill without incurring guilt to some god or other, and especially to the gods of the underworld; this was what Romulus now did. **4** Accordingly, the links between clients and patrons continued for many generations and differed in no way from blood relationships, being handed down to their children's children, and it was a matter of great praise for men from distinguished families to have as many clients as possible, and not only to preserve the continuation of the patronage they inherited but to acquire others by their own merit.

11.1 It was not only in the city itself that the plebs were under the patricians' protection, but also every Roman colony and every city that was joined in alliance and friendship, as well as those conquered in war, had those protectors and patrons among the Romans that they wished. And the senate has frequently referred the controversies of these cities and peoples to their patrons, regarding their decisions as authoritative. **2** Indeed, so secure was the harmony which owed its beginning to the provisions of Romulus that, in 630 years, they never came to bloodshed and mutual killing, even though many great disputes concerning public affairs arose between the people and those in office, as is bound to happen in all cities, great and small.

2.56 Cicero *In Defence of Sextus Roscius of Ameria* 5: Hospitium

In 80 BC, Cicero, in his first criminal case, defended Sextus Roscius on a charge of parricide against the powerful members of Sulla's faction, notably Chrysogonus, one of Sulla's freedmen; see docs 11.24–25. Hospitium (the hospitable entertainment of those from outside Rome) was a hereditary relationship, often exercised by Roman aristocrats over provincial families and communities. When Roscius was proscribed he fled to Caecilia, daughter of Metellus Balearicus (cos. 123), who intervened on his behalf and found Cicero to defend him.

Sextus Roscius, this man's father, was a citizen of the municipality of Ameria and, by his ancestry, noble birth and wealth, was easily the most prominent man, not only of his town but also of the neighbourhood, while his reputation was enhanced by the esteem with which he was regarded by men of the highest rank and his relations of hospitality with them. For he was not only in a relation of hospitality with the Metelli, Servilii and Scipiones but also enjoyed private intimacy and social intercourse with these families, whom, as is right, I mention with the respect due to their high character and consequence. Well, of all these advantages, this is the only one he left to his son: for brigandly members of his family (Titus Roscius Capito and Magnus) have seized and possess his patrimony, while the reputation and life of the innocent son are being defended by the guests and friends of his father.

2.57 Cicero *Letters to his Friends* 13.34: The ties of hospitality

One of Cicero's letters of recommendation to Acilius (written in 46 BC) on the basis of family ties of hospitality and his connections with Sicily. Cicero had been quaestor of Lilybaeum in Sicily in 75 BC, and the Sicilians were his clients.

Cicero to Acilius, proconsul (in Sicily), greetings.
I am bound by ties of hospitality dating back to his grandfather's time with Lyso, son of Lyso, of Lilybaeum, who pays me great respect and whom I have found worthy of both his father and grandfather – for he comes from a very noble family. Accordingly, I commend him to you with more than ordinary urgency, as well as his household; and I beg of you very earnestly to ensure that he realises that my recommendation has been of the greatest assistance in your eyes, as well as a great compliment to him.

2.58 Cicero *Letters to his Friends* 13.4: Cicero and a land comissioner

Cicero is writing in autumn 45 BC to Valerius Orca, one of the commissioners for carrying out Caesar's land grants to his veterans. Cicero had also protected the people of Volaterrae against the Rullan and Flavian land laws (doc. 12.13).

Marcus Tullius Cicero warmly greets Quintus Valerius Orca, son of Quintus, pro-praetorian legate.
1 I have the closest possible connection with the townsmen of Volaterrae. Having received great kindness from me, they have shown their gratitude in return most abundantly; for they have never been found wanting, either in my times in office or in my troubles . . . **4** Were circumstances to give me at the present time power along the lines of the ability I used to have to protect the people of Volaterrae, as I have always looked after my own people, there is no act, no effort, I would omit to be of service to them. But, as I am sure that my influence is no less with you at the present time than I have always possessed with everyone, I ask you in the name of our very close connection and our equal and mutual goodwill towards each other that you serve the people of Volaterrae in such a way that they think that the man who has been placed, as if by some divine plan, in charge of the land commission is the very man on whom, above all others, I – their continual protector – am able to exert the greatest possible influence.

2.59 Cicero *Letters to his Friends* 13.11: Cicero's home town

Cicero is writing in 46 BC to M. Junius Brutus as governor of Cisalpine Gaul. Arpinum, Cicero's home town, owned land there which paid rent to the township. Cicero, of course, has a personal interest here: Arpinum was run by three aediles, and he hopes, through his services to the community, to ensure the election to this position of his son, nephew and friend.

1 Since I have always noticed that you are extremely careful to stay informed of all my concerns, I therefore have no doubt that you know not only which municipality I come from but also how diligently I make it my habit to look after the interests of my fellow townsmen, the inhabitants of Arpinum. Now, indeed, all their revenues and all their means of providing for the worship of the gods and for repairing their sacred dwellings and public buildings are comprised in the rents for the lands they hold in the province of Gaul. To inspect these, and to arrange for the payment of the money owed by the tenants and to investigate and administer the whole business, we have sent a commission of Roman equites, Quintus Fufidius, son of Quintus Fufidius, Marcus Faucius, son of Marcus, and Quintus Mamercus, son of Quintus. **2** I beg you more urgently than usual, in view of our close connection, to concern yourself with this matter and do what you can to see that the town's business is arranged as suitably and quickly as possible, and to treat the men themselves, whose names I have given you, with all possible courtesy and generosity in accordance with your natural disposition. **3** You will find that you have added some excellent men to your close connections and bound a most grateful municipality under obligation to you; indeed, I shall be even more grateful to you, as I have always been accustomed to look after the interests of my fellow townsmen, and this year my attention and services are particularly appropriate because, in order to regulate the town's affairs, I have put my son up for aedile, as well as my brother's son and Marcus Caesius, a very intimate friend of mine – for aediles are the only magistrates we are in the habit of electing in our municipality; you will have done honour to them, and especially to me, if the affairs of the municipality are well managed thanks to your zeal and diligence – and this is what I earnestly ask you again and again to do.

2.60 Plutarch *Life of Pompey* 45.1–5: Pompey as patron of the East

This passage describes Pompey's triumph over Mithridates and the East in September 61 (cf. doc. 12.29). All his conquests came into his clientela.

1 The time was insufficient for the extent of Pompey's triumph, even though it was spread over two separate days, and many of the items prepared for it had to be left out of the spectacle – enough to dignify and adorn another triumph entirely. **2** The nations over which he was triumphing were displayed on posters which went in front. These were: Pontus, Armenia, Paphlagonia, Cappadocia, Media, Colchis, Iberia, Albania, Syria, Cilicia, Mesopotamia, Phoenicia and Palestine,

Judaea, Arabia, and the entire piratical menace which had been overthrown by sea and on land. **3** In these campaigns, according to the posters, he had captured no fewer than 1,000 forts, nearly 900 cities and 800 pirate ships, while founding 39 cities. **4** In addition to all this, the posters stated that, while the public revenue from tax had been 50,000,000 drachmas, they were receiving from his acquisitions for Rome 85,000,000, and that he was bringing the public treasury 20,000 talents in coins and vessels of silver and gold, apart from what had been given to his soldiers, of which he who received the least share had 1,500 drachmas. **5** The prisoners led in the triumph were, apart from the pirate chiefs, the son of Tigranes of Armenia, with his wife and daughter, Zosime, a wife of King Tigranes himself, Aristobulus, king of the Jews, a sister and five children of Mithridates . . .

2.61 Caesar *Spanish War* 42.1–3: Ingratitude in Spain

To Caesar's anger, Hispalis in Further Spain had supported the Pompeian forces in the civil war rather than Caesar's own, though Caesar had governed Further Spain as quaestor (69 BC) and as propraetor (61). Metellus Pius (cos. 80) presumably imposed taxes on Spain following the end of the rebellion of Sertorius (docs 12.2–3).

1 Caesar returned to Hispalis and on the following day summoned an assembly (contio) and reminded them of the following points: that at the start of his quaestorship he had made that province above all other provinces his own special concern and had lavished on it whatever benefits were in his power at that time; **2** that subsequently, after acquiring the rank of praetor, he had requested the senate to rescind the taxes which Metellus had imposed and had freed the province from having to pay that money; that having once adopted the role of their patron he had undertaken its defence by facilitating the introduction of numerous deputations into the senate, as well as representing it in public and private legal actions through which he had incurred the enmity of many; **3** that similarly, during his consulship, he had in his absence granted the province all benefits that were in his power – and he was well aware that, in the current war and in the period preceding it, they were both forgetful of all these benefits and ungrateful for them towards both himself and the Roman people.

2.62 Plutarch *Life of Pompey* 51.1–5: Caesar as patron of Rome's magistrates

Sulla had raised the senate's number to 600; consuls and proconsuls each had 12 lictors carrying the fasces before them, praetors and propraetors (probably) six. Caesar at Luca in 56 BC had a third of the senate and between 10 and 20 current magistrates and promagistrates requesting his patronage; cf. docs 12.69–71.

1 In the meantime, his Gallic wars raised Caesar to eminence . . . **3** By sending back to Rome gold and silver and the other booty and the rest of the wealth gained from his many wars, and enticing people with bribes and assisting with the expenses of aediles and praetors and consuls and their wives, he won the support of many. **4** Consequently, when he crossed the Alps and wintered at Luca, a great crowd of ordinary men and women collected there in haste, while 200 men of senatorial rank, among whom were Pompey and Crassus, and 120 fasces of pro-consuls and praetors were to be seen at Caesar's door. **5** He satisfied all the rest with hopes and money and sent them away; but between himself, Pompey and Crassus the following agreement was made.

LITIGATION AS A WAY OF LIFE

The Romans saw the XII Tables as the beginning of their legal history, though laws were attributed to the kings, such as Romulus: the XII Tables, though increasingly obsolete, were not superseded until the sixth century AD. Magistrates with imperium were the administrators of criminal justice. Trials could take place before the people or in court (quaestio; plural: quaestiones): perpetual quaestiones were set up in the second and first centuries BC. The key legal figure in Rome was the urban praetor, who at the beginning of his term of office published an edict setting out the way he intended to exercise his jurisdiction. Court cases in Rome were a public spectacle, taking place in the forum in the open air, and could be viewed by any interested spectators. Acting as prosecutor or defence counsel was an important way of bringing oneself and one's skills to public notice and acquiring a significant clientele.

2.63 Plutarch *Life of Cato the Elder* 15.3–5: Prosecution as 'pietas'

Cato the Elder was extremely litigious and known for a number of prosecutions during his career: particular targets were Scipio Africanus and his brother L. Cornelius Scipio Asiagenus. Enmities (inimicitiae) could be hereditary, as were friendships (amicitiae). For Galba, see doc. 5.48.

3 It is said that a certain young man, who had got a verdict of loss of citizen rights against an enemy of his dead father, was passing through the forum on the con-clusion of the case, when Cato met him and greeted him with the words: 'These are the offerings we should make to our parents – not lambs or kids, but the tears of their enemies and their condemnation.' **4** However, in his political life he was himself not unscathed, but, wherever he gave his enemies any handle, he was always being prosecuted and in danger of conviction. He is said to have defended nearly 50 cases, the last one when he was 86 years of age . . . **5** And even this one was not the end of his conflicts in the courts, as four years later, when he was 90, he brought a case against Servius Galba.

2.64 Plutarch *Life of Lucullus* 1.1–3: Prosecution as a career move

Lucullus' father, another L. Licinius Lucullus, was governor of Sicily in 103/2 and con-victed of extortion by his successor, Gaius Servilius, and Servilius' cousin Servilius 'the augur'. Lucullus and his brother Marcus brought a charge against this Servilius, apparently of misappropriating public funds.

1 In the case of Lucullus, his grandfather had been consul, and his uncle on his mother's side was Metellus, surnamed Numidicus. But, with regard to his parents, his father had been convicted of fraud and his mother, Caecilia, had a bad reputation as a woman of no discretion in her lifestyle. **2** Lucullus himself, while still a young man, before he had stood for any office or entered public life, made it his first task to prosecute his father's accuser, Servilius the Augur, whom he caught wronging the state. The Romans considered this a splendid achievement, and the case was talked of by everyone, like a great deed of prowess. **3** For, in fact, they thought the business of prosecution, in general and without special excuse, not a sordid action, but were very keen to see their young men clinging to wrongdoers like well-bred dogs to wild beasts. But great animosity was stirred up by the case, so that some people were even wounded and killed, and Servilius got off.

2.65 Cicero *On Duties* 2.49–51: Cicero on prosecution and defence

Cicero is here writing on moral duties to his son, Marcus. Lucius Licinius Crassus, the great orator (cos. 95), had at the age of 21 successfully prosecuted Gaius Papirius Carbo, who committed suicide in 119 to escape condemnation.

49 But while there are many kinds of occasion that require eloquence, and many young men in our Republic have won praise in speaking before the jurors, the people and the senate, it is the speeches in the courts which win the greatest admiration. Speeches in the courts fall into two categories. They are divided into speeches for the prosecution and for the defence; while, of these two, taking the side of the defence is the more praiseworthy, that for the prosecution has also frequently been considered honourable. A short while back I spoke of (Lucius Licinius) Crassus; Marcus Antonius (cos. 99), when a young man, had the same success. It was also a prosecution that brought the eloquence of Publius Sulpicius (tr. pl. 88) to public notice, when he brought an action against that seditious and dangerous citizen Gaius Norbanus (tr. pl. 103). **50** But this should not be done often, and only then for the sake of the state, as in the case of those I have mentioned, or to avenge wrongs, as in the case of the two Luculli, or to protect clients, as I did on behalf of the Sicilians, or as Julius did in prosecuting Albucius on behalf of the Sardinians. The diligence of Lucius Fufius in prosecuting Manius Aquillius (cos. 101) is also well known. Prosecution may be undertaken, then, once or at any rate not often. But if it should have to be undertaken more often, it should be done as a service to the state, for taking vengeance on the state's enemies is not to be considered reprehensible; even then, however, there should be a limit. For it seems the characteristic of a hard-hearted man, or rather of one hardly human, to bring capital charges against many people. It is not only dangerous for the prosecutor himself but damaging to his reputation to allow himself to be called a prosecutor; that happened to Marcus Brutus, who was born of the highest family, and the son of that Brutus who was one of the foremost authorities in civil law.

51 Furthermore, this rule of responsibility should be carefully observed, that you should never bring a capital charge against anyone who might be innocent; for there is no way one can do that without becoming a criminal. For what is so inhuman as to turn the eloquence given by nature for the safety and protection of mankind to the destruction and ruin of good men? Nevertheless, while we have to avoid this, we need have no scruples about defending a guilty person, as long as he is not notoriously wicked or impious; for the people expect it, custom allows it, even humanity accepts it. It is always the job of the judge in a trial to find the truth, and that of the defending counsel sometimes to put forward an approximation to the truth, even if not entirely true; I would not dare to write this, especially when writing about philosophy, were it not also the view of Panaetius, that strictest of Stoics. Then, too, acting for the defence particularly wins one fame and gratitude, and the more so if you should happen to assist one who appears to be oppressed and harassed through the influence of someone in power, as I have done on a number of occasions, for example, when in my youth I defended Sextus Roscius of Ameria against the power of the tyrannical Lucius (Cornelius) Sulla – the speech, as you know, has been published.

THE IMPORTANCE OF ORATORY

Public speaking was an extremely important skill in Rome, whether to influence the assembly, the senate or the jury (and listening public) in a law-court. Latin rhetoric was firmly based on Greek models, and aristocratic Romans trained under Greek teachers and in the Greek language – upper-class Romans being fluent in Greek as well as Latin. Teachers of rhetoric are first mentioned in Rome in the second century BC, with instructional works in Latin, such as the *Rhetorica ad Herennium* and Cicero's *De inventione*, the stock early expositions of rhetorical practices, appearing in the 80s.

2.66 Suetonius *On Rhetoricians* 1: An 'un-Roman' practice

The senatus consultum (decision of the senate) and edict of the censors against Latin philosophers and rhetoricians in 161 and 92 BC are given in doc. 5.60. For Hirtius and Pansa, see doc. 14.9.

Gradually rhetoric itself came to appear useful and respectable, and many devoted themselves to it both in order to defend themselves and to acquire a fine reputation. Cicero used to declaim in both Greek and Latin up to the time of his praetorship, and in Latin even when comparatively elderly, and that in company with the future consuls Hirtius and Pansa (cos. 43 BC), whom he used to call his pupils and 'great big boys'. Some historians state that Gnaeus Pompey (Magnus) resumed the practice of declaiming just before the civil war to argue more easily against Gaius Curio, a very ready-witted young man who was taking up Caesar's cause; and that Mark Antony, and Augustus too, did not give it up even during the war at Mutina . . . Moreover many of the orators even published their declamations. As a result great enthusiasm was generally aroused, and there was a huge influx of practitioners and teachers who prospered to such an extent that some of them advanced from the lowest status to senatorial rank and the highest offices.

But they did not all share the same teaching method, and individuals varied in their practice, since each one trained his pupils in different ways. For they would expound speeches in detail with regard to their figures of speech, incidents and illustrations, now in one way and now in another, and compose narrations sometimes in a brief and summarised form, at other times with greater detail and more expansively; sometimes they would translate Greek works and praise or criticise illustrious men; they would demonstrate that some practices in everyday life were useful and essential, others dangerous and redundant; frequently they defended or attacked the credibility of myths, an exercise which the Greeks call 'destructive' and 'constructive' criticism; finally all these became obsolete, being succeeded by the debate (controversia).

2.67 Cicero *Brutus* 305–11, 314–16, 318–19: Cicero's early career

The *Brutus* was written in early 46 BC to justify Cicero's approach to oratory, which was now being questioned by the younger generation. This work is structured as a dialogue with Atticus and Brutus. Cicero states that nearly every day he heard the top speakers in the popular assemblies, whom he names below. **314**: the main reason for Cicero's leaving Rome after his defence of Roscius was in order to avoid reprisals from Sulla: doc. 11.25.

305 The first disappointment inflicted on my passion for listening struck me when Cotta was exiled. I frequently listened to those who were left, and I continued to write and read and declaim daily with intense diligence but was not satisfied with just oratorical exercises. Then, in the following year, Quintus Varius (tr. pl. 90 BC) went into exile, condemned by his own law; **306** I, however, for the study of civil law, spent much of my time with Quintus (Mucius) Scaevola, son of Quintus, who, although he was not given to teaching anyone, taught those who desired to hear him in his replies to those who consulted him. The next year was that of the consulship of Sulla and Pompeius (88 BC). Publius Sulpicius (Rufus; tr. pl. 88) was then tribune, and I was able to get to know his whole style of speaking inside out as he addressed the popular assemblies on a daily basis; at that same time, when Philo, then head of the Academy, had fled from his home, along with the most reputable Athenians, because of the Mithridatic War and had come to Rome, I was ardently aroused to the study of philosophy and devoted myself to his wonderful teaching, in which I lingered the more attentively, not only because the variety and great magnitude of that subject captured me with its delight but because it then seemed as if the whole justice system had disappeared for all time. **307** In that year Sulpicius had been killed, and in the next year three orators of three different periods were most cruelly slain: Quintus Catulus (cos. 102), Marcus Antonius (cos. 99) and Gaius Julius (Caesar Strabo; aed. 90). In that same year too I devoted my time to study at Rome with Molo of Rhodes, a top-ranking advocate and teacher.

308 For a period of about three years . . . **309** I spent my nights and days in a study of all kinds of learning. I associated with Diodotus the Stoic, who made his home with me and resided with me until a short time ago, when he died at my house. By him, along with other subjects, I was diligently trained in dialectic, which can be thought of as a contracted or compressed form of eloquence . . . But while I devoted myself to his teaching and to the many varied arts he taught, I made sure that no day was spent without rhetorical exercises. **310** I prepared and gave declamations – as they are now called – often with Marcus Piso and Quintus Pompeius, or indeed with anyone, daily, and I used to do this often in Latin but more frequently in Greek, both because Greek rhetoric, providing more opportunities for stylistic ornamentation, produced the habit of speaking similarly in Latin and because the most outstanding teachers, being Greek, were unable to correct or teach me unless I spoke in Greek . . . **311** It was now for the first time that I began to take on both civil and criminal cases, my aim being not to learn in the forum, as most do, but as far as possible to come to the forum already trained. At the same time, I devoted my time to studying with Molo; for when Sulla was dictator Molo came as an envoy to Rome concerning the payments to the Rhodians. In this way, my first criminal case in defence of Sextus Roscius received such commendation that there was no case that appeared to be unworthy of my advocacy. There then followed a series of many others which I presented, carefully worked on as if laboured at through the midnight hours . . .

314 Since I had come to the conclusion that, with relaxation and improved control of my voice and an alteration in my style of speaking, I would be able to avoid risk to my health and deliver speeches with more moderation, the purpose of my leaving for Asia Minor was to change my habit of speaking. And so I left Rome, after having been engaged in cases for two years with my name already well known in the forum. **315** When I arrived at Athens, I spent six months with Antiochus, the most celebrated and skilful philosopher of the old Academy, and I again took up the study of philosophy with the best guide and teacher. Having engaged in the subject from my early youth, I made great strides and never completely abandoned it. At the same time, however, I diligently continued with the practice of rhetoric, under the supervision of Demetrius the Syrian, a teacher of speaking of long-standing and not without reputation. Afterwards I travelled through the whole of Asia Minor, associating with the best orators there, who were generous in giving me the chance to practise with them; of these the leader was Menippus of Stratonicea, in my view the most eloquent man in all Asia at that time . . . **316** The person who associated with me most constantly was Dionysius of Magnesia; there were also Aeschylus of Cnidus and Xenocles of Adramattium. At that time these men were considered as the leading teachers of rhetoric in Asia. Not satisfied with these, I came to Rhodes and attached myself to Molo, whom I had heard in Rome, as he was an advocate in actual cases and an outstanding composer of speeches, as well as extremely skilful in perceiving and correcting mistakes and in his system of instruction and training. He dedicated his time to restraining, if it could be done, what was redundant and excessive in my style, with its youthful rashness and lack of control, and preventing it, as it were, from overflowing its banks. And so I returned two years later, not only with more training but almost transformed – my voice had ceased to be over-strained, my language had come off the boil, and my lungs had gained strength, and my body, weight. . . .

318 Accordingly, in the year after I returned from Asia (76 BC), I engaged in some notable cases when I was standing for the quaestorship, Cotta for the consulship and Hortensius for the aedileship. In the meantime, the next year saw me as quaestor in Sicily, Cotta was sent to Gaul after his consulship, and Hortensius remained the leading advocate both in reality and reputation. When, however, a year later, I returned from Sicily, it was now clear that whatever I had in me was fully developed and had reached a certain maturity. I may seem to be saying too much about myself, especially as I am saying it myself; but the aim of all this part of my talk is for you to perceive not my talent or eloquence, which is far from my purpose, but my hard work and industry. **319** After, therefore, I had been involved in numerous cases with leading advocates for nearly five years, I then, as aedile-elect, engaged in a mighty struggle with Hortensius, the consul-elect, in defence of the province of Sicily (the prosecution of Verres in 70 BC).

2.68 Suetonius *Life of the Deified Julius* 55.1–2: Caesar as a public speaker

Cicero's letters to Cornelius Nepos were published in a collection of two or more books (Macrobius 2.1.14). For Gaius Gracchus' style of oratory, see docs 8.26–27.

1 In eloquence and military skill Caesar either equalled or surpassed the reputations of the most outstanding exponents. After his prosecution of Dolabella he was counted without hesitation among the foremost advocates. Certainly, Cicero, in his enumeration of orators in his *Brutus*, confessed that he had never seen anyone to whom Caesar should yield precedence, and describes his style of speaking as elegant and clear, even dignified and in a sense noble. He also wrote this to Cornelius Nepos about Caesar, **2** 'Well? What orator would you rank before him of those who have concentrated on nothing else? Is there anyone who makes such witty comments or so many of them? Or who uses such attractive and apposite vocabulary?' Caesar seems to have emulated the style, at any rate as a youth, of Caesar Strabo (Gaius Julius Caesar Strabo, aed. 90), some of whose speech *In Defence of the Sardinians* he borrowed word for word for use in one of his own trial orations. It is said that he pitched his voice high in speaking and used impassioned movements and gestures which were not without charm.

2.69 Cicero *Letters to his Friends* 16.21: The education of Marcus junior

In this, one of his many letters to Tiro, his father's freedman, the young Marcus in 44 BC, at the age of 21 or 22, discusses his education at Athens. Marcus had gone to Cilicia with his father, and Cicero had accused him of being extravagant and idle. He nevertheless became consul in 30 BC and governor of Syria and Asia.

3 I should tell you that my close attachment to Cratippus (a philosopher of Mitylene) is not so much that of a pupil as that of a son. For I not only enjoy attending his lectures, but I really find him extremely agreeable. I spend whole days with him, and often part of the night. I even beg him to dine with me as often as he can . . . **5** Besides this, I have begun practising declamation in Greek with Cassius; but I like practising in Latin with Bruttius. I have as daily intimate companions the people whom Cratippus brought with him from Mitylene, men of learning of whom he highly approves.

'BREAD AND CIRCUSES'

The ludi ('games') were intrinsic to Roman culture. There were three types of ludi: the ludi circenses (doc. 2.70), the ludi scaenici (which involved theatrical performances: 2.73–75) and the combatant ludi, involving gladiators and wild-beast displays (docs 2.77–79). Of the ludi scaenici, the Ludi Megalenses established in 191 honoured the arrival of the Magna Mater in Rome (docs 3.61–63). By the end of the Republic there were 57 days devoted to ludi, which were held on fixed dates. Gladiatorial contests (munera) are first mentioned in the third century BC and continued to grow in popularity, being always associated with funerals. They were first held in Rome in 264 BC by two brothers to honour their dead father (Marcus Junius Brutus Pera); three pairs of gladiators were involved. This association of gladiatorial contests with funerals continued throughout the Republic and, before Caesar's games in 46, gladiatorial shows were restricted to funeral games, not public performances (docs 2.78–79). Such shows usually took place in the forum, where the funeral procession had taken place and the eulogy had been delivered, with the spectators on temporary wooden seating. There was opposition to the construction of permanent theatres at Rome on the grounds that it would encourage idleness. The phrase 'bread and circuses' was coined by Juvenal (*Satires* 10.81).

2.70 Dionysius of Halicarnassus *Roman Antiquities* 7.72.1–73.4: The ludi magni (Great Games)

The ludi magni were also known as the Great Games, or Roman Games, and were held in September in honour of Jupiter, Juno and Minerva. Dionysius describes here the procession to the Circus Maximus at the beginning of these games.

72.1 Before starting the games, the most important magistrates conducted a procession in honour of the gods from the Capitol through the Forum to the Circus Maximus. The leaders of the procession were, first, their sons who were approaching manhood and of an age to take part in this ceremony, riding on horseback if their fathers had the property qualifications of equites, while those who would serve in the infantry went on foot; the former were in squadrons and troops, and the latter in divisions and companies, as if they were going to school; this was to show strangers the number and beauty of the state's youths who were near manhood. **2** They were followed by charioteers, some of whom drove four horses abreast, some pairs, and others rode unyoked horses; they were followed by the contestants in both the light and the heavy games, their bodies completely naked except for the covering around their waists . . . **5** The contestants were followed by numerous groups of dancers divided into three sections, the first of men, the second of youths, and the third of boys, and these were accompanied by flute-players, who played ancient, short flutes, as happens even to this day, and by lyre-players, who plucked ivory, seven-stringed lyres and instruments called *barbita*. The Greeks have stopped using these in my time, though their use was traditional, but they are still preserved by the Romans in all their ancient sacrificial ceremonies. **6** The dancers wore scarlet tunics girt with bronze belts, with swords hanging at their sides, and carried shorter than average spears; the men also had bronze helmets adorned with conspicuous crests and plumes. Each group was led by one man who gave the others the figures of the dance and took the lead in expressing the war-like and rapid movements, usually in the proceleusmatic (i.e., four short syllables) rhythms . . . **10** After the groups of armed dancers, other groups of Satyric players took part in the procession enacting the Greek dance called *sicinnis*. The dress of those who represented Sileni consisted of fleecy tunics, which some people call *chortaioi*, and coverings of all sorts of flowers; and those dressed as satyrs had loin-cloths and goatskins, and manes that stood upright on their heads, with other similar things. These mocked and mimicked the serious movements of the others, turning them into more ridiculous performances. . . . **13** After these dancers came a crowd of lyre-players and numerous flute-players, and after them the persons carrying the censers in which perfumes and frankincense were burned along the whole route, as well as the men who carried the vessels made of silver and gold, both those sacred to the gods and those belonging to the state. Last of all in the procession came the images of the gods, borne on men's shoulders, showing the same likenesses as those made by the Greeks, and the same dress, symbols and gifts which they are traditionally shown as inventing and bestowing on mankind: not only images of Jupiter, Juno, Minerva, Neptune and the rest whom the Greeks count among the twelve gods, but also of those still more ancient from whom, in legend, the twelve were sprung, namely Saturn, Ops, Themis, Latona, the Fates, Mnemosyne, and all the rest . . .

73.1 It now remains for me to describe briefly the games which the Romans performed after the procession. First was the race of four-horse chariots, of two-horse chariots, and of unyoked horses . . . **3** After the chariot races were finished, those who contended in their own persons came on, the runners, wrestlers and boxers . . . **4** And, in the intervals between the contests, they observed a practice which was extremely Greek and the best of all customs, that of awarding crowns and proclaiming the honours with which they honoured their benefactors, just as was done at Athens during the festivals of Dionysus, and displaying to all who had assembled for the spectacle the booty they had taken in war.

2.71 Dionysius of Halicarnassus *Roman Antiquities* 3.68.1–4: The Circus Maximus

Traditionally the site of the Circus Maximus was established by Romulus, with stands for viewing built under the Tarquinii; the Tarquinius of this document is Tarquinius Priscus, the fifth king (616–579 BC). Caesar as dictator made substantial improvements to the Circus Maximus, increasing the length of the circus to 620 metres: horses racing seven laps, keeping to the inner side of the spina, would have run over 3 kilometres, while there was seating for some 150,000 spectators. A stade is approximately 600 Greek feet, a plethron 100 feet.

1 Tarquinius also constructed the largest of the hippodromes (the Circus Maximus), which lies between the Aventine and Palatine and was the first to place covered seats around it on scaffolding (for till then the spectators stood), with beams supporting the wooden stands; and dividing the places among the 30 curiae he assigned a section to each, so that every spectator was seated in his proper place. **2** This work was also to become in time one of the most beautiful and spectacular constructions in the city. For the length of the hippodrome is three and a half stades, and the width four plethra; around it on the two longer sides and one of the shorter ones a canal to take water has been dug, ten feet in depth and width. Behind the canal, porticoes three storeys high are built. The lowest of these has stone seats as in the theatres, gradually rising one above the other, and the upper ones have wooden seats. **3** The two longer porticoes are united and joined together into one by means of the shorter one, which has a crescent shape, so that the three of them form a single portico like an amphitheatre eight stades around and capable of holding 150,000 people. The other shorter side is left uncovered and has vaulted starting places for the horses, all opened together by a single machine. **4** Around the outside of the hippodrome there is another one-storey portico which has shops in it and dwellings over them, and through this portico via every shop there are entrances and ascents for those coming to be spectators, so that nothing obstructs the entrance and departure of so many tens of thousands.

2.72 Dionysius of Halicarnassus *Roman Antiquities* 6.13.4–5: Castor and Pollux

At the battle at Lake Regillus (499 or 496 BC), Castor and Pollux appeared to help the Romans against the Latins in response to a vow by the dictator A. Postumius. A procession and annual sacrifices in their honour was still celebrated in Dionysius' time.

4 But above all this there is the procession, which is held after the sacrifice by those who have a public horse, who, arrayed by tribes and centuries, all ride in ranks on horseback, as if they came from battle, crowned with olive branches and dressed in the purple togas with stripes of scarlet, which they call trabeae. They start from a certain temple of Mars built outside the walls and, going through the rest of the city and the forum, pass by the temple of Castor and Pollux, sometimes numbering even as many as 5,000, wearing whatever rewards for valour they have received from their commanders in battle, a wonderful sight and one worthy of the immensity of the Roman empire. **5** These are the things I have learnt to be both related and performed by the Romans as a result of the epiphany of Castor and Pollux.

2.73 Cicero *Letters to his Friends* 7.1.2–3: Pompey's theatre

Cicero is writing to his friend Marcus Marius, who has decided to miss the shows put on by Pompey to celebrate the dedication of his new theatre in 55 BC, during his second consulship; this was the first permanent stone building for theatrical performances constructed in Rome. 500 lions were killed during the shows celebrating the dedication. There was also a display of 20 elephants: the elephants attempted to escape and broke through to the spectators' seats, causing panic. Cicero's attitude to the games is atypical of Romans, as he notes.

2 To be sure, the games (should you want to know) were most splendid, but certainly not to your taste . . . They did not even have the charms which more modest games usually have. The sight of such a sumptuous production destroyed all enjoyment; I am sure you can endure having missed it with equanimity. What enjoyment is there in 600 mules in *Clytemnestra*, or 3,000 mixing-bowls in the *Trojan Horse*, or a variety of infantry and cavalry equipment in some battle or other? These things which won the admiration of the common people would have brought you no enjoyment . . . **3** Or should I imagine that you regret missing the athletes, after scorning gladiators? Actually Pompey himself admits that he had wasted his time and money on them. That leaves the wild-animal hunts, two a day for five days – magnificent, no one can deny it! But what pleasure can a civilised man get out of either a helpless man being torn to pieces by a powerful animal or a magnificent animal being stabbed through with a hunting spear? Even if these were worth seeing, you have seen them often before, and we spectators saw nothing new. The last day was for the elephants. The mob showed great amazement but no enjoyment; in fact, there was a certain sympathy, a feeling that the monsters had some kind of affinity with humans.

2.74 Tacitus *Annals* 14.20.1–21.1: Criticism of Pompey's theatre

Nero in AD 60 instituted four-yearly games at Rome on the Greek model: the reception was mixed, as with Pompey's permanent theatre, before which wooden stages and (later) benches were erected temporarily, usually in the forum, for the occasion.

20.1 Indeed there were some who recalled the criticism of Pompey, too, by his elders for constructing a permanent theatre. For, previously, it had been usual to hold the shows with improvised seating and a stage put up for the occasion or, if you go even further back, for the spectators to stand, in case, if they sat in the theatre, their idleness continue for days on end. . . . **21.1** The majority approved the licence, although they called it by more respectable names. Our ancestors, they said, did not shrink from such public entertainment as their resources permitted: actors (histriones) were brought from Etruria, horse-racing from Thurii; and, with the annexation of Greece and Asia, performances became more ambitious, nor had any respectably born Roman ever demeaned himself by taking to the stage, and 200 years had passed since the triumph of Lucius Mummius (cos. 146), who was the first to put on that kind of show in Rome. Moreover a permanent theatre was far more economical than one which was erected and pulled down every year at tremendous expense.

2.75 Terence *The Mother-in-law: Prologue* 20–40: Problems of a producer

This play was first performed at the ludi Megalenses of 165 BC and then at the funeral games of Aemilius Paullus in 160. The prologue was spoken by the producer-actor Lucius Ambivius Turpio. According to the prologue, Terence has had to compete – unsuccessfully – with

the attractions of boxers, tight-rope walkers and gladiators; the ludi scaenici (performances) and munera (gladiatorial shows), however, were held on separate days and cannot
have conflicted.

20   Now, for my sake, give my plea a fair hearing.
       Once again I am putting the *Hecyra* on before you, a play I have never
       been able to produce without interruption, so greatly has it been beset by
       misfortune.
       This misfortune your understanding
       Can lull, if you will be supportive of our efforts.
25   When I tried to produce it the first time, the report of boxers
       (joined to the belief that a tight-rope walker would appear),
       the throng of their admirers, the shouting, and women's screaming
       forced me off stage before the end.
       I then decided to employ my usual approach on the new play
30   and try it out again; I put it on a second time.
       The first act was going well; then rumour circulated
       That a gladiatorial show was to be put on and the people flocked in,
       Pushing and shouting, fighting for a place,
       Leaving me unable to hold the stage.
35   Now there is no commotion: only peace and silence;
       I now have a chance to put on the play, while you have the opportunity
       To do honour to the stage.
       Do not be responsible for allowing the dramatic art
       To fall into the hands of a few; make sure that your influence
40   Supports and aids my own.

2.76 Suetonius *Life of the Deified Julius* 10.1–2: Caesar's games

The aediles were responsible for the ludi, financed by the state but with the aediles using
their own money as well to provide magnificent celebrations to win political favour with
the populace. Caesar was curule aedile in 65 BC (with Bibulus), producing magnificent
ludi, as well as a huge gladiatorial show in honour of his deceased father.

1 During his aedileship, Caesar decorated not only the comitium and forum with
its basilicas, but even the Capitol, constructing temporary colonnades to display
a large part of the equipment for his games. He put on wild-beast hunts and spectacles, sometimes with his colleague and sometimes on his own, the result being
that he claimed all the credit for the shared expenditure too, so that his colleague,
Marcus Bibulus, openly remarked, 'The same has happened to me as to Pollux:
for just as the temple of the twin brothers in the forum is simply called Castor's,
the joint liberality of myself and Caesar is said to be just Caesar's.' **2** Caesar also
put on a gladiatorial show, but with far fewer pairs than he had intended; for the
vast troop he had collected terrified his enemies, who passed legislation restricting
the number of gladiators that anyone might keep in Rome.

2.77 Cicero *Letters to his Friends* 2.11.2: Caelius needs panthers

Marcus Caelius Rufus (whom Cicero had earlier defended) was elected curule aedile for 50 and importuned Cicero as governor of Cilicia to send him some panthers for his games, as he only had 20; this is Cicero's reply. It was important for Caelius' future career that he should put on a good show at the Circus Maximus.

Regarding the panthers, the accustomed hunters are working diligently on my instructions. But there is a remarkable scarcity, and those that are left are said to be complaining because they are the only beings in my province for whom snares are set. Accordingly they are reported to have decided to leave my province for Caria. The matter, however, is receiving careful attention, especially from Patiscus. Whatever is found will be yours; but what that will come to I really don't know. I swear your aedileship is of great concern to me. The date itself reminds me of it, for I am writing this on the first day of the Ludi Megalenses (4 April).

2.78 Cicero *Tusculan Disputations* 2.41: 'With swords to the death'

Many gladiators were trained at Capua, where the revolt of Spartacus began in a gladiatorial school (doc. 6.50). Gladiators were generally slaves, and lanistae (trainers) bought up slaves or free men (non-Romans) willing to sell themselves. In 49 BC Caesar established a gladiatorial school which housed hundreds of gladiators, foreshadowing the large gladiatorial contests of the imperial age. Noted gladiators were often Samnites.

What of gladiators, who are either ruined men or barbarians, see what blows they can put up with! See how those who have been well trained prefer to receive a blow than disgracefully to avoid it! How often it is made clear that they prefer nothing more than giving satisfaction to their owner or to the populace! Even when they are exhausted by wounds, they send to their owners to ask their wishes – if they have given them satisfaction, they are happy to fall. What ordinary gladiator has ever given a groan or changed countenance? Who has disgraced himself, not only when standing, but even when he falls? Who, after he has fallen, has drawn in his neck when ordered to take the sword stroke? Such is the value of training, practice and habit. So, shall

'The Samnite, low fellow, worthy of that sort of life and place',

have the ability to take this? Shall a man born to renown have any part of his soul so weak that he cannot strengthen it by practice and training? A gladiatorial show is often seen by some as cruel and inhumane, and I rather agree that it is so, in its present form: but, when criminals fought with swords to the death, there could be no better instruction against pain and death, for the eye at any rate, though for the ear there might perhaps be many.

2.79 Suetonius *Life of the Deified Julius* 26.2–3: Caesar buys popular support

The concession was the right to stand for the consulship in absentia (doc. 13.7). The gladiatorial show (munus) for Julia was actually staged in 46 BC, along with Caesar's dedication of his forum and temple of Venus Genetrix. The contests were the first ever celebrated for a woman.

2 On this concession being granted, Caesar set his aims even higher and confidently omitted no kind of expenditure or granting of favours both as a candidate for office and as a private citizen. From his spoils, he began building a forum, and paid more than 100 million sesterces for the site. Then he announced a show and public banquet in memory of his daughter, which was quite unprecedented. To create as much anticipation as possible, he had the banquet, which was leased out to market contractors, also catered by his household. **3** He also proclaimed that any well-known gladiators, who might be fighting in front of a hostile audience, should be forcibly rescued and kept alive. He had new gladiators trained, not in the gladiatorial schools or by professional trainers (lanistae) but in private houses by Roman equites and even by senators, who had experience with weapons, and he begged these, as his letters demonstrate, to train these individually and personally instruct them in their practice. He doubled the legions' pay in perpetuity. Whenever there was an abundance of grain, he would give a distribution to them without measure and sometimes would give every man a slave from the spoils.

2.80 Bruns *FIRA* 122: Caesar's colony, 44 BC

A charter for the colony of Urso in Spain (the Colonia Genetiva Julia) drafted by Julius Caesar in 44 BC and made law by Antony after Caesar's assassination (cf. doc. 13.60). The officials of the colony are the duumvirs, aediles, augurs and priests. One of the main duties of the magistrates was to put on and oversee games and festivals. This inscription is also valuable evidence for the personnel normally employed by the magistrates of municipalities and colonies. HS is the normal abbreviation for sesterces.

62 In regard to the duumvirs, each duumvir shall have the right and power to have two lictors, an assistant, two clerks, two summoners, a copyist, a crier, a soothsayer and a flautist. In regard to the aediles in the aforesaid colony, each aedile shall have the right and power to have a clerk, four public slaves in girded aprons, a crier, a soothsayer and a flautist. Within this number they should employ colonists of the aforesaid colony. The aforesaid duumvirs and aediles, while they hold their magistracy, shall have the right and the power to use the toga praetexta, wax torches and tapers. Regarding clerks, lictors, assistants, summoners, flautists, soothsayers and criers employed by each of these, all the aforesaid persons, during the year in which they perform these duties, shall be exempt from military service. And no such person, during the year in which they perform such duties for magistrates, shall make any such person a soldier against his will, or order him to be so made, or use compulsion, or administer the oath, or order such oath to be administered, or bind such person by the military oath, or order such person to be so bound, except in the case of military unrest in Italy or Gaul. The following is to be the rate of pay for those persons who are in the service of the duumvirs: for each clerk HS 1,200, for each assistant HS 700, for each lector HS 600, for each summoner HS 400, for each copyist HS 300, for each soothsayer HS 500, for a crier HS 300; for persons in the service of the aediles the rate of pay is to be: for each clerk HS 800, for each soothsayer HS 500, for each flautist HS 300, for each crier HS 300. It shall be permitted for the said persons to receive the aforementioned sums without prejudice to themselves. . . .

66 In regard to the pontiffs and augurs created in the colony Genetiva by Gaius Caesar or by the person who by his orders establishes the colony, these are to be pontiffs and augurs of the colony Genetiva Julia and are to have their places in the colleges of pontiffs and augurs within the aforesaid colony, under all the conditions and with all the rights appertaining to pontiffs and augurs in any colony. And the aforesaid pontiffs and augurs who have places in their colleges, and also their children, shall be exempt from military service and from public duties with sacred guarantees, in the same way as a pontiff in Rome has or shall have the same, and all their military campaigns shall be considered as discharged. In regard to the auspices and the matters appertaining to the same: jurisdiction and adjudication shall belong to the augurs. And these pontiffs and augurs at all games publicly celebrated by magistrates and at public sacrifices of the colony Genetiva Julia performed by themselves are to have the right and the power to wear the toga praetexta; and the aforesaid pontiffs and augurs are to have the right and the power to sit among the decurions at the games and the gladiatorial contests. . . .

70 All duumvirs, except those first appointed following this law, in their magistracy are to put on a gladiatorial show or dramatic spectacles to Jupiter, Juno and Minerva, and to the gods and goddesses, over four days, for the greater part of each day, as far as shall be possible, at the discretion of the decurions, and on the aforesaid spectacles and the show each of these persons shall spend from his own money not less than HS 2,000, and from the public money it is to be lawful for each individual duumvir to expend a sum up to HS 2,000, and it shall be lawful for the said persons to do so without prejudice to themselves, as long as no one spends or makes an attribution of any portion of the money, which in accordance with this law shall be given or assigned for those sacrifices which are publicly carried out in the colony or in any other place. **71** All aediles during their magistracy shall put on a gladiatorial show or dramatic spectacles to Jupiter, Juno and Minerva, over three days for the greater part of each day, as far as shall be possible, and games in the circus or forum to Venus on one day, and on the aforesaid spectacles and show these are to expend from their own money not less than HS 2,000, and from the public fund it is to be lawful for each individual aedile to expend HS 1,000, and a duumvir or a prefect is to ensure that that money shall be given and assigned, and it shall be lawful for the aediles to receive this without prejudice to themselves.

3

Religion in the Roman Republic

Most of what is known about Roman religion concerns the official state religion, which was organised and managed for the benefit of the state. Less is known about the personal religion of the Romans as individuals. Politics and religion were intertwined because the Romans saw the gods as aiding and abetting their political success, and the political process took place in religious space. The senate house (curia) was a templum, a piece of inaugurated ground, as was the rostra in the assembly (for templum, see doc. 3.49; for the rostra, doc. 1.65). Roman religion was not an ethical system, and Cicero, for one, is quite blunt on this topic: 'Did anyone ever give thanks to the gods because he was a good man? No, because he was rich, respected, safe and sound. The reason men call Jupiter "Best and Greatest" (Optimus Maximus) is not because he makes us just, temperate and wise, but safe, secure, rich and abundantly wealthy' (Cicero *On the Nature of the Gods* 3.89). The gods, of course, did not condone wrongdoing, but this was not their principal concern: the Romans worshipped the gods to acquire specific benefits, such as their continuing assistance or their help in some crisis.

The state religion was organised by the elite. Nowhere is this made clearer than in the well-known opening to Cicero's speech to the pontiffs, *On his House* (*De domo sua*): 'Among the many divinely inspired expedients devised and instituted by our ancestors, pontiffs, there is nothing more noteworthy than that by which they desired the same individuals to be in charge of the worship of the immortal gods and the highest affairs of state, so that the most important and distinguished citizens might uphold religion by a good administration of the state, and the state by a wise interpretation of religion.' Priests were drawn only from patrician families before 300 BC (doc. 1.56), and it was the senate which outlawed the Bacchanalia (docs 3.65–66) and authorised the introduction of the new cults of Aesculapius (docs 3.59–60) and the Magna Mater (docs 3.61–63). When prodigies occurred, it was the senate that referred the matter to the Etruscan diviners known as haruspices (docs 3.4, 40) or instructed that the Sibylline Books be consulted (docs 3.38–39), and it decided which omens and prodigies of those reported warranted action.

The emphasis on the correct performance of ritual and the various rites which were performed for the state should not lead to the erroneous conclusion that the state religion lacked meaning for the ordinary citizen. The evidence indicates that in the Republic there was a vast array of traditional Roman festivals and cults which satisfied the religious requirements of the Romans as a people and as a state. At the same time, Rome, as its empire grew, naturally came into contact with new deities, and, as in any polytheistic system, room could be made for new gods without compromising the old. New cults filled specific needs, such as that of the healing deity Aesculapius (docs 3.59–60), or, like the fetching of the Magna Mater (docs 3.61–63), were in response to a consultation of the Sibylline Books in an emergency situation. The introduction of new cults and gods, such as that of the Magna Mater, into the religious pantheon was closely controlled by the state (that is, the senate) in the Republican period. In contrast, the cult of Dionysus, which spread to Rome without official sanction, incurred the wrath of the senate (docs 3.65–66).

Religio was a sense of obligation, the relationship by which mortals – both as individuals and as a community – were bound (in the sense of the verb 'to bind', *religare*) to worship the gods. Cicero connects *religio* with the verb *relegere*, 'to go over again, to re-read'. In addition, religious people (*religiosi*) were those who continually go over everything pertaining to the worship (*cultus*) of the gods (doc. 3.68). *Religio*, then, could be said to pertain to the rituals associated with the worship of the gods and the compulsory and binding nature of this worship. The term for the maintenance of the correct relationship between the community of Rome and the gods was *pax deorum*, the 'peace of the gods' (Lucretius 5.1229; Livy 6.41, 7.2.2); it was the gods who guided the res publica (Cic. *Rab. Perd.* 5).

The 'decline' of religion in the late Republic is sometimes postulated (Goar 1972: 29–33 is a good example: in the late Republic, 'the official religion was more and more an empty formality'). There are several areas on which this assumption rests: Augustus' claim that he restored 82 temples (*Res Gestae* 20.4 (doc. 15.1); Horace *Odes* 3.6.1–4; Ovid *Fasti* 2.59–66); the lack of a flamen dialis for several years, from Murena's suicide in 87 until 11 BC; and the 'intellectual' approach to religion, best seen in Cicero's *On Divination*. The first is Augustan propaganda and should not be taken in a literal sense to mean that traditional religion had fallen into decay. The second example points to the problems of the political organisation and its breakdown in this period rather than to a religious decline; and the third is a sign of a new intellectual, rather than religious, climate in which Greek philosophical ideas could be openly discussed without destroying belief. While there are various examples of the blatant use of augury for political ends (doc. 3.76), this was not a new phenomenon, and Cicero expressed it as making use of the gods' assistance to avoid unsuitable legislation (*Laws* 3.27).

The gods themselves were worshipped through prayer (doc. 3.26), sacrifice (doc. 3.32), lectisternia (doc. 3.15) and other rituals presided over by priests. The major Roman gods were Jupiter, Juno and Mars, all of whom held important places in the state religion, with Jupiter *the* major deity of the Romans; he was also an Italian deity worshipped throughout the peninsula. At Rome, he was the supreme god of state presiding over political activities through his role as the sender of *auspicia*, the auspices which were taken before elections, meetings of the assemblies, and any military action (docs 3.49–50). The first meeting of the senate each year took place in his temple on the Capitoline, and on entering office the two consuls sacrificed an ox to him (Livy 41.14.7) His major temple on the Capitoline, that of Jupiter Optimus Maximus, also contained shrines to Juno Regina (Queen Juno) and Minerva; this triad (Jupiter, Juno and Minerva) was probably originally Etruscan. Jupiter was responsible for victories in war, and a huge statue was made of him in the third century BC from the bronze weapons taken from the Samnites (doc. 1.73). The ceremony of the triumph evoked his role as war leader, since the general's face was painted red, like that of Jupiter's statue, and the procession concluded at his Capitoline temple (docs 2.32–35). His priest was the flamen dialis (doc. 3.21), who presided over the Vinalia, the wine festival held in April in Jupiter's honour. He was invoked by and witnessed the rituals of the fetials (doc. 3.14), and the Feriae Latinae (Latin festival) was celebrated in his honour (doc. 3.9).

Juno was also an Italian goddess, a guardian deity, and earned her cult title 'Moneta', she who warns, when her sacred geese gave warning of the Gauls secretly ascending the Capitol, while in another version she earned this title because, in the same crisis, a voice was heard from her temple commanding that an expiatory sacrifice of a pregnant sow be made (geese: Plut. *Rom. Quest.* 98, *Cam.* 27.1–3; voice: Cic. *Div.* 1.101; cf. Ovid *Fasti* 6.183). Her cult as Juno Regina originated in the evocatio of this goddess from Veii (doc. 3.57). She was a goddess of women. Vesta had a crucial role as the goddess of the hearth and, by extension, as a deity of Rome. If her sacred fire in her temple in the forum went out, it was a sign of divine displeasure; prodigies and disasters could be interpreted as meaning that one or more of the Vestals had broken their vows of chastity, and expiation had to be made to correct the relationship between Rome and the gods. The Vestal Virgins (docs 7.88–94) were the only female cult personnel at Rome apart from the wife of the flamen dialis (doc. 3.21).

Worship of Mars was marked by festivals in March and October, the traditional beginning and end of the campaining season respectively (North 1989: 599–600). The Salii performed their rituals in this month to honour the god (doc. 3.13). Most famously, the rite of the October horse (October 15) involved a two-horse chariot race: the right-hand horse of the victorious team was subsequently sacrificed to Mars. Its head was cut off and the inhabitants of the Via Sacra and those of Subura fought for it, while the tail was carried to the Regia and its blood sprinkled on the altar (doc. 3.73). Rome was a militaristic state: the doors of the temple of Janus were closed only when Rome was at peace, and this occurred in the Republic only in 235 BC (doc. 14.60; Varro *Lat. Lang.* 5.165; Livy 1.19.2).

There were also personified concepts of the divine, including Concord (concordia), who had a temple on the lower Capitoline just above the forum. This was of uncertain foundation date (almost certainly not by M. Furius Camillus in 367 BC), and it was famously rebuilt by Opimius on the orders of the senate in 121 after the murder of Gaius Gracchus and his supporters (doc. 8.32). Fides, 'good faith', also had a temple on the Capitoline. Traditional scholarship has placed a great deal of emphasis on the *numina* (spirits) and the gradual development of Roman religion away from numina to anthropomorphic deities. This model is now not accepted, as clearly the Romans always had corporeal gods, chief among whom was Jupiter, and there were various minor deities as well as personifications of entities, often with quite specific roles and functions, such as sowing and rust (docs 3.3, 74), as well as a variety of lesser agricultural deities (doc. 3.2).

Ancient sources: there were numerous sources on religion in the Republic that are now lost. The augurs kept records of their pronouncements (*decreta*) on prodigies. They also maintained books of augural lore (doc. 3.40), and several works on augury were written in the first century BC. The Etruscans had books of divination by entrail inspection (extispicy), and the pontiffs had books of prayers and rituals. In the late Republic, Veranius wrote on augury and the pontifical colleges and Granius Flaccus on the forms of words which the pontiffs used in calling on the gods, both now surviving only as fragments. Varro *Lat. Lang.* 6.86 (doc. 3.24) quotes from the *Censoriae Tabulae*, Censors' Records, when providing information about the lustrum held at the end of the census; Val. Max. 4.1.10 refers to the 'public tables' (publicae tabulae) with respect to the prayer recited by the censor at the lustrum (doc. 3.27). In addition, priests kept records (often of more importance to history as such than religion). The annales maximi, kept by the pontifex maximus, were an annual report posted each year on a whitened board near the Regia, which was wiped clean when the next yearly instalment was ready; the collected annales were published towards the end of the second century BC. They recorded the names of magistrates and also important events. As such the annals were an important primary source for historians.

The main authors on Roman religion, Cicero and Varro, come late in the Republican period. Cicero, in *On the Nature of the Gods* (*De natura deorum*), wrote on the nature and form of the gods; *On Divination* (*De divinatione*) is a discussion on the merits or otherwise of divination; *Laws* (*De legibus*) Book 2 discusses the religious system of his ideal state, analogous to that of the Roman state. In addition, Cicero's various works and letters contain numerous references to the practice of contemporary religion (e.g., docs 3.39–40, 42, 46, 53–54, 68, 81). Varro's 41 books of *Antiquitates rerum humanarum et divinarum* (*Human and Divine Antiquities*), which appeared in 47 BC, comprised 25 books on Roman antiquities and 16 books (dedicated to Julius Caesar as pontifex maximus) on Roman religious themes, namely the priesthoods, sacred places, festivals, rituals and gods. Some quotations from this work survive. Varro mentions various priestly records, such as the books of the Salii (*Lat. Lang.* 6.14). In his *On the Latin Language* (*De lingua Latina*), in dealing with the etymology of various words he reveals a great deal of information (docs 3.2, 17, 19, 24, 49).

Dionysius of Halicarnassus is next in importance after Varro and Cicero (docs 3.7–9, 13, 20, 32, 38, 67), and in his *Roman Antiquities* he preserves a mine of useful information on Roman religion. His account is based not only on his own observations but also on Roman literary sources, such as Varro's works on religion, which he notes at doc. 3.38. One of his concerns is to show that Roman religious practices are based on Greek models or that there are numerous similarities.

Historians such as Polybius and Livy provide information about Roman religion as part of their overall historical treatments. Livy is very interested in omens and religious events. Among these are the condemnation of Vestal Virgins and human sacrifices (docs 4.38, 7.91) and his famous description of the Bacchanalia (doc. 3.65). Polybius, in Book 6, writes about Roman funerary rituals (doc. 3.77) and makes a comment on the political use of religion at the time he is writing (doc. 3.76), but on the whole he does not deal with religious factors in his work.

Ovid's *Fasti* (docs 3.74, 7.79–83) is a month-by-month account – in poetry – of the Roman festival calendar. Unfortunately only half the year survives (January–June), and the other months may never have been written. Ovid (43 BC–AD 17) was writing outside of the Republican period, but most of the festivals he describes belong to the Republic. Important details about dates, aetiological myths and ritual practices are preserved in his extant poems. Plutarch *Roman Questions* asks many (113) questions about Roman customs and practices, most of which concern religion. He cites several Roman authorities for his information. With his interest in delving into the origins of Roman practices he is an important source for details about early Roman religion. Julius Obsequens, of the fourth or early fifth century AD, in his *Book of Prodigies*, dealt with omens and prodigies from 249 to 11 BC, but only that part dealing with 190 to 11 BC survives.

Calendars: Over 40 Roman religious calendars inscribed on stone or painted on walls have survived, sometimes extensively or as fragments, but only one dates from the Republican period (doc. 3.30). These calendars vary in the information they supply, but all list festivals, and some provide information on the gods being honoured and temples whose anniversaries are being celebrated. Inscriptions provide evidence for dedications (e.g., docs 3.25, 55, 60).

EARLY DEITIES AND CULTS

When the Republic was inaugurated in 509 BC, Roman religion had been exposed to Etruscan and, to a lesser extent, Greek influence. The Romans also worshipped similar gods and shared festivals with their Latin neighbours. The basic features of Roman religion had already been established before the early Republic, but by the first century BC the Romans had forgotten the exact meaning of some of their rituals, which they continued to practise out of tradition and piety. Etruscan influence chiefly centred on the haruspices ('soothsayers'), while the major Greek influence includes the introduction of Aesculapius (the Greek Asklepios) and the identification of the Roman gods with the Greek. Yet, despite Greek influences and, in the closing decades of the Republic, the introduction of foreign deities such as the Magna Mater (docs 3.61–63), the cult of Bacchus (docs 3.65–66), and the increasing prominence of the goddess Isis (doc. 3.64), Roman religion had a fundamentally *Roman* character with a major emphasis on agriculture; agricultural festivals remained important to the very end of the Republic and beyond (docs 3.2–3, 12, 74).

3.1 Ennius *Annals* 60–61: The divine council

Ennius (c. 239–169 BC) here catalogues the 12 'Olympian' Roman gods and goddesses, perhaps in connection with a lectisternium ('banquet of the gods': see doc. 3.15) for all 12 great gods held in 217 BC: Jove is Jupiter.

Juno, Vesta, Minerva, Ceres, Diana, Venus, Mars,
Mercury, Jove, Neptune, Vulcan, Apollo.

3.2 Varro *On the Latin Language* 5.74: The early deities

Varro (116–27 BC) is here attempting to determine the linguistic origins of the names of deities. Some of these names are perfectly Roman. Novensides, 'new settlers', is apparently used in opposition to indigetes, 'native gods'; for Feronia: see doc. 3.8. Tatius was king of the Sabines at the time of the 'rape of the Sabine women'.

Feronia, Minerva, the Novensides are from the Sabines. With minor changes, we say the following, also from the same people: Pales (goddess of shepherds), Vesta, Salus, Fortuna, Fons (god of springs), Fides. The altars too which were dedicated at Rome by the vow of King Tatius have the smell of the Sabine language; for, as the *Annals* tell us, he vowed altars to Ops, Flora, Vediovis and Saturn, Sun, Moon, Vulcan and Summanus (responsible for lightning), and likewise to Larunda (a nymph), Terminus, Quirinus, Vertumnus, the Lares, Diana and Lucina; some of these names have roots in either language.

3.3 Servius *On Vergil's Georgics* 1.21: Names and functions of deities

A Fabius Pictor wrote *On the Pontifical Law*; he is probably not the same individual as Fabius Pictor the historian but, rather, an antiquarian of the mid-second century BC. The deities' names reflect their sphere of activity. Clearly the origin of these deities was obscure, but they were closely connected with agricultural activities.

It is quite obvious that names have been given to divine spirits in accordance with the function of the spirit. For example, Occator was so named after the word *occatio*, harrowing; Sarritor, after *sarritio*, hoeing; Sterculinus, after *stercoratio*, spreading manure; Sator, after *satio*, sowing. Fabius Pictor lists the following as deities whom the flamen of Ceres invokes when sacrificing to Mother Earth and Ceres: Vervactor (ploughing fallow), Reparator (replough), Imporcitor (make furrows), Insitor (sow), Obarator (plough up), Occator, Sarritor, Subruncinator (clear weeds), Messor (harvest), Convector (carry), Conditor (store) and Promitor (bring forth).

3.4 Diodorus Siculus *Library of History* 5.40.1–2: Rome's debt to the Etruscans

According to Livy 5.1.6, the Etruscans paid more attention than any other people to religious rites. Etruscan practices involved haruspices (priests who inspected the entrails of victims), the interpretation of thunder and lightning, and prescriptions for rituals involved in the founding of cities and other important events. Miniature fasces have been documented in an Etruscan seventh-century tomb, and the sella curulis (the ivory folding chair used by magistrates, perhaps originally an attribute of the kings) is seen in numerous Etruscan tombs and paintings.

1 The Etruscans also devised the majesty that surrounds rulers, granting them lictors, an ivory stool, and a toga with a band of purple, while with regard to houses they invented the peristyle, a very useful way of avoiding the confusion of crowds of attendants; the Romans copied most of these inventions, improved them and transferred them to their own nation. **2** The Etruscans also perfected literature and the teaching about nature and the gods, and they achieved more expertise than any other race in the art of divination by thunder and lightning, which is why, even up to this present day, the people who rule nearly the entire inhabited world show respect to these men and employ them as interpreters with regard to omens from heaven.

3.5 Ennius *Annals* 125–129: Numa and early religious institutions

Ennius here ascribes to Numa the introduction of several features of religious practice. Varro comments that the deities mentioned here are obscure. Sacrificial cakes: the liba; bakers of offering-cakes: the fictores, who made the liba; the shields refer to those carried by the Salii: doc. 3.13; rush-dummies: the Argei (see doc. 3.7); the tutulati, certain priests who wore a conical head-dress (the tutulus) at sacrifices.

> Numa established the sacrificial banquets, as well as the shields,
> and the sacrificial cakes, bakers of offering-cakes, rush-dummies, and the
>   wearing of conical head-dresses.
> The priests of Volturnus, Palatua, Furrina,
> Flora, Falacer and Pomona were also instituted
> By him.

3.6 Livy *History of Rome* 1.20.1–7: Numa and Roman religion

Vestal Virgins: docs 7.88–94; Salii: doc. 3.13; flamen dialis: doc. 3.21. A feature of Roman religion was its written nature; in the Republic the priests had access to various books in which the precise nature of the rituals which they had to perform were prescribed.

1 Numa then turned his mind to the creation of priests, although he was accustomed to undertake many sacred duties himself, especially those which now pertain to the flamen dialis. **2** But since he thought that in a warlike society there would be more kings like Romulus than like Numa, and that they would take part in wars themselves, he appointed a flamen for Jupiter as his perpetual priest (the flamen dialis), so that the sacred duties of the royal office would not be neglected, and equipped him with a special dress and a royal curule chair. To him he added two more flamens, one for Mars, another for Quirinus; **3** and he chose virgins for Vesta, a priesthood which originated in Alba and which was thus not unsuited to the race of its founder. So that they might be perpetual priests of the temple, he assigned them a salary from the public funds and made them respected and holy through their virginity and other sacred observances. **4** He likewise chose 12 Salii for Mars Gradivus, and gave them the distinction of wearing an embroidered tunic and a bronze breastplate over the tunic, and instructed them to carry the divine shields, which are called ancilia, as they went through the city singing sacred songs to their rhythmic and solemn dance. **5** He then chose from the senators as pontifex (maximus) Numa Marcius, son of Marcus, and entrusted to him the sacred duties written out in full – with what victims, on what days, at what shrines rites should take place and from where money was to be expended to cover their costs. **6** All other public and private rites, too, he placed under the control of the decrees of the pontifex, that there might be someone whom the plebs could come to consult, so that there might be no confusion in divine law through the neglect of ancestral rites and the admission of foreign ones; **7** the pontifex was not merely to teach ceremonies to do with the gods in heaven but correct funerary observances and the propitiation of the spirits of the dead, and what omens shown in lightning or other visible signs were to be dealt with and warded off.

3.7 Dionysius of Halicarnassus 1.38.2–3: Substitute human sacrifices?

Varro (*Lat. Lang.* 5.45, 7.44) gives the number of the effigies known as Argei as 27, while Dionysius has 30. The Argei were made of bulrushes, and the 30 given here would mean one for each curia. The bridge is the Pons Sublicius. A procession visited the shrines on 16 and 17 March, and the Vestals threw the Argei into the Tiber on 14 May, perhaps as a rite of purification.

2 It is said, too, that the men of old used to sacrifice human victims to Cronus (Saturn), as was done in Carthage while that city stood and is still done to this day by the Gauls and some other western peoples, and that Hercules, wishing to put an end to the custom of this sacrifice, erected the altar on the Saturnian hill and began the sacrificial ceremony of unblemished victims burning on a pure fire; and, so that the people might not have any scruples about having neglected their ancestral sacrifices, he taught the natives to appease the wrath of the god by making effigies of the men whom they had bound hand and foot and thrown into the Tiber's stream and to dress these in the same manner and throw them into the river instead of the men, in order that any evil foreboding which remained in the minds of all might be removed, as the appearance of the ancient practice would still be retained. **3** The Romans have continued to do this every year right down to my own time, a little after the spring equinox in the month of May, on what they call the Ides, the day they wish to be the middle of the month; on this day the pontiffs, as they are called – the most important of the priests – offer preliminary sacrifices according to the laws, and with them the virgins who guard the eternal fire, the praetors and those citizens who may lawfully be present at the rites throw 30 effigies made in the form of men from the sacred bridge into the stream of the Tiber; these they call Argei.

3.8 Dionysius of Halicarnassus 3.32.1, 4: Early cult practices

In the reign of Tullus Hostilius (672–641 BC), the Sabines, according to tradition, seized important Romans attending a festival, leading to a further Sabine–Roman war (see Livy 1.30.4–10). Salii: see doc. 3.13; Feronia: a Sabine goddess of uncertain function; the festival of Saturn referred to here is presumably the Saturnalia: doc. 3.71; the Opalia on 19 December celebrated the goddess Ops.

1 After this war another arose from the Sabine people against the Romans, of which the origin and cause was as follows: there is a sanctuary, honoured in common by both the Sabines and Latins and considered as extremely sacred, dedicated to a goddess named Feronia, whom some of those who translate the name into Greek call Anthophoros ('Flower-bearer'), some Philostephanos ('Lover of garlands'), and others Persephone. People from the neighbouring towns used to gather at this sanctuary on the appointed festival days, many of them offering prayers and sacrifices to the goddess, and many with the purpose of doing business during the festival as merchants, craftsmen and farmers, and fairs more splendid than anywhere else in Italy were held here. Some distinguished Romans who had come to this festival were seized, bound and robbed of their money by some Sabines . . . (This led to war, at first with inconclusive results, but a battle was again fought at Eretum in the next year, 160 stades from Rome.)

4 When that battle continued equally balanced for a long period, Tullus, raising his hands to heaven, vowed to the gods that if he conquered the Sabines on that day he would institute public festivals in honour of Cronus and Rhea (Saturn and Ops: the Saturnalia and Opalia), which the Romans celebrate every year after they have gathered in all the fruits of the earth, and would double the number of the Salii, as they are called. These are young men of noble family who, at appointed times, perform dances in full armour to the music of the flute and sing certain traditional hymns, as I have explained in the preceding book.

3.9 Dionysius of Halicarnassus 4.49.1–3: The Feriae Latinae

On entering office the consuls set the date for the Feriae Latinae (the Latin festival) and presided over the sacrifice on the Alban mount to Jupiter Latiaris, identified with Latinus, eponymous ancestor of the Latin race. All the cities of Latium participated.

1 When Tarquinius had acquired sovereignty over the Latins, he sent envoys both to the cities of the Hernici and to those of the Volscians, proposing that they too should enter into a treaty of friendship and alliance. All the Hernici voted to join the alliance, but only two cities of the Volscians, Ecetra and Antium, accepted the invitation. To ensure that the agreements with these cities should last for ever, Tarquinius decided to set up a place of worship in common for Romans, Latins, Hernici and those Volscians who had joined the alliance, so that they should gather together each year at the designated place and jointly celebrate a festival, feast and partake in sacrifices in common. **2** When everyone welcomed the suggestion, he designated, as the place where they should gather, a high mountain lying almost in the middle of these nations and overlooking the Albans' city, on which, he laid down, a festival should be celebrated every year during which there should be a truce to all hostilities and sacrifices should be performed in common to Jupiter Latiaris, as he is called, and joint feasts held. He also assigned what each city was to contribute towards the sacrifices and the share each of them was to receive. Forty-seven cities took part in this festival and sacrifice. **3** The Romans celebrate these festivals and sacrifices to our own time, calling them the 'Latin festivals' (*feriae latinae*); and some of the cities that take part in them bring lambs, others cheeses, or a certain measure of milk, or something similar. One bull is sacrificed in common by all of them and each city receives its designated share of it. The sacrifices are made on behalf of them all and the Romans are in charge of the ceremonies.

3.10 Bruns *FIRA* 283: Regulations for sacred groves, c. 240

These inscriptions were found at Spoleta in Umbria and Lucera in Apulia.

(*lex luci Spoletina*) No person shall desecrate this grove. No one shall either cart away or carry away what belongs to the grove nor shall cut wood within it, except on the day on which the annual divine worship is performed. On that day it shall be permitted without prejudice to cut wood as long as it is done for the purpose of sacred worship. If anyone violates this rule he shall give to Jupiter a sin-offering by means of an ox; if anyone violates this rule with malice aforethought he shall give to Jupiter a sin-offering by means of an ox and shall be fined 300 asses. The exaction of this sin-offering and of this fine shall belong to the dedicator.

(*lex luci Lucerina*) In this grove no person shall deposit dung nor shall cast away a dead body nor shall make solemn sacrifice in honour of his deceased ancestors. If anyone acts contrary to these rules on him, whoever wishes may lay hands on him as on a person adjudged guilty to the amount of 50 sesterces. Or if a magistrate wishes to fine him it shall be lawful to do so.

3.11 Strabo *Geography* 5.3.12: The 'king' of Diana's grove

Mount Albanus was some 16 miles south-east of Rome. The fugitive slave who became the priest was known as the rex Nemorensis (king of the grove). Euripides, in his *Iphigenia in Tauris*, describes the Tauri in the Crimea as sacrificing strangers.

After Mount Albanus there is Aricia, a city on the Appian Way; the distance from there to Rome is 160 stades. The place is in a hollow, but has a strongly positioned citadel. Above it lies, first, Lanuvium, a Roman city, on the right hand side of the Appian Way, from which both the sea and Antium are visible, and then, on the left hand side of the way as you go up from Aricia, the Artemisium, which they call Nemus ('Glade'). The shrine of the Arician goddess (Diana) they say to be a copy of the Tauropolos (the shrine of Artemis as goddess of the Tauri). And indeed a barbaric and Scythian aspect prevails in the sacred customs. For the person who has become the priest is a runaway slave who killed his priestly predecessor with his own hand; so he always carries a sword, keeping a watch out for attacks, ready to defend himself. The shrine is in a grove, with a lake before it like an open sea, and a continuous and lofty mountain ridge encircles it, enclosing both shrine and water in a hollow and deep setting.

EARLY HYMNS AND RITUALS

3.12 *ILS* 5039: Hymn of the Arval Brothers

The song of the 12 Arval brothers, a college of priests, perhaps dates to as early as the sixth century BC. Varro's (doc. 3.19) is the only mention of the Arval brothers in the Republic, but the Hymn has archaic language (such as Lases for Lares) and the Arvals were clearly a Republican institution of some antiquity; by the late Republic the rites had become obscure, and Augustus claims to have revived them (*RG* 7.1: doc. 15.1, cf. 15.20). The hymn invokes the Lares and Mars (Marmar, Marmor), who was originally a protector of farmland (and so repelled invaders; for Mars in agriculture, see doc. 3.23). The Lares were protective deities of the household and crossroads. Leaping here is imitative magic to make crops grow; arva is the Latin word for fields.

Then the priests closed the doors, tucked up their robes, took the books in hand, divided into groups, and danced in three-step rhythm singing in the following words:

> Oh help us, Lares! Oh help us, Lares! Oh help us, Lares!
> Do not let plague or ruin, O Marmar, assail more people.
> Do not let plague or ruin, O Marmar, assail more people.
> Do not let plague or ruin, O Marmar, assail more people.
> Be satisfied, fierce Mars, leap the threshold! Stop! Burn (?)! Be satisfied, fierce Mars, leap the threshold! Stop! Burn (?)! Be satisfied, fierce Mars, leap the threshold! Stop! Burn (?)!
> In turn invoke all the gods of sowing. In turn invoke all the gods of sowing. In turn invoke all the gods of sowing.
> Oh help us, O Marmor! Oh help us, O Marmor! Oh help us, O Marmor! Triumph! Triumph! Triumph, triumph, triumph!

After the triple-rhythmed dance, at a given signal, the public slaves then came in and took the books.

3.13 Dionysius of Halicarnassus 2.70.1–5: The leaping of the Salii

The Salii ('leapers') were two groups of 12 priests. According to tradition, Numa founded the initial group, with Tullus Hostilius later adding the second 12 (doc. 3.8). They sang and danced in honour of Mars, wearing military dress and carrying shields, in March and October. The original shield was said to have fallen from heaven in Numa's reign and it was believed Rome's safety depended on it. The 'martial gods' must be Mars and Quirinus; cf. docs 3.6, 8; doc. 3.51 for the sacred staff.

1 Numa himself appointed the Salii from the patricians, selecting the 12 best-looking young men. Their sacred objects are kept on the Palatine hill, and they themselves are called the *Palatini*. For the (Salii called the) *Agonales*, . . . who have their repository of sacred objects on the Quirinal hill, were appointed by King Hostilius after Numa's reign, fulfilling a vow which he had made in the war fought against the Sabines. All these Salii are a kind of dancers and hymn-singers in honour of the martial gods. 2 The festival takes place . . . in the month of Martius (March). It is celebrated for many days, at public expense, during which time the *Salii* dance through the city to the Forum and the Capitoline Hill and to many other places, public and private. They are attired in embroidered tunics fastened with belts of bronze, and robes with scarlet stripes and a purple border fastened

with brooches. These robes are known as *trabeae*, a peculiarly Roman dress and a mark of the greatest honour. On their heads they wear apices, high caps tapering into a cone shape. . . . **3** Each of the Salii has a sword hung from their belt, and in his right hand a spear or staff or some such thing, and in his left a Thracian shield, an oblong shield which looks like a lozenge, with the sides drawn in to form hollows (i.e., a 'figure of eight shield'). . . . **5** They make rhythmic movements in their armour to the sound of the flute, sometimes all together, sometimes in turns; and while they dance they sing various traditional hymns.

3.14 Livy *History of Rome* 1.32.5–14: The origin of the fetials

Livy is recording a formula for the declaration of war supposedly established by the fourth king of Rome, Ancus Marcius (640–617 BC). The 20 fetials (fetiales) were responsible for the rituals associated with the declaration of war and also the making of treaties. When the enemy territory was not in proximity to Rome, the ritual spear-throwing occurred at Rome itself, near the temple of Bellona.

5 In order that, just as Numa had established religious practices in time of peace, he (Ancus Marcius) might give war its own ceremonial and wars should not only be fought but also declared with some formality, he copied from the ancient tribe of the Aequicolae the law which the fetials now possess, by which redress is sought. **6** When the envoy arrives at the boundary of the people from which redress is sought, he covers his head with a fillet (the covering is woollen) and says, 'Hear, Jupiter! Hear, boundaries of – , naming whichever nation's they are! Let righteousness hear! I am the public messenger of the Roman people; I come rightly and religiously commissioned and let trust be placed in my words.' He then goes through his demands. **7** Then he calls Jupiter to witness: 'If I demand contrary to justice and religion that these men or goods be surrendered to me, then never allow me to share in my country.' **8** He makes this statement, with only a few changes in the formula of the oath, when he crosses the frontier, when the first man encounters him, when he passes through the town's gate, and when he has entered the forum. **9** If those he demands are not surrendered, after 33 days – the established number – he declares war in the following words: **10** 'Hear, Jupiter; and you, Janus Quirinus; and hear, all you gods in heaven, and you on earth and you under the earth. I call you to witness that this people – naming whichever one it is – is unjust and does not make due restitution. But concerning these things we will consult the elders in our country, as to how we may obtain our right.' Then the messenger returns to Rome for consultation. The king would immediately consult the senators (patres) in words such as these: **11** 'Regarding the things, cases, causes about which the pater patratus (fetial priest) of the Roman people of the Quirites has made demands on the pater patratus of the Ancient Latins and the men of the Ancient Latins, which things they have not handed over, fulfilled or done, which they ought to have handed over, fulfilled and done, speak', he would say to the man whose opinion he was accustomed to ask first, 'What is your view?' **12** He would then reply, 'I consider that they ought to be sought in just and righteous warfare and thus I agree and vote.' Then the others would be asked in order; and when the majority of those who were there sided with the same view, war had been agreed. It was usual for the fetial to bear to their opponents' boundary a spear with a head of iron or wood hardened in the fire, and in the presence of not fewer than three adult men proclaim: **13** 'Whereas the peoples of the Ancient Latins and the men of the Ancient Latins have acted and committed offences against the Roman people of the Quirites, and whereas the Roman people of the Quirites has ordered that there be war with the Ancient Latins, and the senate of the Roman people of the Quirites has approved, agreed and voted that there be war with the Ancient Latins, accordingly I and the Roman people hereby declare and make war on the peoples of the Ancient Latins and the men of the Ancient Latins.' After proclaiming this, he would hurl the spear into their territory. **14** It was in this way that redress was sought from the Latins and war declared, and later generations adopted the same custom.

3.15 Livy *History of Rome* 5.13.4–8: The lectisternium, 399 BC

The rite of the lectisternium (plural: lectisternia), the banquet of the gods, was introduced in 399. Lectisternia were held to propitiate the gods after plague and major defeats, as in 218 BC (doc. 3.33). One was held when the cult of the Magna Mater was introduced in 205 BC (doc. 3.61). The duumvirs ('two men') were in charge of the Sibylline Books: doc. 3.38.

4 The severe winter was followed – whether because of the sudden change from such an inclement season to the exact opposite or from some other reason – by a summer that was oppressive and unhealthy to all living creatures. **5** Since nothing could be found to explain the origins of this incurable pestilence or put an end to it, on the senate's advice the Sibylline Books were consulted. **6** The duumvirs in charge of the sacred rites then, for the first time in Rome's history, held a lectisternium and for a period of eight days appeased Apollo, Latona and Diana, and Hercules, Mercury and Neptune, by spreading three couches for them with all the abundance possible at that time. **7** They also celebrated this same sacred rite at their homes. Throughout the whole city, doors were left open, all kinds of goods were placed out in the open for general consumption, strangers were generally welcomed whether known or not, and men spoke courteously and companionably even to their enemies. People refrained from arguments and law-suits; **8** chains were even removed from prisoners during that period; and they later felt it wrong to imprison those to whom the gods had given this assistance.

3.16 Livy *History of Rome* 7.2.1–7: The development of drama

A lectisternium failed to alleviate a plague in 365–364 BC, and a new form of placatory ritual was introduced. The term 'fescennine' was probably derived from Fescennia (a city in Etruria) or from fascinum, a phallus-shaped amulet. Livius Andronicus of Tarentum composed the first Latin comedy, performed in Rome in 240 BC (cf. doc. 7.85).

1 The plague lasted during both this and the subsequent year, the consulship of Gaius Sulpicius Petico and Gaius Licinius Stolo (cos. 364). **2** Nothing worth remembering was done in that year, except that a lectisternium was held for the third time since the foundation of the city, in the hope of entreating the goodwill of the gods. **3** And when the force of the plague was alleviated by neither human counsel nor divine aid, the Romans' minds were overcome by superstition, and, among other practices intended to placate the gods' anger, they are said to have instituted scenic entertainments, a new departure for a warlike people, for their only public spectacle had been that of the Circus. **4** These indeed began in a modest way, as most things do, and were in fact imported from abroad. Without any singing, without any miming of song, players brought in from Etruria danced to the sounds of the flute and performed graceful movements in the Etruscan style. **5** Then the young Romans began to copy them, at the same time exchanging jokes in rude verses, their movements harmonising with the words. **6** Thus the entertainment was accepted and established by frequent usage. The native actors were called *histriones*, because *ister* is the Etruscan word for actor; **7** they no longer, as before, threw at each other rude, improvised lines, such as Fescennine verses, but performed *saturae* (medleys), accompanied by music, with the singing properly arranged to fit the flute-playing and with appropriate movements.

3.17 Varro *On the Latin Language* 5.143: The pomerium

The pomerium ('behind-the-wall') was the boundary line of the city, originally supposed to have been ploughed by Romulus and inaugurated by Servius Tullius. It was a sacred space where auspices were taken, and promagistrates and generals who held imperium had to lay it down on crossing the pomerium into the city.

Many people employed the Etruscan ritual when they were founding a town in Latium – that is, using a team of cattle, a bull with a cow on the inside, they would run a furrow around it with a plough (for religious reasons they would do this on an auspicious day), so they might be defended by a ditch and wall. The place where they ploughed up the earth they called a 'ditch' (fossa), and the earth thrown inside it a 'wall' (murus). The 'circle' (orbis) which was made behind this was the beginning of the 'city' (urbs); because it was 'behind the wall' (post murum), they called this the postmoerium (pomerium), which is the outside limit for auspices taken for the city. Markers of the pomerium stand around both Aricia and Rome.

3.18 Livy *History of Rome* 8.9.4–8, 10.11–11.1: Devotio

The devotio of Decius Mus in 340 BC was the most famous in the Republic but was not a unique example of the ritual, which his own son (doc. 1.70) and grandson were also said to have performed. When in 340 the Romans engaged the Latins in battle near Mount Vesuvius and the left wing was pushed back, Decius undertook the devotio ritual, devoting himself and the enemy to the 'Gods of the underworld (the divine *manes*) and to Earth'; cf. doc. 5.8 for his conduct as military tribune.

9.4 In this moment of confusion the consul Decius cried out to Marcus Valerius in a loud voice: 'Marcus Valerius, we need the gods' help; you are a state pontiff of the

Roman people – come, dictate the words with which I may devote myself to save the legions.' **5** The pontiff told him to put on his purple-edged toga, and, with his head veiled and with one hand protruding from his toga and touching his chin, stand on a spear laid under his feet and repeat as follows: **6** 'Janus, Jupiter, Father Mars, Quirinus, Bellona, Lares, New Gods (divi novensiles), Native Gods (di indigetes), Gods, in whose power are we and our enemies, and you Gods of the underworld (di manes), **7** I supplicate and revere you, I seek your favour and entreat you, that you prosper the might and victory of the Roman people, the Quirites, and afflict the enemies of the Roman people, the Quirites, with terror, fear and death. **8** As I have pronounced the words, so on behalf of the Republic of the Roman people, the Quirites, and on behalf of the army, the legions and the auxiliaries of the Roman people, the Quirites, do I devote myself and, with me, the legions and auxiliaries of the enemy to the Gods of the underworld and to Earth.' . . .

10.11 It seems appropriate to add here that when a consul, dictator or praetor devotes the legions of the enemy, he need not devote himself but may pick any citizen he wishes from an enlisted Roman legion; **12** if the man who has been devoted dies, it is considered that all is well; if he does not die, then an effigy of him is buried 7 feet or more under the ground and a propitiatory sacrifice slaughtered; it is not lawful for Roman magistrates to climb the mound where that effigy has been buried. **13** But if someone chooses to devote himself, as Decius did, and does not die, he cannot perform any religious act either for himself or for the people without desecrating it, whether a sacrifice or anything else he chooses. He who has devoted himself has the right to dedicate his arms to Vulcan or to any other god he chooses; **14** it is not lawful for the spear on which the consul has stood and prayed to fall into the hands of the enemy; if it should, a propitiatory sacrifice must be made to Mars with a pig, sheep and bull (a *suovetaurilia*). **11.1** These details, although the memory of every divine and human practice has been erased by men's preference for the new and foreign in place of what is ancient and traditional, I have considered it not inappropriate to repeat in the very words in which they were handed down and publicly pronounced.

PRIESTHOODS

The basic unit of organised Roman religion was the priesthood. Priests were drawn from the elite, and so, when plebeians became eligible, plebeian priests came from the elite plebeian families. Great social distinction was derived from holding a priesthood. Novi homines are rarely found among the members of priesthoods: only one novus homo (out of 81) is known to have been pontifex maximus, and only two (Marius and Cicero) are among the known augurs. Priests were male; the main exceptions were the Vestal Virgins and the wife of the flamen dialis. There were four major colleges of priests: the *pontifices, augures, quindecimviri sacris faciundis* and *epulones*.

The pontifex maximus was the head of the college of pontifices (pontiffs); Sulla increased their number to 15 (cf. doc. 11.28). There were also 15 flamines (singular: flamen; priest), and each flamen worshipped a single deity. The three most important were the flamen dialis (Jupiter: doc. 3.21), martialis (Mars) and quirinalis (Quirinus). The second major college was that of the augures, the augurs or diviners. The Sibylline Books were kept by two officials (the *duumviri sacris faciundis*), increased under Sulla to 15 (the quindecimviri, or the '15 for performing religious ceremonies'). The epulones organised the epulum Iovis, a feast for Jupiter. Other groups of priests included the fetials, haruspices, Luperci, Fratres Arvales (Arval brothers) and Salii.

3.19 Varro *On the Latin Language* 5.83–86: The priesthoods

Varro's explanation of the etymology of the term pontiffs (pontifices) is to be preferred to Scaevola's. There will have been sacred rites associated with the bridge crossing the Tiber, including that of the Argei; doc. 3.7. **83**: Quintus Scaevola was consul in 95 BC and pontifex maximus c. 89–82 BC. The 30 curiae were the earliest divisions of the Roman people (docs 1.19, 21) and the basis for political and military organisation. **84**: For Furrina and her festival, which was obscure even in Varro's time, see doc. 3.5. Falacer was also obscure, perhaps an old Italian hero.

83 The sacerdotes, priests, were collectively so named from the sacra, sacred rites. The pontiffs, high priests, according to Quintus Scaevola the pontifex maximus, were named from posse, to be able, and facere, to do, as though pontentifices. I actually think the term comes from pons, bridge: for it was by them that the wooden bridge on piles (the Sublicius) was first made and frequently repaired, since in this connection sacred rites are performed on both sides of the Tiber with great ceremony. The curiones, priests of the curiae, were named from the curiae; they are created for the purpose of conducting sacred rites in the curiae.

84 The flamines, flamens, because in Latium they always had their heads covered and bound with a filum, woollen fillet, were called filamines. Individually they have their cognomens from the god whose rites they perform, but some are clear and others obscure: clear such as Martialis and Volcanalis; obscure such as Dialis and Furinalis, since Dialis is from Jupiter (for he is also Diovis) and Furinalis from Furrina, who even has a Furinal festival in the calendar, and the flamen Falacer, too, from the divine father Falacer.

85 The Salii were named from salitare, to dance, because they had the custom and duty of dancing every year in the places of assembly in their sacred rites. The Luperci were named because they make offerings in the Lupercal at the Lupercalia festival. The Arval brothers were so called as they perform public rites to make arva, ploughland, bring forth crops . . . **86** The fetiales, fetial priests, because they were in charge of the state's word of honour between peoples; for it was through them that a war that was declared should be a just war, and through them it was ended so that by a foedus, treaty, the fides, good faith, of the peace might be established. Some of them were sent before war was declared, to demand restitution, and even now it is through them that the foedus, treaty, is made, which Ennius writes was pronounced fidus.

3.20 Dionysius of Halicarnassus 2.73.1–2: The pontiffs

Dionysius sketches the main duties of the pontifices (pontiffs), the most important of the four major colleges of priests.

1 The pontiffs have authority over the matters of greatest importance. 2 They serve as judges in all religious cases concerning private citizens or magistrates or those who minister to the gods, and make laws concerning religious rites which have no written record or established tradition, which they consider appropriate to be sanctioned by law and custom; they inquire into all the magistracies which have duties involving any sacrifice or religious duty as well as all the priesthoods, and ensure that their servants and attendants whom they use in the rituals commit no error in regard to the sacred laws; to the private citizens who are not knowl-edgeable about religious matters concerning the gods and divine spirits, the pon-tiffs are expounders and interpreters; and if they learn that some people are not obeying their instructions, they punish them, examining each of the charges. They themselves are not liable to any prosecution or punishment, nor are they account-able to the senate or people, at any rate concerning religious matters.

3.21 Aulus Gellius *Attic Nights* 10.15.1–30: The flamen dialis

This Fabius Pictor (not the historian) was the author of *On the Pontifical Law.* The flamen dialis was the priest of Jupiter; the origins and meaning of the various taboos affecting this priest are unclear and were probably obscure to the Romans in the late Republic. The flamen dialis was married by the sacred marriage ceremony, confarreatio (doc. 7.10), which involved a sacrifice to Jupiter. His wife, the flaminica dialis, was subject to various restrictions. The rex sacrificulus (or rex sacrorum) succeeded the kings in presiding over sacrifices.

1 Numerous ceremonies are imposed upon the flamen dialis and also many restraints, about which we read in the books written *On the Public Priests* and which are also recorded in the first book of Fabius Pictor. 2 Of these I remember in general the following points: 3 it is unlawful for the flamen dialis to ride a horse; 4 it is likewise unlawful for him to see the 'classes arrayed' outside the pomerium, that is, the army in battle order; for this reason the flamen dialis is rarely made a consul, since wars were entrusted to the consuls. 5 It is likewise unlawful for him ever to take an oath; 6 it is likewise unlawful for him to wear a ring, unless it is perforated and without a stone. 7 It is also against the law to carry out fire from the flaminia (the flamen dialis' dwelling) except for a sacred ritual; 8 if a prisoner in chains enters his house he must be released and the chains must be drawn up through the impluvium ('rainhole') onto the roof-tiles and let down from there into the street. 9 He must have no knot in his cap or girdle or any other part of his clothes; 10 if anyone is being led away to be flogged and falls at his feet as a sup-pliant, it is unlawful for him to be flogged that day. 11 The hair of the dialis may not be cut except by a free man. 12 It is customary for the flamen neither to touch nor even to name a female goat, or uncooked meat, ivy or beans.

13 He must not walk underneath a trellis for vines. 14 The feet of the bed on which he lies must have a thin coating of clay, and he must not be away from the bed for three nights in a row, nor is it lawful for anyone else to sleep in that bed. At the foot of his bed there must be a box containing a little pile of sacrificial cakes and offering-cakes. 15 The clippings of the dialis' nails and hair must be buried

in the ground beneath a fruitful tree. **16** Every day is a holy day for the dialis. **17** He must not go outdoors without his cap; that he is now allowed to do this indoors was decided only recently by the pontiffs, **18** as Masurius Sabinus wrote, and it is also said that some of the other ceremonies have been remitted and he has been excused from them.

19 It is not lawful for him to touch bread made with yeast. **20** He does not take off his inner tunic except in covered places, so he may not be naked under the open sky, as it were under the eye of Jove. **21** No one else reclines above him at a banquet except the rex sacrificulus (the rex sacrorum). **22** If he loses his wife he resigns from the flaminate. **23** The marriage of the flamen may not be dissolved except by death. **24** He never enters a place where bodies are buried, and he never touches a corpse; **25** however, he is not forbidden to attend a funeral.

26 The flaminica dialis has almost the same ceremonies; **27** they say that she observes certain other different ones, for example, that she wears a dyed robe, **28** and that she has a twig from a fruitful tree tucked in her veil, and that it is forbidden for her to go up more than three rungs of a ladder **29** (except what the Greeks call ladders), and also that, **30** when she goes to the Argei, she neither combs her head nor arranges her hair.

3.22 Suetonius *Life of the Deified Julius* 13: Caesar's priesthood

Caesar was elected pontifex maximus in 63 BC, even though he stood against two prominent candidates, P. Servilius Isauricus (cos. 79) and Q. Lutatius Catulus (cos. 78). He was successful even though, at the age of 37, he had not yet been praetor.

After abandoning his ambition of governing the province (Egypt), Caesar stood for the office of pontifex maximus, using the most lavish bribery. It is said that, working out the enormous debts he had contracted, when he went to the comitia that morning he told his mother, as she kissed him, that he would not return unless as pontifex maximus. However, he defeated his two most influential rivals, both of whom were much older and more distinguished, and he won more votes from their own tribes than either won in the entire election.

ROMAN PURIFICATORY RITUALS

A lustratio (lustration) was the performance of a lustrum, a purificatory rite to avert harm and evil in general. It involved a procession finishing at its starting point, invoking divine assistance to keep harm from the area being traversed, and a suovetaurilia (the sacrifice of a pig, sheep and bull; sus, ovis and taurus respectively); cf. docs 3.18, 27. The private suovetaurilia used young beasts, the public ones a full grown male pig, ram and bull. The principal lustration was that at the end of the census: doc. 3.24. There could also be a lustratio of an army (Livy 23.35.5) and fleet (App. *BC* 5.97.401).

3.23 Cato the Elder *On Farming* 141.2–4: The Ambarvalia

The Ambarvalia was celebrated in May, both as a public agricultural festival, designed to purify all fields, and as a private rite, here described by Cato. Manius, here, is a generic name. Mars here has an agricultural role, as in the hymn of the Arval brothers (doc. 3.12), as protector of boundaries; Janus is routinely invoked at the beginnings of prayer. The prayer itself was probably in the form of a hymn. The *strues* and *fertum* are sacrificial cakes.

1 This is the formula to be used for purifying the land. Bid the suovetaurilia to be led around with the words: 'So that, with the goodwill of the gods, our efforts may be successful, take care, Manius, to purify my farm, land and ground with this suovetaurilia, however you think it best for them to be driven or carried around.' **2** First invoke Janus and Jupiter with an offering of wine, then say: 'Father Mars, I pray and entreat you to be kindly and well disposed towards me and our home and household. For this reason I have ordered a pig–sheep–bull procession to be driven around my field, land and farm, so that you will prevent, ward off and turn away diseases, seen and unseen, barrenness and fruitlessness, disasters and storms; and so that you will allow fruits, grains, vines and saplings to grow and achieve fruition; **3** and so that you will protect the shepherds and the flocks and give safety and good health to me and our home and household. For these reasons, therefore, and for the consecration of my farm, land and field, and the offering of a sacrifice for purification, as I have said, accept the sacrifice of the suckling pig–sheep–bull.' Repeat: 'Therefore, Father Mars, accept the suckling pig–sheep–bull sacrifice.'

4 Do it with a knife. Have the *strues* and *fertum* at hand, then make the offering. As you slaughter the pig, lamb and calf, you must say: 'Therefore, accept the sacrifice of the pig–sheep–bull.' Mars must not be named, nor the lamb and calf. If all the offerings are not favourable, say as follows: 'Father Mars, if anything in the suckling pig–sheep–bull sacrifice was not satisfactory to you, I offer this new pig–sheep–bull sacrifice as atonement.' If there is doubt about only one or two, say as follows: 'Father Mars, since that piglet was not satisfactory to you, I offer this piglet as atonement.'

3.24 Varro *On the Latin Language* 6.86–87: The censors' records

A *lustrum* (purification) of the assembly was performed by one of the censors after the census was complete; the act was known as *lustrum condere*, and it took place in the Campus Martius with the citizens drawn up in their centuries. The chief feature of the ceremony was the suovetaurilia. The censor who performed the actual lustrum recited a prayer that the gods might increase the size of Rome's dominions (doc. 3.27).

86 Now, first, I will put down from the *Censors' Records*: When at night the censor has gone into the sacred enclosure (templum) to take the auspices, and a message has come from the sky, he shall command the herald to call the men: 'May this be good, fortunate, happy and advantageous to the Roman people, the Quirites, and to the government of the Roman people, the Quirites, and to me and my colleague, to our good faith and our magistracy. All the citizen soldiers in arms, and private citizens, spokespersons of all the tribes, pronounce an *inlicium* (invitation to a special assembly) in case anyone wishes a reckoning (i.e., a protest against his censor's rating) to be given for himself or for another.'

87 The herald calls it first in the sacred enclosure, afterwards likewise from the walls. When it becomes light, the censors, secretaries and magistrates are anointed with myrrh and ointments. When the praetors and the tribunes of the people and those who have been called to the *inlicium* have come, the censors shall take lots between them to see which shall perform the purification. When the sacred enclosure (in the Campus Martius) has been fixed, then the one who is going to perform the purification holds the assembly.

RITUAL UTTERANCES

The Romans placed a great deal of importance on the correct performance of rituals. There were tabellae, records, of the prayers to be used by magistrates, and these were read rather than recited by heart so that no mistakes were made. The term *religio* in fact embraces the correct performance of religious ritual.

3.25 *ILS* 3124: Correct ritual utterances

This bronze tablet at Falerii was dedicated to Minerva. The inscription is in five lines, read from right to left, while the language is a mixture of Faliscan and Latin.

Sacred to Minerva. Lars Cotena, son of Lars, praetor, by the vote of the senate gave this as a votive gift. When it was given, it was dedicated in the prescribed manner.

3.26 Pliny the Elder *Natural History* 28.10–11: Ritual prayers

The flute drowned out any ill-omened noises so that the efficacy of the prayer was not affected; for flute-players at sacrifices, see also doc. 3.72, cf. 3.8, 13. It was essential that the standard prescription for the prayers was followed, with no changes or hesitations.

10 Of all the remedies which man has discovered, the first gives rise to a most important question which is always unanswered: do words and ritual incantations have any effect? If they do, it would be right and fitting to give man the credit, but individually all our wisest men reject belief in them, although in general the public unconsciously believes in them all the time. Indeed, the sacrifice of victims or due consultation of the gods is thought to have no effect if unaccompanied by a prayer. **11** Furthermore, there is one form of words for seeking favourable omens, another for warding off evil, and another for requesting protection. We also notice that our highest magistrates have adopted set prayers, and, so that no word is omitted or spoken in the wrong place, one attendant reads the prayer from a written text, another is assigned to check it, and a third is put in charge to ensure silence, while a flautist plays so that only the prayer can be heard. There are remarkable cases recorded where the sound of unfavourable omens has ruined the ritual or an error has been made in the prayer, when suddenly the head of the liver or the heart has been missing from the entrails or have been doubled, while the victim was still standing.

3.27 Valerius Maximus 4.1.10: A change in the formula of prayer

Valerius Maximus, in describing the lustrum performed by Scipio Aemilianus as censor in 142 to conclude the census, refers to the scribe reciting the prayer from the records, which Scipio then repeated after him. The incident as recorded is perhaps unhistorical.

When, as censor, the younger Africanus was concluding the census, during the suovetaurilia (solitaurilia) the scribe recited in front of him from the public tablets the formula of prayer in which the immortal gods were requested to make the state of the Roman people better and greater. 'It is good and great enough', stated Scipio, 'So I pray that they keep it safe in perpetuity.' And he thereupon ordered that the formula in the public tablets be emended accordingly. From that time on, the censors have employed this modest form of prayer in concluding the census.

3.28 Cato the Elder *On Farming* 139: Ritual for ensuring an unknown god is not offended

Cato advises that a farmer should placate the deity of a grove before clearing it.

To clear a grove you must use the Roman rite, as follows. Make an expiatory sacrifice of a pig, and say these words: 'Whatever god or whatever goddess you may be to whom this grove is sacred, as it is right to make an expiatory sacrifice of a pig to you for taking this sacred grove, in respect of this, whether I do it or someone else at my orders, may it be rightly done. Therefore, in offering this expiatory sacrifice of a pig to you, I entreat with humble prayers that you will be kindly and propitious to me, my house and household and my children; and so accept this expiatory sacrifice of a pig.'

3.29 *ILS* 4015: Even forgotten cults maintained

On an altar at Rome, c. 90–80 BC.

Whether sacred to god or to goddess, Gaius Sextius Calvinus, son of Gaius, praetor, restored this on a vote of the senate.

THE CALENDAR

Roman religious calendars provide a wealth of information about the dates of festivals. There is only one from the Republic, which includes only brief notices about the deity being honoured. Imperial examples often have both comments about the nature of the festival and historical anniversaries (see docs 14.63, 15.4).

3.30 Inscriptiones Italiae XIII.2, pp. 1–28: A pre-Julian calendar

This calendar (tabula fastorum) for the month Sextilis, written on a wall at Antium (Anzio), a Roman colony south of Rome, is the only surviving Roman calendar from before Caesar's calendar reforms. It measures 1.16 by 2.5 metres and was meant to be clearly displayed to the public. There is an eight-day week (listed here as A–H) and it covers the 12 months of the year, as well as the intercalated month, with each month having its own column. It adds up to a normal Republican year of 355 days. Letters indicated the status of the day with regard to public business. An 'N' after a day indicated *nefastus* (plural: *nefasti*), a day when the assemblies and courts could not be convened; 'F' indicated *fastus* (plural: *fasti*), when courts could convene and business was permitted; 'C' (*comitialis*), when assemblies could be held; 'EN' (*endotercisus*) showed that the day was split between a religious festival and public business, such as day F in the third week.

A   Kalends of Sextilis August. To Hope; to the Two Victories.
B   Business in court.
C   Business in Assembly (?).
D   Business in Assembly (?).
E   Nones. No business. Public holiday. To Safety.
F   Business in court.
G   Business in Assembly.
H   Business in Assembly.

A   Business in court (?).
B   Business in Assembly (?).
C   Business in Assembly.
D   Business in Assembly.
E   Ides. No business. Public holiday. To Diana, Vortumnus, Fortune, Horse-woman, Hercules the Conqueror, Castor, Pollux, Camenae (the Muses).
F   Business in court.
G   Business in Assembly.
H   Business in Assembly.

A   Festival, of God of the Harbour (Portunus). No business. Public holiday (?).
B   Business in Assembly (?).
C   Festival, of Vintage. Business in court in the morning. To Venus.
D   Business in Assembly (?).
E   Festival, of Consus (god of fertility). No business. Public holiday.
F   Midsplit (i.e., nefastus in the morning, fastus for the rest of the day).
G   Festival, of Vulcan. No business. Public holiday. To Vulcan, Hora, Quirinus (or Hora, wife of Quirinus), Maia above the Comitium.
H   Business in Assembly.

A   Festival, of Goddess of Sowing (Ops Consiva). No business. Public holiday (?).
B   Business in Assembly (?).
C   Festival, of Volturnus. No business. Public holiday.
D   Business in Assembly (?).
E   Business in Assembly (?).

3.31 Suetonius *Life of the Deified Julius* 40.1–2: Caesar's calendar reforms, 46 BC

Caesar, in his role as pontifex maximus, reformed the calendar in 46 BC: the shorter months were lengthened to bring the total of calendar days to 365, and every fourth year an extra day was added between 23 and 24 February. To have 45 BC start on the correct solar date, 46 BC was lengthened to 445 days. The calendrical dates of the agricultural festivals were now in tune with the seasons. This Julian calendar, modified by Pope Gregory XIII, is still the basis of today's western calendar.

1 Turning then to domestic reorganisation, Caesar first corrected the calendar which was in a total mess because of the pontiffs' habit of arbitrary insertions, so that the harvest festival no longer coincided with summer or the vintage festival with autumn; he adjusted the year to the course of the sun by making it 365 days, removing the short intercalary month and adding one day every fourth year. **2** Furthermore, so that the correct reckoning should start with the next Kalends of January, he inserted two months between November and December, so that that year, when these changes were made, had fifteen months, including the intercalary one which customarily fell in that year.

SACRIFICE

Sacrifice was *the* most important feature of Roman religion. The participants and the sacrificial victim – always a domestic beast – were purified, and then a procession led the 'willing' victim to the sacrificial altar. The magistrate presiding over the sacrifice wore the cinctus gabinus (see doc. 3.18). The animal's back was sprinkled with mola salsa (salted meal or flour: the immolatio), and a prayer (precatio) was recited to offer the beast to the divinity receiving the sacrifice. Making the mola salsa for sacrifices was one of the chief duties of the Vestal Virgins.

3.32 Dionysius of Halicarnassus 7.72.15, 18: Roman sacrificial practices

Dionysius is describing the ludi magni (Great Games) of 490 (cf. doc. 1.70). Of note in Dionysius' description is the procession, the fact that the consuls preside over the games, the involvement of the priests in the sacrifice, the purifications and the libations. Dionysius was an eye-witness of the ceremonies in his own time but also cites Fabius Pictor as his authority.

15 When the procession was over, the consuls and those of the priests whose duty it was immediately sacrificed oxen, and the way in which the sacrifices were performed was the same as our own. For, after washing their hands and purifying the victims with clean water, they sprinkled the fruits of Demeter on their heads, offered up a prayer, and gave the assistants orders to sacrifice them. Some of these struck the victim on the temples with a club while it was still standing; others placed the sacrificial knives beneath it as it fell. They then flayed and dismembered it and took portions from each organ and every limb as first fruits, which they sprinkled with grains of barley and took in baskets to the sacrificing

priests, who placed them on the altars, lit a fire beneath them, and poured a liba-
tion of wine over them while they were being consumed. . . . **18** I know of these
ceremonies from having seen the Romans performing them in their sacrifices even
in my own time; and, satisfied with this single piece of evidence, I am sure that
the founders of Rome were not barbarians but Greeks who assembled from many
different places.

3.33 Livy *History of Rome* 21.62.1–11: Portents and public sacrifices

Prodigies were considered to indicate that something was amiss between the gods and
mortals. The historical context of this passage is the winter of 218 BC, after the disastrous
defeat by Hannibal at Trebia. More expiations were required after new prodigies following
the disaster of Trasimene in spring 217. **6–8:** For the decemviri and the Sibylline Books,
see docs 3.38–39; for the lectisternium, see doc. 3.15. **9:** Hercules had several places of
worship, but that of Hercules Invictus ('the Unconquered') in the Forum Boarium is presumably meant here. **10:** The genius of the Roman people was the deified entity of the
Roman people.

1 In Rome and the area around the city many queer prodigies occurred that winter, or, as tends to happen when men's minds once turn towards religion, many
were said to have happened and were too easily believed. **2** Among these were a
free-born baby of six months of age who had shouted 'Triumph!' in the vegetable
market, **3** while in the Forum Boarium an ox had climbed, of its own accord, up
to the third storey and then, frightened by the screaming of the occupants, thrown
itself out of the window; **4** shapes like ships had shone in the sky; the temple of
Hope in the vegetable market was struck by lightning; at Lanuvium a sacrificial
victim had moved all on its own, and a raven had flown down into the temple of
Juno and perched on Juno's couch; **5** in the region of Amiternum apparitions of
men, dressed in white, had been seen at a distance in many places, but they did not
approach anyone; in Picenum it had rained stones; at Caere the divination tablets
(*sortes*) had shrunk; and in Gaul a wolf had pulled a sentry's sword from its sheath
and run off with it.

6 For other prodigies the decemvirs were instructed to consult the (Sibylline)
Books, but for the rain of stones at Picenum a nine-day period of sacrifice was proclaimed. Then almost all the citizens took part in expiation of the other portents. **7**
First of all, the city was purified, and greater sacrificial victims (i.e., cattle) were
offered to the gods designated in the *Books*. **8** A gift of gold, 40 pounds in weight,
was carried to Lanuvium for Juno, and the matrons dedicated a bronze statue to
Juno on the Aventine; a lectisternium was ordered at Caere, where the divination
tablets had shrunk, and a supplicatio (expiation ceremony) to Fortune on Mount
Algidus; **9** at Rome, too, another lectisternium was ordered to be made in honour of
Youth (Juventas), as well as a supplicatio at the temple of Hercules, first by named
individuals, then by the whole people before all the couches; **10** five greater victims
were sacrificed to the Genius of the Roman people; and Gaius Atilius Serranus, the
praetor, was commanded to make vows 'if during the next ten years the state should

remain unchanged'. **11** These purifications and vows, prescribed by the *Sibylline Books*, went far to relieve men's minds from their superstitious dread.

3.34 Cato the Elder *On Farming* 75: Cato's recipe for the libum

A libum was a cake often offered to the gods, especially on one's birthday.

Make libum in this way: crush two pounds of cheese in a mortar. When it is thoroughly crushed, add one pound of wheat flour or, if you wish it to be lighter, half a pound of fine flour and mix it well with the cheese. Add one egg and mix together well. Then make it into a loaf, place it on leaves and bake slowly on a hot pan under an earthenware pot.

3.35 Cato the Elder *On Farming* 134.1–4: Pre-harvest sacrifice

Before the harvest the *porca praecidanea* (the pre-harvest piglet) was sacrificed and the entrails were used for divination and then burnt. The rest of the pig was eaten by the participants.

1 Before you harvest, the sacrifice of the *porca praecidanea* should be made in this way. Offer a piglet, as porca praecidanea, to Ceres before spelt, wheat, barley, beans or rape seed are harvested. Make a prayer with incense and wine to Janus, Jupiter and Juno before you kill the piglet. **2** Present an offering-cake (strues) to Janus in these words: 'Father Janus, in offering these cakes I entreat with good prayers that you will be kindly and propitious to me, my children, my house and my household.' Make an offering of an oblation-cake (fertum) to Jupiter with these words: 'Jupiter, in offering this cake I entreat with good prayers that, accepting this cake, you will be kindly and propitious to me, my children, my house and my household.' **3** Then give wine to Janus in these words: 'Father Janus, as I prayed with good prayers in offering the cakes, in the same way accept the wine offered to you.' And then pray to Jupiter in these words: 'Jupiter, accept this cake, accept the wine offered to you.' Then sacrifice the porca praecidanea. **4** When the entrails have been cut out, offer and present an offering-cake (strues) to Janus, making the offering in the same way as before, and offer and present a cake (fertum) to Jupiter, making the offering in the same way as before. In the same way give wine to Janus and give wine to Jupiter as you did before on account of the offering of the strues and the offering of the fertum. Afterwards give the entrails and wine to Ceres.

3.36 Caesar *Gallic War* 6.14, 16–17, 19: Druids and human sacrifice

Despite their gladiatorial competitions and the occasional formal 'sacrifice' of Greeks and Gauls in times of crisis (doc. 4.38), the Romans did not believe in (regular) human sacrifice, and they saw as barbaric those of the Gauls that involved human victims.

14.1 The Druids do not take part in warfare and do not pay taxes like the other Gauls; they are exempt from military service and other such duties . . . **5** Among their teachings they place particular stress on the belief that the soul does not die but passes from one to another after death, and they think that this is the greatest incentive to courage, as it removes fear of death. **6** Furthermore, they hold discussions about the stars and their movements, about the size of the universe and earth, the physical constitution of the world, and the strength and power of the immortal gods and instruct their young men in these subjects. . . .

16.1 As a nation all the Gauls are extremely superstitious, and as a result **2** those suffering from severe illnesses, as well as those exposed to dangers and battles, offer, or vow that they will offer, human sacrifices, employing druids to perform these. **3** For they believe that, unless in place of a man's life another life is offered up, they cannot appease the might of the immortal gods, and they hold regular public sacrifices of the same kind. **4** Some of them have gigantic images made of wickerwork, the limbs of which they fill with living men; these are set on fire and the men burnt to death. **5** They think that sacrifices of those caught in the act of theft or brigandage or guilty of some other offence are preferred by the immortal gods, but if the supply of these runs short they move on to the sacrifice of innocent people. **17.1** The god they reverence most is Mercury. They have numerous images of him and consider him the inventor of all arts, the guide of roads and journeys, and as having the most power in matters of money-making and trade. **2** After him they reverence Apollo, Mars, Jupiter and Minerva . . .

19.3 Husbands have power of life and death over their wives, as over their children; and when the head of a noble family dies his relatives convene; if the circumstances of his death are suspicious, they examine his wives as we do slaves, and should guilt be established they are put to death by fire and other tortures.

DIVINATION

The Romans sought the guidance of the gods in various ways. Augurs took the auspices prior to undertaking military campaigns and before public meetings (docs 3.47–52, 75). At other times, such as at elections and assemblies, the augurs advised magistrates who presided over the auspices by interpreting the flight of birds or lightning and thunder to ascertain what needed to be done to overcome (expiate), by means of rituals, the displeasure of the gods. When the state was confronted by crisis (docs 3.15, 4.38), the Sibylline Books were consulted. These were housed in the temple of Jupiter and consulted only when the senate authorised it.

3.37 Cicero *On Divination* 1.1: Cicero on Roman divination

Cicero's *On Divination* takes the form of a dialogue between Cicero and his brother Quintus at Tusculum. Many of the arguments of Quintus in the first book in favour of divination are based on those of Posidonius the Stoic. Quintus, in his exposition, attempts to reconcile divination with philosophy. In the second book, Cicero ridicules divination. He was himself an augur, and the discussion must reflect ideas that were current among the Roman aristocracy of the time.

There is an ancient belief, handed down to us right from the times of the heroes, and confirmed by the agreement both of the Roman people and of all other nations, that some kind of divination exists among mankind, which the Greeks call mantike – that is, the foresight and knowledge of future events. This is indeed a splendid and beneficial thing, if only it really exists, by which mortal nature can approach very closely to the power of the gods. And just as we have done many things better than the Greeks, so we have given this most extraordinary faculty a name (divinatio), derived from divi (gods), while the Greeks, as Plato interpreted it, derived their term from furor (frenzy).

3.38 Dionysius of Halicarnassus 4.62.4–6: The Sibylline Books

Dionysius 4.62.1–3 relates the story of how Tarquinius Priscus (fifth king of Rome) was offered the nine Sibylline Books: after rejecting the purchase the first time, the woman selling them burned three of them, then offered him the remaining six; when he refused to buy these she burnt another three; the augurs then advised him to buy these three at the same price as the original nine. Two men were chosen to care for them, later increased to ten, and then under Sulla to 15 (the quindecimviri sacris faciundis: the '15 for performing religious ceremonies'), who had to be proficient in the Greek language. The Sibylline oracles (ritual texts and prophecies) were written in Greek hexameters.

4 Tarquinius chose from the citizens two distinguished men, with two public slaves to assist them, to whom he handed over the guardianship of the books, and when one of the two, Marcus Atilius, appeared to have betrayed his trust and was informed upon by one of the public slaves, he had him sewn up in a leather bag and thrown into the sea.

5 After the expulsion of the kings the commonwealth took upon itself the protection of the oracles, appointing two extremely distinguished men as their guardians, who hold this office for life and are exempt from military service and all other state duties, with public slaves assigned to assist them, and without these being present the men are not allowed to consult the oracles. In short, there is nothing, either sacred or profane, which the Romans guard so carefully as the Sibylline oracles. They consult them, whenever the senate decrees, if the state is overcome by discord, or a great misfortune has befallen them in war, or great portents and apparitions, difficult of interpretation, have been seen, as has often happened. Until the time of the Marsian war, as it was called (the Social War), these oracles remained underground in the temple of Jupiter Capitolinus in a stone chest, guarded by ten men. **6** After the one hundred and seventy-third Olympiad (83 BC) the temple was burnt down, either deliberately, as some think, or by accident, and these oracles were destroyed by fire together with the other dedications to the god. Those now in existence have been collected from many places, some brought from the cities of Italy, others from Erythrai in Isaia, where by the senate's vote three envoys were dispatched to copy them; others were brought from other cities, transcribed by private persons. Of these, some are found to be interpolations among the Sibylline oracles, which are recognised by means of the so-called acrostics. My account is based on what (Marcus) Terentius Varro has recorded in his work on religion.

3.39 Cicero *On Divination* 2.110: Cicero on the Sibyl

Cicero is countering his brother Quintus' arguments in favour of divination: cf. docs 3.37, 42. The man described as 'king in face' was Caesar.

We Romans venerate the verses of the Sibyl, who is said to have uttered them while in a frenzy. Recently there was a rumour, which was believed at the time but turned out to be false, that one of the interpreters of those verses was going to declare in the senate that, for our safety, the man whom we had as 'king in face' should be made king also in name. If this is in the books, to what man and to what time does it refer? For it was clever of the author to take care that whatever happened should appear foretold, because all reference to persons or time had been omitted. He also employed a maze of obscurity so that the same verses might be adapted to different situations at different times. Moreover, that this poem is not the work of frenzy is quite evident from the quality of its composition (for it exhibits artistic care rather than emotional excitement), and is especially evident from the fact that it is written in what are termed 'acrostics', wherein the initial letters of each verse taken in order convey a meaning . . . That surely is the work of concentrated thought and not of a frenzied brain. And in the Sibylline Books, throughout the entire work, each prophecy is embellished with an acrostic, so that the initial letters of each of the lines give the subject of that particular prophecy. Such a work comes from a writer who is not frenzied, who is painstaking, not crazy. Therefore let us keep the Sibyl under lock and key so that, in accordance with the ordinances of our forefathers, her books may not even be read without permission of the senate and may be more effective in banishing than in encouraging superstitious ideas.

3.40 Cicero *On the Nature of the Gods* 2.10–12: The 'divinely inspired' art

Tiberius Gracchus (father of Tiberius Gracchus, tr. pl. 133), as consul in 163 BC, was presiding over the elections for the consuls for 162. He was an augur himself, but it was as a magistrate that he took the auspices. As the pomerium was an inaugurated area (docs 1.3, 3.17), he had to take the auspices again when he crossed the pomerium back to where the election was taking place (in the Campus Martius). Cicero notes that the Etruscans had books on interpreting entrails, thunder and lightning, and there were also Roman augural books (Cic. *Div.* 1.72).

10 Why, in the consulship of Publius Scipio and Gaius Figulus, actual fact proved the correctness of the teaching of our augurs and the Etruscan haruspices; when Tiberius Gracchus, consul for the second time, was holding their election, the first polling-officer suddenly fell dead just as he was reporting their names. Gracchus, nonetheless, carried on with the election and, as he noticed that that event had aroused the religious scruples of the people, brought the matter before the senate. The senate decided that it should be referred to 'the customary people'. Haruspices were brought forward who proclaimed that the polling-officer for the elections had not been in proper order. **11** Gracchus thereupon fell into a rage, as my father used to tell me: 'What is this? Was I not in proper order, I who put it to the vote as consul, augur, and after taking the auspices? Do you, Etruscan barbarians, know the Roman people's laws of auspices? Can you be the interpreters of augury for our elections?' And so he then told them to leave; later on, however, he sent a dispatch from his province to the college that, while he was reading the books, he had recollected an irregularity in the auspices when he had chosen Scipio's gardens as the site for his tent, because after this he had crossed the pomerium to hold a meeting of the senate, and when he had crossed the pomerium on his return he had forgotten to take the auspices; therefore there was an irregularity in their election as consuls. The augurs referred the matter to the senate; the senate decided the consuls should resign; they resigned. What more important instances can we look for? A man of the greatest wisdom and, perhaps, supreme distinction preferred to admit his error that could have been concealed rather than to allow the impiety to cling to the commonwealth; the consuls preferred to lay down the highest state office immediately rather than to hold it for a moment of time in violation of religion. **12** The authority of augurs is immense; and surely the art of haruspices is also divinely inspired?

3.41 Livy *History of Rome* 43.13.1–4, 7–8: Portents in Livy's history

Livy routinely includes the prodigies for each year in his history. The year in question is 169 BC (during the Third Macedonian War); only about half of his list has been included here.

1 I am not unaware that, owing to the same disrespect because of which men generally believe in this day and age that the gods foretell nothing, no portents at all are publicly reported or recorded in our histories. **2** But, as I write of ancient matters, not only does my mind in some way become old-fashioned, but certain religious scruples prevent me from regarding what those very wise men considered worthy of public concern as unworthy of being recorded in my history. **3** At Anagnia two portents were reported in that year, a shooting star was seen in the sky, and a cow which spoke; she was being kept at public expense. Also at Minturnae during those same days the sky appeared to be on fire. **4** There was a shower of stones at Reate. At Cumae the Apollo on the citadel shed tears for three days and nights . . . **7** Because of the public portents, the Books were approached by the decemvirs, who proclaimed the gods to whom the consuls should sacrifice 40 larger victims, **8** that a day of prayer (supplicatio) should be held, that all the magistrates should sacrifice larger victims at all the couches of the gods, and that the people should wear wreaths. All this was carried out as the decemvirs prescribed.

3.42 Cicero *On Divination* 1.103–4: Chance remarks as omens

L. Aemilius Paullus, as consul in 168 BC, defeated Perseus of Macedon at Pydna (see docs 5.33–34); Tertia ('third') was presumably his third daughter. Flaccus is probably L. Valerius Flaccus, praetor in 63.

103 I will now give you some well-known examples of omens: when Lucius Paullus was consul for the second time, and it had fallen to his lot to wage war against King Perseus, he returned home in the evening on that very same day and noticed when he kissed his little daughter Tertia, who was still very small, that she looked rather sad. 'What's the matter, Tertia my dear?' he asked, 'Why are you unhappy?' 'Oh, Daddy', she replied, 'Persa has died.' He then embraced her even more closely and said, 'Daughter, I accept the omen.' It was actually a puppy by that name that had died. **104** I heard Lucius Flaccus, the flamen of Mars, tell the story of Caecilia, daughter of Metellus, who wanted to arrange the marriage of her sister's daughter and went to a small sanctuary to receive an omen, according to ancient custom. For a long time, while the girl was standing and Caecilia was sitting on a stool, no word was spoken. The girl then grew tired and asked her aunt to let her sit on her stool for a little while. 'Certainly', replied Caecilia, 'I will let you have my place.' And this was an omen of what followed; she died in a short time and the girl married Caecilia's husband. I realise of course that these omens can be made light of and even laughed at, but to make light of the signs sent by the gods is nothing less than to disbelieve in the gods' existence.

3.43 Suetonius *Life of the Deified Julius* 81.1–3: Omens prior to Caesar's death

Suetonius here discusses the sacrificial omens supposedly recorded before Caesar's death; cf. doc. 13.69.

1 Caesar's death was proclaimed beforehand by unmistakable omens. A few months earlier, the colonists sent to colonise Capua under the Julian law were breaking up old tombs to construct their houses – the more eagerly because they discovered a large number of ancient vases – and came across a bronze tablet in a tomb in which Capys, the founder of Capua, was said to have been buried, which was inscribed in Greek letters and words to the effect that: 'When the bones of Capys are found, his descendant will be murdered by the hand of kinsmen and quickly avenged with great disasters to Italy.' **2** No one should think this fictional or fraudulent, because the authority is Cornelius Balbus (cos. 40), an intimate friend of Caesar's. Shortly afterwards, Caesar learnt that herds of horses, which he had dedicated on crossing the River Rubicon and allowed to wander unguarded, were stubbornly failing to graze and were weeping copiously. Also, while he was performing a sacrifice, the haruspex Spurinna warned him to 'Beware the danger, which will not come later than the Ides of March.' **3** On the day before the Ides, a 'king' bird, with a sprig of laurel, flew into the hall of Pompey pursued by various birds from a nearby grove, which tore it to pieces there. And on that night, on which dawned the day of his murder, he seemed to himself in a dream to be flying above the clouds and to shake hands with Jupiter, while his wife Calpurnia dreamt that the gable ornament of the house collapsed and her husband lay stabbed in her embrace; suddenly the doors of the bedroom opened of their own accord.

3.44 *CIL* I² 2173–89: Oracular responses (1)

Cicero deprecates the use of the sortes, 'lots', at Praeneste (modern Palestrina), which were written on oak and drawn as a form of divination, commenting that only the common people (vulgus) of Praeneste use them and that everywhere else they had gone out of fashion (*Div.* 2.85–87; cf. doc. 3.33). These sortes, inscribed on bronze, generally in hexameters, apparently date to the first century BC. Their place of origin is unknown.

2173 Believe that what has been made crooked can hardly now be made straight.

2174 Do you believe what they say? Things are not so. Don't be foolish.

2175 If you are wise about what is uncertain, take care that things don't become certain.

2176 Don't let lies arise from truth by being a false judge.

2177 That horse is very beautiful, but you can't ride him.

2178 It's an uphill road; you are not allowed to follow by the road you want.

2179 He is afraid of everyone; it is better to follow what he fears.

2180 Many men are liars. Don't believe them.

2181 An untrustworthy enemy (will arise from) a trustworthy man, unless you take care.

2182 I command it; and if he does it for him he will rejoice for ever.

2183 Seek joyfully and willingly, and you will rejoice for ever because it will be granted.

2184 We sortes ('lots') are not the liars you said; you consult like a fool.

2185 Now do you ask me? Now do you consult? The time has now passed.

2186 I help very many; when I have helped, no one thanks me.

2187 After all your hopes have collapsed, do you consult me?

2188 Do not despise what you run away from, what you throw away, what is granted you.

2189 Why do you seek advice after the event? What you ask does not exist.

3.45 *CIL* XI.1129 a, c: Oracular responses (2)

Oracular replies on a bronze tablet, written in prose, found at Forum Novum; they apparently date to the first century BC.

(a) Why do you ask advice now? Be at peace and enjoy your life.
     . . . You have death far from you . . . It is not possible for death to be fastened on you before your fate comes.
     . . . An illness is revealed . . .

(c) She who was previously barren will give birth.

3.46 Cicero *On Divination* 2.98–9: Astrology gains ground

Astrology was not part of traditional Roman beliefs, but Chaldaean astrologers from the East were expelled from Rome in 139 BC, and Cato the Elder advised his bailiff not to consult them.

98 And if it matters under what aspect of the sky or composition of stars every living thing is born, then necessarily the same conditions affect inanimate things; can any statement be more absurd than that? Indeed, Lucius Tarutius of Firmum, our good friend, who was excessively learned in Chaldaean computations, calculating from the fact that our city's birthday was on the Parilia, the date when we are told it was founded by Romulus, asserted that Rome was born when the moon was in Libra, and from this did not hesitate to prophecy Rome's destiny. What incredible power delusion has! . . . **99** But why say more? They are refuted daily. I remember numerous prophecies which the Chaldaeans made to Pompey, to Crassus, even to the late Caesar, saying that none of them would die except in old age, at home, and with great renown!

AUGURY

Magistrates took the auspices ('auspicia'), with an augur present as an advisor. There were five categories: from the sky (lightning, thunder, hailstorms and the like), from the movements of birds (flight, cries and number, as in doc. 3.47), from the sacred chickens (docs 3.52–54), from four-legged animals (any unusual behaviour thereof) and from unusual events. The auspices were taken for all state activities, in particular the elections, and, if pronounced unpropitious, assemblies could be adjourned or their acts declared null and void.

3.47 Ennius *Annals* 80–100: 'A most glorious omen'

According to legend, Rhea Silvia (or Ilia), a Vestal Virgin of Alba Longa who was beloved of Mars, gave birth to twins, Romulus and Remus, who were raised by a she-wolf. Here Romulus, standing on the Aventine, and Remus, on the Remuria, take the auspices at dawn to see who should rule the city and earn the right to have it named after him. The number of the birds, their direction and the fact that they headed towards 'places of favourable and fine omen' are all relevant.

80   Then carefully – with great care – both eager
      For rule, they concentrate on divination and augury;
      . . . on a hill . . .
      Remus dedicates himself to divination and on his own
      Keeps watch for a favourable bird. But handsome Romulus on high
85   Aventine searches, and watches out for the high-flying breed.
      They are contesting whether they should call the city Roma or Remora.
      All men are filled with care as to which should be the ruler:
      Just as when the consul intends to give the signal
      All men wait, eagerly watching the race's starting-gate to see
90   How soon he will dispatch the chariots from the painted mouth:
      Thus the people waited and held their tongues, to learn
      Who should be granted the victory of great kingship.
      Meanwhile the white sun withdrew into the depths of night.
      Then bright light, irradiated, beaming forth –

95   Just then from the height came a most glorious omen,
      A bird flying on the left, just as the golden sun was rising.
      Three times four sacred forms of birds left the sky,
      Taking themselves to places of favourable and fine omen.
      Thence Romulus sees that to him, in due form,
100   By divination, had been granted a kingdom's stable throne and land.

3.48 Dionysius of Halicarnassus 2.5.1–6.2: Romulus and the auspices

Romulus insisted on consulting the auspices when the people wished to grant him sovereignty, and his kingship was confirmed by a flash of lightning from the left to the right, a favourable direction. After this it became the practice that the gods had to sanction any king or magistrate. Lightning was considered unfavourable only during elections.

5.1 As the people approved, he proclaimed a day on which he would consult the auspices about the kingship, and when the time came he rose at daybreak and left his tent. After taking his stand under the open sky in a clear space and offering the customary preliminary sacrifice, he prayed to King Jupiter and the other gods whom he had taken as the leaders of his colony that, if they wished him to be king of the city, favourable signs would appear in the sky. **2** After his prayer lightning flashed across the sky from left to right . . . **6.1** This custom relating to the auspices long continued to be observed by the Romans, not only while the city was a monarchy but also after the overthrow of the monarchy in the election of consuls and praetors and other legal magistrates. **2** It has, however, ceased in our own day, except for a certain semblance of it which remains for form's sake. For those who are about to take up office spend the night outside and, rising at dawn, offer certain prayers under the open sky, and some of the augurs present state that they have seen lightning from the left – which was not there.

3.49 Varro *On the Latin Language* 7.8: An old formula for taking the auspices

In this extract Varro is quoting from the augural books. The trees are boundaries and the four quarters for the auspices set within them. A templum was a rectangular area in the sky that had been marked out, within which the augur or magistrate would look for auspices from birds (see doc. 3.50). It could also be an area of ground so marked out, as here described by Varro. Important templa were the curia, rostra and comitium, since these were places where political decisions were made.

On the earth templum is the name given to a place used for the sake of augury or the taking of auspices and restricted by certain formulaic words. The form of words is not the same everywhere; on the citadel (on the Capitoline hill) it is as follows:

> Temples and wild lands be mine in this way, up to where I have named them
>   rightly with my tongue.

Of whatever kind that truthful tree is, which I consider that I have mentioned, temple and wild land be mine on the left.

Of whatever kind that truthful tree is, which I consider that I have mentioned, temple and wild land be mine on the right.

Between these points, temples and wild lands be mine for direction, observation and interpretation, just as I consider that I have named them rightly.

3.50 Livy *History of Rome* 1.18.6–10, 20.7: The augur marks off the heavens

The lituus, the 'crooked staff without a knot', was a badge of office for augurs. Jupiter was the god of auspices, and so the augur here calls upon him; Jupiter was Elicius because the signs were elicited, 'drawn', from him.

18.6 Summoned to Rome, Numa Pompilius instructed that the gods should be consulted in his case, just as for Romulus, who at the founding of Rome had assumed power after taking auguries. He was therefore conducted by an augur, to whom as a mark of honour a permanent state priesthood was granted from then on, to the citadel, where he sat on a stone facing south. **7** The augur with veiled head took his seat on Numa's left, holding in his right hand the crooked staff without a knot, which they call the *lituus*. Then, looking out over the city and the country beyond, he prayed to the gods and marked off the heavens from east to west, declaring the southward side to be 'right' and the northward side 'left'. **8** He fixed in his mind a point straight in front of him as far away as his eyes could reach, changed the staff to his left hand, placed his right upon Numa's head and prayed in the following words: **9** 'Father Jupiter, if it is Heaven's will that this man, Numa Pompilius, whose head I touch, should be king of Rome, make clear to us specific signs within those limits I have set.' **10** Then he described the auspices that he wished to be sent. When they were sent, Numa was proclaimed king and went down from the augural site (templum). . . . **20.7** Numa consecrated an altar on the Aventine to Jupiter Elicius, whom he consulted by augury as to what signs from heaven it should be proper to regard.

3.51 Cicero *On Divination* 1.30–1: The sacred staff

The temple of the Salii was burnt in the Gallic attack traditionally dated to 390 BC. Attus Navius was the augur of Tarquinius Priscus, the fifth king of Rome.

30 From where did you augurs inherit that staff which is the most conspicuous mark of the office of augurs? It is indeed the one with which Romulus marked out the boundary lines for observing omens when he founded the city. Now this staff of Romulus is a curved wand, slightly bent at the top, which derives its name from its resemblance to the curved trumpet which gives the signal for battle. It was placed in the temple of the Salii on the Palatine, and when the temple was burnt down it was found intact. **31** What historian of antiquity fails to mention that many years after Romulus, in the reign of Tarquinius Priscus, the boundary lines for observations were marked out with this staff by Attus Navius?

3.52 Livy *History of Rome* 6.41.4–10: Patrician control of augury

In 367 BC the tribunes Sextius and Licinius successfully proposed that half of the Board of Ten in charge of the Sibylline Books (*decemviri sacris faciundis*) should be plebeians; Sextius was also to be the first plebeian consul: see docs 1.48–49. This is an extract from Livy's version of the speech made by Appius Claudius Crassus against the tribunes when they sought re-election for the tenth time; cf. doc. 1.56.

4 What am I to say about religious observances and auspices, disregard and insult of which involve the immortal gods? This city was founded under auspices, and who is unaware that all its measures are carried out under auspices, whether in war or peace, at home or on the battlefield? **5** Who then controls the auspices by ancestral tradition? Why, the patricians, for no plebeian magistrate is elected under auspices; **6** and the auspices are ours to such an extent that not only do the patrician magistrates elected by the people have to be elected under auspices but we can ourselves, without the people's vote, take auspices and appoint an interrex. In fact, we can take them in our capacity as private citizens, which plebeians cannot do even when in office. **7** So whoever by creating plebeians as consuls removes auspices from the patricians – who alone can take them – deprives the state of auspices. **8** They can laugh now, if they like, at religious scruples: 'So what does it matter if the chickens will not feed, if they are slow to come out of their hencoop, if a bird squawks an unlucky omen?' These are trivial matters, but it was by not despising these trivial matters that your ancestors built up this great Republic – **9** and now we, as if we no longer had any need of the gods' goodwill, are defiling all the sacred rites. So, let pontiffs, augurs and kings of the sacrifices (the rex sacrorum) be chosen from the common people; let us place the flamen dialis' headdress on anyone's head, as long as he is a man; and hand over the shields, shrines, gods and the gods' service to those whom divine law excludes; **10** let laws be proposed, and magistrates elected, without taking of the auspices; let neither the centuriate nor curiate assemblies be sanctioned by patricians.

THE SACRED CHICKENS

Employing haruspicy or taking the auspices was not always convenient for the commander in battle. Chickens, kept in a cage, provided a mobile divination kit: when they were fed, it was an auspicious omen if they ate greedily and the pellets fell from their beaks; if they did not eat, it was a bad omen. Sacred chickens are depicted on an aes signatum (bronze ingot), minted at Rome c. 260–242 BC: two chickens face each other, eating, so giving a favourable omen.

3.53 Cicero *On the Nature of the Gods* 2.7–8: Do not ignore the chickens!

Publius Claudius Pulcher, as consul in 249 BC, lost his fleet at Drepanum, having previously ignored the unfavourable auspices of the chickens (they were presumably too sea-sick to eat). Because of this he was held responsible for the defeat and charged with perduellio (treason) and fined.

7 Shall we not be moved by the temerity of Publius Claudius in the First Punic War? He was laughing at the gods in jest when the chickens were removed from their cage and would not feed, ordering them to be thrown into the water to drink, as they didn't want to eat. But the joke, when the fleet was defeated, brought many tears to him and a great catastrophe to the Roman people. And did not his colleague Junius in that same war lose a fleet in a storm when he did not obey the auspices? As a consequence, Claudius was condemned by the people and Junius committed suicide. **8** Caelius writes that Gaius Flaminius, after neglecting the dictates of religion (religio), fell at the battle of Trasimene, which gave our state a great blow. The fate of these men demonstrates that our empire was extended by commanders who obeyed the dictates of religion. And if we want to compare our national characteristics with those of others, we shall find that, while in all other respects we are either their equals or even their inferiors, yet in our sense of religion, that is, in reverence for the gods, we are greatly superior.

3.54 Cicero *On Divination* 1.27: Chickens and 'forced augury'

Quintus Cicero is complaining here that the chickens were left hungry and then fed in such a way that a favourable omen was inevitable.

Among us Romans the magistrates make use of auspices which are 'forced'; for, when the pellets are thrown, bits have to fall from the chicken's beak as it is eating. But according to what you augurs have written, if anything falls to the ground, a favourable omen (tripudium) has taken place, and what I spoke of as a 'forced' augury you call the most favourable of omens (*tripudium solistimum*). And so many auguries and auspices, as Cato the Wise complains, have been entirely lost and abandoned by the carelessness of the college.

DEDICATIONS AND VOWS

Dedications were a means of thanking the gods for 'services rendered'. Often such dedications were vowed in moments of crisis and the vow fulfilled when the crisis passed successfully. Dedications could range from small inscribed tablets to temples and monuments. For other dedications, see esp. doc. 3.60 (healing); docs 4.33, 46, 5.33, 42–43 (victory); doc. 6.55 (manumission); docs 7.77, 84–85 (by Roman women).

3.55 *ILS* 4906: A dedication at Furfo, 58 BC

Furfo is 60 miles east of Rome. Since the calendar was then in disarray (doc. 3.30), 13 July 58 BC would actually have been 13 April, in a better season for flowers. A special provision allows iron into the temple, and provision is made that dedications in the temple can be sold, but for the temple's benefit.

Lucius Aienus, son of Lucius, and Quintus Baebatius, son of Sextus, dedicated the temple of Jupiter Liber at Furfo on 13 July in the consulship of Lucius (Calpurnius) Piso and Aulus Gabinius (58 BC), in the month of Flowers, laying down these regulations and these boundaries, that the lowest foundations are to be constructed of stone for the purpose of this temple, **5** and that towards that temple and the staircase, constructed of stone columns on this side of the staircase leading towards the temple, and the posts and beams of this temple are to stand; that it be permissible under human and divine law to touch, repair, cover, remove, drive in, clean out, use iron, push forward and realign. If any gift be given, presented or dedicated to that temple, that it be permitted to use or sell it; when it has been sold, it is to be secular. Let the sale or lease be in the hands of whomever **10** the village of Furfo has elected as aedile, so that they feel that they are selling or leasing that object without crime or impiety; no one else is to have this power. Whatever money is received, that money may be used to buy, lend, put out at interest or give, so that the temple may be improved and more handsome. Any money used for those purposes is to be secular, as there is no fraud involved. Any objects bought with the money, bronze or silver, given for purchase, those things should be subject to the same regulations as if they had been dedicated. **15** If anyone here steals a sacred object, his fining is the responsibility of the aedile, whatever amount he wishes; and if the village of Furfo by majority vote wishes either to acquit or condemn, this is to be allowed. If anyone sacrifices at this temple to Jupiter Liber or to the Genius of Jupiter, the skins and hides are to belong to the shrine.

3.56 Livy *History of Rome* 36.2.1–5: A public vow to Jupiter

When the consuls of 191 BC drew lots for their provinces, Acilius drew Greece, which had been invaded in 192 by Antiochus, king of Syria (docs 5.28–31). The senate decreed that there be a supplicatio to invoke the aid of the gods for the forthcoming war. A supplicatio could be held as an expiation ceremony or, as in this case described by Livy, in connection with a vow, as a thanksgiving. Statues of the gods were placed on couches (pulvinaria), the temples were opened, and the populace was called upon to worship the gods. The consul here repeats the words after the pontifex maximus as part of the procedure to ensure that the exact ritual formulas were used (see doc. 3.26).

1 To Acilius fell Greece, to Cornelius Italy. **2** With the casting of lots determined, the senate passed a decree that, since the Roman people had at that time ordered there to be a war with King Antiochus and those under his authority, the consuls should proclaim a period of prayer (supplicatio) for its success and that the consul Manius Acilius should vow great games to Jupiter and gifts at all the couches of the gods (pulvinaria). **3** The consul made this vow, repeating it after the pontifex maximus, Publius Licinius, in the following words: 'If the war which the people has ordered to be undertaken with King Antiochus shall be brought to a conclusion deemed satisfactory by the senate and people, **4** then the people will hold in your honour, Jupiter, great games for ten consecutive days, and will offer gifts at the couches of the gods of whatever value the senate shall decide. **5** Whatever magistrate shall hold these games, at whatever time and place, let these games be duly celebrated and these gifts be duly offered.' Then the period of prayer, to last for two days, was proclaimed by both consuls.

THE INTRODUCTION OF NEW GODS

The Romans were not in principle opposed to the introduction of new gods, as is indicated by their acceptance of Aesculapius, the Magna Mater and their practice of 'calling out' the gods of states with which they were at war. But the Roman state as represented by the senate had a clear sense of what was appropriate within a Roman context. It was the senate (never the people) which decided which foreign gods gained legitimacy and worship within the formal apparatus of the state religion. The state's interest was active, as can be seen in the Bacchanalia, when the senate took steps to persecute its adherents. Isis began to be popular at Rome in the closing decades of the Republic, but the senate destroyed her temples on more than one occasion in the 50s and 40s BC.

3.57 Livy *History of Rome* 5.21.1–3, 22.3–7: The evocatio of Juno, 396 BC

For the sack of Veii, see doc. 1.61. Evocatio was the procedure by which the Romans would call out the main god of an enemy city, promising them a cult at Rome, and sometimes a temple. The enemy would thus be deprived of divine support. The general in command would undertake the evocatio – in this case the dictator Camillus. Juno's temple was built at Rome on the Aventine Hill in 392 BC; it housed the wooden statue of Juno brought from Veii.

21.1 A great multitude came out and filled the camp. After taking the auspices, the dictator then went out and commanded the troops to arm themselves: **2** 'Under your leadership', he declared, 'Pythian Apollo, and inspired by your divine guidance, I proceed to the destruction of the city of Veii and to you I vow a tenth part of its spoils. **3** And at the same time, Queen Juno, who dwells now in Veii, I pray that you come with us, the victors, to our – soon to be your – city, where a shrine worthy of your greatness will receive you' . . .

22.3 Now that all the wealth belonging to the human residents had been carried out of Veii, they started to remove the gifts to the gods and even the gods themselves, but more in the fashion of worshippers than of looters. **4** For young men were selected from the whole army who washed themselves clean and put on white garments, and these were assigned the task of carrying Queen Juno to Rome. They entered her shrine with reverence and at first were awe-struck at the thought of approaching her with their hands, **5** because the statue by Etruscan custom was to be touched only by a priest of a specific family. Then one of them, whether touched by divine inspiration or a youthful sense of humour, said, 'Do you wish, Juno, to go to Rome?' and the others shouted together that the goddess had nodded yes. **6** It was later added to the tale that her voice had also been heard saying she was willing; at any rate, we are told that she was moved from her station by machines of little power as if she went with them of her own accord and was light and easy to handle during the transfer, and reached the Aventine safe and sound, **7** the eternal home to which the vows of the Roman dictator had summoned her, where Camillus afterwards dedicated to her the temple he had vowed.

3.58 Macrobius *Saturnalia* 3.9.6–9: Carthaginian cults transferred

Serenus Sammonicus was an antiquary killed in AD 211; Furius is thought to be L. Furius Philus (cos. 136 BC), a friend of Scipio Aemilianus. The formulae seem to be of the correct date and would have been spoken by Scipio, the besieging general, in 146 BC. Macrobius at 3.9.3 states that this practice explains why the Romans were careful not to reveal the name of the tutelary god of Rome or the Latin name of the city.

6 We must be careful to make a distinction, unlike some who have incorrectly supposed that a single formula (carmen) is used both to call the gods out of a city and to devote the city itself to destruction. I have found both formulas in the fifth Book of the *Secret World* (*Res Reconditae*) of Sammonicus Serenus, who stated that he had come across them in an extremely ancient book by one Furius.

 7 The formula to call the gods out of a city encircled by a siege is as follows: 'Whether god or goddess, under whose protection are the people and state of Carthage, and to you especially who have been charged with the protection of this city and people, I pray and do reverence and ask a favour of you all, that you abandon the people and state of Carthage, forsake their places, temples, shrines and city, **8** and depart from these; and that you bring fear, terror and bewilderment upon that people and state; and that, once you have abandoned them, you come to Rome, to me and to mine; and that our places, temples, shrines and city may be more acceptable and pleasing to you; and that you take me and the Roman people and my soldiers under your charge that we may know and understand this. If you shall so have done, I vow to you that I shall construct temples and celebrate games.' **9** With these words victims should be sacrificed, and the authority of the entrails examined to see if they predict these events for the future.

3.59 Aesculapius, 292 BC

Following a plague in 293 BC, one of Aesculapius' sacred serpents was brought to Rome by ship and his healing cult established on the island in the Tiber, chosen by the snake itself; a relief of Aesculapius' snake can still be seen there. Healing was by incubation, which was a practice where sick individuals slept overnight in the temple, hoping that the god would appear to them in a dream and heal them.

(i) Livy History of Rome *10.47.6–7*

The year (293 BC) had in many ways been a happy one, but this served as insufficient consolation for one disaster, a plague which raged through both town and countryside; the calamity was considered a portent, and the (Sibylline) Books were consulted to find what limit or remedy the gods proposed for this misfortune. It was discovered in the books that Aesculapius should be summoned from Epidaurus to Rome; nothing, however, could be done in that year, as the consuls were occupied with the war, except that a one-day supplication was held for Aesculapius.

(ii) Livy Periochae *11*

When the state was suffering under a plague, the envoys, who had been sent to fetch the statue of Aesculapius over from Epidaurus to Rome, brought with them a serpent, which came on board their ship of its own accord and in which it was believed that the divinity himself dwelt. When it went ashore on the island in the Tiber, a temple to Aesculapius was built there.

3.60 *ILS* 3833, 3834: Early dedications to Aesculapius

These dedications were discovered in the River Tiber. The first (3833) dates to the third century BC; the second is a little later.

3833 To Aesculapius: a gift dedicated by Lucius Albanius, son of Kaeso.
3834 To Aesculapius: a gift given willingly and deservedly by Marcus Populicius, son of Marcus.

3.61 Livy *History of Rome* 29.14.10–14: The Magna Mater, 204 BC

The Magna Mater, 'Great Mother', was also known as Cybele or the Idaean goddess (from Mount Ida). Frequent showers of stones in 205 BC led to a consultation of the Sibylline Books. An oracle was found there that said, 'If ever a foreign enemy invaded the soil of Italy, he could be driven out of Italy and vanquished, if the Idaean Mother were brought from Pessinus to Rome' (Livy 29.10.5). A delegation was sent to Pessinus in Phrygia to obtain the black meteoric stone of the Idaean Mother, the Magna Mater. P. Cornelius Scipio Nasica (praetor in 194) was chosen to go to Ostia to meet the goddess. She was carried into Rome on 4 April 204; Claudia Quinta's reputation for virtue was in doubt, but, when the ship stuck on a sandbank at the mouth of the Tiber, soothsayers announced that it could only be moved by a virtuous matron. Claudia pulled the ship off, thus proving her innocence (doc. 7.30). The Megalesia in the Magna Mater's honour lasted six days and was first held in 191 BC (the ludi Megalenses, doc. 2.70).

10 Publius Cornelius Scipio was instructed to go to Ostia with all the matrons to meet the goddess; he was to receive her himself from the ship and then hand her, once she was on land, to be carried by the matrons. **11** When the ship arrived at the mouth of the River Tiber, he did as he had been ordered, rowing out to sea, receiving the goddess from her priests, and bringing her to land. **12** The foremost matrons of the city, among whom the name of Claudia Quinta alone is illustrious, received her. Claudia's reputation, which, it is recorded, had before been uncertain, made her virtue, shown by her attendance on the goddess, more noteworthy to posterity. **13** The matrons carried the goddess, passing her from hand to hand one after another; the whole city poured out to meet her, and incense burners were placed in front of the doorways along the route, with people praying, as they lit the incense, that the goddess would enter the city of Rome graciously and propitiously. **14** They carried the goddess into the temple of Victory, which is on the Palatine, on 4 April, and that day was declared a festival. Crowds of people brought gifts to the goddess on the Palatine, and a lectisternium was held and games called the Megalesia.

3.62 Lucretius *On the Nature of the Universe* 2.610–32: The Galli

The activities of Cybele's priests, the Galli, and the rites in her honour were considered to be most un-Roman, especially the self-mutilation (castration) of the priests; here Lucretius (94–55/51 BC) describes a procession in her honour. Roman citizens were not allowed to become Galli or to take part in the procession or worship the goddess in the Phrygian way.

610	Various nations, according to the ancient tradition of her rites, call her
	Idaean mother and assign her bands of Phrygians
	As her attendants, because it was that region first, they say,
	Out of all the earth, which began to produce crops.
	They give her Galli as attendants, to show that those who violate their mother's will
615	And treat their fathers with ingratitude,
	Should be thought unworthy
	Of producing living descendants in the sunlit world.
	Tightly stretched drums thunder out, struck by palms, and curved cymbals,
	And horns threaten with their hoarse-sounding blare,
620	While the hollow flute inspires the heart with Phrygian tunes.
	They carry weapons before her as symbols of violent frenzy,
	That the ungrateful minds and impious hearts of the crowd
	May be terror-struck with fear of the goddess's power.
	So, when she is first carried into a large city
625	And silently bestows wordless blessings on mankind,
	People strew her path along the entire route
	With lavish gifts of copper and silver, with a snow-shower of roses
	Shadowing the Mother and her bands of attendants.
	Next armed group of attendants, called by the Greeks
630	Phrygian Curetes, hold mock battles
	And dance in rhythm, delighted by the bloodshed,
	Shaking, with a nod, the terrifying crests upon their heads.

3.63 Diodorus Siculus *Library of History* 36.13.1–3: The Great Mother's priest

Aulus Pompeius was tribune in 102 BC. Battaces, priest of the Great Mother, arrived from Pessinus in 102 to state that rites of purification were needed; the context is the ongoing wars with the Cimbri and Teutones, concluded in 101.

1 A certain man called Battaces, who was a priest of the Great Mother of the gods, arrived from Pessinus in Phrygia. He stated that he had come on the orders of the goddess and obtained an audience with the consuls and senate, where he

said that the temple of the goddess had been polluted and that rites of purification had to be publicly performed to her at Rome. He wore a robe which, like the rest of his dress, was exotic and totally alien to Roman custom; he had a huge golden crown and a brightly coloured cape interwoven with gold, denoting royal rank. **2** He made a speech to the people from the rostra and inculcated in the populace a feeling of religious awe, and was thought worthy of state lodgings and hospitality. He was, however, forbidden to wear his crown by Aulus Pompeius, one of the tribunes. Brought back to the rostra by another of the tribunes and asked about the purification of the temple, he gave answers which imparted religious awe. When he was attacked on factional grounds by Pompeius and sent back with insults to his lodgings, he did not appear in public again, saying that it was not only he who had been outrageously and impiously treated, but the goddess as well. **3** Pompeius was immediately struck with a burning fever, after which he lost his voice and was seized with quinsy, dying on the third day, and it seemed to the populace that his death was divinely inspired to avenge his actions against the priest and goddess, for the Romans are very much given to religious awe. Accordingly, Battaces was allowed to wear his costume and sacred robe, was honoured with noteworthy gifts, and was escorted by a large crowd of both men and women when he set out on his journey home from Rome.

3.64 Valerius Maximus *On Memorable Doings and Sayings* 1.3.4: Opposition to the cult of Isis

The goddess Isis first made an appearance in Rome in the 50s BC. Her worship was opposed by the senate. Isis was worshipped particularly by women, but the personal soteriology of the cult also attracted men. In 53 and 50 BC the senate had the temples of Isis and Serapis demolished, and Octavian in 28 BC forbade Egyptian cults inside the pomerium.

When the senate decreed that the temples of Isis and Serapis be destroyed, and none of the workmen dared to touch them, the consul Lucius Aemilius (Lepidus) Paullus (cos. 50 BC) took off his toga praetexta, grabbed an axe, and smashed it against the door of that temple.

THE BACCHANALIA, 186 BC

Full narrative at Livy 39.8–19. The Greek cult of Bacchus (Dionysus) spread from southern Italy to Rome, and in 186 BC the senate took action. Possibly the cult was becoming simply too public (note the women going to the Tiber with torches). Livy's account of how the cult came to the attention of one of the consuls, Postumius, is rather dramatic (see doc. 7.63 for the role of Hispala Faecenia), but the details of the senate's treatment of the cult must be correct. According to Livy, 7,000 men and women were involved (39.17.6). Many of the accused committed suicide, and others tried unsuccessfully to escape from Rome. Those convicted of debauchery or murder were put to death, while women were handed over to their family councils for punishment if the death penalty was required (doc. 7.16). The cult was strictly controlled from that date, not only in Rome but throughout Roman Italy.

3.65 Livy *History of Rome* 39.8.3–18.8: 'All crime and lust'

8.3 Both consuls were assigned the duty of investigating secret conspiracies. It started when an obscure Greek arrived in Etruria. He was not with any of those arts which that most learned of all races brought to us in great numbers to cultivate our minds and bodies, but a dealer in sacrifices and soothsaying; **4** nor was he one who imbues minds with falsehood by practising his rites in public and openly proclaiming his profession and doctrine, but a celebrant of secret, nocturnal ceremonies. **5** There were mysteries which were at first divulged only to a few, but which then began to be widely disseminated among men and women. The delights of wine and feasting were added to the religious rites, to allure more people into joining. **6** When their minds were inflamed with wine, and night, and the mingling of men and women, young and old, had annihilated all sense of decorum, all kinds of vice first came into being, since all had at hand the chance to indulge in the pleasure to which nature most inclined them. **7** There was not just one kind of depravity, promiscuous debauchery between free men and women, but false witnesses, forged seals and wills, and perjured informants were all the product of this same workshop, **8** as well as poisonings and murders so secret that sometimes the bodies were not even available for burial. Much was dared by cunning, and more by violence. The violence was concealed because, amid the wailing and the crashing of kettle-drums (tympana) and cymbals, no sound of shrieks could be heard from this scene of debauchery and murders. **9.1** This evil, with all its virulence, spread from Etruria to Rome like the contagion of a plague. At first the size of the city with its greater capacity and tolerance for such evils concealed them: finally information reached the consul (Spurius) Postumius (Albinus). . . .

13.8 Hispala then disclosed the origin of the mysteries. At first, she said, it was a rite for women and it was a rule that no man be admitted to it. Three days had been set aside each year on which, during the day, initiations into the Bacchic rites were conducted; it was customary for the matrons to be made priests in turn. **9** Paculla Annia, a Campanian, when priest, had altered all this, supposedly at the god's behest: for she had been the first to initiate men, her sons Minius and Herennius Cerrinius; she had held the mysteries by night rather than by day, and instead of three days a year had made five days in each month into days of initiation. **10** From the time that the mysteries were held indiscriminately, and with men mixing with women, and with the licence of night-time added as well, no crime or depravity had been omitted. There was more debauchery among men with one another than among women. **11** Any of them who were less tolerant of submitting to outrage or more reluctant to commit crime were sacrificed as victims. To consider nothing to be impious was the highest type of religious belief among them. **12** Men, as if out of their minds, would make prophecies, throwing their bodies about violently as if under divine inspiration; matrons, dressed as Bacchantes, would run, with their hair unkempt, down to the Tiber carrying flaming torches, plunge the torches into the water and (because they contained a mixture of live sulphur and calcium) pull them out with the flame still alight. **13** People were said to have been snatched away by the gods (in fact they were bound to a machine and carried off out of sight to hidden caves): they were the ones who had refused either to join in conspiracies or take part in crimes or suffer sexual violation. **14** The number of adherents was immense, amounting almost to a second nation; among them were some men and women of the nobility. Within the last two years it had been laid down that no one over the age of 20 should be initiated: they sought out young people of this age who would engage in both wickedness and debauchery . . .

14.3 When both witnesses were secured in this way, Postumius brought the matter before the senate, setting out all the points in order, first what had been reported, then what he had himself discovered. **4** The senators were seized with great alarm, both for the public, in case these conspiracies and assemblies might be harbouring some secret treachery or danger, and privately each for himself, in case any connection of their family might be involved in the evil . . . **17.6** More than 7,000 men and women were said to have been involved in the conspiracy. However, it was evident that the ring-leaders of the conspiracy had been Marcus and Gaius Atinius of the Roman plebs and the Faliscan Lucius Opicernius and the Campanian Minius Cerrinius: **7** all the crimes and wickedness had sprung from them, and they were the high priests and founders of the cult. Care was taken that they were arrested at the earliest opportunity. They were brought before the consuls and confessed, asking for no delay in being brought to trial . . .

18.3 Those who had simply been initiated and who had repeated at the priest's dictation, in accordance with the ritual formula, the prayers which contained the impious conspiracy to commit every crime and lust, but had not been involved in any of those deeds against either themselves or others which they had bound themselves on oath to commit, were left in prison; **4** those who had dishonoured themselves by debauchery or murder, who had been polluted by false witness, forged seals, the substitution of wills and other kinds of fraud, suffered capital punishment. **5** More were killed than thrown into prison. There was an immense number of men and women in both categories. **6** Convicted women were handed over to their family, or to those whose authority they were under, so that these could punish them privately: if there was no appropriate person to exact the punishment, it was inflicted by the state. **7** The consuls were then given the task of destroying all forms of Bacchic worship, first in Rome and then through the whole of Italy, except for places where an ancient altar or statue had been consecrated. **8** The senate then decreed that for the future there should be no Bacchanalia in Rome or in Italy.

3.66 *ILS* 18: The senate's resolution, 186 BC

This document is a letter of the consuls of 186, including the actual senatus consultum, written to the people of the Ager Teuranus in Bruttium; it was found on a tablet of brass at Tiriolo in Bruttian territory and was presumably a copy of the letter made to be publicly displayed. It is the oldest extant surviving senatus consultum.

The consuls (Quintus) Marcius (Philippus), son of Lucius, and Spurius Postumius, son of Lucius, consulted the senate on the Nones (7th) of October in the temple of Bellona. Present as witnesses to the record were Marcus Claudius, son of Marcus,

Lucius Valerius, son of Publius, and Quintus Minucius, son of Gaius. Regarding the Bacchanalia, they resolved that the following decree be made known to Rome's allies:

'Let none of them be minded to maintain a place devoted to Bacchus; if there are any people who say that it is necessary for them to maintain a place devoted to Bacchus, they must come to the praetor urbanus at Rome, **5** and, when their words have been heard, our senate shall decide concerning these matters, provided that not fewer than 100 senators are present when the matter is discussed. Let no man, whether Roman citizen or Latin by name, or any of the allies, be minded to attend a meeting of Bacchant women unless they have first approached the praetor urbanus and he has given them authorisation through a vote of the senate, provided that not fewer than 100 senators were present when the matter is discussed.' Passed.

10 'Let no man be a priest; let not any man or woman be a master (magister, i.e., administrator); nor let anyone be minded to keep a common fund; nor let anyone be minded to make any man or woman a master or vice-master; nor henceforward let anyone be minded to swear together, nor vow together, nor make mutual promises, nor pledge to others, nor be minded to plight faith to each other. **15** Let no one be minded to hold sacred rites in secret, whether in public or privately, nor be minded to hold rites outside the city, unless he has first approached the praetor urbanus, and he has given them authorisation through a vote of the senate, provided that not fewer than 100 senators were present when the matter is discussed.' Passed.

'Let no one in a group of more than five, men and women together, **20** be minded to hold sacred rites, and let not more than two men and not more than three women be minded to attend there, unless with the agreement of the praetor urbanus and senate as written above.'

You are to proclaim this in a public meeting (contio) for a period of no fewer than three market-days (seventeen days), and so that you may be acquainted with the vote of the senate, this vote was as follows: 'Should there be any who act contrary to what has been recorded above, **25** the senate resolves that proceedings for a capital crime should be taken against them; and the senate thought it right that you shall inscribe this on a bronze tablet and you shall order it to be put up where it can most easily be seen; and that you ensure that those places devoted to Bacchus which exist be dissolved as recorded above, **30** unless there be anything sacred there, within ten days of the receipt of this letter.' In the Ager Teuranus.

3.67 Dionysius of Halicarnassus 2.19.2–5: Roman worship

Dionysius here compares Roman ritual practices with Greek. Dionysius' point about the Romans' non-acceptance or transformation of foreign cults is borne out by his example of the Magna Mater (the Idaean goddess): docs 3.61–63.

2 No festival is observed by the Romans by the wearing of black or as a day of mourning with women beating their breasts and lamenting over the disappearance of gods, as the Greeks do over the abduction of Persephone or the misfortunes of

Dionysus and other such events; nor may one see among them, even though their customs have now been corrupted, any instances of divine possession, Corybantic frenzies, religious begging rituals, Bacchic rites and secret mysteries, all-night vigils of men and women together in temples or any other trickery of this kind, but there is a reverence in all their words and actions in respect of the gods, which is not seen among either Greeks or barbarians; **3** and the thing that I have marvelled at most of all is that, although the city has attracted tens of thousands of peoples who are compelled to worship their native gods according to the customs of their homelands, it has never publicly adopted any of these foreign practices, as many other cities have done, but, even when she has followed oracles which instructed her to introduce certain rites, she celebrates these according to her own customs after banishing all mythical nonsense, as in the case of the rites of the Idaean goddess. **4** For the praetors perform sacrifices and games for this goddess every year according to Roman customs, but her priest and priestess are Phrygians and they process through the city, begging for alms as is their custom, and wearing images on their breasts and striking their kettle-drums, to the accompaniment of their followers playing songs to the goddess on their flutes; **5** no native-born Roman, however, either ritually begs for alms or processes through the city accompanied by flute-players wearing a multicoloured robe, or worships the goddess with the Phrygian rites – a law and decree of the senate has prohibited this. The city is extremely cautious with respect to religious customs which are not native to Rome and regards as inauspicious all pomp and ceremony which lacks decorous behaviour.

CURSE TABLETS AND SYMPATHETIC MAGIC

Magic was known to the Romans as early as the XII Tables, where the phrases 'whoever shall have bewitched the crops' and 'whoever shall have cast an evil spell' occur (doc. 1.50). Beneficent magic was also practised, as in the cures in which Cato uses common spell techniques, where incomprehensible nonsense words are employed and ingredients (here the reed) are handled and chanted over (doc. 3.70). Curse tablets aimed to gain power over a person, generally for malevolent purposes (as in doc. 3.69), and invoked the deities of the underworld – here the Roman goddess Proserpina (equivalent to the Greek Persephone), wife of Pluto, god of the underworld.

3.68 Cicero *On the Nature of the Gods* 2.71–2: Superstitio versus religio

Cicero distinguishes between the concepts of superstitio and religio. Religio involves rituals handed down over generations and concerned primarily the worship (cultus) of the gods. At *Div.* 2.149, Cicero describes superstitio as listening to a prophet, sacrificing, watching the flight of birds, consulting astrologers or soothsayers, and noting thunder and lightning and prodigies.

71 Religio has been distinguished from superstitio not only by philosophers but also by our forebears. **72** People who passed entire days in prayer and sacrifice so that their children would outlive them were called superstitious (from superstes: survivor), and the word later came to have a wider meaning. Those, however, who diligently reviewed and retraced everything pertaining to the cultus (worship) of the gods were known as religious, from relegere (to retrace, or re-read).

3.69 *CIL* I² 1614, 1615, 2520: Curses

These three inscriptions are curse tablets (defixiones). No. 1614 is a round tablet of lead (an uncommon type), supposedly found at Cumae, written in a mixture of Latin and Oscan; no. 1615 is small bronze plate discovered in a tomb at Cumae. 2520 comprises five thin plates of lead discovered at Rome. Each plate is wrapped around a nail and curses a single person – in the example given here, an individual named Plotius. Each of the five follows the same wording, so that gaps in the curse against Plotius can be filled in from the other plates. They date to the first century BC (between about 80 and 40 BC). These five curses are all inscribed by the one hand.

1614 Lucius Harines, son of Herius Maturus, Gaius Eburius, Pomponius, Marcus Caedicius, son of Marcus, Numerius Andripius, son of Numerius. May the *fancua* of them all stand straight up! May their breath be dry!

1615 To face judgement (among the dead): Naevia Secunda, freedwoman of Lucius, or whatever name she goes under.

2520 Good and beautiful Proserpina, wife of Pluto, unless I ought to call you Salvia ('Saviour'), may you tear from Plotius health, body, colour, strength, vigour. May you deliver him over to Pluto your husband. May he not be able to avoid this by his own devices. May you deliver him to the fourth-day, the third-day, the every-day fever (i.e., malaria), and may they wrestle and struggle it out with him; may they vanquish and overcome him until they tear away his life. Wherefore **10** I deliver this victim to you Proserpina, unless, Proserpina, I ought to call you Acherousia (i.e., goddess of the underworld). May you send, I pray, someone to summon the three-headed dog to tear out Plotius' heart. Promise that you will give him three victims, dates, dried figs, a black pig, if he should have finished before the month of March. These things, Proserpina Salvia, I will give you when you have gratified my wish. I give you the head of Plotius, (slave) of Avonia, **20** Proserpina Salvia, I give you Plotius' forehead, Proserpina Salvia, I give you Plotius' eyebrows, Proserpina Salvia, I give you Plotius' eyelids, Proserpina Salvia, I give you Plotius' pupils, Proserpina Salvia, I give you Plotius' nostrils, lips, ears, nose, tongue, teeth, so Plotius may not be able to say what pains him; his neck, shoulders, arms, fingers, so he may not be able to help himself in any way; **30** his chest, liver, heart, lungs, so he may not be able to feel what gives him pain; his intestines, stomach, navel, sides, so he may not be able to sleep; his shoulder-blades, so he may not be able to sleep soundly; his testicles, so he may not be able to urinate; his buttocks, anus, thighs, knees, shanks, shins, feet, ankles, soles, toes, nails, so he may not be able to stand by his own strength. Should there have been written, **40** whether great or small, any curse, in whatever way Plotius has properly (i.e., according to the laws of magic) written anything (i.e., against me) and committed it, thus I deliver Plotius to you, and commit him that you may deliver and commit that fellow in the month of February. Damn him!, to hell with him!, damn him utterly! May you commit him, may you hand him over, so he may not be able to see, look on or regard any month further!

3.70 Cato the Elder *On Farming* 160: Ritual nonsense performs a cure

Pliny *Nat. Hist.* 28.20 refers to magical prayers with 'foreign unpronounceable words'. Alternative spellings for the incomprehensible words in Cato's spell are given in different manuscripts.

In case of dislocation it may be cured by the following spell. Take a green reed 4 or 5 feet long and split it down the middle, and let two men hold it to their hips. Begin to chant, 'motas vaeta daries dardares astataries dissunapiter' and continue until the pieces meet (another manuscript has 'motas vaeta daries dardaries asiadarides una petes'). Brandish a knife over the pieces and, when they meet so that one touches the other, grasp with the hand and cut at right and left. Bind it to the dislocation or fracture and it will heal. And meanwhile chant every day in the following way in the case of a dislocation, 'huat haut haut istasis tarsis ardannabou dannaustra' (another manuscript has 'huat haut haut ista pista sista dannabo dannaustra').

FESTIVALS

Calendars recorded the dates of festivals and the deities so honoured. The range of gods covered the whole array of the Roman pantheon, from the mighty Jupiter himself to the deity of rust; for women's festivals, see docs 7.75–82.

3.71 Accius *Annals* 2–7: The origins of the Saturnalia

Lucius Accius was born in 170 BC at Pisaurum in Umbria. He states that the annual Roman festival of the Saturnalia began in Greece. However, Saturn is an Italian and Roman deity, his name deriving from *satus*: sowing. His festival commenced on 17 December and lasted for several days. Even the parsimonious Cato the Elder issued extra rations to his farm personnel for the festival (doc. 6.36).

> Most of the Greeks, and especially Athens, celebrate a festival
> In honour of Saturn, which by them is known as the Cronia;
> In celebration of this day, through all the fields and cities,
> They joyfully hold feasts, and each man waits upon
> His own slaves; that same custom has been handed down from there to us,
> So that here, too, slaves feast with their masters.

3.72 Livy *History of Rome* 9.30.5–10: Secession of the flute-players

This incident took place in 311 BC when Rome was concluding a war with the Samnites. For the role of flute-players at sacrifices, see doc. 3.26. The 'period of three days' was the festival of the flute-players celebrated each year on 13–15 June.

5 I would have passed over an incident of the same year as being hardly worthy of mention, had it not seemed to concern religion. The flute-players, annoyed at having been forbidden by the last censors to hold their feast in the temple of Jupiter according to ancient custom, headed off in a body to Tibur, with the result that there was no one in the city to play at sacrifices. **6** Concerned by the religious implications of the incident, the senate sent delegates to Tibur requesting them to try to return the men to Rome. **7** The Tiburtines courteously promised to do so, summoned them to the senate house and urged them to return; when they were unable to persuade them, they handled them with a measure not inappropriate to their natural disposition. **8** On a public holiday, various people invited some of them home on the pretext of celebrating the feast with music, loaded them with wine (to which that type of man is generally well disposed) and got them off to sleep. **9** In this condition they threw them into carts, still fast asleep, and carried them off to Rome. The carts were left in the forum and the players knew nothing about it until daylight found them there – still inebriated. **10** The people then gathered round and prevailed with them to stay, and they were permitted to wander the city in festive dress for a period of three days a year, making music and enjoying the licence which is now customary, while those who played at sacrifices were given back the right of feasting in the temple. This happened at a time of anxiety over two serious wars.

3.73 Festus 190: The October horse

Two-horse chariot races were held on the Ides of October (15 October) in honour of Mars. The head was presumably a symbol of fertility, and, as well as ensuring prosperity for the coming year, the festival marked the end of the campaigning season. The regia was the house of the pontifex maximus at the edge of the forum. The sacred rite might be the Parilia, celebrated on 21 April. This is the only documented example of a horse sacrifice in Rome; cf. Plut. *Rom. Quest.* 97.

The October Horse is so called from the annual sacrifice to Mars in the Campus Martius during the month of October and is the victorious team's right-hand horse in the two-horse chariot races. It was customary for there to be a competition for its head between the residents of the Suburra and those of the Sacra Via, which was taken very seriously. The winners, if the latter, would attach it to the wall of the Regia or, if the former, the Mamilian tower. Its tail was taken to the Regia so speedily that the blood from it could be dripped onto the hearth to become part of the sacred rite.

3.74 Ovid *Fasti* 4.905–42: A dog sacrifice for mildew

The Robigalia (from Robigus or Robigo, the deity of mildew or grain rust) was celebrated on 25 April. The flamen Quirinalis is propitiating the malevolent force of Robigus by presiding over a sacrifice, after first invoking him and offering a prayer. The festival took place on the Via Claudia, at the fifth milestone; the dog-star is Sirius.

905 On that day, as I was returning to Rome from Nomentum,
A crowd of people in white robes blocked the middle of the road.
A flamen was going to the grove of ancient Mildew,
To give to the flames the entrails of a dog and a sheep.
I immediately went closer to learn about the ritual.
910 Your flamen, Quirinus, pronounced these words:
'Harsh Mildew, spare the sprouting grain,
And let their smooth tips quiver on the surface of the ground.
Allow the crops, nurtured by the stars of a propitious sky,
To grow until they become ready for the sickles.
Your power is not slight: the corn, which you have marked,
The farmer sadly gives up as lost.
Neither winds, nor rain storms harm the corn,
Nor the marble-like frost which whitens the brown grain,
As much as does the sun when it warms the wet stalks:
920 Then is the time, dread deity, for you to show your anger.
Spare, I pray, and keep your scabby hands off our harvests.
Do not harm our fields: it is enough that you have the power to do so.
Grasp not tender crops, but hard iron.
First destroy anything which can destroy others.
You will more profitably devour swords and harmful weapons:
There is no need of them – the world is at peace.
Let the hoes and hard mattock and the curved ploughshare,
The farm equipment, shine brightly: but let rust stain weapons,
And when someone tries to pull a sword from its sheath,
930 Let him feel it stick from long disuse.
But do not pollute the corn, and may the farmer always
Be able to offer prayers to you in your absence.'
Thus he spoke: from his right hand hung a loosely woven napkin
And he had a bowl of wine and a casket of incense.
On the fire he placed the incense, wine, sheep's entrails,
And the foul guts of a disgusting dog – we saw him.
Then to me he said: 'Do you ask why these rites are assigned an unusual
victim?'
I had asked that. 'Learn the reason', said the flamen.
'There is a Dog, which they call the Icarian dog, and when that star rises
940 The earth is scorched and dry, and the crops ripen too early.
This dog is put on the altar in place of the starry dog,
And the only reason for this is his name.'

RELIGION AND POLITICS

Roman state religion was dominated by the elite, as shown by Polybius, who suggests that
religion could be manipulated to keep the 'masses' in check (doc. 3.76). The most frequently manipulated area of religion was divination, because an unfavourable declaration

of omens by the presiding magistrate could terminate meetings of the assembly and could stop elections in the comitia centuriata; see docs 12.43, 54.

3.75 Plutarch *Life of Cato the Younger* 42.1, 4–5: Pompey's and the auspices in 55 BC

While presiding over the elections of praetors for 54, Pompey as consul in 55 BC obstructed the election of Cato by claiming to have heard thunder. Similarly, M. Calpurnius Bibulus as consul in 59 BC had attempted to obstruct legislation by his colleague, Julius Caesar, through proclaiming that the omens were unfavourable (doc. 12.43).

1 Cato would not back down, but came forward as a candidate for the praetorship, wanting to have a base of operations for his conflicts against them (Pompey and Crassus) . . . **4** When the first tribe called forward voted for him, Pompey suddenly lied and proclaimed that he heard thunder and then disgracefully dissolved the assembly (since they were accustomed to consider such things as inauspicious and not to ratify anything after a divine sign had occurred). **5** They then resorted again to immense bribery, drove the best citizens from the assembly, and so, by force, got Vatinius elected praetor instead of Cato.

3.76 Polybius *Histories* 6.56.6–12: The political uses of religion

The Roman aristocrats themselves considered that religion was crucial, not for keeping the common people under control but for the state's survival. The Romans' relations with the gods, as expressed in sacrifices and festivals and the expiation of prodigies, assured the support of the gods for Rome's supremacy.

6 But it is in religious belief that the Roman commonwealth seems to me to be vastly superior (to other states). **7** I believe that what is an object of derision among other peoples, namely superstition, is actually the element that holds the state together; **8** for these matters are treated with such pomp, and introduced to such an extent into both public and private life, that they have a place of pre-eminence. This may seem remarkable to many people. **9** My view is that this practice has been adopted for the sake of the common people. **10** If it had been possible to form a state composed of wise men, this approach might not have been necessary; **11** but since the common people is always easily swayed and full of lawless desires, unreasoning anger and violent passions, the only course is to restrain the masses through vague terrors and suchlike dramatisations. **12** For this reason I believe that the ancients were not acting at random or haphazardly when they introduced to the masses notions about the gods and beliefs in the underworld – rather people nowadays are acting at random and foolishly in throwing them out.

FUNERARY PRACTICES

See doc. 1.53 for funerary regulations in the XII Tables. The Romans of the Republic believed that those who died joined the *di manes*, the shades of the deceased, and had no particular 'existence' after death. They were honoured at the Parentalia festival, while at the Lemuria festival the unburied dead were placated. The bodies of the dead and burial places were considered polluting; the flamen dialis could not go to a cemetery or touch a corpse but was allowed to attend funerals (doc. 3.21). Cremation became increasingly common as the Republic progressed.

3.77 Polybius *Histories* 6.53.1–54.3: Funerals and politics

The public funeral procession was the preserve of the nobiles. It celebrated the deeds of the deceased and his ancestors, reminding the public of his services to the state. The masks (imagines) of the ancestors had a 'conspicuous place' in the house. They were made of wax, and each was kept in its own wooden cupboard in the atrium of the house (cf. doc. 2.27).

53.1 Whenever one of their distinguished men dies, as part of his funeral procession he is carried with all honour into the Forum to the so-called Rostra, sometimes conspicuous in an upright position, or, more rarely, reclining. **2** With the whole people standing around, his son, if he has one of adult age to follow him and who happens to be present or, if not, some other relative mounts the Rostra and discourses on the virtues of the deceased and his successful achievements during his lifetime. **3** As a result, the populace, when such facts are recalled to their minds and brought before their eyes – not only those who played a part in these achievements but also those who did not – feel such deep sympathy that the loss seems not to be confined to the mourners but to be a public one which affects the whole people. **4** Next, after burying the body and performing the usual ceremonies, they place the image of the deceased in the most conspicuous place in the house, enclosed in a wooden shrine. **5** This image is a mask fashioned into a remarkable likeness in both its modelling and its painting. **6** On the occasion of public sacrifices, they display these masks and carefully decorate them, and when any distinguished member of the family dies they take them to the funeral, where they are worn by men who seem most to resemble the original in both height and general bearing. **7** These men also wear togas with purple borders, if the deceased had been a consul or praetor, a purple one, if a censor, and a purple one embroidered with gold, if he had celebrated a triumph or performed a similar achievement. **8** They all ride in chariots with the fasces, axes and other insignia appropriate to the dignity of the offices held by each in his lifetime carried before them, and when they arrive at the Rostra **9** they all seat themselves in a row on chairs of ivory. There could be no more edifying sight for a young man who aspires to fame and virtue; **10** for who would not be moved by the sight of the images of men renowned for their excellence, all together as if alive and breathing? What spectacle could be more glorious than this?

54.1 Moreover, the speaker over the man about to be buried, when he has finished his address on the subject of the deceased, goes on to speak of the successes and achievements of each of the others whose images are present, beginning with the oldest. **2** Through this practice, this constant renewal of the fame of brave men, the glory of those who performed some noble deed is made immortal, while the renown of those who served their country well becomes common

knowledge and a heritage for those to come. **3** But the most important consequence is that young men are inspired to endure everything for the common good
for the sake of winning the glory which accompanies brave men.

3.78 *ILS* 6082: Regulations against cremations

This inscription, dating probably to c. 150–120 BC, is a senatus consultum concerning 'the
hill village' and was found on the Esquiline hill in Rome. It effectively bars cremations
from this area and so reserved it for the bodies of the poor (citizen paupers, slaves, the
bodies of executed criminals, and the like). Here the ustrinae are permanent crematoria, the
foci ustrinae causa temporary burning sites, i.e., pyres for a single corpse.

Senatus consultum concerning the hill village:

> . . . and that they should take care and guard it on the decision of the aediles of
> the plebs, whosoever they might be; and that there shall be no burning grounds
> (ustrinae) for corpses on those sites or in the vicinity, nor hearths (foci ustrinae
> causa) **5** for burning the dead, nor shall those who have rented these sites from
> the mountain village choose to make dung-heaps or throw dirt within those
> sites, and if anyone shall have made dung-heaps or thrown dirt in these sites,
> there shall be (a fine of) . . . sesterces, his property shall be confiscated and
> pledges taken.

3.79 *CIL* 1² 2123: Presentation of burial sites (except for gladiators)

A stone tablet found at Sassina in Umbria. Burial sites of a specified size could be chosen
while one was still alive; descendants could use the plot.

> . . . Horatius Balbus, son of . . . , to his fellow townsmen and other residents, at
> his own expense gives burial sites, except for gladiators and those who strangled
> themselves with their own hand and those who **10** followed an unclean profession:
> to each a site 10 feet in front and 10 feet in depth between the bridge over the
> Sapis and the upper monument which is on the edge of the Fangonian estate. In
> those places where no one has been buried, anyone who wishes shall make a tomb
> for himself while still alive. In those places where someone has been buried, **20**
> it will be permitted to have a monument only for him who has been buried there
> and his descendants.

3.80 *CIL* I² 1578: Funerary feast for a father, c. 60 BC

L. Papius Pollio set up this inscription as a memorial to his father. Though in Italian towns
there could be praetors or consuls, it was normal for there to be a duoviri iure dicundo, a
'Board of Two for pronouncing justice'; see doc. 2.11, cf. 2.80. Gladiatorial shows were
originally given at funerals: see docs 2.78–79.

Lucius Papius Pollio, son of Lucius, of the Teretine tribe, member of the Board of Two, in honour of his father Lucius Papius, son of Lucius, of the Falernian tribe, gave a feast of mead and pastry to all the colonists of Sinuessa and Caedex and a gladiatorial show and a dinner to the colonists at Sinuessa and the Papii. He set up a memorial at the cost of 12,000 sesterces **5** by the will and testament (of his father) and with the approval of Lucius Novercinius Pollis, of the Pupinian tribe, son of Lucius.

3.81 Cicero *On the Laws* 2.57: Inhumation practices

'The same fate' which Cicero refers to here is Sulla's scattering of Marius' remains in the River Anio. Before Sulla, the Cornelii had been inhumed.

Maybe it was because he was afraid that the same fate might happen to his body that Sulla, for the first time among the patrician Cornelii, instructed that he be cremated. For Ennius says about Africanus, 'Here he is laid.' And correctly; for 'laid' is used of those who are buried. But their place of burial is not a grave until the proper rites are performed and the pig slaughtered. And the term now in general use for all who are buried, that they are interred, was then restricted to those bodies where earth was thrown on and covered them, and pontifical law confirms this custom. For, until a clod of earth is thrown onto the bones, the place where a body is cremated has no religious character; when the clod is thrown on, the burial has taken place and it is called a grave, and from that point many sacred laws protect it. And so, in the case of a person who has died on a ship and has then been thrown into the sea, Publius Mucius (Scaevola) proclaimed his family free from pollution, because none of the bones lay above the earth; but his heir had to provide the sow, and a holiday of three days had to be kept.

3.82 Crawford *RRC* 385.1: The temple of Jupiter Capitolinus

This denarius of 78 BC depicts the temple of Jupiter Capitolinus, which had burned down during Sulla's capture of the city in 83 BC.

Obverse: Head of Jupiter, facing right, with laurel wreath.

Reverse: Temple of Jupiter Capitolinus. The temple is shown with three closed doors between four columns; Jupiter's thunderbolt is shown in the temple's pediment. The three doors are the entrances to the three cellas (chambers), each devoted to one to the Capitoline triad: Jupiter, Juno and Minerva.

4

The Punic Wars: Rome against Carthage

Rome fought three great wars against the Phoenician city of Carthage in Africa: the First (264–241 BC), the Second (218–201 BC) and the Third Punic War (149–146 BC), which ended with the total destruction of Carthage and the enslavement of its inhabitants in 146 BC, the same year as the Roman destruction of Corinth. The Carthaginians were Phoenicians, Poeni, hence the term 'Punic' Wars. The outbreak of the First Punic War in 264 BC marks the beginning of the Middle Republic. This is because the First Punic War was a watershed in Roman history and dramatically altered Rome. Before the war, Rome dominated Italy but had no overseas possessions: the intervention in Sicily was in fact the first time that the Romans had sent an army overseas. By the end of the Punic Wars, a century later, Rome had possessions in the Mediterranean and was embarked on a round of conquests that continued unabated to the end of the Republic. The First Punic War began the process of territorial expansion; by 146 Rome's chief rival was destroyed, and the Romans had possession of Sicily, Sardinia, Corsica, Carthaginian Africa, parts of Spain and, through activities in the eastern Mediterranean, Illyria, Macedonia and Epirus, with *de facto* control of Greece. Rome was transformed from the dominant city in Italy into the main Mediterranean power, while in the first century BC it would go on to conquer the Greek East.

Carthage was a colony of Tyre, founded about 814 BC, in modern Tunisia, near the city of Tunis. Phoenician ships had been cruising the Mediterranean since about 1000 BC, trading wherever they could. Legend has it that the Libyans offered Elissa, or Dido, the amount of land which an ox-hide could cover: she cut it into very thin strips to encompass more land than the Libyans had bargained for and founded Carthage. The city was ideally positioned, with an eastern peninsula of hills protecting its two harbours. Being strategically situated, it prospered, and it in turn sent out its own colonies; by 246 BC Carthage controlled the North African coastline from Cyrene, a Greek colony, to the Atlantic, as well as western Sicily, Sardinia and Corsica. In the sixth century, in Sicily, the Carthaginians and the Greek colonies, which had been established since the eighth century, became rivals, while Sardinia and Corsica (in neither of which the Greeks had an interest) became Carthaginian. Southern Spain was dominated by Carthage by around 500 BC, and after the First Punic War the Carthaginians extended and tightened their control there. The Carthaginian colonies were established primarily for trade but often involved, as at Carthage, the political and economic domination of the neighbouring indigenous inhabitants. Tribute was levied from the peoples the Carthaginians dominated, and this was a marked difference between Carthage and Rome, though the Romans did levy troops from the Latin allies. The Carthaginian army was made up of their Libyan subjects and mercenaries, again in contrast to Rome; despite this, these troops were generally loyal and in Spain and in Italy proved a match for the Romans. At the beginning of the First Punic War, the Carthaginians had both ships and elephants; the Romans had neither but soon had a navy that eclipsed that of the Carthaginians, who were primarily a maritime power, unlike the Romans, who had previously had no experience at sea.

As evidenced by the three treaties between Rome and Carthage (docs 4.1–3), the relationship between the two cities had been amicable, but once Rome had gained control of southern Italy, including Rhegium, the city across the straits from the island of Sicily, conflict was inevitable. The First Punic War was not sought by either side; rather, it was the result of the escalation of a situation which arose quite fortuitously. The Mamertines, a band of mercenaries from Campania, had gained control of Messana, near the north-eastern tip of Sicily, from which they plundered the north-eastern part of the island (doc. 4.7). When they were opposed by Pyrrhus and Hiero II of Syracuse, they appealed first to Carthage, which installed a garrison, and then to Rome. When the Romans expelled the Carthaginian garrison, Carthage and Hiero united against Messana, and Appius Claudius Caudex (cos. 264) was sent by Rome to raise the siege, after which Rome proceeded to besiege Syracuse. This was the first military expedition made by Rome outside of Italy, and the Romans clearly intended to challenge any further expansion on the part of Carthage and gain possession of as much of the island as possible. Concerned for her possessions there, Carthage then sent an army into Sicily, which was defeated by the Romans, who besieged and violently sacked Agrigentum, Carthage's ally. After inconclusive conflict on land, the Romans decided in 261 that they had need of a fleet to challenge Carthage's supremacy at sea. In 260 they constructed a fleet of 100 quinqueremes equipped with 'ravens', which enabled them to board enemy ships without endangering their own, with which Duilius won the battle at Mylae (docs 4.8–10). The Romans' practical genius had involved the potential rowers practising on dry land prior to taking to sea (doc. 4.8).

When events in Sicily appeared to have resulted in a stalemate, the Romans decided to invade Africa (doc. 4.11). To prevent this, the Carthaginians met them in 256 at a great naval battle off Ecnomus in eastern Sicily. Roman victory ensured that the invasion would go ahead, but after an initial success the army led by the consul M. Regulus Atilius was cut to pieces in 255 by a force of Carthaginian mercenaries led by the Spartan general Xanthippus with the help of a contingent of elephants, while, following this defeat, much of Rome's fleet was destroyed by bad weather off Camarina (doc. 4.13). Again, after a victory over the Carthaginian navy and the capture of Panormus, the Roman fleet was mostly destroyed in a storm in 253 after a raid on Africa; a further fleet was annihilated in 249 at Drepana (apparently because the consul, P. Claudius Pulcher, refused to pay attention to the warning of the sacred chickens). The Carthaginians, after recovering from the Roman invasion of Africa and the effect it had in deterring their allies from participating, sent reinforcements to Sicily in 251, while the impact the elephants had had on the Roman army in Africa led to their employment in Sicily and deterred the Romans from fixed battles, though Rome besieged the city of Lilybaeum from 251 to 240 (docs 4.14–16). With both sides nearing exhaustion, Hamilcar Barca (father of Hannibal) took command in Sicily, waging guerilla warfare on the Romans until 243, when the latter once again committed themselves to naval warfare. In 243, using contributions from wealthy citizens, they raised another fleet, which, led by C. Lutatius Catulus, defeated the Carthaginians in 241 (doc. 4.16). Hamilcar was instructed to negotiate a peace, and the Carthaginians evacuated Sicily, which thus became Rome's first overseas province (except for the kingdom of Syracuse). In reparation, Carthage agreed to pay an indemnity of 3,200 talents over a ten-year period (doc. 4.17).

Carthage took some time to recover from the defeat, especially as its mercenaries, not having been paid, were in a state of revolt. When Rome decided to extend its control over Sardinia, which provided much of Carthage's grain, Carthage in return decided to push further into Spain to secure its silver mines, with the command given to Hamilcar and, after his death in 229, to his son-in-law Hasdrubal. By 226 Hasdrubal had reached the River Ebro, which he gave an undertaking to the Romans not to cross. When in 221 Hannibal took control and took the city of Saguntum in 219 with the approval of Carthage, war was inevitable. Polybius argues that the siege of Saguntum and the crossing of the Ebro were only the beginnings of the war, not its causes, and claims that the agenda of the Barca family, the resentment of the Carthaginains over the peace terms of the First Punic War, and Carthaginain successes in Spain were in fact what provoked the Second Punic War (docs 4.22–28). Rome decided to react to the issue of Saguntum by declaring war, and after a confrontational embassy to Carthage it was agreed that it was inevitable (doc. 4.29). While Roman sources tend to ascribe the war to Hannibal's hatred of Rome and imply that it was undertaken on his own initiative, it is clear that Hannibal sought advice from Carthage over the Saguntum issue and that, at the time of Rome's declaration of war in 218, he had not yet crossed the Ebro.

With war declared, the consuls took command of their armies, P. Cornelius Scipio taking charge of the army in Spain and Ti. Sempronius Longus leaving for Africa to ensure the Carthaginians had no time to reinforce their troops in Europe. While the normal procedure would have been to take ship for Italy, Hannibal, who left his brother Hasdrubal in Spain, defied expectation by leading his army, including some 37 elephants, across the Alps. Longus was recalled and Scipio left his brother Gnaeus in charge in Spain, returning to Italy by sea to confront Hannibal, who crossed the Alps in about 15 days and began besieging cities in Cisalpine Gaul. While sources argue about the number of troops he lost *en route*, after his arrival in Italy Hannibal commanded some 40,000 infantry and 10,000 cavalry: Polybius takes issue with historians who magnify the numbers and difficulty involved (doc. 4.31). When the armies met, Hannibal was victorious at Ticinus in November 218 and again at the River Trebia against an army commanded by both consuls. Now in command of northern Italy, the consuls of

217, C. Flaminius and Gn. Servilius Geminus, were sent to check his approach. Flaminius was trapped in an ambush at Lake Trasimene in June 217 and killed in battle. Of the Roman army, 15,000 men were lost and 10,000 captured, supposedly because, as a novus homo, Flaminius had neglected the auspices (doc. 4.32). As a result of the magnitude of this disaster, the Romans appointed a dictator, Q. Fabius Maximus 'Cunctator' ('Delayer'; doc. 4.34). Hannibal then proceeded south to Campania and Samnium, while Fabius shadowed him but avoided battle, allowing him to plunder Italian cities. However, in 216, at Cannae in Apulia, Hannibal forced the Roman army, again led by two consuls, into meeting him and annihilated it: 70,000 Romans were killed and 10,000 captured, whom Rome refused to ransom (docs 4.35–37). Emergency measures at Rome now included human sacrifice in the Forum Boarium following the conviction of two Vestals for unchastity and, instead of ransoming captured soldiers, the unprecedented purchase of 8,000 slaves to serve in the army. Businessmen at Rome in 215 were also asked to make loans to the state to help supply the army in Spain (doc. 4.38, 40). Much of southern Italy, including Capua, now defected to Hannibal, though central Italy and the colonies remained loyal to Rome. Hannibal achieved little over the next three years (215–213), although he made an alliance with Philip of Macedon in 215 (doc. 4.45), but in 212 he took Tarentum, which led other Greek cities to defect. His attempt to relieve the siege of Capua by threatening Rome was unsuccessful, and he was increasingly pushed south, with Rome regaining Capua in 211 and Tarentum in 209 (docs 4.41–44).

In Spain the Scipio brothers managed successfully to prevent reinforcements reaching Hannibal, capturing Saguntum in 211, but both died in battle, while in Italy Hannibal managed to ambush the Roman army in Lucania in 208, and both consuls, M. Claudius Marcellus, who had recaptured both Syracuse and Tarentum, and T. Quinctius Crispus, were killed (docs 4.46–48). Roman successes continued in Spain, with the younger Scipio (Africanus) capturing New Carthage in 209 and defeating Hasdrubal at Baecula in 208: Scipio was only 24 years of age and a private citizen but had been given consular imperium for the purposes of this campaign. Hasdrubal slipped into Italy in 207 with the intention of joining up with Hannibal, but was defeated and killed at the Metaurus River in June (docs 4.49–50): Hannibal no longer had any hopes of reinforcements, and Scipio drove the Carthaginians from Spain in 206. Scipio, who, despite the successes of Fabius' strategy, has generally been viewed as the Roman commander primarily responsible for the defeat of Hannibal, crossed to Africa in 204 with a relatively small force on account of Fabius' opposition (doc. 4.52) and defeated the Carthaginians twice in 203. Hannibal, who had remained in southern Italy, was now recalled to Carthage and was comprehensively defeated at Zama in 202, after which he persuaded the Carthaginians to make terms (docs 4.53–55). Scipio celebrated a triumph (doc. 4.59), and Carthage retained its possessions in Africa but had to surrender its fleet, prisoners of war and elephants and undertake not to rearm or make war without Rome's permission, as well as pay 10,000 talents in indemnities (doc. 4.58). Hannibal became chief magistrate (suffete) of Carthage and attempted to reorganise the city's finances so that Carthage could pay off the war indemnity, but was accused by his opponents of intriguing with Antiochus III of Syria. In 195 he fled to Antiochus, whom he encouraged to make war against Rome, and then to Prusias of Bithynia, and took poison in 183 or 182 rather than be surrendered to Rome.

Carthage had been weakened but quickly recovered, and this, together with Hannibal's anti-Roman activities, became of concern to Rome, and a pro-war faction began to emerge there. Masinissa of Numidia, Rome's ally, continually encroached on Carthaginian territory, and when Carthage complained to Rome a fact-finding embassy, which included Cato the Elder, was sent in 153. Cato in particular was concerned at how prosperous Carthage had become (doc. 4.61), and when Carthage, unsuccessfully, declared war on Masinissa in 150, in contravention of the peace treaty, this provided the excuse for Rome to declare war in 149. While the Carthaginians were prepared to surrender 'to the faith of Rome', they were not prepared to abandon their city or settle 10 miles from the sea, and the consuls, M. Manius Manilius and L. Marcius Censorinus, were sent to Africa to begin the war. Little was achieved, and to expedite the campaign P. Cornelius Scipio Aemilianus, the son of L. Aemilus Paullus but adopted by P. Cornelius Scipio, the son of Scipio Africanus, was elected consul for 147, although he had not yet held the praetorship and was several years underage (doc. 4.62). Scipio walled off the city and harbour and finally took Carthage by storm under horrific conditions for the inhabitants, calling on its gods to abandon the Carthaginians and remove to Rome (docs 4.63–64, 3.58). The city was destroyed, its territory became the Roman province of Africa, and 50,000 people were taken into slavery. While traces of Carthaginian culture lingered in the Mediterranean (doc. 4.65), a great commercial empire and civilisation had been destroyed to quieten Roman paranoia. Following the sack of Carthage, Scipio Aemilianus celebrated his triumph, and both he and Rome moved on to yet further conquests across the Mediterranean (doc. 5.53).

The three Punic Wars were not an ideological struggle between different cultures and societies. If Rome had not won, Carthage would probably have dominated the Mediterranean. Its imperial system was no better or worse than the Roman; its culture was in significant respects materially richer and it had its own literature, which has not survived. Rome won, and the Mediterranean's history went one way rather than the other. If Hannibal had won, whether that history under Carthage would have been any worse or less successful – or even less bloodthirsty – will never be known.

Ancient sources: it can be no coincidence that it was in the period of the Punic Wars that the Romans began to write their history: there was clearly a sense that Rome's achievements were worth recording. The basic sources for the Punic Wars are Polybius and Livy, who drew on him. Other sources used by Polybius, such as Philinus and Fabius Pictor (see docs 4.4–5, 21), have not survived.

For the First Punic War, the basic narrative is Polybius Book 1. There are also the fragments of both Diodorus 22–4 and Dio 9–11. Livy's account survives only in the *Periochae* 12–19. Philinus of Acragas (Latin: Agrigentum; modern Agrigento) in Sicily, who appears to have been a contemporary witness, wrote a history, which does not survive, in Greek of the First Punic War. He favoured the Carthaginians, understandably given the Roman treatment of his own city. Polybius clearly had access to his account (see doc. 4.4). Naevius' Latin epic *The Song of the Punic War* (*Carmen belli Poenici*; doc. 4.18) on the First Punic War is mainly lost; Naevius served with the army at the close of the war.

The main surviving accounts of the Second Punic War are those of Polybius Books 3–4 and 7–15 and Livy 21–30 (Books 11–20 are lost): note Ridley 2000. Diodorus 25.15–27.18 and Appian *Spanish Wars* (*Iberike*) 1–37, *Hannibalic Wars* and *Punic Wars* (*Libyka*) 1–66 are also relevant. Various other histories no longer survive: the Romans Fabius Pictor and L. Cincius Alimentus both wrote in Greek and were contemporaries of the Second Punic War; Polybius drew on Fabius but tended to be critical of his work (see doc. 4.21). Cato, in his lost *Origines*, dealt with the Second Punic War (incidentally the first history of Rome to be written in Latin), concerning which one sentence survives (Astin 1978: 211–39). Quintus Ennius (239–169 BC), in his poetic *Annals*, covered the foundation of Rome down to his own day; Parts 7–9 of the *Annals* dealt with the Second Punic War. He stressed the role of the gods in Rome's constant expansion. Cornelius Nepos (c. 110–24 BC) also wrote biographies (which survive) of Hannibal and Hamilcar, and Plutarch of Fabius Maximus and Marcellus. Two Greek authors, Sosylus of Sparta and Silenus of Caleacte, both accompanied Hannibal on campaign (Nepos *Hannibal* 13.3) and presumably had a pro-Carthaginian viewpoint. They were stigmatised by Polybius as not historical but as retailing the gossip of the barber's shop (3.20.5; *FGrH* 176 & 177). It is a great loss, as with Philinus' history of the First Punic War, not to have these perspectives. For other references in the ancient sources to these lost accounts, see Walbank I.64–5, 333; Rich 1996: 3–14; Lancell 1998: 25–8; Daly 2002: 17–25.

For the Third Punic War, Polybius was an eye-witness to the destruction of Carthage, but unfortunately his narrative of this event is largely lost (36.1–8, 16; 38.19–22). In addition, nothing of major substance survives from Diodorus and Dio, and Livy's account survives only in the *Periochae* (47–51). Appian *Punic Wars* (*Libyka*) 74–135 is therefore a crucial account (doc. 4.63), especially as he probably used Polybius' lost eye-witness account. Cato the Elder's role is narrated by Plutarch *Cato the Elder* (*Cato Mai.*) 26–7 (doc. 4.61). On the whole, then, the sources are written from the Roman point of view: the Punic side of events is lost. While Polybius could be critical of individual Romans, his perspective is none-theless a Roman one. But his account is credible and reliable and certainly lacks the enthusiastic pro-Roman stance of Livy. For Polybius as a source for the wars: Walbank I.27–9; Lazenby 1996: 2–6; Goldsworthy 2000: 19–23.

This chapter is not a narrative history (which is detailed and complex) of the Punic Wars or a discussion of internal politics at Rome in this period.

ROME'S TREATIES WITH CARTHAGE: 508, 348, 279 BC

Polybius gives the details of three treaties between Rome and Carthage, from the year of the first consuls (509/8) and from 348 and 279 BC. These treaties, in which Rome appears to be the junior partner, safeguarded Carthaginian interests: it is clear that trading interests were crucial to them. In signing these treaties Rome indicated that its interests were land-bound in the Italian peninsula and that there was an absence of a Mediterranean focus or any conception of sea-power at Rome.

4.1 Polybius *Histories* 3.22.1–23.6: The treaty of 508 BC

This treaty of 'friendship between the Romans and the Romans' allies and between the Carthaginians and the Carthaginians' allies' is not mentioned by Livy (7.27.2; cf. Diod. 16.69.1), but its authenticity is guaranteed by Polybius' reference to the text being in an 'ancient' form of Latin and difficult to understand. The kings were expelled in 509/8, and the newly inaugurated Republic may well have been renewing an existing treaty between the kings and Carthage, or the fledgling state may have felt it needed friends. Certainly at this stage Carthage was the more powerful: Carthage regulates Roman trading within its own sphere of interest, and in turn Rome receives a guarantee that Carthage will not inter-fere with Latin towns.

22.1 The first treaty between Rome and Carthage dates to the consulship of Lucius Junius Brutus and Marcus Horatius, the first consuls instituted after the expulsion of the kings, and by whom the temple of Jupiter Capitolinus was founded. **2** This was 28 years before Xerxes' crossing to Greece. **3** I have recorded below as accurate an interpretation as I can. For the difference between the ancient language and that of the Romans today is such that only some of it can be made out by the most intelligent men through careful examination. **4** The treaty is basically as follows: 'On these terms there is to be friendship between the Romans and the Romans' allies and between the Carthaginians and the Carthaginians' allies: **5** the Romans and the Romans' allies are not to sail with long ships beyond the Fair Promontory **6** unless forced by storm or by enemies; if anyone should be forcibly carried beyond it, he is not permitted either to buy or to take anything except for the repair of the ship or for sacrifice, **7** and shall leave within five days. **8** Those coming for trade shall do no business except in the presence of a herald or official secretary. **9** The price of whatever is sold in their presence shall be owed to the seller by the guarantee of the state, if sold in Libya or Sardinia. **10** If any Roman comes to the part of Sicily which is under Carthaginian control, he shall enjoy equal rights. **11** The Carthaginians shall do no wrong to the peoples of Ardea, Antium, Laurentium, Circeii, Terracina or any other of the Latins who are (Roman) subjects; **12** as to those who are not subjects, they shall keep their hands off their cities; if they take one, they shall hand it over undamaged to the Romans. **13** They shall not build a fort in Latium. If they enter the country as enemies, they shall not spend the night in the country.'

23.1 The Fair Promontory is the one which lies in front of Carthage to the north; . . . **5** From the phrasing of the treaty they show that they consider Sardinia and Libya as their own; concerning Sicily they distinctly express themselves otherwise, mentioning in the treaty only the parts of Sicily which are under Carthaginian rule. **6** Similarly the Romans include only Latium in the treaty and do not mention the rest of Italy, because it was not under their authority.

4.2 Polybius *Histories* 3.24.1–15: The treaty of 348 BC

This treaty of friendship is not dated by Polybius but is probably the same as the one which Livy and Diodorus date to 348, and which they incorrectly regarded as the first treaty. As in the treaty of 508, the Carthaginian sphere of interest is clear. Sicily is still only partly in Carthaginian hands, while Carthaginian territory in Libya has increased. Mastia and Tarseum refer not to Spain, as sometimes thought, but to places near Carthage itself; Rome and its allies were being excluded from the western Mediterranean.

1 Later on they made another treaty, in which the Carthaginians include the Tyrians and the people of Utica. **2** It also includes Mastia and Tarseum, in addition to the Fair Promontory, as places beyond which the Romans may not either plunder or found a city. **3** The treaty is basically as follows: 'There is to be friendship on the following terms between the Romans and the Romans' allies, and the Carthaginians, Tyrians and Uticans and their allies. **4** The Romans shall neither plunder or trade nor found a city beyond the Fair Promontory, Mastia and Tarseum. **5** If the Carthaginians capture any city in Latium which is not subject to the Romans, they may keep the property and captives, but shall give up the city. **6** If any Carthaginian captures anyone who is a member of a city with a written treaty of peace with Rome, but which is not subject to them, he may not bring him into Roman harbours; if one should be brought in and a Roman take hold of him (i.e., makes him his slave), he shall be set free. **7** Likewise, the Romans shall not do this. **8** If a Roman takes water or provisions from any country which the Carthaginians control, he shall not use these provisions to wrong anyone whose people have a treaty of peace or friendship with the Carthaginians. **9** Likewise, the Carthaginians shall not do this. **10** If they do so, the person shall not punish them privately; if anyone does this, his wrongdoing shall be public. **11** No Roman shall trade or found a city in Sardinia or Libya . . . (nor remain there) except to take on provisions or repair his ship. If a storm take him there, he shall leave within five days. **12** In the part of Sicily controlled by the Carthaginians and at Carthage he may do and sell anything which is permitted to a citizen. **13** A Carthaginian in Rome may do likewise.' **14** Again in the treaty they lay stress on Libya and Sardinia as their own possessions and close all means of approach to the Romans, **15** but concerning Sicily they clearly state the opposite, mentioning the part subject to them.

4.3 Polybius *Histories* 3.25.1–5: The treaty of 279 BC

Polybius does not date this treaty, but it is clearly the one referred to by Livy (*Per.* 13; Diod. 22.7.5) as being in 279/8 BC. Each side was to support the other against Pyrrhus of Epirus, in western Greece. The Carthaginians did not want Rome making peace with Pyrrhus, who was a principal enemy of Carthage in Sicily, for he would then be free to assist the Greek cities in Sicily against Carthage (see doc. 1.74). The Carthaginians are therefore generous in this treaty, which is no longer concerned only with excluding the Romans from the Carthaginian sphere of interest but offers the use of the Carthaginian navy. Roman seapower was clearly negligible. There were later treaties in 241 and 238 BC: Polyb. 3.27–8 (doc. 4.17).

1 The Romans made another final treaty at the time of the invasion of Pyrrhus, before the Carthaginians had started the war for Sicily; **2** in this they maintain everything in the existing agreements and add the following: **3** 'If they make an alliance with Pyrrhus, both shall make it a written condition that there shall be provision that they shall go to the assistance of each other in the country which is under attack; **4** whichever has the need for help, the Carthaginians shall provide the ships for transport and attack, but each shall provide the pay for their own men. **5** The Carthaginians shall aid the Romans by sea, if necessary. But no one shall force the crews to land against their will.'

4.4 Polybius *Histories* 3.26.1–7: Historical methodology at its worst

The historian Philinus of Akragas accompanied Hannibal on campaign. Polybius rejects Philinus' treaty of 306 BC (3.26.3), perhaps a fabrication to put the Romans in the wrong, as he has seen the treaties between Rome and Carthage on bronze tablets, and Philinus' treaty is not one of them. The location of the quaestors' treasury is unknown.

1 Since the treaties were such, and preserved as they are even today on bronze tablets near the temple of Jupiter Capitolinus in the quaestors' treasury, **2** who cannot reasonably be amazed at Philinus the historian, not because he is ignorant of them – for that is not remarkable, since even in my day the oldest of the Romans and Carthaginians, and even those who seemed to be particularly conversant with public affairs, were ignorant of them – **3** but how and on what grounds did he think to write the exact opposite, that there was a treaty between Rome and Carthage through which the Romans had to keep away from the whole of Sicily and the Carthaginians from the whole of Italy, **4** and that the Romans broke the treaty and their oath when they made their first crossing to Sicily? There is not and never has been such a document at all. **5** But he states this in his second book quite explicitly . . . **6** Of course, if anyone wants to criticise the Romans for their crossing to Sicily, because they accepted the Mamertines into their friendship and afterwards helped them in their need when they had broken their treaty not only with Messana but also with Rhegium, his disapproval would be only reasonable. **7** But if anyone considers that they made their crossing in violation of the treaty and their oath, he is clearly ignorant of the truth.

THE FIRST PUNIC WAR: SICILY

In doc. 4.4, Polybius indicates that the Roman crossing into Sicily to help the Mamertines (doc. 4.7) caused the First Punic War (264–241 BC). This was the first Roman military expedition outside Italy and it was to have enormous implications. The treaties between Rome and Carthage proved inadequate to deal with the situation. The Romans had no real pretext for interfering in Sicily, except perhaps for fears that Carthage might then use an extended control of Sicily to acquire a position in Italy. Once the Romans invaded, they quickly made up their mind to conquer the whole island, and in 23 years succeeded in securing control of it. The main source for the First Punic War is the Greek historian Polybius; the relevant books of Livy are lost.

4.5 Polybius *Histories* 1.14.1–6: Polybius' methodology

Polybius here sets out his historical methodology, imputing bias to the Greek historian Philinus and the Latin Fabius Pictor as being pro-Carthaginian and pro-Roman respectively; while he drew on other sources, these were the most important. Fabius Pictor was the first Roman historian and wrote in Greek, recording a history of Rome from its beginnings down to his own time. Elsewhere Polybius makes clear why the Punic Wars are an attractive topic for historical writing: he can speak to and question those who participated in the events, and he himself lived through some of them (4.2.2, 12.4c.2–5, 12.25e).

1 I have been persuaded to concentrate on this war by a factor equally important to those already mentioned, namely that the historians considered to be the greatest authorities on it, Philinus and Fabius (Pictor), have failed in my view to record the truth as they should have done. **2** I do not want to imply that these men have intentionally lied, judging from their lives and principles; but they do seem to me to have been something in the position of people in love. **3** For, through his convictions and partisan stance, Philinus considers that the Carthaginians acted wisely, well and courageously in every case, and the Romans in the opposite way, while Fabius takes a completely different view. **4** In other spheres of life one should perhaps not rule out such favouritism, for a good man ought to love his friends and his country and share his friends' hatred of their enemies and their love of their friends; **5** but, when a person takes on the role of a historian, he has to forget everything of this sort and often speak well of his enemies and award them the highest praises when their actions demand this, while criticising and severely censuring his closest friends, should their errors of conduct demand this. **6** For, just as a living creature deprived of its eyes is totally incapacitated, so, when history is deprived of truth, nothing is left but an unprofitable tale.

4.6 Polybius *Histories* 6.51.1–8, 52.1–6, 56.1–4: Rome versus Carthage

This passage is from Polybius' discussion of the Roman constitution in Book 6. The 'kings' of Carthage were two annual officials known as suffetes; the Carthaginian senate (gerontion) had 300 members. Aristotle (*Politics* 1273a35–9) also states that at Carthage the highest offices were for sale, resulting in wealth being of more account than merit. 'Although they were totally defeated' (**51.8**) refers to Cannae in 216 BC.

51.1 The Carthaginian constitution appears to me to have been originally well designed in its general features. **2** For there were kings, and the gerontion had aristocratic powers, while the people were supreme in their own sphere; the arrangement of the whole system was similar to that of the Romans and Spartans. **3** But at this time, when the Hannibalic war commenced, that of the Carthaginians was worse and that of the Romans better . . . **5** For, just as Carthage had previously been stronger and more prosperous than Rome, by the same degree Carthage had now begun to decline and Rome was at its peak in its system of government. **6** As a result the people in Carthage had already taken over most of the power of decision-making, while at Rome the senate still possessed this. **7** It was for this reason, with the people making decisions on one side and the most distinguished men on the other, that the Romans' deliberations on public affairs were superior. **8** And, although they were totally defeated, they were finally victorious over the Carthaginians in the war through their wise decision-making.

52.1 To pass to the details, such as the conduct of war to start with, the Carthaginians are superior at sea, as is natural, both in training and in equipment, because from olden times this practice has been their national pastime and they have had much more to do with the sea than any other people, **2** while the Romans are much better exponents of warfare on land than the Carthaginians. **3** For the Romans devote themselves to this entirely, while the Carthaginians completely neglect their infantry, though they do pay some small attention to their cavalry. **4** The reason for this is that they employ foreign and mercenary troops, while the Romans use natives and citizens. **5** So in this respect, too, it must be admitted that Rome's constitution is better than that of Carthage; for Carthage has always to place her hopes of freedom on the valour of mercenaries, but the Romans on their own courage and the support of their allies. **6** As a result, if the Romans are defeated at the outset, they always retrieve their defeat, but the Carthaginians the opposite . . .

56.1 The customs and laws regarding money-making are also better at Rome than at Carthage, **2** for at Carthage nothing is disgraceful which leads to profit, while at Rome nothing is more disgraceful than accepting bribes and making dishonest gains; **3** the Romans' approval of money-making in an honest way is no stronger than their disapproval of profit by forbidden means. **4** Proof of this is that at Carthage they win magistracies by open bribery, but at Rome the penalty for this is death.

4.7 Polybius *Histories* 1.10.1–11.5: The Mamertines

11.2: Polybius writes of the 'gains' that would accrue to the Romans; by this he means the booty and plunder, including (as it turned out) profits from the sale of the 25,000 inhabitants of Agrigentum as slaves and the ransoming or enslavement of the 27,000 people of Panormus (see doc. 6.9). The wealthier citizens who voted for war in the comitia centuriata (to help the Mamertines, not as a vote of war against Carthage) clearly hoped to gain from the enterprise.

10.1 The Mamertines, who had previously lost their support from Rhegium, as I stated above, had now suffered a total defeat on their home territory for the reasons I have just mentioned, and some of them had recourse to the Carthaginians, offering to put themselves and the citadel under their protection, **2** while others sent an embassy to Rome, offering to hand over the city and begging them as a people of the same race to give them assistance. **3** The Romans for a long time were undecided because of the obvious illogicality of giving them assistance. **4** Only a short while earlier, the Mamertines' fellow citizens had suffered the ultimate penalty for breaking their treaty with the people of Rhegium, and now to try to help the Mamertines, who had done exactly the same not only at Messana but at Rhegium as well, was an injustice which it was hard to excuse.

5 The Romans were not unaware of this, but they saw that the Carthaginians had subjugated not only Libya but also large parts of Spain, and that they possessed all the islands in the Sardinian and Tyrrhenian Seas, **6** and were worried that, if they also gained control of Sicily, they might be very difficult and formidable neighbours, encircling them on every side and threatening every part of Italy. **7** It seemed evident that they would soon be in control of Sicily unless the Mamertines received assistance. For, once Messana was in their hands, **8** they would shortly conquer Syracuse, as they were masters of nearly all the rest of Sicily. **9** As the Romans foresaw this and considered it necessary not to abandon Messana and allow the Carthaginians, as it were, to build a bridge for crossing to Italy, they debated the question for a considerable time, **11.1** and the senate even in the end did not authorise the proposal for the reasons just stated. They considered that the illogicality of helping the Mamertines was equally balanced by the advantages of assisting them. **2** The people, however, were worn out by recent wars and in need of all kinds of restorative and, when the generals pointed out that the war would be for the general good for the reasons just stated and the obvious and enormous gains which each of them would privately incur, resolved to send assistance. **3** When the measure had been authorised by the people, they appointed one of the consuls, Appius Claudius, as commander and ordered him to cross with assistance to Messana. **4** The Mamertines threw out the Carthaginian general who already held the citadel, partly by threats and partly by deception; they welcomed Appius and placed the city in his hands. **5** The Carthaginians crucified their general, thinking that he lacked both judgement and courage in abandoning the citadel.

4.8 Polybius *Histories* 1.20.9–21.3: A Roman fleet

Appius Claudius sent a small initial force under C. Claudius to Messana and then moved his two consular legions using ships from Rhegium and other cities. Rome was unprepared for naval warfare, but in 261 decided to construct a fleet. Hiero, tyrant of Syracuse, agreed to aid the Carthaginians. Appius Claudius defeated both Hiero and the Carthaginian commander Hanno. Hiero came over to the Roman side, and most cities revolted from Syracuse and Carthage and joined Rome. But the war against Hanno and the Carthaginians was to go on until 241 BC, as Rome now aimed at the expulsion of the Carthaginians from Sicily.

20.9 Observing how the war was dragging on, the Romans then for the first time undertook the building of ships, 100 quinqueremes and 20 triremes. **10** As the shipwrights were entirely inexperienced in building quinqueremes, since none of the communities of Italy used such ships at that time, the enterprise caused them much difficulty. **11** From this, anyone might see the spirited and reckless nature of the Romans' determination. **12** For it was not that they had reasonable resources for it, but no resources at all, nor had they ever given any thought to the sea, but once they first had the idea they undertook it so boldly that, before they had any experience at all of the matter, they at once undertook a naval battle against the Carthaginians, who had held undisputed command of the sea from their ancestors' time. **13** Evidence for the truth of what I am saying and for their unbelievable daring is this: that when they first undertook to send their forces across to Messana, they not only had not a single decked ship, but no warship at all, not even a single boat, **14** but they borrowed pen-teconters and triremes from the Tarentines and Locrians, and also from the Eleans and Neapolitans, and transported their troops across in them at considerable risk. **15** On this occasion the Carthaginians put to sea to attack them as they were crossing the straits, and one of the decked ships (quinqueremes) advanced too far in its eager-ness and as a result ran aground, falling into the Romans' hands. They then used this as a model, constructing their whole fleet along these lines, **16** so that, had this not happened, it is clear that they would in the end have been prevented from carrying out their plan from lack of experience. **21.1** Thereupon, those who were charged with constructing the fleet were busy with preparation of the ships, while those who collected the crews were teaching them to row on land in the following way. **2** Seating the men on their benches on dry land, in the same order as on their seats on the ships themselves, and stationing the boatswain in the middle, they got them all used to falling back together, bringing their hands back, and again to bending forward, pushing out their hands, and to beginning and stopping these movements at the boatswain's orders. **3** When they had been trained, they launched the ships as soon as they were finished and, after practising for a short time at sea, sailed along the coast of Italy as their general had commanded.

4.9 Polybius *Histories* 1.22.1–11: The 'raven'

Gnaeus Cornelius Scipio Asina (cos. 260 BC) went from Messana with 17 ships to Lipara after receiving an offer to betray the island. When the Carthaginians trapped Scipio's fleet in the harbour he surrendered (Polyb. 1.21.8). Despite receiving the nickname 'Asina' ('donkey'), he went on to another consulship in 254 BC. As the battle of Mylae was to prove (doc. 4.10), the Carthaginians did not know at this stage how to deal with the raven (corvus, plural: corvi), which gave the Romans the advantage of boarding enemy ships without damaging their own.

1 After this the Romans approached the Sicilian coastline and, when they learnt of the disaster that had happened to Gnaeus, immediately sent a message to Gaius Duilius (cos. 260 BC), the commander of the land force, and awaited his arrival, **2** while at the same time, hearing that the enemy's fleet was not far away, began to prepare to fight at sea. **3** As their ships were poorly constructed and hard to manoeu-vre, someone suggested to them the machines which later came to be called 'ravens' as an aid in battle. Their construction was as follows: **4** on the prow stood a round pole 4 fathoms in length and in width 3 palms in diameter. **5** This had a pulley at the top and round it was put a gangway with cross planks nailed to it, 4 feet in width and 6 fathoms in length. **6** In the gangway was an oblong hole, and it went round the pole at a distance of 2 fathoms from its near end. The gangway also had a railing on each of its long sides to the height of a knee. **7** At its end was fastened a piece of iron like a pestle with a point on it with a ring at the other end, so that the whole thing resembled machines for making bread. **8** To this ring was tied a rope with which, when they rammed other ships, they raised the ravens by using the pulley on the pole and let them down on the deck of the enemy ship, sometimes on the prow and sometimes bringing them round when the ships collided side on. **9** Once the ravens were fixed in the planks of the deck, connecting the ships together, if they were broadside on, they boarded from all directions, but if on the prow they attacked by passing over the raven itself two abreast; **10** the leaders covered the front by holding up their shields, and those who followed secured the two flanks by resting the rims of their shields on the top of the railing. **11** So, after adopting this device, they looked out for the opportunity to fight at sea.

4.10 *ILS* 65: Gaius Duilius, consul 260 BC

In 260, with the Roman ships equipped with the ravens, Duilius gave command of the army to the military tribunes and took control of the fleet (Scipio had been taken prisoner). With the enemy ravaging Mylae on the north coast of Sicily, Duilius sailed against the Carthaginians, commanded by Hannibal (not *the* Hannibal of the Second Punic War). The Romans boarded the Carthaginian ships, and it became 'like a land battle' (1.23.7). The Carthaginians surrendered or were slaughtered; the Romans had won their first naval battle, but the bulk of the Carthaginian fleet was still intact. Duilius then raised the siege of Segesta and captured Macela.

. . . and the Segestaeans . . . he delivered from siege; and all the Carthaginian legions and their mighty leader (Hamilcar) after nine days fled their camp in broad daylight; and he took their town Macela **5** by storm. And, in the same command as consul, he had a success with ships at sea, the first to do so, and he was the first to equip and train naval crews and fleets; and with these ships he defeated in battle on the high seas the Punic fleets and likewise all the mightiest forces of the Carthaginians in the presence of Hannibal **10** their commander. And, by force, he captured ships with their crews: namely, one septireme and 30 quinqueremes and triremes, and sank 13. Captured gold: 3,600 . . . pieces. Captured silver, together with booty: 100,000 . . . pieces. **15** Total sum taken in Roman money 2,100,000 . . . He was also the first to give the people booty from a naval battle and the first to lead free-born Carthaginians in triumph . . .

4.11 Polybius *Histories* 1.26.1–3: The Romans invade Africa

The Romans proved unable to press home an advantage in Sicily and resolved to defeat the Carthaginians on their home territory, while the Carthaginians were determined to stop the Romans getting to Africa. A great naval battle was fought at Ecnomus off eastern Sicily in 256, with the Romans, again using the ravens, victorious. This meant that the invasion, the first of the Roman invasions of Carthaginian Africa, could go ahead.

1 The intention of the Romans was to sail to Libya and divert the war there, so that the Carthaginians might find not Sicily, but themselves and their country in danger. **2** The Carthaginians were resolving on doing exactly the opposite, for, knowing that Libya was easily accessible and that all the people in the country would be easily overcome by anyone who once invaded it, they were not able to allow this, **3** but were eager to run the risk of fighting a naval battle.

4.12 Livy *History of Rome* F10: An unusual problem in Africa

The incident of the giant serpent is a curious story which does not appear in Polybius. M. Atilius Regulus, suffect-consul, was sent to Africa in 256 (L. Manlius Vulso was the other consul). After initial success in laying waste to Carthaginian territory, Vulso was recalled to Rome, leaving Regulus with 40 ships, 15,000 infantry and 500 cavalry to continue the campaign into 255.

Let me also mention the serpent described equally carefully and elegantly by Titus Livius. For he states that, in Africa at the Bagradas River, there was a snake of such size that it prevented the army of Atilius Regulus from using the river; many of the soldiers were seized in its huge mouth and large numbers of them crushed by the coils of its tail, nor could it be pierced by weapons hurled at it, but, finally, when it was attacked on all sides by missiles from catapults it collapsed under the frequent, heavy blows from the stones and seemed to everyone, both allied troops and legions, to be more frightful than Carthage itself. With the waters stained with its blood and the area around polluted with the noxious smell of its dead body, it drove the Roman camp away from there. He also says that the beast's skin, which measured 120 feet, was sent to Rome.

4.13 Appian *The Punic Wars* 1.3–4: A Spartan general

Polybius gives a different account of this battle in 255 BC, stressing the role of the elephants which trampled a large part of the Roman army. An important part was also played by the superior generalship of the Spartan Xanthippus and his outflanking tactics; Appian's references to 'heat, thirst and fatigue' are also credible. Regulus was captured and, later in 250, sent on an embassy to Rome, keeping his word that he would return to Carthage whatever the outcome. The Romans had not expected defeat in Africa and, after manning a fleet in 255 BC, defeated the Carthaginian navy, captured 114 ships and rescued the Romans still in Libya, but in Sicily a huge storm off Camarina left only 80 Roman ships out of 364 undamaged.

3 Events began with the Sicilian war when the Romans attacked Libya with 350 ships, took several towns, and left in command Atilius Regulus (256 BC), who captured another 200 towns, which handed themselves over to him through hatred of the Carthaginians, and advanced, ravaging the countryside. The Carthaginians requested a general from the Spartans, thinking that their misfortunes were due to lack of a leader. They sent them Xanthippus, and Atilius, camped beside a lake in the season of burning heat, marched round it against the enemy, his soldiers suffering severely from the weight of their weapons, heat, thirst and fatigue, and under attack from missiles from the heights above them. As he approached towards evening, a river separated them, and he immediately crossed the river in order to terrify Xanthippus, but Xanthippus drew up his forces and sent them from his camp, hoping to overcome an enemy which was exhausted and in such distress and thinking that night would be on the side of the conquerors. Xanthippus was not disappointed in his hope; for, of the 30,000 men led by Atilius, only a few with difficulty escaped to the city of Aspis, while all the rest were killed or taken prisoner. Among the prisoners was the general Atilius, the consul.

4 Not long afterwards (250 BC), the Carthaginians, tired of fighting, sent Regulus together with their own ambassadors to Rome to obtain peace for them or return without it; Atilius Regulus secretly urged the Roman magistrates to continue the war with all their strength and returned to certain torture, for the Carthaginians killed him by shutting him up in a cage full of spikes. Xanthippus' success was the beginning of his misfortunes; the Carthaginians, in order that the credit for the victory might not seem due to the Spartans, pretended to honour him with numerous gifts and escorted him with galleys to Sparta, but instructed the captains to throw him overboard with his Spartan companions. In this way he paid the penalty for his success.

4.14 Polybius *Histories* 1.39.10–12: Beware of elephants

After the great success of the elephants in 255, the Carthaginians took them to Sicily: Hasdrubal, following the destruction of the Roman fleet, crossed to Lilybaeum with 140 beasts (Polyb. 1.38.2). The Romans built a new fleet of about 200 ships and in 254 successfully took Panormus, modern Palermo, the most important Carthaginian possession in Sicily (1.38.7–10), confining the Carthaginians to a small part of western Sicily.

10 The Carthaginians now possessed the secure control of the sea as the Romans had withdrawn from it, and had great hopes of their land forces. **11** This was not unreasonable; for the Romans, when the report got round about the battle in Libya of how the beasts had broken their ranks and killed most of their men, **12** were so terrified of the elephants for the next two years following this period that, even though they were often drawn up in the district of Lilybaeum or that of Selinus 5 or 6 stades from their enemy, they were never bold enough to begin a battle and would never come down to level ground at all, through fear of the charge of the elephants.

4.15 Appian *Of Sicily and the Other Islands* F1: Financial difficulties, 252 BC

By 252 the Romans controlled most of Sicily and in 256 and 253 had invaded Africa.

The Romans and Carthaginians were both at a loss for money, and the Romans were no longer able to build ships, being exhausted by taxes, though they raised an infantry force and sent it to Libya and Sicily year after year, while the Carthaginians sent an embassy to Ptolemy, son of Lagus, king of Egypt, asking to borrow 2,000 talents. He was on friendly terms with both Romans and Carthaginians and tried to reconcile them. Being unable to do so, he said that one should help friends against enemies, but not against friends.

THE LAST YEARS

By 252–251 BC, both sides were exhausted. In 250 Hasdrubal, commander of the Carthaginian forces, attacked Panormus with his elephants, but Rome held the city (Polyb. 1.40). The Romans then besieged Lilybaeum, a Carthaginian stronghold, which withstood the siege from 251 to 240 (holding out beyond the treaty of 241). The Romans suffered their only naval defeat in the First Punic War, under the consul for 249 BC, P. Claudius Pulcher. He decided to attack the Carthaginian fleet at Drepana, setting out at night in an (unsuccessful) attempt to avoid detection. Although the forces were evenly balanced at first, the Carthaginians gained the upper hand: 30 Roman ships, including that of Claudius, escaped; 93 were captured. Back at Rome, Claudius was fined: several sources, but not Polybius, record that the sacred chickens had refused to eat before the battle, a bad omen, so Claudius had them thrown into the sea (doc. 3.53). The other consul, L. Junius Pullus, took charge of the fleet, which was then destroyed by a storm. The Romans now abandoned naval warfare for several years, instead putting their hopes in the siege at Lilybaeum and land warfare.

4.16 Polybius *Histories* 1.58.9–59.8: The final gamble, 243/2 BC

Under their overall commander, Hamilcar, the Carthaginians had from 249 BC kept the Romans at bay, effectively destroying their naval power at the battle of Drepana in 249 and maintaining control of both Drepana and Lilybaeum despite the Roman sieges. In 243 BC the Romans decided to return to naval warfare and built another fleet.

58.9 The Romans and the Carthaginians were worn out with the hard work of coping with a succession of crises and at length began to despair, with their strength paralysed and drained by taxes and expenses continuing over many years. **59.1** Nevertheless, the Romans, as if fighting for their lives, although for nearly five years they had entirely withdrawn from naval operations because of the disasters they had suffered, and because of their belief that they could win the war through their land forces alone, **2** when they saw that their work was not progressing as they had calculated, especially on account of the audacity of the Carthaginian general (Hamilcar), decided for the third time to place their hopes on naval forces, **3** considering that this plan, if they could strike an opportune blow, was the only way of putting a successful end to the war. And this they finally achieved. **4** On the first occasion they had withdrawn from the sea, yielding to the blows of fortune; on the second it was because of their defeat at the battle of Drepana; **5** now they made their third attempt (at Aegusa), through which they won a victory and shut off the Carthaginian legions at Eryx from their supply-line by sea, making a final end to the whole war. **6** It was a struggle for existence rather than an attack. There was no money in the treasury for the purpose; yet through the patriotism and generosity of the leading citizens funds were found to carry it out. **7** By ones, twos and threes, according to their means, they undertook to provide a fully equipped quinquereme, on the understanding that they would be repaid if all went well. **8** In this way 200 quinqueremes were swiftly fitted out, all of them constructed on the model of the 'Rhodian' ship. The Romans then appointed Gaius Lutatius (Catulus) as commander and sent him out at the beginning of the summer.

ROMAN SUCCESS

In 23 years, Rome had passed from having no navy to defeating the Mediterranean's greatest maritime people. This was partially because Rome had greater resources, rebuilding fleets wrecked by storm, though with great financial hardship (doc. 4.16). It also had more manpower because of her allies, who served both in the army and in the fleet as naval allies (*socii navales*). Roman losses were huge: the census figures for before the war were 292,234 adult males, as against 241,212 in 247/6 BC. Naval losses in particular were enormous. All of Sicily except for Hiero's Syracuse now came under Roman administration in 241.

4.17 The peace treaty of 241 BC

In 241, C. Lutatius Catulus (cos. 242) besieged Drepana, as the Carthaginian fleet had returned to Carthage. Hearing of his activities, the fleet went back to Sicily, and battle was joined off Lilybaeum at the Aegates islands. Fifty Carthaginian ships were sunk and 70 captured. The war in Sicily was over. All of Sicily was now under the control of Rome, which had acquired its first overseas territory.

(i) Polybius Histories *1.61.8–63.3*

1.61.8 The Roman general (Lutatius) sailed away to Lilybaeum and the legions and occupied himself with the arrangements for the captured ships and men – a tremendous task, as the prisoners captured alive in the engagement were not many fewer than 10,000. **62.1** After this unexpected defeat, the Carthaginians were still prepared to continue the war under the influence of their passions and ambition but were at a loss with regard to reasoned argument. **2** They were no longer able to provision their forces in Sicily with the enemy in control of the sea; and if they gave these up and, as it were, became their betrayers, they had no other men or leaders whom they could use to continue the war. **3** For this reason they quickly sent to (Hamilcar) Barca, giving him full powers. He acted like an extremely good and sensible leader. **4** While there had been some reasonable hope in events, he had omitted nothing, however reckless or dangerous, but put to the test every hope of success in war, if ever any general did. **5** But, with fortunes reversed, and no reasonable hope left of saving the troops under his command, he showed his intelligence and good sense in yielding to events and sending envoys to negotiate for peace terms. **6** For a general ought to be able to tell both when he is victorious **7** and when defeated. Lutatius gladly accepted the proposals, as he was aware that his side was already worn out and exhausted by the war, and he succeeded in putting an end to the conflict in a treaty in which the terms were basically as follows: **8** 'On the following terms there shall be friendship between the Carthaginians and Romans, if approved by the Roman people. The Carthaginians are to withdraw from the whole of Sicily and not make war on Hiero or bear arms against the Syracusans or the Syracusans' allies. **9** The Carthaginians are to hand over to the Romans all prisoners without ransom. The Carthaginians shall pay the Romans over 20 years 2,200 Euboic talents.' **63.1** When these conditions were referred to Rome, the people did not accept the treaty but sent ten men to investigate matters. **2** On their arrival, they made no great changes to the conditions but imposed slightly more severe terms on the Carthaginians. **3** They reduced the term of payment by half and added 1,000 talents to the sum, and demanded that the Carthaginians withdraw from all the islands lying between Italy and Sicily.

4 This was how the war between Romans and Carthaginians over Sicily ended and these were the peace terms, the war having lasted for 24 years continuously, **5** which is the longest, most continuous and greatest of any I have ever heard of. In it, apart from the rest of the battles and equipment, on one occasion, as I said earlier on, more that 500 quinqueremes in total, and on another close to 700, were engaged in conflict with each other. **6** The Romans also lost about 700 quinqueremes in this war, including those destroyed in shipwrecks, and the Carthaginians about 500.

(ii) Polybius Histories *3.27.1–10*

3.27.1 At the end of the war for Sicily, they made another treaty, with the following conditions: **2** 'The Carthaginians are to withdraw from all the islands which lie between Italy and Sicily. **3** The allies of each are to be secure from attack by the other. **4** Neither is allowed to impose contributions, construct public buildings, or enlist soldiers in the others' territory, nor to make alliances with the allies of the other. **5** The Carthaginians are to pay 2,200 talents within ten years and 1,000 immediately. **6** The Carthaginians are to hand over to the Romans all prisoners without ransom.' **7** Later, at the end of the Libyan war (238 BC), when the Romans had passed a decree declaring war on the Carthaginians, they added an additional clause to the treaty: **8** 'The Carthaginians are to withdraw from Sardinia and pay another 1,200 talents', as I said above. **9** In addition to these, the last agreement was made with Hasdrubal in Spain (226 BC) 'That the Carthaginians are not to cross the river Ebro in arms.' **10** These were the official contracts between Romans and Carthaginians from the beginning up to the time of Hannibal.

4.18 Naevius *The Song of the Punic War*: The first national epic

Naevius was a Roman citizen, born c. 270 BC, who served in the First Punic War and began to produce plays in Rome in 235. His *Song of the Punic War* greatly influenced Ennius and Vergil. **4.31**: Little is known of Regulus' activities in Malta; **6.39**: the reference is perhaps to Hamilcar on Mount Eryx, between Panormus and Drepana, a scene of tussles between the two sides; **7.41–43** refers to the provisional peace of 241 arranged between C. Lutatius Catulus and Hamilcar.

4.31–2   The Roman crosses over to Malta, an island undamaged;
He burns, ravages, lays waste, and puts an end to the enemy's occupation.

6.39   Proudly and disdainfully he wears out the legions.

7.41–3   This also they agree, that their fortifications shall be such
As to conciliate Lutatius; while he agrees
To return the numerous prisoners held as hostages.

THE SECOND PUNIC WAR

Polybius notes that the historians of the Second Punic War provide two reasons for its outbreak (the Carthaginian siege of Saguntum and the crossing of the Ebro, the latter breaking the treaty of 226 BC). He argues that, while these were the beginnings of the war, they were not its causes, and he differentiates between origins and initial incidents, much as Thucydides (1.23.4–6) saw that the pretexts for the Spartans declaring war on the Athenians were not the 'truest cause'.

4.19 Polybius *Histories* 2.24.2–17: Roman manpower, 225 BC

The figures given by Polybius here may derive from Fabius Pictor's account, which probably came from official Roman lists provided by the various communities of Italy; the figures add up to 768,300. The context is a survey of Italian manpower carried out in 225 BC to ascertain available forces when Italy was threatened by a Gallic invasion.

1 To make it clear from the facts how great were the resources that Hannibal dared to attack, and how great was the Romans' empire which he boldly confronted, and on which he so nearly achieved his aim of inflicting major disasters, **2** I must state what resources and number of troops were available to them at that time. **3** Both of the consuls commanded four legions of Roman citizens, each consisting of 5,200 infantry and 300 cavalry. **4** The allied troops in each consular army totalled 30,000 infantry and 2,000 cavalry. **5** The Sabines and Etruscans, who had temporarily come to Rome's assistance, had 4,000 cavalry and more than 50,000 infantry. **6** The Romans massed these troops and stationed them on the border of Etruria, under the command of a praetor. **7** The Umbrians and Sarsinates, who lived in the Apennines, totalled around 20,000, and there were 20,000 Veneti and Cenomani . . . **9** In Rome itself there was a reserve force, prepared for all contingencies of war, of 20,000 Roman infantry and 1,500 cavalry and 30,000 allied infantry and 2,000 cavalry. **10** The lists of men able to fight that were sent back were as follows: Latins, 80,000 infantry and 5,000 cavalry; Samnites, 70,000 infantry and 7,000 cavalry; **11** Iapygians and Messapians, 50,000 infantry and 16,000 cavalry; **12** Lucanians, 30,000 infantry and 3,000 cavalry; Marsi, Marrucini, Frentani and Vestini, 20,000 infantry and 4,000 cavalry. **13** In Sicily and Tarentum there were two reserve legions, each consisting of about 4,200 infantry and 200 cavalry. **14** The total for Romans and Campanians came to 250,000 infantry and 23,000 cavalry; . . . **16** so the total number of Romans and allies able to bear arms was more than 700,000 infantry and 70,000 cavalry, **17** while Hannibal invaded Italy with fewer than 20,000 men.

4.20 Livy *History of Rome* 22.36.1–4: Roman manpower in 217 BC

Livy was clearly frustrated in his attempt to ascertain the precise numbers of combatants following the battle of Trasimene in 217. In 218 there were six legions, and five more were raised before Trasimene in 217, bringing the total to 11 (some 55,000 men). The loss of two legions at Trasimene was immediately made up, and by Cannae there were 13 legions in service. Rome could field 14 legions even after Cannae, and the number peaked in 212 and 211 with 25 legions in the field: the numerical strength of individual legions varied, from 4,500 to 5,500 men.

1 The armies were also increased; the size of the forces added to the infantry and to the cavalry I should hardly venture to say for certain, so greatly do authors differ on both the number and type of forces. **2** Some say 10,000 new troops were conscripted as replacements, others that four new legions were raised so that they took the field with eight; **3** some say that the numbers of infantry and cavalry in the legions were increased by 1,000 infantry and 100 cavalry, **4** so that each was composed of 5,000 infantry and 300 cavalry, and that the allies gave double the number of cavalry but the same number of infantry and that at the time of the battle of Cannae there were 87,200 men under arms.

4.21 Polybius *Histories* 3.6.1–8, 9.6–10.6: The causes of the Second Punic War

Polybius argues that Carthage was justified in going to war because of its loss of Sardinia, but that Rome could put Hannibal in the wrong because he had attacked Saguntum. He probably does not place enough stress on disagreements both at Carthage and at Rome about foreign policy and Hanno's opposition to Hannibal (doc. 4.29). Polybius' account is, however, largely valid: there was genuine anger at Carthage over the loss of their possessions. Rome decided to make the issue of Saguntum a reason for war. **3.9.9**: 'civil disturbances' refers to the mercenaries' revolt at Carthage (237–229 BC).

6.1 Some of those who have written the history of Hannibal and his times, as they wanted to show us the causes that led to this war between Rome and Carthage, put forward as its first cause the Carthaginians' siege of Saguntum **2** and as its second their crossing of the river called by the locals the Iber (Ebro), contrary to treaty. **3** I could agree that these might be called the beginnings of the war, but I can by no means concede that they were its causes. **4** You could just as well say that Alexander's crossing to Asia was the cause of his war against Persia and Antiochus' landing at Demetrias the cause of his against the Romans, neither of which is either plausible or true . . .

9.6 But to return to the war between Rome and Carthage, from which this digression has taken us, we must consider its first cause as being the anger of Hamilcar, surnamed Barca, the father of Hannibal. **7** His spirit was unconquered by the war for Sicily, since he thought that he had kept the army at Eryx under his command with its energies unimpaired, and that he had made peace only through force of circumstances after the defeat of the Carthaginians in the naval battle (at the Aegates islands), and he maintained his resolve, watching for a chance to strike. **8** If the mercenaries' mutiny against the Carthaginians had not occurred, he would soon have found another opportunity and resources, as far as was in his power. **9** He was, however, fully occupied with these civil disturbances which took all his attention. **10.1** After the Carthaginians had put down this mutiny, the Romans declared war against them, and the Carthaginians were at first willing to negotiate on all points, thinking that, as right was on their side, they would win . . . **3** But, as the Romans took no notice, they yielded to circumstances. Though deeply resentful, they were powerless to prevent it, and withdrew from Sardinia as well as agreeing to pay another 1,200 talents in addition to the previous sum, to avoid being forced into another war at that time. **4** This, then, should be taken to be the second and most important cause of the war which followed.

5 Hamilcar added the anger felt by his fellow citizens at this to his own rage and, as soon as he had put down the mutiny of the mercenaries and secured the safety of his country, at once threw all his resolution into the conquest of Spain, with the design of using these resources for the war against the Romans. **6** The success of the Carthaginian project in Spain must be considered as the third cause of the war, for this additional strength caused them to enter into it with confidence.

HANNIBAL

Hamilcar spent nine years in Spain (237–229) and on his death in 229 was succeeded by his son-in-law Hasdrubal; on Hasdrubal's assassination in 221 BC, Hannibal succeeded as Carthaginian commander of military operations in Spain. The Carthaginians acquired great wealth, not just from war but, like the Romans after them, from exploiting the Spanish silver mines. They now needed to pay back the indemnity to Rome and to make up for the financial loss of western Sicily and Sardinia. In 226 BC, the peace treaty of 241 was renewed by Hasdrubal, except that it now took Spain into consideration, indicating a Roman concern with Carthaginian expansion there (docs 4.27–28). In his examination of the issues leading to the outbreak of the war, Polybius does not see Hannibal as a cause, preferring to look further back, to Hamilcar and 241 BC. But Hannibal must be taken into account: he attacked Saguntum, with the blessing of Carthage, despite the Roman request not to do so; without him, there might never have been a Second Punic War.

4.22 Livy *History of Rome* 21.1.3–5: Hannibal's hatred of Rome

Livy's comment on the hatred felt by the Carthaginians ties in with Polybius' first and second causes of the war. Polybius 3.11.5–7 tells the same story of Hannibal's oath, which lends credibility to it. He has the sacrifice made to Zeus, but the actual Carthaginian deity involved will have been Ba'al Shaman, Zeus' equivalent. The oath was religious in nature, and binding.

3 The hatred, too, with which they fought was almost greater than their strength, for the Romans were angry that the conquered should of their own accord be attacking their conquerors, while the Carthaginians believed that the conquered had been treated with arrogance and greed. **4** There is also a story that, when Hannibal was about nine years old, in a childish way he coaxed his father Hamilcar, who had finished the African war and was sacrificing prior to leading the army to Spain, to take him with him. Hamilcar led the boy to the altar and made him swear an oath, touching the offerings, that as soon as he could he would be the enemy of the Roman people. **5** The loss of Sicily and Sardinia tormented Hamilcar's proud spirit; for he believed that Sicily had been surrendered in premature despair and that Sardinia had been wrongly snatched by the Romans during the African revolt with an indemnity imposed on them to make matters worse.

4.23 Polybius *Histories* 3.14.9–15.13: Hannibal and Saguntum, 220/19 BC

3.15.7: Hannibal is referring to the civil dissension that had broken out in 221 BC at Saguntum, in which some of the Saguntines had appealed to Rome against another faction.

Roman ambassadors to Saguntum had organised the execution of the leaders of the other, pro-Carthaginian group. Hannibal made this a ground of complaint against Rome and, to their demand that he keep his hands off the city, made no promises. The Roman envoys saw war as inevitable and sailed to Carthage. The siege of Saguntum began in April or May of 219 BC and went on for eight months, during which time the city received *no* assistance from the Romans. **3.15.8**: 'were behaving unjustly towards some of the people who were subject to Carthage' refers to Saguntine attacks against the Turdenti, allies of the Carthaginians.

14.9 Following their defeat, none of the peoples south of the Ebro River, except the Saguntines, ventured to face the Carthaginians lightly. **10** As far as he could, Hannibal tried to keep his hands off this city, as he wished to give the Romans no acknowledged excuse for war until he had secured possession of the rest of the country, following his father Hamilcar's suggestions and advice.

15.1 But the Saguntines kept sending to Rome, partly because they were anxious on their own account and foresaw what was going to happen, and partly because they wished that the Romans should not be taken by surprise by the Carthaginians' growing power in Spain. **2** The Romans, who had frequently disregarded them, on this occasion sent envoys to investigate the situation. **3** Hannibal at the same time had subdued the tribes he intended and returned with his forces to winter at New Carthage, which was in a way the showpiece and capital of the Carthaginians in Spain. **4** He found there the embassy from Rome and gave them an audience, listening to what they had to say. **5** The Romans affirmed that he should keep away from Saguntum, which lay under their protection, and not cross the River Ebro, in accordance with the treaty made in Hasdrubal's time. **6** Hannibal, who was young and full of martial energy, successful in his plans, and encouraged by his long-time hatred of the Romans, **7** replied to them that he was protecting the interests of the Saguntines and accused the Romans of having unjustly executed some of the leading men, when a short time previously civil conflict had broken out and they were called in as arbiters. The Carthaginians, he said, would not overlook this violation of good faith; for it was an ancestral tradition of theirs to ignore no victim of injustice; **8** and he sent to Carthage asking what action he should take, as the Saguntines, relying on their alliance with Rome, were behaving unjustly towards some of the people who were subject to Carthage. **9** He was wholly influenced by his unreasoning and violent anger, and so did not give the true reasons but took refuge in groundless pretexts, as people generally do when they disregard their duty under the influence of a pre-existing passion. **10** How much better it would have been had he demanded that the Romans restore Sardinia, and at the same time the indemnity which they had unjustly exacted, taking advantage of Carthage's misfortunes and, if this was rejected, to threaten her with war!

11 But now, by keeping silent about the real cause and inventing a non-existent one about the Saguntines, he appeared to be embarking on the war not only without reason but even without justice. **12** The Roman envoys, seeing clearly that war was unavoidable, sailed to Carthage, wishing to make a similar appeal to them; **13** of course they never expected that there would be war in Italy, but in Spain, using Saguntum as a base.

4.24 Polybius *Histories* 3.8.1–8, 11: Hannibal's initiative?

Polybius records Fabius Pictor's view that Hannibal started the war on his own initiative; cf. Livy 21.5.1–3. Polybius, however, makes it clear that Hannibal sent to Carthage for advice on what to do concerning Saguntum (doc. 4.23).

1 Fabius, the Roman historian, says that, besides the injury done to the Saguntines, one of the causes of the Hannibalic war was Hasdrubal's arrogance and love of power. **2** He tells us how, having acquired great power in Spain, he arrived in Africa and tried to dissolve the laws of Carthage and change the constitution into a monarchy. **3** The leading statesmen, however, foresaw his plan and united to oppose him, **4** whereupon Hasdrubal, mistrusting them, left Africa and for the future governed Spain along his own lines, paying no attention to the Carthaginian senate. **5** Hannibal from boyhood had shared and admired Hasdrubal's policy and, when he succeeded to the command of Spain, had used the same approach to dealing with affairs as Hasdrubal. **6** As a result, he now began this war against the Romans on his own initiative and against Carthaginian opinion, **7** with not one of the leading men in Carthage approving Hannibal's conduct towards Saguntum. **8** After saying this, Fabius tells us that, after the capture of this city, the Romans demanded that the Carthaginians should either hand over Hannibal to them or accept war . . . **11** But they were so far from doing any of this that they carried on the war continuously for 17 years in accordance with Hannibal's policy, and did not abandon the war until they had finally lost every hope because of the danger threatening their country and its inhabitants.

4.25 Livy *History of Rome* 21.4.1–10: Hannibal the man, 221 BC

Hannibal went to Spain as a boy of nine with his father Hamilcar in 237. There was clearly interest in Hannibal's character and what made him 'tick'.

1 Hannibal was sent to Spain, where immediately on his arrival the whole army received him with enthusiasm; **2** the old soldiers believed that Hamilcar himself had returned to them as he was when he was young, seeing in Hannibal the same force of expression and energy of glance, the same countenance and features. But soon he brought it about that his likeness to his father was the least consideration in gaining him support; **3** never was the same nature more adaptable to the most diverse things – obeying and commanding. As a result you could not easily tell whether he was dearer to the general or the army; **4** there was no one Hasdrubal preferred more when anything bold or difficult was to be done, nor did the men show more confidence and daring under any other leader. **5** To recklessness in incurring danger he added the greatest judgement when in the midst of the dangers themselves; his body could not be exhausted or his mind overcome by any hard work; **6** he was equally tolerant of cold and heat; his manner of eating and drinking was regulated by natural desire not pleasure; his times of waking and sleeping were not delineated by day and night; **7** what remained when his work was done was given to rest, which he summoned not with a soft bed or silence — he was often seen by many lying on the ground wrapped up in a military cloak among the sentinels and pickets. **8** His clothes were no different from those of his fellows, though his arms and horse did stand out. He was undoubtedly the best of horsemen and infantry; the first to enter battle, and the last to leave once the fighting had begun. **9** These excellent qualities were equalled by his great vices: inhuman cruelty, perfidy more than Punic, no regard for truth or the divine, no fear of the gods, no reverence for an oath, no religious scruples. **10** With this disposition for virtues and vices he served for three years under Hasdrubal's command, omitting nothing that should be done or seen by one who was to become a great commander.

4.26 Polybius *Histories* 9.25.1–4: Hannibal's greed

Polyb. 9.22–6 is taken up with a discussion of Hannibal's character. The Carthaginian sources may have been individuals Polybius had met in Greece or Italy. For the Carthaginians' respect for wealth, see 4.6.

1 Hannibal does seem to have been exceptionally fond of money, as was his friend Mago, who commanded in Bruttium. **2** I obtained this account both from the Carthaginians themselves **3** (for locals know not only in which direction the wind lies, as the proverb says, but also the character of their compatriots) **4** and in more detail from Masinissa, who dwelt at length on the love of money as a characteristic of all Carthaginians, and especially of Hannibal and Mago, who was known as the Samnite.

WHOSE FAULT: ROME OR CARTHAGE?

The background to the Ebro treaty, signed in 226 BC, is sometimes seen as the threat to Rome and Italy from the Gauls, but it is clear that the Romans had become concerned about Carthaginian expansion in Spain. Saguntum was within the area, south of the Ebro River, in which by the treaty of 226 the Carthaginians could operate, but the treaty clearly envisaged the continuing independence of the city.

4.27 Polybius *Histories* 3.30.1–4: Both sides to blame

Polybius argues that the Carthaginians had 'good cause' to go to war but that, if the cause was the destruction of Saguntum, then the Carthaginians were in the wrong for having broken the treaty.

1 It is an undisputed fact that the Saguntines many years before Hannibal's time had placed themselves under Rome's protection. **2** The greatest evidence for this, and one accepted by the Carthaginians themselves, is that, when political conflict broke out in Saguntum, they turned not to the Carthaginians, although they were close at hand and were already involved in affairs in Spain, but to the Romans, and with their help restored the political situation. **3** So, if one were to regard the destruction of Saguntum as the cause of the Hannibalic War, it must be admitted that the Carthaginians were in the wrong in beginning the war, both from the point of view of the treaty of Lutatius, in which the allies of each power were to be secure from attack by the other, and from that of the agreement with Hasdrubal, in which the Carthaginians were not to cross the Ebro in arms. **4** But if we take the cause of the war to have been the annexation of Sardinia and the additional indemnity, then it must certainly be agreed that the Carthaginians had good reason to enter on the Hannibalic war, for, after yielding to circumstances, they were now retaliating with the help of circumstances against those who had wronged them.

4.28 Livy *History of Rome* 21.2.7: Livy's on the Ebro treaty

That the treaty was signed by Hasdrubal rather than the Carthaginian state gave the Carthaginians grounds for arguing that they need not necessarily observe it (doc. 4.29).

It was with Hasdrubal, because of his amazing skill in encouraging the Spanish tribes to join the Carthaginian empire, that the Roman people had renewed their treaty (i.e., that of 241 BC), laying down that the River Ebro should be the boundary for each empire, while the Saguntines, situated between the two empires, should preserve their independence.

4.29 Livy *History of Rome* 21.18.1–19.5: Q. Fabius Maximus as envoy at Carthage

Cf. Polyb. 3.20.6–21.10, 33.1–3. The first Roman embassy to Carthage had met Hannibal to no avail at New Carthage in Spain and then sailed to Carthage, where Hanno 'the Great', commander in the First Punic War, was the lone Carthaginian voice for peace and for observing the treaty (of 226 BC). The Carthaginian council supported Hannibal and his actions in Spain (Livy 21.10.1–11.2). When the Roman embassy returned home, news came that Saguntum had fallen, and the senate, 'ashamed' at not helping the city, prepared for war, though, according to Livy, they did not undertake war lightly, recognising the skill of their enemy (21.16). Before declaring war, a second embassy was sent to Carthage; for Roman ceremonies for declaring war, see doc. 3.14. **2.18.1**: M. Livius Salinator and L. Aemilius Paullus had been the consuls for 219; **2.18.13**: the story of the toga is also in Polyb. 3.33.2–3.

18.1 When these arrangements had been made, to make sure they observed all the due ceremonies before making war, the Romans sent to Africa an embassy of older men, Quintus Fabius, Marcus Livius, Lucius Aemilius, Gaius Licinius and Quintus Baebius, to put to the Carthaginians the question whether Hannibal had attacked Saguntum on the orders of the state, **2** and if, as seemed to be likely, they admitted the act and defended it as state policy, to declare war on the Carthaginian people. **3** After the Romans had arrived at Carthage and the senate granted them a hearing, Fabius put only the single question which they had been instructed to ask. One of the Carthaginians replied: **4** 'Even your previous embassy, Romans, when you demanded that we hand over Hannibal for besieging Saguntum on his own initiative, was somewhat rash; but your present embassy, though expressed up till now more mildly, is in fact more harsh. **5** On that occasion Hannibal was accused and his surrender demanded; now you are trying to extort from us a confession of guilt and immediate reparation as if we had already confessed. **6** Now, in my view, you should be asking not whether Saguntum was attacked on the state's orders or on the decision of an individual, but whether justly or unjustly; **7** the inquiry into the acts of one of our citizens, whether he acted on our authority or his own, and his punishment is up to us; with you we have only one point for discussion – whether what he did was permissible under the treaty. **8** Therefore, since you want there to be a distinction between what commanders do on orders from the state and what they do on their own initiative, consider the treaty made between us and you by Gaius Lutatius, your consul, in which the allies of both sides were protected but nothing was stipulated about the Saguntines, since they were not as yet your allies. **9** But you will perhaps say that in the treaty which Hasdrubal made the Saguntines are especially mentioned. To which I will say only the answer learnt from you. **10** For you have denied that you were bound by the treaty which the consul Gaius Lutatius originally made with us, because it had been made neither on the senate's authority nor the people's command; and so an entirely new treaty was made with the state's approval. **11** If you are not bound by your treaties unless they are made by your authority and command, then neither is Hasdrubal's treaty, which he made without our knowledge, binding on us. **12** So say no more about Saguntum and the Ebro, and produce the thought that has long been developing inside your mind!' **13** At this, the Roman, gathering his toga into a fold, replied, 'Here we bring you peace and war: take which you will!' With his words, they cried out no less aggressively that he might give them what he wished; **14** when he shook out the fold again and said that he gave them war, they all replied that they accepted it and that they would fight in the same spirit in which they accepted it.

WAR IN ITALY

At the Roman declaration of war in 218 BC, Hannibal had not yet crossed the Ebro River and the Romans thought they had the advantage. They appointed one of the consuls of 218, P. Cornelius Scipio, to a command in Spain, with 24,000 men and 60 ships, while the other consul, Ti. Sempronius Longus, was sent to Africa, with 26,000 men and 160 ships. But, as doc. 4.31 indicates, Hannibal was one step ahead. His crossing of the Alps with infantry, horses and elephants has captured the imagination of both modern and ancient writers – too much so on the part of the latter, according to Polybius. Polybius himself made the crossing and his references to eye-witnesses are important: they were one of his main sources for the war. Hannibal's crossing took about 15 days, probably in early November 218.

According to Polybius, Hannibal arrived in Italy with 12,000 African and 8,000 Spanish infantry and about 6,000 cavalry. At the crossing of the Rhône he had 38,000 infantry and 8,000 cavalry (Polyb. 3.60.5), which meant he lost 18,000 men from that point to the descent from the Alps. Hannibal took 37 elephants with him when he crossed the Rhône and presumably the same number across the Alps. They were present at the battle of Trebia; only one survived by 217, but reinforcements reached Hannibal in 215 BC.

4.30 Ennius *Annals* 256–57: The war begins

Sections 7–9 of Ennius' *Annals* dealt with the Second Punic War. These lines here graphically describe Hannibal's advance from New Carthage in spring 218.

> Finally with great force the four-footed horses and riders and elephants
> Hurl themselves forward.

4.31 Polybius *Histories* 3.47.6–9, 48.10–12: Crossing the Alps

Polybius disparages writers exaggerating the difficulties Hannibal faced in crossing the Alps. Livy's numbers for the losses (28.31.3–5) are unrealistic, particularly given that Hannibal had native guides and that the inhabitants were opposed to the Romans; they were to supply warm clothing and footgear and food to the Carthaginian army (Polyb. 3.48.10–12). After being joined by Gauls from northern Italy, Hannibal had 40,000 infantry and 10,000 cavalry at Cannae (Livy 22.46.6–7).

47.6 Some of those who have written about this crossing, because they wanted to astonish their readers with their marvellous tales about these places already mentioned, have, unnoticed, fallen into the two vices most alien to all writing of history – for they are forced into the making of false statements and self-contradiction. **7** On the one hand, they describe Hannibal as a general unrivalled in courage and foresight, but at the same time they present him to us as totally without judgement **8** and are unable to find a solution or way out of their falsehood except by introducing gods and the children of gods into a pragmatic history. **9** For they show the impassability and rugged character of the Alps to be such that not only horses and troops accompanied by elephants but even active infantrymen would have difficulty in crossing them, while at the same time they describe to us the desolation of the country as being such that, unless some god or hero had met Hannibal and shown him the way, his whole army would have been lost and utterly perished, unquestionably falling into both the above mentioned vices. . . .

48.10 Of course Hannibal did not act as these writers suggest but conducted his enterprise with great common sense. **11** For he had clearly ascertained the natural wealth of the country into which he planned to descend and the resentment of its people towards the Romans, and to deal with the difficulties of his route he employed native guides and scouts who were going to share his aims. **12** I can speak with confidence on such matters because I made inquiry about what happened from men who were present on these occasions, and have inspected the country and crossed the Alps to see and learn for myself.

CATASTROPHE FOR ROME

Hannibal had evaded Scipio, who decided not to pursue him by land. He left the army with his brother Gnaeus in command to proceed to Spain, and himself went by sea to northern Italy (Polyb. 3.49.1–4; Livy 21.32.1–5). Hannibal arrived in Italy, took Taurini (Turin), and began besieging cities in Cisalpine Gaul. Rome was astir: talk of the sack of Saguntum had only just ended, and Hannibal was already in Italy, attacking cities. Tiberius Sempronius

Longus, the other consul, who had got as far as Lilybaeum in Sicily on his expedition to Africa, was recalled. In November 218 the armies met in a skirmish at Ticinus, and Hannibal was victorious; Scipio was wounded but saved by his son (doc. 4.51). The first real battle came in December, at the River Trebia which flows into the Po. The Romans suffered a major defeat under the other consul, Longus, and most of the army was annihilated. Hannibal now dominated northern Italy.

4.32 Polybius *Histories* 3.83.1–84.7: Trasimene, 21 June 217 BC

In 217, the consuls Gaius Flaminius and Gnaeus Servilius Geminus were sent to guard the Apennines (Italy's mountainous backbone). In June, the Romans under Flaminius, who was killed in battle, were again defeated, losing 15,000 men in an ambush at Lake Trasimene, 140 kilometres north of Rome; the defeat was put down to Flaminius' neglect of the auspices (as a novus homo). Hannibal could now move freely in central Italy.

83.1 The road led through a level defile with high hills on each side all along its length, while in front crossways was a steep ridge, difficult to climb, and behind was the lake, with only a narrow access to the defile between the lake and the hillside. **2** Hannibal skirted the lake and passed through the defile, occupying the ridge in front and encamping on it with his Spaniards and Libyans, **3** while he brought his slingers and pikemen round to the front and stationed them in an extended line under the hills lying to the right of the defile. **4** Similarly, taking his cavalry and Celts in a circle round the hills on the left, he deployed them in a continuous line, so that the last of them were at the entrance to the defile which lay between the lake and the hillside. **5** After making these preparations in the night and surrounding the defile with troops in ambush, Hannibal stayed quiet. **6** Flaminius followed behind him, eager to engage with him; **7** he had encamped on the previous day at a very late hour close to the lake itself, and on the next day, as soon as it was dawn, he led his vanguard beside the lake into the above-mentioned defile, wanting to keep in touch with the enemy. **84.1** It was an unusually misty morning, and Hannibal, as soon as the greater part of the enemy's column had entered the defile and the vanguard had already made contact with him, gave the signal for battle and sent messages to the men waiting in ambush, attacking the enemy simultaneously from all sides. **2** Their sudden appearance took Flaminius totally by surprise, and, as the condition of the air made it still very difficult to see clearly and the enemy were charging at and attacking them from above in many different places, the Romans' centurions and military tribunes were not only unable to do anything necessary to help the situation but could not even understand what was going on. **3** They were being attacked simultaneously from the front, from the rear and from the sides, **4** and, as a result, most of them were cut down in marching order, not able to protect themselves, and as if betrayed by their commander's lack of judgement. **5** For, while they were still considering what they ought to do, they were being killed without knowing how. **6** It was at this point that some of the Celts attacked and killed Flaminius himself, who was in the greatest distress and difficulty. **7** So in the defile nearly 15,000 Romans fell, unable either to yield to circumstances or to do anything, but considering it their most important duty to adhere to their tradition of not fleeing or leaving their ranks.

4.33 *ILS* 11: Marcus Minucius, dictator

This dedication is on the side of an altar found at Rome. The disaster at Trasimene led to the appointment by the comitia centuriata of a dictator, Q. Fabius Maximus; they also appointed as his master of horse M. Minucius Rufus (cos. 221). Minucius, who did not keep to Fabius' delaying tactics, was killed in battle at Cannae.

Marcus Minucius, dictator, son of Gaius, vowed this dedication to Hercules.

4.34 Ennius *Annals* 360–62: Fabius Maximus 'Cunctator'

'Cunctator' means the delayer. Upon appointment as dictator in 217 after the disaster at Trasimene, Fabius carried out extensive religious rites and restored confidence at Rome. His policy was to avoid pitched battle, but the policy of allowing the Carthaginians to pillage and loot Roman and Latin territory and property was unpopular. In 216 consuls were elected as usual: L. Aemilius Paullus (cos. 219) and the novus homo C. Terentius Varro. Cicero (*Off.* 1.84) quotes these lines by Ennius in praise of Fabius.

One man by his delays restored our state for us.
He put no rumours before our safety;
Therefore in after times – even today – this hero's glory shines forth, more than once it did.

4.35 Polybius *Histories* 3.113.1–118.5: Cannae, 216 BC

The Romans refused to adhere to Fabius' delaying strategy and confronted Hannibal at Cannae; the result vindicated Fabius. The Roman army of eight legions and an additional 40,000 allied troops (80,000 men all told) was commanded on alternate days by each of the two consuls (Varro on the day of the battle). Hannibal, with about 40,000 foot and 10,000 cavalry, was clearly outnumbered. The battle was an outstanding military disaster of the first order for the Romans: one consul, L. Aemilius Paullus died, while the other (C. Terentius Varro) escaped, 70,000 Romans were killed and 10,000 were captured. This was probably the greatest casualty rate in a day for any European army in history. Hannibal lost 6,700 men. But the loss of the men was not Rome's greatest problem, for it refused to ransom its surviving defeated soldiers (doc. 4.36); rather, the defection of allies and loss of territory was the greatest blow.

113.1 On the very next day it was Gaius Terentius Varro's turn to take command, and at the first sign of sunrise he moved his troops out of each encampment, **2** crossing the river with those from the larger camp, whom he drew up at once in battle-order, while he stationed those from the other camp alongside them in the same line, all facing south. **3** The Romans' cavalry he positioned near the river on the right wing and the infantry next to them in the same line, placing the maniples more closely together than had been done before and making the depth of the maniples many times greater than the front; **4** he drew up the allied cavalry on the left wing; and in front of the whole army and some distance away he drew up the light-armed troops. **5** Counting the allies, there were 80,000 infantry and a little more than 6,000 cavalry. **6** At the same time, Hannibal sent his slingers and pikemen across the river and placed them in the front of his army, while he led the rest of his troops out of camp, crossing the river in two places and drawing them up facing the enemy. **7** On his left, near the river, he put his Spanish and Celtic cavalry opposite the Roman cavalry, and alongside these half of his heavy-armed Libyans, then his Spaniards and Celts. Beside these he positioned the other half of his Libyans and put his Numidian cavalry on the right wing. **8** When he had drawn up his whole army in a straight line, he took the middle companies of the Spaniards and Celts and brought them forward, keeping the rest in contact with these but making the front crescent-shaped and thinning the line of battle, intending to have his Libyans as a reserve force in the battle, and let the Spaniards and Celts bear the brunt.

114.1 The Libyans were armed in the Roman style, as Hannibal had equipped them all with selected spoils from earlier battles; **2** the Spaniards' and Celts' shields were similar, but their swords totally different; **3** the thrust of the Spaniards' swords was no less effective than their cut, but the Gallic sword was able only to cut, and not at close quarters. **4** With their companies drawn up alternately, the Celts naked and the Spaniards in their national costume, short tunics edged with purple, they were a strange and awe-inspiring sight. **5** Altogether the Carthaginian cavalry numbered about 10,000 and their infantry, including the Celts, not much more than 40,000. **6** Aemilius commanded the Romans' right wing, Gaius (Terentius) the left, and Marcus (Atilius) and Gnaeus (Servilius Geminus), the previous year's consuls, the centre. **7** Hasdrubal commanded the Carthaginian left, Hanno the right; Hannibal himself the centre, with his brother Mago. **8** As the Roman line looked south, as I said before, and the Carthaginians north, neither was troubled by the rising sun.

115.1 The advance guards were the first to engage, and at first, with only the light-armed troops involved, the conflict was even, but, as soon as the Spanish and Celtic cavalry on the left met the Romans, the conflict was truly barbaric; **3** for there were none of the customary wheeling movements, but having once engaged they dismounted and fought hand to hand. **4** When the Carthaginians prevailed and killed most of the enemy in the engagement, with all the Romans fighting with great bravery, they started driving the rest along the river, slaughtering them without mercy, and then the heavy infantry took over from the light-armed troops and fell on each other. **5** For a short time, the ranks of the Spaniards and Celts stayed firm and fought bravely with the Romans; then, under the pressure, they gave way and fell back, losing the crescent shape. **6** The Romans' maniples bravely pursued them and easily cut through the enemy's line, as the Celts were drawn up thinly, while the Romans had crowded together from the wings to the middle where the action was; **7** for the wings and the centres did not engage simultaneously, but the centres first, as the Celts were drawn up in a crescent shape, a long way in advance of their wings, with the convex front of the crescent facing the enemy. **8** The Romans, pursuing these and putting pressure on the centre and that part of the enemy's line that was giving way, pushed so far forward that on each side of their flanks they now had the Libyans in their heavy armour; **9** of these, those on the right wing faced left and charged the enemy flank from the right, **10** while those on the left faced right and, re-forming, did the same from the left, the situation making it clear how to act. **11** As a result, as Hannibal had planned, the Romans, in their pursuit of the Celts, were caught in the middle of the Libyans. **12** They no longer kept formation, but turned either singly or in companies and fought the enemy who were attacking their flanks . . .

116.7 At this point Hasdrubal seems to have acted with great skill and common sense; seeing that the Numidians were very numerous and most skilful and formidable against a fleeing enemy, he allowed them to deal with those in flight (i.e., the Roman cavalry) and led his men to the conflict between the infantry, eager to assist the Libyans. **8** Falling on the Roman legions from the rear and making successive attacks with his companies simultaneously from various points, he encouraged the Libyans and subdued and terrified the spirits of the Romans. **9** It was at this point that Lucius Aemilius, after several severe wounds, lost his life in hand-to-hand combat, a man who did his duty to his country, if ever anyone did, both during the whole course of his life and on this final occasion. **10** As long as the Romans could turn and present a front to the enemy that surrounded them, they held out; **11** but, while the outer ranks kept falling and they were increasingly hemmed in, they were all finally killed, including Marcus and Gnaeus, the previous year's consuls, who in this conflict had acted like brave men worthy of Rome.

117.1 This was the outcome of the battle between the Romans and Carthaginians at Cannae, a battle which had the bravest men as both victors and vanquished. **2** This was clear from events. For, of the 6,000 cavalry, 70 escaped to Venusia with Terentius, and around 300 of the allied horse found safety in the cities in scattered groups; **3** of the infantry, some 10,000 were captured fighting, but not in the battle itself, and perhaps only 3,000 escaped from the conflict to the neighbouring cities. **4** All the rest, some 70,000, died bravely, the main contribution to the Carthaginians' victory, both on this occasion and formerly, being the number of their cavalry . . . **6** Of Hannibal's army, about 4,000 Celts fell, 1,500 Spaniards and Africans, and 200 cavalry . . .

118.2 The Carthaginians, through this action, came into immediate control of nearly all the rest of the coast; **3** the Tarentines at once surrendered, while the Argyrippans and some Campanian towns invited Hannibal to them, while all the rest now looked towards the Carthaginians. **4** These had great hopes of becoming masters of Rome itself at the first attempt; **5** the Romans at once gave up hopes of keeping their supremacy in Italy because of this defeat and were in great fear and danger on their own account and that of their ancestral city, expecting Hannibal to arrive at any moment.

4.36 Polybius *Histories* 6.58.2–13: Conquer or die!

Following the defeat, the senate refused to ransom the 8,000 men who had been guarding the Roman camp, even though it was not their fault that they had not engaged in the battle; it preferred to enrol slaves in the army (doc. 6.1). The reason was partly to avoid giving Hannibal monetary resources with which to carry on the war (Livy 22.26.1–2), but at the

same time they were upholding the doctrine of 'no surrender' on any terms. Hannibal therefore sold the prisoners into slavery.

2 When, after his victory at Cannae, the 8,000 men who were guarding the camp
came into Hannibal's hands, he took them all prisoner and allowed them to send
a deputation home on the subject of ransom and release. **3** They chose ten of their
most distinguished men and he sent them off, after making them swear an oath
that they would return to him. **4** One of the men selected, as he was going out
of the camp's palisade, said he had forgotten something and went back, leaving
again after collecting what he had left behind, and thinking that by his return he
had kept his faith and absolved himself of the oath. **5** When they arrived in Rome,
they begged and entreated the senate not to begrudge the prisoners their release
but allow each of them to pay 3 minas and return to their families; for Hannibal,
they said, had allowed this; **6** they were worthy of release: for they had not been
guilty of cowardice in the battle, or done anything unworthy of Rome, but had
been left behind to guard the camp and, when all the others had been killed in
the battle, had been forced by circumstances to surrender to the enemy. **7** But the
Romans, despite having encountered serious defeats in their battles and having
now, so to speak, lost all their allies, and despite the fact that they were expecting
Rome itself to be threatened any day, **8** listened to what they said but neither disregarded their dignity under the pressure of disasters nor neglected any necessary
step in their consideration, **9** but, seeing that Hannibal's purpose was, through
this action, both to obtain funds and to deprive the men opposed to him in battle
of their high spirit, by showing that if defeated they might still hope for safety,
10 were so far from agreeing to this request that they took no account either of
pity for their relatives or of the future value which these men would be to them,
11 but thwarted Hannibal's calculations and the hopes he had placed in them and
refused to ransom the men, while they imposed a law on their troops that, when
they fought, they must either conquer or die, as there was no hope of safety for
them if they were defeated. **12** Consequently, after deciding this, they sent away
the nine envoys, who returned willingly according to their oath, while they put the
man who had tried to trick his way out of the oath into chains and returned him
to the enemy, **13** so that Hannibal's pleasure at his victory in the battle was not so
great as his disappointment, when he saw with amazement the steadfastness and
high spirit of the Romans in their resolutions.

4.37 Ennius *Annals* 276–77: Ennius on Cannae

Propertius *Odes* 3.3.9–10: 'and (Ennius) sang . . . of the victorious delays of Fabius, and the
unlucky battle at Cannae, and the gods being turned (to hear) our pious prayers.' Hannibal's
African and Spanish mercenaries were remarkable for their loyalty and discipline; here
Hannibal is offering his troops Carthaginian citizenship.

He who will strike an enemy, I promise, will be a Carthaginian,
Whoever he may be, whatever country he comes from . . .

4.38 Livy *History of Rome* 22.57.2–6, 9–12: Emergency measures

Polyb. 3.112.8–9 comments on the religious activity at Rome just before Cannae and notes that the Romans considered no rites unseemly or undignified which would propitiate the gods. In 228, 216 and 113 BC, a Gallic couple and a Greek couple were buried alive in the Forum Boarium at Rome after a consultation of the Sibylline Books. In 216 and 113 the burials occurred after Vestal Virgins were convicted of unchastity. On this occasion, in 216, two Vestals had been convicted of unchastity, a great pollution. Their conviction was not unusual as a response to Roman disasters (cf. doc 7.93).

2 The Romans were terrified, moreover, not only by these immense disasters but also by numerous prodigies, and in particular because two Vestals in that year, Opimia and Floronia, had been convicted of fornication, and one of them had been buried alive, as the custom is, near the Colline Gate, while the other had committed suicide; **3** Lucius Cantilius, a pontifical secretary (one of those who are now called lesser pontiffs), who had slept with Floronia, was scourged so harshly in the comitium by the pontifex maximus that he died under the lashes. **4** Since this impious crime, being in the midst of so many disasters, was, as often happens, converted into a portent, the decemvirs were ordered to consult the (Sibylline) Books, **5** and Quintus Fabius Pictor was sent to Delphi to ask the oracle what prayers and supplications they should use so as to appease the gods and what the end of these immense disasters would be. **6** Meanwhile, on the instructions of the Books of Fate, some extraordinary sacrifices were made, among which a Gallic man and woman and a Greek man and woman were buried alive in the Forum Boarium in a place enclosed with stone, which had even on an earlier occasion been saturated with the blood of human victims, a rite most untypical of Roman practice . . . **9** On the senate's authority a dictator, Marcus Junius (Pera), was appointed, with Tiberius Sempronius (Gracchus) as his master of horse, and after proclaiming a levy they enlisted young men over the age of 17 and some still wearing the toga praetexta. **10** From these they made up four legions and a thousand horsemen. They also sent to the allies and the Latins to supply their soldiers according to agreement. They ordered that armour, weapons and other things be prepared and took down old enemy spoils from the temples and porticoes. **11** The levy had a novel appearance owing to the scarcity of free men and the crisis: they bought with state money 8,000 young, strong slaves and armed them, asking each first if he were willing to serve. **12** They preferred these as soldiers, though at less expense they could have redeemed the prisoners of war.

4.39 Livy *History of Rome* 22.51.1–4: Hannibal fails to march on Rome

The story of Maharbal (son of Himilco), commander of the Libyan cavalry, urging Hannibal on the battlefield of Cannae to march on Rome, is not found in Polybius. It is possibly an invention of Livy or one of his sources in order to express amazement that after such a spectacular victory Hannibal did not march on the city. If Hannibal had done so, the outcome of the war might have been markedly different. Hannibal did march on Rome in 211 to draw off Roman forces from their siege of Capua but did not settle down to besiege the city.

1 While the other officers had crowded round Hannibal, congratulating him on his victory and counselling him, now that he had brought so great a war to an end, to rest himself and allow it to his exhausted soldiers for what remained of that day and the following night, 2 Maharbal, the cavalry commander, considered that now was least of all the time for inactivity: 'On the contrary', he said, 'that you may understand what has been achieved in this battle, on the fifth day you will banquet, as victor, in the Capitol! Follow – I will go on ahead with the cavalry so the Romans may know that you have arrived before they know you are coming.' 3 The suggestion seemed to Hannibal too delightful and immense for his mind to be able to grasp it all at once. So he said that he praised Maharbal's goodwill but needed time to think about his advice. 4 To which Maharbal replied, 'Truly, the gods do not give the same man all their gifts: you know how to win battles, Hannibal, but you do not know how to use victory.' That day's delay is generally believed to have saved Rome and the empire.

4.40 Livy *History of Rome* 23.48.4–49.3: Appeals to businessmen, 215 BC

In this emergency situation, businessmen, especially those who had profited from the business of war, were asked in 215 to make loans to the state, with deferred repayment, and to supply the army.

48.4 At the end of summer, a letter came from Publius and Gnaeus Scipio, reporting the extent and success of their campaign in Spain, but that the army needed money for pay, clothing and grain, while allies in the navy were in need of everything. 5 With regard to the pay they would, if the treasury was empty, find some way of obtaining it from the Spaniards; the rest had certainly to be sent out from Rome or else neither the army nor the province could be kept. 6 When the letter was read out, there was no one among them all who did not admit that the statements were true and the demands reasonable . . . 9 Therefore, the senate came to the conclusion that, unless the state could be supported by credit, its assets were insufficient to keep it going. 10 They decided that the praetor, Fulvius, should appear before the assembly, inform the people of these public needs, and urge those who had increased their family property through state contracts to allow the state, from which they had acquired their wealth, 11 time to make payment and to contract to supply what was needed for the army in Spain, on condition that they be the first to be paid when there was money in the treasury. 12 The praetor put this to the assembly and named a day on which he would let the contracts for providing clothing and grain to the Spanish army and whatever else was needed for the allies in the navy. 49.1 When that day came, three companies of 19 men came forward to take up the contracts, but they had two demands: 2 one, that they should be exempt from military service while they were engaged in this public business, the other, that the cargoes on their ships should be at the risk of the state as regards the threats of enemies or storms. 3 When both these demands were agreed to, they took up the contracts, and the state was carried on with private money.

THE IMPACT ON THE ALLIES

Hannibal's attempt to stir up revolt and 'free' the Italians after the battles of Trebia (218 BC) and Trasimene (217) had not led to any defections, perhaps because of the length of time many of the Italian peoples had been allies of Rome. Moreover, the outcome of the contest was not yet clear. But even after Cannae the Latin allies remained firm, despite the fact that Hannibal let the allied troops return home without ransom, as he had after Trebia and Trasimene – clearly in order to win over their communities.

4.41 Polybius *Histories* 3.77.3–7: Hannibal and the allies, 218–217 BC

Hannibal told the captured allies after Trebia and Trasimene that he had come not to fight them but to free them: he was in Italy fighting for (not against) the Italians. Capua took up his offer but emphasised its independence of the Carthaginians (doc. 4.42). Hannibal, according to Livy (34.60.3), had expected the allies' support and defection from Rome.

3 Hannibal, while wintering in Cisalpine Gaul, kept the Romans whom he had captured in battle imprisoned, giving them just enough to eat, **4** but he continued to show great kindness to those from the allies and later called them to a meeting and spoke to them, stating that he had not come to make war on them but on the Romans on their behalf. **5** So, if they were sensible, they should accept his friendship, **6** for he had come primarily to restore the freedom of the Italian people, as well as to help them recover the cities and territory which had been taken from each of them by the Romans. **7** Having spoken in this way, he sent them all to their homes without ransom, as he wished by doing so to win over the inhabitants of Italy to his side and at the same time to turn their loyalties against Rome, while inciting to revolt those who thought their cities or harbours had suffered decline under Roman rule.

4.42 Livy *History of Rome* 23.4.6–8, 6.5–8, 7.1–3: Capua secedes, 216 BC

Following Cannae, the situation in Campania changed. Capua, an Oscan city, produced the most spectacular of the revolts against Rome, which included the Samnites, Bruttians, Lucanians, Uzentini, and almost all the Greek coastal cities and the Cisalpine Gauls. Despite these defections, the Romans did not consider peace, even though allies made up about 50 per cent of Roman manpower. Hannibal had gained more allies, but he had also acquired responsibilities, among them the need to protect these cities, especially Capua, which was recovered by Rome in 211 (doc. 4.44), as well as Tarentum in 209, Locri in 205 and Croton in 203.

4.6 To the Campanians' contempt for the laws, magistrates and senate, there was now added, after the disaster at Cannae, scorn too for the power of Rome, for which they used to have some respect. **7** The only thing which held them back from immediate secession was that the ancient right of connubium (intermarriage) linked many distinguished and powerful families with the Romans, **8** and the strongest bond was that 300 horsemen, the most noble of the Campanians, were serving in the Roman army, chosen by the Romans and sent to garrison Sicilian cities . . . **6.5** Finally the majority view prevailed that the same envoys who had gone to the Roman consul should be sent to Hannibal. **6** Before they went, and before the plan to secede was settled, I find in some annals that envoys were sent to Rome by the Campanians, with the demand that, if they wished them to aid the Roman state, one of the consuls should be a Campanian; **7** anger was aroused and they were ordered to be removed from the senate house, and a lictor was sent to lead them from the city and order them stay for the rest of that day outside Roman territory. **8** There was once a very similar demand made by the Latins, and because Coelius and other writers have with some reason omitted it I have been afraid to set this down as certain.

7.1 The envoys came to Hannibal and made peace on these conditions: that no Carthaginian general or magistrate should have any jurisdiction over a Campanian citizen and no Campanian citizen should be forced to serve in the army or perform any other service; **2** that Capua was to have its own laws and magistrates; that the Carthaginians should give the Campanians 300 of their Roman prisoners, whom the Campanians were to choose, with whom there would be an exchange for the Campanian cavalry who were serving in Sicily. **3** These were the terms; in addition to this agreement, the Campanians committed the following crimes: for the populace suddenly seized prefects of the allies and other Roman citizens, some of them on military duty, others engaged in private business, and ordered them all to be shut up in the baths, as if under guard, where they might die in a terrible way, suffocated by the extreme heat.

4.43 Livy *History of Rome* 24.1.13: Hannibal and the Locrians, 215 BC

Livy includes Locri and the other Greek cities among the defectors, but in 216 these cities initially opposed Hannibal: the Locrians surrendered to Hannibal in 215 but allowed the Roman garrison to leave secretly; they finally made peace with Rome in 204.

By Hannibal's order, the Locrians were given peace: they were to live in freedom under their own laws, their city should be open to the Carthaginians, their harbour was to be in the control of the Locrians, and the alliance was to stand on the condition that the Carthaginians should help the Locrians and the Locrians the Carthaginians in peace and war.

4.44 Livy *History of Rome* 26.16.5–10, 13: The fate of Capua, 211 BC

In 215, Rome's activities in Spain prevented reinforcements reaching Hannibal; the Romans hemmed him into southern Italy with some success. In 214, the consuls M. Claudius Marcellus and Q. Fabius Maximus 'Cunctator' (also consul in 215, and his son in 213) pushed Hannibal further south. But 213 saw several Greek cities go over to Hannibal, including Tarentum, which was recaptured in 209. The year 212 saw preparations for the recapture of Capua, which occurred in the following year; 53 Capuan senators were beheaded (because, as Roman citizens, they were traitors).

5 From Cales the Romans returned to Capua and the surrender of Atella and Calatia was received. There too punishment fell on the leaders responsible. **6** Thus some 70 leading senators were executed, while approximately 300 Campanian nobles who were imprisoned, and others who were sent under guard to cities of the Latin allies, died in various ways: the rest of the citizens of Capua were sold. **7** Discussion continued about the city and the remaining land, some being of the opinion that a city so powerful, so close and so unfriendly ought to be destroyed. But present advantage triumphed; on account of the land, which was well known to be the most fertile of any in Italy, the city was saved so there might be a home for the farmers. **8** To populate the city, the foreign residents, freedmen, and retailers and craftsmen were allowed to stay: all the land and buildings became the public property of the Roman people. **9** But it was decided that Capua should remain a city only in the sense of a place of habitation, and it was to have no political body — no senate, no assembly of the people, no magistrates: **10** without a public council, without military authority, they thought the mob, having nothing in common with each other, would be incapable of agreement; a praetor would be sent each year from Rome to administer justice . . . **13** The enemy had to admit what power the Romans possessed to exact punishment from disloyal allies and how helpless Hannibal was to guard those whom he had taken under his protection.

THE TIDE TURNS

4.45 Polybius *Histories* 7.9.1–17: The alliance between Hannibal and Philip of Macedon, 215 BC

Cf. Livy 23.33.10–12; App. *Mac.* 1. Philip V of Macedon approached Hannibal after Cannae for this alliance; Rome knew of the alliance through capturing Xenophanes, Philip's ambassador, who was returning to the king with the treaty (this may be the source of Polybius' copy). The alliance brought Hannibal no material value, but its psychological effect and propaganda value in Sicily and southern Italy among the Greek cities which had rebelled might have been important. It is clear that there was no Carthaginian intention to destroy Rome, only to limit its power.

1 The sworn treaty made between Hannibal the general, Mago, Myrcan, Barmocar, and all the Carthaginian senators with him and all the Carthaginians serving under him, and Xenophanes the Athenian, son of Cleomachus, the envoy whom King Philip, son of Demetrius, sent to us on behalf of himself, the Macedonians and the allies.

2 In the presence of Zeus, Hera and Apollo; in the presence of the god of Carthage, Heracles and Iolaus; in the presence of Ares, Triton and Poseidon; in the presence of the gods who battle for us and of the sun, moon and earth; in the presence of rivers, harbours and waters; **3** in the presence of all the gods who possess Carthage; in the presence of all the gods who possess Macedonia and the rest of Greece; in the presence of all the gods of the army who preside over this oath.

4 Hannibal the general, and all the Carthaginian senators with him, and all the Carthaginians serving under him, propose that, in respect of what seems good to you and to us, we should make this sworn treaty of friendship and goodwill to be friends, kinsmen and brothers, **5** on the following conditions: That King Philip and the Macedonians and the rest of the Greeks who are their allies shall protect the Carthaginians, the sovereign people, and Hannibal their general and those with him and those subject to the Carthaginians who have the same laws; also the people of Utica, and all cities and peoples subject to the Carthaginians, and our soldiers and allies; **6** also all cities and peoples in Italy, Gaul and Liguria, with whom we are in alliance and those in this country with whom we may hereafter be in alliance;

7 That King Philip and the Macedonians and the other Greeks who are their allies shall be protected and guarded by the Carthaginians who are serving with us, by the people of Utica, and by all cities and peoples that are subject to Carthage, by our allies and soldiers, and by all peoples and cities in Italy, Gaul and Liguria, who are our allies and such other as may hereafter become our allies in Italy and the neighbouring regions;

8 That we shall make no plots against each other, nor set ambushes against one another, but with all zeal and goodwill, without guile or treachery, we will be enemies of those who make war against the Carthaginians, excepting the kings, cities and harbours with whom we have sworn treaties and friendships;

9 That we shall also be the enemies of those who make war against King Philip, excepting the kings, cities and peoples with whom we have sworn treaties and friendships;

10 That you will be our allies in the war which we now wage against the Romans, until the gods grant victory to us and to you, **11** and you will give us such help as we need or as we agree on;

12 That when the gods have granted us victory in the war against the Romans and their allies, if the Romans ask us to make terms of peace, we shall make such an agreement that shall include you also, **13** on the following conditions: That the Romans shall never be permitted to make war on you; that the Romans shall no longer have authority over Corcyra, Apollonia, Epidamnus, Pharos, Dimale, Parthini or Atintania; **14** and that they shall hand back to Demetrius of Pharos all those of his friends who are in Roman territory;

15 That if the Romans should make war on you or on us, we shall help each other in the war, as may be required by either side; **16** that we shall do the same if any others do so, excepting the kings, cities and peoples with whom we have sworn treaties and friendships; **17** that, if we decide to withdraw from or add to this sworn treaty, we will withdraw or add such conditions as are agreed by both.

4.46 *ILS* 12, 13: Marcus Claudius Marcellus in Sicily

Below are two dedications found at Rome, dated to 211 BC; at 13, *vovit*, vowed, was originally inscribed and replaced by *dedit*, gave, when the vow was fulfilled. M. Claudius Marcellus (271–208 BC, five times consul) was victorious in Sicily between 214 and 212. Consul for the first time in 222 BC, he had defeated the Gauls, killing their chief in single combat (thus winning the spolia opima) and capturing their capital. In 214 Marcellus took up the command against Syracuse, which had revolted on the death of Hiero, and conquered it in 211 BC. Most Sicilian cities now joined Rome, with the notable exception of Agrigentum. In 208 Marcellus, his son, and his fellow consul (T. Quinctius Crispinus) were mortally ambushed by the Cathaginians at Venusia. For his descendant and namesake, Augustus' nephew, see doc 15.36.

12 Marcus Claudius, son of Marcus, consul, took this (as booty) from Enna (in Sicily).

13 To Mars, Marcus Claudius, son of Marcus, consul, gave this.

4.47 Plutarch *Life of Marcellus* 30.6–9: Marcus Claudius Marcellus and Greek art

Archimedes, the great mathematician, was killed in the capture of Syracuse, to Marcellus' regret; his many inventions had aided the defence of the walls. Plut. *Marcell.* 21.1–6 tells how Marcellus brought Syracuse's works of art to Rome to adorn the capital, the first massive influx of Greek art into Rome.

6 The monuments which Marcellus dedicated, besides those in Rome, were a gymnasium at Catana in Sicily and statues and tablets from Syracuse in the temple of the gods named the Cabiri in Samothrace and in the temple of Athena at Lindos. **7** On his statue there, as Posidonius tells us, the following epigram was inscribed:

> **8** This man, stranger, was the great star of his country, Rome,
> Claudius Marcellus, of distinguished ancestors,
> Seven times consul he protected her in warfare
> Through which he launched plentiful death at the enemy.

9 The rank of pro-consul, which he held twice, the writer of the epigram has counted with his five consulates.

4.48 Plutarch *Life of Fabius Maximus* 22.5–6, 23.1: Tarentum recaptured, 209 BC

The Romans had lost Tarentum in 213 through the revolt of the aristocrats. According to Plutarch, Q. Fabius Maximus 'Cunctator' took the city by treachery with the help of a Bruttian contingent (whom he then slaughtered); Livy 27.16 says that the Bruttians were killed because of a feud with Rome.

22.5 At that point Fabius' love of honour appears to have taken a nose dive: he ordered his men to kill the Bruttians first, to hide the fact that he took the city by treachery; however, he failed to win credit for this and incurred a charge of bad faith and savagery. **6** Many of the Tarentines were slaughtered too, 30,000 were sold as slaves, and the city was sacked by the Roman army, while 3,000 talents found their way into the treasury . . . **23.1** It is said that Hannibal had arrived within only

40 stades of the city, and in public remarked, 'The Romans have another Hannibal; we have lost the city of Tarentum as we took it' – though in private he then told his friends for the first time that he had seen for a long while that it would be difficult for them to conquer Italy with their existing forces, and now he saw it was impossible.

THE METAURUS, 22 JUNE 207 BC

The Carthaginians had other military commitments in Spain and Sicily, and briefly in Sardinia (215), and Hannibal had had essentially to manage with the force he brought in 218 plus some additions from Italy. Mago Barca's contingent intended for Italy had been deployed instead in Spain because of Roman activities there. Hasdrubal, the son of Hamilcar Barca and Hannibal's brother, left in command of Spain by Hannibal in 218 BC, crossed the Alps and entered Italy in 207 BC. The brothers planned to join forces in Umbria. Taking 6,000 infantry and 1,000 cavalry, the consul C. Claudius Nero marched north and joined the other consul, M. Livius Salinator, at the Metaurus River. Polybius gives 10,000 Carthaginians and Gauls and 2,000 Roman dead (11.3.3); Livy expands this to 56,000 enemy dead and 8,000 Romans and allies, and makes it a second Cannae, this time for the Carthaginians. Hannibal could now expect no more reinforcements and was bogged down in Italy.

4.49 Polybius *Histories* 11.1.1–3, 3.3–6: Hasdrubal fails to reinforce Hannibal

1 Hasdrubal's arrival in Italy was much easier and swifter than Hannibal's had been. Rome had never before been so expectant and terrified, awaiting the outcome . . . **2** None of this pleased Hasdrubal, but with circumstances no longer permitting delay, since he saw the enemy advancing in battle formation, he was forced to draw up his Spaniards and the Gauls who were with him. **3** Positioning his elephants, who were ten in number, at the front, he increased the depth of his line, making his whole army very narrow, and then, taking up his position in the centre of the line of battle behind the elephants, he made his onslaught on the enemy's left, having resolved that in this crisis he had either to conquer or die . . .

3.3 No fewer than 10,000 Carthaginians and Gauls and about 2,000 Romans were killed in the battle. Some distinguished Carthaginians were captured alive, and the rest were slain. **4** When the news reached Rome, they did not believe it at first, because they had so badly wanted to see this happen; **5** when more messengers came, not only reporting the event but giving exact details, the city was full of surpassing joy, and every shrine was decorated, every temple full of offerings and sacrificial victims, **6** and they generally became so confident and bold that everyone thought that Hannibal, of whom they had been so terrified earlier, was now not even in Italy.

4.50 Livy *History of Rome* 27.51.11–12: Hasdrubal's head

It was common for Romans to behead traitors, such as the Capuan senators who had allied the city with Hannibal (doc. 4.44). The Gauls were head-hunters: after the battle of Ticinus, some Gallic troops deserted Scipio and brought Hannibal the heads of the Roman soldiers who had been camped near them (Polyb. 3.67).

11 After the consul Gaius Claudius (Nero) had returned to his camp, he ordered that the head of Hasdrubal, which he had kept carefully and brought with him, be thrown in front of the enemy's outposts and that captured Africans be displayed, just as they were, in chains . . . **12** Hannibal, under the impact of so great an affliction, both public and private, is reported to have said that he could see the fate of Carthage.

SCIPIO AFRICANUS

The Scipio brothers had died in Spain in 211. According to Livy, none of the leading men put themselves forward for the command, when Publius Cornelius Scipio, 24 years old, suddenly did so (Livy 26.18). Duly appointed commander by the people, the younger Scipio continued the war as a private citizen, privatus, invested with imperium pro consule, the first privatus to be so invested. In late 210 he arrived in Spain and made for New Carthage, where the Carthaginians kept huge amounts of supplies, and took it in 209. In 208 he defeated Hasdrubal Barca at the battle of Baecula; Hasdrubal took his remaining forces for Italy, to bring reinforcements to Hannibal (see doc. 4.49). After a battle at Ilipa in 206, Carthaginian control of Spain was at an end. Scipio had, in a few years, captured Carthage's main overseas possession.

4.51 Polybius *Histories* 10.3.1–7: Scipio Africanus

The battle near the Po River was the battle of Ticinus in 218 (see Polyb. 3.64). Laelius was an important source for Polybius on Scipio, having served with him in Spain and Africa.

1 It is widely agreed that he (Scipio) was beneficent and magnanimous, but that he was also shrewd and discreet, with a mind always concentrated on the object in view, would be admitted only by those who had been closely associated with him and who had scrutinised his character, as it were, by the light of day. **2** One of these was Gaius Laelius (cos. 190), who from his boyhood until the end of his life had shared in his every word and deed, and who has produced this belief in me because his account seemed probable and in agreement with Scipio's actual achievements. **3** He says that Publius' first distinguished act was during the cavalry battle between his father and Hannibal near the river called the Po. **4** At the time he was 17 years of age and, this being his first campaign, his father had put him in command of a troop of picked cavalry to keep him safe and sound, but when he saw his father in danger, surrounded by the enemy with only two or three horsemen and badly wounded, he at first tried to urge his companions to assist his father, **5** and, when they hung back for a while because of the large numbers of enemy surrounding them, he is said to have recklessly and audaciously charged on his own against those encircling them. **6** Thereupon the others were also compelled to attack, and the enemy broke up in terror, while Publius, so unexpectedly saved, was the first to address his son as his preserver in the hearing of everyone. **7** Having won a universally acknowledged reputation for bravery through this service, for the future he seldom exposed himself to danger when the hopes of his entire country depended on him – which is a characteristic not of a leader who relies on luck but of one who possesses intelligence.

4.52 Plutarch *Life of Fabius Maximus* 25.1–27.1: Fabius' disapproval

Once elected to the consulship for 205 BC, Scipio requested Africa as his allocated province. Fabius opposed this, probably because he was focusing on driving Hannibal from Italy, while Scipio wanted to defeat both Hannibal and Carthage. He was given the two legions in Sicily (the troops who had survived Cannae) and raised volunteers. The recall of Hannibal in 202 BC meant the end of his plan to capture Italy; for several years since 216 he had really been active only in southern Italy and was eventually more or less confined to Bruttium and the Lacinian promontory.

25.1 Cornelius Scipio had been sent to Spain, defeating the Carthaginians in numerous battles and driving them from the country, as well as winning for the Romans the support of many tribes, large cities, and splendid victories. When he returned to Rome, he possessed more goodwill and a better reputation than anyone ever before and was elected consul (205 BC). Recognising that the people demanded and expected a great exploit from him, he decided that the strategy of engaging with Hannibal in Italy was quite out of date and over-cautious; he resolved immediately to pour troops and armies into Libya and ravage Carthage herself, so transferring the war scene from Italy to Africa, and he encouraged the people to support this plan with all his enthusiasm. **2** Fabius, however, did his best to spread fear through the city, on the grounds that they were being led into extreme risks by a thoughtless young man, and spared neither words nor deeds which he thought might deter his fellow citizens. He convinced the senate, but the people thought that he was jealous of Scipio's success and afraid that, if Scipio achieved some great and splendid success and either completely ended the war or took it out of Italy, he himself might appear to be lazy and cowardly for having let the war drag on for so long. **3** It seems likely that, originally, Fabius' drive to oppose Scipio was on account of his great caution and foresight, fearing the risks, which were indeed great, while his effort to prevent Scipio's increasing influence made him more violent and extreme and brought in an element of rivalry and competition. He even tried to persuade (P. Licinius) Crassus, Scipio's fellow consul, not to hand over the army but to lead it across himself, if the resolution was taken, and did not allow Scipio to be given money for the war. **4** Scipio was therefore forced to find the money himself and raised it privately from the cities in Etruria, as they were personally devoted to him; Crassus was kept at home partly by his nature, as he was not quarrelsome but mild, and partly on religious grounds, as he held the highest priesthood . . .

26.2 Fabius managed to frighten the Romans, and they voted that Scipio should use only the troops already in Sicily and take with him 300 of the men who had served him loyally in Spain. Fabius appears to have followed this policy through his innate caution. **3** But when Scipio crossed to Libya (204 BC), news of wonderful achievements and victories, splendid in both size and glory, immediately reached Rome, and immense booty followed as proof of these reports, including the king of Numidia as a prisoner and the burning and destruction of two enemy camps together with numerous men, weapons and horses, and envoys were sent to Hannibal by the Carthaginians, asking and begging him to leave his fruitless hopes in Italy and come to help them at home . . . **27.1** Not long afterwards, Scipio defeated Hannibal in a pitched battle (Zama), overthrowing fallen Carthage's pride and trampling it underfoot, thus giving his fellow citizens a joy greater than any they had hoped for and restoring their supremacy.

4.53 Polybius *Histories* 15.14.1–9: The Battle of Zama, 202 BC

Scipio had marched his troops out to the Great Plains and Hannibal encamped nearby at Zama, about 160 kilometres south-west of Carthage. After a conference, requested by Hannibal, they proceeded to battle. Hannibal had 36,000 infantry, 4,000 cavalry and 80 elephants, outnumbering Scipio's 29,000 infantry and 6,000 cavalry. There was so much carnage that Scipio re-formed his troops and the battle proceeded as Polybius describes below. The arrival of the cavalry of Masinissa and Laelius 'in the nick of time' was critical for the Roman victory.

1 The space between the remaining armies was full of blood, slaughter and corpses, and this obstacle to his pursuit of the enemy put the Roman general in a great quandary; **2** for the slippery nature of the corpses, which were covered in blood and had fallen in heaps, and the piles of arms, which had been thrown away at random along with the bodies, would make it difficult for his men to remain in their ranks while crossing the ground. **3** Nevertheless, after moving the wounded to the rear of the army and calling back by trumpet those of the hastati who were pursuing the enemy, he placed these in the front of the battle opposite the enemy's centre **4** and, getting the principes and triarii to close their ranks on each wing, ordered them to advance through the dead. **5** When these had got across and were in a line with the hastati, the phalanxes engaged with each other with the greatest eagerness and enthusiasm. **6** As both sides were a good match in numbers, spirit, courage and armour, the battle was for a long time undecided, with men falling honourably where they stood, **7** until Masinissa and Laelius returned from pursuing the cavalry and joined battle fortuitously at the right moment. **8** When they fell on Hannibal's men from the rear, most of them were cut down in their ranks, while few of those who fled managed to escape, as the cavalry were nearby and the region was level. **9** More than 1,500 Romans fell, and more than 20,000 Carthaginians, with nearly as many being taken prisoner. **15.1** This was the outcome of the final battle between the two aforementioned commanders, the one which decided everything in the Romans' favour.

4.54 Livy *History of Rome* 30.35.3–11, 37.13: Livy praises Hannibal

35.4: Hadrumentum was Hannibal's base (Livy 30.29.1). **35.10**: Hannibal was nine years old when he left Carthage for Spain. **37.13**: Hannibal was elected as one of the two suffetes in 196. He did not leave Carthage until 195 and thereafter spent several years with Antiochus III (doc. 5.30) and the years 187 to 183 with King Prusias of Bithynia. He committed suicide in 183 when Prusias decided to surrender him to Flamininus.

35.3 Over 20,000 of the Carthaginians and their allies were killed on that day; about the same number were captured, with 132 military standards and

11 elephants; about 1,500 of the victors fell. **4** In the commotion Hannibal escaped with a few of his cavalry and fled to Hadrumentum. He had tried everything possible both before the battle and during it before he left the fighting, **5** and even by Scipio's admission and that of all the military experts he deserved praise for having drawn up his battle-line that day with remarkable skill . . .

10 After performing this as his last act of military skill, Hannibal fled to Hadrumentum but was summoned from there to Carthage, returning in the thirty-sixth year since he had left it as a boy. **11** In the senate house he admitted that he had been conquered not only in the battle but in the war and that there was no hope of safety except in treating for peace . . . **37.13** Some authors relate that Hannibal went straight from the battle to the coast and then, on a ship prepared for him, sailed immediately to King Antiochus, and that, when Scipio demanded that Hannibal be surrendered to him before everything else, the answer was that Hannibal was not in Africa.

4.55 Lucilius *Satires* 29.3.952–3: Lucilius on Hannibal

This quotation probably concerns Hannibal's defeat at Zama (202 BC), when Scipio's tactics neutralised Hannibal's elephants.

> . . . that in this way, I say, that old fox, that old wolf
> Hannibal was taken in.

4.56 Ennius *Scipio* 1–6: Scipio Africanus the hero

Ennius devoted a whole poem to the African campaigns of his friend Scipio, who was given the cognomen 'Africanus' for his victories there. This was the highpoint of his career: he was censor in 199 and consul again in 194.

> From the rising sun above the marshes of Maiotis
> There is no one able to match his deeds . . .
> If it is right for anyone to ascend to the regions of the gods
> To me alone heaven's great gate lies open . . .
> Here lies that man to whom no citizen or enemy
> Will be able to render a recompense befitting his services.

4.57 Naevius *Fragment*: Satires on the Roman commanders

An unassigned fragment from a fabula togata (comedy). Naevius was less generous than Ennius and appears to have retailed scandal about Scipio; for Scipio's Hellenising dress (the pallium), see doc. 5.54.

> Even he, who often with his hand gloriously achieved great exploits,
> Whose deeds now live and flourish, pre-eminent among all nations,
> He, with just a single cloak (pallium), was dragged by his father from his mistress.

PEACE TERMS

The peace treaty came into effect in 201 BC. After Zama, the defeat of all their forces and of their last hope, Hannibal, the Carthaginians had to surrender or else endure a long siege. Hannibal was instrumental in arguing for peace (Polyb. 15.19.1–9, Livy 30.37.7–10). The Second Punic War was over.

4.58 Polybius *Histories* 15.18.1–8: Peace terms offered to Carthage

The conditions that Rome had proposed in 203 were a little more lenient. The terms were crushing, but Carthage would survive.

1 The main points of the terms proposed were as follows: Carthage was to retain all the cities she had earlier possessed in Africa before entering on the last war against the Romans, and all her former territory, all flocks and herds, slaves and other property; **2** from that day onwards the Carthaginians were to suffer no further injury, they were to be governed by their own laws and customs and not have a garrison. **3** These were the lenient conditions; the others of an opposite nature were as follows: the Carthaginians were to pay reparation to the Romans for all acts of injustice during the truce; prisoners of war and deserters who had come into their hands at any time were to be handed over; all ships of war, with the exception of ten triremes, were to be handed over, **4** as were all elephants; they were not to make war on any people outside Libya at all, and on none in Libya without the Romans' consent; **5** they were to restore to King Masinissa all the houses, territory, cities and other property which had belonged to him or to his ancestors within the boundaries which were to be assigned to him; **6** they were to provide the Roman army with corn for three months and with pay until a reply should be received from Rome concerning the treaty; **7** they were to pay an indemnity of 10,000 talents of silver over a period of 50 years in instalments of 200 Euboic talents each year; **8** and they were to hand over as a guarantee of good faith 100 hostages, to be chosen by the Roman commander from the young men between the ages of 14 and 30.

4.59 Livy *History of Rome* 30.45.1–7: Scipio's triumph, 201 BC

This is the first time Livy mentions Polybius (cf. 33.10.10: 'a not unknown author'). Scipio celebrated his triumph over Hannibal, the Poeni (Carthaginians) and Syphax. (Scipio had not been given a triumph for his Spanish success because he was a privatus, private citizen, at that time.) Culleo was a senator, captured in Africa.

1 With peace made by land and sea, and his army embarked on ships, Scipio crossed to Lilybaeum in Sicily. **2** After sending a large proportion of his soldiers on board ship, he made his way to Rome through Italy, which was enjoying peace just as much as the victory, while not only cities poured out to honour him but crowds of countryfolk also blocked the roads, and on his arrival he rode into the city in the most distinguished of all triumphs. **3** He brought into the treasury 123,000 pounds of silver in weight. To his soldiers he distributed 400 asses each from the booty. **4** Syphax by his death was removed rather from the sight of the spectators than from the glory of the triumphing general; he had died not long before at Tibur, where he had been taken from Alba. However, his death attracted general notice because he was given a state funeral. **5** Polybius states that this king was led in the triumph, and he is an authority not to be lightly dismissed. Following Scipio as he triumphed was Quintus Terentius Culleo, wearing a liberty cap, who for the rest of his life, as was proper, honoured Scipio as the author of his freedom. **6** Whether his popularity with the soldiers or the favour of the people first gave him the honorific surname of Africanus, just like Felix for Sulla and Magnus for Pompey in our fathers' time, I cannot say. **7** He was certainly the first general to be distinguished by the name of a nation conquered by him; later, following his example, men who were in no way his equals in victory won eminent superscriptions for their masks and glorious surnames for their families.

4.60 Livy *History of Rome* 31.13.1–9: War bonds, 200 BC

In 210, businessmen had loaned money to the state to enable Rome to continue the war against Hannibal, to be repaid in three instalments. The third instalment of this loan, due in 200, was not actually repaid until 196; even though the Punic War was over, Rome was still involved in war against Philip of Macedon.

1 When the consuls were ready to set off to their provinces, **2** a number of private citizens, who were owed this year the third instalment of repayment on the loans made in the consulship of Marcus Valerius (Laevinus) and Marcus Claudius (Marcellus), appealed to the senate, **3** as the consuls had stated that, because the treasury had hardly enough funds for the new war, which was to be waged with a great fleet and great armies, there was no money at present to make them this payment. **4** The senate could not withstand their complaints: if the state wanted to use for the Macedonian War the money lent for the Punic War, with one war arising after another, what would happen except that, in return for their generosity, their money would be confiscated, as if it had been a crime? **5** Since these private citizens were making a reasonable request, but the state was nevertheless unable to pay back the loan, **6** the senate decided on a middle course halfway between justice and expediency: that, because many of the creditors said there was land for sale everywhere, land which they would like to buy, they should be given the opportunity to receive public land within the fiftieth milestone from the city. **7** The consuls were to give a valuation on the land and impose a rent of one *as* per iugerum to show that it was still public land; **8** when the state was able to pay its debts, if any of them preferred to have the money rather than the land, he could give the land back to the people. **9** The private citizens happily accepted this arrangement.

THE THIRD PUNIC WAR, 151–146 BC

Rome and Carthage made peace in 201 BC. By the 150s Carthage was once again prosperous. Its main problem was with Masinissa, king of Numidia (c. 238–148 BC), who continually encroached on Carthaginian territory. The Carthaginians complained to Rome in 153, and an embassy, including Cato, was sent from Rome, which saw how prosperous and populous Carthage had become. Upon his return, therefore, Cato ended every senatorial speech with 'Delenda est Carthago': 'Carthage must be destroyed' (doc. 4.61). The Carthaginians eventually declared war on Masinissa in 151/50 BC, which provided an excuse for the Romans. The Third Punic War saw the deaths or enslavement of thousands of Carthaginians and the destruction of a city with a long history and vibrant culture; it was almost certainly unnecessary and counts as one of the great tragedies of Mediterranean history. But Scipio won his gloria (reputation), a great triumph was celebrated, and Rome moved on to its next round of conquests.

4.61 Plutarch *Life of Cato the Elder* 26.1–27.5: Carthage must be destroyed!

Carthage was of course usually much more than three days by sea from Rome; Cato was a decisive influence in the declaration of war, but whether he was the foremost articulator of senatorial fears or actually moulded senatorial policy is unclear. He died in 149 BC.

26.1 The last of Cato's public services is said to have been the destruction of Carthage. It was actually Scipio the Younger who completed the work, but the war was undertaken mainly on the counsel and advice of Cato, in the following way. **2** Cato was sent to the Carthaginians and Masinissa the Numidian, who were at war with each other, to inquire into the reasons for their conflict. Masinissa had been a friend of the Roman people from the beginning, and the Carthaginians had entered into a treaty with Rome after their defeat by Scipio (Africanus), which deprived them of their empire and imposed a heavy monetary indemnity. **3** Finding, however, that the city was not, as the Romans thought, in a poor and unprosperous state, but well populated with good fighting men, teeming with immense wealth, full of all kinds of arms and provisions for war, and not a little proud of this, Cato thought that it was not the time for the Romans to be organising the affairs of the Numidians and Masinissa; rather, if they did not now put a stop to the city which had always been their most hostile enemy and was now grown to so unbelievable an extent, they would once more be in danger as great as before. **4** So he quickly returned to Rome and advised the senate that the former defeats and disasters of the Carthaginians had lessened not so much their power as their foolishness, and that these were likely to make them in the end not weaker, but more skilful in warfare, while their conflict with the Numidians was a prelude to conflict with the Romans, and peace and treaty were just names for a war which was waiting for a suitable opportunity to arise . . . **27.1** In addition to this, it is reported that Cato arranged to drop a Libyan fig in the senate when he shook out the folds of his toga. To the senators who admired its size and beauty, he remarked that the country where it grew was only three days' sail from Rome. **2** And in one respect he was even more violent, in that, whenever he gave his vote on any issue whatever, he would add the words: 'In my view Carthage must be destroyed!' . . . **5** In this way Cato is said to have brought about the third and last war against the Carthaginians.

4.62 Appian *Punic Wars* 17.112: Scipio Aemilianus' first consulship

The Carthaginians refused to accede to Rome's demand that they abandon their city and settle at least 10 (Roman) miles from the sea, and the consuls began the war. P. Cornelius

Scipio Aemilianus, the second son of L. Aemilius Paullus but adopted by P. Cornelius Scipio, the son of *the* Scipio (victor of 201 BC), was then elected to the consulship for 146 BC, though he had not held the aedileship or praetorship; he was also several years under age. He restored morale in the Roman army in Africa and campaigned as relentlessly as he did later in 134 at Numantia (docs 5.49–50).

When Piso's failure and the Carthaginians' preparations were reported at Rome, the people were angry and apprehensive over the escalating war – immense and relentless as it was – with such a close neighbour, and they could not expect any peaceful resolution, as they had been the first to contravene the agreement. Remembering the recent achievements of Scipio while still a military tribune in Libya, and comparing them to current events, and bearing in mind the reports written to them by their friends and relatives in the army, they passionately wanted to send Scipio to Carthage as consul. The elections were approaching, and Scipio was a candidate for the aedileship (as, because of his age, the laws did not allow him to hold the consulship) – and the people elected him consul. This was illegal, and the consuls pointed out the law to them, but they implored and hectored them, shouting that by the laws of Tullius and Romulus the people had jurisdiction over the elections and that they could annul or ratify any of the electoral laws as they chose. Finally one of the tribunes stated that he would strip the consuls of the right to hold elections unless they submitted to the people's demand. The senate then permitted the tribunes to revoke this law and enact it again after one year – just as the Spartans did when, out of necessity, they freed from dishonour those who were captured at Pylos, stating, 'Let the laws sleep today.' In the same way, Scipio, while standing for the aedileship, was elected consul, and when his colleague, Drusus, told him to cast lots to decide which of them would have Africa, one of the tribunes proposed that the decision regarding this command should be in the hands of the people – and the people chose Scipio. He was granted by conscription an army as numerous as those who had been killed and as many volunteers as he could attract from the allies, and to send to kings and cities, as he chose, letters written in the name of the Roman people which would bring him assistance from the cities and kings.

4.63 Appian *Punic Wars* 8.128–30.610–17, 620: The end of Carthage

Polybius was with Scipio and an eye-witness of the city's destruction. Hasdrubal, the Carthaginian commander, surrendered to Scipio in person, and what was left of Carthage was destroyed on the senate's orders.

610 Scipio's energies were directed towards an attack on Byrsa; this was the most strongly fortified part of the city, and most of the inhabitants had taken refuge there. There were three streets leading up to it, with densely packed, six-storey houses on all sides, from which the Romans were targeted, but they captured the first houses and from them attacked those on the neighbouring houses. **611** When they had taken these over, they placed planks and boards over the narrow passages between and crossed as if on bridges. **612** While one battle was taking place up on the roofs, another was going on in the streets as opponents met each other. Everywhere was full of groaning, shrieks, cries and all kinds of suffering; some were killed hand-to-hand, others were thrown alive down from the roofs to the pavement, some falling onto the points of spears, or other sharp points, or swords. **613** No one as yet began lighting fires until Scipio had reached Byrsa; then he set fire to the three streets altogether and ordered that the burning streets be made passable so that the troops as they moved position might pass through freely. **614** After this came new horrific scenes, as the fire consumed and ravaged everything, with the soldiers destroying the houses not little by little, but demolishing them all at once. **615** The crashing became much louder, and with the stones fell heaps of corpses. Others were still living, especially old men and children and women, who had hidden in the recesses of houses, some wounded, others half-burnt, uttering hideous cries. **616** Still others, being hurled and falling from so great a height along with stones and timbers and fire, were torn into various horrible shapes, smashed and broken. **617** Nor was this the end of their sufferings; for the stone movers, who were removing the rubbish with axes, mattocks and poles and clearing the streets to make them passable, removed the dead and those still living into holes in the ground, some with axes and mattocks, others with the hooks on their poles, sweeping them like timber or stones, or turning them over with iron tools — and humans were used for filling up ditches . . . **620** Six days and nights were spent in such labours, with the soldiers working in rotation so they might not be worn out with sleeplessness, toil, slaughter and hideous sights.

4.64 Strabo *Geography* 17.3.14–15: The site of Carthage

Most of these details are taken from App. *Pun.* 13–14. Ten ships, not 12, were mentioned in the Second Punic War treaty. Strabo here refers to the numbers of arms surrendered at the demand of the consuls for 149 BC.

14 Carthage, too, is situated on a kind of peninsula which comprises a circuit of 360 stades, this circuit having a wall, while 60 stades of its length are taken up by the neck itself from sea to sea, which is where the Carthaginians had their elephant stalls and is a spacious place. Near the centre of the city was the acropolis, which they called Byrsa, a fairly steep hill inhabited all around, with at the top the temple of Asclepius, which the wife of Hasdrubal burnt during the sack, along with herself. The harbours lie below the acropolis, as does Cothon, a circular island surrounded by a strait which has ship sheds all around on both sides.

15 . . . The Carthaginians' power should appear evident from the last war, in which they were defeated by Scipio Aemilianus and their city utterly destroyed. For when they began to wage this war, they possessed 300 cities in Libya and had 700,000 people in the city, and, when they were under siege and compelled to turn to surrender, they gave up 200,000 suits of armour and 3,000 catapults, on the understanding that there would not be a war again; but when they decided to recommence the war, they suddenly organised weapons manufacture, and each day produced 140 fitted shields, 300 swords, 500 spears and 1,000 catapult missiles, and the women slaves provided the hair for the catapults. Moreover, though they had only 12 ships from 50 years earlier, in accordance with the treaty made in the second war, they then, although they had already fled for refuge into the Byrsa, constructed 120 decked ships in two months, and, since the mouth of Cothon was being guarded, they dug another mouth, from which the fleet unexpectedly sailed out; for old timber had been stored away and a large number of craftsmen were in waiting and maintained at public expense. But despite all this, Carthage was still captured and razed to the ground.

4.65 *CIL* I² 2225: Carthaginians continue in Sardinia

A marble pedestal inscribed in both Latin and Punic, found on Sardinia, dating to not earlier than the time of Sulla.

To Himilco, son of Idnibal, who superintended the construction of this temple by the state's decree, his son Himilco set up this statue.

5

Rome's Mediterranean Empire

Rome's first encounter with Macedon (the First Macedonian War) took place following Philip V's alliance with Hannibal in 215 BC (doc. 4.45); Philip hoped to force the Romans to withdraw from the Illyrian coast. It was in this context that the Romans sent envoys to Greek states hostile to Macedon, and Marcus Valerius Laevinus made a treaty with the Aetolians against Philip in 212/11 BC (doc. 5.22). This was Rome's first alliance in the eastern Mediterranean. Before 205, Antiochus III of Syria (223–187) was occupied with restoring Seleucid control of Armenia and Iran (Polyb. 11.39.11–16), after which he adopted the title of Great King and attempted to regain control of western Asia Minor. He then took advantage of the death of Ptolemy Philopator of Egypt in 204 to invade Coele Syria and seize the Egyptian possessions of Phoenicia and Palestine. The peace of Phoenice was made between Philip and Rome in 205, but from 203 Philip, after some incursions into Illyria, continued his expansion in the Aegean, defeating Rhodes, capturing Miletus and attacking Pergamum. In 201 Rhodes and Attalus, king of Pergamum, requested Roman aid (Livy 31.2.1–3). Envoys were sent to Philip demanding that he make war against no Greek states and pay compensation to Attalus (Polyb. 16.27.2–3); the envoys then proceeded to Egypt to request Ptolemy's support should war eventuate against Philip (Livy 31.2.3–4; cf. Polyb. 16.34.2–3). Rome decided on war, despite an initial vote against it in the assembly (which suggests that it was less popular with the people than with the magisterial class), to be under the command of Publius Sulpicius Galba, one of the consuls for 200, who received Macedonia as his province (Livy 31.6.1–8.2); Philip meanwhile was ravaging Attica and besieging Abydus to gain control of the Hellespont. The Aetolians again joined Rome in 199, and in 198 the Achaean league broke its alliance with Macedon and defected to Rome. Flamininus, consul in 198, promoted the image of Rome as liberator of Philip's Greek possessions from Macedon and won the support of southern and central Greece by early 197. Philip was defeated at the battle of Cynoscephalae in 197 and agreed to withdraw from Greece, including the 'Three Fetters' of Greece: Demetrias, Chalcis and Acrocorinth (doc. 5.23). In 196, at the Isthmian Games, Flamininus proclaimed the unrestricted freedom of the Greeks (doc. 5.24), and in 194 all Roman troops were finally withdrawn.

Antiochus III had taken advantage of Rome's war against Philip to recover coastal territories in Asia Minor in 197, attacking Smyrna and Lampsacus in the winter or spring of 196 and crossing to Europe, where he rebuilt the town of Lysimachia on the Thracian coast. Hannibal fled from Carthage to Antiochus in 195, which intensified Rome's concern. Envoys were sent to Antiochus at Lysimachia to demand that he leave the autonomous cities of Asia Minor alone and withdraw from those that had belonged to Ptolemy; if he did not withdraw from Europe, Rome would interfere on behalf of the freedom of the Greeks in Asia (Polyb. 18.49.3–51.10). Antiochus continued military activities in Thrace in 193 and 192; meanwhile the disgruntled Aetolians captured Demetrias but failed to take Sparta and Chalcis (Livy 35.31–9). At their invitation Antiochus crossed to Demetrias in the autumn of 192, thus provoking war with Rome. In spring 191, the consul Manius Acilius Glabrio took charge with 20,000 men. With little support from within Greece, Antiochus decided to make a stand at Thermopylae, and his army was totally defeated. Lucius Scipio (brother of Africanus) and Gaius Laelius were elected consuls for 190; after arranging a truce with the Aetolians, in autumn 190 the Scipio brothers led the first Roman army into Asia, where Antiochus was defeated at Magnesia. He agreed to the Romans' terms at the peace of Apamea, signed in 188 (doc. 5.30).

In 184 or 183 Philip was instructed to withdraw his garrisons from Thracian cities claimed by Eumenes of Pergamum (Polyb. 22.13.1–2, 23.1.1–4, 3.1–3; Livy 39.33.1–34.1, 46.6–9, 53.10). Demetrius, Philip's younger son, who had been a hostage in Rome, returned in 183 and was murdered in 180 for supposedly plotting with the Romans to seize the throne (Livy 40.20.3–6, 24.1–8, 54.1–55.8). Following Philip's death in 179, his son Perseus tried to reassert Macedon's position against the background of increasing intransigence from Rome. When Eumenes of Pergamum brought charges against Perseus in 172, the latter was declared an enemy, and the war (the Third Macedonian War) was entrusted to the consuls of 171 (Livy 42.11.1–13.12, 18.1–5). After some Macedonian successes, Perseus was finally manoeuvred by Lucius Aemilius Paullus (cos. 182 and 168) into giving battle at Pydna (Livy 44.41.1–42.9); his army was defeated. He later surrendered at Samothrace and featured in Paullus' triumph.

Rome was involved in new theatres of war in the 150s, such as Dalmatia, c. 155 (according to Polybius, to check the effeminacy at Rome caused by 12 years of peace: 32.13.6–8; Livy *Per.* 46–47); Spain, from 154 to 133; Macedonia, where a pretender, Andriscus, had initial successes in 149 but was captured in 148 (Polyb. 36.10.2–7; Livy *Per.* 49–52); and Carthage and mainland Greece in 146, when Corinth was sacked and enslaved by the consul Lucius Mummius (doc. 5.41). The destruction of Carthage by Scipio Aemilianus ended the long tension between Rome and Carthage (docs 4.62–64), while the sack of Corinth saw Greece, with Macedonia, become a Roman province. Asia Minor was to follow with the death of Attalus III in 134/3 (doc. 5.45). In the West, from 201 to 190, one or both consuls had been assigned to the Gallic region to reconquer the tribes that had regained their freedom with the arrival of Hannibal. These were finally subdued by Publius Scipio Nasica as consul in 191. The Latin colonies of Cremona and

Placentia (both established in 218) were resettled in 206 and reinforced in 190 (Livy 37.46.9–47.2), with further colonies such as Bononia, Forum Livii, Regium Lepidum, Parma and Mutina, and Aquileia established in the 180s. Spain, at the beginning of the second century, consisted of cities of Punic or Greek character on the coast with numerous independent peoples in the interior. The Romans initially became involved in Spain to drive out the Carthaginians. Following Scipio Africanus' victory at Ilipa, two Spanish provinces (Hispania Ulterior, 'Further', and Citerior, 'Nearer') were created, signifying that control and conquest of Spain had become government policy (Livy 32.28.11). In 198 two new praetorships were created for these Spanish provinces (Livy 32.27.6). Cato was to serve in Spain as consul in 195 (doc. 5.46), while both Tiberius Sempronius Gracchus (the elder) and Lucius Aemilius Paullus governed one of the Spanish provinces. Roman misgovernment led to escalating warfare from the middle of the century (docs 5.48–49), until the last real stronghold of Spanish resistance, Numantia, was finally destroyed by Scipio Aemilianus in 133 (docs 5.52–53).

Ancient sources: most valuable is the extensive epigraphic evidence, from the Hellenistic East and elsewhere, recording treaties (docs 5.22), edicts (docs 5.25, 47), dedications by victorious commanders (docs 5.33, 42–43) and senatus consulta and letters (docs 5.29, 32, 44–45). Of literary sources, Polybius (c. 200– c. 118 BC) is the earliest: he was a Greek historian concerned with chronicling Rome's rapid rise to power between 220 and 167 (he later continued the work down to 146) and contemporary with much of the material about which he writes: he was an eye-witness of certain important events, such as the sack of Carthage in 146. He consulted all types of sources, was well travelled, spoke with eye-witnesses and is often critical of other more 'slip-shod' historians. He is biased towards Scipio Aemilianus and his family and, as an Achaean, against the Aetolian league, yet he attempts to discover the facts and interpret them scientifically. He frequently quotes or paraphrases treaties (docs 5.23, 28–31, 38). Only books 1–5 of the 40 books of his *Histories* remain intact; others are represented by excerpts made by later writers or are extensively used by Livy. Books 21–45 of Livy's *Ab urbe condita* cover the period 218–167 BC, with book 31 beginning the account of Rome's domination of the Greek East and focusing through to book 45 on the conflicts with Philip V of Macedon, Antiochus and Perseus. Livy relies on literary sources, and from book 31 onwards he clearly used Polybius as his main source, though he also looked at the works of the first-century writers Q. Claudius Quadrigarius, Valerius Antias and L. Coelius Antipater and perhaps others; for missing books of Livy there are the *Periochae*, fourth-century AD summaries of the text (see doc. 5.50), which may not always reflect entirely accurately the contents of Livy's books. His account generally tends to be pro-Roman. Livy gives a description of the Roman army c. 340 BC, while Polybius records detailed information (docs 5.7, 11–20) on the army and its practices in his own day. Appian of Alexandria was writing in the second century AD; his book on the *Spanish Wars* preserves valuable material for the Roman conquest of Spain (docs 5.46, 48, 52–53), especially because many of the sources he used (Polybius was one of them) are now lost. Pausanias (c. AD 150) wrote a *Description of Greece*, concentrating particularly on monuments and monumental art before 150 BC; his account of the sack of Corinth (doc. 5.41) is a useful supplement to Polybius.

Plutarch's *Lives* have been used minimally in this chapter, though his biographies of Flamininus, Philopoemen and Aemilius Paullus help to flesh out portrayals of some of the main characters of the time; Plutarch's primary aim, however, is a moralising one. His *Life of Titus* (Flamininus) preserves a hymn to Flamininus sung at his festival on Chalcis (doc. 5.26). The 20 books of Aulus Gellius, the *Attic Nights*, written in the second century AD, are concerned particularly with matters of Latin grammar and expression; his discussion of usages often includes valuable citations of passages of text otherwise lost (e.g., doc. 5.37).

THE IDEOLOGY OF ROMAN MILITARY SUPREMACY

Military glory was always the highest form of prestige in Rome – after all, the Romans believed that they were descended from the god Mars himself (doc. 5.6). The greatest honour for any Roman magistrate was the victorious command of an army and the award of a triumph (docs 2.32–35); military virtues were seen as those most essential for any Roman, and Rome's destiny was to rule the inhabited world.

5.1 Plutarch *Life of Coriolanus* 1.6: Valour as the highest virtue

Gnaeus Marcius Coriolanus supposedly received his surname for taking Corioli from the Volsci in 493 BC. Plutarch contrasts the Greek terms *arete*, virtue, and *andreia* (from *aner*: the qualities belonging to a man, hence bravery). The Latin *virtus* (from *vir*, man) means manliness or the excellences of a man, particularly that of bravery in combat.

In those days Rome honoured most highly that aspect of virtue concerned with warlike and military achievements, and proof of this can be seen by the fact that the Romans have only one word for virtue, which is *virtus* (valour), and use the specific virtue of valour to stand for virtue in general.

5.2 Livy *History of Rome* 9.4.10–14: The army *is* Rome

When the Romans were trapped at the Caudine Forks by the Samnites in 321, the Samnites proposed that the Roman army should pass under the yoke (unconditional surrender). Here Lucius Lentulus (cos. 328) reacts to the suggestion; Rome went into mourning at the news of this disgrace (doc. 1.67).

10 Indeed I confess that death on behalf of one's country is a glorious thing, and I am ready either to devote myself on behalf of the Roman people and legions or to throw myself into the midst of the enemy; **11** but it is here I see my country, here are all Rome's legions, and, unless they choose to rush upon death for their own sakes, what have they to save by dying? **12** 'The roofs and walls of the city', someone might say, 'and the multitude by whom the city is inhabited.' But, by Hercules, all these are betrayed, not saved, once this army is annihilated! **13** For who will protect them then? The common folk, unwarlike and unarmed, I suppose! — just as it preserved them from the Gallic attack . . . **14** Here are all our hopes and resources, and if we save these we save our country, whereas if we give them up to death we abandon and betray it.

5.3 Livy *History of Rome* 9.16.16: Papirius Cursor makes a joke!

Papirius Cursor routed the Samnites in 319 and made them pass under the yoke in revenge for the Roman defeat at the Caudine Forks (cf. docs 1.67, 2.33). No general was harder on his men.

Indeed, a story is told how his cavalrymen once dared to ask him to let them off some task in return for a job well done, and that he replied to them, 'So you won't be able to say that I don't let you off anything, I excuse you from patting your horses' backs when you dismount.'

5.4 Lucilius *Satires* 26.708–11: Rome's invincibility

One of Lucilius' earliest books of satire, perhaps written c. 131. For Viriathus, see docs 5.48, 50, for Hannibal, docs 4.22–26.

> ... the Roman people has often been defeated by force and overcome in many battles
> But never in an actual war, on which everything depends –
> No, we do not know the disgrace of being defeated in war by a barbarian
> Viriathus or Hannibal.

5.5 Cicero *In Defence of Murena* 22: Military excellence

L. Licinius Murena (cos. 63; cf. doc. 12.17) had served with Lucullus in Asia and been propraetor of Transalpine Gaul in 64. Cicero is defending him for electoral bribery.

Excellence in military service outranks all other forms of excellence. It is this that has won the Roman people its fame, that has won this city its everlasting glory; it is this that has made the whole world obey this government; all the activities within this city, all these glorious pursuits of ours, the applause and the labours here in the forum, all lie under the care and protection of excellence in warfare.

5.6 Vergil *Aeneid* 1.275–88: Rome's great destiny

Jupiter here prophesies to the goddess Venus, mother of Aeneas, 'ancestor' of Julius Caesar and Augustus (here called 'Julius'), the future military success of Rome, including the conquest of Greece. Mars was the father of Romulus and Remus; the house of Assaracus means the Trojans and their Roman descendants; Julus, son of Aeneas, was supposedly the ancestor of the Julian gens; cf. doc. 15.36 for Augustus' nephew Marcellus.

> 275 Then, joyful in the tawny skin of the she-wolf, his nurse,
> Romulus will inherit the line and found the walls of Mars,
> Calling his people 'Romans' after his own name.
> For these I limit their empire by no boundaries or periods of time;
> I have granted them dominion without end. Yes, even fierce Juno,

280   Who now with fear wearies both sea and earth and sky,
           Shall turn to better counsels, and with me cherish
           The Romans, masters of the world, nation of the toga.
           This is my decree. As the years slip by, an age will come
           When the house of Assaracus shall crush with servitude
285   Phthia and famed Mycenae and hold dominion over conquered Argos.
           From this glorious line shall be born the Trojan Caesar,
           To make Ocean his limit of empire, the stars the limit of his fame,
           A Julius, his name descended from great Julus.

THE IDEOLOGY OF THE MILITARY HERO

Roman citizens were by definition soldiers and liable for service from the age of 17 to 46 (at 46 men joined the seniores). Citizens were called up by the dilectus (levy), for which the consuls, as commanders, were responsible; the maximum number of annual campaigns was probably between 16 and 20, while the equites needed to serve only ten. Until Marius, it was those with property who served (doc. 9.10).

5.7 Polybius *Histories* 6.39.1–10: Awards for valour

Decorations for wounding or killing the enemy were awarded only for courage above and beyond the call of duty. The armour of an enemy commander killed in single combat by the general – known as the spolia opima – was dedicated on the Capitol.

1 The Romans also have an excellent way of encouraging the young soldiers to face danger. **2** Whenever some of them distinguish themselves in action, the general summons the army to an assembly, brings forward those whom he considers to have conducted themselves with conspicuous excellence, and first makes a speech in praise of the courageous actions of each one, and of anything else in their conduct worthy of commendation, **3** and then hands out the following rewards: to the man who has wounded an enemy, a javelin; and to the man who has killed and despoiled an enemy, a cup, if he is in the infantry, and horse-trappings, if in the cavalry – although originally the reward was only a spear. **4** These rewards are not given to men who have wounded or stripped enemies in a pitched battle or the capture of a city but only to those who have done so in skirmishes or other similar situations, in which there was no need to hazard themselves in single combat, but who threw themselves into this voluntarily and by their own choice.

    5 When a city is stormed, the first man to scale the wall is awarded a crown of gold. **6** In the same way, those who have shielded and saved any of the citizens or allies receive honorary gifts from the consul, and those whom they saved present them of their own free will with a crown; if not, the tribunes who judge the case compel them to do so. **7** A man preserved in this way also reveres his preserver like a father for the rest of his life and must treat him in every way like a parent. **8** By such incentives, they incite to emulation and rivalry in times of danger not only those who are present and witness what takes place but those who stay at home as well; **9** for the recipients of such gifts, apart from their prestige in the army and their fame soon afterwards at home, are especially distinguished in religious processions after their return to their native land, for in these no one is allowed to wear decorations except those honoured for their bravery by the consuls, **10** and they hang up the spoils they have won in the most conspicuous places in their homes, considering them as the tokens and evidence of their valour.

5.8 Livy *History of Rome* 7.37.1–3: The grass crown

In a conflict against the Samnites in 345/3 BC the military tribune Publius Decius Mus (cos. 340) took and held a hilltop; in the Roman victory 30,000 Samnites were killed. Both consuls celebrated a triumph, with Decius given a place of honour in the procession. Pliny *Nat. Hist.* 22.6–13 records eight recipients of the grass crown (the last being Augustus).

1 After the engagement had terminated in this way, the consul called an assembly (contio) and not only completed the praises of Publius Decius he had begun before but recounted those due to his recent deeds of bravery, and besides other military gifts he gave him a golden crown and a hundred oxen, plus one exceptionally fine fat white one with gilded horns. **2** The soldiers in his troop with him were granted a double ration of grain for life and, for the time being, an ox each and two tunics. Following the consul's presentation, the legions placed on Decius' head the wreath of grass for delivering them from a siege, accompanying the gift with cheering; another wreath, a mark of the same honour, was put on him by his own troops. **3** Wearing these insignia, he sacrificed the fine ox to Mars and gave the other hundred to the soldiers who had been with him on the expedition. To these same soldiers the legions contributed a pound of spelt and a pint (a *sextarius*) of wine each; all this was done with great enthusiasm, the soldiers' cheering demonstrating unanimous approval.

5.9 Livy *History of Rome* 42.34.5–14: Spurius Ligustinus

This incident took place in 171 BC, when there was dissatisfaction because some Romans who had previously served as centurions were drafted as common soldiers. Ligustinus, being over 46, was enlisting voluntarily. He had been on campaign for 22 of the last 30 years, though he had a small farm and eight children.

5 I became a soldier in the consulship of Publius Sulpicius and Gaius Aurelius (200 BC). I spent two years as a common soldier in the army which was taken to Macedonia against King Philip; in the third year, because of my bravery, Titus Quinctius Flamininus made me centurion of the tenth maniple of hastati. **6** After Philip and the Macedonians had been defeated and we were brought back to Italy and discharged, I immediately set out for Spain as a volunteer soldier with the consul Marcus Porcius (Cato, in 195). **7** Those who have had experience of him and other commanders through long service know that, of all the generals now alive, none was a keener observer and judge of bravery. This general judged me worthy to be made centurion of the first century of the hastati. **8** I became a volunteer soldier again for the third time in the army which was sent against the

Aetolians and King Antiochus (191). Manius Acilius made me centurion of the first century of the principes. **9** When King Antiochus had been driven out and the Aetolians beaten, we were brought back to Italy; twice after that I served in campaigns where the legions served for a year. I then campaigned twice in Spain, once when Quintus Fulvius Flaccus was praetor (181) and again when Tiberius Sempronius Gracchus was praetor (180). **10** I was brought back by Flaccus to appear with him along with others whom he brought back from the province for his triumph because of their valour; I went back to the province because Tiberius Gracchus asked me. **11** Four times within a few years I was chief centurion; 34 times I was rewarded by my generals for valour; I have received six civic crowns. I have served 22 years in the army and I am over 50 years old. . . . **13** For myself, as long as anyone who is enrolling armies considers me a suitable soldier, I will never try to be excused from service. **14** Of whatever rank the military tribunes think me fit, that is their decision; I shall make sure that no one in the army surpasses me in bravery; and, that I have always done so, both my generals and those soldiers who served with me are my witnesses.

5.10 Pliny the Elder *Natural History* 7.101–6: The most courageous Roman

Pliny is here discussing the Roman who most demonstrated outstanding courage. He also mentions M. Manlius Capitolinus, who repelled the Gauls from the Capitol in 390, but in Pliny's view his attempt at kingship negated his achievements.

101 Lucius Siccius Dentatus, who was tribune of the plebs in the consulship of Spurius Tarpeius and Aulus Aternius (454 BC), not long after the kings had been expelled, gets an extremely large number of votes for having fought in 120 battles, been the victor in eight challenges to single combat, and having the distinction of 45 scars in front and none on his back. **102** He also captured spoils 34 times, was given 18 spear-shafts, 25 badges of honour, 83 torques, 160 armlets, 26 crowns (including 14 civic crowns, eight of gold, three for being the first to scale the walls, and one for rescuing others from a siege), a bag of money, ten prisoners and with them 20 cows, followed in the triumph of nine generals whose victories were due primarily to him, and furthermore (which I think to be the finest of his achievements) **103** had one of his generals, Titus Romilius, at the end of his consulship, convicted of maladministration. . . .

104 In these cases, indeed, there are great achievements of courage, but even more of fortune: while no one, in my view at any rate, can justly rank any man above Marcus Sergius, even though his great-grandson Catiline lowers his name's fair repute. In his second campaign Sergius lost his right hand, and in two campaigns he was wounded 23 times, with the result that he was disabled in both hands and both feet, with only his spirit unwounded; although crippled, he served afterwards in numerous campaigns. He was twice taken prisoner by Hannibal – he was engaged not just with any old enemy – and twice escaped from Hannibal's incarceration, although he was kept in chains or fetters every single day for 20 months. He fought four times with his left hand alone, and two horses on which he was mounted were cut from under him. **105** He had a right hand of iron made for himself and, going into battle with it tied on, raised the siege of Cremona, saved Placentia, and took 12 enemy camps in Gaul, all of which are known from his speech during his praetorship when he was barred by his colleagues from the sacrifices as disabled – a man who with a different enemy would have heaped up piles of crowns! . . . **106** Others have indeed conquered men, but Sergius conquered Fortune too.

THE ROMAN ARMY

The army was a crucial component of Roman culture and civilisation. The Roman ability to wage war successfully allowed their city-state to emerge from the status of just another community in Italy to become master of the Mediterranean world. Polybius' *Histories* were written to explain Rome's rise as the major power, with a long discussion on the Roman army. He gives the earliest contemporary description of the Roman army, that of the second century BC (docs 5.12–16), including the equipment of the soldiers of his day, while Livy describes the army of the fourth century BC (doc. 5.11).

The legion, first with its maniples and later with its cohorts, was flexible and manoeuvrable, as opposed to the Greek phalanx, with its emphasis on a fixed line. The size of the legion in 340 BC was 5,000 infantry with 300 cavalry (doc. 5.11), while its size in the middle Republic varied between 4,200 or 5,000 infantry (doc. 5.13). Rome's allies – the Latins and Italians – provided her with troops; this was their main obligation to Rome. Cavalry does not appear often in the sources; it seems mainly to have been provided by the allies and fought in Sicily and in Africa.

5.11 Livy *History of Rome* 8.8.3–14: Early army organisation, 340 BC

Livy here notes the change in types of shield: the clipeus (plural: clipei) was round and made of bronze; the scutum (plural: scuta) which replaced it was oval (oblong) and made of wood covered with bull's hide. In the mid-fourth century BC the first two lines of the battle formation were the hastati and principes, each having 15 maniples. Livy divides the last three lines into the triarii, rorarii and accensi (the last two do not appear in Polybius' account, indicating that the army had changed by that time). The 15 maniples of the hastati included 20 light-armed men with the rest being more heavily armed with body armour and the scutum; the 15 maniples of the principes were all heavily and better armed. These 30 maniples were the antepilani. Behind them, the structure became more complicated. Here there were 15 companies (ordines, sing: ordo; Livy does not use the word maniples in describing them), each company having three parts (*vexilla*); the names of the three parts were the triarii, rorarii and accensi, placed in that order within the companies (there were thus 15 ordines, each made up of three vexilla). Livy does not indicate the size of the maniple in 340 BC, but from his description of the ordines they must have had 60 to 70 men each.

3 The Romans had earlier used round shields (clipei), but after they began to serve for pay they made oblong shields (scuta) instead of round ones; and what had earlier been a phalanx, like the Macedonian ones, afterwards began to be a battle-line formed in maniples, **4** the troops in the rear being drawn up in a number of companies (ordines). **5** The first line, the hastati, consisted of 15 maniples, stationed a short distance apart; the maniple included 20 light-armed soldiers, the remainder carrying oblong shields – those who were called light-armed carried only a spear and javelins. **6** This front line of the battle-order contained the pick of the young men who had reached the age for military service. Behind these came a similar number of maniples made up of men of more mature age, who were called the principes, all with oblong shields and especially splendid arms. **7** This body of 30 maniples was called the antepilani, because right behind the standards were positioned another 15 companies, each of which had three sections, the first section of each being named the pilus; **8** a company consisted of three vexilla (standards), a vexillum having 60 soldiers and two centurions, with one standard-bearer (vexillarius), making 186 men altogether. The first standard led the triarii, veteran soldiers of proven courage, the second the rorarii, younger and less experienced men, the third the accensi, the least reliable group, who were for that reason assigned to the line furthest back.

9 When an army had been drawn up in this order, the hastati were the first of all to open the battle. If the hastati were unable to overcome the enemy, they slowly retreated and were received through the gaps between the principes. The fighting was then the job of the principes with the hastati following them. **10** The triarii knelt under their standards with the left leg in front, shields resting against their shoulders, holding their spears fixed in the ground with the point facing upwards, just as if the battle-line was bristling with a protective fortification. **11** If the principes were also unsuccessful in their fighting, they fell back slowly from the front line to the triarii (from which comes the proverb, when things are going badly, 'to have reached the triarii'). **12** The triarii, rising up when they had allowed the principes and hastati to pass through the gaps in their lines, would at once compress their ranks, just as if they were blocking the pathways, and in one unbroken body, with no more reserves behind, would fall upon the enemy; **13** this was especially disconcerting for the enemy, who had followed up those they thought defeated only to see a new line suddenly rising up with increased numbers. **14** There were generally about four legions enlisted, each with 5,000 foot-soldiers and 300 horse to each legion.

POLYBIUS ON ROME'S MILITARY SYSTEM

Polybius' description of the Roman army falls into two overall sections: (a) 6.19–26 on the army itself and its various features, such as the enrolment of troops (doc. 5.13), length of service (doc. 5.12), pay (doc. 5.14) and equipment (doc. 5.15), and (b) 27–42 on the Roman camp (docs 5.16, 18). These details apply to the time at which Polybius was writing, and the army he describes is generally thought to be that which had come about as a result of the Second Punic War.

5.12 Polybius *Histories* 6.19.1–5: Length of service

Roman citizens who were 17 years old were eligible for military duty. The length of time required for military service before political office could be sought indicates the martial character of Roman society and its political institutions. In this document, the military tribunes should not be confused with the plebeian tribunes (for which, see docs 1.23–24). Polybius' Greek for the years of service of the infantry is corrupt, and is usually emended by editors to read 16 years, though six years seems more probable. Under Augustus the term of service was 16 years, but this reflects a period when long service in the armies of the civil war and the professionalisation of the army had taken place.

1 After electing the consuls, they appoint military tribunes, 14 from those who have served for five years **2** and ten from those who have served for ten. With regard to the rest, a cavalryman must complete ten years' service and an infantryman six before reaching the age of 46, **3** except for those whose property was assessed at less than 400 drachmae; all these are assigned to naval service. In the case of a pressing emergency, **4** the infantry are obliged to serve for 20 years. No one is able to hold political office **5** before he has completed ten years' service.

5.13 Polybius *Histories* 6.19.5–21.4: Enlistment of troops

Enlistment took place on the Capitol at Rome. While Polybius refers to an initial day for recruitment, it is clear that enlistment might take several days, which would be understandable given the numbers involved. The tribunes mentioned here are the military tribunes, of whom there were 24.

19.5 When the consuls are about to enrol soldiers, they announce at a meeting of the assembly the day on which all Roman citizens of military age must present themselves. **6** They do this annually. On the appointed day, when those liable for service have arrived in Rome **7** and assembled on the Capitoline Hill, the junior military tribunes divide themselves into four groups in the order in which they have been appointed by the people or consuls, as the main and original division of the Roman forces was into four legions. **8** The four first appointed are allocated to the first legion, the next three to the second, the next four to the third, and the last three to the fourth. **9** Of the senior tribunes, the first two are assigned to the first legion, the next three to the second, the next two to the third, and the last three to the fourth.

20.1 Once the division and appointment of the tribunes has been made so that each legion has the same number of officers, **2** those of each legion take their seats apart and draw lots for the tribes one by one, summoning each in the order of the lottery. **3** From each tribe they select four youths who resemble each other as far as possible in age and physique. **4** When these are brought forward, the officers of the first legion have the first choice, those of the second legion second choice, those of the third third, and those of the fourth last. **5** When the next batch of four are brought forward, the officers of the second legion have first choice, and so on, with those of the first legion last. **6** Then, when another batch of four are brought forward, the officers of the third legion have first choice and those of the second last. **7** By giving each legion the first choice in turn, every legion gets men of roughly the same standard. **8** When they have chosen the required number, that is, when each legion has 4,200 infantry, or 5,000 in times of especial danger, **9** they then used in earlier times to choose the cavalrymen after the 4,200, but now they choose them first, the censor selecting them on the basis of their wealth, and 300 are assigned to each legion.

21.1 When the enrolment has been completed in this way, those tribunes whose duty it is in each legion collect the enrolled soldiers and, picking out of them all one who seems the most suitable, **2** make him take the oath that he will obey his officers and carry out their commands to the best of his ability. **3** Then the others come forward and each in turn swears that he will do the same as the first man. **4** At the same time the consuls send orders to the allied cities in Italy which they wish to contribute allied troops, stating the number required and the day and place at which those selected should present themselves. The cities select the men and administer the oath in a manner similar to the one described and send them off, after appointing a commander and paymaster.

5.14 Polybius *Histories* 6.39.12–15: Army pay

The army was at first a volunteer one, but Rome's continual wars meant that pay had to be introduced for Roman legionaries by the middle Republic. A Greek drachma (6 obols) was roughly equivalent to the Roman denarius. At this stage, deductions for expenses were taken from the pay; a cavalryman's pay was higher to cover the costs of keeping a horse. Allies were not paid by the Roman state but received a food allowance.

12 As their pay the infantrymen each receive two obols a day, centurions twice this, and cavalrymen a drachma. **13** The infantry are each allowed about two-thirds of an Attic medimnus of wheat a month, and the cavalry seven medimni of barley and two of wheat. **14** Of the allies, the infantry get the same, and the cavalry one and one-third medimni of wheat and five of barley. **15** These are provided free to the allies, but in the case of the Romans the quaestor deducts from their pay the price fixed for the grain and their clothes and any additional arms they might need.

5.15 Polybius *Histories* 6.22.1–23.15: Army equipment

The Spanish sword – gladius Hispaniensis – was a short weapon used for chopping and stabbing at close range and adopted from the Spanish; the surviving example is 76 mm long. It differs from the long Gallic sword which was used for slashing and needed room to do so. The legionaries also carried a dagger. While the Roman soldier made use of the *pilum* in the initial stages of a battle, he was primarily a swordsman; Polybius records that each of the hastati had two pila.

22.1 The youngest soldiers, the velites, are ordered to carry a sword, javelins and shield (parma). **2** The shield is strongly constructed and of sufficient size for protection; it is circular and 3 feet in diameter. **3** They also wear a plain helmet (i.e., with no crest), sometimes covered with a wolf's skin or something of that sort, both for protection and as a distinguishing mark by which their officers can recognise them and observe whether or not they show bravery in battle. **4** The wooden shaft of the javelin measures about 2 cubits in length and a finger's breadth in thickness, and the head is a span long and is so thinly hammered out and finely sharpened that it is necessarily bent by the first impact and the enemy are unable to hurl it back; otherwise the weapon could be used by both sides.

23.1 The next in seniority, who are called hastati, are ordered to wear a full set of armour (panoply). **2** The Roman panoply consists, first, of a shield, the convex surface of which measures 2½ feet (5 hemipodia) in width and 4 feet in length, **3** with the depth at its rim being the width of a palm, which is made by gluing two planks together and covering the outer surface first with canvas and then with calf-skin. **4** Its upper and lower edges have a shield-rim which helps it to ward off descending swordblows and protects it when fixed in the ground. **5** An iron boss is also attached to it which protects it from violent blows from stones, pikes and heavy weapons generally. **6** Besides the shield they also carry a sword, which is worn on the right thigh and called a Spanish sword. **7** This has a sharp point and an effective cutting edge on both sides, as the blade is very strong and firm. **8** In addition they have two throwing spears (*pila*), a bronze helmet and greaves. **9** Some of the pila are thick, others thin. Of the thicker kind, some are round and a palm's breadth in diameter, others a palm square. Those of the thin type that they carry, in addition to the others, are like moderate-sized hunting-spears, **10** the length of the wooden shaft of all of these being about 3 cubits. Each is fitted with an iron head which is barbed and of the same length as the shaft; **11** this is fastened securely by attaching it right along the shaft up to the middle and fixing it with numerous rivets, so that in battle the iron will break rather than the fastening come loose, although its thickness at the bottom, where it touches the wood, is the width of one and a half fingers — they take such great care to attach it securely. **12** Finally they wear as an ornament a circle of feathers with three upright black or purple feathers, **13** about a cubit in height. With these placed on the helmet on top of the rest of the armour, every man looks twice his real height, and it gives him a fine appearance which strikes terror in the enemy. **14** The common soldiers also wear in addition a bronze breast-plate a span square, which is placed over the heart and called a heart protector, which completes their armaments, **15** but those who are rated above 10,000 drachmas wear a coat of chain-mail instead of this heart protector. **16** The principes and triarii are armed in the same way except that, instead of pila, the triarii carry thrusting spears (*hastae*).

MILITARY TECHNOLOGY

5.16 Polybius *Histories* 6.27.1–3, 6.31.10–14, 6.34.1–6:
The Roman camp

This is an extract from a lengthy discussion of the Roman army camp (Polyb. 6.27–42). Polybius describes a two-legion camp, half of the larger camp when the two consular armies (i.e., four legions) were together – that is, each two-legion consular army had its own camp but shared one side of it with the other army. The Roman army would encamp each night, and such camps were generally temporary, occupied for that night alone, or for longer periods if outside a besieged town or city. The camp had the appearance of a town, as Polybius notes, with several streets, including the via principalis ('main street'), along which was the praetorium (general's tent), the quaestorium (quaestor's quarters) and the forum.

27.1 Their method of laying out a camp is as follows. Once the site for the camp has been chosen, the position in it most suitable for obtaining a general view and issuing orders is allocated to the general's tent (praetorium). **2** They plant a standard on the spot where they intend to pitch the tent and measure off around the standard a square plot, each side of which is 100 feet from the standard, so that the whole area measures 4 plethra (one plethron = 10,000 square feet). **3** Along one side of this square, in the direction which seems to offer the best facilities for watering and foraging, the Roman legions are stationed . . .

31.10 The result of these arrangements is that the whole camp forms a square, and its division into streets and its general plan gives it the appearance of a town. **11** The rampart is dug on all sides at a distance of 200 feet from the tents, and this empty space serves a number of important uses. **12** To begin with, it provides the suitable facilities necessary for marching the troops in and out; for they all march out into this space via their own streets rather than converging into one street en masse and jostling and trampling each other. **13** It is here, too, that they collect any cattle brought into camp and booty taken from the enemy and guard them safely during the night. **14** But most important of all is that, in night attacks, neither fire nor weapons can reach them, apart from a very few, which are almost harmless because of the distance and the space left in front of the tents . . .

34.1 As regards the construction of the ditch and stockade, the two sides along which their two wings are quartered are the responsibility of the allies, the other two being that of the Romans, one for each legion. **2** Each side is divided into sections, one for each maniple, and the centurions stand by and supervise each section, with two of the military tribunes superintending the work as a whole on each side. **3** They also supervise all other work to do with the camp; they divide themselves into pairs, drawing lots for their turn, and each pair is on duty for two months out of every six, supervising all field operations. **4** The prefects of the allies use the same procedure in dividing their duties. **5** At dawn all the cavalry officers and centurions parade at the tents of the tribunes, and the tribunes report to the consul. He gives the necessary orders to the tribunes, **6** and the tribunes pass them on to the cavalry officers and centurions, and they convey them to the soldiers when the proper time comes.

5.17 Caesar *Gallic War* 2.30–31: Siege works in Gaul

Caesar is here engaged in campaigns in Gaul in 57 BC: the Aduatuci were coming to the aid of the Nervii, but on hearing of their defeat returned home and collected together in a town of great strength on high rocks with a double wall and only one approach.

30 On the arrival of our army, they made frequent sorties from the fortress and engaged with our troops in minor skirmishes; later, when they were enclosed by a rampart 12 feet high, 15,000 feet in circumference, and with forts at frequent intervals, they stayed inside the town. When the mantlets had been pushed forward and a ramp constructed, and they saw a siege tower being erected at some distance, they first made fun of us from the wall and loudly criticised us for having set up so great a machine at such a distance: by what handiwork and what strength, they cried, could men of such short stature (for our stature, short when compared to their own gigantic build, is generally despised by the Gauls) expect to place so heavy a tower on the wall? **31** When, however, they saw the tower moving and approaching the walls, they were dismayed at such a novel and unusual sight and sent envoys to speak to Caesar about peace, in the following way: they considered, they said, that the Romans did not make war without divine assistance, as they could move forward with such speed machines of such height: they therefore submitted themselves and all their possessions to the Romans' power.

MILITARY DISCIPLINE

Roman military discipline was severe and uncompromising. There was no appeal against standard punishments to be inflicted for various offences. But to balance the discipline was the system of rewards (see docs 5.7–10) and the fact that soldiers could not be arbitrarily punished. The punishments for delinquency on the night-watch are clearly understandable: this type of laxness endangered the safety of the camp and the lives of all the men within it.

5.18 Polybius *Histories* 6.34.7–12: The watchword

7 The way they ensure the safe passing round of the watchword for the night is as follows: **8** from the tenth maniple of every class of cavalry and infantry, the maniple which is encamped at the lower end of the street, a man is selected who is relieved from guard duty and who presents himself every day at sunset at the tent of the tribune. He receives the watchword – that is, a wooden tablet with the word inscribed on it – and takes his leave. **9** When he returns to his maniple he hands over the tablet and watchword, in the presence of witnesses, to the commander of the next maniple, who in turn passes it on to the one next to him. **10** All in turn do the same until it reaches the first maniples, the ones near the tents of the tribunes. These men have to return the tablet to the tribunes while it is still light. **11** If all the tablets issued are returned, he knows that the watchword has been given to all the maniples and has passed through them all on the way back to him; **12** if one is missing, he makes inquiry immediately, being able to tell from the inscription from what quarter the tablet has not returned. The person responsible for the hold-up meets with the punishment he deserves.

5.19 Polybius *Histories* 6.37.1–3, 6: Delinquency on the night-watch

Death by beating with cudgels and stoning (the fustuarium) was also the punishment for those who stole in camp, gave false evidence or were homosexuals (doc. 7.59), as well as for anyone punished for the same offence three times.

1 A court-martial composed of the tribunes immediately meets to try him, and if found guilty he is punished by being beaten to death. This is carried out as follows: **2** the tribune takes a cudgel and just touches the condemned man with it, **3** whereupon all those in camp strike him with clubs and stones, usually killing him in the camp itself. **4** But even those able to escape have no hope of safety – how could they? They are not allowed to return to their homes, and no relative would dare to receive such a man in his house. So those who have once fallen into this misfortune are utterly ruined . . . **6** Consequently, because of the severity of this inescapable penalty, the night-watches of the Roman army are kept impeccably.

5.20 Polybius *Histories* 6.38.1–4: 'Decimation'

Decimation was the traditional penalty for desertion or abandoning the standards; Crassus imposed this penalty on the army defeated by Spartacus (doc. 6.50). Death was by the fustuarium (doc. 5.19).

1 If it ever happens that a large body of men behave in the same way (i.e., run away or throw away their weapons) and whole maniples leave their posts under heavy pressure, they reject the possibility of beating to death or executing all who are guilty, but find a solution to the problem which is both effective and terrifying. **2** The tribune assembles the legion and brings out to the front those who left the ranks, reprimands them severely and finally chooses by lot sometimes five, sometimes eight, sometimes 20 of the offenders, calculating the number so that it represents as far as possible a tenth of those guilty of cowardice. **3** Those who are chosen by lot are mercilessly beaten to death in the manner described above, and the rest are given rations of barley instead of wheat and are ordered to make their quarters outside the safety of the rampart. **4** The danger and the fear of drawing the lot threatens everyone equally, as there is no knowing on whom it might fall, and, as the shame of receiving rations of barley falls on all alike, the practice adopted is the one best adapted to inspire fear and correct such faults.

5.21 Aulus Gellius *Attic Nights* 16.4.2–4: Military oaths

Laelius and Lucius Cornelius Scipio Asiaticus were consuls in 190 BC. Booty was an important incentive for the troops: no more than half the total force was sent to collect it, the rest remaining on the alert, and after it was sold it was the responsibility of the military tribunes to ensure that it was equitably distributed.

2 Also in the fifth book of the same Cincius' *On Military Science* there is written: 'When a levy was made in ancient times and soldiers were enrolled, the military tribune compelled them to take an oath in these words: "In the army of the consul of Gaius Laelius, son of Gaius, and the consul Lucius Cornelius, son of Publius, and for 10 miles around, you will not commit a theft with malice aforethought, either alone or with others, of greater value than a silver sesterce on any one day; and except for a spear, spear-shaft, firewood, fruit, fodder, wineskin, sack and torch, if you find or carry off anything there which is not yours, which is worth more than one silver sesterce, you will bring it to the consul Gaius Laelius, son of Gaius, or Lucius Cornelius, son of Publius, or to whomsoever either of them should order, or within the next three days you will reveal whatever you have found or carried off by malice aforethought, or you will return it to its owner, whomever you think that to be, as you wish to do what is right."

3 'When the soldiers had been enrolled, a day was appointed on which they should appear and answer the consul's summons; then an oath was taken that they should be present, **4** with the following exceptions added: "Unless there be any of the following reasons: a family funeral or days of purification (but not if they have been appointed for that day in order that he might not appear on that day), or a serious disease, or an omen which could not be passed by without expiation, or an anniversary sacrifice which could not be properly celebrated unless he himself were there on that day, or violence or enemies, or a stated and appointed day with a guest; if anyone shall have any of these reasons, then on the day following that for which he is excused for these reasons, he shall come and serve the one who made that district, village or town subject to levy."'

ROME'S CONQUEST OF THE MEDITERRANEAN

5.22 *SEG* 13.382: Treaty between Rome and the Aetolian league

This treaty made by Marcus Valerius Laevinus with the Aetolians against Philip in 212/11 BC was Rome's first alliance in the eastern Mediterranean. The earliest extant Roman official document found in Greek, this formal bilateral agreement sets out arrangements for conducting the war, the division of booty and the terms of peace.

5 If the Romans take by force any cities of these peoples, as far as the Roman people are concerned the Aetolian people shall be permitted to keep these cities and their territories; anything else, apart from the cities and territories, that **10** the Romans take, the Romans shall keep. If the Romans and the Aetolians in concert capture some of these cities, as far as the Roman people are concerned the Aetolians shall be permitted to keep those cities and their territories; anything they take apart from the cities shall belong jointly **15** to both. If any of these cities submits or surrenders to the Romans or the Aetolians, as far as the Roman people are concerned the Aetolian people shall be permitted to take these people and their cities and territories **20** into their league.

5.23 Polybius *Histories* 18.44.1–7: Peace settlement with Philip

The Second Macedonian War ended with Philip's defeat at Cynoscephalae in Thessaly in 197. The peoples named in the treaty had been part of Philip's empire in Greece. Livy has two additional clauses, that Philip should have no more than 5,000 soldiers and no elephants, and that he should wage no war outside Macedonia without the senate's permission.

1 At this time the ten commissioners came from Rome to deal with affairs in Greece, bringing with them the senate's decree about peace with Philip. **2** The decree's main points were as follows: all the rest of the Greeks in Asia and Europe were to be free and subject to their own laws; **3** Philip was to hand over to the Romans all Greeks under his rule and all towns with garrisons before the start of the Isthmian games (June 196 BC); **4** he was to leave free, after withdrawing his garrisons from them, the towns of Euromus, Pedasa, Bargylia and Iasus, as well as Abydus, Thasus, Myrina and Perinthus; **5** in accordance with the senate's decree, Titus (Flamininus) was to write to Prusias (of Bithynia) about the liberation of the Ciani; **6** within the same time period, Philip was to restore to the Romans all prisoners of war and deserters and all his decked ships, with the exception of five light vessels and his ship with 16 banks of oars; **7** he was to pay them 1,000 talents, half immediately and half by instalments over ten years.

5.24 Polybius *Histories* 18.46.1–47.2: Flamininus 'liberates' Greece

Titus Quinctius Flamininus was less than 30 years of age as consul in 198 BC, having held neither the curule aedileship nor the praetorship. This universal declaration of freedom for Greeks included Greeks in Asia Minor, doubtless with a view to curbing Antiochus' activities there; the motive was not 'philhellenism' but rather the wish to weaken Macedon. Many Greek cities honoured Flamininus as a benefactor, while, according to Plutarch, he was granted divine honours at Chalcis and Argos (the cult of the 'Titeia'; doc. 5.26).

46.1 With the Isthmian games now approaching, and the most distinguished men from nearly the whole world gathered there owing to their expectation of what would take place, many different rumours were current during the whole festival, **2** with some saying that it was impossible for the Romans to withdraw from certain places and cities, while others declared that they would withdraw from the places considered to be famous but would keep those which had less appeal but which were equally useful to them. **3** They even named these on the spot out of their own heads and competed with each other in their ingenious guesswork. **4** This was everyone's current concern, and, when the crowd had gathered in the stadium to watch the games, the herald came forward and, after silencing the crowds with his trumpeter, made the following announcement:

 5 'The senate of Rome, and Titus Quinctius (Flamininus) the proconsul, having overcome King Philip and the Macedonians, leave free, without garrisons, subject to no tribute, and governed by their ancestral laws, the Corinthians, Phocians, Locrians, Euboeans, Achaeans, Magnesians, Thessalians and Perrhaebians.' **6** At the very start an incredible shout immediately went up, with some people not having heard the announcement, while others wanted to hear it again. **7** The great majority of the audience, unable to believe it and thinking that they heard the words as if in a dream because of the unexpected nature of the event, **8** each moved by a different impulse shouted to the herald and trumpeter to come forward into the middle of the stadium and repeat the proclamation, wishing, I think, not only to hear the speaker but to see him on account of the unbelievable nature of his announcement. **9** When the herald came forward into the middle and silenced the uproar with his trumpeter, once more reading out the same proclamation as before, such a tremendous outburst of cheering arose that those who hear of the event today cannot easily conceive it. **10** When the noise finally died down, no one took any further account of the athletes, but all talked away, some to each other, some to themselves, as if quite out of their senses. **11** Indeed, after the festival was over, they were so grateful that they almost killed Titus through their excessive joy; **12** some of them wanted to look him in the face and call him their saviour, others were anxious to take his hand, and most people threw garlands and fillets on him, so he was almost torn in pieces. **13** But, however extravagant their gratitude was, one may say with confidence that it was far inferior to the importance of the event. **14** It was remarkable that the Romans and their general Titus should be there for this purpose and incur every expense and danger for the sake of the Greeks' freedom; it was also a great thing that they employed a force adequate to realise their purpose; **15** but greatest of all was that no mischance occurred to oppose their design, with everything leading to that one moment when, by a single announcement, all Greeks living in Asia and Europe were free, without garrisons, subject to no tribute, and governed by their ancestral laws.

47.1 When the festival was over, the commissioners first gave an audience to the envoys from Antiochus, instructing him with regard to the cities in Asia to keep his hands off those which were autonomous and make war on none of them, and to withdraw from those he had just captured which had been subject to Ptolemy and Philip. **2** In addition they declared that he should not cross with an army to Europe; for none of the Greeks was now being made war on by anyone or subject to anyone.

5.25 *SIG*³ 593: Chyretiae, 194 BC

Flamininus' command in Greece was prorogued (extended) until 194. This document concerning the people of Chyretiae in Thessaly demonstrates the kind of settlement made by Flamininus before the Romans' departure and his wish to ensure Greek support or neutrality for Rome's forthcoming confrontation with Antiochus III. 'Persons who are not accustomed to act according to the highest standards of behaviour' are the Aetolians who had sacked Chyretiae in 199. Flamininus in this document returns Chyretian property currently in Rome's possession, which had been taken by the Aetolians. The tagoi are Flamininus' newly appointed magistrates.

Titus Quinctius, consul of the Romans, to the magistrates (tagoi) and people of Chyretiae, greetings. Just as in all other matters also I have made clear my personal policy and that of the Roman people, which we have towards you in general, I have decided **5** in the following matters also to demonstrate in every respect our support for what is honourable, so that not even in these matters can persons who are not accustomed to act according to the highest standards of behaviour have the opportunity to criticise us.

For any of your possessions, in land or buildings, that may still be in the possession of the treasury **10** of Rome, I grant them all to your city, that you may recognise our magnanimity in this respect too and to show we have no desire for financial profit in any matter at all, since we value goodwill and a good reputation above all else. If any do not recover what belongs to them, **15** if they prove to you and appear to you to be speaking reasonably, as long as you adhere to the decisions given by me in writing, I consider that these should in justice be restored to them. Farewell.

5.26 Plutarch *Life of Flamininus* 16.7: The girls of Chalcis honour Flamininus

This paean was sung by the girls of Chalcis in Euboea in 191 BC to honour Flamininus and Roman *fides* (Greek *pistis*, 'good faith'). Flamininus was to be honoured as Chalcis' patron, and his cult, the Titeia, was established with an elected priest. Plutarch here cites the last lines of the long cult hymn of praise. This is the earliest extant hymn which mentions the goddess Roma (see doc. 5.35, 15.55–56); 'Great Zeus' may be an attempt in Greek to reproduce Jupiter Optimus Maximus.

> We revere the fides of the Romans,
> Which we have solemnly sworn to cherish;
> So celebrate, girls, in song and dance
> Great Zeus, and Roma, and Titus and the Romans'
> Fides; hail, all hail,
> Titus our saviour.

5.27 *IG* XI.4.712: The Delians honour Scipio Africanus, c. 193 BC

A stele from Delos. There is a crown of leaves above the text to the left and a staff or baton on the right. The Apollonia was a festival at Delos with competitions in drama and music.

Decreed by the council and people. Antilakos son of Simides proposed the motion: since Publius Cornelius, son of Publius, Scipio, Roman, being proxenos and benefactor **5** of the temple and the Delians, bestows all care on the temple and the Delians, the council and the people decree that Publius Cornelius, son of Publius, Scipio, Roman, is to be crowned **10** at the Apollonia with the sacred crown of laurel; the sacred herald is to announce in the theatre, when the children's choruses are conducted, the proclamation as follows: The people of Delos crown Publius **15** Cornelius Scipio, Roman, with the sacred crown of laurel because of his excellence and his piety towards the temple and his goodwill towards the people of Delos. Lysanias son of Kaibon put the motion to the vote.

ANTIOCHUS III 'THE GREAT'

Antiochus III of Syria (223–187 BC) had taken advantage of Rome's war against Philip to appropriate coastal territories in Asia Minor and had also conducted military activities in Thrace, especially in 193–192. Hannibal fled to him in 195, which concerned Rome. In the autumn of 192 Antiochus provoked war with Rome, and in spring 191 the consul Manius Acilius Glabrio took the field with 20,000 men. Antiochus decided to make a stand at Thermopylae, and his army was totally defeated. Lucius Scipio (brother of Africanus) and Gaius Laelius were elected consuls for 190; after arranging a truce with the Aetolians, the Scipio brothers led the first Roman army into Asia in autumn 190, where Antiochus was defeated at Magnesia. He agreed to the Romans' terms at the peace of Apamea, signed in 188 (doc. 5.30).

5.28 Polybius *Histories* 21.32.1–15: Treaty with the Aetolian League

En route through Greece in 190 BC the Scipio brothers arranged a six-month truce with the Aetolians, Antiochus' main supporters in Greece. In 189 the consul M. Fulvius Nobilior marched against them and they surrendered. They had to pay 500 talents over six years and restrict the membership of the Aetolian league. The terms were not reciprocal and the Aetolians had to agree to 'uphold the empire and sovereignty of the Roman people'. The sections in square brackets are supplied from Livy.

1 When the senate had passed a decree and the people had voted in favour of it, the peace was ratified. The detailed conditions of the treaty were as follows: **2** 'The Aetolian people [shall uphold in good faith] the empire and sovereignty of the Romans. **3** They shall not permit any enemies making war against the Romans or their allies or friends to pass through their country, nor shall they provide any supplies by public consent. **4** [They shall have the same enemies as the Roman people] and if the Romans make war on anyone, the people of Aetolia shall make war likewise. **5** The Aetolians shall surrender all deserters, fugitives and prisoners belonging to the Romans and their allies, **6** excepting those who were taken in war, returned to their own country and again captured, and excepting those who were enemies of the Romans at the time when the Aetolians were fighting in alliance with Rome. All of these are to be surrendered, within 100 days of the peace being sworn, to the magistrate on Corcyra; **7** if any are not found before that date, they shall be surrendered without fraud when they are discovered; and they are not to return to Aetolia after the peace is sworn. **8** The Aetolians are to hand over at once to the consul in Greece 200 Euboic talents, in silver not inferior to Attic money, paying a third of the sum in gold, if they wish, at the rate of one gold mina for ten silver minae, **9** and, for the first six years after the swearing of the peace, 50 talents a year; the money is to be brought to Rome. **10** The Aetolians are to give the consul 40 hostages, not younger than 12 years of age or older than 40, for six years, whom the Romans are to choose, none of them being a general, hipparch, public secretary or one of those previously a hostage in Rome. These hostages are to be brought to Rome: **11** if any of the hostages dies they are to replace him with another. **12** Cephallenia is not to be included in the treaty. **13** Of the villages, cities and people previously subject to the Aetolians who were captured or became friends of the Romans in or after the consulship of Lucius Quinctius (Flamininus) and Gnaeus Domitius Ahenobarbus (192 BC), none of these cities or their inhabitants is to be annexed by the Aetolians. **14** The city and territory of Oeniadae is to belong to Acarnania.' **15** When the oaths were taken, peace was finalised on these conditions. This was the settlement of affairs in Aetolia and Greece generally.

5.29 *SIG*³ 612: Delphian privileges, 189 BC

This inscription suggests that envoys from Delphi had been sent to discuss their rights of asylum and to request immunity from tribute or exemption from military requisitions by Rome during the war against Antiochus III. Spurius Postumius was the urban praetor in 189 BC.

A . . . concerning the freedom of the city and the right of sanctuary for the temple . . .

B Spurius Postumius, son of Lucius, praetor of the Romans, to the Delphian League, greetings. The envoys sent by you, Boulon, Thrasycles and Orestas, have discussed with us the question of sanctuary for your temple and city, omitting no mark of respect, and made a request concerning freedom and exemption from tribute, so that the city and territory of Delphi may be autonomous and immune from taxation. Know then that the senate has resolved that the temple of Apollo and the city shall have the right of sanctuary, **5** that the city and territory of Delphi shall be exempt from taxation, and that its citizens shall be autonomous in every respect . . . being free, administering their own government by themselves and being responsible for the temple and its precinct, as has been their ancestral right from of old. For your information, I am sending you a copy.

C May 4. Spurius Postumius, son of Lucius, praetor, consulted the senate in the comitium . . . Gaius Atinius, son of Gaius, Tiberius Claudius, and . . . assisted in the drafting. Whereas the Delphians spoke about the right of sanctuary for the temple, the freedom of the city, the exemption of its territory from taxation, and autonomy, regarding this matter the senators **5** resolved as follows: 'Whereas it was the decision of Manius Acilius (Glabrio) that Delphi should possess those privileges which had earlier been hers, it was resolved to abide by this decision.'

5.30 Polybius *Histories* 21.41.6, 9–43.1–3: The treaty of Apamea, 188 BC

The Romans demanded that Antiochus evacuate all of Asia Minor and pay the full cost of the war. Negotiations failed and Antiochus was defeated near Magnesia, probably in December 190 or January 189. Antiochus had already made a payment of 3,000 talents; a further indemnity of 12,000 Euboic talents was imposed (as well as 540,000 modii of grain), and Antiochus was to surrender most of his fleet and elephants, hand over Hannibal (who went to Bithynia), pay compensation to Pergamum, and evacuate all Asia north and west of the Taurus Mountains. Antiochus agreed to these terms at Apamea. Gnaeus Manlius Vulso (cos. 189) succeeded L. Cornelius Scipio in the command of the war in Asia. The treaty between Rome and Antiochus was sworn at Apamea and Antiochus was confined to Syria. The section in square brackets is supplied from Livy.

41.6 The ten commissioners and King Eumenes reached Ephesus by sea in early summer; they rested there for two days after their journey and went up country to Apamea . . . **9** On arriving at Apamea and meeting Eumenes and the ten commissioners, Manlius Vulso took counsel with them about the situation. **10** They decided first of all to ratify the sworn treaty with Antiochus, about the conditions of which I need say no more, but will give the document itself.

42.1 The conditions in detail were as follows: 'There is to be friendship between Antiochus and the Romans for all time, if he keeps to the conditions of the treaty. **2** King Antiochus and his subjects shall not permit the passage through their territory of any enemies making war against the Romans and their allies, nor provide any supplies for them; **3** the Romans and their allies shall undertake to do likewise towards Antiochus and his subjects. **4** Antiochus is not to make war on the inhabitants of the islands **5** or on those of Europe. **6** He is to withdraw from all cities, villages, [lands and forts on this side of Taurus as far as the River Halys, and all between the valley of Taurus and the mountain ridges that descend to Lycaonia]; he is to take away nothing except the arms carried by his soldiers; if anything should be carried away it is to be restored to the same city. **7** He is not to receive soldiers or anyone else from the kingdom of Eumenes. **8** If any men in the army of Antiochus are from the cities which the Romans take over, they shall be brought to Apamea. **9** If there are any men from the kingdom of Antiochus with the Romans and their allies, they are permitted to stay or leave as they wish. **10** Antiochus and his subjects are to hand over the slaves of the Romans and of their allies, both those who were captured in war and those who deserted, and any prisoners they may have taken. **11** Antiochus is to give up, if it is in his power, Hannibal son of Hamilcar the Carthaginian, Mnasilochus the Acarnanian, Thoas the Aetolian, Eubulidas and Philo the Chalcidians, and all Aetolians who have held public office, **12** as well as all the elephants now in Apamea, nor is he to have any for the future. **13** He is to give up his long ships and their equipment and fittings and is not to have more than ten decked ships for the future; nor is he to have any galley rowed by more than 30 oars, nor a ship with one bank of oars for any war in which he is the aggressor. **14** His fleet is not to sail beyond the Calycadnus and the Sarpedonian promontory, unless carrying tribute, envoys or hostages. **15** Antiochus is not to be permitted to hire mercenaries from territory subject to the Romans or to receive fugitives. **16** All houses of the Rhodians or their allies in the territory subject to Antiochus shall belong to the Rhodians, as they did before he began the war. **17** If any money is owed to them, it shall likewise be recoverable; and if anything has been taken away from them, it may be sought and handed back. Goods meant for Rhodes are to be free of duty, as before the war. **18** If Antiochus has given to others any of the cities which he has to hand over, he is to remove the garrisons and men from these as well. And if any later wish to desert (to him) he is not to receive them.

19 Antiochus is to pay to the Romans 12,000 talents of the best Attic silver over 12 years, paying 1,000 talents per year, the talents weighing not less than 80 Roman pounds, and 540,000 modii of corn. **20** He is to pay to King Eumenes 350 talents in the next five years, 70 a year, at the time appointed for his payments to the Romans, **21** and in place of the corn, as King Antiochus estimated it, 127 talents and 1,208 drachmas, which Eumenes has agreed to receive as an acceptable payment. **22** Antiochus is to give 20 hostages not younger than 18 years of age and not older than 45 and send others in exchange every three years. **23** If there is any discrepancy in his payments of money, he shall hand it over in the following year. **24** If any of the cities or nations against whom Antiochus is forbidden to make war should first make war on him, he is allowed to make war. **25** He is not to have sovereignty over these cities or nations or bring them into his alliance. **26** Any wrongs committed by one party against another are to be taken to court. **27** If both parties wish to add clauses to this treaty or remove them by mutual decree, they may do so.'

43.1 When this was sworn to, the proconsul immediately sent Quintus Minucius Thermus and his brother Lucius, who had just brought the money from Oroanda, **2** to Syria, with instructions to receive the king's oath and ensure that each detail of the treaty was carried out. **3** He sent letter-carriers to Quintus Fabius (Labeo), the commander of the fleet, ordering him to sail back to Patara, seize the ships there, and burn them.

5.31 Polybius *Histories* 21.45.1–3, 9–11: The final settlement of Asia Minor

The Romans' settlement laid down that, of Antiochus' non-Greek territories, Lycia and Caria were to belong to Rhodes, the rest to Eumenes II of Pergamum; Greek cities which joined Rome before the battle of Magnesia were to be free, the others were to be divided between Rhodes and Eumenes. The Romans at this point did not claim territory in Asia Minor.

1 At Apamea the ten (commissioners) and Gnaeus (Manlius Vulso) the Roman proconsul listened to all those who presented themselves and, where the dispute was about land, money or something else, assigned cities upon which both parties were agreed where they could settle the matters under dispute. The general settlement that they made was as follows. **2** All autonomous towns which had formerly paid tribute to Antiochus, but had then remained loyal to Rome, they freed from tribute; all that paid contributions to Attalus were instructed to give the same sum as tribute to Eumenes. **3** If any had withdrawn from the Roman alliance and fought with Antiochus, they ordered them to give to Eumenes the tribute imposed on them by Antiochus ... **9** Regarding King Eumenes and his brothers, they had made all possible provision for them in the treaty with Antiochus, and they now added, in Europe, the Chersonese, Lysimachia and the adjoining forts and territory, which Antiochus had ruled, **10** and, in Asia, Hellespontic Phrygia, Greater Phrygia, the part of Mysia which Prusias had earlier taken from Eumenes, Lycaonia, the Milyas, Lydia, Tralles, Ephesus and Termessus. **11** These were the gifts they gave Eumenes; regarding Pamphylia, as Eumenes declared it was on this side of the Taurus, and Antiochus' envoys said it was on the other, they were unable to reach a decision and referred the question to the senate.

ROME AS MASTER OF THE MEDITERRANEAN

Following Philip's death in 179, his son Perseus tried to reassert Macedon's position but was declared an enemy of Rome in 172. After some Macedonian successes in the Third Macedonian War, Perseus was finally manoeuvred by Lucius Aemilius Paullus (cos. 182 and 168) into giving battle at Pydna; his army was defeated and he later surrendered at Samothrace and featured in Paullus' triumph. From the late third century, Roman attitudes towards conquests and allies became increasingly aggressive and autocratic. From 182, Rome is seen in honorific inscriptions as the 'common benefactor' of the Greeks and is considered the superior power even when it is not directly the subject of the inscriptions.

5.32 *SIG*³ 643: The Romans instruct Delphi

This edict or letter presents Roman charges against Perseus made before the Amphictyons at Delphi after Rome had declared war on Perseus of Macedon in 171, to encourage them to assist Rome. Macedonian agents had supposedly attempted to assassinate Eumenes II of Pergamum at Delphi.

1 . . . you shall administer, as it concerns Perseus, who in violation of what is fitting came to Delphi with an army in the truce of the Pythian games; it was not at all right to allow him either to come forward or to share in the oracle or the sacrifices or the games or the Amphictyonic Council, in which all the Greeks participate. **2** For he **(10)** brought barbarians who dwell beyond the Danube and who, once before, gathered for nothing good but for the enslavement of all Greeks, and invaded Greece and marched against the Temple of Pythian Apollo at Delphi intending to plunder or destroy it, but met with fitting punishment from the god, and most of them perished. **3** He also broke the oaths, made by us to his father, and the treaty, which he himself had renewed. **4 (15)** He also made war against the Thracians, our friends and allies, and made them home-less. **5** Abrupolis, whom we included as our friend and ally in a treaty with him, he expelled from his kingdom. **6** Envoys sent from the Greeks and the kings to Rome about an alliance with the Thebans he drowned, and others in other ways he attempted to put out of the way. **7** He also reached such a degree of folly that he had it in mind to kill our council by poisons. **8** The Dolopians **(20)** were deprived of freedom through his attacks. **9** In Aetolia he planned both war and slaughter and brought their whole people into upheavals and discord. **10** Also against all Greece he continues to do the worst things, both by devis-ing other evils and by receiving fugitives from cities. **11** Also, by destroying the leading men and at the same time courting the masses, he both promised cancellations of debts and brought about revolutions, making clear his policy towards both the Greeks and the **(25)** Romans. **12** As a result, it has happened that the Perrhaebians and the Thessalians and the Aetolians fell into incurable misfortunes and the barbarians have become still more terrible to the Greeks. **13** Desiring war against us for a long time, that he might catch us without aid, when no one was opposing him, and enslave all the Greek cities, **14** he bribed Genthius the Illyrian and set him against us. **15** He plotted to kill King Eumenes, our friend and ally, by means of Evander, **(30)** at the time when Eumenes was going to Delphi to pay a vow, without considering at all the safe conduct given by the god to all who come to him and without taking into account that the sanctity and inviolability of the city of Delphi, for both Greeks and barbarians, acknowledged by all men, has existed for all time . . .

5.33 *ILS* 8884: Lucius Aemilius Paullus

After Pydna in 168 BC, Aemilius replaced Perseus' statue on a monument at Delphi with one of himself on horseback. The frieze recorded scenes from the battle of Pydna. Significantly the inscription was in Latin, not Greek.

Lucius Aemilius, son of Lucius, imperator, took this (as booty) from King Perseus and the Macedonians.

5.34 Livy *History of Rome* 45.33.1–34.6: Booty from Epirus, 167 BC

Cf. Polyb. 30.15 (doc. 6.9). The Molossians of Epirus had taken the side of Perseus: following a senatorial decree, 70 towns were sacked to provide booty for the army and as an object lesson. Strabo 7.327 notes that over 100 years later the area was still a desert. Paullus paid so much into the treasury that all citizens were relieved from the annual *tributum*, or land tax. Macedon was eradicated and formed into four separate republics without the rights of intermarriage or trade. Perseus died in prison, following Paullus' triumph.

33.1 After the public games had been held (at Amphipolis) and the bronze shields had been piled onto the ships, the rest of the arms of all kinds were heaped into a huge pile, and the general, after praying to Mars, Minerva, Mother Lua, and the rest of the gods to whom it is right and lawful to dedicate the spoils of the enemy, personally used a torch to kindle it . . . **5** The gaze of the crowd which came was no more drawn to the stage spectacle, the athletic contests or the chariot races, than to all the booty of Macedonia which was put on show – statues, paintings, textiles, vessels of gold, silver, bronze and ivory made with great pains in the palace (at Pella), **6** not only for immediate show, like the things with which the palace at Alexandria was filled, but for constant use. **7** These were loaded onto the fleet and given to Gnaeus Octavius to transport to Rome . . .

    34.1 Paullus sent dispatches to Anicius so that there should be no disturbance over what was going to take place, saying that the senate had granted to his army the booty from the cities of Epirus which had defected to Perseus, **2** and sent centurions to the individual cities, to say that they had come to remove the garrisons so that the people of Epirus might be free like the Macedonians. He also summoned ten leading men from each city and told these to have all the gold and silver brought into the public square, while cohorts were sent to all the cities. **3** Those to the cities further away were sent before those to the nearer ones, so that they would all arrive on the same day. **4** The tribunes and centurions had been instructed as to what to do. Early in the morning all the gold and silver was collected; at the fourth hour the soldiers were given the signal to plunder the town; **5** there was so much booty that a distribution was made of 400 denarii to each of the cavalry and 200 to the infantry, and 150,000 people were led into slavery. **6** Then the walls of the plundered cities were torn down; there were about 70 communities. All the booty was sold and from this the amounts given above were paid to the army.

5.35 Melinno F1: Melinno 'of Lesbos' on the might of Rome

Stobaeus 3.7.12. Roma, Rome, is here portrayed as a warrior goddess whose rule is both eternal and unique. Melinno's date and origins are not known, but the poem is generally now dated to the early second century BC and was possibly written for performance at a local festival in honour of Roma. For the later cult of Roma and Augustus, see docs 15.53–54.

Hail, Roma, daughter of Ares,
Golden-crowned warrior queen
You who live on earth on holy Olympus,
For ever indestructible.

5   To you alone, most revered one, has Fate
Granted royal glory of unbreakable dominion,
So that, with your sovereign power,
You might lead the way.

Under your yoke of strong leather straps,
10   The chests of earth and grey sea
Are tightly bound together; with firm hand you govern
The cities of your peoples.

The longest eternity, which overthrows everything
And shapes the course of life first in this way, then in that,
15   For you alone does not change the wind
Which fills the sails of empire.

Indeed, out of all, you alone give birth to
Strong men, wielders of spears,
Sending forth a well-aiming crop of men
20   Like the fruits of Demeter.

ROME'S IMPERIALIST STANCE

Successful warfare generated prestige (dignitas) and popularity – as well as personal wealth. According to Cicero (when defending a military man), true gloria was won only in war (4.5.5) and was the attribute most desired by Roman nobles. A general's military success was signalled by the senate's award of a triumph, in which the commander was able to show off booty and captives. Such perceptions naturally added to the intense rivalry for office among the very competitive magisterial class.

5.36 Polybius *Histories* 29.26.1, 27.1–11: Rome decides peace or war

In this episode in 168 BC, Gaius Popillius Laenas (cos. 172) prevented Antiochus IV Epiphanes from making war on Ptolemy VI Philometor. Antiochus had invaded Egypt and in early 168 was close to capturing Alexandria. An Egyptian embassy to Rome led to direct Roman intervention: Gaius Popillius Laenas, leader of a Roman commission, threatened that whichever king failed to withdraw from the war would lose Rome's friendship.

26.1 Forgetting all that he had written and said, Antiochus was preparing for war against Ptolemy . . . **27.1** As Antiochus was approaching Ptolemy in order to occupy Pelusium, **2** Popillius, the Roman commander, when greeted from a distance by the king, who held out his right hand, gave him the tablet which he had ready, containing the decree of the senate, and ordered Antiochus to read it first, not thinking it right, **3** it seems to me, to give this usual mark of friendship before he knew whether the intentions of the person greeting him were friendly or hostile. **4** When the king had read it, he said that he wanted to consult his friends about this information, but Popillius, on hearing this, acted in a manner thought to be harsh and extremely arrogant; **5** he had with him a staff cut from a vine, with which he drew a circle round Antiochus and ordered him to give his decision about the letter while still inside the circle. **6** The king was startled at this assumption of authority, but, after a few moments of doubt, said he would do all that the Romans demanded. Popillius and his entourage then all took his hand and greeted him warmly. **7** The letter told him to cease his war against Ptolemy immediately. **8** As a result, since a specific number of days were granted him, he led his forces back to Syria, unhappily and with complaints, but giving way to circumstances for the present. **9** Popillius arranged matters in Alexandria and instructed the Egyptian kings to agree, telling them to send Polyaratus to Rome, and then sailed to Cyprus, wanting to use all expedition in expelling the troops there from the island. **10** When he arrived and found that Ptolemy's generals had been defeated in battle and that things in Cyprus were generally all upside down, he soon made the (Syrian) army withdraw from the country and stayed there until the troops had sailed to Syria. **11** In this way the Romans saved Ptolemy's kingdom, or at least as much of it as had not already been reduced . . .

5.37 Aulus Gellius *Attic Nights* 6.3.16, 38, 48–50: Cato and the Rhodians, 167 BC

When the economy of Rhodes suffered during the Third Macedonian War against Perseus, the consul of 169, Marcius Philippus, seems to have suggested that the island attempt to negotiate between Perseus and Rome. The Rhodian envoys arrived at Rome only after Perseus' defeat and were almost declared an enemy of Rome. War was averted by a speech from Cato (censor 184). This speech was subsequently introduced into Cato's history (*Origines* F95). Gellius is here disagreeing with Tiro, Cicero's freedman, who wrote a letter to Quintus Axius criticising this speech of Cato's.

16 And Tiro gives Cato's own words as follows: 'And I really think that the Rhodians did not want us to put an end to the war as we did, or to conquer King Perseus. But the Rhodians were not the only people who felt like that: in fact I believe many peoples and many nations felt the same. I rather think that some of them did not desire our success, not for the sake of making us look small, but because they were afraid that, if there was no one whom we feared, we would do whatever we liked. I think that they held that opinion for the sake of their own liberty, so they would not be entirely subject to our empire and in servitude to us. Also, the Rhodians never publicly aided Perseus. Consider how much more cautiously *we* deal with each other as individuals. For each of us, if he thinks anything is being done against his interests, tries as hard as he can to prevent it; they, however, let it happen.' . . . **38** Later on Cato continues: 'But if it is not right for honour to be won because someone says that he wanted to do well, but did not do so, shall the Rhodians suffer not because they did wrong, but because they are said to have wanted to do wrong?' . . . **48** The charge of arrogance, which was brought at that time particularly against the Rhodians in the senate, he evades and disposes of it in a brilliant and almost divinely inspired reply. **49** I will give Cato's actual words, since Tiro has omitted them: **50** 'They say the Rhodians are arrogant, accusing them of something which I should certainly not want to have brought against me or my children. Suppose they are arrogant? What is that to do with us? Are you going to be angry, just because someone is more arrogant than we are?'

5.38 Polybius *Histories* 30.32.6–12: Decree on Achaean exiles, c. 165 BC

After Perseus' defeat, 1,000 'pro-Macedonian' Achaeans (from the north-west Peloponnese) were deported to Italy while others were murdered or exiled. The 1,000 were sent as hostages and remained for 17 years; one of these was Polybius, who was lucky enough to win the friendship of Scipio Aemilianus. This is one of the occasions on which the exiles' return was refused. Charops was in charge of a pro-Roman government in Epirus, while Callicrates had been responsible for the deportation of the 1,000 Achaeans in the first instance. The issue was finally settled in 150, when Scipio Aemilianus enlisted Cato's support; at this point only 300 of the exiles were still alive.

6 The senate listened to what the envoys said in accordance with their instructions and found it difficult to make a decision, as they were met by objections on every side; **7** they did not think it was their duty to pronounce judgement, while setting the men free without trial would, they considered, involve the certain destruction of their friends; **8** so under force of circumstances, and with the intention of dispelling entirely the hope of the populace for the restoration of those in detention, in order to make them obey in silence the party of Callicrates in Achaea and in the other states thought to be friends of Rome, they wrote the following answer: **9** 'We are not of the opinion that it is in the interests either of the Romans or of your peoples that these men shall return home.' **10** When this reply was delivered, not only did utter despair and helplessness fall upon those who had been summoned to Italy, but all the Greeks went, as it were, into mourning, as the reply seemed to deprive **11** the poor men of all hope of restoration. And when the reply given about the accused to the Achaeans was announced in Greece, the people's spirit was crushed and a kind of hopelessness came over everyone, **12** while the supporters of Charops and Callicrates and all the defenders of their policy were again in high spirits.

5.39 Polybius *Histories* 31.10.1–3, 6–10: The partitioning of Egypt

When in 164 Ptolemy VI Philometor was expelled from Egypt by his brother Ptolemy VIII Euergetes II, he went to Rome. As Euergetes' reign was unpopular, it was agreed that Philometor should have Egypt and Cyprus and Euergetes should have Cyrene. In 162, however, Euergetes came to Rome and asked for Cyprus, which was granted to him. One of these Ptolemies, presumably Euergetes, was said to have offered marriage to Cornelia, mother of the Gracchi: doc. 8.1.

1 After the two Ptolemies had partitioned the kingdom, the younger Ptolemy (Euergetes) arrived in Rome, as he wanted to cancel the division which had been effected between himself and his brother, **2** stating that it was not of his own free will but by compulsion and under pressure of circumstances that he had done what he had been ordered to do. **3** He therefore begged the senate to assign him Cyprus, for, even with this, his share would still be greatly inferior to his brother's . . . **6** As the senate saw that the divisions had been quite unjust, and as it wanted to partition the kingdom in an effective way, with themselves responsible for the partition, they agreed to the requests of the younger brother, as this coincided with their own interests. **7** For, nowadays, many of the Romans' decrees are of this kind, and they effectively increase and build up their own empire through the mistakes of their neighbours, simultaneously granting a favour and appearing to confer benefits on those who commit the mistakes. **8** Accordingly, since they perceived the importance of Egypt's kingdom and were afraid that, should it acquire a protector, he might think more highly of himself than he should, **9** they appointed Titus Torquatus and Gnaeus Merula to accompany Ptolemy as envoys to Cyprus and put his plan and their own into execution. **10** They immediately dispatched them, with instructions to reconcile the brothers and establish the younger brother in Cyprus without warfare.

5.40 1 Maccabees 8.17–32: Treaty with the Jews, 161 BC

In 162 the Seleucid ruler Demetrius (I Soter), nephew of Antiochus IV Epiphanes (175–164), in Rome as a hostage, escaped to Syria and took the throne. Rome allowed him to rule but later supported opposition against him. The Jews had rebelled under Antiochus IV, and, after defeating Demetrius' army in 161, Judas Maccabaeus sent an embassy to Rome to secure an alliance, which was granted by the senate. No practical help resulted: Demetrius' army again attacked Judaea and Judas was killed.

17 And Judas chose Eupolemus, son of John, son of Accus, and Jason, son of Eleazar, and sent them to Rome to establish friendship and alliance with the Romans **18** and to request that they would take the yoke from them, for they saw that the kingdom of the Greeks was reducing the Jews to slavery. **19** And they went to Rome, a very great journey, and came into the senate, where they spoke and said, 'Judas Maccabaeus and his brothers and the people of the Jews have sent us to you to establish with you an alliance and peace, and for us to be enrolled as your allies and friends.' And the speech pleased the senate. **22** And this is the copy of the letter which the senate wrote in reply on bronze tablets and sent to Jerusalem to be for them there a memorial of peace and alliance: **23** 'May it be well for the Romans and the nation of the Jews by sea and land forever, and may the sword and enemy be far from them. **24** But if war comes first upon Rome or any of their allies in all their dominion, **25** the nation of the Jews will fight alongside them with all their heart, as the occasion prescribes for them. **26** To those making war they shall not give or supply grain, arms, money or ships, as seems good to the Romans; and they shall keep their covenants without receiving anything for them. **27** In the same way, if war is made on the nation of the Jews first, the Romans shall fight alongside them wholeheartedly, as the occasion prescribes. **28** And grain, arms, money or ships shall not be given to those fighting against them, as seems good to Rome; and they shall keep their covenants and that without deceit.

29 'According to these words the Romans have made a covenant with the people of the Jews. **30** And if after these words one side or the other should wish to add or subtract anything, they shall do so as they choose, and whatever they add or take away shall be ratified. **31** And concerning the wrongs that King Demetrius is committing against them, we have written to him saying, "Why have you made your yoke heavy on our friends and allies the Jews? **32** If, therefore, they appeal any more against you, we shall give the decision for them and shall make war against you by sea and land."'

ROME'S CONQUEST OF GREECE

The Achaean exiles returned in 150 BC to find that Sparta was again on bad terms with the rest of the Achaean league. When Sparta seceded, Achaea was determined to force her back, ignoring the advice of Roman embassies and of Quintus Caecilius Metellus, the Roman commander in Macedonia. When the Achaean league declared war on Sparta, Lucius Mummius (cos. 146) was already on his way with an army to prevent the attack, while Metellus marched south from Macedonia. The Achaean forces were routed and Corinth was sacked. Macedonia, including southern Greece, became a Roman province.

5.41 Pausanias *Description of Greece* 7.16.1, 7–10: The sack of Corinth, 146 BC

Mummius has gained a reputation as a complete philistine: Polybius himself was present at the sack of Corinth, and tells us (39.2.1–2) that Mummius' soldiers played dice on masterpieces of Greek art. The majority of the artworks, however, did end up at Rome. Mummius celebrated a magnificent triumph in 145.

1 Mummius brought with him Orestes, who had earlier been sent to deal with the conflict between the Spartans and the Achaeans, and reached the Roman army at dawn. After sending Metellus to Macedonia, he waited at the Isthmus for his whole force to assemble. 3,500 cavalry arrived, while the infantry numbered 23,000; then came Cretan archers and Philopoemen, who led troops from Attalus, sent from Pergamum on the Caicus . . . **7** At nightfall, the Achaeans, who had taken refuge in Corinth after the battle, escaped from the city; most of the Corinthians escaped with them as well. Mummius at first held back from entering Corinth, though the gates were open, suspecting that an ambush had been set inside the walls; however, on the third day after the battle, he took Corinth by storm and burnt it. **8** The Romans slaughtered most of those they captured, but Mummius sold the women and children as slaves; he also sold all the slaves who had been set free and had fought on the Achaean side and who had not immediately fallen on the battlefield. Mummius carried off the dedications, which were especially admired, as well as other works of art, while he gave the lesser ones to Philopoemen, the general sent by Attalus; in my time there was still Corinthian booty at Pergamum. **9** Mummius razed the walls of all the cities that had fought against Rome and seized their arms, even before commissioners were sent from Rome; when these arrived to act with him, he began to put down democracies and establish governments where magistrates were chosen for their property qualifications; tribute was imposed on Greece and those with property were forbidden to acquire property abroad; all confederacies based on race, whether Achaeans, Phocians, Boeotians or any other Greeks, were all put down in the same way. **10** A few years later, the Romans began to feel sorry for Greece and restored the various ancient racial confederacies and the right to acquire property abroad, and removed the penalties Mummius had imposed; for he had ordered the Boeotians to pay 100 talents to the people of Heraclea and Euboea, and the Achaeans 200 to the Spartans. Although these impositions on the Greeks were removed by the Romans, a governor was sent out even down to my time; the Romans call him governor not of Greece, but of Achaea, because they subjugated Greece on account of the Achaeans, the leaders at that time of the Greek world.

5.42 *ILS* 20: Lucius Mummius (1)

This tablet was found at Rome on the Mons Caelius and was dedicated by Mummius in 142. He also made dedications at Delphi, Olympia and many other sites.

1 Lucius Mummius, son of Lucius, consul.

Under his leadership, auspices, and command, Achaea was captured and Corinth **5** destroyed and he returned to Rome for a triumph. On account of these successful achievements, this temple and statue of Hercules the Conqueror (Victor), which he had vowed during the war, **10** he dedicates as imperator.

5.43 *ILS* 21d: Lucius Mummius (2)

Here Mummius makes a dedication at Italica in Spain for the capture of Corinth. He had been praetor in Hispania Ulterior (Further Spain) in 153.

Lucius Mummius, son of Lucius, imperator, gave this on the capture of Corinth to the town of Italica.

5.44 *SIG*³ 684: Letter of Q. Fabius Maximus to the people of Dymae

Mummius settled Greece with the help of a commission of ten; democracy was no longer to be the normal form of government and, according to Pausanias (doc. 5.41), governments were based on a census qualification. Reactionaries in Achaean Dymae revolted later, with the aim of cancelling debts, and the pro-Romans appealed to the proconsul Quintus Fabius Maximus. The proconsul may have been Q. Fabius Maximus Eburnus (cos. 116).

1 In the priesthood of Leon, when Stratocles was secretary of the council. Quintus Fabius Maximus, son of Quintus, proconsul of the Romans, to the magistrates, councillors and city of Dymae, greetings.

Since the councillors, led by **5** Cyllanius, have notified me of the crimes committed in your city, that is, the burning and the destruction of the archives and the public records, in which the leader of the entire disturbance was Sosus, son of Tauromenes, who also drafted the laws in opposition **10** to the constitution given to the Achaeans by the Romans, which I have already discussed in detail with my advisory council at Patrae; since, therefore, in committing these actions they seem to me to be devising a condition of the worst kind of political disorder and upheaval for all the Greeks, not only by disaffection towards one another and by cancellation of private debts **15** but also by acting contrary to the freedom granted to the Greeks in common and our policy; and since the accusers have provided genuine proofs, I judge Sosus, the leader in what was done and the framer of the law for the abolition of the constitution granted by us, **20** to be liable to the death penalty, and similarly Phormiscus, son of Echesthenes, one of the demiurgi, who co-operated with those who burned the archives and the public records, as he himself confessed.

But since Timotheus, son of Nicias, who drafted the legislation with Sosus, seems less guilty, **25** I have ordered him to proceed to Rome and have exacted an oath that he shall be there on 1 September, and I have informed the praetor peregrinus that he shall not be allowed to return home until . . .

5.45 *OGIS* 435: Attalus III of Pergamum

Attalus III, the son of Eumenes II of Pergamum, died probably in September 134, leaving his kingdom to Rome. A committee of five envoys, with the pontifex maximus Scipio Nasica in charge, went out to settle affairs in 133/132. A pretender to the throne, Aristonicus, was defeated and sent to Rome, and the Roman province of Asia was created (see doc. 8.23). This inscription appears to confirm an earlier senatorial decree, with governors being instructed to adhere to the proposals of the earlier commissioners, and tacitly abolishes anything done in the name of the rebel Aristonicus.

Decree of the senate. The praetor Gaius Popillius, son of Gaius, consulted the senate . . . on the . . . **5** of . . . ember.

Whereas there was a discussion about affairs in Pergamum as to what instructions should be given to the praetors being dispatched to Asia regarding whether the regulations, gifts, concessions and fines that had been made by the kings in Asia up to the death of Attalus **10** should remain in force, the senate resolved as follows in regard to this affair: 'Concerning the matters brought up by the praetor Gaius Popillius, son of Gaius, the senators resolved as follows in regard to this affair: any regulations and fines or gifts and concessions which were made by King Attalus and the other kings, **15** and which took place at least one day before the death of Attalus, shall be valid, and the praetors dispatched to Asia shall alter nothing without good reason, but shall allow these to remain in force in accordance with the senate's decree.' **20** Public Servilius . . . assisted in drafting the decree.

THE WESTERN MEDITERRANEAN

Cato the Elder, as consul in 195, was sent to Hispania Citerior (Hither Spain) after the proconsul Gaius Sempronius Tuditanus had been killed in battle there in 196. Cato took with him two legions, supported by 15,000 allies, 800 cavalry and 20 warships. However, the conflict there was not resolved, though between 197 and 180 there seems to have been little systematic conquest. Tiberius Sempronius Gracchus (the Elder) was governor of Nearer Spain from late 180 and returned in 178 with 40,000 pounds of silver, although he was long remembered for his integrity. In 171, several peoples from both Spanish provinces sent delegates to Rome to complain of the misconduct of governors. Spain was a profitable possession for Rome: there were 40,000 slaves in the silver mines at New Carthage (originally organised by Cato), bringing Rome 25,000 denarii a day in revenue.

5.46 Appian *The Spanish Wars* 6.40–41.161–70: Cato the Elder in Spain

Cato's only active army command was during his time as consul in Spain in 195, for which he was awarded a triumph.

161 When Cato sailed to Spain and arrived at the place called Emporion, the enemy gathered against him from all sides to the number of 40,000. **162** He quickly trained his army and, when he was about to engage in battle, he sent away the ships that he possessed to Marseilles and told the army: 'Do not be afraid that the enemy will overwhelm us with their numbers – for a brave spirit will always overcome superior numbers – but because we have no ships, unless we win, we have nothing – not even safety . . . ' **165** When he saw that the centre of his forces were in particular difficulties, he rushed among them, putting himself at risk, and threw the enemy into confusion by his deeds and cries, and was the first to begin the victory. **166** He pursued them all that night, capturing their camp and killing many of them. On his return, the soldiers embraced him and celebrated with him as leader of the victory. After this he rested the army and sold the booty.

167 When all sent embassies to him, he demanded more hostages and sent sealed letters to each, telling all those who carried them to hand them over on the same day; he fixed the day by estimating when the letters would reach the furthermost town. **168** The message instructed all the magistrates of the towns to destroy their walls on the same day, that on which they received the letters; if they postponed the day, he threatened them with enslavement. **169** Having recently been defeated in a great battle, and being ignorant whether these orders had been given to them alone or to everyone, they were afraid, if they were the only ones, that they would be powerless, and, if they were with others, that they would be the only ones to delay, and, as they had no time to send round to each other and were wary of the soldiers who had come with the letters and were standing right in front of them, they all considered their own safety to be of prime importance and hastily dismantled their walls. Once they had decided to obey, they competed against each other to complete the task quickly. **170** And in this way the towns along the River Ebro themselves destroyed their own walls on a single day, as the result of just one stratagem, and, because the Romans could easily attack them, they remained mostly at peace.

5.47 *ILS* 15: L. Aemilius Paullus in Spain, 189 BC

Paullus was in charge of Further Spain as propraetor (191–189 BC), defeating the Lusitanians in 189. This decree on a bronze plate frees the serfs of the city of Hasta and allows them to retain the lands they worked, presumably an attempt to weaken Hasta economically. The town was captured by the Romans in 186.

1 Lucius Aemilius, son of Lucius, commander-in-chief, decreed that the serfs of the people of Hasta, who live in the tower of Lascuta, are to be free; he ordered that the land and town **5** which they possessed at that time they are to possess and hold as long as this is the wish of the Roman people and senate. Enacted in camp, 19th day of January.

5.48 Appian *The Spanish Wars* 6.51–52, 59–60 (215–20, 247–55): Massacre in Spain, 151–150 BC

In 154 the Lusitanians in Further Spain invaded Roman territory and defeated two praetors, even crossing to North Africa. Though M. Claudius Marcellus, consul for the third time in 152, was successful in Spain and urged that peace be made, the senate wanted military triumphs and continued the war. Marcellus' successor, L. Licinius Lucullus (cos. 151), without authority, attacked the Vaccaei, a Celtiberian tribe, despite the fact that they were not at war with Rome; he ordered the killing of 20,000 men at the Vaccaenan city of Cauca in 151, even though they had surrendered. Sulpicius Galba, praetor in Hispania Ulterior in 151 and prorogued for 150, defeated and accepted the surrender of 8,000 Lusitanians, who were then butchered. He was brought to trial for his misconduct in Spain but still became consul in 144. Viriathus survived Galba's massacre and became the hero of the resistance, until assassinated by treachery in 139.

215 The war against the Belli, Titthi and Arevaci had in this way come to an end before Lucullus' time, but Lucullus, who was eager for glory and needed money because of his poverty, attacked the Vaccaei, another Celtiberian tribe, neighbours of the Aravaci, though no vote on this had taken place, nor had the Vaccaei made war on the Romans or wronged Lucullus himself in any way. **216** He crossed the river called the Tagus and arrived at the town of Cauca and made camp beside it . . . **218** On the next day the elders, wearing crowns and carrying olive branches, again asked Lucullus what they should do to be friends. He demanded that they give hostages and 100 talents of silver and ordered that their cavalry fight on his side. **219** When he had received all this, he demanded that a garrison enter the town. The Caucaei accepted this too, and he led in 2,000 men, chosen for their courage, whom he told to take up positions on the walls once they were inside. When the 2,000 had taken the walls, Lucullus led in the rest of the army and with a trumpet blast signalled that they should kill all the Caucaei of age. **220** The Caucaei, calling on their guarantees and the gods as witnesses of their oaths, and cursing the Romans for their bad faith, were savagely slaughtered, with only a few of the 20,000 men escaping through difficult passages; Lucullus sacked the town and brought the Romans into disrepute . . . **247** Lucullus had made war without authority on the Vaccaei and was at that point wintering in Turditania. Learning that the Lusitanians were making attacks on the neighbouring regions, he sent out his best commanders and killed about 4,000 of them. **248** He also killed about 1,500 others as they were crossing the straits near Cadiz, and, when the remainder took refuge on a hill, he fenced them off with a ditch and captured a vast number of them. He also invaded Lusitania and ravaged it bit by bit. **249** Galba also ravaged it on the other side. When some of their envoys came to Galba, wanting to confirm the treaty they had made with Atilius, the previous general, and then broken, he received them and made a truce, pretending to feel sympathy with them because they were compelled by poverty to plunder, make war and break treaties. **250** 'For', he said, 'the poverty of your soil and your penniless condition force you to do these things; I will divide you into three and give you, my poor friends, good land, settling you in fertile country.'

251 Expecting this to happen, they left their own country and gathered at the place Galba had appointed; he divided them into three groups and showed each a certain plain, commanding them to remain on this plain until he came and told them where to settle. **252** When he came to the first division, he instructed them as friends to put down their arms, and, when they had done so, he fenced them off with a ditch and sent in men with swords who slaughtered them all, as they lamented and called on the names of the gods and their guarantees of good faith. **253** In the same way he rushed to the second and third divisions and slaughtered them, while they were still ignorant of what had happened to the first, repaying treachery with treachery and imitating barbarians in a way not worthy of the Romans. **254** A few of them escaped, among them Viriathus, who not long afterwards became leader of the Lusitanians, killing many Romans and achieving great successes. But I shall speak later of these subsequent events. **255** Galba, who was more avaricious than Lucullus, then distributed a small amount of the booty to his troops, and a little to his friends, but kept the rest for himself although he was already one of the wealthiest of the Romans; but they say that even in peace he did not stop lying and breaking his word for the sake of gain. Although hated and brought to court, he escaped because of his wealth.

5.49 Cicero *Brutus* 89–90: Servius Sulpicius Galba as orator

Despite his breaking faith with the Lusitanians and the disapproval of Cato the Elder, Galba was still able to avoid condemnation for the massacre in 150 BC by his clever rhetoric and appeal to family sympathies. Gaius Sulpicius Gallus was a friend of Lucius Aemilius Paullus and fought at Pydna.

89 From this account of Rutilius, one may deduce that, of the two greatest qualities an orator may possess – that of arguing shrewdly in order to convince, the other of speaking impressively in order to sway the hearts and minds of his auditors – the man who inspires the jurors is far more successful than he who instructs them: in other words, Laelius possessed craft, Galba forcefulness. This power was indeed most clearly realised when Servius Galba, as praetor, was accused of massacring Lusitanians in violation – as it was believed – of his good faith. Lucius

Libo, tribune of the plebs, aroused the people and brought forward a measure against Galba personally, while Marcus Cato, though extremely elderly (as I have mentioned before), spoke in favour of making a vehement attack on Galba; this speech he included in his *Origines* a few days or months before he died. **90** Galba then, requesting no favours for himself, but calling on the faith of the Roman people, entrusted to their care, weeping as he did so, his own children as well as the son of Gaius (Sulpicius) Gallus (cos. 166), whose orphaned condition and tears inspired remarkable compassion on account of the recent memory of his illustrious father. In this way Galba snatched himself from the flames, as Cato wrote, by stirring up the populace's compassion for young children.

5.50 Livy *Periochae* 54–56: Rome repudiates treaties

From 144, Celtiberian revolt centred on the town of Numantia. Resistance was exacerbated by the Romans' constant repudiation of peace agreements. **54**: the treaty made by Pompeius, consul in 141, was not ratified by the senate. Viriathus defeated at least four Roman armies, and in 141/0 he surrounded a Roman army and terms were made. Fabius' treaty was ratified but then disowned at the instigation of Q. Servilius Caepio, the new governor (cos. 140).

C. Hostilius Mancinus (cos. 137), in attempting to withdraw from Numantia by night, was trapped and surrounded; terms made by the quaestor Ti. Sempronius Gracchus (tr. pl. 133) saved the lives of the 20,000 Romans but were repudiated by the senate. D. Junius Brutus (cos. 138) reconquered tribes in 137–136; his Gallaeci campaign in north-west Spain was in 134. His gift of land was perhaps to soldiers (i.e., veterans) who had fought *against* Viriathus, not under him. Aemilius Lepidus Porcina undertook his campaign on his own initiative and was fined by the senate after his return.

54 The consul Quintus Pompeius conquered the Termestini in Spain (141 BC). He made a peace treaty with them and the Numantines which was repudiated by the Roman people . . . Quintus Fabius, as proconsul, won successes in Spain but spoiled his record by making peace with Viriathus on equal terms (140 BC). Viriathus was assassinated by traitors at the instigation of Servilius Caepio and was greatly mourned by his army and given a noble burial. He was a great man and a great leader, and, in the 14 years in which he waged war against the Romans, he got the better of them more often than not. **55** The consul Junius Brutus in Spain gave those who had served under Viriathus land and a town, called Valentia. Marcus Popillius, after a peace treaty with the Numantines had been repudiated by the senate, was routed and put to flight by them together with his army. When the consul Gaius Hostilius Mancinus was sacrificing, the chickens flew out of their enclosure; later, when he was going on board his ship to set out for Spain, the cry, 'Stay. Mancinus', was heard; that these omens were unfavourable was proved by the outcome. For he was defeated by the Numantines and his camp was despoiled, and, when there was no hope of saving his army, he made a ignominious peace with them which the senate refused to ratify. 40,000 Romans were defeated by 4,000 Numantines. Decimus Junius totally subdued Lusitania by storming its cities right up to the Atlantic Ocean. **56** Decimus Junius Brutus waged a successful campaign in Further Spain against the Gallaeci. A different outcome resulted when the proconsul Marcus Aemilius Lepidus made war on the Vaccaei, and he suffered a similar disaster to that at Numantia. To release the Roman people from the sanctity of the Numantine treaty, for which he was responsible, Mancinus was handed over to the Numantines, who would not accept him.

5.51 Livy *Periochae* 56: Scipio's second consulship

The Numantine war had dragged on for two decades and Scipio Aemilianus was sent out in 134 to end the conflict. He recruited four legions and allies, including Numidian cavalry led by Jugurtha with 12 war elephants. Recruitment had been slow, but, when Scipio Aemilianus volunteered for service, recruits put themselves forward enthusiastically. Despite a law against second consulships, perhaps passed in 151 BC, the situation was serious enough for the constitution to be put aside.

As the Numantine war was dragging on because of the failure of the generals, and not without public shame, the consulship was therefore offered to Scipio Aemilianus by the senate and Roman people; he was not permitted to accept this on account of a law which forbade anyone to become consul for a second time, but was exempted from the laws as in his earlier consulship.

5.52 Appian *The Spanish Wars* 6.84–85 (363–70): Scipio Aemilianus ejects camp followers

By 134 only the northern peoples of Spain and the Aravaci of the Numantia region remained unsubdued. Scipio Aemilianus, as consul in 134, tightened up discipline in the Spanish troops and evicted all unnecessary camp followers and equipment (including, according to Livy *Per.* 57, 2,000 prostitutes).

363 In Rome the people, tired of the Numantine issue, as the war had been much longer and more difficult than they had expected, chose Cornelius Scipio, the conqueror of Carthage, to be consul for a second time, as the only person able to overcome the Numantines. **364** Even at that point he was still younger than the age limit for consuls, and so the senate, just as when he was elected to fight against the Carthaginians, once more decreed that the tribunes should repeal the law about the age limit and bring it in again the next year . . . **367** When he arrived, he drove out all the merchants, prostitutes, diviners, and fortune-tellers, whom the soldiers constantly consulted in their anxiety over their lack of success; and, for the future, he prohibited the importation of anything superfluous, not even a victim prepared for divination. **368** He also ordered that the wagons and the superfluous items loaded on them, and the draft animals, except for those he exempted, be sold. Furthermore, no one was permitted to have any equipment for cooking, except a spit, a bronze pot and one drinking cup. Their food was restricted to boiled and roast meat. **369** He forbade them to have beds, and was the first to lie down to rest on a straw mattress. He also forbade them to ride on mules while marching: 'For what can be expected in war', he said, 'from a man unable to walk on foot?'

When they rubbed themselves with oil and when they were in the baths, they put on their own oil, as Scipio joked that it was those, like mules, who had no hands, that needed others to rub them down. **370** In this way he converted them all to self-restraint and got them used to respect and fear, as it was difficult to get access to him and he was averse to granting favours, especially those against regulations.

5.53 Appian *The Spanish Wars* 6.97–98 (419–24): Numantia, 133 BC

Scipio surrounded Numantia with seven camps and a massive stone wall 9 kilometres in length and some 3 metres high, starving it out in 133 BC after a siege of eight months. The populace, which had resorted to cannibalism, were sold as slaves, but Scipio allowed a day in which those who wished could commit suicide.

419 Such was the love of freedom and of courage in a city that was both barbarian and small in size. In peace time there were only about 8,000 inhabitants, yet they inflicted such numerous great defeats on the Romans, made such treaties with them on terms of complete equality (though the Romans never agreed to make such treaties with anyone), and frequently challenged in battle such a great general, the last to be sent against them, who surrounded them with 60,000 men. **420** He was, of course, a better general than they were, and would not come to grips with wild beasts, but exhausted them through starvation, an evil which cannot be fought, through which alone it was possible to take the Numantines and through which alone they were taken. **421** This is what I have to say about the Numantines, looking at their small numbers, their ability to bear hardship, their many achievements, and the length of time they held out; **422** first of all, those who wished killed themselves, each in his own way; the rest came out on the third day to the appointed spot, an appalling sight and a completely inhuman one, with their bodies unwashed, full of hair, nails and filth, smelling dreadfully, with their clothes foul and stinking no less than they did. **423** To their enemies, this made them seem pitiable, but their expressions made them terrifying; for they looked at the Romans in a way that displayed their anger, their grief, their suffering, and their consciousness of their cannibalism. **424** Scipio chose 50 of them for his triumph, sold the rest and destroyed the city.

THE IMPACT OF GREEK CULTURE ON ROME

Between 211 (Marcellus' capture of Syracuse) and 146 BC (Mummius' sack of Corinth and Scipio Aemilianus' sack of Carthage), Rome was flooded with the spoils of war; this included Greek art, as well as goods such as precious metals, gems, money and slaves. Vast sums were acquired through conquests in both the East and the West.

5.54 Livy *History of Rome* 29.19.10–13: Scipio Africanus in Syracuse

Fabius Maximus and other senators attacked Scipio for his conduct while he was preparing for war in Africa. Scipio is here criticised not for his interest in Greek activities *per se*, but because he pursues them so openly; he is not behaving in a manner befitting a Roman commander on duty. Scipio was a lover of Greek culture and was granted honours by Greek communities; for satire on his behaviour, see doc. 4.57.

10 Not all the senators' opinions could be asked on that day because of the party spirit which was inflamed for and against Scipio. **11** In addition to the crime of Pleminius and the disastrous situation of the Locrians, even the general's appearance was the subject of attack, not only as un-Roman but even as unsoldierly: **12** he was said to stroll about in the gymnasium in Greek mantle (*pallium*) and sandals; to give his attention to books and exercising in the palaestra; his entire staff was enjoying the amenities of Syracuse in idleness and relaxation; **13** Carthage and Hannibal had been entirely forgotten; and the whole army was being spoiled by lack of discipline, just as had happened at Sucro in Spain and currently at Locri, and was to be feared more by allies than by the enemy.

5.55 Livy *History of Rome* 39.6.3–7.5: Gnaeus Manlius Vulso, 186 BC

Vulso (cos. 189) as proconsul took 40,000 prisoners from the Galatians of central Asia Minor at Mount Olympus (who were sold to neighbouring tribes) and levied large sums from different cities for Rome's 'friendship'. He celebrated a triumph over the Galatians, whom he defeated in two battles, and his booty was used to reimburse citizens for their war loans. Cistophoroi were Asiatic coins worth approximately 4 drachmas; philippei were Macedonian gold coins worth 20 drachmas.

6.3 At the end of the year, when the magistrates had already been elected, on the third day before the Nones of March, Gnaeus Manlius Vulso triumphed over the Gauls (i.e., the Galatians) who live in Asia. **4** The reason for his leaving the celebration of his triumph so late was to avoid making his defence under the *lex Petillia* before the praetor Quintus Terentius Culleo and being consumed in the flames of another's trial, where Lucius Scipio had been condemned, **5** in as much as the jurors were far more hostile to him than to Scipio, because rumour stated that he, as Scipio's successor, by allowing all kinds of licence, had ruined the military discipline which Scipio had strictly preserved. **6** Nor was this the only grounds on which he was criticised – hearsay accounts of what had occurred in his province far out of sight – but more damning was the evidence seen daily in the conduct of his soldiers. **7** For the army which returned from Asia introduced the beginnings of foreign luxury into the city. They brought to Rome, for the first time, bronze couches, valuable robes as coverings, tapestries and other textiles, and – what was at that time considered to be splendid pieces of furniture – tables with one foot and ornate sideboards. **8** Female lute-players and harpists and other entertaining acts became a feature of banquets; moreover, the banquets themselves began to be prepared with both greater care and expense. **9** It was then that the cooks – to the men of olden times the most worthless of slaves in both monetary valuation and practical value – began to be worth something, and what had been merely an occupation now came to be seen as an art-form. But even these imports, which were then seen as remarkable, were hardly even the seeds of the luxury which was to follow.

7.1 In his triumph, Gnaeus Manlius bore 212 golden crowns, 220,000 pounds of silver, 2,103 pounds of gold, 127,000 Attic 4-drachma pieces, 250,000 cistophori, and 16,320 gold philippei, **2** as well as arms and many Gallic spoils carried in wagons, while 52 enemy leaders were led before his chariot. He gave the soldiers 42 denarii each, twice that to each centurion, three times that to each eques, and doubled their pay; **3** many soldiers of all ranks, who had been given military awards, followed his chariot. Songs which were sung by the soldiers about their general clearly showed that they were sung about an indulgent commander who courted their goodwill, and that the triumph was conspicuous more by the applause of the soldiers than that of civilians. **4** But Manlius' friends were able to win popularity with the people as well; **5** at their urging, the senate passed a decree that the arrears of the tax contributed by the people into the treasury should be paid out of the money which had been carried in the triumph. The city quaestors scrupulously paid 25 and one half asses for every thousand asses.

5.56 Livy *History of Rome* 41.28.8–10: Gracchus dedicates a painting

In 174 BC Tiberius Sempronius Gracchus (the Elder) commissioned a huge painting, including a map, as a memorial of his victory in Sardinia. This was placed in the temple of Mater Matuta at Rome and dedicated to Jupiter.

8 In the same year a tablet was placed in the temple of Mater Matuta with the following inscription: 'Under the command and auspices of the consul Tiberius Sempronius Gracchus, the legion and army of the Roman people conquered Sardinia. In that province more than 80,000 of the enemy were killed or captured. **9** After the state had been successfully organised, the allies freed, and the revenues restored, he brought the army back home safe and unimpaired and loaded with booty; for the second time he entered the city of Rome in triumph. To commemorate this he dedicated this tablet to Jupiter.' **10** It had the shape of the island of Sardinia and on it depictions of the battles were painted.

5.57 Diodorus Siculus *Library of History* 37.3.1–6: Aristocratic extravagance

Diodorus is here referring specifically to the period following the Third Macedonian War (171–168 BC). Paullus brought home after Pydna and his Greek tour huge amounts of spoils, as well as an artist, Metrodorus, to decorate his triumph. The criticism here is directed especially against extravagance and epicureanism (qualities very much opposed to the Romans' traditional view of their own ancestral frugality). For Cato's remark, see Diod. 31.24; cf. Scipio Aemilianus' disapproval of long-sleeved tunics in his speech against Sulpicius Gallus: doc. 7.57.

1 In olden days the Romans, by employing the best laws and customs, gradually increased their power to such an extent that they gained the greatest and most glorious empire within memory. In more recent times, when most nations had been subjugated and peace was of long duration, love of ancient custom at Rome turned to perdition. **2** For, with the end of warfare, the youth turned to luxury and licentiousness, using their wealth to obtain their desires. Extravagance was preferred throughout the city to frugality, leisure to the practice of warlike deeds; the man considered blessed by the populace was not the man who was ornamented by his excellences but the man who spent his whole life enjoying the most enticing pleasures. **3** Accordingly, elaborate dishes at expensive dinner parties became fashionable, and the perfumes of wondrous unguents, the provision of costly, coloured draperies and the construction of dining-couches from ivory and silver and the other most expensive materials by the most skilful artisans. With wines, one that only moderately delighted the palate was rejected, while Falernian, Chian and every wine which gave similar pleasure to these were consumed without restraint, as were those fish and other delicacies which were most highly prized for enjoyment. **4** In line with this, the young men would wear garments of incredible softness in the Forum, so fine as to be transparent, something similar to women's clothes. And since they were providing themselves with everything relating to pleasure and ruinous ostentation, they soon raised the price of these commodities to unbelievable heights. **5** A jar of wine sold for 100 drachmas, a jar of Pontic preserved fish for 400 drachmas, chefs especially gifted in the arts of cookery for four talents, and male catamites of exceptional beauty for many talents . . . **6** Marcus Cato, a prudent man distinguished for his good conduct, denounced in the senate the prevalence of luxury at Rome, saying that only in this city were jars of Pontic preserved fish worth more than men who drove a yoke of oxen, and pretty boys more than farmland.

5.58 Polybius *Histories* 31.25.2–8: The social impact of conquest

Polybius is here praising Scipio Aemilianus, his friend and patron; Scipio was 18 years old at the time to which this passage refers (c. 167/6). With the wealth in money and slaves that poured into Rome in the first half of the second century, many upper-class Romans acquired a taste for Greek pursuits, artefacts and extravagance.

2 The first object of Scipio's desire to lead a good life was to win a reputation for temperance and in this respect to surpass all the young men of his age. **3** This is a great prize and one difficult to attain, but was one easy to win in Rome at this time because of the tendency of most of the young men towards vice. **4** For some of them had given themselves up to homosexual relationships with boys or to affairs with courtesans, many to musical entertainments and drinking-parties and the extravagance these involve, having swiftly become attached to the Greeks' laxity during the war against Perseus. **5** So unbridled was the licence into which the youth had fallen in such matters that many paid a talent for a favourite boy and many 300 drachmas for a jar of Pontic pickled fish. Marcus (Cato), indignant at this, once said in a speech to the people that the best sign that the state was degenerating was when lovely boys fetched more than fields and jars of pickled fish more than ploughmen. **6** It was at the time of which we are speaking that the current tendency became obvious, first of all because, after the Macedonian kingdom fell, they thought that their universal sovereignty was uncontested, **7** and next because, after the wealth of Macedonia had been brought to Rome, there was a great parade of riches both in private life and in public. **8** Only Scipio set out to follow the opposite lifestyle, combating all his desires and shaping his life to be in all respects uniform and harmonious, gaining in about the first five years a universal reputation for self-discipline and temperance.

5.59 Aulus Gellius *Attic Nights* 2.24.2–4: Sumptuary legislation, 161 BC

At the Megalesia nobles gave dinner parties to each other on 4 April; the ludi Romani (in Cicero's time) lasted from 5 to 19 September; the plebeian games from 4 to 17 November; the Saturnalia, originally on 17 December, later lasted for seven days. The *lex Fannia* in 161 (sponsored by the consul C. Fannius Strabo) prohibited the private entertainment of more than three people outside of the family, or five on nundinae (market-days), while laying down the maximum expenditures for daily and limits on annual purchases.

2 Just recently I read in Ateius Capito's *Miscellanies* an old senatorial decree passed in the consulship of Gaius Fannius and Marcus Valerius Messala, in which the leading citizens, who by ancestral custom 'interchanged' at the Megalesian games – that is, hosted banquets for each other in turn – were instructed to take an oath in front of the consuls in set terms: that they would spend no more on each dinner than 120 asses, excepting vegetables, bread and wine; that they would not serve foreign wine, but only that produced locally; and that at a banquet they would not use more than 100 pounds of silverware. **3** But, following that senatorial decree, the *lex Fannia* was introduced, which allowed 100 *asses* a day to be spent at the Roman games, plebeian games and Saturnalia and, on other specific days, 30 *asses* a day on ten further days in each month, and only ten on all other days. **4** It is this law to which the poet Lucilius refers, when he says, 'Fannius' miserable 100 asses'.

5.60 Aulus Gellius *Attic Nights* 15.11.1–2: Edicts on Latin rhetoricians

Cf. Suet. *Rhet.* 1 (doc. 2.66). Following the Third Macedonian War many Greek intellectuals were imported to Rome, and the lectures given by the Greek philosopher Carneades in Rome in 155 were to prove highly popular (to Cato's dismay: doc. 5.61). As most rhetoricians and philosophers would have been part of private households, this edict in 161 BC was intended primarily to reassert Roman native traditions. The edict of 92 also aimed at moral censure rather than the closing of schools of Latin rhetoric.

1 In the consulship of Gaius Fannius Strabo and Marcus Valerius Messala, this decree of the senate was passed concerning Latin-speaking philosophers and rhetoricians: 'The praetor Marcus Pomponius put a motion before the senate. Following a discussion about philosophers and rhetoricians, they resolved as follows, that Marcus Pomponius, the praetor, should take heed and ensure in whatever way seemed to him to be in the interests of the state and the dignity of his office that they should not remain in Rome.'

2 Then some years after that senatorial decree Gnaeus Domitius Ahenobarbus and Lucius Licinius Crassus, the censors, proclaimed the following edict for repressing Latin rhetoricians: 'It has been reported to us that there are men who have introduced a new kind of training, whose schools the youth frequent; that these men have adopted for themselves the title of Latin rhetoricians; that young men sit idle there for whole days. Our ancestors laid down what they desired their children to learn and to what schools they wished them to go. These innovations, which are contrary to our ancestors' customs and principles, neither please us nor appear proper. Wherefore, it appears to be our duty that we should declare our opinion, both to those who hold these schools and to those who are in the habit of attending them, that they displease us.'

5.61 Plutarch *Life of Cato the Elder* 2.5–6, 22.1–23.6: Cato and the Greeks

Cato was consul in 195 and censor in 184; he posed as a champion of austerity and old Roman standards but was not totally opposed to Hellenic culture. In 155 BC, Cato heard Carneades' speeches in Rome. Athens had suffered a damaging judgement in her dispute with Oropus (which was heard by Sicyon, which imposed a fine of 500 talents). Athens appealed to the senate, using as spokespersons the heads of three major philosophical schools, who also offered public lectures. These were extremely popular, and this popular appeal was Cato's major concern.

2.5 It is said that he did not learn Greek until later in life and was quite old when he took to reading Greek books, when his oratory benefited a little from Thucydides but more from Demosthenes. **6** However, his writings are fairly well adorned with Greek opinions and stories, and many literal translations from Greek can be found in his maxims and proverbs . . . **22.1** When he was already an old man, Carneades the Academic and Diogenes the Stoic philosopher came as envoys from Athens to Rome (155 BC) to request the reversal of a judgement against the Athenian people . . . **2** The most scholarly of Rome's young men immediately thronged to them and became their admiring audience . . . **4** This delighted the other Romans, and they were pleased to see their young men acquiring Greek culture and associating with such remarkable men; **5** but Cato, from the time when this zeal for eloquence had poured into the city, was unhappy, fearing that the young men, through turning their ambition in this direction, would come to desire a reputation for speaking more than one based on exploits and campaigns. And when the philosophers' fame rose even higher in the city and their first speeches to the senate were interpreted by that distinguished man Gaius Acilius, at his own desire and request, Cato resolved to have all these philosophers removed from the city on a decent pretext. **6** So, in the senate, he criticised the magistrates for detaining for so long an embassy of men who could easily achieve through persuasion anything they wished; **7** they ought to make a decision and vote on the embassy as quickly as possible, so that they could return to their schools and lecture to the young men of Greece, and the youth of Rome could listen to their laws and magistrates as before.

23.2 . . . In an attempt to prejudice his son against Greek culture, he employs a dictum too bold for an old man, stating like a prophet or visionary that the Romans will lose their empire once they are infected with Greek learning. **3** But time has shown these words of evil omen to be groundless, for when the city was at its peak of empire she adopted every type of Greek learning and culture. He not only hated Greek philosophers but was also suspicious of Greeks who practised medicine at Rome. **4** It would seem that he had heard of Hippocrates' answer, who told the Great King, when asked for his services for a fee of many talents, that he would never work for barbarians who were enemies of Greece. Cato said all Greek doctors had taken a similar oath and urged his son to beware of all of them; **5** he had himself written a book of medical notes, which he used in treating and regulating the diet of any of his household who were sick. He never prescribed fasting for anyone but fed them on vegetables, or bits of duck, pigeon or hare; **6** this diet was light and suitable for invalids, except for often causing dreams in its eaters, and by employing such treatment and diet he was in good health himself and kept his family healthy.

5.62 Pliny *Natural History* 29.14: Cato to his son Marcus

Pliny here cites an extract from a work supposedly addressed by Cato to his son, though it was perhaps a collection of axioms for a wider audience. For Cato's home remedies, see doc. 2.17.

I shall speak about those Greek fellows in their proper place, Marcus, my son, making clear what I learnt at Athens and convincing you what good comes of looking at their literature, but without thoroughly studying it. They are a totally good-for-nothing and incorrigible race of people – take my words as prophetic! When that race gives us its literature it will corrupt everything – and still worse, if it sends us its doctors! They have conspired among themselves to murder all 'barbarians' with their drugs, and, what's more, do this for a fee, to gain our confidence and easily dispose of us. Moreover, they keep calling us barbarians and bespatter us even more obscenely than others by giving us the nickname of 'Opici' (Oscans).

5.63 Cicero *Tusculan Disputations* 4.70–71: Nudity and pederasty

Cicero is here referring not to homosexuality *per se* but to pederasty practised with citizen youths. There was no moral stigma about relationships with young male prostitutes and slaves, though it was considered shameful to be the passive partner. One of the main issues involved in the Bacchanalia was the seduction of young freeborn male adults (*stuprum*), and homosexual relationships in the army were severely dealt with (because between citizens): doc. 7.59; cf. 8.22 for Gaius Gracchus. Laius was a character in a lost play of Euripides, the *Chrysippus*.

70 Why is it that no one is ever in love with an unsightly youth or a handsome old man? My view is that this custom appears to have grown up in the gymnasia of the Greeks, in which such loves were free and permissible; it was well said by Ennius (F107),

'Nudity amongst citizens is the beginning of disgrace.'

Even when such relationships are, as I see they can be, within the bounds of propriety, they cause uneasiness and anxiety – all the more because they are a law
unto themselves and are subject to no outside control. **71** Again, leaving aside
love for women, to which nature has allowed greater licence, who can either doubt
the poets' meaning in the tale of the rape of Ganymede or fail to understand Laius'
speeches and desires in Euripides' play?

5.64 Plutarch *Roman Questions* 40: Roman athleticism

Moralia 274de. This passage gives the Romans' view rather than Plutarch's. He is here discussing why the flamen dialis was forbidden to anoint himself with oil in the open air (doc. 3.21).

The Romans used to be very suspicious of rubbing themselves down with oil,
and they believe that nothing has been more responsible for the enslavement and
effeminacy of the Greeks than their gymnasia and wrestling schools, which give
rise to much idleness and waste of time in their cities, as well as bad practices and
pederasty and the ruin of the bodies of the young men by a regimen of sleeping,
walking, rhythmical movements and strict diet. Through these practices they have
unconsciously left off the practice of arms and have become happy to be called
nimble, beautiful athletes instead of excellent foot-soldiers and horsemen.

5.65 Cicero *Tusculan Disputations* 1.1–3: Roman native qualities

In his *Tusculan Disputations*, written in 45, Cicero is trying to make Greek philosophy
accessible to the general reader. He argues that areas of study may be Greek, but virtues
and morals are Roman and the Romans have improved on what they have borrowed. Livius
Andronicus, a Greek, came from Tarentum; he was commissioned by the government in
240 to adapt Greek drama to celebrate the end of the First Punic War (cf. doc. 7.85).

1 I have always been convinced that our fellow countrymen have in every field
shown themselves to be wiser than the Greeks, whether in what they have discovered for themselves or in the ways they have improved upon what they had taken
over from the Greeks, at any rate in those areas which they considered worthy of
their exertions. **2** For we undoubtedly uphold standards of morality, regulate our
lives, and run our families and households in a much better and more honourable fashion, while our forefathers organised government with better practices
and laws than anyone else. What shall I say about the science of warfare? In
this our countrymen have shown their superiority, not only through their excellence but even more by their disciplined practice. As for those qualities which are
attained by nature, not through books, they cannot be compared with those of the
Greek or any other race. For where has such dignity, such firmness of character,
such greatness of spirit, such integrity, such trustworthiness – where has such
pre-eminent excellence in every respect been found in any races which could bear
comparison with that of our ancestors? **3** Greece was superior to us in learning
and all kinds of literature, and it was easy for them to win with no competition.
For, while, among the Greeks, the most ancient learned class is that of the poets,

since Homer and Hesiod lived before the founding of Rome and Archilochus in the reign of Romulus, we acquired poetry at a later date. About 510 years after the foundation of Rome Livius (Andronicus) produced a play in the consulship of Gaius Claudius, son of Caecus, and Marcus Tuditanus, in the year before Ennius was born, who was older than Plautus and Naevius.

5.66 Varro *On Farming* 2.1.1–3: The decline of Roman standards

Varro here demonstrates the degree to which Romans could adopt Greek habits and architecture within their private villas: cf. doc. 2.20 for Scipio Africanus. The ninth days refer to the market-days (nundinae) on the last day of the eight-day market week.

1 Not without reason did those great men, our ancestors, put those Romans who lived in the country before those who lived in the city. For, as in the country, those who live in the villas are lazier than those who are engaged in doing work on the land, so those who resided in town they thought to be more slothful than those who dwelt in the country. As a result, they divided up their year in such a way that they saw to their city affairs only on the ninth days and dwelt in the country for the remaining seven. **2** As long as they kept up this practice they achieved both objects – keeping their fields extremely productive through cultivation and themselves fitter in health and not in need of the city gymnasia of the Greeks. Nowadays one gymnasium is hardly enough, nor do people consider they have a villa unless it resounds with many Greek terms for individual locations, called procoetion (ante-room), palaestra (exercise-room), apodyterion (dressing-room), peristylon (colonnade), ornithonon (aviary), peripteros (veranda) and oporotheca (fruit-room). **3** As, therefore, almost all heads of families have nowadays crept inside the walls, abandoning the sickle and plough, and prefer to employ their hands in the theatre and circus than in the wheat-fields and vineyards, we hire a man to bring us grain from Africa and Sardinia so our stomachs can be filled, and the vintage we store up comes in ships from the islands of Cos and Chios.

ROME AND THE PROVINCES

The term 'province' originally implied the area in which a magistrate functioned: by the second century, provinces had come to mean overseas territories permanently administered by the Romans. The first was Sicily, mostly acquired in 241 BC following the First Punic War, which became a unified province in 211, followed by Sardinia and Corsica in 227, and then in 198/7 by the two Spanish provinces. Macedonia was annexed in 146, Asia in 129, Transalpine and Cisalpine Gaul after 100, Cilicia c. 80, and Bithynia and Pontus, Crete, Cyprus and Syria in the 70s, 60s and 50s. While provinces were initially allocated to magistrates and promagistrates by the senate and then by lot, in 123 Gaius Gracchus legislated that the senate was to decide, before the consular elections (and hence before the election results were known), which provinces would be consular (i.e., would be held by the successful consular candidates as promagistrates after their year of office): doc. 8.28.

Promagistrates were often motivated by personal gain (the expenses of election were immense) and the desire for gloria (and possibly a triumph). Governors could be subject to prosecution for extortion on their return to Rome, but in practice convictions were rare.

5.67 Cicero *On the Agrarian Law* 2.45: The unpopularity of Roman imperium

Cicero, as consul in 63, is speaking against Rullus' proposal of a commission of ten who would be given powers to sell state lands and purchase land for distribution in Italy: doc. 12.13.

Foreign nations can hardly stand our ambassadors, men with slight authority, who go on free embassies for the sake of their own private affairs. For the name of imperium is oppressive and feared even when its possessor is insignificant, because it is your name, not their own, that they abuse when they have left Rome.

5.68 Cicero *Against Verres* 2.3.66, 120–1, 2.4.1–2: Verres in Sicily

Praetor urbanus in 74, Verres had then been propraetorian governor of Sicily; his term extended to 71. His governorship is a fine illustration of the abuses perpetrated by many Roman governors. Cicero had served as quaestor in Sicily and had connections and clients there, hence his taking the side of the prosecution against Verres. The fine was accessed at 750,000 denarii (a low assessment: Plut. *Cic.* 8.1), and Verres went into exile at Marseilles.

3.66 You observe, jurors, how great a blaze swept at the tax-gatherers' approach not only through the farmers' fields but even through their remaining possessions, and not only through their possessions but even through their rights as free men and citizens, with Verres as governor. You could see some of the farmers hanging from trees, others being beaten and flogged, still more held as prisoners, others made to remain standing through banquets, others being convicted by the governor's personal doctor and herald; the goods of all of them being meanwhile despoiled and swept away from their farms. What does all this mean? Is this the government of Rome? Are these the laws a governor administers? Are these the courts that judge our loyal allies, our closest province? ... **120** How then can all this be proven? By this fact, most of all, that the tax-paying lands of the province of Sicily were deserted owing to his greed. It was not merely that those who did stay on their land continued farming on a much smaller scale, but that a great many wealthy men, important and diligent farmers, abandoned their broad and fertile properties and left their entire farms derelict. The fact can easily be made clear from the communities' public records, since by a law of Hiero a return of the number of farmers is officially made to the magistrates every year. Read out now the total of farmers in the Leotini district when Verres arrived in the province: 84. The number who made a return in his third year: 32. So we see that 52 farmers were thrown out in such a way that no one even came in to take their places. How many farmers were there in the Mutyca district while you were *en route* to Sicily? Let us see from the public records: 187. Well now, in your third year? 86. Owing to his iniquities, a single district feels the lack of 101 farmers – indeed, our own nation, since the revenues are those of the Roman people, feels the lack of all these men and their families and demands their restitution. The district of Herbita in his first year had 252 farmers, 120 in his third; 132 of its householders were driven from their homes and fled elsewhere. The Agyrium district – what fine, well-regarded, substantial inhabitants! – had 250 farmers in the first year of your governorship. And now? How many in your third year? 130, as you have heard, jurors, from representatives of Agyrium who read it from their public records. **121** Immortal gods! If you had driven out 170 farmers from the whole of Sicily, could you be acquitted by a serious court? It is this single district of Agyrium which is emptier by 170 farmers – can you not then, jurors, hazard a guess regarding Sicily as a whole?

4.1 I come now to what he himself calls his favourite occupation, his friends a foolish obsession, and the Sicilians highway robbery; what name I should give it, I do not know. I will place the facts before you, and you can judge it by its nature, not its name. First, listen to its general characteristics, jurors, after which you will, perhaps, have no difficulty in deciding what you think it should be called. I maintain that, in the whole of Sicily, such a wealthy, ancient province, in all its towns, in all its very substantial households, there was not one vessel of silver, not one of Corinthian or Delian bronze, no precious stone or pearl, nothing made of gold or ivory, no bronze, marble or ivory statue, no painting or embroidered textile that he did not seek out, examine and, if he liked it, appropriate . . . **2** In no man's house, even though he be his host, in no public place, even though it be a sacred shrine, in the possession of no man, whether Sicilian, or even Roman citizen, nowhere, to be brief, has he left anything which struck his eyes or taste, whether private or public property, belonging to men or gods, in the whole of Sicily.

5.69 Cicero *Letters to his Brother Quintus* 1.1.8, 13, 22: Provincial corruption

Part of a letter of advice written by Cicero to Quintus in 60 or early 59 BC, when Quintus was governing Asia as propraetor (he governed Asia 61–58). Cicero is here clearly concerned with subordinates (and perhaps slaves) accepting bribes to influence the governor's judgement; cf. doc. 6.53 for his concerns over Quintus' freedman.

8 It is a mark of great distinction that you have been two years in Asia in supreme command and that no statue, picture, dish, garment, slave, beautiful face or offer of money – all of which that province has in abundance – has caused you to deviate from the highest integrity and moderation. What can be found so outstanding or desirable as that your virtue, self-restraint and self-control should not lie hidden and out of sight in shadow but be displayed to the light of Asia, to the eyes of that most illustrious province, and to the ears of all races and nations? That these men are not terrified by your official visits? That they are not exhausted by your expenditure? That they are not anxious at your approach? That, wherever you arrive, there is the greatest public and private happiness, since it appears that their city has received a protector, not a tyrant, the home a guest, not a despoiler? . . . **13** Finally let it be public knowledge that you will be severely displeased not only with those who have taken a bribe but with those who have given one, if you come to know of it. Nor indeed will anyone give a bribe, when it is made perfectly clear that nothing can be got out of you by those people who pretend to have great influence with you . . . **22** If such courtesy is welcome at Rome, where there is so much arrogance, such unrestricted freedom, such infinite licence generally, and in short so many magistrates, so many sources of aid, such popular power, such senatorial authority, how welcome then must the courteousness of a praetor be in Asia, where so great a multitude of citizens and allies, so many cities, so many states watch for the nod of a single man? Where there is no legal help, no chance to complain, no senate, no assembly? It must therefore always be the role of a great man, and one controlled not only by his own nature but also by the knowledge and study of the finest of the arts, so to conduct himself in a position of such power that the existence of no other power may be desired by those over whom he rules.

5.70 Cicero *Letters to his Brother Quintus* 1.1.32–3: The problems of being a governor

G. Gracchus in 122 had arranged for the indirect taxes of Asia to be sold to publicani on five-year contracts, and their rapacity led to the rebellion in Asia of 88 BC (docs 11.8–10). In this case, the syndicate of publicani had obviously overbid on the contract and demanded its cancellation (cf. doc. 12.35).

32 To all your goodwill and diligence the publicani present a serious problem; if we oppose them, we will alienate both from ourselves and from the government a class which has deserved the best from us and which has, through our efforts, been brought into association with the government; if, however, we give in to them in every situation, we will be permitting the total ruin of those people whose safety and advantage we are bound to consider. If we want to consider the matter truthfully, this is the one problem in your whole administration. For, as to being temperate, controlling your passions, keeping your staff in check, maintaining a fair system of justice, showing yourself to be courteous in investigating cases and in listening to and giving audiences to men – all this is a matter of splendour rather than difficult. For it depends not on any hard work but on making up your mind and willingness to carry it out. **33** How much bitterness this question of the publicani causes among our allies we have appreciated from our own citizens, who recently, when harbour dues were abolished in Italy, complained not so much of the tax as of certain offences by the collectors. I am therefore aware of what happens to our allies in far-off lands when I hear such complaints from citizens in Italy. And for you to behave in such a way that you satisfy the publicani, especially when their contract for tax collection has proved unprofitable, yet not allow our allies to be ruined, seems to require a certain divine excellence – such as you possess, of course.

5.71 Cicero *Letters to Atticus* 5.16.2: The desperate state of Cilicia

Cicero wrote this letter to Atticus on his arrival in his province of Cilicia in 51, when he heard numerous complaints about his predecessor, Appius Claudius Pulcher, who had supported the publicani against the provincials.

I must tell you that on 31 July I made my eagerly awaited arrival in this desperate and, in fact, totally and permanently ruined province . . . I have heard about nothing but inability to pay the mandatory poll tax, the universal sale of taxes, the groans and laments from the communities, monstrous deeds, as of some savage beast, not of a human being. In short, these people are absolutely weary of life.

5.72 Cicero *Letters to Atticus* 6.1.5–6: The (ig)noblest Roman of them all

Cicero as governor of Cilicia in 51–50 BC discovered that M. Junius Brutus (Cicero's friend and later one of Caesar's assassins), under cover of two agents, Scaptius and Matinius, was loaning money to the people of Salamis on Cyprus at a rate of 48 per cent per annum (Cicero as governor had set interest rates at 12 per cent, 1 per cent per month: *Att.* 5.21). Cyprus was under the control of the governor of Cilicia. Because of his connection with Brutus, Cicero left the problem to his successor and ignored the Salaminians' difficulties.

5 Now let me tell you about the Salaminians: I see that it came as a surprise to you as much as it did to me. I never heard him (Brutus) say that the money was his; in fact, I even have a memorandum of his in which it is stated: 'The Salaminians owe money to Marcus Scaptius and Publius Matinius, friends of mine.' He recommends them to me; he even adds, as an extra spur to me, that he had gone surety for them for a large sum of money. I had arranged that the Salaminians should pay off their debt at 1 per cent a month, with interest to be added annually. But Scaptius demanded 4 per cent. I feared, if he got it, that I would lose your regard; for I would have had to renege on my own edict and totally ruin a community under the patronage of Cato and Brutus himself, and one on which I had bestowed favours.

6 And at this very moment Scaptius hands me a letter from Brutus stating that he, Brutus, was the person concerned, a fact which Brutus had never told me or you, and requesting that I give Scaptius a prefecture. But I had already told him, through you, that one would not be given to a businessman: even if I did, it would surely not be to him. He had been prefect under Appius (Claudius Pulcher) and had cavalry squadrons with which he locked the senate of Salamis in their senate house and besieged them, so that five senators died from starvation! And so, on the very day on which I reached my province . . . I sent a letter ordering the cavalry to leave the island immediately. For these reasons, I suppose, Scaptius has written Brutus some injurious remarks about me. However, this is what I have decided: if Brutus is going to think that I ought to have imposed 4 per cent interest, even though I recognised 1 per cent throughout the whole province and had stated this in my edict, with the approval of even the most grasping moneylenders; if he is going to complain because I refused a prefecture to a businessman; . . . if he is going to be annoyed because I ordered the cavalry recalled, I shall be sorry, of course, to have angered him, but much sorrier that he is not the man I thought he was.

5.73 Cicero *Letters to his Friends* 15.4.2–4: A governor's duties

Cicero is here writing to Cato the Younger from Tarsus during his governorship of Cilicia in January 50 BC. He had achieved some successes against the Parthians and clearly felt he deserved a triumph. Here he is trying to persuade Cato to support a supplicatio; for Cato's reply, see doc. 13.19.

2 When I arrived at my province on the last day of July and saw that, on account of the time of year, I should join my army as quickly as possible, I spent two days in Laodicea, then four days at Apamea, three days at Synnada, and the same number at Philomelium. I held large courts of law in these towns and freed many communities from excessively harsh taxation, exorbitant interest payments and false claims of debt. As the army had been scattered before my arrival by a near mutiny, and five cohorts, without a legate, without a military tribune, and even without a single centurion, had encamped at Philomelium, while the rest of the army was in Lycaonia, I ordered my legate Marcus Anneius to bring those five cohorts to join the rest of the army, and after the army was assembled in one spot to make camp at Iconium in Lycaonia. **3** When all this had been diligently carried out, I arrived at the camp on 24 August, having in the meantime, in the preceding days, in accordance with the decree of the senate, collected a trustworthy band of veterans, a quite sufficient cavalry corps, and volunteer auxiliaries from the free peoples and allied kings. Meanwhile, after I had reviewed the army and begun the march into Cilicia, some envoys sent to me by the king of Commagene reported on 28 August in a state of panic, but not untruthfully, that the Parthians had crossed into Syria. **4** On hearing this, I was seriously concerned about Syria as well as my province and in fact about the whole of Asia . . . I therefore made camp on the border on Cappadocia, not far from Mount Taurus at the town Cybistra, in order to protect Cilicia and by holding Cappadocia to prevent any new schemes on the part of our neighbours.

5.74 Diodorus Siculus *Library of History* 38.11: An inflammatory governor

C. Fabius Hadrianus, governor of Africa since 84, was so unpopular that the Roman citizens in Utica burned his headquarters with him inside it in 82. Roman officials must often have inflamed local sensibilities: at some time between 60 and 56 BC, Diodorus was present when an Egyptian mob lynched a visiting Roman official for killing a cat, perhaps accidentally (Diod. 1.83.8–9).

Hadrianus, the propraetor governing Utica, was burnt alive by the Uticans. Although the deed was terrible, no charges were brought because of the wickedness of the victim.

6

Slaves and Freedmen

Slavery was a social institution in Rome from the earliest times, and slaves are included in the lawcode of the XII Tables (doc. 1.32, cf. 1.53), though slaves and the institution of slavery as such are not defined in the Republic; such definitions were to be the work of the imperial jurists. To the Romans of the Republic, a slave was a piece of property and slavery an institution in which human beings owned by others fulfilled labour requirements for their owners. Slaves, whether acquired as booty in warfare or raised within the household, were items of property, *res mancipi*, a term applied to other types of property such as land and animals, and so wholly in the ownership of their masters, who had the power of life and death over them. Slaves were not considered fully competent beings: a master could be sued for his slave's wrongs. Slave status depended on that of the mother: if the mother was a slave so was the child, even if one of the citizen males of the household was the father.

Rome became a true 'slave-owning society' only in the second century BC, when slaves, both in the mines and, especially, on the latifundia (large landed estates) became a vital aspect of Roman production. Rome can be said to have become reliant on slave labour from this time on. The crucial factor was not simply the acquisition of large numbers of slaves through conquest but the control by an aristocratic elite which could afford to buy large numbers of slaves to work the land: Sicily, in particular, came to be dominated by the latifundia of this elite in the second century BC. Agriculture became a major absorber of slaves, displacing peasant farmers, with social, political and military consequences (see docs 8.5–9). In this sense, Roman slavery best approximates to that of the other major historical slave-owning society, the United States of America. But, while agriculture in both of these societies provided the bulk of employment for slaves, their uses in ancient Rome were widespread. Slaves are found in a variety of domestic situations (doc. 6.14–23), with Greek slaves employed as secretaries and in other educated roles within the household (docs 6.12, 51, 58), and it was these slaves, in close contact with their masters and having the possibility of reward for their service and loyalty, who stood the most chance of being manumitted. Slaves also carried out a wide variety of tasks in manufacturing and industrial concerns such as the silver mines (docs 6.28–30) and on the landed estates (docs 6.35–40). The 'entertainment industry' also made use of slaves, as actors and mimes (docs 6.31–32), while the great playwright Terence himself, born in Carthage, came to Rome as a slave (doc. 6.59). Gladiators were also slaves, and Spartacus' slave revolt began in the gladiators' barracks in Capua (doc. 6.50).

As in all slave societies, there were important variables in how slaves were treated in Republican Rome; the most important of these were their occupations and the character of their masters. The Roman system in the Republic allowed for slaves on the latifundia to work in chain gangs and those in the Spanish silver mines to be brutally treated by their overseers (doc. 6.30) – on the other hand, Cicero could free his trusted slave Tiro, who continued in his former owner's employment, and gladly address him as 'my dear' (doc. 6.51–54). Cato the Elder, in contrast, advised selling off old and useless slaves along with other equipment past its prime (doc. 6.35). Slaves could be and were tortured for evidence in judicial cases (docs 6.42–43) and, if Cicero is to be believed, sometimes with shocking results, even by Roman 'standards', while those who did not want to punish their own slaves could contract the torture out to professionals (docs 6.43–44).

Slaves could resist their enslavement in various ways, by disobedience and laziness, much caricatured by Plautus but probably reflecting their tendency, if they could, to work slowly and inefficiently as a means of resisting and ameliorating their status (doc. 6.24). Another method was to run away, but such slaves could be recaptured (docs 6.46–47). Those with a tendency to run off were provided with a slave collar (doc. 6.45). The slave rebellions which broke out in Sicily and Italy are clearly indicative of the problems associated with slavery (docs 6.48–50). In all three cases, the slaves that rebelled seemed largely to have been free men who had been enslaved in Rome's wars of conquests and who did not accept their servile status. These rebellions took the Roman authorities some time to suppress but led to no reflection on the nature of slavery or any improvement in the treatment of slaves, despite their appeal in modern times: Spartacus' rebellion and the film based on his activities has almost made him a modern household name.

There is little actual information about Roman attitudes to slavery in the Republic. There were certainly none of the discussions, such as those that occurred in the Greek world of the fourth century BC, about the institution of slavery and whether it was legal or moral. For Cicero, the human booty of war was simply a welcome addition to his workforce (doc. 6.11). An understanding of Roman slavery during the Republic is inhibited by a lack of legal sources for this period, with much of the best evidence coming from the imperial period. More importantly, a freed slave such as Tiro has left behind no autobiographical information about life as a slave – all the sources accept the system and show minimal if any concern for the slave's perspective. Publilius Syrus (doc. 6.21) proves perhaps a partial exception, though his maxims depend on the role being played by the character that speaks them in his mimes. What is missing most is, of course, accounts of enslavement and the resulting servile experience from the point of view of the slaves themselves – men, women and children – who were captured by the Romans in the extra-Italian conflicts of the third to first centuries BC, though epitaphs by freedpersons show the relief and gratitude of those who had managed to escape the system and acquire Roman citizenship (docs 6.60–65, 7.33). The economic effects of slavery are difficult to assess. While not essential to the development of the latifundia, the available numbers of slaves not only squeezed out the labour of the native citizenry but ensured that the owners of the land received higher profits.

Ancient sources: for the history of the Sicilian slave revolts (135–132, 104–100 BC) there is the narrative of Diodorus, which depends greatly on Posidonius (c. 135–51 BC): Diodorus used Posidonius definitely for the first slave revolt and probably for the second. Unfortunately, Diodorus' account of the first revolt survives not intact but in two summaries, one by the ninth-century Byzantine patriarch Photius and the second by the tenth-century Byzantine emperor Constantine VII Porphyrogenitus. That of Constantine is longer and more detailed. Both accounts agree that it was the cruelty and arrogance of the masters that caused the revolt. For the revolt of Spartacus, the narrative of Appian *Civil Wars* 1.116–20 is particularly important (see doc. 6.50). While ancient Greek authors, especially philosophers, wrote about slavery, there is no body of similar writings for Roman slavery. While some legal material about Roman slavery in the Republic survives, as in the XII Tables and in scattered literary sources, the main body of legislation comes from the imperial period. The evidence for slavery is scattered among the literary sources. The playwrights give an indication of popular opinions about slaves in general (docs 6.24–25), while Cicero makes clear how the relationship between a master and slave could be close (docs 6.51–52). However, while slave characters speak in plays, the genuine 'voice' of a slave and their feelings is never heard in Republican Rome: it is the masters who record their feelings.

SLAVE NUMBERS IN REPUBLICAN ROME

The XII Tables include a number of laws pertaining to the institution of slavery, and slavery was obviously an accepted institution in the fifth century BC, though Rome was not yet a slave-owning society on a large scale. When conquering communities in Italy, such as the city of Veii, large-scale enslavements such as were later practised do not seem to have taken place (despite Livy 5.22.1; doc. 1.61) and awards of citizenship were Roman policy (Livy 6.4.4). Slave numbers did not assume significant proportions until Rome entered upon its wars of conquest outside of the Italian peninsula in the second century BC.

6.1 Valerius Maximus 7.6.1a: Slaves used in war

Valerius refers to the property qualification for serving in the Roman army, which excluded free but property-less citizens: the Roman state, in its desperation after the disastrous defeat at Cannae in 216 BC (docs 4.35–36), enrolled slaves. Like the Greeks, the Romans preferred free men who would fight with unquestioned loyalty and could afford their own equipment. The Tiberius Gracchus here is the consul of 215 BC, great-uncle of the Tiberius Gracchus who was tribune in 133. With an army which included these slaves, Gracchus raised the siege of Cumae and captured the envoys of Philip V of Macedon to Hannibal. Because of manpower shortages, slaves were used by the Romans as rowers in the Second Punic War (Polyb. 10.17.11–13; Livy 24.11.7–9).

During the Second Punic War, when the Roman youth of military age had been reduced by a number of unfavourable battles, the senate, on a motion of the consul Tiberius Gracchus, decreed that slaves should be bought out of public moneys for use in war and in repulsing the enemy. After a bill about this was put to the people by the tribunes of the plebs and passed, three commissioners were appointed to purchase 24,000 slaves. These were bound by an oath that they would give strenuous and courageous service and that they would bear arms as long as the Carthaginians were in Italy, and were sent to camp. In addition, from Apulia, from the Paediculi, 270 slaves were bought as replacements for the cavalry . . . . The city, which up to this time had scorned to have as soldiers even free men without property (the *capite censi*), added to its army as its main support persons taken from slave quarters and slaves gathered from shepherd huts.

6.2 Athenaeus *Deipnosophistae* 6.272de, 273ab: Slave numbers of 'traditional' Romans

The setting for this discussion about slavery is Alexandria, c. AD 200. In the Republic, important Romans did not own large numbers of slaves simply for the purposes of ostentatious show. Scipio Aemilianus was sent by the senate to the east in 140 BC.

272d But every Roman (as you know very well, my dear Masurius) **272e** owns the greatest number of slaves he can; in fact numerous people own 10,000, 20,000 or even more, not for the sake of income, like the extremely wealthy Greek Nicias – the majority of Romans keep the largest numbers to accompany them when they go out . . . **273a** The Romans of olden days were moderate and superior in every respect. Scipio Africanus (Aemilianus), for example, when sent by the senate to organise all the kingdoms of the world so that they would submit to their rightful rulers, took only five slaves with him, as Polybius and Posidonius tell us, **273b** and, when one of them died on the trip, he wrote to his relatives telling them to buy and send him out another one in his place. Julius Caesar, the first of all men to cross over to the British Isles, had a thousand ships but took with him only three slaves, as Cotta, who was serving under him, relates in his work on the *Roman Constitution* in our native language.

6.3 Pliny *Natural History* 33.47: Total slave numbers?

Gaius, in the second century AD (*Inst.* 1.43), envisages that it was possible for an individual to own more than 500 slaves, but this is for the imperial period. That elite Romans owned dozens if not hundreds of slaves in the last decades of the Republic does not seem improbable. For Italy in 28 BC, 3,500,000 citizens and 2,000,000 slaves appears to be a reasonable estimate of the population.

Marcus Crassus (cos. 70, 55) used to say that nobody was rich unless he could maintain a legion on his annual income. He owned property worth 200,000,000 sesterces – being the richest citizen after Sulla . . . In later times we have seen many freed slaves who were even richer – three equally so, quite recently, during Claudius' reign: Callistus, Pallas and Narcissus. And, to leave these aside, as if they were still in power, there was the case of Gaius Caecilius Isidorus, freedman of Gaius, who, in the consulship of Gaius Asinius Gallus and Gaius Marcius Censorinus (8 BC), stated in his will dated 27 January that, in spite of great losses in the civil war, he left 4,116 slaves, 3,600 pairs of oxen, 257,000 other cattle, and 60,000,000 sesterces in money, and he ordered 1,100,000 to be spent on his funeral.

6.4 Lucilius *Satires* 6.2.278–81: Urban poverty and self-sufficiency

Gaius Lucilius (c. 180–102/1 BC) was from a senatorial family and served with Scipio Aemilianus at Numantia (134/3 BC). His poetry was satirical and often attacked political figures.

> He who has no beast of burden, slave, or any companion
> Keeps with him his purse and any coins he might have;
> He eats, sleeps and washes with his purse; the man's whole property
> Is in the one purse; this purse is tied onto his upper arm.

6.5 Lucilius *Satires* 30.3.1053–56: A well-equipped household

The varied use of slaves within the household is made clear in this passage. Obviously even in the late second century BC there were households with numerous specialist slaves.

> Take care that there are at home
> A weaver, maidservants, slave-boys, a belt-maker, a wool-weaver.
> And if you should have enough money, you should add
> A large-sided female baker who knows about all sorts of Syrian breads.

6.6 Pliny *Natural History* 7.128: Top slave prices

Pliny, writing in the first century AD, contrasts these Republican prices with the 50 million sesterces Clutorius Priscus paid for Sejanus' attractive eunuch Paezon in Tiberius' reign. M. Aemilius Scaurus was consul in 115 BC, and the price of 700,000 he paid (below) was considerable (though cf. doc. 6.44); Cato the Elder would spend at most 1,500 denarii on a slave (doc. 6.38, cf. 6.33), and most slaves in the later Republican period cost in the range of 1,200 to 1,500 sesterces.

The highest price paid up till now for a man born in slavery, as far as I have been able to ascertain, was when Attius of Pesaurum was selling the grammarian Daphnis and the princeps senatus, Marcus Scaurus, offered 700,000 sesterces. In our own time this figure has been exceeded – and quite considerably – by actors buying their freedom with their earnings; even in the days of our ancestors the actor Roscius is said to have earned 500,000 sesterces a year.

SOURCES OF SLAVES

In the Republic, the greatest source of slaves was warfare. From the second century BC, Rome's wars of expansion resulted in large numbers of enslaved persons, but even in the fourth century wars in Italy provided significant numbers of slaves (doc. 6.7). The 150,000 persons enslaved by the Romans when they captured Epirus (doc. 6.9) shows how war easily outweighed all other sources, though this was an exceptional total; at the sack of Corinth, Mummius sold all the women and children into slavery; Scipio Aemilianus also sold all the Numantines, except 50 kept for his triumph (docs 5.41, 53). Freelance slave traders contributed previously free persons to the slave market, and, according to Plutarch, Sulla's settlement of Asia was so harsh that people had to sell their children into slavery (doc. 11.10).

6.7 Livy *History of Rome* 9.42.7–8: Italians enslaved in 307 BC

In 307 BC, during the Second Samnite War, the Romans enslaved the allies of the Samnites after Q. Fabius Maximus (cos. 308) confined the Samnite army in its camp near Allifae.

7 The next day, before it was properly light, they started to surrender, and the Samnites among them asked to be allowed to go in just their tunics; they were all sent under the yoke. **8** The allies of the Samnites were protected by no guarantee, and 7,000 of them were sold into slavery.

6.8 Polybius *Histories* 10.17.6–15: Slaves captured in war

Captives could be distributed to troops and sold by them to dealers, or all could be sold *en bloc* to dealers and the proceeds divided among the soldiers. Here, at Scipio's capture of New Carthage in Spain, in 210, some of the prisoners became state property but with the prospect of manumission.

6 While the military tribunes were organising the collection and distribution of booty, the Roman general, when the crowd of prisoners, numbering a little less than 10,000, had been collected, ordered first the citizens with their wives and children to be set apart, and next the craftsmen. **7** When this had been done, he called on the citizens to be favourably disposed to the Romans and remember how well they had been treated and dismissed them to their own houses. **8** Simultaneously weeping and rejoicing at the unexpectedness of their deliverance, they prostrated themselves before the general and departed. **9** He told the craftsmen that, for the present, they were public slaves of Rome, but, if they showed goodwill and hard work in their various crafts, he promised them freedom if the war against Carthage proceeded successfully. **10** He ordered them to enrol themselves with the quaestor and appointed a Roman supervisor for every group of 30; their total number was about 2,000. **11** From the other prisoners he chose the strongest, best looking and youngest and mixed them in with his crews, **12** thus acquiring half as many sailors again as he had before and manning the captured ships. In this way the crews of the ships were a little under double what they had been – **13** there were 18 captured ships and he originally had 35. **14** He promised these men too their freedom, once they had won the war against Carthage, if they showed goodwill and hard work. **15** By this treatment of the prisoners he made the citizens well disposed and loyal, both to himself and to Rome, and the craftsmen hard-working in the hope of being set free.

6.9 Polybius *Histories* 30.15 (Strabo 7.7.3): Aemilius Paullus takes 150,000 slaves

This passage reflects the huge influx of slaves into Roman Italy in the second century BC. Aemilius Paullus was the victor in the Third Macedonian War in 168 BC against Perseus (see docs 5.33–34).

Polybius says that, after his defeat of Perseus and the Macedonians, Aemilius Paullus destroyed 70 cities in Epirus, most of these belonging to the Molossians, and sold 150,000 people into slavery.

6.10 Caesar *Gallic War* 2.33.1–7: A job lot in Gaul

In 57 BC, after the defeat of the Nervii, the Aduatuci retreated to their stronghold; they took part in negotiations, but then broke the truce. Caesar clearly handed the inhabitants over to the slave-dealers who followed the armies.

1 Towards evening Caesar ordered the gates to be closed and the soldiers to leave the town so that the inhabitants might receive no injury at night at the hands of the soldiers. **2** The townsfolk, it appeared, had formed a plan, believing that, following the surrender, our troops would leave their posts or at least man them less carefully . . . In the third watch they suddenly sallied out with all their forces, on the side where the ascent to our defences seemed less steep. **3** The signal was swiftly given by flares, as Caesar had instructed beforehand, and troops from the nearest forts rushed there. **4** The enemy fought bravely, as might have been expected of brave men in a crisis, when all hope of deliverance lay in bravery alone, fighting on unfavourable terrain against troops who could hurl weapons at them from rampart and towers. **5** About 4,000 men were killed and the rest were driven back into the town. **6** On the next day, the gates were smashed open, for there were now no more defenders, and, after our soldiers had been sent in, Caesar sold the whole town as one lot at auction. **7** The purchasers informed him that the number of persons was 53,000.

6.11 Cicero *Letter to his Brother Quintus* 3.9.4: Slaves from Gaul for Cicero

Cicero is writing from Rome to Quintus in Gaul in December 54. There is no moral or ethical consideration on Cicero's part of these slaves as human beings who are to be transported against their will to an alien culture: Cicero simply appreciates the offer of more hands.

I thank you most gratefully for the slaves, which you promise me; I am indeed, as you say in your letter, short-handed both at Rome and on my estates. But take care, my dear brother, that you do not consider doing anything for my convenience, unless it is entirely convenient for you and totally within your means.

6.12 Pliny *Natural History* 35.199–200: Rome imports educated slaves

Pliny is here discussing different medicinal earths. The proscriptions referred to are those of Sulla in 82 BC and of the 'Second Triumvirate' in 43 BC (docs 11.19–25, 14.20); for Publilius, see doc. 6.21.

199 There is another kind of chalk called 'silversmith's' because used for polishing silver, but the cheapest kind is that which our ancestors set the custom of using to denote the victory-line in the circus and mark the feet of slaves brought from overseas when up for sale; examples are Publilius (Syrus) from Antioch, the founder of the mimic stage, and his cousin Manilius Antiochus the founder of astronomy, and Staberius Eros the first grammarian – all of whom our great-grandfathers could see arrive on the same ship. **200** But why mention these men, recommended as they are by their literary honours? Other examples they saw up for public sale were Sulla's Chrysogonus, Quintus Catulus' Amphion, Lucius Lucullus' Hector, Pompey's Demetrius, Demetrius' Auge (although she was also believed to have belonged to Pompey), Mark Antony's Hipparchus, and Menas and Menecrates, who belonged to Sextus Pompeius – as well as a list of others whom this is not the occasion to enumerate, who enriched themselves by the bloodshed of Roman citizens and the licence permitted by proscriptions.

6.13 Suetonius *Life of the Deified Julius* 4.1–2: Caesar and the pirates

Piracy in the eastern Mediterranean provided another major source of slaves. Pirates' activities became so notorious that Pompey was empowered under the *lex Gabinia* of 67 BC to deal with them (see docs 12.8–9).

1 After Lepidus' revolt had been suppressed, Caesar brought a charge of extortion against Cornelius Dolabella (cos. 81), an ex-consul who had held a triumph; when he was found not guilty, Caesar decided to withdraw to Rhodes, both so the ill-feeling would have time to die down and so that he could, while at leisure, study under Apollonius Molo, the most distinguished teacher of rhetoric at that time. The winter months had already arrived while he was on his way to Rhodes, and he was captured by pirates near the island of Pharmacussa. He remained with them, not without the greatest indignation, for nearly 40 days, accompanied by only a doctor and two valets. **2** For he had at once sent off his companions and other slaves to procure the money by which he might be ransomed. Once the 50 talents had been paid and he was left on the shore, he raised a fleet without delay and went off in pursuit of them. Once they were in his power he put them to death, as he had often threatened to do to them in jest.

DOMESTIC SLAVES

Slaves were used in a wide variety of contexts: mining, domestic service, education, and as secretaries to officials. They were barred only from political office and army service, though they could be enrolled as soldiers and rowers in a crisis (doc. 6.1).

6.14 *CIL* I² 560: Kitchen slaves on a bronze casket, c. 250 BC

The casket, dated to c. 250–235 BC, on which this inscription appears depicts a countrified kitchen scene and shows two or more slave cooks having an animated discussion while preparing a meal. Some of the meanings are obscure.

A: Prepare the fish (shown cutting up a fish).
B: I have collected the garlic (taking down part of a pig).
B: I have prepared it (holding dish and knife).
A: Beat it some more (holding dish out to B).
B: Boil for me properly (addressing a cauldron).
A: Mix well (stirring the cauldron and holding a plate).
B: I'm here, coming (walking away).

6.15 Varro *On the Latin Language* 8.6, 10, 21, 83: Naming slaves

For the ease of naming a single slave, see doc. 6.16, where 'Marcipor' is the slave ('puer') of Marcus. Roman masters chose not to use the original name of the slave because a new name was a means of asserting ownership.

6 For example, those who have recently been bought as slaves in a large household quickly learn to inflect the names of all their fellow slaves in the oblique cases when they have heard only the nominative . . . **10** In those matters in which usage was simple, the inflection of the name was also simple, just as in a house with only one slave there is need for only one slave name, but in a house with numerous slaves there is need of numerous names . . .

21 There are two kinds of word derivation, voluntary and natural; voluntary derivation is when an individual of his own accord chooses a word derivation. So, when three men have brought a slave each at Ephesus, one sometimes derives his name from that of the seller Artemidorus, and calls his Artemas, another names his slave from the region where he bought him, so Ion from Ionia, and the third calls him Ephesius because he bought him at Ephesus. In this way each derives the name from a different cause, as he chooses . . .

83 Most freedmen set free by a town (municipium) have their names from the town, though in this matter the slaves of associations and temples have not observed the rule in a similar way, and the freedmen of the Romans ought to be called Romanus, like Faventinus from Faventia and Reatinus from Reate. In this way freedmen whose fathers were public slaves would be named Romanus if they had been manumitted before they began to take the names of the magistrates who set them free.

6.16 Pliny *Natural History* 33.26: 'Marcipors and Lucipors'

Pliny is here talking about the need to use seal rings to protect possessions. Marcipor and Lucipor mean 'Marcus' boy' and 'Lucius' boy' – an easy way of denoting a single slave. Pliny is here recalling the Republic when individual masters had far fewer slaves than in his time.

To think what life was like in olden days, and what innocence there was when nothing was sealed! Nowadays even articles of food and wine have to be protected from theft by a ring. This has been brought about by our legions of slaves, the crowd of outsiders in our homes, and the fact that we have to employ a nomenclator even to tell us the names of our own slaves! In times of old things were different – there were just single slaves, Marcipors and Lucipors, part of their masters' families, who took all their meals in common with the family, and there was no need to keep a watch in the house over the household slaves.

6.17 Macrobius *Saturnalia* 1.11.36–40: Juno Caprotina

Female slaves, like free women, celebrated the festival of Juno Caprotina on 7 July; caproficus is a wild fig tree.

36 It is well known that the Nones of July is the festival of female slaves, and both the origin and the reason for the celebration are common knowledge. For on that day free women and female slaves both sacrifice to Juno Caprotina under a wild fig tree in commemoration of the generous spirit which was displayed by female slaves in preserving Rome's public honour. **37** For, after the city had been captured and the Gallic onslaught had subsided, the state was reduced to such weakness that her neighbours were on the watch for the chance to attack Rome; they appointed as their leader Postumius Livius, the chief magistrate of Fidenae, and he sent instructions to the senate demanding that, if they wished the remnants of their state to survive, they should hand over to him their married women and unmarried girls: **38** when the senators were wavering in anxious debate, a female slave named Tutela, or Philotis, promised that she and the other slaves would go to the enemy under the names of their mistresses, and in the dress of married women and girls they were handed over to the enemy with the tears of those accompanying them as proof of their grief. **39** When they had been allocated in the camp by Livius, they tempted the men with copious wine, pretending it was a festival day at Rome, and after making them drowsy they gave a signal to the Romans from a wild fig tree near the camp. **40** These were victorious in their sudden attack, and the senate, grateful for the service, ordered all the female slaves to be manumitted, gave them dowries from the treasury and permitted them to wear the type of dress they had assumed. The senate named the day itself 'Nonae Caprotinae', after the wild fig tree from which the signal leading to victory was received, and it resolved that there should be an annual festival and sacrifice, when the juice of the wild fig tree should be offered in commemoration of this deed I have narrated.

6.18 Suetonius *On Rhetoricians* 27: A lucky doorkeeper

Slave doorkeepers served in chains so that they were unable to run away. From a mere doorkeeper, Voltacilius became an historian, though Suetonius' comment 'is said to have been' might indicate his disbelief in this background.

Lucius Voltacilius Pilutus is said to have been a slave and even to have served as a doorkeeper in chains, according to ancient custom, until he was manumitted for his talents and interest in literature and helped his patron prepare for his work as prosecutor. Then he became a teacher of rhetoric and taught Pompey the Great, and wrote a history of his father's achievements, as well as those of Pompey himself, in numerous volumes; in the view of Cornelius Nepos he was the first freedman who undertook the writing of history, which up to that time had always been written by men of the highest rank.

6.19 Lucilius *Satires* 22.624–5: A favourite slave

Books 22–25 of Lucilius apparently consisted mainly of epigrams and epitaphs on his slaves and freedmen in their own dialects.

A slave neither unfaithful to his master nor useless in any respect.
A little pillar of Lucilius' household lies here – Metrophanes.

6.20 Papyrus *BGU* 4.1108 (*EJ* 262): Contract with a wet-nurse, 5 BC

A papyrus found in Alexandria, Egypt. A long list of conditions follows, including the provision that Erotarion is not to sleep with a man, become pregnant or nurse another child.

To Artemidorus, chief judge, in charge of the circuit judges and other judges, from Marcus Sempronius, son of Marcus, of the tribe Aemilia, soldier of the Legion XXII, cohort . . . and from Erotarion, daughter of . . . with as guardian and protector my relative Lucius . . . **5** son of Lucius . . . Erotarion agrees that for 15 months from Phaophi of the present 26th year of Caesar she will nurse and suckle outside at her own home in the city, with her own milk, pure and unadulterated, the slave baby named Primus whom Marcus entrusted to her from as long ago as Epeiph in the previous year, the pay per month for milk and nurture being 10 drachmas and two jars of oil.

6.21 Publilius Syrus *Maxims* 414, 489, 596, 616: Maxims of Publilius Syrus

Publilius was brought to Rome from Antioch as a slave in the late 80s BC. He became a composer of mimes and performed at Caesar's games in 46 BC. Pithy sayings by his characters were collected in the first century AD.

414   There are fewer risks in being tame, but it makes you a slave.
489   It is glorious to die instead of being degraded as a slave.
596   If you serve wisely you will have a share in the master's role.
616   If you don't like being a slave, you will be miserable; but you won't stop being a slave.

6.22 Appian *Civil Wars* 2.120.505: Slaves indistinguishable from their masters

Appian is here stressing the 'degeneration' of the plebs at Rome in the context of Caesar's assassination and the speeches of the 'tyrannicides'. There was clearly no special clothing for slaves.

The plebs are now very much intermingled with alien blood, while a freedman has the same citizen rights as a citizen has, and a man who is still a slave wears the same clothes as his master; for, except for the senatorial class, the dress of the rest of the citizens is the same as that of the slaves.

6.23 Pliny *Natural History* 7.56: Identical twins

The 'twin' boys purchased by Antony were obviously status symbols, perhaps as dining-room attendants. The value of such attractive young slaves to an owner is reflected in the extremely high price paid for them as decoration in their own right rather than for any specific services.

While Antony was one of the triumvirs, a slave-dealer, Toranius, sold him two boys of outstanding beauty as twins, because they looked so alike, though one of them was born in Asia and the other beyond the Alps. When the deception was afterwards uncovered from the boys' accents, the furious Antony violently abused the dealer, complaining, among other things, of the enormity of the price (which was 200,000 sesterces). The wily dealer, however, replied that was the reason why he was selling them at so high a price, since there would have been nothing remarkable in the boys' similarity of appearance if they had been born of the same mother, but, as it was, to find boys so exactly like each other from different countries put them above all market value. He conveyed such fervent admiration to the mind of 'the proscriber' that, from being incensed about the injury done him, he instead considered that he had nothing in his possession of greater value.

THE TREATMENT OF SLAVES

Cicero (*Off.* 1.41) believes that masters have an obligation to treat their slaves properly, as if they were hired workmen ('the lowest station and fortune is that of slaves, and those who tell us to treat them like hired workers are quite right to do so: work must be exacted, their dues paid'). In Plautus' *Pseudolus* (doc. 6.24) the punishments of slaves are made an object of comedy: the slaves are so hardened that the owner hurts himself more than the slave when he undertakes to flog them. But beneath the humour lies the ugly reality of the whipped and beaten slave, ordered, bullied and threatened by the master, all over a meal designed to impress. Note in particular the stock complaints of masters about their slaves, the main one being that of servile idleness, which was probably an important form of passive servile resistance to slavery. The passage makes clear that the master had physical control of the slave.

6.24 Plautus *Pseudolus* 133–70: Treatment of household slaves

Plautus was writing between c. 205 and 184 BC. Here Ballio, a relatively well-off if uncultured householder, is giving instructions to his slaves and threatening to punish them for their laziness. Slavery was implicit in Roman society, and that slaves had to be forced to work was widely accepted.

Ballio: Get out, come on, out with you, you lazy things, kept at a loss and bought at a loss,
    None of you ever thinks at all of doing anything right;
    I can't get any use out of you, unless I try this treatment!
    I've never seen any men more like donkeys, your ribs are so hardened with blows!
    If you flog any of them you hurt yourself the most – they actually wear out the whip,

And all they think of when they get the chance is to rob, steal, pinch,
    loot, drink, eat and run away: this

140   Is their idea of work, and you'd rather leave wolves in charge of sheep,
Than these in charge at home.

I will say that when you look them over they don't seem too bad:
It's their work which is no good.

Now – unless you all pay attention to this pronouncement,
Unless you get that sleep and laziness out of your chests and eyes,
I'll whip your sides till they're really colourful,
They'll have more colours that Campanian coverings
Or clipped Alexandrian tapestries with their embroidered beasts.

I gave you all your orders and 'assigned your provinces' yesterday,
But you're so good at being cunning and worthless,

150   I must remind you of your duties with a good thrashing.

True, that's the way you're made: your toughness is too much for
    me – and this!

Look at that, will you? They're not even paying attention! Attend to
    this, concentrate on this,

Turn your ears here to what I'm saying, you race of men born to be
    flogged!

By Pollux! Your hide will never be tougher than my rawhide here.
Now what? Does it hurt? That's for a slave who ignores his master.
All line up in front of me and pay attention to what I tell you.
You there, with the pitcher, fetch the water, and make sure the cook's
    pot is filled.
You with the axe, I appoint you to the province of wood-chopping.

Slave: But the axe is blunt.

Ballio: Well, what if it is? You're all blunted with thrashings, too:

160   But is that any reason why I shouldn't get work out of you all?

Now you – I order you to make the house shine. You've got your
    job, hurry up, go on in!

You, put the couches straight. You, clean the silver, and put it away.

Now, when I come back from the forum, make sure I find everything
    ready:

Swept, sprinkled, polished, smoothed, cleaned and all as it should be.
Today's my birthday and you all ought to celebrate it.

Make sure the ham, skin, sweetbreads and udder are put to soak in
    water, do you hear?

I want to entertain some classy gentlemen in high style so they think
    I've got money.

Get indoors and hurry along with all this quickly, so there's no delay
    when the cook comes;

I'm off to market to see what sort of fish I can buy.

170   Boy, you go on in front: we must take care no one cuts a hole in my
    purse.

6.25 Plautus *The Two Menaechmuses* 966–84: A sensible slave

A household slave, Messenio, is soliloquising; his master (Menaechmus Sosicles) is one of the brothers of the play's title.

> This is the proof of a good slave, who looks after his master's business,
> Sees to it, gives it his care, and thinks about it,
> That when his master is away he cares for his master's business diligently,
> Just as if he were present, or even more so.
970 > His back rather than his appetite, his legs than his stomach,
> Ought to concern a fellow whose heart is in the right place.
> He should remember what good-for-nothings
> Get from their masters – lazy, worthless fellows:
> Whippings, fetters,
> The mill, weariness, hunger, bitter cold –
> These are the rewards of laziness.
> That's what I'm really afraid of; that's why it's better to be good than be bad.
> I can much more easily stand a telling-off; but I hate floggings,
> And I'd much rather eat the meal than do the grinding.
980 > That's why I follow master's orders, carry them out properly and quietly;
> And I find it pays.
> Others can do as they think proper; I'll be just where I should be:
> Let me keep a sense of fear, and avoid making mistakes, so I'll always be
>   there when master wants me.
> I shan't have much to fear. Master will soon reward me for my service.

6.26 Seneca the Younger *On Anger* 3.40.1–4: Man-eating lampreys

Vedius Pollio, an equestrian, was a friend of Augustus and, at some point, proconsul in Asia. He died in 15 BC and left his enormous villa and part of his estate to Augustus in his will.

1 To rebuke someone who is angry and to lose your temper in return serves only to provoke him. **2** You would do better to change your approach and behave affably, unless you happen to be a person of such importance as to be able to restrain his anger, as the god Augustus did when dining with Vedius Pollio. One of the slaves had broken a crystal goblet: Vedius ordered him to be seized and experience an unusual type of death – he commanded that he be thrown to the lampreys, of which he had huge specimens in his fishpond. Who would not think that he did this as a demonstration of extravagance? It was cruelty! **3** The boy shook off their hands and took refuge at Caesar's feet, begging only that he might suffer some other death than being eaten. Caesar was disgusted at this innovation in barbarity and ordered that he be released, that all the crystal goblets be smashed in his presence, and that the fishpond be filled in. **4** Caesar was able to censure one of his friends in this way and used his authority wisely: 'Do you give commands for human beings to be snatched from a dinner party and be torn to pieces by a new kind of punishment? If a cup of yours has been broken, is that any reason why a person should be disembowelled? Are you so pleased with yourself that you order that someone be killed in the very presence of Caesar?'

6.27 Suetonius *Life of the Deified Augustus* 67.1–2: Augustus' household

For Augustus' legislation on slavery and manumission, see docs 15.61–64.

1 As patron and master, Augustus was no less strict than friendly and forgiving, and he honoured many of his freedmen and was very intimate with them, for example Licinus, Celadus and others. His slave Cosmus, who spoke most disrespectfully of him, he only had put in irons. When he was walking with his steward Diomedes, who hid behind him out of fear when they were charged by a wild boar, he preferred to accuse him of timidity rather than malicious intent and turned a matter of some danger into a joke, as there was no harm intended. **2** However, he forced one of his favourite freedmen, Polus, to commit suicide, after he was found to have been having affairs with married women, and broke the legs of his secretary, Thallus, because he accepted 500 denarii for betraying the contents of a letter. He also had the paedagogus and servants of his son Gaius, when they took advantage of his illness and death to behave with arrogance and greed in his province, thrown into a river with heavy weights tied around their necks.

SLAVES IN INDUSTRY AND MANUFACTURE

Slaves were employed widely in Italian agriculture, though the degree to which they were employed in industry and manufacture is unclear. Republican Rome was hardly a consumer society: there was no mass market of consumers, and production and consumption of manufactured items was largely limited to functional, everyday items.

6.28 *CIL* I² 412, 416, 2487: Early inscriptions denoting slave or freedman manufacture

Inscriptions by slaves on pottery items made before 220 BC at Cales, north of Naples; Cales was known for its pottery, which has been found in various parts of Italy. Pottery was the ancient equivalent of modern plastic; a patera is a shallow dish.

(i) On a patera found at Tarquinii: I, Retus Gabinius, slave of Gaius, made you at Cales.

(ii) On a patera: Kaeso Serponius made this at Cales in the Esquiline quarter. A slave of Gaius.

(iii) On a clay vessel: Marcus, at Cales. A household slave (verna).

6.29 *CIL* I² 889–90, 2663a: 'Tesserae consulares'

These pieces of bone or ivory (sing.: tessera) with a handle or hole for attachment to some item give a slave or freedman's name, his master or patron, the word 'spectavit', 'inspected' (or an abbreviation thereof), and date by day, month and consulship. They have been argued to record the official checking of coins for weight and genuineness as opposed to counterfeit. These particular tesserae date to the 90s.

(i)   Inspected by Capito, slave of Memmius, in November in the consulship of Gnaeus Domitius and Gaius Cassius (cos. 96).
(ii) Inspected by Menophilus, slave of Lucius Abius, in the consulship of Gaius Valerius and Marcus Herennius (cos. 93).
(iii) Inspected by Philoxenus, servant of the association of iron-smiths, on the Nones of April in the consulship of Gaius Coelius and Lucius Domitius (cos. 94).

6.30 Diodorus Siculus *Library of History* 5.36.3–4, 38.1: Slaves in Spanish mines

The silver mines in Spain were owned by the Roman state but worked by individual operators, who turned over a proportion of the profits to the state. Polybius writes that there were 40,000 workers involved in the mines outside New Carthage (34.9.9); Diodorus is here citing the Stoic philosopher Posidonius (*FGrH* 87 F117).

36.3 Initially any individuals who came along used to work the mines, and these acquired great wealth because the silver-bearing earth was accessible and abundant; later, when the Romans took control of Spain, a large number of Italians took over the mines and acquired great wealth through their love of profit. **4** They purchase a large number of slaves and hand them over to the overseers of the mining operations, who open shafts in numerous places and dig deep into the ground in search of its seams rich in silver and gold; they not only go a long way into the ground but extend their digging to the depth of many stades, with galleries twisting and turning in all directions, thus bringing from the depths the ore which provides their profits. . . .

38.1 The men engaged in the mining operations procure unbelievably large revenues for their masters, but through their excavations under the earth both by day and by night they wear out their own bodies, many of them dying because of the exceptional hardships; they are not allowed any relaxation or rest, but are compelled by the beatings of their supervisors to endure these terrible evils and throw away their lives in this wretched manner, although some of them who can endure it suffer their misery for a long time because of their bodily strength or sheer willpower; but they prefer dying to surviving because of the extent of their suffering.

SLAVES AND THE ENTERTAINMENT INDUSTRY

The entertainment 'industry' was an important one at Rome, and slaves were prominent in it. Slaves could be actors and mimes, gladiators and prostitutes. Unlike the freedman of Lucius (doc. 6.32), Protogenes had apparently not been freed, nor had Panurgus (docs 6.30, 32). Some 11 Republican actresses, the majority of them slaves, are known by name: see docs 7.62–65.

6.31 *ILS* 5221: An entertaining slave

Found in a wall at Preturo, near Amiternum, perhaps dating to c. 165–160 BC. The inscription is clearly not the work of a professional.

Here is laid the delightful mimic actor Protogenes, slave of Clulius,
Who gave great enjoyment to people through his jesting.

6.32 *CIL* I² 1378: An entertaining freedman

A first-century BC epitaph from a grave at Rome.

For . . . freedman of Lucius, a professional jester (*scurra*),
A most respectable and excellent
Freedman of utmost trustworthiness,
His patron made this.

6.33 Cicero *In Defence of Quintus Roscius the Comedian* 28–29: A comedian's market value

Quintus Roscius, the famous actor, and Gaius Fannius Chaerea jointly owned a slave, Panurgus, whom Roscius was training as a comic actor (histrio). When Panurgus was murdered, Roscius accepted a farm worth 100,000 sesterces in lieu of his half of the slave. However Fannius brought an action that half the farm ought to be his in compensation for his part-ownership of Panurgus. Cicero argues that the value of the slave was the result of his training by Roscius; for Roscius, see docs 6.6, 11.39.

28 You state, Saturius, that Panurgus was the property of Fannius. But I maintain that he belonged entirely to Roscius. For what part of him belonged to Fannius? His body. What part belonged to Roscius? His training. It was not his appearance but his skill that was worth money. The part that belonged to Fannius was worth no more than 4,000 sesterces; the part that belonged to Roscius was worth more than 100,000 sesterces, for no one judged him by his bodily physique, but valued him by his skill as a comedian. His limbs by themselves could not earn more than 12 asses, but his training, received from this man, brought in no less than 100,000 sesterces . . . **29** The hopes and expectations, the devotion and favour that Panurgus won on the stage were because he was the pupil of Roscius! Those who loved Roscius supported him, those who admired Roscius approved of him – in short, those who had heard Roscius' name considered Panurgus excellent and accomplished.

6.34 Lucilius *Satires* 4.2.172–81: A satire on gladiators

This is a satire on a famous gladiatorial fight. Anyone who fought in the arena was either a slave or a free man who gave up his rights as a free person; for gladiators, see docs 2.74–75.

In the gladiatorial show put on by the Flacci
Was a certain Aeserninus, a Samnite, a vile chap, worthy of that life and station.
He was matched with Pacideianus, best by far
Of all gladiators since the birth of mankind.

Pacideianus speaks:

> 'Indeed I'll kill him and win, if that's what you want', he said.
> 'But I think it will happen like this: first I'll take it on my face,
> Then I'll fix my sword in that blockhead's stomach and lungs.
> I hate the fellow, I'll fight in a temper, and we'll wait no longer
> Than it takes each of us to adjust our sword to our right hand –
> So furiously am I carried away by my passion, anger and hatred for him.'

FARM SLAVES: THEIR OCCUPATIONS AND TRAINING

Slaves had been used in large numbers on landed estates, such as the latifundia, since the second century BC (doc. 8.6). Their presence there had been an important factor in the Gracchan land reforms. As is clear from both Cato the Elder and Varro's agricultural treatises, slaves were important in farming and were in fact the 'backbone' of agriculture. Varro makes clear that slave-breeding occurred (doc. 6.39), while Cato allowed the male slaves to purchase sexual gratification as a means of keeping them under control. Slave families thus came into existence, though legally slaves could not marry, and therefore their families had no legal status.

6.35 Cato the Elder *On Farming* 2.2–4, 7: Slave duties on an old-fashioned farm

Even in antiquity, Cato was viewed as a hard master. His manual, written for the farming gentry c. 160 BC, provided advice on how to make a profit from farming. Clearly agricultural slaves, even when they grew old, did not expect manumission.

2 If the amount of work does not seem to the master to be sufficient, but the overseer says that he has been industrious, but the slaves have not been well, the weather has been bad, slaves have run away, he has had public work to do – when he has given these and many other reasons, call the overseer back to the calculation of the work and workmen. **3** If the weather has been rainy, mention the work which could have been done during rain: washing out the wine vats, pitching them, cleaning the farmhouse, moving grain, carrying out manure, making a manure-pit, cleaning seed, mending ropes and making new ones; and that the slaves ought to have mended their rag-coverings and hoods. **4** On festivals, too, old ditches might have been cleaned out, road work done, brambles cut back, garden dug, meadows cleared, wood bundled, thorns weeded, grain husked, and cleaning-up done. When the slaves were sick, such large rations ought not to have been issued . . . **7** Inspect the livestock and hold a sale: sell the oil, if the price is right, and sell surplus wine and grain; sell old oxen, defective cattle, defective sheep, wool, hides, an old cart, old tools, an elderly slave, a sickly slave, and anything else superfluous. The paterfamilias (master of the household) ought to be fond of selling, not of buying.

6.36 Cato *On Farming* 56–59: Rations for slaves

The slave diet consisted mainly of bread and wine with some relishes. The rations are daily amounts and are sufficient for daily needs. A hemina is half a sextarius, and a congius is 6 sextarii or approximately 6 pints (3 litres). A modius is a measure of corn (16 sextarii); a quadrantal a liquid measure (8 congii). Cato's 'pound' (libra) is actually 13 ounces (0.325 kg). **56**: The slaves shackled together receive their ration as bread rather than as grain, as they cannot make their own bread. **57**: The Saturnalia involved a degree of licence on the part of slaves; the Compitalia was in honour of the Lares Compitales, the lares of the cross-roads. Three litres were allowed for each slave for these festivals.

56 Rations for the slaves. For the workers 4 modii of wheat through winter and 4½ through summer; for the overseer, housekeeper, superintendent and shepherd 3 modii; for the slaves shackled together 4 pounds of bread through the winter, 5 from when they begin to dig the vineyard until the figs come, then return to 4. **57** Wine ration for the slaves. For three months after the harvest let them drink after-wine; in the fourth month give them a hemina (half a pint) a day, that is 2½ congii a month; in the fifth, sixth, seventh and eighth month a sextarius (a pint) a day, that is 5 congii a month; in the ninth, tenth, eleventh and twelfth month 3 heminae a day, that is an amphora a month; in addition give out a congius per person for the Saturnalia and Compitalia: total of wine for each person per year . . . . For the shackled slaves issue an additional amount in proportion to their work; it is not too much for them to drink 10 quadrantals of wine each year. **58** Relish for the slaves. Conserve as many windfall olives as possible. Later conserve the ripe olives from which you will get the least oil and be sparing with them, so they will last as long as possible. When the olives are eaten up, give out fish-paste and vinegar. Issue each person with a pint of oil a month. A modius of salt per person per year is sufficient. **59** Clothing for the slaves. A tunic 3½ feet long and a coat every other year. Whenever you give out a tunic or coat to anyone, first take the old one and make rag-coverings of it. You should issue heavy boots every other year.

6.37 Cato *On Farming* 143.1–3: Supervising the housekeeper

Cato here instructs the overseer on the role of the slave housekeeper. Must is new wine boiled thick.

1 Take care that the housekeeper performs her duties. If the master has given her to you as your wife, be satisfied with her. Ensure that she respects you. Make sure she is not too extravagant. She should visit the neighbouring and other women as little as possible and not invite them to the house or her part of it. She should not go out to meals or be fond of going out. She should not take part in religious worship or get others to do it on her behalf without the orders of the master or mistress: she should remember that the master sees to religious worship for the whole household. **2** She should be clean; and she should keep the whole farm-house clean; she should sweep the hearth every day before she goes to bed. On the Kalends, Ides and Nones – whenever there is a holy day – she should place a garland on the hearth, and on those days she should pray to the household gods as much as she is able. She should take care to have cooked food available for you and the household. **3** She should keep many hens and eggs. She should have stores of dried pears, sorbs (berries), figs, dried grapes, sorbs in must, pears, grapes and sparrow-quinces preserved in jars and raisins preserved in grape pulp and in pots buried in the ground, as well as fresh Praenestine nuts buried in a pot in the ground. She should keep Scantian apples in jars and other fruits that are usually preserved, as well as crab apples. All these she should make sure she has stored away diligently every year. She should also know how to make good flour and fine spelt.

6.38 Plutarch *Life of Cato the Elder* 4.5–5.2, 21.1–3, 7–8: Cato – a typical slave owner?

Huge numbers of slaves were imported from the third century BC to the end of the Republic, but it is also clear that the slave population reproduced itself to some degree, as Cato's and Varro's comments about allowing sexual relationships between slaves makes clear.

4.5 He tells us that he never paid more than 1,500 drachmas for a slave, as he wanted not the delicate or handsome types but tough workmen like grooms and herdsmen; and, when they got older, he thought that he ought to sell them and not feed useless workers. **6** On the whole, he considered nothing was cheap if you didn't need it, and what a man didn't need was expensive even if it cost only an *as*; and that you should buy land for tilling and grazing rather than for watering and sweeping. **5.1** Some people put this down to stinginess on his part, while others accepted that he kept within his means to make others mend their ways and learn some moderation. For myself, I consider his conduct towards his slaves in getting full use out of them like pack-animals, and then, when they got old, driving them off and selling them, as the mark of a thoroughly inflexible character, unable to recognise any dealings between man and man except necessity . . . . **2** A good man will take care of his horses even when age has worn them out and look after his dogs not only when they are puppies but when they need care in their old age . . .

21.1 Cato acquired a great many slaves whom he bought as prisoners of war, particularly the young ones, who could still be raised and trained, like pups and colts. None of these ever entered into another person's house unless sent there by Cato himself or his wife. If any one of them were asked what Cato was doing, he answered only that he did not know. **2** At home, a slave had either to be doing his work or be asleep, and Cato greatly preferred the sleepy ones, thinking them to be both more mild-tempered than those who were wakeful and better workers at anything when they had enjoyed a sleep than those who had not. **3** Considering also that the greatest reason for misconduct in slaves was their sexual passions, he arranged at a fixed price for them to sleep with the females, and none of them was allowed to associate with a woman outside the household . . . **7** He also lent money to those of his slaves who wished it; they would buy boys and, when they had trained and taught them at Cato's expense, would sell them again after a year. **8** Cato kept many of these for himself, accounting to the trainer the highest price offered. To encourage his son to such practices, he used to say that lessening the value of an estate was the mark not of a man but of a widow woman.

6.39 Varro *On Farming* 1.17.3–7: Varro on slave labour

Varro emphasises rewards rather than punishments and encourages loyalty among the slaves.

3 Slaves ought to be neither timid nor high-spirited. **4** They ought to have men over them who have had some training in letters and a degree of education, who are honest and older than the labourers I have mentioned . . . **5** They are not to be allowed to control the men with whips instead of words, as long as you can achieve the same result. You should not acquire too many slaves of the same nation; for that is the strongest cause of domestic hatreds. The foremen are to be made more eager by rewards, and care must be taken that they have some property of their own and are mated to fellow slaves, from whom they can have children, for from such treatment they become steadier and more attached to the estate. It is on account of such relationships that slave households from Epirus are more highly regarded and more expensive than others. **6** The goodwill of the foremen should be acquired by showing them some consideration, and those of the labourers who are superior to the others should also be spoken to about the work to be done, since, when this is done, they are less inclined to think that the master despises them and to believe that he holds them in some regard. **7** They are made to take more interest in their work by being treated more liberally in regard to food, or more clothing, or exemption from work, or by being allowed to graze some livestock of their own on the estate, or something of the same kind, so that, if some punishment or heavier labour than usual is imposed on them, their goodwill and friendliness towards their master may be restored by the consolation derived from such concessions.

6.40 Varro *On Farming* 2.10.2–8: Varro on herdsmen and their acquisition

Varro refers to six different ways in which possession of slaves can be legally obtained. Mancipium was a formal purchase, and cession was when someone 'ceded' the ownership of an item to another; the other four ways were inheritance, possession (usus), as war booty and through purchase at a public sale. Note the reference to the slave's peculium, which was transferable with the slave.

2 The herdsmen should be made to stay on the pasture land the whole day and feed the herds together, but on the other hand each should spend the night with his own herd . . . **3** The type of men selected for this should be those that are tough and swift, nimble, with supple limbs, who are able not only to follow the herd but protect it from wild beasts and robbers, who can lift loads onto pack animals, run with speed, and throw the javelin. **4** Not every race is fitted for herding duties, and neither a Bastulan nor a Turdulan (from southern Spain) is suitable, while Gauls are ideal, especially for draught animals. In purchasing them there are some six ways of acquiring legitimate ownership: by legal inheritance; by receiving them, in proper form, through mancipium from one who had a legal right to do so; by legal cession, from one who had the right to give them up, and at the proper time;

by right of possession (usus); by purchase from war booty; or at a public sale among other property or confiscated property. **5** In the purchase of slaves it is usual for the peculium to go with the slave, unless specifically excepted, and for a guarantee to be given that he is sound and has not committed theft or damage; or, if mancipium is not granted, double the amount is guaranteed, or, if agreed on, just the purchase price. They should have their food apart during the day, each with his own flock, but in the evening all those under one supervisor should eat together . . .

6 Regarding the breeding of herdsmen, it is easy in the case of those who stay all the time on the farm, because they have a female fellow slave in the farm-house, and the pastoral Venus looks no further than this. But, for those who tend the flocks in mountain valleys and wooded country and escape rain storms not in the farmhouse but in hastily constructed sheds, many have thought it advisable to send them women to follow the herds, prepare victuals for them and make them harder working. **7** But these women have to be tough and not ugly, and in many ways they are as good as the men in their work, as can be seen generally in Illyricum, for they can tend the herd, carry the firewood and cook the food, or look after the equipment in the huts. **8** As to nursing their babies, I say only this, that generally they can feed them as well as bear them. At the same time turning to me, he said, 'I have heard you say that when you were in Liburnia you saw mothers carrying firewood and children whom they were nursing at the same time, sometimes one, sometimes two, showing that our mothers who lie for days under their mosquito nets after giving birth are weak and contemptible.'

SLAVES AND THE LAW

The slave was a *res mancipi* in the ownership of his master, and in the Republic there were no constraints on how masters treated slaves. Slaves were routinely tortured in law-suits in Rome (as in Greece; cf. doc. 15.64 for Augustus' legislation). The rationale was that they could not be trusted to tell the truth in any other circumstances. Slavery is not defined in the XII Tables, though manumission is mentioned in Table 5.8. Table 12.2 (doc. 1.45) points to the legal inca-pacities of slaves: a slave was without rights, and only a person with rights (sui iuris) could be party to a legal action (legis actio). Therefore slaves themselves could not be sued for any actions they committed or damage they caused. The master had to pay the prescribed penalty for his slave's wrongdoing or hand the slave over for punishment to the wronged party.

6.41 Gaius *Institutes* 1.52: The legal position of slaves

The legal, codified definitions of slavery come from the imperial period. Writing in the second century AD, Gaius records details which are nevertheless true for the Republic. The slave-owner had 'dominium' over his slave, including the power of life and death.

Slaves are in the potestas of their masters, and this potestas is acknowledged by the laws of all nations, for we know that, in all nations alike, the master has the power of life and death over his slaves, and whatever a slave acquires is acquired by his master.

6.42 Cicero *In Defence of Roscius of Ameria* 77–78: **Roscius' slaves**

Roscius was accused in 80 BC of parricide by family members supported by Sulla's freedman Chrysogonus. Roscius' advocates may have been P. Cornelius Scipio Nasica (praetor 94 or 93 BC) and M. Metellus (praetor 69 BC). In this case, the accusers have decided that to submit the slaves of Roscius to torture is too risky, whereas in doc. 6.43 the accuser depends on the slaves breaking down under torture and agreeing to false charges; cf. docs 6.54, 7.91.

77 There remains the possibility that he committed the crime using the agency of slaves. O ye immortal gods! What a wretched and calamitous affair! That which in an accusation of such a kind is generally the salvation of innocent men – that they should offer their slaves up for examination – is not permitted to Sextus Roscius! You, the accusers of this man, have all his slaves; not a single boy out of so large a household has been left to see to his daily meals. I appeal to you now, Publius Scipio, and you Metellus, when you were counselling him and acting on his behalf, Sextus Roscius several times demanded two of his father's slaves from his opponents for examination; do you not remember that Titus Roscius refused? Well? Where are those slaves? Jurors, they are part of the household of Chrysogonus, by whom they are honoured and valued . . . **78** Jurors, everything in this case is lamentable and scandalous, but nothing more severe or unjust than this can be pronounced – that a son should not be allowed to examine his father's slaves about his father's death!

6.43 Cicero *In Defence of Cluentius* 175–78: **Slaves remain firm under torture**

Cluentius was charged with having poisoned his stepfather, Oppianicus, who had married his mother, Sassia. Two of the slaves examined were hers, but the third had belonged to the deceased Oppianicus, now in the possession of his son, the young Oppianicus (176). Despite two separate days of the 'severest tortures' (177), the slaves would not incriminate Cluentius. What arouses Cicero's condemnation is that the slaves were tortured with the intention of providing false evidence: the use of torture on slaves as such is not condemned.

175 While wandering from place to place as a vagrant and exile, everywhere rejected, Oppianicus took himself to Lucius Quinctius in Falernian territory, where he first fell sick and remained seriously ill for some time. Sassia was with him and was more intimate with a certain tenant farmer called Sextus Albius, a fine healthy fellow, than even the most dissolute husband could tolerate while his own fortunes were intact. She thought that the requirements that a marriage be chaste and lawful no longer applied now her husband had been convicted. It is said that a trusty slave-lad of Oppianicus' called Nicostratus, who was inquisitive and totally truthful, used to report much of this to his master. Meanwhile Oppianicus, who was beginning to recover and was unable to put up with the Falernian tenant's misbehaviour any more, set off for Rome – he used to rent somewhere to stay outside the city gate – but is said to have fallen from his horse and, being already unwell, hurt his side seriously; he arrived at Rome with a fever and died a few days later. The manner of his death, jurymen, is such as to admit no suspicion; if any should be admitted, it has to be confined to the household within those four walls.

176 After his death that wicked woman Sassia immediately began to plot against her son and decided to hold an investigation into her husband's death. She bought a slave called Strato from Aulus Rupilius, whom Oppianicus had employed as a doctor, as if intending to do the same as Habitus when he bought Diogenes. She said that she was going to interrogate this Strato and one of her own slaves called Ascla. Furthermore she demanded that young Oppianicus here should hand over for interrogation the slave Nicostratus, who, she thought, had been too talkative and loyal to his master. Since he was a boy at the time, and the investigation was supposedly being held to inquire into his father's death, he did not dare refuse, although he believed that this slave was well intentioned towards himself, just as he had been towards his father. Many friends and associates both of Oppianicus and of the woman herself were summoned, respectable men distinguished in every way. The interrogation was carried out extremely rigorously with every form of torture. The slaves were tempted with both promises and threats to make them say something under interrogation, but, encouraged, I believe, by the high rank of those summoned to witness the inquiry and the violence of the tortures, they stood by the truth and said they knew nothing.

177 The interrogation ceased for that day on the advice of the friends. Some considerable time later they were summoned again. The interrogation was held over again: the severest tortures were vigorously employed. The witnesses objected, unable to bear it any longer, while the cruel and savage woman was furious that her schemes were not proceeding as she had hoped. When the torturer and even his instruments of torture were exhausted and she still did not want to bring proceedings to a close, one of the witnesses, a man of eminent public rank and the highest character, proclaimed that he considered that the purpose of the proceedings was not to find the truth but to force the slaves to say something false. The others agreed, and it was the view of them all that the interrogation had gone far enough.

178 Nicostratus was returned to Oppianicus, while Sassia went to Larinum with her people, grieving over the thought that her son would now certainly be safe, since neither a true accusation nor even a fabricated suspicion could touch him, and not only his enemies' open hostility but even his mother's secret plots had been unable to harm him. When she got to Larinum, although she had pretended that she was convinced by the story that her husband had earlier been poisoned by Strato, she immediately gave him a well set-up and fully stocked shop at Larinum so that he could practise medicine.

6.44 *AE* 1971 88: An exacting business

At Puteoli, during the reign of Augustus, a firm of undertakers ran a torture and execution business as a sideline. The undertakers' contract, including details of their rates, was displayed on a huge inscription some 2.5 metres wide. They performed public punishments as part of their contract, while offering similar services to citizens wanting their slaves privately punished or executed. The charge for these services was 4 sesterces for each workman employed.

II 8 Should anyone wish to have a male or female slave privately punished, the person who wishes to have this exacted shall do as follows: if he wishes to put the slave on the cross or fork, the contractor shall supply the posts, chains, ropes for scourgers and the scourgers themselves. The person having the punishment exacted is to pay 4 sesterces for each of the workers who carry the fork and the same for the scourgers and the executioner.

11 The magistrate shall give orders for those punishments that he exacts in his public capacity, and, whenever it is ordered, the contractor shall be ready to exact the punishment; he shall set up crosses and supply for free nails, pitch, wax, candles and whatever else is necessary to deal with the person under examination.

RUNAWAYS AND FUGITIVES

There were three basic forms of slave action against their servitude: deliberate destruction of property and obstruction of whatever work had to be undertaken; flight; and – the most radical option – revolt against their masters, as in Sicily and with Spartacus. When slaves ran away, masters took steps to recover their property (doc. 6.47), and the state took an interest as well (doc. 6.46). Running away was especially common in times of disturbance: Augustus later claimed to have returned 30,000 slaves to their masters after defeating Sextus Pompeius; the 6,000 whose masters could not be found were crucified: *RG* 4.25 (doc. 15.1).

6.45 Lucilius *Satires* 29.917–18: A collar and chain

Owners could fit iron collars on their slaves, which stated the names of the slave and the owner, the address to which to return him, and the promise of a reward; cf. Plaut. *Capt.* 357.

> . . . when I bring him back home like a runaway in manacles and a dog-chain and dog-collar.

6.46 *ILS* 23: Runaway slaves recovered as a public duty

This milestone near Forum Popillii in Lucania records the achievements either of Publius Popillius Laenas (cos. 132) or of T. Annius Rufus (cos. 128, propraetor 131) relating to the serious slave-rising which began in 135. The Via Popillia (or Via Annia) continues the Via Appia from Capua to Rhegium; 'the men from Italy' were perhaps resident in Sicily.

I made the road from Rhegium to Capua and on that road I positioned all the bridges, milestones and signposts. From here there are 51 miles to Nuceria, 84 to Capua, **5** 74 to Muranum, 123 to Consentia, 180 to Valentia, 231 to the strait at the statue (at the straits of Messina), 237 to Rhegium: total from Capua to Rhegium 321. Also as praetor in **10** Sicily I sought out the runaways belonging to men from Italy and returned 917 people. I was also the first to cause cattle-breeders to retire from public state land in favour of ploughmen. **15** Here I put up a market and public buildings.

6.47 Cicero *Letters to his Friends* 13.77.3: One of Cicero's slaves decamps

Cicero wrote this letter to P. Sulpicius Rufus in Illyricum in 46 BC. It seemed credible to Marcus Bolanus and others that Cicero had manumitted his slave Dionysius, when in fact he had not done so (he was still at large in 44 BC). Despite doc. 6.46, it is quite clear that there was no state apparatus in the Republic for helping owners to recover their runaway slaves.

I beg of you with more urgency than usual, in view of our friendship and your continual devotion to me, that you particularly exert yourself in the following matter: my slave Dionysius, who had charge of my library, which is worth a great deal of money, stole a large number of books and, believing he would not get away with it unpunished, ran away. He is in your province. Both my friend Marcus Bolanus and many others saw him at Narona, but they believed him when he asserted that I had manumitted him. If you should see to returning him to me, I can't tell you how grateful I would be. It is a small thing in itself but has made me very upset. Bolanus will tell you where he is and what can be done. If I should receive the fellow back through your agency I shall consider that you have done me a very great favour.

SLAVE REVOLTS

Individual slaves could run away and desert their masters, but there was another phenomenon in the Roman world, not evident in classical Greece, and that was the slave revolt, when large numbers of slaves rose up against their masters. The most famous rebellion was that of Spartacus (73–71 BC), but there were two revolts on a considerable scale in Sicily (135–132, 104–100 BC). All three major uprisings were crushed ruthlessly. Punishment of slaves and severity towards them was seen as the best defence against revolt.

6.48 Diodorus Siculus *Library of History* 34.2.1–23: Rebellion in Sicily, 135–132 BC

Sicily was finally unified as a Roman province in 211 BC, and Rome's conquests in the eastern Mediterranean provided a huge influx of slaves to work the Sicilian estates. Under harsh conditions, the slaves were impelled to revolt. Diodorus gives the slave numbers as 200,000; other sources have 60,000–70,000, which, given the population of Sicily at the time, is more probable. The revolt commenced in 135 (perhaps earlier) and was finally quashed in 132, after the Romans had suffered some notable defeats; Rupilius, the consul who terminated the rebellion, was the third consecutive consul sent out to deal with it. The second slave revolt followed the same pattern: large numbers of the newly enslaved, and harsh working conditions, led the slaves to rebel.

1 When Sicily, after the Carthaginian collapse, had enjoyed 60 years of prosperity in every respect, the slave war arose for the following reason: the Sicilians had become so prosperous and acquired such great wealth that they began purchasing a great number of slaves, on whose bodies they put identifying marks and brands when they had dragged them home in herds from the slave depots. **2** They used the young men as herdsmen and the others in whatever way they happened to be useful. But they treated them harshly in their service, and thought that they deserved only the very slightest care in terms of food and clothing. As a result, most of them made a living from robbery, and there was bloodshed everywhere, as the robbers were like scattered armies. **3** The praetors tried to stop them but did not dare to punish them because of the power and influence of the masters who owned the robbers, and they were forced to overlook the plundering of the province . . . **4** The slaves, oppressed by their hardships and often quite unreasonably mistreated by beatings, could not endure it. When opportunity offered they got together and discussed the subject of revolt, until they put their plan into action. **5** There was a certain Syrian slave (Eunus), belonging to Antigenes of Enna, from Apamea by birth, and given to magic and wonder-working. He claimed to foretell the future through commands from the gods in his sleep and deceived many by his skill in this direction. Going on from there, he not only prophesied through dreams but even pretended to see visions of the gods and hear the future from them while awake . . .

10 There was a certain Damophilus of Enna, a man of great wealth and property, but very arrogant in his behaviour. He maltreated his slaves to excess, and his wife Megallis closely rivalled her husband in her punishments and other inhumanity towards the slaves. Reduced by this savage treatment to the level of animals, they agreed to revolt and kill their owners. Going to Eunus, they asked him if their decision was approved by the gods. With his usual marvels, he promised the gods' approval and persuaded them to engage in the undertaking at once. **11** They immediately, therefore, gathered together 400 of their fellow slaves and, having armed themselves as opportunity presented, fell upon the city of Enna with Eunus leading them and working his miracle with flames of fire for their benefit. They broke into the houses and committed great bloodshed, sparing not even breast-feeding babies. **12** Instead they tore them from the breast and dashed them to the ground; I am unable to say how they insulted and outraged the women – and this with their husbands watching. They were joined by a great number of slaves from the city, who first did their worst to their masters and then turned to the slaughter of others. (Damophilus and his wife are captured, but their daughter spared because of the humanity she had shown. Damophilus was killed in the theatre.)

14 After that Eunus was chosen as king, not because of his courage or military leadership but only because of his marvels and because he had started the revolt, as well as for his name, which seemed to suggest the favourable omen that he would bear 'goodwill' towards his subjects. **15** Established as master of the rebels in all respects, he summoned an assembly and put to death all the citizens of Enna who had been captured, except for those skilled in manufacturing weapons, and these he put to work in chains. He gave Megallis to the female slaves to deal with as they wished; they tortured her and then threw her over a cliff. He himself put to death his own owners, Antigenes and Python. **16** He wore a diadem and adorned himself with all the other attributes of royalty, proclaimed the woman living with him as queen – she was a Syrian and from the same city as himself – and appointed as counsellors men who seemed to be especially gifted with intelligence, one of whom was Achaeus (Achaeus by name and an Achaean by birth), a man exceptionally gifted both in planning and in action. In three days Eunus had armed, as best he could, more than 6,000 men, as well as leading others who had single- and double-edged axes, slings, sickles, fire-hardened stakes, or even cooking spits. He went about plundering the whole countryside, and since he kept being joined by a countless number of slaves he even ventured to do battle against Roman generals, and in the engagements frequently overcame them by weight of numbers, as he already had more than 10,000 soldiers.

17 Meanwhile a man named Cleon, a Cilician, began a revolt of other slaves. Everyone was buoyed up with hopes that the two groups of revolutionaries would come into conflict with each other and that the rebels would liberate Sicily from strife by destroying themselves, but against expectations they joined forces, with Cleon subordinating himself to Eunus merely at his command and carrying out the duties of a general towards his king. His personal following consisted of 5,000 soldiers; it was now about 30 days since the beginning of the revolt. **18** Shortly afterwards they engaged in battle with a praetor, Lucius Hypsaeus, who had arrived from Rome and commanded 8,000 Sicilian soldiers, and the rebels were victorious, being now 20,000 in number. In a short time their total reached 200,000, and in many battles against the Romans they acquitted themselves well and were seldom beaten. **19** As this news spread, a revolt of a band of 150 slaves flared up in Rome, and of more than 1,000 in Attica, and of others on Delos and in many other places; because of the speed with which forces were brought against them and the severity of the punishments inflicted, the magistrates of the communities in each case quickly put an end to the rebels and brought to their senses anyone on the point of revolting. **20** In Sicily, however, the situation continued to deteriorate, and cities were captured with all their inhabitants and many armies cut to pieces by the rebels, until Rupilius (cos. 132 BC), the Roman commander, recovered Tauromenium for the Romans, after besieging it severely and confining the rebels under conditions of unspeakable hardship and starvation, which resulted in their beginning by eating their children and progressing to their womenfolk, and finally not entirely abstaining from eating each other; it was on this occasion that Rupilius captured Comanus, Cleon's brother, as he was trying to escape from the besieged city. **21** In the end, after Sarapion, a Syrian, had betrayed the citadel, the general seized all the runaways in the city, whom he tortured and threw over a cliff. From there he went to Enna and besieged it in much the same way, bringing the rebels into extreme hardship and dashing their hopes. Their leader, Cleon, came out from the city and fought heroically with a few men until Rupilius displayed him dead, covered with wounds, and took this city too by betrayal, since it was impregnable to force of arms because of its strength. **22** Eunus took his bodyguard of 1,000 men and fled in a cowardly fashion to a precipitous region. The men with him, however, realised that their fate was unavoidable, for the general Rupilius was already marching against them, and killed each other with their swords by beheading. Eunus, the wonder-worker and king, who had through cowardice taken refuge in certain caves, was dragged out with four others – a cook, a baker, the man who massaged him in his bath, and a fourth who used to entertain him when he was drinking. **23** Placed in prison, his body disintegrated into a mass of lice, and he died at Morgantina by a death appropriate to his villainy. Thereupon Rupilius marched throughout Sicily with a few picked men and liberated it from every band of robbers sooner than anyone expected.

6.49 Crawford *RRC* 401.1: The second Sicilian slave revolt

A denarius of 71 BC. The reference is to Manius Aquillius and his suppression of the second slave revolt in Sicily as consul in 101 BC and proconsul in 100; the coin was issued by the consul's grandson (as indicated by the left and right legends). The soldier may be taken to represent the consul himself. Issued after the suppression of Spartacus' revolt, the coin reminded the public of the achievements of Aquillius' grandfather in a previous slave insurrection.

Obverse: Bust of Virtus wearing helmet; legend on right rim: 'Virtus'.

Reverse: Standing soldier, with shield in left hand; with right hand he raises up a prostrate kneeling woman.

Legend below: 'SICIL'; on right rim of denarius: 'MN AQUIL'; on left: 'MN F MN N'.

6.50 Appian *Civil Wars* 1.116.539–120.559: Spartacus, 73–71 BC

Spartacus had been a free man before he became a slave gladiator (one specialist occupation of slaves); he and the other escaping gladiators preferred to 'endanger their lives in pursuit of freedom' rather than in the 'public spectacle' of the arena. His aim was to lead his troops north through the Alps, and his decision not to march on Rome, like Hannibal's, was perhaps a grave error. He defeated the two consuls of 72 BC. Crassus, probably praetor in 73, was then given proconsular imperium and was successful in driving Spartacus into the toe of Italy. **554**: Crassus clearly had the situation in hand, but in 71 the senate also appointed Pompey, who had returned from Spain, to the command. Pompey overcame 5,000 slaves fleeing from the battle and informed the senate that, while Crassus had defeated the gladiators, he (Pompey) had rooted out the slave revolt. Pompey received a triumph for his success against Sertorius in Spain; but, as he had fought against slaves, Crassus was entitled only to an *ovatio*.

539 At the same time (as the murder of Sertorius, and Perperna's conquest by Pompey) there were in Italy some gladiators who were being trained at Capua to appear in public shows. Spartacus, a Thracian, who had at one time served with the Roman army but who had become one of the gladiators after being imprisoned and sold, persuaded about 70 of them to endanger their lives in pursuit of freedom rather than in a public spectacle, and with them he overcame the guards and escaped; **540** they armed themselves with clubs and daggers belonging to some travellers and fled to Mount Vesuvius, where, after being joined by many runaway slaves and some free men from the fields, he plundered the neighbouring region, having as his subordinates gladiators named Oenomaus and Crixus. **541** As he divided up the plunder equitably, he soon had plenty of men; Varinius Glaber (actually the praetor Gaius Claudius Glaber) was the first sent against him, and after him Publius Valerius (actually the praetor Publius Varinius), but not with regular armies, just any men they could gather quickly on their route (for the Romans did not yet consider this a war, but a raid similar to banditry), and when they attacked they were defeated. Spartacus himself even captured Varinius' horse – so close did the Roman general himself come to being a gladiator's prisoner. **542** After this even more people rushed to join Spartacus, until his army totalled 70,000 and he was making weapons and gathering equipment, when the Romans sent out the consuls with two legions.

543 Crixus, leading 30,000 men, was defeated by one of the consuls near Mount Garganus, and both he and two-thirds of his army perished; **544** Spartacus was making haste through the Apennines to the Alps and the Gauls beyond, but one of the consuls got ahead of him and cut off his chance of flight, while the other pursued him. He turned on them one after another and successively defeated them. **545** They retreated from there in disorder, and Spartacus sacrificed 300 Roman prisoners to Crixus and marched on Rome with 120,000 foot-soldiers, after burning any useless equipment, killing all his prisoners and butchering his pack-animals so he could move unhindered; many deserters approached him, but he refused to accept any of them. **546** The consuls met him again in the region of Picenum, and there was another great conflict and another great defeat, too, for the Romans.

547 Spartacus changed his mind about marching on Rome, on the grounds that he was not yet powerful enough for that and his whole army was not properly armed (for no city had joined him, only slaves and deserters and rabble), but he occupied the mountains around Thurii and took the city itself, and prohibited merchants from bringing in gold or silver and the possession of these by his men, but they bought a great deal of iron and bronze and did no harm to those who imported them. **548** Supplied in this way with abundant material, they prepared themselves well and went out frequently on plundering expeditions. When they next engaged with the Roman forces they were again victorious and returned laden with booty.

549 This war was now in its third year and terrible for the Romans, though ridiculed and despised at first because it was against gladiators. When it was time for the election of new praetors, everyone was overcome by cowardice and no one stood, apart from Licinius Crassus, distinguished among the Romans by birth and wealth, who accepted the command and marched against Spartacus with six legions; when he reached the front he also took over the two legions of the consuls. **550** Of these he immediately chose by lot and executed one man out of every ten for having been so often defeated. Some say instead that, after engaging in battle with his whole army and having himself been defeated too, he chose by lot and executed a tenth, about 4,000, of them, undeterred by the number involved. **551** Whatever he did, after demonstrating to the army that he was more to be feared than defeat by the enemy, he overcame 10,000 of the Spartacans who were encamped by themselves, killed two-thirds of them, and marched contemptuously against Spartacus himself. He won a glorious victory over him and pursued him as he fled to the sea, where he intended to sail to Sicily; catching up with him, he hemmed him in with ditch, wall and palisade.

552 Spartacus tried to break out and get into Samnite territory, but Crassus killed about 6,000 of his men in the morning and about the same number towards nightfall, with only three of the Roman army being killed and seven wounded – so great a change in their confidence of victory had come about as a result of their punishment. **553** Spartacus, who was expecting cavalry to join him from somewhere, no longer went into battle with his whole army but frequently harassed the besiegers from different sides with sudden and continuous attacks, throwing bundles of wood into the ditch and setting light to them and making their job difficult. He also crucified a Roman prisoner in the area between the two armies, to show his own men the sight of what they would suffer if they did not win. **554** When the Romans in the city learnt of the siege, they thought it would be disgraceful if the war against gladiators went on any longer and appointed Pompey too, who had just arrived from Spain, to the command, as they believed that the task of confronting Spartacus was still a great and formidable one.

555 As a result of this vote Crassus tried in every way to come to grips with Spartacus, so that the glory of the war might not be Pompey's, and Spartacus, wanting to anticipate Pompey's arrival, invited Crassus to come to terms with him. **556** When this was scornfully rejected he decided to risk a battle, and, since his cavalry had now arrived, he broke out through the besieging wall with all his army and fled to Brundisium with Crassus pursuing him. **557** When Spartacus learnt that Lucullus too had just arrived at Brundisium after his victory over Mithridates, he despaired of everything as hopeless and engaged his forces, which were even then very numerous, against Crassus; there was a long and hard-fought battle, to be expected of tens of thousands of desperate men, and Spartacus, wounded in his thigh with a spear, fell onto his knee and fought against his attackers holding his shield in front of him until both he and the great number of those with him were surrounded and killed. **558** The rest of his army broke ranks and were cut down in crowds, the slaughter being so great that no one could count them; the Romans lost about 1,000 men, and the body of Spartacus was not found. **559** A large number of his men fled from the battle to the mountains, where Crassus went after them. They divided themselves into four parts and kept fighting until all perished except for about 6,000, who were captured and crucified along the whole road (the Via Appia) from Capua to Rome.

THE MANUMISSION OF SLAVES

Freed slaves retained obligations towards their ex-master and became his clients. These freedmen became Roman citizens and joined one of the four urban tribes, but they were ineligible for magistracies and could not hold senatorial or equestrian rank. Priesthoods were also closed to them. However, these disabilities did not carry through into the second generation, and sons, if born after their father's manumission, were free. Various restrictions on manumission were introduced by Augustus, suggesting that it was a largely unrestricted process until then (docs 15.60–61).

6.51 [Cicero] *Letters to his Friends* 16.16.1–2: Cicero's favourite slave

In this letter from to his brother Marcus in 54 or 53 BC, Quintus Cicero expresses his joy that Marcus has freed his trusted slave secretary Tiro, who is a classic example of a valued slave playing an important role in the household, as is Statius (doc. 6.53).

1 With regard to Tiro, my dear Marcus, as surely as I hope to see you and my son Cicero and my darling Tullia and your son, you have done what gave me the very greatest pleasure when you preferred that he, who did not deserve his bad fortune, should be our friend rather than our slave. Believe me, when I had read your letter and his, I jumped for joy. I both thank you and congratulate you. **2** For if Statius' faithful service is such a source of great pleasure to me, how valuable should such qualities be in Tiro, especially when we take into account his literary skills, his conversational powers and his refinement, which outweigh even the personal services he can perform.

6.52 Cicero *Letters to his Friends* 16.18.1, 3: Cicero writes to Tiro

For the first time, in this letter (written after October 47) Cicero addresses Tiro as an equal, using the address 'Tullius Tironi (Tullius to Tiro)': only intimates were addressed without using the praenomen (i.e., Marcus).

1 Well, what about it? Isn't it quite right? I certainly think it is – and even that I ought to add 'dear'. But, as you wish it, let criticism be avoided – although I have often treated it with contempt. I'm pleased that perspiring has done you good. But if my place at Tusculum has helped, merciful gods!, how much more charming I will find it! But, as you love me – as indeed you either do or make a good pretence of it, in which, it is true, you succeed very well – however that may be, look after your health, which, indeed, you have not sufficiently seen to up to now because you have been devoting yourself to me. You are not unaware of what it demands – good digestion, proper rest, moderate walking, massage and proper movement of the bowels. Make sure you return in good health – and I will love not only you but also my place at Tusculum . . .

3 I will send you the sundial and books, if we have nice weather. But about yourself, do you have no light reading with you? Or are you composing something Sophoclean? Show me what you've been working on. Aulus Ligurius, Caesar's friend, is dead, an excellent man and a friend of mine. Make sure I know when to expect you. Look after yourself carefully. Goodbye.

6.53 Cicero *Letters to his Brother Quintus* 1.2.3: An overbearing freedman

This letter was written by Cicero in late 59 BC advising his brother Quintus not to leave any incriminating records behind in his province. Quintus' freedman and secretary Statius was considered somewhat overbearing.

But what used to irritate me most was when I kept on being told that he had more influence over you than was called for by the weight of your years and your experience in government – how many people do you think have pleaded with me to recommend them to Statius? How many times when talking to me has he naively used terms such as, 'I didn't agree with that', 'I warned him', 'I urged him', 'I discouraged him'? Although all this demonstrates the highest loyalty (and

I quite believe it, since that is what you think), nevertheless the very appearance of a freedman or slave enjoying such favour is totally undignified – and indeed I maintain (for I should neither speak rashly nor keep anything back designedly) that all the subject matter of the gossip of those who wish to denigrate you has been provided by Statius; previously nothing could be understood but that some people were angry with you for your severity; now, with his manumission, those who were angry have plenty to talk about.

6.54 Cicero *In Defence of Milo* 57–58: Milo frees his slaves

Milo was put on trial in 52 for the murder of Publius Clodius Pulcher and was defended by Cicero (docs 13.1–5). Milo manumitted all his slaves before the trial, and it was clearly thought that he was worried about what they would reveal under torture. Cicero counters with the idea that Milo was rewarding his slaves by manumitting them. Milo was convicted and went into exile.

57 Then why did Milo manumit them? Of course, it was because he feared they might incriminate him, that they might be unable to endure the pain, that they might be compelled by torture to confess that Publius Clodius was murdered on the Appian Way by Milo's slaves. Why would you need a torturer? What fact are you looking for? Whether he killed him? He did kill him. Was it justified or not? That is nothing to do with a torturer. . . . **58** What reward can be great enough for slaves, so devoted, so brave and so loyal, who saved their master's life? . . . Had he not manumitted them, they were to be handed over to torture – the saviours of their master, the avengers of crime, the averters of death. Indeed, amid all his misfortunes, there is nothing which Milo views with more pleasure than the fact that, whatever may befall him, these have been given a well-deserved reward.

6.55 *ILS* 3491: A freedman pays his vow

On an altar at Rome, dating to before 80 BC. Trypho has made a vow and, now free, fulfils it.

Quintus Mucius Trypho, freedman of Quintus, vowed this as a slave and paid it willingly and deservedly when free; sacred to the Good Goddess.

6.56 Dionysius of Halicarnassus *Roman Antiquities* 4.24.1–6: Manumission

Here Dionysius comments on slavery under Servius Tullius, though his remarks on warfare as the most important method of obtaining slaves obviously relate to his own time. He gives various reasons why slaves might be manumitted, particularly because the ex-slaves could receive and give their ex-masters the grain dole for which they would now be eligible (since Gaius Gracchus' reforms of 122 BC). The liberty cap was worn by freedpersons.

1 As I have come to this section of my narrative, I think that I ought to give the details of the customs of the Romans of that time with regard to their slaves, to prevent anyone blaming either the king, who was the first to undertake to make citizens of those who had been slaves, or those who accepted the law, for rashly casting aside traditions. **2** The Romans acquired their slaves by the fairest means: they either bought them from the state under the spear (i.e., at an auction) from the spoils of war, or the general allowed them to keep the prisoners they had taken as well as the rest of the booty, or they obtained the slaves by purchasing them from others who had acquired them by these same means. **3** Neither Tullius who established the custom, nor those who accepted it and kept it up, thought that they were doing anything shameful or harmful to the public interest if those who had lost their country and their freedom in war and who had served well those who had enslaved them, or those who had purchased them from these people, were granted country and freedom by their masters. **4** Most of them received their liberty as a free gift for their good conduct, and this was the best method of discharge from their masters, but a few paid a ransom which they had collected by lawful and honest labour.

In our day, however, this is not the case, but affairs have come to such a state of confusion, and the traditions of the Roman commonwealth have become so dishonoured and sordid, that some buy their freedom with money acquired from robbery, housebreaking, prostitution and every other corrupt means and are Romans on the spot; **5** others who have been their masters' collaborators and accomplices in poisonings, murders and crimes against the gods or state receive from them their freedom as their reward. Some are freed so that, when they receive every month the corn given at public expense and any other liberality donated by the powerful to the poorer citizens, they can bring it to those who granted them their freedom; and others owe it to the lightmindedness of their master and his thirst for popularity. **6** At any rate, I know of some who have allowed all their slaves to be freed after their deaths, so that, when dead, they might be called good men and many people with felt skullcaps (i.e., liberty caps) on their heads might follow their funeral biers; some of those taking part in these processions, as could be heard from those in the know, were criminals, just released from prison, who had committed crimes deserving ten thousand deaths. But most people are unhappy when they look on these stains that can hardly be washed away from the city, and condemn the custom, considering it not appropriate for a pre-eminent city, which thinks itself fit to rule the whole world, to make such people citizens.

THE OCCUPATIONS OF FREEDMEN

Educated slaves, and those who had served their masters well in other professional capacities or in domestic service, might be manumitted and follow the same occupations after manumission (as did Tiro). Many freedpersons, by necessity and because of the demands of the patron–client system and manumission obligations, will have remained in their master's employ. Agricultural and mining slaves were not usually manumitted; many of the craftsmen and shopkeepers at Rome were freedmen; for freedwomen prostitutes and actresses, docs 7.62–65.

6.57 *CIL* I² 2519: An association of Greek actors

This is from a tablet of stone dedicated by a society of Greek actors. It was discovered in a tomb near the Praenestine gate. The second part of the inscription was added when the tomb was later restored by Philo.

Belonging to the association of Greek actors who are in this company (synodos), out of their common fund. Maecenas Mal . . . , son of Decimus, master of ceremonies and patron of the company approved it. Marcus Vaccius Theophilus, freedman of Marcus, and Quintus Vibius Simus, freedman of Quintus, chairman of the company of Decumiani, **5** superintended the purchase of a site for the tomb and its construction.

   Lucius Aurelius Philo, freedman of Lucius, chairman for the seventh time of the company of the association of Greek singers and those who are members of this association, superintended the restoration from his own funds.

6.58 Suetonius *On Grammarians* 7, 10, 13, 15, 17, 21: Freedmen as literary figures

Educated Greek slaves were an indispensable component of elite family households, where they served as teachers, doctors, readers, secretaries and even astrologers. Roman education, with its strong Greek flavour, required slaves from that country. Staberius was able to purchase his own freedom through his peculium at a public sale (13), but slaves could not purchase their own freedom without their master's consent, even if the peculium was of sufficient value.

7 Marcus Antonius Gnipho was born free in Gaul but disowned; he was manumitted by his foster-father and educated (in Alexandria, according to some, and in close association with Dionysius Scytobrachion; but I am unable to believe this for reasons of chronology). He is said to have been a man of great talent, of unexampled memory, and educated in Greek no less than in Latin; moreover his character was affable and good-natured, never stipulating any fees, with the result that he received all the more from the generosity of his pupils. He first taught in the house of the Deified Julius (Caesar) when the latter was still a boy, and then in his own home. He taught rhetoric, too, and gave instruction in the art of speaking every day, but in declamation only on market-days (i.e., once a week). It is said that distinguished men also attended his school, among them Marcus Cicero, even when he was holding office as praetor.

   10 Lucius Ateius Philologus was a freedman born at Athens. The well-known jurist Ateius Capito calls him 'a rhetorician among grammarians and a grammarian among rhetoricians'. Asinius Pollio, in the book in which he criticises the writings of Sallust for being flawed by a striving after archaisms, writes as follows: 'In this he was especially encouraged by Ateius Praetextatus, a famous Latin grammarian, later a critic and teacher of declamation, who finally styled himself Philologus.' He himself wrote to Laelius Hermas that he had made great progress in Greek literature and some in Latin, had been a pupil of Antonius Gnipho, and then a teacher; also that he had instructed many eminent young men, among them the brothers Appius and Claudius Pulcher, whom he had also accompanied to their province. He appears to have assumed the name Philologus ('lover of literature') because, like Eratosthenes, who was the first to claim the surname, he considered himself a man of extensive and varied learning. This is certainly evident from his commentaries, although very few survive; he gives some idea of their number in another letter to Hermas: 'Remember to recommend my *Hyle* to others, in which, as you know, I collected all kinds of material in 800 books.' He was afterwards a great friend of Gaius Sallustius (Sallust) and, after his death, of Asinius Pollio, and when they began writing history he provided one with a summary of all Roman history from which he could select what he wished, the other with rules on the art of writing.

13 Staberius Eros was purchased by his own savings at a public sale and manumitted because of his commitment to literature; he taught Brutus and Cassius among others. Some people say that he was so generous that in the times of Sulla he admitted the children of the proscribed to his school free and without any fees.

15 Lenaeus, freedman of Pompey the Great and his companion on nearly all his campaigns, on the death of Pompey and his sons supported himself by a school, teaching in the Carinae, near the temple of Tellus, the quarter where the Pompeys' house had been, and was so devoted to his patron's memory that he tore the historian Sallust to pieces in a savage satire because he had described Pompey as being of honest face but shameless character . . . It is also said that, when he was still a boy, he was stolen from Athens but escaped and returned to his homeland and, after acquiring a liberal education, offered the price of his freedom to his former master, but was manumitted for free on account of his talents and learning.

17 Marcus Verrius Flaccus, a freedman, was renowned for his method of teaching. To stinulate the intellects of his pupils he used to set those at the same level against each other, choosing not only the topic on which they were to write but a prize to be won by the victor. This would be some beautiful and rare antique book. As a result he was selected by Augustus as well as tutor for his grandsons and moved to the Palatine with his whole school, but on the understanding that he would take no more pupils. He taught in the house of Catulus, which was then part of the palace, and was paid 100,000 sesterces a year. He died in old age during the reign of Tiberius.

21 Gaius Melissus was born a free man at Spoleto but exposed because of a disagreement between his parents. However, through the care and efforts of the man who brought him up, he received a higher education and was presented as a gift to Maecenas as a grammarian. Finding that Maecenas appreciated him and treated him as a friend, even though his mother claimed his freedom, he kept the status of a slave and preferred this present condition to his real origins. As a result he was soon freed and became friendly with Augustus. It was Augustus who appointed him to supervise the arrangement of the library in the portico of Octavia.

6.59 Suetonius *Life of Terence* 1–5: Terence: a success story

Publius Terentius Afer was born at Carthage, according to Suetonius, and came to Rome as a slave of Terentius Lucanus. He was the author of six comedies in the 160s BC and was supported in his work by his patrons Scipio Aemilianus (cos. 147, 134) and Scipio's friends C. Laelius (cos. 140) and L. Furius Philus (cos. 136). Note that there are various versions of his death given here: clearly no one actually knew where he retired.

1 Publius Terentius Afer, born at Carthage, was the slave at Rome of the senator Terentius Lucanus, by whom, on account of his talent and appearance, he
was not only given a liberal education but quickly manumitted. Some think that
he was captured in war, but Fenestella shows that this cannot possibly have
been the case, since Terence was born and died between the end of the Second
Punic War (201 BC) and the beginning of the third (149 BC); and if he had
been captured by the Numidians and Gaetulians he would not have been able to
come into the hands of a Roman commander, as commerce between the Italians
and Africans did not begin until after the destruction of Carthage. He lived
on familiar terms with many men of the nobility, and particularly with Scipio
Africanus and Gaius Laelius. It is even thought that he won their favour through
his appearance, which Fenestella also denies, arguing that he was older than
both, although Nepos records that they were all of the same age and Porcius
raises a suspicions of love affairs with these words:

'While he sought the lusts of noble men and their false praises,
While he drank in the divine voice of Africanus with greedy ears,
While he thought it glorious to dine constantly with Furius and Laelius,
While he was often taken to the villa at Alba for his youthful charms,
Later he found he had lost everything and was in total penury.
So he withdrew from the sight of all to the furthest part of Greece,
Dying at Stymphalus, a town in Arcadia. Neither Publius
Scipio, nor Laelius, nor Furius benefited him,
The three most comfortably well-off nobles of that time.
He did not even have with their assistance a rented house,
Where his little slave could at least announce his master's death.'

2 He wrote six comedies, and when he offered the first of these, the *Andria*, to the
aediles, he was told to read it to Caecilius (Statius). When he arrived, he found
Caecilius at dinner, and it is said that because of his humble dress he read the
beginning of the play sitting on a bench near Caecilius' dining couch, but after
a few lines he was invited to recline at table, and later went through the rest of
the play to Caecilius' great admiration. Furthermore this play and the other five
delighted the people equally . . . The *Eunuch* was even acted twice in the same
day and earned more than any previous comedy of this type had ever done, that is
8,000 sesterces; the sum is even included on the title-page . . .

4 After publishing these comedies before he had passed his twenty-fifth year,
either to avoid the gossip about his publishing other people's work as his own or
to study Greek manners and customs, in case he had not depicted them quite successfully in his writings, he left Rome and never returned. Concerning his death,
Vulcacius writes as follows:

'But when Afer had presented six comedies,
He journeyed from here to Asia, and from the time
He went on board, he was never seen again; thus he vanished from life.'

5 Quintus Cosconius writes that he died at sea while returning from Greece with 108 plays adapted from Menander. The others record that he died at Stymphalus in Arcadia or at Leucadia in the consulship of Gnaeus Cornelius Dolabella and Marcus Fulvius Nobilior (159 BC), after becoming ill from grief and irritation when his luggage was lost, which he had sent on in advance by ship, and with it the new plays he had written. He is said to have been of medium height, slender figure and dark complexion. He left a daughter, who afterwards married a Roman eques; also gardens of 20 iugera on the Appian Way near the villa of Mars.

FUNERARY INSCRIPTIONS

While the vast majority of funerary inscriptions (epitaphs) and reliefs relating to freedpersons (and slaves) in the city of Rome come from the imperial period, there are examples from the late Republic. These inscriptions are invaluable in attesting both to individual manumissions and to the occupations of the manumitted slaves. It is clear that there was a high frequency of manumission at Rome and that freedpersons constituted a sizeable proportion of the population in the first century BC. The open attitude to citizenship via manumission distinguished the Romans from other ancient peoples and ensured that, by the end of the Republic if not earlier, large numbers of the citizen residents of Rome were ex-slaves or descended from slaves.

6.60 *ILS* 8341: A doctor's family in Rome

The doctor freedman of this inscription had clearly been successful enough to afford a tomb large enough to contain so many occupants (it was common to include in the inscription the tomb's dimensions). The marital relationships mentioned are important: it was often the case that freedmen married freedwomen (often from the same household) and included other freedpersons in their tomb.

Gaius Hostius Pamphilus, a doctor, freedman of Gaius, bought this memorial for himself and for Nelpia Hymnis, freedwoman of Marcus, and for all their freedmen and freedwomen **5** and their descendants. This is our home for evermore, this our farm, this our gardens, this our memorial. Frontage 13 feet, depth 24 feet.

6.61 *ILS* 7642: Quintus the butcher

For another freedman butcher, see doc. 7.33.

Here lie the bones of Quintus Tiburtius Menolavus, freedman of Quintus, who slaughtered animals for sacrifice.

6.62 *ILS* 8417: Farewell, be well!

A memorial from New Carthage in Spain (probably first century BC), erected as reward for Plotia's good conduct ('how she behaved').

Here lies Plotia (often called Phryne), freedwoman of Lucius and Fufia. This memorial shows how she behaved towards her patron and patroness, her father, and her husband. **5** Farewell, be well.

6.63 *ILS* 1932: Aulus the auctioneer

From Rome, dating to c. 100 BC.

This silent stone asks you, stranger, to stop
While it reveals to you what he, whose shade it covers, entrusted it to reveal.
The bones of a man of honour and great trustworthiness,
Aulus Granius, the auctioneer, lie here.
5 That is all. He wanted you to know this. Farewell.
Aulus Granius Stabilio, freedman of Marcus, auctioneer.

6.64 *ILS* 8432: Two inseparable slaves

An inscription found at Rome on the Appian Way.

For Aulus Memmius Clarus.
Dedicated by Aulus Memmius Urbanus to his fellow freedman and his dearest companion.
5 I cannot remember, my most honoured fellow freedman, there having been any quarrel between us. By this epitaph, I call the gods of heaven and of the underworld as witnesses that **10** together we stood on the slave-dealer's platform, that in the same household we were made freedmen, and that nothing ever separated us until this your fatal day.

6.65 *CIL* I² 1570: Grave of a freedwoman

Larcia Horaea was freed by Publius Larcius Nicia and Saufeia, both of whom were themselves freedpersons (libertini), and became the wife of Publius Larcius Brocchus, their son. This inscription was found at Traiectum (on the Liris) and may date to c. 45 BC.

Publius Larcius Nicia, freedman of Publius; Saufeia Thalea, freedwoman of a matron; Lucius Larcius Rufus, son of Publius; Publius Larcius Brocchus, son of Publius; Publia Horaea, freedwoman of Publius and his wife.

I was respected by the good and hated by no honourable woman.
I was obedient to my aged master and mistress, but to him I was dutiful,
For they gave me my freedom and he married me.
From when I was a girl I supervised the house for twenty years –
The whole of it. My final day gave its judgement,
And death took my spirit, but did not remove the splendour of my life.

SLAVES AND FREEDMEN OF THE IMPERIAL HOUSEHOLD

The Monumentum Liviae, a subterranean burial site on the Appian Way, gives some indication of the numbers of slaves and freedmen who served the imperial household. The site, which was overseen by an association of slaves and freedmen and could hold well over

1,000 urns, contains the remains of some 90 persons who are specifically stated to belong to Livia herself, not including their own children and slaves. Most of the staff were men, except for Livia's dressers and masseuse, and their named occupations show how specialised the staff positions could be. Among the personnel were a steward, financial and secretarial officials, dressers and wardrobe-keepers, cooks, footmen, doctors, craftsmen and jewel-setters, wetnurses and midwives, and individuals in charge of furniture and pictures, as well as a pet child ('delicium') named C. Julius Prosopas, who had been freed and died at the age of nine years.

6.66 Dio *Roman History* 53.30.3: Augustus' doctor

Unfortunately, after Augustus' recovery during the epidemic in the first half of 23 BC, Musa was unable to cure Augustus' son-in-law Marcellus, who had the same symptoms (see doc. 15.36).

Even though he had lost the ability to deal with even the most essential matters, a certain Antonius Musa cured him by using cold baths and drinks of cold water. In return he received much money from Augustus and the senate and the right to wear gold rings (he was a freedman), as well as immunity from taxation both for himself and his fellow doctors, not only for those currently alive but for ones in the future.

6.67 CIL 6.4035: A statue-keeper

Agrypnus Maecenatianus, slave of Caesar Augustus, in charge of statues.

6.68 CIL 6.4045: A masseuse

Galene, slavewoman of Livia, masseuse.

6.69 *ILS* 1795: Augustus' food-taster

To the genius of Coetus Herodianus, taster of the divine Augustus, afterwards also bailiff in the gardens of Sallust, died 5 August in the consulship of Marcus Cocceius Nerva and Gaius Vibius Rufinus. Julia Prima for her patron.

6.70 *ILS* 1877: Octavia's ex-slave

Gaius Octavius Auctus, freedman of Octavia, sister of Augustus, records clerk; Viccia Gnome, freedwoman of Gaius, his wife.

6.71 *ILS* 7888: Agrippa's freedmen

Marcus Vipsanius Zoticus, freedman of Marcus, three times curator of the burial club, gave urn 14 for himself and for Vipsania Stibas, freedwoman of Marcus, club-member.

Vipsania Acume, freedwoman of the Marci, wife of Zoticus, slave of Marcus Agrippa, who was in charge of the monuments of Marcus Agrippa.

6.72 *ILS* 1926: A family of freedmen

Quintus Fabius Cytisus, freedman of Africanus, quaestorian summoner (viator) of the treasury, tribunician records clerk, quaestorian records clerk of the three decuries.

Gaius Calpetanus Cryphius, freedman of Gaius, summoner of the sacred chickens, first husband of Culicina.

Lucius Nymphidius Philomelus, freedman of Lucius, quaestorian records clerk of the three decuries, dutiful and loyal brother of Cytisus.

Gaius Proculeius Heracleo, freedman of Gaius, father of Culicina.

Proculeia Stibas, mother of Culicina and of Livia Culicina, freedwoman of the divine Augusta.

Plasidiena Agrestina, daughter of Lucius, wife of Calpetanus Livianus, chief centurion.

7

Women, Sexuality and the Family

The Roman family was typically an extended one, under the authority of the eldest male (the paterfamilias, or 'father of the family'), and included all descendants
except those who had been emancipated (given their independence by the paterfamilias). Hence the family might comprise not only the head of the household
but children and grandchildren, the wives of married sons and grandsons, adopted
children, and slaves (doc. 7.1). The paterfamilias had almost total control over all
members of the household and was the only one to own property, unless he had
specifically allowed any of his sons a peculium, or fund, of their own or to enter
into legal contracts. This authority over family members was called patria potestas
(doc. 7.2). While he had total power to kill slaves as and when he chose, it appears
that his power of 'life or death' over his children was tempered by the custom of
consulting a family council beforehand. However, should the advice of the council be in favour, then the offending family member would be put to death with no
guilt incurred by the father (docs 7.12, 14–15, 17). Should the paterfamilias wish,
he could emancipate any of his children, and a son would then be a paterfamilias
in his own right, just as if his father had died (doc. 7.4).

The status of wives varied and, while women needed a male guardian (doc.
7.5), they could either be in the power (manus, or 'hand') of their husband or
remain members of their original family and so under the control of their father
or brother. If married by coemptio (a pretend sale), the wife, together with her
property, came into the manus of her husband, giving her the status of one of her
husband's daughters. However, if married by usus, or cohabitation, the wife could
avoid coming into her husband's manus if she absented herself from his household for three nights in the year, and in this case her property remained entirely
separate from that of her husband; nor, should her husband die intestate, was she
considered a member of his family for inheritance purposes (docs 7.10–11). This
form of marriage was referred to in the XII Tables in the fifth century BC, and
by the first century at least it seems to have been the most common form. Where
a wife was not 'in manu' to her husband, it was the duty of the wife's own relatives, not her husband, to exact punishment if she were found guilty of criminal
behaviour, as with those women initiated into the Bacchanalia (docs 7.16–17).
Divorce was relatively easy in Rome (except for those married by confarreatio,

which was the religious form of marriage restricted to patricians) for both parties, though the wife's dowry had to be returned (with certain deductions for children or misconduct: doc. 7.13).

In being financially independent of her husband, and in possessing far greater freedom within the household than the citizen women of ancient Athens (doc. 7.28), the materfamilias ('mother of the family') had a significant role in the upbringing of children and grandchildren and in the running of the home generally. In addition, women were not excluded from meeting men outside their own families (docs 7.22–23). Stereotypical descriptions of the 'ideal' wife, especially in funeral eulogies and epitaphs, do not disguise the great respect often felt for wives and mothers and the influence they had over their children (docs 7.30–37). The relationship between parents and daughters could be extremely close and indicative of great affection and respect on either side (docs 7.24–27). Anecdotes regarding marital disagreements, as with Cicero's brother Quintus and his wife Pomponia, suggest that many women also felt free to express their views (docs 7.38–41), while their freedom of movement and active social life is confirmed by the evidence of numerous adulterous liaisons engaged in by upper-class Roman women, as well as by their involvement in outlawed or non-mainstream religious rites (docs 7.42–46, 52).

While adultery on the part of the wife was clear grounds for divorce (doc. 7.18), Roman men were free to engage in heterosexual love affairs, as long as they steered clear of citizen women (docs 7.47–56), and there was no stigma involved in visiting prostitutes (docs 7.62–64). Following the successful conquests of the second century BC, many young men engaged in a luxurious and dilettantist lifestyle, and the cost and availability of high-class prostitutes rose accordingly, as did that of handsome young boys. While the Romans considered that passive homosexuality degraded a citizen and made him, at best, an object of ridicule (doc. 7.60), it was considered normal that Romans should use young male slaves or prostitutes as passive sexual objects (docs 7.57–61). Indeed, the best-known love poet of the Republic, Catullus, not only chronicled his supposed affair with the faithless 'Lesbia' but eulogised the attractions of certain young boys (docs 7.47–49, 51, 61).

While women of the early Republic were given both a *praenomen* (first name) of their own and the family *nomen*, by the middle Republic women are distinguished only by the female form of their father's nomen (e.g., Tullia, daughter of Marcus Tullius Cicero). Where there were numerous daughters they could be identified by numerals, such as Claudia *Quinta* ('fifth') and Aemilia *Tertia* ('third'), see docs 3.42, 7.30. However, by the late Republic, women could also adopt the female form of their father's cognomen and were beginning to be noticed by historians as individuals, worthy of comment or criticism in their own right (as with Sempronia: doc. 7.44). By the late Republic, women were well-documented property owners, and, although historians were in the habit of trivialising their interests because of their apparent desire for ornaments and cosmetics (docs 7.66–68), it is clear that ornaments served as conspicous status symbols for the wives and their husbands in certain religious contexts, such as festivals and processions (doc. 7.70). In addition, women could wield significant power as consumers as well as exercise *de facto* control over considerable financial investments – for example, Cicero's wife Terentia and Hortensia, the daughter of the orator Hortensius (docs 7.69, 71–72, 74–75).

Roman women also played an extremely significant role in the worship of the gods, with numerous festivals restricted to women-only participation, including the important cult of the 'Bona Dea' (docs 7.86–88). Many of these cults were concerned primarily with childbirth and fertility (docs 7.78–81, 83), while others involved citizen women and prostitutes alike (docs 7.83). Women could also play an important role in making supplication on behalf of the state in times of crisis (docs 7.84–85). The six Vestal Virgins not only guarded the 'sacred things' in the temple of Vesta and prepared the mola salsa (meal) for sacrifices but took part in various state religious ceremonies (docs 7.88, 90). The welfare of the state was bound up with the preservation of their chastity, and should a Vestal break her vows it was seen as threatening the security of Rome itself (docs 7.89–91, 93).

Ancient sources: it is the jurists of the imperial period, such as Gaius, Ulpian and Pomponius, who give definitions of the Roman family and the status of the persons within it (docs 7.1–7, 9–10, 13). Otherwise, information on Roman families and their lifestyles has to be gleaned from a variety of literary and historical sources, namely Livy and Dionysius for early Rome and Plutarch and Valerius Maximus for anecdotal evidence for family life and the position of women. Cicero's *Letters* reveal details of relationships within his own family, while epitaphs for wives and daughters (docs 7.23–5, 31–33, 37) also show the ways in which they were valued by husbands and fathers. Comic dramatists (docs 7.38, 7.68) present humorous depictions of married life, and Catullus (docs 7.46–51) sheds some light on heterosexual love in first-century Rome. The *Fasti* of Ovid (43 BC–AD 17) provide a valuable survey of women's religious festivals in the first half of the year (docs 7.79–83).

FAMILY LAW

In early Rome, gentes (sing.: gens), or clans, were formed by a number of related families who possessed a common name and shared a common family cult (such as the Julian gens or Claudian gens). In the absence of closer family members, the XII Tables laid down rules on guardianship and intestate inheritance within such gentes (1.35).

Should a paterfamilias (plural: patres familiarum) die intestate (i.e., without a will), the order of inheritance was, firstly, direct heirs, such as children, grandchildren, and his wife (if 'in manu', i.e., in the power of her husband); then the closest agnate (family member in the male line of succession), who was linked to the deceased through males (siblings and paternal uncles); and, finally, *gentiles*, or clansmen, of the same name. In the first century BC, cognates were increasingly recognised, so the order of inheritance then became children, then husband or wife.

7.1 The definition of a Roman family

In theory the paterfamilias possessed unlimited power over his entire household until he either died or emancipated his children. Until then, whatever the age of his children or grandchildren, he was the only one with the right to own property, although he could allow his offspring to have control of a fund called a peculium and incur financial obligations. After his death his descendants (should there be no other direct male ancestor living) became sui iuris (independent) and the sons were in their own turn patres familiarum.

(i) *Justinian* Digest *50.16.195 (Ulpian)*

1 Let us see how the word 'familia' should be understood, for it is understood in various ways, as it refers to both property and persons; to property, as in a Law of the XII Tables, where it is said, 'Let the nearest agnate (the next of kin on the father's side) have the estate (familia).' The term 'familia' also refers to persons, as when the same law referring to a patron and his freedman says, 'from this familia into that familia'. In this instance, it is understood that the law refers to persons.

2 The term 'familia' also refers to a collection of persons, connected either by their own legal rights vis-à-vis each other or by a more general kinship relationship. We say that a family is connected by its own legal bond when several persons are either by nature or by law subjected to the potestas of one person — for example, the paterfamilias, materfamilias, and son and daughter under paternal control, as well as their descendants, such as grandsons, granddaughters and their successors. The person who has authority over the household is designated the paterfamilias, and he is properly called so even if he has no son, for we designate not merely him as a person but also his legal right. We even style a minor the paterfamilias when his father dies, and each of the persons who were under the father's control begins to have a separate household and take on the title of paterfamilias. The same thing happens in the case of a son who is emancipated, for he also begins to have his own familia when he becomes independent (sui iuris). We also use the term 'familia' of all the agnates, because, even though the paterfamilias may have died and each of them has a separate familia, still all who were under the potestas of this one man can properly be said to belong to the same familia, as they have sprung from the same house and gens (clan).

3 We are also accustomed to use the term familia for groups of slaves . . . In the interdict 'On violence', the term familia includes not only all the slaves but the children as well. **4** Again the term familia is used of all those persons who are descended by blood from a single ancestor (as we speak of the Julian family), referring as it were to persons derived from a single remembered origin. **5** A woman, however, is the beginning and end of her own familia.

(ii) *Gaius* Institutes *1.196 (*On the Provincial Edict *XVI)*

The head of the family is himself included in the term 'familia'. It is clear that children do not belong to the wife's family, because anyone who is born to a father does not belong to his mother's family.

7.2 Gaius *Institutes* 1.48–49, 52, 55: Patria potestas

While technically the paterfamilias had the right of 'life and death' over members of his household, in practice, a paterfamilias would not exercise the right of life and death over his sons without consultation with a family council (consilium). A paterfamilias, however, was quite free to disinherit his children (though, in general, feelings were against this).

48 Some persons are legally independent (sui iuris), others are subject to another person (alieni iuris). **49** Of those subject to another person, some are in potestas and others in manus to a husband. **52** Slaves are in the potestas of their masters . . . **55** Similarly, any of our children whom we have begotten in lawful marriage are in our potestas. This right is peculiar to Roman citizens, for there are almost no other peoples who have such power over their children as we have . . .

7.3 Gaius *Institutes* 1.97–107: Adoption

The law distinguished between the transfer of a son by his natural father to a new family and adrogatio (where a person sui iuris, i.e., independent in his own right, placed himself under another's potestas). Both practices required public ratification, while testamentary adoption, such as the adoption of Scipio Aemilianus and his brother Q. Fabius Maximus Aemilianus, was a purely private practice. The families of P. Scipio Africanus and Q. Fabius Maximus would otherwise have died out in a generation had they not adopted two of the sons of L. Aemilius Paullus and Papiria.

97 It is not only natural children, as we have stated, who are in our potestas, but also those whom we adopt. **98** Adoption takes place in two ways: either by the authority of the people or by the imperium of a magistrate – as, for instance, a praetor.

99 We adopt, by the authority of the people, those who are their own masters, and this kind of adoption is called 'arrogation', for the reason that he who does the adopting is asked, that is to say 'arrogated', whether he desires to have the person whom he intends to adopt as his lawful son; and he who is adopted is asked whether he is willing for this to take place; and the assembled people are asked whether they direct this to take place. By the command of the magistrate we adopt those who are under the potestas of their parents, whether they are in the first degree of descendants, such as a son or a daughter, or whether they belong to an inferior degree, such as a grandson, a granddaughter, a great-grandson or a great-granddaughter.

100 Adoption by the authority of the people can take place only at Rome, while the other method generally takes place in the provinces before the provincial governors. **101** The prevailing view is that women cannot be adopted by the authority of the people; but women may be adopted in the tribunal of the praetor at Rome or in the provinces in the tribunal of the proconsul or legate . . . **103** It is a rule common to both kinds of adoption that persons who are incapable of begetting children, such as eunuchs, can adopt. **104** Women, however, cannot adopt other persons in any way because they do not have potestas even over their natural children. **105** Similarly, if anyone adopts another person, either by the vote of the people or by the consent of the praetor or provincial governor, he can give the son he has adopted in adoption to another. **106** It is debatable, however, with reference to both forms of adoption, whether a person can adopt someone who is older than himself.

107 It is peculiar to that kind of adoption which takes place by the vote of the people that, if he who gives himself to be adopted has children under his control, he will not only himself be subject to the authority of the adopter, but his children will also be under the latter's authority, as grandchildren.

7.4 Gaius *Institutes* 1.116–20: Emancipation of family members

Sons could be disadvantaged by emancipation because they would lose their chance of inheritance if their father died intestate.

116 We now have to explain which persons are subject to mancipation (in mancipio). **117** All children, whether male or female, who are under the potestas of their father, can be mancipated by him in the same way as slaves.

118 The same rule of law applies to anyone who is in the control of another, and they can be mancipated in the same way by those to whom they have been sold, just as children may be mancipated by their father; also, while a woman who is married to the purchaser may occupy only the place of his daughter, even if she should not be married to him, and not occupy the position of his daughter, she can still be mancipated by him. **118a** In general, mancipation takes place either by parents or by those who obtain possession by coemptio, when the parents and the so-called purchasers wish to free the persons from their authority, as will appear more clearly below.

119 Mancipation, as stated above, is a kind of fictitious sale, and the law governing it is peculiar to Roman citizens. The ceremony is as follows: not fewer than five witnesses (who must be Roman citizens above the age of puberty) are assembled, plus another person of the same status who holds a brass balance in his hand and is styled the 'balance-holder.' The so-called purchaser, holding a piece of bronze in his hands, then states:

'I declare that this man belongs to me by my right as a Roman citizen. Let him be purchased by me with this piece of bronze and bronze balance.' Then he strikes the scales with the piece of bronze and gives it to the so-called seller as purchase money.

120 In this way both slaves and free persons are mancipated, as well as any animals that are subject to sale, including oxen, horses, mules and donkeys, and also urban and country estates.

7.5 Ulpian *Rules* 11.1, 27: Guardianship

All women, if they had no father living or were not in manu to a husband, had a tutor. Freedwomen had their patron as their guardian. Even widows could not have potestas over their children, so their children needed a tutor. Women who were *sui iuris* could inherit and receive legacies, and, while in early Rome women were unable to make a will, later they could do so with their guardian's consent. For the will of Hispala, a freedwoman, see doc. 7.63.

1 Guardians are appointed for both males and females: only for males who have not yet reached the age of puberty, because of their infirmity of age, but for females both before and after puberty because of the weakness of their sex, as well as their ignorance of business matters.

27 A woman needs the approval of her guardian in transactions of this kind – that is, if she wishes to bring a legal action; if she accepts a legal or financial obligation; if she permits a freedwoman of hers to cohabit with another's slave; or if she wishes to alienate property transferable by mancipation. The guardian's approval is also required by wards for the alienation of property which is not transferable by mancipation.

7.6 Justinian *Digest* 50.17.2 (Ulpian *On Sabinus*): Second-class citizens

Women are excluded from all civil and public offices; as a result they cannot sit on juries, or perform the duties of magistrates, or bring actions in court, or be guarantors for others, or act as advocates. Similarly children should not hold any public office.

THE FORMALITIES OF MARRIAGE

The reason for matrimony was, in legal terms, in order to have children. Adult males were asked by the censors, 'To the best of your knowledge and belief, do you have a wife?' (Gell. 4.20.3). There were three types of marriage in Rome: confarreatio, supposedly established by Romulus, was the only religious marriage performed and allowed no divorce. Certain priests, such as the rex sacrorum and flamen dialis, had to be married by confarreatio (as did their parents), and it was presumably restricted to patricians. Coemptio was a fictitious sale of a girl to her husband which brought the wife in 'manus', giving her the status in her new family of a daughter, subject to her husband's potestas (see doc.7.10, cf. 7.4). In 'usus', the normal form of marriage in the late Republic, cohabitation for a year was changed into a manus form of marriage. The wife could, however, avoid passing into her husband's manus if she stayed away for three nights during the year (a provision laid down by the XII Tables: doc. 1.38).

7.7 Justinian *Digest* 23.1.4, 12 (Ulpian *On Sabinus*): Betrothal

The minimum legal age at marriage for girls was 12 and for boys 14, and before Augustus (doc. 15.23) betrothals could take place at any age. Though many aristocratic girls may have married young (between 12 and 15), those outside the elite seem to have married later. Verbal consent between the parties and patres familiarum was all that was necessary, though a written contract and dowry arrangements might be formalised.

4 Mere consent is sufficient in contracting a betrothal. It is laid down that parties who are absent can be betrothed, and this takes place every day.

12 A girl who does not obviously resist the will of her father is understood to give her consent. A daughter is allowed to refuse her consent to her father's wishes only where he selects someone for her husband who is unworthy because of his habits or because he is of infamous character.

7.8 Livy *History of Rome* 38.57.5–8: A materfamilias is affronted

Cornelia, younger daughter of Scipio Africanus and Aemilia (daughter of L. Aemilius Paullus who died at Cannae), was betrothed to Ti. Gracchus the elder in 187. This extract suggests that a wife expected to be consulted on the selection of a husband for her daughter.

5 The story goes that the senate, which had happened to dine that day on the Capitoline hill, rose up and begged that during the banquet Africanus should betroth his daughter to Gracchus. **6** When the betrothal contract had been duly made on this public occasion, Scipio returned home and told his wife Aemilia that he had betrothed their younger daughter. **7** She, indignant as any woman would naturally be at not being consulted about their daughter, who was hers as well as his, added that the mother ought to be consulted on the matter, even if his choice were Tiberius Gracchus. **8** Scipio, pleased that they agreed on this, replied that it was to Gracchus that he had betrothed her.

7.9 Justinian *Digest* 23.3.6 (Pomponius *On Sabinus*): The dowry

While the husband (or his paterfamilias) became the owner of the wife's dowry, this was returnable on death or divorce. Deductions could be made from the dowry for the wife's misconduct (i.e., one-sixth for adultery) or to provide for children (one-sixth for each child up to one half of the total). While the dowry could be used to help underwrite some household expenses, it remained the wife's, and any non-dotal property the wife inherited or received remained under her own control as long as she was not in manu. Scipio Africanus gave each of his daughters a dowry of 50 talents.

Relief is granted to the father by law, for, when he has lost his daughter, he is entitled to the return of the dowry which he provided, and this is done for his consolation, so he may not suffer the loss of both his daughter and the money.

7.10 Gaius *Institutes* 1.108–15b, 136–37a: Marriage with manus

The paterfamilias' power over his wife and daughter(s)-in-law was called manus. For a Roman girl, marriage in manu meant she became part of her husband's family with rights equivalent to those of his daughters (i.e., if he died intestate she succeeded as if she were an agnate). Everything she owned belonged to her husband, being counted as dowry, but any property, together with her dowry, had to be returned on divorce or the husband's death. If a wife was under her husband's manus, he could appoint a tutor for her in his will or allow her to choose one for herself. If there were children, the property was divided between widow and children equally. However, if they were married by free marriage, the wife did not inherit unless specific provisions were made in the will, and her property remained entirely separate from that of her husband.

108 Let us now consider persons who are in manus, which is another right peculiar to Roman citizens. **109** While both males and females are found in potestas, only females can come into manus. **110** In olden days, women passed into manus in three ways, by usus, confarreatio and coemptio. **111** A woman used to pass into her husband's manus by usus if she cohabited with him continuously for a year, the rationale being that she, as it were, had been acquired by usucapio through possession during one year and so passed into her husband's family, where she occupied the place of a daughter. Accordingly it was provided by the law of the XII Tables that any woman who did not wish to come into her husband's manus in this way should absent herself from him for three nights in each year and thus interrupt the usus during each year. But the whole of this institution has been abolished partly by statutes and partly by disuse.

112 Women come into the manus of their husbands by confarreatio, through a kind of sacrifice made to Jupiter Farreus, in which the spelt cake (*far*), from which the ceremony obtains its name, is employed. Additionally, in the course of the ceremony, many other rituals are performed and enacted, accompanied by special formal words, in the presence of ten witnesses. This institution is still in existence today, for the major flamens – that is, those of Jupiter, Mars and Quirinus, as well as the rex sacrorum – can be selected only from persons born of marriages celebrated by confarreatio. Further, these persons themselves cannot serve as priests unless they are married by confarreatio.

113 When women come into the manus of their husbands by coemptio, it takes the form of a mancipation, that is, a sort of fictitious sale, in which the man purchases the woman who comes into his manus in the presence of not fewer than five witnesses, who must be Roman citizens over the age of puberty, and also of a balance-holder.

114 Through this act of sale a woman can perform a coemptio not only with her husband but also with a stranger: that is to say, the coemptio takes place for the purpose of either marriage or a trust. A woman who disposes of herself in this way to her husband for the purpose of occupying the place of his daughter is said to have performed a coemptio for matrimonial purposes; but where she does this for some other purpose, either with a husband or with a stranger, for instance in order to avoid a guardianship, she is said to have made a coemptio for fiduciary purposes.

115 What takes place is as follows: if a woman wishes to get rid of her existing guardian and obtain another, she makes this coemptio of herself with their authority; her purchaser then sells her again to the person she chooses as her guardian, and he manumits her by the ceremony of the praetor, and by this means becomes her guardian. He is designated a fiduciary guardian, as shown below. **115a** Formerly fiduciary coemptio was performed for the purpose of acquiring power to make a will, for women, with certain exceptions, did not then have the right to make a will unless they had made a coemptio and been resold and manumitted . . . **115b** Even if a woman makes a fiduciary coemptio with her husband, she still occupies the place of his daughter; for if a wife comes into the manus of her husband for any reason whatsoever, it is accepted that she acquires the rights of a daughter.

136 A woman placed in the manus of her husband by confarreatio is not, for this reason, currently released from paternal potestas unless coemptio has been performed . . . However, a woman placed in the manus of her husband by coemptio is freed from her father's potestas; and it is the same whether she is placed in the manus of her husband or that of a stranger, although only those who are in the manus of their husbands are considered to occupy the place of daughters.

137 Women placed in the manus of their husbands by coemptio cease to be subject to this authority in the same way as daughters under their father's potestas – that is, either through the death of the person in whose power they are or because he has been forbidden water and fire (i.e., exiled).

137a They also cease to be in the manus of their husbands by a single mancipation; and if emancipated by a sale they become independent (*sui iuris*). A woman who has concluded a coemptio with a stranger can compel him to sell her again to anyone whom she chooses, but a woman who has been sold to her husband, in whose manus she is, cannot compel him to do so, any more than a daughter can compel her father, even if adopted. A woman, however, can, by serving notice of divorce, force her husband to release her, just as if she had never been married to him.

7.11 Aulus Gellius *Attic Nights* 17.6.1, 9–10: A wife's property

In his support for the Voconian law (169 BC, doc. 7.69), Cato criticises the economic power held by wives who are clearly not married in manu. The wife and husband's fortunes were entirely separate and the husband was not responsible for his wife's debts if she was not 'in manu'.

1 Marcus Cato, when supporting the Voconian law, spoke as follows: 'To start with, the woman brings a large dowry; then she retains a large sum of money, which she doesn't entrust to her husband's control but instead lends to him. Then, later on, when she is angry with him, she orders a slave of her own to follow him around and hound him for the money back . . . ' **9** So, from that property of her own, which she retained after the dowry was given, she lent her husband money. **10** When she happens to be angry with her husband, she appoints to dun him for it a slave of her own – that is, a slave in her possession whom she had kept back with the rest of the money and not given as part of her dowry, but retained; for it would be inappropriate for the woman to give such an order to her husband's slave, but only to her own.

7.12 Dionysius of Halicarnassus *Roman Antiquities* 2.25.6–27.1: Romulus' laws

Carvilius Ruga was not of course the first to divorce his wife, but it appears that this episode, in 231 BC, was the first legal case in Rome over the return of a wife's dowry. For the selling of sons into slavery, see doc. 1.34.

25.6 These offences (of a wife) were judged by her relatives together with her husband: among them were adultery and, what would seem to the Greeks to be the least of all faults, if a wife was found to have drunk wine. For Romulus allowed them to punish both these offences with death, as the worst crimes women could commit, considering adultery the beginning of madness and drunkenness of adultery. **7** And both these continued for a long time to be met by the Romans with implacable wrath. The length of time is witness to the excellence of the law concerning women. For it is agreed that in 520 years no marriage was dissolved at Rome; and in the 137th Olympiad, when Marcus Pomponius and Gaius Papirius were consuls (231 BC), the first man to divorce his wife was Spurius Carvilius, a man of distinction, who was compelled by the censors to swear that he had married his wife for the sake of children (his wife was barren), and who was hated for this deed by the people for ever after, although it was done out of necessity.

26.1 These, then, are the excellent laws which Romulus brought in regarding women, by which he made them behave better towards their husbands, but those which he introduced with regard to the respectful and dutiful behaviour of children, so that they should honour their parents by doing and saying whatever they might order them to do, were even more honourable and dignified than these and greatly superior to our own laws . . . **4** The Romans' law-giver granted the Roman father almost total power over his son, valid through the whole of his life, whether he chose to imprison him, to whip him, to put him in chains to work in the fields, or even to kill him, even if the son was already involved in public affairs, counted among the highest magistrates, and lauded for his zeal towards the state . . . **27.1** And the Romans' law-giver did not even stop the father's power at that point, but allowed the father to sell his son, without worrying whether this permission might be considered as cruel and harsher than natural affection would warrant. And – what anyone who has been educated in the relaxed customs of the Greeks would marvel at as savage and tyrannical – he even permitted the father to make a profit by selling his son up to three times, thus giving more power to a father over his son than to a master over his slaves.

7.13 Justinian *Digest* 17.24.1, 2, 10: Divorce

It appears that in the early Republic divorce was permitted only in specific cases (doc. 7.12). The XII Tables (4.3) recognised divorce, but there is no evidence on what grounds. Persons who were sui iuris could terminate their own marriage, but those in potestas needed the consent of their paterfamilias. A paterfamilias could bring about a son's divorce, even against his son's wishes.

(i) Paulus On the Edict *35*

Marriage is dissolved by divorce, death or captivity, or by any other kind of servitude which may happen to be imposed upon either of the parties.

(ii) Gaius On the Provincial Edict *11*

The word divorce is derived either from difference of opinion or because those who dissolve their marriage go different ways. **1** In cases of repudiation, that is to say, in renunciation of marriage, the following words are employed: 'keep your property' or 'keep the management of your property'. **2** For the purpose of dissolving betrothals, it is certain that a renunciation must be made, in which case the following words are used, namely: 'I will not accept your conditions.' **3** It makes no difference whether the renunciation takes place in the presence or in the absence of the person under whose control one of the parties may be, or of him who is under that control.

(iii) Modestinus Rules *1*

A freedwoman who has married her patron cannot divorce herself from him without his consent, unless she has been manumitted under the terms of a trust, and then she can do so even though she is his freedwoman.

OLD-FASHIONED FAMILIES

7.14 Valerius Maximus *On Memorable Deeds* 5.8.1–3: Traditional fathers

Here are three examples of severe fathers from 509, 485 and 140 BC. L. Junius Brutus was one of the Republic's first consuls, holding the office in 509 BC; Spurius Cassius was father of Sp. Cassius Vicellinus, consul (not tribune) in 486 (also in 502 and 493). Brutus, an example of parental severity, executed his son as consul, not as a father, and so did not consult a family consilium; T. Manlius Torquatus, as consul in 340 (doc. 7.15), put his son to death for disobeying orders. In this passage his descendant convicted his son of misgovernment in 140 BC and drove him to suicide.

1 Lucius Brutus' glory is equal to that of Romulus, since the latter founded the city, while the former established its freedom. While he held supreme authority, his sons attempted to restore the rule of Tarquin, whom he had himself driven out – he ordered that they be arrested, beaten with rods in front of the tribunal, tied to a stake, and beheaded with an axe. He divested himself of the role of father to take on that of consul and chose to live childless rather than to fail to exact public retribution. 2 Cassius emulated his example. When his son, Spurius Cassius, who, as tribune of the plebs, had been the first to propose agrarian legislation and gain popular support in many other ways, laid down his office, Cassius summoned a council of relatives and friends and condemned him in his house on the charge of aiming at kingship. He ordered him to be flogged and executed and dedicated his property to Ceres. 3 In a similar case Titus Manlius Torquatus, a man of unprecedented prestige on account of his many exceptional qualities, as well as highly knowledgeable in both civil law and priestly rituals, did not believe that he needed even a counsel of relatives and friends: for when Macedonia presented to the senate via envoys complaints against his son Decimus Silanus, who had governed that province, he asked the senators to come to no decision on that matter before he had himself looked into the case of the Macedonians and his son. Then, undertaking his inquiry with the fullest approval both of that most august order and of those who had come with the complaint, he sat in his house alone and for two whole days listening to both sides, and on the third day, after the most detailed and exhaustive hearing of witnesses, he gave his verdict as follows: 'Since it has been proved to my judgement that my son Silanus accepted bribes from our allies, I adjudge him unworthy of our state and of my house and command him immediately to leave my sight.' Shocked by his father's awful verdict, Silanus could not endure to look any longer on the light of day and killed himself by hanging the following night. Torquatus had now enacted the part of a severe and conscientious judge, the state had been satisfied, Macedonia had its revenge, and the father's severity could have been alleviated by the son's repentant death – but he did not take part in the young man's last rights, and, at the exact time when the funeral was being conducted, gave his attention to those wishing to consult him: for he saw that the mask of Torquatus the Imperious himself, conspicuous in its severity, was displayed in the very atrium in which he was sitting, and as a very sagacious

man he realised that the effigies of one's ancestors, with their designations, are usually placed in the first part of the house to ensure that their descendants should not only read of their virtues but imitate them.

7.15 Livy *History of Rome* 7.4.4–7: An imperious paterfamilias

Lucius Manlius 'Imperiosus' was dictator in 363 BC. His son grew up to be the famous Titus Manlius Torquatus, who as consul put his own son to death for disobeying orders in 340.

4 Among other charges, the tribune brought up Manlius' treatment of his son, who, though found guilty of no misconduct, had been banished from his city, home and household gods, from the forum, public view, and the company of his equals, and consigned to servile labour, all but in a prison or penitentiary, **5** where this young man of the highest rank and son of a dictator could learn by daily misery how truly 'imperious' his father was. And what was his fault? **6** That he was not sufficiently quick with words and not ready with his tongue! Should his father not have tried to help this natural infirmity, if he had any humanity in him, rather than chastising it and making it conspicuous by his persecution? . . . **7** But Lucius Manlius aggravated his son's difficulties by adding to them, putting heavier pressure on his natural backwardness, and, if there were any spark of natural ability in him, quenching it by his uncultivated lifestyle and rustic upbringing among cows and sheep.

7.16 Livy *History of Rome* 39.17.5–6, 18.5–6: The Bacchanalia

For the full narrative of the events of 186 BC, see doc. 3.65.

17.5 The names of many suspects were reported to the authorities, and some of these, both men and women, committed suicide. **6** More than 7,000 men and women were said to have been involved in the conspiracy . . . **18.5** More were killed than thrown into prison. There was an immense number of men and women in both categories. **6** Convicted women were handed over to their family, or to those whose authority they were under, so that these could punish them privately: if there was no appropriate person to exact the punishment, it was inflicted by the state.

7.17 Valerius Maximus *On Memorable Deeds* 6.3.8–9: Wife-beating

Both Publicia and Licinia were supposed to have poisoned their husbands and were put to death by their own relatives. This took place c. 154–150 BC. As with the Bacchanalia, it appears that husbands had no right to kill their wives without the consent of their blood relatives, even if they were only in manu. Wine-drinking by women was thought to lead to adultery (cf. docs 7.12, 18).

8 Publicia, who had poisoned her husband, the consul Postumius Albinus (cos. 154), and Licinia, who had done the same to her husband, Claudius Asellus, were strangled by the decree of their relatives: for those men of severity did not think that in so obvious a crime they should wait for a lengthy public enquiry. And so they made haste to punish the guilty, whom they would have defended had they been innocent. **9** Their severity was aroused to exact punishment by a great crime, that of Egnatius Mecennius, for a far slighter reason. He beat his wife to death with a cudgel because she had drunk some wine, and his action found no one to prosecute or even criticise it, for all the best men considered that the penalty she had paid to injured sobriety was a good precedent. For assuredly any woman who desires to drink wine without moderation closes the door to all virtues and opens it to all vices.

7.18 Aulus Gellius *Attic Nights* 10.23.1–5: Alcohol and adultery

This passage cites a speech of Marcus Porcius Cato the Elder. For adulterous wives and their punishments, see docs 7.42–46; Cato here highlights the double standards of morality in Rome.

1 Those who have written about the life and culture of the Roman people say that the women of Rome and Latium 'lived an abstemious life' – that is, that they always abstained from wine, which in the early language was called *temetum*, and that it was customary for them to kiss their relations for the purpose of detection, so that, if they had been drinking, the smell would give this away. **2** But they say that the women were accustomed to drink the second pressing, raisin wine, myrrhed wine and other drinks of that kind which taste sweet. **3** Indeed, these things are related in those books which I have mentioned, but Marcus Cato states that women were not only censured but also punished by a judge no less severely if they had drunk wine than if they had committed a heinous act such as adultery. **4** I have copied the words of Marcus Cato from his speech *On the Dowry*, in which it is also stated that husbands had the right to kill wives caught in adultery: 'When a husband', he says, 'divorces his wife, he judges the woman as a censor does, and has full powers if she has committed any wrong or disgraceful act; she is punished if she has drunk wine; if she has done wrong with another man, she is condemned to death.' **5** However, regarding the right to put her to death, he wrote as follows: 'If you should catch your wife in adultery, you may with impunity put her to death without a trial; but, if *you* should commit adultery or indecent acts, she should not dare to lay a finger on you, nor is it lawful.'

7.19 Livy *Periochae* 68: The parricide's punishment

The summary of Livy is presumably referring to the first historical occasion (in 101 BC) on which this punishment was inflicted; Tarquinius Superbus used this punishment for crimes against religion (doc. 3.38). The penalty for parricide was to be sewn alive in a sack with a dog, cock, ape and viper and thrown in the river.

Publicius Malleolus, who had killed his mother, was the first to be sewn up in a sack and thrown into the sea.

311

FAMILY RELATIONSHIPS

Child mortality in the first week of life was very high; as a result girls were not named until their eighth day, boys on their ninth, before which they were 'more like a plant than an animal' (Plut. *Rom. Quest.* 102). Perhaps some 25 to 30 per cent of those born alive died in their first year and 50 per cent before they were ten. Legally speaking, children under 12 months were not to be mourned. The XII Tables laid down that an especially deformed child was to be quickly killed (doc. 1.34). The poor were often constrained by poverty to abandon children: see doc. 8.10 for the poor before 133 BC. It was the father's decision whether to keep or abandon the new baby by 'picking him up' and thus accepting him into the family: see doc. 1.35.

7.20 Plutarch *Life of Cato the Elder* 17.7, 20.1–3: Cato's family

This provides an interesting sidelight on the austere Cato (234–149 BC): a reactionary, he represented old Roman virtues and respect for traditional practices. His wife was Licinia; for Cato's regulation of public morals as censor, cf. doc. 7.58.

17.7 Cato expelled another person from the senate who was thought to have a good chance of winning the consulship, Manilius, because he kissed his wife in daytime with his daughter watching. For his own part, he said, he never kissed his wife except during loud thunder; and it was a joke of his to say that he was a happy man when it thundered.

20.1 He was also a good father, a kindly husband, and a manager not easily to be despised, nor did he give only a subsidiary attention to this, as a matter of little or no importance. So I think I should recount appropriate episodes of his conduct in such matters. **2** He married a wife who was more well-born than rich, considering that, although both alike may possess dignity and pride, the high-born in their fear of disgrace are more obedient to their husbands in all that is honourable. **3** He used to say that the man who struck his wife or child laid hands on the most sacred of objects. He also used to say that he thought it was more praiseworthy to be a good husband than a great senator; and that there was nothing else to admire in Socrates in olden times except that he always treated his bad-tempered wife and stupid sons with kindness and gentleness.

7.21 Plutarch *Life of Cato the Elder* 20.4–7: Cato's son

Cato's history, the *Origines*, covered the history of towns in Italy, especially Rome. This was the first history of Italy in Latin; only fragments survive today.

4 Once his son was born, Cato considered no business so urgent, except government duties, as to prevent him from being there while his wife was bathing and swaddling the baby. **5** She nursed it with her own milk and often gave her breast to her slaves' infants, so that from this common nurture they should develop goodwill towards her son. And when the child was old enough to learn, Cato himself took him in hand and taught him to read, even though he had an accomplished slave, called Chilon, who was a teacher and had taught many boys; **6** Cato, however, did not think it right, as he himself says, for his son to be told off by a slave, or to have his ears pulled when he was slow at learning, or to owe so priceless a thing as his education to a slave. Therefore, he was himself his reading teacher, his law teacher, his athletics coach, teaching his son not only to hurl a javelin, fight in armour, and ride a horse but also to box, endure both heat and cold, and swim strongly through the eddies and surges of the river. **7** He also says that he wrote his history with his own hand and in large letters so his son might have the chance to become acquainted at home with Rome's ancestral traditions; and he states that he was careful to avoid indecent language no less in his son's presence than in that of the holy virgins who are called Vestals.

7.22 Cicero *Brutus* 210–11: Women's role as educators

See doc. 8.25 for fragments of a letter attributed to Cornelia. Laelia is the daughter of Gaius Laelius (cos. 140 BC and friend of Scipio Aemilianus). She married Q. Mucius Scaevola 'the Augur' (cos. 117). One of her daughters, the Muciae, married M'. Acilius Glabrio, the other Lucius Licinius Crassus (cos. 95); one of her granddaughters, the Liciniae, married P. Cornelius Scipio Nasica and was the mother of Q. Caecilius Metellus Pius Scipio (cos. 52).

210 It makes a great difference what kind of speakers one hears at home every day, the people whom one has been talking with from childhood, and the way in which fathers, tutors and even mothers speak. **211** I have read the letters of Cornelia, mother of the Gracchi; it is clear that her sons were not so much raised at her breast as through her conversation. I have often frequently heard Laelia, daughter of Gaius, speak; clearly her speech was coloured by her father's refinement, and I have also heard her daughters, both Muciae, whose speech I knew well, and her granddaughters the Liciniae, one of whom, the wife of Scipio, I expect you, Brutus, have also sometimes heard speak. 'Yes, with pleasure', replied Brutus, 'and the more so, as she was Lucius Crassus' daughter.'

7.23 *ILS* 8394: Eulogy for Murdia, a perfect mother

This first-century BC marble tablet in honour of Murdia records a funerary eulogy by the son of her first marriage. On her death she left her money to her second husband but ensured that her son by her first husband received the money she had inherited from his father and that all her sons were treated equally in her will.

She made all her sons equal heirs and gave her daughter a share. Her maternal love was demonstrated by her care for her children and their sharing equally. She left a specified sum to her husband so that the dowry, which was his right, should be increased by the acknowledgement of her good opinion. Recalling the memory of my father, and following the advice of that and her own trustworthiness, she left me a legacy after a valuation had been made, not to show preference for me over my brothers **10** and insult them but because, mindful of my father's generosity, she thought what she had, at her husband's discretion, received from my patrimony ought to be returned to me, so that, after preserving it in her *usus*, she might restore it to my ownership.

This was typical of her behaviour; she was married by her parents to worthy men; she safeguarded her marriages by her obedience and probity; as a wife, she was the more welcome for her merits, the more beloved for her fidelity, and left the more honoured for her discretion. After her death, she was unanimously praised by the citizens for the division of her property, which demonstrated her gratitude and trustworthiness towards her husbands, her fairness towards her children, and her genuine love of justice.

20 Eulogies of all good women are generally straightforward and similar to each other, because the innate merits women safeguard require very little variety of expression, and it is enough that all of them have behaved in the same way deserving of good repute. As it would be a hard task to discover new praises for a wife, since her life is troubled by less diversity, stock phrases have necessarily to be employed, in case any of the proper maxims be left out and discredit all the rest.

My mother, who was dearer to me than anything, deserved all the more praise for being the equal of all respectable women with regard to her modesty, probity, chastity, obedience, skill at wool-working, diligence and trustworthiness, nor was she second to anyone when her virtue, **30** industry and wisdom were put to the test, showing herself to be outstanding. . . .

7.24 *CIL* I² 1837: A beloved daughter

This epitaph was discovered at Monteleone; cf. doc. 3.42 for Aemilius Paullus and Tertia.

Posilla Senenia, daughter of Quartus, and Quarta Senenia, freedwoman of Gaius.
Stranger, stop and at the same time read through what is written here:
A mother was not permitted to enjoy her only daughter,
On whom some god or other, I believe, cast an evil eye.
Since it was not permitted for her to be adorned by her mother while she was
    alive,
She did this after her death, as was right, at the end of her time,
And honoured with a monument the girl whom she had loved.

7.25 *CIL* I² 1222: A beloved daughter (2)

A marble tablet found at Rome.

If anyone has a grief to add to mine,
Let him stand here and weep with not a few tears.
A sorrowful parent has here laid to rest his only daughter,
Nymphe, whom he cherished and enjoyed with tender love,
While the shortened time of the Fates allowed it.
She, so dear to her family, has now been snatched from her home and is cov-
    ered with earth.
Her lovely face and figure praised as lovely
Are all now insubstantial shadow and her bones just a little ash.

314

7.26 [Cicero] *Letters to his Friends* 4.5.1, 4–6: A letter of condolence

Tullia, Cicero's only daughter and eldest child, born sometime between 79 and 76/5 BC, was married to C. Calpurnius Piso Frugi between 63 and 58, to Furius Crassipes in 56 (divorced in 51), and then to P. Cornelius Dolabella in 50. Servius Sulpicius Rufus (governor of Greece) is writing a letter of condolence to Cicero in mid-March 45, on the death of Tullia after the birth of her second son by Dolabella: both boys subsequently died. Her death devastated Cicero.

Servius to Cicero, greetings.

1 After the news about the death of your daughter Tullia reached me, I was really, as I ought to have been, deeply and painfully sorry, and I felt that this calamity had struck us both. If I had been in Rome, I would have been with you and shown my grief to you in person. . . .

4 Recently, so many distinguished men died at the same time, so great a weakening of the power of the Roman state occurred, all our provinces were shaken to their depths; can you be moved so deeply by the loss of the poor soul of one poor woman? Even if she had not died now, she must nevertheless have died in a few years because she was mortal. **5** You too must remove your mind and your thought from these things and dwell instead on matters which are worthy of your character: that she lived as long as was good for her, that is, she lived while there was a Republic; she saw you, her father, praetor, consul and augur; she was married to young men from noble families; she enjoyed almost all of life's blessings; and, when the Republic died, she left life. How then, can you or she quarrel with Fortune on this account? . . .

6 There is no grief which the passage of time does not lessen or soften. It is unworthy of you to wait for the time to pass rather than anticipating it with your own good sense. If any consciousness remains in those below, her love for you and her dutiful devotion to all her family were such that she certainly does not wish you to act like this. Yield to your dead daughter, yield to others, your friends and family, who are distressed because of your grief, yield to your country so that, if need arises, it can use your service and counsel.

7.27 Cicero *Letters to Atticus* 12.46: Tullia's death

Tullia died at Cicero's villa at Tusculum in mid-February 45 BC, a month after giving birth to her second son. Cicero wrote this letter from his house at Lanuvium on 15 May 45.

I think I shall overcome my feelings and go from Lanuvium to Tusculum. For I must either give up my property there forever (since my sorrow will remain the same, although it may be better hidden) or else realise that it doesn't matter in the slightest whether I go there now or in ten years. Certainly it will not possibly remind me of her any more than do the thoughts that consume me perpetually, day and night. You will ask, 'Is there no help in books?' In this case, I am afraid, they actually make it worse; perhaps I would have been tougher without. For in an educated mind there is nothing rough or unfeeling.

WIVES AND THEIR ROLE

As with Murdia (doc. 7.23), stereotypes of women's epitaphs include the terms old-fashioned, domestic, chaste, obedient, charming, not extravagant or given to ornamentation, religious, and devoted to household work. The term univira (married to only one man) was a point of especial honour.

7.28 Cornelius Nepos *Great Generals* Preface 6–7: Roman versus Greek women

While the Roman matron might spend much of her time at home, she was not secluded there or kept from the sight of visitors.

6 Much of what we consider to be respectable the Greeks think to be disgraceful. What Roman, for example, would be embarrassed at taking his wife to a dinner party? What wife (materfamilias) does not hold the place of honour in her house and circulate in full public view? **7** Things are very different in Greece; there women are not admitted to dinner parties, except for ones with just family members, and she stays in the more retired part of the house called the 'women's apartments', to which no man has access unless he is a close relative.

7.29 Valerius Maximus *On Memorable Deeds* 6.7.1: A blind eye

A 'good' wife obviously considered it beneath her to comment on her husband's love affairs within the household (whether with male or female slaves); Aemilia is here unusual, not in the fact that she ignores the liaison, but because she rewards the girl of her own accord. Africanus died in 183 BC.

To touch on wifely fidelity too, Tertia Aemilia, wife of the elder Africanus and mother of Cornelia of the Gracchi, was so accommodating and forbearing that, although she knew that one of her slave girls was having an affair with her husband, she pretended not to know of it, so that she, a woman, should not accuse the great hero, conqueror of the world, of lack of self-control. And she was so little interested in revenge that, after Africanus' death, she freed the slave girl and married her to one of her own freedmen.

7.30 Pliny *Natural History* 7.120: Selecting the best

Sulpicia was chosen, c. 215 BC, as the most chaste woman in Rome, to dedicate a statue of Venus Verticordia, 'changer of hearts', which was erected to improve female morals; the festival day was 1 April. Claudia Quinta was accused of unchastity: in 204 a ship carrying the black stone of Cybele (the Magna Mater) from Pessinus to Rome was grounded, and the soothsayers announced that only a chaste woman could move it; Claudia was able to pull it free (cf. doc. 3.61).

The first time a woman was judged the most chaste by the vote of all the matrons was Sulpicia, daughter of Paterculus and wife of Fulvius Flaccus, who was selected from a previously chosen 100 to dedicate the statue of Venus in accordance with the Sibylline Books; and on another occasion, in a test of her piety, Claudia, when the Mother of the Gods was being brought to Rome.

7.31 *ILS* 8403: The perfect wife (1)

This epitaph is now lost, but it probably dates to 135–120 BC.

> Stranger, my message is short; stand by and read it through.
> This is the unlovely tomb of a lovely woman.
> Her parents gave her the name of Claudia.
> She loved her husband with her whole heart.
> She had two sons, of whom one
> She leaves on earth, the other she has placed under the earth.
> Her conversation was charming, yet her bearing correct.
> She kept the house, she made wool. I have spoken. Depart.

7.32 *ILS* 8398: The perfect wife (2)

Found at Rome, dating to the first century BC.

> Here lies the renowned, dutiful, virtuous, chaste
> And modest Sempronia Moschis,
> To whom thanks for her merits
> Are here returned by her husband.

7.33 *ILS* 7472: The perfect wife (3)

A stone slab now in the British Museum, found at Rome near the Via Nomentana. It dates to c. 80 BC; the couple were Greek ex-slaves who served the same family.

> Lucius Aurelius Hermia, freedman of Lucius, a butcher on the Viminal Hill.
> She who preceded me in death, my only wife, chaste in body, a loving woman
> possessed of my heart, lived faithful to her faithful husband. Equal in devotion,
> she never in bitter times shrank from her duties.
> Aurelia, freedwoman of Lucius.

> Aurelia Philematium ('Little Kiss'), freedwoman of Lucius.
> In life I was called Aurelia Philematium,
> Chaste and modest, not knowing the crowd, faithful to my husband.
> My husband was a fellow freedman, whom I've now lost, alas!,
> And was in real truth more than a father to me.
> He took me to his bosom when I was seven years old,
> And at the age of forty I am in death's power.
> He always flourished through my constant care. . . .

317

7.34 Catullus 96: Calvus and Quintilia

Gaius Licinius Calvus, an orator and poet, was a friend of Catullus and a colleague of Cicero (Cic. *Fam.* 15.21.4). Poems 14 and 50 are also addressed to Calvus.

> If anything welcome or acceptable from our grief
> Is able to reach the dumb grave, Calvus,
> By the longing with which we renew our old loves
> And weep for friendships lost in times past,
> Surely Quintilia does not grieve so much for her premature death
> As much as she rejoices in your love.

7.35 Plutarch *Life of Julius Caesar* 5.1–5: Eulogies for Caesar's women

Caesar had previously refused to divorce his first wife, Cornelia, daughter of Cinna, despite Sulla's orders. Both his aunt Julia (the widow of Marius; doc. 9.5) and his wife died in 69 BC. The first person to deliver a eulogy for a woman was Q. Lutatius Catulus (cos. 102), for his mother Popilia. The next were for Caesar's wife and aunt.

1 The first proof Caesar received of the people's goodwill towards him was when he competed for the post of military tribune against Gaius Popilius and was elected (for 71 BC). **2** A second and much clearer proof was when, after the death of his aunt Julia, the wife of Marius, he delivered a brilliant eulogy of her in the forum and was daring enough to bring out in the funeral procession images of Marius, which were then seen for the first time since Sulla's regime, when the Marians had been declared public enemies.

3 Some people cried out against Caesar for this, but the populace answered them enthusiastically, welcomed Caesar with applause, and admired him for having brought back into the city after so long, as if from the dead, the honours due to Marius. **4** It was an ancient Roman tradition to give funeral orations for older women, but it was not customary for young women, and Caesar was the first to make a funeral oration when his own wife died. **5** This also brought him popular favour and gained the sympathies of the populace, who loved him as a tender-hearted man, full of feeling.

7.36 Cicero *Letters to his Friends* 14.1.1: Cicero to Terentia

Cicero divorced Terentia for extravagance and dishonesty in 46 BC after a marriage lasting some 33 years. This letter was written to her in mid-November 58 BC after he was exiled in November 58 and shows his affection for Terentia and their daughter. Numerous affectionate letters are addressed to her during this period.

Many people's letters and everyone's conversation tell me about your amazing courage and fortitude, and that you are not exhausted by your hardships of mind and body. Woe is me! That you, with such courage, loyalty, probity and generosity, should have fallen into such great tribulations on my account! And that our darling Tullia should receive such grief from a father in whom she used to take such delight! . . .

7.37 *ILS* 8393: the Laudatio 'Turiae'

An inscription discovered in Rome, which presents an oration in a deceased wife's honour, probably delivered over the grave. Cicero records that families preserved funeral orations, as they did ancestral masks (imagines): *Brut.* 61. The woman is known as 'Turia' because of a conjectured identification with the wife of Quintus Lucretius Vespillo (perhaps cos. 19 BC). The inscription is evidence for women's involvement in legal and political issues, since it appears that, after her father and mother had been murdered in 49, she brought the killers to justice, secured her inheritance, and saved her husband during the proscriptions of the Second Triumvirate (docs 14.20).

I.3 You were suddenly orphaned before the day of our marriage, when both your parents were murdered together in a lonely part of the countryside. It was mainly through you, since I was on my way to Macedonia and **5** your sister's husband Gaius Cluvius on his way to the province of Africa (49 BC), that the death of your parents did not go unavenged. You put so much energetic work into this act of duty in asking questions and demanding punishment that we would not have been able to do any more, even had we been there. The credit is due to you and that most devoted lady your sister.

10 While you were involved in this and ensured that the guilty be punished, you left your father's house in order to protect your virtue and took yourself to my mother's house, where you awaited my return. Both of you were then pressured to state that your father's will, in which we were the heirs, had been invalidated, since he had married his wife by coemptio, which would have made it necessary for you, with all your father's property, to pass into the guardianship of those who were **15** bringing the case. Your sister would have got no share at all, because she had passed into the manus of Cluvius, and, although I was not there, I heard about the courage with which you heard their proposals and the presence of mind with which you resisted them.

18 You defended our common interests by the truth: that the will had not been invalidated, and in order that we both be the heirs, rather than you alone possess-ing the entire property, you were determined to **20** uphold your father's actions in the same way that, if you had not won your point, you intended to share with your sister and were not going to let yourself pass into the guardianship of someone who had no legal right over you, and for whom no relationship of clan (gens) with your own family could be proved, which might force you to do that. For even if your father's will had been invalidated, nevertheless that right did not belong to those who claimed it, since they did not belong to the same clan. **25** Because of your persistence they gave up and did not take the case any further; by this deed of duty towards your father, devotion towards your sister, and loyalty to me, you single-handedly succeeded in the defence you had undertaken.

27 Marriages of such length, which are ended by death and not broken by divorce, are rare. In our case our marriage lasted till its forty-first year, without a disagreement. Would that the final ending had come about through me instead, since it would have been more appropriate for me, as the elder, to yield to fate!

30 Why should I mention your domestic virtues – your modesty, obedience, kindliness, good nature, dedication to wool-making, piety without superstition, inconspicuous dress and understated elegance. Why speak about your affection for your relatives and your devotion towards your family, for you looked after my mother just like you did your own parents and gave her the same care, you who have innumerable other merits which you share with all matrons who care for their reputation? The merits which I claim for you are your very own, and few women have encountered such situations **35** in which they have had to undergo such trials or demonstrate such merits: fortunately fate has ensured that women rarely face these.

37 We have preserved all the patrimony you received from your parents with mutual diligence, for you did not want to make your own what you had transferred completely to me. We divided our duties so that I had guardianship of your property, and you the preservation of mine. On this subject I shall omit much so that I do not take a share in what is properly yours – **40** let it be enough that I have indicated your feelings on this matter.

42 Your generosity has been demonstrated both to your numerous intimates and especially to your beloved family. One could praise by name other women on this same count, but your sister is the only real equal you have had, for you brought up your own female relatives **45** who deserved such treatment in our own household. So that they might make marriages worthy of your family, you presented them with dowries, and when you had decided on these I and Gaius Cluvius by common consent took it upon ourselves to pay them, as we approved of your generosity, but so that your patrimony did not suffer we made use of our own properties and gave our own estates as dowries. I have not mentioned this to glorify ourselves, but so it is clear **50** that we considered it a matter of honour to carry out the plans which stemmed from your liberality and devotion to your family.

52 I have decided to pass over many other examples of your generosity . . . (several lines missing)

II.2 You provided many kinds of immense support during my exile and bestowed ornaments on me when you gave me gold and jewellery taken from your body, and then, after outwitting the guards posted by our opponents, continually enriched my absence with slaves, money and provisions. **6** Your courage urged you to beg for my life in my absence, and, overcome by your words, the clemency of those for whom you prepared them protected me. Whatever you said was always uttered with firmness of mind. **8** Meanwhile, when a troop of men collected by Milo, whose house I had purchased when he was in exile, tried to make the most of the opportunities of civil war to break in and loot, you successfully resisted and defended our house . . . (several lines missing)

11 . . . that I was brought back to my homeland by him, for, if you had not by taking care for my safety kept something he might save, he would have promised his help in vain. And so I owe my life no less to your devotion than to Caesar.

14 Why should I now reveal our private and secret plans and personal conversations – how I was saved by your advice when I was called by unexpected reports to face present and imminent dangers? How you did not allow me imprudently to risk the situation too rashly, but when I took a more sensible approach prepared a safe hiding place for me and selected as assistants in your plans to save me your sister and her husband Gaius Cluvius, all united in taking the risk? There would be no end **20** if I tried to give all the details – it is enough for me and for you that I was hidden in safety.

21 I declare, however, the bitterest event that ever happened to me in my life is the way you were treated when I had returned home as a citizen through the good-will and judgement of the absent Caesar Augustus, when his colleague Marcus Lepidus, who was in Rome, was troubled by you over my recall, when you threw yourself to the ground at his feet and were not only raised up but **25** dragged away forcibly like a slave. Though your body was covered in bruises, your spirit was quite undaunted, and you continued to urge him about Caesar's edict and his pleasure at my recall – even when you had heard the most insulting words and suffered cruel wounds, you openly persisted so it should be apparent who was the person responsible for my perils. This was soon to be damaging to him. **29** What could have been more effective than courage like this – to present Caesar with the opportunity for clemency, while, together with protecting my life, branding Lepidus' hateful cruelty with your outstanding endurance?

32 Why should I continue? Let us spare my speech, which should and can be brief, so that, in narrating your very great deeds, I should treat them less worthily than they deserve, when in demonstrating your services to me I present to the eyes of all commemoration of a life saved.

35 With the world pacified and the state restored, then peaceful and happy times came upon us. We wanted to have children, which some fate begrudged us. If Fortune had agreed to continue to look on us favourably, what could either of us have wanted? But it continued otherwise and put an end to our hopes. What you undertook to do for this reason, and the measures you attempted to take might perhaps have been outstanding and praiseworthy in some women, **40** but in you were not especially remarkable when compared to your other virtues, and I will pass over them. **41** You despaired over your lack of fertility and grieved because of my lack of children, in case by remaining married to you I would lose the hope of having children and be miserable for that reason; so you spoke of divorce and suggested handing over our empty household to another woman who was fertile, and that you would yourself find and **45** arrange for me someone worthy of our well-known love; you declared that you would treat future children as joint and as your own and would not divide up our inheritance, which until now had been held in common: it would remain, if I wanted, under my control and, if I wished, under your management. You would have nothing kept apart or separated from me, and you would from now on perform the duties and role of my sister or my mother-in-law.

50 I have to admit that I was so infuriated that I lost my mind and was so horrified by your suggestions that I could hardly regain control of myself. How could you consider a separation before it was dictated by fate! How could your mind even conceive any reason that, while still alive, you should cease to be my wife, you who had remained so loyal to me when I was in exile and all but dead! How could the desire or need for children be so great that I would consequently **55** break faith with you, that I would change certainties for doubts? But why continue? You stayed with me; for I could not have given in to you without disgrace to myself and misery for us both. But, for your part, what have you done more worthy of praise than the effort you made in your sense of duty towards me that, as I could not have children by yourself, you wanted me to have them through your agency and that, in your despair of bearing children, **60** you should make available to me the fertility of another wife?

62 If only the lifetimes of each of us had permitted our marriage to continue until I, as the elder, as would have been more fair, was carried out for burial, and you had performed my last rites, and that I had died leaving you as the survivor to be my daughter in place of my childlessness! **64** Fate decreed that you should precede me. You left me grief through my longing for you but did not leave me children to comfort me in my loneliness. But I, too, shall moderate my feelings in accordance with your judgement and shall follow your advice.

66 Let all your opinions and prescriptions give way to your praises, so these may be my comfort and prevent me from yearning too much for what I have consecrated to immortality for eternal remembrance. What you achieved in life will not be lost to me, and, fortified by the thought of your renown and instructed by your actions, may I oppose Fortune, which has not robbed me of everything **70** since it has allowed your memory to blossom through praise. But with you I have lost my state of repose, and when I think of you, my sentinel and first defence against dangers, I break down under the calamity and cannot keep to my promise. Natural sorrow deprives me of my power of self-control; I am overwhelmed by grief and cannot stand my ground against either the grief or fear that torment me. When I look back to my previous misfortunes and envisage what the future may have in store, **75** deprived as I am of such great and valuable protection, my courage fails, and as I gaze on your reputation I do not so much have the strength to endure as seem destined to longing and sorrow.

77 The conclusion of my oration will be this: you deserved everything, but I was never able to give you everything as I should. I have considered your commands as my law. I will continue to do for you whatever else I still can. **79** I pray that your departed spirit lets you rest and so watches over you.

MARITAL DISCORD

According to Gellius (1.6.1–6), Metellus Numidicus (cos. 102 BC) urged men to marry, saying that, 'If we were able to exist without wives, fellow Romans, we would all be free from that troublesome matter; but since nature has so ordained that it is impossible to live very comfortably with them, and utterly impossible to live without them, we must consider our long-term welfare rather than our short-term pleasure.' Spurius Carvilius Ruga was supposedly the first to divorce his wife (for childlessness), c. 231 (doc. 7.12). This was a new kind of divorce with the return of the dowry and without laying criminal blame on the wife. Unhappy marriages are attested, such as that of Scipio Aemilianus and Sempronia, sister of the Gracchi (docs 8.21, 7.39).

7.38 Caecilius Statius *Plocium* 136–55: A domineering wife

Caecilius was a Gaul brought to Rome c. 195 BC; he died in 168. A friend of Ennius, he wrote comedies from Greek models (fabulae palliatae).

A.   Indeed, he is a wretch who doesn't know how to hide his misery
        Out of doors; for my wife, even if I keep quiet, gives the game away by her
            looks and actions –
        My wife, who has everything you don't want – except a dowry.
        Anyone who's wise will learn from me . . .
        While I long for her death, I live as a corpse among the living.
        She says that I secretly consorted with my maidservant; that's what she charges
            me with,
        And so by begging, and pleading, and threatening, and scolding she forced me
        To sell her.

B.   But, tell me, is your wife bad-tempered?
A.   Well, what a question!
B.   Well, how then?
A.   It upsets me just talking about it!
        Whenever I come home and sit beside her, the first thing she does
        Is give me a kiss with that awful breath of hers.
B.   She makes no mistake with that kiss –
        She wants you to vomit up what you've been drinking outside.

7.39 Cicero *Letters to Atticus* 5.1.3–4: A quarrelsome wife

Written at Minturnae, 5/6 May 51 BC. Pomponia, sister of Cicero's friend Atticus, was married to Cicero's brother Quintus. The couple were clearly experiencing difficulties because of expenditure and Quintus' dependence on his freedman Statius (see docs 5.66, 6.51, 53). They divorced in 44.

3 Now I come to the line written crossways at the end of your letter, in which you mention your sister. These are the facts of the case. When I reached Arpinum, and my brother met me, we first had a long talk about you. I then brought the conversation round to the discussion you and I had about your sister at Tusculum. I have never seen anything gentler or kinder than my brother's behaviour at that time towards your sister, which was such that, if there was any quarrel about expenditure, there were no signs of it. So passed that day. On the next day we left Arpinum. Quintus had to stay at Arcanum for a festival, while I went to Aquinum, but we lunched at Arcanum. You know his property there. When we arrived, Quintus said most politely, 'Pomponia, you invite the women and I'll ask the men.' Nothing, as far as I could see, could have been gentler than his words or his intention and expression. But she, in everyone's hearing, said, 'Oh, but I'm just a stranger here!' I suppose because Statius had been sent ahead to see to the arrangements for our lunch. Then Quintus said to me, 'There! I have to put up with that every day!'

4 You will say, 'So, what's wrong with that?' A lot! She really upset me, she answered with such unnecessary rudeness in word and look. I hid my annoyance and we all took our places except her. Quintus sent her some food from the table: she refused it. In short, it seemed to me that nothing could have been more tolerant than my brother and nothing more rude than your sister; and I have passed over many incidents that upset me more than they did Quintus. I then went on to Aquinum. Quintus stayed at Arcanum and met me the next morning and told me that she had refused to sleep with him and that, when she was leaving, she was as bad-tempered as when I had seen her. Actually, you may tell her that in my opinion she behaved with a total lack of courtesy that day.

7.40 Cicero *Letters to his Friends* 14.20: His last letter to Terentia

This is Cicero's last extant letter to Terentia, written in October 47. Following his divorce in 45, after 33 years of marriage, Cicero married his ward Publilia, mainly for her money. He divorced her the next year because she showed little grief at Tullia's death. The tub (labrum) was a large container in which the bathers washed before immersing themselves.

I think I shall arrive at the Tuscan estate either on the Nones (the 7th) or the day after. See that everything is got ready. I will perhaps have several others with me and I expect that we shall stay there for a considerable time. If there is no tub in the bath, see that there is one – the same regarding everything else necessary for life and health. Goodbye. 1 October, Venusia.

7.41 Valerius Maximus *On Memorable Deeds* 2.1.6: A consultation for marital harmony

Viriplaca, 'pleaser of men', was an epithet of the goddess Juno, goddess of marriage.

Whenever there was some little argument between husband and wife, they used to go to the shrine of the goddess Viriplaca on the Palatine hill. There each in turn stated what they wanted; and, after they had put aside their quarrelsome feelings, they went back home in harmony. The goddess is said to have obtained this name because of her power to placate husbands; she certainly deserves to be venerated and honoured with some outstanding and exceptional sacrifices as the guardian of peace in everyday and household affairs, who by her very title grants the respect owed by wives to the superior rank of husband within the yoke of equal affection.

ADULTERY, CONSPIRACY AND SORCERY

The husband, or the wife's father, was allowed to kill the wife if caught in the act of adultery (doc. 7.18), while the seducer could be punished by whipping, castration or rape. Before Augustus (doc. 15.25), the seduction of wives and daughters was the concern of the family, though a number of public trials are recorded, presumably where there were no male relatives to take action.

7.42 Livy *History of Rome* 8.18.2–11: Sorceresses anonymous

This story, which Livy affects to disbelieve, took place in the context of a bad plague in 331 BC. As with the Bacchanalia, women are shown as 'out of control' (see docs 7.16–17). Only those who had no kinsfolk were punished by the state. While this story is probably apocryphal, adultery and poisoning were linked in the Roman mind.

2 One thing, however, I should be glad to believe has been falsely handed down – and not all the authorities mention it – namely that those whose deaths made the year notorious for the plague were in fact killed by poison; **3** still, I must set down the story as it has been handed down, lest I destroy confidence in any of my sources. **4** When leading citizens were suffering from the same kind of disease which ended in nearly every case with their death, a certain maidservant came to Quintus Fabius Maximus, the curule aedile, and declared that she would reveal the cause of this general pestilence if she were given a promise by him that her evidence would not injure her. **5** Fabius immediately referred the matter to the consuls, and they to the senate, and with its agreement the promise was made to the informer. **6** She then disclosed that the city was suffering from the crimes of its women, and that these poisons were being prepared by married women who could be caught in the act if they were willing to follow her at once. **7** They followed the informer and found certain women brewing poisons and others that were stored away. **8** These were brought to the forum, and some twenty matrons in whose houses they had been found were summoned there by an apparitor. Two of these, Cornelia and Sergia, both from patrician families, asserted that they were salutary medicines, but when the informer refuted this and told them to drink and prove her wrong in the sight of all, **9** they took time to confer, and when the crowd had been sent away referred the question to the rest; finding that, like themselves, they would not refuse to drink, they swallowed down the poison, and all perished by their own evil practices. **10** Their attendants were immediately arrested and informed against a large number of married women, of whom 170 were found guilty. **11** Before that day there had never been a trial for poison in Rome.

7.43 Valerius Maximus *On Memorable Deeds* 6.1.12–13: Punishments for adultery

Most of those mentioned below are unknown; Memmius was married to Sulla's daughter Fausta, whom he divorced in 55 BC; for Lusius, see doc. 7.59.

12 The general Gaius Marius pronounced Gaius Lusius, his sister's son and military tribune, rightly killed by Gaius Plotius, a private soldier, because he had dared to solicit him sexually. **13** But to run through those who in avenging chastity made their own injury into a stand for public law: Sempronius Musca whipped Gaius Gallius, whom he had caught in adultery, with lashes; Gaius Memmius beat Lucius Octavius, caught under the same circumstances, with thigh bones; Carbo Attienus and Pontius were seized and castrated by Vibienus and Publius Cerennius, respectively; the man who seized Gnaeus Furius Brocchus gave him to his slaves to be raped. None of these suffered a penalty for indulging their anger.

7.44 Sallust *The Catilinarian Conspiracy* 24.3–25.5: An unconventional woman

Sempronia, wife of Decimus Junius Brutus (cos. 77 BC), is an example of an educated aristocratic woman in the republic; she was one of Catiline's adherents in 63. This passage demonstrates the independence open to noble women. For the negative connotations of dancing, see doc. 8.20.

24.3 At that time (the news that Cicero and Antonius were to be consuls for 63) Catiline is said to have gained numerous supporters of every class, and even of some women who had at first supported their excessive extravagance by prostitution and then, when their age put an end to their income, though not their luxurious tastes, had piled up huge debts. **4** With their help, Catiline believed, he would be able to rouse the city slaves to his side and set fire to the city, and either get their husbands to join him or murder them.

    25.1 Now among their number was Sempronia, a woman who had often committed many crimes of masculine daring. **2** In birth and beauty, as well as in her husband and children, the woman had been well gifted by fortune. Well educated in Greek and Latin literature, she was more skilled at playing the lyre and dancing than a respectable women need be, having many other accomplishments which minister to extravagant tastes. **3** But there was nothing that she valued less than decency and chastity; you would find it difficult to say whether she was less sparing of her money or her reputation; her desires were so ardent that she more often made advances to men than they did to her. **4** Even before this she had often broken her word, repudiated debts on oath, and been an accessory to murder; extravagance and poverty combined had sent her headlong. **5** Nevertheless, her talents were not negligible; she could write poetry, crack jokes, and converse with modesty, tender feeling or wantonness; in fact she possessed great wit and considerable charm.

7.45 Suetonius *Life of the Deified Julius* 50.1–2: Caesar's love-life

Suetonius also relates Caesar's affairs in Gaul and the queens who had been his mistresses. Eunoe, wife of Bogudes, was supposed to be one and Cleopatra another (52.1). Servilia, wife first of M. Junius Brutus and then of D. Junius Silanus (cos. 62 BC), was Cato the Younger's older half-sister and mother of M. Junius Brutus. In Greek myth, Aegisthus was the lover of Clytemnestra, wife of Agamemnon.

1 It is generally believed that Caesar was much disposed to love affairs and to extravagant behaviour within these affairs, and that he seduced a great many well-born women, among them Postumia, wife of Servius Sulpicius, Lollia, wife of Aulus Gabinius, Tertulla, wife of Marcus Crassus, and even Gnaeus Pompey's wife, Mucia. Certainly Pompey was reproached by both Curio the Elder and Curio the Younger and many others for having married Caesar's daughter for political gain, when it was on Caesar's account, whom Pompey had often named in his laments as 'Aegisthus', that he divorced his wife after she had given him three children.

2 But above all others he loved Marcus Brutus' mother Servilia the best, and in his first consulship he bought her a pearl worth 6,000,000 sesterces, and gave her many presents during the civil war, as well as letting her buy certain lavish estates at auction for a trifle; when many wondered at the low price, Cicero quipped: 'It was an even better bargain than you think, because a third (tertia) was discounted' – Servilia, you see, was also thought at the time to be prostituting her daughter Tertia to Caesar.

7.46 Catullus 67: A front door tells all

A dialogue with the front door of a house in Verona reveals the gossip relating to the household, especially the fact that the new bride, after earlier indiscretions, was no virgin and had been seduced by her father-in-law.

Catullus
    Dear to a beloved husband and pleasing to his father,
    Greetings, and may Jupiter preserve you with kindly help,
    House door, whom they say used once to do kind service to Balbus,
    When the old man himself owned the house,
    And which they say since then has been doing evil service to his son,
    Now the old man's been laid out and you've become the door of married people.
    Come, tell us why you're said to have changed
    And abandoned your old loyalty to your master.
House door
    It is not (so may I please Caecilius, to whom I've been handed over)
10   My fault, though it is said to be mine,
    Nor can anyone speak of any wrong done by me:
    But people will say that the door does it;
    Whenever any ill deed is discovered
    They all shout at me, 'Door – it's your fault!'
Catullus
    It's not enough for you to say it with a single word,
    But to do it so that anyone may know and see it.
House door
    How can I? No one asks or is concerned to know.
Catullus
    I want to know: don't hesitate to tell me.

House door
First then, that she was handed over to us a virgin, as is said,
20   Is a lie. It was not her husband who was the first to touch her
Whose 'little dagger' hangs more listless than a young beetroot
And never erects itself to mid-tunic.
Instead his father is said to have dishonoured his son's bed
And polluted the wretched house;
Either because his impious mind burned with blind lust,
Or because the son was impotent, with barren seed,
So they had to find one more vigorous
Who could unloose her maiden tie.

Catullus
You speak of a father distinguished by remarkable affection,
30   Who comes in the lap of his own son.

House door
And yet Brixia under the cliffs of Cycnea,
Brixia, which golden Melo runs through with its soft stream,
Brixia, beloved mother of my own Verona,
Says he isn't the only one known to have had her;
But she tells about Postumius and the love of Cornelius,
With whom she was involved in wicked adultery.

Catullus
Here someone might say, 'What? How do you, door, know all this?
You who are never allowed to be away from your master's threshold,
Nor to listen to the people, but fixed under this lintel
40   Are only accustomed to close and open the house?'

House door
I have often heard her talking in a secretive voice
Alone with her maids about these crimes of hers,
Speaking by name of those of whom I spoke, as if
She thought that I had neither tongue nor ear.
Moreover, she added someone, whom I don't want to mention
By name, lest he should raise his red eyebrows.
He is a tall man, once troubled by a great lawsuit
About a false womb and a lying pregnancy.

HETEROSEXUAL LOVE: CATULLUS AND LESBIA

'Lesbia' has generally been supposed to have been the pseudonym of Clodia Metelli, one of the three sisters of the tribune P. Clodius Pulcher. This Claudia (Clodia) was married to Quintus Caecilius Metellus Celer (cos. 60 BC). Metellus died in March 59, and shortly afterwards Clodia is supposed to have begun an affair with M. Caelius Rufus. In April 56 Clodia Metelli was in court as a witness against Caelius, whom she claimed owed her money. Cicero, who defended him, concentrates on a character assassination of Clodia as an ageing prostitute who might have poisoned her husband, and who had an incestuous relationship with her brother. Lesbia, however, is probably a poetic construct, compiled from stereotypes of Roman women rather than a real-life lover of Catullus.

7.47 Catullus 7: An idyllic relationship

In Roman eyes this picture of Catullus would have been uncontrolled and inappropriate, and the poem is deliberately intended to shock his readership.

> You ask how many kissings of you,
> Lesbia, will be enough and to spare.
> As great a number as the grains of Libyan sand
> That lie on silphium-bearing Cyrene,
> 5 Between the desert oracle of Jupiter Ammon
> And the sacred tomb of legendary Battus,
> Or as many as are the stars, in the silent night,
> That see men's clandestine loves –
> To kiss you with so many kisses
> 10 Is enough and to spare for your infatuated Catullus,
> Which busybodies could not count up
> Nor an evil tongue bewitch.

7.48 Catullus 85: Love and hate

> I hate and love. Why I do so, perhaps you will ask.
> I do not know, but I feel it to be so, and I am in torment.

7.49 Catullus 43: A less than gallant address

Catullus also addresses Mamurra's girlfriend, Amaena, in poem 41, where she propositions him for the price of 10,000 sesterces. Clearly the poem is yet another attack on Caesar's architect Mamurra: cf. poems 29 and 57 (doc. 12.89).

> Greetings, girl without a tiny nose
> Without a pretty foot or black eyes
> Or long fingers or a dry mouth,
> Not to mention, in truth, a tongue of minimal refinement,
> 5 Lady friend of the bankrupt of Formiae (Mamurra).
> Are you beautiful, as the province (Cisalpine Gaul) declares?
> Is our Lesbia compared with you?
> O what a world! So stupid! So undiscriminating!

7.50 Catullus 45: Septimius and Acme

Septimius is not known, but the name Acme suggests a Greek freedwoman. In Roman divination the left was the fortunate side, while in Greek the right was favourable; for Roman divination, see docs 3.37–54.

> Septimius, holding his love Acme in his arms, says, 'My Acme,
> If I do not love you desperately and if I am not prepared to go on loving you
>   everlastingly all my years

5   As much as the most devoted of lovers ever could, may I in Libya or parched
        India
     Encounter on my own a green-eyed lion.' As he said this, Love, on the left, as
        before
     On the right, sneezed approbation. Then Acme, slightly tilting her head
11   And kissing the love-drunk eyes of her sweet boy with those rosy lips,
     Says, 'As I hope, my life, my dear Septimius, that we may to the end serve
        this one master,
15   The passion that burns in my tender marrow is far greater and fiercer than in
        yours.'
     As she said this, Love, as before on the left, sneezed approbation on the right.
     Now starting with a good omen, they love and are loved with interchanged hearts.
21   Poor love-sick Septimius prefers Acme to any Syria or Britain:
     In Septimius alone his faithful Acme takes her pleasure and desires.
     Who ever saw people more blessed? Who ever saw a more auspicious love?

7.51 Catullus 58: Disenchantment

Many of Catullus' poems to Lesbia are works of invective, accusing her of deceit and
shameful affairs with others: cf. poems 11, 37 and 36 (where Lesbia, 'my girl', wants him
to stop writing invective against her).

     Caelius, my Lesbia, well-known Lesbia,
     Lesbia whom Catullus alone loved
     More than himself and all his own,
     Now in the street-corners and alley-ways
     Performs oral sex with the descendants of high-minded Romulus.

7.52 Cicero *In Defence of Caelius* 32–35, 47–49: Lesbia by another name

Clodia was, according to Cicero, one of the forces behind Calpurnius Bestia's prosecution of Marcus Caelius Rufus on a charge of attempted murder and robbery in 56 BC;
49: Lucius Herennius Balbus was one of the prosecutors. Cicero shows Caelius as a
naive, pleasure-loving young man and Clodia as a seductress and quasi-prostitute. Appius
Claudius Caecus, her ancestor, was censor in 312 and consul in 307 and 296. Baiae was a
fashionable resort and spa near Cumae.

32 And indeed I never thought I should have to engage in quarrels with women,
especially with one whom all have generally considered to be a 'friend' to everyone rather than anyone's enemy. **33** But first I will ask her whether she prefers me
to deal with her severely, solemnly, and in an old-fashioned way or indulgently,
mildly and politely. If in that serious traditional fashion I will have to raise up from
the dead one of those bearded men of old, not with a little trimmed beard, such as
she takes delight in, but with one of those rough ones, as seen on old statues and
busts, who can rebuke the woman and speak on my behalf, so she may perhaps not

be enraged with me. Let me conjure up, therefore, some member of her own family, and particularly the venerable Appius Claudius the Blind (Caecus) – for he will feel less sorrow than anyone else because he will not be able to see her. **34** If he should appear, this is certainly how he would speak and what he would say: 'Woman, what business have you with Caelius, who is a young man and unrelated to you? Why have you been so friendly with him that you lend him gold, or so hostile that you are afraid of poison? Have you not seen that your father, have you not heard that your uncle, your grandfather, your great-grandfather, your great-great-grandfather and your great-great-great-grandfather were consuls? Finally, did you not know that you were recently married to Q. Metellus, an illustrious and courageous man, totally committed to his country, who had only to set foot out of doors to surpass almost all his fellow citizens in excellence, reputation and rank? When you had married from a house of the greatest importance into a most illustrious family, why was Caelius so closely linked with you? Was he a blood relative? A marriage connection? A close friend of your husband? He was none of these things. What therefore could it have been except some uncontrollable passion?'

35 As for you, woman (for now it is I and not a fictional person who is addressing you), if you plan to prove the truth of what you did, said, asserted, designed and alleged, you will need to account for and explain the reason for such familiarity, such intimacy, such a close friendship. Indeed, the prosecutors are hurling at us the words debauchery, love-affairs, adultery, Baiae, beach resorts, dinner parties, revels, singing, music, boat trips, and at the same time tell us that all this is said with your approval. And since in some kind of mad and reckless frame of mind you have wanted all these matters to be brought into the forum and the court, you must either disprove them, and demonstrate them to be untrue, or admit that neither your accusation nor your evidence is to be believed . . .

47 So, does that well-known neighbourhood not put us on the scent? Does general rumour, does Baiae itself tell us nothing? Baiae not only tells us something, it even resounds with the news that the passions of one woman are so degraded that she not only does not seek privacy and darkness and such veils for disgraceful deeds, but rejoices in her shameless activities in well-frequented gatherings and broadest daylight . . . **49** If a woman without a husband opens her house to the desires of all men and openly conducts herself like a prostitute, if she is in the habit of taking part in dinner parties with men totally unconnected with her, if she does this in the city, in the gardens, in those crowds at Baiae, if, finally, she so behaves that not only her walk, her dress and her companions, not only the ardour of her glances and the freedom of her speech, but even her embraces, kisses, days at the beach, sailing trips and dinner parties show her to be not only a prostitute but one who is wanton and shameless – if a young man should happen to consort with her, would you, Lucius Herennius, consider him an adulterer or a lover? Would you think that he wanted to storm her chastity or satisfy his passion?

7.53 [Tibullus] 3.13 (4.7): Sulpicia on her lover

Sulpicia, who was the daughter or granddaughter of Servius Sulpicius Rufus (cos. 51 BC) and niece of Marcus Valerius Messalla Corvinus (cos. 31), belonged to the group of poets associated with Messalla. Her elaborately constructed poems, addressed to a young man whom she calls Cerinthus, have been preserved in the collection of Tibullus. As an educated aristocratic woman she is highly unusual in publishing poetry supposedly relating her personal emotional experiences.

> At last love has come, of a kind which to conceal through modesty
> Would be more of a scandal than to bare it to anyone.
> Cytherea, won over by my poetic Muses,
> Has brought him and placed him in my arms.
> 5   Venus has fulfilled her promises: let those talk about my joy,
> Who, it is said, have none of their own.
> I would not choose to entrust anything to sealed tablets,
> So that no one could read it before my lover did –
> I delight in offending, and to wear a mask for scandal's sake
> 10   Bores me: let me declare that I, a worthy woman, am linked with a worthy man.

7.54 *CIL* I² 2540a, c: A lover's graffiti

These graffiti were scratched in the same hand on a wall of the smaller theatre at Pompeii, c. 90–80 BC; (i) may be a quotation from a poem; (iii) is unfinished; 'da veniam ut veniam' (give me leave to come) is a clever play on words.

(i)   'What's the matter?
    After your eyes have forcibly drawn me into the fire . . .
    with your copiously flowing cheeks.'
(ii)   'But tears cannot put out the flame;
    look, they burn the face and waste away the heart.'
    The composition of Tiburtinus.
(iii)   If you know how strong love is, if you know that you are human,
    take pity on me, give me leave to come.
    May Venus' flower (be given) to me . . .

7.55 Lucretius *On the Nature of the Universe* 4.1121–40, 1278–87: The folly of love

Lucretius (c. 94–c. 55 BC) is here condemning romantic love from the Epicurean standpoint (to Epicureans, tranquillity was the greatest goal). He derides lovers for turning their mistresses' defects into charms in their imagination (1155–70).

1121   Add to this that they consume their strength and perish under the strain;
    Add to this that their time is passed at the whim of another.
    Meanwhile their wealth slips away and is converted into Babylonian brocades,
    Duties are neglected and reputation wavers and sickens.
    Fine perfumes and Sicyonian slippers smile on his lady's feet;
    Yes, huge emeralds flashing with green light
    Are clasped in gold, and sea-coloured garments are worn away

With constant use in which they absorb Venus' perspiration;
The hard-won wealth of his father turns into head-bands and turbans,
1130   Or perhaps into a robe and garments from Alinda and Ceos.
Banquets with magnificent trappings and food, entertainments,
Wine in abundance, perfumes, garlands, wreaths of flowers are got ready –
In vain, since from the middle of the fountain of delights
Rises a taste of bitterness that causes torment among the very flowers,
Either when a guilty conscience happens to sting the lover with the thought
That youth is being spent in sloth and perishing in debauchery,
Or perhaps she has let fly and left rankling a word of doubtful import,
Which fixes in his passionate heart and glows there like fire,
Or because he thinks that she is making eyes and gazing at another man,
1140   While he sees the traces of mockery in her face.

1278   Nor is it due to divine intervention or the arrows of Venus
When a woman deficient in beauty happens to be beloved;
For the woman herself sometimes manages by her own conduct,
By her compliant manners and by keeping herself fresh and neat,
To make it easy for a man to get used to spending his life with her.
Furthermore, it is habit that produces love;
For whatever is struck by frequent blows, however light,
1285   Yields in the long run and gives way.
Do you not see that even drops of water falling on a stone
In the long run wear the stone through?

7.56 Lucilius *Satires* 17.1.567–73: The idealisation of noble women

The satirist Gaius Lucilius served with Scipio Aemilianus at Numantia (doc. 5.53). His sister was grandmother of Pompey the Great. Here he parodies epic stereotypes of characterisation; Alcmena was the wife of Amphitryon, prince of Tiryns and leader of the Thebans; Zeus was enamoured of her and she gave birth to twins, Heracles (Hercules) to Zeus and Iphicles to Amphitryon. Helen of Troy was, of course, a whore or adulteress because she ran away with Paris, abandoning her husband and daughter.

Surely you don't believe that any 'lovely-locked', 'lovely-ankled' girl
Can't possibly have her breasts touching her stomach and navel,
Or that Amphitryon's wife Alcmena couldn't have been knock-kneed or bowlegged,
And that others, even Helen herself, could not have been – I can't say it;
See to it yourself and choose any two-syllable word you like –
That a daughter of a noble sire could not have had some distinguishing mark,
A wart, mole, mark, one slightly projecting tooth?

HOMOSEXUALITY

There was no stigma for adult male Romans attached to penetrating both women and young boys. Cato the Elder fulminates on the prices of young boys after the Third Macedonian

War (docs 5.57–58) and Catullus writes love poems interchangeably to women and boys (see poem 99: to Juventius, doc. 7.61). Sulla's relationship with the female impersonator Metrobius (docs 11.1, 32) is unusual primarily in that it continued throughout Metrobius' career, not only while he was a youth. However, there was great shame attached to passive homosexuality (passive partners should be young slaves or male prostitutes), and Cicero uses such accusations to tarnish the reputations of Catiline. Homosexuality was particularly outlawed in the army, and Marius honoured the soldier who killed an officer who attempted to seduce him: docs 7.43, 59.

7.57 Aulus Gellius *Attic Nights* 6.12.1–7: P. Sulpicius Gallus

Scipio Aemilianus delivered this speech against P. Sulpicius Gallus when Scipio was censor in 142 BC, as part of the yearly review of the equites. He comments on Gallus' depilation, mirrors, tunics with sleeves, perfumes, and plucking of eyebrows. Traditional Romans wore a toga without a tunic or with a sleeveless tunic; Caesar was unusual in wearing a tunic with fringed wrist-length sleeves: doc. 13.61.

1 For a man to wear tunics coming below the elbow, right up to the wrist and nearly to the fingers, was considered inappropriate in Rome and all Latium. **2** Our countrymen called these tunics by the Greek name 'chiriotae' (long-sleeved) and considered that a long and flowing robe was suitable only for women, in that it protected their arms and legs from sight. **3** Roman men, however, at first wore just the toga without tunics; later on, they had tight, short tunics ending at the shoulder, which the Greeks call 'exomides' (sleeveless). **4** Accustomed to this traditional practice, Publius Africanus, son of Paullus, a man endowed with all great arts and every excellence, rebuked Publius Sulpicius Gallus, a man addicted to luxury, with the accusation that, among many other things, he wore tunics which completely covered his hands. **5** These are Scipio's words: 'For one who daily perfumes himself and dresses in front of a mirror, whose eyebrows are plucked, who walks around with his beard pulled out and smooth thighs, who, though a young man, has reclined on the inner side of a couch in a long-sleeved tunic with a lover, who is not only a wine-lover but a man-lover too, does anyone doubt that he acts as pathics generally act?'

7.58 Plutarch *Life of Cato the Elder* 17.1–5: A shameful relationship

T. Quinctius Flamininus conquered Philip of Macedon at Cynoscephalae in 198 BC (cf. doc. 5.23); his brother Lucius was praetor urbanus in 199 and then Titus' legate in charge of the navy (198–194); Lucius became consul in 192, but was expelled from the senate in the censorship of Cato the Elder and Valerius Flaccus in 184 for the incident described below. Livy calls the boy Philippus a Carthaginian male prostitute. The outrage is inspired not by the prostitute's sex but by the inapposite use of imperium at a banquet while under the influence of alcohol.

1 Cato named Lucius Valerius Flaccus, his colleague and friend, princeps senatus, and expelled many others from the senate, including Lucius Quinctius, who had been consul seven years earlier and, what contributed more to his reputation than his consulship, was brother of the Titus Flamininus who defeated Philip. **2** The reason for his expulsion was as follows: Lucius kept a youth who, ever since his boyhood, had been Lucius' favourite, keeping him with him and taking him on campaigns with greater honour and influence than any of Lucius' closest friends and relatives. **3** While he was administering his consular province, at a certain banquet the lad, as was his custom, reclined beside him and started flattering a man who was easily led when under the influence of wine, saying he loved him so much that 'when there was a gladiatorial show back at Rome, something I had never seen, I rushed away to join you, though I really desired to see a man killed.'

4 Lucius responded affectionately, 'Well, don't lie there distressed with me over that, for I can put that right.' And after ordering that one of the men sentenced to death be brought to the banquet and that a lictor with an axe stand beside him, he asked his beloved again if he wanted to see the man struck dead. When he said he did, Lucius ordered the man's head to be cut off.

5 This is the version which most writers narrate, and so Cicero has represented Cato himself as recounting it in his dialogue *On Old Age*. But Livy says the man killed was a Gallic deserter, and that Lucius did not have the man slain by a lictor but did it with his own hand, and that this is the version in a speech of Cato's.

7.59 Plutarch *Life of Marius* 14.4–8: Death for seduction

In his campaign against the Cimbri, Marius excused the homicide of his own nephew by a soldier whom he had propositioned (doc. 7.58). Homosexual relationships were strictly forbidden in the army, with offenders being clubbed to death (the fustuarium; cf. docs 5.19–20, 7.43).

4 Gaius Lusius, Marius' nephew, had been assigned an army command under him, and, while in all other respects he was a man of good repute, he had a weakness for good-looking boys. **5** He was attracted by one of the young men who served under him, called Trebonius, and had often unsuccessfully attempted to seduce him; at length he sent a servant at night to summon Trebonius. **6** The youth, being unable to disobey a summons, went, but when he was conducted into the tent and found himself the object of Lusius' violence he drew his sword and killed him. **7** This took place in Marius' absence, but on his return he brought Trebonius to trial. **8** As there were many accusers but no one speaking in his defence, Trebonius boldly took the stand and recounted what had happened, bringing witnesses to show that he had frequently refused Lusius' solicitations and that he had never prostituted his body to anyone, despite offers of expensive gifts. Marius in admiration and delight ordered the traditional crown for bravery to be brought and himself crowned Trebonius with it, declaring that, in a time that was in need of noble examples, he had performed the noblest deed of all.

7.60 Suetonius *Life of the Deified Julius* 49.1–2, 4: Caesar and Nicomedes

Caesar, while serving as a young man in Asia, was sent to Nicomedes IV of Bithynia in 81 BC to acquire ships for the siege of Mitylene. He was rumoured to have been successful because of a homosexual relationship with the elderly king. Dio comments (43.20.4) that Caesar welcomed all his soldiers' jokes except for these allusions to Nicomedes. The charges of passive homosexuality were damaging to Caesar in a way that rumours of his affairs with married women (doc. 7.45) could never be. The orator and poet Gaius Licinius Calvus was a close friend of Catullus: doc. 7.34.

1 The only charge that damaged his reputation for virtue was that of his intimacy with Nicomedes, which was, however, a serious and continuous stain on his character exposing him to general censure. I say nothing of the notorious verses of Licinius Calvus:

> 'Whatever Bithynia had
> and Caesar's sodomiser.'

I also pass over the attacks of Dolabella and the elder Curio, in which Dolabella calls him 'the queen's rival, inner partner of the royal bed', and Curio 'Nicomedes' brothel and Bithynian bagnio'. **2** I ignore the edicts of Bibulus in which he published his colleague as 'queen of Bithynia, who previously desired a king, and now a kingdom' ... **4** Finally, at Caesar's Gallic triumph, his soldiers, among other songs, such as are usually sung in jest as they follow the chariot, declaimed this one which became notorious:

> 'Caesar mastered Gaul, and Nicomedes Caesar:
> look, Caesar now celebrates his triumph, who mastered Gaul,
> but Nicomedes celebrates no triumph, though he mastered Caesar.'

7.61 Catullus 99: To Juventius

Compare this stanza with Catullus' poem to Lesbia (doc. 7.47).

> I stole a sweet kiss while you played, honey-sweet Juventius,
> One sweeter than sweet ambrosia.
> But I did not take it unpunished – for more than an hour,
> I remember, I hung at the top of the gallows
> 5   While I justified myself to you, though with all my tears
> I couldn't lessen your anger the tiniest bit;
> No sooner was it done than, your lips rinsed,
> With plenty of water, you wiped it away with all your fingers
> So no contagion from my lips might remain,
> 10 As though it were the foul spit of a polluted whore.
> Worse, you handed me in my misery over to vengeful love
> And have not failed to torment me in every way,
> So that that sweet kiss was now changed for me from ambrosia
> And became more bitter than bitter hellebore.
> 15 Since you lay down such punishments for my unhappy love,
> I'll never after this steal any kisses again.

PROSTITUTION

There was no stigma attached to frequenting prostitutes of either sex; indeed, visiting a prostitute could be seen to divert a male's sexual drives away from citizen women. Women prostitutes were supposed to wear a coloured (masculine) toga to distinguish them from respectable citizen women who wore the stola, but often they wore more spectacular clothing. According to Lucilius, charges for visiting a prostitute could be minuscule (doc. 7.62), though some could become wealthy: Sulla's initial wealth was said to have derived from a bequest by a prostitute: doc. 11.1.

7.62 Lucilius *Satires* 9.1.359–60: An old professional

Book 9 of Lucilius' satires was probably written towards the end of his life; he died c. 102 BC.

If she's nothing to look at, and if she was once a prostitute and whore,
A cent (an as) is all it takes and she's yours.

7.63 Livy *History of Rome* 39.9.5–7: Hispala Faecenia

For the Bacchanalia, see doc. 3.65. As a woman *sui iuris* after the death of her patron, Hispala needed a tutor to perform any legal act, such as making a will (doc. 7.5). As a reward for their information, the senate passed a decree that both Hispala and Aebutius should be given 100,000 asses out of the treasury, Aebutius should be exempt from military service, and Hispala should be given the right to give and alienate property, marry outside her gens, chose her own tutor, and marry a man of free birth (Livy 39.19.3–6). Marriage of a freeborn person with a prostitute was otherwise banned.

5 There was a noted prostitute, a freedwoman called Hispala Faecenia, not worthy of the profession to which she had grown accustomed while just a slave, who made her living in the same way even after she had been manumitted. **6** She had commenced a sexual relationship with Aebutius, a young man in the neighbourhood, which was in no way damaging to his property or reputation: this was because she had loved him and sought him out of her own accord, and, since his family made quite insufficient provision for him, he was supported through the generosity of the prostitute. **7** Even more, matters actually reached the point that, under the influence of their relationship, when she found herself in manu to no one after her patron's death, she applied to the tribunes and praetor for a guardian and made her will, naming Aebutius as her sole heir.

7.64 Plutarch *Life of Lucullus* 6.2–5: A powerful courtesan

L. Licinius Lucullus was Sulla's lieutenant; P. Cornelius Cethegus was a popular politician powerful during the 70s: Cic. *Brut.* 178. Lucullus (cos. 74 BC) wanted the province of Cilicia to conduct the war against Mithridates: docs 11.10–11, 12.10.

2 A certain woman called Praecia, one of those renowned for beauty and wantonness, who in other respects was in no way better than a courtesan but who used her associates and companions to further the ambitions of her friends, thus adding to her other attractions the reputation of being a good and effective friend, and acquiring the greatest influence, was at that time in Rome. **3** And when she won over Cethegus too, who was then at the peak of his reputation and in control of the city, and gained him as her lover, political power passed totally into her hands; no public measure was passed unless Cethegus approved it, and he did nothing except at Praecia's bidding. **4** So Lucullus won her over by presents and flattery – it was no doubt a great prize for a woman so arrogant and ostentatious to be seen sharing Lucullus' ambitions – and he immediately had Cethegus praising him and soliciting Cilicia for him. **5** But, once he had obtained this, he no longer needed to appeal to the assistance of Praecia or Cethegus, but everyone was unanimous in entrusting him with the Mithridatic war, on the grounds that no one else was better qualified to bring it to an end.

7.65 Pliny *Natural History* 7.158: The longevity of women

Pliny (7.156–57) notes that M. Perperna lived to 98 years of age and Gorgias to 108, while M. Valerius Corvus (reputedly cos. 348, 346, 343, 335, 300, 299 BC) reached 100 years. Sixty-year-olds, while they were no longer able to vote and were freed from public duties, still retained legal control over their familia.

Among women, Livia, wife of Rutilius, lived more than 97 years, Statilia, a lady of noble family under the emperor Claudius, 99, Terentia, wife of Cicero, 103, Clodia, wife of Ofilius, 115, and she also bore 15 children. The mime Lucceia gave a recitation on the stage at the age of 100. Galeria Coppiola, the actress of interludes, was brought back to the stage in the consulship of Gaius Poppaeus and Quintus Sulpicius (AD 9) at the votive games given for the recovery of the god Augustus in her 104th year; she had been brought out at her first appearance by Marcus Pomponius, aedile of the plebs, in the consulship of Gaius Marius and Gnaeus Carbo 91 years before (82 BC), and as an old woman was brought back to the stage as a curiosity by Pompey the Great at the dedication of his great theatre.

WOMEN AS OWNERS AND CONSUMERS

Aristocratic women possessed jewellery and money in their own right even in the early Republic. When Rome was threatened by the Gauls in 390 BC, the women of the city, according to Livy (5.50), offered to make up the ransom sum: they were therefore granted the right to be honoured by eulogies at their funeral. In 215, taxes were imposed on wealthy widows to provide for military pay, while the *lex Oppia* restricted their ornaments and forbade them to ride in carriages (Livy 34.3–5). In 207, to expiate unfavourable omens and a lightning strike on the temple of Juno on the Aventine, the augurs declared that married women had to make an offering to placate the goddess (Livy 27.37.7–10); doc. 7.85.

7.66 *ILS* 8562: A toilet casket

A large bronze casket (the Ficoroni cista) with an inscribed lid, found in a tomb at Praeneste (Palestrina), dated to c. 315 BC. The lid is decorated with statues of Dionysus and two satyrs and is engraved with athletic scenes taken from the *Argonautica* of Apollonius Rhodius. Under one of the legs the name Macolnia is also inscribed.

> Dindia Macolnia gave this to her daughter.
> Novius Plautius made me at Rome.

7.67 Livy *History of Rome* 34.2.8–3.1: Women lobby for luxury goods

Following the battle of Cannae, the Oppian law, proposed by the tribune Gaius Oppius in 215 BC, restricted women's use of luxury items such as jewellery and expensive clothing. In 195 there was a proposal to repeal this law, and women turned out in force to persuade the men to vote for its repeal. Cato the Elder is here portrayed as showing his disapproval of the women's conduct. As censor in 184 he taxed luxuries, including women's clothes, jewellery and vehicles.

8 'Indeed, it was not without some embarrassment that I made my way a short time ago to the forum through a throng of women. If respect for the dignity and modesty of them as individuals had not held me back, so they should not be seen to be rebuked by a consul, I would have said: **9** "What kind of behaviour is this, running around in public and blocking the streets and talking to other women's husbands? Could not each of you have asked your own husband the same thing at home? **10** Are you more persuasive in public than in private, and with other women's husbands rather than with your own? And yet, even at home, if modesty kept matrons within their proper limits, it's not your place to concern yourselves about what laws should be passed or repealed here."

11 'Our ancestors allowed no woman to transact business, even private business, without a guardian in control, and wanted them to be under the control of their fathers, brothers and husbands. We, in heaven's name!, now allow them to get involved in politics and to mingle with us in the forum and to attend formal and informal assemblies (*comitia* and *contiones*) . . . **14** What they want is complete freedom – or, to speak the truth, total licence! **3.1** And if they win in this, what will they not attempt?'

7.68 Plautus *Pot of Gold* 505–22: Early second-century extravagance

Megadorus (a bachelor) is here speaking to his potential father-in-law Euclio, imagining the extravagances that a rich wife demanded as a normal part of her lifestyle; compare doc. 7.55 for women's extravagant tastes.

505   Wherever you go nowadays, you see more wagons in front of city homes
       Than you do in the country when you go to a farm.
       But even this is a fine sight compared to when they come round for their money.
       There stands the fuller, the dyer, the goldsmith, the wool weaver;
       Salesmen of flounces, lady's underwear,
510   Veils, in purple dye, in yellow dye,
       Muffs, balsam-scented shoes,

Retailers of linen, shoemakers,
Squatting cobblers, slipper-makers,
Sandal-makers, mallow-dyers,
515 Dealers in breast-bands, and corset-makers alongside them.
Now, you may think you've paid them all off: along with more demands come
Three hundred more, who stand like doorguards in your atrium –
weavers, fringe-makers, casket-makers.
520 You bring them in and pay them off.
Now, you think, I've paid them all, when in come saffron-dyers
And all sorts of other pests who are always demanding something.

7.69 Cicero *Republic* 3.17: The *lex Voconia*

The Voconian law in 169 BC, proposed by the tribune Voconius Saxa, limited women's
rights of inheritance, preventing men in the highest property class from making daughters
their heirs or from leaving them more than half their fortune: in other words, no woman
could be left more than half an estate by someone in the first census class. Cicero's *Republic*
is set as a dialogue between Scipio Aemilianus, Laelius, and some of their friends in c. 129;
it was actually written in 54–51. The daughter of the wealthy Publius Crassus Mucianus
Dives, Licinia, was married to Gaius Gracchus; Mucianus presumably died intestate and
therefore his daughter could inherit as an only child (cf. doc. 8.33).

But if I wished to describe the conceptions of justice, and the principles, customs and
habits which have existed, I could show you not merely differences in all the different
nations, but that there have been a thousand changes in a single city, even in our own
in regard to these matters. For example, our friend Manilius here, being an interpreter
of the law, would give you different advice about the rights of women in regard to
legacies and inheritances from that which he used to give in his youth before the
passing of the Voconian law. In fact that law, passed for men's advantage, is full of
injustice to women. For why should a woman not have money of her own? Why may
a Vestal Virgin have an heir, while her mother may not? Why, on the other hand, if it
was necessary to limit the amount of property a woman could own, should the daughter of Publius Crassus, if she were her father's only child, be permitted by law to have
a hundred million sesterces, while mine is not even allowed three million?

7.70 Polybius *Histories* 31.26–27: Cultic paraphernalia

Aemilia was the wife of Scipio Africanus and grandmother by adoption of Publius Scipio
Aemilianus, Polybius' friend. As sister of his natural father, Lucius Aemilius Paullus, she
was also Aemilianus' aunt; she died in 162 BC. The elder Scipio had died in 183, leaving
his wife and sons as heirs in his will. His daughters did not inherit equally with their mother
and brothers but took 50 talents each into their marriages. The sum of 25 talents paid to the
daughters is described as the second instalment of their dowry; dowries were generally paid
in three instalments over a period of three years.

26.1 The first occasion (on which Scipio Aemilianus displayed generosity in
money matters) was when the mother of his adoptive father died, the sister of

his own father Lucius (Aemilius) and wife of his grandfather by adoption, the great Scipio. **2** He inherited from her a large fortune, and his handling of it was to give the first proof of his principles. **3** For the lady, whose name was Aemilia, used to display immense magnificence whenever she left her house to take part in women's ceremonies, having shared the life and fortune of Scipio (Africanus) at the height of his success; **4** apart from her own attire and the decorations of her carriage, all the baskets, cups and other sacrificial vessels were made of silver or gold and were carried in her train in such illustrious processions, **5** while her retinue of maids and menservants was proportionately large. **6** Immediately after Aemilia's funeral, he gave all this equipment to his mother (Papiria), who had been separated from Lucius for many years, and whose means were insufficient to maintain an appearance suitable for her birth. **7** Before this she had stayed away from these solemn processions, but now, when an important public sacrifice took place, she drove out in Aemilia's splendid equipage, and when, in addition, the muleteers and pair and carriage were the same, **8** the women who saw it were astonished at Scipio's kindness and generosity and lifted up their hands, praying for every blessing on him . . . **27.1** After this he had to pay the daughters of the great Scipio, the sisters of his adoptive father (the Corneliae), the second half of their dowries. **2** Their father had agreed to give each of the daughters 50 talents, **3** and their mother had given half of this to their husbands immediately on their marriage, but left the other half owing when she died. **4** As a result Scipio had to pay this debt to his father's sisters. **5** By Roman law the part of the dowry still owing had to be paid within three years, with personal property being handed over within ten months according to Roman custom, **6** but Scipio straightaway instructed his banker to pay each of them in ten months the whole 25 talents.

7.71 Pliny the Elder *Natural History* 34.11–12: An expensive lampstand

In his discussion of bronzeware, Pliny discourses on the construction and cost of Corinthian lampstands, which could clearly cost immense sums in the Republic. The funerary inscription of the lucky slave hunchback below (Clesippus Geganius) dates to the first half of the first century BC.

At the sale of such a lampstand, on the instructions of Theon the auctioneer, a fuller named Clesippus, a hunchback of hideous appearance, was thrown in. It was bought by Gegania for 50,000 sesterces. She threw a party to display her purchases, and for the entertainment of her guests she had the man appear with no clothes on; struck with outrageous passion for him, she admitted him to her bed, and later made him her heir. He thus became extremely rich and worshipped the lampstand as a divinity – thus attaching this story to Corinthian lampstands generally – though his character was vindicated by his erecting a noble tomb to perpetuate the memory of Gegania's shame throughout the world.

7.72 *ILS* 3423: A business-like woman

This inscription on a stone tablet was found at Rome, dated to before 80 BC.

Publicia, daughter of Lucius, wife of Gnaeus Cornelius son of Aulus, built a temple and folding-doors for Hercules and had it adorned, and restored an altar sacred to Hercules. She superintended the performance of all these works out of her own and her husband's estate.

7.73 *CIL* I² 2685: Forewomen of Minturnae

In the early first century BC, 'forepersons' of religious colleges at Minturnae, located at the north-west of the ager Campanus, dedicated 29 slabs to serve as altars (destroyed by fire, c. 50 BC). A number of these were dedicated by women forepersons (magistrae). Tertia Domatia is clearly freeborn, unlike the other dedicants of these altars. Each vicus, or 'quarter', probably elected annually a college of 12 forepersons for each cult, who may have had other duties concerned with the maintenance of the relevant crossroads or street-corner or with the celebration of the Compitalia festival.

In the year of office of . . . Members of the Board of Two. These forewomen present this as an offering to Venus: Tertia Domatia, daughter of Spurius; Alfia Flora, freedwoman of a matron; Cahia Astaphium, freedwoman of a matron; Dosithea, slave of Numerius Calidius; and others. . . .

7.74 Cicero's friend Caerellia

In writing to P. Servilius Vatia Isauricus, governor of Asia, in 46 BC, Cicero talks of Caerellia's estates, investments and possessions in Asia. He borrowed money from her, which Atticus thought 'undignified' (*Att.* 12.52.3). Q. Fufius Calenus (cos. 47 BC) used Caerellia – whose friendship with Cicero must have been widely known – as ammunition against him in 43 in his defence of Mark Antony. His other vicious jibes included Cicero's incest with his daughter, the prostitution of his wife, and his son's constant inebriation (46.18.6; cf. doc. 14.47) – which gives a clear idea of the very personal and vitriolic nature of Roman oratory.

(i) Cicero Letters to his Friends *13.72.1–2*

1 Regarding the estate, investments and possessions in Asia of my very close friend Caerellia, I recommended them to your notice as carefully as I could when I was with you in your garden; and you, in accordance with your usual practice and your continual, immense services to me, most generously promised that you would do all that was in your power. I expect that you remember it; I know you generally do. However, Caerellia's agents have written that, because of the size of your province and your multitudinous business, you have had to be reminded over and over again. **2** So I beg you to remember that you told me that you would do everything your honour permitted with all liberality. Indeed, I think you have a great opportunity of assisting Caerellia (though it is a matter for you to consider and decide) following the senate's decree which was passed about the heirs of C. Vennonius. You will employ your own wisdom in interpreting that decree. For I know that the authority of that class has always been of great weight with you. Concerning what still has to be done, I would like you to believe that, in whatever ways you show kindness to Caerellia, you will be doing me the greatest possible favour.

(ii) Dio Roman History *46.18.1–4*

1 This is what Cicero, or Cicerculus, or Ciceracius, or Ciceriscus, or Graeculus, or whatever you like being called, the uneducated, the naked, the perfumed man (Antony) achieved; **2** and none of it was done by you – the clever, the wise, the user of much more lamp-oil than wine, the one who lets his clothing drag round his ankles, not, by heaven, like the dancers do who instruct us in the intricacies of arguments by their gestures, but just to conceal the ugliness of your legs! **3** Oh no, it's not from modesty that you act like this, you who spoke at such length about Antony's lifestyle! Who is there who doesn't notice those delicate mantles you wear? Who is there who doesn't smell your grey hair, so very carefully arranged? Who does not know that you divorced your first wife, who had given you two children, and married instead in your old age a young girl, just so you could pay your debts out of her property? **4** And yet you didn't even hang onto her either, in order to have the liberty to consort with Caerellia, with whom you had an affair, though she was as much older than you as the girl you married was younger, and despite this you still write such letters to her as a babbling jester might write to a woman of 70 of whom he was enamoured.

7.75 Appian *Civil Wars* 4.5.31–34: Protest by wealthy women, 42 BC

Hortensia was the daughter of the great orator Q. Hortensius Hortalus, Cicero's rival in the courts. In 42 BC the triumvirs Octavian, Antony and Lepidus needed to raise funds for the civil war against the assassins of Julius Caesar. When they decided to place a tax on Rome's 1,400 wealthiest women, Hortensia spoke publicly on their behalf.

31 Accordingly the triumvirs who had hoped to acquire enough funds for the preparations for the war still had a shortfall of 200 million drachmas. **32** They addressed the people and published a decree relating to 1,400 of the wealthiest women: these had to have their property valued and contribute to the needs of the war as much as the triumvirs required from each. It was also laid down that any of these women who concealed any of their property or made a fictitious valuation would be fined, and rewards would be given to any informers regarding this, whether free persons or slaves. The women decided to beg the support of the triumvirs' womenfolk. They were not unsuccessful with Caesar's sister and Antony's mother, but when driven away from the door of Fulvia, Antony's wife, they took her outrageous treatment badly. They forced their way into the forum, to the triumvirs' tribunal, with the people and guards making way for them, and declared, through Hortensia, whom they had chosen as their spokesperson: 'As is appropriate for women of our rank in petitioning you, we had recourse to your womenfolk; but, after undergoing treatment that was not appropriate from Fulvia, we have been driven by her to the forum. You have already deprived us of our fathers, sons, husbands and brothers, whom you have claimed to have wronged you; if you also take away our property, you downgrade us to a position unbecoming and unworthy of our birth, lifestyle and female nature. If we have wronged you in some way, as you say our menfolk have, proscribe us as well as them. But if we women have not declared any of you a public enemy or pulled down your house or destroyed your army or led another one against you – if we have not pre-vented you from obtaining your offices or honours, why do we share the penalties when we did not participate in the offences?

33 'Why should we pay taxes when we have no share at all in the magistracies, honours, commands or politics over which you struggle with each other with such dire outcomes? Because it's wartime, you say? And when have there not been wars? And when have women ever been taxed – we whose nature exempts us among all persons? Our mothers on one occasion did rise above their nature, when you were at great risk over the whole empire and the city itself, during the conflict with the Carthaginians. At that time they contributed willingly, not from their land or fields, their dowries or their houses, without which life is impossible for free women, but only from their personal jewellery at home, and even these were not valued, were not given up in fear of informers or accusers, were not the result of compulsion or force, but whatever they themselves wanted to donate. What threat is now looming over you regarding the empire or country? Let there be war with the Gauls or Parthians, and we shall not be less anxious than our mothers for the safety of the state. But may we never contribute to civil wars or assist you against each other! We did not pay taxes to Caesar or Pompey, and neither Marius nor Cinna compelled us to – nor even Sulla the tyrannical ruler of this country: while your claim is that you are restoring the state!'

34 While Hortensia was delivering this speech, the triumvirs were angry that women should be so bold and hold a public meeting while the men were silent, that they should inquire into magistrates' actions and, while the men were on cam-paign, not even contribute money. They ordered the lictors to drive them away from the tribunal until cries were raised from the mob outside, at which point the lictors desisted and the triumvirs stated that they would put the matter off to the following day. On the next day they reduced the number of women who had to assess the value of their property from 1,400 to 400, and decreed that all men who possessed more than 100,000 drachmas, both citizens and strangers, freedmen and priests, and men of all nationalities, with no exception, under the same fear of penalties and of similar denouncements, should lend them immediately a fiftieth of their property and contribute a year's income as a tax for the war.

7.76 Valerius Maximus *On Memorable Deeds* 8.3.1–2: Women in court

Valerius cites the cases of three women (including Hortensia: cf. doc. 7.75) who repre-sented themselves in court. Like Sempronia (doc. 7.44), Carfania (sometimes known as Carfinia or Afrania) oversteps the conventional line allowed to women.

1 Maesia of Sentinum defended her own case, with the praetor L. Titius in charge of the court, and in the presence of a great throng of people, carrying out all the usages and stages of a defence, not only thoroughly but even with spirit, and was acquitted at the first hearing and almost unanimously. Because under her wom-an's guise she possessed a man's resolve they called her Androgyne. **2** Carfania, the wife of the senator Licinius Buccio, was quick to engage in law-suits and always spoke on her own behalf before the praetor, not because she could not find advocates but because she was overflowing with effrontery. By constantly plaguing the tribunals with her unprecendented yapping in the forum, she became the most notorious example of female mud-slinging, to such an extent that the name Carfania is used as a reproach to taunt women who behave inappropriately. She lived through until the second consulship of Gaius Caesar which he held with P. Servilius (48 BC). For such a monstrosity, the date of death rather than that of birth is the one that should be remembered.

WOMEN AND THE GODS

While, in Greek religion, goddesses tended to have women priests, in Rome goddesses had male priests: there were male flamines for the goddesses Ceres, Flora, Furrina and Pomona. This deprived women of religious roles which they might otherwise have played. Though sacrifices were made in women's rites (such as at the festival of Fortuna Muliebris: doc. 7.84), men would have performed these for them, and women had no role in most sacrifices: the presiding magistrates and priests were male. The exception to this rule was the Vestal Virgins, who attended various sacrifices and also had an important role in preparing the sacrificial flour (the mola salsa: see below), but this in effect denied other women even this supporting role. Their status as Vestals was not as women but as females whose sexuality was denied (because of the cultural construction of the definition of gender at Rome and in the ancient world generally). Other women supported the state in times of crisis through their worship, but in passive ways: taking part in supplicationes (doc. 7.85), praying to divinities, and making offerings, which could involve the use of splendid cultic paraphernalia (doc. 7.70).

Women, however, participated in a number of festivals. Most is known about rites concerning women's role as childbearers and mothers, though little is articulated in the sources except for what is known about the Lupercalia (doc. 7.78). But women did have festivals which concerned them, and even rituals from which men were excluded – most explicitly for the Bona Dea (docs 7.86–87) but also for the Pudicitia (doc. 7.77), Veneralia (doc. 7.81), Matralia (doc. 7.83) and Fortuna Muliebris (doc. 7.84), festivals in which the sources mention the participation of women but not of men.

WOMEN'S FESTIVALS

7.77 Livy *History of Rome* 10.23.1–10: The Pudicitia

Livy has the Pudicitia, which celebrated the chastity of Roman women, 'passing into oblivion', but Festus in the late second century AD knew of it. L. Volumnius Flamma was consul in 296 BC (also cos. 307) and proconsul in 295. His wife, Verginia, had clearly been married without manus, as she retained her patrician status; cf. doc. 7.10.

1 In that year (295 BC) there were many portents, to avert which the senate decreed supplications for two days; **2** wine and incense were provided at public expense; crowds, of both men and women, were to offer prayers. **3** The supplication was made memorable by a quarrel which arose between matrons in the temple of Patrician Chastity, which stands in the cattle-market by the round temple of Hercules. **4** The matrons had excluded from their ceremonies Verginia, Aulus' daughter, a patrician girl married to a plebeian, the consul Lucius Volumnius, because she had married outside her patrician rank. A short altercation followed, which, as a result of the sex's hasty temper, blazed up into a passionate dispute, **5** Verginia boasting, with reason, that she had entered the temple of Patrician Chastity both as a patrician and as a chaste woman, who was the wife of the man to whom she had been married as a virgin, and that she was ashamed neither of her husband nor of his honours and achievements.

6 She then followed up her proud speech with a deed which did her credit: in the Vicus Longus, where she lived, she shut off a part of her house, which was spacious enough for a shrine of reasonable size, and erected an altar there. She summoned the plebeian matrons and, after complaining of the insult by the patrician women, said, **7** 'I dedicate this altar to Plebeian Chastity and exhort you that, just as the men in this city compete for the prize of courage, **8** you as matrons do the same with regard to chastity, and strive that this altar may, if possible, be said to be tended more reverently than that one, and by women who are more virtuous.' **9** This altar was tended with nearly the same rites as the more ancient one, so that no woman except one of proven chastity, who had been married to only one man, should have the right to sacrifice. **10** Later on the cult was cheapened by polluted participants, not only matrons but women of every status, and eventually passed into oblivion.

7.78 The Lupercalia (15 February)

The Lupercalia, celebrated on 15 February, was a ceremony concerned both with the purification of the city and with women's fertility. It was at the Lupercalia in 44 BC that Antony as one of the Luperci offered a diadem to Julius Caesar: cf. doc. 13.55; the scene is immortalised in Shakespeare's *Julius Caesar*, Act 1, Scene 1.

(i) *Varro* On the Latin Language 6.13

The Lupercalia is so called because the Luperci sacrifice at the Lupercal. When the rex sacrorum announces the monthly festivals on the Nones of February, he calls this day 'februatus': for the Sabines call a purification 'februm', and this word is not unknown in our rites, for a goat hide, with a thong of which young women are flogged at the Lupercal, the men of old called a 'februs', and the Lupercalia was called Februatio (festival of purification), as I have shown in my *Books of Antiquities*.

(ii) *Plutarch* Life of Julius Caesar 61.1–3

1 It was the festival of the Lupercalia, regarding which many writers say that in olden days it was celebrated by shepherds and also connected in some way with the Arcadian festival of Lycaean Zeus. **2** Many of the well-born youths and magistrates run through the city naked, striking those they encounter with rough thongs to invoke sport and laughter; **3** many noble women deliberately get in their way and put out their hands, like schoolchildren, for the blows, believing that this assists the pregnant in childbirth and the childless in conceiving.

7.79 Ovid *Fasti* 3.241–58: The Matronalia (1 March)

The Matronalia marked the anniversary of the temple of Juno Lucina. The emphasis of these rites was on aiding pregnancy, and on this day husbands prayed for their wives and gave them presents, and the rites of the Salii were also celebrated (doc. 3.13). Here Mars (Juno's son) answers a question of Ovid's. The Matronalia should not be confused with the Matralia (June 11).

> 'Now the field is fertile, now is the time for breeding stock,
> Now the bird on the branch prepares a house and home:
> It is proper that Latin mothers should celebrate the fertile season,
> For in their childbirth they engage in conflict and prayer.
> 245 Add that, where the Roman king kept watch,
> On the hill which now bears the name of Esquiline,
> A temple to Juno was founded by Latin married women
> At public expense on, if I remember correctly, this very day.
> Why should I make a long story of it and weary your mind with various reasons?
> 250 What you seek, look – it stands there before your eyes.
> My mother loves brides: a crowd of mothers throngs my temple:
> So pious a reason particularly becomes us both.'
> Bring the goddess flowers: flowering plants
> Delight this goddess: wreathe your heads with fresh flowers;
> 255 Say, 'You have given us, Lucina, the light of life.'
> Say, 'You are there to help those who pray in childbirth.'
> But whoever is pregnant, let her pray with loosened hair,
> So the goddess may gently loose her childbirth.

7.80 Varro *On the Latin Language* 6.14: The Liberalia (17 March)

This festival celebrated Liber Pater, an Italian god of fertility and of wine and a Roman equivalent to Dionysos. Liber shared Ceres' games (*ludi Ceriales*) on 19 March; it was also on this day that Roman boys who had attained puberty donned the *toga virilis* (Ovid *Fasti* 3.771–2).

The Liberalia is so called because on that day, throughout the whole city, old women sit crowned with wreaths of ivy, as priestesses of Liber, with cakes and a brazier on which they offer them up on behalf of those who buy them.

7.81 Ovid *Fasti* 4.133–9, 145–50: The Veneralia (1 April)

The Veneralia honoured Fortuna Virilis (Virile Fortune). Those who 'do not wear the fillets and long robe' are women who are not matrons, i.e., prostitutes; the place of 'warm water' is the baths. Presumably men were not present at the baths when this festival was celebrated.

> With due religious observances you worship the goddess, Latin matrons old and young,
> And you, who do not wear the fillets and long robe.

135 Remove the golden necklaces from the marble neck,
  Remove the rich adornments: the goddess must be completely bathed.
  Return the golden necklaces to her neck, now dried:
  She must now be given other flowers, now the blooming rose.
  She herself commands you too to bathe under the green myrtle . . .
145 Now learn why to Fortuna Virilis you offer
  Incense in the place which is damp with warm water.
  All women remove their coverings when they enter that place
  And it sees every blemish of their naked bodies;
  Fortuna Virilis undertakes to conceal this and hide it from men
150 And for this service asks only a little incense.

7.82 Ovid *Fasti* 4.863–72: The Vinalia (23 April)

The Vinalia was celebrated on both 23 April and 19 August. Ovid describes the festival of 23 April, when an offering of new wine was made to Jupiter, and emphasises the role played by prostitutes. The Praeneste calendar (AD 6–9) notes 24 April as a holiday for prostitutes. The temple next to the Colline gate, taking its name from the Sicilian hill (Eryx), was the aedes of Venus Erycina, vowed by L. Porcius Licinus (cos. 184 BC) during wars in Sicily and opened in 181.

  I have spoken of Pales, and now I will speak of the Vinalia;
  One day, however, separates the two festivals.
865 Girls of the streets, celebrate the divine majesty of Venus:
  Venus is very appropriate for those who earn their wages as prostitutes.
  Offer incense and pray for beauty and popularity,
  Pray for charm and witty speech,
  Give the mistress the wild thyme she loves and her own myrtle
870 And chains of rushes concealed in bunched roses.
  It is now the proper time to frequent her temple
  Near the Colline gate, which takes its name from the Sicilian hill.

7.83 Ovid *Fasti* 6.475–80: The Matralia (11 June)

Cf. Varro *Lat. Lang.* 5.106 (for the crusty golden cakes the women baked in heated earthenware). The Mater Matuta was honoured in her temple in the Forum Boarium at this festival. There had been a temple on the site, according to tradition, since Servius Tullius, and it was restored after the siege of Veii.

475 Go, good mothers (the Matralia is your festival),
  Offer the Theban goddess her yellow cakes.
  Adjoining the bridges and great Circus is a famous
  Space, which takes its name from the ox statue there:
  Here, on this day, they say Servius dedicated to Mother Matuta
480 A temple with his own sceptre-bearing hands.

7.84 Dionysius of Halicarnassus *Roman Antiquities* 8.39.1, 8.55.3: Fortuna Muliebris (6 July)

The traditional (but almost certainly fictitious) aetiology of this cult, 'Fortune of Women', is that the successful general Coriolanus, while exiled from Rome, led a Volscian army against it in 493 (or 488) BC. His wife and mother, accompanied by large numbers of matrons, persuaded him to lead the army away. A temple was built on the site of the confrontation with Coriolanus, 4 miles south of Rome on the Via Latina (cf. doc. 15.22).

39.1 As the danger was now close at hand, their wives threw to the winds the propriety of staying at home and ran with lamentations to the shrines of the gods, prostrating themselves before the statues; and every sacred place was filled with the wailing and supplication of women, especially the temple of Jupiter Capitolinus . . . (A noble woman, Valeria, persuades the women to supplicate Coriolanus' wife and mother to entreat him to make peace. The women succeed and the senate and people grant them praise and an eternal remembrance.) **55.3** The women deliberated and decided to request a gift which would not cause jealousy, but to ask the senate for permission to found a temple to the Fortune of Women (Fortuna Muliebris) on the place where they had made their prayers on their city's behalf, and for them to assemble there every year and sacrifice to her on the day that they had ended the war. The senate and people decreed, however, that a precinct should be purchased from public monies and dedicated to the goddess, and that a temple and altar be built in it, in whatever way the pontiffs might prescribe, and that sacrifices should be conducted at the public expense, with a woman commencing the rites, whomever the women themselves should decide upon as the celebrant.

7.85 Livy *History of Rome* 27.37.7–15: The supplicatio of 207 BC

The women of Rome are here expiating various prodigies, including the birth of an hermaphrodite child. This involvement of women in supplicationes was a feature of Roman history.

7 The pontiffs also decreed that thrice nine virgins should go through the city singing a hymn. While they were learning the hymn, composed by the poet Livius (Andronicus), in the temple of Jupiter Stator, the temple of Juno the Queen on the Aventine was struck by lightning; **8** as the haruspices' interpretation was that this portent concerned the matrons and that the goddess should be appeased by a gift, **9** an edict of the curule aediles summoned to the Capitol all matrons who resided in the city of Rome or within 10 miles of the city, and these chose from among themselves 25, to whom they should bring a donation from their dowries. **10** From these donations a golden basin was made as a gift and carried to the Aventine, and after proper purification the matrons offered a sacrifice.

11 A day was immediately named by the decemvirs for another sacrifice to the same goddess, the procedure for which was as follows: two white cows were led from the temple of Apollo through the Porta Carmentalis into the city; **12** after them were carried two cypress-wood statues of Juno the Queen; then came 27 virgins, dressed in long robes, singing the hymn to Juno the Queen, **13** which at that time perhaps seemed praiseworthy to their uncultivated minds, but which now would seem rough and uncouth, if recited. The group of virgins were followed by the decemvirs, crowned with garlands of laurel and wearing the toga praetexta. **14** From the gate they came along the Vicus Iugarius into the forum. The procession stopped in the forum, and the virgins, passing a rope from hand to hand, moved forwards, accompanying the sound of their voices by beating time with their feet. **15** Then, via the Vicus Tuscus and the Velabrum, through the Forum Boarium, they continued to the Clivus Publicius and the temple of Juno the Queen. There the two victims were sacrificed by the decemvirs and the cypress-wood statues carried into the temple.

THE BONA DEA

Bona Dea was the 'Good Goddess'. She had two rites, on 1 May and, more importantly, on 3 December. Men were not permitted to know her real name and her rites were secret. The December ceremony was held at night in the house of the consul (Cicero in 63 BC) or the praetor (Julius Caesar in 62). Cicero describes the December sacrifice as 'ancient and secret' and performed by the Vestals 'on behalf of the Roman people'.

7.86 Plutarch *Life of Cicero* 19–20: Terentia and the Catilinarian conspiracy

This incident took place on 4 December 63, the day before the debate in the senate on the fate of the Catilinarian conspirators (doc. 12.21).

19.4 As it was now evening and the people were gathered waiting, Cicero went out and told the citizens what he had done and with their escort went to the house of a friend and neighbour, since his own was occupied by the women who were celebrating the secret rites of the goddess whom the Romans call 'Bona Dea' and the Greeks 'Gynaeceia' (Women's). **5** Every year a sacrifice is made to her in the consul's house by his wife or mother, with the Vestal Virgins present. On entering the house, Cicero, with only a few people present, deliberated with himself what he should do with the conspirators . . . **20.1** While Cicero was making up his mind what to do, a sign was given to the women as they were sacrificing. For the altar, on which the fire seemed to have totally died down, sent out from the ash and burnt bark an immense, brilliant flame. **2** The other women were terrified by this, but the sacred virgins instructed Terentia, Cicero's wife, to go with all speed to her husband and tell him to carry out his resolutions for his country's good, as the goddess was giving him a great light on his road to safety and glory. **3** So Terentia, who was generally not of a mild and retiring disposition but an ambitious woman and, as Cicero himself states, more inclined to share in his political concerns than to share her domestic concerns with him, told him this and urged him to take action against the conspirators.

7.87 Plutarch *Life of Julius Caesar* 9.1–10.9: Clodius and the Bona Dea

As Caesar was praetor in 62 BC, the rites of the Bona Dea were held in his house. Clodius' intrusion was raised in the senate and referred to the Vestals and the pontifices, who decreed that it was 'nefas' (sacrilege); the rites had to be celebrated anew. Clodius was tried for sacrilege and Cicero disproved his alibi, but the bribed jurors acquitted him. In revenge, Clodius eventually succeeded in having Cicero banished; for this incident and Clodius' trial, see docs 12.54–56.

9.1 There were no disturbances in Caesar's praetorship, although he met with a disgraceful misfortune in his own household. **2** Publius Clodius was a patrician by birth, distinguished for both his wealth and his eloquence, but second to none of the noted profligates of the time in insolence and audacity. **3** He was in love with Caesar's wife, Pompeia, and she was not unwilling. But strict watch was kept on the women's apartments, and Caesar's mother, Aurelia, a discreet woman, kept her eye on her daughter-in-law and made any meeting difficult and risky. **4** The Romans have a goddess whom they call 'Good', whom the Greeks call 'Gynaeceia' . . . **6** It is not lawful for a man to be present, or even in the house, while the rites are being celebrated; the woman are said to perform by themselves rites during their worship which are Orphic in nature.

7 So, when it is time for the festival, the husband, who is either consul or praetor, and every other male, leaves the house, while the wife takes it over and sets it in order. **8** The most important ceremonies are celebrated at night, when the all-night celebrations are mingled with fun and games and with much music, too, as a feature.

10.1 As Pompeia was at that time conducting the festival, Clodius, who had as yet no beard, and so thought he would pass unnoticed, put on the dress and accessories of a lute-girl and went there in the guise of a young woman. **2** Finding the door open, he was brought in without any difficulty by the maid, who was in the know. She ran on to tell Pompeia, but, as there was a long wait, Clodius had not the patience to remain where he had been left and wandered around in the large house, trying to avoid the lights, when an attendant of Aurelia's encountered him and asked him to play with her as one woman would another. When he refused, she dragged him forward and asked who he was and where he came from. **3** Clodius replied that he was waiting for Pompeia's maid Abra (this was her name) and was detected by his voice, whereupon the attendant sprang away with a scream to the lights and the crowds, crying out that she had caught a man. The women were terrified, and Aurelia put a stop to the rites of the goddess and covered up the ritual objects, ordering the doors to be closed and going around the house with torches looking for Clodius. **4** He was found to have taken refuge in the room of the girl who had let him in, and when they saw who he was the women drove him out of doors. **5** At once, that same night, the women went and told their husbands, and in the morning the report was all over the city that Clodius had committed sacrilege and should be punished for his crimes, not only against those he had directly offended, but against the city and the gods as well. **6** One of the tribunes therefore prosecuted Clodius for impiety, and the most powerful senators leagued against him, giving evidence about his adultery with his sister, who was married to Lucullus, and other dreadful acts of licentiousness. **7** The people opposed their efforts and defended Clodius and were of great assistance to him with the jurors, who were terrified and afraid of the mob. **8** Caesar immediately divorced Pompeia, but when summoned as a witness at the trial said he knew nothing of the matters with which Clodius was charged. **9** As his statement appeared strange, the prosecutor asked him, 'Why then did you divorce your wife?' 'Because', he replied, 'I thought that my wife should not even be suspected.'

THE VESTAL VIRGINS

The Vestal Virgins were six women devoted since childhood exclusively to the service of the goddess Vesta, who presided over the hearth in Roman homes. They served for 30 years, and their main role, besides officiating at various state religious ceremonies, was to keep alight the sacred fire of Vesta and guard the 'sacred things', including the ancient palladium, the image of Minerva rescued from Troy when the Greeks sacked it, referred to by Livy as the 'pledge of Roman imperium' (26.27.14; doc. 2.29). According to tradition, the Vestals were established by Numa (docs 3.6, 7.90). Vesta's festival, the Vestalia, was celebrated on 9 June. The Vestals participated at various rites and prepared enough mola salsa for all Rome's official sacrifices (i.e., they ground the first ears of grain for the season and baked this with salt to make mola salsa, salted flour).

7.88 Dionysius of Halicarnassus *Roman Antiquities* 2.67.1–2: A Vestal's life

Dionysius (3.67.2) records that Tarquinius Priscus added two Vestals to the initial four, and that the number of Vestals up to Dionysius' own day had remained six.

1 The Vestal Virgins live in the sanctuary of the goddess, which no one who wishes can be prevented from entering during the day, though it is not lawful for any man to stay there at night. **2** They were required to remain undefiled by marriage for 30 years, offering sacrifices and performing other religious rites in accordance with the law. During the first ten years they had to learn these rites, during the second ten to perform them, and during the remaining ten to teach others. When the period of 30 years had been completed, there was nothing which prevented those who so wished from putting aside the headbands and other insignia of their priesthood and marrying. And some, though only a few, have done so, but the ends of their lives were unenviable and not at all happy, and in consequence, taking their misfortunes as ominous, the rest remain virgins in service to the goddess until their deaths, when another is again appointed by the pontiffs to fill the vacancy.

7.89 Dionysius of Halicarnassus *Roman Antiquities* 8.89.3–5: A Vestal's death, 481 BC

Cf. Livy 2.42.10–11 for Livy's account. Describing a similar incident in 471 BC, Dionysios states that the Vestal was also scourged (9.40.3–4).

3 In Rome many portentous signs, in the form of unusual voices and visions, occurred as evidence of divine wrath. **4** The augurs and expounders of religious matters shared their experiences and proclaimed that some of the gods were wrathful because they were not receiving their customary honours, since their rites were not being conducted in a pure and holy manner. A great inquiry was then held by everyone, and eventually the pontiffs received information that one of the virgins who guarded the sacred fire, whose name was Opimia, had lost her virginity and was polluting the rites. **5** By tortures and other proofs, the pontiffs discovered that the information was correct, and they took the headbands from her head and, carrying her in procession through the forum, buried her alive inside the city walls. The two men who were convicted of seducing her were flogged in public and then immediately executed. After this, the sacrifices and the auguries became favourable, as if the gods had remitted their anger against them.

7.90 Plutarch *Life of Numa* 9.8–10.13: Plutarch on the Vestals

After the Gallic victory at the battle of the Allia, traditionally dated to 390 BC, the Vestals removed the fire of Vesta and other sacred objects in their care from Rome. These objects were thought to include the palladium brought from Troy by Aeneas, the Samothracian images, and two small jars (one open and one sealed).

9.8 The chief of the pontiffs (the pontifex maximus) had the duty of expounding and interpreting or, rather, presiding over sacred ceremonies, not only being in charge of public rites but overseeing private sacrifices, too, and ensuring that established custom was not transgressed, as well as giving instructions as to whatever was necessary for the worship or propitiation of the gods. **9** He was also the overseer of the holy virgins, who are called Vestals. **10** To Numa is attributed the consecration of the Vestal Virgins and the care and worship of the perpetual fire which they guard, either because he considered the essence of fire to be pure and uncorrupted, and so entrusted it to chaste and undefiled persons, or because he saw fire as barren and unfruitful and so analogous to virginity. **11** Yet, wherever fire is unquenched in Greece, as at Delphi and Athens, not virgins but women past the age of marriage have care of it . . . **15** Some consider that nothing other than the perpetual fire is guarded by the holy virgins; others say that certain sacred objects are kept in concealment by them, which no one else may see: what may be learnt and told about these things I have written in my *Life of Camillus*.

10.1 Initially, they say, Gegania and Verenia were consecrated by Numa, and then Canuleia and Tarpeia; and two others were later added by Servius, making up the number which has continued to this day . . . **5** He granted them great privileges – for example, the right to make a will while their father was still alive and the power to manage their other affairs without a guardian, like mothers of three children. **6** When they appear in public, the fasces are carried in front of them, and if they meet someone being led to execution, he is spared – the Vestal has to swear that the encounter was involuntary and accidental, not contrived. If anyone passes underneath the litter on which they are being carried he is put to death. **7** For other

offences the Vestals' punishment is flogging, the pontifex maximus carrying it
out, with the offender sometimes naked, in a dark place, with a curtain pulled
between them; **8** but if one has broken her vow of chastity, she is buried alive
near the gate called the Colline; there a little mound of earth lies within the city,
extending for some distance: in the Latin language it is called choma, 'agger'. **9**
A small underground room has been constructed there, with steps leading down
from above. In it is placed a bed with coverings and a lighted lamp and small
portions of the necessities of life, such as bread, water in a bowl, milk and oil, as
though they are absolving themselves from killing by hunger a person consecrated
to the highest religious duties.

    10 The offender is placed on a litter, which they throw coverings over and tie
down with cords, so that no cry she makes can be heard, and take her through the
forum. **11** Everyone stands aside in silence and escorts it noiselessly with dreadful
gloom: no other sight is more frightful, and the city observes no more awful day
than this. **12** When the litter has been carried to the spot, the attendants undo the
cords, and then the high priest, uttering certain silent prayers and raising his hands
to the gods before the act, brings her out still covered and places her upon the steps
that lead down to the room. **13** He then averts his face with the other priests; when
she has descended, the ladder is drawn up and the room's entrance is concealed
with a quantity of earth heaped up over it, so as to make it level with the rest of the
mound. This is the punishment for those who break their vow of virginity.

7.91 Livy *History of Rome* 8.15.7–8: A Vestal's punishment

Livy dates this incident to 337 BC. Minucia was not allowed to free her slaves because
slaves could be tortured to give evidence. On her punishment, Ennius wrote, 'Since no law
ever demanded anything more horrible' (*Annals* 474).

In that year the Vestal Minucia, suspected initially because of her dress, which
was more elegant than was fitting, was accused before the pontiffs on the evidence
of a slave and was ordered by their decree to abstain from performing sacrifices
and to retain her slaves in her own power. After her conviction, she was buried
alive near the Colline gate on the right of the paved road in the Polluted Field – a
place named, I believe, for her unchastity.

7.92 Pliny the Elder *Natural History* 28.12–13: A Vestal's miraculous powers

For the devotio rituals of the Decii, see doc. 3.18; for runaway slaves, docs 6.45–47.

12 As an important example of ritual there has survived that used by the Decii,
father and son, to devote themselves; also extant is the Vestal Tuccia's plea of
innocence when accused of unchastity, when she carried water in a sieve in the
year 609 of the city (145 BC). **13** We believe today that our Vestals are able, with
a prayer, to root runaway slaves to the spot, providing that they have not yet left
the city.

COINAGE AND THE VESTALS

7.93 Crawford *RRC* 428.1–2: Condemnation of Vestals in 113 BC

This denarius of 55 or 53 BC was minted by Q. Cassius Longinus, commemorating his great-grandfather L. Cassius Longinus Ravilla. In 114 BC, the virgin daughter of a Roman eques was struck dead by a lightning bolt. The omen was interpreted to mean that the Vestals had broken their vows. Aemilia was condemned but the other two were acquitted by the pontiffs (the Aemilia is not the same as in doc. 7.94). With L. Cassius Longinus Ravilla as prosecutor (quaesitor), in 113 the two Vestals previously acquitted, Licinia and Marcia, were also condemned to death, as well as several equites. The curule seat shown on the coin is a reference to Ravilla's official position as quaesitor.

Obverse: Head of the goddess Vesta.

Reverse: Temple of Vesta (which was in the forum). Within the temple of Vesta there is a curule chair. On the left of the temple, a voting urn, and on the temple's right a voting tablet inscribed with the letters A and C, for absolvo (I acquit) and condemno (I condemn). The coin shows the temple's circular construction, as well as a statue, presumably Vesta, on the roof (not to be confused with the ancient statue within the temple itself).

7.94 Crawford *RRC* 419.3: The Vestal Virgin Aemilia honoured for her virtue

This denarius was minted by the moneyer M. Aemilius Lepidus in 61 BC. The reverse shows the *Basilica Aemilia et Fulvia*, a two-storey portico constructed in the forum in 179 BC by his ancestor M. Aemilius Lepidus (cos. 187) with his fellow censor M. Fulvius Nobilior. On the obverse is a woman attired as a Vestal Virgin, whom scholars identify as the Vestal Aemilia, who is reported to have rekindled the fire in the temple of Vesta (which had gone out) by throwing one of her loveliest garments onto it (Val. Max. 1.1.7).

Obverse: Head of a veiled woman, wearing laurel wreath.

Reverse: Basilica Aemilia and Fulvia, two storied, with legend *Aimilia* above building (ignoring the Fulvia); portrait shields are attached to the columns; on the left the letters *REF* (*refecta*, 'rebuilt') and on the right *SC* ('by decree of the senate'). The legend M(arcus) Lepidus underneath the building.

7.95 Cicero *On his House* 109: Home is where the hearth is

The demolition of a house was a symbolic destruction of the offender and all his family. When Cicero was exiled, his house on the Palatine was destroyed by Clodius by decree and replaced by a monument to Liberty; Cicero was recalled in 57 BC and made a case before the pontiffs that the consecration was null and void; his house was then rebuilt (docs 12.60–61).

What is more holy, what more protected by every kind of sanctity than the home of every individual citizen? There are his altars, his hearths, his household gods, his sacred rites, observances, rituals: it is a sanctuary so holy in the eyes of all that it is sacrilege to drag a person from it.

8

Tiberius and Gaius Gracchus

Land and its distribution and redistribution was an issue in late Republican politics from the time of the Gracchi down to Caesar, with Saturninus, Drusus (the
younger), Sulla and Caesar all concerned with land redistribution (Stockton 1979:
16). It is not an understatement to say that the demise of the Republic began with
the Gracchi, plebeians with impeccable family backgrounds whose ancestors had
been conspicuous in their military service (docs 8.1, 5.56). They attempted to deal
with pressing economic and social problems – and failed. The violence that was
to mark the late Republic (133–44 BC) began in 133, when members of the senate shattered the concordia of the state by murdering Tiberius Gracchus. It was
acknowledged by Appian – and accepted by modern historians – that the period of
the Gracchi saw the beginning of the decline of the Republic: Tiberius' tribunate
is the point at which Appian began his *Civil Wars*, part of his history of Rome
(doc. 8.4).

Scholars agree less on the precise nature of the problems facing Rome which
Tiberius, as tribune in 133, and then his brother Gaius, as tribune in 123 and 122,
sought to overcome and on what their motives were. But the overall aim presented
by the sources for Tiberius is that he wanted to settle Roman citizens on ager publicus (public land) so that they would become eligible for military service (docs
8.6, 9). Whether he did this from pure altruism, to 'get even' with the senate, to
pursue gloria and advance his political career, or a combination of these, is up to
the reader to decide. But it is clear that he did not, in proposing his law, deliberately seek to alienate the senate or to destroy its power. However, their obstruction
of the workings of the land commission led him to a decision, the use of funds
from Pergamum, which would interfere in senatorial prerogatives. Events led on
from there to a disastrous conclusion (doc. 8.15).

Roman conquests of the third and second centuries, during which farmers were
often away from their farms serving in the army, combined with the increase in
the number of slaves, had resulted in much of the land of peasant farmers being
concentrated in the hands of the few and being worked by slaves. These were not
yet latifundia – huge farms (such as could be found in Sicily at this time); rather,
the rich tended to own a 'patchwork' of smaller estates run as independent units.
To be eligible for military service, citizens had to belong to one of the property

356

classes. When they lost their farms, and perhaps the use of ager publicus through the encroachments of the rich, they were no longer eligible for service in the army. A property census rating of 11,000 sesterces was necessary for military service; with small farmers replaced by slaves, it became difficult to raise recruits, and slaves themselves were a danger (docs 1.20, 8.6). During the tribunate of Tiberius the slave revolt in Sicily (135–132 BC) was in full swing (doc. 6.48).

Both Appian and Plutarch agree that Tiberius' main concern was to increase the number of soldiers by distributing the ager publicus. Rome owned large amounts of ager publicus, particularly in southern Italy, from confiscations from communities that had gone over to Hannibal in 216 or soon after (see doc. 4.42). By 167 a law limited possession of ager publicus to 500 iugera per individual, but the senators resented this law, and, as with the much earlier fourth-century Licinio–Sextian law which disallowed private possession of ager publicus (doc. 1.48), it seems to have been largely ignored. Certainly by Tiberius' time much of this land was treated as private property, and this was the cause of his conflict with the rich. But it was when Tiberius proposed that the plebeian assembly legislate on the bequest of Attalus III's kingdom of Pergamum to Rome, interfering in the senate's traditional prerogatives of foreign affairs and finance, that his opponents had a basis for blocking his measures, further aggravated by his decision to stand for a second time as tribune when the opposition to him became clear (doc. 8.15). The charge made against Tiberius, that he was aiming at kingship, was clearly not credible in anyone's eyes but was a deliberate attack on him.

The urban and rural poor alike were interested in Tiberius' proposed agrarian law and flocked to the assembly to support it, while the rich, who had much to lose, opposed it. Tiberius' tribunate marks the beginning of the trend towards violence in Republican politics: there had been the occasional imprisonment of consuls by tribunes, but no political assassinations. The murder of Tiberius, together with 300 of his supporters (doc. 8.15), and his brother Gaius, with 3,000 (doc. 8.32), even if these numbers were exaggerated, did not mark a single aberration in the history of the Republic; rather, it was a signal of what was to come – bloody proscriptions, civil wars and devastation on a scale unheard of in Italy. The tribunates of the Gracchi did not automatically lead to the destruction of the Republic, nor can they even be said to have set the process in train. Rather, the Gracchi and the problems which they sought to overcome, and the ways in which they reacted to opposition, which provoked the senate to respond with force, exposed fundamental flaws in the Roman political apparatus and demonstrated its inability to deal peacefully with these problems.

While Tiberius started out with several influential supporters in the senate, including his father-in-law Appius Claudius Pulcher (cos. 143), who was princeps senatus (doc. 8.11), it was the assembly which became his, and Gaius', mainstay, though it was not as loyal as might have been expected. Gaius discovered this in 122, when the assembly was won over by Drusus' proposals to support his opponents. The Gracchi created a power base independent of the senate and, particularly in Gaius' case, family connections. Marius and Sulla did not follow in the footsteps of the Gracchi or appreciate the lesson that the senate was not absolute, but they also exposed the same fundamental political problem of who ruled Rome – senate or people. Nevertheless the Gracchi hardly caused the collapse of the Republic, and the view that 'they precipitated the revolution that overthrew the Republic' (Scullard *GN* 38) is simplistic in the extreme. Rome was 'quiet' for two decades after Gaius' murder, and the forces that brought down the Republic had origins other than the problems Tiberius and Gaius sought to address.

Tiberius' younger brother, Gaius, born 154, also had influential friends and connections. He was married to Licinia, the daughter of P. Licinius Crassus Dives Mucianus (cos. 131). He served in Numantia with Scipio Aemilianus, his cousin and brother-in-law, and was elected to serve on Tiberius' land commission in 133. He clearly followed the policies of his brother and was a highly accomplished orator (docs 8.26–27). He was elected tribune for 123, though returned fourth out of ten, showing that he was not immediately popular, and was re-elected for 122. His tribunates were to see a vast legislative programme, his first aims being to put fresh life into his brother's agrarian reform (docs 8.28–29) and to seek justice – though limited – against the latter's murderers (doc. 8.29). His legislation cannot always be firmly dated to one tribunate or the other, but it generally benefited either the people or the equites, such as the reforms of the extortion court and tax collection, both of which benefited the equites (doc. 8.28), and he may have been concerned not so much to court their support as to show that the people were an important source of authority: the laws about these two matters emanated from the people's assembly and challenged senatorial control of foreign affairs and state finance. The extortion court ties in with his attacks on the corruption of Roman officials (docs 8.22–4). His road-building and granary projects (doc. 8.28) prob-ably also benefited the equites, as well as the people. Like Tiberius, he resorted to a makeshift bodyguard when his fortunes were reversed and, like Tiberius, died violently along with his supporters (docs 8.30–33). The success of his legisla-tion is uncertain, and Appian judged his agrarian law a failure (doc. 8.35), but the *lex agraria* of 111 BC conferred ownership of the land on those to whom the Gracchan land commission had apportioned it (doc. 8.36). Cicero's verdict on the Gracchi was negative (doc. 8.37) except when circumstances demanded it (doc. 8.39), while Sallust, who favoured the populares, was supportive and pointed out that the senate's use of force endangered the state (doc. 8.40).

Ancient sources: there were several contemporary writers on the Gracchi: Calpurnius Piso (cos. 133; *HRR* I² 120–38), C. Fannius (cos. 122 and son-in-law of Laelius: *HRR* I² 139–41) and Sempronius Asellio (military tribune in 133; *HRR* I² 179–84) all held office in the crucial period, though none of their works survive intact. Sempronius' history probably began in 146 and dealt with events at least down to Drusus' assassination; apparently L. Cornelius Sisenna's history was a continuation of Asellio's from this point (*HRR* I² 276–97). Posidonius (c. 135–51: *FGrH* 87), an eastern Greek, wrote a world history from 146 BC down to the mid-80s; it is no longer extant, but his material on the slave revolts was used heavily by Diodorus (see chapter 6). Both Tiberius and Gaius Gracchus were excellent orators, and fragments of Gaius' speeches survive (*ORF*⁴ 174–98; docs 8.22–24). Cicero provides valuable references to the Gracchi, and his study of oratory would have included them. Of historians proper, Livy, Plutarch and Appian are the most important, but Livy's relevant books survive only in the abbreviated form of the fourth-century AD summaries (the *Periochae*) of Books 58, 60 and 61. Plutarch's *Life of Tiberius Gracchus* and *Life of Gaius Gracchus* are invaluable, closely following the Roman annalistic tradition, and his main source is the same as used by Appian: Books 1.9.35 to 26.113 of Appian's *Civil Wars* deals with the Gracchi. He made use of the hostile account of C. Fannius (one fragment of a speech made by him survives: doc. 8.28), as well as the political pamphlet which Gaius had written about his brother. The historical record for the Gracchi is, then, quite considerable, and Appian and Plutarch are largely reliable witnesses. Diodorus 34/5.24–27 provides judgemental comments of little value. In this chapter, the sources are taken as an essentially correct view of the period. Modern critics can and do disagree, but the sources must form the backbone of any historical reconstruction of this controversial period. The evidence of epigraphy is invaluable: mainly the surviving boundary stones set up by the agrarian commission, the *lex Acilia*, and the *lex agraria* of 111 BC.

FAMILY BACKGROUND

8.1 Plutarch *Life of Tiberius Gracchus* 1.1–7: Parents of the Gracchi

Cornelia was the daughter of *the* great Scipio Africanus, who defeated Hannibal at Zama in 202 BC. The younger Scipio, Scipio Aemilianus, Tiberius' and Gaius' brother-in-law, was responsible for the destruction of Carthage in 146 BC. His marriage to Sempronia, sister of the Gracchi, was not a success (doc. 8.21).

The father of the Gracchi was Ti. Sempronius Gracchus the Elder, who held two consulships (177 and 163), was censor in 169, and celebrated two triumphs. His uncle, also a Ti. Sempronius Gracchus, was consul in 215 and 213. The family, though plebeian, was therefore distinguished. **1**: Both Agis IV and Cleomenes were third-century BC Spartan kings who attempted to increase the number of citizens by land redistribution. **6**: A tale of the elder Tiberius finding two serpents on his bed; whichever he killed first would mean the death of that spouse; he chose to kill the male. **7**: Possibly Ptolemy VIII Euergetes II (cf. doc. 5.39).

1 Now that I have completed the first part of my account (the *Lives* of Agis and Cleomenes), I have to turn to the equally unfortunate story of the Roman pair Tiberius and Gaius Gracchus, whom I have chosen as their parallel. **2** They were the sons of Tiberius Gracchus, who was renowned more for his personal excellence than for having been censor and twice consul and having celebrated two triumphs. **3** It was for this reason that he was thought worthy to marry Cornelia, daughter of that Scipio who conquered Hannibal, after Scipio's death, even though they were not friendly and were on different sides in politics . . . **5** Tiberius died shortly afterwards (c. 150 BC), leaving Cornelia with 12 children by him. **6** Cornelia took charge of both the children and the household and showed herself to be so discreet, devoted to her children and high-minded that Tiberius was considered to have made no bad decision in choosing to die instead of such a wife;

7 for when King Ptolemy asked her to share his crown and marry him she refused. While a widow she lost all her other children except for a daughter who married Scipio (Aemilianus) the younger, and two sons, Tiberius and Gaius, concerning whom this *Life* is written, whom she brought up so zealously that, although it is admitted that they were the most naturally gifted of all Romans, their virtues were thought to be owed more to their education than to nature.

8.2 Valerius Maximus *On Memorable Deeds and Sayings* 4.4 pref.: Cornelia

Cornelia's marriage occurred sometime between 175 and 165. She was the second daughter of P. Cornelius Scipio Africanus and aunt by adoption of Scipio Aemilianus (who was her cousin). The date of the *Collecta* of Pomponius Rufus is not known.

That children are a mother's greatest adornments we find as follows in Book . . . of Pomponius Rufus' anthology: when a Campanian lady was a guest in her house and showed off her jewellery, the very finest there was at the time, Cornelia, the mother of the Gracchi, detained her in conversation until her children returned home from school and then said, 'These are *my* jewels'.

8.3 Plutarch *Life of Gaius Gracchus* 2.2–5, 3.1–2: The two brothers

For Gaius needing a pitch-pipe to guide him while speaking, see doc. 8.27. The dolphins were presumably furniture ornaments.

2.2 First of all Tiberius was mild and sedate in his facial appearance, glance and demeanour, while Gaius was eager and vehement, so when they spoke to the people Tiberius did so decorously, remaining on the same spot, while Gaius was the first Roman to walk up and down on the rostra and pull his toga off his shoulder while he was speaking, just as Cleon the Athenian is said to have been the first demagogue to pull at his garment and strike his thigh. **3** Gaius' oratory was awe-inspiring and passionate to the point of exaggeration, while Tiberius' was more pleasant and productive rather of pity in the hearer. His style was pure and accurately cultivated, while Gaius' was persuasive and glamorous. **4** It was the same with regard to their way of life and eating habits, for Tiberius' was inexpensive and simple, while Gaius', though moderate and austere when compared with that of others, was extravagant and epicurean in comparison with that of his brother: evidence for this is Drusus' charge that he bought silver dolphins at a cost of 1,250 drachmas a pound. **5** The same distinction was apparent in their characters as in their oratory, with Tiberius being reasonable and mild and Gaius harsh and hot-tempered, in consequence being often, against his judgement, carried away by anger while speaking, when his voice would become high-pitched, and he would become abusive and confuse his argument. . . .

3.1 These were the differences between them but, with regard to courage in the face of the enemy, justice towards subjects, diligence in government, and restraint in their pleasures, they were indistinguishable. Tiberius was the elder by nine years; **2** and this meant that their careers were divided by a period of time, which was an important element in weakening their actions, as they did not come to prominence together or wield power at the same time, for their power would have been immense and unsurpassable had both worked together.

8.4 Appian *Civil Wars* 1.2 (4–5): The emerging conflict

Appian sees the period of the Gracchi as the beginning of violent conflict in the Republic. Scholars follow him in dating the beginning of the disintegration of the Republic from this period.

4 And this is the only occurrence of armed conflict that one might find in the ancient struggles, and this was brought about by an exile (Coriolanus), but the sword was never brought into the assembly, nor was there any civil killing, until Tiberius Gracchus proposed laws as tribune. **5** He was the first to lose his life in internal strife, and with him many others, who were gathered on the Capitol round the temple, were also slain. Nor did the internal strife come to an end with this dreadful deed . . .

THE TRIBUNATE OF TIBERIUS, 133 BC

Tiberius Gracchus came to the tribunate after creditable military service and could ordinarily have expected a political career. He served in the Third Punic War as quaestor under his brother-in-law Scipio Aemilianus, who sacked Carthage in 146 BC. He was quaestor in Spain in 137 BC and extricated the army of Hostilius Mancinus from disaster by negotiating a treaty; see docs 8.8, 5.50. *En route* to Spain, Tiberius had observed the number of slave-operated farms and decided to distribute the ager publicus among Roman citizens and increase the population liable for military service.

8.5 Appian *Civil Wars* 1.7 (26–31): Slaves versus citizens

The Romans had acquired a great deal of land in their conquest of Italy; much of this became public land, ager publicus, leased out for a tax or toll. But the rich took up the land and farmed it using slaves, causing the Italian population to decline and the slave population to grow. This passage refers to the period of the third and second centuries.

26 As the Romans subdued Italy in war bit by bit, they used to seize a part of the Italians' lands and build towns there or to choose colonists of their own to occupy towns which were already there. **27** Their intention was to use these as garrison towns, while on each occasion they immediately distributed to the colonists the cultivated part of the land acquired by conquest, or sold or leased it; as for the part which was then lying idle because of the war – which tended to be the greater proportion – as they did not have the time as yet to divide it up, they used to proclaim that, in the meantime, those who wished to work it might do so in return for a tax on the crops every year, a tenth of the grain and a fifth of the fruit. It was laid down that those who farmed animals should pay tolls on both the larger and smaller stock animals. **28** They did all this in order to increase the Italian population, which they considered very tough, so that they would have home-grown allies. But the very opposite occurred. **29** For the rich took over most of the unassigned land and, being confident in time that no one would ever dispossess them, absorbed small plots adjoining theirs and those of their poor neighbours, purchasing some through persuasion and taking others by force, and ended up farming great plains rather than individual properties, using purchased slaves as farm-workers and herdsmen, as free men might be diverted from farm-work into the army. In addition, the ownership of slaves brought them great gain from their abundance of children, who multiplied free from danger because they were not liable for military service. **30** In this way, powerful men became extremely rich and slaves as a class multiplied throughout the country, while the Italian population dwindled, worn down by poverty, taxes and military service. **31** If they had any respite from these, they had to spend their time in idleness because the land was held by the rich, who used slaves as their farm-workers instead of free men.

8.6 Appian *Civil Wars* 1.8–9 (32–7): Military recruitment

The Licinio–Sextian legislation of 367 (doc. 1.48) attempted to prevent the ager publicus from coming into private ownership. Either in 367 or after, a provision was enacted that no one was to hold more than 500 iugera (c. 300 hectares or c. 150 acres). In addition, there was the recent attempt of Laelius, consul in 140, to reform the abuse of the ager publicus.

Tiberius in 133 attempted to put the ager publicus into the hands of small-scale peasant farmers, drawn from the Roman citizen class, who would become the soliders Rome needed. There was no food shortage at Rome; it was a question of who was producing food – slaves and not free citizens.

32 On this account, the people were concerned in case they should no longer have a good supply of allies from Italy and that their government might be at risk on account of so great a number of slaves; and, since they could come up with no solution, **33** as it was neither easy nor at all fair to take away from so many men so much property that they had held for so long, including their own plantations, buildings and equipment, they finally and with difficulty passed a law introduced by the tribunes that nobody should occupy more than 500 iugera of this land or pasture more than 100 large stock (cattle) or 500 smaller stock (sheep). To enforce this they determined that there should be a number of free men whose job it was to keep a watch and report what happened. **34** Having enshrined these measures in a law, they took an oath over and above it and set penalties for breaking it, believing that the rest of the land would soon be distributed in small lots among the poor; but there was no concern for the laws or oaths, and those who seemed to respect them made the land over dishonestly to their relations, while the majority completely ignored them, **35** until Tiberius Sempronius Gracchus, a distinguished and most ambitious man, an extremely powerful speaker and well known to everyone for these reasons, spoke eloquently as tribune about the Italian people and the way that, though they were very good at warfare and related to the Romans, they were slowly declining into penury and depopulation with no hope of a solution. **36** He criticised the slave body as being of no use for military service and never faithful to its masters, bringing forward as an example of this the disaster owners in Sicily had recently suffered at the hands of their slaves, whose numbers had swelled from agriculture, and the fact that the Romans' war against them was neither easy nor short, but long drawn out and full of dangers of all kinds. **37** When he had said this he proposed the renewal of the law that no one should hold more than the 500 iugera (of public land). But he added to the ancient law that their sons might hold half that amount; three elected men, changed annually, should divide the remainder of the land among the poor.

8.7 Plutarch *Tiberius Gracchus* 5.1–6, 7.1–7: Tiberius' motives (1)

Plutarch discusses the effect on Tiberius of the repudiation of his treaty in 137 with the Numantines. Numantia in Spain withstood six Roman attempts to take it and it was captured only in 133 by Scipio Aemilianus (docs 5.50–53). Tiberius' diplomacy saved 20,000 Roman citizens.

5.1 After the war against Carthage, Tiberius was elected quaestor, and it fell to him to serve in a campaign against Numantia under the consul Gaius (Hostilius) Mancinus (137 BC), who was not a bad man, but more unfortunate than any other Roman as a general. **2** Nevertheless, amid unexpected misfortunes and adverse encounters, not only did Tiberius' intelligence and courage shine out all the more brightly but also, which was remarkable, his respect and honour towards his commander, who, under the misfortunes of the campaign, even forgot that he was general. **3** After being defeated in major battles, Mancinus tried to break camp, withdrawing the army during the night; the Numantines noticed this and immediately seized the camp, attacking the men as they fled, and killed the rearguard. They then encircled the whole force and drove them to difficult terrain with no chance of escape. Mancinus, who had given up hope of forcing his way to safety, sent heralds to propose a truce and peace terms. **4** The Numantines declared that they had no confidence in anyone except Tiberius and ordered that he be sent to them. **5** They came to this decision both because of the young man himself (for he had an excellent reputation among their troops) and because they remembered his father Tiberius, who had fought against the Spaniards, and subdued many of them, but made a peace with the Numantines, which he had always ensured that the people kept scrupulously and justly. **6** So Tiberius was sent to negotiate with the enemy, and, after persuading them to accept some terms and accepting others himself, he arranged a truce and unarguably saved the lives of 20,000 Roman citizens, without counting slaves and camp followers. . . .

7.1 When he returned to Rome, the whole transaction was being criticised and denounced as a terrible disgrace to Rome, although the relatives and friends of the soldiers, who formed a large part of the people, came running to Tiberius, blaming the disgrace of what had happened on his commander and declaring that it was through Tiberius that so many citizens' lives had been saved. **2** Those, however, who were unhappy at what had been done urged that they should imitate the actions of their forefathers, who had thrown naked to the enemy the very generals who had been content to be released by the Samnites, and similarly throw out those who had had a part and share in the treaty, such as the quaestors and military tribunes, placing on their shoulders the perjury and repudiation of the agreement. **3** It was on this occasion that the people particularly demonstrated their good-will and affection towards Tiberius. **4** For they voted that the consul should be handed over to the Numantines stripped and in chains, but spared all the others for Tiberius' sake. **5** It appears that Scipio (Aemilianus), at that time the greatest and most powerful man at Rome, also helped; but nonetheless he was criticised because he had not saved Mancinus and had not insisted that the treaty, negotiated by his relative and friend Tiberius, should be kept. **6** It seems most likely that the difference between the two men arose through the ambition of Tiberius and from the friends and sophists who encouraged him; but this difference led to no irremediable break. **7** My own view is that Tiberius would never have met with his misfortunes if Scipio (Aemilianus) Africanus had been at Rome during his political career; but he was already at Numantia and waging war there when Tiberius undertook his programme of proposed reforms.

8.8 Cicero *On the Responses of the Soothsayers* 43: Cicero's view

Cicero, like Plutarch, sees the resentment (*dolor*) of Tiberius as crucial to his decision in 133 to press for reform of the ager publicus. Cicero reflects the senatorial element that opposed Tiberius, although he had some senatorial support: his law did not aim to 'wage war' on the senate.

Tiberius Gracchus had been involved in concluding a treaty with the Numantines when he was serving as quaestor to the consul Gaius Mancinus. The unpopularity he gained from this and the inflexibility of the senate in refusing to ratify it inspired Tiberius with resentment and fear, and these forced that brave and distinguished man to break away from the authority of the senate.

8.9 Plutarch *Tiberius Gracchus* 8.6–10: Tiberius' motives (2)

Plutarch adduces several other motives for Tiberius. The extent to which Cornelia was an influence on her sons is unclear. She did persuade Gaius to desist from his attack on Octavius (doc. 8.29), and there is no reason to assume that she was not ambitious for her sons (doc. 7.22).

6 As soon as Tiberius became tribune he put his plans straight into action, under the encouragement, as most report, of Diophanes the orator and Blossius the philosopher. Diophanes was an exile from Mytilene, while Blossius was a native Italian from Cumae and had been a close friend at Rome of Antipater of Tarsus, who had honoured him by dedicating to him some of his philosophical treatises. **7** But some also put the blame on his mother Cornelia, since she often reproached her sons, because the Romans still referred to her as the mother-in-law of Scipio and not yet as the mother of the Gracchi. **8** Others say that a certain Spurius

Postumius was responsible. He was the same age as Tiberius and a rival of his for reputation as an advocate, and, when Tiberius returned from the campaign and found Postumius had far surpassed him in reputation and influence and was widely admired, he decided, it seems, to outdo him by undertaking a bold political programme which would give rise to widespread expectations. **9** But his brother Gaius has written in a certain pamphlet that, as Tiberius was travelling through Etruria on his way to Numantia, he observed the depopulated nature of the country, and that the farmers and herders were imported barbarian slaves, and that it was then that he first thought of the programme which was to bring countless ills on the two brothers. **10** But it was the people themselves who most of all kindled his energy and ambitions, who called on him by means of graffiti on porticoes, house walls and monuments to recover the public land for the poor.

8.10 Appian *Civil Wars* 1.10 (38–42): The reaction of the wealthy

The senatorial reaction was reasonable. There had been an understanding that the ager publicus could be farmed, and Tiberius had made no provision for reimbursement or compensation. But the provision that the wealthy retain 500 iugera, and more depending on children, was very generous, especially as the lots distributed to the poor were a maximum of 30 iugera.

38 What particularly upset the wealthy was that they were no longer able to ignore the law, as they had before, because of the commissioners, nor could they buy the land from those to whom it was allocated, because Gracchus had foreseen this and forbidden it to be sold. **39** They banded together in groups and aired their grievances, accusing the poor of robbing them of their work of many years, their plantations and houses, while some had paid their neighbours for the land and would lose their money with the land, while others had ancestral tombs on land that had been allotted to them in the division of their fathers' properties; others had spent their wives' dowries on their estates or given the land as dowries to their daughters; some could show debts contracted to moneylenders with their land as surety, and there was widespread lamentation and anger. **40** On the other hand, the poor complained in their turn that they had been reduced from comfort to utter poverty and from there to childlessness, since they were not able to bring up their children. They enumerated how many campaigns they had served for the acquisition of this land and were angry at the suggestion that they might be deprived of their part of the common land, while they abused their opponents for choosing to use slaves instead of free men, citizens and soldiers, since slaves were always an untrustworthy and hostile race and for that reason of no use in the army. **41** While the two sides were making such complaints and mutual recriminations, another large group of those who lived in the colonies or free towns, or who were in some way or other concerned with this land and had similar fears, flooded in (to Rome) and took the part of one side or the other. **42** Taking heart because of their numbers, they grew exasperated and kindled numerous conflicts while they waited for the voting on the law, with one party determined by any means to prevent its being enacted, the other to have it passed at all costs.

8.11 Plutarch *Tiberius Gracchus* 9.1–6: Tiberius' rhetoric

(*ORF* 4 F149.) Tiberius relied mainly on the people's support, though he also had supporters in the senate drawn largely from his family connections. Here he refers to landless
soldiers, who had perhaps lost their farms while on service. P. Licinius Crassus (cos. 131)
was pontifex maximus from 132; Mucius Scaevola was consul in 133.

1 He did not draft the law on his own but followed the advice of the citizens
who were most eminent in merit and reputation, among whom were Crassus the
pontifex maximus, Mucius Scaevola the jurist, who was then consul, and Appius
Claudius, Tiberius' father-in-law. **2** And it did seem that no law against such
injustice and greed had ever been put in more mild and gentle terms . . . **3** Despite
the restitution being so conciliatory, the people were content to leave the past
alone as long as the injustice would come to an end in the future, but the wealthy
and landowners hated the law out of greed and the law-giver out of rage and con-
tentiousness and tried to turn the people against it on the grounds that Tiberius
was introducing a redistribution of land to overthrow the state and stir up a revolution. **4** They had no success; Tiberius was striving for a policy which was just
and good in itself and employing oratory which would have adorned a less worthy subject. He was formidable and insuperable when, with the people crowding
around the rostra on which he was mounted, he would speak on behalf of the poor:
5 'The wild beasts that dwell in Italy have their homes, with each having a lair
and a hiding place, but the men who fight and die on behalf of Italy have a share
of air and light – and nothing else. Without houses or homes they wander aim-
lessly with their children and wives, and their generals deceive them when they
urge the soldiers on the battlefield to drive off the enemy to protect their tombs
and temples; **6** not one of these Romans has a family altar, not one an ancestral
tomb; instead, they fight and die to protect the luxury and wealth of others. They
are called masters of the earth yet have not a single clod of earth that is their own.'

8.12 Cicero *Brutus* 103–4: Tiberius as public figure

Cicero again sees the *invidia* (animosity) over the repudiation of the Numantine treaty as
being a major stimulus for Tiberius' legislation. He is incorrect in stating that Tiberius was
'put to death by the state itself' (103); he was murdered by senators who took the law into
their own hands. C. Papirius Carbo (cos. 120) was a member of Tiberius' land commission.

103 If only Tiberius Gracchus and Gaius Carbo's attitude towards conducting the
affairs of state properly had equalled their genius for speaking well! – Indeed, no
one would have surpassed them in reputation (gloria). Gracchus, as a result of the
tempestuous violence of his tribunate, to which he proceeded enraged with
the 'honest men' (the boni) over the animosity aroused by (the repudiation of) the
Numantine treaty, was put to death by the state itself; Carbo, as a result of his
constant irresponsibility in popular politics, saved himself from the condemnation
of a jury only by a death at his own hands. But each was a top-class orator **104** –
and I can state this with our fathers' memory of their speeches as my evidence;
for we possess speeches of both Carbo and Gracchus in which the language does

not yet achieve brilliance, but which are to the point and skilful in the extreme. Through the diligence of his mother Cornelia, Gracchus had been educated from boyhood and was thoroughly versed in Greek literature. For he had always had excellent teachers from Greece, one of whom, from his youth, being Diophanes of Mytilene, who was considered to be the most eloquent speaker in Greece at that time. But Gracchus' time for developing and displaying his talent was short-lived.

8.13 Appian *Civil Wars* 1.11–13 (43–57): Octavius' deposition

Tiberius' proposal was to renew the law that no one should hold more than the 500 iugera of public land, while their children might each hold half that amount, and that a commission of three men should divide the remaining land among the poor (cf. doc. 8.6). He has 500 iugera and half again for each son, with no limit on the number of sons (or children). Tiberius took the legislation directly to the comitia tribute, and the opposition of the tribune M. Octavius to the agrarian proposal was clearly unexpected. No tribunician veto had been imposed between 287 and 133 BC, and Octavius, in opposing the clear wishes of the assembly, went against established practice.

43 Gracchus' intention in proposing the bill was to effect a plentiful supply not of money but of men, and, being particularly enthused by the useful nature of the work, believing that Italy could experience nothing greater or more glorious, he paid no consideration to the attendant difficulties. **44** When it was the time for voting, he brought forward many other arguments at length and inquired of them whether it was not just that the common property should be divided in common and whether a citizen was not always more a legitimate concern of theirs than a slave, a soldier more useful than one who had no part in warfare, and a man who shared in the common property more devoted to the public welfare than one who did not. **45** Without spending much time on this comparison as being demeaning, he went straight on to a consideration of their country's hopes and fears, pointing out that they held most of their territory through conquest in war and hoped to possess the remainder of the inhabited world, and that now was the critical moment, as to whether they would have plenty of men and obtain the rest or lose what they had to their enemies through weakness and jealousy. **46** After exaggerating the glory and prosperity of the one and the danger and fear of the other, he told the wealthy to consider all this and to give this land as a gift, if necessary, from themselves to those who would bring up children to bring these hopes about. They should not, by disputing about trifles, overlook the larger picture, especially as they were getting sufficient compensation for the work they had put in, with each of them getting, without payment and for all time, undisputed possession of 500 iugera, and also half of this again for each of their children, should they have any. **47** After making a long speech along these lines and stirring up the poor and those others who were motivated by reason rather than the desire for gain, Gracchus ordered the clerk to read out the proposed law.

48 Marcus Octavius, however, another tribune, who had been induced by those in occupation of the lands to interpose his veto – for among the Romans the veto is always the more powerful – ordered the clerk to be silent. **49** Gracchus thereupon severely censured him and adjourned the meeting to the next assembly day. He stationed beside himself a sufficient guard, as if he were going to force Octavius against his will, and ordered the clerk with threats to read the bill out to the people. He began to read, but on Octavius' forbidding it fell silent. **50** The tribunes began to abuse each other, and the people were in considerable uproar, when the leading citizens asked the tribunes to submit the matter under debate to the senate, and Gracchus seized on the suggestion, as he believed that his law would be accept-able to all well-disposed people, and hurried to the senate house. **51** But since he had few supporters there and was insulted by the rich, he ran back to the forum and said that at the next meeting of the assembly he would put a vote both about the proposed law and about Octavius' magistracy, to decide whether a tribune who acted against the interests of the people should continue to hold office. **52** And this he did; for when Octavius, not at all browbeaten, again interposed his veto, Gracchus put the vote about him first.

When the first tribe voted to depose Octavius from his magistracy, Gracchus turned to him and begged him to change his mind. As he would not be persuaded, he put the vote to the other tribes. **53** There were 35 tribes at that time, and, after the first 17 angrily concurred with the motion, Gracchus, as the eighteenth, was about to give the decisive vote, again, in the sight of the people, when he urgently begged Octavius, whose position was now critical, not to render null and void a work that was extremely fair and useful to all Italy, nor to overturn the people's earnest wish, especially since it was only right for him as tribune to give in to their desires and not to seek to have his office taken away by the people's condemnation. **54** After saying this and calling on the gods to witness that it was not willingly that he was dishonouring a colleague, as Octavius did not give in, he went on taking the votes. Octavius immediately became a private citizen and went off unnoticed.

55 Quintus Mummius was elected tribune in his place, and the agrarian law was passed. The first commissioners elected to allocate the land were Gracchus him-self, the law's proposer, his brother of the same name (Gaius) and his father-in-law Appius Claudius, as the people were still very afraid that the law might not be put into effect unless Gracchus and his whole family began the work. **56** Gracchus was highly thought of by the people because of this law and was escorted home as if he were the founder, not of a single city or race, but of all the nations in Italy. **57** After this the victors returned to their fields, from where they had come for this purpose, while the losers who remained in the city took it badly, saying that once Gracchus was a private citizen again he would be sorry that he had insulted the sacred and inviolable tribunate and had given Italy such an occasion for conflict.

TIBERIUS AND THE SENATE

8.14 Plutarch *Tiberius Gracchus* 13.2–14.3: Tiberius offends the senate

The senate cannot have been unduly upset at Tiberius' act in taking agrarian legislation direct to the comitia tributa, and some senators supported him (doc. 8.11). However, the loss of so much ager publicus was obviously a blow to many senators, and they attempted to frus-trate the land commission through allocating it a paltry allowance. Tiberius did encroach on senatorial prerogatives when he proposed to make use of the money available from the bequest of Attalus III of Pergamum (doc. 5.45): this gave rise to violent opposition.

13.2 Tiberius succeeded in carrying all these measures peaceably and without opposition, and in addition had a replacement tribune elected, not a man from a distinguished family, but Mucius, a client of his. The wealthy, angered at all of this and afraid of Tiberius' increasing power, kept insulting him in the senate, **3** and when, as was the custom, he requested a tent at the public expense for his work in dividing up the land, they did not grant it, though others had often received one for less important duties, and assigned him an expense allowance of 9 obols a day on the proposal of Publius Nasica, who had utterly given himself up to hatred of Tiberius; for he possessed a very great deal of public land and bitterly resented being obliged to give it up. **4** This enraged the people still more; and when a certain friend of Tiberius' died suddenly, with malignant eruptions apparent all over the corpse, they cried out that he had been poisoned . . . **6** Whereupon, Tiberius incited the people still further by going into mourning and bringing his children before the people and begging them to take care of them and of their mother, as if he had given himself up for lost.

14.1 When Attalus Philometor died and Eudemus of Pergamum brought his will to Rome, in which the king had named the Roman people as his heir, Tiberius immediately, to win popularity, proposed a law that the king's money be given to those citizens who had been allocated land, to use for equipping and cultivating their farms. **2** As regarded the cities which were part of Attalus' kingdom, Tiberius said that it was not a matter to be decided by the senate, but that he himself would propose a motion to the people. **3** By this he gave extreme offence to the senate, and when Pompeius got up to speak he declared that he was Tiberius' neighbour and so knew that Eudemus of Pergamum had given him a diadem and purple robe out of the royal treasure, as the future king of Rome.

8.15 Appian *Civil Wars* 1.14–17 (58–72): Tiberius' death

Tiberius sought re-election to the tribunate to safeguard himself, as his enemies were threatening to prosecute him once his tribunate was over (Plut. *Ti. Gracchus* 16.1; App. 1.13). This decision to stand again was also an object of attack, and his methods caused all of the tribunes, with the exception of the replacement for Octavius, to desert him: Tiberius occupied the Capitol, drove the rich from the assembly, and the tribunes fled. Nasica, the pontifex maximus, took the matter into his own hands, and Gracchus and his supporters were bludgeoned to death with bench legs, staves and clubs.

58 It was now summer, and the tribunician elections were at hand; as the day for voting approached, it was very clear that the rich had been earnestly supporting the election of those especially hostile to Gracchus. He was afraid as the danger came closer that he might not be tribune for the following year, and he summoned the people from the fields to the election. **59** As they were busy with the harvest, he was compelled by the nearness of the day appointed for voting to have recourse to the plebeians in the city, and he went round to them all individually asking them to elect him tribune for the next year, since he was at risk on their account. **60** When the voting took place, the first two tribes voted for Gracchus, but the rich objected that it was not legal for the same man to hold the office twice in succession, and the tribune Rubrius, who had been chosen by lot to preside over the assembly, was in doubt as to the matter . . . **62** As there was much argument over this question, and Gracchus was losing, he postponed the election till the next day, and in total despair dressed himself in black, though still in office, and for the rest of the day led his son around the forum, introducing him to everyone and committing him to their care, as if his destruction at the hands of his enemies was close at hand.

63 On reflection, the poor were seized with great sorrow, both for themselves, believing that they would no longer be treated equally as citizens under the laws but would be compelled to work for the rich, and for Gracchus himself, who was in such fear and suffering on their account, and they all escorted him to his house that evening with lamentation, bidding him to take courage for the next day. **64** With renewed confidence, Gracchus assembled his supporters before dawn and told them the signal, should fighting be necessary. He then occupied the temple on the Capitoline hill, where the voting was to take place, and the middle of the assembly. **65** Obstructed by the tribunes and the rich, who would not allow the votes to be taken on this issue, he gave the signal. A sudden shout arose from those in the know, and violence broke out, with some of Gracchus' supporters protecting him like bodyguards, and others girding up their togas, grabbing the rods and staves in the hands of the lictors, and breaking them into pieces. They then drove the rich from the assembly **66** with such uproar and wounds that the tribunes fled from their central position in fear, and the priests closed the temple. Many ran away in confused flight, spreading false rumours, some that Gracchus had deposed the other tribunes from their office (this was believed because they could not be seen), others that he had declared himself tribune for the next year without an election.

67 While this was going on, the senate met in the temple of Fides. It seems amazing to me that it did not occur to them at that juncture to appoint a dictator, though they had often been protected in such dangers by the rule of one man, but an action which had been so useful in earlier times did not occur to the people, either then or later. **68** After taking their decisions, they made their way up to the Capitol. The first, who led the way, was the pontifex maximus, Cornelius Scipio Nasica; he cried in a loud voice,

'Those who wish to save their country, follow me!' . . . **69** When he reached the temple and advanced on Gracchus' men, they gave way out of respect for such a distinguished man, and because they saw the senate accompanying him; but the senators grabbed the clubs from Gracchus' men and smashed the benches and other pieces of equipment which had been provided for the assembly, and began to strike the Gracchans, pursuing them and driving them over the cliff. **70** In this uproar, many of Gracchus' men died, including Gracchus himself, who was pressed up against the temple and slain at the door near the statues of the kings. All these bodies were thrown at night into the River Tiber. **71** In this way

Gracchus, son of the Gracchus who was twice consul and of Cornelia, daughter of the Scipio who had taken its supremacy away from Carthage, was killed on the Capitol while still in office as tribune, as a result of an excellent proposition which, however, he pursued too violently. This was the first occasion on which a heinous crime of this sort took place in the assembly, and similar incidents were to be encountered on a regular basis from thenceforth. **72** The city was divided on the issue of Gracchus' death into grief and delight, with some people lamenting both for themselves and for him, as well as for the current state of affairs, for they considered that the state was no longer in existence and that it had been replaced by force and violence, while the others felt that all their wishes had been granted.

BOUNDARY STONES OF THE GRACCHAN PERIOD

Despite Tiberius' murder, the activities of the land commission proceeded and the distribution of land went ahead, with the senate proposing that a new commissioner be chosen in place of Tiberius (Plut. *T. Gracchus* 21.1), implying that their opposition was not to his agrarian legislation. Several boundary stones set up by the commissioners have survived, from Campania, the territory of the Hirpini, Lucania and Picenum.

8.16 *ILS* 26: Gracchan boundary stones of 132 BC

A small pillar found between Pisaurum and Fanum, dating to 82/81 BC; the boundary stones laid by Tiberius' commission were being replaced.

Marcus Terentius Varro Lucullus, son of Marcus, acting as praetor, **5** by a resolution of the senate superintended the re-establishment of boundary stones where Publius Licinius, Appius Claudius and Gaius Gracchus, Board of Three for adjudging and assigning lands, established them.

8.17 *CIL* I² 639: Land-surveying boundaries, 131 BC

A pillar marking the corner of a century, found at Atina in Lucania, dated to 131 BC. A century was a large block of land which was then divided into individual plots.

(On shaft) Gaius Sempronius Gracchus, son of Tiberius; Appius Claudius, son of Gaius; Publius Licinius, son of Publius; Board of Three for adjudging and assigning lands. Seventh hinge-baulk.

8.18 *ILS* 25: Land-surveying boundaries, 123 BC

A pillar marking an angle at the boundary of the estate of an established occupier, found at Rocca San Felice, dated to 123 BC.

(On shaft) Marcus Fulvius Flaccus, son of Marcus; Gaius Sempronius Gracchus, son of Tiberius; Gaius Papirius Carbo, son of Gaius; Board of Three for adjudging and assigning lands. (On top) To established occupier; allowed free of charges.

THE AFTERMATH OF TIBERIUS' LEGISLATION

8.19 Appian *Civil Wars* 1.18 (73–7): The land commission continues

Tiberius' death did not end the matter, and actions against his supporters continued. Nasica, however, was very unpopular and was sent off to Pergamum to organise the province. The consuls for 132 (P. Rupilius and P. Popillius Laenas) established a senatorial court, and some of Tiberius' supporters were executed, others banished without a trial.

73 After Gracchus was killed and Appius Claudius died, Fulvius Flaccus and Papirius Carbo were appointed as commissioners in their place, together with the younger Gracchus, to divide the land. Since those who possessed land neglected to register it, the commissioners proclaimed that informers should testify against them. **74** There was soon a huge number of difficult law-suits; for whenever a field which adjoined this land was sold or divided among the allies, it all had to be accurately investigated because of the measurement of this field, as to how it was sold or divided, though not all the owners still had their contracts or allotment deeds – even those which were found were ambiguous. **75** When the land was resurveyed, some owners were transferred from orchards and farm-buildings to bare ground, others from cultivated to uncultivated land or to swamps or marshes, since the survey had never been done accurately in the beginning, as the land was won in battle. **76** The original proclamation, that anyone who wished might farm the unallocated land, had encouraged many to work land adjoining their own and blur the status of both; the passing of time had also confused everything. **77** And so the injustice done by the rich, though great, was hard to identify. There was nothing but a complete resettlement, with everyone being transferred from their own and settled on other people's property.

8.20 Macrobius *Saturnalia* 3.14.6–7: The judiciary law

Scipio Aemilianus made it clear that he disapproved of Tiberius' actions and thought his death justified (Plut. *T. Gracchus* 21.7). Scipio also attacked Tiberius' judiciary law, giving the land commissioners powers of adjudication, in a speech to the senate in 129 BC. Scipio was successful, and the jurisdiction over the land distribution was given to C. Sempronius Tuditanus (cos. 129) and not the land commissioners.

6 However, we certainly know that the sons and – though it is a dreadful thing to say – the unmarried daughters of noble families as well regarded the practice of dancing as one of their accomplishments, our witness being Scipio Africanus Aemilianus, who states as follows in his speech against the judiciary law of Tiberius Gracchus: **7** 'They are taught disreputable feats, and, in the company of male dancers (cinaeduli) and zither and lute, they go to a school for actors, they learn to sing songs which our ancestors considered disgraceful in the freeborn – freeborn girls and boys go, I say, to a dancing school and mix with male dancers. When someone told me this I could not bring myself to believe that men of noble birth taught their children such things: but when I was taken to the dancing school, I saw, on my oath, more than 50 boys and girls in that school and among them – and this more than anything else made me pity the state – a boy wearing the amulet of a freeborn child, the son of a candidate for office, a boy not less than 12 years old, dancing with castanets a dance which even a shameless little slave could not decently perform.'

8.21 Appian *Civil Wars* 1.19–20 (78–85): The allies, 129 BC

While Scipio Aemilianus did not attempt to interfere in the agrarian legislation, he successfully proposed that the land commission not deal with cases of disputes between the commissioners and allies, as the allies did not have confidence in the commission. Much of the ager publicus throughout Italy will have been farmed by Italians. When Scipio was found dead, suspicions were raised, since he had taken the side of the allies against the activities of the land commission.

78 The Italians were unable to tolerate this situation, especially the pressures arising from the law-suits brought against them, and chose Cornelius Scipio, the destroyer of Carthage, to be their defender against these injustices. **79** As they had been his eager supporters in his wars, he was reluctant to ignore their request, and in the senate, while he did not openly criticise Gracchus' law because of the people, he spoke against the hardship it caused and proposed that the law-suits should no longer be adjudicated by the commissioners, since the litigants had no confidence in them, but be settled by others. **80** As his suggestion seemed reasonable, the proposal was adopted, and Tuditanus the consul was appointed to judge the cases. But when he had begun on the task and saw its difficulties, he went off to fight the Illyrians, making this an excuse for not serving as judge, while the land commissioners stayed idle, since no one brought them cases for judgement. **81** As a result Scipio became a target for the hatred and anger of the people, because they saw the man for love of whom and on whose behalf they had often opposed the nobility and aroused their enmity, and whom they had twice elected consul, though illegally, now acting in the interests of the Italians in opposition to their own. **82** When Scipio's enemies noticed this, they cried out that he was completely determined to abolish Gracchus' law, and to this end was going to bring about widespread slaughter and armed strife.

83 When the people heard this they took fright, until Scipio, after putting a writing tablet beside him, on which he intended during the night to write the speech he was going to make to the people, was found dead without a wound – perhaps the deed of Cornelia, mother of the Gracchi, so that Gracchus' law might not be abolished, aided and abetted by her daughter Sempronia, who was married to Scipio in a mutually loveless relationship because she was deformed and childless, or perhaps, as some believe, he committed suicide because he saw that he would not be able to fulfil what he had promised. **84** Some say that slaves under torture stated that strangers, who were brought through the back door of the house at night, suffocated him, and that those who knew of it shrank from revealing it because the people were still angry with him and pleased at his death. **85** So Scipio died and was not thought worthy of a public funeral, though he had made great contributions to Rome's supremacy; in this way present anger outweighs past gratitude. And this event, important as it was, took place as if an unimportant incident in the strife brought about by Gracchus.

THE CAREER OF GAIUS GRACCHUS

Gaius had served in Numantia under Scipio Aemilianus, his cousin and brother-in-law. In 126 he was a supporter of M. Fulvius Flaccus, and he had been on the land commission from 130 BC. Fulvius proposed awarding the Italians citizenship, which would make them eligible for possession of the Roman ager publicus; he was elected as consul for 125, but the senate sent him to protect Massilia against the Salluvii. Gaius served as quaestor in Sardinia from 125. His desire to avenge his brother encouraged him to stand for the tribunate for 123, ten years after his brother's tribunate; he held a second in 122. As tribune Gaius passed numerous laws; his was the most comprehensive legislative programme ever undertaken by a tribune. He did not want to overthrow the senate or even curtail most of its powers, though he did act in the interests of the people and subjected the senate to new controls; much of his legislation remained in force.

8.22 Aulus Gellius *Attic Nights* 15.12.1–4: Gaius' return, 124 BC

Gaius served in Sardinia as quaestor in 125; he returned to Rome in 124 before his consul (L. Aurelius Orestes, cos. 126), no successor having been appointed because the nobles wanted to keep him out of Rome. He defended himself on the charge of leaving his province early and was elected tribune for 123. His criticism of the behaviour of Roman governors is perhaps an indirect attack on Orestes.

1 When Gaius Gracchus returned from Sardinia, he made a speech to the people in the assembly in the following words: **2** 'My conduct in my province', he said, 'was such as I thought would be to your benefit, not such as would contribute to my own ambition. My establishment had no cook-shop or any slave boys of outstanding appearance, and at any entertainment of mine your sons were treated with fewer temptations than at military headquarters.' **3** Later on, he states: 'My conduct in my province was such that no one could say with truth that I received an *as*, or more than that, as a present, or that anyone was put to any expense on my account. I spent two years in my province; if any prostitute entered my house or any slave boy was solicited on my behalf, then consider me the most worthless and iniquitous of mankind. Since I conducted myself with such continence towards their slaves, then you are able to judge on what terms I lived with your sons.' **4** After an interval he continues: 'Accordingly, citizens, when I set out for Rome I brought back empty from the province the money-belts which I took there full of money. Others have brought home overflowing with money the amphorae which they had taken out full of wine.'

8.23 Aulus Gellius *Attic Nights* 11.10.2–6: The veniality of politicians

Manius Aquillius (cos. 129), with a commission appointed by the senate, organised the province of Asia; part of Phrygia was awarded to Mithridates V of Pontus and not to Nicomedes of Bithynia. Gaius' comments about bribery were to be reflected in Sallust's remarks (docs 9.3, 9.7). Aquillius was prosecuted in the mid-90s for extortion in Asia but was acquitted despite being guilty.

2 Fellow citizens, if you wish to be advised wisely and honestly, when you consider the matter carefully you will find that none of us presents himself here without a price. All of us who make speeches are after something, and no one appears before you with any purpose other than to carry something away. **3** I myself, who am advising you to increase your taxes, by which you will be more easily able to administer your government and communal interests, do not come forward for free; but I ask you not for money but for your good opinion and respect. **4** Those who come forward to dissuade you from accepting this law are seeking not respect from you but money from Nicomedes; those who advise you to accept it, these too are seeking not your good opinion but a reward and increase in their possessions; those, however, of the same rank and status who are silent, these are the most grasping, for they take money from everyone and deceive you all. **5** Because you think that they distance themselves from such matters, you give them your good opinion; **6** but the embassies from the kings, since they think that they are silent for their sake, present them with lavish and immense sums of money. In the same way, in the land of Greece, at a time when a Greek tragic actor was boasting that he had been given a silver talent for one play, Demades, the most eloquent man of his country, is said to have replied to him: 'Does it appear wonderful to you that you have made a talent by speaking? I received 10 talents from the king for my silence.' In the same way, these men are now receiving an immense price for keeping quiet.

8.24 Aulus Gellius *Attic Nights* 10.3.2–5: Gaius on Roman magistrates

This speech may have been delivered in the context of his proposal in 122 to award citizenship to the Italians. But the incident in (**5**) also shows that his target was the misconduct of Roman officials in general (cf. doc. 8.23). The three towns mentioned in the first anecdote are on the Via Latina; Venusia is in Apulia.

2 I recently read the speech of (Gaius) Gracchus *On the Promulgation of Laws*, in which he complains with all the passion he can command that Marcus Marius and other respectable men of the Italian municipalities were unlawfully beaten with rods by magistrates of the Roman people. **3** These are his words on the subject: 'Recently a consul came to Teanum Sidicinum (in Campania). His wife said that she wished to bathe in the men's baths. The Sidicinian quaestor, Marcus Marius, was given the job of seeing that those who were washing in the baths were driven out. The wife reports to her husband that the baths were not handed over to her quickly enough and that they were not sufficiently clean. On that account a stake was set up in the forum and Marcus Marius, the most illustrious man in his city, was led to it. His clothes were removed and he was beaten with rods. The people of Cales, when they heard this, passed an edict that no one should wash in the baths when a Roman magistrate was in the town. At Ferentinum our magistrate ordered the quaestors to be arrested for the same reason: one threw himself from the wall, the other was taken and beaten with rods.'

5 Gracchus in another place also speaks as follows: 'I will give you a single example of the degree of passion and lack of self-control possessed by our young men. Within these last few years a young man was sent from the province of Asia on behalf of his governor, not having to that time held a magistracy. He was carried in a litter. A ploughman, one of the Venusian peasants, encountered him and, as a joke, since he was unaware who was being carried, asked whether they were carrying a corpse. When the young man heard this, he ordered the litter to be put down and ordered him to be beaten with the straps with which the litter was tied together until he expired.'

8.25 Cornelius Nepos *On the Latin Historians* F59: Cornelia's advice

Cornelia's letters were preserved after she died; here she writes to her son Gaius. Cornelius Nepos was a Republican biographer and might have had access to a collection of her letters. The setting is 124 BC, when Gaius was a candidate for his first tribunate.

You will say that it is a noble deed to avenge oneself on enemies. To no one does this seem finer and more noble than to me, as long as no harm is done to the state. But, since that is not possible, it will be far better that our enemies should not perish and remain as they are now, rather than that the state be overthrown and perish.

I would swear a solemn oath that, except for those who killed Tiberius Gracchus, no enemy has given me as much trouble and hardship as you have in this affair – you who should have taken the part of all those children I used to have and should have seen to it that I had as little anxiety as possible in my old age. Whatever you were doing, your main object should have been to please me, and you should consider it criminal to do anything important against my will, especially since I have only a short time to live. Can you not do your duty even for that short time without going against my will and overthrowing the state? Where will it ultimately end? Will our family ever leave off its madness? Will a limit ever be put to it? Will we ever stop taking and giving offence? Will we ever feel great shame at creating uproar and disturbance in the state? Well, if that is not a possibility, stand for the tribunate when I am dead; feel free to do as you please when I will not know about it. When I am dead, you will sacrifice to me and call upon the spirit of your parent. At that time will you not be ashamed to summon the spirits of those whom you abandoned and deserted when they were alive and with you? If only heavenly Jupiter would not permit you to continue on this path or such insanity to enter your mind! And if you carry on, I fear that, through your own fault, you will have to suffer such hardship through your whole life that you yourself will not at any time be able to be satisfied with your conduct.

8.26 Cicero *Brutus* 125–26: Gaius as orator

Cicero here praises Gaius as an orator but is swayed by his views of Gaius' political activities.

125 Now, however, there comes a man of outstanding ability, extreme dedication and education from his boyhood, Gaius Gracchus. Do not imagine, Brutus, that anyone was ever more fully or more richly qualified for oratory.

I think exactly the same, he replied, and he is almost the only one of our earlier speakers that I read.

Yes, I certainly think that you should read him, Brutus. For with his early death the Roman state and Latin literature incurred a great loss. **126** If only he had chosen to display as much loyalty to his country as to his brother! How easily with such talent, if he had lived longer, would he have rivalled the reputation of his father or grandfather! Indeed, I believe that in eloquence he would have had no equal. He is lofty in diction, wise in ideas, impressive in his whole style. His works have not received the final touch; much is begun admirably but, clearly, has not received the final polish. Indeed, he is an orator to be read by our youth, Brutus, if anyone is; for he can not only sharpen but nourish their talents.

8.27 Aulus Gellius *Attic Nights* 1.11.16: Gaius' oratorical devices

In Cicero's account (*De orat.* 3.225), the musician stood behind Gaius to modulate his delivery. Gellius (1.11.10–16), however, believes 'more reliable authorities', who say that the musician was in the audience, his purpose being to restrain Gracchus' energy as orator.

So this same Gracchus, Catulus, as you can hear from your client Licinius, an educated man who was Gracchus' amanuensis, used to have an experienced musician with an ivory pitch-pipe standing concealed behind him when he was addressing the assembly, who could quickly blow a note to rouse him up if lethargic or restrain him from over-vehemence.

GAIUS' LEGISLATION

8.28 Appian *Civil Wars* 1.21–3 (86–101): Gaius' laws (1)

Appian and Plutarch date the grain, land and military laws to 123. The laws concerning the equites, law-courts and colonies clearly belong to the second tribunate of 122, as do those for roads. The citizenship proposal must also belong to 122.

1.21.86 *Land legislation*: Gaius' first aim was to re-establish his brother's land legislation dividing the ager publicus among Roman citizens. **1.21.89** *The grain distribution* (the *lex frumentaria*): The state bought up large quantities of grain, had granaries built at Rome for storing it, and offered it for sale at 6⅓ asses for a modius, slightly below the usual market rate. Gaius' reorganisation of tax collection in Asia was initiated to pay for this and his other measures.

1.21.90 *Re-election to the tribunate*: Gaius was easily elected because of a lack of a tenth candidate. Fulvius Flaccus, the Gracchan land commissioner and consul of 125, was also elected in 123 as a tribune for 122. **1.22.91** *The extortion law*: Belonging to early in the second tribunate, this dealt with the recovery of money which Roman magistrates illegally extracted from Latins, allies and foreigners subject to Rome (it is sometimes referred to as the *lex Acilia repetendarum*). He gave the equites judicial rights and responsibilities that had hitherto been the province of the senate.

1.21.86, 23.99–101 *The citizenship issue*: Flaccus' failure to enfranchise the allies had led to the revolt of Fregellae. The Latins were now to be offered full citizenship; the Italians were offered voting rights but not full citizenship. The election of Lucius Opimius, the destroyer of Fregellae, as consul for 121, was a signal that there was opposition to this. **1.23.101** *M. Livius Drusus* was one of the tribunes for 122. He proposed 12 colonies in a successful attempt to outbid Gaius' colony proposal. *Lex de provinciis consularibus*: The two provinces to which the consuls were to be assigned were to be decided by the senate before the election of the consuls themselves; this removed personal considerations from the allocation of provinces. *The province of Asia*: This measure arranged for tax collection in the province of Asia (Attalus of Pergamum's bequest). The censors would, every five years, farm out by auction the right to collect taxes in the province.

86 The occupiers of the land still put off its division for a considerable time on all kinds of pretexts. Some people even proposed that all the Italian allies, who were offering the most resistance about the land, should be enrolled as Roman citizens, since in return for this greater favour they would no longer make difficulties about the land. **87** The Italians welcomed this proposal, since they preferred Roman citizenship to the possession of the fields. Fulvius Flaccus, who was both consul and land commissioner, supported them in this to the utmost. The senate, however, was angry at the thought of making their subjects equal citizens with themselves.

88 And so this undertaking was abandoned, and the people, who had been in hopes of land for so long, lost heart. While they were in this condition, Gaius Gracchus, who had gained their favour as a land commissioner, stood for the tribunate – he was the younger brother of Gracchus the law-maker and had stayed out of politics for some time after his brother's death; but, as many of the senators treated him with scorn, he stood for the tribunate. **89** After an electoral triumph, he immediately started devising plans against the senate, proposing that a monthly distribution of grain be made to each citizen at the public expense, which was quite unprecedented. **90** Thus by one political ploy, in which Fulvius Flaccus co-operated, he quickly won over the people. Straight afterwards he was elected tribune for the next year as well; for a law permitted the people to choose a tribune from the body of citizens if there were not enough candidates for the office.

91 In this way Gaius Gracchus was tribune for the second time; already having the people in his pay, as it were, he now began to win over by a similar political ploy the so-called equites, who hold the middle status between senate and people. **92** He transferred the law-courts, whose reputation had been lost because of bribery, from the senators to the equites, reproaching the former in particular because Aurelius Cotta, Salinator, and third in the list, Manius Aquillius, who conquered Asia – all notorious bribe-takers – were acquitted by the judges, although ambassadors sent to complain about them were still in Rome going around making impassioned accusations against them. The senate was ashamed of such conduct and gave in to the law; and the people ratified it. **93** In this way the law-courts were transferred to the equites from the senate; it is said that, just after the law was passed, Gracchus stated that he had overthrown the power of the senate completely, and the train of events made his remark appear more and more significant. **94** For their role in passing judgement on all Romans and Italians, even on the senators themselves, to an unlimited degree, in cases which involved property, civil rights and exile, exalted the equites to the status of being, as it were, their rulers, while it put the senators on the level of subjects. **95** Since the equites leagued with the tribunes in elections, and in return got from them whatever they wanted, they were a cause of great anxiety to the senators; soon it happened that the control of government was reversed, with the senate retaining only the dignity, while the equites held the power. **96** Indeed, they went so far that they not only possessed the power but also insulted the senators beyond what was right. They started taking bribes, and, when they had had a taste of the enormous profits, they used them even more wickedly and immoderately than the senators had done. **97** They set suborned accusers on the wealthy and completely did away with suits involving bribery, partly by agreement among themselves and partly by force, so that the practice of this kind of inquiry completely disappeared and the judiciary law gave rise to another long-standing factional struggle, of no less impact than the earlier ones.

98 Gracchus also constructed lengthy roads throughout Italy and got the support of a large number of contractors and workers, who were ready to do whatever he told them. He also proposed the foundation of numerous colonies. **99** He called on the Latins to demand full citizen rights, as the senate could not decently refuse them to men of the same race; to the other allies, who were not permitted to vote in Roman elections, he proposed to give the right to vote, so that he might have their support too in voting for his laws. **100** The senate was greatly concerned at this and ordered the consuls to proclaim that: 'No one who does not have a vote shall stay in the city or approach within 40 stades of it while the voting on these proposals is taking place.' **101** It also persuaded Livius Drusus, another tribune, to veto Gracchus' proposed laws without stating his reasons to the people; it was not necessary that a vetoing tribune give his reasons. They also gave him the opportunity to conciliate the people by proposing 12 colonies; the people were so very pleased with this that it despised Gracchus' proposed laws.

8.29 Plutarch *Gaius Gracchus* 4.1–6.5: Gaius' laws (2)

Gaius proposed two laws in 123 BC designed to address his brother's death: that magistrates deposed by the people could not hold office again (aimed at Octavius, which was withdrawn at Cornelia's instigation) and that only the Roman people could authorise a death sentence against a citizen (P. Popillius Laenas as consul in 132, who had presided over the execution of Tiberius' supporters, went into self-exile when the law was passed). **5.1**: The military law (*lex militaris*; not mentioned by Appian) attempted to promote army recruitment.

4.1 After stirring up the people with such rhetoric – and he had a powerful voice and was a very forceful speaker – he proposed two laws, one stating that if the people had deposed any magistrate from office he was not allowed to hold office a second time; the other, that if any magistrate banished a citizen without trial he could be prosecuted by the people. **2** The first of these laws had the clear object of disqualifying Marcus Octavius, who had been deposed from the tribunate by Tiberius, while the second attacked Popillius: for as praetor he had banished Tiberius' friends. **3** Popillius did not stand trial and fled from Italy; Gaius himself withdrew the first law, stating that he had spared Octavius at his mother Cornelia's request. **4** The people were pleased that the motion was withdrawn, since they honoured Cornelia no less for her sons than for her father, and they later erected a bronze statue of her with the inscription, 'Cornelia, mother of the Gracchi'. . . .

5.1 Of the laws which he proposed to please the people and undermine the senate, one concerned the allotment of land, dividing the public land among the poor; another dealt with the army, laying down that clothing be supplied at public expense, with nothing being subtracted from soldiers' pay for this purpose, and no one younger than 17 years of age being conscripted; **2** another concerned the allies, giving the Italians voting rights equal to those of citizens; a grain law lowered the market price for the poor; while, through a jury law, he most severely undermined the power of the senate. **3** They alone had judged law-suits and, by this, had been formidable both to the people and to the equites; but Gracchus chose an additional 300 equites to add to the 300 senators, and juries were drawn from these 600. . . .

6.1 When the people not only passed this law but granted him the power to select the judges from the equites, a kind of kingly power was invested in him, so that even the senate accepted his advice. His advice was always in favour of measures which did the senate credit; **2** an example of this is the very fair and honourable decision concerning the grain sent by Fabius (Q. Fabius Maximus Allobrogicus, cos. 121), the propraetor, from Spain, when Gracchus persuaded the senate to sell the grain and return the money to the cities, as well as to censure Fabius for having made Rome's rule oppressive and burdensome to her subjects; this added greatly to his reputation and gained him goodwill in the provinces. **3** He also proposed laws to send out colonies, to construct roads and to establish granaries, making himself the director and organiser for all these undertakings, and was never worn out by any of these numerous and weighty projects – rather, he carried out each one with amazing speed and application, as though it were his only concern, so that even those who most hated and feared him were thunder-struck at the way everything was accomplished and brought to completion. **4** The people were amazed at the mere sight of him when they saw him attended by a mob of contractors, craftsmen, ambassadors, magistrates, soldiers, scholars – all of whom he handled with ease, still maintaining his dignity in his courtesy and giving each his proper consideration. He thus showed up as malicious slanderers those who called him terrifying or utterly arrogant or violent. **5** In this way he was more effective as a popular leader when he associated with others and dealt with business than in his speeches from the rostra.

8.30 Appian *Civil Wars* 1.24 (102–6): Loss of popular support

Because of Drusus' legislation in 122 BC, Gaius lost popularity, and he set off to establish a colony at Carthage ('Junonia'), which had been destroyed in 146 (doc. 4.63). In 122 he stood for a third tribunate but was not elected. The Latin citizenship proposal had been vetoed, and in 121 one of the tribunes, Minucius Rufus, proposed the repeal of the legisla-tion for Junonia. The (fabricated) omens indicate the aristocracy's control of religion: see docs 3.75–76.

102 After the failure of this attempt to win popular favour, Gracchus sailed to Africa together with Fulvius Flaccus, who, after his consulship, had been chosen tribune for the same reasons as Gracchus. A colony in Africa had been voted for on account of its reputation for fertility, and these men had been specifically chosen as its founders so the senate might have a brief rest from popular politics in their absence. **103** They laid out the colony's city on the spot where Carthage had once stood, without considering that when Scipio destroyed it he had laid curses on the site that it should stay sheep pasture for ever more. **104** They assigned 6,000 colonists, instead of the smaller number given in the law, hoping in this way to gain the support of the people. When they returned to Rome they summoned the 6,000 from all of Italy. **105** The officials who were still in Africa, laying out the site of the city, sent word that wolves had torn up and scattered the boundary markers of Gracchus and Fulvius, and the soothsayers considered the colony ill-omened. The senate therefore summoned the assembly, in which it was proposed to repeal the law about this colony; **106** when Gracchus and Fulvius saw they were failing in this matter as well, they were enraged and declared that the senate had lied about the wolves. The boldest of the plebs joined them, carrying daggers on their way to the Capitol, where the assembly about the colony was to be held.

8.31 Gaius Gracchus *ORF* 4 F47: A plea to the people, 122 BC

This fragment of a speech appears to belong to a period when Gaius felt insecure, presumably late in his second tribunate.

If I had wanted to speak to you and to ask you, as a member of an eminent family and one who had lost my brother on your account, and seeing that there is no descendant of the families of Publius Africanus and Tiberius Gracchus left apart from myself and my young son, that you would permit me to lead a quiet life uninvolved in politics for the present, so that my family might not utterly die out but that some offshoot of my family might survive, I believe you would have granted my request not unwillingly.

ASSASSINATION AND REPRISALS

8.32 Appian *Civil Wars* 1.25–6 (107–20): Gaius' death

The outbreak of violence was sparked off by the use of force on the part of a Gracchan supporter. Antyllus, in Plut. *G. Gracchus* 13.3, was an attendant of the consul Opimius, and Plut. 14.3 has the senate pass the *senatus consultum ultimum* (cf. doc. 1.70) that Opimius as consul should 'save the state', the first time it was passed. Strangulation was usually reserved for common criminals.

107 The people had already assembled, and Fulvius was beginning to speak about the matters in hand, when Gracchus came up to the Capitol accompanied by a bodyguard of his supporters. **108** Troubled by his conscience over his portentous plans, he turned aside from the assembly's meeting-place, went into the portico, and walked around waiting on what was to happen. **109** A plebeian called Antyllus, who was making a sacrifice in the portico, saw him in this state of disturbance and, putting his hand on him, either because he knew or suspected something or was motivated to speak by some other reason, begged him to spare his country. **110** Gracchus, even more disturbed, and alarmed like a criminal caught in the act, looked sharply at him; one of those who accompanied him, although there had been no signal or order given, supposed merely from Gracchus' fierceness towards Antyllus that the time had come, and, thinking that he would do Gracchus a favour by being the first to act, drew his dagger and killed Antyllus. **111** A cry went up, the dead body was seen in the middle of the crowd, and everyone rushed from the temple in fear of a similar fate.

Gracchus went into the assembly wishing to excuse himself from what had happened, **112** but no one would even listen to him and everyone turned from him as if he were polluted. He and Flaccus had no idea what to do, as through this premature act they had lost the opportunity to carry out their wishes, and they hurried to their homes, their supporters with them. The rest of the crowd occupied the forum after midnight as if in expectation of some disaster. **113** Opimius, the consul who was present in the city, ordered some armed men to gather at the Capitol at dawn and summoned the senate through heralds, while he waited on what was to happen in the temple of the Dioscuri in the centre of the city.

114 Matters stood like this when the senate summoned Gracchus and Flaccus from their homes to the senate house to defend themselves, but they ran out with their weapons to the Aventine hill, hoping that, if they took it first, the senate would make some terms with them. **115** As they ran through the city, they offered the slaves freedom, but none of them listened to them. With the men that they had, however, they seized the temple of Diana and sent Flaccus' son Quintus to the senate, requesting some form of agreement and harmonious co-existence. They were told to lay down their arms, come to the senate house and state their wishes, or not to send any more messengers.

116 When they sent Quintus a second time, the consul Opimius arrested him, since he had been warned he was no longer an ambassador, and sent his armed men against Gracchus' supporters.

117 Gracchus fled across the river by the wooden bridge (the Pons Sublicius) to a grove accompanied by a single slave and, being on the point of arrest, presented his throat to the slave; **118** Flaccus took refuge in the workshop of an acquaintance, and as his pursuers did not know the house they threatened to burn the whole row. The man who had given him shelter shrank from pointing out the suppliant but told another man to give him away. Flaccus was seized and killed. **119** The heads of Gracchus and Flaccus were taken to Opimius, and he gave those who brought them the equivalent weight in gold; the plebs plundered their houses and Opimius arrested their sympathisers, threw them in prison, and ordered them to be strangled. **120** However, he allowed Quintus, Flaccus' son, to die as he chose. He then purified the city from the killings, and the senate ordered a temple of Concord to be erected in the forum.

8.33 Plutarch *Gaius Gracchus* 17.5–9: The aftermath

This is apparently the first time a reward was paid for a head; cf. Sulla's proscriptions (docs 11.19–23). Licinia was the daughter of the wealthy P. Licinius Crassus Dives Mucianus, a member of the land commission and consul in 131 (cf. doc. 7.69). According to Plutarch, 3,000 died. This might be an exaggeration, but this was a much bloodier incident than the murder of Tiberius and his supporters.

17.5 Gaius' head was brought by Septimulius to Opimius stuck on the point of his spear, and when it was placed on the scales it weighed 17⅔ pounds, for Septimulius had acted not only abominably but criminally, having removed the brain and poured in molten lead. The men who brought in Fulvius' head – they were of less importance – got nothing. **6** The bodies of these two and of the others who were killed, 3,000 in all, were thrown into the river, and their property was confiscated by the state; their wives were forbidden to go into mourning, and Licinia, Gaius' wife, was deprived of her dowry. **7** The most inhuman treatment was that of Fulvius' younger son, who had neither used violence nor been among those who fought, but whom they had arrested when he came to propose a truce before the battle, and whom they killed after the fighting was over. **8** But what annoyed the people more than this or any of the other events was the erection by Opimius of a temple of Concord; for he appeared to be priding himself and exultant, and even in some way to be celebrating a triumph over the killing of so many citizens. **9** As a consequence some people during the night carved this verse under the inscription on the temple: 'This temple of Concord was made by an act of Discord.'

18.1 Opimius was the first person to use dictatorial powers during his consulship and to have 3,000 citizens put to death without a trial, among them Gaius Gracchus and Fulvius Flaccus, one of whom was an ex-consul and had celebrated a triumph and the other the most eminent man of his time in merit and reputation. Nor did he avoid fraud but, when he was sent as envoy to Jugurtha the Numidian, took bribes from him (116 BC); **2** and, after being convicted of the most heinous charge of bribery (109 BC), he grew old in disgrace, hated and insulted by the people, who were humbled and downcast by these events, though they soon made clear how much they wanted and missed the Gracchi. **3** For they set up statues of them in a prominent place, and they consecrated the sites where they were killed and offered them the first fruits of all the seasons, while many people sacrificed to them on a daily basis and worshipped them as if they were visiting the gods' shrines.

19.1 Furthermore Cornelia is said to have borne this further disaster nobly and magnanimously and to have said regarding the sacred sites where the killings had taken place that the dead had worthy tombs. **2** She went to live at the place called Misenum and made no change in her customary way of life. She had many friends and showed great hospitality to guests, and Greeks and scholars were her constant visitors, while all the kings received and sent presents to her. **3** She would please her visitors and friends greatly by recounting tales of the career and lifestyle of her father (Scipio) Africanus, but what they admired most was when she recalled without grief or tears the fates and achievements of her sons, relating them to anyone who asked as if she was speaking of men of olden days. **4** From this some people thought that she had lost her mind from old age or the weight of her troubles, and that she was insensible of her misfortunes, but it was these who were truly insensible of how much a noble disposition, and good ancestry and upbringing, can shield men against grief, and of how fate, while it may often defeat virtue's attempts to ward off misfortunes, cannot take away the power to bear this with equanimity.

8.34 Cicero *Brutus* 128: Gracchan anti-senatorial reprisals

The Mamilian commission was established by the tribune C. Mamilius Limetanus in 109 to look into the Jugurthine affair: many senators were accused of taking bribes; for Mamilius, see doc. 9.7. P. Scipio Nasica (cos. 111) was the son of the Nasica involved in killing Tiberius. Opimius was acquitted in 120 of killing Gaius but convicted of bribery in 109 by this commission.

Publius Scipio Nasica's colleague in his consulship, Lucius Bestia, made a good beginning to his tribunate, for, through the measure which bears his name, he recalled Publius Popillius (Laenas), who had been banished by the violence of Gaius Gracchus and was a keen-witted man and not ineloquent, though the end of his consulship was a sad one. For, under that hateful Mamilian law, Gaius Galba, an ex-quaestor and priest, and four ex-consuls, Lucius Bestia (cos. 111), Gaius Cato (cos. 114), Spurius Albinus (cos. 110) and that most pre-eminent citizen Lucius Opimius (cos. 121), the killer of Gracchus, who was acquitted by the people even though he had made a stand against the people's wishes, were got rid of by Gracchan jurors.

FAILURE OF THE GRACCHAN REFORMS

8.35 Appian *Civil Wars* 1.27 (121–3): Further agrarian legislation

Appian mentions three laws passed after Gaius' assassination: first, those who had received land allotments could sell them (probably in 121); second, Thorius' law that distribution of the ager publicus was to cease (probably in 111); and, third, rent payable on ager publicus was abolished. The allotments must have been inalienable under Tiberius' legislation. The colony at Carthage continued, the work of the land commission went on until 111 BC, and nearly all of Gaius' legislation remained in force.

121 In this way the strife caused by the second Gracchus came to an end. Not long afterwards, a law was passed which permitted the occupiers to sell the land under dispute; for even this had been forbidden by the law of the elder Gracchus. The rich immediately started buying from the poor or forcibly seized the land on a number of pretexts. **122** So, for the poor, their condition became even worse than before, until Spurius Thorius, a tribune, introduced a law that the allocation of the land was no longer to be continued, and that the land would belong to those who occupied it, who should pay rent for it to the people, and that this money was to be distributed. This distribution gave some relief to the poor but was of no help in increasing the population. **123** Gracchus' law, which was excellent and extremely useful if it could have been put into practice, was once and for all undermined by such devices, and shortly afterwards another tribune abolished the rent, and the people lost absolutely everything.

8.36 *CIL* I² 585 (selections): The *lex agraria*, 111 BC

This is the agrarian law introduced by Thorius (doc. 8.35). All the ager publicus, except the land which the legislation had made exempt (1, 4), which had been allotted or retained by the possessor up to the limit allowed under the Gracchan legislation, was confirmed as private, as were any buildings (7) and the land entered in the censors' lists as private (8). Ownership was guaranteed, but the Gracchan limits were to be observed (13–14).

1 . . . tribunes of the plebs duly brought a bill before the plebs and the plebs duly voted in the forum on the . . . day of . . . ; the . . . tribe voted first; the first to vote in the name of his tribe was Quintus Fabius, son of Quintus.

Regarding the state land in the country of Italy belonging to the Roman people in the consulship of Publius Mucius and Lucius Calpurnius (133 BC), not including the land which by a clause under the law or plebiscite introduced by Gaius Sempronius (Gracchus), son of Tiberius, tribune of the plebs, was exempted from division . . . **2** whatever land or ground out of that land or ground any long-standing occupier by law or plebiscite took or kept for himself, provided that its size not be greater than the amount one man was allowed by law or plebiscite to take or retain for himself.

Regarding the state land in the country of Italy belonging to the Roman people in the consulship of Publius Mucius and Lucius Calpurnius, not including the land which by a clause under the law or plebiscite introduced by Gaius Sempronius, son of Tiberius, tribune of the plebs, was exempted from division . . . **3** whatever land or ground out of that land or ground a member of the Board of Three has granted or assigned by law or plebiscite to any Roman citizen selected, provided that it is not included in that land or ground beyond . . .

4 Regarding the state land in the country of Italy belonging to the Roman people in the consulship of Publius Mucius and Lucius Calpurnius, not including the land which by a clause under the law or plebiscite introduced by Gaius Sempronius, son of Tiberius, tribune of the plebs, was exempted from division, whatever land or ground out of that land or ground was granted, given in exchange or confirmed by a member of the Board of Three to any person who exchanged public land for private. . . .

7 All land, ground or building which is recorded above . . . not including such land as has been exempted by a clause above, is to be private . . ., **8** and there is to be right of purchase and sale of that land, ground or building in the same way as for other private grounds, land or buildings; and a censor, whoever is in office, shall cause that land, ground or building, which has been made private by this law, to be entered in the censor's lists in the same way as other private lands, grounds or buildings . . . ; **9** and no one shall so act as to prevent any person to whom under law or plebiscite that land, ground, building or holding belongs or shall belong from using, enjoying, holding or possessing that land, ground, building or holding . . . nor is anyone to bring a motion before the senate in relation to this matter . . . **10** nor is any person by virtue of a magistracy or imperium to express an opinion or bring a motion by which any of those to whom under law or plebiscite any such land, ground, building or holding belongs or shall belong . . . shall be prevented from using, enjoying, holding or possessing that land, ground, building or holding, or by which possession shall be taken away against his will or, if he be deceased, against the will of his heirs . . .

13 Regarding the state land in the country of Italy belonging to the Roman people in the consulship of Publius Mucius and Lucius Calpurnius, not including the land which by a clause under the law or plebiscite introduced by Gaius Sempronius, son of Tiberius, tribune of the plebs, was exempted from division . . . and not including that land, which a long-standing occupier took or retained for himself by law or plebiscite, provided that its size not be greater than the amount one man was allowed to take or retain for himself, if any person at any time when this law shall be introduced **14** shall have entered into that land for the purpose of cultivation and possess or hold not more than 30 iugera of that land, that land is to be private.

Any person who shall send to pasture on common pasture land not more than ten head of larger cattle and any of their young less than a year old . . . or who shall send to pasture there not more than . . . head of smaller cattle and any of their young less than a year old, that person shall not owe impost or pasture tax for those cattle **15** to either people or tax-farmer and shall not be required to make any return or payment in relation to this matter.

LATER VIEWS OF THE GRACCHI

8.37 Cicero *On Duties* 2.73–85: Cicero's views

In this essay dedicated to his son Marcus in 44 BC, Cicero is giving his opinion about agrarian and debt laws and expressing the optimates' concern about the distribution of public land.

73 A person who holds public office must make it his first duty to see that each man keeps what belongs to him and that private citizens suffer no loss of property through an act of government . . . It was for this reason in particular that governments and states were instituted: so that each man might keep what belonged to him. For, although men banded together under nature's guidance, it was in hope of keeping their possessions safe that they sought the protection of cities. . . . **78** Indeed, men who wish to be populares, and who for that reason either try to bring in some agrarian reform so that the occupants may be driven out of their residences or think that money which has been loaned should be made over to the borrowers, are undermining the foundations of the state, for they are disrupting, firstly, public harmony (*concordia*), which cannot exist when money is taken away from some people and made over to others and, secondly, justice, which is completely done away with if each man is not allowed to keep what belongs to him . . . **79** How can it be just that a man who has never had any property should now hold land which had been occupied for many years or even generations, while the man who had had it should lose it? **80** It was by reason of this kind of wrongdoing that the Spartans banished their ephor Lysander and put to death their king Agis, which had never before happened in Sparta, and from that time on immense conflicts occurred and tyrants rose up, the optimates were driven out, and the excellently constituted state fell apart; nor indeed did it fall on its own, but, through the contagious nature of the evils which started in Sparta and then spread more widely, it overturned the rest of Greece too. What can we say of our own Gracchi, the sons of that eminent Tiberius Gracchus and grandsons of Africanus, but that it was strife over agrarian reform that destroyed them? . . . **85** And so men whose job it is to look after the state must refrain from that kind of generosity which takes property from some people to give it to others, and they should take especial care that each man keeps what belongs to him through the just administration of the law and courts and that the poorer classes should not be oppressed because of their humble status, while envy should not prevent the wealthy from holding onto or recovering what belongs to them.

8.38 Cicero *In Defence of Sestius* 96–7, 103: Cicero on the optimates

In this defence of Sestius (tr. pl. 57), delivered in 56 BC, Cicero divides senators into two groups.

96 There have always been two groups of men in this state who have been eager to participate in government and thus to distinguish themselves. Of these groups one wished to be, and to be thought to be, populares, 'popular'; the other, optimates, 'best'. Those who wanted everything they did and said to be agreeable to the masses were considered populares, but those who so acted that their policies won the approval of all the best citizens were considered optimates . . . **97** All are optimates who are neither criminal, nor disgraceful in disposition, nor insane, nor embarrassed by troubles in their family. It follows, therefore, that these men, whom you have called a 'breed', are honest and of sound mind and have their domestic circumstances comfortably organised . . .

103 Tiberius Gracchus proposed an agrarian law. The people were pleased: it looked as if the situation of the poorer classes would be relieved. The optimates, however, opposed it because they saw that it would give rise to dissension, and they also thought that, if the wealthy were evicted from land they had long occupied, the state would be stripped of its champions. Gaius Gracchus proposed a grain law. The people were delighted, as it provided plenty of food with no need to work. The 'good men' fought against it because they thought the masses would be drawn away from hard work towards idleness, and they saw that the treasury would be drained.

8.39 Cicero *On the Agrarian Law* 2.10: Cicero praises the Gracchi

Cicero's speech, as consul in 63, against the Rullan land bill was delivered before the people, which accounts for his pro-Gracchan sentiments here. Elsewhere he shows no sympathy for the Gracchi (docs 8.34, 37, 38).

For – I will speak frankly, Romans – I cannot disparage agrarian laws in themselves. I recall that those two most distinguished and most gifted men, the greatest friends of the Roman people, Tiberius and Gaius Gracchus, settled the plebs on public land, which had previously been privately owned. I am not one of those consuls who, like the majority, think it wrong to praise the Gracchi, whose advice, wisdom and laws, I see, have regulated many aspects of the administration.

8.40 Sallust *Jugurthine War* 42.1–4: Sallust on the Gracchi

Sallust, a supporter of Marius and a critic of the optimates, provides a positive assessment of the Gracchi to contrast with Cicero's views. A triumvir: one of the three men on the land commission.

1 So when Tiberius and Gaius Gracchus, whose ancestors had done much in the Punic and other wars to increase Rome's power, tried to defend the liberty of the plebs and expose the crimes of the few, the guilty nobility were shocked and opposed the Gracchi's proceedings, using now the allies and Latins and now the Roman equites, whom hope of an alliance had detached from their support of the plebs. First they butchered Tiberius, and then Gaius a few years later, because he was engaging in the same issues, the one a tribune, the other a triumvir for founding colonies, along with Marcus Fulvius Flaccus. **2** Certainly the Gracchi's desire for victory had led them to behave with insufficient moderation. **3** But a good man should prefer to be beaten than to defeat injustice by doing wrong. **4** As it was, the nobility used their victory arbitrarily and killed or banished a number of people, which added more to their fears during the rest of their lives than to their powers. This is what generally destroys great states, when each side will do anything possible to overcome the other and then avenge themselves harshly on their defeated opponents.

8.41 Plutarch *Agis and Cleomenes and the Gracchi Compared* 1.1–2, 5.4–6: The Gracchi as reformers

This passage comes from Plutarch's comparison of his life of the Gracchi and that of Agis IV and Cleomenes III of Sparta, who both attempted to reform Sparta in the face of domestic crisis.

1.1 Now that this biography is also finished, it remains for me to take a survey of all the lives in parallel. As for the Gracchi, not even those who totally abuse and hate them on other grounds have dared to deny that, of all Romans, they were the best equipped by nature for the practice of virtue and enjoyed an excellent upbringing and education; **2** the natural gifts of Agis and Cleomenes appear to have been more formidable than theirs, in so far as, though they did not receive correct training and were brought up in customs and ways of life by which their elders had long since been corrupted, they made themselves leaders in economy and moderation. . . . **5.4** Those who criticise their characters blame the two Greeks for having been despotic and aggressive from the beginning and the two Romans for having naturally been immoderately ambitious, though their enemies had nothing else to charge them with; in fact, they agree that it was because they were roused by the conflict with their opponents and by passions not natural to them, as if by blasts of wind, that they launched the state into such a dangerous crisis. **5** For what could have been more fair or just than their original proposals – had not the wealthy, in their attempts to obstruct the law by violence and factionalism, involved both of them in conflict, Tiberius through fear for his life and Gaius in his attempt to avenge his brother who had been killed without justice, without a decree of the senate, and without even the approval of a magistrate? **6** So, from what has been said, you will perceive the difference between them; but if I am to state my view of them separately, I should say that Tiberius was the most pre-eminent of them all in excellence, that Agis as a young man made the fewest mistakes, and that, in achievements and courage, Gaius was far behind Cleomenes.

9

Marius

Following Gaius Gracchus' death, the senatorial oligarchy re-established its influence, until increasing dissatisfaction with bribery, corruption and military incompetence brought change. One of the tribunes for 120 BC, P. Decius Subulo, prosecuted Opimius before the assembly for executing Roman citizens without a trial, which Gaius' *lex Sempronia* had prohibited. Opimius argued that he had carried out the senatorial decree calling upon him as consul to take measures to defend the state. He was acquitted, and P. Popillius Laenas, who had organised the witch-hunts of 132, returned from exile (*MRR* I.524; docs 8.19, 8.29). The senate's triumph seemed complete.

The next major phase in Roman politics came with the Jugurthine War. Sallust's *Jugurthine War* 5 sees it as the first time a challenge was made to 'the arrogance of the nobility' and also as the beginning of a struggle which ended with the civil war between Pompey and Caesar. It was the Jugurthine War, or rather the senate's poor handling of this, that gave Marius his chance to run for the consulship.

Marius' background was that of an equestrian from Arpinum. While he had not had the benefit of a thorough Greek education (docs 9.1–2), he clearly was not from an impoverished or obscure family. Arpinum possessed Roman citizenship, and Marius began his adult life with a military career typical of Roman equites. His military competence stood out, and he was elected to a military tribunate on the basis of his service in Spain (doc. 9.4), as well as holding the quaestorship. But his early political career was chequered. His tribunate of 119 was gained with the support of L. Caecilius Metellus (cos. 119), whom Marius threatened with violence over opposition to his voting law (docs 9.4, 36). Only with difficulty did he later obtain a praetorship after missing out on an aedileship (see doc. 9.4), though his marriage to Julia connected him with an aristocratic Roman family (doc. 9.5). Sallust overlooks these electoral difficulties in his presentation of Marius (doc. 9.6).

By 109 Marius was in favour again with the Metelli and accompanied Q. Caecilius Metellus (cos. 109) to Numidia, clearly on the basis of his military skills. The death of the king of Numidia, Micipsa, in 118 had left two sons (Hiempsal and Adherbal) and their cousin Jugurtha as heirs to the Numidian throne. Jugurtha had Hiempsal killed and defeated Adherbal, who fled to Rome. Opimius was sent to divide the kingdom, but Jugurtha continued to attack Adherbal and ignored the Romans, killing Adherbal and his Italian supporters in 112. Bestia (cos. 111) and Albinus (cos. 110) were sent out to Numidia, but both were incompetent against Jugurtha. Widespread bribery by Jugurtha of senators at Rome was suspected and clearly did occur. At about the same time, in 113, the army of Gnaeus Papirius Carbo (cos. 113) was destroyed by the Cimbri. This military incompetence and the failure to defeat Jugurtha led to widespread dissatisfaction at Rome, and Mamilius' law as tribune in 109 BC established a *quaestio extraordinaria* to deal with those accused of having been bribed by Jugurtha or who had otherwise aided him: Opimius, Albinus and Bestia were all convicted (doc. 9.7).

Metellus initially refused to let Marius return from Numidia to Rome in 108 to campaign for the consulship of 107, but Marius gained the support of Italian businessmen in Africa and the Roman troops, who wrote home supporting his consular candidacy. Metellus finally allowed him to go (doc. 9.9), and he was elected, probably because of dissatisfaction with the general performance of the nobility on the military front, and also because he had promised an end to the war, claiming that Metellus was protracting hostilities; the support of the equites must have been crucial (docs 9.7–9). The senate had already reassigned Numidia to Metellus, but one of the tribunes proposed a bill to grant the command to Marius. Metellus was furious but was granted a triumph and the title 'Numidicus'.

Marius wanted more troops than the senate had authorised, so he changed the recruitment procedure, including members of the *capite censi*, the landless poor, in his army (docs 9.10–11). The Gracchi's concern with military recruitment in attempting to restore small landholders is relevant here. Marius recruited from even the poorest, and so created a client army dependent on its general for land at the end of its period of service.

Sulla acted as Marius' quaestor in Numidia. They clearly worked well together, and Sulla was to be Marius' legate in the German wars. At this stage there was no animosity between them (doc. 9.12), and it was only in 88 BC that real rivalry between the two manifested itself. In Numidia as consul, Marius took several years to defeat Jugurtha and, when he was on the point of doing so, Bocchus, ruler of Mauretania, surrendered the king to Sulla (docs 9.13, 11.50).

Reforms to the army itself followed with the campaigns against the Germanic tribes, the Teutones and Cimbri (docs 9.23–6), with Roman fears of these migrating hordes leading to an unprecedented five consecutive consulships for Marius (104–100 BC). There had been a series of disasters against the Germans (doc. 9.14) and, with panic in Italy (doc. 9.16), Marius was a logical choice; the generals who had failed were prosecuted (doc. 9.19). The first years were quiet, and Marius reformed the army (docs 9.21–2), but great victories were then won against the Germans in 102 and 101 and Italy was safe (docs 9.23, 9.26, 9.37). Marius had the support of populares and optimates alike (docs 9.24–5). In 104 he had had the support of a tribune for 103, L. Appuleius Saturninus, in seeking the consulship. Saturninus' tribunate in 103 was not altogether remarkable. In 100 he was tribune for a second time as a result of the murder of the tribune Nonius, whom Saturninus replaced. His land legislation, passed for Marius' veterans during 100, violently and against the omens, aroused opposition and led to Metellus going into exile. A grain law is also usually dated to this year (doc. 9.38).

Saturninus was elected for a third tribunate with the impostor L. Equitius, who claimed to be a son of Tiberius Gracchus. Saturninus, with Glaucia, who was hoping for the consulship, organised the killing of one of the consular candidates for 99, Memmius, to ensure the election of Glaucia, who was praetor in 100 (and so ineligible for election as he was holding a magistracy and so could not seek election to another). The senate acted and an emergency decree was passed, with the consuls (C. Marius and L. Valerius) empowered to 'preserve the imperium and majesty of the Roman people' (doc. 9.30). Marius as consul presided over the distribution of weapons. The senate and equites acted together and arms were given to the plebs. Saturninus and his supporters were besieged on the Capitol, and the water pipes were cut off until they surrendered. Saturninus and his supporters were then held in the senate house, but the crowd broke in and stoned them; Glaucia was dragged from his house and his neck broken. Saturninus, Glaucia and Equitius were thus all killed on the first day of the tribunate, 10 December 100. Marius apparently tried to save their lives but was unable to oppose the angry mob. His attitude towards Saturninus was unclear, but he had obtained his land grants for his veterans and as consul clearly felt his interests lay more with the senate. Plutarch has Marius fall into obscurity for the 90s; this may be an exaggeration, but certainly there was little scope for his military talents in this period. He was involved in the Social War (docs 10.14, 18, 23). One last consulship awaited him. The command against Mithridates was awarded to Sulla as consul for 88, but Marius intrigued with the tribune P. Sulpicius Rufus to replace Sulla in the command (doc. 9.32). Sulla did not accept this, marched on Rome, had Sulpicius killed and Marius exiled, and left for the East (doc. 9.33). Marius returned to Rome amid bloodshed (doc. 9.34) and was elected to a final consulship for 86, but he died after a few days in office, on 13 January.

Any assessment of Marius' career must reflect not so much on his victory against Jugurtha – which may well have belonged to Metellus if he had been allowed to retain his command – but on his five consecutive consulships and the victories against the Germans for which he was largely responsible. His reforms of the army were to play a crucial role from 88 to 44 BC, with generals able to rely on the support of their armies in their struggle for pre-eminence. Sulla was to reap the first benefits of the dependent relationship between a general and his client army.

Ancient sources: the main sources are Sallust's *Jugurthine War*, which deals only with Marius' career in that conflict, and the unsatisfactory *Marius* of Plutarch. Sallust's *Jugurthine War* (references to this work are abbreviated as *BJ*, *Bellum Jugurthinum*) deals with Marius' campaigns in Africa. His portrait of Marius and Sulla in their early political careers is favourable, but he condemned Sulla's later career (Marius: *BJ* 84.2, 86; Sulla: *BJ* 95–6; docs 9.10, 12). Metellus' leadership of the army is reported positively (*BJ* 45.1–3), but his aristocratic *superbia* (arrogance) – which leads him to treat Marius' consulship aspirations with scorn – is also noted (doc. 9.6). Sallust's treatment of Marius, as the ultimate *popularis*, is

often seen as extremely favourable (note Marius' denunciations of the aristocracy:
BJ 85; doc. 9.2), but the portrait is not totally flattering, and Sallust can be critical
(doc. 9.6); Syme, however, overemphasises its negative aspects (1964: 159–4).
Sallust clearly realises the significance of the support of the equites in obtaining for Marius the consulship and command which was absolutely crucial for his
future political career and without which he might have remained a minor politician (*BJ* 64.5–6), but he neglects the details of Marius' early chequered career.

Plutarch *Marius*, esp. 7–12; *Sulla* 3–4, 6.1–2, 7–10: for Marius, Plutarch used
the writings of the philosopher Posidonius, who wrote a universal history from
146 down to the 80s; Posidonius was a contemporary and actually spoke to Marius
in his last days (*FGrH* 87 FF37, 60). Posidonius dealt with the Cimbri (Strabo
7.2.2 = *FGrH* 87 F31), and Plutarch presumably used him for Marius' northern
campaigns. Otherwise, Plutarch mentions Sulla, Rufus and Catulus as sources
and probably used Sisenna and Scaurus, none of whom presented a sympathetic
portrait, as well as Sallust. Sulla in his *Memoirs* denigrated Marius' achievements,
while other contemporary writers – the princeps senatus M. Aemilius Scaurus
(cos. 115), P. Rutilius Rufus (cos. 105) and Q. Lutatius Catulus (cos. 102) – who
would have been read by both Sallust and Plutarch, were hostile to him, and L.
Cornelius Sisenna's account of Sulla can hardly have favoured Marius (*HRR* I[2]
276–97). Plutarch's *Marius* is far from satisfactory as an historical account, not
merely because of its hostility to its subject and its moralising nature but because
it does not attach any significance to Marius' army reforms, and its lack of understanding of the political situation of the time is made clear at *Mar.* 8.5–9.4, where
Plutarch fails to consider how Marius wrested the war against Jugurtha from
Metellus.

Cicero is generally favourable to Marius (though he calls him 'omnium
perfidiosissimus', 'more untrustworthy than anyone else': *Nat. Deor.* 3.80): both
were novi homines, from the same town (Arpinum), and were in fact related. But
Cicero might have had ulterior motives: Marius had been involved in the violent
deaths of Saturninus and Glaucia and their supporters, just as Cicero himself had
put citizens to death without a trial: see Carney 1960. Cicero refers to an account
of Marius' campaign against the Cimbri written by Archias the poet which won
Marius' approval (Cic. *Arch.* 19–20), but the accounts of those hostile to him were
too strong. Licinianus 13–14 is important for Mallius (cos. 105) and the disastrous
defeat by the Cimbri in 105 BC. Appian *BC* 1.28–32.125–45 (Appian's *Celtica*
13, now only fragmentary, presumably dealt with Marius' campaigns) is quite
brief and a narrative with no interpretative material. For an inscription dealing
with Marius' career, see doc. 9.35.

MARIUS' EARLY CAREER

9.1 Plutarch *Life of Marius* 2.1–2: Marius the man

Plutarch's *Marius* is less than satisfactory as a source, and this passage gives a good indication
of the moralising in which it indulges. Like Cato the Elder (doc. 5.61), Marius could of course
speak Greek, but would not use it for important official occasions; cf. doc. 9.2.

1 As for Marius' appearance, I have seen a stone statue of him at Ravenna in Gaul, which fits well with the roughness and harshness supposed to have been characteristic of him. He was naturally brave and warlike, his education having been in the military rather than the civil sphere, and when in power he was unable to control his anger. **2** It is said that he never learnt Greek literature and never used the Greek language on any important occasion, on the grounds that it was ridiculous to study a literature whose teachers were subjects; and after his second triumph (in 101 BC), when at the consecration of a temple he put on some Greek performances, he just went into the theatre and sat down before immediately leaving. Plato often used to say to the philosopher Xenocrates, whose character seemed to have been rather too uncouth, 'My dear Xenocrates, sacrifice to the Graces' – and if anyone had persuaded Marius to sacrifice to the Greek Graces and Muses he would not have brought his career, so distinguished in military commands and public magistracies, to an end so unsightly, and would not have run aground upon an extremely bloodthirsty and cruel old age under the force of his anger, untimely ambition and uncontrollable arrogance.

9.2 Sallust *Jugurthine War* 85.31–35: Marius' self-portrait

Sallust describes Marius after his election to the consulship of 107 BC as encouraging the people to enlist for the war in Numidia, with much abuse of the *nobiles*. The speech is deliberately laconic and unsophisticated, and Marius stresses both his readiness to endure the same hardships as his troops and the ways in which, as a novus homo, he differs from the nobility.

31 My words are not carefully chosen; I care little for that. Merit demonstrates itself sufficiently on its own. It is they (the *nobiles*) who need skill to cover up their shameful deeds with rhetoric. **32** Nor have I studied Greek literature; I had little interest in studying this, as it had not improved the characters of its teachers. **33** But I have learnt the best lessons by far for the good of the state: to smite the enemy, mount guard, fear nothing except disgrace, suffer heat and cold alike, sleep on the ground, and endure at the same time lack of food and hard work. **34** With these lessons I shall encourage my soldiers, and I shall not subject them to short rations while living sumptuously myself or win my glory through their hard work. **35** This is the profitable way, this is the way for a citizen to lead his fellows.

9.3 Sallust *Jugurthine War* 8.1–2: Intrigue in Rome, c. 134 BC

Jugurtha, nephew of Micipsa, was sent to Spain by his uncle in 134, became intimate with Publius Scipio Aemilianus, under whom he served at Numantia (docs 5.52–53), and employed wholesale bribery to get his own way at Rome (see doc. 9.7). Both the novi homines and the nobiles, according to Sallust, were out for enrichment.

1 At that time in our army there were a great many new men and nobles to whom riches meant more than virtue and integrity, who were party intriguers at home, influential with Rome's allies, and notorious rather than respected, who fired

Jugurtha's ambitious spirit by promising that, should king Micipsa die, he alone would wield power in Numidia, since his merits were pre-eminent, while everything at Rome could be bought for money. **2** When Numantia had been destroyed, Publius Scipio decided to disband his auxiliary troops and return home. After making gifts to Jugurtha and commending him highly before the assembled soldiers, Scipio took him into his tent and there privately advised him to cultivate the friendship of the Roman people in general rather than that of individuals and not to form the habit of offering bribes – it was dangerous to buy from the few what belonged to the many. If Jugurtha would continue in his good conduct, glory and a kingdom would come to him of their own accord, but if he acted too hastily his own money would bring about his downfall.

9.4 Valerius Maximus *On Memorable Deeds and Sayings* 6.9.14: Marius' changing fortunes

Both Marius and Cicero were born in Arpinum in central Italy, Marius probably in 157 BC. Marius was a novus homo in every sense, and this could account for the difficulty he had in entering Roman politics: there had not been a novus homo consul since 132 BC (see docs 9.9, 2.39–40). He was of equestrian rank, and very little is known about his early career, though he served under Scipio Aemilianus at Numantia in Spain. He became quaestor, perhaps in 121, and stood for election as a plebeian tribune in 119 with the support of Caecilius Metellus, there being a patron–client relationship between the Metelli and the Marii. However, his activities as tribune upset his relationship with the Metelli, although he was connected with them again in the Numidian campaign.

Next comes Gaius Marius, Fortune's great contest: for with extreme bravery he stood up to all her blows by his strength both of body and mind. Judged unworthy of the honours of Arpinum, he dared to stand for the quaestorship at Rome. Then, by his patience under repulses, he rather broke into the senate than entered it. In his candidature for the tribunate and aedileship too he experienced a similar electoral disgrace, and as a candidate for the praetorship clung to the last place, which, however, he won not without danger, for, accused of bribery, he obtained an acquittal from the jurors with the greatest difficulty. From that Marius, so lowly at Arpinum, so obscure at Rome, so disdained as a candidate for office, emerged the Marius who conquered Africa, who drove king Jugurtha before his chariot, who annihilated the armies of the Teutones and Cimbri, whose two trophies are seen in the city, whose seven consulships are read in the Fasti, and whose fate it was to be made consul after exile and to hold a proscription after having been proscribed. What could be more fickle or changeable than his position? If you were to put him among the wretched, he would be found the most wretched of all, if among the fortunate, the most fortunate.

9.5 Plutarch *Life of Marius* 6.3–4: Marriage to Julia

After his praetorship of 115, Marius went to Further Spain as governor. He had almost certainly enriched himself there both in 134–33 and in 114. Soon after his return he married

Julia (as his second wife), and a son was born in 109 or 108. This marriage connected him with the Roman aristocracy. Julia was to be the aunt of Julius Caesar, born 100 BC.

3 When he returned to political life he lacked both wealth and rhetorical skill, which the most prestigious men of that time used in their control of the people. **4** His steadfast spirit, persistence in hard work and plain lifestyle gained him popularity with the citizens, and he approached more closely to power through his reputation, so he was able to make a brilliant marriage to Julia, from the distinguished family of the Julii Caesares, who was the aunt of that Caesar who was later to become the greatest man in Rome and who, to some extent, imitated Marius because of this family relationship, as I have written in my *Life* of him.

MARIUS IN AFRICA

9.6 Sallust *Jugurthine War* 63.1–64.6: Gaius Marius – Sallust's view

The Caecilii Metelli had held numerous consulships (123, 119, 117, 115, 113, 109) and had assisted Marius to his tribunate. Q. Caecilius Metellus, as consul in 109 BC, took Marius to Africa with him. Masinissa, as king of Numidia, had been a loyal ally of Rome. When he died in 148, Micipsa gained the throne, and on his death in 118 BC bequeathed the kingdom to his two sons (Hiempsal and Adherbal) and to Jugurtha, his nephew. Hiempsal and Adherbal refused to recognise Jugurtha, who had Hiempsal assassinated, while Adherbal fled to Rome. **63.7** The term novus homo (also as homo novus) applied strictly to a consul from an equestrian family.

63.1 At about the same time it happened that, when Gaius Marius was offering a sacrifice to the gods at Utica, the haruspex (soothsayer) declared that it portended a great and wonderful future; accordingly, whatever he had in mind, he should rely on the gods and carry it out and make trial of his fortune as often as possible, since everything would turn out successfully. **2** Even before this Marius had been driven by an intense desire for the consulship, for acquiring which he had all the qualifications in abundance, except the antiquity of his family: a capacity for hard work, integrity, great military skill, and a spirit mighty in warfare, temperate in private life, unaffected by passionate desire for wealth, and covetous only of glory. **3** He had been born and spent his boyhood at Arpinum, and when he first reached the age of military service he trained himself in the performance of military duties, not in Grecian eloquence or the niceties of city life; engaged thus in wholesome occupations, his unspoiled character quickly matured. **4** As a result, when he was a candidate before the people for the rank of military tribune for the first time, even though the majority did not know him by sight, he was known by his deeds and elected by all the tribes. **5** Then from that office he won one after another, always conducting himself in such a way that he seemed worthy of a higher position. **6** However, although he had shown himself so exceptional a man up to that point – for later on he was driven headlong by ambition – he still did not dare attempt the consulship. For even at that time, although the plebs could bestow the other magistracies, the nobility passed the consulship from hand to hand among themselves. **7** No 'new man' was so distinguished or his achieve-ments so splendid that he was considered worthy of that honour, and he was looked on as if he were unclean.

64.1 Therefore, when Marius saw that the words of the soothsayer pointed in the same direction as that in which his heart's desire was urging him, he asked Metellus to grant him leave of absence to stand for office. Although Metellus pos-sessed in abundance courage, the love of glory and other qualities desired by good men, he also had a proud, disdainful spirit, a common weakness in the nobility. **2** At first, therefore, he was disturbed by the unusual situation, expressed his amaze-ment at Marius' intention, and advised him, as if motivated by friendship, not to attempt so irregular a proceeding or entertain ideas above his station: all things are not to be desired by all men, said Metellus, and Marius should be content with his own lot; and, finally, he should beware of asking from the Roman people some-thing which they would be justified in refusing.

3 After he had made this and similar comments and Marius' determination remained unshaken, he finally replied that, as soon as public business permitted him, he would do what Marius requested. **4** Later, when Marius often made the same request, he is said to have replied, 'Don't be in such a hurry to go to Rome – you'll be old enough to stand for the consulship when my son does.' The son, at that point, was serving there on his father's staff and was about 20 years of age. This kindled both Marius' desire for the office to which he aspired and his hatred towards Metellus. **5** As a result he allowed himself to be motivated by desire and anger, the worst of all counsellors, abstained from no word or deed that might be of any use in gaining him popularity, and was less of a disciplinarian than before with the soldiers under his command in the winter quarters, while in discussing the war with the businessmen, of whom there was a large community at Utica, he made simultaneous accusations and boasts: if half the army, he proclaimed, would be entrusted to him, in a few days he would have Jugurtha in chains; his commander was deliberately dragging things out because, as a man of vain and despotic pride, he was too fond of power. **6** All these comments seemed all the more reliable to his listeners, because their businesses had been ruined by the lengthy duration of the war and because nothing moves fast enough for eager men.

9.7 Sallust *Jugurthine War* 40.2–3, 75.4–5: The *lex Mamilia*

After the murder of Hiempsal, Jugurtha sent envoys to Rome, who bribed senators to take up his cause but were unable to win over enough senators. Opimius (cos. 121; cf. docs 8.33–34) was sent out at the head of a commission of ten: as a result of bribery, he awarded Jugurtha the better half of Numidia. Jugurtha in 112 attacked Adherbal's capital Cirta and murdered him along with Italian traders there. L. Calpurnius Bestia (cos. 111) was sent out with an army, but was bribed by Jugurtha and granted him a lenient peace; Spurius Postumius (cos. 110) prosecuted the war against Jugurtha, but, when he returned to Rome to hold elections, his brother Aulus was easily defeated by Jugurtha and the Romans surrendered and passed under the yoke (*BJ* 36–9). In 110 Metellus was elected as one of the two consuls for 109 and was awarded Numidia as his province. G. Mamilius Limetanus (tr. pl. 109) proposed proceedings against those bribed by Jugurtha; several prominent senators were successfully prosecuted, including Opimius. **75.4**: Gauda: a grandson of Masinissa with the Roman army; Marius promised him the Numidian throne.

40.2 Measures to oppose the bill (of Mamilius) were taken both by those conscious of their guilt and by others afraid of the dangers arising from factional ill-will, and, since they were unable to resist it openly without admitting their approval of these and similar actions, they did so secretly through their friends and especially through men of Latin and Italian allied towns. **3** But the people passed the bill with incredible eagerness and decisiveness rather out of hatred for the nobility, against whom these measures were being directed, than out of concern for the state – so high were party passions running.

75.4 In this way Marius induced Gauda and the Roman equites, both those in the army and the businessmen, some by his personal influence, but most of them by the hope of peace, to write to their connections in Rome criticising Metellus' conduct of the war and demanding Marius as commander. **5** Accordingly many people canvassed for Marius' candidature for the consulship in a show of support that was highly flattering. Moreover, at that time the plebs, with the nobles frustrated by the law of Mamilius, were trying to promote novi homines (new men). Thus everything worked in Marius' favour.

9.8 Cicero *On Duties* 3.79: **One novus homo on another**

Cicero here is talking about the wrongs that stem from overreaching ambition. Generally, as a fellow townsman from Arpinum and because of family links with the Marii, he is quite pro-Marius.

Gaius Marius had long lacked the hope of a consulship and had now been out of office for six years following his praetorship, nor did he seem to have any chance of even being a candidate for the consulship, when he was sent by Quintus Metellus, one of our most outstanding men and citizens, whose legate he was, to Rome. There he accused Metellus before the Roman people of protracting the war; if they would make him consul, he promised, he would in a short time deliver Jugurtha alive or dead into the power of the Roman people. And so he was elected consul, it is true, but he had forsaken good faith and justice in that, by bringing a false charge, he had subjected one of the best and most respectable citizens, although he was his legate and on a mission for him, to the people's ill-will.

9.9 Sallust *Jugurthine War* 73.1–7: **Marius gets his heart's desire**

Marius was elected to the consulship of 107. **73.1**: Bomilcar was executed by Jugurtha for complicity in an attempt to assassinate him. **73.7**: Although many novi homines had held lesser offices, there had not been a novus homo consul since P. Rupilius in 132; cf. doc. 2.44. Numidia had again been allotted to Metellus by the senate, but the comitia centuriata elected Marius consul (the support of the equites will have been crucial) and the people gave him Numidia as his province).

1 When Metellus learned from deserters of the fate of Bomilcar and the discovery of the plot, he again hastened to make all his preparations as if starting a completely new war. **2** As Marius kept on importuning him about his leave of absence, he sent him home, thinking that a subordinate who was simultaneously discontented and at odds with his commander would be of little value. **3** At Rome as well, the plebs, on hearing the letters which had been sent regarding Metellus and Marius, readily accepted what was said about both. **4** The commander's noble birth, which had previously been counted as an honour, became a source of ill-will, while in Marius' case his humble origins added to his popularity. In both cases, however, factional zeal had more weight than the good or bad qualities of the men involved. **5** Furthermore, seditious magistrates (tribunes) whipped up the mob, in every assembly charging Metellus with treason and exaggerating Marius' virtues. **6** At length the plebs were so inflamed that all the craftsmen and farmers, those whose prosperity and credit depended on the work of their own hands, left their work to attend Marius, considering their own necessities of life less important than his success. **7** And so the nobles were beaten, and after many years the consulship was granted to a *novus homo*. Afterwards, when the people were asked by the tribune of the plebs, Titus Manlius Mancinus, in a packed assembly whom they wished to lead the war against Jugurtha, they appointed Marius. Shortly before this the senate had assigned Numidia to Metellus: their decision was rendered null and void.

9.10 Sallust *Jugurthine War* 84.1–2, 86.1–4: The capite censi

For Marius' later army reforms: docs 9.22–23. The Roman army was made up of soldiers whose ownership of property was felt to bind them to the interests of the state and its defence. Livy 1.43 states that Servius Tullius established classes based on property qualifications (cf. doc. 1.20); the capite censi, who were without property, were exempt from military service and entered on censors' lists only regarding their person (caput; cf. doc. 9.11). Marius now did away with property qualifications entirely and, by enrolling these, created the beginning of the 'client army'.

84.1 Marius, as I said above, had been elected consul with the enthusiastic support of the plebs; while he had already been hostile to the nobles before this point, after the people assigned him the province of Numidia he threatened them with persistence and boldness, attacking now individuals, now the entire class, asserting that he had defeated them and taken the consulship as spoils, as well as other remarks intended to glorify himself and cause them annoyance. **2** Meanwhile he gave priority to preparations for the war, demanding reinforcements to bring the legions up to strength, summoning auxiliaries from foreign nations and kings, and in addition calling up the bravest members of the Latins and allies, most of whom he knew from military service and a few only by reputation, while by personal solicitations he also induced veterans who had finished their service to join his force. **86.1** After Marius had made a speech in these terms and seen that it aroused the spirits of the plebs, he made haste to load his ships with provisions, money, arms and other useful items and ordered his legate Aulus Manlius to set sail with these. **2** Meanwhile he himself enrolled soldiers, not, according to ancestral custom, by property classes but by taking any man who volunteered, mostly the capite censi. **3** Some stated that he did this through lack of good men, others to win popularity, as it was from that class he had gained his status and rank – and to someone seeking power the poorest man is the most useful, for he is not concerned about his property, not having any, and considers anything respectable for which he receives pay. **4** As a result Marius set sail for Africa with a much greater force than had been authorised and arrived at Utica in a few days. The army was handed over to him by the legate Publius Rutilius. **5** Metellus had avoided meeting Marius, so that he might not see what he had been unable to bear even hearing about.

9.11 Aulus Gellius *Attic Nights* 16.10.10–11, 14: Removal of property qualifications

10 Those of the Roman plebs who were the humblest and poorest, and who reported no more than 1,500 asses at the census, were called proletarii, while those who were assessed as having no property at all, or next to none, were termed capite censi, 'counted by head', and the lowest rating of the capite censi was 375 asses. **11** But since property and money were seen as being a hostage or pledge to the state, and since there was in them a sort of guarantee and basis for patriotism, neither the proletarii nor the capite censi were enlisted as soldiers, unless in an extreme emergency, because they had little or no property or money . . . **14** Gaius Marius is said to have been the first man to have enrolled the capite censi, according to some in the war against the Cimbri at a time of great crisis for the state, or, more probably, as Sallust says, in the Jugurthine War, an act unheard of before that time.

MARIUS AND SULLA

9.12 Sallust *Jugurthine War* 95.1–96.3: Sulla enters military life

Despite Marius' earlier complaints against Metellus, the war against Jugurtha continued after Marius' consulship expired, and he continued the war as proconsul. Jugurtha was captured in 105, and Marius returned to Rome and celebrated his triumph on 1 January 104; 3,007 pounds of gold, 5,775 pounds of uncoined silver and 287,000 drachmas in coins were said to have been carried in the triumphal procession: Plut. *Mar.* 12.6. Sulla was chosen by Marius as his quaestor for 107 BC and would also serve under him in 104 as legate and in 103 as military tribune. For Sulla's background: see doc. 11.1.

95.1 In the meantime the quaestor Lucius Sulla arrived in camp with a large force of cavalry, which he had been left behind to raise from Latium and the allies. **2** Since the event has brought that great man to my attention, it seems appropriate to say a few words about his character and style of life. For I shall not speak elsewhere about matters pertaining to Sulla, and Lucius Sisenna, who has given the best and most careful account of him, does not seem to me to have spoken with sufficient frankness.

3 Sulla, then, was a noble of patrician descent, but his family was by this point buried in almost total oblivion because of the worthlessness of his ancestors. He was well educated alike in Greek and Latin literature and was of great mental capacity, devoted to pleasure, but more devoted to glory, spending his leisure time in extravagant living – though his enjoyments never interfered with his duties, except that he could have behaved more honourably as a husband. He was eloquent, clever and good at making friends; his mind was incredibly deep in its ability to disguise his plans; and he was generous with many things, especially money. **4** He was the most fortunate of all men before the civil war, but his good fortune was never greater than his assiduous efforts, and many have doubted whether his courage or good luck were the greater. As to what he did afterwards, I am unsure whether one should speak of it more with shame or with disgust.

96.1 After Sulla, as I have said above, reached Africa and Marius' camp with his cavalry, although he was without training and experience in war, he became in a short time the most skilful soldier in the whole army. **2** In addition he spoke in a friendly manner to the soldiers and granted favours to many at their request and to others of his own accord, though he was unwilling to accept favours himself and paid them back more promptly than a debt of money. He never asked anyone for repayment but, rather, worked hard to have as many people as possible in his debt; **3** he would exchange jokes or serious conversation with the humblest and spent much time with the men at their work, on the march and on guard duty, but in the meantime he did not try, like those whom corrupt ambition motivates, to harm the reputation of the consul or any other respectable man. His only concern was to make sure that no one was before him in counsel or action, and that he surpassed nearly everyone. Such character and behaviour endeared him in a short time to Marius and the soldiers.

9.13 Plutarch *Life of Marius* 10.3–9: Rivalry with Sulla

Plutarch dates the enmity between Marius and Sulla to the incident involving Bocchus, but the deadly rivalry between the two men was as yet many years away. Sulla negotiated Jugurtha's betrayal, but Marius would not – rightly – have seen this as crucial in bringing the war to a conclusion. For a coin showing Bocchus delivering Jugurtha to Sulla: doc. 11.46. Jugurtha appeared in Marius' triumph in 104 BC and was killed in the state prison: doc. 12.22 (the prison).

3 The king of the natives in the interior was Bocchus, Jugurtha's son-in-law . . . **4** He sent for Lucius Sulla, Marius' quaestor, who had been useful to Bocchus during the campaign. **5** Sulla trusted him and made the journey up country to see him, but the native changed his mind and regretted his action, deliberating for several days the options of handing Jugurtha over or detaining Sulla. **6** Finally he carried out his original betrayal and surrendered Jugurtha alive to Sulla. **7** This was the first seed of their incurable and savage conflict which came close to destroying Rome. **8** For there were many who wanted to give the credit to Sulla, out of jealousy of Marius, while Sulla himself used to wear a signet ring he had had made, engraved with Jugurtha being surrendered to him by Bocchus. **9** He used this ring constantly, irritating Marius, who was an ambitious man, disinclined to share glory with anyone else, and given to quarrels. He was led on by Marius' enemies, who attributed the first and greatest achievements of the war to Metellus and its final stages and conclusion to Sulla, in an attempt to put an end to the people's admiration of and total devotion to Marius.

MARIUS AND THE GERMANS

The Romans suffered several defeats at the hands of the Germans in the last decade of the second century; there was also a particularly spectacular debacle when in 107 the Tigurini, a group of the Helvetii (Celts), killed Marius' fellow consul L. Cassius Longinus in battle and sent the Romans under the yoke. The Germanic defeat of the Romans by the Cimbri in 105 BC was also catastrophic. Marius was elected to a second consulship to deal with the German tribes – then to a third, fourth, fifth and sixth. The people awarded him the command against the Germans, bypassing the senate. Marius spent 104 and 103 in military preparations. In 102 the tribes were active again but divided their forces, and Marius won his great victory over the Teutones at Aquae Sextiae in Transalpine Gaul, while in 101 the Cimbri were defeated by the combined armies of Marius and Catulus at Vercellae in Cisalpine Gaul, north of the Po River. Marius was elected to his sixth consulship for 100 BC.

9.14 Livy *Periochae* 65, 67: Disasters in Gaul

Q. Servilius Caepio (cos. 106) had not co-operated with Cn. Mallius Maximus (cos. 105), and at Arausio, now Orange (France), the Romans were disastrously defeated in 105 BC. This propelled Marius to his second consulship, for 104, to deal with the crisis. In 105 Caepio's imperium was cancelled; and Longinus' law in 104 as tribune expelled from the senate anyone whose imperium had been abrogated (doc. 9.19). C. Norbanus prosecuted Caepio over the treasure which had been captured at Tolosa in 106 and which had disappeared (doc. 9.18), and Caepio was convicted over his role in the Arausio disaster. He went into exile at Smyrna in Asia Minor.

Marius went straight from his triumph to the Capitol, where he had convened a meeting of the senate, but changed into an ordinary toga when he saw that he was giving offence: see doc. 9.35. Cn. Manlius is Cn. Mallius Maximus (cos. 105). He, like Caepio, was prosecuted and convicted for his role in the defeat at Arausio.

65 The consul Marcus Junius Silanus (cos. 109) lost a battle against the Cimbri (108 BC). The senate refused the request of envoys from the Cimbri for a dwelling place and land on which they might settle. The proconsul Marcus Minucius (cos. 110) fought successfully against the Thracians (109/08). The consul Lucius Cassius was slaughtered with his army in the territory of the Nitiobroges by the Tigurine Gauls, who had left that state (107). The soldiers who were left after this slaughter made a treaty with the enemy that they be released unharmed after giving up hostages and half of all their possessions . . .

67 Marcus Aurelius Scaurus, a consular legate, was taken prisoner by the Cimbri when his army was routed; when he was summoned to their council, he tried to deter them from crossing the Alps to enter Italy, on the grounds that the Romans could not be defeated, and was killed by Boiorix, a savage youth (105). The consul Gnaeus Manlius and proconsul Quintus Servilius Caepio were defeated in battle by these same enemies at Arausio, both their camps were plundered, and 80,000 soldiers and 40,000 servants and camp-followers were killed, according to Antias. Caepio, through whose rashness the disaster had been incurred, was condemned and his property was confiscated by the state, for the first time since King Tarquin, and his imperium was taken away (104). In the triumph of Gaius Marius, Jugurtha with his two sons was led before his chariot and killed in prison (104). Marius came into the senate in his triumphal clothes, which no one had previously done; because of anxiety about the war against the Cimbri, his consulship was renewed for several years. The second and third times he was elected consul in his absence, and he won a fourth consulship by pretending not to campaign for it.

9.15 Licinianus 13–14: Panic in Italy

Following the catastrophic defeat at the hands of the Cimbri (doc. 9.14), Saturninus established the court (quaestio) before which Mallius and Caepio were prosecuted.

Gnaeus Mallius was exiled by the people from Rome on the same charge as Caepio through the bill brought in by Lucius Saturninus (103 BC). The consul Rutilius, Mallius' colleague, was left in sole charge of the state. And so, with fear of the advancing Cimbri shaking the whole country, he made all men of military age take an oath that they would not leave Italy, and messengers were sent through all Italy's coasts and ports to proclaim that no one less than 35 years of age should be taken on board a ship . . . (105 BC).

9.16 Sallust *Jugurthine War* 114.1–4: The man of the hour

The defeats of Carbo near Noreia in 113, Silanus in 109, Cassius Longinus in 107, and Cn. Mallius (here Manlius) Maximus and Caepio in 105 by the Germanic tribes invading Gaul roused fear at Rome. Marius was elected consul in 104 although in absentia (absent from Rome), violating the *lex Villia annalis* (180 BC), with its stipulation of a ten-year gap between consulships; however, this would pale in comparison with his successive run of consulships (II–VI, 104–100 BC). The Gauls mentioned in the passage below are the Cimbri, a Germanic tribe, and the defeat was at Arausio in October 105.

1 At the same time the Gauls inflicted a defeat upon our commanders Quintus Caepio and Gnaeus Manlius, 2 which made all Italy tremble with fear. The Romans of the time, and from then even down to our own day, believed that everything else would fall before their valour, but that a war against the Gauls was a struggle for survival, not for glory. 3 But when it was announced that the war in Numidia was over and that Jugurtha was being brought to Rome in chains, Marius was elected consul in his absence and Gaul was assigned to him as his province. On the first day of January (104 BC) he held a triumph in great state as consul. At that time the hope and welfare of the state depended on him.

9.17 Florus *Epitome* 1.38 (3.1–6): The Germanic tribes seek land

1 The Cimbri, Teutones and Tigurini, refugees from the extremities of Gaul as the Ocean had inundated their lands, started to look throughout the world for new places where they could settle, and, **2** being excluded from Gaul and Spain, migrated into Italy and sent representatives to Silanus' camp and then to the senate requesting that the people of Mars grant them some land, as if for payment for military service, and employ their hands and weapons for any purposes it might wish. **3** But what land could the Roman people give them when it was on the point of conflict over agrarian legislation? And so, rebuffed, they began seeking by force what they had failed to gain by entreaties. **4** Silanus was unable to withstand the barbarians' first onslaught, nor Manilius their second, nor Caepio their third: all were routed and their camps despoiled. **5** Rome would have been finished if Marius had not belonged to that age. Even he did not dare to meet them at once but kept his soldiers in camp until the invincible frenzy, which the barbarians possess instead of courage, had worn off. **6** The barbarians, therefore, withdrew, mocking our men and advising them – such was their confidence that they would capture Rome – to give them any message they had for their wives.

9.18 Orosius *History* 5.15.25: The Tolosa treasure disappears

The outcome of Caepio's trial over the Tolosa treasure is unknown; he went into exile at Smyrna after being prosecuted over the Arausio debacle (see doc. 9.14).

The proconsul Caepio captured a Gallic town called Tolosa and removed 100,000 pounds of gold and 110,000 pounds of silver from the temple of Apollo. He sent this off with guards to Massilia (Marseilles), a city on good terms with the Roman people, and, after those to whom he had entrusted its protection and conveyance had been – as some state – secretly killed, he is said to have criminally stolen the whole of it. This resulted in a large-scale enquiry being held at Rome.

9.19 Asconius *Commentaries on Cicero* 78, 80: Prosecutions for failure

Longinus (tr. pl. 104 BC) was chiefly targeting Caepio, though his legislation reflects popular dissatisfaction not just with Caepio but with the general conduct of the wars against the Gallic and German tribes. Domitius: Cn. Domitius Ahenobarbus, who was to be consul in 96. M. Junius Silanus (cos. 109) was acquitted, probably in 104.

78 Lucius Cassius Longinus, son of Lucius, as tribune of the plebs in the consulship of Gaius Marius and Gaius Flavius, carried a number of laws aimed at reducing the power of the nobles, among which was the one that anyone condemned by the people or stripped of his office by them should not remain a member of the senate. This stemmed from his conflict with Quintus Servilius (Caepio), consul two years earlier, who had been stripped of his office by the people after his failure against the Cimbri (105 BC).

80 Marcus Silanus had been consul five years before Domitius' tribunate and had also failed against the Cimbri (109 BC); on these grounds, Domitius

prosecuted him before the people. The charge against him was that he had conducted his campaign against the Cimbri without the authority of the people, and
that this had been the origin of the disasters which the people had suffered in
the war against them; he also produced a document about this. But Silanus was
acquitted decisively, as only two tribes, Sergia and Quirina, voted for conviction.

9.20 *ILS* 8887: A rare triumph

Marcus Minucius Rufus (cos. 110) triumphed over the Scordisci and Triballi in 109 as
proconsul in Macedonia; he celebrated a triumph at Rome in 106 BC; this inscription
comes from the pedestal of a statue at Delphi. The Roman military record as a whole in this
period, however, consisted mostly of a series of defeats.

Marcus Minucius Rufus, son of Quintus, imperator. The people of Delphi dedicated (this statue) on account of his valour in defeating the Galli, Scordisti, Bessi
and the rest of the Thracians.

ARMY REFORMS

Marius had not actually reformed the army itself for his Numidian campaign of 107 BC
by abolishing the property qualification. But reforms to the legion took place at about
this time, though not all are necessarily to be attributed to Marius. These improved the
efficiency of the Roman soldier and legion. Many Roman armies had been serving for
long periods, as in Spain, but Marius' recruitment of the capite censi certainly hastened
the development of standing professional armies in which experience and expertise were
retained from year to year. For the army before Marius, see docs 5.11–21.

9.21 Valerius Maximus *On Memorable Deeds and Sayings* 2.3.2: Gladiatorial training

This type of training is not attested elsewhere. However, it is also possible that this was one of
Marius' reforms which, through hostility to him, was attributed instead to Rutilius (cos. 105).

Practice in handling weapons was given to the soldiers by Gnaeus Mallius' colleague as consul, Publius Rutilius (105 BC): for, following the example of no
previous general, he called in gladiatorial instructors from the troop of Gaius
Aurelius Scaurus and implanted in the legions a more skilful technique of avoiding and giving blows, and mingled valour with skill and skill, in turn, with valour
to make the former stronger by the force of the latter and the latter more cautious
by the knowledge of the former.

9.22 Plutarch *Life of Marius* 13.1–3: Marius' 'mules'

When Marius was appointed consul for the second time, for 104 BC, he instituted army
reforms. These included replacing the previous five standards of each legion (boar, eagle,
wolf, horse, minotaur) with a single eagle standard. He may have introduced the cohortal

legion (changing the basic unit of the legion from the maniple to the cohort), though this may have been a gradual innovation (cf. docs 5.11, 5.15); now each legion consisted of ten cohorts, a cohort having three maniples each of two centuries, with each century having 80 men. The 'mules': that the soldiers carried their own baggage gave greater mobility to the army with less reliance on the baggage train.

1 During the campaign he kept training the army *en route*, practising the men in all kinds of running and long marches, and compelling every man to carry his own baggage and prepare his own meals, hence the later expression 'Marius' mules' for those who enjoyed hard work and followed orders cheerfully and in silence. **2** However, others think there was a different origin for the expression. They say that, when Scipio was besieging Numantia and wanted to inspect not only the weapons and horses but also the mules and wagons to see whether the men were keeping them in proper condition and ready for action, Marius brought out his horse, which was beautifully kept, and a mule very different from all the others in condition, sleekness and strength; **3** the general was so pleased with Marius' animals, and so often mentioned them, that those who wanted to make a joke would praise any persevering, patient and hard-working soldier by calling him one of Marius' mules.

9.23 Plutarch *Life of Marius* 15.1–4, 25.2–3: Weapons innovation

The years 104 and then 103, despite the fears of the Roman people, were quiet. Marius was elected to a fourth consulship for 102 with the nobilis Q. Lutatius Catulus. Prior to the defeat of the Cimbri in 102, Marius altered the construction of the javelin (pilum), which now broke and so could not be hurled back by the enemy; if it struck an enemy's shield, it would droop downwards, making the shield heavy and useless to the enemy. It was about 2 metres long, had a range of 30 metres, and was thrown in unison at the approaching enemy.

In 102, Marius won a decisive victory over the Ambrones and Teutones in southern Gaul at Aquae Sextiae (now Aix-en-Provence) and, as consul again in 101, with Catulus as proconsul, defeated the Cimbri, another Germanic tribe, at Vercellae in Cisalpine Gaul. Marius shared the triumph (for the victories of 102 and 101) with Catulus.

15.1 When Marius learnt that the enemy was nearby, he swiftly crossed the Alps and, after constructing a camp by the river Rhone, brought into it abundant provisions so that he should never be forced to give battle to the army's disadvantage because of his lack of supplies. **2** He made the transportation of supplies by sea to the army, which before this had been slow and expensive, easy and swift. **3** For the mouths of the Rhone, where it met the sea, had been silted up with a great deal of mud and obstructed with sand and deep clay brought in by the tide, and this made it difficult, laborious and slow for the transport ships to sail in. **4** As the troops were at leisure, Marius brought them here and dug a great canal, diverting a large part of the river into this and bringing it round to a suitable part of the coast where the river mouth was deep and navigable for large ships, as well as being smooth and calm for entering the sea. This canal still bears his name today.

25.2 It is said that, in preparation for the battle with the Cimbri, the innovation to the javelin (*pilum*) was first made by Marius. **3** Previously the shaft was fastened into the iron head with two nails of iron, but Marius now, leaving one of the nails where it was, removed the other and put in instead an easily breakable wooden pin so that when the javelin struck the enemy's shield it would not stay upright, but, with the wooden pin broken, would droop from the iron head and drag the spear downwards, due to the spear's crooked shape.

MARIUS AND THE OPTIMATES

9.24 Cicero *On the Consular Provinces* 19: Marius was indispensible

A speech in 56 regarding the allocation of provinces for 54 for the consuls of 55, in accordance with Gaius Gracchus' law (doc. 8.28; Pompey and Crassus were to be elected: doc. 12.72). Cicero is arguing that personal hatreds (i.e., against Caesar) should not outweigh the needs of the state and argues for the replacement of Gabinius and Piso.

Who ever had more enemies than Gaius Marius? Lucius Crassus and Marcus Scaurus were antagonistic to him, all the Metelli were his enemies. Yet not only did they not attempt to have that enemy of theirs recalled from Gaul, but, in view of the importance of the Gallic war, they assigned him the province as an extraordinary command.

9.25 Dio *Roman History* 27 F94.1: The nobility support Marius

According to Dio, Marius in his election to his fifth consulship (101 BC) may have had senatorial support as well as that of the people.

In the barbarians' defeat, even though casualties in the battle had been heavy, a few were saved. Accordingly, Marius, to encourage and reward these at the same time, sold them all the booty very cheaply so it would not appear as if he had bestowed favours on any individual. By doing this Marius, although he had previously been well regarded only by the populace, because he came from that class and had been brought to power by it, now also won the support of the nobles by whom he had been hated, so that he was praised equally by everybody and received the consulship for the following year, to enable him to finish off his campaign, from an enthusiastic and unanimous electorate.

9.26 Livy *Periochae* 68: Victories, 102–101 BC

The consul Gaius Marius defended his camp, which was assaulted with the greatest force by the Teutones and Ambrones. He then destroyed these same enemies in two battles near Aquae Sextiae, in which it is recorded that 200,000 of the enemy were killed and 90,000 captured. In his absence, Marius was elected consul for the fifth time (in 102 for 101). He postponed the triumph offered to him until he should conquer the Cimbri as well. The Cimbri drove back from the Alps and put to flight the proconsul Catulus, who was trying to block the Alpine passes and had left a fort on high ground at the River Atesis garrisoned with a cohort. This cohort, however, got itself out of difficulty by its own bravery and caught up with the fleeing proconsul and the army. The Cimbri had now crossed into Italy and were defeated in battle by the combined armies of the same Catulus and Gaius Marius. In this battle it is recorded that 140,000 of the enemy were killed and 60,000 captured. Marius was welcomed with the unanimous consent of the whole state, but instead of the two triumphs which were offered him he was satisfied with one. The leading men of the state, who for some time had had a grudge against him as a 'new man' elevated to positions of such importance, were now admitting that the state had been saved by him.

9.27 Cicero *In Defence of Balbus* 46–49: Marius rewards good service

Lucius Cornelius Balbus, from southern Spain, served with the Romans in the war against Sertorius (79–72 BC). With Pompey's support he was granted citizenship in 72, and he was taken to Spain by Caesar in 61 as his chief engineer. Balbus was prosecuted in 56 for illegally claiming citizenship, under the *lex Papia* of 64. Cicero, who was one of Balbus' advocates (along with Crassus and Pompey), cites Marius as a precedent. Marius had granted citizenship to two allied cohorts at Vercellae (in 101 BC).

46 Can we therefore submit for your approval, as an authority for a precedent and for the action which is criticised by you, Gaius Marius? Do you ask for anyone more venerable, more steadfast, more pre-eminent in courage, wisdom and integrity? Good! He bestowed citizenship upon Marcus Annius Appius of Iguvium, an extremely courageous man endowed with the highest merits, while he also bestowed citizenship upon two whole cohorts from Camerinum, although he was aware that the treaty with the Camertes was one of the most inviolable and just of all treaties . . . **48** Accordingly, when a few years after this grant of citizenship the matter of citizenship was intensively investigated under the Licinian and Mucian law, who was there from the allied states, which had been granted citizenship, who was brought to trial? Titus Matrinius of Spoletium, from a Latin colony which was especially strong and illustrious, was the only one of those to whom Gaius Marius had granted citizenship who had to defend himself. His prosecutor, that eloquent man Lucius Antistius, did not say that the people of Spoletium had not approved it . . . , but since the colonies under the Appuleian law had not been founded – the law which Saturninus had brought in for Gaius Marius, allowing him to create three Roman citizens in each colony – he maintained that this grant should be invalid, as the measure itself had been repealed. **49** That prosecution has no resemblance to this case; but Gaius Marius possessed such prestige that, without employing Lucius Crassus, his relative by marriage, a man of amazing eloquence, he undertook the defence of that case and won it in a few words through the weight of his own personality. Who could there be, jurors, who would want to deprive our generals of the power to select the most courageous in war, in the battle-line and in the army, or our allies and federates of the hope of rewards in the defence of our state? But, if the countenance of Gaius Marius, if his voice, if the commanding flash of his eyes, if his recent triumphs, if his bodily presence had such power, let his prestige, let his achievements, let his memory, let the everlasting name of the bravest and most illustrious hero have the same power now!

SATURNINUS AND THE LAND LAW

9.28 Appian *Civil Wars* 1.28–31 (126–40): Saturninus' land law

As tribune in 103, L. Appuleius Saturninus successfully proposed a law to settle Marius' veterans from the Numidian campaign in Africa. Land for the capite censi serving with Marius now emerged as an issue and caused great conflict in Saturninus' second tribunate in 100. Saturninus' support had been important, according to Plut. *Mar.* 14.12–13, for Marius gaining his fourth consulship (102 BC). In 100, in Marius' sixth consulship, Saturninus as tribune successfully proposed that Marius' veterans from the campaigns of 102–101 be settled in Transalpine Gaul. As with the legislation of 103, many of Marius' veterans were from the capite censi and were rewarded with land grants.

Saturninus in 103 or 100 passed the *lex Appuleia de maiestate* to deal with the crime of treason, maiestas, against the Roman people. In 100 he passed a grain law which perhaps restored Gaius Gracchus' original grain law. The price for grain would be 6⅓ asses a modius, subsidised as in Gaius' law by the state, but under Saturninus' provision it was to be cheaper by ⅓ a modius. This law was opposed by the quaestor for 100, Q. Servilius Caepio, who was prosecuted under the *lex Appuleia de maiestate* but was acquitted and minted coins 'For the purchase of wheat by senatorial decree': doc. 9.38. **126**: The Metellus here is the consul of 109 BC; Glaucia: C. Servilius Glaucia, tribune, perhaps in 101, and praetor in 100 BC. He proposed and had carried a repetundae law (*lex Servilia Glauciae*) restoring the juries of the extortion courts to the equites. **128**: Nonius (actually Aulus Nunnius) was elected tribune but was murdered, and Saturninus took his place. **140**: Metellus went into exile on Rhodes but was allowed to return in 99 BC, against Marius' wishes (cf. doc. 9.29).

126 The censor, Quintus Caecilius Metellus, tried to demote Glaucia, a senator, and Appuleius Saturninus, who had already been tribune, for their disgraceful lifestyles, but did not succeed; for his colleague would not agree. **127** Shortly afterwards Appuleius, to revenge himself on Metellus, stood for another tribunate, using the opportunity of Glaucia's being praetor and presiding over the tribunician elections. Nonius, a man of distinguished birth, who employed blunt speech against Appuleius and reproached Glaucia severely, was elected tribune. **128** Glaucia and Appuleius, fearing lest he should take revenge on them once he was tribune, attacked him in an uproar with a mob of men as he was leaving the assembly and killed him after he had fled into a tavern. As this murder appeared pitiful and awful, Glaucia's supporters, before the people had assembled, elected Appuleius tribune at dawn. **129** In this way the murder of Nonius was hushed up because of Appuleius' tribunate, as people were afraid that he might convict them.

Metellus was also banished by them with the help of Gaius Marius, who was then holding his sixth consulship and was Metellus' secret enemy. Thus they all co-operated with each other. **130** Appuleius introduced a law to divide all the land that the Cimbri, a Celtic race, had seized in what the Romans now call Gaul. Marius had recently driven them out and made the land which had been theirs into Roman territory. **131** The law also provided that, if the people should ratify the law, the senate should swear within five days that it would obey the law, and that anyone who did not swear should no longer belong to the senate and pay the people a fine of 20 talents. Their motive was to revenge themselves on whose who were displeased with it, especially Metellus, who was not going to give in to the oath because of his high spirit. **132** This then was the proposed law, and Appuleius appointed the day for voting and sent out men to inform people in the country, in whom he had special confidence since they had served under Marius. The people were dissatisfied, however, because the Italians gained more than they did under the law. . . .

138 Metellus alone did not swear, but persisted fearlessly in his decision. Appuleius immediately sent his attendant for him and tried to drag him from the senate house. **139** When the other tribunes defended him, Glaucia and Appuleius rushed to the country people and told them that the land would not be theirs nor the law enacted unless Metellus were banished. They proposed a decree of exile against him and instructed the consuls to proclaim that no one was to share fire, water or shelter with him; and they appointed a day for the enactment of this decree. **140** The city people were terribly angry and attended Metellus constantly, daggers and all. Metellus thanked them and praised them for their determination, but said he could not allow any danger to happen to the country on his account. After this statement he left the city, and Appuleius had the decree ratified and Marius had its contents proclaimed.

9.29 Livy *Periochae* 69: **Marius changes sides**

Livy here records the story that Marius won his sixth consulship (for 100 BC) with bribes. According to Plutarch, Rutilius' account was that Marius used bribes to secure the election of Valerius Flaccus as his consular colleague for 100 BC to prevent Metellus being elected (Plut. *Mar.* 28.7–8); for Memmius, see doc. 9.30. The slave war referred to here was the second great uprising in Sicily: cf. doc. 6.49; Manius Aquillius had been consul with Marius in 101.

Lucius Appuleius Saturninus, who had the support of Gaius Marius, and whose rival Aulus Nunnius was killed by the soldiers, was elected tribune of the plebs by violence and conducted his tribunate no less violently than his campaign for office; after he had passed a land law by violence, he indicted Metellus Numidicus because he had not sworn to support it. Metellus was defended by the better citizens (the *boni*), but, to avoid being the occasion for strife, he went into voluntary exile at Rhodes and there found diversion in hearing and reading distinguished philosophers. With Metellus gone, Gaius Marius, the man responsible for the civil strife, who had bought his sixth consulship with money distributed among the tribes, banned him from fire and water. The same Appuleius Saturninus, tribune of the plebs, killed Gaius Memmius, a candidate for the consulship, because he was afraid of him as an opponent of his proceedings. The senate was aroused at these deeds, and Gaius Marius too, a man of varying and changeable nature whose policy followed the dictates of fortune, had come over to its side. Saturninus, together with the praetor Glaucia and other associates in the same madness, was put down by armed force and killed in a sort of war. Quintus Caecilius Metellus was brought back from exile to the great applause of the whole state. The proconsul Manius Aquillius ended a slave war which had arisen in Sicily.

9.30 Cicero *In Defence of Gaius Rabirius* 20–21: The senatus consultum 'ultimum'

Cicero here gives the terms of the senatus consultum ultimum passed to suppress Saturninus; cf. doc. 1.60. Cicero is defending, in 63, the senator Rabirius on a charge of treason for the murder of Saturninus 36 years earlier in a riot. This attack on Rabirius was orchestrated by Caesar and the populares. Saturninus was elected in 100 to a third tribunate for 99; Glaucia was seeking the consulship for 99; Marcus Antonius was chosen as one of the consuls. Glaucia and Memmius were rivals for the second position, and Glaucia and Saturninus had Memmius beaten to death with clubs in the comitia centuriata (see doc. 9.29). A reaction set in against Saturninus: he seized the Capitol, with the praetor Glaucia and the quaestor for 99, Gaius Saufeius. The ex-prisoner Gracchus (i.e., Equitius), who pretended to be Ti. Gracchus' son, was elected tribune with Saturninus for 99 and was killed with him on the first day of his office, 10 December 100.

20 A decree of the senate was passed that the consuls, Gaius Marius and Lucius Valerius, should summon those tribunes of the plebs and praetors whom they thought fit and take steps to preserve the imperium and majesty of the Roman people. They summoned all the tribunes of the plebs except Saturninus and all the praetors except Glaucia, and they ordered those who desired the safety of the state to take arms and follow them. Everyone obeyed; weapons from public buildings and armouries were issued to the Roman people, with Gaius Marius, as consul, in charge of the distribution. I will, at this point, leave aside other matters, Labienus, to put a question to you personally. When Saturninus was in armed occupation of the Capitol, and with him Gaius Glaucia, Gaius Saufeius and even that ex-prisoner Gracchus (i.e., Equitius) – I will add, since you insist on it, that Quintus Labienus, your father's brother, was there too – while in the forum were Gaius Marius and Lucius Valerius Flaccus, the consuls, and with them the entire senate – and such a senate as even you are accustomed to praise to help in your detraction of the senate of today; there was also the equestrian order – and what equites they were, immortal gods! who in our fathers' time played a great part in government, including charge of the entire dignity of the law-courts – who had taken up arms alongside all men of all classes who believed that their own safety was tied in with the safety of the state; I ask you again personally, Labienus, what was Gaius Rabirius to do?

21 When, acting on a decree of the Senate, the consuls had issued a call to arms, when Marcus Aemilius (Scaurus), the princeps senatus, had armed himself and taken up his stand in the assembly, who, though he could hardly walk, thought that his lameness would be no hindrance in pursuit but only in flight, when even Q. Scaevola (the augur), worn out by old age, dreadfully ill, infirm, crippled and feeble in every limb, leaned on his spear, displaying both his mental vigour and bodily weakness and strength of spirit, when Lucius Metellus, Servius Galba, Gaius Serranus, Publius Rutilius, Gaius Fimbria, Quintus Catulus, and all the other ex-consuls of the time had taken up arms for the common safety; when all the praetors and everyone of high birth and military age were hastening to help, such as Gnaeus and Lucius Domitius, Lucius Crassus, Quintus Mucius, Gaius Claudius, Marcus Drusus; when all the Octavii, Metelli, Julii, Cassii, Catones, Pompeii . . . and in fact every man of pre-eminence was with the consuls – what then was Gaius Rabirius to do?

9.31 Appian *Civil Wars* 1.32–3 (141–46): Sedition, 100 BC

Plut. *Mar.* 30.4: Saturninus and his supporters were slaughtered as they made their way down into the forum. Marius' association with Saturninus tarnished his career, and he did not stand for the next censorship, although he was expected to do so (*Mar.* 30.5). Glaucia was praetor in 100 and so could not legally seek election to the consulship for 99. His involvement in the murder of Nunnius and senatorial hostility (doc. 9.28) told against him. **143**: Saufeius had been elected as quaestor for 99 and entered office on 5 December 100. Saturninus' legislation was declared invalid by the senate after his murder.

141 In this way Metellus, a most well-respected man, went into exile, and Appuleius (Saturninus) was tribune for the third time. One of his colleagues (Equitius), who was considered to be a runaway slave, claimed that the elder Gracchus was his father. The mob supported him in the election because they missed Gracchus so much. **142** When the consular elections came round, Marcus Antonius was indisputably elected to one of the consulships, while the other was contested between Glaucia and Memmius. As Memmius was by far the more illustrious, Glaucia and Saturninus were anxious about the result and sent some men with clubs to attack him at the election itself, who struck Memmius in the middle of the assembly and cut him down in the sight of everyone. **143** The assembly broke up in turmoil, with neither laws nor law-courts nor any shame remaining; the people were enraged and on the following day rushed in anger to kill Appuleius. He had, however, gathered another mob from the country and with Glaucia and Gaius Saufeius, the quaestor, seized the Capitol. **144** When the senate voted for their destruction, Marius was vexed but nevertheless reluctantly issued arms to some people; and, while he was delaying matters, some other people cut off the water which ran to the temple. Saufeius, dying of thirst, suggested burning the temple, but Glaucia and Appuleius, in hopes that Marius would assist them, surrendered themselves, followed by Saufeius. **145** With everybody at once demanding that he put them to death, Marius locked them up in the senate house as if he intended to deal with them more legally. The people thought this just a pretext, took the tiles from the senate house roof, and battered Appuleius and his companions to death, including a quaestor and a tribune and a praetor, still wearing their official insignia. **146** A great crowd of others were killed in the sedition, including another tribune, supposedly the son of Gracchus, on his first day as tribune, while freedom, democracy, laws, reputation and magisterial rank were no longer of any use, as even the tribunate, which had been created to hinder wrongdoers and protect the plebs, and was sacred and inviolable, was now committing and suffering such outrages.

MARIUS' LATER CAREER

9.32 Appian *Civil Wars* 1.55–56 (240–50): The command against Mithridates

Doc. 11.5 continues this extract from Appian. In 100 Marius had opposed the recall of Metellus, and he preferred to set sail for Asia rather than see Metellus return. In the Social War, which broke out in 91, Marius played a limited but important role (doc. 10.18). Immediately after the Social War, conflict between Marius and Sulla led to the outbreak of civil war for the first time at Rome. Sulla was elected to a consulship for 88 and was to have the command against Mithridates, but in 88 Marius manoeuvred to deprive Sulla of the command. Sulla led his army against Rome and exiled Marius (doc. 11.5). So commenced the Marius–Sulla civil war.

Publius Sulpicius Rufus (tr. pl. 88) sought to address the problem of the distribution of the newly enfranchised Latin and Italian citizens in the tribes (see docs 10.17, 21, 26). His proposal to distribute them among all of the tribes rather than eight aroused fierce opposition, because the Italians would potentially outnumber the Romans in the people's assembly. The law about citizenship was passed, and Marius supported him in return for the Mithridatic command. The revoking of Sulla's command (cf. doc. 11.5) led to Sulla's march on Rome, after which Sulla had Sulpicius executed and his laws revoked. Sulla enacted some laws in the tribal assembly, but these were repealed when Marius and Cinna gained control of the city; these laws foreshadowed some of the reforms Sulla passed as dictator.

240 Up till now the murders and seditions had remained internal and not widespread; but after this the party leaders attacked each other with great armies according to the rules of war, and the country was the prize which lay between them. The beginning and origins of these took place immediately after the Social War, in the following way. **241** When Mithridates, king of Pontus and other nations, invaded Bithynia and Phrygia and the part of Asia which neighbours these, as I recounted in my previous book (*Roman History* 12), the consul Sulla was chosen as governor of Asia and commander of the Mithridatic War (he was still at Rome). **242** Marius, thinking it would be an easy and very profitable war, wanted the command, and with many promises got the tribune Publius Sulpicius to work with him to obtain it. He also led the new Italian citizens, who had little influence in elections, to hope to be distributed among all the tribes, suggesting nothing openly about the benefits to himself in that he would be able to use them as loyal adherents in everything. **243** Sulpicius at once introduced a bill for this purpose; if this were enacted, Marius and Sulpicius would have achieved everything they wanted, since the new citizens would far outnumber the old. **244** The older citizens, however, saw this and fought with the new citizens with all their strength. They used clubs and stones against each other, and the evil continually increased until the consuls, afraid as the day for voting approached, proclaimed a vacation of several days, as was usual on the occasion of festivals, in order to delay the voting and the evil . . . (the son of the consul Quintus Pompeius, Sulla's son-in-law, is killed by the Sulpicians). **248** Sulla cancelled the vacation and hurriedly left for Capua, where his army was, as if to cross from Capua to Asia for the war against Mithridates, for he was not yet aware of what was being done in opposition to him. **249** Sulpicius, with the vacation cancelled and Sulla out of the city, enacted the law, and Marius, for whose sake all this had taken place, was immediately elected commander of the war against Mithridates instead of Sulla. **250** When Sulla learnt this he resolved that the matter should be decided by war and summoned his army to an assembly . . .

9.33 Appian *Civil Wars* 1.60 (269–71): Marius banished from Rome

After Sulla took Rome by force, Marius was banished and barely escaped. Sulpicius was put to death.

269 This was the first army of citizens to invade Rome as an enemy country. **270** From now on seditions were to be decided only by armies, and there were frequent attacks on Rome and battles for the walls and all other warlike activities, with no longer any sense of shame, whether for the laws, institutions or country, to restrain violence. **271** On this occasion Sulpicius, who still held the office of tribune, together with Marius, who had been consul six times, and his son Marius, Publius Cethegus, Junius Brutus, Gnaeus and Quintus Granius, Publius Albinovanus, Marcus Laetorius and others with them, about 12 in number, were banished from Rome on the grounds that they had aroused sedition, fought against the consuls, and proclaimed freedom for slaves to incite them to rebellion, and were voted to be enemies of the Romans, while anyone who met them was permitted to kill them with impunity or bring them before the consuls; their goods had been confiscated.

9.34 Plutarch *Life of Marius* 43.4–8, 44.9, 46.6–9: Marius' return, 87 BC

Sulla, deprived of his command, fled but returned with six legions and captured Rome (doc. 11.5). Marius escaped from Rome with difficulty, going to Africa, where many of his veterans were settled; he returned with Cinna (elected consul for 87) to take revenge after Sulla had left for Asia Minor.

Cinna agitated for the distribution of the new citizens in all the tribes (he was opposed by the other consul for 87, Gnaeus Octavius: doc. 10.26); violence erupted, and Octavius (illegally) deprived Cinna of his consulship. Fleeing to Campania, Cinna won over the army there and was joined by Sertorius and Cn. Carbo (who was to be consul with Cinna in 85 and 84 BC), while Marius and his son returned from Africa. The senatorial forces were led by Octavius (cos. 87), P. Licinius Crassus (cos. 97), Caecilius Metellus Pius (later to be consul in 80) and Cn. Pompeius Strabo (cos. 89). The senate negotiated with Cinna – recognising him as consul – and he and Marius entered Rome. Crassus committed suicide and Octavius was murdered just before Marius entered the city. In the bloodshed that followed, both equites and senators were killed. Marius did not live long into his seventh consulship; the younger Marius was consul in 82 BC.

43.4 The people was summoned into the forum, but before three or four tribes had given their votes Marius left off the pretence, giving up his sophistic definition of himself as an exile and entering the city with his bodyguard, a picked band of slaves who had joined him and whom he called 'Bardyiae'. **5** These killed many on his command, many simply at his nod, and finally Ancharius, a senator and ex-praetor, who met Marius and was not spoken to, was cut down with their swords in front of him. **6** After this, whenever anyone greeted Marius and was not addressed or replied to, they took this as a sign to slaughter him immediately in the street, so that even each of his friends was full of terror and fear whenever he approached to speak to Marius. **7** When many had been killed, Cinna's desire for bloodshed was satiated, but Marius' rage and thirst for blood kept increasing day by day, and he removed anyone against whom he had any grudge. **8** Every road and every city was full of men who were fleeing and men hunting down those who were escaping or in hiding. . . . **44.9** Despite the headless bodies thrown into the street and trampled on, there was no pity, only general fear and terror at the sight. The people found the brutality of the so-called Bardyiae particularly hard to endure. **10** For they slaughtered householders in their houses, dishonoured their children and raped their wives, and were unbridled in their plundering and bloodletting until Cinna and Sertorius' parties got together and took action against them when they were asleep in their camp, shooting them all down with javelins . . .

46.6 Marius died 17 days after becoming consul for the seventh time; and immediately in Rome there was a great feeling of delight and confidence, in that they were rid of a savage tyrant. **7** But in a few days they realised that they had exchanged an old master for a new one in his prime; Marius the son now revealed such savagery and bitterness in killing the noblest and most respected men . . . **9** Finally (in 82 BC) he was trapped in Praeneste by Sulla and, after many vain attempts to save his life, when the city was captured and escape impossible, he killed himself.

9.35 *ILS* 59: Marius' career inscription

Marius' career inscription, now lost, but reconstructed by Mommsen from fragments and Renaissance transcriptions, was one of the elogia of illustrious Romans erected in the Forum of Augustus. For the triumphal robe: doc. 9.14.

Gaius Marius, son of Gaius, seven times consul, praetor, tribune of the plebs, quaestor, augur, military tribune, contrary to the rule concerning the allocation of provinces waged war against Jugurtha king of Numidia as consul, captured him, and, when celebrating a triumph in his second consulship, ordered him to be led before his chariot. He was made consul for the third time in his absence and in his fourth consulship destroyed an army of the Teutones. In his fifth consulship he routed the Cimbri. He again celebrated a triumph over these and the Teutones. In his sixth consulship he freed the state when it was in chaos from the seditions of a tribune of the plebs and a praetor, who had armed themselves and occupied the Capitol. At more than 70 years of age, he was expelled from his country by civil strife and was restored by force and made consul for a seventh time. From the spoils of the Cimbri and Teutones he built a shrine to Honour and Virtue. In triumphal robe and patrician shoes he entered the senate.

COINAGE

9.36 Crawford *RRC* 292.1: Marius' voting reform as tribune

A denarius (silver) coin dated to 119, 113 or 112, or c. 105 BC.

Obverse: Bust of the goddess Roma.

Reverse: A voting scene in the comitium. A voter on the left-hand side of the coin, just entering onto the voting bridge (pons), receives a voting tablet (tabella) from an attendant below, shown behind the pons, while at the end of the bridge another voter is depositing his voting tablet into a ballot box (cista). A voting tablet is itself shown in the upper right, perhaps with the traces of the letter 'P' signifying one of the tribes (either Pupinia or Papiria). Two parallel horizontal lines on the coin probably represent a marked-off voting area. The name of the moneyer, P. (Licinius) Nerva, appears prominently.

9.37 Crawford *RRC* 322.1: Triumph over the Germans

A denarius of 102 BC. A priest of the 'Great Mother', identified with Cybele, had foretold the victories over the Germans, and so Cybele's presence on this coin and in the chariot is taken as referring to his victories (Plut. *Mar.* 17.9–11; cf. Diod. 36.13). The Syrian prophetess, called Martha, accompanied Marius on campaign: Plut. *Mar.* 17.1–5; cf. doc. 9.6.

Obverse: Bust of the goddess Cybele.

Reverse: The deity Victory in a biga (two-horse chariot).

9.38 Crawford *RRC* 330.1: Saturninus' grain bill

A denarius of 100 BC. This coin presumably refers to the grain law of Saturninus, passed in 100 BC. Caepio had opposed the law with violence but apparently saw no difficulty in then advertising his role in putting it into effect. Struck by L. Calpurnius Piso and Q. Servilius Caepio.

Obverse: Head of Saturn, with the names 'Piso' and 'Caepio' and the abbreviation 'Q', indicating that they are quaestors.

Reverse: Two figures sitting on a bench, facing left; an ear of grain on either side of the coin, with the inscription 'AD.FRU.EMV.EX.S.C.': 'for the purchase of grain by decree of the senate.'

10

The Social War

The Social War between Rome and the Italian allies broke out in 91 BC and was largely over by 89 BC, though resistance to Rome continued (doc. 10.28). The Italian allies (the *socii*, hence the name given to the war) desired Roman citizenship and all the various benefits which this conferred. The Romans refused to enfranchise them, and war broke out. The seriousness of the situation then caused the Romans to enfranchise the Latins and those Italian allies who had not revolted (doc. 10.17).

The Romans had over a period of centuries granted Roman citizenship to individuals in Latin and also allied Italian communities, but there was opposition at Rome to the enfranchisement of the Latins and a proposal about this had been rejected by the senate even in the emergencies of the Second Punic War (see doc. 4.40). The issue of citizenship for the allies became important in the last decades of the second century BC. According to Velleius Paterculus (2.2.2), Tiberius Gracchus promised citizenship to the whole of Italy: 'in the consulship of Publius Mucius Scaevola and Lucius Calpurnius (133 BC), 162 years ago, he split away from the senatorial party and promised citizenship to all of Italy.' This is debated, for it is not mentioned by Plutarch or Appian, and in fact Tiberius did not promise the allies citizenship but actually exacerbated relations with them. Cicero *Rep.* 3.41 notes, 'Tiberius Gracchus kept faith with the citizens but disregarded the treaty rights of our allies and the Latins.' This presumably refers to the distribution of ager publicus to Roman citizens; Scipio Aemilianus therefore stepped in to defend the allies against the appropriation of ager publicus in their territories (doc. 8.21). Tiberius did not raise the idea of citizenship for the allies, and it probably was not an issue in 133 BC.

The question of citizenship was first introduced in the 120s. A law was passed in 126 BC by the tribune M. Junius Pennus to prevent non-citizens from living in Rome and to expel those already doing so. In 125 BC, the consul M. Fulvius Flaccus (a friend of Gaius Gracchus and member of the Gracchan agrarian commission) proposed that all Italian communities should receive full franchise or the right of appeal against Roman magistrates, the *ius provocationis*, but this was opposed by the senate (doc. 10.6). The Latin town of Fregellae revolted and was razed to the ground by Opimius (cf. doc. 8.28). This revolt could be taken as an indication that there was some desire among the Latin allies for citizenship. But the fact that only Fregellae rebelled could point to specific local grievances on its part, and the character of its population had in fact changed and was now more Oscan, i.e., Italian, in character. The Italians had been allies of Rome for two centuries and contributed heavily to the success against Hannibal and in Rome's extensive wars in the second century BC. A law granting Roman citizenship to magistrates in Latin colonies might have been passed at about the time of the revolt of Fregellae as a 'half-way' measure.

The next major move in this matter came with Gaius Gracchus: allies of Latin status were to be given full franchise and other allies were to be raised to Latin status (this was defeated by the senate through the counter-proposals of the tribune Livius Drusus: doc. 8.28). This proposal and Livius Drusus' counter-colony measures were largely responsible for Gaius' loss of support among the body of Roman citizens (docs 8.28, 30). Some 25 years later, in 100 BC, Saturninus raised Italian hopes by offering the franchise to a select number of Marius' allied veterans, but the law was declared invalid by the senate after his murder. To what extent Gaius and Saturninus had in mind a Latin and Italian interest in citizenship is unclear, and it may well have been the case that they stimulated hopes for citizenship. Roman opposition to an extension of citizenship is clear from the *lex Licinia Mucia* of 95, which set up a *quaestio* on all aliens claiming to be citizens (doc. 10.2).

By 91 BC, however, there was clearly an overwhelming desire among Latins and Italians for Roman citizenship, and the Social War broke out on this very issue. The tribunate of the younger Livius Drusus in 91 brought this to the forefront of Roman politics (docs 10.4–9). He was – by one of the peculiar twists of history that sometimes occur – the son of the tribune Livius Drusus who had opposed Gaius Gracchus in 122 BC. His proposal to give citizenship to the Italians was part of a broader programme (doc. 10.6) aimed at giving senators a role in the juries, dominated under Gaius Gracchus' legislation exclusively by the equites (doc. 8.28). This proposal may also have been influenced by the unfair conviction by an equestrian jury of his uncle Rutilius Rufus for extortion in Asia (doc. 10.5). But Drusus' citizenship proposal lost him support, and he was assassinated in his own home (doc. 10.9). The 'oath' which the Italians were supposed to have sworn to Drusus (doc. 10.8) is clearly an invention of the latter's enemies; it was meant to create an impression that Drusus was aiming at a huge Italian clientela which would overshadow the smaller clientela relationships that Romans serving abroad had established.

Drusus' murder, like that of the tribunes Tiberius and Gaius Gracchus, Fulvius Flaccus and Saturninus, was a forerunner of the internal violence about to descend upon Rome with Sulla's march in 88 (doc. 11.5). Drusus' attempted reforms and his association with the leader of the Marsi (Q. Poppaedius Silo: doc. 10.4, cf. 10.7, 10.18) led to a law in the following year (90 BC), successfully proposed by the tribune Varius, to try anyone suspected of collusion with the allies. When in 91 the allies revolted in frustration, the initial Roman response had been to deny them citizenship (doc. 10.11). Then, in an acknowledgement of the seriousness of the situation (freedmen were enrolled as soldiers) and of the fairness of the Italian demands, citizenship was offered to the Latins and the Italian communities that had not revolted (doc. 10.17). The rebels who surrendered (and so became *dediticii*) were enfranchised later, possibly in 87. The allies' demands could be seen as fair: 'every year and in every war they were providing . . . cavalry and infantry' (doc. 10.13); they fought, as Cicero observed, 'to be received' into the Roman state (doc. 10.14).

After Poppaedius had led an abortive march on Rome (doc. 10.7), actual war between Rome and the Italian allies broke out in 91. Numerous allied communities rebelled, particularly the Marsi and the Samnites (docs 10.10–11). The revolt began at Asculum (doc. 10.10) and quickly spread. The rebels established a capital city, at Corfinium, renamed Italia, with a constitution along Roman lines, and minted their own coins (doc. 10.12). They had initial successes against the Romans, but the Latin allies remained loyal, as did the Etruscans and Umbrians (doc. 10.17), and Marius, Sulla and Gnaeus Pompeius Strabo served as legates under the consuls (docs 10.18–20).

As noted, citizenship was extended to the Latins and loyal Italians. The law enacting this, the *lex Julia*, was passed in 90 BC (doc. 10.21). The Latin and Italian communities were enfranchised and their citizens became Roman; their communities were given the status of *municipia* and were governed by four officials, as at Tarentum in southern Italy (doc. 10.22). The Italians' distribution among the tribes was not effected immediately: P. Sulpicius Rufus' attempt to have them distributed fairly among all 35 tribes was rescinded by Sulla, but by the censorship of 70 BC some form of distribution had finally taken place and the censors counted 910,000 Roman citizens (doc. 10.24; *MRR* II.127). All of Italy south of the River Po (Cisalpine Gaul was north of the Po) now had Roman citizenship and became one political unit.

Ancient sources: these are largely the narratives of Appian *Civil Wars* 1.34–53.150–231 and Diodorus 37.1–25 (fragments), as well as Velleius Paterculus 2.13–17 and Livy *Periochae* 70–76. Plutarch deals with Marius and Sulla's involvement: *Mar.* 33, *Sulla* 6; see also *Cato Min.* 2; *Cic.* 3.2 (Cicero saw service under Sulla in the Social War).

THE RESTRICTION OF ROMAN CITIZENSHIP

10.1 Valerius Maximus *On Memorable Deeds and Sayings* 3.4.5: An embarrassing consulship

Perperna was consul in 130 BC; he died in 129 before celebrating a triumph for his victory over and capture of the pretender to the throne of Pergamum (cf. doc. 5.45). Perperna's family was Etruscan, and the fact that he lacked Roman citizenship was discovered only when his father was named in a list of people whose return was demanded by their native cities. The Papian law was passed in 65 against the illegal assumption of citizenship: Valerius here has probably confused the Papian and Pennan laws (126 BC). The Crassian 'carnage' refers to the defeat and death of P. Licinius Crassus Dives Mucianus (cos. 131) in Asia in 130.

No small embarrassment to the consulship is Marcus Perperna, seeing that he was consul before he was a citizen, though in the conduct of war he was a far more useful general to the state than Varro: for he captured King Aristonicus and avenged the Crassian carnage, but, while his life triumphed, his death was condemned under the Papian law. For his father had taken on the rights of a Roman citizen with no justification, and the Sabelli forced him after a trial to return to his former residence. So Marcus Perperna's shadowy name, false consulship, misty command and fleeting triumph resided unlawfully in an alien city.

10.2 Cicero *On Duties* 3.47: The *lex Licinia Mucia*, 95 BC

In 126 BC the tribune L. Junius Pennus set up a commission to examine the rights of allies to be in Rome and to eject those there illegally. He may have been motivated by Fulvius Flaccus' proposals canvassed in 126 while seeking the consulship of 125 (doc. 8.28). For the *lex Licinia Mucia*, passed by the two consuls of 95, Q. Mucius Scaevola and L. Licinius Crassus, see doc. 9.27, where one of Marius' grants of citizenship was challenged under this law.

They also do wrong who prohibit foreigners from enjoying the use of a city and exclude them from it, as Pennus did in our forefathers' time, and Papius recently. It is of course right that a non-citizen not be allowed to exercise citizen rights; the law on this was brought in by those extremely wise consuls Crassus and Scaevola. However, to prohibit foreigners from enjoying the use of a city is certainly barbarous.

10.3 Asconius *Commentaries on Cicero* 67–68: The impact of the *lex Licinia Mucia*

67 'With regard to the lex Licinia Mucia, concerning the reduction of citizen numbers, I consider that all are agreed that, although it was passed by two consuls who were the wisest of all we have known, it was not only ineffective but seriously harmful for the state.' Cicero is referring to the orator Lucius Licinius Crassus and Quintus Mucius Scaevola, the pontifex maximus, orator and jurist. In their consulship, they brought in the law to which Cicero is referring, which restored the allies to their own states. For **68** the peoples of Italy desperately wanted Roman citizenship, and because of this a large number of them were passing themselves off as Roman citizens; accordingly it seemed necessary to pass a law to restore everyone to the jurisdiction of their own states. But this law so alienated the leaders of the peoples of Italy that it may have been the main cause of the Italian war which broke out three years later.

MARCUS LIVIUS DRUSUS

Marcus Livius Drusus was tribune in 91 BC. The Marsi of central Italy, who spoke Oscan, were prominent among the rebels in the Social War, and the Romans called the war after them (the Marsic War): Diod. 37.1. Drusus attempted to deal with several problems: senatorial dissatisfaction at the control of the law-courts by the equites was his primary aim, but also colonies for the landless poor and a grain law presumably concerned with cheap distribution. Like his father, he was using the tribunate to advance the interests of the aristocracy. He was the grandfather of Livia Drusilla, wife of Augustus. For Servilius Caepio, who organised the equites against Drusus, see docs 9.14, 18.

10.4 Plutarch *Life of Cato the Younger* 2.1–4: Drusus' Italian friends

Cato the Younger and his siblings, including his older half-brother Caepio, were brought up in the home of their uncle Livius Drusus, tribune in 91 BC: Cato would have been four years old in 91. Poppaedius led the Marsi, and his forces ambushed and killed Caepio, Drusus' brother-in-law, in 90 BC.

1 While Cato was still a child, the Romans' allies were trying to acquire Roman citizenship; and one of them, Pompaedius (Poppaedius) Silo, a man of great experience in war and of the highest reputation, a friend of Drusus, was spending several days at his house, during which time he came to be friendly with the children. 'Come', he said to them, 'Ask your uncle to help us in our struggle for citizenship.' **2** Caepio agreed with a smile, but, when Cato made no reply and gazed at the strangers with a stubborn, fierce glare, Pompaedius said to him, 'And you, young man, what do you say? Are you not able to join your uncle in helping the strangers like your brother?' **3** When he said nothing, but appeared through his silence and facial expression to refuse the request, Pompaedius lifted him through a window as if he would let him go, and ordered him to agree or he would drop him . . . **4** When Cato had put up with this treatment for some time without fright or fear, Pompaedius put him down, saying quietly to his friends, 'What a piece of luck for Italy that he is a child! If he were a man, I do not think we would get a single vote among the people.'

10.5 Livy *Periochae* 70–71: Drusus makes enemies

70: The 'largesse' comprised agrarian laws and grain distribution. Quintus Mucius Scaevola (not Gaius, as here) (cos. 95 BC) was proconsul of Asia (probably in 94 BC) with Publius Rutilius Rufus, Drusus' uncle, as his legate. Rutilius (cos. 105), who had angered the publicani, was condemned in 92 BC for extortion in a court manned with equites as jurors (cf. docs 8.28–29).

70 Publius Rutilius, a man of the greatest integrity, was hated by the equestrian order because, as legate of the proconsul Gaius Mucius, he had protected Asia against the wrongs of the publicani, and, since the law-courts were in their power, Rutilius was condemned for extortion and sent into exile (92 BC) . . . The senate refused to bear the equestrian order's lack of restraint in running the courts and began to make every effort to transfer the courts to themselves, with their cause supported by Marcus Livius Drusus, tribune of the plebs, who roused the plebs with the ruinous hope of largesse in order to strengthen his position . . .

71 In order to gain greater strength in his attempt to support the senate's cause, Marcus Livius Drusus, tribune of the plebs, tried to win over the allies and the peoples of Italy with the hope of Roman citizenship; with their help he passed agrarian and corn laws by violence and also brought in a law on the courts, that control of the courts should be shared equally by the senate and the equestrian order. But when, at last, it was not possible to give the allies the citizenship they had been promised, the Italians were furious and began to stir up a revolt. Their gatherings and conspiracies, and the speeches of their leading men in counsels, are recorded. Because of these events, Livius Drusus was hated even by the senate as being responsible for promoting rebellion among the allies, and he was killed in his own home by a person unknown.

10.6 Appian *Civil Wars* 1.34.152–35.161: The pro-Italian legislation of Drusus, 91 BC

To gain support for the jury law, Drusus sought popular support through a law for colonies in Italy and Sicily, presumably the colonies legislated for in his father's tribunate (doc. 8.28). This raised the opposition of the allies (doc. 10.9), because the colonies in Italy would use ager publicus which they held. The promise of citizenship was not enough to counter the opposition to his colonies. Drusus had his measure passed in the assembly with violence, but senatorial opposition to the inclusion of equites in the senatorial order and the enfranchisement of the Italians was led by one of the consuls for 91, L. Marcius Philippus. He had all of Drusus' laws annulled by a single decree of the senate as having been passed despite inauspicious omens.

152 Fulvius Flaccus in his consulship (125 BC) was the first and foremost to arouse openly in the Italians the desire for Roman citizenship – that they should be partners in the empire instead of subjects. When he introduced the idea and strongly persisted in it, he was sent off because of this on some military command by the senate. **153** During this, his consulship came to an end, but he later obtained the tribunate and managed to have as his colleague the younger Gracchus, who helped him to bring in other measures in the Italians' favour. **154** When they were both killed, as I narrated earlier, Italy was aroused even more; for they did not think it right that they be considered subjects instead of partners, or that Flaccus and Gracchus should have suffered such misfortunes while working on their behalf.

155 After them the tribune Livius Drusus, a man of most distinguished family, promised the Italians, at their own request, that he would introduce another law to grant them citizenship; they especially desired this because, at a stroke, they would become rulers instead of subjects. **156** In order to gain the people's support for this measure he tried to win them over with many colonies in Italy and Sicily, which had been voted long before but not yet been carried out. **157** He attempted to reconcile by an impartial law the senate and the equites, who had serious differences with each other at that time over the law-courts. As he was unable to transfer the courts back to the senate openly, he devised the following compromise: **158** as there were now hardly 300 senators on account of the conflicts, he introduced a law that an equal number, chosen according to merit, should be added to their number from the equites, and that the courts of justice should for the future be made up from the entire body. He added a clause that they should make investigations into cases of bribery, as accusations of that kind were almost unknown, because bribery was such a common practice. **159** This was his plan for a compromise, but it turned out quite the opposite to what he expected. The senators were furious that so large a number should be added to their body all at once and be transferred from the equites to the highest rank, considering that it was not unlikely that they would form their own separate senatorial party and contend against the former senators more strongly than ever. **160** The equites for their part suspected that, by this treatment, the law-courts would for the future be transferred from the equites to the senate on its own, and, as they had acquired a taste for the immense wealth and power, they did not bear this suspicion without grief. **161** The majority of them, too, were worried and suspicious of each other as to who seemed the more worthy to be enrolled in the 300; and jealousy towards their betters infected the remainder. The equites were angry primarily at the charge of bribery being revived, which they thought they had already firmly and completely suppressed on their own account.

10.7 Diodorus Siculus *Library of History* 37.13.1: A pre-emptive strike planned

Q. Poppaedius Silo (Pompaedius) was dissuaded from this attack on the way to Rome in 91 BC by Domitius, perhaps Cn. Domitius Ahenobarbus (cos. 96). Presumably the investigations they feared were connected with the *lex Licinia Mucia* and the problems Drusus was having in passing his legislation. This was the Poppaedius who had stayed with Drusus.

The Marsic leader, Pompaedius, commenced a great and hazardous enterprise. He assembled 10,000 men from those who feared the investigations and led them against Rome with swords hidden under their clothes. His intention was to surround the senate with armed men and demand citizenship, or, if he failed, to destroy Rome's rule with fire and sword.

10.8 Diodorus Siculus *Library of History* 37.11.1: The 'oath' of the Italians

This oath, supposedly sworn by Drusus' Italian supporters, was circulated by his enemy L. Philippus and was presumably composed to discredit Drusus on the grounds that it would have given him unrivalled clientela and influence in Italy.

I swear by Jupiter Capitolinus, and Roman Vesta, and Rome's ancestral god Mars, and Sun the Founder (i.e., Sol Indiges), and Earth the benefactress of animals and plants, and also by the demi-gods who founded Rome and the heroes who have increased her empire, that the enemy and friend of Drusus shall be my enemy and friend, and I shall not spare my property, nor the lives of my children and parents, unless it benefit Drusus and those who swear this oath. And if I become a citizen by Drusus' law, I will consider Rome my country and Drusus my greatest benefactor. And I will transmit this oath to as many of my countrymen as I can. May all good things come to me if I keep the oath, and the opposite if I break it.

10.9 Appian *Civil Wars* 1.36.162–37.165: Drusus' assassination

The Umbrians and Etruscans were clearly opposed to Drusus' agrarian legislation, due to the fact that these communities (most particularly the aristocracies there) had large amounts of ager publicus they were not willing to trade for citizenship.

162 And so it happened that the senate and equites, despite their differences, were united in their hatred of Drusus, and only the people were happy with their colonies. Even the Italians, on whose especial behalf Drusus was devising these measures, had concerns about the law on colonies, worried that the Roman public land, which was still undistributed and which they were still farming, some in open violation and others clandestinely, would immediately be taken away from them, and that they might also be disturbed in their own lands. **163** The Etruscans and the Umbrians shared the Italians' fears, and, when they were, as was believed, summoned to the city by the consuls to overthrow Drusus, which was their true aim, though the pretext was to make their complaints, they opposed the law publicly and remained for the day of voting. **164** Aware of this, Drusus did not go out much but regularly transacted his business in the poorly lit atrium of his house, when one evening, as he was sending the crowd away, he suddenly cried out that he was wounded, and fell down while still saying the words. A shoemaker's knife was found thrust into his thigh.

165 In this way Drusus too was killed while tribune. The equites, to make his policy grounds for accusation against their enemies, persuaded Quintus Varius, a tribune, to introduce a law to prosecute anyone who helped the Italians acquire citizenship, whether openly or secretly, hoping that they might bring all the senators under a dreadful accusation and themselves sit in judgement on them, and with them out of the way be even more powerful in their rule of Rome.

THE SOCIAL WAR

The war, which ran from 91 to 89 BC, with the main confrontation being in 91–90, began in Asculum. The allies had not been interested in citizenship when Gaius Gracchus had proposed this, but by 91 a consciousness of its importance may have come about through the activities of the Gracchan land commission, against which Scipio Aemilianus had defended them in 129. There had also been grants of citizenship to allies, such as Marius' grant to two cohorts of Camertes (doc. 9.27), and the aristocracies in allied communities were presumably aware that Latin aristocrats possessed Roman citizenship. The issue of the ager publicus, revisited by Drusus in 91, was also a reminder both of Roman dominance of the allies and of the steady encroachment of Romans on Italian land and Roman expansionism. After the Social War the allied aristocracies, now that they had acquired citizenship, entered the political life of Rome in full, surely reflecting the aspirations they had in 91 which drove them to revolt when these were ignored. The fact that most of the allies would never be able to exercise their voting rights as citizens effectively at Rome was irrelevant.

10.10 Livy *Periochae* 72: Secession

The Italian allies who revolted fell into two main groups of peoples: the Marsi and the Samnites. The rebels as a whole were from central and southern Italy. Servilius was actually a praetor or propraetor who attempted to threaten the Asculans, and so the revolt started prematurely.

The commencement of the war was occasioned by the Picentes, when the proconsul Quintus Servilius was killed in the town of Asculum along with all the Roman citizens who were in the town. The Roman people adopted military dress.

10.11 Appian *Civil Wars* 1.38.169–39.177: Full-scale war

When an Italian embassy to Rome was rebuffed, the last chance for peace was wasted, and a significant number of allies rebelled.

169 When the Italians learnt of the murder of Drusus and of the pretext for banishing the others (for supporting the Italians), they considered that they could no longer endure that those bringing measures on their behalf should suffer in such a way, and, seeing no other chance of their acquiring the citizenship, they decided to rebel against the Romans and make war against them with all their power. **170** They sent envoys to each other in secret, formed a league, and exchanged hostages as a pledge of loyalty. For a considerable time the Romans remained unaware of this because of their law-suits and internal strife in Rome; when they did find out, they sent men around to the cities, who knew them well, to discover secretly what was happening. **171** One of these saw a youth from Asculum being taken as a hostage to another city and informed Servilius, who was proconsul in that region. **172** There were, it appears, at that time, magistrates governing parts of Italy as pro-consuls . . . **173** Servilius hastened to Asculum and delivered a threatening speech to the people who were celebrating a festival, whereupon, supposing that the plot had been discovered, they killed him. Fonteius, his legate, was also killed (for this is what they call those of senatorial rank who accompany provincial governors as assistants). **174** With these killed, there was no mercy shown to any of the other Romans, and the people of Asculum fell on them all and stabbed them and plundered their belongings.

    175 Once the revolt had started, all the peoples bordering Asculum joined in – the Marsi, Paeligni, Vestini and Marrucini, who were followed by the Picentes, Frentani, Hirpini, Pompeiani, Venusini, Apulians, Lucanians and Samnites, peoples who had been hostile to Rome in earlier times, and all the other peoples between the River Liris (now, I think, the Liternus) and the end of the Adriatic, both maritime and inland. **176** They sent ambassadors to Rome to complain that, though they had helped the Romans in every way to build up their empire, they had not thought their helpers worthy of citizenship. The senate sternly replied that, if they repented of what they had done, they could send envoys, otherwise not. **177** In despair of any other remedy, they went on with their preparations; and, in addition to the soldiers stationed as garrisons at each city, there was a communal force amounting to some 100,000 cavalry and infantry. The Romans sent against them a force of equal size, made up of Roman citizens and of the Italian peoples who were still their allies.

10.12 Diodorus Siculus *Library of History* 37.2.4–7: The Italian constitution

The Italians' constitution was not a true federalist structure but, rather, a government modelled on Roman lines for the conduct of the war. One of the allies' silver coins has Pompaedius Silo's name on it, with the reverse showing a sacrificial pig with, on either side, four warriors swearing an oath over the pig. By minting such coins, the rebels challenged Rome's monopoly on the issuing of silver coinage (docs 10.29–31).

4 At war with the Romans were the Samnites, the Asculans, the Lucanians, the Picentes, the people of Nola, and other cities and nations; their most notable and largest city was Corfinium, recently established as the Italians' federal capital, where they had set up, among all the other things which strengthen a large city and government, a good-sized forum and a senate house, and abundant supplies of everything needed for a war, including a large amount of money and a plentiful supply of provisions. **5** They also set up a joint senate of 500 men, from whom men worthy to rule the country and able to devise measures for the common safety would be selected, and they entrusted the management of the war to these, though they gave the senators full powers to make decisions. They ruled that two consuls and 12 praetors should be elected every year.

6 The men put into power as consuls were Quintus Pompaedius Silo, a Marsian by birth and the outstanding man of his nation, and secondly Gaius Aponius Motylus, of the Samnite race, who was also a man pre-eminent in reputation and achievements in his nation. They divided the whole of Italy into two parts and assigned them as consular provinces and districts. **7** To Pompaedius they assigned the region from what is called Cercola to the Adriatic Sea, the section towards the west and north, and granted him six praetors; the rest of Italy, that towards the east and south, they assigned to Gaius Motylus, providing him also with six praetors. When in this way they had organised their government skilfully, and for the most part in imitation of the long-standing Roman model, they then devoted themselves even more earnestly to the war which was to come, after naming their federal capital Italia (Italica).

BROTHERS-IN-ARMS

10.13 Velleius Paterculus *Compendium* 2.15.1–2: The Italians' grievances

Velleius states why the allies deserved citizenship: they fought for a state but had no share in its citizenship. Even though his ancestors fought on the Roman side (see doc. 10.18), he recognised that the allied cause was not unjust.

1 One hundred and twenty years ago, in the consulship of Lucius Caesar and Publius Rutilius (90 BC), the whole of Italy took up arms against the Romans. The revolt began with the people of Asculum, who had killed the praetor Servilius and his deputy Fonteius, and was next taken up by the Marsi and made its way into all districts of Italy. **2** The fate of the Italians was as cruel as their cause was just, for they were seeking citizenship in the state whose power they were defending by their arms: every year and in every war they were providing a double number of men, both of cavalry and of infantry, and yet were not admitted to citizen rights in the state which, through them, had reached so high a position that it was able to look down upon men of the same race and blood as foreigners and aliens.

10.14 Cicero *Philippics* 12.27: The allies' aims

Gnaeus Pompeius Strabo was consul in 89 BC, and Cicero served under him in 90–89.

I can remember conferences with both the bitterest enemies and the most deeply rebellious citizens. The consul Gnaeus Pompeius, son of Sextus, held a conference in my presence, when I was a new recruit in his army, with the Marsian leader, Publius Vettius Scato, between the two camps. I recall the consul's brother, Sextus Pompeius, a learned and wise man, coming to this conference from Rome. Scato greeted him and asked, 'How shall I address you?' 'As a guest, if I had the choice', said Pompeius, 'but as an enemy by necessity.' It was a fair conference: no fear, no underlying suspicion, not even a lot of hatred. For the allies were seeking not to rob us of our state but to be received into it themselves.

10.15 Appian *Civil Wars* 1.48.207–10: Heroic suicide at Asculum

Vidacilius, Lafrenius and Vettius had defeated Pompeius, but later Sulpicius defeated Lafrenius, who was killed in the battle; Lafrenius' troops fled to Asculum (see 10.11). Vidacilius then went to Asculum's assistance; the city was besieged by the Romans for some time, and it fell in November 89 BC, after Vidacilius' suicide. He must have realised that the allied cause was lost: App. 1.47.204–6; Vell. 2.21.

207 Asculum was the home town of Vidacilius, and, fearing for its safety, he hurried there, taking eight cohorts. . . . **208** he forced his way into the town through the middle of the enemy with what forces he could get and reproached the citizens for their cowardice and disobedience. **209** As he gave up hope that the town could be saved, he killed all his enemies, who had been in conflict with him and who through jealousy had recently prevented the people from carrying out his orders; he then built a pyre in the temple, placed a couch on the fire, and held a feast with his friends. At the height of the drinking he swallowed poison and, throwing himself onto the pyre, told his friends to set light to it. **210** So perished Vidacilius, a man who was proud to die for his country.

10.16 *CIL* I² 848, 857–61, 875, 877: Inscriptions found on sling-shots

Lead sling-shots found at Corropoli (848) and Asculum, dated to 90–89 BC. Pompeius is Pompeius Strabo, sent to besiege Asculum in 91 BC. In 860 there is a pun on *pica* (magpie) and Picentes; woodpecker, *picus* (the bird connected with Picenum) may have been intended. In 877, the allusion is perhaps to the Samnite bull, stamped on Samnite coins struck; for inscribed sling-shots at Perusia in 41–40, see doc. 14.31.

848 (a) The Italians (b) Titus Lafrenius, praetor.
857 Hit Pompeius!
858 Bring safety for Pompeius (right to left).
859 For the Asculans!
860 Hit a magpie!
861 Runaways, you are doomed!
875 Evil's coming to you, evil one!
877 (a) Swallow the bull and go to hell! (b) But you'll vomit up the lot!

10.17 Appian *Civil Wars* 1.49.211–15: The senate learns to compromise

Umbria and Etruria, hearing of the scale of the revolt, were on the brink of joining. Rome found itself so short of troops that it enrolled freedmen, which it had not done even in the worst days after Cannae (but see doc. 6.1). The Roman reliance on its allies for infantry and cavalry is made clear here (see doc. 10.13).

211 While these events were taking place on the Adriatic side of Italy, the inhabitants of Etruria and Umbria and other neighbouring peoples on the other side of Rome heard of them and were all roused to revolt. **212** The senate was afraid that they might be surrounded by war and unable to protect themselves and garrisoned the coast from Cumae to the city with freedmen, who were then for the first time enrolled in the army because of the lack of troops. They also decreed that those of the Italians who had kept to their alliance should become citizens, which they practically all desired more than anything. **213** They sent the news round the Etruscans, who gladly accepted the citizenship. By this gift, the senate made the faithful more faithful, made sure of those who were indecisive, and undermined those at war through the hope of similar treatment. **214** The Romans did not enrol these new citizens in the 35 existing tribes, in case they outvoted the old citizens in the elections, but enrolled them in ten new tribes, which voted last. **215** So it often happened that their vote was useless, since a majority was obtained from the 35 tribes that voted first. Either this was not noticed initially or the Italians were pleased even with this, but when it was observed later it caused another political conflict.

10.18 Velleius Paterculus *Compendium* 2.15.3–16.4: The bitter outcomes of the conflict

Velleius stresses the roles of three Roman commanders: Pompeius, Sulla and Marius. Marius' role in the Social War was initially much more limited than might have been expected; he had not recovered from the Saturninus affair and, despite the loss of two Roman consuls and the seriousness of the situation, Rome did not at first rely on him. He served as legate under P. Rutilius Lupus (cos. 90 BC). When Rutilius was killed, after having neglected Marius' advice, the senate appointed Marius and Q. Servilius Caepio to the command; when Caepio was killed in an ambush, Marius was given full command of the consul's army. Sulla and Marius then together in a battle defeated the Marsi.

C. Papius Mutilus and Q. Poppaedius Silo were chosen as the two consuls of the new confederacy. Mutilus was defeated by L. Julius Caesar (cos. 90) and by Sulla in 89.

Poppaedius in 89 BC defeated and killed one of the consuls of that year, L. Porcius Cato. However, Cn. Pompeius Strabo defeated him, after which he abandoned Corfinium. In 88 he was defeated and killed by Q. Caecilius Metellus Pius. The Marsi were a spent force, and the war was more or less over.

15.3 The war wiped out more than 300,000 of the youth of Italy. The most distinguished Roman commanders in the war were Gnaeus Pompeius, father of Pompey the Great, Gaius Marius, whom I have already mentioned, Lucius Sulla, who had held the praetorship in the previous year, and Quintus Metellus, son of Metellus Numidicus . . . **16.1** The most celebrated Italian leaders were Silo Popaedius, Herius Asinius, Insteius Cato, Gaius Pontidius, Telesinus Pontius, Marius Egnatius and Papius Mutilus. **2** Nor should I, through modesty, deprive my own family of glory, especially when I am recording the truth, for much is due to the memory of my great-grandfather, Minatius Magius of Aeculanum, grandson of Decius Magius, leader of the Campanians, a man of great renown and loyalty, who showed such loyalty to the Romans in this war that, with a legion which he had himself enlisted among the Hirpini, he took Herculaneum along with Titus Didius, besieged Pompeii with Lucius Sulla, and occupied Compsa. **3** Others have recorded his services, but the longest and clearest account is that of Quintus Hortensius in his *Annals*. The Roman people made full repayment for his loyalty by a grant of citizenship to him and by making his sons praetors at a time when they elected only six. **4** So changeable and savage was the fortune of the Italian war that in two successive years two Roman consuls, Rutilius (Publius Rutilius Lupus, cos. 90) and then Cato Porcius (Lucius Porcius Cato, cos. 89), were killed by the enemy, the armies of the Roman people were routed in many places, and the Romans were compelled to adopt military dress and retain it for a long time. The Italians chose Corfinium as their capital and named it Italica. Then gradually the strength of the Romans was augmented by admitting to citizenship those who had not taken up arms or who had been quick to lay them down again, and Pompeius, Sulla and Marius restored the wavering and sinking power of the Roman people.

THE EMERGENCE OF L. CORNELIUS SULLA

10.19 Livy *Periochae* 75: Sulla's victories, 89 BC

Sulla's victories against the allies ensured him a consulship when he stood in 89 for 88 BC. Q. Pompeius Rufus (not to be confused with Gnaeus Pompeius Strabo (cos. 89 BC), who was the father of Pompey the Great) was also awarded a consulship for 88. Pompeius Rufus' son married Sulla's daughter. The Romans' success was due primarily to the superior generalship of Pompeius Strabo and Sulla and to the fact that the Latins and many Italian communities remained loyal and supplied Rome with troops.

Lucius Cornelius Sulla, as legate, defeated the Samnites in battle and stormed two of their camps. Gnaeus Pompeius received the surrender of the Vestini . . . Lucius Sulla overcame the Hirpini, routed the Samnites in several battles and received the surrender of several peoples. After achievements rarely equalled by anyone else before becoming consul, Sulla set out for Rome to stand for the consulship.

10.20 Velleius Paterculus *Compendium* 2.17.1–3: Sulla receives his rewards, 88 BC

For Sulla's praetorship, see doc. 11.2.

1 With the Italian war ended for the most part, except for the remnants of revolt which continued at Nola, the Romans, who were exhausted, agreed to grant citizenship to the conquered and humiliated rather than giving it to them as a whole at a time when their own strength was still unimpaired. **2** Quintus Pompeius (Rufus) and Lucius Cornelius Sulla entered upon the consulship, Sulla being a man who, up to the end of his victory, cannot be sufficiently praised and who, after his victory, cannot be adequately censured. He was born from a noble family, the sixth in descent from Cornelius Rufinus, who had been one of the famous leaders in the war against Pyrrhus, and, as his family's splendour had waned, for a long time he behaved as if he had no thought of standing for the consulship. **3** Then, after his praetorship, when he had gained renown in the Italian war, as he had earlier in his Gallic command under Marius in which he routed the most pre-eminent leaders of the enemy, he stood for the consulship, encouraged by his success, and was elected by the vote of almost all the citizens. But he did not achieve this honour until his forty-ninth year.

CITIZENSHIP FOR THE ITALIANS

The *lex Julia* of October 90 BC offered full citizenship to all Latins and to the allied communities (not individuals) that had not revolted, as well as to those who had surrendered (the dediticii) or who were willing to do so within a given time. The allied communities that continued fighting were finally enfranchised in 87 BC. By the end of 89 most of the Italians had surrendered, but not the Samnites, Lucanians and Nola. The Samnites still fighting in 87 refused citizenship. The enfranchisement of all the communities south of the Po River in Italy led to the Romanisation of the peninsula; Italy north of the Po received Roman citizenship and was incorporated into Italy by 42 BC. Latin soon became the accepted language, and, although many communities retained their ethnic identity in the short term, within two generations Italy was Roman. Although censors (L. Julius Caesar and P. Licinius Crassus) were appointed in 89, progress in registering the new citizens was initially slow, though the census of 70–69 recorded some 900,000 citizens.

10.21 Cicero *In Defence of Balbus* 21: Rome makes the offer

Citizenship was awarded to communities as a whole: citizens belonged to a particular municipium but were also citizens of Rome. The aristocracies of these communities, if they visited Rome, could vote in the comitia centuriata, where voting took place according to wealth classification, and could stand for magistracies. As Greek colonies, both Heraclea and Naples had considerable Greek populations.

Finally came the Julian law, by which citizenship was given to allies and Latins, laying down that communities that had not ratified the offer should not have the citizenship. As a consequence, there was a serious dispute among the citizens of

Heraclea and Naples, since a large proportion of the people in those two cities preferred to keep the freedom enjoyed under their treaty of alliance rather than Roman citizenship.

10.22 *ILS* 6086: A constitution for Tarentum (after 90 BC)

Following the grant of Roman citizenship by the *lex Julia* in 90 BC to the Italians not in arms (doc. 10.21), the municipium of Tarentum was granted this constitution (though this may not have taken place immediately: spelling and style suggest a later date). It was engraved on a bronze tablet found at Tarentum. Curiae survived in Italian towns as voting units; the Board of Four consisted of the duoviri (Board of Two) and two aediles.

Ninth table of the law:

. . . nor shall he be allowed to be . . . nor shall anyone steal by fraud or misappropriate any money, public, sacred or concerned with religion, belonging to that municipium, nor act in such a way whereby any of the above might ensue; nor shall he with evil intent lessen funds through mishandling public accounts or public fraud. Whoever should act thus shall be fined four times the amount involved **5** and be condemned to pay that sum to the municipium, and the demand and exaction of that sum shall be the responsibility of whoever shall be at that time a magistrate in the municipium.

The Board of Four, including the aediles, who shall be the first to serve under this law, whoever of them shall have come to Tarentum, shall, within the next 20 days after his first coming to Tarentum after the passing of this law, take steps to stand as surety for himself and present bondsmen and their estates (as sureties) to the Board of Four, **10** sufficient that any money, whether public, sacred or concerned with religion, belonging to that municipium, which should come into his hands during his term of office, shall be properly secured to the municipium of Tarentum, and he shall give an account of that matter in whatever way the senate shall decide. And that member of the Board of Four to whom surety shall be given shall accept it and shall have it recorded in the public records (tabulae); and whoever shall hold a public assembly (comitia) to propose for election the members of the Board of Two and aediles, **15** he shall, before a majority of the curiae shall return any of those who are seeking office at that assembly, accept bondsmen from the candidates sufficient that any money, whether public, sacred or concerned with religion, belonging to that municipium, which should come into their hands during his term of office, shall be properly secured to the municipium of Tarentum, and he shall give an account of that matter **20** in whatever way the senate shall decide, and he shall have it recorded in the public records. With regard to those to whom public business in the municipium shall be given by a vote of the senate, or who shall have performed public business, and who shall have paid or exacted public money, he to whom that business shall have been given, or who has performed public business, or paid or exacted public money, shall give and present in good faith an account of that matter to the senate within the next ten days **25** following the decision of the senate of the municipium.

Anyone who is or shall be a decurion (member of the senate) of the municipium of Tarentum, or shall have voted in the senate in the municipium of Tarentum, shall possess in good faith in the town of Tarentum or within the boundaries of that municipium a house (aedificium), which shall be roofed with not fewer than 1,500 tiles. Whoever of the above who does not possess such a house of his own, **30** or who shall have bought a house or received one by formal purchase in such a way that he would fraudulently evade this law, shall be condemned to pay the municipium of Tarentum money amounting to 5,000 sesterces for each year of the offence.

No one in the town which belongs to that municipium shall take the roof off a house or demolish or destroy one, unless he is going to restore it to a state no worse (than before) or unless by a vote of the senate. If anyone acts in opposition to this, he shall be condemned to pay the municipium **35** money equal in value to that of the house, and anyone who wishes may bring an action for the payment of that sum. The magistrate who exacts the sum shall pay one-half into the public treasury and spend one-half on the games which he will put on publicly during his term of office, or if he wishes to spend the money on a public monument to himself he shall be permitted, and shall be permitted to do so at no liability (to penalty) to himself.

If any member of the Board of Four, whether a member of the Board of Two or an aedile, shall be minded publicly, for the sake of the municipium, **40** to make, lay, alter, build or pave within those boundaries belonging to that municipium, he shall be permitted to do so, provided that it shall be done without injury (to any person).

Anyone who does not owe money to the municipium of Tarentum, and who is a citizen of the municipium and has not in the six years previous to his wish to leave (the municipium) been a member of the Board of Two or aedile, who wishes to leave the municipium of Tarentum, shall be permitted to do so at no liability (to penalty) to himself. . . .

10.23 *ILS* 8888: Spanish horsemen given citizenship

Through the *lex Julia*, Gnaeus Pompeius Strabo (cos. 89 BC) here grants citizenship to Spanish horsemen 'for valour'; the date is 17 November of either 90 or 89, while at Asculum. This inscription was found on fragments of a bronze tablet at Rome and demonstrates that individual commanders could award citizenship for service in the field (cf. doc. 9.27). A turma (squadron of horse) was one-tenth of an ala: first 30 and then 32 men. The Salluitan squadron was from Salduba, Spain (Iberia); from their names, some of the Iberians were clearly partly Romanised already. Along with their names are those of 60 members of Pompeius Strabo's *consilium* (advisory council), including his son Pompey, Lepidus (cos. 78) and Catiline.

(a) GNAEUS POMPEIUS, SON OF SEXTUS, IMPERATOR, ON ACCOUNT OF THEIR VALOUR, made Spanish horsemen Roman citizens in camp at Asculum on 17 November according to the lex Julia. At the council (*consilium*) were . . . Lucius Gellius, son of Lucius, of the Tromentine tribe, Gnaeus Octavius, son of Quintus . . . (there follows the names of some 60 staff officers).

(b) THE SALLUITAN SQUADRON

(col. 1)	(col. 2)
Sanibelser, son of Adingibas	*Ilerdans*
Illurtibas, son of Bilustibas	Ootacilius, son of Suisetarten
Estopeles, son of Ordennas	Gnaeus Cornelius, son of Nesille
Tersinno, son of Austinco	Publius Fabius, son of Enasagin
(. . . others . . .)	*Begensians*
	Turtumelis, son of Atanscer
	Segiensians
	Sosinaden, son of Sosinasa
	(. . . others . . .)

(col. 4) Gnaeus Pompeius, son of Sextus, imperator, in camp at Asculum, presented the Salluitan squadron on account of their valour with a helmet horn, plate, collar, armlet, chest-plates, and a double ration of corn.

10.24 Cicero *In Defence of Archias* 6–7: The *lex Plautia Papiria*, 89 BC

M. Plautius Silvanus and C. Papirius Carbo as tribunes in 89 BC passed the *lex Plautia Papiria*. This gave citizenship to any individual who belonged to an Italian city which had a treaty with Rome, who was permanently resident in Italy, and who reported himself to a praetor within 60 days of the passing of the law. It benefited those who belonged to communities which received citizenship under the *lex Julia* but who themselves were not living in their communities of origin when the law was passed. The poet Archias, a protégé of the Luculli, was attacked as a non-citizen by the Pompeians and defended by Cicero in 62. Metellus Pius was praetor in 89.

6 After a long period of time, after going to Sicily with Marcus Lucullus and returning with him from that province, Archias went to Heraclea; this city had been granted full civic privileges by the terms of its treaty with Rome, and Archias wanted to be enrolled among its citizens. His own merits would have sufficiently recommended him, even without the prestige and influence there of Lucullus, and his request was granted by the people. 7 Roman citizenship was granted by the law of Silvanus and Carbo, which extended citizenship to 'all who have been registered in allied communities, if they were resident in Italy at the time of the passing of this law, and if they have reported themselves to the praetor within sixty days.' Archias had resided at Rome for many years, and had reported himself to the praetor Quintus Metellus, his great friend.

10.25 *CIL* I² 588: Sailors discharged with honour, 78 BC

A decree of the senate in 78 BC, concerning Asclepiades of Clazomenae, Polystratus of Carystus and Meniscus of Miletus in Asia Minor, on a bilingual tablet of bronze found at Rome (Latin and Greek). The three Greek naval captains from Asia Minor and Euboea had loyally served the Republic and now were honourably discharged. The 'Italian War' is presumably the Social War (or possibly Sulla's war in Italy of 83–82). Various privileges are granted to the men, ensuring that they suffer no material loss because of their absence, but not the right to vote.

In the consulship of Quintus Lutatius Catulus, son of Quintus, and Marcus Aemilius Lepidus, son of Quintus, grandson of Marcus, and the urban praetorship and praetorship 'for aliens' of Lucius Cornelius Sisenna (i.e., he was praetor urbanus and praetor peregrinus), son of . . . in the month of May.

Quintus Lutatius Catulus, son of Quintus, consul, consulted the senate in the meeting-place (the curia) on 22 May. Present as witnesses were Lucius Faberius, son of Lucius, of the Sergian tribe, Gaius . . . son of Lucius, of the Poblilian tribe, Quintus Petillius, son of Titus, of the Sergian tribe.

With regard to the matter on which Quintus Lutatius, son of Quintus, consul, reported, that Asclepiades, son of Philinus, of Clazomenae, Polystratus, son of Polyarces, of Carystus, and Meniscus, son of Irenaeus, of Miletus, who had been known as Meniscus son of Thargelius, served on our ships as captains at the beginning of the Italic war, that they served our state valiantly and loyally, and that he wished them to be discharged to their homes by senatorial decree, should it seem right to the senate that such honour be accorded them in return for their successful campaigns and valiant deeds on behalf of our state: on this matter the senators resolved the following:

That Asclepiades, son of Philinus, of Clazomenae, Polystratus, son of Polyarces, of Carystus, and Meniscus, son of Irenaeus, of Miletus, who had been known as Meniscus son of Thargelius, be called upright men and our friends; that the senate and Roman people considered that they had served our state valiantly and loyally; on account of which the senate resolved that they, their children, and their descendants be free and exempt from all things (i.e., dues) in their own countries; that, if any taxes have been exacted from their properties after they had left in the service of our state, that these be returned and restored to them, and, if any fields, houses or property of theirs have been sold after they left their homes in the service of our state, that all of these be restored in their entirety; and, if any deadline has expired after they left their homes in the service of our state, that that fact should not injure them, and that for that reason they should be owed no less, and that they shall be permitted no less to claim and exact such a debt, and they may have, possess and enjoy any inheritances which have come to them or their children; . . .

That any judgements which have been made against them in their absence after they had left their homes shall be rendered void and judgements be made afresh in their entirety by decree of the senate. If their states publicly owe any moneys, they shall not be required to contribute towards these moneys. If any of our magistrates lease out Asia and Euboea, or impose tax on Asia or Euboea, they shall take care that these men shall not be required to pay anything. Also the consuls Quintus Lutatius and Marcus Aemilius, either or both as they should see fit, shall take care that they be entered in the official list of friends; and that they be permitted to erect a bronze tablet to Friendship on the Capitol and make a sacrifice; and that they instruct the city quaestor to send a gift according to official regulations and to make arrangements for their quarters and entertainment (as for foreign ambassadors). And that, if they should wish to send ambassadors about their affairs to the senate or to come as ambassadors, they, their children and their descendants shall be permitted to send ambassadors or come themselves. And that the consuls Quintus Lutatius and Marcus Aemilius, either or both as they should see fit, shall send a letter to our magistrates who hold the provinces of Asia and Macedonia, and to their magistrates that the senate wishes and thinks right, that these things be done in such as way as seems to them advantageous to our state and to their own dignity. Passed.

10.26 Velleius Paterculus *Compendium* 2.20.2–3: Pro-Italian legislation, 88 BC

For P. Sulpicius Rufus, tribune in 88 BC, and his pro-Italian and pro-Marian legislation, see doc. 9.32. His proposal to distribute Italians among all the tribes caused riots from the existing citizens. The consul Cinna was driven out in 87 for the same reasons. The Italian rebels who did surrender (i.e., became dediticii) probably gained citizenship in 87 or perhaps 84, but some held out until 80 BC (see doc. 10.28).

2 Cinna was no more restrained than Marius or Sulpicius. Though the citizenship had been given to Italy in such a way that the new citizens were to be distributed among eight tribes so that their power and numbers might not weaken the position of the old citizens and the beneficiaries should not receive more power than the benefactors, Cinna promised to distribute them among all the tribes. For this purpose he had brought together into the city a vast crowd from all over Italy. **3** Because of this he was driven out by the strength of his colleague (Gnaeus Octavius) and the optimates and set out for Campania, while his consulship was taken away by the authority of the senate, and Lucius Cornelius Merula, the flamen dialis, was appointed in his place.

10.27 Licinianus 20–21: Cinna courts the Italians, 87 BC

Cinna and Marius took Rome in 87 BC and were proclaimed consuls for 86. Q. Caecilius Metellus Pius was attempting to crush the Samnite resistance; he recognised Cinna as consul but, as a result of the Marian takeover, went into exile in Africa.

Legates were sent by Metellus to consult the senate about the attitude of the Samnites, who were refusing to make peace unless they and all deserters were granted citizenship and their property returned. The senate refused . . . when Cinna learnt of this through Flavius Fimbria he acceded to all their requests and added them to his troops . . . Citizenship was granted to all who had surrendered who had promised many thousands of soldiers, but who sent scarcely 16 cohorts.

10.28 Velleius Paterculus *Compendium* 2.27.1–3: Italian resistance, 82 BC

Most of the fighting in the Social War was over by 87 BC, and the Roman war against Mithridates proceeded despite the remnants of Italian opposition. When Cinna marched against Rome in 87 BC, the consuls recalled Q. Caecilius Metellus from fighting the Samnites: he would not agree to the Samnites' demands, but Cinna and Marius did. Sulla, on his return from the East in 82, recognised the grants of citizenship to the Italian communities, but the Samnites held out, and a great battle was fought outside Rome at the Colline gate. This defeat of the Samnite opposition to Rome in 82 BC was not the last, and the Samnites held out at Nola until 80 BC.

1 In the consulship of Carbo and Marius (the Younger), 109 years ago, Pontius Telesinus, a Samnite leader, who was brave in spirit and deeds and who deeply loathed the very name of Rome, collected about 40,000 of the bravest and most unyielding youth who still retained arms, and on 1 November fought with Sulla near the Colline gate a battle which was so critical as to bring both Sulla and the city into the greatest danger. **2** Rome had not faced a greater danger when the camp of Hannibal was visible within the third milestone than on this day, when Telesinus flew around the ranks of his army exclaiming that 'The Romans' last day is at hand!' and shouting that the city should be overthrown and destroyed, adding that, 'The wolves who stole Italian liberty will never disappear until the woods in which they are accustomed to take refuge are cut down!' **3** It was only after the first hour of the night that the Roman army was able to take breath and the enemy withdrew. On the next day Telesinus was found half-dead, with the expression rather of a conqueror than a dying man. His head was cut off and Sulla ordered it to be fixed on a spear and carried around Praeneste.

COINAGE IN THE SOCIAL WAR

No Roman coins specifically address the Social War. Coins of the allies were sometimes modelled on Roman coins, as in the case of the oath scenes, and have themes relating to the war. The allies minted on the Roman denarius standard and paid their soldiers in it. The allies' coins had Latin legends as well as Oscan, the language of the southern belligerents.

10.29 Grueber II.323–324.10, 327, 329: Allied soldiers swear an oath

A denarius on which the allied soldiers swear an oath to the cause of allied liberty (the number eight could indicate the number of groups engaged in war against the Romans when the coin was minted or simply be used to fill up the coin; some coins with a similar scene have two, four or six soldiers). The coins discussed in docs 10.29–30 are representative of the allied Social War coinage generally. Grueber II.329 has the name of the allied general Q. Silo (Q. Poppaedius Silo: docs 10.4, 10.7, 10.18) on the reverse, under the oath-taking scene.

Obverse: Head of the goddess Italia with wreath, facing left, with legend 'Italia' on right rim of coin.

Reverse: Eight warriors, four on either side of a pig which is held by an attendant; the eight warriors point their swords at the pig; behind the attendant, a standard.

10.30 Grueber II.327.19–329.30: Italian warrior and bull

A denarius depicting a bull, which stands for Italia and the allied cause: see coin at doc. 10.31.

Obverse: Head of the goddess Italia.

Reverse: A standing warrior, with spear and sword, and a reclining bull. The warrior's left foot is set upon a Roman standard.

10.31 Grueber II.327.18: The Italian bull gores the Roman wolf

A denarius depicting the god Bacchus, who was identified with the Italian deity Liber Pater.

Obverse: Head of the god Bacchus.

Reverse: A bull tramples a wolf, goring it with a horn; underneath, an Oscan inscription: Vitelliu (Italia).

11

Lucius Cornelius Sulla 'Felix'

Sulla first became prominent when he served with Marius in Africa in 107–105 (as quaestor in 107, then as proquaestor) and, specifically, when he arranged for the surrender of Jugurtha by Bocchus in 105 (docs 9.13, 11.50); his career until then had been unremarkable. His background was obscure and his family had not been prominent for some generations, though details concerning his poverty are probably exaggerated to highlight his subsequent rise to the position of Rome's most powerful man (docs 9.12, 11.1). He next worked with Marius in the northern campaigns in 104–103 (see Plut. *Sull.* 4, where the account of opposition between the two at this stage is clearly a later invention of Sulla's which Plutarch found in Sulla's *Memoirs*) and was obviously trusted by Marius on the strength of his African credentials. In fact it was only the issue of who was to hold the command against the king of Pontus, Mithridates, that led to the struggle between them, unless Plutarch's story about Marius' anger directed against Sulla on the occasion of King Bocchus' erection of a statue group showing Jugurtha being surrendered by Bocchus to Sulla is to be accepted (Plut. *Mar.* 32.4–6, *Sull.* 6.1–2). Little is known of Sulla's career in the 90s (doc. 11.2), but he was praetor in 93, and in 92 he was in Cilicia *pro consule* and returned to Rome in time for the breaking out of the Social War, in which he played a prominent role in Campania and Samnium (docs 10.18–20). His election to the consulship for 88 BC would have been on the strength of these military successes. The consulship brought with it the province of Asia and command against Mithridates, who was expanding his kingdom into Asia Minor, where at his instigation 80,000 Italians were massacred (doc. 11.4). At this point events took a turn that had serious ramifications – the agitation of the tribune Sulpicius to have the newly enfranchised Italians distributed among all the tribes. In return for Marius' support for his enfranchisement proposal, Sulpicius then had legislation passed that the command against Mithridates be transferred to Marius, who saw the war against Mithridates as 'an easy and very profitable' one (doc. 9.32). But so too did Sulla, who had left to join his army at Capua and who clearly saw this command as a crucial stage in his career. Marius obviously had not thought through the consequences of his attempt to take the command against Mithridates. After all, Marius had done the same to Metellus, depriving him of his command, and actually with Metellus in the field of operations (doc. 9.10).

In 88 BC, much depended on Sulla. He decided – rightly or wrongly – that he was not going to be deprived of his command, and that the way to do this was to march upon Rome. His officers had some scruples, but his soldiers (and his fellow consul) did not: the war promised plunder, and they were worried Marius would use troops other than themselves (doc. 11.5). This march on Rome and its capture by a magistrate with imperium was extraordinary. The murder of a tribune, Sulpicius, and the mob violence that followed were in themselves disastrous but not unprecedented (as in the cases of Tiberius and Gaius Gracchus, Drusus and Saturninus). Sulla introduced some political reforms and then set off for the East. Cinna, consul in 87, was driven from Rome by his fellow consul Octavius, deprived of office, and declared an enemy. Cinna decided not to accept this but raised an army; he was joined by Marius, who, after initial fighting, had fled the city at Sulla's entry. With others, he had been declared a public enemy, to be killed with impunity (doc. 9.33). Marius fought his way into the city, and the violence now rose to an exceptional level as he settled old scores; he was elected for a seventh consulship for 86 (with Cinna, consul for the second time in 86, and again in 85 and 84) but died within a few days of taking office. There was now peace at Rome. But Sulla, despite being declared a *hostis* (and technically therefore without imperium), had gone to his province and commenced war against Mithridates. He was able to return to Rome in 83, having arranged a peace treaty after decisive victories at Chaeronea and Orchomenus in Greece (docs 11.7–10).

Cinna (cos. 87–84 BC) had remarkable influence at Rome, but little is known of his policies. Significantly, the enfranchised Italians seem to have been finally distributed among all the tribes. When Valerius Flaccus was elected as consul in 86 BC to replace Marius and was sent out to Asia Minor (see doc. 11.7), he took an offer to Sulla that if he would submit to the senate he would cease to be a public enemy. Whether this was a senatorial initiative or simply a Cinnan one is unclear. Sulla dealt first with Mithridates, then with Fimbria, who as legate led a mutiny against Flaccus, in which the latter was killed, and took over his army (doc. 11.8; there are two individuals called L. Valerius Flaccus in this period: one took over Marius' consulship in 86 and was killed by Fimbria in Asia Minor, the other was the princeps senatus who led the senate in a policy of reconciliation towards Sulla and had been Marius' colleague in his sixth consulship of 100). Sulla, possibly in late 85, wrote to the senate reminding them both of his past victories and his present successes against Mithridates and of the fact that those exiled by Cinna had fled to him, and saying that he was returning to Rome to take vengeance (doc. 11.13). The princeps senatus (L. Valerius Flaccus) successfully proposed the sending of emissaries to Sulla, and the senate ordered Cinna and Carbo (consuls for 85) to stop recruiting an army until he replied. Cinna and Carbo, however, declared themselves consuls again for 84, and Cinna raised an army against Sulla, but was murdered by his own troops; Carbo continued to oppose Sulla (doc. 11.12; App. *BC* 1.77).

Sulla returned to Italy. The consuls for 83 BC, C. Norbanus and L. Cornelius Scipio, were overcome, and many desertions took place to the Sullan camp; civil war broke out. The optimates largely supported Sulla and joined him, among them

Crassus and Pompey (docs 11.14–15). The younger Marius and the Samnites held out but were dealt with at Praeneste (doc. 9.34) and at the battle of the Colline gate (doc. 10.28). Sulla now turned his attention to Rome and his enemies, and there occurred the infamous proscriptions, in which hundreds – perhaps thousands – perished in addition to the thousands who had lost their lives in the civil war (docs 11.19–23). Sulla's reform programme of 88 was revived, with special attention being paid to strengthening the senate and disempowering the tribunate, which had challenged optimate control (docs 11.26–38). Sulla voluntarily laid down his dictatorship sometime in 80 BC, when he held his second consulship. With his death in 79 some ill-feeling was expressed about his reforms; though they survived his death, changes weakened their effect, and in 70 Crassus and Pompey, who had benefited under him, restored the tribunate (doc. 12.4). But his judicial and administrative reforms remained in force (docs 11.39–40). Pompey first emerges at this point as an important figure, as he raised (as a private citizen: *privatus*) three legions for Sulla and was then sent to deal with the Marians in Africa and Sicily. He managed to extract the concession of a triumph from Sulla and ensured, against the wishes of Lepidus, that Sulla had a state funeral (docs 11.17–18, 44), but his political stance changed in the 70s. Opinions concerning Sulla vary as to the extent to which his dictatorship and actions as dictator were constitutional. What is clear is that he showed what was possible for a promagistrate invested with imperium and an army: this army returned with Sulla to Italy to do his bidding; 'his army was devoted to him, well trained and immense, and elated by its successes' (App. *BC* 1.76.347). In addition, for the first time, there had been a major civil war at Rome, as opposed to the civil dissensions and bloodshed centred around the tribunate.

Ancient sources: Appian 1.55–106.240–443 provides the basic narrative framework, and, as for other periods such as that of the Gracchi, is crucial given the loss of Livy, which survives for this period only in the form of summaries (*Periochae*). Livy *Periochae* 77–90 preserves a chronological framework and important, though brief, details of the dictator's constitutional reforms. Sulla is in fact presented as preferring peace to civil war (doc. 11.14). Livy is decidedly anti-Marian; his criticisms of Sulla come with the capture of Rome and the proscriptions. Plutarch's *Sulla* is unfortunately, but not surprisingly, almost totally lacking in detail about Sulla's constitutional reforms, but for details of the Mithridatic Wars, the overall narrative and various other points he is important. Other *Lives* provide details: *Marius* 10, 26, 35, 41, 45; *Pompey* 5–16; *Crassus* 6; *Caesar* 1. Plutarch made use of Sulla's *Memoirs*; despite clear criticism of Sulla's proscriptions, his account, with its hostile portrait of Sulpicius Rufus (*Sull.* 8) and Cinna and Carbo (*Sull.* 22.1), must owe something to Sulla's own narrative. Cicero *Pro Roscio Amerino* (esp. 2–3, 6, 125–6), delivered in Sulla's lifetime, is an important source dealing with the proscriptions, but he was careful not to attack Sulla himself, arguing that abuses such as the confiscation of the elder Roscius' property were not countenanced by Sulla. Cicero in several works condemns the confiscation of the property of the proscribed but is less concerned with the proscriptions themselves, for he too, in 63 BC, put men to death without a trial; see especially Dowling 2000: 306–13.

Sulla himself wrote his *Memoirs* (*Commentarii*: HRR I² 195–204), which were edited by L. Licinius Lucullus (cos. 74). Lucullus was the only officer, as quaestor in Sulla's army, to support his march on Rome in 88 (*MRR* II.52n.5 with Appian 253: doc. 11.5). The memoirs have not survived, but Plutarch refers to them, and his sources and those of Appian will have made use of them. In these memoirs, Sulla denigrated Marius' achievements against the Cimbri, attributing the victory to himself (see also docs 9.23, 26). He emphasised his own *virtus* (courage) as a general and his *felicitas*, the good fortune bestowed upon him by the gods. Also important was the history (*Historiae*) written by L. Cornelius Sisenna (praetor 78) and used by Appian and Livy. Sisenna's account focused on the Social War and Sullan period (see *HRR* I² 276–97), and his history probably commenced where that of Sempronius Asellio ended; Sallust seems then to have started his writing from the end of Sisenna's history. Sallust refers to Sisenna's work and appears to criticise Sisenna for not being critical enough of Sulla (*BJ* 95), whom he presents as possessing the various qualities of a good soldier in the Jugurthine War but as a cruel and tyrannical dictator; for Sallust, his dictatorship is the beginning of the final collapse of the Republic, which, for him, had begun with the sack of Carthage in 146 BC: Sall. *Cat.* 5, *BJ* 95–6 (doc. 9.12), *Hist.* 1.34–53. In addition, there are Licinianus and the fragments of Diodorus 38–39.

SULLA'S EARLY CAREER

11.1 Plutarch *Life of Sulla* 1.1–2.8: Sulla as a young man

Cf. Sallust's description: doc. 9.12. Sulla's consular ancestor was P. Cornelius Rufinus, who had been consul twice (290, 277 BC) and dictator; this was the height of the family's fortunes until the arrival of Sulla himself. For statues of Sulla, see docs 11.31, 11.48. Sulla when he died was still in love with Metrobius the actor (doc. 11.39; cf. docs 7.57–61).

1.1 Lucius Cornelius Sulla came of a patrician or, as one might say, noble family. It is said that one of his ancestors, Rufinus, held the consulship, though his disgrace is better known than his holding this honour. For it was discovered that he had obtained more than 10 pounds of silver plate, which was against the law, and for this reason he was expelled from the senate. **2** After him the family continued in its lowly position and Sulla's own family was poor. . . . **7** This is what is recorded of Sulla's fortunes in his youth. **2.1** What his personal appearance was like can be seen from his statues, but his facial complexion made the terribly sharp and dominating blueness of his eyes even more formidable, **2** for the pale skin was blotched here and there with angry patches of red; it was because of this, it is said, that he got his name describing his skin, and one of those insulting him at Athens made up a mocking verse which went: 'Sulla is a mulberry sprinkled with barley.'

3 It is not out of place to use this kind of evidence for Sulla, whom they say was by nature a lover of jokes, as a result of which, while he was still young and unknown, he used to spend his time living dissolutely with actors and comedians **4** and, when he held supreme power, collected around him the most outrageous personages of stage and theatre, with whom he would drink and crack jokes all day, so that he appeared to be acting in a manner very ill-suited to his age and lowered the reputation of his magistracy by dismissing those who wanted his attention . . . **6** He was in love with Metrobius, an actor, while he was still young, and remained so. **7** Another experience of his was when he began by falling in love with a well-off prostitute called Nicopolis, who, as she got used to his society and to the charm he had as a youth, ended up falling in love with him and left him as her heir at her death. **8** He also inherited from his stepmother, who loved him as though he were her own son; and from these legacies he was moderately well-off.

11.2 Plutarch *Life of Sulla* 5.1–4: Sulla's political career

Sulla's political career actually took a long time to develop. He did not become consul until he was 48 or 49 years of age, and on the strength of his Social War victories (not 'suo anno'). He had been unsuccessful in standing for the praetorship in 98 BC, but through bribery succeeded in becoming praetor urbanus in 93, not having held the aedileship. In 92 he was in Cilicia *pro consule* (with the military powers of consul). On his return the incident over Bocchus' dedication of statues supposedly occurred (see doc. 10.18). Sulla was then involved in the Social War.

1 Sulla, thinking that his reputation in war should serve him well in politics, left the army and went straight into public life, but when he stood as a candidate for the praetorship he was proved wrong. **2** He assigns the reason for this to the plebs; for he says that they knew of his friendship with Bocchus and looked forward, if he served as aedile before becoming praetor, to some splendid hunts and wild animal combats from Libya, and so they appointed other candidates as praetors to force him to become aedile. **3** It appears, however, from later events that Sulla is not giving the real reason for his failure. **4** For in the next year he achieved the praetorship after winning over the people, partly by flattery and partly also by money.

MITHRIDATES VI OF PONTUS

Mithridates VI (also spelt as Mithradates) was king of Pontus (120–63 BC) and an enemy of Rome for the 40 years before his death. After murdering his mother and brother, Mithridates effected the conquest of the Crimea and northern shore of the Black Sea, and while Rome was engaged in the Social War conquered Cappadocia and Bithynia. In Asia, he conquered the Greek cities and massacred the Italian residents (doc. 11.4). Greece, in particular Athens, came over to him. Defeated but not destroyed by Sulla, who was anxious to return home upon Cinna's death in 84, Mithridates engaged the Romans in a further two wars, being finally dealt with by Pompey.

11.3 Appian *Mithridatic Wars* 20–1 (76–81): Mithridates

Mithridates and Tigranes, king of Armenia, had divided Cappadocia between them, but the senate sent Sulla to put Ariobarzanes I on the throne. In 91 BC Mithridates conquered Bithynia, driving out Nicomedes IV, who had previously been an ally of Rome, while Tigranes drove Ariobarzanes out of Cappadocia. Manius Aquillius (cos. 101, with Marius) restored Nicomedes and Ariobarzanes in 90 BC and Mithridates and Tigranes withdrew.

Aquillius had Nicomedes attack Mithridates, who unsuccessfully protested; Mithridates retaliated by deposing Ariobarzanes (again), sparking off the First Mithridatic War (89–85) and capturing and killing Aquillius.

76 After having conquered the whole kingdom of Nicomedes by this one assault, Mithridates took it over and organised the cities. He then invaded Phrygia and stayed at the inn where Alexander had lodged, thinking it a good omen that Mithridates should be quartered where once Alexander had stayed. **77** He then overran the rest of Phrygia, as well as Mysia and the areas of Asia which the Romans had recently acquired, sending his officers to the neighbouring provinces and subjugating Lycia, Pamphylia and the country as far as Ionia . . . **80** Shortly afterwards he captured Manius Aquillius, who was primarily responsible for this embassy and the war, and led him around bound on a donkey, proclaiming to all who saw him that he was Manius and, as a criticism of the Roman's taking of bribes, finally poured molten gold down his mouth at Pergamum. **81** He appointed satraps over the different peoples and proceeded to Magnesia, Ephesus and Mitylene, all of which gladly welcomed him, while the Ephesians destroyed their Roman statues, for which they were punished not long afterwards.

11.4 Appian *Mithridatic Wars* 22–3 (85–7, 91–2): The First Mithridatic War

Mithridates' conquest of the Greek cities of Asia Minor and his invasion of Greece points to great ambition and perhaps the desire to create a Hellenistic-style kingdom. 80,000 Italians were supposedly killed in Asia Minor in 88. The Greek cities were ready to go over to Mithridates because of the tax-collecting activities of the publicani.

85 The conflict in Rome delayed Sulla for some time, as I have written in my *Civil Wars*; in the meantime Mithridates built a large number of ships to attack Rhodes and wrote in secret to all satraps and city governors that, on the thirtieth day, they should all attack the Romans and Italians in their towns, the men, their women and children and their freedmen of Italian birth, kill them and throw out their bodies unburied, and share their possessions with King Mithridates. **86** He proclaimed punishment to anyone who buried them or concealed them and rewards to informers and those who killed anyone in hiding, as well as freedom to slaves who did this to their masters and remission of half their debt to debtors who did this to their creditors. **87** These orders Mithridates sent in secret to all the cities at the same time . . .

91 These were the dreadful fates met by the Italians and Romans in Asia, men, children and women all together, and their freedmen and slaves who were of Italian blood. From this it was extremely clear that the actions of the inhabitants of Asia were motivated not only by fear of Mithridates but also by hatred of the Romans. **92** But they paid a double penalty, at the hands of Mithridates himself, who not long afterwards broke his word and ill-treated them, and later at the hands of Cornelius Sulla.

LUCIUS CORNELIUS SULLA 'FELIX'

THE ORIGINS OF THE CIVIL WAR

11.5 Appian *Civil Wars* 1.57–59 (250–53, 258–68): The command against Mithridates

This passage follows on from doc. 9.32. Sulla fled from Rome to Nola, where his army was preparing to cross to Asia for the war against Mithridates; he then proceeded to march on Rome, the first Roman to do so. His senior officers deserted him (his quaestor and relative L. Licinius Lucullus was the only exception), though he was joined by the other consul, Q. Pompeius Rufus. With six legions he quickly overcame Marius and Sulpicius; Sulpicius' measures were annulled because they had been passed by violence, and he was murdered; Marius fled. Support for Sulla's actions in the city was non-existent: he had done the unthinkable by marching on Rome itself.

Sulla then introduced several reforms. The Italians were no longer distributed among all the tribes, no proposal was to go before the people before it had been to the senate, voting was not to be by tribes but by centuries in the comitia centuriata, so giving voting power – as Appian noted – to the wealthy and conservatives, and 300 men were enrolled in the senate as its numbers had become depleted. This legislation was all annulled when Sulla left Rome but foreshadowed that when he was dictator. Cinna was elected as consul for 87; Marius returned in an orgy of revenge after Sulla had gone to the East (doc. 9.34); Sulla (but not yet his army) was voted a public enemy, a *hostis*.

250 When Sulla learnt this, he resolved that the matter should be decided by war and summoned his army to an assembly. The army was eager for the campaign against Mithridates because it would be profitable, and they thought that Marius would enlist for it other soldiers than themselves. **251** Sulla spoke of the way he had been insulted by Sulpicius and Marius, and, without clearly alluding to anything else (for he did not as yet dare to mention this kind of war), he urged them to be ready to carry out his orders. **252** They understood what he meant, and, as they were afraid on their own account in case they should lose the chance to go on the campaign, they laid bare Sulla's intention and told him to lead them to Rome with all confidence. **253** Sulla was delighted and took six legions there straightaway. All his senior officers, however, except one quaestor, fled to the city, because they could not undertake to lead an army against their country; envoys who met him on the road asked him why he was marching with armed forces against his country. His reply was: 'To liberate her from her tyrants.' . . .

258 Marius and Sulpicius went to meet them (Sulla and Pompeius Rufus, the consuls) near the Esquiline forum with as many men as they had been able to arm. **259** And here a battle took place between the enemies, the first in Rome no longer under a factional banner but unambiguously under trumpets and standards according to the rules of war; to such a degree of evil had the irresponsibility of factionalism now progressed . . . **261** Sulla called for fresh troops from his camp and sent others around by the Suburran road to outflank the enemy in the rear. **262** The Marians fought feebly against the new arrivals and, fearing that they might be surrounded, summoned the other citizens who were still fighting from their houses and proclaimed freedom to the slaves if they would share their dangers. **263** When no one came forward they despaired and fled at once from the city, along with the nobles who had co-operated with them. . . .

265 At dawn Sulla and Pompeius summoned the people to an assembly and lamented over the government's having so long been in the hands of demagogues, stating that what they had done had been out of necessity. **266** They proposed that nothing should be brought before the people which had not already been discussed by the senate, as had been done in earlier times but long since abandoned, and that voting should be not by tribes but by centuries, as King Tullius had laid down, thinking that through these two measures, with no law being brought before the people until it had gone to the senate and voting not being in the hands of the poor and audacious but rather in those of the wealthy and prudent, no opportunity would be given for sedition to arise. **267** They diminished the power of the tribunes in many other ways, as it had become extremely tyrannical, and enrolled all at once 300 of the best citizens into the senate, which had been reduced to a very small number and become despised for that reason. **268** All the measures enacted by Sulpicius after the vacation from business had been proclaimed by the consuls were cancelled as not legal.

SULLA AND MITHRIDATES

Sulla arrived in Greece in 87 BC with five legions. Mithridates' general Archelaus had taken most of central Greece. Sulla marched to Athens, which he besieged but mercifully spared in 86 BC. He defeated Archelaus in two battles in Greece, at Chaeronea and Orchomenus. In 84 he went to Asia Minor and, in order to return to Rome now that Cinna was dead (84 BC), made peace with Mithridates.

11.6 *CIL* I² 712: Dedication to Sulla, 87 BC

On the pedestal of a statue at Delos, dated to 87 BC. The collegia are presumably business corporations, perhaps connected with the slave trade, of which Delos was an important centre (cf. doc. 6.13) before it was sacked in 88 BC by one of Mithridates' generals.

Lucius Cornelius Sulla, son of Lucius, proconsul. From the money which the collegia contributed by general subscription.

11.7 Livy *Periochae* 81–83: Sulla's victories in Greece

Lucius Valerius Flaccus replaced Marius as consul upon the latter's death in 86. He was given Asia as his province and the command against Mithridates, but was killed by his legate Gaius Flavius Fimbria in 85. Fimbria played a major role in dealing with Mithridates, winning several battles and, finally, a great victory over four generals at the River Rhyndacus. His success might have continued, but Sulla, hearing of Cinna's murder in 84, was eager for a peace.

81 Lucius Sulla besieged Athens (87 BC), which Archelaus, Mithridates' commander, had occupied, and captured it after great difficulty (86 BC), leaving the town its liberty and property. Magnesia, the only city in Asia which had remained loyal, was defended against Mithridates with the greatest courage . . . **82** (86 BC)

Sulla defeated in battle the king's forces, which had seized Macedonia and entered Thessaly, with 100,000 of the enemy killed and their camp captured as well. When the war then recommenced, he again routed and destroyed the king's army. Archelaus surrendered himself and the royal fleet to Sulla. Lucius Valerius Flaccus, the consul, Cinna's colleague, was sent to replace Sulla, but, hated by his army because of his greed, he was killed by his own legate Gaius Fimbria, a man of the utmost daring, and his command transferred to Fimbria. The storming of cities in Asia by Mithridates and the brutal plundering of the province . . . is also narrated. **83** Flavius Fimbria routed in battle several of Mithridates' commanders and captured the city of Pergamum, all but capturing the king during the siege. He stormed the city of Ilium, which was waiting to hand itself over to Sulla, destroyed it, and recovered a large part of Asia . . . After crossing to Asia, Sulla made peace with Mithridates on condition that he evacuate the following provinces – Asia, Bithynia and Cappadocia. Fimbria was abandoned by his army, which crossed to Sulla; he stabbed himself and offered his throat to his slave, telling him to kill him.

11.8 Plutarch *Life of Sulla* 22.8–25.5: Peace terms with Mithridates

After his successes against Archelaus in Greece, Sulla concluded the 'Peace of Dardanus' with Mithridates. He then attacked Fimbria, whom he clearly saw as a rival and an enemy, arguing that Flaccus' army, which Fimbria had taken over, was intended to be used against him.

22.8 After this Archelaus (Mithridates' general) knelt down and begged Sulla to put an end to the war and to make peace with Mithridates. **9** Sulla granted his request, and the terms were that Mithridates was to give up Asia and Paphlagonia, restore Bithynia to Nicomedes and Cappadocia to Ariobarzanes, pay the Romans 2,000 talents, and give them 70 bronze-armoured ships together with their equipment; **10** Sulla was to guarantee to Mithridates the rest of his empire and have him voted an ally of Rome. (Mithridates tries to renege on the terms, but is concerned about Fimbria, who after killing Flaccus marches against him) . . .

24.7 Sulla realised that his soldiers were aggrieved at the cessation of hostilities (for they considered it dreadful that they should see this most hostile of kings, who had had 150,000 Romans in Asia massacred on the same day, sailing away with the wealth and spoils of Asia, which he had continuously plundered and taxed for four years). He defended himself to them by saying that, if Fimbria and Mithridates had joined forces, he could not possibly have fought them together. . . . **25.1** He set out from there against Fimbria, who was encamped near Thyateira, and, after making camp nearby, started encircling his camp with a ditch. **2** But Fimbria's soldiers came out from their camp unarmed, welcomed Sulla's men, and willingly helped them out with their work. **3** Fimbria saw them changing sides and, fearing that Sulla would not be open to reconciliation, committed suicide in his camp. **4** Sulla now imposed on Asia as a whole a penalty of 20,000 talents, while he ruined private families by the brutal behaviour and arrogance of the troops quartered on them. **5** Orders were given that every host should give his lodger 4 tetradrachms a day and should provide an evening meal for him and as many friends as he liked to invite, while an officer should receive 50 drachmas a day and two suits of clothes, one to wear at home and one to wear to the forum.

11.9 Appian *Mithridatic Wars* 61–63 (250–52, 259–61): Sulla punishes the province

The misery of the Greek cities which had led most of them to welcome Mithridates now returned with Sulla's arrangements for the province.

250 After having settled Asia, Sulla granted freedom to the Ilians, Chians, Lycians, Rhodians, Magnesians and some others, either rewarding them for their allegiance or compensating for what they had suffered from their goodwill towards him, and inscribed them as friends of the Romans, sending his army around to all the rest. **251** He also proclaimed that slaves, to whom Mithridates had given freedom, were to return immediately to their masters. As many disobeyed, and some cities revolted, there were numerous massacres of both free men and slaves on various excuses, the walls of many towns were razed, they were plundered and their inhabitants enslaved. . . . **252** After this a proclamation was circulated that the high-ranking citizens from each city were to meet Sulla at Ephesus on a stated day. When they had assembled, he addressed them from the platform as follows: . . .

259 'To spare even now the Greek race, name and reputation throughout Asia, and for the sake of the good name which is so dear to the Romans, I will impose on you only five years' of taxes to be paid immediately, together with whatever the war has cost me and anything else to be spent in restoring the province. **260** I will assign these to each of you city by city and will lay down the deadline for payments, and those who do not keep to this I will punish as enemies.' After this speech, Sulla divided up the fine between the envoys and sent men for the money. **261** The cities were desperate and borrowed at high rates of interest, mortgaging to the lenders their theatres, gymnasia, walls, harbours and every piece of public property under pressure from the soldiers, who urged them on with insults. In this way the money was collected and brought to Sulla, and Asia had nothing but misery.

11.10 Plutarch *Life of Lucullus* 4.1, 20.1–6: The taxation of Asia

In 84 BC, as proquaestor, Lucullus was responsible for carrying out Sulla's measures. As consul in 74 he acquired the command against Mithridates and, once in Asia, attempted to ameliorate Sulla's impositions. Plutarch (*Luc.* 23.1) records that the cities celebrated festivals called Lucullea to honour him. However, his organisation of Asia provoked hostility from those at Rome who had lost financially in the process, and he was eventually superseded by Pompey (docs 12.10–11).

4.1 After peace had been made, Mithridates sailed away into the Black Sea, and Sulla fined Asia 20,000 talents, commissioning Lucullus to collect this money and coin it, and it seemed to the cities to be some abatement of Sulla's harshness when Lucullus showed himself not only honest and just but even mild in his performance of so heavy and disagreeable a duty . . .

20.1 Lucullus now turned his attention to the cities in Asia, in order that, while he was at leisure from warfare, he might contribute in some way to justice and law, from a long lack of which unspeakable and incredible misfortunes gripped the province, which was ravaged and enslaved by the tax-gatherers and moneylenders, with families forced to sell their handsome sons and virgin daughters, and cities their votive offerings, pictures and sacred statues. **2** At last men had to surrender to their creditors and become their slaves, but what preceded this was far worse – tortures of rope, barriers and horses, of standing under the open sky in the heat of summer, and in winter being thrust into mud or ice – so that slavery seemed in contrast to be a removal of burdens and peace. **3** Such were the evils which Lucullus found in the cities, and in a short time he freed the oppressed from them all.

First he ordered that the rate of interest (per month) should be reckoned at 1 per cent and no more; second, he cut off any interest that exceeded the principal; third, and most important of all, he laid down that the lender should receive no more than the fourth part of his debtor's income, and any lender who added interest to principal lost the lot. As a result, in less than four years all debts were paid off and the properties restored to their owners free of encumbrances. **4** This public debt arose from the 20,000 talents which Sulla had fined Asia; twice the amount had been paid back to the moneylenders, by whose reckoning of the interest the debt amounted to 120,000 talents. **5** These men consequently made an outcry against Lucullus at Rome as to the terrible hardships they had suffered and bribed some of the tribunes to work against him, as they were men of great influence who had many politicians under obligations to them. **6** Lucullus, however, was not only beloved by the peoples whom he had well treated, but other provinces also longed to have him, and congratulated those who were lucky enough to have such a governor.

11.11 *CIL* I² 714: Lucullus in Asia

This inscription on two fragments of a statue pedestal was found at Delos, presumably dedicated by grateful businessmen.

Lucius Licinius Lucullus, son of Lucius, proquaestor. Set up by the Athenian people, men from Italy, and Greek businessmen on the island.

EVENTS IN ROME

11.12 Livy *Periochae* 83–84: Waiting for Sulla, 85–84 BC

There was clearly a party in the senate that favoured an accommodation with Sulla; their spokesman was L. Valerius Flaccus, princeps senatus since 86 BC. He was later to be instrumental in the appointment of Sulla as dictator and was made his master of horse (magister equitum). Cn. Papirius Carbo (cos. 85, 84) had less authority in the senate and less overall power than the more ruthless Cinna, but, along with the consuls for 83, L. Cornelius Scipio Asiaticus and Gaius Norbanus, he rallied opposition to Sulla. The provision that all armies be disbanded was aimed against Sulla, whose power resided solely with his troops. However, many joined Sulla on his return because he represented the optimates, while the Marians were connected with the populares and the tribunician violence of Sulpicius. Pompey, Crassus, Q. Metellus Pius and, perhaps, Cicero were among those that joined Sulla.

The right to vote granted to new citizens referred to here (**84**) may mean that enfranchisement of the Italians was finally put into place, or that the new citizens were finally distributed throughout all 35 tribes.

83 When Lucius Cinna and Gnaeus Papirius Carbo, who had made themselves consuls for a two-year period, were preparing for war against Sulla, it was brought about by Lucius Valerius Flaccus, the princeps senatus, who made a speech in the senate, and by the others who were desirous of concord, that envoys be sent to Sulla to discuss peace. Cinna was killed (84 BC) by his own army when he was trying to force it to embark to fight Sulla against its will. Carbo remained as sole consul . . .

84 Sulla replied to the envoys who had been sent by the senate that he would place himself in the power of the senate if the citizens, who had taken refuge with him after being driven out by Cinna, were reinstated. Although this condition seemed just to the senate, Carbo and his party prevented it from taking effect, as they thought war would be of more service to them. The same Carbo wished to demand hostages from all the towns and colonies in Italy, to compel their loyalty against Sulla, but this was prevented by a unanimous decision of the senate. By decree of the senate, the right to vote was granted to new citizens. Quintus Metellus Pius, who had taken the side of the optimates, started stirring up war in Africa but was beaten by the praetor Gaius Fabius (84 BC), and a decree of the senate that all armies everywhere should be disbanded was passed owing to the party of Carbo and the Marians. Freedmen were distributed through the 35 tribes. It also contains the preparations for the war which was being aroused against Sulla.

11.13 Appian *Civil Wars* 1.76–77, 79 (347–48, 350–51, 363): Sulla invades Italy, 83 BC

Sulla's decision to march on Italy was determined partly by the murder of Cinna by his troops in 84; Cinna had dominated Roman politics since 87. In his letter to the senate, Sulla stressed his military achievements. The exiles who returned with him to Italy were displayed to great effect in his triumph, calling upon him as 'saviour' and 'father': Plut. *Sull.* 34.1–2.

347 Sulla now hurried on his return to deal with his enemies, having quickly put an end to the war with Mithridates, as I related earlier. In less than three years he had killed 160,000 men, recovered Greece, Macedonia, Ionia, Asia and many other nations for the Romans that Mithridates had seized, taken the king's fleet away from him, and, from such a great area, restricted him just to his ancestral kingdom. He returned with an army which was well disposed to him, well trained, immense, and inspired by his successes. **348** He commanded a vast number of ships, money and equipment suited to all contingencies, and was an object of fear to his enemies: indeed, Carbo and Cinna were so afraid of him that they sent throughout Italy to gather money, troops and supplies . . . **350** Sulla wrote spiritedly to the senate, relating what he had achieved in Libya against Jugurtha the Numidian while still a quaestor, and against the Cimbri as a legate, and as praetor in Cilicia, and as consul, boasting of his recent achievements against Mithridates and listing for them the many nations whom he had recovered en masse from Mithridates for the Romans. He particularly stressed that those who had been banished from Rome by Cinna had fled to him and that he had received them in their desperate condition and assisted them in their misfortunes. **351** In return for this, he said, his enemies had declared him a public enemy and razed his house and killed off his friends, and his wife and children had with difficulty escaped to him . . .

363 Bringing with him five legions of troops from Italy and 6,000 cavalry, together with other troops from the Peloponnese and Macedon, altogether some 40,000 men, Sulla sailed from the Piraeus to Patrae and from Patrae on to Brundisium in 1,600 ships. The Brundisians received him without a fight, in return for which he later gave them exemption from taxation, which the town still enjoys.

SULLA'S SUPPORTERS

11.14 Livy *Periochae* 85: Sulla's return welcomed

Clearly Sulla with his five legions was in a superior military position to the 'Marians' (a convenient term for the supporters of Marius, Cinna and then Carbo and the younger Marius). From Brundisium Sulla marched to Campania, where he defeated the consuls of 83; in 82 Carbo and the younger Marius recruited in Etruria and Cisalpine Gaul.

Sulla crossed to Italy with his army and sent envoys to discuss peace terms. When these were treated with violence by the consul Gaius Norbanus, he conquered this same Norbanus in battle. And when he was about to assault the camp of the other consul, Lucius Scipio, with whom he had done everything possible to come to terms, but unsuccessfully, the consul's entire army, invited by soldiers sent by Sulla, carried their standards over to Sulla. Although Scipio might have been killed, he was released. Gnaeus Pompey (the Great: cos. 70, 55, 52), son of that Gnaeus Pompeius (Strabo: cos. 89) who had taken Asculum, enlisted an army of volunteers and came with three legions to Sulla, to whom all the nobles were making their way, and as a result of this migration to his camp Rome was deserted.

11.15 Appian *Civil Wars* 1.80 (365–68): The young Pompey

Pompey recruited three entire legions as a private citizen. His father fought against Cinna and Marius, though he was negotiating with Cinna when his own death intervened. Q. Caecilius Metellus Pius (praetor in 89), who had defeated Poppaedius in the Social War, had gone to Africa but joined Sulla on his return to Italy. He was rewarded with a consulship for 80 and the position of pontifex maximus. Crassus joined Sulla with an army of 2,500 raised in Spain, where he had been in hiding from the Marians.

365 Caecilius Metellus Pius met him . . . and spontaneously offered himself as an ally along with the force he had with him, being still a proconsul – for those who have been selected for this rank retain it until they return to Rome. **366** After

Metellus came Gnaeus Pompey, who not long after was called Magnus ('the Great'), the son of that Pompeius (Strabo) who had been killed by lightning and who was not considered to have been a friend of Sulla's, but the son removed this suspicion, arriving with a legion which he had collected in Picenum on the basis of his father's reputation, which was still high there. **367** Shortly afterwards he raised two more legions and became the most useful of all Sulla's lieutenants; consequently, though he was still very young, Sulla treated him with honour, and he was the only man, they say, that Sulla rose to greet when he approached. **368** When the war was nearly over Sulla sent him to Libya to drive out Carbo's supporters and replace Hiempsal on his throne, as he had been overthrown by the Numidians.

11.16 Livy *Periochae* 86–88: The Marian last stand, 82 BC

In 82, Sulla and the younger Marius fought at Sacriportus, near Praeneste, to which the latter retreated after a heavy defeat (doc. 9.34). In a series of battles in 82, Metellus, Pompey and Crassus, along with Sulla, crushed Carbo and Norbanus. The final battle occurred on 1 November 82 BC at the Colline gate, outside Rome, where Sulla and Crassus clashed with the Marian allies, the Samnites and the Lucanians (doc. 10.27); the Samnites and Lucanians not killed in battle were later massacred. The younger Marius at Praeneste killed himself, and the siege of that city by Q. Lucretius Afella ended with a massacre of the inhabitants. The Marians were pursued into Sicily and Africa by Pompey.

86 Gaius Marius, son of Gaius Marius, though not yet 20 years old, was made consul unconstitutionally . . . Sulla made terms with the peoples of Italy to prevent them being afraid of him as a threat to their citizenship and recently granted right to vote . . . The praetor Lucius Damasippus, on the decision of Gaius Marius the consul, assembled the senate and slaughtered all the nobles in Rome. Among their number was Quintus Mucius Scaevola, the pontifex maximus, who was killed as he fled in the forecourt of the temple of Vesta . . .

87 Sulla besieged Gaius Marius, whose army he had routed and destroyed at Sacriportus, in the town of Praeneste, and recovered Rome from the hands of his enemies. When Marius tried to break out, Sulla drove him back . . . **88** Sulla slaughtered Carbo's army at Clusium, Faventia and Fidentia and drove him out of Italy; he fought it out with the Samnites, who alone of the Italian peoples had not yet put down their arms, near the city of Rome in front of the Colline gate . . .

11.17 Plutarch *Life of Pompey* 13.1–9: Pompey wants his quid pro quo

In 82 the young Pompey was given a senatorial grant of extraordinary propraetorian imperium and six legions by Sulla and sent first to Sicily and then in 81 to Africa, where he defeated and killed Cn. Domitius Ahenobarbus (Cinna's son-in-law). Sulla then requested that Pompey dismiss five of his six legions and return to Rome as a private citizen, but Pompey declined; with his legions camped outside Rome, he gained a triumph from Sulla and an unwilling senate (cf. doc. 11.18). Sulla called him Magnus ('the Great'), perhaps ironically.

1 When he returned to Utica (81 BC), Pompey received letters from Sulla ordering him to discharge all the rest of his troops and remain there with one legion to await his successor. **2** At this Pompey was aggrieved and upset, but hid his feelings, while his army was openly indignant, and, when he requested them to return to Italy before him, they shouted out against Sulla and declared that they would never desert him and refused to allow him to trust the tyrant. **3** Pompey first tried to calm the men down and comfort them, but, as he was unable to convince them, he came down from the platform and went away to his tent in tears, while they seized him and set him on the platform again; **4** this took up a great part of the day, with the soldiers telling him to remain and stay in command, and Pompey asking them to obey orders and not mutiny, until, after they continued to harangue him and shout, he swore that he would kill himself if they forced him, and in this way, with reluctance, they put a stop to it. **5** The first report that Sulla had was that Pompey had revolted . . . **6** but when he learnt the truth of the matter and saw everyone rushing out to welcome Pompey and show their goodwill by escorting him to Rome, he sought to go one better: **7** he went out to meet him and, after greeting him in the warmest manner possible, addressed him in a loud voice as 'Magnus' and told everybody else there to do the same; 'Magnus' means great. **8** Others say that Pompey was first given this title by the whole army in Africa, but that it gained strength and force when Sulla confirmed it. **9** Pompey himself was the last person to use it, and only a long time afterwards, when he was sent to Spain as a proconsul against Sertorius (77 BC), did he begin to sign himself in his letters and decrees as 'Pompeius Magnus'; for it was no longer likely to cause jealousy and had become a matter of course.

11.18 Licinianus 31: The young Pompey's triumph, 81 BC

Pompey had not been a praetor or a consul and so could not technically hold a triumph; Sulla gave ground, not simply because of Pompey's assistance, but also because a marriage alliance was arranged between them, with Pompey divorcing his wife to marry Sulla's stepdaughter Aemilia, already married and pregnant (leading to the sorry saga related at Plut. *Pomp.* 9). So Pompey, at the age of 24 (Livy *Per.* 89), still an eques, celebrated a triumph on 12 March 81 for his successes in Africa.

At the age of 25, while still a Roman eques, which was totally unprecedented, Pompey as propraetor celebrated a triumph from Africa, on 12 March. On this day, it is said, the Roman people saw elephants in his triumph. But when he entered the city the triumphal gate was smaller than the four elephants yoked to his chariot, although he made the attempt twice.

SULLA'S PROSCRIPTIONS

Widespread proscriptions followed Sulla's gaining control of Rome: those whose names were on the proscription lists could be put to death, with no judicial procedure involved (doc. 11.20). The victims were senators and equites who had supported the Marians and opposed Sulla. Their property was confiscated, leading to numerous abuses, in which Sulla's associates added names to the lists of the proscribed in order to gain their property. The sons and grandsons of the proscribed could not hold political office until Caesar as dictator allowed this (docs 11.22, 13.56).

11.19 Livy *Periochae* 88: Sulla's brutality

Marius' ashes were disinterred and scattered into the Anio River (Pliny *Nat. Hist.* 7.187). Marcus Marius Gratidianus, twice praetor, son of a sister of Marius, was killed by Catiline, his brother-in-law, at the tomb of Quintus Lutatius Catulus, whom Gratidianus had prosecuted, leading Catulus to commit suicide. The Villa Publica was the rendezvous for military recruits in the Campus Martius. The survivors from the battle of the Colline gate were gathered there; Plut. *Sull.* 30.3–4, 32.1 has 6,000 plus 12,000 Praenestians killed.

With the state restored, Sulla polluted a most glorious victory by cruelty such as no man had ever shown before. He slaughtered 8,000 men, who had surrendered, in the Villa Publica; he set up a proscription list and filled the city and all Italy with slaughter, and among these killings ordered all the people of Praeneste, who were unarmed, to be cut down and had Marius (Marcus Marius Gratidianus), a man of senatorial rank, killed after having his legs and arms broken, his ears cut off and his eyes gouged out.

11.20 Appian *Civil Wars* 1.95–96 (440–48): Sulla's 'iron fist'

Carbo (cos. 82) was executed, Norbanus (cos. 83) committed suicide, and their supporters, both in Rome and in the Italian communities, were all punished with death. **442**: The estimates of the proscribed vary. Appian gives 'some 40 senators and 1,600 equites', with the names of further senators added to these; Plutarch (doc. 11.21) has 80 individuals proscribed, with two further lists of 220 names; Orosius (doc. 11.23) puts the figure as high as 9,000. **448**: Sulla's violence was also visited on the Italians, and land confiscated from them was awarded to his veterans.

440 Pompey was sent to Libya against Carbo and to Sicily against Carbo's friends there; **441** Sulla himself summoned the Romans to an assembly and made a speech boasting about his achievements and making a number of menacing statements to inspire terror, ending up by saying that he would bring about some changes beneficial to the people if they would obey him, but that he would spare none of his enemies, and that he would deal with them with the utmost severity and take vengeance with all his might on praetors, quaestors, military tribunes and anybody else who had co-operated with his enemies, after the day on which the consul Scipio did not adhere to the agreements made with him. **442** After saying this, he immediately published a proscription list of some 40 senators and 1,600 equites. He was apparently the first man to draw up a list of those whom he punished with death, to offer prizes to killers and rewards to informers, and to lay down punishments for those who hid the proscribed. **443** Not long afterwards he added the names of other senators to these. Some of these were captured unawares and killed where they were caught, in their houses, the streets, or shrines; some were borne through mid-air to Sulla and thrown at his feet; others were dragged and trampled on, with all the observers so terrified that they were unable to utter a word against these injustices. **444** Exile was the fate of some and confiscation of their possessions that of others. Investigators searched everywhere for those who had escaped from the city, and whomever they caught they killed.

445 There was also much slaughter, banishment and confiscation among the Italians who had obeyed Carbo or Norbanus or Marius or any of their subordinates. **446** There were vicious judgements against them throughout all Italy and various charges – of taking command, of army service, of contributing money or other services, even of giving counsel against Sulla. Hospitality, friendship, lending money – for both borrower and lender – were all crimes, and one might be arrested for willingness to help someone or even for being his companion on a journey. These accusations targeted particularly the rich. **447** When accusations against an individual failed, Sulla took vengeance on cities and punished these instead, destroying citadels, razing walls, imposing general fines, or crushing the people with severe taxes; **448** and among most of them he settled his ex-troops to hold Italy by means of garrisons, while he took away their land and houses and shared them among his men, by which he made the latter well disposed to him even after he was dead; as these could not possess their holdings securely unless Sulla's measures were secure, they fought on his behalf even after he had died.

11.21 Plutarch *Life of Sulla* 31.1–9: The proscription lists

The proscription lists had been preceded by butchery on a scale unprecedented at Rome, even during Marius' bloody return. Those who aided the proscribed also risked death.

1 Sulla now devoted himself to butchery, and the city was filled with murders without number or limit. Many people with whom Sulla had no concerns were killed out of private enmity, which Sulla permitted as a favour to his supporters, **2** until one of the young men, Gaius (Caecilius) Metellus, ventured in the senate to ask Sulla what end there would be to these evils . . . **3** Sulla replied that he did not know yet whom he would spare, and Metellus answered, 'Then tell us whom you intend to punish.' Sulla said that he would do this. **4** Some say this last speech was made not by Metellus but by one of Sulla's associates called Fufidius. **5** Sulla at once published a list condemning 80 men, without consulting any of the magistrates; everybody was indignant, but the next day but one he proscribed another 220, and on the third day again no fewer. **6** He made a speech to the people on the subject and told them that he had proscribed as many men as he could remember, but that he would proscribe later any who had now slipped his mind . . . **8** What seemed most unjust of all, Sulla deprived the sons and grandsons of the proscribed of their civil rights and confiscated all their property. **9** The lists were published not only in Rome but in every city of Italy.

11.22 Velleius Paterculus *Compendium of Roman History* 2.28.4: The 'sins of the fathers'

Nor was his ferocity directed only towards those who had borne arms against him but towards many of the innocent. Furthermore, the goods of the proscribed were sold, and their children were not only deprived of their fathers' property but also prohibited from the right of standing for magistracies, and, at one and the same time, the greatest injustice of all, the sons of senators had both to bear the burdens of their rank and lose its privileges.

11.23 Orosius *History* 5.21.1–5: 'Butchery was unrestrained'

1 Shortly after Sulla had entered Rome as conqueror, he violated religion and good faith by killing 3,000 unarmed and unsuspecting men who had surrendered through intermediaries. After this, an immense number of people were also killed – I will not say of innocent men, but even some of Sulla's own supporters – who are reported to have numbered more than 9,000. Murders took place unrestrained throughout the city, with assassins roaming far and wide motivated by anger or plunder. **2** With everyone openly murmuring what each individually feared for himself, Q. Catulus at last asked Sulla openly, 'Whom are we going to live with if we kill armed men in war and unarmed men in peace?' **3** Sulla then, at the suggestion of the first centurion L. Fursidius, was the first to bring in his infamous proscription list. The first proscription was of 80 people, who included four ex-consuls, Carbo, Marius, Norbanus and Scipio, and with them Sertorius, the greatest cause of fear at that time. **4** A second was then brought out with 500 names – Lollius was reading this, quite unconcerned and aware of no wrongdoing, when he suddenly came upon his own name, and while he was making in agitation for the forum, his head covered, he was murdered. **5** But confidence and an end to wickedness was not provided even by these lists, for some were murdered after being proscribed, while others were proscribed after they had been murdered.

11.24 Plutarch *Life of Cicero* 3.4–6: Making a quick profit

Many enriched themselves through the proscriptions. Crassus in particular benefited from acquiring at low prices the property of the proscribed (Plut. *Crass.* 6.8). Sextius Roscius of Ameria in southern Umbria was murdered, and, in order to acquire the property cheaply, two of his relatives in conjunction with Chrysogonus had his name included among the proscribed. Cicero defended the son, Sextus Roscius (*pro Sexto Roscio Amerino*); cf. doc. 2.56.

4 At this time Chrysogonus, Sulla's freedman, put up for auction the estate of a man who, so it was said, had been on one of Sulla's proscription lists and been killed. Chrysogonus bought it himself for 2,000 drachmas. **5** At this Roscius, the son and heir of the deceased, was indignant and made it known that the real value of the estate was 250 talents. Sulla was furious at being found out and, after Chrysogonus fabricated a case, charged Roscius with parricide. No lawyer could be found to defend him, but everyone kept clear, fearing Sulla's severity . . . **6** Cicero undertook the defence of Roscius and succeeded to everyone's admiration, but as he was afraid of Sulla he went overseas to Greece (79–77 BC), after spreading the word that it was for the sake of his health.

11.25 Cicero *In Defence of Sextus Roscius* 21: Cicero defies Sulla's freedman

Although the proscription was no longer mentioned, and even those who were previously afraid returned, believing that they were now out of danger, the name of Sextus Roscius (the father), a very great supporter of the nobility, was entered on the proscription lists; the purchaser was Chrysogonus; three estates, perhaps the most notable, were given to Capito (Titus Roscius Capito) as his own property, which he still possesses to this day; as for the rest of the property, this Titus Roscius, as he says himself, seized it in Chrysogonus' name. This property, worth 6,000,000 sesterces, was purchased for 2,000 sesterces. All this, I am sure, jurors, was done without Sulla's knowledge.

DICTATORSHIP AND CONSTITUTIONAL REFORMS

When Sulla entered Rome in 82 his imperium technically lapsed (from the point of view of his opponents it had lapsed when he was declared a *hostis* by Cinna). The senate proceeded to confirm all his acts as consul (88 BC) and proconsul (87–82 BC) and voted him an equestrian statue to be erected before the rostra. This was the first occasion such an honour had been voted. As both the consuls for 82 had been proscribed and were dead (Carbo and the younger Marius at his own hand), Sulla ordered the senate to appoint an interrex, and it chose the princeps senatus, L. Valerius Flaccus (cos. 100). Flaccus introduced the *lex Valeria* to the comitia, which elected Sulla dictator 'to make laws and reform the constitution'. Sulla now had supreme authority unchecked by any veto and with no fixed term (doc. 11.26); although there was an election, Plutarch was correct to write that Sulla 'appointed himself dictator' (doc. 11.27). He had Flaccus appointed his master of horse (magister equitum). As dictator he carried out various reforms (docs 11.27–29, 31), extended the pomerium of Rome, and carried out a modest building programme in Rome and Italy.

11.26 Appian *Civil Wars* 1.98–99 (456–62): Unlimited dictatorship

459: It was actually 120 years since the last dictatorship. **462**: Appian states that the dictatorship of Sulla was 'unlimited' compared to the previous short dictatorships of fixed periods, but Appian (459) also indicates, as did events, that Sulla (unlike Julius Caesar) did not seek a lifelong dictatorship.

456 Sulla became *de facto* king, or tyrant, not through election but by power and force, but, as he needed the pretence of being elected, he contrived this as follows . . . **457** If by some chance there should not be a consul, an interrex was appointed to hold a consular election. **458** Sulla made use of this custom. As there were no consuls, since Carbo had died in Sicily and Marius (the Younger) at Praeneste, he went out of the city and ordered the senate to choose an interrex. **459** They selected Valerius Flaccus, expecting that he would soon hold a consular election; but Sulla wrote to Flaccus instructing him to present his view to the people that Sulla considered it expedient that, for the present, there be in the city the position which they call the dictatorship, a custom which had ceased for 400 years; he ordered them that their appointee should not rule for a fixed period but until he should have stabilised the city and Italy and the whole government, which had been shaken by seditions and wars. **460** That his intention in this proposal referred to Sulla himself was not at all doubtful; and Sulla did not hide it, revealing at the end of his letter that, in his own opinion, he could be particularly useful to the city in that role.

461 This was Sulla's message, and, while the Romans were unwilling, they were no longer electing people according to law and considered that this action was no longer within their power, so in the general confusion they welcomed the charade of an election as a show and pretence of freedom, and they elected Sulla to be their tyrant and master for as long as he chose. **462** In earlier days the rule of dictators had been autocratic but limited to a short period of time; now for the first time it became unlimited and so a complete tyranny. However, they added for the sake of appearances the condition that they appointed him dictator to enact whatever laws he might think fit and to restore the constitution.

11.27 Plutarch *Life of Sulla* 33.1–2: Sulla's powers

1 He appointed himself dictator, reviving this type of magistracy after 120 years. **2** He was voted immunity for all his past actions and, for the future, the power of life and death, confiscation, founding colonies or cities, sacking cities, and the making and deposing of kings as he chose.

11.28 Livy *Periochae* 89: Sulla's 'reforms'

Fasces: It was customary for dictators to have 24 fasces carried by 24 attendants (lictors) before them. *Tribunes*: see docs 11.30, 32. *Senate*: Sulla first brought the senate up to its traditional number of 300 members by enrolling those with distinguished military service. To increase the size of the senate further – to 600 members – he drew upon the equites, who could provide men of sufficient wealth to join this body. *Priesthoods*: Sulla increased the numbers of priests, augurs and officials in charge of the Sibylline Books to 15.

Sulla was made dictator and appeared in public with 24 fasces, which had never happened before. He strengthened the constitution of the state by new laws, weakened the power of the tribunes of the plebs, and took from them all power of introducing legislation. He added to the colleges of pontiffs and augurs so there were 15 members in each college; he recruited the senate from the equestrian order; he took away from the sons of the proscribed the right to stand for magistracies, and he sold off their goods, of which he seized the largest part for himself. The proceeds were 350,000,000 sesterces.

11.29 Velleius Paterculus *Compendium of Roman History* 2.32.3: The law-courts

With the senate increased to 600 members, the juries could be transferred to that body and adequately manned by it; Gaius Gracchus had given the equites sole control of the courts, but in the most recent law concerning the juries, the *lex Plautia iudiciaria* of 89, all classes of citizens were eligible. Sulla now granted the senate a monopoly of jury membership. In addition, Sulla reorganised the law-courts (quaestiones); there were to be seven quaestiones: murder and poisoning, extortion, peculation, assault, treason, electoral bribery and forgery.

The right of acting as jurors, which Gaius Gracchus had taken from the senate and given to the equites, Sulla gave back to the senate.

11.30 Appian *Civil Wars* 1.100 (465–70): Power returned to the senate

465: The election of consuls for 81 BC was part of Sulla's overall plan to restore the constitution and establish normality. **466**: This refers to the cursus honorum, a strict progression of office, from quaestor to praetor to consul, which had held since the lex Villia Annalis of 180 BC and which was now reinforced by Sulla. Age criteria were also put in place (e.g., 42 years for the consulship). Sulla himself had been consul in 88 and was to be elected again for 80, laying down the dictatorship in 81. He therefore broke the provisions of his own law requiring a ten-year lapse before holding the same office for a second time.

467: For the tribunate, see also docs 11.29, 11.32. The tribunate lost its legislative character, and the tribunician power of veto was taken away or severely restricted. **469**: The enfranchisement of the 'youngest and the strongest' of the slaves perhaps points to the intended use of these freedmen as intimidators in the voting process and as voters. They and the 12,000 Sullan veterans who had received land and money were formidable support for Sulla. **470** (cf. **448**: doc. 11.20) According to Appian, Sulla distributed land to 23 legions in order to provide him with support throughout Italy.

465 However, in a pretence of maintaining the country's constitution, he allowed them to appoint consuls, and Marcus Tullius (Decula) and (Gnaeus) Cornelius Dolabella were elected (for 81 BC); but, like a king, Sulla was dictator over the consuls; for 24 axes were carried in front of him, the same number carried before the kings of olden days, and he also had a large bodyguard. **466** He repealed laws and added others; and he forbade anyone to become praetor before he had been quaestor, and to be consul before he had been praetor, and he prohibited anyone from holding the same office for a second time until ten years had passed. **467** He reduced the power of the tribunes to such an extent that it seemed to be insignificant and passed a law preventing a tribune from going on to hold any other office – for which reason all those of reputation or family who used to seek the office avoided it for the future . . . **468** To the senate itself, which had been greatly reduced in number by the seditions and wars, he added about 300 of the best equites, allowing the tribes to vote on each of them. **469** He freed more than 10,000 slaves of proscribed persons, choosing the youngest and the strongest, made them Roman citizens, and added them to the people, calling them Cornelii after himself, thus ensuring that he could make use of 10,000 of the plebeians who were ready to carry out his orders. **470** With the intention of doing the same throughout Italy, he distributed to the 23 legions who had served under him a large amount of land in the different communities, as I have already related, some of which was still unallocated, and some of which he took away from the communities as a penalty.

11.31 *ILS* 881: Dedication by freedmen

This dedication dates to 82–79 BC and is inscribed on a pedestal, presumably surmounted with a statue of Sulla. Seven Latin inscriptions survive for Sulla from Italy, probably part of statue bases honouring him.

To Lucius Cornelius Sulla Felix, dictator, son of Lucius, from his freedmen (*leiberteini*).

11.32 Cicero *On the Laws* 3.20–22: Sulla and the tribunate

Cicero's brother Quintus is speaking here (Marcus follows with a more balanced view). The repeal of Sulla's laws concerning the tribunate began in 75 and was completed by Pompey as consul in 70 (docs 12.4–5). Cicero here refers to the tribunes' continued right of protecting plebeians and their property, the ius auxilii. For Clodius, see docs 12.54–56.

20 Indeed, was it not the overthrow of Gaius Gracchus and the daggers, which he himself said had been cast into the forum so that citizens could use them to stab each other, that totally altered the stability of the state? Why should I go on to mention Saturninus, Sulpicius and the rest, whom the state was unable to remove without a sword? . . . **22** And what ruin and destruction did he (Clodius) bring about, ruin such as could have been brought about only by the frenzy of a foul beast without reason or hope inflamed by the frenzy of a mob! Consequently, I greatly approve of Sulla's laws on this subject, which removed from the tribunes of the plebs the power of doing wrong through their legislation but left them their right of assistance (*ius auxilii*). And as for our friend Pompey, though in all other matters I always praise him in the highest possible terms, I am silent about the power of the tribunes; for I should not criticise him and am unable to praise him.

LEGISLATION

From Appian it is clear that Sulla had a comprehensive legislative programme (doc. 11.30). The increase in the number of senators, the diminution in the powers of the tribunes, the transfer of the courts to the senate, and the enforcement of the *lex Villia Annalis* clearly strengthened the position of the senate while weakening the populist element. In addition, Sulla abolished the position of princeps senatus, presumably so that no individual senator had undue influence.

11.33 Crawford *Statutes* 14: The quaestors

Sulla increased the number of quaestors to 20, with the quaestorship giving direct entry into the senate. This is a fragment of Sulla's quaestorship law of 81 BC on a bronze tablet which was to be set up on a wall by the temple of Saturn, the storehouse of state records. This fragment makes arrangements for the appointment and employment of extra *viatores* (messengers, or official summoners) and *praecones* (heralds) to assist the elected quaestors. These viatores and praecones held their posts for annual terms.

Lucius Cornelius, son of Lucius, dictator . . . duly proposed to the people, and the people duly resolved in the forum . . . on the day of . . . tribe voted first; for his tribe the first to vote was . . .

   Eighth tabula of the law: Concerning the Twenty Quaestors. . . .

   7 The consuls now in office shall, before the first day of next December, select from those who are Roman citizens one viator (messenger) who shall attend as messenger in that group which is or will be **10** required to attend on the quaestors at the treasury on and after the fifth day of next December. And the same consuls shall, before the first day of next December, select from those who are Roman citizens one praeco (crier) who shall attend as crier in that group which is or will be required to attend on the quaestors at the treasury on and after the fifth day of next December. . . .

32 And they shall select all those messengers and criers whom they shall consider to be worthy of that rank. For whichever group each messenger shall have been selected in this way, **35** he is to be a messenger in that group just as others in that group are to be messengers. And for whichever group each crier shall have been selected in this way, he is to be a crier in that group just as others in that group are to be criers. And law and statute in all matters are to apply to those messengers and to a quaestor concerning those messengers, **40** just as if those messengers had been formerly selected for or substituted as one of three messengers for that group, for which group any of them shall have been selected as messenger under this law. And law and statute in all matters are to apply to those criers and to a quaestor concerning those criers, just as if those criers **45** had been formerly selected for or substituted as one of three criers for that group, for which group any of them shall have been selected as crier under this law.

Whichever of the quaestors shall be obliged by law or plebiscite to select or substitute messengers, those quaestors **50** shall select or substitute four messengers according to the law and statute by which those now in office have selected or substituted three messengers; and whichever of the quaestors shall be obliged by law or plebiscite to select or substitute criers, those quaestors shall select or substitute four criers according to the law and statute **55** by which those now in office have selected or substituted three criers . . .

11.34 Crawford *Statutes* 50: *Lex Cornelia de sicariis et veneficiis*

One of Sulla's seven law-courts was that for 'murder and poisoning'. This law remained in force as the statute for murder (except for parricide) into the principate.

1 The praetor or judge of the investigation, to whom the investigation concerning murderers shall have fallen by lot, in respect of what has or shall have occurred in the city of Rome or within one mile, with those jurors who shall have fallen by lot to him according to this statute, is to make investigation concerning the capital crime of that person who has been or shall have been armed with a weapon for the purpose of killing a man or perpetrating a theft, or has or shall have killed a man, or by whose malice aforethought that has been or shall have been done.

5 The praetor or judge of the investigation . . . with those jurors who shall have fallen to him by lot according to this statute is to make investigation concerning the capital crime of that person who, for the purpose of killing a man, has or shall have prepared or has or shall have sold or has or shall have bought or has or shall have had or has or shall have administered a poisonous drug.

6 The praetor or judge of the investigation . . . is to make investigation concerning the capital crime of the person who has or shall have been military tribune in the first four legions . . . , quaestor, tribune of the plebs . . . , or has or shall have given his opinion in the senate, whoever of them has or shall have conspired, or has or shall have combined, or has or shall have plotted, . . . or has or shall have given false witness with malice aforethought, . . . in order that someone might be condemned on a capital charge in a public court.

11.35 *RDGE* 18, lines 1–22, 49–131: Autonomy for Stratonicea, 81 BC

This is a decree of the senate, proposed by Sulla as dictator, renewing an earlier grant of autonomy to the city of Stratonicea, recognising the arrangements Sulla had made concerning the city when he was in the East; it had supported the Romans in the Mithridatic War. The people of Stratonicea had asked permission to dedicate to the senate a golden crown worth 200 talents.

Lucius Cornelius Sulla Felix (Epaphroditus), son of Lucius, dictator, to the magistrates, council and people of Stratonicea, greetings; we are aware that you, through your ancestors, have always done your duty towards our empire and that on every occasion you have sincerely preserved your loyalty to us; and that in the war against Mithridates you were the first of those in Asia to oppose him, and for that reason most eagerly took upon yourselves many dangers of all kinds on behalf of our state . . . **10** both public and private, on account of your friendship, goodwill and gratitude towards us, and on the occasion of the war sent envoys to the other cities of Asia and to the cities of Greece . . .

Lucius Cornelius Sulla Felix, dictator, to the magistrates, council and people of Stratonicea, greetings. I have handed over to your envoys the following resolution by the senate: Lucius Cornelius Sulla Felix, son of Lucius, dictator, consulted the senate on 27 March **20** in the comitium; Gaius Fannius son of Gaius . . . Gaius Fundanius son of Gaius . . . were present at the writing (of the decree) . . .

49 . . . And Lucius Cornelius Sulla Felix, dictator, decreed . . . that they make use of the same laws and customs as they did before, and that whatever decrees they made because of the war which they declared against King Mithridates, that all these remain in force; that they keep possession of Pedasus, Themessus, Ceramus, and the lands, villages, harbours and revenues of the cities which the commander Lucius Cornelius Sulla assigned and granted them as a mark of their excellence; that the shrine of Hecate, most manifest and greatest goddess, which has long been revered . . . and the precinct be inviolate; **60** that, regarding what they lost in the war, the senate give instructions to the magistrate setting out for Asia to give care and attention to ensuring that their actual property be restored to them, that they recover their prisoners of war, and that concerning everything else they receive their due; and that any envoys who come to Rome from Stratonicea be granted by the magistrates audience with the senate out of turn.

Concerning this matter it was resolved (by the senate) as follows: it was resolved to reply in a friendly manner in their presence to the envoys of Stratonicea in the senate, to renew goodwill, friendship and alliance with them, and **70** to address the envoys as good and honourable men and our friends and allies from a good and honourable people, our friend and ally. And concerning the matters on which the envoys and Lucius Cornelius Sulla Felix, dictator, spoke, that it was well known to the Romans from the letters sent by the governors of Asia and Greece and by the legates who had been in those provinces that the Stratoniceans had always consistently preserved their friendship, loyalty and goodwill towards the Roman people in time of war and peace, **80** and had always taken care to protect with enthusiasm the interests of the Roman people with soldiers, grain, and great expenditures . . . (and) because of their high sense of honour had waged war alongside them and had most bravely opposed the generals and armies of King Mithridates on behalf of the cities of Asia and Greece.

Concerning these matters it was decreed as follows: that the senate is pleased to remember good and just men and to provide that Lucius Cornelius Sulla Felix, **90** dictator, should instruct the proquaestor to give them gifts of hospitality according to the ordinance; and that they should make use of the same laws and customs as they did before; and that whatever laws and decrees they passed because of this war against Mithridates, that all these remain in force for them; and that whatever states, revenues, lands, villages and harbours the commander Lucius Cornelius Sulla assigned and granted them in consultation with his council as a mark of their excellence, they be permitted to keep possession of these; and that the Roman people . . . ; **100** and that Lucius Cornelius Sulla Felix, dictator, if he wishes, take note of the states, villages, lands and harbours which he as commander assigned to Stratonicea, and allocate the tax which each is to pay to Stratonicea; and, if he so allocates, that he send letters to those states which he assigned to Stratonicea, for them to pay a tax of so much to Stratonicea; **110** and that those who may at any time be governors of the provinces of Asia and Greece see to it and ensure that these things are carried out in this way: that the shrine of Hecate be inviolate; that whatever proconsul may govern the province of Asia take note of the properties the Stratoniceans are missing, who seized these, and who are in possession of them, so that he may ensure that these are given back and restored; that they are able to recover their prisoners of war, and that in all other **120** matters they receive their due, as he considers most in keeping with the interests of the state and with his own good faith. Resolved.

And with regard to the crown sent to the senate by the people, that the people be permitted to dedicate it wherever Lucius Cornelius Sulla Felix, dictator, considers it appropriate and that, if they wish, they be allowed to offer sacrifice on the Capitol. And to the envoys who come from Stratonicea **130** to Rome that they be granted by the magistrates audience with the senate out of turn. Resolved.

11.36 *RDGE* 23 lines 5–69: Tax exemption for sanctuaries

A dispute arose between the sanctuary of Amphiaraus, a healing deity, at Oropus (north of Athens) and tax-collectors (publicani) in 73 BC. It was claimed that Sulla had exempted the sanctuary from taxation. The case was investigated by the consuls for 73, M. Terentius Varro Lucullus and G. Cassius Longinus, with a board of 16 senators, who confirmed the tax exemption. The tax-farmers had suggested that Amphiaraus was not a god (technically he was a hero, a demi-god) and therefore not exempt from taxation.

5 October 14 in the Basilica Porcia. Present on our council were . . . (16 names). Concerning the matters on which Hermodorus, son of Olympichus, priest of Amphiaraus, who was previously named ally by the senate, and Alexidemus, son

of Theodorus, and Demaenetus, son of Theoteles, envoys of the Oropians, spoke: that since in the law on tax-farming those **20** lands were exempted which Lucius Sulla granted for the sake of preserving the sacred precincts of the immortal gods, and that these revenues which are under dispute were assigned by Lucius Sulla to the god Amphiaraus, so that no revenue should be paid to the tax-farmer for these lands. And concerning the matters on which Lucius Domitius Ahenobarbus spoke on behalf of the tax-farmers, that in the law on tax-farming those lands were exempted which Lucius Sulla granted for the sake of preserving the sacred precincts of the immortal gods, but that Amphiaraus, to whom these lands are said to have been granted, is not a god, so that the tax-farmers should be permitted to collect taxes on these lands.

On the advice of our council we declared our resolve: we shall lay before the senate our findings, **30** which we have recorded also in the minutes: 'Concerning the territory of Oropus, about which there was a dispute with the tax-farmers, this had been exempted by the law on tax-farming, so that the tax-farmer may not collect taxes on it. We investigated in accordance with the decree of the senate.

'In the law on tax-farming it appears to have been exempted as follows: "excluding those, which in accordance with a decree of the senate, a commander or commanders of ours, for the sake of honouring the immortal gods and preserving sacred precincts, granted and left them to enjoy, and excluding those which the commander Lucius Cornelius Sulla on the advice of his council, for the sake of the **40** immortal gods and the preservation of sacred precincts, granted to them to enjoy, which same the senate ratified and which was not subsequently made invalid by a decree of the senate."

'Lucius Cornelius Sulla appears to have made this decision on the advice of his council: "For the sake of repaying a vow I assign to the sanctuary of Amphiaraus land extending 1,000 feet in every direction, so that this land too may be inviolable." Similarly for the god Amphiaraus he seems to have consecrated all the revenues of the city, the territory and the harbours of the Oropians to the games and sacrifices which the Oropians perform for the god Amphiaraus, and likewise also to all those which they may perform in the future for the victory and empire of the Roman people, **50** with the exception of the lands of Hermodorus, son of Olympichus, priest of Amphiaraus, who has remained a consistent friend of the Roman people.

'Concerning this matter a decree of the senate appears to have been passed in the consulship of Lucius Sulla Felix and Quintus Metellus Pius (80 BC), which decree the senate worded as follows: "Whatever Lucius Cornelius Sulla on the advice of his council assigned or granted to the god Amphiaraus and to his sanctuary, these same the senate considered to have been given and granted to this god."

'In (Sulla's) council were present the same people as in the first record of deliberations, fourteenth page.' The following decree of the senate was passed: **60** October 16 in the comitium. Present at the writing were (3 names) . . . Concerning the matters which the consuls Marcus Lucullus and Gaius Cassius investigated and reported that they had investigated concerning the territory of Oropus and the tax-farmers, that the territory of the Oropians appeared to have been exempted by the law on tax-farming, and that it did not seem right that the tax-farmers should collect taxes on it, it was so decreed, as they deemed best in keeping with the interests of the state and with their own good faith.

11.37 Sumptuary legislation, 81 BC

(i) Gellius Attic Nights *2.24.11*

There had been previous sumptuary legislation in 161 and c. 143 prescribing the amounts that could be spent per day or on a dinner: cf. docs 5.59, 2.22–24, 13.56.

Afterwards, Lucius Sulla as dictator, at a time when these laws were consigned to forgetfulness through dust and old age, and numerous people with ample patrimonies were squandering and dissipating both family and fortune into whirlpools of dinners and banquets, brought a law before the people in which it was stated that, on the Kalends, Ides and Nones, on days of games and on certain solemn festivals, it was proper and legal to spend 300 sesterces on a dinner but on other days no more than 30.

(ii) Macrobius Saturnalia *3.17.11–12*

11 These laws were followed by the Cornelian law, another sumptuary law, which was brought in by Cornelius Sulla as dictator, which did not restrict the magnificence of banquets or set a limit on gourmandising, but it lowered the prices of things. Ye gods! What foods they were, the choice and almost unheard of kinds of delicacies! What fish and titbits it names and yet lays down cheaper prices for them! I would venture to say that the cheapening of foodstuffs encouraged people into the preparation of an abundance of dishes and allowed even the less well-off to cater to their gluttony. **12** I will say clearly what I think. A person, at whose banquet such dishes are served up seems to me to be extravagant and prodigal beyond all others, even if they cost him nothing. And so it is clear that this age of ours is much more disposed to practise complete self-control in this matter, since most of the delicacies included in the Sullan law as being generally well known, none of us knows even by name.

11.38 *RDGE* 49: Privileges for actors

In the winter of 85/4 BC Sulla had billeted troops in the towns which had supported Mithridates and imposed an indemnity of 20,000 talents (docs 11.9–10). The actors' guild in the region appealed, and Sulla confirmed a pre-existing agreement exempting them from such obligations. In 81 Sulla allowed the actors to erect a marble stele recording this. A citharist is a harp player.

With good fortune!

A Lucius Cornelius Sulla Felix, son of Lucius, dictator, to the magistrates, council and people of Cos, greetings; to the citharist Alexander of Laodicea, a good and honourable man and our friend, envoy of the joint association of the theatrical artists of Ionia and the Hellespont and the theatrical artists of Dionysus our Leader, I have granted permission to erect a stele in your most prominent place **10** on which will be inscribed the privileges I have given to the artists; as, following his embassy to Rome, the senate passed a decree approving of this, I therefore wish you to ensure that a most prominent place be provided, where the stele concerning the artists may be erected. I attach below copies of my letter (to the artists) and of the decree of the senate.

B ... together with the goodwill you bear us, I therefore wish you to know that, on my council's advice, I have proclaimed my decision that you shall keep whatever privileges, offices and exemptions from public service our senate, consuls and proconsuls have given and granted you as a mark of honour to Dionysus, the Muses and your association; and that, just as before, you shall be exempt from all public service and military service, **10** you shall not pay any tax or contribution, you shall not be troubled by anyone for supplies or lodging, and you shall not be forced to have anyone billeted on you ...

SULLA IN RETIREMENT

It is not known exactly when Sulla laid down his dictatorship; presumably he held it down to the moment of his retirement in 79 BC – that is, he remained dictator during his term as consul in 80, retiring into private life in 79 BC. In that year, he allowed the consular elections for 78 to run their course to the extent that he permitted the election of Lepidus as consul.

11.39 Plutarch *Life of Sulla* 36.1–4: Sulla's love life

Valeria made a pass at Sulla at an exhibition of gladiators, and they soon married: *Sull.* 35.5–11. Sulla had divorced his previous wife, Metella, when she became fatally ill, so that his house would not become polluted (he was augur), but he gave her a magnificent funeral, despite his own sumptuary legislation (*Sull.* 35.2–4). For Roscius, see docs 6.6, 29.

1 Nevertheless, even though he had Valeria at home, he still associated with women who were actresses or cithara-players and with musicians from the theatre, who used to lie drinking on couches all day long. **2** Those who were at this time most influential with him were Roscius the comedian, Sorex the leading comic actor, and Metrobius the female impersonator, who was now past his prime, but Sulla throughout everything insisted that he was in love with him. **3** By living in this way he aggravated a disease which had not originally been serious, and for a long time he was not aware that he had ulcers in the intestines, which resulted in the whole flesh being corrupted and turning into worms, so that, although a number of people spent day and night removing them, it was nothing compared with the way they multiplied: all his clothing, baths, washing water and food were overrun with that flux and corruption, so greatly did it keep breaking out. **4** To counter it, he frequently immersed himself in water to wash off and cleanse his body. But it was of no benefit: the transformation quickly overcame him, and the immensity of their number prevented all attempts at purgation.

SULLA'S ABDICATION, 79 BC

11.40 Appian *Civil Wars* 1.103–4 (478, 480–83, 487–89): Why abdicate?

Sulla held the consulship for 80 BC with Q. Caecilius Metellus Pius. Having passed numerous laws and reorganised the courts, he must have felt that he had carried out what he had been appointed as dictator to achieve: he had 'stabilised the city and Italy and the whole government' (doc. 11.26), and the holding of consular elections emphasised the return to normality. Sulla clearly felt confident in his 10,000 freedmen and his veterans, while there were many senators who owed their rank to him. Caesar was to comment that Sulla did not know his political 'ABC' (Suet. *Jul*. 77), but Sulla may not have considered a perpetual dictatorship.

478 The following year (80 BC) Sulla, although dictator, consented to become consul for the second time with Metellus Pius to provide a pretence and facade of democratic government . . . **480** The next year (79 BC) the people, to flatter Sulla, chose him again as consul, but he refused it and appointed Servilius (Vatia) Isauricus and (Appius) Claudius Pulcher and of his own accord willingly laid down supreme power, although no one was troubling him. **481** This act of Sulla's seems amazing to me, that he should have been the first and only person up to that time to lay down such immense power with no one compelling him to do so, not to sons (like Ptolemy in Egypt and Ariobarzanes in Cappadocia and Seleucus in Syria) but to the very people who were the subjects of his tyranny; **482** and it is incredible that, after recklessly forcing his way to power, once he was in possession of it he should have laid it down. It is also strange beyond everything that he was not afraid, though in this war more than 100,000 young men had died and of his enemies he had removed 90 senators, 15 consuls and 2,600 equites, including those who were banished; **483** the property of these men had been confiscated and the bodies of many thrown out without burial, yet Sulla, worried neither by those at home nor by the banished, nor by the cities whose citadels, walls, land, houses, money and privileges he had done away with, proclaimed himself a private citizen . . .

487 In my view Sulla – in every respect the same strong and powerful man – set his heart on becoming a tyrant when a private citizen and a private citizen when a tyrant, and after that on spending his time in rural isolation. **488** For he went off to his own estate at Cumae in Italy and there occupied himself in solitude with the sea and hunting, not because he wanted to avoid private life in Rome, nor because he was too frail to do what he wished – **489** he was still at a robust time of life and sound in health, and throughout Italy there were 120,000 men who had recently served under him and had received large grants of money and plenty of land from him, while in the city there were 10,000 Cornelii, besides the rest of his party, devoted to him and still formidable to everyone else, all of whom relied on Sulla for their immunity for the acts they had committed in co-operation with him. But my view is that, tired of war, tired of power and tired of Rome, he fell in love with the countryside.

11.41 *CIL* I² 2646: Dedication to his sister

On the fragment of an architrave found at Verona.

Lucius Cornelius Sulla, son of Lucius, built this in the name of his sister Cornelia.

LATER VIEWS OF SULLA

11.42 Pliny *Natural History* 7.137–38: Pliny the Elder's view

The temple of Jupiter Capitolinus which had burnt down in 83 was rebuilt and dedicated in 69 BC by Q. Lutatius Catulus (cos. 78). Despite the survival of Sulla's *Memoirs*, the fact that many of his political reforms were overturned and his initial rule so bloody ensured that his actions aroused many criticisms.

137 The only person to have assumed the surname 'Fortunate' is Lucius Sulla, who actually won the title by shedding the blood of fellow citizens and making war on his native country. And what proofs of good fortune inspired him? Was it his ability to proscribe and slaughter so many thousands of his fellow citizens? What a corrupt interpretation of the word! How unfortunate he was to be in the future! Were they then at their deaths not more fortunate, whom today we pity, while there is no one who does not hate Sulla? **138** Come now, was not the end of his life more cruel than the calamity of all the proscribed, when his body ate itself away and gave birth to its own torments? Although he kept up a good pretence, and although we believe from that last dream, when he was almost on the point of death, that he alone was able to conquer hatred by glory, nevertheless he admitted that his happiness was lacking one thing – that he had not dedicated the Capitol.

11.43 Dionysius of Halicarnassus *Roman Antiquities* 5.77.4–6: Dionysius on Sulla's dictatorship

Dionysius is discussing the first dictatorship at Rome, that of Titus Larcius Flavus (cf. doc. 1.14); Spurius Cassius was his master of horse. The sentiments are very much like those of Pliny; Sallust, too, criticises Sulla for bringing everything to a bad end and demoralising the army (*Cat.* 11.4–6).

4 But in our fathers' time, a full 400 years after Titus Larcius' dictatorship, the institution was discredited and became hateful to all men under Lucius Cornelius Sulla, the first and only dictator who exercised his power as dictator cruelly and severely; as a result the Romans then noticed for the first time that of which they had previously been unaware, that the rule of a dictator is a tyranny. **5** For Sulla made up the senate from just about anybody, reduced the power of the tribunate to the minimum, depopulated whole cities, abolished some kingdoms and created others, and committed many other arbitrary actions which it would be a lengthy task to recount; and of the citizens, besides those who died in battle, he killed not fewer than 40,000 after they had surrendered to him, and some of these after first torturing them. **6** Whether all these acts of his were necessary or beneficial to the state it is not now the time to inquire; what I have tried to show is that, on their account, the name of dictator was loathed and appeared terrible.

11.44 Plutarch *Life of Sulla* 38.6: Sulla on himself

Sulla died in 78, at the relatively young age of only 60. Lepidus (cos. 78), with some support, wanted to deprive Sulla of funeral honours, but he received a sumptuous state funeral.

His monument is in the Campus Martius; it is said that the inscription on it is one that he wrote for himself. The purport of it is that none of his friends had outdone him in doing good and none of his enemies in doing harm.

COINAGE, 87–81 BC

Sulla's name appeared on four issues of coins (Crawford *RRC* 359, 367, 368, 381). While there are some difficulties of interpretation, they were clearly meant to serve Sulla's propaganda purposes, as on the coins appear Roma, Venus, the palm branch of victory, the triumphal chariot, trophies, and symbols of Sulla's position as augur.

11.45 Crawford *RRC* 351.1: Cinna and grain distribution

A denarius, 86 BC. This coin probably refers to a free distribution of grain.

Obverse: Bust of Ceres, goddess of agricultural growth.

Reverse: Ear of wheat. Two male figures sitting on a bench (*subsellium*), facing right, with an ear of grain on the far right.

11.46 Crawford *RRC* 367: Sulla triumphant

This coin is an aureus (gold coin) of c. 82 BC. It hails Sulla as imperator, and the following coin (doc. 11.47) has him as imperator for a second time. This type forms the bulk of Sulla's coinage.

Obverse: Bust of the goddess Roma.

Reverse: Sulla, wearing toga, in triumphal quadriga (four-horse chariot), facing right; Victory flies above him, facing left, and carrying a victory wreath; inscription: L. Sulla Imperator. Sulla carries in his right hand a laurel branch (Grueber, Sydenham *CRR*) or a caduceus, herald's staff (Crawford *RRC*); a laurel branch of victory is the best interpretation. He holds the reins in his left hand.

11.47 Crawford *RRC* 359.1: Sulla and Venus

An aureus of c. 84–83 BC, minted by Sulla outside Italy. The jug and lituus refer to Sulla's role as augur. Which two acclamations as imperator are being referred to is debated: as the Colline gate battle involved a victory over citizens, a coin representing two major events of his career, Cilicia and his victory over Mithridates, is to be preferred.

Obverse: Head of the goddess Venus, with diadem, facing right, with standing Cupid (holding a palm branch, the sign of victory) facing left; inscription: Sulla.

Reverse: Jug and lituus (augur's staff; the jug and lituus were symbols of the augurate), with a trophy on either side; inscription: Imperator iterum (a second time).

11.48 Crawford *RRC* 381: Sulla's equestrian statue

An aureus of c. 80 BC.

Obverse: Bust of the goddess Roma.

Reverse: Equestrian statue of Sulla, facing left, right hand raised; inscription: L. Sull(a) Feli(x) Dic(tator).

11.49 Crawford *RRC* 381: Establishment of Sulla's colonies (?)

A denarius of 81 BC. This coin is sometimes taken to be related to Sulla's military colonies.

Obverse: Bust of the goddess Ceres.

Reverse: Ploughman, holding a staff, with pair of oxen, facing left.

11.50 Crawford *RRC* 426.1: The coinage of Sulla's son

Sulla's son Faustus Cornelius Sulla issued silver denarii c. 60 BC (perhaps in 63 BC) commemorating the surrender of Jugurtha by Bocchus to Sulla. The coin may represent the signet ring which Sulla had cut to commemorate the occasion (doc. 9.13).

Obverse: Bust of the goddess Diana wearing diadem.

Reverse: Sulla seated, facing left; Bocchus kneels before him, handing an olive branch (vertical) to Sulla. Jugurtha, facing left and with his hands bound, kneels behind the seated Sulla.

12

The Collapse of the Republic

Pompey's career to 78 BC had been extraordinary, for he thrived under Sulla. Though he disregarded Sulla's constitution both in Sulla's lifetime and after his death, he was nevertheless the defender of the Sullan senate against both Lepidus and then Sertorius: when Sulla died Pompey had ensured he had a magnificent funeral (doc. 11.44). Cicero in the 70s was pursuing his oratorical training and gaining increasing experience in the law-courts (doc. 2.67), while Caesar, who was to be quaestor in 69, avoided embroilment with Lepidus (doc. 12.2), whose insurrection almost immediately followed Sulla's death in 78 BC. As consul for that year, Lepidus may have desired to emulate Sulla and seize control of the state. In 79 Pompey had not opposed the election of Lepidus as consul, although Sulla apparently objected to his candidature (doc. 11.39). Lepidus' revolt was put down by Catulus (cos. 78) with Pompey's involvement (doc. 12.2). Pompey then refused to disband his army and was granted imperium to go to Spain in 77 to help Caecilius Metellus Pius (cos. 80) against Sertorius; after initial setbacks, and lack of support from Rome, Pompey sent a letter to the senate in 75 BC requesting reinforcements (doc. 12.3). Following Sertorius' assassination by Perperna, who had brought remnants of Lepidus' army to join Sertorius, Pompey defeated and killed Perperna and organised Spain into provinces. The senate's ability to deal with the revolts of Lepidus and Sertorius (and Spartacus' slave revolt) indicates the success of Sulla's constitutional reform: the senate as a united body opposed both men, and successfully.

Pompey was recalled by the senate in 71 to assist Crassus in suppressing Spartacus' uprising (doc. 6.50) and was awarded a triumph. With Crassus, he then stood successfully for the consulship of 70: Pompey had at this stage held no other civic magistracies. The two apparently disagreed at the beginning of their consulship, but they did restore tribunician powers, reform the law-courts, and organise the census of Roman citizens to be taken (docs 12.4–7). The last time a tribune and the popular assembly had conferred a military command was in 88 BC in the case of Sulpicius Rufus, who transferred Sulla's command against Mithridates to Marius (doc. 9.32). Pompey benefited directly from the restoration of the tribunate through the *lex Gabinia* (67) and then the *lex Manilia* (66). These commands gave him imperium on an unrivalled scale; despite the senate's opposition to the *lex Gabinia*, Pompey received a three-year command and in fact was to deal with the pirates infesting the Mediterranean in a few months (docs 12.8–9). In 66, through the *lex Manilia*, he was awarded Lucullus' command in the East against Mithridates, where Lucullus had had some spectacular success: the campaign had, however, dragged on, Clodius Pulcher had encouraged Lucullus' troops to mutiny, and the publicani were unhappy with Lucullus' favourable treatment of the provincials (docs 11.10, 12.10). Cicero spoke in favour of Pompey receiving the command, and Lucullus, deprived of his command, as a result became Pompey's implacable enemy. Pompey defeated Mithridates in the same year and spent until 62 reorganising the East (docs 12.11–12).

In Pompey's absence, Cicero had held the praetorship in 66 and reached the consulship in 63. In this year the Catilinarian conspiracy broke out; despite Cicero's palpable desire to emphasise the enormity of Catiline's threat to the state, it does seem in fact to have been a serious threat (docs 12.14–23). Cicero, with the authority of the senate, put five of the chief conspirators to death: Caesar had spoken against this in the senate, but Cato the Younger had successfully urged their execution. As the conspirators were Roman citizens, they should have been tried, and Cicero would pay dearly for this with exile in 58–57 BC. In 62 BC, the scandal of Clodius' profanation of the rites of the Bona Dea occurred: he was put on trial, and Cicero disproved his alibi, incurring Clodius' political enmity as a result (docs 7.87, 12.38, 48, 56).

Pompey had enjoyed great successes in the East (docs 12.28–31), and his return was viewed with apprehension, but he disbanded his troops when he landed at Brundisium in 62 BC. There was tension between him and Cicero, who felt slighted that Pompey was not effusive enough over Cicero's role in squashing Catiline (docs 12.32–34). Pompey's victories were duly celebrated in his (third) triumph in 61 (docs 12.29, 2.60). He sought ratification for his reorganisation in the East and land for his veterans. But he had miscalculated: the senate obstructed both measures (doc. 12.36). Another issue developed: the equites had bid too much for their contract to collect taxes and wanted the contract renegotiated; Crassus supported them in this. The senate, led principally by Cato, refused. The proposal that equites be liable to prosecution for accepting bribes in judicial cases also caused friction between senate and equites (doc. 12.35). These two issues played a role in the next major development at Rome, with far-reaching consequences – the events of the consulship of Caesar (59 BC). Caesar had used massive bribery to gain election as pontifex maximus in 63 BC against more senior senatorial contenders (doc. 3.22), as praetor-elect for 62 he had opposed in 63 the execution of Catiline's chief supporters (doc. 12.21), and in 61 BC he had been successful as governor in Further Spain, where he had earned a triumph which he planned to celebrate on his return to Rome in 60. He requested that he be allowed to stand in absentia (a magistrate with imperium could not enter the pomerium of the city, and he had to retain his imperium in order to celebrate his triumph); on Cato's urging the senate refused to grant this permission (doc. 12.39).

The election of Caesar as consul brought three men – Caesar, Crassus and Pompey – together in what is often known as 'the First Triumvirate'; the initiative came from Caesar, the most junior of the three. Cicero was offered a close relationship with them but, true to his republican ideals, refused (doc. 12.40), as he later did a place on Caesar's land commission (doc. 12.46). He would also in 58 turn down a position on Caesar's staff in Gaul which might have saved him from exile. Pompey married Caesar's daughter Julia to cement the alliance (docs 12.41, 45). During his consulship Caesar effected the ratification of Pompey's Eastern settlements (acta) and land for his veterans, while the publicani received relief from their contract (docs 12.43–45). He was able to act unopposed: Caesar's fellow consul was M. Calpurnius Bibulus, Cato's son-in-law, who with Cato opposed Caesar's agricultural legislation. Violence in the forum led to Bibulus spending the remainder of the year in his house proclaiming unfavourable omens; he was inactive to the extent that jokes apparently circulated about the 'Consulship of Julius and Caesar' (doc. 12.43).

Fearing that Caesar might achieve the consulship, the senate had assigned the 'woods and pastures' as the consular provinces for the consuls of 59 (doc. 12.43). Caesar therefore ensured that he was awarded the governorship of the two Gauls and Illyricum (north-east of the Adriatic) for five years. Opposition to the triumvirate grew in 59, led largely by the younger Curio, who, however, was to be tribune of the plebs in 50 BC and, as such, a chief supporter of Caesar (docs 12.50–52, 13.14–16). Cicero complained about 'certain political matters' in 59 (doc. 12.48), and in his opinion this led to the adoption of Clodius by a plebeian; Clodius was duly elected to the tribunate for 58 and carried out an extensive legislative programme; he also attacked Cicero, who went into exile (docs 12.54–56), arranged for Cato to go on an official mission to Cyprus (docs 12.57–59) and began attacks on Pompey, who as a consequence then supported the moves for Cicero's recall. Cicero describes his triumphant return to Italy and Rome (docs 12.60–62), where he proposed that Pompey be given powers to deal with the city's grain crisis (docs 12.63–65). Caesar had meanwhile been busy conquering, pillaging and massacring in Gaul (docs 12.66–68), gaining enormous amounts of wealth with which to pursue his political aims at Rome. Cicero was soon speaking with his customary freedom, attacking Caesar in the hope of separating him from Pompey. This, along with growing antagonism between Crassus and Pompey, resulted in a realliance of the triumvirs, with Caesar meeting Crassus at Ravenna and then Pompey at Luca in April 56 (docs 12.69–72). It was agreed that Crassus and Pompey should share the consulship again for 55 and be granted five-year provincial commands to follow, while Caesar's command in Gaul would also be extended for another five years. Cicero was 'brought to heel' and, as part of his 'palinode' in 56 opposed the proposal to deprive Caesar of his command (doc. 12.73), while he was also forced to defend old enemies at the behest of the triumvirs (doc. 12.77). This rapprochement was undercut by the death of Julia in childbirth (Pompey turned down another marriage alliance with Caesar) and Crassus' death in Parthia (docs 12.79–84). Caesar meanwhile continued amassing wealth from his conquests in Gaul and Britain (docs 12.85–91). In his absence, ongoing factional violence in Rome between Clodius and Milo was to set the stage for Pompey's sole consulship in 52, his acceptance by the optimates and the outbreak of civil war, which it could be argued was brought about by senators whose main aim was Caesar's downfall. Tacitus (doc. 12.1) associates Pompey with Marius and Sulla as individuals who were part of the process of the transformation from political liberty to the 'sole dominion' of Augustus. Like the other four major protagonists in this period, Pompey was to meet a violent death: Crassus was killed in battle, Pompey was murdered, Cato committed suicide, Caesar was assassinated and Cicero was proscribed.

Ancient sources (for 78–44 BC): for this period, on account of the writings of Cicero and Caesar, there is a degree of contemporary information unrivalled for any other period in Roman history. In addition, the biographies of Plutarch and the histories written in the imperial age are important, as they provide the overall chronological framework within which Cicero's more detailed information can be placed. Caesar's *Gallic War* is an account of his campaigns in Gaul; it is in seven books with an eighth by Hirtius continuing the account. Caesar's *Civil War* provides his perspective on events: needless to say, this is hardly objective. Caesar presents himself and his actions in the way he wants these to be viewed and interpreted. However, along with Cicero's letters, Caesar's *Civil War* provides a personal and contemporary perspective on the conflict. The *Alexandrian War*, *Spanish War* and *African War* dealing with these campaigns are not by Caesar, but they provide detailed accounts, starting with Caesar's arrival in Alexandria in 48 BC and concluding with his return to Rome in 45 BC. Cicero delivered various speeches in this period, not all of which survive; there are 57 speeches in all for the period 81 to 43 BC: those delivered by his opponents are no longer extant. He could clearly be tendentious, and he cannot be accepted as giving the 'whole truth and nothing but the truth'. There is also the commentary of Asconius on five of these speeches. Particularly important is his commentary on Cicero's *Milo* (doc. 13.1), which shows that Cicero, in defending Milo on the charge of killing Clodius, was not being completely accurate. Cicero's correspondence is also crucial. He wrote letters to his close friend Atticus (*Att.*), to his brother Quintus (*Quint.*), to Brutus, and to others (*Fam.*), and among the collection of letters to friends are some written to him. Some 912 letters survive. These letters, usually dated, provide detailed information about the unfolding of events, though many contain contemporary allusions which are difficult to understand.

Another contemporary source is Sallust. He wrote two important historical monographs, one concerning the war against Jugurtha (see chapter 9) and the other concerning the conspiracy of Catiline (docs 12.14–16, 19–23). In addition, his *Historiae* (*Histories*) dealt with the period from 78 BC (perhaps continuing the history of Sisenna, but Sulla's death in that year marked a logical place to begin). The last dated fragment (in Book 5) refers to 67 BC, but Sallust's intention must have been to continue his account beyond that date. An important fragment is Pompey's dispatch from Spain to the senate (doc. 12.3). As in his two historical monographs, there is an overriding emphasis on attacking the nobiles and emphasising the decline of Rome.

Lucan (AD 39–65) wrote the Pharsalia (*De bello civili*), a poetic epic which commences with Caesar crossing the Rubicon and ends with Caesar in

Alexandria (48–47 BC) but is unfinished. He almost certainly drew on Livy's lost books for this period. There are also the historians of the imperial period. None of Livy's works on this period survive, but they are summarised in *Periochae* 90–116. Velleius Paterculus in Book 2.29–58 deals with the period in a brief but important continuous chronological treatment; there is a reasonably long section on Caesar (2.41–59). Appian *Civil Wars* 1.107–21, 2.1–117 is also very important in presenting a chronological framework. As in other parts of his *Civil Wars* he uses sources now lost. For Lucullus' and Pompey's campaigns against Mithridates, his *Mithridatica* 67–121 is vital. Dio, books 36–44, also covers this period, and there are various biographies. The beginning of Suetonius' biography of Caesar, the *Divus Julius*, is lost and in its current state the *Life* commences in Caesar's sixteenth year. His approach, after sketching the details of Caesar's life, is (as in the other biographies) to develop themes rather than to use a chronological approach. He is certainly interested in the personal characteristics of his subject, but the account is reliable. Plutarch wrote several biographies of the individuals involved: Antony, Brutus, Caesar, Cato the Younger, Cicero, Crassus, Lucullus, Pompey and Sertorius. The number of relevant biographies indicates the importance of the period. They are of mixed quality and offer the author's usual moral observations. But he drew heavily on lost historians, and in many of the *Lives* there is a wealth of detail about individual historical events (such as the account of Cato in Africa). In the *Lives* of those involved in the events of 52–44 BC, however, there is a frustrating lack of detail concerning the main events.

THE AFTERMATH OF SULLA

12.1 Tacitus *Histories* 2.38: Tacitus on Republican history

Tacitus alludes to the tribunes Ti. and G. Gracchus, Saturninus and Drusus. Otho was hailed emperor by the praetorians in AD 69 but committed suicide when his troops were defeated; Vitellius was proclaimed emperor by his troops in 69; his forces were defeated by those of Vespasian and he was killed by the mob in December 69.

The old lust for power, long ingrained in mankind, came to maturity and erupted as the empire became great; for equality was easily maintained while Rome's power was moderate. But when, with the conquest of the world and the destruction of rival cities or kings, there was the freedom to desire the secure enjoyment of wealth, the struggles between senators and people first blazed up. At one time the tribunes stirred up trouble, at another the consuls were in control, and the city and forum saw the first attempts at civil war; then Gaius Marius, from the lowest ranks of the plebs, and Lucius Sulla, the most ruthless of the nobles, conquered liberty by arms and turned it into tyranny. After them came Gnaeus Pompey, who was no better, though cleverer at concealing his aims, and from then there was no other aim but autocracy. Legions of Roman citizens did not shrink from fighting at Pharsalus or Philippi, and it was even less likely that the armies of Otho and Vitellius would have made or abandoned war of their own accord: the same divine wrath, the same human madness, the same criminal purposes drove them to conflict.

12.2 Appian *Civil Wars* 1.107.501–4: Lepidus' revolt, 78–77 BC

M. Aemilius Lepidus (cos. 78) had supported Sulla and benefited financially from the proscriptions; though Sulla (according to Plutarch) did not support him as a consular candidate (doc. 11.39), he was elected. Lepidus' measures undermined Sulla's settlement: exiles were to be recalled, confiscated land was to be returned to its original owners, and grain distributions resumed. An uprising broke out in Etruria on Sulla's death, and Lepidus and the other consul of 78, Q. Lutatius Catulus, were authorised to suppress it; Lepidus decided to support the rebels. The senate nevertheless assigned him Transalpine Gaul for 77. When the senate recalled him to Rome to hold the consular elections, he marched on the city in 77 and demanded both a second consulship and the restoration of tribunician powers; when the tribunes had asked this of the consuls in 78, Lepidus had refused. Caesar, though invited, did not join the revolt. A *senatus consultum ultimum* (*SCU*) was passed on the motion of L. Marcius Philippus (cos. 91), and Pompey was appointed to support Catulus in squashing the revolt. Lepidus retreated to Etruria and then to Sardinia, where he died. The remnants of his army, under Perperna (M. Perperna Veiento), joined Sertorius in Spain. Lepidus' legate M. Junius Brutus (the father of Brutus, Caesar's assassin), was killed by Pompey after he had surrendered.

501 This was the end of Sulla, and as soon as the consuls returned from the funeral they began engaging in a heated quarrel, while the citizens started to side with one or the other. Lepidus, who wanted the support of the Italians, stated that he would return the land taken from them by Sulla. **502** As the senate was afraid of both parties, it made them take an oath that they would not resort to war. When Lepidus was assigned Transalpine Gaul by lot, he did not return to the assembly because in the following year he would be free from his oath not to make war on the Sullans, as it was considered that the oath was binding only during the year of office. **503** As his plans did not escape observation, he was summoned by the senate, and as he well knew the reasons for the summons he came with his entire army, with the intention of bringing it into the city with him. When this was prevented he ordered his men to take up arms, and Catulus on the other side did the same. **504** A battle took place not far from the Campus Martius in which Lepidus was beaten, and with no further attempt at resistance he sailed off to Sardinia, where he died of a consumption. His army gradually melted away, with the greater part of it taken by Perperna to Sertorius in Spain.

12.3 Sallust *Histories* 2.98: Pompey's letter and the senate, 75 BC

Quintus Sertorius (c. 126–73 BC) served against the Cimbri under Q. Servilius Caepio and Marius and as military tribune under T. Didius in Spain from 97 to 93. As quaestor in 90 he saw service in the Social War, and in either 89 or 88 he stood for the tribunate; however, as Sulla effectively prevented his election, he turned to Cinna. As praetor (in 83) he was allotted Roman Spain, where he went when it was clear that Sulla would be victorious.

Initially driven out of Spain by the proconsul C. Annius, Sertorius returned at the invitation of the Lusitanians in 80; by 77 he controlled most of Roman Spain, where he set up a Roman-style senate and government. The consuls of 77 declined to go to Spain, and Pompey, who had again refused to disband his army, was sent with proconsular imperium to assist Q. Caecilius Metellus Pius (cos. 80) against Sertorius and Perperna. After various successes by the Roman generals, Sertorius counter-attacked, in 75 cutting off their supplies. Pompey, still an eques, wrote the following letter to the senate for reinforcements. In 72 Perperna assassinated Sertorius (doc. 12.4) and in the same year was defeated and executed by Pompey. Val. Max. 6.2.8: Helvius Mancia described Pompey as *adulescentulus carnifex* (youthful butcher) on account of his murders of Cn. Domitius Ahenobarbus, M. Brutus, Cn. Carbo and Perperna.

1 'If I had undertaken such hardships and dangers in a war against you, my country and my country's gods – and frequently from my early youth the most abominable enemies have been routed under my leadership and your safety assured – you could have taken no worse measures against me in my absence than you are doing at present, Fathers of the Senate, for, after dispatching me, despite my youth, to a most savage war, you have destroyed me, together with an excellent army, as far as you could, by starvation, the most wretched of all deaths. **2** Is it with such expectations that the Roman people sends its sons to war? Are these the rewards for wounds and blood so often shed on the state's behalf? Wearied by writing letters and sending legates I have exhausted all my own resources and even my hopes, and in the meantime you have given me barely a year's expenses over a three-year period. **3** By the immortal gods! Do you think I can perform the function of a treasury or maintain an army without provisions and pay?

4 'I admit that I entered this war with more zeal than prudence, for within 40 days of receiving the mere title of general from you I had raised and prepared an army and driven the enemy, who were already at the throat of Italy, from the Alps into Spain; through those mountains I opened up another route than that of Hannibal, and one more convenient for us. **5** I recovered Gaul, the Pyrenees, Lacetania and the Indigetes, and withstood with newly enrolled soldiers and far inferior numbers the first attack of the conqueror Sertorius, and spent the winter in camp surrounded by the most savage enemy, not in the towns or in pursuit of my own popularity.

6 'Why, then, should I enumerate the battles or winter campaigns, the towns destroyed or recovered? Actions speak louder than words: the capture of the enemy's camp at Sucro, the battle at the River Turia, and the destruction of the enemy leader Gaius Herennius, together with his army and the city of Valentia, are known to you well enough; in return for which, grateful senators, you have given me want and hunger. As a result, the condition of my army and the enemy's is the same; for neither is given pay, **7** and both can march as victor into Italy. **8** I warn you of this and beg you to give it your attention, rather than compelling me to take care of the army's necessities in a private capacity. **9** Whatever of Hither Spain is not held by the enemy has been ravaged either by ourselves or by Sertorius to the point of utter devastation except for the coastal cities, so that it is actually an expense and burden on us; last year Gaul provided Metellus' army with pay and provisions, and now it can scarcely keep itself because of a bad harvest; I have exhausted not only my property but even my credit. **10** You are all that is left – unless you come to our aid, the army, albeit against my will and with advance warning on my part, will cross over into Italy, and with it all the war in Spain.'

This letter was read in the senate at the beginning of the following year (74 BC). But the consuls distributed between themselves the provinces decreed by the senate, Cotta taking Hither Gaul and Octavius Cilicia. Then the next consuls (for 74 BC), Lucius Lucullus and Marcus Cotta, greatly disturbed by Pompey's letters and messages, both for the sake of the state and because if the army was led into Italy they would have neither glory or status, provided him with money and reinforcements by every means possible, with the nobility especially exerting themselves, the majority of whom were already giving him their support and backing up their words with deeds.

THE CONSULSHIP OF 70 BC

Pompey returned to Italy in 71 BC at the request of the senate to assist in crushing the revolt of Spartacus, who had defeated the two consuls of 72 (L. Gellius Publicola and Cn. Cornelius Lentulus Clodianus), both separately and then with their armies combined. Crassus was appointed proconsul against Spartacus and in six months in 72–71 BC defeated the slave rebels. Pompey returned in time to kill 5,000 fugitives from Crassus' last engagement against the slaves and wrote to the senate that he (Pompey) had finished the war (see doc. 6.50). Crassus nevertheless asked for Pompey to stand for the consulship with him, and the two men kept their armies under arms outside Rome, awaiting their triumph (Pompey for his victory in Spain) and ovatio (Crassus), and were elected to the consulship in absentia.

Restoration of tribunician powers: Sulla had stripped the tribunate of its powers (doc. 11.30). Lepidus had proposed to restore these in 78 BC (doc. 12.2), and in the 70s there had been various other attempts opposed by the senate, such as that of L. Licinius Macer in 73 (apparently with Pompey's support). In 75 BC, the prohibition from holding further office after the tribunate was removed. The full restoration of the tribunate came with Pompey and Crassus in 70 BC, which was an important qualification of the Sullan constitution. That same year, however, Pompey failed to gain land for the veterans who had served with him in Spain, and neither Pompey nor Crassus took up a provincial command.

12.4 Livy *Periochae* 96–97: The events of 72–70 BC

96 (72 BC) The praetor, Quintus Arrius, killed Crixus, leader of the runaways, along with 20,000 men. The consul Gnaeus Lentulus lost a battle to Spartacus. The consul Lucius Gellius and the praetor Quintus Arrius were defeated in battle by the same man. Sertorius was murdered at a banquet by Marcus Perperna, Manius Antonius and other conspirators, in his eighth year as leader, a great commander and more often than not the victor over two generals, Pompey and Metellus, but towards the end cruel and spendthrift. The command of his faction was transferred to Marcus (Perperna), whom Gnaeus Pompey conquered, captured and killed; Pompey recovered Spain in about the tenth year after the war had started. The proconsul Gaius Cassius and praetor Gnaeus Manlius lost a battle to Spartacus, and the war was entrusted to the praetor Marcus Crassus.

97 (72–70 BC) The praetor Marcus Crassus first won a battle against part of the runaways, composed of Gauls and Germans, with 35,000 of the enemy's soldiers killed, including their leaders Castus and Gannicus. He then fought the matter out with Spartacus, who was killed with 60,000 of his men. The praetor Marcus Antonius undertook a campaign with little success against the Cretans and closed it with his death. The proconsul Marcus Lucullus subdued the Thracians. Lucius Lucullus won a battle against Mithridates in Pontus, with more than 60,000 of the enemy's soldiers killed. Marcus Crassus and Gnaeus Pompey were made consuls (Pompey by senatorial decree, while a Roman eques and before he had held the quaestorship) and restored the power of the tribunes. The courts were also transferred by the praetor Marcus Aurelius Cotta to the Roman equites. Mithridates was forced by the hopelessness of his circumstances to take refuge with Tigranes, king of Armenia.

12.5 Appian *Civil Wars* 1.121.560–61: 'Neither praetor nor quaestor'

The senate passed a law to exempt Pompey from the Sullan *lex annalis*, the provisions of which prescribed that the quaestorship and praetorship be held prior to the consulship, with a minimum age (42 years) for election to the consulship (doc 11.30).

560 Crassus accomplished this (the defeat of Spartacus) in six months, and as a result was immediately at loggerheads with Pompey over which of them deserved the greatest prestige. He did not disband his army, for neither had Pompey. Both were candidates for the consulship, but, while Crassus had held the praetorship in accordance with Sulla's legislation, Pompey had held neither praetorship nor quaestorship and was only 34 years old. He had, however, promised the tribunes that he would restore their magistracy to much of its traditional power. **561** Once elected consuls, they still did not disband their armies, keeping them close to the city. Each made an excuse: Pompey that he was waiting for the return of Metellus for his Spanish triumph, Crassus that Pompey should be the first to do so.

12.6 Cicero *Against Verres* 1.37–40: Reform of the law-courts, 70 BC

Sulla had handed the courts over to the senators, overturning Gaius Gracchus' reform (docs 11.29, 8.28). Lucius Aurelius Cotta (brother of the Cottas who were consuls in 75 and 74 BC), as praetor in 70 BC, introduced a law (the *lex Aurelia*) to give membership of the juries to three groups: the senators, the equites and the tribuni aerarii ('treasury officials'), who belonged to the same census qualification as the equites. Pompey's role in the reform as consul-elect is not attested.

37 I shall not only remind you, but deal with, corroborating every detail, the entire account of judicial wickedness and corruption which has occurred during the ten years since the courts have been transferred to the senate. **38** The Roman people will learn from me, jurors, how it was that, for nearly 50 successive years, while the equestrian order made the decisions in the courts, not even the slightest suspicion of receiving money as a bribe fell upon a single Roman eques when acting as a juror; how it was that, when the courts were transferred to the senatorial order and the power of the people over you as individuals had been removed, Quintus Calidius declared, after his conviction, that someone of praetorian rank should not in all fairness be convicted for less than 3,000,000 sesterces; how it was that, when Publius Septimius, the senator, was convicted, with Quintus Hortensius as praetor in charge of the extortion court, the penalty was specifically calculated with regard to the fact that he had taken a bribe when acting as juror; **39** how it was that, in the cases of the senators Gaius Herennius and Gaius Popilius, who were both convicted of embezzlement, and in that of Marcus Atilius, who was convicted of treason, it was clearly established that they had taken bribes as jurors; how it was that senators were found, when Gaius Verres as city praetor was appointing jurors, who would vote against a defendant, whom they were convicting, without knowing anything about the case; how it was that a senator was found who, when acting as juror, in the same case took money from the defendant to bribe the other jurors and from the prosecutor to convict the defendant. **40** And now, in what terms can I bewail that humiliating and calamitous blot on the whole order, the fact that in this country, when the senatorial order served in the courts, the voting tablets of jurors under oath were marked with different colours? I promise you that I shall deal with all these facts with diligence and severity.

12.7 Enrolment of the Italians as Roman citizens

After the enfranchisement of the Italians nearly one million Roman citizens were registered in 70 BC. The censors, Gnaeus Lentulus and Lucius Gellius, were the first elected since 86 BC. Cicero, in delivering his oration against Verres, notes that the census coincided with elections and ludi (games).

(i) Livy Periochae *98*

The censors, Gnaeus Lentulus and Lucius Gellius, conducted a harsh censorship, with 64 members removed from the senate. When they closed the lustrum, 900,000 citizens were registered.

(ii) Cicero Against Verres *1.54*

I will not allow the case to be decided only when this concourse from all over Italy, which has gathered from all parts at one and the same time for the elections, games and census, shall have left Rome.

POMPEY'S EXTRAORDINARY COMMANDS

12.8 Cicero *On the Command of Gnaeus Pompey* 52–53: The *lex Gabinia*, 67 BC

Aulus Gabinius (tr. pl. 67, cos. 58) legislated that the consul M'. Acilius Glabrio be given command over Bithynia and Pontus and part of Lucullus' army, signalling the beginning of the end of the latter's Eastern command. He also proposed the *lex Gabinia*, which gave Pompey extensive control of the Roman Mediterranean world to deal with the pirates who threatened Rome's commerce and food supply. Previous commands against the pirates had been held by M. Antonius (cos. 99) in 101 and 100 and by his son as praetor in 74 BC (cf. doc. 12.4). Cicero here, in speaking in 66 BC on the proposal to grant Pompey the command against Mithridates, refers to the *lex Gabinia* and Hortensius' opposition to it.

52 So what does Hortensius say? That if supreme command is to be bestowed on one man, Pompey is the best choice by far, but that supreme command should not be granted to one man. That argument is now out of date, proved wrong far more by events than by words. For it was you yourself, Quintus Hortensius, who, to the very best of your abilities and with your unique eloquence, gave a lengthy, authoritative and brilliant speech in the senate against that courageous man Aulus Gabinius, after he had proposed a measure concerning the appointment of a single commander against the pirates, while from this very spot you likewise made a lengthy speech against the same proposal.

53 Well, by the immortal gods, if your judgement had had more weight with the Roman people than their own safety and their real interests, would we today possess this our present glory and worldwide empire? Or did you think our empire existed at a time when envoys, quaestors and praetors of the Roman people were being taken prisoner, when we were prevented from private and public communication with all our provinces, when all seas were so closed to us that we were even unable to engage in either private or public business overseas?

12.9 Plutarch *Life of Pompey* 25.1–26.4: A piratical command, 67 BC

Pompey had taken no command after his consulship of 70, presumably awaiting another opportunity for military service. Gabinius initially proposed the appointment of a consular without mentioning Pompey, to whom the people (opposing the wishes of the senate) turned when the law was passed, granting him greater forces than the law had proposed: imperium for three years over the Mediterranean and 400 stades inland (50 miles or 80 kilometres), 500 ships (200 were originally proposed), and 15 legates who had been praetors and were now invested with propraetorian imperium. The whole campaign lasted three months ('in 40 days he had expelled them from the entire sea': Livy *Per*. 99).

25.1 The pirates' power had spread throughout the whole of our Mediterranean Sea, rendering it unnavigable and impassable to all trade. **2** It was this which primarily induced the Romans, who were suffering from a shortage of food supplies and anticipating a great scarcity, to send Pompey out to clear the sea of pirates. **3** Gabinius, one of Pompey's intimate friends, proposed a law giving him not command of the sea, but complete autocracy and unlimited power over all men. **4** The law gave him command over the sea up to the pillars of Hercules (Gibraltar) and over all the mainland up to 400 stades from the sea. **5** Not many places within the Roman world were outside these limits, and the greatest nations and most powerful kings were included within them. **6** In addition, he was given power to select 15 legates from the senate to be assigned specific tasks, to take as much money from the treasury and taxation officials as he wished, and to command 200 ships, with full authority over the number and levying of soldiers and crews of rowers.

7 When these provisions were read out, the people received them with great enthusiasm, though the most important and influential members of the senate thought this undefined and limitless power too great for envy but still something to be feared. **8** They therefore opposed the law, except for Caesar; he supported the law, not in the least because of any concern he felt for Pompey, but because from the beginning he was trying to gain the favour of the people and win their support. **9** All the rest violently attacked Pompey, and when one of the consuls (Gaius Calpurnius Piso) told him that if he wanted to be a second Romulus he would not escape Romulus' fate, he only narrowly escaped being torn to pieces. **10** When (Quintus Lutatius) Catulus came forward to speak against the law, the people respected him enough to keep quiet for a time, but when after speaking at length in generous praise of Pompey he advised them to spare such a man and not to keep on exposing him to continuous dangers and wars and asked, 'Whom else will you have, if you lose him?', with one voice they all shouted out, 'You!' **11** So Catulus, as he couldn't convince them, retired, and when Roscius came forward to speak no one would listen to him . . . **26.1** When Pompey heard that the law had been passed, he entered the city by night, to avoid the envy that would be caused by the people rushing to meet him. **2** He appeared at daybreak and conducted a sacrifice; and at an assembly held for him he arranged that he was given many other powers besides those already voted, almost doubling his forces. **3** Five hundred ships were manned for him, and 120,000 infantry and 500 cavalry raised. Twenty-four men who had held commands or served as praetor were chosen by him from the senate, and he was also given two quaestors. **4** The fact that the price of foodstuffs fell straightaway allowed the people in their delight to say that the very name of Pompey had put an end to the war.

12.10 Plutarch *Life of Lucullus* 28.7–9: Victory in the East, 69 BC

The Second Mithridatic War (83–81 BC) was fought by L. Licinius Murena, who was defeated by Mithridates. The Third Mithridatic War (73–66) was more serious, prosecuted at first by L. Licinius Lucullus (cos. 74) and then by Pompey. Lucullus in 73 drove Mithridates out of Asia and Bithynia and invaded Pontus, driving Mithridates from there in 72; in 71 he organised tax relief in Asia (doc. 11.10). In 69 BC he scored a spectacular success against Tigranes II of Armenia, Mithridates' son-in-law (100,000 enemy infantry and most of the cavalry perished; the Romans lost five men), and sacked Armenia's capital, Tigranocerta. Lucullus' army, however, encouraged by Publius Clodius Pulcher, his brother-in-law, mutinied in Armenia in the winter of 68–67, and at Rome he was accused of lengthening the war for his own gloria. The *lex Manilia* of 66 BC replaced him with Pompey, and Lucullus did not celebrate his triumph until 63 (doc. 2.34); he opposed the ratification of Pompey's Eastern acta (doc. 12.28).

7 It is said that over 100,000 of Tigranes' infantry were killed and only a few of all his cavalry escaped. Only 100 of the Romans were wounded, and five were killed. **8** Antiochus the philosopher mentions this battle in his treatise *Concerning*

Gods and says that the sun never beheld such a battle as this. And Strabo, another philosopher, in his *Historical Commentaries*, says that the Romans themselves were ashamed and laughed at one another for needing arms against such slaves. Livy has also stated that the Romans had never been so numerically inferior when they faced an enemy; for the victors were hardly even a twentieth part of the conquered, but less. **9** The Roman generals who were most skilful and experienced in war praised Lucullus for this in particular, that he outgeneralled two kings who were most pre-eminent and powerful by two very opposite tactics, speed and slowness. For he used up Mithridates, who was at the height of his power, by long delays; but crushed Tigranes by his speed, being one of the few generals ever to use delay for success and boldness for safety.

12.11 Plutarch *Life of Pompey* 30.1–2: Pompey and Mithridates

Manilius, as tribune for 66 BC, proposed that command of the war against Mithridates be given to Pompey, with the provinces of Cilicia, Bithynia and Pontus, plus the imperium he had already been granted under the *lex Gabinia*. There was opposition from Hortensius and Catulus, but supporters of the law included four consulars.

Pompey quickly defeated Mithridates and received the submission of Tigranes in 66; he campaigned in the Caucasus region in 66–65 and annexed Syria in 64 and Judaea in 63. Mithridates committed suicide in 63. Pompey organised Bithynia-Pontus as a province; Syria (including Judaea) became a province, and that of Cilicia was enlarged. Several client kingdoms liable to pay tribute to Rome were created, including Armenia, Galatia, Palestine, Cappadocia and Commagene (doc. 12.29, cf. doc. 2.60).

1 When it was reported at Rome that the war against the pirates was over and that Pompey, being at leisure, was visiting the Eastern cities, one of the tribunes, Manlius (Manilius), proposed a law that Pompey should be given all the territory and forces under the command of Lucullus, with the addition of Bithynia as well, which was under the command of Glabrio, to make war on the kings Mithridates and Tigranes, keeping also the naval forces and command of the sea he had originally been granted. **2** This meant that the entire Roman empire was placed in the hands of one man, for the only provinces which could be thought to be outside his control by the earlier law – Phrygia, Lycaonia, Galatia, Cappadocia, Cilicia, Upper Colchis and Armenia – were now added to it, along with the armies and troops which Lucullus had used in his conquest of Mithridates and Tigranes.

12.12 Cicero *On the Command of Gnaeus Pompey* 27–28: The *lex Manilia*, 66 BC

Cicero as praetor in 66 BC was enthusiastic in this speech on the appointment of Pompey (they had served together in the Social War: doc. 10.14). This passage sums up Pompey's career and makes clear that, at this stage, Cicero was a supporter of his.

27 If only, Quirites, you had so large a supply of brave and honest men as to make this a difficult decision of yours regarding who, in your view, should be put in total authority over such important matters and so great a war! But, as the case stands, as Gnaeus Pompey is unique as one whose merit has surpassed not only the glory of the men of today but even the memory of olden days, what consideration is there that could make anyone hesitate at this point? **28** For my point of view is that a very great commander must have these four qualities – knowledge of warfare, courage, reputation and luck. Who, therefore, has there ever been or ought to have been more knowledgeable than Pompey here? – who left school and boyhood studies for his father's army and the study of warfare in a dangerous campaign with the fiercest of enemies; who, in his earliest youth, served in the army of a very great commander, while at the approach of manhood he was himself the commander of a huge army; who has engaged more often with the nation's enemy than any other man has disputed with his own, who has fought more wars than others have read of, who has held more offices than other men have longed for; whose youth was instructed in the knowledge of warfare not by the teachings of others but by his own commands, not by defeats but by victories, not by campaigns but by triumphs? To sum up, what kind of warfare can there be in which the fate of his country has not exercised his talents? The Civil, African, Transalpine, Spanish, Slave and Naval wars, various and dissimilar types of wars and of opponents, not only waged by himself without aid but even carried through to a successful conclusion, make it clear that there is nothing in the military sphere which is outside Pompey's experience.

THE CATILINARIAN CONSPIRACY, 63 BC

The main issue of 63 BC, the year of Cicero's consulship, was the conspiracy of Catiline. Cicero as quaestor in Sicily in 75 BC had organised for grain to be sent to Rome to alleviate a shortage, but he made his mark chiefly in his prosecution of Verres after the latter's corruption in Sicily. In 66, as praetor, Cicero defended Manilius in a case of extortion. With Catiline and C. Antonius Hibrida he was a candidate in 64 for the consulship of 63; Sallust (doc. 2.44) suggests that Catiline's candidature benefited Cicero, who was elected with Antonius. Catiline, praetor in 68 BC, had been propraetor in Africa in 67–66 BC. His extortion there was such that his candidature for a consulship for 65 was denied on those grounds, and he could not stand for 64 as he was awaiting trial; the senators on the jury voted for conviction, the equites for acquittal: he was acquitted. Catiline finally stood in 64 for the consulship for 63 BC.

Failing to gain the consulship for a second time in 63 (for 62), Catiline's conspiracy emerged as a threat to the state; his main supporters were Lentulus, Cethegus, Statilius and Gabinius (not the tr. pl. 67), who, with Caeparius, were to be executed by Cicero. P. Cornelius Lentulus Sura (cos. 71) had been expelled by the senate in 70 but was elected praetor again for 63. Fulvia, through Q. Curius, made known the details of Catiline's plot and a *senatus consultum ultimum* was passed when news arrived that Catiline's forces planned to march on Rome (doc. 12.17). Nevertheless, on 8 November 63 Catiline attended the senate, where Cicero delivered the *In Catilinam I* against him; Catiline fled, leaving in Rome his fellow conspirators, who planned to assassinate Cicero while Catiline organised his army in Etruria.

At the beginning of 63 P. Servilius Rullus as tribune proposed a land law to establish a commission of ten men for five years to settle colonies in Italy and the provinces (primarily for

Pompey's veterans), with the land purchased with public money. Cicero successfully opposed the bill; agrarian legislation continued to arouse conservative opposition (doc. 12.13).

12.13 Cicero *On the Agrarian Law* 1.21–23: Cicero on agrarian legislation

This speech was delivered to the senate on the first day of Cicero's consulship (1 January) against the tribune Rullus, who had proposed to sell all state lands (with some exceptions) to purchase land for distribution in Italy. Those 'feared more than Rullus' are Crassus and Caesar. For Cicero's speech on this occasion, cf. doc. 2.45.

21 I am speaking now of the danger to our safety and freedom. **22** For what in the state, or in your independence and prestige, do you think will be left for you untouched once Rullus – and those whom you fear far more than Rullus – with his band of needy and rascally settlers, with all his forces, with all his silver and gold, has occupied Capua and the surrounding cities? Such plans, conscript fathers, I will vehemently and fiercely resist, nor shall I, while I am consul, permit men to bring forward the designs they have long been formulating against the state. **23** You were greatly in error, Rullus, you and some of your colleagues, when you hoped that, by opposing a consul who was popular in real truth, not just in show, you could make yourself look popular in overthrowing the government.

12.14 Sallust *Conspiracy of Catiline* 5.1–8: Sallust's view of Catiline

Unsavoury details of Catiline's early career are also sketched at 15.1–2. In 73 Catiline was acquitted of involvement with the Vestal Virgin Fabia, half-sister of Cicero's wife, Terentia, and in 64 BC he was charged with the murder of those proscribed by Sulla but acquitted. He promised the abolition of debts, proscription of the rich and, for his supporters, offices, priesthoods and plunder.

1 Lucius Catiline was of noble birth and possessed great vigour of both mind and body but an evil and depraved nature. **2** From his youth he delighted in civil wars, murder, robbery and political strife, and in these he spent his early manhood. **3** His body was able to endure hunger, cold and want of sleep to an incredible degree. **4** His mind was daring, crafty, untrustworthy, capable of any pretence or dissimulation, covetous of other men's property, prodigal with his own, violent in its passions; he possessed more than enough eloquence but insufficient wisdom. **5** His insatiable mind always desired things which were excessive, incredible, out of his reach. **6** After the dictatorship of Lucius Sulla, he had been seized with the overpowering desire to take over the government, with little consideration of the means by which he should achieve it, provided that he acquire sovereignty on his own account. **7** His headstrong spirit was tormented more and more every day by poverty and by the consciousness of guilt, both of which he had aggravated by those practices I mentioned earlier. **8** He was further incited by the corruption of a society troubled by two great and opposing evils, extravagance and avarice.

12.15 Sallust *Conspiracy of Catiline* 23.1–4: Fulvia as informant

Fulvia's role may not have been as significant as Sallust suggests, but clearly the optimates saw Cicero's candidature as more acceptable than Catiline's: see doc. 2.44.

1 Among the conspirators was Quintus Curius, a man not of low birth but steeped in disgrace and crime, whom the censors had expelled from the senate because of his immorality. **2** This man was just as reckless as he was untrustworthy; he could neither keep quiet about what he had heard nor even hide his own heinous deeds; he was absolutely heedless as to what he said or did. **3** He was engaged in an intrigue of long-standing with Fulvia, a well-born woman, and when he started to fall out of favour with her, because poverty forced him to be less generous, he quickly started boasting and promising her 'seas and mountains' and occasionally threatening her with a weapon unless she submitted to him, and generally behaved more savagely than before. **4** Fulvia, however, when she learned the reason for Curius' arrogance, had no intention of covering up such danger to the state, but without mentioning her source recounted to a number of people what she had heard about Catiline's conspiracy.

12.16 Sallust *Conspiracy of Catiline* 26.1–27.2: Catiline's plans

According to Sallust, Catiline's failure in the consular elections in 64 BC led him to plot his revolution in detail, but he also stood in 63 for the consulship of 62. Sulla's veterans were motivated to support Catiline by the hope of plunder and booty. They had clearly not made good soldier settlers. Antonius had been granted Cisalpine Gaul as his province, but Cicero allowed him to take Macedonia, a more attractive option, and declined a province for himself (26.4).

26.1 After these preparations, Catiline nonetheless stood for the consulship for the next year (62 BC), hoping that, should he be elected, he could easily do what he liked with Antonius. In the meantime he was not idle but kept working on all kinds of plots against Cicero, **2** who, however, was not lacking in the guile and astuteness to evade them. **3** For at the very start of his consulship, by numerous promises made through Fulvia, Cicero had persuaded Quintus Curius, whom I mentioned a short while ago, to lay bare Catiline's plots to him. **4** He had also persuaded his colleague Antonius not to harbour designs against the state by agreeing to let him have his province, and he had secretly stationed around himself bodyguards of friends and clients. **5** When election day came, and Catiline was successful neither in his candidature nor in the plots he had made against the consuls in the Campus Martius, he decided on war and resorting to extreme measures, since his undercover attempts had met with failure and dishonour. **27.1** He therefore dispatched Gaius Manlius to Faesulae and that area of Etruria, a certain Septimius of Camerinum to the Picene district, Gaius Julius to Apulia, and others to any other places he believed might suit his purpose. **2** In the meantime he was busy with many plans at once: laying traps for the consul, preparing to set fires, stationing armed men in strategic places, and himself went armed, ordering the others to do the same, and urging them to be always alert and ready.

12.17 Cicero *In Defence of Murena* 52–53: Cicero threatened

In September 63 BC, on Cicero's motion, the consular elections were postponed, when Cicero accused Catiline of a plot against the state. When D. Junius Silanus and L. Licinius Murena were elected on the next day Catiline equipped armed followers throughout Italy. Cicero informed the senate on October 21 that Manlius was to march on Rome on October 27, and on 22 October an *SCU* was passed. An attempt to assassinate Cicero was foiled on 6 November, and on 8 November Cicero made the first of his four speeches against Catiline. Catiline left Rome that night, joining Manlius in Etruria. Murena, consul-elect for 62, had been accused of bribery by Ser. Sulpicius Rufus (cos. 51) and M. Porcius Cato (tribune-elect). Cicero is arguing that, if Murena were to be convicted, Catiline would be elected in his place.

52 Impelled by his actions, and by the awareness that Catiline was bringing men who were already members of the conspiracy into the Campus Martius armed with swords, I entered the Campus with an unshakeable bodyguard of the very bravest men and wearing that broad and conspicuous breastplate, not so it should protect me – for I was aware that Catiline generally aimed not at the side or the stomach but at the head and neck – but so that all the 'honest men' should notice it and, when they saw their consul in such a fearful danger, rush to his aid and defence, as indeed they did. And so, Servius, when they thought that you were rather lethargic in your candidature and saw Catiline inflamed with hope and desire, all those who wanted to eject this pest from the state at once went over to Murena. **53** Indeed, a great change of support can happen suddenly at consular elections, particularly when the trend is towards a respectable man who is distinguished in his candidature by numerous other advantages.

12.18 Cicero *Against Catiline* 2.7–9: Cicero's portrait of Catiline

This speech was delivered before the people on 9 November, after Catiline had left Rome, and demonstrates the latitude of expression allowed orators (cf. doc. 7.76). Compare the characterisation of Catiline's followers at Sall. *Cat.* 14.1–7.

7 Of what imaginable or conceivable wickedness and criminality has he not been the instigator? In all of Italy can any poisoner, gladiator, robber, assassin, parricide, forger of wills, cheat, glutton, spendthrift, adulterer, woman of notoriety, corrupter of youth, corrupted youth or desperate character be found who does not admit that they have lived on the most intimate terms with Catiline? What murder has been committed through all these years without his involvement? What abominable act of lechery has been accomplished, if not through his agency? **8** Who, indeed, has ever presented such great allurements for young men as this fellow? He has made love to some of them in the most disgusting fashion, while he has most disgracefully allowed others to make love to him, promising some the satisfaction of their wanton passions, others the murder of their parents – and in this he not only encouraged them but even gave them a hand. And now how swiftly he has assembled an immense number of desperate men, not only from the city but also from the country! There was no one overwhelmed by debt, whether from Rome or any corner of the whole of Italy, that he did not admit into this incredible league of crime. **9** And note his various interests in a wide range of activities: there is no one in a gladiatorial school a little too inclined towards crime who does not claim he is Catiline's intimate friend, no one on the stage too inconsequential or good-for-nothing who does not affirm that he has been almost his sworn companion. . . .

10 And if these comrades of his will go after him, if these dissolute swarms of desperate men will leave the city, how happy we shall be, how fortunate the state, how illustrious the praise for my consulship! For the wanton behaviour of these men is no longer moderate – their temerity has become inhuman and unendurable! They think of nothing but murder, arson and robbery. They have squandered their patrimonies, they have mortgaged their properties; their money has run out long ago, and now their credit is beginning to fail – and yet the wanton tastes they had in abundance still remain. If they, in their drinking and gambling, desired only revels and prostitutes, they would indeed be hopeless cases, but we could at least put up with them; but who can bear that idle fellows should be setting an ambush for the bravest of men, idiots for the prudent, drunkards for the sober, the somnolent for the watchful? These, I tell you, reclining at their banquets, embracing their prostitutes, drowsy with wine, stuffed with food, garlanded with wreathes, smothered with unguents and weakened by vice, belch forth in their talk the slaughter of good men and the conflagration of the city!

12.19 Sallust *Conspiracy of Catiline* 43.1–2, 44.1–3: The Allobroges

The Allobroges of Transalpine Gaul, oppressed by their governor and Roman moneylenders, had sent ambassadors to Rome. Lentulus, in charge of the conspiracy at Rome, attempted to draw them in. Initially tempted, the Allobroges decided that the rewards of informing the senate would be more beneficial. They passed the information on to Q. Fabius Sanga, their patron at Rome, who informed Cicero.

43.1 At Rome, Lentulus and the others who were leading the conspiracy, who had organised what seemed to them a huge body of troops, had arranged that, when Catiline reached the locality of Faesulae with his army, the tribune Lucius Bestia should call a public meeting (contio) and, by vilifying the actions of Cicero, throw the blame for a catastrophic war on that best of consuls; that was to act as the signal for the rest of the large body of conspirators each to carry out his own duties on the following night. **2** Their responsibilities are said to have been divided up in this way: Statilius and Gabinius with a large gang were to start fires at 12 strategic sites in the city, while the resulting confusion would make it easier to gain access to the consul and the others against whom their conspiracy was directed; Cethegus was to station himself outside Cicero's door and use violence against him, while others were assigned their own targets; the sons of various families, mostly of the nobility, were to kill their fathers; lastly, taking advantage of the disorder caused by the slaughter and arson, they were all to rush to join Catiline . . . **44.1** The

Allobroges, on Cicero's instructions, were introduced to the others by Gabinius. They demanded that Lentulus, Cethegus, Statilius and Cassius too give them an oath, which they would send sealed to their countrymen, as otherwise they would be reluctant to be drawn into so grave an affair. **2** The others gave it without suspicion, though Cassius promised to come to Gaul himself soon and left Rome before the envoys. **3** Lentulus sent a certain Titus Volturcius from Croton with them, so that before they proceeded homewards the Allobroges might confirm the alliance by exchanging pledges with Catiline.

12.20 Sallust *Conspiracy of Catiline* 49.1–4: An attack on Caesar

Cicero made arrangements for the conspirators to be arrested at the Mulvian bridge in the early hours of 3 December. On that day, Cicero delivered his *Against Catilinam III* before the people. In the senate on 4 December, Crassus was implicated in the plot by one of the conspirators, but on the motion of Cicero the senate voted that the information was false. Enemies of Caesar, such as Catulus (cf. doc. 3.22), tried to implicate him as well.

1 At the same time Quintus Catulus (cos. 78) and Gaius Piso (cos. 67) tried in vain, by entreaties, influence and bribes, to persuade Cicero to have a false accusation brought against Gaius (Julius) Caesar either through the Allobroges or through some other witness. **2** For both were bitter personal enemies of Caesar; Piso, when on trial for extortion, had been charged by him with unjustly executing a man from Transpadane Gaul, while Catulus' hatred arose out of his candidature for the pontificate, because he had reached a ripe old age and attained the highest offices but was beaten by Caesar, who was still a young man. **3** Moreover, it seemed an opportune time as Caesar, through his pre-eminent generosity in private life and lavish entertainments in office, was heavily in debt. **4** But they were unable to incite the consul to so monstrous a crime . . .

12.21 Sallust *Conspiracy of Catiline* 51.43: Caesar on the conspirators

Cicero was unsure how to deal with the conspirators, and Plutarch has Cicero's wife, Terentia, bringing him news of a good omen that decided him (doc. 7.86). The senate on 5 December voted that the conspirators were guilty of treason. The consul-elect, Junius Silanus, argued that they should be executed, as did subsequent speakers, but he changed his mind after Caesar, as praetor-elect, argued for confiscating their property and sentencing them to life-long imprisonment in Italian cities; Cato then successfully argued for their execution, emerging as a leader of the optimates on this issue. On Cato's motion, Cicero was acclaimed *pater patriae*, Father of his Country.

'Am I then advising that the prisoners be allowed to leave and augment Catiline's army? Certainly not! My view is this, that their properties should be confiscated and that they should be kept imprisoned in the strongest municipia, and that no one in future should refer the matter to the senate or bring it before the people; should anyone act against this, they should be considered by the senate as conspiring against the state and public safety.'

12.22 Sallust *Conspiracy of Catiline* 55.2–6: The public prison (carcer)

On the night of 5 December the principal conspirators met their deaths. Cicero announced to the crowd in the forum, 'They have lived' (Plut. *Cic.* 22.4). The prison (Rome's only public one) was located on the west side of the comitium; it was of stone and had two levels, one underground, of 7 metres diameter, reached only through an opening in the ceiling. It was a place of execution, primarily for non-citizens; defeated enemy leaders would be incarcerated here after being paraded in a triumph and then were usually strangled.

2 Cicero himself, after setting guards, led Lentulus to the prison; the praetors did the same for the others. **3** In the prison there is a place which is called the Tullianum, when you have gone up a little way towards the left, about 12 feet below ground. **4** Walls enclose it on all sides and it has a vaulted stone roof: its neglected condition, darkness and stench make it hideous and terrifying to behold. **5** After Lentulus was let down into this place, the executioners carried out their orders and strangled him with a noose. **6** Thus that patrician, from the illustrious family of the Cornelii, who had held consular authority at Rome, met an end befitting his character and actions. Cethegus, Statilius, Gabinius and Caeparius suffered the same punishment.

12.23 Sallust *Conspiracy of Catiline* 60.7–61.9: Catiline's stand

News of the execution of the conspirators led many in Catiline's force to desert. He attempted to escape with the remainder, by forced marches, to Cisalpine Gaul, but Q. Caecilius Metellus Celer (proconsul of Cisalpine Gaul in 62) blocked his escape with three legions. On the approach of C. Antonius, Catiline decided to meet him in battle.

60.7 When Catiline saw his troops routed and that he was left with just a few men, he rushed, mindful of his family and former rank, into the thickest of the enemy and was pierced through and through as he fought. **61.1** Once the battle was over, you could clearly perceive the audacity and resolution possessed by Catiline's army. **2** For almost every man covered with his lifeless body the position he had taken when alive at the start of the fighting. **3** True, a few in the centre, whom the praetorian cohort had dispersed, were lying a little way away from the rest, but all their wounds were in front. **4** Catiline, indeed, was found far in advance of his men among the corpses of his enemies, still breathing slightly and retaining on his face the ferocity of spirit he had possessed in his lifetime. **5** Finally, out of the entire army, no free-born citizen was captured either during the battle or in flight; **6** all of them put the same value on their own lives as on those of the enemy. **7** The army of the Roman people had won a victory that was neither a cause for rejoicing nor bloodless. All the best fighting men had either fallen in battle or had come away with serious wounds. **8** Indeed, many, who had left the camp to view the battlefield or to look for booty, when they turned over the enemy's corpses, found now a friend, now a guest, now a relative; similarly some recognised their personal enemies. **9** And so the entire army was moved with joy and sorrow, mourning and rejoicing.

CICERO AND HIS TIMES

12.24 Pliny *Natural History* 7.116–17: Pliny's view of Cicero

Pliny is here reviewing Romans of intellectual eminence, such as Ennius, Vergil and Varro. L. Roscius Otho in 67 (as tr. pl.) reserved 14 rows in the theatre for the equites; this was always unpopular and in 63 led to rioting.

116 But on what grounds could I be silent about you, Marcus Tullius? By what distinctive mark can I make known your supreme eminence? By what, in preference to the most abundant testimony of the decree of that whole nation, selecting out of your whole life just the achievements of your consulship? **117** Your oratory induced the tribes to reject the agrarian law – their own livelihood; your persuasion induced them to excuse Roscius, the proposer of the law about the theatre, and to endure with equanimity being marked out by a distinction of seats; your plea made the children of the proscribed ashamed of standing for office; your genius turned Catiline to flight; you proscribed Mark Antony. Hail, you who were the first to be titled Father of your Country (*pater patriae*), first winner of a civilian triumph and crown of honour for oratory, and parent of eloquence and of Latin letters, and – as your former enemy, the dictator Caesar, wrote of you – winner of a laurel crown greater than that of any triumph, since it is much more important to have advanced the frontiers of the Roman mind than those of Rome's empire.

12.25 Macrobius *Saturnalia* 2.1.10–13, 3.2, 3.5: Cicero's human side

Vatinius (tr. pl. in 59) was elected consul with Q. Fufius Calenus in September 47 for the remainder of that year. For Cicero's biting wit, see also doc. 13.54.

1.10 First I would like to remind you of two very eloquent men of olden times, the comic poet Plautus and the orator Tullius (Cicero), who were both outstanding in the wittiness of their jokes . . . **12** What Cicero could do in this way is well known to anyone who has taken the trouble to read the collection his freedman (Tiro) made of his patron's jokes, which some ascribe to Cicero himself. Similarly, who does not know that his enemies used to call him that 'consular buffoon'? – as Vatinius actually does in his own speech. **13** Indeed, would it not take too long, I would remind you of the cases in which, in his defence of the most guilty clients, he won victory by a joke; for example, when he was defending Lucius Flaccus, accused of extortion, and got him off clearly proved charges through an opportune witticism . . .

3.2 When Marcus Cicero was dining with Damasippus, who produced a mediocre wine with the words 'Try this Falernian – it's 40 years old', Cicero replied, 'It carries its age well.' . . . **5** The consulship of Vatinius, which lasted only a few days, gave Cicero plenty of opportunities for exercising his sense of humour in some widely publicised sayings: 'A great portent has occurred in Vatinius' term of office', he said, 'because in his consulship there has been neither winter, spring, summer nor autumn.' And when Vatinius asked him why it had been too much trouble for Cicero to visit him when he was ill, he replied, 'I intended to come when you were consul, but night overtook me.' However, Cicero was thought to have been getting his revenge here, recalling the retort made by Vatinius to his boast that he had returned from exile carried in triumph on the shoulders of the people: 'Then where did you get those varicose veins?'

12.26 Cicero *On Divination* 1.20–21: Cicero 'On his consulship'

Prophecies of disaster made in 65 were supposedly fulfilled during Cicero's consulship; here Quintus quotes his brother's poem *On My Consulship* to prove the value of divination (the Muse Urania is speaking).

Then who, perusing the records and volumes of the diviners' art,
Failed to bring to light the mournful prophecies written by the Etruscans?
All seers uttered warnings to beware the destruction and ruin
Plotted against the nation by men of aristocratic birth
Or proclaimed the overthrow of law in continual prophecies,
And ordered that the temples of the gods and city
Be snatched from the flames and frightful butchery and slaughter be feared;
And these would be fixed and resolved by inexorable destiny
Unless first, high on a column, with handsome form,
A sacred statue of Jupiter faced to the east;
Then would the people and revered senate be able to discern
Hidden plans, if, turned to the rising sun,
It should behold from its station the seats of the senators and people.
This statue was long postponed with many delays
Till with you as consul it was placed at last in its lofty position,
And just at the moment of time fixed and predicted
Jupiter exhibited his sceptre on his elevated column
And the destruction prepared for our fatherland by flame and sword
Was revealed to senate and people by Allobrogian voices.

12.27 Cornelius Nepos *Life of Atticus* 1.1–2.6, 4.3–5.2, 6.1–7.3:
Titus Pomponius Atticus

Atticus, banker, editor and patron of literature, was a lifelong friend of Cicero and other statesmen. He remained an equestrian, never accepting a magistracy or political position, but was hugely influential because of the sums of money he loaned to individual politicians and municipalities and as business manager to luminaries such as Cicero, Hortensius and Cato. Cicero's *On Friendship* was dedicated to him, and he wrote a book on Cicero's consulship (now lost). Born in 109, he died in 32, deliberately starving himself to death in a terminal illness. His sister was wife to Quintus Cicero, his daughter wife of Agrippa. For his long-term friendship with both Augustus and Mark Antony, see doc. 14.38.

1.1 Titus Pomponius Atticus, who was descended from the earliest Roman families, always maintained the equestrian rank he had inherited from his ancestors.

2 His father was committed to business and, for those times, rich, as well as especially devoted to literature. Because of his own love of letters, he educated his son in all the areas of study in which the young should be engaged. **3** The boy, moreover, possessed, in addition to an aptitude for learning, an extremely attractive enunciation and mode of speaking, so that he not only learnt his tasks quickly but also declaimed them superbly. Consequently in childhood he was pre-eminent among his peers and outshone them more noticeably than his aristocratic fellow students were able to accept with unconcern. **4** He therefore inspired them all by his own application, among whom were Lucius Torquatus, Gaius Marius the son, and Marcus Cicero, and with all of these he formed so great an intimacy that no one was ever dearer to them than he.

2.1 His father died early. While a youth, because of his relationship by marriage with Publius Sulpicius, who was killed while tribune of the plebs (88 BC), he was himself liable to the same danger, for Anicia, Pomponius' cousin, had married Servius, Sulpicius' brother. **2** After Sulpicius was killed, however, as he saw that the state was in dissension as a result of Cinna's rebellion, and that no opportunity would be given him of living in accordance with his rank without offending one faction or the other – since the views of the citizens were polarised, with some supporting Sulla's party and the others Cinna's – he considered it an ideal time for pursuing his studious tastes and betook himself to Athens. Nonetheless, he did aid the young Marius from his funds when he was proclaimed a public enemy, and facilitated his flight with money. **3** So that his living out of Rome should not have any detrimental impact on his property, he transferred a large part of his fortune to Athens. He lived there in such a way that he endeared himself greatly to all the Athenians, and rightly so, **4** as, apart from the favours he could perform for them, which were considerable even when he was still a youth, he often used his funds to relieve their impoverishment. As an instance, when the state needed to raise money to cover a debt, and they could not do so on reasonable terms, he always stepped in and in such a way that he never charged them inequitable interest and did not let them remain in debt beyond the agreed time. **5** Both of these were to their benefit, as he did not permit their debt to grow old out of leniency or grow through the accumulation of interest. **6** He added to this service by yet another liberal gesture, for he made a distribution of grain to all of them, giving everyone 6 modii of wheat, which is equal to the measure at Athens called a medimnus. . . .

4.3 While residing here for many years, he gave his property as much care and attention as was the duty of a conscientious paterfamilias and spent all the rest of his time either on literature or on the Athenians' public business, while nonetheless neglecting services at Rome for his friends – **4** for he always used to come to Rome when they were candidates for magistracies and was present for any important undertaking. To Cicero, for example, in all his dangers he demonstrated exceptional loyalty, and when on his journey into exile gave him 250,000 sesterces. **5** When calm once again prevailed at Rome, he returned there, I believe, when Lucius Cotta and Lucius Torquatus were consuls (65 BC), and when he departed from Athens the entire citizen body of Athenians escorted him (to the ship), showing by their tears the grief at losing him for the future. **5.1**

His mother's brother was Quintus Caecilius, a Roman eques and a close friend of Lucius Lucullus, a wealthy man but hard to get on with. Atticus handled his abrasive temper so well that, although no one else could bear him, he retained his goodwill without offending him right up to extreme old age. By such behaviour he reaped the fruits of his dutifulness. **2** Caecilius at his death adopted him by will and made him his heir to three-quarters of his estate, and he received from this inheritance around 10 million sesterces. . . .

6.1 In public life he so behaved as always to be and to be considered one of the optimates faction, though he did not commit himself to the turbulence of civil disturbances, as he thought that those who gave themselves up to them had no more control over themselves than people tossed by the sea's waves. **2** He did not look for magistracies, although they were open to him through either his influence or his prestige, because they could not be canvassed for in the traditional manner or won without breaking the law because of the inordinate distribution of bribes, or conducted for the good of the state without hazard, at a time when public moral values were so perverted. **3** He never went to a public auction. He never acted as a surety or contractor of taxes. He never brought an action against anyone either in his own name or in conjunction with someone else, never went to law about his own property, and never presided over a court of law. **4** He accepted the prefectures offered him by a number of consuls and praetors on condition that he did not accompany anyone to his province, being satisfied with the honour and scorning the opportunity to increase his property; he even refused to go to Asia with Quintus Cicero (61 BC), although he could have held the position of his deputy – he did not think it appropriate that after refusing to hold a praetorship he should become a praetor's attendant. **5** In this decision he was consulting not only his reputation but also his peace of mind, as he thus avoided all suspicion of misconduct. Consequently his services were more appreciated by everyone, since they saw that they stemmed from genuine courtesy rather than from fear or hope.

POMPEY'S RETURN FROM THE EAST

In 63 BC, the tribunes proposed various honours for Pompey as conqueror of the East, and Cicero organised a vote of thanksgiving. In January 62, Nepos as tribune proposed that Pompey should both be recalled to deal with Catiline and his army and be allowed to stand for the consulship in absentia. Cato as tribune opposed both measures, while Caesar as praetor supported them; violence broke out, the senate passed an *SCU* and Nepos fled to Pompey.

In 62 Clodius apparently violated the rites of the Bona Dea on 3 December, and Caesar, in whose house the rites had been conducted as praetor, divorced his wife, Pompeia (see doc. 7.87). Clodius was acquitted, but Cicero had disproved his alibi, and Clodius became his inveterate enemy. Caesar then left for Further Spain, his propraetorian province for 61. Towards the end of 62 BC, Pompey, after a public dispatch (doc. 12.32), arrived in Italy; he celebrated his triumph in 61 (doc. 12.29) and disbanded his army. He needed ratification of his Eastern acta, as well as land for his veterans (doc. 12.36). He met with considerable opposition from the senate, especially from one of the consuls for 60, Metellus Celer. By the end of 60, Pompey had failed to achieve both aims and the stage was set for his co-operation with Caesar.

12.28 Velleius Paterculus *Compendium of Roman History* 2.40.4–5: Pompey's golden crown

T. Ampius Balbus and T. Labienus were tribunes in 63 BC; Caesar supported these honours, Cato opposed them. Both Lucullus (cos. 74) and Metellus Creticus (cos. 69) had reason to feel that Pompey had robbed them of their 'gloria'.

4 In Gnaeus Pompey's absence, Titus Ampius and Titus Labienus, tribunes of the plebs, proposed a law that Pompey should be allowed, at the Circus games, to wear a golden crown and the full dress of triumphators and, at the theatre, the toga praetexta and the golden crown. But he did not venture on this privilege more than once, and this indeed was too often. For Fortune raised this man to the summit by such great leaps, triumphing first over Africa, then over Europe, and then over Asia, and the divisions of the world became so many monuments of his victory. Greatness never lacks jealousy. **5** Both Lucullus and Metellus Creticus, who remembered the affront he had received – indeed his complaint was not unjust, for Pompey had robbed him of the captive generals who were to adorn his triumph – opposed him, along with a section of the optimates, who tried to prevent Pompey's promises to the cities and the rewards for good service to him being carried out according to his wishes.

12.29 Pliny *Natural History* 7.96–99: Pompey's victories

Pompey in Pliny's view was equal not only to Alexander but even (nearly) to Hercules. Pompey's triumph lasted for two days, 28–29 September 61 BC; cf. doc. 2.60 for Pompey's immense clientela.

96 Well then, after the recovery of Sicily, he first, as one of Sulla's supporters, rose up as the state's champion, and, after the subjugation of the whole of Africa and its reduction to Roman domination, and with the title Magnus acquired as one of the spoils, though an equestrian – a thing which no one had ever done before – rode in a triumphal chariot and immediately afterwards crossed over to the West, and after erecting trophies in the Pyrenees added to his victories the subjection to Roman domination of 876 towns, from the Alps to the borders of Further Spain, and, with greater magnanimity, refrained from mentioning Sertorius. After extinguishing the civil war which was on the point of stirring up all our foreign relations, he again led triumphal chariots into Rome as an equestrian, having twice been imperator before serving as a common soldier. **97** Following this, he was sent to every sea and then to the East and brought back unending titles for his country, in the manner of those who conquer in the sacred contests (i.e., panhellenic games) – for these are not crowned themselves but crown their country; accordingly he bestowed these honours on the city in the shrine of Minerva that he dedicated from the proceeds of the spoils: Gnaeus Pompeius Magnus, imperator, after ending a 30 years' war, scattering, routing, killing and receiving the surrender of 12,183,000 persons, sinking or capturing 846 ships, receiving the surrender of 1,538 towns and forts, and subduing the lands from the Maeotians to the Red Sea, duly fulfils his vow to Minerva.

98 This is his summary of his deeds in the East. The announcement of the triumph which he held on 28 September in the consulship of Marcus Piso and Marcus Messalla (61 BC) was as follows. After liberating the sea coast from pirates and restoring the command of the sea to the Roman people, he celebrated a triumph over Asia, Pontus, Armenia, Paphlagonia, Cappadocia, Cilicia, Syria, the Scythians, Jews and Albanians, Iberia, the island of Crete, the Basternae, and in addition to these over King Mithridates and Tigranes. **99** The greatest achievement in these glorious exploits was (as he himself said in the assembly when he was speaking of his successes) to have found Asia the remotest of the provinces and to have made her a central possession of his country. If, on the other side, anyone wants to survey in a similar fashion the achievements of Caesar, who showed himself greater than Pompey, he would truly have to enumerate the whole world, which, it will be agreed, would be a task without end.

12.30 Diodorus *Library of History* 40.4: Pompey's dedication to Minerva

Pompey had his achievements in Asia inscribed and set up as a dedication; a copy of the inscription follows: Pompey the Great, son of Gnaeus, Imperator, liberated the coastline of the inhabited world and the islands this side of Ocean from the war against the pirates, having also saved from siege the kingdom of Ariobazanes (king of Cappadocia), Galatia and the lands and provinces beyond it, Asia, and Bithynia; he protected Paphlagonia and Pontus, Armenia and (Scythian) Achaea, as well as Iberia, Colchis, Mesopotamia, Sophene and Gordyene; he subdued Darius, king of the Medes, Artoles, king of the Iberians, Aristobulus, king of the Jews, Aretas, king of the Nabataean Arabs, Syria bordering on Cilicia, Judaea, Arabia, the province of Cyrene, the Achaeans, the Iozugi, the Soani, the Heniochi, all the other tribes along the coastline between Colchis and the Maeotic Sea, with their kings, nine in number, and all the nations dwelling between the Pontic and the Red Seas; he extended the frontiers of the empire to the limits of the earth; and protected, and in some cases increased, the revenues of the Roman people. After confiscating the statues and the other images of the gods, as well as the other valuables taken from the enemy, he has dedicated to the goddess 12,060 pieces of gold and 307 talents of silver.

12.31 Pompey honoured in the Greek East (67–62)

(i) ILS 9459 (from Miletopolis, Asia Minor)

The people honour Gnaeus Pompeius, son of Gnaeus, the Great, imperator for the third time, saviour and **5** benefactor of the people and of all Asia, guardian of land and sea, because of his excellence and goodwill towards them.

(ii) SIG³ 751 (from Mytilene)

The people honour their saviour and founder Gnaeus Pompeius, son of Gnaeus, the Great, imperator for the third time, who **5** destroyed those who had seized the inhabited world by his wars on both land and sea. Dorotheus, son of Hegesandros, of Olynthos made this.

CICERO AND POMPEY

12.32 Cicero *Letters to his Friends* 5.7: A letter to Pompey, April 62 BC

Pompey's reply to Cicero's letter informing him of his role in suppressing Catiline's conspiracy did not mention Cicero's actions, and Cicero here shows his disappointment; he is tactful, however, as he clearly desires to be politically close to Pompey. Cicero's 'own great goodwill' was manifested in his support for the *lex Manilia*, with its retrospective approval of the *lex Gabinia*, and in moving as consul a ten-day supplicatio for Pompey on the news of Mithridates' death and another on receipt of Pompey's dispatch.

1 From Marcus Tullius Cicero, son of Marcus, to Gnaeus Pompeius Magnus, son of Gnaeus, Imperator, greetings. I hope all is well with you and your army, as it is with me. I received immeasurable pleasure, like everyone else, from your public dispatch; for you display such a hope of peace as I, relying on you alone, have always been promising everyone. But I must tell you that your letter dealt a severe blow to your old enemies, now your new friends, who despond, cast down from their high hopes. **2** Although the letter you sent to me displays only slight indication of your regard for me, I must tell you that it was most welcome to me anyway. For in nothing do I generally take such pleasure as in the consciousness of my services to others; if these do not receive a mutual response, I am quite content that the balance of the service lies with me. I do not doubt that, if my own great goodwill towards you has not sufficiently attached you to me, the public interest will unite and bind us together.

3 So that you are not unaware of what I missed in your letter, I will write plainly, just as is demanded both by my character and by our friendship. My achievements were such that I expected some congratulatory comment in your letter for the sake of both our close relationship and the commonwealth; I suppose that you left it out for fear of giving anyone offence. But I must tell you that what I did for the country's safety is approved by the judgement and testimony of the whole world; when you arrive back, you will recognise that I acted with such policy and magnanimity as to make you well content to have me as your political ally and friend, a not much lesser Laelius to a much greater Africanus.

12.33 Cicero *On Duties* 1.77–78: Cicero compares himself and Pompey

Writing in 44 BC, Cicero quotes from his poem on his consulship, praising himself by quoting Pompey's opinion of him.

77 The truth, however, is in the verse which, I am told, the dishonest and envious attack: 'Arms, yield to the toga, victory laurels, to civic praise.' Not to mention other examples, did not arms yield to the toga when I was piloting the state? For never was the state in more serious danger or greater peace. So, as a result of my advice and diligence, the weapons, of their own accord, fell suddenly from the hands of the most desperate citizens. What achievement in war was ever so great? What triumph can be compared to it? **78** For I may boast to you, son Marcus, as to you belong the inheritance of this glory and the necessity of imitating my deeds. Indeed it was to me that Gnaeus Pompey, a man overwhelmed with praises for his exploits in war, paid this compliment in the hearing of many when he said that his third triumph would have been won in vain, unless by my services to the state he were to have somewhere to celebrate it.

12.34 Cicero *Letters to Atticus* 1.13.4: Relations cool, January 61 BC

The 'dear friend' is Pompey. Cicero's opinion will have been motivated largely by Pompey's tardiness in praising Cicero's role in the suppression of the Catilinarian conspiracy.

Your dear friend (do you know whom I'm talking about? The person about whom you wrote to me that he began to praise once he no longer dared to find fault) declares his great regard, his esteem, his affection for me, with praise on the surface, though underneath, but still visible, lies his jealousy. Without courtesy, sincerity, political influence, integrity, courage or plain speaking – but I'll write in more detail at another time, as I don't yet know enough on the subject and I dare not entrust a letter on such important matters to any sort of unknown chap.

12.35 Cicero *Letters to Atticus* 1.17.8–9: The equites and their tax contract

Cicero is writing in December 61 BC. In 62, after the Catilinarian conspiracy, in which the equites and senators had united against Catiline, Cicero developed his concept of the concordia ordinum ('concord of the orders'). In 61, two issues affected this, as Cicero describes – dispute over the law-courts and the tax contract in Asia. The request of the equites, championed by Crassus (censor in 65), who had overbid on the tax contract in Asia, was in Cicero's estimation simply 'disgraceful'.

8 We are living in a commonwealth which is feeble, unhappy and unstable. I suppose you have heard that our friends, the equites, have almost broken with the senate; for a start, they took great exception to the pronouncement under senatorial decree of a bill authorising investigation in the case of jurors who had taken bribes. While this was being voted on, I happened to be away, and, realising that the equestrian order was very annoyed, though they said nothing publicly, I criticised the senate using, as I felt, the whole weight of my reputation, giving an extremely authoritative and eloquent speech in a rather disreputable cause. **9** Now, here come further pretensions of the equites, which are almost unendurable! – and I have not only borne with these but even given them my support. Those who bought the taxes of Asia from the censors complained in the senate that they had been induced by their cupidity to make too high a bid; they asked that their contract be cancelled. I was their chief supporter, or rather first but one, for it was Crassus who urged them to make this bold demand. The whole thing is invidious – the demand is disgraceful, a confession of reckless conduct! There was terrible risk that, if they were made no concessions, they would openly break with the senate. Here, again, it was I in particular who came to their assistance and ensured that they found the senate fully attended and feeling generous, and on the Kalends of December and the following day I spoke at length about the dignity and concord of the orders (concordia ordinum). The business has still not yet been settled, but the senate's wishes are obvious. The only one who spoke against it was Metellus, the consul-elect; our hero Cato was going to speak but lost his chance as the day was not long enough.

THE EVENTS OF 60 BC

12.36 Dio *Roman History* 37.49.1–50.6: Pompey's setbacks, 60 BC

Pompey on his return to Italy divorced his wife, Mucia, and proposed marriage to the elder of Cato's nieces and the hand of the younger for his son. Cato rejected this proposal. Unfortunately, Mucia was half-sister to Metellus Celer, who, with L. Afranius, was to be one of the consuls for 60. Afranius, a novus homo from Picenum, had been a legate of Pompey's in Spain. Pompey wanted land for his veterans and employed the tribune L. Flavius to secure this. Ager publicus was to be used as well as land purchased with the Eastern revenues and was to be made available to veterans and other citizens in order to win their support. Metellus opposed the measure, and it had gone 'quite cold' by mid-60 (doc. 12.38). Metellus' opposition was such that he was dragged off to prison by Flavius, but was released when he summoned the senate there. At the end of 60, Pompey's veterans were without land and his acta in the East unratified.

49.1 Pompey arrived in Italy at this time and had Lucius Afranius and Metellus Celer appointed consuls (for 60 BC), hoping vainly that through them he would be able to achieve all that he wanted. **2** He particularly wanted some land to be granted to his soldiers and all his settlements to be ratified, but at the time he failed to achieve either of these. For the optimates, who even before this had not been on good terms with him, prevented a vote being taken; **3** and, as for the consuls themselves, Afranius (who knew more about dancing than about business) was of no assistance at all, and Metellus, angry that Pompey had divorced his sister, although he had children by her, opposed him violently in everything . . . **5** And since Pompey had annulled some of Lucullus' acts, Lucullus demanded that an investigation be made in the senate into the acts of both of them, so it could ratify whichever ones they approved of. **50.1** Cato and Metellus and all the others of the same mind strongly supported him. Accordingly, when the tribune (Lucius Flavius) who was proposing that land be granted to Pompey's men added to this measure the proposal that land be granted to all the citizens as well, so that they would more readily vote for this and ratify Pompey's acts, Metellus met every point with such opposition that, when the tribune had him thrown into prison, he then desired the senate to assemble there . . . **5** So, when Pompey could effect nothing because of Metellus and the others, he said they were jealous of him and that he would reveal this to the people, but, as he was afraid that they too might fail him and cause him greater shame, he withdrew his demands. **6** In this way he realised that he possessed no real power, but just the name and envy arising from his former authority, while in reality he received no profit from this and repented of having dismissed his legions and having put himself in his enemies' power.

12.37 Cicero *Letters to Atticus* 1.19.4–7: Cicero's stance, 60 BC

Flavius' agrarian legislation, discussed here by Cicero (15 March 60), who supported it while ensuring occupiers of the land were not disadvantaged, was thwarted by the consul Metellus Celer and other optimates. Herennius' attempts to transfer Clodius to the plebs were vetoed by the other tribunes.

4 Affairs in the city are as follows. The agrarian law is being enthusiastically pushed by the tribune Flavius, with Pompey's support, though there is nothing 'popular' about it but the proposer. From this law, with the approval of an assembly, I tried to remove everything that disadvantaged private interests; I wanted to remove from its control such land as was state land in the consulship of Publius Mucius and Lucius Calpurnius (133 BC), confirm the holdings of Sulla's settlers, and leave the people of Volaterra and Arretinum, whose land was confiscated but not allocated, in possession of their land; I did not reject one motion, that the land should be bought out of the money from abroad received from the new taxes over a five-year period. The entire proposal for land distribution is being opposed by the senate, which suspects that some new power for Pompey is sought: in truth, he has set his heart on the bill being passed. To the great gratitude of all those who are to receive the land, I am ensuring that the possessions of all private owners be confirmed; after all, this is my army, as you are well aware, the well-to-do. However, for the people and Pompey I am meeting their wishes (as I also wish to do) through purchase, which, if carefully organised, I believe could drain off the dregs of the city and repopulate Italy's desolation. But the whole affair has gone cold with the interposition of war. Metellus is certainly a good consul and a good friend of mine. The other one (L. Afranius) is such a nonentity that he doesn't know what he's purchased.

5 That is all about politics, unless you think it relates to politics that a certain Herennius, a tribune and tribesman of yours, and a totally worthless and needy chap, has begun making regular attempts to have Publius Clodius transferred to the plebs. He gets a lot of vetoes. That is all, I believe, about the commonwealth. **6** However, since the great Nones of December (5 December 63 BC), when I reached extraordinary and undying glory, joined with the ill-will and hostility of many, I have not ceased to involve myself in politics with that same greatness of mind, or to maintain the prestige I then won and undertook; but when I afterwards noted the light-mindedness and weakness of the courts, through Clodius' acquittal, and then saw how easily our friends, the tax-farmers, were separated from the senate, although not estranged from myself, and moreover how some wealthy men, I mean the fish-lovers (piscinarii), friends of yours, were not able to hide their jealousy of me, I thought I should look for greater resources and more stable protection. **7** And so, I drew Pompey, who had kept quiet for too long about my achievements, into choosing to give me in the senate, not once but on a number of occasions and at length, the credit for saving our empire and the world. That was not of such importance to me (for my achievements are neither so unknown as to need witnesses nor so doubtful as to need praise) as to the state, as there were some scoundrels who considered that some disagreement out of all this discord might arise between Pompey and myself. I have united myself with him in so close a relationship that both of us can feel safer as individuals and politically stronger by our alliance.

12.38 Cicero *Letters to Atticus* 2.1.6–8: Cicero approaches Pompey and Caesar

Cicero is writing in June 60 BC. The agrarian law is that of Flavius (tr. pl. 60). While senators were covered by provisions concerning judicial bribery, the equites were exempt from these, and Cato proposed a law in the senate to investigate jurors who had taken bribes; it was strongly opposed by the equites and dropped. Cato also opposed the equites' demand for tax relief. In 60 Caesar achieved successes in Further Spain, and Cicero hoped that he could influence Caesar, just as he felt he could influence Pompey, who had finally acknowledged Cicero's achievements of 63 (doc. 12.37).

6 You mention the agrarian law – it seems to have gone quite cold. And in a gentle sort of fashion you criticise me for my friendly relations with Pompey, though I wouldn't want you to think that I have become allied with him for my own protection; but circumstances were so constituted that any disagreement that arose between us would inevitably have occasioned major conflicts in the state. If I have in this way foreseen and taken measures against this, it is not that I have departed from my constitutionalist policy, but that he is now more constitutionally minded and has relaxed somewhat from his attempts to win popular favour. As for my achievements, which many had tried to stir him up to attack, you should be aware that he commends them far more flatteringly than his own, proclaiming that he served the state well, but that I saved it. I do not know how much his doing this is of benefit to me, but it is certainly advantageous for the state. And what if I can even make Caesar, who is certainly at the moment sailing with a favourable wind, more constitutionally minded? **7** Would that harm the state so much? Even if no one bore me any ill-will, if everyone was well disposed to me, as would be reasonable, nonetheless medicines for healing the corrupt parts of the state ought to be tried instead of cutting them out. But now, when the equites, whom I stationed on the Capitoline slope with you as their standard-bearer and chief, have abandoned the senate, with our leaders thinking that they've reached the summit of human fortune if they have bearded mullet in their fishponds which will swim up to their hands, and neglecting all other business, don't you think that I have done enough good if I succeed in stopping those who have the power from wanting to do harm?

8 Regarding our friend Cato, you do not feel for him more warmly than I do, but despite all his principles and integrity he is sometimes a nuisance politically; he voices his opinion as if he were in Plato's *Republic*, not in the sewers of Romulus' city. What can be more proper than that any juror who takes a bribe be brought to trial? Cato brought this motion and the senate agreed: the equites declare war on the senate house – not on me, for I disagreed. What could be more shameless than tax-farmers reneging on their contract? Yet the loss was worth incurring to keep the order on our side. Cato opposed and carried his point. And so, a consul is confined in prison, and one riot follows another, while not one of those who used to back me or the consuls who succeeded me in the defence of the state is of any assistance. 'So then', you ask, 'shall we keep these as mercenaries?' Why not, if we are unable to do so in any other way? Or should we act as the servants of our freedmen and even our slaves? But, as you would say, enough serious talk.

12.39 Appian *Civil Wars* 2.8.26–30: Caesar loses his triumph

When Caesar returned to Rome in mid-60 BC, Pompey's agrarian law was more or less dead, his acta had not been ratified, and his friendship with Cicero had brought no dividends. The senate, particularly Cato, had been hostile to Pompey, and Cato took the lead in opposing Caesar's request to stand for the consulship in absentia in order to hold his triumph. Caesar therefore had to disband his army and forego the triumph in order to stand for the consulship.

26 After being selected as praetor for Spain, Caesar was detained in Rome by his creditors, as he owed much more than he was able to pay off because of his expenses connected with holding office. He was reported to have said that he needed 25,000,000 sesterces in order to have nothing. **27** However, he settled with those who were importuning him, as far as he could, and went to Spain, where he paid no attention to administering the cities, arbitrating on legal cases and all other matters of that kind, as he thought these of no use in furthering his plans, but raised an army and attacked the remainder of the Spanish tribes one after another, until he had made the entire country of Spain pay tribute to the Romans. He also sent a large amount of money to Rome to the public treasury. **28** As a result, the senate granted him a triumph, and he made arrangements outside the walls for a magnificent triumphal procession during the days in which candidates for the consulship were being invited to stand and had to be present in person – anyone who entered the city was not allowed to leave again to celebrate his triumph. **29** He was extremely eager to attain the magistracy, and, as his procession was not yet ready, he sent to the senate requesting that he be allowed to work through his friends and stand in his absence, knowing that it was illegal but that it had been done by others. **30** Cato spoke in opposition and spent the final day for the presentation of candidates in making speeches. Caesar, therefore, ignored his triumph, presented himself as a candidate and waited for the election.

12.40 Cicero *Letters to Atticus* 2.3.3–4: Caesar sounds out Cicero, December 60 BC

Cicero had supported Pompey's agrarian law but opposed Caesar's (also to provide land for Pompey's veterans). The quotation is from Cicero's poem on his consulship; 'one omen is best': Hector in Homer *Iliad* 12.243.

3 The matter needs careful consideration. Either I strongly oppose the agrarian law, which will involve something of a struggle, though a praiseworthy one, or I keep quiet, which is almost the same as leaving for Solonium or Antium, or I even give it my assistance, as they say Caesar unhesitatingly expects me to do. Cornelius, Balbus I mean, came to visit me, Caesar's friend. He declared that Caesar will follow my advice and Pompey's in everything and will work to unite Crassus and Pompey. **4** This would mean my intimate association with Pompey, and even with Caesar, should I wish, reconciliation with my enemies, peace with the populace, relaxation in my old age. But I'm affected by that conclusion of mine in Book Three:

'Meanwhile the paths, which from your earliest youth
And which as consul, with courage and spirit, you sought,
Keep to these and increase your prestige and good men's praise.'

Calliope herself dictated this to me in that book in which there are many aristo-cratic sentiments, so I do not think I ought to hesitate; may I always feel: 'one omen best – to fight for your country.'

THE FIRST TRIUMVIRATE

Pompey still needed ratification of his Eastern acta and land for the veterans of his campaigns, Crassus wanted financial relief for the equites, and Caesar needed the consulship followed by a lucrative province. Caesar played the key role in bringing Crassus and Pompey together in this relationship, now known as the 'First Triumvirate', to pursue various ends. Overtures were made to Cicero but he would not join them. This association allowed the three men involved to achieve their political ends. The association lasted until Julia, Caesar's daughter, died in 54 and Crassus was killed in Parthia in 53. Pompey and Caesar remained on good terms, but Pompey's political position shifted, and his appointment with the optimates' blessing as sole consul in 52 marks the beginning of the real change in his relationship with Caesar.

12.41 Velleius Paterculus *Compendium of Roman History* 2.44.1–3: The 'First Triumvirate'

Modern scholars have referred to this alliance as the 'First Triumvirate', but this is not an ancient term: Cic. *Att.* 2.13.2 refers to a regnum (kingship), Velleius uses the term societas (partnership), and Livy *Per.* 103, speaks of a conspiratio (secret agreement). Cicero refers to Pompey's marriage to Julia as recent in a letter of May 59 (*Att.* 2.17.1).

1 It was in Caesar's consulship that the partnership in political control between him and Gnaeus Pompey and Marcus Crassus was formed which was to be so destructive to the city, to the world and, no less, at different periods, to the men themselves. Pompey's reason for supporting this plan was **2** so that his settlements in the overseas provinces, which, as I have said already, many were opposing, should finally be ratified by Caesar as consul; Caesar's was because he realised that, in making this concession to Pompey's prestige, he would increase his own and, by putting onto Pompey the ill-will arising from their joint political control, he would strengthen his own power; Crassus' was so that he might achieve, through the influence of Pompey and the power of Caesar, the pre-eminent place which he had not been able to reach on his own. **3** In addition, a marriage connection was made between Caesar and Pompey, in that Gnaeus Magnus married Julia, Gaius Caesar's daughter.

12.42 Plutarch *Life of Crassus* 7.1–4: Relations between Crassus and Pompey

Crassus and Pompey had held a joint consulship in 70 BC (docs 12.4–5). Though they were not on the best of terms, their various needs would be met by their association with Caesar.

1 Crassus was annoyed by Pompey's success in his campaigns, by the fact that he celebrated a triumph before becoming a senator, and by his being called Magnus, which means 'Great', by his fellow citizens. When on one occasion someone said, 'Pompey the Great is coming', Crassus laughed and asked 'As great as what?' **2** Accordingly he gave up all attempts to equal Pompey in military achievements and threw himself into politics, and through his hard work, advocacy in the courts, loans of money and his help in canvassing and supporting candidates for office he obtained influence and prestige rivalling that won by Pompey from his many great military expeditions. **3** They both had their own special position: when Pompey was away he had the greater reputation and influence in the city on account of his campaigns, but when he was at home he was often less important than Crassus because, owing to the arrogance and pretence of his way of life, he would avoid crowds, retire from the forum and assist only a few of those who asked him, and then with no great eagerness, so as to retain his influence the more unimpaired for use on his own behalf. **4** Crassus, on the other hand, was continually ready to be of use, never aloof or difficult to get hold of, and was always actively involved in whatever was going on, and so, by his kindness to everyone, gained the advantage over Pompey with his haughty reserve. Both men, it is said, were similarly gifted with dignity of appearance, persuasiveness of speech and grace of countenance.

CAESAR'S CONSULSHIP

Caesar's consulship was marked by a legislative programme 'more fitting for a radical tribune than a consul' (doc. 12.45). He carried through the wishes of Pompey and Crassus and then his own agenda: a military command in the West, proposed by the tribune P. Vatinius. Cicero refused to accept Caesar's overtures and did not support his land legislation or accept any of his invitations to official posts (doc. 12.46, 12.56). His opposition seems to have been a decisive factor in the adoption of Clodius as a plebeian, which paved the way for the latter's tribunate of 58 and Cicero's exile (docs 12.54–56). The triumvirate became unpopular throughout the course of the year (docs 12.50–52), with Curio prominent among the critics, and Cicero complains about the general loss of liberty (doc. 12.51).

12.43 Suetonius *Life of the Deified Julius* 19.2–20.2: 'The consulship of Julius and Caesar'

The senate, fearing that another military command would increase Caesar's popularity, assigned as provinces to the consuls of 59 the 'woods and pastures'. Bibulus' opposition to Caesar took the form of obnuntiatio (declaration of unfavourable omens) at meetings of the assembly: cf. doc. 3.75. Caesar did not allow this to interfere with his legislative programme, and Bibulus' consulship was therefore ineffective, his main achievement being to postpone the consular elections for 58.

19.2 Caesar was therefore made consul with Bibulus. For the same reason, the optimates took care that the provinces assigned the consuls-elect would be of the most trivial importance; that is, woods and pastures . . . **20.1** After taking office, Caesar's first enactment was that the daily proceedings of both the senate and the people should be collected and published. He also revived an ancient custom that, in the months when he did not have the fasces, a state officer should walk in front of him while the lictors followed behind. He proposed an agrarian bill and used force to drive his colleague from the forum when he pronounced that the omens were unfavourable, and, when his colleague made a complaint in the senate on the following day, no one could be found who was bold enough to bring a motion or express their opinion about such a disruption, although decrees had often been passed regarding lighter disturbances. Bibulus was driven to such a degree of desperation that, until the end of his magistracy, he stayed at home, merely issuing edicts that the omens were unfavourable. **2** From that time on, Caesar handled all matters of state on his own and on his own judgement, so that some humorists, when they were acting as witnesses to documents, wrote as a joke not 'done in the consulship of Caesar and Bibulus' but 'in the consulship of Julius and Caesar', putting the same man down twice by name and surname, while the following verses were soon widely circulated:

'A deed took place recently, not in Bibulus' year but Caesar's –
For I don't remember anything happening in Bibulus' consulship!'

12.44 Dio *Roman History* 38.1.1–7, 7.4–6: Caesar's agrarian legislation

Caesar as consul passed land legislation, though the tribune Flavius had failed to do so the previous year. He established a committee of 20, which Cicero refused to join (doc. 12.46). Caesar left the state property in Campania out of his initial legislation, but in May the ager Campanus was added to the legislation for distribution to 20,000 citizens. **7.4**: Caesar finally dealt with the request of the equites in 61 BC for a reduction in the price contracted for the taxes for Asia Minor, organising this through the assembly. Pompey's Eastern acta were also ratified in the assembly.

1.1 The next year Caesar wanted to grant favours to the whole people in order to make them even more firmly attached to his side. As he also wished to appear to be supporting the optimates, to avoid incurring their enmity he told them frequently that he would not propose any measure that was not in their interests; **2**

indeed, he framed a law about the land, which he wished to distribute to the whole populace, in such a way that not the slightest fault could be found with it, though he pretended that he would not introduce it if they did not wish for it. No one was able to criticise him in any way over this law, for the swollen city mob, **3** which was primarily responsible for the constant disturbances, would be channelled into work and agriculture, and most of Italy, which was now desolate, would be recolonised, so that not only those who had endured the hardships of campaign but all the others too would have sufficient means to live on, while this would involve no expense for the city or loss to the optimates, many of whom would acquire both dignity and office. **4** He wished to allocate all the public land except for Campania (which he advised them to keep separate as state property because of its excellence) and told them to purchase the rest, not from anyone who was unwilling nor for a price desired by the land commissioners, but firstly from those willing to sell and secondly for the same price as that assessed in the tax registers. **5** He stated that they had a large amount of surplus money from the booty taken by Pompey and from the tributes and taxes recently established, and that they should, in so far as it had been acquired through the dangers faced by citizens, spend it on these same persons. **6** In addition, he proposed that there should be not just a few land commissioners, so as to appear like an oligarchy, nor should they be people who had to give an account of their conduct in office, which might displease someone, but firstly that there should be 20, so the honour should be shared, and secondly that they should be the most suitable men, except for himself. **7** For he insisted on this at the beginning, so he might not be thought to be proposing a measure to his own advantage; he himself was satisfied, so he said, with planning and proposing the measure, though he was clearly doing a favour to Pompey, Crassus and the rest. . . .

7.4 In this way Caesar won the support of the populace, while he gained that of the equites by releasing them from one-third of the taxes for which they had contracted; they were responsible for all tax collection and, though they had often asked the senate for some satisfaction, had not been successful because Cato and others opposed it. **5** When Caesar had won over this class, encountering no protests, he first ratified all Pompey's settlements, with no opposition from Lucullus or anyone else, and then enacted many other measures without resistance. **6** Not even Cato objected, although, when he was praetor a little while later, he would never mention the title of Caesar's laws, because they were called 'Julian'; for, although he followed them in allocating the courts, he most ridiculously concealed their name.

12.45 Plutarch *Life of Julius Caesar* 14.1–13: Caesar's methods as consul

When Caesar's land legislation (the *lex Julia agraria*) was opposed in the senate, he took it to the comitia tributa. Bibulus (with the assistance of three tribunes) unsuccessfully opposed it. The legislation was passed with violence, while Cato was almost hauled off to prison. On the next day Bibulus attempted to have the law annulled in the senate, but it would not act. He then kept to his house, observing the omens for the remainder of his consulship and declaring them unfavourable, so that technically the assembly could not meet (the obnuntiatio) and Caesar's legislative activities were therefore invalid.

1 So Caesar, supported and defended by the friendship of Crassus and Pompey, put himself forward for the consulship; **2** once he was triumphantly elected with Calpurnius Bibulus and had entered upon his office, he immediately proposed laws more fitting for a radical tribune than a consul, bringing forward measures for the allocation and distribution of land. **3** When the respectable elements in the senate opposed him, this gave him just the pretext he needed and, protesting loudly that he was being driven to the assembly against his will, and forced by the insolence and intransigence of the senate to pay court to it, he hurried there. **4** After placing Crassus on one side of himself and Pompey on the other, he asked them if they approved of his laws. When they declared that they did, he called on them to assist him against those who were threatening to oppose him with swords. **5** They promised to do this, and Pompey added that he would meet swords with a sword and shield too. **6** The nobility were irritated by this rash and childish speech, unworthy of his own dignity and unsuited to the respect due to the senate, but the people were delighted.

7 Caesar went on to obtain an even greater claim to Pompey's influence, as he had a daughter, Julia, engaged to Servilius Caepio, whom he now engaged to Pompey, saying that he would give Servilius Pompey's daughter, though she too was not unengaged, but had been promised to Faustus, son of Sulla. **8** And shortly afterwards Caesar married Calpurnia, Piso's daughter, and had Piso made consul for the following year, at which Cato protested violently, crying out that it was unendurable to have the government prostituted by marriage alliances and men promoting each other to provinces, armies and offices by the means of women.

9 As Caesar's colleague Bibulus achieved nothing in his efforts to obstruct Caesar's laws and was often in danger, with Cato, of being killed in the forum, he shut himself up at home for the rest of his term. **10** Straight after his marriage, Pompey filled the forum with armed men and assisted the people in ratifying the legislation and granting Caesar Gaul on both sides of the Alps for five years, along with Illyricum and four legions. **11** When Cato tried to speak against these measures, Caesar had him led off to prison, imagining that he would appeal to the tribunes; **12** but when he walked off without a word and Caesar saw that not only were the nobles displeased, but that the people out of respect for Cato's excellent qualities were following him in silence with downcast faces, he secretly asked one of the tribunes to have him released. **13** Of the rest of the senators, only a very few used to attend Caesar's meetings in the senate; the rest showed their disapproval by staying away.

12.46 Cicero *On the Consular Provinces* 40–41: Cicero rebuffs Caesar

There was to be a board of 20 on the land commission (doc. 12.44), which Cicero was invited to join. He here refers to a Board of Five, presumably a sub-committee of the 20.

He had refused to join the triumvirate in December 60 (doc. 12.40) and now refused to join the Five, considering that it was this refusal that aroused Caesar's hostility towards him. Cicero also refused the position of Caesar's legate in Gaul and, in April 59, the offer of an ambassadorship to Egypt.

40 I think it relevant here, to prevent my being frequently interrupted by some people or condemned in the thoughts of those who are silent, to explain briefly the nature of my relations with Caesar. In the first place I will make no mention of that time when we were all young men and were very intimate with him – myself, my brother and my cousin Gaius Varro. After I became deeply involved in politics, my opinions differed from his, but, despite our differences, we still remained united by friendship. **41** As consul he brought in measures in which he wanted me to participate; while I did not approve of these, I had, however, to feel pleased with his opinion of me. He asked me to be one of the Commission of Five; he wanted me to be one of the three consulars most closely allied to himself; he offered me any ambassadorial role I wished, with whatever privileges I might choose. I rejected all these offers, not because I was ungrateful, but because I remained true to my own convictions.

12.47 Cicero *Letters to Atticus* 2.16.2: Cicero on Caesar's consulship

This letter dates to late April or early May 59 BC. The three tribunes who opposed Caesar's land legislation were entitled to veto it but did not have the chance to do so because of the violent nature of the assembly. Pompey refused to comment on the issue; Cicero's quotation is from a play by Sophocles.

I have absolutely no idea what our friend Gnaeus (Pompey) is planning at the moment,

'For he no longer blows on little pipes,
But with wild gusts without a mouthband'

since it's been possible to bring him even to these lengths. Until now he has quibbled, saying that he approves of Caesar's laws but that Caesar himself has to be responsible for his own actions; that he was in favour of the agrarian bill, but whether vetoes were possible or not was in no way his concern; that he was in favour of finally settling the case of the Alexandrian king, but whether Bibulus had been observing the sky was not for him to inquire into; regarding the tax-farmers, he had wanted to do that order a favour, but wasn't able to foretell what might happen if Bibulus went down to the forum on that occasion.

12.48 Cicero *On his House* 41: 'Certain political matters'

Publius Clodius Pulcher had been quaestor in Sicily in 61–60 BC. His transfer to the plebeians from the patrician class in 60, so he could stand for the tribunate, proposed by the tribune C. Herennius, had been vetoed by other tribunes and opposed by his brother-in-law Metellus Celer as consul (doc. 12.37). Cicero claimed that it was something which he himself had said in his defence of his colleague Antonius Hibrida (cos. 63), who was being prosecuted for extortion as proconsul in Macedonia (62–61 BC), that led Caesar to engineer the adoption of Clodius. Cicero later complained that the transfer was illegal (and hence Clodius' legislation was invalid: doc. 12.49).

It was perhaps at the sixth hour of the day that, in a case in which I was defending Gaius Antonius, my colleague, I made a complaint about certain political matters which seemed to me to impact on my poor client's case. Scoundrels reported this to certain worthy gentlemen in terms very different from those I had actually used. At the ninth hour of that very same day your adoption occurred.

12.49 Cicero *In Defence of Sestius* 15–16: 'This loathsome and monstrous beast'

Caesar and Pompey presided over the adoption as a means of silencing Cicero, who immediately retired to his country estates. Cicero here claims that Pompey bound Clodius not to harm Cicero's interests, but he later stated that Pompey 'showed more concern for restoring me (from exile) than for keeping me here' (doc. 13.35).

15 Gnaeus Pompey, a most illustrious man and one who had been extremely friendly to me at a time when many people were showing me hostility, had bound Clodius by every kind of pledge, agreement and sacred oath not to act against me in any way during his tribunate . . . **16** This loathsome and monstrous beast, though bound by the auspices, tied down by ancestral custom, fettered by sacred law, was suddenly freed by a consul through a law in the comitia curiata, either, as I believe, because he was prevailed on by entreaties or, as many people considered, because he was angry with me, but certainly unaware of and not foreseeing the great crimes and evils which were hanging over our heads.

12.50 Cicero *Letters to Atticus* 2.15.1–2: 'Publius is our only hope'

This letter dates to c. 28 April 59 BC. Bibulus delayed the elections for the consulship of 58 in an attempt to undermine the triumvirate, but two associates of the triumvirs were to be finally elected in October: Gabinius (who had proposed the *lex Gabinia*) and L. Calpurnius Piso Caesoninus (Caesar's father-in-law). Publius is Clodius. Cicero earlier in April had met on the Appian Way Gaius Scribonius Curio (Curio the Younger), who told him that Clodius was standing for the tribunate as the enemy of Caesar, and Cicero was hopeful that this would change the current political situation.

1 One thing I can't understand is how a scheme can be devised to provide enough land without anyone objecting. **2** Bibulus has shown great nobility of mind in delaying the (consular) elections, but what does it achieve except an expression of his personal opinion without any solution for the state's problems? No doubt about it, Publius is our only hope. Alright, let him become tribune, if for no other reason than to bring you back from Epirus more quickly. I don't see how you could bear to miss him, especially if he wants to pick a quarrel with me. But if anything of that kind happens, I'm sure you will fly back. Even if it doesn't, whether he wrecks or revitalises the state, I anticipate a splendid show, as long as I can watch it with you sitting beside me!

12.51 Cicero *Letters to Atticus* 2.18.1: Curio and 'our masters'

Here in June 59 Cicero laments the servitude of the times with the 'triumvirate' in place (cf. doc. 12.52). Curio the Younger was the son of the consul of 76; despite his opposition to the triumvirs in 59, in 50 he became Caesar's man.

We are mastered on all sides, and no longer object to being in servitude, but fear death and exile as worse evils, though they are much less serious. This is the present state of affairs, lamented by one universal groan but alleviated by no one's actions or words. The aim of our masters, I suspect, is to leave nothing for anyone else to bestow. The only one to speak or oppose them openly is young Curio. He gets great rounds of applause, a most prestigious amount of greetings in the forum, and a multitude of other signs of goodwill from the 'honest' men.

12.52 Cicero *Letters to Atticus* 2.19.2–3: The unpopularity of the triumvirate

In July 59 Pompey was at Capua, possibly overseeing the distribution of the ager Campanus. The ringmaster (dominus) at the gladiatorial show is unknown, perhaps Gabinius as a candidate for the consulship for 58. The Roscian law passed in 67 reserved the first 14 rows of seats in the theatre for the equites (cf. doc. 12.2–4). The grain law could be the *lex Terentia Cassia* (73 BC), dealing with the price of grain from Sicily. The threatened rescindments would punish the equites and the plebs; for the quotation from Ennius on Fabius Maximus 'Cunctator', see doc. 4.34.

2 You should be aware that there has never been anything so infamous, humiliating and uniformly hateful to all types, classes and ages of men as this current state of affairs – more, I assure you, than I wished, let alone what I expected. Those 'popular' politicians have now taught even mild-tempered people to hiss. Bibulus is in heaven, I don't know why, but he is praised as though 'one man alone by his delays restored for us the state (Ennius)'. My very dear Pompey has brought about his own ruin, which is a great grief to me. They hold no one by goodwill; I am afraid that they may find it necessary to employ fear. For my part, however, I neither fight with their party on account of my friendship with him nor assent to it, or I should be condemning all that I did earlier. I take a middle path. **3** The feeling of the people has been evident at the great theatre and shows. For, at the gladiators, both the ringmaster and his friends were greeted with hissing, and at the Games of Apollo (ludi Apollinares) the tragic actor Diphilus impudently attacked our dear Pompey: 'To our misery you are Great' – he had to encore this numerous times. 'The time will come when you will deeply rue that same manliness' – he spoke that to the applause of the entire theatre, and the rest the same. Actually these verses are such as to seem to have been written for the occasion by an enemy of Pompey. 'If neither laws nor customs can compel' and the rest were recited to immense noise and shouting. When Caesar arrived, applause died. The younger Curio followed him and got the kind of applause that Pompey used to receive in the time when all was well with the state. Caesar took it badly. A letter is said to be flying to Pompey at Capua. They are at loggerheads with the equites, who stood up to applaud Curio, they are at war with everyone; they threaten the Roscian law, even the grain law. Matters are certainly in a bad way. I would actually have preferred their undertaking to pass in silence, but I fear that that may not be possible. People won't endure it, though it seems it must be endured. But now there is just one universal cry, though united by hatred rather than the ability to oppose them.

12.53 Cicero *Letters to Atticus* 2.24.2–3: The Vettius affair

Written probably in August 59, and certainly before the consular elections in October. L. Vettius in 62 had accused Caesar of complicity in the Catilinarian conspiracy. In 59 Vettius confessed before the senate that he was plotting to kill Pompey and that the younger Curio was associated with him in the plot. He was incarcerated and died in prison, strangled or poisoned, according to the sources, on the orders of the very men who put him up to the incident. Caesar was able to exploit the affair to strengthen his relationship with Pompey and keep him apart from the optimates.

2 That chap Vettius, my old informer, clearly promised Caesar that he would find a way to bring the younger Curio under suspicion of some crime. So he wormed his way into the young man's friendship and became a close associate of his, as events make clear. He finally brought things to the point where he told him that he had decided with the help of his slaves to make an attack on Pompey and kill him. Curio carried this information to his father, and he to Pompey. **3** The affair was brought to the senate's attention. When Vettius was brought in, he denied that he had ever been friendly with Curio, at least not for a long time; he then requested a public guarantee of safety. This was shouted down. Nevertheless he related that a band of young men existed, with Curio as leader, which initially included Paulus, Caepio (that is Brutus) and Lentulus, the flamen's son, his father being aware of this; later on Gaius Septimius, Bibulus' clerk, had brought Vettius a dagger from Bibulus. This was totally laughed down – as though Vettius could not have had a dagger unless the consul gave him one! His story was all the more disbelieved, because on the 13th Bibulus himself had informed Pompey to watch out for a plot, for which Pompey had thanked him. When the younger Curio was brought in, he replied to Vettius' statements, and Vettius was particularly criticised for stating that the plan of the young men had been to attack Pompey during Gabinius' gladiatorial show in the forum, and that Paullus was one of the leaders, as it was well known that he was then in Macedonia. A senatorial decree was passed that Vettius, since he had admitted to having a weapon, should be put in chains and any person who let him go would be acting against the interests of the state. The general view is that the original idea was for Vettius to have been arrested in the forum with his dagger, together with his slaves with their weapons, and that he would then have asked to turn informer. And that's what would have happened if the Curios had not taken the affair to Pompey beforehand.

CLODIUS AND CICERO

In assisting Clodius' transfer to the plebs, Pompey and Caesar must have realised that he would stand for the tribunate (cf. docs 12.49–50). But it appears that they did not want him to stand for 58 BC. In April, Clodius was promised an embassy to Egypt (it actually went to someone else) and offered another to Tigranes (possibly to have him out of Rome for the tribunician elections in July). He did not take it up and did not receive a place on the agrarian commission of 20. Cicero in April sees Pompey and Caesar as keeping Clodius' tribunate in reserve for the time when it will suit them and hears hints from Curio that there might be a falling out among the triumvirs and their associates. However, there was no substantial rift between Pompey, Caesar and Clodius at this stage. Clodius supported the legislation of Vatinius as tribune in 59 arranging the special five-year command for Caesar (App. *BC* 2.14.53), but this law, though early in the year, cannot be precisely dated. He was elected as tribune for 58 and was to pursue an extensive legislative programme. Clodius was in no way a puppet or agent of the triumvirs: he was independent from the beginning of his tribunate and by its end had attacked and alienated Pompey and, to a lesser extent, Caesar.

12.54 Dio *Roman History* 38.12.5–13.1, 13.6: Clodius as tribune

Clodius' legislation was introduced on 1 January 58 BC and became law on 4 January. Sulla had abolished Gaius Gracchus' grain law, and the *lex Terentia Cassia* of 73 BC had revived it in some form; Cicero emphasises the cost of Clodius' law to the treasury. Many of the guilds, collegia, were abolished in 64 by the senate; they could play an important role in elections. Censors had the right to revise the roll of senators and to expel members; Clodius' law meant that the senator involved had to be present, allowing the senator the right of defending himself (clearly designed to seek senatorial support). Gabinius and Piso had become consuls for 58, and both supported Clodius: Gabinius was given command of Cilicia (later changed to Syria) and Piso of Macedonia. Clodius also abolished the taking of the auspices for assemblies, permitting assemblies to meet on dies fasti (see doc. 3.30), obviously in reaction to Bibulus' activities in 59.

12.5 Cicero irritated numerous people with his speeches, and those whom he helped were not so much won over to his side as those who were injured were alienated . . . **6** he also made himself some very bitter enemies by always trying to get the better of even the most powerful men and by always employing an uncontrolled and excessive freedom of speech towards everyone alike in his pursuit of a reputation for intellect and eloquence above anyone else's, even in preference to being thought a worthy citizen. **7** As a result of this, and because he was the greatest boaster alive and considered no one his equal, but in speeches and life alike despised everyone and thought no one on the same footing as himself, he was a trial and a burden to others and was accordingly envied and hated even by those who were otherwise in sympathy with him. **13.1** So Clodius hoped that he could soon deal with him if he first won over the senate, equites and people, and straightaway started distributing free grain (for now Gabinius and Piso had become consuls he introduced a bill for its being handed out to the poor) and revived the associations called collegia in Latin, which had existed in ancient times but been disbanded for some time; he also forbade the censors to remove anyone from any order or censure anyone without his being tried and convicted before both censors . . . **6** Clodius also, afraid that if he indicted Cicero some people might use this method of postponing or delaying the trial, introduced a measure that none of the magistrates might observe signs from the heavens on days on which the people had to vote on anything.

12.55 Dio *Roman History* 38.17.1–6: Cicero leaves town

After Clodius had passed his legislation, he turned on Cicero, who had preferred to stay in Rome rather than join Caesar's staff, and had a law passed forbidding fire and water to anyone who had put citizens to death without a trial. Cicero therefore went into voluntary exile, and Clodius immediately passed a law which both mentioned Cicero explicitly by name and forbade any further discussion of the matter. Cicero's house was demolished, and a shrine to Libertas (Liberty) was erected on the site by Clodius.

1 However, Caesar (who was outside the walls, as he had already taken charge of his army, so Clodius assembled the populace there to allow him to arbitrate on the proposal) condemned the illegality of the actions taken regarding Lentulus **2** but did not approve the proposed punishment; he stated that everyone knew what he had thought about events at the time (for he had voted to spare their lives), but it was not appropriate for such a retrospective law to be drawn up now. **3** This was Caesar's view, and Crassus gave some support to Cicero through his son but sided himself with the populace. Pompey kept promising Cicero help but, by making various excuses at different times and deliberately leaving town on frequent trips, did nothing to assist him. **4** When Cicero perceived this, he was afraid and again attempted to carry weapons (among other things openly castigating Pompey), but was prevented from doing this by Cato and Hortensius in case a civil war should eventuate, and he departed unwillingly with the disgrace and dishonour of having chosen to go into exile. **5** Before he left, he went up to the Capitol and dedicated a small statue of Minerva, whom he called 'Protectress'. He slipped away to Sicily, for he had been governor there and had great hopes of honourable treatment from its towns and citizens. **6** On his departure the law came into force, not only with no opposition but, once he was out of the way, with the support among others of those who had seemed to be Cicero's chief adherents. His property was confiscated, and his house destroyed, as though an enemy's, and its site dedicated for a temple to Liberty. A decree of exile was passed against Cicero himself, and his stay in Sicily was prohibited; he was banished 3,750 stades from Rome, and it was proclaimed that, should he ever be found inside this limit, both he and those who received him could be killed with impunity.

12.56 Velleius Paterculus *Compendium of Roman History* 2.45.1–2: Clodius' hatred for Cicero

For Clodius' profanation of the rites of the Bona Dea, see doc. 7.87; Cicero disproved his alibi, but he was acquitted. For Caesar's invitation to Cicero to join the land commission, see doc. 12.46.

1 At about the same time Publius Clodius, a man of noble family, a skilful speaker and man of audacity, who knew no limits in speech or action except his own wishes, passionate in the execution of his evil schemes, notorious too for his affair with his sister, and who had been brought to trial for his profanation of the Roman people's most sacred rites, since he felt a violent hatred for Marcus Cicero (for what friendship could there be between men so different?) and had had himself transferred from the patricians to the plebs, proposed a law as tribune that whoever had put a Roman citizen to death without a trial should be forbidden fire and water (i.e., exiled): although Cicero was not expressly named, he alone was the target. **2** And so this man, who had deserved the best from the state, won the calamity of exile as his reward for saving his country. Caesar and Pompey were not free from the suspicion of having been involved in Cicero's downfall. Cicero seemed to have brought this on himself by having refused to be one of the commission of 20 men in charge of distributing the land in Campania.

CATO THE YOUNGER IN CYPRUS

Before Cicero's exile, Clodius had proposed that Cyprus, the property of Ptolemy, the brother of Ptolemy XII Auletes of Egypt (recognised by Rome in 59 BC), be annexed. A little later (the chronology is imprecise), Clodius moved a second law to send Cato to Cyprus to administer the annexation of the island and to reinstate exiles at Byzantium (docs 12.58, 59). The revenues from Cyprus would offset the cost of his grain law. Cicero states that Clodius chose Cato because he wanted both Cicero and Cato out of the way (doc. 12.58), but Plutarch's comment that Cicero's exile would be effected only with Cato's absence is incorrect (doc. 12.59). Cato had counselled Cicero to acquiesce in going into exile, to avoid a civil war, and had not objected to Clodius' legislative programme.

12.57 Cicero *In Defence of Sestius* 59–63: Cato in Cyprus

The commission to Cyprus was clearly a prestigious one, and Cato went to Cyprus willingly as quaestor pro praetore. Ptolemy committed suicide in Cyprus, and Cato realised nearly 7,000 talents for Rome, receiving a triumphant reception on his return to the city. **63**: Cato, along with other senators, had not attended senate meetings called by Caesar as consul in protest against the violence of the latter's methods.

59 That unfortunate king of Cyprus, who had always been our friend, our ally, about whom no damaging suspicion had ever been brought to the attention of the senate or our commanders, saw himself with his own eyes, as they say, being auctioned off with every scrap of food and clothing . . . **60** Their aim in this business was to put a blot on the reputation of Marcus Cato, being unaware of what strength lies in seriousness of character, in integrity, in greatness of soul and, lastly, in that excellence which remains calm in tempestuous storms, which shines in darkness, which, even when shaken, remains unmoved and steadfast in its proper place, and which always gleams with its true light and is never diminished by other people's baseness. Their intention was not to honour Marcus Cato but to exile him, not to entrust that task to him but to impose it on him, for they openly stated in the assembly (contio) that they had torn out Marcus Cato's tongue, which had always spoken unrestrainedly against extraordinary commands . . . **61** When I was consul, at which time he was tribune-elect of the plebs, he put his life in hazard; he expressed that opinion for the unpopularity of which, he saw, he would have to take responsibility at the risk of his life; he spoke with vehemence, he acted with spirit; he expressed clearly what he felt; he was leader, instigator, prime mover of those measures – not that he did not see the danger to himself, but in such a storm threatening the state he thought that he should consider nothing but the danger to his country . . . **62** If he had refused the command, do you doubt that violence would have been done to him, since all the measures of that year would have seemed in the process of being overthrown by that one man? . . . **63** For could a man who had failed to attend senate meetings in the previous year – though if he had attended, he could at least have seen me as one of the supporters of his political opinions – could he have remained calmly in Rome once I had been banished and in my name the entire senate and his own stance been condemned?

12.58 Cato and Cicero as exiles

Cicero paints Cato as an exile like himself, believing that his own exile redounded to his credit because it came about through his role in suppressing the Catilinarian conspiracy. While deploring Caesar's refusal to interfere with his exile, Cicero here in (iii), in April 49 BC, puts the blame on Pompey.

(i) Cicero On his House *65*

So the hated Marcus Cato is banished to Cyprus, as if in receipt of a favour. Scoundrels were unable to endure the sight of two people, and these were driven out, one by being granted a distinction which was the deepest insult, the other by a disaster which redounded very much to his credit.

(ii) Cicero In Defence of Sestius *56*

Exiles who had been convicted were brought back from Byzantium at a time when citizens who had not been convicted were driven out of Rome.

(iii) Cicero Letters to Atticus *10.4.3 (14 April 49 BC)*

The one (Caesar) who once would not even raise me up when I prostrated myself at his feet declared that he could do nothing against the other's (Pompey's) wishes.

12.59 Plutarch *Life of Cato the Younger* 34.3–7: Cato neutralised?

3 Clodius could not expect to overthrow Cicero with Cato in Rome, but, as he was plotting for this more than anything else, when he entered on the tribunate he summoned Cato and told him that, as he considered him the man of most integrity among all the Romans, he was ready to prove this by his actions. **4** Though many were requesting the command concerning Cyprus and Ptolemy and begging to be sent, he considered only Cato worthy of it and offered him this favour with pleasure. **5** When Cato protested that the affair was a trick and an insult, not a favour, Clodius replied with arrogance and contempt, 'Well, if you do not consider it a favour, you will go on it as a disfavour', and he immediately went before the people and had a law passed sending Cato on the mission. **6** And when he set out, Clodius gave him not a ship, nor a soldier, nor an assistant, but only two secretaries, one of whom was a thief and total rascal and the other one of Clodius' clients. **7** And, as if he had imposed just a small task on him with Cyprus and Ptolemy, he also instructed him to restore the exiles of Byzantium, as, while he was tribune, he wished Cato to be out of the way for as long as possible.

CICERO'S RETURN

With Cicero exiled and Caesar absent, Clodius in 58 began attacking Pompey's acta. Clodius' arrangements for Cyprus had interfered with Pompey's Eastern settlement but at that stage were not the cause of any friction. However, Clodius freed Tigranes, the son of the king of Armenia, held hostage for Pompey in the house of L. Flavius (doc. 12.60). A skirmish on the Appian Way in which Pompey's adherents attempted to regain the hostage resulted in the death of Papirius, one of Pompey's followers. A riot broke out at Rome, and Gabinius' fasces as consul were smashed, his followers were wounded, and Clodius consecrated his property to the gods. The other consul, Piso, supported Clodius and was himself wounded. On 11 August, a slave of Clodius was apprehended with a dagger outside the senate and confessed to attempted murder: Pompey thereafter retired to his house. Clodius also brought Bibulus into the assembly to affirm that he had been observing the heavens when Caesar's legislation was passed, therefore technically invalidating it.

Pompey, in reaction to Clodius' attacks, sought to recall Cicero to help him against Clodius, hoping that Cicero would not speak against the triumvirate. Already in 58 (unsuccessful) moves had been made by two tribunes (Ninnius and Culleo) to recall Cicero from exile, and on 29 October eight tribunes supported his recall, but the tribunician veto was applied. Cicero's recall from exile was effected in 57 through the agency of eight of the tribunes, with two tribunes once again opposed (Serranus and Numerius Rufus): he returned to a tumultuous welcome on 4 September 57.

12.60 Dio *Roman History* 38.30.1–39.8.3: Cicero recalled

On 1 January 57 a senatorial resolution concerning Cicero's recall was frustrated by a tribune, and on 23 January a tribunician bill put to the assembly ended in bloodshed when Clodius' brother Appius Claudius supplied gladiators he had on hand for funeral games. For the rest of the year there were clashes between Milo and Clodius and their followers; Milo also made use of gladiators. The senate decreed in July that a law about Cicero's recall be brought before the comitia centuriata (doc. 12.61); the senate, attended by 417 members, was unanimous except for one vote, that of Clodius, who spoke against Cicero when the bill was put to the comitia on 4 August 57, but it was passed. There is a lacuna (gap) in the manuscript at 39.6.2.

38.30.1 Cicero was not in exile for long but was recalled by Pompey, the very man who had been mainly responsible for his banishment. The reason for this was that Clodius had been bribed to seize and release Tigranes the Younger, **2** who was still imprisoned at the home of Lucius Flavius, and when Pompey and Gabinius were annoyed at this he treated them with contempt, inflicted blows and wounds on their followers, and broke the consul's fasces and confiscated his property. **3** Pompey, enraged at this, especially because of the way Clodius was using against him the authority which he had himself restored to the tribunes, determined to recall Cicero and immediately began to work through Ninnius for his restoration . . .

39.6.1 While this was happening in Gaul, Pompey had put Cicero's return to the vote. The man he had used Clodius to drive out he now brought back to help him against that very same person! – so swiftly does human nature sometimes alter, with men receiving the very opposite treatment from those people from whom they expect assistance or injury. **2** He was supported by some of the praetors and tribunes, including Titus Annius Milo, who brought the proposal before the populace. Spinther the consul was acting partly as a favour to Pompey and partly to take vengeance on Clodius for a private enmity . . . **3** Clodius, on his side, was supported by various magistrates, including his brother Appius Claudius, a praetor, and the consul Nepos, who had a private reason for disliking Cicero. **7.1** So now they had the consuls as leaders, these men caused even more disorder than before, as did the other people in the city as they took one side or the other. Consequently, many other forms of anarchy took place, **2** including that of Clodius, who, during the voting, as he knew the people were going to recall Cicero, got hold of the gladiators that his brother had organised for the funeral games of Marcus, his relative, and charged into the gathering, wounding many and killing many others. **3** As a result the proposal was not passed and Clodius was feared by all, both as the associate of gladiators and for other reasons. He then stood for the aedileship, hoping to avoid paying the penalty for his violence if he were elected . . . **8.1** Milo's contesting this caused great disturbance, and in the end he also gathered some gladiators and others with the same aims as himself and kept coming to blows with Clodius, with killings occurring through practically the whole city. **2** Nepos was afraid of his colleague, and of Pompey and the other leading men, and changed his stance, so the senate decreed on Spinther's motion that Cicero be recalled. The populace, on the motion of both consuls, passed the measure. **3** Clodius of course spoke against it, but with Milo as his opponent could commit no violence, and Pompey among others spoke in support of the law so that that side was much the stronger.

12.61 Cicero *Letters to Atticus* 4.1.4–5: Cicero's account of his return

Written c. 10 September 57 BC. The nomenclator was the slave employed by wealthy Romans to remember the names of associates, voters and clients. Cicero arrived in Rome on 4 September, deliberately timing his arrival to coincide with the celebration of the ludi Romani, and the next day, the Nones, he delivered his speech to the senate, in which he prided himself on the general support for his recall (cf. doc. 1.8).

4 I set out from Dyrrachium on 4 August, the very same day the law about me was voted upon. I arrived at Brundisium on the Nones of August. My dear little

Tullia was there to meet me, and it was her birthday ... On 11 August, while I was at Brundisium, I learnt from a letter from my brother Quintus that the law had been passed in the comitia centuriata to astounding demonstrations of enthusiasm from all ages and ranks and with an incredible assemblage of people from Italy. I then set out, after receiving the most distinguished attention from the people of Brundisium, and, as I journeyed, deputations gathered from all sides with their congratulations. **5** My arrival at Rome was such that there was no man of any rank known to my nomenclator who did not come to meet me, except for enemies who were unable to conceal or deny that they were my enemies. When I arrived at the Porta Capena, the temples' steps were crowded with ordinary citizens, and their welcome was marked by immense applause, while similar crowds and applause accompanied me right up to the Capitol – in the forum and on the Capitol itself the number of people was astonishing. In the senate, on the following day, the Nones of September, I expressed my thanks to the senators.

12.62 Cicero *On the Responses of the Soothsayers* 57–59: Cicero's view of Clodius

This speech was delivered in 56 BC. A strange noise had been heard near Rome, and the haruspices (soothsayers) had given interpretations of why it had occurred: Cicero argued in this speech that it was because of Clodius. He had, according to Cicero, extinguished the rites of the Claudii Pulchi by being adopted by Fonteius: this was not true, as Fonteius emancipated Clodius and he never ceased being a Claudian (Clodius also had two brothers). The Aelian and Fufian laws, of the mid-second century, regulated the use of obnuntiatio; Clodius' law to allow senators to defend themselves against expulsion from the senate is construed by Cicero as an abolition of the censorship: see doc. 12.54. The 'generals' refers to Clodius' tampering with the loyalty of Lucullus' army in Asia Minor.

57 By taking the name of Fonteius, Clodius has consigned the name, religion, memory and family of his parents to oblivion; by his inexpiable crime, he has overthrown the gods' fires, their thrones, tables, concealed and inmost hearths, and secret rites forbidden not only to the sight but even to the hearing of men; he has set on fire the shrine of those very goddesses whose aid is used in combating fires elsewhere. **58** And what can I say about his dealings with his country? Firstly, by violence, weapons and threats he drove from the city, from all the protection of his country, a citizen whom you have consistently proclaimed to be that country's saviour: next, after achieving the downfall of one whom I have always stated to be the senate's partner and whom he kept stating was its leader, he overthrew the senate itself, the originator of the state's well-being and policy, by violence, massacre and fire; he abolished two laws, the Aelian and Fufian, which were of the greatest benefit to the state; he did away with the censorship; he removed the right of veto; he annulled the auspices; he furnished consuls who were his partners in crime with funds, provinces and an army; those who were kings he sold, those who were not he named so; he drove Gnaeus Pompey from his house by armed violence; he overturned generals' monuments; he demolished his enemies' houses; he inscribed his own name on your monuments. The crimes he committed against his country are endless. And what of the individual citizens he has put to death? The allies he has severed from us? The generals he has betrayed? The armies where he has stirred up trouble? **59** Still worse, how grievous are those crimes he has committed against himself, against his own family! Who has ever treated an enemy camp worse than he has all the parts of his body? What ship on the public river has ever been so open to all traffic than his youth has been? What wastrel has ever wallowed so unrestrictedly with prostitutes as he has with his sisters? And, last of all, what Charybdis so monstrous has the creative talent of poets been able to paint which could gulp down oceans so great as the plunder of Byzantines and Brogitaruses he has swallowed up? Or what Scylla ever had dogs so conspicuous and famished as those you see him using, wretches such as Gellius, Clodius and Titius, to devour the very rostra themselves.

POMPEY'S GRAIN COMMAND, 57 BC

Cicero became reconciled with Pompey and showed his gratitude by helping to secure him an extraordinary command (the *cura annonae*) to deal with the grain shortage. After Cicero's return on 4 September, the plebs had blamed him, because of the large numbers of Italians who had come to Rome to welcome him, for a shortage of grain in Rome, and there was violence in the forum and on the Capitol; on 7 September the consul Metellus Nepos was stoned and stabbed by two of Clodius' supporters. On the next day, at a meeting of the senate which most of the consulars avoided because of the violence of the day before, Cicero proposed powers for Pompey to deal with the grain shortage. The tribune Messius' proposal of even greater powers was not accepted, though possibly reflecting Pompey's wishes. On 9 September, the senate was well attended and approved the grain law; it gave him broad powers, and he was granted 15 legates, the only known ones being Cicero and his brother Quintus. Pompey himself visited Sicily, Sardinia and Africa, collecting grain for Rome. He is known as active in this capacity for the years 57–54 (there is no evidence for 53).

12.63 Cicero *Letters to Atticus* 4.1.6–7: Pompey's command

This passage follows on from doc. 12.61 above. The 'one praetor and two tribunes' referred to here are Appius Claudius and the two tribunes opposed to Cicero's recall. Cicero was waiting for the pontiffs to rule whether Clodius' consecration of his house was valid, and so kept out of the issue as to whether Pompey should have wider powers than those proposed by the consuls. Messalla and Afranius were supporters of Pompey.

6 Two days after that (Cicero's return on 4 September), when the price of grain was extremely high and people had gathered first at the theatre and then at the senate, shouting, on Clodius' instigation, that the shortage of grain was my doing, the senate held meetings during those days about the grain supply, and Pompey was called on to superintend it, not only by the populace but also by the honest men (boni). As he himself wanted it and the crowd called on me by name to make the proposal, I did so in an elaborate speech. In the absence of all the consulars, except Messalla and Afranius, on the pretext that they thought it was not safe for them to voice an opinion, a senatorial decree ratified my proposal that Pompey should be asked to take on the commission, and a law was brought in to that effect. The decree was immediately read out, and the people applauded in the new absurd fashion when my name was mentioned. I then addressed the meeting, with the consent of all the magistrates present except for one praetor and two tribunes.

7 On the following day the senate was crowded, with all the consulars there. Nothing Pompey requested was refused. When he asked for 15 legates, he named me first and said that I should be his second self in all matters. The consuls drew up a law which gave Pompey total control over grain supplies throughout the world for a five-year period; Messius proposed another one which gave him control over all moneys and added on a fleet, an army and authority in the provinces overriding that of their governors. Our consular law now appears quite moderate; Messius' one is felt unendurable. According to himself, Pompey prefers the first, according to his friends the second. The consulars, led by Favonius, are furious. I keep quiet, all the more because the pontiffs have not yet given any reply about my house. If they declare it no longer sacred, I have an outstanding site, and the consuls, by senatorial decree, will make an estimate of the value of the building; if not, they will demolish it, let out a contract in their own name, and make an estimate for the whole.

12.64 Plutarch *Life of Pompey* 49.4–8: A secret agenda?

4 Pompey was won over by the arguments of those who thought that he ought to bring back Cicero, Clodius' greatest enemy and a great favourite with the senate, **5** and he escorted Cicero's brother, who was petitioning on his behalf, with a large force into the forum, where people were wounded and some killed, though he got the better of Clodius. **6** The law was passed, and Cicero returned and immediately reconciled Pompey to the senate, and, by his advocacy for the grain law, made him once again almost total master of all the Romans' possessions by land and sea. **7** For all harbours, trading centres, crop distributions – in a word, all goods carried by sea or produced on land – were put under his control. **8** Clodius attacked it on the grounds that the law had not been proposed because of the scarcity of grain, but that the scarcity of grain had been contrived so that the law might be proposed and Pompey's power, which was, as it were, withering away as a result of his depressed spirits, might be revitalised and restored by a new office.

12.65 Dio *Roman History* 39.9.1–3: The plebs riots

1 Cicero set aside the hatred he felt for Pompey as a result of his exile and was reconciled to him, paying him back at once for his good services. **2** A severe famine had broken out in the city, and the whole populace rushed into the theatre . . . and then to the Capitol where the senators were meeting, and threatened at first to slaughter them with their own hands and then to burn them alive, along with the temples, **3** but Cicero persuaded them to appoint Pompey as superintendent of the grain supply and also to give him for this purpose proconsular imperium for five years, both within Italy and outside of it. So now, as earlier in the matter of the pirates, Pompey was again to rule the whole world then under the power of Rome.

CAESAR IN GAUL

Events in 60 BC shifted the focus of attention towards Gaul. A revolt in 62 in Transalpine Gaul of the Allobroges, oppressed by debt (cf. doc. 12.19), was crushed in 61 by Pomptinus, the province's governor. In 60 BC, the Helvetii defeated the Aedui (allies of Rome) and planned a large-scale migration into Gaul. The senate reacted by altering the provinces allocated to the consuls, arranging that they govern the Gauls (Cisalpine and Transalpine); Metellus Celer died (April 59) without going to his province. Caesar as proconsul in 58 was allocated Cisalpine Gaul and Illyricum for five years under the *lex Vatinia*; the senate was to add Transalpine Gaul. When he arrived in Gaul in 58, the situation was at first peaceful. On 28 March 58 BC, the Helvetii (based in what is modern Switzerland) and other tribes began a mass migration. Caesar succeeded initially in blocking them by destroying the bridge across the Rhone, but they crossed the river through the territory of the Sequani. They were not in the Roman province, but Caesar pursued them. He had five legions, including two raised by recruitment in Cisalpine Gaul (bringing the total number of legions in Gaul to six). He defeated the Helvetii and forced them to resettle the lands they had abandoned.

In 57 BC, Caesar conquered most of Gaul and was voted, on the proposal of Cicero, an unprecedented 15-day supplicatio for his victories (Pompey had been awarded a ten-day supplicatio: doc. 12.31). Most of the year was spent campaigning against the Belgic tribes in north-west Gaul. Caesar's campaigns in 56 brought the rest of Gaul under Roman authority, in particular the tribes of the Atlantic coast, especially the Veneti. The following year (55) saw German tribes advance into Gaul across the Rhine; Caesar defeated them and made a show of force across the Rhine into German territory. This year and the next (54) he went to Britain, but in 54 there was an uprising in northern Gaul among the Treviri and the Eburones which continued into 53, when Caesar marched across the Rhine again. The following year, 52 BC, saw the revolt of Vercingetorix (doc. 12.91).

12.66 Cicero *Letters to Atticus* 1.19.2–3: The Gallic scare

Cicero, writing on 15 March 60, refers to three ambassadors chosen to persuade Gallic tribes not to link up with the Helvetii, who were planning their migration. The description of Lentulus as 'perfume on lentils' reflects his inadequacy for the task.

2 In politics the most important issue at present is the scare of a Gallic war. The Aedui, our brothers, have recently suffered a defeat, and there is no doubt that the Helvetii are in arms and making raids into the province. The senate has decreed that the consuls should draw lots for the two Gauls, a levy be held, all exemptions from service be cancelled, and ambassadors with full powers be sent to address the communities of Gaul and attempt to stop them uniting with the Helvetii. The ambassadors are Quintus Metellus Creticus, Lucius Flaccus and, 'perfume on lentils', Lentulus, son of Clodianus. **3** While I am on the topic, I cannot omit mentioning that, when the first lot drawn from among the consulars was mine, a crowded senate unanimously proclaimed that I ought to be kept in Rome. The same thing happened to Pompey after me, so that it appeared as if we two were being kept as guarantees for the Republic's safety. Why, anyway, should I wait for flattering comments on myself from other people when I am so good at it myself?

12.67 Caesar *Gallic War* 1.29.1–3: Massacre in Gaul

1 In the camp of the Helvetii were found records written in Greek which were brought to Caesar, which included a detailed list stating what number of them had left their homes, how many were able to bear arms, and a separate list of children, old men and women. 2 The total of all of these amounted to 263,000 Helvetii, 36,000 Tulingi, 14,000 Latobrigi, 23,000 Rauraci and 32,000 Boii; of these there were about 92,000 able to bear arms. 3 The grand total was 368,000. A census was held of those who returned home, at Caesar's order, and the number was found to be 110,000.

12.68 Caesar *Gallic War* 2.15.2, 27.3–28.3: Caesar and the Nervii, 57 BC

This passage concerns his campaign against the Nervii, one of the Belgic tribes, in 57; he was almost defeated by them at the River Sambre.

15.2 Caesar came to the borders of the Ambiani, who surrendered themselves and their belongings to him without delay. 3 Their nearest neighbours were the Nervii. When Caesar inquired about their character and lifestyle, he was informed as follows: 4 traders had no access to them; they allowed no wine or any other luxuries to be imported because they believed that such things enfeebled their spirits and diminished their courage. 5 They were fierce men of great courage, who reproached and accused the rest of the Belgians for surrendering to the Roman people and renouncing their ancestral courage; 6 they proclaimed that they would send no envoys nor accept any peace terms . . .

27.3 The enemy, even when all hope of safety was lost, displayed immense courage; when their first ranks had fallen, the next stood on them as they lay there and fought from their bodies; 4 when these were thrown down and the corpses heaped up, the remainder, as if from a mound, threw their missiles at our men and intercepted and returned our javelins. 5 It was clear, therefore, that they were to be judged men of immense courage, who had dared to cross a very broad river, climb huge banks, and advance over very unfavourable terrain; the greatness of their spirit made such immense difficulties easy. 28.1 With the battle over and the nation and name of the Nervii almost brought to extermination, the elders, whom I said earlier were hiding with the children and women in the creeks and marshes, believed, when the outcome was reported, that there was nothing to hinder the conquerors, 2 nothing to save the conquered, and sent, with the consent of all the survivors, envoys to Caesar and surrendered to him, stating, in relating the disaster which had befallen their state, that they had been reduced from 600 senators to three, and from 60,000 men who could bear arms to 500. 3 To show compassion to these wretched suppliants, Caesar was careful to leave them unharmed, ordering them to keep their lands and towns and commanding their neighbours to restrain themselves and their associates from any injuries or crimes against them.

THE CONFERENCE AT LUCA, 56 BC

12.69 Cicero *Letters to his Brother Quintus* 2.3.2–4: Pompey's unpopularity

A letter written to Quintus mid-February 56. On 7 February Milo had been tried in the forum, prosecuted by Clodius for the violence in 57. Pompey's speech in Milo's favour was interrupted by Clodius' gang, and when Clodius spoke he too was heckled and insulted by obscene verses about his relationship with his sister (cf. 12.60 for further insults). Pompey told Cicero that he was suspicious of a plot against his life and of Crassus' support for C. Porcius Cato (not Cato the Younger), a tribune who supported Clodius. Pompey was also suspicious that Crassus was financing Clodius.

Ptolemy XII Auletes, having paid 6,000 talents in 59 to be recognised as king of Egypt, was deposed by the Egyptians and took refuge in one of Pompey's villas. Cicero proposed that Lentulus Spinther (cos. 57) should restore Ptolemy when he became proconsul of Cilicia in 56, with force if necessary. However, following a Sibylline oracle that the Romans not assist the king of Egypt 'with a multitude', it was proposed by Crassus that a commission of three effect the king's restoration. Pompey's friends made it clear that Pompey wanted the commission. The senatorial debate lasted for three days, and the matter then came before the assembly, inconclusively. Finally the senate voted not to restore Ptolemy at all, but this decision was vetoed. Pompey's opponents in the senate had nevertheless won out, and he was not chosen to restore Ptolemy.

2 Milo's trial took place on 7 February. Pompey spoke, or rather attempted to speak, for as soon as he stood up Clodius' gang put up a great clamour and kept interrupting him throughout his speech, not only with shouting but with loud insults and abuse. As he came to a conclusion (and I must say that he showed courage, and was not put off, but said all he had to and occasionally even won silence by the force of his personality) – when he concluded, Clodius got up. Our side made such a noise (for we wanted to return the favour) that it affected his thoughts, tongue and countenance. That was finished by the eighth hour, as Pompey had spoken till just after the sixth hour, when all sorts of abuse and lastly some extremely obscene verses were thrown at Clodius and Clodia. Pale and furious, Clodius started asking his supporters in the middle of the shouting who it was who was starving the people to death; his gang replied, 'Pompey!' Who wanted to go to Alexandria? They replied, 'Pompey!' Whom do you want to go? 'Crassus!' (He was there in support of Milo but with little goodwill.) . . . **4** So I think great things are afoot. Pompey is aware, and passes the information on to me, that there is a plot on hand against his life, that Gaius Cato is being backed by Crassus and supplying Clodius with money; and that both are being supported by Crassus and Curio, Bibulus and his other critics; he says he has to keep well on guard not to be got the better of, with the crowd who attend public meetings just about alienated from him, the nobility hostile, the senate against him, and the youth misconducting themselves. So he is getting prepared and collecting men from the countryside, while Clodius is strengthening his gangs and getting them ready for the festival of the Quirinalia. With a view to the same occasion, we are far superior with Milo's personal forces, but a large band is expected from Picenum and Gaul to help us stand up to Cato's bills about Milo and Lentulus.

12.70 Cicero *Letters to Friends* 1.9.7–9, 11–12: Cicero on Luca

In December 54 Cicero wrote to Lentulus in his province of Cilicia explaining how he came 'to include Caesar' (1.9.12) in his policy: friendly relations with him were necessary because of Caesar's connections with Pompey, and he mentions the promises made by Pompey to Caesar, and by Quintus, Cicero's brother, to Pompey, that Cicero would, in effect, 'behave himself'. The letter is a justification for Cicero's activities after Luca.

Caesar's activities as consul had come under scrutiny in 58, when L. Domitius Ahenobarbus (cos. 54) as praetor had unsuccessfully attacked his legislation; Ahenobarbus was now threatening to renew these attacks. On 5 April 56 BC the issue of the Campanian land was hotly debated in the senate, and Cicero at this senate meeting successfully proposed that the issue of the Campanian land 'should be referred to a full senate on the Ides of May', which was an attack on Caesar's land legislation; his speech to this effect 'caused a sensation', 'not only where I had intended (presumably Caesar), but even with people I had never imagined (Pompey)'. A few weeks previously Cicero had subjected Vatinius (tr. pl. 59) to a hostile cross-examination as a witness in the prosecution of Sestius: Vatinius as tribune in 59 had been a major ally of the triumvirs and had passed legislation granting Caesar his commands. Both of these attacks angered Caesar.

Pompey left on a trip to Sardinia as grain comissioner, but went via Luca. Caesar had already seen Crassus at Ravenna, where Caesar 'complained a great deal' about Cicero's planned debate. Cicero makes it quite clear that Caesar met with Crassus at Ravenna and with Pompey at Luca. Later sources – Plutarch, Suetonius and Appian – have a three-man meeting at Luca, but Cicero is clearly correct. Pompey's thinly veiled accusation in the senate that Crassus was trying to kill him indicated that all was not well between him and Crassus, but Caesar was able to organise a reconciliation between them.

7 My entire cross-examination was in fact nothing but a criticism of Vatinius' tribunate. In it I spoke throughout with the greatest independence and spirit regarding the use of violence, the auspices and the grants of kingdoms, and not only indeed in this case but consistently and frequently in the senate. **8** In the consulship of (Cn. Cornelius Lentulus) Marcellinus and (L. Marcius) Philippus, on the Nones of April, the senate adopted my proposal that the matter of the Campanian land should be referred to a full senate on the Ides of May. Could I have done more to invade the citadel of that clique or been more forgetful of my past difficulties or more mindful of my past career? My speech caused a sensation, not only where I had intended but even with people I had never imagined. **9** After the senate had passed a decree on my motion, Pompey, without showing me any sign of being angry, left for Sardinia and Africa and *en route* joined Caesar at Luca. There Caesar complained a great deal about my motion (he had been stirred up against me by Crassus, whom he had seen beforehand at Ravenna). Pompey was said to be extremely upset; although I heard this from other people, I learnt this primarily from my brother. Pompey met him in Sardinia a few days after he had left Luca. 'You're the man I want', he said. 'Nothing could be more fortunate than our meeting. If you don't speak seriously to your brother Marcus, you're going to have to pay up on that pledge you made me on his behalf.' In short, he made a serious complaint, mentioned what he had done for me, recalled the talks he had had so frequently with my brother himself about Caesar's legislation and what my brother had pledged to him about me, and called my brother himself to witness that his actions over my return had had Caesar's approval. He asked that he commend Caesar's cause and prestige to me, requesting that I should not attack them if I was unwilling or unable to defend them . . .

11 If I had seen the state in the control of reprobates and villains, as we know happened in Cinna's time and some other periods, no rewards (which have not the slightest weight with me) or dangers (which can influence even the bravest men) would have made me join their side, however great their services to me. However, the chief man in the state was Gnaeus Pompey, who had won this power and glory through services to the state of the greatest importance and the most outstanding military achievements, and whose successful reputation I had promoted from my youth, while in my praetorship and consulship I had visibly supported it. For his part he had himself assisted me with his authority and by voicing his opinion in the senate and by plans and hard work in conjunction with you. He had only one enemy in Rome who was also mine, so I did not think that I need be afraid of the reputation of inconsistency if, in sometimes voicing my opinion, I had changed direction a little and shown my desire to enhance the reputation of a great man who had performed many services on my behalf. **12** In this policy I had to include Caesar, as you will see, since his interest and prestige were bound up with Pompey's. The long-standing friendship, which you are aware existed between Caesar and my brother and myself, was here of great value, as was Caesar's courtesy and generosity, which we soon clearly observed in his letters and his services to us. Concern for the state also influenced me strongly, as it seemed to me that it did not desire a conflict with these men, especially after Caesar's immense achievements, and strongly objected to one. But what had most influence on my decision were the promises on my behalf which Pompey had given to Caesar and my brother to Pompey.

12.71 Appian *Civil Wars* 2.17.61–63: Caesar's clientela at Luca

Pompey and Crassus were to be consuls for 55 BC and to have, respectively, Spain and Syria as their provinces for five years; Caesar was to be proconsul in Gaul and Illyricum for another five years and to appoint ten legates. While the story of the 120 lictors and 200 senators at Luca might be an exaggeration (cf. doc. 2.62), clearly various magistrates did make their way to Luca, and, among them, specifically named as present were Appius Claudius Pulcher (cos. 54) (Clodius' brother) and Metellus Nepos (cos. 57) (Plut. *Caes.* 21.2; cf. Suet. *Jul.* 24.1). This second double consulship of Pompey and Crassus was supported by Clodius, and to cement their alliance Pompey's son married Appius' daughter.

Appius Claudius' and Clodius' brother Gaius was praetor in 56; Clodius himself was aedile. What Clodius stood to gain is unclear: perhaps it was simply a case of family advancement to the consulship. Clodius made a public speech to win Pompey's approval and inveighed against the opposition of Marcellinus (cos. 56) to the candidature of Pompey and Crassus (Dio 39.29.1). He did not, however, desist from his hatred of Cicero (as Cic. *Har. Resp.* indicates). Appian on Caesar and the Celts [Gauls]: *Gallic History* FF xv–xxi.

61 Caesar, who had achieved numerous brilliant successes in Gaul and Britain, which I have recounted in my book on the Celts, returned loaded with wealth to Cisalpine Gaul on the River Po to allow his army a short rest from constant warfare. **62** From here he dispatched large amounts of money to many people in Rome, and those who were the magistrates for that year and others who had achieved distinction as governors or generals went in turn to meet him; so many of them were there that 120 lictors could be seen around him at a time and more than 200 senators, some of them thanking him for what they had already received, and others hoping to get money from him or trying to gain some other benefit from the same source. Caesar could now manage anything as a consequence of his huge army, the immensity of his wealth, and his eagerness to oblige everyone. **63** Pompey and Crassus, his partners in the regime, also came at his invitation. In their deliberations it was resolved that Pompey and Crassus should hold the consulship again, and that Caesar's governorship over his provinces should be extended for another five years.

12.72 Dio *Roman History* 39.31.1–2: Pompey and Crassus re-elected

Pompey and Crassus still had to be elected as consuls in the comitia centuriata. They declared their candidature after the date for nominations closed and then prevented the consul Marcellinus from holding elections, employing C. Cato as tribune to interpose his veto; the elections were finally held early in 55. L. Domitius Ahenobarbus also stood as a candidate for the consulship, encouraged by his brother-in-law M. Porcius Cato, but withdrew when his slave was killed and he, Cato and other supporters were wounded. Crassus' son Publius brought soldiers from Caesar to assist in the election.

1 After this Pompey and Crassus were appointed consuls following an interregnum, since none of those who had previously announced their candidature put up any opposition, though Lucius Domitius, who had canvassed right up to the very last day, set off from his house for the assembly in the dark but, when the slave carrying the light in front of him was murdered, took fright and proceeded no further. **2** Accordingly, as no one opposed their magistracy, and, what is more, as Publius Crassus, who was Marcus' son and at that point one of Caesar's officers, brought soldiers into Rome to ensure this, they were elected without difficulty.

12.73 Cicero *On the Consular Provinces* 19, 29, 34–35: Caesar's command

Cicero delivered this speech following the conference of Luca, after Pompey's talk to Cicero's brother Quintus (doc. 12.70) had forced Cicero to adopt a more moderate political line. The debate in June 56 concerned the assignation of four provinces: the two Gauls, Macedonia and Syria. Cicero successfully spoke against the proposal to deprive Caesar of the command of one or both of the provinces of Gaul with fulsome praise of Caesar and his conquests. This speech, *On the Consular Provinces*, might be Cicero's 'palinode' to which he refers (doc. 12.74), but not all agree. He stresses that it is for the good of the state that Caesar should remain in control of Gaul (esp. 34–35).

19 A vitally important war has been fought in Gaul; mighty races have been subdued by Caesar, but they are not yet bound to us by laws, by established rights, by
a sufficiently stable peace. We see that the war is nearly at an end and, to speak
truth, almost completed, but it is only on condition that the same man who began
the war follows it up to the end that we may presently see it brought to a final conclusion, and, if he is succeeded, there is a danger that we may hear of the remnants
of that important war being revived and renewed.

28 Recently the matter of pay for his army was referred to us; not only did I
vote for it, but I even worked hard to persuade you to do so too; I gave lengthy
replies to those who disagreed; I was part of the committee that drafted the resolution. At that point, too, I conceded more to the man than to any kind of necessity.
For my view was that, even without this monetary assistance, he was able to
maintain his army by booty already won and conclude the war; but I did not think
that the honour and glory of a triumph should be diminished by any parsimony
on our part. We passed a resolution about ten legates, whom some totally refused
to grant, while others asked for precedents, others wanted to postpone the discussion, and others wanted to grant them but omitting any flattering terms; I spoke
on this matter too in such a way that everyone could understand that I did what I
felt was in the interests of the state all the more lavishly on account of the prestige
of Caesar himself. **29** But, now it is a matter of allocating provinces, I am interrupted, though I expressed my views on those other questions to a silent audience.
In the former cases honours for Caesar were at issue, but now my only concern
is military considerations and the highest benefits to the state. For why should
Caesar wish to remain in his province, unless to hand over to the state the work he
has on hand completely finished?

34 One or two summers more, with fear or hope, punishment or rewards, arms
or laws, can bind the whole of Gaul to us with everlasting chains. But, if the work
of conquest is abandoned prematurely and without finishing touches, although the
power of our enemies has been truncated, it will at some point come to life again
and result in the renewal of the war. **35** And so let Gaul stay under the protection
of the person to whose loyalty, courage and good fortune it has been entrusted.
For if he, who has already been adorned with Fortune's richest gifts, were unwilling to risk tempting that goddess too often, if he were in haste to return to his
country, his household gods, the honour which he sees waiting for him at Rome,
his delightful children, his illustrious son-in-law, if he were longing to ride to the
Capitol in triumph with that distinguished mark of honour, if, finally, he feared
some set-back which could not add to his glory as much as it could take away,
it would however still be incumbent on us to wish that all those tasks should be
completed by the same man by whom they have been so nearly brought to an
end. But, as what he has achieved at this point is enough for his own glory but
not enough for the state, and as he prefers to postpone his enjoyment of the fruits
of his labours rather than not fulfil the duty he has undertaken for the commonwealth, we ought neither to recall a general who is so dedicated to successful
service of the state nor to disturb and impede the whole policy relating to the war
in Gaul which is now so nearly finalised.

12.74 Cicero *Letters to Atticus* 4.5.1–2 Cicero's 'palinode':

Cicero refers in this letter of June 56 BC to his palinode, in which he said goodbye to 'principles, truth and honour' in his support of the triumvirate.

1 I feel my palinode was something which doesn't do me credit. But farewell to principles, truth and honour! . . . **2** The truth is I wanted to forge an unbreakable connection for myself with this new alliance to make it totally impossible for me to slip back to those people who, even when they should feel sorry for me, won't stop being jealous of me . . . Since those who have no power do not wish to be my friends, let me try to make myself liked by those who do possess power.

THE CONSULSHIP OF CRASSUS AND POMPEY

12.75 Plutarch *Life of Pompey* 52.3–5: The second consulship of Crassus and Pompey

C. Trebonius, tribune in 55 BC, passed a law to provide for two five-year proconsular commands – Syria and the provinces of Spain – with the governors to make peace and war as they saw fit. Syria went to Crassus, Spain to Pompey, who, contrary to Plutarch, did not obtain Libya (Africa) as part of his command. Pompey and Crassus then successfully proposed in the assembly an extension of Caesar's command for five years. Bribery and violence had been used to ensure the election of Vatinius, rather than M. Porcius Cato, to the praetorship for 55.

3 By such means they made their way into office, and even then they did not behave any more appropriately. First, while the people were in the act of voting for Cato's election to the praetorship, Pompey dissolved the assembly on the grounds of inauspicious omens, and, after bribing the tribes, they proclaimed Vatinius praetor instead of Cato. **4** They then, by means of Trebonius, a tribune, brought in laws which, according to their agreement, continued Caesar's command for a second term of five years and gave Crassus Syria and the expedition against the Parthians, and Pompey himself the whole of Libya, both Spanish provinces and four legions, two of which he lent to Caesar at his request for the war in Gaul. **5** While Crassus went out to his province at the end of his consulship, Pompey opened his theatre and put on gymnastic and musical contests at its dedication, as well as wild-beast combats in which 500 lions were killed, and above all an elephant fight, a most astounding spectacle.

12.76 Dio *Roman History* 39.33.1–34.1: Jobs for the boys

Dio incorrectly gives Caesar's extension of command as three years, not five. The picture of Caesar's supporters does not tally with the accounts of Plutarch and Appian above, who record prearranged deals for 55 BC to benefit all three men. Favonius (praetor in 49) was a supporter of Cato and an opponent of the triumvirate.

1 With the magistrates appointed, Pompey and Crassus started working to achieve their aims. They did not speak on their own behalf either in the senate or in the assembly but seriously pretended that there was nothing else they desired; **2** however, one of the tribunes, Gaius Trebonius, put forward a proposal that one of them should be given Syria and the neighbouring regions as his province and the other the two Spains (where there had been recent disturbances), both for a five-year period, and that they were to have the use of as many troops as they wished, both citizens and allies, and the power to make war or peace with whomever they chose. **3** Many people disapproved of this, especially Caesar's friends, because, after attaining their own aims, Pompey and Crassus were bound to prevent Caesar from holding power for much longer, and some of them therefore prepared themselves to oppose the proposal. The consuls were then afraid that they might fail to achieve their object and gained their support by extending Caesar's command too for another three years, to give the correct figure. **4** They did not, however, bring anything before the people on his behalf until their own position was secured. Caesar's supporters were in this way won over and stayed quiet, and most of the others were too subdued by fear to say anything, satisfied, by so doing, to preserve their lives. **34.1** On the other hand, Cato and Favonius opposed all their projects, with two tribunes and some others working with them, but, as they were a few struggling against a large number of opponents, they spoke out in vain.

12.77 Cicero defends his enemies in court

Cicero had to defend followers of Pompey and Caesar in 56–54 BC. Particularly galling for Cicero were the defences he made at Pompey's request of both Vatinius and Gabinius. Vatinius was prosecuted for misconduct in his election to the praetorship for 55; with Cicero defending him, he was acquitted; for Gabinius, see doc. 12.78.

(i) Cicero Letters to his Friends 7.1.4 (to M. Marius, (?) September 55)

I was weary of it (forensic oratory) even at the time when youth and ambition led me on and when I could indeed turn down a case I did not wish to defend, but now life is just not worth living. I have no reward to expect for my hard work, and I am sometimes obliged to defend persons who have deserved none too well of me, at the entreaty of those who have deserved well.

(ii) Cicero Letters to his Brother Quintus 3.5.4 (October or November 54)

Some of my enemies I have not attacked, others I have actually defended. Not only my mind but even my hatred is not free.

THE EVENTS OF 54 BC

In December (probably) of 55 BC, Domitius Ahenobarbus was elected to the consulship and Cato to the praetorship for 54, both of which had been prevented earlier by Pompey and Crassus (cf. doc. 3.75). Clodius' brother Appius Claudius Pulcher was the other consul elected for 54, with Pompey and Caesar's support. The enmity between Cicero and Clodius remained, and Ahenobarbus as consul renewed his attacks on Caesar's legislation of 59, again unsuccessfully.

In 54 BC Messalla Rufus and Aemilius Scaurus were prosecuted for misconduct in their campaigns for the consulship of 53, but the outcome is uncertain. In 52 Scaurus was prosecuted again for the same offence and convicted. Gabinius on 23 October was acquitted of *maiestas* (treason) for his restoration of Ptolemy without the authorisation of the senate, but one hour later he was convicted of extortion in his province of Syria, where he had upset the publicani. Gabinius as consul in 58 had ignored Cicero's plea to prevent Clodius exiling him, and Cicero had attacked his proconsulship in Syria. Nevertheless he appeared as a witness for his defence in the trial for *maiestas* and defended him in the trial for extortion.

12.78 Electoral scandal in 54 BC

In the course of 54, evidence of an electoral scandal broke: Memmius, one of the candidates for 53, revealed with Pompey's connivance, but to Caesar's annoyance, that he and a fellow candidate, Cn. Domitius Calvinus (tr. pl. 59; not to be confused with Domitius Ahenobarbus, cos. 54), had made a pact with the consuls in office during that year. The elections for 53 were therefore continually postponed, and all four candidates were to be prosecuted for bribery. This election scandal delayed the election of consuls for 53 until July 53; Calvinus and Messalla Rufus were elected and then took office.

(i) Cicero Letters to Atticus *4.17.2–3, 5 (1 October 54)*

2 The consuls are embroiled in a dreadful scandal because Gaius Memmius, one of the candidates, read out in the senate an agreement which he and his fellow competitor Domitius made with the consuls, that they would both give the consuls 4,000,000 sesterces if they were elected, unless they had found three augurs who would state that they had been present when a *lex curiata* was passed, which had not been passed, and two consulars, who would state that they had been present at a decree arranging for the consular provinces, even though the senate had not met. This agreement, as was stated, was not an oral one but with names and details in many people's notebooks, and was produced by Memmius at Pompey's instigation with the names erased. This meant nothing to Appius; he hasn't lost anything. His colleague is ruined and totally finished. **3** Memmius' chances, now the coalition is dissolved against the wishes of Calvinus, have gone cold, all the more because we now understand that his revelation has seriously displeased Caesar. Our friend Messalla and his fellow competitor Domitius have treated the populace very liberally, and hence are very popular. They were sure to become consuls . . . **5** Three of the candidates are expected to face prosecution, Domitius by Memmius, Messalla by Quintus Pompeius Rufus, Scaurus by Triarius or Lucius Caesar. 'What can you say on their behalf?' you may ask. I'll be damned if I know!

(ii) Cicero Letters to his Brother Quintus *3.3.2–3 (21 October 54 BC)*

2 Now hear what has been going on in politics. Day after day election days are cancelled by the declaration of inauspicious omens, to the great joy of all honest men, as the consuls are extremely unpopular because of the suspicion of their having arranged to take bribes from the candidates. All four consular candidates have been charged. Their cases are difficult, but I shall do my best to save our friend

Messalla, which involves the safety of the others too. Publius Sulla has charged Gabinius with bribery, with his stepson Memmius, his brother Caecilius and his son Sulla as co-prosecutors. Lucius Torquatus put in a rival claim to prosecute, but to everyone's delight failed to get it. **3** You will be interested to know what is going on with Gabinius: we shall know about the treason in three days' time; in that trial he is disadvantaged by the dislike felt for him by all classes and is greatly damaged by the witnesses, while his case is handled by unenthusiastic prosecutors. The jury is a diverse one, the president Alfius is reliable and solid, and Pompey urgently trying to influence the jurors. What will happen I don't know, but I see no place for him in the community, am very unworried by the thought of his ruin, and am perfectly at ease as to how things will turn out.

12.79 Plutarch *Life of Julius Caesar* 23.5–7: The death of Julia

While Pompey did not renew the marriage alliance with Caesar after the death of Julia, no real break between the two men can be dated to this point; it was Pompey's sole consulship of 52 and his reconciliation with the senate that saw the beginning of the breakdown in the relationship. Caesar was in Britain and received the letters advising him of Julia's death on his return; he staged a gladiatorial show in her honour in 46 (doc. 2.79).

5 (On returning to Gaul from Britain) Caesar found letters from his friends in Rome which were about to be sent across to him, informing him of his daughter's death. She had died in childbirth at Pompey's house. **6** Both Pompey and Caesar were greatly distressed at this, and their friends were very disturbed, as the relationship which preserved the otherwise troubled state in peace and harmony was now dissolved. And the baby also died, only a few days after its mother. **7** As for Julia, the people took her body and carried her, in spite of the tribunes, to the Campus Martius, where her funeral was held and where she lies buried.

12.80 Suetonius *Life of the Deified Julius* 27.1: A proposed marriage alliance

Pompey in fact married Cornelia, daughter of Q. Metellus Scipio, soon after entering his sole consulship in 52. Cornelia's husband had been the younger Crassus, killed in Parthia on his father's staff. Pompey chose Metellus as his consular colleague in July.

To maintain his relationship and goodwill with Pompey, Caesar offered him as his wife Octavia, his sister's granddaughter, who was married to Gaius Marcellus (cos. 50), and for himself asked for Pompey's daughter in marriage, who was betrothed to Faustus Sulla.

12.81 Cicero *Letters to his Brother Quintus* 3.1.17, 3.6.3: Cicero feels for Caesar

Written in September and November 54. For Cicero's affection for his own daughter, Tullia, see docs 7.27–28.

3.1.17 While I was still folding up this letter, letter-carriers arrived from you on 20 September, the twenty-seventh day after you sent it. How worried I was! And how distressed I was by Caesar's charming letter! The more charming it was, the more distress I felt for the misfortune which has befallen him.

    3.6.3 I got great pleasure in learning from your letter of the courage and dignity with which Caesar conducts himself in his immense sorrow.

CRASSUS IN PARTHIA

12.82 Plutarch *Life of Crassus* 15.7–16.3: **Crassus' Parthian aims**

While Pompey remained in Rome and administered Spain through legates, Crassus set out for Syria in November 55 to make war on Parthia. In 54 BC he carried out punitive raids into Mesopotamia and seized the Temple treasures of Jerusalem, and in 53 he invaded Parthia. At the River Balik the Parthians defeated the Romans, decapitating his son Publius and displaying the head, fixed to a spear, to Crassus. The survivors retreated to Carrhae, where on 9 June Crassus and some 30,000 of the army were killed – one of the most spectacular defeats the Roman army had ever experienced.

15.7 When the lots were cast, Crassus received Syria and Pompey the Spanish provinces. **16.1** Everyone was pleased with the way the lot turned out. Most people did not want Pompey to be far from Rome, and Pompey, who loved his wife, intended to spend most of his time there, while as soon as the lot took place Crassus showed by his delight that he considered that no more glorious piece of good fortune than this had ever happened to him, and he could hardly keep quiet among strangers and in public, while to his intimate friends he made many empty, childish boasts unsuited to his age and temperament, since before this he had been anything but boastful or pompous. **2** Now, however, frantic with excitement and out of his senses, he did not intend Syria or the Parthians to be the limit of his success but wanted to make Lucullus' campaigns against Tigranes and Pompey's against Mithridates look like child's play, in his hopes seeing himself reaching as far as Bactria and India and the Outer Sea. And yet in the decree passed concerning his command there was no mention of a Parthian war. **3** But everyone knew that Crassus was obsessed with this idea, and Caesar wrote to him from Gaul approving the project and encouraging him to start the war.

12.83 Cicero *On Duties* 1.25, 3.75: **Cicero's views of Crassus**

At *Off.* 1.109 Cicero links Crassus with Sulla as examples of those who would stoop to anything to achieve their aims.

1.25 In those with greater ambitions, the love of riches leads them to strive for power and patronage, as in the case of Marcus Crassus, who recently stated that no amount of money was enough for the man who wished to be the leading citizen in the state, unless he could keep an army on the income from it.

    3.75 But if you were to give Marcus Crassus the power to get himself named as an heir, though he was not truly an heir, by snapping his fingers, believe me, he would dance in the forum.

12.84 Ovid *Fasti* 6.463–68: The death of Crassus

Augustus was of course to negotiate the return of Crassus' standards, which he presented as one of his greatest achivements (docs 15.1 (*RG* 19.2), 15.18, 15.96).

> Of course, grief is sometimes mixed with joy,
> Lest festivals prove an unmixed delight for the people:
> Crassus at the Euphrates lost his eagles, his son, and his soldiers,
> And was himself the last to perish.
> 'Parthian, why do you rejoice?' said the goddess.
> 'You shall return the standards, while there will be an avenger who shall take
> vengeance for the death of Crassus.'

CAESAR AND BRITAIN

In 55 and again in 54 BC, Caesar invaded Britain. His declared motive was the assistance given by the British to the Gauls; there was also the allure of another conquest, and presumably the desire for booty (and pearls: Suet. *Jul*. 47). There were no territorial gains from either expedition, and no garrisoning force was left behind; it is hardly likely that any of the tribute imposed was paid, although it was presented as a triumphal achievement. Actual conquest of Britain began only in the reign of the emperor Claudius.

12.85 Dio *Roman History* 39.50.1–53.2: Caesar in Britain, 55 BC

50.1 Caesar was at this time the first Roman to cross the Rhine, and afterwards, in the consulship of Pompey and Crassus, he crossed over to Britain . . . **51.1** Caesar wanted to cross to this country at this time because the rest of Gaul was at peace and he had won over the Morini. He made the crossing with his infantry by the best possible route but did not land at the most suitable spot, as the Britons, who had learnt of his voyage, had seized all the landing-places facing the mainland. **2** He therefore sailed around a certain projecting promontory and along the other side of it, where he disembarked in the shallows, overcoming those who engaged with him and gaining a foothold before more help could arrive, afterwards driving back these attackers too. **3** Only a few of the barbarians were killed (being chariot-drivers and cavalry, they easily escaped the Romans, whose cavalry had not yet arrived), but, panic-stricken at the reports about the Romans which had come from the mainland, and at the fact that they had dared to cross at all and been able to set foot in their country, they sent some of the Morini, friends of theirs, to Caesar to treat for peace. When he requested hostages, they were at that point willing to give them to him, **52.1** but when the Romans meanwhile faced problems because of a storm, which damaged the fleet they had there and the one which was joining them, they changed their minds and, while they did not attack them openly (for the camp was heavily defended), captured some men who had been sent out to forage for supplies in the belief that the country was friendly and killed them all, except a few, for Caesar swiftly came to their rescue, after which they attacked the Romans' defences. They achieved nothing, but suffered reverses, though they would not make peace terms until they had been defeated a number of times. **3** Caesar would not have considered coming to terms with them, except that the winter was approaching and he did not possess a sufficient force to continue to make war at that time of year, as the force which was coming to back him up had been damaged and the Gauls had revolted as a result of his absence, so he reluctantly made peace with the Britons, this time demanding numerous hostages but getting only a few.

53.1 He sailed back to the mainland and put an end to the uprisings, having gained nothing from Britain, either for himself or for Rome, except the prestige of having made an expedition against the Britons. He took great pride in this, and the Romans at home extolled this achievement to a marvellous degree. Because they saw that what had formerly been unknown was now familiar, and the formerly unheard of accessible, they considered the hopes for the future aroused by these deeds as actual facts and rejoiced at all their anticipated future gains as if they already possessed them. Because of this they voted the celebration of a thanksgiving (supplicatio) lasting 20 days.

12.86 Cicero *Letters to his Brother Quintus* 2.16.4–5: Quintus in Britain

Written in late August 54 at Rome to Quintus, who was serving as Caesar's legate. Cicero wrote a literary account of Caesar's expedition to Britain. He had also written a poem, 'On my vicissitudes', and was hoping for further favourable comments from Caesar.

4 I come now to what should perhaps have been first. How happy I was to get your letter from Britain! I dreaded the Ocean, I dreaded the island coastline; not that I am making light of what is still to come, but there is more to hope than fear, and I am more troubled by anticipation than by anxiety. I see that you have some really splendid literary material – places, nature, topography, customs, peoples, fighting, and of course the general himself! I shall be pleased to help you, as you request, in any way you like, and I shall send you the verses you ask for (an owl to Athens!)

5 But, look here, you seem to be keeping something from me. Brother, what does Caesar think of my poem? He wrote to me earlier that he had read the first book and had never read anything better than the first part, even in Greek; the rest to a certain point he thought more slipshod (the word he used). Tell me the truth: is it the content or the style he doesn't like? Don't worry at all – I won't think a whit less of myself. Just tell me the truth frankly and, as you always do, like a brother.

12.87 Cicero *Letters to Atticus* 4.18.5: Mail from Britain

Written in October or November 54 BC. In a letter to Trebatius, *Fam.* 7.7.1, Cicero wrote in June 54, 'I hear there is no gold or silver in Britain; in that case I suggest you get a war chariot and hurry back to us as soon as possible.'

From my brother Quintus and from Caesar I received letters on 24 October sent from the shores of nearer Britain on 25 September. Britain has been subdued, hostages taken, no booty, but tribute has been imposed and they are bringing the army back from Britain.

12.88 Cicero *Letters to his Brother Quintus* 3.6.1: Quintus as Caesar's legate

Quintus had clearly been bemoaning conditions in Gaul; Marcus in November 54 reminds him of the advantages which will accrue to both of them from Caesar's patronage and support.

Marcus to his brother Quintus, greetings. I have nothing to reply to your earlier letter, which is full of irritation and complaining (you write that you gave another too in the same vein to Labeo the day before, which hasn't arrived yet), but your more recent letter removed all my annoyance. I only advise and beg you to remember amid these annoyances and labours and deprivations our reason for your going there. We were not, after all, looking out for slight or trivial benefits. What was it that we thought worth buying at the cost of our separation? We were in search of solid support from the goodwill of a great and extremely powerful man for every aspect of our public standing. We are relying more on hope than on money; if that is lost, the rest will have been accumulated just to be thrown away. So, if you keep on carrying your mind back to the purpose behind our former decision and hope, you will find it easier to put up with those military labours and the other annoyances.

12.89 Caesar's engineer, Mamurra

This was written before Julia's death and after the first invasion of Britain, with Catullus seeing Pompey and Caesar (here called 'Romulus') as associates. Mamurra was of an equestrian family and had served both with Pompey against Mithridates and with Caesar in Spain in 61; he was Caesar's engineer in Gaul. He had made an immense fortune and indulged in luxurious living, but he must have been capable to have been serving with Caesar in Gaul; for cinaedi (sodomites), see docs 7.57–60.

(i) Catullus 29

Who can see it, who can endure it,
Unless a shameless, greedy gambler,
That Mamurra owns the wealth that once belonged to long-haired Gaul
And Britain at the end of the world?
5   Romulus, you sodomite, can you put up with the sight?
And shall that arrogant, overbearing chap
Now wander through everyone's bedrooms
Like a white dove or an Adonis?
Romulus, you sodomite, can you put up with the sight,

10   You shameless, greedy gambler?
      Surely this isn't why, O egregious one,
      You went to the furthest island in the West,
      So this worn-out prick owned by you two
      Could squander two or three hundred times its worth?
15   What is this but perverse generosity?
      Hasn't he finished off or got through enough?
      First he went through his inherited property,
      Then the plunder from Pontus, then thirdly
      Spain's, as the gold-bearing Tagus River knows:
20   Now fears are felt for Gaul and Britain.
      Why on earth do you coddle him? What can he do
      But eat up rich inheritances?
      Surely this wasn't why you, the city's wealthiest men –
      Father-in-law, son-in-law – have ruined the entire world?

(ii) Catullus 57

      They suit one another well, those shameless sodomites (cinaedi),
      Mamurra that pathic and Caesar.
      And no wonder! Identical stains,
      Picked up by one in the city, by the other at Formiae,
5   Mark them, which cannot be washed away,
      Equally diseased, just like twins,
      Both learned scholars on one little bed,
      Neither a more voracious adulterer than the other,
      Friendly rivals even of young girls.
      Yes, they suit one another well, those shameless sodomites.

12.90 Caesar *Gallic War* 5.12.1–6, 14.1–5: Caesar on Britain

12.1 The interior of Britain is inhabited by natives who state that, according to their tradition, they are indigenous to the island, **2** the coastal region by people who crossed over from Belgium for the purposes of plunder or warfare, who after the invasion settled there and began to cultivate the land. Nearly all of these are called by the names of the states from which they came before their journey to Britain. **3** There is a vast population and very numerous farm buildings similar to those in Gaul, with an immense number of cattle. **4** They use either bronze or gold coins or, instead of coins, iron rods of a standard weight. **5** Tin is found in the midland regions of Britain, iron in the coastal regions, but of the latter the supply is small; they use imported bronze. There is timber of all kinds, as in Gaul, except for beech and fir. **6** They consider it wrong to eat hare, chicken and goose but keep these for diversion and pleasure. The climate is more temperate than that of Gaul, with milder cold seasons . . . **14.1** Of all the inhabitants, the most civilised by far are those who live in Kent, a completely coastal region, whose lifestyle differs little from that of the Gauls. Most of the inland dwellers do not plant corn **2** but live on milk and meat and dress in skins. Indeed, all the Britons dye themselves with woad, which produces a blue colour and gives them a more frightful appearance in battle; **3** they wear their hair long and shave their whole body except for the head and upper lip. **4** Ten or 12 men have wives in common, especially brothers with brothers and fathers with sons; **5** but the offspring are considered to belong to the family to which the girl was first taken in marriage.

12.91 Caesar *Gallic War* 7.1.1–8, 3.1–4.2: Vercingetorix

Caesar's campaigns had until now been against a disunited Gaul, which he and his legates had conquered piecemeal. At the beginning of 52 BC, the Gauls united in one great revolt against the Romans led by Vercingetorix, in which even the Aedui joined. Caesar deals with this revolt in *BG* 7, probably the most dramatic and exciting part of the *BG*. After various incidents, Caesar besieged Vercingetorix in Alesia. He in turn was surrounded by a Gallic force and had to build two walls, one around Alesia, and one on the outside of his position against the besieging Gauls. Their attack failed, and Alesia surrendered. Vercingetorix was to appear in his triumph and then be executed. A 20-day supplicatio was decreed by the senate. Caesar had to fight some last battles, but in 51 Gaul was pacified and Caesar could turn his attention elsewhere.

1.1 When Gaul was quiet, Caesar, as he had decided, sets out for Italy to hold the assizes. There he learns of the murder of Clodius and, on being informed of the senate's decree that all younger men should be called up and sworn in, he resolves to hold a levy throughout his province. **2** These events are quickly reported to Transalpine Gaul. The Gauls invent and add to the rumours, a matter which the situation seemed to demand, that Caesar was detained by disturbances at Rome and, because of such great discord, was unable to join his army. **3** Excited by this opportunity, those who even before this were bemoaning their subjection to the rule of the Roman people begin to make war plans with greater freedom and audacity. **4** Assemblies were summoned by arrangement between the Gallic chiefs in wooded and remote areas and they complain of the death of Acco; they point out that his fate could next fall upon them; **5** they pity the misfortune suffered by the whole of Gaul; with all kinds of promises and rewards they call upon men to begin the war and champion the freedom of Gaul at the risk of their lives. **6** First of all, they say, they must find a way, before their secret plans become generally known, to cut Caesar off from his army. **7** That was easy, because the legions would not dare to leave their winter quarters in their commander's absence, nor could the commander reach his legions without an escort. **8** Finally, it was better to die in battle than to fail to win back their former prestige in warfare and the liberty handed down by their forefathers . . . **3.1** When the day comes, the Carnutes, under the leadership of two desperate men, Cotuatus and Conconnetodumnus, rush at a given signal against Cenabum, put to death the Roman citizens who had settled there for trading purposes, among them Gaius Fufius Cita, a respected Roman eques who by Caesar's order was in charge of the corn supply, and seize their possessions. **2** The report is swiftly carried to all the states of Gaul – for whenever any more important or glorious event occurs, they proclaim it loudly through the fields and localities; others then take it up and hand it on to their neighbours, as happens on this occasion. **3** For the deeds done at Cenabum at sunrise were heard before the end of the first watch on the borders of the Arverni, a distance of some 160 miles.

4.1 In a similar way there, Vercingetorix, son of Celtillus, an Arvernian, a youth of the highest influence, whose father had held the chieftainship of the whole of Gaul, and consequently, because he aimed at kingship, had been put to death by the state, summons his dependants and easily inflames their spirits. **2** As soon as his plan is known there is a general rush to arms.

13

Civil War and Dictatorship

The 'First Triumvirate' had survived in 56 BC, much to Cicero's disappointment, but events soon paved the way for the breakdown of the alliance. The deaths of Julia and Crassus left only two partners, who were no longer joined by family ties, and Pompey gradually began to align himself with the optimates. During Caesar's absence in Gaul, factional violence led by Milo and Clodius reached such heights that the consular elections in 54 were so delayed that the consuls for 53 did not enter office until July; elections for 52 were continually postponed, and bribery was rampant. As a result there was increasing talk of making Pompey dictator, until a confrontation between Milo and Clodius on the Appian Way on 18 January 52 resulted in Clodius' murder and riots in Rome in which the senate house was burned down (docs 13.1–2). In consequence, Pompey was made sole consul for 52, a position the optimates, led by Cato, were more willing to allow him than a dictatorship (docs. 13.3–4). Later he took his new father-in-law, Q. Caecilius Metellus Pius Scipio (one of the declared candidates for 52), as colleague in the consulship for the last five months of the year (doc. 13.6). Milo was convicted and Pompey took the opportunity to introduce more stringent anti-violence and anti-bribery laws (doc. 13.5). He was granted a further five-year governorship in Spain, and his increased influence and favour with the optimates widened the breach with Caesar, whose supporters wished to ensure that he could safely hold a second consulship, which he wanted after his Gallic command (doc.13.7). In contrast, the 'hardline' optimates such as Cato the Younger wanted to see Caesar brought to trial for his actions as consul in 59 before he should be elected to such a second consulship, and he attempted to replace him in Gaul with a successor: this issue and the resulting ongoing debate were to lead directly to civil war.

The Marcelli (consuls in 51, 50 and 49) were to be particularly opposed to Caesar, and senatorial hostility towards him continued to grow during 51. Pompey was pressured into requesting from Caesar a legion he had lent him to deal with a crisis in Gaul (docs 13.9–10) and, though this legion and another of Caesar's own were withdrawn in 50 to deal with the Parthian crisis, they in fact remained in Italy under Pompey's command, a situation which then seemed to present a threat to Caesar (docs 13.10, 13, 21). On 29 September 51 the senate passed a resolution (doc. 13.12) that the question of Caesar's successor should take precedence over all other government business from 1 March 50. However, Caesar, with the immense wealth gained in Gaul, was not without supporters, most notably one of the consuls for 50, L. Aemilius Lepidus Paullus, who presented obstacles to this discussion, and the tribune C. Scribonius Curio, one of Caesar's most notable critics in 59, now won over to his side by payment of his immense debts, who demanded joint disarmament by both Caesar and Pompey (docs 13.14–16).

During 50 Pompey moved inexorably closer to the optimates and supported attempts to terminate Caesar's command. The breach between the two had widened to such an extent by August that, to Cicero's friend and correspondent M. Caelius Rufus, war appeared inevitable (docs 13.16–18). Nevertheless, war was only the direct choice of a few 'diehard' optimates: when Curio managed on 1 December 50 to divide the senate on a vote for joint disarmament, only 22 senators voted against, while, in order to avoid civil war, 370 were in favour of Pompey laying down his command as well as Caesar. At this point C. Claudius Marcellus as consul entrusted the safety of the state to Pompey (docs 13.22–24). When in January two of the tribunes for 49, M. Antony and Q. Cassius Longinus, attempted to veto the *senatus consultum ultimum* outlawing Caesar, they were obstructed and fled to Caesar at Ravenna (docs 13.24–25). On the night of 10 January 49 Caesar crossed the River Rubicon into Italy, making civil war inevitable, justifying himself on the grounds that his command had been terminated unfairly and insultingly (docs 13.26–27). Suetonius, however, considers that his main motive was to escape the prosecution by his enemies for his acts in 59, which Cato had been continually threatening (doc. 13.28).

To the surprise of Cicero, at least, Pompey decided to abandon Rome and withdrew first to Brundisium and then to western Greece, where Cicero was to join him, despite overtures from Caesar. Caesar pursued Pompey down the Italian peninsula and then returned to Rome before proceeding to Spain (Pompey's province), where he dealt with Pompeian opposition (docs 13.29–38). Now, as later, Caesar was to deal with his defeated opponents with clemency. After returning from Spain, he held the dictatorship for 11 days to preside over the consular elections; after he himself was elected for 48, he followed Pompey to Greece (doc. 13.42). Pompey's supporters were riven with jealousy of each other and hatred of Caesar, and his forces were inadequately trained (doc. 13.43). Following an initial defeat in an attempt to blockade the army at Dyrrachium, Caesar overwhelmingly overcame the Pompeian forces at Pharsalus in August 48 (docs 13.43–44). Pompey fled and was assassinated in Egypt by advisors of the Egyptian king, to Caesar's great regret (docs 13.46, 53). After a stay in Egypt with Cleopatra, Caesar had to engage in further military campaigns in Asia (against Pharnaces: doc. 13.48), in Africa (against Metellus Scipio, Cato and other Pompeians) and, finally, in Spain (against Pompey's sons). With this final success at Munda in Spain in 45 his victory was complete.

From 46 in particular Caesar began an intensive programme of political reform (colonies, debt relief and grain distribution: doc. 13.56). Despite his clemency and his practice of placing defeated opponents in key positions (docs 13.52–53, cf. 13.62), he was unpopular with the optimates because of his neglect of Republican values and his increasing autocracy (docs 13.51, 54). He received numerous unprecedented honours from the senate and people (doc. 13.55). The granting of a perpetual dictatorship in February 44 BC led to a conspiracy of more than 60 senators to murder him before he left for his Parthian campaign on 18 March (docs 13.66–67); Caesar was assassinated on the Ides (15th) of March 44. The conspirators, however, did not take advantage of their position, as Cicero laments (doc. 14.4), and Caesar's popularity and the unpopularity of the 'tyrannicides' was enhanced by the generosity of Caesar's will (doc. 13.68), in which he adopted his great-nephew Octavian, who was to complete the demise of the Republic. It could be argued that it was the intransigence of the senatorial aristocracy towards Caesar (particularly of the 22 optimates – among whom Cato was conspicuous – who voted against peace on 1 December 50 BC), Pompey's attitude, and Caesar's own personality and the legacy of his own actions in his consulship of 59 BC that led to the events of 50 and the outbreak of the war between Caesar and Pompey. For the ancient sources and background reading for this period, see the introduction to chapter 12.

ANARCHY IN ROME

Cn. Domitius Calvinus and M. Valerius Messalla Rufus had finally entered office as consuls in July 53, but three of the consular candidates for 52 caused various disruptions for the rest of the year: Q. Caecilius Metellus Pius Scipio (who was to become Pompey's father-in-law in July 52), T. Annius Milo and P. Plautius Hypsaeus. In addition, Clodius was a candidate for a praetorship. Not only did widespread bribery take place on an unprecedented scale, but these candidates had armed gangs in their employ, and the consul Calvinus was wounded in one incident.

Milo had spent extravagantly on ludi in 53 to ensure election; he had put on immensely expensive games and squandered three patrimonies in so doing. Clodius, on the other hand, could expect election to the praetorship, given his popularity with the plebs and sections of the senate and the support of Pompey, and he naturally supported Milo's rivals Scipio and Hypsaeus. These two were also Pompey's choice, as his own rapprochement with Clodius now made Milo dispensable. The year 53 ended without elections having been held, and the increasing anarchy was giving rise to calls that Pompey should assume the dictatorship.

13.1 Asconius *Commentaries on Cicero* 30–36: The murder of Clodius

This incident took place on 18 January 52 BC. Marcus Lepidus is M. Aemilius Lepidus (cos. 46 and 42, praetor 49), a member of the second triumvirate; he was the son of the consul of 78 who led a revolt against the state (doc. 12.2). While he was interrex (he took up office on 20 January), an attack on his house was carried out by the gangs of Clodius and he was trapped there for five days. The interrex under whom the elections were actually held was Ser. Sulpicius Rufus (cos. 51). Pompey assumed the sole consulship on the 24th of the intercalary month before March.

30 Titus Annius Milo, Publius Plautius Hypsaeus, and Quintus Metellus Scipio were candidates for the consulship, supporting their candidature not only by lavish and open bribery but also by gangs of armed men. There was a bitter feud between Milo and Clodius, because Milo was a close friend of Cicero's and as tribune had worked strenuously to have Cicero recalled, while Publius Clodius still remained violently hostile to him after his recall and therefore enthusiastically supported Hypsaeus and Scipio against Milo. Milo and Clodius frequently came to blows with each other in Rome at the head of their own gangs: they were both equal in recklessness, but Milo was on the side of the optimates. Moreover, while Milo was standing for the consulship, Clodius was a candidate, in the same year, for the praetorship, which he realised would be crippled with Milo as consul. The consular elections had been long delayed and could not be completed because of these **31** desperate squabbles between the candidates, and for this reason in January there were still no consuls or praetors, and the election day was being put off by the same means as before; Milo in fact wanted the elections to be completed as soon as possible and was confident of the support both of the 'honest' men, since he was opposing Clodius, and of the people, because of the largesse he had widely distributed and his immense expenditure on theatrical performances and gladiatorial shows, on which Cicero informs us he spent three patrimonies, while his opponents preferred to postpone them, and so Pompey, Scipio's son-in-law, and the tribune Titus Munatius had not allowed a proposal to be put to the senate for an assembly of patricians to choose an interrex – the traditional procedure in such a situation being to appoint an interrex. On 18 January (for I consider it best to follow the official records and this very speech which agrees with the official records, rather than Fenestella who gives the date of 19 January) Milo set out for Lanuvium, his home town, where he was dictator, to appoint a flamen on the following day. At about the ninth hour, he was encountered by Clodius, a little past Bovillae, the spot being close to a shrine of the Bona Dea; Clodius was returning from Aricia, where he had been addressing the town officials. Clodius was riding on horseback; he was accompanied by some 30 slaves, the usual practice when making a journey at that time, who were lightly equipped and armed with swords. Moreover Clodius had three friends with him, of whom one was a Roman eques called Gaius Causinius Schola, and two were well-known plebeians, Publius Pomponius and Gaius Clodius. Milo was travelling in a carriage with his wife Fausta, daughter of the dictator Lucius Sulla, and a relation called Marcus Fufius. Accompanying them **32** was a large band of slaves, including some gladiators, among whom were the two well-known figures Eudamus and Birria. They were at the far end of the column, moving more slowly, and began a brawl with the slaves of Publius Clodius. When Clodius looked back threateningly at this uproar, Birria threw a spear through his shoulder. With the fight in progress, more of Milo's men hurried up. The wounded Clodius was conveyed into a nearby tavern in Bovillae.

When Milo heard that Clodius had been wounded, he decided that it would be more dangerous for himself to leave him alive, while his death would be a great relief, even if he had to undergo a penalty, and ordered him to be turned out of the tavern. The leader of Milo's slaves was Marcus Saufeius. Clodius, who was hiding, was then dragged out and finished off with a number of wounds. His body was left in the road, because Clodius' slaves were either dead or in hiding with serious injuries . . . To Clodius' house hurried the tribunes Titus Munatius Plancus, brother of the orator Lucius Plancus, and Quintus Pompeius Rufus, grandson of the dictator Sulla through his daughter. **33** At their urging, the ignorant mob carried the body to the forum, naked and trampled, on the couch as it had been laid, so that the wounds could be seen, and placed it on the rostra. There Plancus and Pompeius, who supported Milo's opponents, held a public meeting and whipped up hostility to Milo. Under the leadership of the clerk Sextus Cloelius the people carried the body of Publius Clodius into the senate house and cremated it there, using benches, tribunals, tables and secretaries' notebooks; the senate house itself caught fire and the Basilica Porcia next door to it was also damaged. The crowd of Clodius' supporters also attacked the house of Marcus Lepidus, the interrex (for he had been appointed to this office), and that of Milo, who was absent, but was driven back with arrows. Then they seized the axes from the grove of Libitina and carried them to Scipio's house and Hypsaeus' and finally to Pompey's gardens, calling on him now as consul, now as dictator.

The conflagration of the senate house gave rise to a good deal more anger among citizens than the murder of Clodius. And so Milo, who was thought to have gone into voluntary exile, reassured by his opponents' unpopularity, returned to Rome on the night of the burning of the senate house. Undeterred, he still campaigned for the consulship; he even openly gave each man 1,000 asses according to tribe. Some days later the tribune Marcus Caelius held a public meeting on his behalf and Cicero himself pleaded his case to the people. Both stated that Milo had been ambushed by Clodius.

In the meantime, one interrex after another was appointed, because consular elections could not be held **34** on account of the disturbances caused by the candidates and the same armed bands. So, as a first step, a senatorial decree was passed that the interrex, tribunes and Gnaeus Pompey, who was proconsul and near the city, should see to it that the state suffered no harm, and that Pompey should hold a levy throughout Italy . . . **35** During all this, as the feeling was increasing that Gnaeus Pompey should be appointed dictator as the only way to solve the state's problems, **36** it seemed safer to the optimates that he should be created consul without a colleague, and, when the matter had been debated in the senate, in a senatorial decree on the motion of Marcus Bibulus, Pompey was appointed consul by the interrex Servius Sulpicius on the 24th of the intercalary month and took up office immediately. Three days later he moved new laws, two promulgated by senatorial decree, one on violence, which specifically mentioned the murder on the Appian Way, the burning of the senate house and the attack on the house of the interrex Marcus Lepidus, and the other on bribery, in which the penalties were intensified and the court procedure made shorter.

POMPEY AS SOLE CONSUL, 52 BC

After Clodius' murder there were calls for Pompey to become dictator and a military levy was held throughout Italy. The level of violence and corruption in 53 and 52 BC had become unacceptable, even by Roman standards. Cato and his supporters felt that it would be better if Pompey had a more regular office, and Bibulus (Cato's son-in-law) therefore proposed that he be made sole consul. This marks the change in the relationship between Pompey and Caesar, which up to that point had been relatively amicable.

13.2 Cicero *In Defence of Milo* 27: Clodius at fault

Meanwhile, as Clodius was aware – nor was it difficult to be aware of it – that Milo, as chief magistrate (dictator) at Lanuvium, had, under the obligation of sacred and civil law, to take a journey to Lanuvium to proclaim the appointment of a flamen, he suddenly left Rome the day before so he might, as was clear from the event, lay an ambush for Milo in front of his estate.

13.3 Dio *Roman History* 40.50.3–5: The optimates turn to Pompey

Pompey had been invited by the senate to become sole consul and was increasingly reconciled with the optimates. He now emerges as the supporter of law and order, though not in any sense a tool of the senate. But Pompey's good relationship with the senate was established and would develop.

3 The city was in a state of suspense over who were to be its magistrates, with some people saying that Pompey should be elected dictator, others that Caesar should be consul . . . 4 As they were afraid of both men, the rest of the senate, as well as Bibulus, who was the first to be asked for his opinion, anticipated the populace's enthusiasm by giving Pompey the consulship, so he would not be named dictator, and as sole consul, so that Caesar might not be his colleague. 5 This novel action was without precedent, yet they appeared to have made the right decision; as Pompey was less supportive of the populace than Caesar, they hoped to detach him from them completely and make him one of their own. And this worked out: elated at this new and unexpected honour, he no longer made any plans to please the people but tried to carry out in every respect the wishes of the senate.

13.4 Plutarch *Life of Pompey* 54.5–8: Bibulus and Cato support Pompey

5 When, later on, Rome was again without consuls and more people now brought up more vigorously the question of a dictatorship, Cato and his party were afraid that they would be forced to give way and so decided to let Pompey have some sort of legal magistracy to prevent his holding the absolute authority of a dictatorship. 6 In fact Bibulus, Pompey's enemy, was the first to propose in the senate that Pompey should be elected sole consul, arguing that in this way Rome would either be saved from its current chaos or at least be enslaved to its best citizen. 7 The proposal appeared incredible, bearing in mind its advocate, and Cato got up, giving rise to the belief that he would oppose it, but, when everyone fell silent, declared that he would not personally have proposed the measure but, as it had been proposed by someone else, he recommended that they adopt it, as he preferred any government to no government, and thought that Pompey would govern better than anyone else in times of such chaos. 8 The senate accepted the measure and decreed that Pompey, if elected consul, should govern without a colleague, but that if he himself should want a colleague he could choose whomever he thought suitable at the end of two months of office.

13.5 Dio *Roman History* 40.54.1–2: Milo's conviction

Pompey as sole consul introduced various measures, including two laws on violence and electoral bribery. Milo was charged with murder and other offences and tried on 4–7 April. Pompey had already indicated that he would not support him, and he was defended by Cicero and M. Claudius Marcellus (cos. 51); the prosecution was carried out by Mark Antony and Appius Claudius Pulcher. Milo was condemned to exile for the murder; he was also tried and convicted under Pompey's law for electoral bribery. Hypsaeus, the second of the two consular candidates supported by Pompey in 53, was also convicted. Pompey's law on bribery was retrospective, covering events back to his own first consulship in 70 BC. This led Caesar's supporters to be suspicious that Caesar was being targeted.

1 The courts met peacefully as a result of these measures and many were convicted on a variety of charges, including Milo among others for the murder of Clodius, even though he had Cicero speaking for the defence. **2** For when the orator saw the unprecedented sight of Pompey and the soldiers in the court he was so panic-stricken and overwhelmed with fear that he said nothing of the speech he had prepared, but merely with difficulty uttered a few words that died away and gladly retired. The speech now extant, which purports to have been delivered on Milo's behalf at the time, was written later at leisure, when he had recovered his confidence.

13.6 Appian *Civil Wars* 2.24–25 (92, 95): Pompey's fellow consul

Appian (doc. 13.7) has those exiled from convictions under Pompey's laws about violence and ambitus going to Caesar. The son of Scipio Nasica, Q. Caecilius Metellus Pius Scipio had been adopted by Q. Caecilius Metellus Pius.

92 All those condemned were exiled and Gabinius was fined in addition to being exiled. The senate praised these proceedings loudly, voted Pompey two more legions, and extended the term of his provincial government . . . **95** Pompey, as if he had corrected all the problems which had necessitated one-man rule, made Scipio his consular colleague for the rest of the year. But even after this, when others had been appointed to the office, Pompey nonetheless remained the overseer and ruler and main power in Rome; for he possessed the senate's goodwill, particularly on account of their jealousy of Caesar, who had not consulted them at all during his consulship, and because Pompey had swiftly helped the state recover from its illness and not annoyed or offended any of them during his magistracy.

13.7 Appian *Civil Wars* 2.25 (96–97): A second consulship for Caesar?

Caesar wanted to be allowed to stand in absentia for a later consulship: all ten tribunes passed a law allowing him to do so. Pompey supported the law, but soon after he had a law passed that candidates for office had to announce their candidature in person in Rome. However, he then exempted Caesar from it. Caesar would be eligible to stand for a consulship for 48, and hence needed his command to run to the end of 49, to stand in absentia for the consular elections in summer of that year and step immediately into a consulship without any intervening period as a private citizen. For himself, Pompey took another five-year command in Spain, governing it through legates.

96 Those who were exiled went to Caesar in droves, warning him to watch out for Pompey, as Pompey's law on bribery was aimed at him in particular, but Caesar encouraged them and spoke favourably of Pompey, and persuaded the tribunes to introduce a law to allow him to stand for the consulship a second time in his absence. Pompey was still consul when this was ratified and made no objection to it. **97** As Caesar suspected that the senate would oppose this and was afraid that he might become a private citizen and vulnerable to his enemies, he worked towards keeping his power until elected consul and requested the senate to allow him a little more time in his current governorship of Gaul or of part of it. When Marcellus (cos. 51), who succeeded Pompey as consul, prevented this, Caesar is recorded as replying to the person who informed him, with his hand on his sword-hilt, 'This shall give it to me.'

THE LEAD UP TO CIVIL WAR

M. Claudius Marcellus and Servius Sulpicius Rufus were elected consuls for 51 BC. (M. Claudius Marcellus was consul in 51, another Marcellus, C. Claudius Marcellus – his first cousin – was consul for 50 BC, and yet another Marcellus, also a C. Claudius Marcellus – brother of Marcus – for 49: all three were opposed to Caesar.)

It is unclear when Caesar's command in Gaul was due to expire, but M. Claudius Marcellus began moves against him early in 51 BC. He proposed that a successor to Caesar be appointed before the latter's tenure as proconsul of Gaul expired, arguing that the war in Gaul was over and that Caesar not be allowed to stand *in absentia* for the consulship. Marcellus also argued that Pompey's additional clause exempting Caesar from the decree requiring candidates for the consulship to be present was not valid, as it had been added by Pompey and was not part of the decree itself. Caesar used the tribunes to veto Marcellus' proposals; the other consul, Ser. Sulpicius Rufus, also acted in Caesar's interests to resist Marcellus. Marcellus showed his personal hostility to Caesar by having one of the citizens of Novum Comum scourged (docs 13.8–9).

Pompey did not support Marcellus, in particular opposing his plan to terminate Caesar's command. It was decided to hold a debate later, on 13 August, which was postponed until 1 September; on 1 September 51 Pompey in the senate argued that no decree could be passed about the Gallic provinces, but Metellus Scipio (Pompey's father-in-law) proposed the motion that the Gallic provinces should be discussed (before any other item of business) in the senate on 1 March 50 BC. Later, on 29 September 51, Pompey indicated that a debate about the consular provinces could take place in March 50 (docs 13.12, 13.35). These attempts to have Caesar recalled were the first steps to civil war.

In addition, in 53 the senate had resolved that there should be a five-year gap between holding an office and taking up a provincial command, and Pompey in 52 had this made into law (the *lex Pompeia de provinciis*). Until five years had elapsed and magistrates currently in office could take up these governorships, governors were to be chosen by lot from consulars and praetorians who had not previously held a province. Under this law Cicero was chosen by lot as governor (proconsul) of Cilicia, and he left Rome in May 51 to take up his post. This law meant for Caesar that after his consulship there would be five years during which he did not have imperium and could be prosecuted for his acts as consul in 59.

13.8 Cicero *Letters to Atticus* 5.11: Marcellus has a Transpadane Gaul flogged

Written on 6 July 51. 'Our friend' here is Pompey: he was patron of the Transpadani. The colony had been founded under legislation authored by Vatinius as tribune in 59 BC. Marcellus was showing his opposition to Caesar's activities during his consulship of 59.

2 Marcellus behaved with cruelty over the man from Comum. Even though he may not have held a magistracy, he was still a Transpadane; so I imagine Marcellus has irritated our friend no less than Caesar. But that's his business.

13.9 Appian *Civil Wars* 2.26 (98–100): Growing hostility to Caesar, 51 BC

Novum Comum: doc. 13.8. Marcellus refused to accept as legal Caesar's grant by the *lex Vatinia* in 59 of Latin rights to Comum.

98 Caesar founded the town of Novum Comum at the foot of the Alps and granted it Latin rights, one of which was that whoever held the magistracies each year should become Roman citizens; for this is a condition of Latin status. Marcellus (cos. 51) had one of the men of Novum Comum, who had been a magistrate and who was accordingly considered a Roman, beaten with rods for some reason, in defiance of Caesar, something which does not happen to Romans. Marcellus in his anger revealed his true purpose that the blows should be the mark of the alien – he instructed the man to carry them to Caesar and show them to him. **99** As well as insulting Caesar in this manner, he also proposed to send successors to take over his provinces before the appointed time; but Pompey prevented this with a specious pretence of goodwill, saying that they should not insult a distinguished man who had been so very useful to his country in a dispute over a short period of time, while he made it clear that Caesar's command must be terminated immediately it expired. **100** For this reason Caesar's greatest enemies were elected consuls for the following year (50 BC), Aemilius Paullus and Claudius Marcellus, cousin of the Marcellus already mentioned, while Curio was made tribune, who was Caesar's bitter enemy and very popular with the people and a very skilled speaker. Of these Caesar was unable to win over Claudius by money but bought Paullus' neutrality for 1,500 talents and the cooperation of Curio with an even larger sum, as he knew he was encumbered by numerous debts.

13.10 Caelius in [Cicero] *Letters to his Friends* 8.4: Pressure is put on Pompey

Cf. doc. 13.12. Written by M. Caelius Rufus to Cicero in Cilicia on 1 August 51. Caelius (tr. pl. 52 and aedile in 50) kept up a regular correspondence with Cicero while the latter was in Cilicia, and these letters provide an invaluable source for the events of 51 and 50. The temple of Apollo was outside the pomerium in the Campus Martius and therefore Pompey, who was invested with imperium, could be present at the meeting. The consuls-elect for 50 were L. Aemilius Lepidus Paullus and C. Claudius Marcellus. Pompey had lent Caesar a legion in 53.

4 In politics we had ceased to expect anything new; but when the senate met in the temple of Apollo on 22 July (51 BC) and the question was put about pay for Pompey's troops, the matter of the legion which Pompey had lent to Caesar was brought up, whom it belonged to and how long Pompey would let it stay in Gaul. Pompey was compelled to state that he would remove the legion, but not straightaway in response to the remarks and outcry from his detractors. Then there was a question put about the replacement of Gaius Caesar, regarding which (that is, on the question of the provinces) it was agreed that Pompey should return to the city as quickly as possible so that a debate on the replacement of governors could be held with him present – Pompey was on the point of going to his army at Ariminum and left at once. I think the debate will take place on the Ides (13th) of August. Either a decision will be reached or it will be disgracefully vetoed – for during the discussion Pompey made the comment that everyone ought to pay attention to the senate's dictates. I, however, am looking forward to nothing so much as Paullus, as consul-elect, being the first to give his views on the issue.

13.11 [Caesar] *Gallic War* 8.53.1–2: Marcellus tries to end Caesar's command

The law of Pompey and Crassus was the *lex Licinia Pompeia* in 55 BC, extending Caesar's command for another five years in Gaul.

1 In the previous year (51 BC), in an attack on Caesar's position, Marcellus, contrary to a law of Pompey and Crassus, had brought prematurely before the senate a motion on Caesar's provinces. Opinions were voiced, and when Marcellus, who wanted any position for himself which could be gained from the ill-will felt towards Caesar, called for a division, the crowded senate crossed over in support of the 'No' side. **2** This did not alter the resolution of Caesar's enemies but incited them to come up with more compelling reasons, which could be used to force the senate to approve what they themselves had resolved.

13.12 Caelius in [Cicero] *Letters to his Friends* 8.8: Pompey's views on Caesar's command

In this letter of early October 51 BC, Caelius gives an account of the senatorial proceedings of 29 September 51 and quotes decrees of the senate (8.8.5–8). The senate resolved, with Pompey's agreement, that the consuls elected for 50 (Paullus and C. Marcellus) would on 1 March in their year of office (50) bring the matter of Caesar's command before the senate and bring no other matter to the senate until this issue was resolved. Another decree of the same day, that no one with the power of veto should prevent the discussion about the provinces taking place on that day, was vetoed by four tribunes (but the resolution itself about the provinces was not).

4 Finally, after frequent postponements and much serious discussion, it became clear that Gnaeus Pompey wanted him (Caesar) to leave his command after the Kalends of March. The senate approved and I send you a copy of the decree and recorded resolutions. **5** 'On this day, 29 September, in the temple of Apollo, . . . In as much as M. Marcellus, consul, did address the senate on the matter of the consular provinces, it was resolved: that L. Paullus and C. Marcellus, consuls, on entering their office, should on or after the Kalends of March in their year of office (50 BC) refer the question of the consular provinces to the senate, and that from the Kalends of March they should bring no business before the senate, either previously or in conjunction; moreover for the same purpose they might hold a meeting of the senate on comitial (assembly) days and pass decrees . . . '

9 Furthermore the confidence of the public has been greatly enhanced by some comments made by Gnaeus Pompey, in which he remarked that before the Kalends of March he could not justly make any decision about Caesar's provinces, but after the Kalends of March he would have no hesitation. When he was asked what would happen if any vetoes were interposed at that stage, he said that it was of no importance whether Gaius Caesar was not going to follow the senate's decree or if he was getting someone ready to prevent the senate from passing a decree. 'And what', asked someone else, 'if he wants to be consul and keep his army?' Pompey replied mildly: 'What if my son wants to take his stick to me?' As a consequence of these remarks, people think that Pompey is having trouble with Caesar.

13.13 Caelius in [Cicero] *Letters to his Friends* 8.10: Parthian problems

Written on 17 November 51. After Crassus' defeat in Parthia, his quaestor Cassius (C. Cassius Longinus, one of the conspirators against Caesar) had regrouped the survivors in Syria. In September 51 the Parthians crossed the Euphrates towards Roman Syria. Pompey wanted the command, but for the moment Cassius, then Cicero and Bibulus as governors in 51–50 of Cilicia and Syria, dealt with the situation (cf. doc. 5.73).

2 The reports about the Parthian crossing have given rise to a lot of talk. One view is that Pompey should be sent, another that Pompey ought not to be taken away from Rome, another that Caesar should go with his army, another the consuls, but no one wants *privati* sent by senatorial decree. Moreover the consuls, who are afraid that the senate may not approve their military appointment and that the job might go shamefully over their heads to someone else, are unwilling to have senate meetings at all, to the point where they appear to be neglecting government. But whether due to negligence or inertia or the fear I suggested, it is respectably obscured under the belief that they are men of moderation who have no wish for a province . . . **3** It's now the end of the year – I am writing this letter on 17 November. I can clearly see that nothing can be done before the Kalends of January. You know (M. Claudius) Marcellus, how slow and ineffectual he is, and Servius (Sulpicius Rufus) too, a real procrastinator. What do you think of their behaviour, what do you see as their ability to get something done which they are not interested in, when they are dealing so feebly with something they do want as to make it look as if they are not interested? When the new magistrates come in, if there is going to be a Parthian war, that issue will take up the first months, but if there's not going to be a war there, or if it's small enough for you two (Cicero and Bibulus) or your successors to cope with with a few reinforcements, I can see Curio being active in two directions, first taking something away from Caesar, then giving something to Pompey, any little gift, however trifling. Paullus, too, is talking unjustifiably about a province. Our friend Furnius (tr. pl. 50) is ready to put up resistance to his greed.

THE EVENTS OF 50 BC

One of the tribunes elected in 51 for 50, Servaeus, was convicted of electoral bribery under the *lex Pompeia de ambitu*, and C. Scribonius Curio was elected in his place. Curio had been opposed to the triumvirate in 59 (docs 12.51–53) and was viewed as a friend of the optimates. He was popular with the plebs and had married Fulvia, Clodius' widow. He had been massively in debt but was bailed out by Caesar and served his interests, though at first he concealed his change of alliance, moving formally over to Caesar in February 50 when his request for a month to be intercalated was refused.

The main issue of this year was the terminal date of Caesar's Gallic command. Scholars disagree both on the exact date when his second term as governor of Gaul was due to expire and whether the dates set for the discussion of termination of his command (1 March 50) and, later, for its actual termination (13 November 50) were reasonable: Pompey thought the 13 November date 'fair' and accused Curio of simply making trouble (doc. 13.16). But Caesar (doc. 13.27) states that the *SCU* of 7 January 49 deprived him of six months of his command (i.e., it was due to expire in mid-49). Pompey's insistence in 51 that Caesar's command should not be debated until 1 March 50 could be taken to indicate that the extension of the latter's five-year command as arranged by Crassus and Pompey in their consulship (55 BC) under the *lex Pompeia Licinia* was due in fact to expire on or soon after that date. The first year Caesar could hold a second consulship was 48, as he himself notes (doc. 13.42). It was essential for Caesar that his command should be extended until he was elected to his second consulship, or he would be liable for prosecution for events in his first; Pompey was anxious, however, that there *should* be such a gap (docs 13.16, 13.18).

The consuls elected for 50 BC were one of M. Marcellus' cousins, C. Claudius Marcellus, and L. Aemilius Lepidus Paullus, who was thought to have been bribed by Caesar. In 50 Paullus did support Caesar, who had helped him financially to complete his rebuilding of the Basilica Aemilia in the forum at the cost of 1,500 talents. The debate about consular provinces was due to take place on 1 March 50, but the matter was apparently postponed, and Paullus, as presiding consul, clearly played a key role. Caelius in a letter of April notes that Pompey had now decided, along with the senate, that Caesar was to step down from his command on or before 13 November 50 (doc. 13.16).

13.14 Caelius in [Cicero] *Letters to his Friends* 8.6: Curio changes sides

Written in February 50 BC. Cicero in his province had heard of disturbances in Curio's tribunate. Appian sees Curio's road bill (he planned to be superintendent for five years) and the expected optimate opposition to it as a deliberate move to excuse his change of allegiance from Pompey. In 50 Caelius was curule aedile. For the panthers, see doc. 2.77.

3 We have really industrious consuls! – up till now they'd not managed to get a single decree through the senate except about the (date of the) Latin Festival. **4**

Our friend Curio's tribunate is a total frost. I just can't tell you how dormant everything is here. If it weren't for my battle (as aedile) with shopkeepers and water-pipe inspectors, the whole city would be fast asleep . . . **5** Regarding my remark above about Curio's frozen inactivity, he's now warmed up – and is being enthusiastically torn to pieces! Most irresponsibly, because he didn't get his own way about intercalation, he's gone over to the populace and begun talking in support of Caesar. He's declared a road bill, rather like Rullus' agrarian bill, and a food bill, which instructs the aediles to make distributions. He'd not started any of this when I wrote the first part of my letter . . . You'll be in disgrace if I don't have any Greek panthers!

13.15 Appian *Civil Wars* 2.27 (103–5): Joint disarmament

If Caesar planned to stand in summer 49 for the consulship of 48, there would have been ample time for him to be prosecuted for his activities as consul in 59 BC if he stood down from his governorship on 13 November 50. In this case, he would need to rely on Pompey in any confrontation with Cato and other optimates, or face prosecution and its serious consequences for his career. Curio proposed early in the year that *both* Caesar and Pompey lay down their arms. On 1 December 50 Curio made the same proposal, this time successfully: it produced a dramatic vote in favour of peace (docs 13.22–23).

103 Matters turned out as Curio had anticipated, and he had an excuse for taking an opposing line. Claudius proposed the sending of successors to Caesar to take over his provinces, for his term was coming to an end. Paullus kept silent. **104** Curio, who was believed to disagree with both, supported Claudius' motion but added that Pompey ought to lay down his provinces and army like Caesar, for in this way Rome's government would be free and without fear on all sides. **105** Many argued with this as unfair, as Pompey's term had not yet ended, at which Curio showed himself more openly and decidedly against sending successors to Caesar unless the same applied to Pompey – as they were suspicious of each other, he stated, the city could enjoy no definite peace unless they all became private citizens. He said this because he was aware that Pompey would not lay down his command and saw that the people were now angry with Pompey over his prosecutions for bribery.

13.16 Caelius in [Cicero] *Letters to his Friends* 8.11: Curio opposes Pompey

Caelius in April 50 BC here indicates that Pompey had expressed his unwillingness that Caesar be elected consul while still in control of Gaul and his army. This highlights Caesar's predicament, as he did not wish there to be an opportunity for his enemies to prosecute him for the events of 59. Pompey was presumably envisaging that Caesar would stand for the consulship of 48 BC.

3 As for politics, all dispute is centred on just one issue, that of the provinces. The current state of play is that Pompey appears to be supporting the senate on Caesar having to lay down his command on the Ides of November (50 BC). Curio would put up with anything rather than allow that, and has put aside the rest of his programme. Moreover our friends, whom you know well, don't dare to take the matter to outright conflict. This is how the scene for the whole issue is set: Pompey acts as if he is not attacking Caesar but settling the issue so as to be fair to him; he says Curio is deliberately stirring up trouble. Yet he strongly disapproves and clearly is afraid of Caesar becoming consul-elect before he has handed over his army and province. He is getting fairly rough treatment from Curio and the whole of his third consulship is being subjected to criticism. I can tell you this: if they use every means to restrain Curio, Caesar will protect his veto-giver; if, as seems likely, they are too scared, Caesar will stay as long as he likes.

13.17 Appian *Civil Wars* 2.28 (107–11): Pompey confronts Caesar

Pompey's attitude towards Caesar may have been encouraged by the support he received throughout Italy when he fell ill.

107 While sick in Italy, Pompey wrote a disingenuous letter to the senate praising Caesar's achievements and narrating his own from the beginning – that he had not sought his third consulship or the provinces and army which followed but had been granted them after he had been called on to cure the state. Regarding the powers he had unwillingly accepted, he said, 'I will willingly lay them down for those who wish to take them back and will not wait for the designated date on which they expire.' **108** The disingenuousness of his letter created an impression of sincerity for Pompey and prejudice towards Caesar, as not going to give up his command even at the fixed time. When he reached the city, Pompey made similar statements to the senators and then promised to lay down his command. **109** As a friend and kinsman of Caesar, he said that Caesar would very gladly do the same, for he had had a lengthy and difficult campaign against very warlike peoples, had added a great deal of territory to his country, and would now come back to his honours, sacrifices and relaxations. He said this so that Caesar would immediately be assigned successors, while he had only made a promise.

    110 Curio exposed his deviousness, stating that promises were not enough and that he should immediately lay down his command and Caesar should not disarm until Pompey was a privatus. Because of their private enmity, it would not be advantageous either for Caesar or for the Romans that such great power be held by one man, but that each of them should have power against the other in case either should use violence against Rome. **111** With no further attempt at concealment, he ceaselessly attacked Pompey as aiming at tyranny and stated that, if he did not lay down his command now through his fear of Caesar, he would never do so. He proposed that, if they did not obey, both should be voted public enemies and an army be raised against them, for by doing this he concealed that he had been bought by Caesar.

13.18 Caelius in [Cicero] *Letters to his Friends* 8.14: Caelius forecasts war

Written c. 8 August 50.

2 On important political matters, I have often written to you that I cannot see peace lasting another year; and the closer the inevitable conflict approaches, the plainer the danger seems. The question on which the great powers will come into conflict is that Gnaeus Pompey is determined not to allow Gaius Caesar to become consul unless he gives up his army and provinces, while Caesar is sure he cannot be safe if he leaves his army; he has, however, proposed that both should give up their armies. This is what their love affair and scandalous alliance have come to – not sliding into secret disparagement but breaking out into war! For my own position, I cannot decide what course to take; I don't doubt the same question is going to trouble you too. I have obligations and friendly relations with the men on one side; on the other side I love the cause and hate the people . . . **3** In the present conflict I see that Gnaeus Pompey will have on his side the senate and those who sit on juries, while all who live in fear and gloomy expectations for the future will join Caesar; his army is without comparison. At all events, there is still enough time to weigh up their respective forces and choose which side to join . . .

4 To sum up, what do I think will happen? If one or the other does not go to the Parthian war, I see great dissension ahead, to be settled by steel and force. Both are well prepared with resolution and troops. If only it could happen without personal risk, Fortune would be preparing a great and entertaining show for your benefit.

13.19 Cato in [Cicero] *Letters to his Friends* 15.5: Cato on Cicero's supplicatio

In this very characteristic letter of late April 50 BC – brief, to the point and surely heavily ironic – in reply to one of Cicero's, Cato explains why he voted against the successful motion of mid-April for a supplicatio in Cicero's honour for his defeat of brigands on Mount Amanus. Bibulus, hopeless governor of Syria, was Cato's son-in-law, and Cato had arranged for him to have a 20-day supplication. Caesar had also written congratulating Cicero and commenting gleefully on Cato's attitude (Cic. *Att.* 7.1.7, 7.2.7). For a similar request to C. Marcellus, as consul-elect for 50, see doc. 2.49.

1 That which the public interest and our friendship encourage me to do, I do willingly, that is, rejoice that the courage, integrity and diligence, which it is well known were displayed by you as a civilian in a grave crisis at home, are being put to good use with equal assiduity by you as a soldier. As a result, that which I was able to do according to my own judgement, that is, to praise by both vote and speech the fact that the province was protected by your integrity and judgement, that the kingdom of Ariobarzanes, and the king himself, were saved, and that the hearts of our allies were brought back to an enthusiastic acceptance of our rule, this I did.

2 As to the supplicatio being decreed, if you, in a matter in which the safety of the state was secured, not in any way by chance but by your own judgement and moderation, would prefer that we should thank the immortal gods rather than give the credit to you, I rejoice at it. But if you think a supplicatio automatically leads to a triumph, and this is the reason you prefer fortune to get the praise rather than yourself, I should say that a triumph does not always follow a *supplicatio*, and that it is far more glorious than a triumph to have the senate resolve that a province was secured and preserved by the clemency and integrity of its governor rather than by the force of soldiers and the goodwill of the gods; that was my view when I gave my vote.

3 I have written to you at length against my usual practice to make you believe (as I very much wish you to do) that I am making every effort to convince you, both that I supported the course that I thought most conducive to your honour and that I rejoice that your own preference was adopted. Goodbye, retain your affection for me, and, following the road you have begun, continue to demonstrate to the allies and the state your responsibility and diligence.

13.20 Cicero *Letters to Atticus* 7.7: Cicero returns to Italy

Dated to 19(?) December 50 BC. Cicero returned to Rome in January 49 but, despite his wishes, was not awarded a triumph. **6**: Caesar was planning to be a candidate for the consulship of 48. His tribunes for 49 were Mark Antony and Q. Cassius Longinus (not to be confused with the later conspirator C. Cassius Longinus, also tribune that year). Pompey's 'council' was made up of his close associates. The 'man from Gades' refers to the adoption of L. Cornelius Balbus (earlier Caesar's engineer) by the wealthy Theophanes of Mytilene; for Mamurra, see doc. 12.89.

4 Regarding my triumph, unless Caesar attempts something underhand through his tribunes, all seems to be plain sailing; but calmest of all is my own mind, which takes the whole thing in a spirit of acquiescence, all the more because I hear from a number of people that it has been decided by Pompey and his council to send me to Sicily because I have imperium. That's just stupid! Neither the senate nor the people has authorised me to hold imperium in Sicily, and, if the state refers this to Pompey, why send me rather than a private individual? And so, if this imperium is going to be troublesome, I'll make use of the first gate I see. **5** You state that the anticipation of my arrival is astounding, but that none of the honest, or reasonably honest, men have doubts about what I will do. I don't understand whom you mean by 'honest men'. I know of none – that is, if we are looking for classes of good men. There are some honest men individually, but in political conflicts you need to look for classes and species. Do you consider the senate 'honest',when it is their doing that the provinces have no governors? – Curio would never have held out if discussion had begun with him, but the senate refused to support the proposal and as a consequence there are no governors to succeed Caesar. What of the tax-farmers, who are never reliable and are now Caesar's greatest friends, or the moneylenders, or the farmers, who desire peace above anything else? – unless you think they are afraid of living under an autocracy, but they would never have worried about that as long as they were left in peace.

6 You may ask whether I approve of accepting the candidature of a man who retains his army after the legal date has passed. I disapprove even of his candidature in absence, but, once that was granted, the other was granted with it. Do I approve of his ten years' command and the way it was put in place? I then approve of my exile, of the loss of the Campanian lands, of a patrician being adopted by a plebeian, and of a man from Gades by someone from Mytilene, and of the wealth of Labienus and Mamurra and Balbus' gardens and estate at Tusculum. The source of all these evils is the same. We should have opposed him when he was weak and it was easy; now we are facing 11 legions, all the cavalry he might want, the Transpadane Gauls, the urban populace, so many tribunes, our desperate young men, and a leader of such prestige and daring. We must either fight it out with him or allow his candidature according to law. 'Fight', you'll say, 'rather than be a slave.' **7** For what? If you're defeated, proscription; if you win, you'll still be a slave. . . . I can see clearly what would be best in these terrible circumstances: no one can be certain what will happen if it comes to war, but we all assume that, if the honest men are defeated, he'll be no more merciful than Cinna in slaughtering the leading men and no more moderate than Sulla in robbing the wealthy . . .

13.21 [Caesar] *Gallic War* 8.54.1–55.2: Caesar loses two legions

In 50 the senate decreed that two legions be prepared for the Parthian campaign; the question of Caesar's return of a legion loaned by Pompey had already been the subject of senatorial discussion in August 51 (doc. 13.10).

54.1 The senate then decreed that one legion was to be sent by Gnaeus Pompey and a second by Gaius Caesar for the Parthian campaign, and it was quite clear that the two legions were to be taken off only one man. **2** For Gnaeus Pompey gave up the First Legion, which he had sent to Caesar as it was raised by a levy in Caesar's province, as if one of his own. **3** Caesar, however, although there was no doubt at all about the intentions of his enemies, returned the legion to Pompey and from his own troops ordered the Fifteenth, which he had kept in Nearer Gaul, to be handed over in accordance with the senate's decree . . . **5** He himself set out for Italy. **55.1** When he arrived, he learnt that, through the agency of the consul Gaius Marcellus, the two legions he had sent back, which in accordance with the senate's decree should have been led off for the Parthian campaign, had been handed over to Gnaeus Pompey and kept in Italy. **2** Although this action left no doubt in anyone's mind what was in train against Caesar, Caesar still decided to put up with everything as long as some hope was left to him of the issue being resolved constitutionally rather than through military conflict.

13.22 Plutarch *Life of Pompey* 58.1–9.2: Caesar's friends – and enemies

Plutarch here summarises the events of 50 BC. Curio's support came from Piso, Caesar's father-in-law, and his friend Mark Antony (tr. pl. 49). Curio's suggestion on 1 December that both men lay down their command was considered by many in the senate as unfair, as Pompey's command had three years yet to run (doc. 13.15). But the mood for peace was clear: only 22 senators sided with Marcellus and the rest with Curio. Marcellus therefore went to Pompey's Alban villa and entrusted him with the two legions that were stationed in Italy in preparation for the aborted Parthian campaign (doc. 13.21).

58.1 Caesar, too, was now becoming more actively involved in public affairs and no longer stayed at a distance from Italy's borders, but was always sending his soldiers to Rome to vote in elections and using money to win over and bribe numerous magistrates. **2** Among these were the consul Paullus, who changed sides for 1,500 talents, and the tribune Curio, who was relieved from irretrievable debt by Caesar, plus Mark Antony, who out of friendship for Curio had become involved in his debts. **3** It was actually said of one of Caesar's centurions, who had come back to Rome and was standing near the senate house, when he heard that the senate would not give Caesar a prolongation of command, that he clapped his hand on his sword and said, 'But this will give it to him.' **4** And all of Caesar's actions and preparations had this end in view. Nevertheless Curio's demands and requests on Caesar's behalf seemed very fair. **5** He demanded one of two alternatives: either that Pompey as well should be required to disband his army or that Caesar should not – on the grounds that, whether they became private citizens on equal terms or remained rivals with their present forces, they would cause no disturbance, but whoever made one of the two weak doubled the power he feared. **6** When Marcellus, the consul, replied to this by calling Caesar a robber, and urging that he be voted a public enemy if he did not lay down his arms, Curio, supported by Antony and (L. Calpurnius) Piso, got his way in having the matter put to the senate's vote. **7** He proposed that those who wanted only Caesar to lay down his arms and Pompey to retain his command move to one side; the majority did so. **8** When he a second time made the proposal that all those who wanted both men to lay down their arms and neither retain command move to one side, only 22 sided with Pompey and all the rest with Curio. **9** He felt that he had won and rushed joyfully to the assembly, which welcomed him with applause and pelted him with garlands and flowers. Pompey was not in the senate, as commanders of armies are not allowed into the city.

10 Marcellus, however, got up and said he was not going to sit there listening to speeches, but, as he could see the imminent arrival of ten legions marching over the Alps, he was personally going to dispatch someone to oppose them in his country's defence. **59.1** At this everyone put on mourning as if for a national disaster, while Marcellus, with the senators following him, marched through the forum on his way to see Pompey and, standing in front of him, declared, 'I order you, Pompey, to come to your country's aid, to make use of the forces already prepared for action and to levy others.' **2** Lentulus (L. Cornelius Lentulus Crus) too, one of the two consuls elected for the following year (49 BC), said the same. But when Pompey began to raise troops, some refused to obey the order and others showed up only reluctantly and without enthusiasm, while most people demanded a settlement.

13.23 Appian *Civil Wars* 2.29–31 (112–23): Pompey 'the better Republican'

C. Claudius Marcellus as consul divided Curio's motion of 1 December 50 into two separate motions, one to send out successors to Caesar (which passed) and one to deprive Pompey of his command, which was not carried, which was what Marcellus had intended. But Curio reintroduced his motion, and the senate voted 370 to 22 to preserve the peace by decreeing that both were to lay down their arms. Marcellus then entrusted the state to Pompey, who clearly had made up his mind for war. Curio's tribunate ended on 10 December, and he left to join Caesar at Ravenna.

112 Pompey was enraged with him (Curio) and threatened him, immediately withdrawing to the suburbs in indignation. The senate was now suspicious of both men but considered Pompey the better Republican, while they hated Caesar for behaving towards them with contempt during his consulship; some of them considered that it was really not safe to remove Pompey's power until Caesar should have laid down his, since he was outside the city and possessed of more sweeping ambitions than Pompey. **113** Curio gave the opposite viewpoint, that they needed Caesar against Pompey, or that everyone should be disbanded together. As he did not carry his point, he dismissed the senate with the whole affair still unresolved – tribunes are able to do this. Pompey thus had cause to regret restoring the tribunate to its former powers after it had been reduced to insignificance by Sulla. **114** Despite being dismissed, however, they voted on just one issue, that Caesar and Pompey should each send one legion of soldiers to Syria to defend it after the disaster incurred by Crassus. **115** Pompey was devious and demanded back the legion which he had recently lent to Caesar to compensate for the disaster suffered by Caesar's two generals, Titurius and Cotta. Caesar made each man a present of 250 drachmas and sent the legion to Rome with another of his own. As the anticipated emergency in Syria did not eventuate, these legions spent the winter at Capua, **116** while the people sent by Pompey to Caesar spread many reports hostile to Caesar and assured Pompey that Caesar's army was worn out by long, hard service and longing for home, and that it would defect to him as soon as it crossed the Alps. **117** Though they gave these reports, either from ignorance or because they had been bribed, every soldier enthusiastically supported and laboured for Caesar from being used to serving in his campaigns and from the rewards accorded by war to the victors and all the other things they received from Caesar – for he gave lavishly to ensure their support for his plans – and, though they were well aware of these, they stood by him nonetheless. **118** Pompey, however, relied on this information and did not collect either an army or equipment appropriate for so great an enterprise. The senate asked each man for his opinion, and Claudius (Marcellus) cunningly divided the question into two and asked for their views separately, whether successors to Caesar should be sent and whether Pompey should be deprived of his command. The majority voted against the latter motion but in favour of successors for Caesar. **119** Curio then put it to the vote whether both should lay down their commands: 22 senators voted against and 370 went back to Curio's view to avoid civil war, whereupon Claudius dismissed the senate with the cry: 'Have it your own way – with Caesar as your master!'

120 When a false report suddenly came to hand that Caesar had crossed the Alps and was marching against the city, there was immense confusion and fear on all sides, and Claudius proposed that the army at Capua should go to engage Caesar as an enemy. When Curio opposed him on the grounds that the report was false, he declared: **121** 'If I am hindered by a vote from taking steps for the public safety, I shall do so on my own authority as consul.' With these words, he ran from the senate with his colleague to the suburbs, where he presented a sword to Pompey, saying, 'My colleague and I instruct you to march against Caesar on your country's behalf, and we give you for this purpose the army now at Capua or in any other region of Italy and whatever troops in addition you should yourself wish to levy.' **122** Pompey undertook to obey the consuls' orders, but added, 'If there is no better way', whether being disingenuous or still making a pretence of decency. **123** Curio had no authority outside the city (for tribunes are not allowed to go outside the walls), but publicly lamented what had occurred and demanded that the consuls should proclaim that no one had to obey Pompey's levy. He was unsuccessful, and, as his period of office was coming to an end and he was afraid for himself, as well as having given up any hope of being able to assist Caesar any longer, he left in haste to join him.

THE FLIGHT OF THE TRIBUNES

In 50 BC the consuls elected for 49 BC were C. Claudius Marcellus, brother of the consul of 51 BC, and L. Cornelius Lentulus Crus; both were opposed to Caesar, and Caesar's candidate Servius Galba was defeated. Antony, however, was elected to the college of augurs on the death of Hortensius and also as one of the tribunes for 49. Caesar used the rights of the tribunes as a major pretext for war (cf. doc. 1.23). On 21 December Antony, as tribune, attacked Pompey's entire career and spoke for those condemned under the laws of 52. On 1 January 49 matters came to a head with a dispatch from Caesar read to the senate.

13.24 Caesar *Civil War* 1.1.1–5.5: Caesar's view of events in January 49

Caesar's *Civil War* (*BC*) commences with a reference to a dispatch brought by Curio from Caesar at Ravenna and read out in the senate, despite opposition. Caesar proposed that both Pompey and he should give up their armies; if Pompey would not, neither would Caesar, and he would defend his position with arms. On 7 January the optimates, especially Lentulus and Cato, successfully had a senatus consultum ultimum passed and warned Pompey not to be deceived by offers from Caesar.

1.1 When the consuls had been handed Caesar's dispatch, permission was obtained from them with difficulty, and after a great struggle on the part of the tribunes, that it be read in the senate; they could not, however, gain permission for a motion to be brought before the senate regarding the dispatch. The consuls propose a motion concerning the Republic. **2** The consul Lucius Lentulus urges on the senate, promising that he will not fail the Republic if they are prepared to speak their views boldly and resolutely; **3** but, if they consider Caesar and try to win his favour, as they have done on earlier occasions, he will consider his own interests and not submit to the senate's authority: he, too, could take refuge in Caesar's favour and friendship. (Q. Caecilius Metellus Pius) Scipio voices the same view: **4** that Pompey is of a mind not to fail the Republic if the senate supports him; if it delays and acts in a more conciliatory fashion, the senate will vainly request his assistance, should it choose to do so at a later date.

    2.1 This speech of Scipio's, as the senate was meeting in the city and Pompey was close by, appeared to come from Pompey's own mouth. **2** Some had voiced more moderate views, such as, initially, Marcus Marcellus, who gave a speech to the effect that the matter should not be referred to the senate until levies had been held throughout Italy and armies enlisted, under whose protection the senate could venture, safely and freely, to make whatever decrees it wished; **3** and such as Marcus Calidius, who gave his view that Pompey should set out for his provinces, so that there should be no reason for hostilities: Caesar was afraid, he said, now two legions had been extorted from him, that it might appear that Pompey was holding them back and keeping them near the city to use them against him; such as Marcus Rufus, too, who supported Calidius' view with a few minor changes. **4** All these were vehemently and abusively attacked by the consul Lucius Lentulus. **5** Lentulus totally refused to put Calidius' motion. Marcellus, frightened by the abuse, abandoned his proposal. **6** And so most of them were forced by the language of the consul, fear at the presence of the army, and the threats of Pompey's friends, against their will and under pressure, to support Scipio's proposal: that Caesar should disband his army before a certain date; if he did not do this, he should be considered to be planning acts against the Republic. **7** Mark Antony and Quintus Cassius, tribunes, interpose their veto. The question of their veto is at once brought to the senate. **8** Violent opinions are voiced, and the more violent and fierce the speech, the more loudly the speaker is applauded by Caesar's enemies.

3.1 When the senate was dismissed in the evening, all its members are summoned out by Pompey. Pompey praises the brave and encourages them for the future and reproaches and rouses the unenergetic. **2** Many from the old armies of Pompey are called up from all sides with hope of rewards and promotions, and many are summoned from the two legions handed over by Caesar. **3** The city and comitium itself are full of tribunes, centurions, volunteers . . . **4.4** Pompey himself, urged on by Caesar's enemies, and by his wish to have no one his equal in prestige (dignitas), had completely turned away from Caesar's friendship and become reconciled with their common enemies . . . **5.3** That final and ultimate decree of the senate is resorted to which had never previously been called upon, except when the city was on the point of destruction and when, through the temerity of evildoers, everyone despaired of safety: the consuls, praetors, tribunes and any men of proconsular rank near the city are to take measures that the Republic suffer no harm. **4** This resolution is recorded by the senate's decree on 7 January. And so, on the first five days on which the senate could meet from the day Lentulus took up his consulship, excepting two election days (i.e., up to 7 January), the most severe and harsh decrees are passed regarding Caesar's command and those most important persons, the tribunes of the plebs. **5** The tribunes immediately flee from the city and take themselves to Caesar. At that time he was at Ravenna and awaiting replies to his very moderate requests, in case men's sense of justice might be able to bring matters to a peaceful conclusion.

13.25 Cicero *Letters to his Friends* 16.11: Cicero on the flight of the tribunes

The tribunes fled to Caesar at Ravenna, where he made their treatment a pretext for war (doc. 1.23). Caesar's view that his proposals were moderate is not one shared by Cicero, who saw them as belligerent. Cicero is writing here on 12 January 49 BC to Tiro.

2 True that our friend Caesar has sent a sharp, threatening letter to the senate and continues to declare that he will keep his army and province against the senate's wishes, and my friend Curio is encouraging him. Our friend Antony and Quintus Cassius, without being forcibly expelled, left to join Caesar together with Curio, after the senate had given the consuls, praetors, tribunes and us proconsuls the duty of seeing to it that the state took no harm. **3** Never has the state been in greater danger, never have wicked citizens had a leader more ready for action. True that on our side, too, preparations are very earnestly under way. This is happening through the authority and enthusiasm of our friend Pompey, who has begun, rather late, to be afraid of Caesar.

CROSSING THE RUBICON

13.26 Appian *Civil Wars* 2.34 (134–40): 'The die is cast'

News of the senatus consultum of 7 January reached Caesar by 10 January, and he made the decision to defend his position with arms. On the night of 10–11 January he crossed the Rubicon, bringing his troops into Italy. Ariminum, the first town in Italy proper, was taken. The phrase 'Let the die be cast!' is from a play by the Greek playwright Menander.

134 Although the war had now started on both sides, being already openly declared, the senate considered that Caesar's army would take some time in arriving from Gaul and that he would not rush into such a venture with only a few men, and so ordered Pompey to raise 130,000 men from Italy, particularly veterans who would have experience of war, and to enlist as many brave men as possible from neighbouring provinces. **135** They voted him for the war the entire public treasury straightaway and their private fortunes in addition, if needed for the soldiers' pay. In their anger and partisanship, they sent round to the allies for additional funds with the greatest possible haste. **136** Caesar had sent for his own army, but, being used to depend on the surprise caused by his speed and the terror caused by his audacity rather than on the immensity of his preparations, he decided, with his 5,000 men, to be the first to attack in this great war and to seize the strategic positions in Italy before the enemy. **137** Caesar, therefore, sent the centurions, with a few of their most courageous soldiers, dressed in civilian clothes, to enter Ariminum and take the city by surprise; this is the first town in Italy after you leave Cisalpine Gaul. **138** As evening approached, Caesar withdrew from a drinking party, on the grounds that he was not feeling well, leaving his friends to continue feasting, and, mounting his chariot, drove towards Ariminum, with his cavalry following at a distance. **139** On his journey he came to the Rubicon River, which forms Italy's frontier, where he stopped and, gazing at the stream, revolved in his mind a consideration of each of the evils that would result if he crossed this river in arms. **140** He recovered himself and said to those with him, 'My friends, my not crossing will bring about evils for me – my crossing will for all mankind.' With these words, he crossed with a rush like one possessed, uttering this well-known phrase, 'Let the die be cast!'

13.27 Caesar *Civil War* 1.8.1–11.4: Caesar's justification

The proposal of Pompey's father-in-law, Metellus Scipio, in the senate on 1 January that Caesar dismiss his army (doc. 13.24) and so become a private citizen would have meant that he would be open to prosecution by his enemies. This was a situation he had to avoid. At Ariminum, Caesar received the praetor Roscius and Lucius Caesar, as public envoys, with a communication from Pompey. Caesar replied with his own proposals for peace, presented to Pompey on 23 January at Capua; Pompey replied in turn, but Caesar argues here that he could not accept Pompey's conditions. Preparations for war continued. To Caesar his right to stand *in absentia* for the consulship while retaining his Gallic command was the crucial issue, and in his speech to his troops in January 49 he exhorted them to defend his dignitas.

8.1 After learning the wishes of the soldiers he sets out for Ariminum with the Thirteenth Legion and there meets the tribunes who had fled to join him; he summons the remaining legions from their winter quarters and orders them to follow him. **2** To Ariminum comes the young man Lucius Caesar, whose father was one of his legates. When their first greetings were over, he reveals the reason for his coming, that he has instructions for him from Pompey on a private matter: **3** he says that Pompey wants to clear himself in Caesar's eyes, and that Caesar should not take as an attack on himself what he had done for the sake of Rome. He had always put the good of Rome before private friendships. Caesar, considering his high position, should also for the benefit of Rome give up his partisanship and grievances and not be so bitterly angry with his enemies as to harm the state in his desire to harm them. **4** He adds a few remarks of the same kind together with excuses for Pompey. The praetor Roscius puts before Caesar nearly the same proposals in the same words, explaining that they came from Pompey.

9.1 Although these proceedings appeared to do nothing towards alleviating the wrongs that had been committed, now, however, that he had obtained suitable men to convey his wishes to Pompey he asks of both, as they had brought him Pompey's instructions, that they not object to taking his terms in reply back to Pompey, in case they might be able, by a little trouble, to put a stop to serious conflict and free all Italy from fear. **2** As for himself, he said, his prestige (dignitas) had always been of prime importance to him and preferable to life itself. He had been grieved that a kindness bestowed on him by the Roman people should be insultingly wrested from him by his enemies, and that he should be dragged back to the city deprived of six months of command, when the people had decreed that he could be a candidate in absentia at the next elections. **3** However, for Rome's sake he had endured with equanimity the loss of this privilege: when he sent a dispatch to the senate suggesting that everyone should give up their armies, he had not even been granted that. **4** Levies were being held throughout Italy, two legions, taken from him on the pretence of a Parthian war, were being kept back, the state was in arms. What was the aim of all this but his destruction? **5** He was, however, prepared to agree to anything and to put up with anything for the sake of Rome. Let Pompey set out for his provinces, let them both disband their armies, let everyone in Italy lay down arms, let the state be freed from fear, and let free elections and the control of the whole state be entrusted to the senate and Roman people. **6** That this might be done more easily and on definite conditions and be ratified by an oath, either let Pompey come nearer or allow him to approach Pompey: in this way all conflict would be settled through discussion.

10.1 After accepting the commission Roscius arrives at Capua with Lucius Caesar where he finds Pompey and the consuls; he reports Caesar's demands. **2** After deliberation they reply and send them back to him with instructions, of which the gist was as follows: **3** Caesar should return to Gaul, leave Ariminum and disband his army; if he did so, Pompey would go to the Spanish provinces. **4** Meanwhile, until a pledge be received that Caesar would do as he promised, the consuls and Pompey would not pause in levying troops. **11.1** It was an unfair condition to demand that Caesar should leave Ariminum and return to his province, while he himself (Pompey) kept not only his provinces but someone else's legions; to desire Caesar to disband his army, while he was holding levies; **2** to promise to go to his province and not to fix a deadline by which he must go, so that, even if he set out when Caesar's consulship had finished, he would still appear guiltless of breaking his oath; **3** furthermore, failure to make an opportunity for a conference or promise to approach Caesar meant that all hopes of peace should be abandoned. **4** Accordingly, he sends Mark Antony from Ariminum to Arretium with five cohorts; he himself stays at Ariminum with two cohorts and arranges the holding of a levy there; he occupies Pisaurum, Fanum and Ancona, each with one cohort.

13.28 Suetonius *Life of the Deified Julius* 30.1–4: Caesar's motives

1 But when the senate would not interfere and his enemies declared that they would come to no compromise over matters affecting the state, he crossed into Cisalpine Gaul, held the assizes, and stopped at Ravenna, intending to resort to war should the senate take more serious action against the tribunes of the plebs who used their vetoes on his behalf. **2** This was his excuse for civil war, but it is thought that he had other reasons. Gnaeus Pompey used to state that, because Caesar's private wealth was not sufficient to finish the works he had undertaken or to fulfil on his return the expectations he had raised in the populace, he wanted general mayhem and anarchy. **3** Others say that he was afraid of being called to account for what he had done in his first consulship contrary to the auspices, laws and vetoes, for Marcus Cato habitually proclaimed, and on oath, that he would prosecute Caesar the instant he dismissed his army. It was also publicly said that, if he returned as a privatus, he would have to defend his case before jurors surrounded by armed men, as Milo did. **4** Asinius Pollio renders this more probable when he states that Caesar at Pharsalus looked on his enemies as they lay dead on the battlefield or fled with these actual words: 'They wanted it like this; with all my great achievements, I, Gaius Caesar, would have been condemned if I had not looked to my army for help.'

CICERO'S VIEW OF EVENTS

13.29 Cicero *Letters to Atticus* 7.11, 7.13: Pompey abandons Rome

Written on 21(?) and 23 January 49 BC. Caesar had the Thirteenth Legion with him at Ravenna (doc. 13.27) and eight legions in Gaul, of which two were on their way to him.

Pompey had seven legions in Spain and three in Italy. Though Pompey controlled Rome and had the backing of the senate, he abandoned the city on 17 January and retired to Capua, ordering the consuls and the senate to join him there, unless they wanted to be declared enemies of the state. On 17 March, despite Caesar's attempted blockade, he sailed to Epirus and established his forces at Dyrrachium. Caesar then went to Rome for two weeks, having a meeting with Cicero on the way at Formiae (see doc. 13.37). At Rome, while he made it clear that he was no Sulla or Marius, when he was debarred from the treasury by one of the tribunes, Caesar took the money by force.

11.3 Let's return to our friend. What do you think, for heaven's sake, of Pompey's plan? I mean why has he abandoned Rome? I'm totally at a loss. At that point nothing seemed more stupid. Abandoning Rome? Wouldn't you have done the same if the Gauls were on their way? 'The state isn't made up of house walls', he might say. But it is of altars and hearths . . . **4** The complaints from the public are amazing (as to Rome I don't know, but you will tell me) at the city being without magistrates, without the senate. What's more, the idea of Pompey as a runaway affects people amazingly. And so, the situation is completely changed. They now think there should be no concessions to Caesar. You will have to explain to me what all this means.

13.1 But you see what kind of a war it is: a civil war, true, but one originating not from conflict from among the citizens but from the recklessness of one desperate citizen. He, however, is strong in his army, has won many to his side by hopes and promises, and has coveted every man's entire possessions. The city has been delivered to him, without protection, full of resources. What might you not fear from a man who considers our temples and homes not as his native land but as plunder? But what he will do or how, without senate or magistrates, I have no idea; he certainly won't be able to maintain any pretence of behaving constitutionally.

13.30 Cicero *Letters to his Friends* 16.12: Caesar's terms

According to Cicero in this letter to Tiro on 27 January 49 BC, Caesar offered the following terms after the flight of Pompey and the optimates from Rome.

2 As Caesar, driven by some insanity and unmindful of his name and honours, has seized Ariminum, Pisaurum, Ancona and Arretium, we have abandoned Rome – how wisely or courageously there is no point in arguing. **3** You see our situation. True, he is offering terms, that Pompey go to Spain, that the levies which have been raised and our forces be disbanded, while for his part he will hand over Transalpine Gaul to Domitius and Cisalpine Gaul to Considius Nonianus (who have been allocated them); he will come to Rome to canvass for the consulship and no longer wants his candidature to be accepted in absentia; he will canvass for three market-days in person. We have accepted his terms, as long as he withdraws his troops from the places he has occupied, so a senate meeting can be held in Rome to discuss these terms without fear. **4** If he does this, there is hope of peace, though not an honourable one (for the terms are imposed on us), but anything is better than to be in our current situation.

13.31 Appian *Civil Wars* 2.38 (152): Pompey marshals his forces

Cicero disapproved of the departure from Italy, but Pompey had considerable resources in the East. His clients, gained during his Eastern campaigns (cf. doc. 2.61), sent troops, and he collected a fleet. Pompey was perhaps regarding Sulla as an example, as he had returned from the East to triumph over his enemies and capture Rome.

Pompey hastened from Capua to Nuceria, and from Nuceria to Brundisium to cross the Adriatic to Epirus and there finish his preparations for war. He wrote to all the provinces and to their kings, cities, governors and leaders to send him assistance for the war as speedily as possible. While they were all doing this, Pompey's own army was in Spain and ready to set out to any place where it might be needed.

13.32 Cicero *Letters to Atticus* 8.3: Cicero's indecision

Cicero on 22 January 49 had expressed to Atticus his doubts about whom to join in the conflict; while still undecided, here, on 18–19 February, his preference for Pompey comes through. He did join Pompey, even after personal solicitation from Caesar (docs 13.36–37).

1 Troubled as I am by most serious and unhappy events, and not having the opportunity to consult with you in person, I would still like your advice. The whole matter at issue is this: if Pompey leaves Italy – which I think he will – what do you think I should do? You may be able to advise me more easily if I briefly set out what comes to my mind in favour of each side. **2** As well as the greatest obligations which I owe to Pompey regarding my restoration and the friendship I have with him, the state's cause itself leads me to feel that my policy should be joined to his policy and my fortune to his. There is something else: if I remain and abandon that band of most upright and distinguished citizens, I have to fall into the power of one man. While he demonstrates in many ways that he is my friend (and you are aware that I endeavoured long ago to make him such, because I suspected that this storm was imminent), two things, however, have to be considered – how much confidence can be placed in him and, however definitely he is a friend of mine, whether the role of a brave man and good citizen should be to stay in the city, in which he has held the highest offices and commands, has achieved great things, and has been endowed with the most glorious priestly office, with reduced status and with danger to be undergone, together, perhaps, with some dishonour, should Pompey ever restore the constitution. So much on this side.

  3 Now see what lies on the other. Our friend Pompey has done nothing which has not lacked wisdom and courage and, I should add, nothing which hasn't been contrary to my advice and influence. I say nothing of the past, how he promoted, aggrandised and armed Caesar against the state, supported his laws passed by violence and contrary to the auspices, added on Transalpine Gaul, became his son-in-law, acted as augur at Publius Clodius' adoption, showed more concern for restoring me than for keeping me here, extended Caesar's command, consistently supported him during his absence, exerted himself, even in his third consulship after he had taken on the role of defender of the state, to see that the ten tribunes brought in their law that Caesar could stand in absentia, which he confirmed in some way by a law of his own, opposed the consul Marcus Marcellus, when he was trying to end Caesar's command in Gaul on the Kalends of March – saying nothing of all this, what could be more disgraceful or more confused than this departure from Rome or, rather, this shameful flight in which we are now engaged? What terms would not have been accepted in preference to abandoning our country? The terms were bad, I admit, but what could be worse than this?

4 Alright, he will restore the constitution. When? What provision has been made for such hope? Hasn't Picenum been lost? Hasn't the road to Rome been opened? Has not all money, public and private, been handed over to the enemy? What's more, there is no party, no strength, no base to draw those who wish to defend the constitution. Apulia was chosen, the least populated part of Italy and the most distant from the onset of this war, perhaps in despair as on the coast and opportune for flight.

13.33 Pompey in [Cicero] *Letters to Atticus* 8.11c: Pompey summons Cicero

Pompey wrote this to Cicero on 20 February 49 BC. Cicero in fact procrastinated about joining Pompey in Apulia and did not sail with him to Dyrrachium in Epirus. His leaving Italy was then delayed by Caesar's control of the peninsula, and he sailed to Dyrrachium only in June.

Greetings. I read your letter with pleasure; I recognised your former qualities still active for the public welfare. The consuls have joined the army I command in Apulia. I urge you very strongly, in view of your unrivalled and constant concern for our country, to join us so that we may work together to bring aid and assistance to our afflicted country. I suggest that you travel by the Appian Way and come quickly to Brundisium.

CIVIL WAR

13.34 Caesar in [Cicero] *Letters to Atticus* 9.7c: Caesar to Oppius and Balbus

This letter was written c. 5 March 49 on the march through Italy. Domitius Ahenobarbus, appointed Caesar's successor in Transalpine Gaul, had defended Corfinium against Pompey's advice and was defeated. Caesar released the captured senators and equites. Caesar's policy of clemency contrasted strongly with Pompey's attitude that senators who did not join him would be enemies of the state and the talk in Pompey's camp of proscriptions and confiscations of property (doc. 13.43). The Spanish-born L. Cornelius Balbus (cos. 40) had been Caesar's officer of engineers (praefectus fabrum) and, along with C. Oppius, an eques, was one of his main supporters.

1 I am extremely pleased that you express in your letter how strongly you approve of the events at Corfinium. I will willingly follow your advice, all the more willingly because I had of my own accord decided to show as much clemency as possible and work hard towards a reconciliation with Pompey. Let us try to see whether in this way we can regain everyone's goodwill and enjoy a long-lasting victory, since all others by their cruelty have been unable to escape hatred or to make their victory last, except for only Lucius Sulla, whom I am not going to imitate. Let this be the new type of conquest, to defend ourselves with clemency and generosity. Regarding how this can be done, I have a few ideas and many more can be found. I ask you to turn your thoughts to such matters. **2** I captured Numerius Magius, Pompey's prefect. Of course I followed my usual practice and released him at once. Two prefects of engineers of Pompey's have now come into my power and have been released by me. If they wish to show their gratitude, they should urge Pompey to prefer to be my friend rather than the friend of those who have always been his and my bitter enemies, whose intrigues have brought Rome to its present condition.

13.35 Cicero *Letters to Atticus* 5.6, 7.8: Cicero's debts to Caesar

Two letters of Cicero's on 19(?) May 51 and 25/26 December 50 referring to his indebtedness to Caesar; he owed him some 800,000 sesterces (200,000 denarii; *Att.* 5.5.2: 15 May 51). Despite Cicero's constant criticisms of Caesar, he had had little compunction in borrowing money from him. Caesar's successes in Gaul had enabled him to give financial support to numerous senators (cf. docs 12.70–72).

5.6.2 But I shall keep persisting in one matter as long as I think you are in Rome, and that is in asking you about Caesar's loan, that you leave it settled.

    7.8.5 But what annoys me most is that Caesar's money must be repaid and the provision for my triumph be used for that purpose; it has an ugly look to be in debt to a political opponent. But this and much else when we are together.

13.36 Caesar in [Cicero] *Letters to Atticus* 9.6a: Caesar to Cicero

Written by Caesar on the way to Brundisium c. 5 March 49 BC. Caesar was to see Cicero at his estate at Formiae (doc. 13.37). C. Furnius was tribune in 50.

Although I have just seen our friend Furnius and was unable to speak or hear his news at my leisure, since I am hurrying and on the march with my legions already sent on ahead, I could not, however, omit writing to you and sending him to express my thanks, as I have often done and expect to do even more often: you have done me such services. I especially request you, since I expect to come soon to Rome, that I may see you there so I can make use of your advice, influence, prestige and help in everything. I must return to my purpose: you will overlook my haste and the brevity of this letter. You will learn all the rest from Furnius.

13.37 Cicero *Letters to Atticus* 9.18: Caesar visits Cicero

Ten days after Pompey fled from Italy, Caesar called on Cicero (28 March 49). He wanted Cicero to attend the senate at Rome, but Cicero insisted on his own freedom of speech or non-attendance. Caesar was displeased and advised him to stay out of the conflict (*Att.* 10.8.3, 10.8b). Antony refused to allow Cicero to leave Italy, but he managed to join Pompey's forces at Dyrrachium in June.

1 On both points I took your advice; my words were such that he thought well of me rather than thanked me, and I was adamant on the matter of not going to Rome. But we were mistaken in thinking him compliant – I have never seen anyone less so. He said that in my judgement I was convicting him, that the rest would be slower to come if I did not. I replied that their case was not the same as my own. After a long discussion, 'Come on, then, and work for peace.' 'At my own discretion?' I asked. 'Would I dictate to you?' he replied. 'Well', I said, 'I shall work along the lines that the senate does not approve of an expedition to the Spanish provinces or of armies being transported to Greece, and', I went on, 'I shall have a lot to say commiserating with Gnaeus.' His response to that was, 'But I don't want those sorts of things said.' 'That's what I thought', I replied. 'But that is why I do not want to be there, as I must either make those kind of remarks or not come to Rome – with much else, which I could not keep quiet about, were I there.' The conclusion was that he asked me to think things over, as if looking for a way to end the conversation. I could not refuse. That's how we parted. I believe, therefore, that he is not pleased with me. But I was pleased with myself, a feeling I have not had for some time.

13.38 Caesar *Civil War* 1.32.1–33.4: Caesar addresses the senate

32.1 After carrying out these arrangements Caesar withdraws his soldiers into the nearest towns so they might for the remainder of the time have some rest from labour; he himself sets out for Rome. **2** Having summoned the senate, he reminds them of the injuries done him by his personal enemies. He declares that he had not sought any extraordinary position but, in waiting for the proper time for his consulship, had been content with the privileges open to all citizens. **3** A proposal had been brought forward by the ten tribunes and passed, though his enemies spoke against it, and Cato in particular bitterly opposed it, using his old delaying tactics of making the discussion drag on for days, that he should be allowed to stand for the consulship in absence, Pompey himself being consul at the time; if Pompey disapproved, why had he allowed it to be passed? If he approved, why did he prevent him from making use of the people's kindness? **4** He points out his own patience, when of his own accord he suggested that the armies be disbanded, although this would have meant a sacrifice for himself of prestige and position. **5** He comments on the vindictiveness of his enemies who, what they demanded in the other case, refused in his, and preferred total upheaval to giving up their imperium and armies. **6** He relates the way they wronged him in taking away his legions, their cruelty and insolence in impinging upon the rights of the tribunes; he reminds them of the terms he proposed, the meetings requested and refused. **7** Under these circumstances he urges and desires them to take up the government and administer it alongside himself. If fear makes them shun this, he will not put the burden on them but administer the state on his own. **8** Envoys should be sent to Pompey regarding a settlement, nor was he frightened by what Pompey had said a little earlier in the senate, that the prestige of those to whom envoys are sent is enhanced, while fear is attributed to those who send them. **9** Such considerations seemed to belong to a weak and feeble spirit. His wish was, just as he had striven to outdo others in achievements, to surpass them too in justice and equity. **33.1** The senate approves the proposal to send envoys, but no one who could be sent was found, everyone refusing the duty of the embassy, primarily through fear. **2** For Pompey, on leaving the city, had said in the senate that he would take the same view of those who remained in Rome and those who were in Caesar's camp. **3** So three days were spent in discussion and excuses. Moreover Lucius Metellus, a tribune, is put up by Caesar's enemies to thwart this proposal and prevent everything else he might propose to enact. **4** When his aim was understood, with several days already having been wasted, Caesar, in order to avoid spending any more time, having failed to achieve the business he had intended to transact, leaves the city and goes to Further Gaul.

13.39 Cicero *Letters to Atticus* 10.7.1: The battle for autocracy

This letter was written on 22(?) April 49 BC. Cicero foresaw a repetition of Sulla's takeover of Rome in 82.

The Republic is not the question at issue. The struggle is over who is to be autocrat, in which the king who has been expelled is the more moderate, honourable and blameless, and unless he is the winner the name of the Roman people must inevitably be wiped out, but, if he is the winner, his victory will follow Sulla's practice and example. So, in this conflict, you should support neither openly and adapt yourself to events. But my case is different, because I am tied by an obligation and cannot be ungrateful.

13.40 Velleius Paterculus *Compendium of Roman History* 2.33.3: Pompey endured no equal

Cf. Caesar *BC* 1.4 (doc. 13.24): Pompey wished to have no one his equal in prestige (dignitas).

From the time Pompey first went into public life, he could endure no equal at all, and in those affairs, in which he ought to have been first, he desired to be the only one. No one craved all other things less, or glory more, than he did; he was unrestrained in grasping at magistracies, though extremely diffident once in office, while he entered into them with the greatest eagerness, only to lay them down without concern, and, although he appropriated of his own free will whatever he desired, he would resign it at the wish of other people.

13.41 Cicero *Letters to Atticus* 10.4.4: Cicero blames Pompey and Caesar

Written to Atticus from Cumae on 14 April 49.

I do not rank the achievements of these top commanders above my own, nor even their very fortune, though they seem to be at the peak of prosperity, and my fortune appears more turbulent. For can anyone be fortunate and happy who has either abandoned his country or oppressed it?

13.42 Caesar *Civil War* 3.1.1–2.2: Caesar's first dictatorship

After swiftly overrunning Italy, Caesar then proceeded to Spain, where he defeated Pompey's legates Afranius (cos. 60) and Petreius. While at Massilia he was named dictator after a law to this effect was passed by the praetor Lepidus, and on returning to Rome in 49 he presided over the consular elections in which he himself was elected consul for 48. He resigned the dictatorship after eleven days and made his way to northern Greece (leaving Lepidus in charge of Rome). His legislation during this short period as dictator included debt relief and the restoration of exiles and sons of the proscribed, and he ensured the celebration of the Latin Festival.

1.1 Caesar as dictator held the elections, and Julius Caesar and Publius Servilius (Isauricus) were made consuls, for this year (48 BC) was the first in which Caesar was legally able to become consul. **2** Once this was done, as credit throughout Italy was fairly tight and debts were not being repaid, he decided that arbitrators should be appointed to make assessments of property and possessions at pre-war values, and that the creditors should be paid at these rates. **3** He thought that this was the best way to remove or lessen the fear of the abolition of debts, which often accompanies wars or civil strife, and to preserve the debtors' honour. **4** Furthermore, in motions brought before the people by praetors and tribunes, he restored to their former status several persons who, in the period when Pompey had kept troops in the city as a bodyguard, had been convicted of bribery under the Pompeian law, in whose trials, which were completed in a single day, one set of jurors had heard the evidence and another given their votes . . . **2.1** He allowed 11 days for these measures and for holding the Latin festival and all the elections, and then resigned the dictatorship, left the city and went to Brundisium. **2** He had ordered 12 legions and all the cavalry to meet there. However, he found only enough ships to transport scarcely 15,000 legionaries and 500 cavalry. This one thing, shortage of ships, prevented Caesar from quickly concluding the war.

POMPEY AND HIS FOLLOWERS

13.43 Cicero *Letters to his Friends* 7.3: Cicero regrets his actions

In this letter, written in mid-April 46 to M. Marius, Cicero recalls his views of Pompey's followers at Dyrrachium. Caesar's opinion was along the same lines (doc. 13.44): Pompey's followers were not the boni, the 'honest men', after all, and the only thing good was the cause itself, not its adherents. The 'certain engagement' that gave Pompey false confidence was his defeat of Caesar at Dyrrachium in July. But Caesar lifted the siege and moved his troops, and Pompey pursued him: the 'pitched battle' that resulted was Pharsalus in August 48, in which Pompey and his forces were thoroughly routed.

1 Since I very frequently ponder the general miseries in which we have lived for so many years and, as I see it, in which we will continue to live, I have been in the habit of bringing to mind the last time we were together; I even remember the actual day. It was on 12 May in the year Lentulus and Marcellus were consuls (49 BC) and I had come down that evening to my Pompeian place, and you were there to see me, very worried in your mind. You were worried by considerations of my duty on the one hand and my danger on the other: if I stayed in Italy, you feared I would be failing in my duty; if I left for the war you were concerned about the danger to me. On that occasion you doubtless saw that I, too, was in such confusion that I could not decide what was best for me to do. But I preferred to give in to honour and reputation rather than to weigh up chances of personal safety. **2** I came to repent of my action, not so much on the grounds of danger to myself as on those of the many evils with which I was struck when I arrived (at Dyrrachium): first of all, that the troops were neither numerous nor warlike; secondly, that, apart from the commander and a few others (I mean among the chief figures), all the rest were greedy for plunder in the war itself and so bloodthirsty in the way they talked that I shuddered at the thought of their victory; finally, the most distinguished among them were deep in debt. In short – nothing good except the cause. After seeing all this, I despaired of victory and began trying to persuade them to make peace, of which I had always been a supporter; then, when Pompey was strongly opposed to that view, I set to persuading them to delay the war. Sometimes he approved of this and seemed to be going to follow this policy, and perhaps he would have done had he not started, after a certain engagement, to have confidence in his troops. From that time, that pre-eminent man was no longer a general. With an inexperienced and hastily collected army he fought a pitched battle against the toughest of legions. He was defeated, even his camp was lost, and he fled shamefully and alone. **3** As far as I was concerned that was the end of the war, and I could not see how we, who had been no match for the enemy with our forces intact, would be superior with our forces shattered.

13.44 Caesar *Civil War* 3.82.2–83.4: Pompey's supporters

L. Domitius Ahenobarbus, as consul in 54, had opposed the triumvirate; he was to command Pompey's left wing at Pharsalus and was killed in the battle; Q. Caecilius Metellus Pius Scipio (cos. 52, Pompey's father-in-law) had been responsible for the proposal at the beginning of 49 that Caesar disarm; he escaped from Pharsalus to Africa and died at Thapsus; P. Cornelius Lentulus Spinther (cos. 57) was the older brother of Lentulus Crus (cos. 49), one of the Pompeians released by Caesar after Corfinium who rejoined Pompey. He died shortly after Pharsalus.

82.2 With this addition to Pompey's forces and the uniting of two great armies, the former view of everyone was confirmed and their hope of victory increased, so that whatever interval lay before them seemed only a delay in their return to Italy, and, whenever Pompey acted with some slowness or deliberation, they proclaimed that it was the business of only a day, but that he was making the most of his command and behaving to men of consular and praetorian rank as though they were slaves. **3** They were already openly fighting over rewards and priesthoods and allocating the consulship for years ahead, while others were demanding the houses and other property of those who were in Caesar's camp . . . **83.1** Domitius,

Scipio and Lentulus Spinther were already in daily contention for Caesar's priesthood and openly sinking to the worst invective in their speech, as Lentulus paraded the distinction of his age, Domitius boasted his influence with the people and prestige, and Scipio trusted in his kinship with Pompey . . . **4** In short, all were concerned about potential honours for themselves or monetary rewards or prosecuting private enmities, and they reflected not on the ways in which they could conquer the opposition but on how they ought to use their victory.

13.45 Dolabella in [Cicero] *Letters to his Friends* 9.9: Cicero's son-in-law

This letter was written, in May 48 BC from Caesar's camp outside Dyrrachium, by Dolabella (tr. pl. 47), one of Caesar's legates, to his father-in-law Cicero. Dolabella argued that it was time for him to abandon his adherence to Pompey. It is usually thought that Caesar was instrumental in having this letter written. Dolabella commanded a fleet for Caesar in 49 but was defeated.

2 You can see Gnaeus Pompey's position – he is defended neither by the glory of his name and achievements nor by his status as patron of kings and nations, which he used frequently to boast about, and does not have the chance, which the most lowly people have, of being able to flee with honour. Driven out of Italy, Spain lost, his veteran army taken, and now finally blockaded, which I don't think has ever happened before to any of our generals! And so, use your common sense to consider what he can hope for or what good you can do him; you will then find it easiest to make the decision which would be most advantageous for you. But I beg you that, if he does get out of his current predicament and takes refuge with his fleet, you consider your own interests and be, at long last, your own friend rather than anyone else's. You have now done enough for duty and friendship; you have done enough for your party and the kind of state of which you approved. **3** It is now time to take our stand where the state is at present rather than, by longing after its old form, to find ourselves nowhere.

13.46 Plutarch *Life of Pompey* 79.1–80.3: Pompey's death

Pompey and his forces fled, and Pompey made for Egypt via Lesbos, where his wife Cornelia joined him. The advisors (Achillas, Potheinus and Theodotus) of the young king Ptolemy XIII decided to kill Pompey rather than earn Caesar's hostility by receiving him. Achillas took Septimius and sailed out to Pompey's trireme: Septimius had been Pompey's military tribune in 67 BC and was serving in Egypt in this capacity from 55 to 48. Philip, who cremated the remains of the corpse, was Pompey's freedman. Pompey's remains were later retrieved and buried by Cornelia at his Alban villa; Caesar arrived in Egypt three days after Pompey's death, on 2 October, and was presented with his head and signet ring; he had Achillas and Potheinus executed. Theodotus escaped but was later killed by Brutus or Cassius.

79.1 As it was a long distance to land from the trireme, and none of those in the boat with him had a friendly word for him, he looked at Septimius and asked,

'Surely I am not mistaken? Were you a comrade-in-arms of mine?' He only nodded his head, without saying anything or showing any friendliness. **2** As there was deep silence again, Pompey took a small roll containing a speech written by him in Greek, which he had prepared for his address to Ptolemy, and started to read it. **3** As they approached the shore, Cornelia, along with his friends, watched from the trireme with great anxiety as to what would happen and began to take courage when she saw many of the royal entourage at the landing place, as if to give him an honourable reception. **4** But at this point, while Pompey was holding Philip's hand so he could stand up more easily, Septimius first ran him through with his sword, and then Salvius next and Achillas drew their daggers and stabbed him. **5** Pompey drew his toga over his face with both hands, without saying or doing anything unworthy of himself, only groaning and enduring their blows, having lived one year less than 60 and ending his life only one day after his birthday.

80.1 When the people on the ships saw the murder, they gave such a cry of lamentation that they could be heard from the shore and fled, quickly weighing anchor. A strong wind assisted them as they ran out to sea, so that the Egyptians, though they wanted to pursue them, turned back. **2** But they cut off Pompey's head and threw the rest of his body naked from the boat and left it there for anyone who wanted to see such a sight. **3** But Philip remained by him until they had had their fill of gazing at it; he then washed the body in seawater and wrapped it in one of his own tunics, as he had no other, and looked along the shore until he found the remains of a small fishing boat, old but sufficient for a funeral pyre for a body which was naked and not intact.

13.47 Cicero *Letters to Atticus* 11.6: Cicero on Pompey's death

Written to Atticus on 27 November 48.

5 I never had any doubt regarding Pompey's fate. The hopelessness of his situation was such that all rulers and peoples were totally convinced of it, so that, wherever he went, I thought this would happen. I cannot help grieving over his wretched fate; I knew him to be a man of integrity, clean living and good character.

13.48 Plutarch *Life of Julius Caesar* 49.10–50.4: 'Veni, vidi, vici'

In Alexandria, Caesar supported Cleopatra in the power struggle against her brother-husband Ptolemy, and Caesar's son by Cleopatra, Caesarion (Ptolemy XV), was born in 47 BC. Caesar then moved north to deal with Pharnaces, king of the Crimea, whom he defeated on 2 August 47 at Zela. The Domitius here is Cn. Domitius Calvinus (cos. 53).

49.10 Leaving Cleopatra as ruler of Egypt – who a little while afterwards had a son by him, called Caesarion by the Alexandrians – he set out for Syria. **50.1** After leaving Syria, he learnt while crossing Asia that Domitius had been defeated by Pharnaces, son of Mithridates, and had fled from Pontus with a few troops, while Pharnaces was making full use of his victory to occupy Bithynia and Cappadocia, attempting to take over the country called Lesser Armenia and stirring up revolt among all the kings and tetrarchs there. **2** Accordingly Caesar immediately marched against him with three legions, fought a great battle against him near the city of Zela, and drove him in flight from Pontus, while utterly destroying his army. **3** When he reported how swift and speedy this battle had been in writing to one of his friends, Amantius, at Rome, he used just three words, 'Came, saw, conquered!' **4** In Latin, the words have the same inflectional ending and thus an impressive brevity.

13.49: Caesar honoured after Pharsalus, 48 BC

Inscribed pedestals at Ephesus and Pergamum, dedicated in honour of Caesar in 48 BC.

(i) SIG³ 760 (Ephesus)

The cities in Asia and the peoples and tribes (dedicated this statue of) Gaius Julius, son of Gaius, Caesar, pontifex maximus and imperator **5** and consul for the second time, (descendant) of Ares and Aphrodite, god manifest and common saviour of human life.

(ii) IGRR 4.305 Pergamum

The people (dedicate this statue of) Gaius Julius, son of Gaius, Caesar, imperator and pontifex maximus, consul for the second time, their patron and benefactor, **5** saviour and benefactor of all the Greeks, because of his piety and justice.

13.50 Cicero *Letters to Atticus* 11.9: Cicero again regrets his position

Written to Atticus on 3 January 47. When Cicero returned to Italy after Pharsalus, Antony informed him that Caesar was reviewing on an individual basis the cases of those who had supported Pompey and wished to return to Italy. Cicero was 'pardoned' in September and arrived in Rome in October. L. Cornelius Balbus managed Caesar's affairs in Rome.

1 As you write, I did indeed act incautiously and more hastily than I should have, and I have no hope, now that I am being kept back by the exemptions in the edicts. If these had not been effected by your zeal and goodwill, I would have been able to retire to a place of solitude. Now even that is forbidden. But why should I be pleased to have come before the beginning of the tribunate, if I am not pleased to have come at all? What am I to hope for from a person who was never my friend, now I am legally ruined and crushed? Every day Balbus' letters to me grow less warm, and perhaps many letters from many writers are going to Caesar against me. I am destroyed by my own fault; nothing in my wretched state is owing to chance – it can all be laid on my shoulders. When I saw what kind of war it was, with total lack of preparation and weakness against an excellently prepared opposition, I decided what to do and determined on a plan which was not so much courageous, but permissible, especially in my case.

CAESAR'S DICTATORSHIPS

Shortly after Pharsalus, Caesar was named dictator for the second time, for 12 months, by his fellow consul for 48 BC, P. Servilius Isauricus. Antony, master of the horse in late 48 and 47 (and so second-in-command to the dictator), temporarily lost Caesar's support in 47 as a result of his mishandling of the situation in Italy. Dolabella (Cicero's son-in-law), as tribune for 47, had agitated for a cancellation of debts which led to riots at Rome; Antony had difficulty in restoring order and in dealing with mutinous soldiers in Campania. After his defeat of Pharnaces in 47, Caesar returned to Rome in September and dealt with the debt problem and mutiny. Antony remained out of favour until Caesar's return from Munda. Dolabella was forgiven, served under Caesar in Africa and Spain, and was chosen by Caesar to replace him as consul for 44 BC when he went to Parthia.

In Africa, Caesar defeated the Pompeians led by Metellus Scipio (cos. 52) at Thapsus on 6 April 46 (Scipio committed suicide, as did Cato a few days later at Utica). Probably in late April 46, Caesar (also consul for the third time in 46) was made dictator for the third time, now for ten successive years. His fourth dictatorship of 45 was to be converted into a lifetime dictatorship in February 44 BC; he had held the consulship in 48, 46, 45 and 44. In Rome he celebrated four triumphs (for Gaul, Egypt, Pontus and Africa) in 46 BC (doc. 2.35). Made consul for the fourth time for 45, Caesar proceeded to Spain, defeating Pompey's sons at Munda in March 45 BC: Gnaeus was later captured and killed, while Sextus continued the revolt in Further Spain. A triumph for Munda was celebrated in October 45.

Rex ('king'): Before February 44, when he was made perpetual dictator, Caesar's position was still within Republican norms. It is possible that, with the Lupercalia incident (doc. 13.55), when Antony offered him a diadem, Caesar was testing public opinion to see what the reaction would be to his becoming king: Antony's offer could hardly have been spontaneous. However, his planned departure on 18 March roused the conspirators to act on 15 March. **God**: In the Hellenistic and Roman East, Caesar, like Hellenistic kings and other Roman generals, had already been accorded divine status. After Munda, temples were dedicated to him; statues of him were to be placed in all the temples in Rome; and a statue of him was placed in the temple of Quirinus and inscribed: 'To the Unconquered God'. Antony was a member of the college of the recently established Luperci Juliani (it was probably in this capacity that he participated in the Lupercalia: doc. 7.78) and was appointed as the first flamen of Caesar, though he did not take up this appointment until 40 BC. Caesar was allowed triumphal dress (and so appear as Jupiter) for all public occasions; like the gods, he had a couch (pulvinar) on which his image was placed; his house was to have a pediment, like a temple. Formal deification came after his death. But he was in 45 and 44 clearly approaching divine status, even if outright worship was not yet practised in Rome.

13.51 Cicero *Letters to his Friends* 9.15: Cicero to L. Papirius Paetus

One of several amusing letters written by Cicero to his wealthy friend Paetus at Naples in 46 BC. Q. Lutatius Catulus was consul in 78 and defeated by Caesar for the position of pontifex maximus in 63 (doc. 3.22).

3 You speak to me of Catulus and those times. What is the resemblance? Then, indeed, I did not like to be away too long from protecting the state; for I was sitting in the stern in charge of the helm. But now I hardly even have a place in the hold! **4** Do you think there will be any fewer decrees of the senate if I am in Naples? When

I am in Rome and often in the forum, decrees of the senate are written at the home of your admirer, my intimate acquaintance; indeed, when it occurs to him, I am put down as present at their drawing up, and I hear of a senatorial decree, said to have been passed on my motion, reaching Armenia and Syria, before I hear so much as a mention of the matter itself. And I don't want you to think that I am joking. I should tell you that letters have been brought to me from kings at the ends of the earth, in which they thank me for proposing the motion to give them the title of kings, when I was unaware not only of their royal appellation but even of their very existence!

13.52 Cicero *In Defence of Marcellus* 13, 15: Caesar's pardons

M. Claudius Marcellus (cos. 51), who had scourged a magistrate of Novum Comum (docs 13.8–9) and attempted to have Caesar replaced in Gaul before his term expired, resided at Mytilene after Pharsalus. In 46, the senate requested that he be pardoned, and in this speech Cicero praises Caesar's clemency during the civil war.

13 Note, conscript fathers, the far-reaching effects of Caesar's decision: all of us who went to war impelled by some wretched and calamitous fate which attends the state, though we can be charged with culpability on the grounds of human error, have assuredly been acquitted of criminality. When Caesar preserved Marcus Marcellus for the state at your intercession, and when he restored me both to myself and to the state without any intercession, and all these other renowned men, too, to themselves and to their country, whose number and eminence you can see at this very meeting, he did not bring enemies into the senate but decided that most people had been induced by ignorance and false and groundless fears to go to war, not by greed or bloodthirstiness . . . **15** No critic of events will be so unjust as to question Caesar's wishes with regard to war, since he has without loss of time decided on the restitution of those who advocated peace, though showing more resentment to the rest. That was perhaps less to be wondered at when the outcome and fortune of war was undecided and doubtful, but when a victor treats the advocates of peace with respect, he is surely proclaiming that he would have preferred not to fight at all rather than to win.

13.53 Cicero *Letters to his Friends* 6.6: Caesar fails to bear grudges

Written in October(?) 46 BC to A. Caecina, a Pompeian exiled after Pharsalus, who had written a 'libellous' book against Caesar (Suet. *Jul.* 75.5); he later produced a book of *Remonstrances*, dwelling on Caesar's clemency. He had surrendered to Caesar in 46 and was in Sicily awaiting permission to return to Italy.

8 In Caesar we see a mild and merciful disposition, just as you portrayed in your outstanding book of *Remonstrances*. He is also amazingly impressed by remarkable talents such as your own, and moreover gives way to widely held opinions, as long as these are fair and inspired by duty and not petty or self-interested . . . **10** No one is so hostile to the cause, which Pompey embraced with more enthusiasm than preparation, as to dare to speak of us as bad citizens or reprobates. In this respect I always have to admire Caesar's sense of responsibility, fairness and wisdom. He never mentions Pompey except in the most respectful terms. Perhaps he acted with harshness towards Pompey on numerous occasions – but those were the acts of war and victory, not of Caesar himself. Look how he has welcomed us! He made Cassius his legate, put Brutus in charge of Gaul and Sulpicius (cos. 51) of Greece, while Marcellus, with whom he was particularly angry, has been restored in the most honourable way.

13.54 Cicero *Letters to his Friends* 7.30: Cicero to Manius Curius

In 45, Caesar was sole consul until the beginning of October; he then resigned and was replaced by Q. Fabius Maximus and C. Trebonius; when Fabius Maximus died on the last day of the year, Caesar replaced him with C. Caninius Rebilus. Cicero quipped that no one had breakfast in Caninius' consulship (cf. his comments on Vatinius: doc. 12.25). Cicero is here writing at the beginning of 44 BC to a friend of his, a businessman in Patrae (western Greece).

1 It is unbelievable how disgraced I feel in living in today's Rome. You show yourself to have been far more farsighted about events when you took flight from here. Although things here are still disagreeable when you hear them, nevertheless to hear them is more bearable than to see them. You at least were not in the Campus when the elections to the quaestorship started at the second hour. An official seat had been put out for Quintus Maximus, whom these men used to call consul; at the report of his death, the seat was taken away. He (Caesar), however, having taken the auspices for a comitia tributa, held a centuriate assembly, and at the seventh hour he proclaimed a consul elected, to remain in office until the Kalends of January – the morning of the following day. So I can tell you that in the consulship of Caninius no one had any breakfast! However, no crime was committed in his consulship; his vigilance was amazing – **2** he did not close an eye in the whole of his magistracy! You'll find all this laughable; that's because you are not here. If you were to see it, you couldn't keep from tears. What if I told you the rest? There are countless examples in the same vein.

13.55 Suetonius *Life of the Deified Julius* 76, 78.1–80.1: Exceptional honours

After Munda in April 45 BC, Caesar was voted a supplicatio of an unprecedented 50 days and granted the right to wear a laurel wreath, *Imperator* as a hereditary title, and the name *Liberator*. He was to manage the army and public finances, and to have a public palace. Annual races were to be held in the Circus on 21 April in his honour; the month Quintilis, in which he was born, was renamed July; and he was named 'Father of his Country' (*parens patriae*).

76.1 Not only did he accept excessive honours: a continuous consulship, a perpetual dictatorship, the censorship of morals, as well as the praenomen 'Imperator' and the cognomen 'Father of his Country', a statue among those of the kings, and a raised seat in the orchestra, but he also allowed honours too great for the mortal condition to be bestowed on him: a golden seat in the senate house and on the tribunal, a chariot (for carrying divine images) and litter in the circus procession, temples, altars, statues next to those of the gods, a couch, a flamen, a college of the Luperci, and the naming of a month after him; indeed, there were no honours that he did not receive or grant at will. **2** His third and fourth consulships he held in name only, satisfied with the power of the dictatorship, which was voted him at the same time as the consulships, and in both years he substituted two consuls for himself for the three final months, in the meantime holding no elections except for tribunes and plebeian aediles and designating prefects instead of praetors to administer the city's affairs in his absence. When a consul died suddenly on the day before the Kalends of January, he gave the vacant magistracy for a few hours to someone who asked him for it. **3** With the same licence and disdain for ancestral custom, he appointed magistrates for several years ahead, bestowed decorations of consular rank on ten ex-praetors, and admitted to the senate men who had been granted citizenship and even some half-barbarous Gauls. In addition, he placed his personal slaves in charge of the mint and public revenues. He entrusted the supervision and command of the three legions he had left at Alexandria to his favourite Rufio, son of one of his freedmen . . .

78.1 However, the incident that particularly aroused deadly hatred against him was when all the conscript fathers approached him with numerous high honours that they had voted him, and he received them before the temple of Venus Genetrix without rising from his seat. Some people believe that he was held back by Cornelius Balbus when he attempted to rise; others, that he made no such attempt at all, but instead glared at Gaius Trebatius when he advised him to stand up. **2** This action of his seemed the more intolerable, as when, in one of his triumphs, he rode past the tribunician benches, he was so furious that one of the college, Pontius Aquila (tr. pl. 45), did not stand up, that he cried out, 'Go on then, Aquila, make me restore the Republic, tribune!' and for several successive days would not promise anything to anyone except with the rider, 'That is, if Pontius Aquila will permit it.'

79.1 To this insult, which so obviously showed his disdain for the senate, he added a deed of far greater arrogance, for, at the Latin festival, as he was returning to Rome, among the extravagant and unheard-of acclamations of the populace, someone in the crowd placed a laurel wreath on his statue with a white fillet tied to it, and when the tribunes Epidius Marullus and Caesetius Flavus (tr. pl. 44 BC) ordered that the fillet be removed from the wreath and the man taken off to prison, Caesar sharply reprimanded them and deposed them from office, grieved either that the suggestion of monarchy had been so unenthusiastically received or, as he stated, because he had been deprived of the prestige of refusing it. **2** From then on, however, he was unable to dispel the ill-repute of having aspired to the title of king, although, when the plebs greeted him as king, he replied that his name was Caesar and not Rex (King), and when, at the Lupercalia, the consul Antony attempted a number of times to place a diadem on his head, he refused to accept it and sent it to the Capitol as an offering to Jupiter Optimus Maximus. **3** Indeed, the rumour had even spread widely that he was going to move to Alexandria or Troy, taking the wealth of the state with him and leaving Italy exhausted by levies and his friends in charge of Rome, while, at the next meeting of the senate, Lucius Cotta was going to announce the view of the Fifteen in charge of the Sibylline Books that, since it was written in the books of fate that the Parthians could be conquered only by a king, Caesar should be given the title of king. **80.1** It was for this reason that the conspirators hurried on their plans, to avoid having to assent to this.

CAESAR'S LEGISLATION

Caesar's main reforms, which date to 46, concerned the calendar, grain distribution and debt relief. Sumptuary legislation was also introduced to limit personal expenditure and extravagance.

13.56 Suetonius *Life of the Deified Julius* 41.1–43.2: Caesar's reforms

In addition to the measures described in this passage, Caesar's plans included constructing a temple to Mars, a theatre, a highway from the Adriatic, a canal through the Isthmus and libraries, restructuring the law code, draining the Pomptine marshes, and waging war against Dacian and Parthian.

41.1 He filled the vacancies in the senate, enrolled more patricians, and increased the number of praetors, aediles and quaestors, as well as that of the minor officials; he also reinstated those who had been stripped of their privileges by action of the censors or had been condemned for bribery by a jury. **2** He shared elections with the people on the basis that, except for the candidates for the consulship, the people should choose half the magistrates and he should personally nominate the other half. These he announced by circulating brief notes around the tribes: 'Caesar the Dictator to tribe such-and-such. I recommend to you so-and-so to hold their magistracies by your votes.' He even admitted to office the sons of those who had been proscribed. He restored the right of jury service to two classes, the equites and senators, disqualifying the third class, the tribunii aerarii. **3** He registered the people for the corn dole by a new method and locale, street by street, using the owners of apartment buildings, and reduced the number of those who received free grain from 320,000 to 150,000; so that new meetings did not have to be called in the future to enrol people, he laid down that the places of those who died were to be filled by lot every year by the praetors from those who were not registered. **42.1** Since 80,000 citizens had been assigned to overseas colonies, he enacted a law to rebuild the population of the depleted city which laid down that no citizen older than 20 or younger than 40 years of age, unless he was serving in the army, should absent himself from Italy for more than three years in succession; that no senator's son should go overseas except as one of a magistrate's household or staff; and that graziers should have among their herdsmen at least one-third who were free-born. He also granted citizenship to all medical practitioners and teachers of liberal arts at Rome to induce them to stay in the city and encourage others to settle there. **2** Regarding debts, he disappointed those who wanted them cancelled, which was frequently called for, but finally decreed that debtors should satisfy their creditors through a valuation of their property at the price for which they had purchased it before the civil war, with whatever interest they had paid in cash or pledged in writing being deducted from the total; by this arrangement, about a quarter of the loan was wiped out. **3** He dissolved all guilds except those founded in ancient times. He increased penalties for crimes; and, since the wealthy had less compunction about committing crimes because they were merely exiled with their property intact, he punished murderers of fellow citizens, as Cicero records, by the confiscation of their entire property and the rest by the confiscation of half of it.

43.1 He administered justice with great conscientiousness and severity. He even removed those convicted of extortion from the senatorial order. He annulled the marriage of an ex-praetor who had married a woman the day after her divorce from her husband, although there was no suspicion of adultery. He imposed duties on foreign goods. He forbade the use of litters and the wearing of scarlet robes or pearls to everyone except those of a certain standing and age and on specific days. **2** He particularly enforced his law against luxury by placing watchmen in parts of the market to seize and bring him delicacies which were on sale in violation of his prohibition, while he sometimes sent his lictors and soldiers to take from a dining-room items which his watchmen had failed to confiscate, even after they had been served.

13.57 Dio *Roman History* 43.50.1–51.9: Better than Sulla

Caesar was clearly attempting reconciliation with the Pompeians and ensuring the people's support for a large-scale three-year expedition against Parthia. His great-nephew Octavian (later the princeps Augustus) now enters the historical record. The two patrician aedileships that Caesar created in 44 BC, the aediles cereales, had the especial role of overseeing the grain supply.

50.1 Caesar also brought in laws and extended the pomerium. In this, as well as in other matters, he appeared to be acting like Sulla. Caesar, however, removed the penalties from the survivors of those who had fought against him and granted them immunity on fair and equal terms: **2** he promoted them to magistracies and returned their dowries to the wives of those that had been killed, while to their children he granted a proportion of their properties, putting Sulla's bloodthirstiness in a very bad light and winning an outstanding reputation for himself not just for valour, but also for magnanimity – although it is generally difficult for the same man to excel both in war and in peace. **3** He prided himself on this, and also on the fact that he had restored Carthage and Corinth . . . **51.1** These cities, then, just as they had earlier been razed together, so they now revived at the same time and looked like prospering once more. While Caesar was involved with this, the desire to avenge Crassus and those who died with him overcame all the Romans together, along with the hope that now, if ever, they could defeat the Parthians. With one impulse they voted the war to Caesar and made extensive preparations for it. **2** Among other matters, they resolved that he should employ a large number of subordinates and, so that the city would not be without magistrates in his absence, and by deciding them on their own they should not relapse into civil strife, that magistrates should be appointed for the next three years, the period that they thought necessary for the campaign, although they did not nominate them all beforehand. **3** Ostensibly Caesar chose half of them, having some legal right to do so, but in fact he chose them all. For the first year, too, 40 quaestors were elected, as happened previously, and now two patrician aediles for the first time, as well as four from the plebs. Of these, two have their title from Demeter (Ceres), and this has remained in force to the present time. **4** Sixteen praetors were also appointed. . . .

6 All those to hold magistracies in the first year after that were appointed in advance, and for the second year just the consuls and tribunes. They were far from appointing anyone for the third year. **7** Caesar intended to hold the rank of dictator for both these years and nominated those who were to be masters of the horse, someone else and Octavian, although he was still a lad. **8** For the time being, while this was taking place, he appointed Dolabella consul in place of himself, while Antony was to continue in power for the whole year. He assigned Gallia Narbonensis and Hither Spain to Lepidus, and two men as masters of horse in his place, each acting separately. **9** Owing favours as he did to many people, he paid them back by such appointments and by priesthoods, adding one extra to the Board of Fifteen and three to the Board of Seven, as they were called.

13.58 Josephus *Antiquities of the Jews* 14.10.2.190–95: Privileges for Hyrcanus

A covering letter attached to Caesar's decree on privileges of Hyrcanus, the high priest of the Jews, in 47 BC. The Jews had originally signed a treaty of friendship with Rome in 161. The final sentence may refer to all the Jews, not just Hyrcanus.

190 Gaius Julius Caesar, imperator and pontifex maximus, dictator for the second time, to the magistrates, council and people of the Sidonians, greetings.

If you are well, it is well; I with the army am also well. **191** I send to you the copy of the decree on a tablet, regarding Hyrcanus, son of Alexander, high priest and ethnarch of the Jews, so that it may be placed among your public records. It is my wish that this shall be erected on a bronze tablet in both Greek and Latin. **192** It is as follows: Julius Caesar, imperator, [dictator] for the second time and pontifex maximus, with my council have decided thus. Whereas the Jew Hyrcanus, son of Alexander, both now and in former times in both peace and war, demonstrated both loyalty and zeal towards our affairs, as many generals have born witness to regarding him, **193** and in the most recent war in Alexandria came as an ally with 1,500 soldiers, and when sent by me to Mithridates surpassed in courage all the regular troops, **194** for these reasons I order that Hyrcanus, son of Alexander, and his children are to be ethnarchs of the Jews and hold the priesthood of the Jews in perpetuity according to their ancestral customs, and he and his children are to be our allies and are also to be counted among our individual friends, **195** and that he and his children are to possess whatever high priest's privileges exist according to their own laws. And if in this period there should be any investigation concerning the Jews' way of life, it is my pleasure that the decision should rest with them. I do not approve that winter billeting or money shall be exacted.

13.59 Bruns *FIRA* 102: Regulations for local magistracies

In this law for municipalities in Italy and their officials (the *lex Julia municipalis*), Julius Caesar lays down the qualifications for magistracies and membership of the local senate. These colonies and other towns were generally governed by a Board of Two or a Board of Four. This law was in draft form at Caesar's death and taken by Mark Antony to the senate for ratification; other sections of the law deal with grain distribution, local censuses and the repair of Rome's streets (doc. 2.8).

88 After the Kalends of January (1 January), in the second year after this law is passed, in a municipality, colony or prefecture, no person less than 30 years of age **90** shall be a candidate for, accept or administer the office of duumvir, quattuorvir or any other magistracy, unless he has served three campaigns in the cavalry or six campaigns in the infantry of a legion. These campaigns he shall have served in a camp or in a province for the greater part of a year. Alternatively, two half-years may count as separate years if allowed by laws and plebiscites. If someone has exemption from military service by laws, plebiscites or treaty, whereby he should not properly serve against his will, he is not bound by this restriction. Nor shall anyone who is an auctioneer, master of funerals or undertaker, while engaged in this business, **95** be a candidate for, accept, administer or hold the office of duumvir, quattuorvir or any other magistracy, nor shall he be a senator, decurion or conscript or give his vote in a municipality, colony or prefecture. If any of those listed above acts contrary to this law he shall be liable for a fine of 50,000 sesterces to the people, and anyone who wishes is entitled to bring a case for this sum.

If anyone holds elections in a municipality, colony or prefecture after the next Kalends of July (1 July) for the election or substitution of duumvirs, quattuorvirs or any **100** other magistrates, he shall not proclaim or order to be proclaimed as elected to any of these magistracies anyone who is less than 30 years of age unless he has served three campaigns in the cavalry or six campaigns in the infantry of a legion, and who has served these campaigns in a camp or in a province for the greater part of a year, or alternatively two half-years counting as separate years, if allowed by laws and plebiscites, or unless he has exemption from military service by laws, plebiscites or treaty, **105** whereby he should not properly serve against his will. Nor shall he proclaim the election of anyone who is an auctioneer, master of funerals or undertaker, while engaged in his business, as duumvir, quattuorvir or whoever may be the magistrate. Nor shall he select, substitute or co-opt such persons either into the senate or into the decurions and conscripts. Nor knowingly with malice aforethought shall he ask such a person for his opinion or order him to speak or cast his vote. If anyone acts contrary to this law, he shall be liable for a fine of 50,000 sesterces to the people, and anyone who wishes is entitled to bring a case for this sum.

Nor among the decurions and conscripts in the senate of a municipality, colony, prefecture, forum or meeting-place of Roman citizens shall anyone be admitted or be permitted to speak his opinion or **110** cast his vote who has been or is condemned for theft committed by himself or who compounds such a theft; anyone who has been or is condemned in a case relating to trusteeship, partnership, guardianship, mandate, bodily injury or malice aforethought; anyone who has been or is condemned either by the Plaetorian law (before 184 BC) or for something he has done or does contrary to that law; anyone who has bound or binds himself to fight in the arena; anyone who has denied or denies a debt on oath or who has sworn or swears that he is financially sound; anyone who has declared or declares to sureties or creditors that he is not able to repay his debt **115** or compounds with them on his failure to pay; anyone whose debt is settled for them; anyone whose goods are seized in accordance with the edict of the magistrate in charge of administering the law, except for those who were under guardianship or absent on public business, as long as they had not fraudulently contrived to be absent for this reason; anyone who has been or is condemned in a public trial at Rome, with the ruling that he is not permitted to remain in Italy, and has not been or is not restored to full status; anyone who has been or is condemned in a public trial in the municipality, colony, prefecture, forum or meeting-place to which he belongs; **120** anyone who has been or is found guilty of having made a false accusation or done something from collusion; anyone who has been or is stripped of army rank because of disgrace; anyone whom a general has ordered or orders to leave the army because of disgrace; anyone who has taken or takes money or another reward for the head of a Roman citizen; anyone who has made or who makes a profit from prostituting his body; anyone who has become or becomes a gladiator or stage actor or who keeps a brothel. If, against the terms of this law, anyone takes his place or gives his vote **125** among the decurions or conscripts in the senate, he shall be liable for a fine of 50,000 sesterces to the people, and anyone who wishes is entitled to bring a case for this sum . . . .

135 Those who by this law are not permitted to be senators, decurions or conscripts of their municipality, colony, prefecture, forum or meeting-place shall not stand for or accept the position of duumvir, quattuorvir or any other magistracy from which they would pass into the senatorial order; nor shall such a person take their seat at the games, or when gladiators are fighting, in the senatorial seating for decurions and conscripts, or to take part in public banquets. If such a person is declared elected against the terms of this law, he shall not become duumvir or quattuorvir **140** or hold any other magistracy or office. If anyone acts contrary to this law, he shall be liable for a fine of 50,000 sesterces to the people, and anyone who wishes is entitled to bring a case for this sum.

13.60 Bruns *FIRA* 122: A charter for Urso

This law, officially the *lex Colonia Genetiva Julia*, a colony in southern Spain, appears to have been drafted in the office of Julius Caesar shortly before his assassination and later enacted by Mark Antony. Government is clearly in the hands of the senate and officials (duumvirs, aediles, augurs and priests) rather than the people: cf. doc. 2.80. A new fragment lays down that a decurion has to possess a building with no fewer than 600 roof-tiles (and a citizen one with no fewer than 300 roof-tiles).

102 No duumvir who is conducting an investigation or holding a trial in accordance with this law, unless that trial is bound by this law to be completed in one day, shall conduct the investigation or hold the trial before the first hour or after the eleventh hour of the day. The duumvir, with regard to the different prosecutors, shall allow the chief prosecutor four hours and each subsidiary prosecutor two hours. Where a prosecutor concedes some of his time to another person, this person will be allowed as much additional time for speaking as has been conceded to him. Likewise he will allow the person who has conceded some of his time to another person that much less time for speaking. However many hours in total the entire prosecution has for speaking in each individual case, he shall allow to the defendant or whoever speaks in his defence twice that number of hours in each individual case. **103** Whenever the majority of the decurions present resolve to draft men in arms for the sake of defending the territories of the colony, the duumvir or prefect charged with jurisdiction in the colony of Genetiva shall be permitted without prejudice to draft colonists and native inhabitants assigned to its jurisdiction. And that duumvir, or whoever the duumvir has placed in command of those men in arms, shall have the same right of punishment as a military tribune of the Roman people in the army of the Roman people, and he shall exercise that right and power without prejudice, as long as his actions are in accordance with the resolve of the majority of the decurions who were present.

130 No duumvir or aedile or prefect of the colony Genetiva Julia shall propose to the decurions of the colony Genetiva, or consult the decurions, or carry a decree of the decurions, or enter or order to be entered such a decree in the public records, and no decurion, when this matter is being discussed, shall announce a vote to the decurions, or draft a decree of the decurions, or enter or order such a decree to be entered in the public records, by which any senator of the Roman people or son of that senator shall be adopted, chosen or made patron of the colony Genetiva, unless three-quarters of the decurions agree using voting tablets, and unless that person, at the time the decree of the decurions is under discussion, is a private person in Italy without imperium. If anyone in contravention of this proposes to the decurions, or carries or causes to be carried a decree of the decurions, or enters or orders such a decree to be entered in the public records, or if anyone proclaims a vote to the decurions, or drafts a decree of the decurions, or enters or orders such a degree to be entered in the public records, he shall be condemned to pay to the colonists of the colony Genetiva Julia, for every individual act in contravention of this law, 100,000 sesterces, and anyone who wishes shall have the right and power to bring an action, claim and prosecution for that sum in accordance with this law before a duumvir, interrex or prefect.

132 No person in the colony Genetiva, after the passing of this law, who is a candidate or standing for election to any magistracy in the colony Genetiva Julia, in that year in which he stands or intends to stand for a magistracy, shall put on entertainments, or invite anyone to dinner, or with malice aforethought put on or hold a banquet or cause another person to hold a banquet or invite anyone to dinner with regard to his candidature, except for the candidate himself during that year in which he is seeking election, who may invite to dinner if he wishes, and without malice aforethought, no more than nine persons daily. No candidate seeking election shall with malice aforethought make a gift or give handouts or anything else with regard to his candidature. No person with regard to the candidature of another person shall put on entertainments or invite anyone to dinner or hold a banquet, or with malice aforethought make a gift or give handouts or anything else with regard to another person's candidature. If anyone acts in contravention of this law he shall be condemned to pay to the colonists of the colony Genetiva Julia 5,000 sesterces, and anyone who wishes shall have the right and power to bring an action, claim and prosecution for that sum in accordance with this law in an action for recuperation before a duumvir or prefect. **133** As to those persons who will in accordance with this law be colonists of the colony Genetiva Julia, their wives who are in the colony Genetiva Julia in accordance with this law shall obey the laws of the colony Genetiva Julia, like their husbands, and shall possess all those rights laid down in this law without prejudice.

CAESAR AND HIS IMAGE

13.61 Suetonius *Life of the Deified Julius* 45.1–3: Caesar's appearance

45.1 Caesar is said to have been tall, with a fair complexion, shapely limbs, a rather full face, and keen black eyes, and to have had sound health, except that towards the end of his life he was subject to sudden fainting fits as well as nightmares. He also had two attacks of epilepsy while on campaign. **2** He was fastidious in the care of his person, and so not only kept his hair carefully trimmed and shaved but even had his body hair plucked – some people accuse him of that at any rate – while he was extremely vexed by the disfiguring effect of his baldness, since he found it exposed him to the ridicule of his opponents. As a result he used to comb his receding hair forward from the crown of his head and, of all the honours voted him by the senate and people, there was none that pleased him more or that he made use of more gladly than the privilege of wearing a laurel wreath on all occasions. **3** They say, too, that his dress was unusual: his purple-striped tunic had fringed sleeves down to the wrist and he always wore a belt over it, though it was rather loosely fastened. This, it is said, was the reason for Sulla's frequent warning to the optimates to beware of the 'ill-girt boy'.

13.62 Sallust *Conspiracy of Catiline* 53.6–54.6: Caesar versus Cato

Sallust's comparison of the virtues of Caesar and Cato was written c. 42 BC. He may have been intending a tacit criticism by 'extreme good qualities' in the first line – both overdid their excellences (Caesar his liberality, and Cato his 'justice').

53.6 Now within my living memory there have been two men of extreme good qualities but very different characters, Marcus Cato and Gaius Caesar. Since the subject has come up, it is not my intention to pass them by in silence but to disclose the nature and character of each, as far as my ability permits. **54.1** Well, their descent, age and eloquence were very similar, their greatness of spirit equal, and likewise their glory, but in other respects they were different. **2** Caesar was considered great in kindnesses and liberality, Cato in the integrity of his life. The former became noted for his clemency and compassion, while severity added to the latter's dignity. **3** Caesar won glory by giving, helping and pardoning, Cato by making no gifts. In the one there was a refuge for the wretched, in the other the destruction of evildoers. The former's good nature, the latter's firmness were the subjects of praise. **4** Finally, Caesar had trained himself to work hard, to stay vigilant; intent on his friends' affairs, to neglect his own, to refuse nothing worth giving; for himself he longed for great imperium, an army, a new war in which his virtue could shine forth. **5** But Cato's pursuit was moderation, what was fitting, and most of all gravity. **6** He did not try to rival the rich in richness nor the ambitious in politics, but the active man in virtue, the moderate in modesty, the blameless in self-control; he preferred rather to be than to seem good; thus the less he sought glory, the more it followed him.

13.63 Catullus 93: Catullus on Caesar

Suet. *Jul.* 73: Caesar invited Catullus to dinner after the latter had apologised for his invective against Caesar and Mamurra (cf. doc. 12.89).

I have no very great desire, Caesar, to try to please you –
Or even to know whether you are white or black.

13.64 Suetonius *Life of the Deified Julius* 56.1–7: Caesar's literary abilities

Caesar's oratory was highly praised by Cicero (doc. 2.68), and he wrote a treatise on *Analogy*. Of his works, the three books on the *Civil War* and seven books on the *Gallic War* (the eighth was written by Hirtius) survive; see doc. 16.6.

1 He left memoirs of his deeds in the *Gallic War* and the *Civil War* against Pompey. The author of the accounts of the Alexandrian, African and Spanish campaigns is unknown: some think it was Oppius, others Hirtius, who also completed the last book of the *Gallic War* which Caesar left unfinished. Regarding Caesar's memoirs, Cicero, also in the *Brutus*, comments: **2** 'He wrote memoirs which should be highly praised; they are simply, straightforwardly and gracefully composed, with all the clothing of rhetorical ornamentation removed; but, while his aim was to provide material for others who wanted to write history to draw upon, he has perhaps gratified several fools, who may choose to touch up his writings with curling-tongs, but has deterred all sensible men from writing on it.' **3** Concerning these memoirs, Hirtius (*BG* 8, pref. 5–6) stresses that: 'These memoirs are so highly regarded in all men's judgement that he seems to have deprived writers of an opportunity rather than offered them one, while our admiration for this is greater than that of others, for they know how beautifully and faultlessly he wrote, while we also know how easily and rapidly he completed the task.'

4 Asinius Pollio considers that the memoirs were composed with insufficient care and accuracy, since in many cases Caesar put too much trust in reports given by others of their deeds and records his own actions incorrectly, either deliberately or through forgetfulness; and he believes that Caesar intended to revise and correct his work.

5 He also left a two-volume work *On Analogy*, two more volumes *In Answer to Cato*, and a poem entitled *The Journey*. Of these, he wrote the first while crossing the Alps when returning to his army after holding assizes in Cisalpine Gaul, the second at roughly the time of the battle of Munda, and the last during the 24 days he was travelling between Rome and Further Spain. **6** Some letters of his to the senate are also extant, and he appears to have been the first to convert them to pages and the form of a notebook, while, previously, consuls and generals sent their reports written right across the sheet. Some letters of his to Cicero are also extant, as well as others to his close friends on personal matters, in which, if anything had to be conveyed confidentially, he wrote in cipher, that is with the order of the letters changed, so that no word can be understood: if anyone wishes to decipher these and find out their meaning, he has to change the fourth letter of the alphabet, that is, D for A, and so on with the rest. **7** Certain writings of his boyhood and early youth are mentioned, such as *Praises of Hercules* and a tragedy *Oedipus* and *Collected Sayings*; but Augustus forbade the publication of all these minor works in a very brief and frank letter sent to Pompeius Macer, whom he had chosen to organise his libraries.

13.65 Pliny *Natural History* 7.91–94: Caesar's outstanding intellect

91 The most outstanding example of mental vigour I consider to be the dictator Caesar; I am not now thinking of courage and perseverance, or of an elevation of mind able to embrace all that the heavens contain, but of native vigour and quickness winged as if with fire. We are told that he was accustomed to read or write and dictate or listen simultaneously, and to dictate to his secretaries four letters at the same time on matters of great importance, **92** or, if not otherwise occupied, seven. He also fought 50 pitched battles and was the only one to beat Marcus Marcellus (cos. 222), who fought 39 – for I would not count it to his glory that, in addition to victories over fellow citizens, he killed 1,192,000 persons in his battles, a huge, if unavoidable, injury to the human race, as he himself admitted it to be by not publishing the number slaughtered in the civil wars.

93 It would be fairer to credit Pompey the Great with the 846 ships he captured from the pirates: unique to Caesar, in addition to what was mentioned above, was the distinction of his clemency, in which he surpassed all others – even to the point of regretting it later; he also presented an example of magnanimity with which no other can be compared. **94** To count under this label the spectacles that he put on and the wealth he poured out, or the magnificence of his public works, would condone extravagance, but it demonstrated the genuine and unparalleled elevation of an unsurpassed mind that, when Pompey the Great's letter cases were captured at Pharsalus and Scipio's at Thapsus, he showed the highest integrity and burnt them instead of reading them.

THE IDES OF MARCH

By the time Caesar became perpetual dictator in February 44, many of those he had pardoned were reconciled to his prominence – others were not, and in becoming dictator for life it was made clear that he had no intention of restoring the Republic. Though probably predisposed to resist monarchy, M. Junius Brutus was won over to the conspirators' cause by C. Cassius Longinus. Brutus and Cassius, both pardoned by Caesar after Pharsalus (doc. 13.52), were the most prominent assassins ('tyrannicides'); all told, more than 60 senators were involved. Brutus joined Pompey's forces in the civil war as representing the state, but requested Caesar's pardon after Pharsalus; he was made governor of Cisalpine Gaul in 46 and urban praetor for 44 BC and was designated as consul for 41.

Cassius had been quaestor under Crassus in Syria; he survived Carrhae and organised the defence of Syria, where he served as proquaestor in 52–51, inflicting a major defeat on the Parthians in the latter year. Tribune in 49 (not to be confused with another tribune of 49, Q. Cassius Longinus), he was an adherent of Pompey's and commanded a fleet, but after Pharsalus surrendered it to Caesar and was pardoned; he served with him as a legate against Pharnaces. Other assassins included Decimus Brutus, chosen as consul for 42, and Trebonius (tr. pl. 55, cos. suff. 45). The assassination took place on the Ides of March (15 March) 44 BC. Caesar went to the senate house on the Ides despite ill omens, a dream of Calpurnia (his wife) and an illness – all perhaps post-eventum inventions of the sources. On the way he was handed a scroll with details of the plot but did not read it (perhaps another invented detail). His assassination heralded the return of civil war.

13.66 Plutarch *Life of Julius Caesar* 66.4–14: Caesar's assassination

Cicero has Trebonius detaining Antony, and he later writes to him that he wished that Antony too had been killed (doc. 14.16).

4 Now Antony, who was a close friend of Caesar's and physically fit, was detained outside (the senate house) by Brutus Albinus (Trebonius in Plut. *Brutus* 17.1), who deliberately engaged him in a lengthy conversation. **5** Caesar went on in and the senate rose in his honour, while some of Brutus' partisans went and stood behind his seat and others went to meet him, as though they were going to support the petition being made by Tillius Cimber on behalf of his brother in exile, and they joined him in his entreaties, accompanying Caesar as far as his seat. **6** When, after sitting down, Caesar continued to reject the requests and started to grow angry with one or another as they importuned him more urgently, Tillius grasped his toga with both hands and pulled it down from his neck – the signal for the attack. **7** It was Casca who gave the first blow with his dagger, in the neck, a wound which was neither mortal nor even deep, probably because he was nervous at the beginning of such a bold venture, and Caesar, as he turned, was therefore able to grab the knife and hold on to it. **8** At nearly the same moment both cried out, the victim in Latin, 'You villain, Casca, what are you doing?', the aggressor to his brother in Greek, 'Brother, help!' **9** This was how it began, while those who were not in the plot were thunderstruck and terrified at what was being done, not daring to flee or go to Caesar's help, or even to utter a word. **10** All of those who had prepared themselves for the murder produced their naked daggers, and Caesar was encompassed by them all, wherever he turned confronting blows and dagger aimed at his face and eyes, driven here and there like a wild beast and entangled in the hands of them all – **11** for they all had to participate in the sacrifice and taste his blood. It was for this reason that Brutus too gave him one blow in the groin. **12** And some say that Caesar fought back against all the others, darting this way and that and crying out, but, when he saw that Brutus had drawn his dagger, he covered his head with his toga and sank down, either by chance or because he had been pushed there by his murderers, against the pedestal on which the statue of Pompey stood. **13** The pedestal was drenched with blood, so as to appear that Pompey himself was presiding over this vengeance on his enemy, lying at his feet and struggling convulsively under numerous wounds. **14** He is said to have received 23, and many of the conspirators were wounded by each other as they tried to direct so many blows into one body.

13.67 Suetonius *Life of the Deified Julius* 82.1–2: 'Et tu, Brute?'

Brutus' mother, Servilia, was Cato's sister, and Caesar was rumoured to be Brutus' father through an early liaison with Servilia: cf. doc. 7.45 for the affair.

1 As he took his seat, the conspirators gathered round him as if to pay their respects, and straightaway Tillius Cimber, who had taken the lead, came closer as if to ask a question. When Caesar shook his head and put him off to another time, he seized his toga by both shoulders. Then, as Caesar cried out, 'This is violence', one of the Cascas wounded him from behind just below the throat. **2** Caesar seized Casca's arm and ran it through with his stylus, but, as he tried to leap up, he was stopped by another wound; when he saw that on every side he was confronted by drawn daggers, he covered his head with his toga and at the same time drew its fold down to his feet with his left hand to fall more decently, with the lower part of his body also covered. Like this he was stabbed with 23 blows, without uttering a word, except for a groan at the first stroke, though some have recorded that when Marcus Brutus came at him he said (in Greek), 'You, too, my child?'

13.68 Suetonius *Life of the Deified Julius* 83.2: Caesar's will

The reading of Caesar's will with its bequest to the people of Rome incited popular opposition to the tyrannicides. In the will, ratified by the senate on 18 March, Octavian, Caesar's great-nephew and the future princeps Augustus, was adopted as Caesar's heir in September 45.

In his last will he named as his three heirs his sisters' grandsons, Gaius Octavius to three-quarters of the property and Lucius Pinarius and Quintus Pedius to the remaining quarter; at the very end he also adopted Gaius Octavius, who was to take his name, into his family; and he named several of his assassins among the guardians of his son, if one should be born to him, Decimus Brutus even among the heirs in the second degree. To the people he bequeathed for their public use his gardens near the Tiber and 300 sesterces to each man.

13.69 Cicero *On Divination* 1.118–19: Omens of Caesar's assassination

For the omens preceding Caesar's death and the soothsayer (haruspex) Spurinna, see Suet. *Jul.* 81 (doc. 3.43).

118 If we concede the proposition that there is a divine power which pervades men's lives, it is not difficult to apprehend the principle which directs those signs which we see come to pass. For it is possible that, in the choice of a sacrificial victim, there is some intelligent force that guides us which is diffused through the whole world, or that when you are about to make the sacrifice a change takes place in the vitals so that something is either taken away or added; for in a moment nature adds or changes or diminishes many things. **119** The clearest proof, which shows that this cannot be doubted, is what happened just before Caesar's death. When he was offering sacrifices on that day on which he first sat on a golden throne and showed himself in a purple robe, no heart was found in the vitals of the fat ox. Now do you think that any animal that has blood can exist without a heart? Caesar was not perturbed by the strangeness of this occurrence, even though Spurinna said that he should beware lest both thought and life desert him; for, he said, both of these stemmed from the heart. On the following day there was no head on the liver of the sacrificial beast. These omens were foretold to Caesar by the immortal gods so he might foresee his death, not so that he might be on his guard against it. So when those organs without which the victim could not have lived are not found in the vitals, we should understand that the absent organs disappeared at the moment of sacrifice.

13.70 Cicero *On Divination* 2.22–23: The fates of the 'triumvirs'

Cicero here argues against his brother Quintus that divination is of no use if events are ruled by Fate, and, if they are, then knowledge of the future is a disadvantage.

22 Leaving aside the men of earlier days, do you think that it would have been of any advantage to Marcus Crassus, when he was at the peak of his wealth and fortune, to know that he was going to perish beyond the Euphrates in shame and dishonour after the death of his son Publius and the destruction of his army? Or do you think that Gnaeus Pompey would have found happiness in his three consulships, in his three triumphs and in the fame of his pre-eminent achievements if he had known that, after losing his army, he would be slaughtered in a lonely Egyptian spot, and that there would follow, after his death, events of which we cannot speak without tears? **23** What indeed do we think of Caesar's case? If he had foreseen that in the senate, which he for the most part had chosen himself, in Pompey's hall, in front of the statue of Pompey himself, with so many of his own centurions looking on, he would be slaughtered by the most noble citizens, some of whom owed everything they possessed to him, and so little honoured that not only none of his friends would approach his corpse but not even any of his servants, in what torment of mind would he have spent his life?

COINAGE

13.71 Crawford *RRC* 452.2: Victory over the Gauls

An aureus (gold coin) of 48–47 BC.

Obverse: Female head (a goddess, perhaps Pietas?), facing right and wearing a diadem and an oak wreath.

Reverse: A trophy of arms, made up of Gallic weapons, helmet, shield and armour. Legend: Caesar.

13.72 Crawford *RRC* 458.1: Caesar and Venus

A denarius of c. 47 BC. Anchises and Venus were the parents of Aeneas, legendary founder of the Julian family. The coin is usually dated generally to after the defeat of Pompey at Pharsalus or to 47–46 BC.

Obverse: Bust of Venus, wearing diadem.

Reverse: Aeneas, holding the palladium (see docs 2.29, 7.90) and carrying his father on his flight from Troy.

13.73 Crawford *RRC* 480.7a: Perpetual dictator

A denarius of February–March 44 BC. The veil presents Caesar as pontifex maximus, showing the official importance he attached to this position.

Obverse: Head of Caesar with veil (face visible); legend: *Caesar Dict. Perpetuo* (Caesar, Perpetual Dictator).

Reverse: Standing Venus, facing left, with a sceptre in her right hand and a Victory deity in the palm of her left hand.

13.74 Crawford *RRC* 508.3: The assassination of Caesar

A denarius of 43–42 BC. The assassination of Caesar is represented as emancipation for the Roman people; this is the only contemporary portrait of Brutus.

Obverse: Head of Brutus. Legend: *Brut. Imp.* (Brutus imperator).

Reverse: A freedom cap, as worn by emancipated slaves, between two daggers. Legend: *Eid. Mar.* (*Eidibus Martiis*: on the Ides of March).

14

Octavian's rise to power

Following the assassination of Julius Caesar, his fellow consul and protégé, Mark Antony, was in an unparalleled position of power once it became clear that the 'liberators' did not enjoy popular support. He had considerable political and military experience, far more so than the young Octavian, Caesar's great-nephew, who was shortly to arrive on the scene. Antony had served with Gabinius in Egypt and Syria (57–54) and with Caesar in Gaul. As tribune in 49, his flight from Rome had given Caesar a pretext for invading Italy, and he had played an important role as Caesar's magister equitum during the civil war, while Caesar had intended leaving him in charge at Rome during his own Parthian campaign. While clearly a flamboyant character, he was an experienced general, and accounts of his dissipation and intemperance owe much to later Augustan propaganda (doc. 14.1). In contrast, Octavian was only 19 years of age at Caesar's death and little known in Rome. Despite his relationship with Caesar, his family had had little experience in political life: his father, Gaius Octavius, was a novus homo who was praetor in 61 BC, though his stepfather, Philippus, had been consul in 56. Octavian had served in Spain with Caesar and had ridden behind him at his African triumph. He had been studying at Apollonia, where the Parthian expedition was assembling, at the time of the assassination (doc. 14.2). On hearing the news that he was Caesar's primary heir and had been adopted by him posthumously, he returned to Italy and took the name Gaius Julius Caesar, even though his mother and stepfather advised him against this, so positioning himself as Caesar's son whose main object was to avenge his death. Despite senatorial support, the liberators were unpopular, and Brutus and Cassius had been forced to leave Rome. They had then begun raising troops to secure Macedonia and Syria, the provinces they had been assigned by Caesar but which had been reallocated to Antony and his fellow consul, Dolabella (doc. 14.3).

In the meantime Cicero provided full details of his reactions to events to his correspondent Atticus, often at almost daily intervals, regretting that the liberators had not seized their opportunity properly and that Antony had taken the opportunity to have all Caesar's draft acta ratified, including some laws that may not have actually been Caesar's (doc. 14.4). Octavian arrived at Brundisium in early April and *en route* to Rome began encouraging Caesar's veterans to support him as Caesar's son. He soon attracted a significant following and also appears to have had access to state monies arriving into Brundisium, including taxes from the East (docs 14.5–7). At Puteoli he met Cicero, as well as his mother and stepfather and the consuls-designate for 43, Hirtius and Pansa. Despite the fact that his accepting the adoption and taking Caesar's name clearly implied that he would be taking action against Caesar's assassins, Cicero seems to have viewed him, if he could be separated from Antony (doc. 14.9), as a potential political asset. In Rome, Antony attempted to frustrate Octavian's plans, and, when Antony refused to release the bequest given by Caesar to all citizens (300 sesterces per person), Octavian raised the money by selling property, thus reinforcing the popular support he enjoyed as Caesar's son and heir, while Antony was criticised for coming to terms with the 'liberators'. There was also conflict over Octavian's wish to stand for the tribunate and his attempt to place a golden chair and wreath for Caesar at the games in honour of his victories held in July, while Octavian's adoption was not formally ratified by a *lex curiata* until late in 43 (docs 14.8, 10). Antony had made the most of his opportunities following Caesar's death and was thought to have abstracted the latter's funds, some 700 million sesterces, from the treasury in the temple of Ops (docs 14.10, 14.15). In June he decided that Cisalpine Gaul, with its command of the northern border of Italy, would be a more strategic province than Macedonia and had irregular legislation passed exchanging his province for Cisalpine and Transalpine Gaul, while retaining five of the six Macedonian legions which were recalled to Italy: however, the governor of Cisalpine Gaul, Decimus Brutus, refused with the senate's approval to give up his province. In October Antony also accused Octavian of attempting to assassinate him with the help of his (Antony's) own bodyguard, and he then made for Brundisium to meet his legions and ensure their loyalty (docs 14.10–11).

Octavian, painfully aware that he had little real support as yet, toured the colonies of Caesar's veterans in November, offering large bounties (2,000 sesterces apiece) and presenting himself as Caesar's avenger, while he persuaded Cicero to support him in the senate. Cicero's letters to Atticus detail his painful indecision in early November over what to reply to Octavian's letters and whether or not to go to Rome to support him (he was 'still obviously a boy') in the senate (doc. 14.12). Octavian's agents also managed to effect the desertion of two of Antony's Macedonian legions to his cause to add to the two legions of veterans he had already raised, and he offered these to the senate to use against Antony, who was preparing to attack Decimus Brutus in Cisalpine Gaul. Octavian gave them a bounty of 2,000 sesterces apiece and promised 20,000 on demobilisation. Antony, hearing of his legions' defection, had left for Cisalpine Gaul in late November to besiege Decimus Brutus in Mutina, and, despite his unpopularity with much of the senate, most of the senators and equites had come to him at Tibur to offer their loyalty and support (doc. 14.13). Without legions under its own command until the consuls of 43 took office, the senate perforce accepted Octavian's troops, and, at the 'request' of his army, granted him propraetorian imperium at the urging of Cicero, who, however violent his denunciations of Antony in the *Philippics*, was unable to persuade the senate to declare him a public enemy, though he did encourage Decimus

Brutus to resist him at all costs (docs 14.13–15). From December 44, while disdaining Antony's claims and requests, Cicero constantly presented Octavian to the senate as the saviour of the state against Antony's aggression and brutality, and when Octavian was granted imperium at the beginning of 43 he positioned himself with Cicero's approval as the senate's champion alongside the two new consuls. At this point Cicero was still regretting that Antony had not been eliminated along with Caesar and considered Octavian as an 'extraordinary boy' (doc. 14.16). Even as late as April Cicero was congratulating himself on his political sagacity, when, after relieving the siege of Mutina, the consuls and Octavian finally defeated Antony and he was declared a public enemy. Both consuls had been killed in the conflict, but Cicero's proposal of a triumph and 50-day thanksgiving in Octavian's honour was opposed, and Cicero, who even considered the possibility of holding the consulship with Octavian, was warned by Decimus Brutus and Plancus that the boy was equivocating rather than following up the victory and retaining troops that had been promised elsewhere (docs 14.17–18).

By July Octavian had clearly decided that he would achieve more by siding with Antony than with the senate, and in early August 43 he marched on Rome with eight legions, paying his men from public funds half the bounties promised them. He was appointed consul in his twentieth year, never having held a magistracy (doc. 14.19). Lepidus had joined Antony in late May, and the three met on an island near Bononia in October 43 to settle their differences and plan for the future. This alliance is known as the 'Second Triumvirate'. It was decided that they should wage full-scale war against the 'liberators', and they shared the Western provinces among themselves for a five-year period, with Antony taking the most strategic provinces in Gaul. Octavian at this point was still apparently the junior partner. They also decided that, in order to raise funds to pay all the veterans due to be demobilised, they would expropriate the property of 18 Italian cities, impose severe taxes, and draw up a list of proscribed whose property would be confiscated. Approximately 300 senators and 2,000 equites were named, including Cicero. On 27 November the senate formally appointed the triumvirs to restore the state, with powers to make laws, appoint magistrates and exercise jurisdiction unchallenged. Octavian then resigned the consulship, and Lepidus was appointed consul for 42 (doc. 14.20). While Octavian was said to have argued to spare Cicero, the triumvirs were not reluctant to give up members of their own families, and Cicero, who had been totally hoodwinked by 'the extraordinary boy', was executed at Caieta, one of his many country houses, in December 43 – to Antony's intense satisfaction. Livy pays credit to his courage in the face of death (docs 14.21–22).

During 43 BC the tyrannicides had been consolidating their support in the East. Cassius had taken control of Syria and four legions from Egypt, while Brutus controlled Macedonia and Greece. Their troops had also been promised 20,000 sesterces apiece in the event of victory. The propaganda against the liberators was intensified by the deification of Julius Caesar, which gave Octavian the status of 'son of the god' and the war a new religious dimension (docs 14.23–24). Brutus and Cassius in their turn were honoured in the East in the hope that they might liberate Greece from the Romans (doc. 14.25). The armies met at Philippi in two engagements, on 3 and 23 October. The victory was due to Antony's generalship (Octavian, who was unwell, was reported to have spent three days hiding in a marsh) and to the fact that Cassius committed suicide on believing that Brutus had been defeated; Brutus committed suicide after the second battle. Appian reports that Rome's government, and the fate of the Republic, was explicitly decided by the outcome.

Octavian returned to Italy to oversee the allocations of land to the veterans being discharged, while Antony took charge in the East to restore stability after the rapacious demands of the tyrannicides (docs 14.26–27). While the triumvirs had agreed on the confiscation of the property of 18 Italian towns for colonies of veterans, nearly double that number had to be sequestered, and the redistribution of land brought great hardship to many areas. This was exacerbated by the piratical activities of Sextus Pompeius, Pompey's younger son, which caused intermittent famine at Rome (doc. 14.28). In 41, Lucius Antonius, one of the consuls and Antony's brother, and Antony's wife, Fulvia, considered that Octavian was settling his own veterans in preference to Antony's and stirred up unrest in Italy. Lucius had the support of the senate and briefly gained control of Rome, but was then besieged in Perusia and defeated by Octavian in March 40. It is unclear to what extent Antony himself knew what was happening, and his generals in the West did not interfere on Lucius' behalf. Fulvia may also have been inspired by Octavian's breaking of his betrothal with her daughter Clodia Pulchra, which took place after Bononia at the troops' request, since she now had no ties of relationship with the young man. Octavian's obscene lines attacking Fulvia and her sexuality are quoted by Martial, while slingshots from both sides preserve the insults hurled by the troops at each other (docs 14.29–31).

From 42 Antony toured the East, establishing client kings, settling disputes, and raising resources to pay for the settlement of veterans and their promised bounties, as well as overturning decisions made by Cassius in Syria (doc. 14.33). Another pressing issue was the prosecution of the war against the Parthians, planned by Caesar, not only to restore Roman honour after Crassus' defeat but to protect the Eastern provinces from Parthian incursions (doc. 14.35). One of the most important client rulers in the East was Cleopatra VII of Egypt, who was summoned to meet Antony at Tarsus. The resources of Egypt were important to Rome. Antony dealt with all threats to her position and spent the winter of 41–40 in Egypt: their twins were born in the following year (doc. 14.34). In mid-40 Antony returned to Italy to patch up any differences with Octavian; to seal the reconciliation, Antony and the younger Octavia, Octavian's sister, were married, Fulvia having recently died in Athens. Following a meeting at Brundisium, probably in September, the generals went to Rome, where they were awarded ovations. The empire was again portioned out, this time between East and West, with Lepidus, who was clearly being sidelined, given only Africa. Octavian was to make war on Sextus Pompeius and his fleet, and Antony on the Parthians. Because of Pompeius' activities Rome was again suffering famine, and new taxes had to be introduced. These were so unpopular that Octavian's life was endangered by rioting and he had to be rescued in the forum by Antony and his troops (docs 14.36). The famine and riots demonstrated Pompeius' position of strength, and in 39 Antony, Octavian and Pompeius signed a treaty at Misenum, by which Pompeius was granted Sicily, Sardinia and other territories for a five-year period and was designated consul for 33 alongside Octavian. Consuls for the next four years were also selected, with Antony to be consul in 34 and Octavian to hold the consulship with him in 31. This agreement was greeted with enthusiastic fervour in Rome and Italy (doc. 14.37).

As part of the negotiation with Pompeius, Octavian had married Scribonia (Pompeius' nearest possible female relation: she was the sister of Pompeius' father-in-law). Octavian divorced her in October 39, the day that she gave birth to his only child, Julia, in order to marry a young noblewoman, Livia Drusilla. She was heavily pregnant at the time, but her husband kindly divorced her so that she could marry Octavian. They were to remain together for over 50 years (doc. 14.39). Italy was still threatened by Pompeius, and in 38 Octavian's fleet was twice defeated. Antony returned to Italy again in 37 and met Octavian at Tarentum: the triumvirate, which had lapsed, was renewed for a further five-year period. Pompeius was finally conclusively defeated by the talents of Octavian's admiral Agrippa, off Naulochus in September 36, and Lepidus, after trying to take control of the land forces, lost his command and membership of the triumvirate. Octavian was seen as the saviour of Italy; he was awarded an ovation, tribunician sacrosanctity, and a golden statue in the forum, and he flagged that the Republic would be restored on Antony's return from Parthia (doc. 14.41).

During Antony's absence in Italy, his legate Ventidius had defeated the Parthians and killed the Parthian king. Antony returned to Cleopatra in 37, giving Egypt a number of territories, including Cyprus and Cyrene. He was not to see Octavia again, and Cleopatra bore another son, Ptolemy Philadelphus, in 36. Antony made war on Parthia on his own account that year, invading from Armenia to the north, but was forced to retreat when Artavasdes of Armenia and his cavalry deserted, and he lost more than 20,000 men, a third of the army, to starvation and disease. This was his first real military catastrophe, and it contrasted badly with Octavian's promotion of himself as the defeater of Pompeius (doc. 14.42). Octavian was also to follow this up with a successful campaign against the Dalmatians and Pannonians, while Antony, rather than taking another military force north, entrapped Artvasdes of Armenia, which he publicised as a conquest of Armenia, heralding it as such on his coinage. Cleopatra was also depicted, titled 'queen of kings and of her sons who are kings', reflecting the 'Donations of Alexandria', a public spectacle in 34 in which Antony proclaimed Cleopatra (who appeared as Isis), Caesarion, and their three young children rulers of Eastern provinces and client kingdoms of the Roman empire. Such actions caused consternation in Rome, while Octavian refused to allow Antony to raise troops in Italy and tried to make capital out of the latter's divorce of his sister (docs 14.43–46). Both sides engaged in invective and propaganda: Antony was portrayed as having 'gone native' and living a dissolute and un-Roman lifestyle under the influence of an arrogant and ambitious foreign queen, while Octavian in turn was shown as a hypocrite and gambler with a murky past, whose morals were no better than Antony's (docs 14.47–49).

The term of the triumvirate expired in December 33, and when in the new year Octavian surrounded himself with an armed guard in the senate, the two new consuls, Sosius and Domitius Ahenobarbus, fled to Antony, who formed an alternate senate from his numerous senatorial supporters. New and unpopular taxes were instituted in Italy in 32 to cover the costs of the preparations for war. When two of Antony's legates, Titius and Plancus, deserted to Octavian (supposedly because of their dislike of the presence of Cleopatra), he removed Antony's will from the keeping of the Vestals and supposedly read it in the senate, stressing in particular that Antony had expressed the wish for his body after his death to be sent to Cleopatra (doc. 14.50). War was then declared on Cleopatra as a foreign enemy, and Antony and Cleopatra took their stand on the west coast of Greece and waited for Octavian. At this point again Agrippa was to be Octavian's greatest asset, and his actions in weakening Antony's naval contingent and capturing supply bases prior to the actual battle at Actium played a significant role in the outcome. The battle itself took place on 2 September 31. Antony broke out through the encircling fleet with about one-third of his ships and followed Cleopatra to Egypt, abandoning his infantry, who surrendered to Octavian. When Octavian's troops reached Alexandria in 30, Antony's entire navy deserted and he committed suicide. Cleopatra killed herself nine days later to avoid being taken in triumph to Rome (docs 14.51–53). In a poem to the literary patron Maecenas, Octavian's childhood friend and, like Agrippa, 'right-hand' man, Horace acclaims Octavian's victory at Actium over Roman soldiers in 'a woman's power', surrounded by wrinkled eunuchs and mosquito-nets (doc. 14.52). Egypt was an important acquisition, far too important to be governed by a senator in the normal way, and Octavian was to ensure that the governor of Egypt would answer directly to him and be, not a senator, but an equestrian. C. Cornelius Gallus had played an important part in Octavian's campaign after Actium and was appointed as first prefect of Egypt. His governorship was a success, in that he put down a revolt in Thebes and led his army beyond the First Cataract. However, his trilingual inscription at Philae in 29 recording his achievements was hardly modest, and when he had statues of himself erected throughout Egypt and inscriptions placed on the pyramids he found himself recalled. It appears that the senate called on him to answer charges of treason, and he committed suicide in 26 BC (docs 14.55–57).

Octavian had returned briefly to Italy after Actium, though not to Rome, but it was his arrival in August 29 BC that led to great celebrations. At this point he was still only 32 years of age. In his absence in January 29, the senate had ratified all his acta, given him the right to use 'Imperator' as a first name, and declared that the doors of the temple of Janus should be closed, signifying that the empire was finally at peace for the first time since 235 BC. On his return, as the 'restorer of the Republic' and Rome's saviour from civil strife, he held three triumphs, over Dalmatia, Cleopatra (Actium) and Egypt, between 13 and 15 August. Triumphal arches were also erected in Rome and Brundisium, and the coinage celebrated his wide-ranging victories. From the vast wealth of Egypt he was able to distribute 400 sesterces to every citizen, and 1,000 to every veteran, over and above the bounties promised. The rate of interest fell sharply and everyone rejoiced (docs

14.58–62). There were still, however, issues to be addressed, most notably the discharge of veterans: following Actium, Octavian was in command of some 70 legions and had to find appropriate settlements for tens of thousands of veterans. The problem was ameliorated by many of them being paid out in money rather than in land, and he may have settled 150,000 to 200,000 soldiers, leaving Rome with 28 legions (*RG* 3.3: doc. 15.1). His birthday and victories were quickly incorporated into the calendar, while Antony's birthday, 14 January, became unlucky (nefastus) (doc. 14.63). In general, however, the fact that the conflict had been against Antony was downplayed, with Cleopatra put centre stage as the empire's enemy.

With opposition removed, it was important to Octavian that he be seen to 'restore the state' and facilitate the return to constitutional government. He held the consulship every year between 31 and 27 BC, in the last two years in conjunction with Agrippa, which gave him a constitutional position from which to work. In 28 the two of them had a full census carried out, and the membership of the senate was revised and reduced to some 800 members, while constitutional normality was apparently being restored. It was also in this year that Octavian boasted that he had restored 82 temples in Rome (docs 14.58, 15.1; *RG* 20.4). As the conclusion of this programme of 'restoring the state' during 28 and 27 BC, Octavian on 13 January 27 in a speech to the senate made a carefully prepared gesture of resigning his powers into the hands of the senate and people. The senators naturally responded with horror and begged him to retain power. He later states that he came to be princeps by popular consent (*RG* 34.1; doc. 15.1), but even so he was careful to avoid any suggestion of a perpetual position; while he did hold supreme power, he did so in carefully defined five- or ten-year periods which had to be renewed at the appropriate point. He now took control of any provinces where unrest or warfare was a possibility, including of course their armies, while leaving to the senate governorships of the more pacified provinces. This was initially for a ten-year period. The governors he nominated would answer directly to him and hold the rank of propraetor. At the same time he continued to hold the consulship down to 23 BC. As Dio comments (doc. 14.64), since Octavian had control of the armies and finances, in reality he had 'absolute control of all matters for all time', even if the pretence and forms of Republican government were retained. This, in Dio's view, was the beginning of the monarchy. To signify his personal authority and eminence, the princeps was also awarded the name 'Augustus' at the motion of Plancus, previously one of Antony's supporters. Tacitus considers that Octavian, while 'parading himself as consul', had gradually accumulated powers and functions so quietly and unobtrusively that all opposition was at an end and that the nobility and provinces welcomed the ensuing stability, even if it did border on slavery (docs 14.65–66).

Ancient sources: apart from the *Res Gestae*, Augustus' own account of his achievements, the main sources for his early reign are Appian's *Civil Wars* books 3–5 and Dio's *Roman History* 45–56. Appian's history, much of which is based on sources now lost, unfortunately breaks off just before the final confrontation between Octavian and Antony. The fragmentary *Life of Augustus* by Nikolaos of Damascus presents some valuable material for Octavian's early years and arrival in Rome in 44, and this is especially useful, as it appears to be based on Augustus' own (lost) autobiography. Plutarch's *Life of Antony* retells much of the anti-Antony propaganda current before the battle of Actium but preserves some interesting anecdotes, some of which may be accepted. Suetonius' thematic biography covers the main aspects of the reign, occasionally citing Augustus' own letters. The letters of Cicero also provide a detailed account of affairs at Rome, and Cicero's view on them, down to December 43. His *Philippics*, attacking Antony, encapsulate the worst possible view of the latter's aims and actions in an attempt to pressure the senate into declaring him a public enemy of the state, but they are magnificent rhetoric and evidence that senate meetings could be highly charged and intellectually enjoyable.

ANTONY AND OCTAVIAN

Despite the term 'Second Triumvirate' (rule of three men), which is often used to label the period between the death of Julius Caesar and the establishment of the principate, of the three, Lepidus was in many ways a cipher. Events between 44 and 30 BC were centred around two men in particular, Mark Antony and Caesar's young great-nephew Octavian, 20 years Antony's junior and, at the age of 19, almost entirely without experience of politics or warfare. Mark Antony had, in contrast, been one of Caesar's legates, was Caesar's consular colleague in 44, and had a distinguished military reputation, even if later sources are careful to accuse him of a rather disreputable past as a youth. In 44 no one would have believed that, of the two, it would be Octavian who would rise to sole power and portend the demise of the Republic.

14.1 Plutarch *Life of Antony* 2.1–4.4: The young Antony

Mark Antony was probably born in 83 BC. He served as cavalry commander under Gabinius in 57–54 BC and then with Caesar in Gaul. He commanded Caesar's left wing at Pharsalus in 48 and was his consular colleague in 44. At Caesar's death he was the most powerful man in Rome.

2.1 Antonius Creticus' wife was Julia of the house of the Caesars, who rivalled the best and most prudent women of her time. Her son Antony was brought up by her, and after the death of his father she married Cornelius Lentulus, whom Cicero executed for being a member of Catiline's conspiracy. **2** This seems to have been the reason and origin of Antony's violent hatred towards Cicero. At any rate, Antony says that Lentulus' dead body was not even given over to them until his mother had begged it from Cicero's wife. **3** This is, however, admittedly incorrect, for none of those punished by Cicero was denied burial. **4** Antony in his youth showed brilliant promise, they say, until his friendship and intimacy with Curio had a disastrous effect on him, for Curio was undisciplined with regard to pleasures, and to make Antony more pliant got him involved in drinking sessions, women, and expensive and unbridled extravagances – **5** which resulted in a serious debt, especially serious for one of his age, of 250 talents. When Curio pledged himself as security for all of it and his father learnt of it, he banished Antony from their house. **6** Antony then for a short time became intimate with the gang of Clodius, the most brazen and loathsome of the demagogues of that time, which was disrupting the entire government of the state; **7** but he soon had enough of that man's insanity and, in fear of the faction that was forming against Clodius, left Italy for Greece and spent his time exercising his body for military service and in studying oratory. **8** He adopted the extravagant, so-called Asiatic, style of speaking, which was at the peak of its popularity at that time, which bore a strong similarity to his own lifestyle, being boastful and arrogant and full of pride and perverted ambition.

3.1 When Gabinius, a man of consular rank, was sailing for Syria, he tried to persuade Antony to be part of the expedition, and, while he said that he would not participate as a private citizen, he accompanied him on campaign once made master of the horse. **2** And when he was sent against Aristoboulos, who was inciting the Jews to a revolt, he was himself the first man to ascend the highest of the fortifications and drove Aristoboulos from them all; **3** he then joined battle with him, routed with his handful of troops their far more numerous forces, and killed all but a few of them: Aristoboulos himself with his son was captured. . . . **4.1** His physique gave him a noble bearing and he had an imposing beard, a breadth of forehead and an aquiline nose, which were thought to mirror the virility depicted in the portraits and statues of Herakles. **2** There was also an ancient account that the Antonii were Herakleidai, as descendants of Anton, son of Herakles. **3** He also believed that he authenticated this account by his physique, as I have said, and his manner of dressing. For, whenever he was going to be seen by a number of people, he would always have his tunic girt to his thigh, a great sword hung at his side and a cloak enveloping him. **4** And even things others found offensive, such as his boasting and jests and his drinking vessel in clear view and his sitting beside someone who was eating, and eating standing at a soldiers' table – it is remarkable to find how much goodwill and affection towards him this inspired in his soldiers.

14.2 Suetonius *Life of the Deified Augustus* 3.1–4.2, 8.1–3: Octavian's family

Octavian, Caesar's great-nephew, was born in 63 BC. At the time of Caesar's assassination he was at Apollonia with Caesar's army waiting to depart for the Parthian expedition. C. Cassius Parmensis was one of Caesar's assassins and was put to death by Octavian after Actium. **3.2**: Cicero's letter is to his brother Quintus (1.1.21).

3.1 His father, Gaius Octavius, was from the beginning of his life a man of wealth and reputation, and, indeed, I wonder that some have said that he was also a money-changer and even employed to distribute bribes and perform other electioneering jobs in the Campus: in fact, being brought up in affluence, he easily attained magistracies and performed in them with distinction. He obtained Macedonia by lot as his province after his praetorship and on his way there wiped out a band of runaway slaves, the remnants of Spartacus and Catiline's armies, who were in possession of the area around Thurii, a special commission given him by the senate. **2** He governed his province with no less justice than courage: for, as well as routing the Bessi and other Thracians in a great battle, he so dealt with our allies that letters of Marcus Cicero are still extant, in which he urges and counsels his brother Quintus who at the time was serving as proconsular governor of Asia – with little credit to himself – to copy his neighbour Octavius' behaviour in winning the good opinion of our allies.

4.1 He died suddenly on his return from Macedonia (59 BC) before he could stand as a candidate for the consulship, leaving three children: an elder Octavia by Ancharia and a younger Octavia and Augustus by Atia. Atia was the daughter of Marcus Atius Balbus and Julia, sister of Gaius Caesar. Balbus came from Aricia on his father's side, with many senatorial portraits (imagines) in his family, and on his mother's side had a very close connection with Pompey the Great. After holding the office of praetor, he was one of the Commission of Twenty under the Julian law which divided up the Campanian land for the plebs. **2** Indeed Antony, who tried to disparage Augustus' maternal line as well, taunts him by saying that his great-grandfather Balbus was of African birth and that he owned first a perfumery and then a bakery at Aricia. Cassius of Parma similarly sneers at Augustus in one of his letters as the grandson of both a baker and a money-changer: 'Your mother's flour came from a wretched bakery at Aricia, and was kneaded into shape by a money-changer from Nerulum whose hands were tarnished with currency exchange!'

8.1 He lost his father when he was four. In his twelfth year he delivered to the people the eulogy for his grandmother Julia. Four years later, after adopting the adult toga, he received military rewards at Caesar's African triumph (46 BC), although he had not taken part in the war because of his youth. When shortly afterwards his uncle went to Spain to deal with the sons of Pompey, although he had barely recovered from a serious illness he followed him through roads infested with the enemy, with minimal companions, and even after suffering a shipwreck. By this undertaking he greatly recommended himself to Caesar, who quickly formed a high opinion of his character over and above the efforts he had put into his journey. **2** After the recovery of the Spanish provinces, Caesar, in his plans for an expedition against the Dacians and then the Parthians, sent him on ahead to Apollonia, where he devoted his time to study. As soon as he heard that Caesar had been assassinated and that he was his heir, he hesitated for a while as to whether to call on the nearest legions but decided against that plan as precipitate and premature. However, he returned to the city and claimed his inheritance, despite his mother's doubts and the strong discouragement of his stepfather, the ex-consul Marcius Philippus. **3** From that time he raised armies and ruled the state, first with Mark Antony and Marcus Lepidus, then with Antony alone for nearly 12 years, and finally on his own for 44.

THE AFTERMATH OF CAESAR'S ASSASSINATION

After Caesar's assassination on 15 March 44 BC, there was general panic. Antony, the other consul, fled home to hide; the troops of Lepidus, Caesar's magister equitum, seized the forum that night, and the conspirators, aided by a band of gladiators belonging to

Decimus Brutus, occupied the Capitol. On 17 March the senate, summoned by Antony, voted for an amnesty, and that Caesar should have a public funeral while his laws and will were to remain in force. On 20 March Caesar's will was publicly read and his corpse displayed to the crowd by Antony, which enraged the people against the conspirators; his body was cremated in the forum, and by the middle of April Brutus and Cassius had to flee from Rome. On Antony's proposal, the senate abolished the dictatorship, and Antony was thought to have fabricated many documents and new laws on the pretence that they were found among Caesar's papers. According to Cicero (doc. 14.15), Antony had also seized Caesar's funds, 700 million sesterces, from the temple of Ops.

14.3 Appian *Civil Wars* 4.8.57–58: Appian's overview of 44–43 BC

57 When Gaius Caesar was assassinated, his murderers seized the Capitol, coming down when an amnesty was decreed. The people were greatly affected at his funeral and ran through the city searching out the assassins. These defended themselves from their roofs, and those who had been appointed by Caesar himself as provincial governors left Rome immediately. Cassius and Brutus were still in office as praetors in the city, though Cassius had been selected by Gaius Caesar as governor of Syria and Brutus of Macedonia. As they were not yet able, for the time being, to take up their governorships of these provinces, but were unable to ride out the disturbing situation in the city patiently, they left while still praetors; to put a good face on this, the senate put them in charge of the grain supply so that they did not appear to have to have made a run for it during this intervening period. When they had gone, Syria and Macedonia were reassigned to the consuls Antony and Dolabella, very much to the disapproval of the senate, although Cyrene and Crete were given in exchange to Cassius and his fellow conspirator. They disdained these because of their relative unimportance and began to raise troops and funds to invade Syria and Macedonia. **58** While they were engaged in doing this, as Dolabella had put Trebonius to death in Asia and Antony was besieging Decimus (Brutus) in (Cisalpine) Gaul, the indignant senate decreed Dolabella and Antony to be public enemies and reinstated Brutus and Cassius in their former commands, adding Illyria to that of Brutus, while instructing everyone else who held commands of provinces or armies from Rome, from the Adriatic (Ionian) to Syria, to obey any orders given by Cassius or Brutus.

14.4 Cicero *Letters to Atticus* 14.4–5, 14.9–10: Cicero on the Ides of March

Cicero saw the conspirators as tyrannicides or liberators and the senate on the whole sympathised with them, but by April they were unpopular enough to be almost house prisoners. Cicero had proposed the vote that Caesar's acta should stand because he believed that the liberators' cause was already lost, and his frustration at events is clear. Octavian arrived at Brundisium in April; the consuls-designate for 43 were Hirtius and Pansa.

14.4.2 (Lanuvium, 10 April 44) The Ides of March are our consolation. Our heroes achieved all that rested with themselves gloriously and magnificently; what remains needs money and men, none of which we have.

14.5.2 (Astura, 11 April 44) Those who ought to be guarded by all mankind, not only for their protection but also for their glorification, are praised and loved, but that is all, and are confined within their houses. Yet they are happy under any circumstances, while the state is wretched. **3** I would really like to know how Octavian's arrival went off, and whether anyone is rallying to him or if there is any hint of a *coup*. I don't suppose there is, but in any case I would like to know.

14.9.2 (Puteoli, 17 April 44) There is a great crowd here and will be, as I hear, a greater, including the so-called consuls-designate. Great gods! The tyranny lives on, the tyrant is dead! We rejoice at the death of a murdered man whose acts we defend! So . . . criticises us severely, so as to make us ashamed of being alive, and not wrongly! It would have been better to die 1,000 times rather than put up with all this – and it looks to me as if this will be of long duration!

14.10.1 (Cumae, 19 April 44) And so, was this what my – and your – dear Brutus worked for, that he should stay at Lanuvium, that Trebonius should set out on byways for his province, that everything done, written, said, promised and planned by Caesar should have more weight than if he himself were alive? Do you remember my crying out on that first day on the Capitol that the senate should be summoned to the Capitol by the praetors? Immortal gods! What could have been effected then to the rejoicing of all good men – even the reasonably good – with the power of the bandits broken! You blame the Liberalia (17 March). What could have been done then? We were long done for by that point. Do you remember how you cried out that the cause was lost if he had a state funeral? But he was even cremated in the forum and given a pathetic eulogy, and slaves and paupers were sent against our houses with torches. Then what? That they dare to say, 'Are you opposing Caesar's wishes?' This and the like I am unable to endure. So I am planning a trip to 'land beyond land'; your land, however, is out of the gale.

14.5 Livy *Periochae* 117: The events of 44 BC

After the assassination, Antony had Lepidus, Caesar's magister equitum, made pontifex maximus in place of Caesar and married his daughter to Lepidus' son.

Gaius Octavius came to Rome from Epirus (for Caesar had sent him there ahead as he was planning a war in Macedonia), and on receiving favourable omens took the name Caesar. In the political disruption and insurrection, Marcus Lepidus appropriated the office of pontifex maximus. The consul Mark Antony governed with violence, carried by force a law concerning changes in the provinces, and inflicted great injuries on Caesar (Octavian), too, when he asked for his support against the assassins of his great-uncle. Caesar both for his own interest and for that of the state began readying resources to use against Antony and called upon the veterans who had been settled in colonies.

OCTAVIAN ARRIVES IN ITALY

At the time of Caesar's murder, Octavian (whom Caesar had adopted by will in September 45 BC) was studying at Apollonia in Illyria, where the army was stationed in readiness for Caesar's planned Parthian campaign. When the will was read, and it was learnt that he had been left as Caesar's principal heir, Octavian hastened to Italy in April 44, with some caution in case he might meet with opposition. During his journey from Brundisium to Rome he began to encourage Caesar's veterans to support him as Caesar's son, and even though the adoption was not yet officially approved by the senate he called himself Gaius Julius Caesar (Octavianus), son of Caesar.

14.6 Appian *Civil Wars* 3.2.11–13: Octavian's reaction to Caesar's murder

On his journey from Brundisium, Octavian was escorted by crowds of veterans and other supporters, and by June he had raised an army of some 3,000 veterans. On 21 April he met Cicero at Puteoli, as well as his mother Atia and stepfather L. Marcius Philippus, who advised him to decline the inheritance (doc. 14.9). On arrival at Rome he met the consul Mark Antony, who resented the young man's arrival and his claim to be Caesar's son and heir.

11 When more accurate information about the murder and public mourning reached Octavian, together with copies of the will and the senate's decrees, his relatives cautioned him even more strongly to be wary of Caesar's enemies as he was his son and heir, and advised him to reject the adoption along with the inheritance. However, he thought that to do so and not to avenge Caesar would be shameful, and went to Brundisium after sending in advance to make sure that none of the murderers had set any trap for him. When the army there advanced to meet him and welcomed him as Caesar's son, he took courage, offered a sacrifice, and immediately took the name Caesar (it is usual among the Romans for adoptees to take the name of their adopted fathers). He not only assumed it but even changed his own name and patronymic completely, instead of Octavian son of Octavius, calling himself Caesar son of Caesar, and continued this usage from that day on. Straightaway crowds of men flocked to him from all sides as the son of Caesar, some out of friendship for Caesar, others freedmen and slaves, as well as soldiers who were transporting supplies and money to Macedonia or money and tribute from other countries to Brundisium. **12** Encouraged by the crowds that were joining him, and by the prestige given to Caesar's name and the goodwill of everyone towards himself, he travelled to Rome with an impressive multitude which grew greater day by day like a torrent, though, while protected from open plots by the crowds, he was even more on guard against surprise attacks because of this circumstance, since nearly all those accompanying him were recent acquaintances. Some of the towns did not give him their entire support, but the soldiers who had served under Caesar and been distributed into colonies flooded from these to greet the youth, and lamented Caesar's death and cursed Antony for not taking action against such an abominable crime, saying that they would themselves avenge it if anyone would lead them. Caesar praised them, but put the matter off for the present and sent them away. When he was at Tarracina, about 400 stades from Rome, he heard that Cassius and Brutus had had Syria and Macedonia taken away by the consuls and that they had received as compensation the smaller provinces of Cyrene and Crete; in addition, some exiles had returned, Sextus Pompeius had been recalled, and new members had been enrolled in the senate in accordance with Caesar's memoranda, as well as many other events.

13 When he arrived at the city, his mother, Philippus, and all his other connections were worried about the senate's estrangement from Caesar, the decree that Caesar's murder should not be punished, and the disdain shown him by Antony, who was now in total control, and who had neither gone to meet him on his approach as Caesar's son nor sent anyone. He calmed their fears, saying that he would himself go to meet Antony, as the younger man to the elder and the private individual to the consul, and would pay all due respect to the senate. With regard to the decree, he said, it had gone through because no one had as yet prosecuted the assassins, but, when someone did have the courage to bring a prosecution, the people and the senate would give him their assistance as one who was law-abiding, and the gods as one who was upholding justice, while Antony would equally support him. He broke off his remarks to declare that it was honourable not only for him to incur danger but even to meet death, if after being selected out of everyone in this way by Caesar he wanted to show himself worthy of one who had himself courted every danger. He thereupon quoted the words of Achilles, which were then particularly apposite, turning to his mother as if she were Thetis: 'Might I straightway die, who was not able to defend his slain comrade!' (Homer *Iliad* 18.98). After this quotation, he added that it was this speech in particular, and the subsequent action, that gave Achilles eternal renown; that he called on Caesar not as a companion but as a father, not as a fellow soldier but as a general, not as one who had fallen under war's laws but as one who had been sacrilegiously assassinated in the actual senate house.

14.7 Nikolaos of Damascus *Life of Augustus* 18.54–57: Octavian's assets

Nikolaos implies that Octavian may have appropriated the taxes from Asia – state moneys – as well as Caesar's funds for his Parthian campaign; cf. Appian (doc. 14.6), who suggests he also had access to revenue from the East coming into Brundisium. Nikolaos records that Philippus strongly advised his stepson not to accept the legacy and adoption. Octavian's friends doubtless included his schoolfriends Agrippa and Maecenas.

54 Atia allowed him to use the name Caesar and was the first in fact to agree. **55** Caesar inquired what all his friends thought about this as well and then immediately accepted both the name and the adoption, with good fortune and favourable auspices. This was the beginning of great things both for himself and for all mankind, but in particular for the state and Roman people as a whole. He sent off at once to Asia for the money and assets that Caesar had previously sent there for the Parthian war, and when he received it, together with a year's tribute from the people of Asia, he kept for himself just the amount that had belonged to Caesar and handed what was public property over to the state treasury. **56** Some of his friends at this point urged him, as they had earlier at Apollonia, to visit Caesar's colonies and raise an army, inciting the men to join an expedition on his behalf by making use of the prestige inherent in the renowned name of 'Caesar'. They declared that the soldiers would happily follow the leadership of Caesar's son and would do anything they could for him, as they still felt a tremendous loyalty and goodwill towards Caesar. They remembered what they had achieved with him during his lifetime and longed to win under the auspices of the name of 'Caesar' the power which they had previously conferred on Caesar himself. **57** However, the time for this did not seem to be ripe. Accordingly he sought instead to acquire legally, through a decree of the senate, the honours his father had held, and not to gain the reputation of being ambitious rather than trustworthy. He therefore listened closely to the eldest of his friends and those with most experience, and set out from Brundisium for Rome.

14.8 Plutarch *Life of Antony* 16.1–6: Tension between Octavian and Antony

When Antony returned to Rome in May 44 BC, tension soon developed between him and Octavian when he refused to hand over the money bequeathed by Caesar to each member of the plebs (300 sesterces per person). Octavian raised the money by selling property, gaining great popularity in so doing. Antony also opposed Octavian's desire to stand for the tribunate and his placing a golden chair and wreath for Caesar in July at the Ludi victoriae Caesaris (games in honour of Caesar's victories, held 20–30 July), as decreed in 45 BC. In addition, Antony delayed the passing of a *lex curiata* to ratify Octavian's adoption officially. There was a brief reconciliation between the two in July.

16.1 With affairs in this state, the young Caesar arrived at Rome. He was son of the dead Caesar's niece, as said earlier, and left as heir to his property, and had spent some time at Apollonia, which is where he was when Caesar was killed. **2** He at once greeted Antony as his father's friend and reminded him of the money left in his hands – for he was under obligation to give each Roman 75 drachmas as Caesar had decreed in his will. **3** Initially disdaining him as a mere youth, Antony said that he was foolish and that in the total absence of good judgement and good friends he was taking up an unmanageable burden in seeking to succeed Caesar. **4** When he would not listen to this, but kept demanding the money, Antony still kept on addressing him and treating him with arrogance. **5** He opposed him when he stood for the tribunate, and when he was attempting to dedicate his father's golden chair, as had been decreed, he threatened to send him off to prison if he did not stop currying favour with the people. **6** But when the young man attached himself to Cicero and the others who hated Antony and with their help conciliated the senate, while winning over the people and gathering the soldiers from their colonies, Antony grew alarmed, and they held a meeting on the Capitol which led to their reconciliation.

14.9 Cicero *Letters to Atticus* 14.11–12, 15.12: Cicero's reactions, April–June 44 BC

At Puteoli, on his way to Rome, Octavian met Cicero and the consuls-designate for 43, Hirtius and Pansa, as well as his mother and stepfather. Octavian apparently flattered Cicero, though Cicero was aware that, by accepting the adoption, Octavian would be hostile towards the conspirators ('our friends'). Marcellus (cos. 50) married Octavian's sister. In April Antony was proposing measures, supposedly intended or drafted by Caesar, such as citizenship for the whole of Sicily.

14.11.3 (Puteoli?, 21 April 44) Balbus, Hirtius and Pansa are with me here. Octavian has just arrived, in fact is staying at the villa next door, that of Philippus, and pays me the highest respect. Lentulus Spinther is staying with me today, but off early tomorrow.

14.12.1 (Puteoli, 22 April 44) My dear Atticus, I am afraid the Ides of March have brought us nothing but joy and a recompense for our hatred and grief. What news of events in Rome has reached me! And what I see here! – 'a good deed, but incomplete'. You know what affection I have for the Sicilians and what an honour I judge it for them to be my clients. Caesar was generous to them, which pleased me (though their Latin status was not to be endured – but be that as it may). Well, behold Antony putting up a law (in return for an enormous bribe), a law 'carried by the dictator in the assembly' by which they become Roman citizens – a thing never mentioned when he was alive! . . . . **2** Octavius is here with me – extremely respectful and friendly. His own people call him Caesar, but Philippus does not, so neither do I. I don't think he can be a good citizen: there are too many people with him who threaten death to our friends and say that matters cannot remain in this state. What do you think will happen when the boy comes to Rome, which isn't safe for our liberators? They will always be famous, as well as happy in the consciousness of what they did; but as for us, unless I am mistaken, we will not be appreciated. So I long to be away – 'where no more of Pelops' line . . . ', as the poet says. Nor am I fond of these consuls-designate, who have even made me give them oratory lessons, so I'm not allowed to have a rest even here at the waters! But this comes of my being too easy-going!

15.12.2 (Astura?, c. 10 June 44) Octavian, as I saw, does not lack intelligence or spirit and seemed to be as disposed towards our 'heroes' as I could wish. But how much we can depend on one of his age, name, heredity and educational background is an important question. His stepfather in fact thinks nothing at all (I saw him at Astura). But he's to be encouraged, and if nothing else kept away from Antony. If Marcellus is recommending my works, that's excellent: Octavian appeared to be to be very attached to him. He wasn't particularly inclined to trust Pansa and Hirtius. A good character – if he can hold his ground.

OCTAVIAN AND POPULAR SUPPORT

With Caesar dead, the main players in Roman politics were looking to improve their own positions and further their own interests. The consuls made use of their magistracy to have themselves voted valuable provinces for five-year periods: in June Antony put irregular legislation before the people, exchanging his province of Macedonia for a five-year governorship of Cisalpine and Transalpine Gaul (so he would be in a position to dominate Italy) while retaining five of the six legions currently in Macedonia; Dolabella, with the other legion, was to hold Syria for five years. The Macedonian legions were summoned back to Italy, and Antony went to meet them at Brundisium in October. Brutus and Cassius, who had senatorial support, which Antony did not, had refused first control of the grain supply, then the relatively unimportant provinces of Crete and Cyrene, and were intent on taking over the powerful Eastern provinces of Macedonia and Syria for themselves. Decimus Brutus, another of the conspirators, refused to give up his province of Cisalpine Gaul to Antony. At this point Octavian had no power base, and according to Nikolaos felt threatened by Antony, who was blocking all his moves (such as ratification of his adoption and paying honours to Caesar at the games in honour of his victories in July). In October Antony also alleged that Octavian had tried to use Antony's own bodyguard to assassinate him. In November, therefore, Octavian toured colonies of Caesar's veterans to raise his own army, promising large bounties and vengeance on Caesar's murderers, and tried to ensure Cicero's support in the senate. His position was strengthened when two of the Macedonian legions deserted to him in late November and enabled him to offer to the senate the use of his legions against Antony, who was preparing to attack Decimus Brutus in his province of Cisalpine Gaul.

14.10 Nikolaos of Damascus *Life of Augustus* 28.108–13: Jostling for position

Octavian was at this point in an invidious position; he was not supported by the consuls, who had control of the treasury, with the result that he did not have access to the money he was to distribute to the people according to Caesar's will. His main rallying point was the desire to avenge the murder of Caesar, though the 'liberators' had strong senatorial support.

108 Caesar, however, not at all cowed on account of his high spirit, put on some spectacles on the occasion of the festival of Aphrodite (Venus Genetrix), established by his father. He approached Antony again with a number of his friends, asking to be allowed to set up the seat and wreath in his father's honour. Antony made the same threat as before, if he did not drop the idea and keep quiet. Caesar backed off and did not oppose the consul's refusal. But when he entered the theatre the people loudly applauded him, and his father's soldiers, angry because he had been hindered from renewing these honours for his father, kept giving him, as a mark of their approval, one round of applause after another throughout the performance. **109** He then paid out the people's money, which won their great goodwill. **110** From that day on, Antony was clearly even more hostile towards Caesar, as an obstacle in the way of the people's support for himself. Caesar saw (what had become very plain to him from the current situation) that he was in need of political authority. He also saw that the consuls, using the strength of their position, were openly resisting him and appropriating even more power for themselves. Even the city treasury, which his father had filled with large amounts of money, they had emptied within two months of Caesar's death, withdrawing huge sums on any excuse in this unstable situation, and were also on good terms with the assassins. Octavian was therefore the only one left to avenge his father, for Antony let everything go by and even approved of an amnesty for the assassins. While many men joined Octavian, not a few joined Antony and Dolabella and their supporters . . . **112** Lepidus, who had broken away part of Caesar's army and who was trying to seize power for himself, was in Nearer Spain and also possessed the part of Gaul which borders on the upper sea. Lucius (Munatius) Plancus, the consul-elect, held Gallia Comata with another army. Gaius Asinius, with another army, was in charge of Further Spain. Decimus Brutus held Cisalpine Gaul with two legions, and Antony was getting ready to march against him. Gaius Brutus was claiming Macedonia and was just about to cross over there from Italy, while Cassius Longinus was claiming Syria, though he had been appointed praetor for Illyria. **113** There were so many armies in service at that time, and with such men in charge, each of whom was determined to acquire complete power for himself, regardless of all law and justice, with everything decided upon according to the force each wielded. Caesar alone, to whom all authority had legally been bequeathed, in accordance with the authority of him who had acquired it earlier, and because of their relationship, was without any share of power whatever, and he was suspended between the political jealousy and greed of men who were lying in wait for him and for supreme power. God and Good Fortune were later to ensure that all this turned out appropriately. But for the present Caesar feared for his life, as Antony's stance towards him was clear, and as he was unable to change it in any way he stayed at home awaiting his chance.

14.11 Cicero *Letters to his Friends* 12.23, 11.28: Cicero to his friends (October 44 BC)

12.23: Cicero is referring to Octavian's supposed attempt in October to assassinate Antony (cf. App. *BC* 3.39). Cornificius was one of Caesar's legates and governor of Africa 44–42; Matius was a friend of Caesar's who had served with him in Gaul and had helped to organise the celebrations of the Ludi victoriae Caesaris (Caesar's victory games) in July 44.

12.23.2 (Rome, c. 10 October 44: to Cornificius) I am sure that news of city matters is sent to you. If I thought otherwise I would write you all the details myself, especially regarding Caesar Octavian's venture. The general public think that Antony has trumped up the accusation so he can possess himself of the young man's money; men of sense, however, and honest men both believe in the fact and approve of it. In short, great hopes rest on him. It is thought that there is nothing he will not do for praise and glory. As for our friend Antony, he is so conscious of the hostility towards him that, after seizing the assassins in his house, he doesn't dare to publicise the matter. So on 9 October he set off for Brundisium to meet the four Macedonian legions, whose support he intended to buy and then march them to the city and place them on our necks. **3** You now have the outline of how the republic stands at present, if there can be a republic in an army camp. I often feel sorry for you, as your age has prevented you from ever being able to experience the Republic in a state of health and security. Earlier it was at least possible to hope; now even that has been denied us. What hope remains, when Antony dares say in a public meeting that Cannutius (tr. pl. 44) is trying to get standing with people who can have no place in the state while he – Antony – is alive and well!
    11.28.2 (Rome, mid-October 44: Matius to Cicero) I am well aware of the criticisms people have made against me following Caesar's death. They count it as a failing that I should find it difficult to bear the death of a friend and that I am angry

that the man I loved should have been killed; for they say that country should be ranked before friendship, just as if they have already demonstrated that his death benefited the state. But I shall not argue like a debater – I admit that I have not yet arrived at that stage of philosophy. In the civil conflict I followed not Caesar but a friend, whom, although I did not approve of his actions, I did not desert. I never approved of civil war or even of the cause of the conflict, which I did my very best to quench in its infancy. And so, in my friend's (Caesar's) victory, I was allured by the delights of neither office nor money, rewards of which others, whose influence with him was less than mine, took unfair advantage. My property was even lessened by one of Caesar's laws, thanks to which many who rejoice at Caesar's death continue to live in Rome. I exerted myself to ensure that our con-quered fellow citizens be treated with forbearance, as if to save my own life. **3** Can I, then, who wanted everyone unharmed, not be angry at the killing of the man who brought it about, especially when the same men were responsible for both his unpopularity and his death? 'You will pay, then', they insist, 'since you dare to disapprove of our action!' What unheard-of arrogance! Some may take pride in an act, while others are not even allowed to grieve with impunity! Even slaves have always had the freedom to hope or fear, to rejoice or grieve of their own free will, not that of someone else; those 'authors of our liberty', as these people like to call themselves, are now trying to use fear to wrest this freedom from us. **4** They will get nowhere. I will never deviate from duty or compassion through any threats of danger. For I never considered an honourable death a thing to be avoided, and often would even have desired it. . . . **6** So – I organised the games for Caesar's victory given by young Caesar. That was as a private service and had nothing to do with the state. However, it was a duty that I owed to the memory and status of an intimate friend, even after his death, and one which I could not deny at the request of a most promising young man entirely worthy of the name of Caesar. Also I have often called at the house of consul Antony to pay my respects, to whom you will find those who consider me inadequately dedicated to my country keep thronging to make some request or carry off a favour. What presumption! – considering Caesar never stopped my associating with anyone I chose, even those he did not like, that those who robbed me of my friend should try to stop me by their grumbling from liking the people I choose!

14.12 Cicero *Letters to Atticus* 16.8, 16.9, 16.11, 16.15: Cicero envisages a rapport (November 44)

Octavian in November toured colonies of veterans in Campania to win their support; he offered them 2,000 sesterces apiece and raised a body of 3,000, supposedly to protect himself from Antony. The Alaudae were the famous Legion V (the 'Larks' – a Celtic word – raised by Caesar in Transpadane Gaul). P Servilius Casca, one of Caesar's assassins, was to be tribune in 43.

16.8.1 (Puteoli, 2 or 3 November 44) A letter to me from Octavian on the even-ing of the first. He has a big undertaking in hand. He has won the veterans at

Casilinum and Calatia over to his point of view. No wonder – he's giving them 500 denarii a head. He's thinking of going round the rest of the colonies. Clearly he's looking towards war with Antony with himself as commander. So it looks to me as if in a few days we will be in arms. But whom are we to follow? Look at his name, look at his age. And he's asking me first to have secret talks with him at or near Capua. This is childish if he thinks it can be done secretly. **2** I told him by letter that this was neither necessary nor possible. He sent me a certain Caecina from Volaterra, a friend of his, who brought the news that Antony is heading for the city with the Alaudae legion, requisitioning funds from the towns and marching the legion in battle formation. He asked my advice on whether he should set out for Rome with 3,000 veterans, or hold Capua and block Antony's approach, or go to join the three Macedonian legions which are marching along the Adriatic coast, which he hopes will be on his side. They refused to take a bounty from Antony – that's his story, anyway – threw violent abuse at him, and left him while he was still haranguing them. In a word, he is putting himself forward as our commander and is expecting me to support him. I advised him to head for Rome. I believe he will have the urban mob on side, and, if he can make them trust him, the honest men as well. Oh, Brutus – where are you? What a great opportunity you are missing! I couldn't actually predict *this*, but I thought something of the kind would happen.

Now I ask your advice. Do I go to Rome, or stay here, or flee to Arpinum (which offers safety)? Probably Rome, in case I am missed if something seems to have been achieved. So solve this – I have never been less able to make up my mind.

16.9 (Puteoli, 4 November 44) Two letters for me in one day from Octavian! He now wants me to come to Rome at once – he wants to handle matters through the senate. I told him that I didn't think the senate could meet before 1 January, which I believe is the case. He adds 'with your advice'. In short, he's pressing and I'm stalling. I have no confidence in his age, and I don't know what he's thinking. I don't want to do anything without your friend Pansa. I'm worried about Antony's power and I don't want to leave the sea. But I'm afraid of some 'valiant deeds' while I'm not there. Varro doesn't like the boy's plan: I disagree. He's got a powerful army and can have (Decimus) Brutus. And he's pursuing matters openly, organising companies at Capua and paying bounties. I can see war at any minute. Reply to all this. I'm surprised that your courier left Rome on 1 November without a letter from you.

16.11.6 (Puteoli, 5 November 44) I did not hide myself down at Pompeii, as I wrote to you I would, partly because of the weather, which is dreadful, and then because I'm getting daily letters from Octavian saying that I should get busy, come to Capua, save the Republic once again, or at any rate come to Rome. 'Do not refuse out of shame, out of fear accept!' (*Iliad* 7.93). He has definitely shown, and is still showing, plenty of energy, and will come to Rome with a large following; but he is still obviously a boy. He thinks the senate will meet immediately. Who will come? And if he does come, who will want to upset Antony with things so uncertain? Perhaps he may be some protection on 1 January, or it may in fact all have been fought out by then. The towns are coming out in favour of the boy in a remarkable way. On his way to Samnium he went through Cales and stayed at Teanum. Astounding turn-outs and support. Would you have expected it? In consequence I'll be back in Rome earlier than I planned. As soon as I decide, I shall write.

16.15.3 (Arpinum, after 12 November 44) The boy is keeping Antony in check very nicely for the moment, but we had better wait and see what eventuates. But what an address! – a copy was sent to me. He swears 'that he may be permitted to attain his father's honours' – while stretching his right hand out to the statue! 'Better destruction than such a rescuer!' But, as you write, I think the most reliable touchstone will be our friend Casca's tribunate, as in fact I said to Oppius when he was urging me to embrace the young man – and his whole cause and band of veterans into the bargain – that I could do no such thing unless I was positive that he would be not only no enemy but an actual friend to the tyrannicides. When he said he would be, then 'In that case why should we hurry?' was my reply. 'He doesn't need my help until 1 January, and we shall learn his attitude over Casca before the Ides of December.' He agreed wholeheartedly. So much for this then!

14.13 Appian *Civil Wars* 3.7.45–48: Senatorial wavering

Two of the Macedonian legions deserted to Octavian *en route* from Brundisium to Rome in November 44 BC. Octavian gave them 2,000 sesterces apiece, promising 20,000 on demobilisation, and stressed Antony's reluctance to avenge Caesar; he also captured Antony's elephants (doc. 14.15), which was a great publicity item. Antony had called a meeting of the senate on 24 November but postponed it to 28 November, after which he left for Cisalpine Gaul (on 2 June the assembly had passed a law transferring the province of Cisalpine Gaul to Antony for five years). Decimus Brutus (with the senate's support) refused to surrender the province to him, and Antony besieged him in Mutina in December. In early December Octavian offered his legions to fight against Antony on behalf of the senate.

45 Antony chose from them all a praetorian cohort of the men who were best in physique and character and marched to Rome, from there intending to make for Ariminum. He entered the city arrogantly, encamping his troop of horse in front of the town, but the men he kept with him were equipped for war and mounted guard over his house at night in full armour; he also gave them passwords, and the watch changed regularly as if in camp. He convened the senate to protest about Caesar's actions and, while he was actually entering, heard that, of his four legions on the march, the one called 'Martian' had gone over to Caesar. Moreover, when he was waiting at the entrance considering his options, he was told that the so-called Legion IV had, like the Martian, gone over to Caesar. In this state of perturbation he entered the senate house, as if he had convened them on other matters, spoke briefly, and immediately departed to the city gates and from there to the town of Alba to persuade the deserters to change their minds. But when he was shot at from the walls he withdrew and sent to the other legions 500 drachmas per person, while with the ones he had with him he marched to Tibur, taking with him the usual equipment for those going into war: it was obvious now that there would be a war, since Decimus had not given up Gaul. **46** While Antony was there, nearly the entire senate and most of the equites, as well as the most important members of the plebs, came to pay him their respects; they arrived when he was swearing in the soldiers who were present, as well as the veterans who had flocked to him (and there were a great number), and they voluntarily swore the oath as well that they would not fail in goodwill and loyalty towards Antony, so that it would have been hard to know who were the men who shortly before at Caesar's assembly were the ones bad-mouthing Antony. After this splendid demonstration, Antony set out for Ariminum, which lies on the border with Gaul. His army, apart from the new recruits, comprised three legions summoned from Macedonia, the rest of which had now arrived, and one of discharged veterans who, though old, nevertheless appeared to be worth twice the new levies. So Antony had four legions of experienced men and the assistance that normally accompanies them, apart from his bodyguard and the new recruits. Lepidus, who had four legions in Spain, Asinius Pollio, with two, and Plancus in Further Gaul, with three, seemed likely to take Antony's side.

47 Caesar had two equally valuable legions, those that deserted to him from Antony, as well as one of new recruits and two of veterans, which were not complete in numbers or arms but were brought up to the full total by new recruits. He led them all to Alba and sent a message to the senate, which congratulated Caesar to such an extent that one would now have been at a loss to know who those were who had earlier paid their respects to Antony – though it was concerned that the legions had not come over to the senate but to Caesar. Nevertheless, it praised both them and Caesar and said that it would shortly vote them everything necessary, once the new magistrates had taken up their duties. It was clear that they would use these against Antony; having no army of their own and being unable to raise one without consuls, they put off everything till the consuls took office. **48** Caesar's army provided him with lictors equipped with fasces and urged him to take the title propraetor, as he was in charge of the war and themselves, and they were always marshalled under magistrates. He thanked them for the honour but deferred this matter to the senate. When they wanted to go before the senate in a body, he prevented them as well as restraining them from sending envoys, as the senate would vote these for him on their own account – and all the more, he stated, if they perceive your enthusiasm and my hesitation.

CICERO AND ANTONY

Cicero was fanatically opposed to Antony and openly regretted that he too had not been assassinated with Caesar on the Ides of March, blaming Trebonius for merely distracting him rather than having him killed as well. In his *Philippics* (so named after the speeches of Demosthenes against Philip II of Macedon), he pictured Antony as implacably opposed to sound government and in total pursuit of personal power to the detriment of all that Rome and the senate stood for. An initial version of the *First Philippic* was delivered against Antony in the senate on 2 September 44 BC. The *Second Philippic* was never actually delivered, only circulated in written form, but its denunciations of Antony's conduct and lifestyle since boyhood made any chance of co-operation between the two impossible for the future. In the *Third Philippic* on 20 December, Cicero urged the senate to back Decimus Brutus (who was refusing to stand down from his province) against Antony by confirming all governors, and to reward Octavian and the two legions that had deserted to him. He was, however, unable to persuade the senators to name Antony a public enemy.

14.14 Cicero *Letters to his Friends* 11.7.2–3: Decimus Brutus must resist Antony

Cicero here urges Decimus Brutus to remember his aims as a tyrannicide and to resist Antony and his army.

(Rome, mid-December 44: to Decimus Brutus) The main point is this, which I want you to grasp very carefully and keep in mind: that in protecting the liberty and well-being of the Roman people you should not wait for the authorisation of a senate which is not yet free, or you would be condemning your own deed (for it was not by any public decision that you liberated the Republic, which makes that achievement both more significant and more glorious). You would also be suggesting that the young man – or, rather, the boy – Caesar had acted indiscreetly in venturing to undertake so momentous a public cause on his own initiative. Moreover, you would be suggesting that the country-folk (who are of course very brave men and the most loyal of citizens) had lost their senses – firstly the veterans, your own fellow soldiers, and then the Martian and Fourth legions, who judged their consul to be a public enemy and rallied to defend the welfare of the Republic. The will of the senate should be acted on instead of its authority when its authority is constrained by fear. **3** Finally, you have twice taken up the cause, so you are already committed – first on the Ides of March, and then recently when you raised a new army and troops. And so you must be prepared and motivated, not that you will do nothing unless told to, but that you will so act as to receive the greatest praise and commendation from everyone.

14.15 Cicero *Philippics* 3.2, 5.16–17, 8.8: Cicero denounces Antony

In the *Third Philippic*, on 20 December 44, Cicero was already presenting Octavian as the saviour of the state against Antony's brutality and bloodthirstiness and urged that he be given official authorisation to continue this role. The senate met on 1 January 43 to discuss war with Antony, and the new consul, Pansa, began a debate which was to give Octavian propraetorian imperium and a place in the senate with the right to speak among the consulars. Octavian now became the senate's champion against Antony, while the two consuls started recruiting armies. **3.2.4**: Antony had killed some of the centurions of the Martian legion for mutiny at Brundisium. Gallia togata: Cisalpine Gaul; Gallia comata: 'long-haired' Gaul.

3.2.3 (20 December 44) Gaius Caesar, a young man – or, rather, almost a boy – of incredible and nearly superhuman intelligence and courage, just at the time when Antony's ferocity raged most hotly and when his cruel and destructive return from Brundisium was causing terror, though we were neither requesting, nor considering, nor even hoping for it – as it seemed an impossibility – gathered a most reliable army of that indomitable class of veterans and lavished his patrimony on this – although I have not used the word I should, for he did not lavish it; he invested it in the preservation of the state. **4** And although we cannot repay him to the extent we are indebted, we should feel a gratitude greater than our minds can imagine. For who is so ignorant of events, who so uncaring for the state, that he does not realise that, if Mark Antony had reached Rome as he was threatening, with the forces he expected to have, he would have left undone no kind of cruelty? He who, in the house of his host at Brundisium, commanded the bravest of men and best of citizens to be slaughtered, with whose blood as they were dying at his feet it was well known that his wife's face was spattered? Imbued with such cruelty, since he was becoming much more incensed against us than he had been against those he murdered, which – I ask you – of us, or which honest man at all, would he have spared? **5** From this disaster, on his own initiative (for it could not have happened otherwise), Caesar has liberated the state. And if he had not been born in our state, through Antony's criminality we would now have no state at all. For this is my view and my judgement, that, had not a single youth stood out against the attack and most callous endeavours of that madman, the state would have perished to its very foundation. Indeed on this very day, conscript fathers – as we are now for the first time assembled with the opportunity, thanks to his good services, to speak our views with freedom – we must grant the authority to enable him to defend the state, a task not only undertaken by him but entrusted to him by us.

5.16.42 (1 January 43) I come now to Gaius Caesar, conscript fathers, and, if he had not lived, which of us would be surviving today? Flying from Brundisium to the city was a man of exceptional ferocity, inflamed with hatred, with a mentality hostile to all honest men, with an army – Antony! What could have been used to counter his brazenness and villainy? We did not yet have any commanders, any troops; there was no public senate meeting, no freedom; our necks lay open to his iniquitous savagery; we were all looking towards flight, which itself offered no escape. **43** What deity at that point granted us, granted the Roman people, this god-like young man? – who, when everything tending to our destruction was wide open to that malevolent citizen, suddenly, beyond everyone's expectations, arose and assembled an army with which he opposed the frenzy of Mark Antony, before anyone had any suspicion of these intentions? . . . **45** So let us give Caesar imperium, without which no military matters can be conducted, no army held together, no war waged; let him be propraetor, with all official authority. That rank is an exceptional one for his age but is demanded by the force of circumstances, not just for the sake of his prestige. So let us ask for that, which is as much as we will attain today.

5.17.45 But I do hope that both we and the Roman people will often be able to distinguish and honour this young man. For the moment, however, I propose that the following be decreed: **46** 'Whereas Gaius Caesar, son of Gaius, pontifex, propraetor, in a grave state emergency exhorted the veteran soldiers to defend the liberty of the Roman people and enlisted them; and whereas the Martian legion and the Fourth with the highest zeal and greatest unanimity towards the state under the leadership and authority of Gaius Caesar are defending and have defended the liberty of the Roman people; and whereas Gaius Caesar, propraetor, has set out with his army to relieve the province of Gaul, has brought under his authority and that of the Roman people cavalry, archers and elephants, and has come, at a most critical time for the state to aid the preservation and dignity of the Roman people – for these reasons it is the desire of the senate that Gaius Caesar, son of Gaius, pontifex, propraetor, be a senator and participate in debates with the standing of praetor and that, whatever magistracy he may try for, the same computation be made of his eligibility as would be permissible by law if he had been quaestor in the preceding year.'

8.8.25 (4 or 5 February 43) But how modest are Antony's commands! We must be made of iron, senators, to deny him anything! 'Both provinces', he states, 'I give up, I dismiss my army, I do not refuse to be a private citizen': these are his words – he seems to be coming to himself. 'I forget everything, I am prepared for reconciliation.' But what does he add? 'If you give bounties and land to my six legions, to my cavalry, to my praetorian cohort.' He even demands rewards for men, for whom it would be totally presumptuous to request a pardon. Moreover he adds that 'those to whom he and Dolabella granted lands should remain in possession' – **26** this is the Campanian and Leontine lands, both of which our ancestors considered to be sanctuaries for our grain. . . . Additionally he demands that 'his own and his colleague's (Julius Caesar) decrees in handwriting and notebooks should stay in force'. Why is he concerned that each buyer should keep what he bought if he who sold it keeps the money? And 'that the accounts in the temple of Ops should not be tampered with' – that is, that 700 millions of sesterces should not be recouped, and that 'the Commission of Seven should not be indicted for their actions' . . . **27** However, he does not urge on us more 'commands': he makes some compromises and concessions. 'Gallia togata', he states, 'I resign, but demand Gallia comata' – so he wishes to remain in peace – 'with six legions, and these brought up to strength from Decimus Brutus' army' – not from his own levies – 'and hold it as long as Marcus Brutus and Gaius Cassius hold their provinces as consuls and proconsuls'. The way this man runs an election, his brother Gaius (for it is his year) has already been defeated! 'And that I shall hold my province', he goes on, 'for a five-year period' – but Caesar's law forbids that, and you defend his acts!

14.16 Cicero *Letters to his Friends* 10.28, 12.25: Cicero's accusations

Cicero obviously felt that he was a major player in politics in 44–43 BC, his aim being to undermine Antony's position at all costs. As events proved, those he thought he was manipulating were better and more ruthless players than he himself. During Caesar's assassination Trebonius had distracted Antony; Trebonius as governor of Asia had been killed by Dolabella in January 43. **12.25.4**: Cicero is referring to his *First Philippic* (2 September 44).

10.28.1 (Rome, early February 43: to Trebonius) Cicero to Trebonius, greetings! **1** How I wish that you had invited me to that splendid banquet on the Ides of

March! We would then have had no left-overs! And now these are causing us so many problems that the god-sent service to the Republic effected by you and your colleagues leaves some room for complaint. And due to the fact that it was by you, you excellent creature, that this cursed pest was drawn aside, and because of you that he still lives on, I am almost infuriated with you, which in me is hardly right – though you have left me more trouble to deal with than you have everyone else put together. As soon as the senate was able to meet freely after Antony's disgraceful departure (for Cisalpine Gaul, 28 November), I reverted to that former spirit of mine, that spirit which you and that dedicated citizen your father always praised and admired. **2** For when the tribunes called a meeting of the senate on 20 December and brought forward another issue, I ran through the entire political situation, dealing with it in a very pointed manner, and recalled the lethargic and burnt-out senate to its former customary vigour more by passion than by strength of character. This day and my exertion and performance brought the Roman people the first hope of recovering their liberty. And from that point I have used every moment, not only in thought but in action too, on behalf of the state. **3** If I didn't think that all city matters and proceedings were reported to you I would run through them myself, although hampered by a huge amount of important business. But you will learn all that from others – from me a few items and those in outline. We have a brave senate, but of the consulars some are fearful and others on the wrong side. There was a great loss in Servius. Lucius Caesar holds sound views but, as his (Antony's) uncle, doesn't express his opinions very forcefully. The consuls are extraordinary: Decimus Brutus is splendid, the boy Caesar extraordinary, and I at least have great hopes for him in the future; at any rate you can certainly take this as a fact that, if he hadn't quickly enlisted veterans, if two legions of Antony's army hadn't put themselves under his command and, if Antony hadn't been faced with this threat, he would have left no crime and no cruelty undone. Although I thought you would have heard all this I wanted you to know it in more detail. I will write more when I have more free time.

12.25.3 (Rome, c. 20 March 43: to Cornuficius) A contrary tempestuous southerly brought me back to your fellow tribesmen at Rhegium, and from there I hastened to my homeland with all speed of winds and oars, **4** while the following day I was the one free man in a gathering of servile lackeys. I delivered an attack on Antony which he was unable to bear and poured out all his drunken fury on me alone, at one point trying to provoke me into giving him a pretext for bloodshed, at another trying to ensnare me with traps. I cast him, belching and vomiting, into Caesar Octavian's snares. This extraordinary boy has furnished the protection of an army in the first place both for himself and for us, and then for the very survival of the Republic itself. Unless he had done so, Antony's return from Brundisium would have meant the destruction of our country.

CICERO AND OCTAVIAN

Even in April 43 BC Cicero was still convinced of Octavian's trustworthiness and his own ability to manipulate him as an inexperienced politician in need of support, continuing to present him to the senate as their saviour against Antony. After an initial panic in Rome, when the first victory over Antony was reported, Cicero was treated as a hero.

14.17 Octavian as saviour

After a lengthy siege of Mutina by Antony, the battle of Forum Gallorum had taken place on 14 April: Antony defeated Pansa but was in turn defeated by Hirtius; on 21 April Hirtius was again to defeat Antony, who was finally declared a public enemy on 27 April. In thanks for the first victory, on 21 April, Cicero proposed that Octavian be given the title imperator and that there be 50 days of thanksgiving in honour of Octavian and the two consuls. Decimus Brutus was awarded a triumph, but Cicero's proposal of an ovation for Octavian was opposed (Octavian had also asked for a triumph). The three brothers are the Antonii (Mark Antony, Lucius and Gaius). This letter to Brutus was written c. 21 April 43 BC.

(i) *Cicero* Letters to Brutus *1.3*

From Cicero to Brutus, greetings. **1** Our affairs seem to be in a better shape. I'm sure you have been sent letters of all that has happened. The consuls have proved themselves just as I have often written to you. As for the young Caesar, his natural manly qualities are quite extraordinary. I only hope that when he achieves his position and influence I will be able to guide and control him with the same ease as I do now. Of course that will be more difficult, but I don't despair of it. The young man's convinced, mainly through me, that his job is to see to our survival – and, for sure, if he had not turned Antony back from the city, all would have been lost.

2 Three or four days before this magnificent outcome the whole city was thrown into a panic and poured out with wives and children to go and join you. On 20 April they recovered and decided they wanted you to come here, rather than go to you. On that day in fact I received the most splendid rewards for my great labours and late-night vigilance – if there is any reward in genuine, wholehearted glory! A huge crowd – the whole population of our city – thronged to my house and then escorted me up to the Capitol and placed me on the rostra to the accompaniment of the most remarkable cheering and applause. There is nothing vain about me – there is no need; but the unanimity of all classes, with their thanks and congratulations, does move me, for it is illustrious to be popular for having ensured the people's well-being – but I would prefer that you heard this from others! **3** Make sure that you are meticulous in keeping me informed of your plans and actions, and bear in mind that your generosity does not appear to be weakness. The senate and the Roman people both consider that no enemies ever deserved harsher punishment than those citizens who took up arms against their native country in this war. Of course I retaliate and attack them whenever I express my opinion with the support of all right-minded men. Your opinion on this is for you to decide. Mine is that the three brothers are three of a kind!

(ii) *Cicero* Philippics *14.10.28–29*

28 (21 April 43) Will anyone really hesitate to call Caesar imperator? His age will assuredly not dissuade anyone from such a decision, seeing that through valour he has overcome his age. And in my view the services of Gaius Caesar have always seemed the greater in that, because of his age, they were the less to be demanded of him. For when we gave him imperium (1 January 44, as propraetor) we at the same time bestowed on him the hopes which that name implies, and since he has fulfilled them he has by his own actions justified the authority of our edict. So this young man, of the highest spirit, as Hirtius most correctly writes, defended a camp made for many legions with only a few cohorts and fought a successful battle. And so, by the valour, judgement and good fortune of three generals of the Roman people on a single day and in many locations, the state has been preserved. **29** Accordingly I propose, in the name of those three, 50 days of thanksgiving.

14.18 Cicero *Letters to his Friends* 11.20, 10.24: Warnings from Cicero's friends

Some of Cicero's friends felt more concern about Octavian's intentions than did Cicero, who ignored their hints. The Ten: set up by the senate after the battle of Mutina to review Antony's acts as consul. From May 43 Octavian was in communication with Antony and Lepidus, who joined forces in late May. Decimus Brutus was killed in June trying to flee to Macedonia. He had joined Plancus and his army in Gaul, but in late July or early August Plancus made the decision to join Antony.

11.20.1 (Eporedia, 24 May 43: Decimus Brutus to Cicero) My regard for you and your services to me make me feel for you something I do not feel for myself – fear! For I have often been told this, and have not dismissed it – most recently by Labeo Segulius, who always acts in character and who tells me that he had been with Caesar and that you were much spoken of. It's true that Caesar made no complaints about you except for the remark which he said you made about him – 'The young man should be praised, honoured – and disposed of' – and he went on to say that he had no intention of being 'disposed of'. I believe that the remark was repeated to him, or made up by Labeo, not by the young man. Labeo wants me to believe that the veterans are complaining bitterly and that you are in danger from them, as they are especially upset that neither Caesar nor I have been made members of the Board of Ten and that everything has been left to the judgement of you chaps. . . . **3** You should meet with the veterans in any way possible. Do first whatever they want about the Board of Ten and then about the bounties; if you agree, you should propose that the lands of those soldiers who were Antony's veterans should be given to them by the two of us. As regards cash payments, say that the senate will make a decision in time depending on finances. I think that the four legions who have been allocated grants of land can be provided for out of the . . . and Campanian land. In my view the lands should be allocated to the legions either in comparable amounts or by lot. **4** It is not my insight that encourages me to write this to you but my regard for you and my desire for peace, which cannot come about without you. Unless it is absolutely necessary I shall not leave Italy. I am arming and preparing my legions. I trust I shall not have the least successful of armies in meeting all contingencies and enemy attacks. Regarding the army, Caesar is not returning me the legion of Pansa's. Reply at once to this letter and send one of your people if there is anything more confidential that you think I might need to know.

10.24.3 (Camp in Gaul, 28 July 43: Plancus, consul-elect, to Cicero) To this point we have conserved our situation here entirely unchanged. I hope this decision meets with the approval of you all, although I realise how great is the longing for a victory (against Antony), as is only to be expected, as it would be so desirable an outcome. Should these armies meet with a defeat, the state has no large reinforcements at hand to put up a resistance to any sudden attack or skulduggery by these traitors. I think you know what our forces consist of: in my camp there are three veteran legions and one of recruits, the best of them all, while in (Decimus) Brutus' camp there is one veteran legion, another that has served two years, and eight of recruits. So the total army is numerically strong but weak in terms of reliability. We've seen only too often how much trust can be put in a formation of recruits. **4** If the veteran African army or Caesar's were to be added to the strength of our forces we would confidently put the fate of the Republic to the test; and we have noticed that, in Caesar's case, there is less distance involved. I have not stopped sending him letters urging him, and he has not ceased asserting that he is coming without delay, though I realise that in the meantime he has been side-tracked from that intention towards other plans. I have, however, sent our friend Furnius to him with messages and letters, in case he may be able to achieve something. **5** You are aware, my dear Cicero, that where regard for Caesar is concerned you and I are colleagues, and as part of my intimacy with the late Caesar during his lifetime I was bound to feel a regard and esteem for *him*, and, as far as I could tell, he was of an extremely tolerant and obliging disposition. Considering the very marked friendship between myself and Caesar and the fact that he was considered as his son both by Caesar's own decision and that of you all, I think I would look bad if I did not treat him as such. **6** However – and, by Hercules!, anything I write to you is written more in a spirit of grief than of hostility – the fact that Antony is still alive today, that Lepidus has joined him, that they have armies that are not to be sneezed at, that they have high hopes and audacity – for all this they can thank Caesar! I will go back no further than the time when he himself declared to me that he was on his way, and if he had decided to come the war would either have been entirely over by now or have been pushed back into Spain, which is very opposed to them, with great losses on their side. What he has in mind and whose advice has made him turn away from so glorious an undertaking, indeed one which is necessary and advantageous for himself, and deflected him instead to this idea of a six-month consulship which he is pursuing to the alarm of everyone with such absurd perseverance, I simply cannot imagine. . . . **8** Meanwhile we are enduring the full impact of the war in very difficult conditions, as we see no chance of a decisive engagement in the immediate future and will not commit ourselves to a withdrawal which could bring even greater ruin on the state. If Caesar were to be mindful of his own best interests, or if the African legions arrive quickly, we will make you safe on this side. Please keep up your regard for me and be assured that I am all your own. 28 July, from camp.

TRIUMVIRATE AND PROSCRIPTIONS

With the consuls for 43 BC both dead following the battles against Antony, Octavian demanded one of these vacant consulships, using his army to pressure the senate into offering him the position. At this point Cicero still supported Octavian, and there was some suggestion that they might share the consulship together. However, when the senate failed to appreciate his services and tried to entice away the loyalty of his veterans, he, like his great-uncle before him, marched on Rome, in early August 43, with the support of his eight legions. Once appointed consul, he gave his men half the amount promised for bounties (10,000 sesterces each) from public funds and had Caesar's legacy to the people finally paid in full. He also patched up his differences with Antony, and, together with Lepidus, they formed the 'Second Triumvirate' and began to proscribe their opponents.

14.19 Appian *Civil Wars* 3.12.87–88: Octavian crosses the Rubicon

Octavian is here addressing his troops after the senate has proposed that they serve a second campaign before receiving the promised bounty of 5,000 drachmas per man. The senate had also sent messengers to the two legions that had deserted from Antony to advise them to trust in the senate rather than a single commander. Following his *coup d'état*, Octavian was appointed consul on 19 August, along with Pedius, Caesar's nephew, for the remainder of 43 BC. Antony and Dolabella were now no longer public enemies, and Caesar's assassins were condemned and outlawed.

87 'I shall accept my fate, whatever it may be (for it is honourable to suffer anything in a father's service), but I have concerns for you, who are so deserving and numerous, who have put yourself into danger for my sake and that of my father. You know that I am not corrupted by ambition, since the time when I refused the praetorship and its insignia which you offered me. I can now see only one safe path for both of us: that I should procure the consulship with your assistance. Should that occur, all my father's grants to you will be confirmed, the colonies that are still owed you will eventuate, and all your rewards will be paid in their entirety, while I shall bring the murderers to justice and exempt you from all further wars.'

88 At these words the army eagerly applauded and at once sent their centurions to demand the magistracy for Caesar. When in response the senate brought up the matter of his age, the centurions argued as instructed that, in earlier times, Corvinus was younger when he held the office, and later the Scipios, both the Elder and the Younger, and that the country had greatly benefited from the youth of each. They also mentioned the case just recently of Pompey the Great and Dolabella, and that Caesar himself had been allowed to stand for the magistracy ten years before the legal age. While the centurions were arguing this with great confidence, some of the senators who could not stomach the fact that centurions could enjoy such freedom of speech censured them for being more audacious than was proper for soldiers. When the army learnt this they grew even more enraged and demanded that they be led immediately to the city, stating that, because he was Caesar's son, they would hold a special election to give him the consulship, and they eulogised the elder Caesar without restraint. When Caesar saw them so passionate, he led them straight from the assembly, eight legions of infantry and a corresponding number of cavalry, as well as the auxiliaries serving with the legions. After crossing the River Rubicon from the province of Gaul into Italy, which his father similarly crossed at the beginning of the civil war, he divided his army into two: one of these he instructed to follow in their own time, while the better, hand-picked division he had make a forced march, hastening to take the city still unprepared.

14.20 Appian *Civil Wars* 4.1.2–11: The 'Board of Three'

After a three-day meeting near Bononia, the triumvirate was formed in October 43 BC. The troops insisted Octavian marry Antony's stepdaughter, Fulvia's daughter Clodia, and the senate agreed to promote the campaign against Brutus and Cassius and their 20 legions. The *lex Titia* on 27 November appointed the three 'to restore the state': they could make or annul laws, appoint magistrates and exercise jurisdiction unopposed. Octavian then resigned as consul, with Ventidius appointed instead, and Lepidus was to be consul in 42. **4.1.7**: for the tax on women, see doc. 7.75.

2 Caesar and Antony transformed their enmity into friendship near the city of Mutina, on a small low-lying island in the river Lavinius. Both had five legions of soldiers, and they stationed these opposite each other while they made their way with 300 men each to the bridges over the river. Lepidus went in front, searched the island, and signalled with his military cloak for the other two to approach. They left their 300 soldiers on the bridges under the control of friends and advanced in full view to the centre, where they met in council, Caesar positioned in the middle because of his office. Their meeting lasted for two days from morning till night, and they reached the following decisions: Caesar would resign the consulship and Ventidius take it over for the rest of the year; a new magistracy would be brought in by law to deal with the civil dissensions, which Lepidus, Antony and Caesar would hold for five years with powers equal to those of consuls – they thought it better to call it this than dictators, perhaps because of Antony's decree abolishing dictators for the future; they would immediately nominate the city's yearly magistrates for the next five-year period; they would allocate the governorships of the provinces, with Antony to have the whole of Gaul except that part bordering the Pyrenees, which was called Old Gaul; Lepidus was to govern this in addition to Spain; Libya, Sardinia and Sicily and any other islands in that region were to be Caesar's. **3** In this way the three divided the Romans' empire among themselves, postponing only the division of the areas beyond the Adriatic because these were still under the control of Brutus and Cassius, against whom Antony and Caesar were to make war. Lepidus was to be consul for the following year and remain in the city to deal with any emergencies there, while governing Spain through others. Lepidus was to have three legions of his army to keep control of Rome and divide the other seven between Caesar and Antony, so that each could lead 20 legions to the war. To encourage the army with promises of war booty, they would give them, apart from other gifts, 18 of the Italian cities as colonies, cities renowned for their wealth and the beauty of their estates and houses, which would be divided among them – estates and houses included – just as if they had been captured from an enemy in battle. . . .

5 As soon as the three men were by themselves they collaborated in writing a list of those who were to be executed – the powerful because they suspected them – while each selected their personal enemies, and they exchanged their own relatives and friends with each other for slaughter, both then and later. For various persons were added to the list from time to time, some from enmity, some only for an offence or because they were friends of their enemies, or enemies of their friends, or because of their wealth – for they needed a great deal of money for the war, since all the revenue from Asia had been given to Brutus and Cassius, who were still in receipt of it, and the kings and satraps were still paying their contributions. They, however, were insolvent, as Europe and especially Italy were exhausted with wars and taxes. In consequence they imposed very harsh taxes both on the plebeians and even on women and intended taxes on sales and rents. Some people were already on the proscription list as a result of the beauty of their country or town house. All those from the senate who were condemned to death and confiscation numbered about 300, and from those known as 'knights' some 2,000. Both their brothers and uncles were among the proscribed, as well as some of the officers serving under them who had points of disagreement with the leaders or other officers. . . .

7 A tribune, Publius Titius, proposed a law setting up a new magistracy to sort out the present situation for five years comprising three men, Lepidus, Antony and Octavian, to have the same powers as consul . . . with no time allowed for consideration nor a proper day fixed for voting on it – the law was ratified immediately. That same night, in addition to the first 17 victims, 130 other men were proscribed in various parts of the city and shortly afterwards another 150. Names of those who were condemned retrospectively or had been killed earlier by mistake kept being added to the tablets, so that all the executions appeared to be legitimate. It was proclaimed that the heads of all the victims should be brought to the three for a fixed reward: this was paid in money to a free man and in freedom and money to a slave. Everyone had to allow their private property to be searched. Anyone who harboured or hid victims or refused the search was liable to the same penalties. Anyone who informed on these was entitled to receive the same rewards.

8 The proscription was made in the following words: 'Marcus Lepidus, Marcus Antonius and Octavius Caesar, who have been elected to govern and regulate affairs of state, proclaim as follows: if the traitors (to Julius Caesar) had not duplicitously begged for mercy, and once obtaining it acted as the enemies of their benefactors and conspired against them, they would not have assassinated Gaius (Julius) Caesar – they whom he captured in war and then saved by his clemency, whom he made his friends and promoted to magistracies, honours and gifts without number; nor should we have been forced to make such widespread use of our powers against those who have insulted us and proclaimed us public enemies. Now, seeing that the evil intentions of those who have plotted against us and at whose hands Gaius Caesar met his death cannot be pacified by benevolence, we prefer to take pre-emptive measures against our enemies rather than put up with the situation without protest. No one should consider our action unjust, harsh or excessive who sees what both Gaius and ourselves have had to endure. Although Gaius was both supreme commander and pontifex maximus, although he had conquered and added to our possessions the peoples most menacing to Rome, although he was the first man to attempt to sail the unnavigated sea beyond the pillars of Hercules and the discoverer of a land unknown to the Romans, in the centre of the senate house – designated as sacred space – under the eyes of the gods, 23 men murdered him with their villainous butchery, men whom he had captured in war and spared, while some of them had been named as heirs of his wealth; then the rest, in response to such an abominable crime – instead of punishing the malefactors! – dispatched them to magistracies and commands, which they made use of to seize hold of public funds. Even now they are raising an army against us and trying to obtain another from barbarians who have always been the enemies of our empire, while cities under Roman rule that have not obeyed them have been burned or destroyed or razed to the ground, and others they have terrorised and forced to bear arms against their native land and ourselves. **9** We have taken punishment on some of them already, while others, with god's help, you will soon see paying the penalty. The greatest part of this undertaking has already been accomplished and is well in hand, in Spain and Gaul and matters here at home, but there is still one mission remaining – to march against Gaius' assassins over the sea. Since we are on the point of fighting this overseas war on your behalf, we do not consider it safe, either for your interests or for our own, to leave other enemies behind who will take advantage of our absence and be in wait for opportunities presented by the war, nor should we delay on their account in a matter of such great urgency, but ought rather to obliterate them once and for all, since they were the ones who began the war against us when they voted that we and the armies under our command were public enemies. . . . **10** But we shall avenge ourselves only against those who are most guilty and most reprehensible. And this is on your behalf no less than on our own. While we are fighting our wars, you will all necessarily be facing dangers all around you, while we will have to pacify the army which has been insulted, provoked and proclaimed a public enemy by our common adversaries. Although we could have arrested immediately those whom we decided to, we prefer to proscribe them rather than arrest them unawares: this too on your account, so that the enraged soldiery will not have the power to exceed their instructions by taking action against the innocent, but with their victims enumerated and identified by name should spare the rest as ordered.

11 With good fortune! No one is to receive in his house any persons whose name appears on this list, nor conceal them, nor send them away anywhere, nor accept bribes. Anyone who is found saving or assisting or colluding with them we shall add to the list of the proscribed without taking into account any mitigation or pardon. Those who take part in the executions are to bring the heads to us – free men for 25,000 Attic drachmas per head, and slaves for their freedom and 10,000 Attic drachmas and their masters' citizen status. The same rewards will be in place for informers. And no one who receives a reward will be recorded in our archives, so they will remain anonymous.' This was the wording of the three's proclamation, as closely as it can be translated from Latin into Greek.

14.21 Plutarch *Life of Cicero* 45.1–49.2: The end of Cicero's career

In the first round of proscriptions, depending on the source, 12 or 17 victims were chosen, including, at Antony's insistence, Cicero. The proscriptions were to raise money to pay the troops the promised rewards, but even so the triumvirs had to give them 18 of Italy's richest towns, and heavy and unprecedented taxes were imposed on the wealthy in Italy (Brutus and Cassius controlled the resources of the East). Cicero was murdered on 7 December 43 BC (cf. App. 4.19). Fulvia was said to have pulled out Cicero's tongue and stabbed it with a hair-pin (Dio 47.8).

45.1 It was Cicero's hatred for Antony in the first place, and then his innate partiality for prestige, that attached him to Caesar (Octavian), as he thought to enhance his own political standing through Caesar's power. **2** Indeed, the young man bowed down to him to the extent that he even addressed him as father. Brutus was exceptionally angry at this, and in his letters to Atticus attacked Cicero on the grounds that, in making up to Caesar through fear of Antony, he was clearly not achieving freedom for his country but currying favour for himself with a benevolent master. **3** However, Brutus took up with Cicero's son, who was studying in Athens, gave him a command and achieved a great deal through his agency. **4** Cicero's power in the city was at its peak at this point, and, since he could do whatever he pleased, he raised a faction against Antony and drove him from the city, and dispatched the two consuls, Hirtius and Pansa, to make war on him, while he persuaded the senate to vote Caesar lictors and praetorian insignia on the grounds that he was fighting to defend their country. But when Antony had been defeated and the forces had united under Caesar, with the two consuls having died as a result of the battle, **5** the senate became afraid of the young man who had enjoyed this splendid good fortune and attempted to entice his troops away from him with honours and gifts and strip him of his power, arguing that there was no need to defend the country now that Antony had taken flight. Caesar in consequence became alarmed and sent emissaries in secret to Cicero to beg and persuade him to secure the consulship for them both, and to handle affairs as he thought best once he had taken office and act as a guide to him as a youth who was striving for name and prestige. **6** Caesar himself admitted that it was through fear of his army being disbanded and the danger of isolation that he made use in this crisis of Cicero's love of authority and urged him to seek the consulship with his collaboration and assistance in canvassing.

46.1 It was at this point indeed, more than at any other time, that Cicero was inveigled and tricked, an old man by a young one. He assisted Caesar's canvassing and got the senate on his side, for which he was immediately blamed by his friends, while shortly afterwards he realised that he had brought ruin on himself and betrayed the people's freedom. **2** For when the young man's power had increased and he won the consulship, he gave Cicero the cold shoulder, made friends with Antony and Lepidus, united his forces with theirs, and divided up rule with them, just like any other piece of property. And they drew up a list of more than 200 men who had to be put to death. **3** The proscription of Cicero generated the greatest disagreement in their debates, with Antony refusing to come to terms unless he was the first to be executed and Lepidus being in agreement with Antony, while Caesar opposed them both. **4** They held secret meetings on their own near the city of Bononia for three days, getting together at a place some distance from the camps and surrounded by a river. **5** It is reported that for the first two days Caesar kept up his fight to save Cicero, but gave in on the third day and threw him over. The compromise reached was as follows: Caesar was to abandon Cicero, Lepidus his brother Paulus, and Antony Lucius Caesar, who was his uncle on his mother's side. **6** In this way any human considerations were driven out by the presence of anger and rage or, rather, they demonstrated that no wild beast is more savage than man when in passionate pursuit of power. . . .

47.4 Only a few days afterwards Quintus (Cicero) was betrayed by his servants to those searching for him and was put to death along with his son. Cicero was brought to Astura and, finding a ship there, immediately embarked and sailed along the coast as far as Circaeum, making use of the wind. **5** From there the steersmen wanted to set sail at once, but whether he feared the sea or had not yet entirely given up his confidence in Caesar he disembarked and travelled 100 stades on foot as far as Rome. **6** Once again undecided, he changed his mind and went down to the sea at Astura. There he spent the night in terrible and desperate calculations, with the result that he actually decided to make his way secretly to Caesar's house and commit suicide on the hearth to set an avenging spirit on Caesar – **7** but then the fear of tortures impelled him away from this course as well. Turning over in his mind numerous muddled and contradictory resolutions, he put himself in his servants' hands to be taken by sea to Caieta, where he had an estate and a pleasant refuge in the summer when the Etesian winds blow most agreeably. . . .

48.6 Meanwhile his assassins arrived, Herennius a centurion and Popillius a tribune, whom Cicero had once defended when he was charged with parricide, along with assistants. On finding the door closed they broke in: Cicero was not to be seen, and those inside said they did not know where he was, though it is reported that a youth called Philologos, who had been educated by Cicero in liberal studies and other lessons and who was a freedman of his brother Quintus, told the tribune that the litter was being carried through the wooded and shady walks to the sea. So the tribune, taking a few men with him, ran round towards the exit, while Herennius hurried at a run down the walks. When Cicero saw him he told the servants to put the litter down where they were. He, clasping his chin with his left hand, a typical gesture of his, gazed steadily at his murderers, unwashed and unkempt and his face wasted with worry, causing most of them to cover their faces while Herennius was killing him. He stretched out his neck from the litter and was killed, being at that point in his 64th year. Herennius, at Antony's orders, cut off his head and his hands, with which he wrote the *Philippics*. For Cicero himself titled his speeches against Antony *Philippics*, and so the books are called to this day. **49.1** When these appendages were brought to Rome, Antony happened to be conducting an election, but when he heard of their arrival and caught sight of them he cried out, 'Now let our proscriptions have an end!' **2** He ordered the head and hands to be placed above the ships' beaks on the rostra, a spectacle which was hideous to the Romans because they thought they saw there not the face of Cicero, but a likeness of Antony's soul.

14.22 Livy *F* 50 (book 120): Livy's estimation of Cicero

Marcus Cicero had left the city before the arrival of the triumvirs, convinced, as was the case, that he could no more escape Antony than Cassius and Brutus could Caesar. He fled first to his Tusculan estate and from there set out by indirect routes for his property at Formiae, as he planned to set sail from Caieta. From there he put out to sea several times, but sometimes contrary winds drove him back, and at others he was unable to endure the way the ship plunged under the heaving of the waves, and finally a weariness for both flight and life overcame him. He returned to his upper villa, which is little more than a mile from the sea, and said, 'I shall die in the native land I have so often saved.' It is definitely known that his slaves were prepared to fight bravely and loyally in his defence, but he ordered them to set down the litter and endure patiently what a hostile fate was forcing upon them. He put his head out of the litter and held his neck steady and was decapitated. Nor was this sufficient for the savage brutality of the soldiers: they also cut off his hands, upbraiding them for having written anything against Antony.

So the head was brought back to Antony and placed between the two hands on the rostra, where as consul and often as ex-consul, and even in that same year in opposing Antony, he had been listened to with so much acclaim for his eloquence as no other human voice had won. People could hardly raise their eyes for tears to gaze on his butchered appendages. He lived for 63 years, so that if there had been no violence his death would not have seemed to be unseasonable. His character was fortunate, both in its achievements and in its rewards for achievements. He enjoyed a considerable period of good fortune and a long course of prosperity, at intervals being struck by serious blows – his exile, the downfall of the party whom he represented, his daughter's death, and his own most grievous and bitter demise – bearing none of these misfortunes in a manner worthy of a true man except his death, which, if given its true weight, should seem the less undeserved because he suffered from a victorious opponent nothing crueller than he would have done himself had he achieved the same success. If, however, one were to weigh his faults against his virtues, he was a man of greatness, dynamism and pre-eminence – and one that would need a Cicero as eulogist to relate in detail the entirety of his merits.

14.23 Livy *Periochae* 118–20: The events of 43 BC

118 In Greece, on the pretext of the welfare of the state and the campaign against Mark Antony, Marcus Brutus gained control of the army commanded by Publius

Vatinius as well as the province. Gaius Caesar (Octavian), who as a private citizen had taken up arms for the state, was given propraetorian imperium by the senate plus consular insignia and also became a senator. Mark Antony besieged Decimus Brutus in Mutina; envoys sent to him by the senate to negotiate for peace had little success in arranging it. The Roman people put on military cloaks. Marcus Brutus in Epirus overcame the praetor Gaius Antonius and his army. **119** Gaius Trebonius was killed in Asia by the treachery of Publius Dolabella. For this crime Dolabella was declared a public enemy by the senate. When the consul Pansa was beaten by Antony, consul Aulus Hirtius came up with his army, routed Mark Antony's forces, and equalised the fortune of both sides. After being defeated by Hirtius and Caesar, Antony fled into Gaul and gained the support of Marcus Lepidus and the legions he commanded. He was declared a public enemy by the senate together with all those in his camp. Aulus Hirtius, who after his victory had fallen in the actual camp of the enemy, and Gaius Pansa, who died of a wound he received in his unsuccessful battle, were buried in the Campus Martius. The senate showed little gratitude to Gaius Caesar, the only survivor of the three commanders, as it decreed a triumph for Decimus Brutus, who had been delivered from his siege at Mutina by Caesar, but made an inadequate statement of their gratitude to Caesar and his soldiers. Consequently Gaius Caesar, once friendly relations between him and Mark Antony were restored though the agency of Marcus Lepidus, came to Rome with his army, catching his opponents off-guard by his arrival, and was made consul at the age of 19 years. **120** Gaius Caesar as consul passed a law to bring to trial those by whose deed his father had been murdered; Marcus Brutus, Gaius Cassius and Decimus Brutus were cited in that law and condemned in absentia. Asinius Pollio and Munatius Plancus also joined Mark Antony with their armies, thus enlarging his forces, and Decimus Brutus, whom the senate had instructed to pursue Antony, fled when abandoned by his legions and was killed on Antony's orders after coming into his power, struck down by Capenus, a Sequanian. Gaius Caesar came to terms with Antony and Lepidus with the provisions that he, Lepidus and Antony should be a Board of Three for governing the state for a five-year period and that each of them should proscribe their personal enemies. An immense number of Roman knights and the names of 130 senators were included in this proscription, among them Lucius Paulus, the brother of Lepidus, Lucius Caesar, the uncle of Antony, and Marcus Cicero. Cicero was executed by Popillius, a legionary solder, at the age of 63, and his head and right hand were also placed on the rostra.

THE 'LIBERATORS' AND CIVIL WAR

One of the agreements made at Bononia in October 43 BC was that Octavian and Antony were to unite forces to make war on Brutus and Cassius to avenge Caesar's death and were to share the command with 43 legions (only 19 fought at Philippi). In January 42, Julius Caesar was consecrated as a god. This gave the war against the liberators a new religious dimension, and Octavian now had the status of divi filius ('son of the god'); a temple was built to Caesar in the forum. Brutus had taken Macedonia peaceably at the end of the term of the retiring proconsul, Hortensius (his uncle), and also controlled Greece and most of the troops in Illyricum. Pansa, urged by Cicero, had had Brutus ratified as governor, and

Brutus crossed to Asia in mid-43. Cassius succeeded in taking over Syria and was joined by the four legions from Egypt. Trebonius, one of the conspirators, was governor of Asia. The 'liberators' possessed huge armies and enormous resources from their Eastern provinces which they governed rapaciously, and according to Plutarch (*Brutus* 38) the armies that met at Philippi were the greatest Roman forces that had ever fought each other. To encourage commitment in fighting against other Romans, the soldiers had been promised the (now standard) 20,000 sesterces a head in case of victory.

14.24 Dio *Roman History* 47.18.1–19.2: Caesar's deification

A comet which appeared during the Ludi victoriae Caesaris (July 44 BC: doc. 14.8) had been publicly interpreted by Octavian as Caesar's soul ascending to heaven and was later depicted on his coinage; in 38 a gold coin was issued depicting the head of the deified Caesar with a star on the obverse. The Ludi Apollinares were celebrated from 6 to 13 July.

18.1 These three men at the same time venerated the former Caesar to the highest degree, for, in as much as they were aiming at and striving for monarchy, they furiously pursued the rest of the assassins, **2** in so doing organising immunity in advance for themselves for their actions and security, and they eagerly undertook anything that contributed to his honour in the hope that one day they might be thought worthy of the same. For this reason they glorified him, both by the distinctions that had already been voted him and by others they now appended. **3** So, on the first day of the year (42 BC), they took an oath and made everyone else take one too that they would consider all his acts unchangeable (this still happens today in honour of all those who come to supreme power and of those who have held it and not been dishonoured). **4** They also laid the foundation of a temple (heroon) to him in the forum in the place where he was cremated and had a statue of him carried round at games in the circus, together with another of Aphrodite. If a victory anywhere was reported, they granted the honour of a thanksgiving both to the victor and to Caesar, though deceased. **5** They forced everyone to celebrate his birthday by wearing laurel and making merry, and legislated that anyone who failed to do so was accursed in the sight of Jupiter and Caesar himself and, if senators or their sons, were to be fined 250,000 denarii. **6** It happened that the Ludi Apollinares fell on the same day, and so they decreed that his birthday should be celebrated on the day before, as there was a Sibylline oracle prohibiting a festival of any god on that day except Apollo. **19.1** As well as granting these honours, they laid down that the day on which he was assassinated, when there had always been a sovereign meeting of the senate, was unlucky. They closed the room in which he was murdered for the time being and afterwards changed it into a lavatory; they also built the Curia Julia, named for him, alongside the place known as the Comitium, as had been decreed. **2** Furthermore, they prohibited any image of him, as if he really were a god, to be carried at the funerals of his relatives, though this was a very ancient custom and still taking place.

14.25 The people of Greece honour Brutus, 44–43 BC

i: This is a white marble base from Athens. Brutus had been adopted by his uncle, Quintus Servilius Caepio, though he retained his own cognomen. ii: This inscribed base of a pedestal from Delos held four statues; according to Dio 47.20.4, the Athenians voted Brutus and Cassius bronze statues and set them up next to Harmodius and Aristogeiton, while the inhabitants of Greece and Macedonia generally hoped Brutus would liberate them from the Romans, as he had the Romans from Caesar (47.21.2). Quintus Hortensius was proconsul of Macedonia (44–43 BC). iii: This is a white marble base, from Oropos in Boeotia.

(i) SEG 17.75; Raubitschek 15

The people (erected this statue of) Quintus Servilius, son of Quintus, Caepio Brutus.

(ii) ILS 9460; Raubitschek 17

The people of the Athenians and those who live on the island (dedicated this statue) of Quintus Hortensius, son of Quintus, uncle of Caepio, because of Caepio's own benefactions to the city (of Athens), to Apollo.

(iii) SEG 17.209; IG 7.383; Raubitschek 16

The people of the Oropians (dedicated this statue of) Quintus Caepio, son of Quintus, Brutus, their own saviour and benefactor, **5** to Amphiaraos.

14.26 Livy *Periochae* 121–24: The battles of Philippi, 42 BC

The first battle of Philippi, when Cassius committed suicide, took place on 3 October; the second on 23 October. The final victory was due to Antony's generalship: Octavian was conspicuously absent much of the time and, according to Pliny, spent three days hiding in a marsh (doc. 15.116). Antony had Hortensius (Brutus' uncle), who had killed Antony's brother Gaius, executed over his brother's tomb, but sent Brutus' ashes to his mother, Servilia.

121 Gaius Cassius, who had been instructed by the senate to conduct a campaign against Dolabella after he was declared a public enemy, gained control of Syria supported by the authority of the state and, with the three legions which were in that province, besieged Dolabella in the city of Laodicea and compelled his death. By the orders of Marcus Brutus, Gaius Antonius was also captured and executed. **122** For a short time Marcus Brutus successfully conducted a campaign against the Thracians, and, when all the overseas provinces and armies had been brought into the control of himself and Gaius Cassius, both men met at Smyrna to decide on their plans for the coming war. They pardoned by common consent their prisoner Publicola, the brother of Marcus Messala. **123** Sextus Pompeius, the son of Magnus, gathered the proscribed and runaway slaves from Epirus and for a considerable time used his force to engage in piracy without possessing any particular base. First of all, he seized the town of Messana in Sicily, and then the whole province, killed the praetor Pompeius Bithynicus, and finally defeated Caesar's legate Quintus Salvidenus in a naval battle. Caesar and Antony with their armies crossed over to Greece to make war on Brutus and Cassius . . . **124** Gaius Caesar and Antony fought at Philippi against Brutus and Cassius with a disparate outcome, in that the right wing of each was successful and the victors on each side captured the enemy camp. The death of Cassius tipped the balance between the two sides, as he was on the wing which had been routed and committed suicide, believing that the whole army had been vanquished. Then on the following day Marcus Brutus was also defeated and put an end to his life, entreating Strato, his companion in flight, to drive a sword through him. His age was about 40 . . . , among whom Quintus Hortensius was killed.

14.27 Appian *Civil Wars* 4.17.137–38, 5.1.3: The aftermath of Philippi

Antony now took control of the Eastern provinces, raising monies to pay the triumvirs' soldiers. Octavian returned to Italy after another severe illness to oversee the settlement of the veterans and continue the war against Pompeius.

137 In this way Caesar and Antony achieved through the audacious taking of risks and two infantry battles an outcome so successful that it was totally without precedent. Never had such large or powerful Roman military forces come into conflict with each other before this time, nor had these been enlisted by normal conscription methods but were hand-picked; they were not inexperienced recruits, but disciplined and hardened over a long period, and turned on each other rather than fighting against foreign or barbarian peoples. Sharing the same language and military proficiency, alike in training and endurance, they were reciprocally invincible against each other for these reasons. Nor had there ever been such rage and daring shown in war as now, when citizens were fighting against citizens, relatives against relatives, and fellow soldiers against each other. Proof of this is that the number of the slain, across each of the battles, was apparently no fewer for the conquerors than for the conquered.

138 The army of Antony and Caesar validated the forecast of its generals, on one day and with one engagement exchanging the utmost peril of famine and fear of annihilation for splendid wealth, total security and glorious victory. Furthermore, the outcome came about that they had predicted to the Romans as they were going into battle: Rome's government was explicitly decided by that one action, and it has not yet returned to being a democracy, nor was there any further necessity for similar conflicts against each other, except for the civil war between Antony and Caesar not long afterwards, which was the last engaged in by the Romans . . . .

5.1.3 After the victory at Philippi, Caesar and Antony performed a magnificent sacrifice and praised their army. To arrange for the allocation of the rewards of victory, the former went to Italy to divide up the soldiers' land and to settle them in the colonies (he chose this himself because of his sickness), while Antony went to the peoples beyond (the Aegean) to collect the money the soldiers had been promised. They divided the provinces between them as before and added those of Lepidus. It was decided on Caesar's advice that Gaul within the Alps (Cisalpine) be independent, as the elder Caesar had intended, while Lepidus had been accused of betraying matters to (Sextus) Pompeius. They agreed that, if Caesar considered the accusation against Lepidus to be false, he would be given other provinces. They dismissed from service those who had completed their full period except for 8,000 who asked to continue to serve; these were taken back and divided between them, formed into praetorian cohorts. The remainder of their army, including those who had come over from Brutus, comprised 11 legions of infantry and 14,000 cavalry. Of these Antony took six legions and 10,000 cavalry for his campaign overseas, while Caesar had 4,000 cavalry and five legions, but he gave two of these to Antony in exchange for those left in Italy by Antony under the command of Calenus.

DISPOSSESSION, FULVIA AND LUCIUS ANTONIUS

With huge numbers of veterans due to be disbanded, the need for land on which to settle colonies was of paramount importance following the triumvirs' victory at Philippi. Although the triumvirs had agreed following the conference at Bononia that the lands of 18 Italian cities were to be appropriated for this redistribution, in the event the holdings of some 40 cities in Italy were confiscated; an allotment of 50 iugera seems to have been the norm for soldiers, and 100 for officers: senatorial estates were exempted. Vergil's own family was said to have lost its land near Mantua until an appeal was made to Octavian by the poet's powerful friends. This redistribution of land, the effects of which were heightened by occasional famine at Rome because of the activities of Sextus Pompeius, was to cause unrest over the next decade. Mark Antony's brother Lucius, consul in 41, together with Antony's wife, Fulvia, considered that Antony's veterans were not receiving fair treatment and stirred up enough resentment to spark off war with Octavian in Italy, which ended with their defeat at Perusia in 40 BC.

14.28 Vergil *Eclogue* 1: Discontent in Italy

The redistribution of land in Italy to veterans caused great hardship, reflected in Vergil's *Eclogues* 1 and 9. In *Eclogue* 1 (written probably in 41 BC), Meliboeus represents the dispossessed farmer, Tityrus (singing love songs at his ease) one who has been exempted from dispossession by 'god-like' Octavian.

Meliboeus

    Tityrus, here lying under cover of the spreading beech
    You practise the woodland Muse on your slim reed-pipe
    While I must leave my native land and my sweet fields:
    I am driven from home – you, Tityrus, at ease in the shade
5   Teach the woods to echo 'sweet Amaryllis'.

Tityrus

    Meliboeus, a god has granted me this leisure:
    For to me he will always be a god, and his altar
    A tender lamb from my sheepfolds will always drench with blood.
    It is he, as you see, that allows my cattle to ramble and myself
10   To play as I choose on this rustic pipe . . .

Meliboeus

26   What then was this special cause of your seeing Rome? . . .

Tityrus

40   What else could I do? My slavery allowed of no escape,
    Nor were there elsewhere any other gods at hand to help.

    Here I saw that youth, Meliboeus, in whose praise
    Twelve days a year my altars will give smoke:
    He was the first to answer my request with,
    'Pasture your cattle, as before, and raise your bulls.' . . .
    So, sooner will nimble deer graze on open sea

60   And seas abandon fish uncovered on the shore,
    Sooner migrating across each other's borders, will the exiled
    Parthian drink the Araris, or Germany the Tigris,
    Than his countenance will ever fade from my heart!

Meliboeus

    While the rest of us must leave, some to thirsty Africa,
    To Scythia and the turbulent Oxus,
    Or Britain far separated from the whole earth!
    When shall I ever see again my native lands after long years,
    Or the turf-heaped roof of my poor cottage,
    Or in after times gaze wondering at the ears of grain – my only kingdom!

70   Some godless soldier will now possess my well-tilled fallow,
    A foreigner these crops! What misery civil strife
    Has brought us! For these we have sown our fields!

14.29 Livy *Periochae* 125–26: The siege of Perusia

In 41 BC, following Octavian's confiscation of land for his veterans, there was extensive rioting, as well as famine, as Pompeius was blockading Italy. Antony's wife, Fulvia, and his brother Lucius, as consul, made political use of the concerns of the dispossessed. Lucius had the support of the senate and briefly gained control of Rome with his army, but he was besieged at Perusia and defeated by Octavian in March 40. Antony, who may not have been fully aware of events, and Octavian were reconciled later in 40 at Brundisium.

125 Antony was left overseas (the provinces lying in that part of the empire had submitted to him), and Caesar returned to Italy and distributed lands to his veterans. Mutinies in his army against their general by soldiers incited by Fulvia, the wife of Mark Antony, he put down at great risk. The consul Lucius Antonius, brother of Mark Antony, on the advice of that same Fulvia, made war on Caesar. The people whose lands had been assigned to the veterans were enlisted on his side, and he routed Marcus Lepidus, who with his army was in charge of the defence of Rome, and made a hostile foray into the city. **126** When Caesar was 23 years of age, he besieged Lucius Antonius in the town of Perusia and repulsed several attempts by him to break out. When he was forced by hunger to surrender, Caesar pardoned him and all his soldiers but destroyed Perusia. With all the armies of the other side brought under his command, he put an end to the war without bloodshed.

14.30 Martial *Epigrams* 11.20: Octavian's elegiacs on Fulvia

Antony placed Glaphyra's son Archelaus IV on the Cappadocian throne after Philippi (it was rumoured that Glaphyra and Antony were lovers). Manius was one of his agents in

Italy, working with Fulvia in 41–40 BC. Octavian in this poem, emphasising his masculinity and down-to-earth Roman moral standards, is clearly focusing on Fulvia rather than on the Antonii as being responsible for the conflict. Octavian had recently divorced Fulvia's daughter Clodia Pulchra, which would have encouraged Fulvia to fight for Antony's rights against those of Octavian. Martial is here comparing his own 'lewdness' with the language used by Augustus in his youth.

> Malicious reader, these six bawdy lines of Caesar Augustus
> Peruse, you who read Latin words with ill-humour:
> 'Because Antony is fucking Glaphyra, this punishment
> Fulvia laid down for me, that I should fuck her as well.
> 5 That I should fuck her too? What if Manius begged me
> To bugger him – would I do it? I don't think so, if I had any sense!
> "Either fuck me or we fight", she says. What – if my prick
> Was more precious to me than life? Let the war trumpets sound!'
> Caesar, you certainly absolve *my* naughty little books from censure –
> 10 *You* who know how to express yourself with Roman bluntness.

14.31 *CIL* 11.6721.5, 7, 9a, 11, 14: Flying insults from Perusia

ILLRP 1106–18. The term for a slingshot was glans (plural: glandes), which meant both acorn and the head of the penis. These slingshots are known as the glandes perusinae. Many slingshots were inscribed with insults (cf. 10.16 for examples in the Social War). Lucius' coins show that he did in fact suffer from hair loss, as did Julius Caesar.

> 5   I'm heading for Fulvia's cunt!
> 7   I'm heading for Octavian's ass!
> 9a Greetings Octavian, you suck!
> 11 You pansy Octavian, sit on this one!
> 14 Bald Lucius Antonius, and you too Fulvia, open up your assholes!

ANTONY'S REORGANISATION OF THE EAST

Antony made a tour of the Eastern provinces, some of which had suffered severely under the 'liberators', arbitrating disputes, installing client kings, raising resources and removing tyrants. Although Brutus and Cassius had made great exactions throughout the East to finance their war, Antony also needed to raise funds to pay for the settlement of the triumvirs' veterans. Many of the Eastern provinces had supported the liberators and so needed careful handling, and he showed leniency to all except those who had been involved in Caesar's assassination, granting privileges to Athens and other cultural centres. One of the most important client rulers was Cleopatra, whom he met (again) at Tarsus in 41 BC. She had already supported the triumvirs by sending four legions to oppose Cassius. While the campaigns against the Parthians were seen as expeditions honour bound to take revenge for earlier defeats and retrieve captured Roman standards, it is clear that the Eastern provinces could be devastated by their incursions, as in 40–39, and that the Parthians had to be dealt with as a very real threat, and not just to cities on the frontier.

14.32 *RDGE* 57: Antony honours festival winners

A letter of Antony's found on papyrus in Egypt dated to 42–41 BC (or perhaps 33–32 BC), the two occasions on which he was known to be in Ephesus. The grant refers to members of a professional organisation of those who had won wreaths for events at sacred festivals, both athletes and performers. Artemidoros is Antony's physical trainer (his 'anointer'), and his name shows that he owed his citizenship to Antony. The purple stripe was granted to distinguished citizens in Greek cities.

Mark Antony, imperator, triumvir for the restoration of the state, to the koinon (association) of Greeks in Asia, greetings. **5** Earlier I was met in Ephesus by Marcus Antonius Artemidoros, my friend and trainer, along with the eponymous priest of the society (synodos) of crowned victors at sacred festivals worldwide, **10** Charopeinos of Ephesus, with regard to the previous privileges of the society that they may remain unchanged, and that I should agree to write to you immediately concerning the other honours and immunities which they requested from me, such as exemption from military service **15** and exemption from all liturgies and exemption from billeting, and a sacred truce and inviolability during festivals, and the purple stripe. **20** I willingly, both because of my friend Artemidoros and for the sake of their eponymous priest, grant this favour for the honour of the society and for its growth. And now Artemidoros has again met me, requesting that they be allowed to dedicate a bronze tablet and to inscribe on it the immunities written above, and I, choosing in no way to fail Artemidoros when he came to me about these issues, granted the dedication of the tablet as he requested me. I have confirmed this in a letter to you.

14.33 Josephus *Antiquities of the Jews* 14.12.4.301–23: Antony and the Jews, 41 BC

Antony here makes provisions for Jews who suffered under the government of Brutus and Cassius in the East. Hyrcanus was high priest and ethnarch of Judaea; in 37 BC Antony and the senate declared Herod king of Judaea.

301 Antony and Caesar had defeated Cassius near Philippi, as has been recounted by others. After the victory, Caesar went to Italy and Antony marched off to Asia, and while he was in Bithynia embassies from all parts came to address him. **302** Those in authority among the Jews also came to accuse the factions of Phasaelus and Herod, stating that Hyrcanus had the semblance of ruling, but that these men had all the power. **303** Antony showed great respect to Herod, who had come to him to defend himself against his accusers, and consequently his opponents could not even obtain an audience – Herod gained this from Antony through bribery. **304** When Antony arrived at Ephesus, Hyrcanus, the high priest, and our people sent an embassy to him bearing a crown of gold and requested that he would write to the provincial governors to release those Jews who had been taken by Cassius as prisoners of war, although they had not fought against him, and to return to them that country which, under Cassius, had been taken from them. **305** Antony considered that the Jews' requests were just and wrote immediately to Hyrcanus and the Jews, and also sent a decree to the Tyrians, which stated that decision.

306 'Mark Antony, imperator, to Hyrcanus the high priest and ethnarch and to the people of the Jews, greetings. If you are well, it is good; I too, with my army, am in health. **307** Lysimachus, the son of Pausanias, Josephus, the son of Menneus, and Alexander, the son of Theodorus, your ambassadors, met me at Ephesus and have renewed the embassy on which they had formerly served at Rome; they have diligently carried out the present embassy on behalf of you and your people and have made clear the goodwill you have towards us. **308** Since I am convinced, therefore, both by your actions and by your words, that you feel friendship towards us, and as I understand that your lifestyle is steadfast and god-fearing, **309** I regard you as one of our own. When those enemies to us and to the Roman people overran the whole of Asia, sparing neither cities nor shrines, and did not keep the oaths they had given, it was not only on account of our own conflict with them but on account of everyone jointly that we took vengeance on those responsible for the offences against men and wickedness towards the gods, the reason why, we suppose, that the sun turned away his light, it too being loath to view their abominable crime against Caesar. **310** We have also overcome their conspiracies, aimed against the very gods themselves, which Macedonia experienced, as a climate peculiarly appropriate for their unholy and reckless deeds, and (have overcome) that assemblage of half-mad depravity which they mustered at Philippi in Macedonia, when they took possession of terrain that was well situated and walled round with mountains to the very sea, and where the approach was controlled through only a single gate – and we succeeded because the gods had condemned them for their wicked machinations. **311** And Brutus, when he had fled to Philippi and had been corralled by us, shared in Cassius' destruction. Now these have received their punishment, we hope that we may enjoy peace for the future and that Asia may have a rest from war. **312** We therefore ensure that the peace which god has granted us includes our allies as well, with the whole of Asia restored as if from an illness through our victory. Therefore, with regard to both you and your people, I shall take care of what will augment your well-being. **313** I have also sent letters to the cities, that if anyone, whether freemen or slaves, has been sold under the spear by Gaius Cassius or his subordinates, they shall be set free, and I desire that you make use of the privileges granted you by myself and Dolabella. I also forbid the Tyrians to use any violence against you and order them to restore whatever places of the Jews they now hold. The crown that you sent me I have accepted.'

319 'Mark Antony, imperator, to the magistrates, senate, and people of Tyre, greetings. I have sent you my decree, which I desire you to take care to inscribe on the public tablets, in Roman and Greek letters, and that you position it inscribed in the most prominent place so that it can be read by all. **320** "Mark Antony, imperator, one of the triumvirate for restoring public affairs, made this declaration: Since Gaius Cassius, in his revolt, plundered that province, which was not his, and which was overrun with armies, as well as our allies, and made the Jewish people – a friend of the Roman people – capitulate; **321** and since we have overcome his rebellion by arms, we now restore by our decrees and judgements what he has plundered, so that these may be returned to our allies. And whatever Jewish possessions have been sold, whether they be Jewish persons or property, let them be released, the persons into their original state and the property to its former owners. **322** I also desire that anyone who does not obey this decree of mine shall suffer punishment; and, if caught, I will take care to prosecute the offender according to his deserts."' **323** He wrote the same to the Sidonians, Antiochians and Aradians. I have presented these opportunely as evidence for what I have stated: that the Romans showed consideration towards our people.

14.34 Appian *Civil Wars* 5.1.8–11: Antony meets Cleopatra

As one of Rome's client rulers, Cleopatra was summoned to meet Antony in 41 BC while he was in Cilicia. According to Plutarch (*Ant.* 26) she sailed up the River Cydnus in a barge with gilded stern, oars of silver and sails of purple, dressed like Venus and fanned by boys like Cupids. Antony spent the winter of 41–40 in Egypt with Cleopatra, and their twins were born in 40, a year after their meeting.

8 Antony was struck with her intelligence as well as her appearance and was immediately taken with her, just as if he were a young man, although he was now 40 years of age. It was said that he was always very susceptible in such matters and that he had developed an interest in her at first sight long ago, when she was still a girl, when he was serving as a young man as master of horse under Gabinius' command at Alexandria (55 BC). **9** Antony's concern for public affairs up to this point immediately vanished, and whatever Cleopatra ordered transpired, with no regard for sanctity or justice. Though her sister Arsinoe was a suppliant at the temple of Artemis Leukophryne at Miletus, Antony sent there and had her put to death, and Serapion, Cleopatra's governor in Cyprus, who had fought alongside Cassius and was now a suppliant at Tyre, he ordered the Tyrians to hand over to her, and he instructed the Aradians to hand over another suppliant who, when Cleopatra's brother Ptolemy disappeared at the sea battle against Caesar on the Nile, said he was Ptolemy and whom the Aradians held. . . . **10** He did not wait for the troubles in Syria to settle but distributed his army to winter in the provinces while he himself went to Egypt to Cleopatra. **11** She received him with magnificence, and he spent the winter there without any of his insignia as a commander, adopting the dress and lifestyle of an ordinary person, either because he was in a country under foreign sovereignty in a royal city or because he considered his winter stay as a holiday, as he even laid aside the concerns and retinue of a general and wore the square-cut Greek garment instead of that of his own country and the white Attic shoe which the Athenian and Alexandrian priests wear, called the phaikesion. His excursions were made only to the temples, gymnasia and debates of the philosophers, and under Cleopatra's influence he spent his time with Greeks, to whom he dedicated the whole period of his stay.

14.35 *RDGE* 60: Parthians devastate the East

According to hostile sources, the Parthians took opportunity of Antony's stay in Egypt to attack Roman Asia Minor and took Syria, Palestine and even parts of northern Asia Minor.

This letter of Octavian's, written to the city of Mylasa in Caria in 31 BC, highlights its sufferings during the Parthian invasion in 40–39 led by Labienus. The city was still in a critical financial condition in 31.

A Imperator Caesar, son of the god Julius, installed as consul for the third time, to the Mylasan magistrates, council and people, greetings. If you are well, **5** it is good. I too, with my army, am in health. You sent to me formerly concerning the adversity that oppresses you, and now your **10** envoys have come to me, Ouliades, ... **B** of the enemy to have fallen, and your city conquered, and many of your citizens lost as prisoners of war, not a few murdered, and some burnt along with the city, **5** with the brutality of the enemy sparing neither the shrines nor the most sacred temples. They have informed me about your plundered land and the farm buildings that have been torched, **10** resulting in your meeting with every misfortune. With regard to all these, I am aware that you who have suffered this are men who deserve every honour and favour from the Romans . . .

EVENTS IN ITALY

In 40 BC both armies were keen for compromise. At Brundisium the terms after Philippi were mostly replicated, except that Octavian was now recognised as controlling Gaul. Essentially Lepidus had been sidelined and the empire was divided into East and West, with Antony in control of the East but with Octavian having the advantage of being clearly based in Italy, even though he had the almost impossible task of combatting Sextus Pompeius and his fleet. As Fulvia had died, to ratify this arrangement Antony married Octavian's sister Octavia Minor. Both Antony and Octavian went to Rome, where they were awarded ovations, and coins were struck featuring them both, together with the head of Concordia.

14.36 Appian *Civil Wars* 5.7.64–8.68: The treaty of Brundisium, 40 BC

The pact of Brundisium took place in 40 BC, probably in September (Dio 48.28.3–29.1). However, heavy taxation was again imposed, including an inheritance tax and one on slaves, and Pompeius continued his blockade of grain ships. Riots took place in November 40 BC, and Antony's intervention was necessary to save Octavian from being stoned by the mob. Ahenobarbus, who had been in charge of the liberators' fleet, had joined Antony.

7.64 When Caesar's army learnt these facts they chose envoys and sent the same ones to both commanders, taking no notice of accusations because they had been selected not to decide between them but to make peace. They added Cocceius to their number as a friend of both, as well as Pollio from Antony's side and Maecenas from Caesar's, and determined that there should be an amnesty for the past between Caesar and Antony and friendship for the future. Furthermore, as Marcellus, who had married Octavia, Caesar's sister, had only just died, the adjudicators decided that Caesar should betroth Octavia to Antony, which he did straightaway. The two men embraced each other, and shouts and good wishes to each of them went up from the army without ceasing throughout the whole day and night. **65** Caesar and Antony once again partitioned the whole Roman empire between them, their boundary being at Scodra, an Illyrian city supposed to be halfway up the Illyrian gulf. All nations and islands east of this as far as the River Euphrates were to be Antony's and all west of it as far as the Ocean to Caesar. Lepidus was to govern Africa, as Caesar had given it to him. Caesar was to make war on Pompeius, unless they came to terms, and Antony on the Parthians to avenge their treachery towards Crassus. Caesar was to make the same agreement with Ahenobarbus that Antony had. Each could raise an army in equal numbers in Italy without interference. These were the last peace terms in place between Caesar and Antony. Each of them immediately sent his friends to deal with crisis situations, Antony dispatching Ventidius to Asia against the Parthians and Labienus, son of Labienus, who with the Parthians had invaded Syria and reached as far as Ionia in the recent hostilities. . . .

8.67 The Romans were now oppressed with famine, since the Eastern merchants were unable to put to sea for fear of Pompeius and his Sicilian base, and those of the West for fear of Sardinia and Corsica, which were under the power of Pompeius' officers, while those from the African coast were prevented by both of these as they controlled both coastlines. The prices of everything rose, and the people put this down to the conflict between the leaders and abused them, urging them to make peace with Pompeius. As Caesar would not comply with this, Antony counselled him to hurry up the war because of the shortage. As there was no money for this, a decree was published that the owners of slaves should pay a tax for each of them of one-half of the 25 drachmas that had been laid down for the war against Cassius and Brutus, and that anyone receiving a testamentary legacy should contribute a proportion. The people tore down this document with violent rage, infuriated that, after draining the public treasury, stripping the provinces bare, and loading Italy itself down with imposts, taxes and confiscations, not for foreign wars or for expanding the empire but against personal enemies and to increase their own power – which was why the proscriptions and executions and horrific famine had come about – they should rob them of whatever they had left. Thronging together, they shouted their protest and stoned those who did not join them, threatening to ransack and set fire to their houses, **68** until the whole populace was enraged and Caesar with his friends, and a few attendants came among them intending to make them see sense and reason away their grievances. As soon as they caught sight of him they started stoning him unmercifully and were not even ashamed of themselves when he patiently tolerated this and allowed them to continue even though he was wounded. When Antony heard of this he came urgently to his assistance. When they saw him coming down the Via Sacra they did not stone him, because he was in favour of making peace with Pompeius, but told him to go away – when he refused they stoned him as well. He called in more troops who were outside the walls. As they still would not let him pass through, the troops divided to each side of the street and forum and attacked from the narrow ways, killing those they met: the people were unable to escape easily, being hemmed in by the crowd and no longer having an exit route, while there transpired a scene of slaughter and wounds with laments and cries from the rooftops. Antony made his way through with difficulty and snatched Caesar away from the obvious danger he was currently facing and got him safe to his house.

When the populace dispersed, the corpses were thrown into the river to prevent the sight of them causing too much distress. A further reason for lamentation was the sight of them floating down the river and of the soldiers, along with certain malefactors, stripping the bodies and carrying off the better quality clothing as their own. This affair was terminated at the cost of fear and hatred of the leaders, while the famine grew worse and the people kept up their complaints – but quietly.

14.37 Appian *Civil Wars* 5.8.72–74: The treaty of Misenum, 39 BC

Following the riots in Rome, in 39 BC Octavian, Antony and Pompeius signed a treaty at Misenum (also known as the treaty of Puteoli). Pompeius now had a fleet of some 250 vessels, and in this agreement he was granted Corsica, Sicily, Sardinia and the Peloponnese for five years, as well as the consulship for 33. The reaction of the people, who sacrificed to Antony and Octavian 'as if to saviours', shows the hardships which the ongoing conflict had caused.

72 Finally, at the urging of Pompeius' mother Mucia and his wife Julia, the three men met on the mole at Puteoli, washed on both sides by the waves, with ships anchored round it as protection, and agreed to the following terms: that the war between them both by land and sea should be terminated and that trade should be unhindered everywhere; that Pompeius should remove whatever garrisons he had in Italy and no longer receive runaway slaves or blockade the coast of Italy with his ships; that he should govern Sardinia, Sicily and Corsica, and all islands then in his possessions, as long as Antony and Caesar governed the others; that he should send to the Romans the grain that had long been laid down as tribute from these islands, and possess the Peloponnese as well as these; that he should hold the consulship in absentia through any friend he might designate; and that he should be listed among the priests of the highest college. These conditions pertained to Pompeius: the aristocrats still in exile could return, except those condemned by vote of the senate or a court ruling as involved in the murder of Gaius Caesar; the property of the rest, who had gone into exile through fear and whose possessions had been seized by violence, were to be restored in their entirety except for moveable property, while the proscribed would receive a fourth of theirs. Slaves who had served in Pompeius' army were to be free, and free persons, on their discharge, were to receive the same gratuities as those serving under Caesar and Antony. **73** These were the agreed terms, which they signed and sealed, and sent to Rome to be guarded by the Vestal Virgins. . . . The daughter of Pompeius (the granddaughter of Libo) was betrothed to Marcellus, the stepson of Antony and nephew of Caesar. On the following day they designated the consuls for the next four years: first Antony and Libo (34 BC), with Antony able to substitute anyone he chose for himself, then Octavian and Pompeius (33 BC), Ahenobarbus and Sosius (32 BC) and, finally, Antony and Octavian again (31 BC), and, as they would both have been consuls a third time, it was hoped that they would then restore the government to the people. **74** When this was completed, they went their different ways: Pompeius sailed to Sicily, and Caesar and Antony travelled to Rome. When the city and Italy learnt of this, there was immediate and universal praise for the restoration of peace, as they had been released from civil war, the conscription of their sons, the arrogance of guards, the running away of slaves, the plundering of fields, the devastation of agriculture and, above all, the famine, which had utterly oppressed them. In consequence, as they made their journey, sacrifices were offered to them as if to saviours, and the city would have received them illustriously had they not entered Rome by night and secretly to avoid resentment.

14.38 Cornelius Nepos *Life of Atticus* 19.4–20.5: Octavian, Antony and Atticus

Atticus remained a close friend and adviser to both Antony and Octavian despite their political differences; cf. doc. 14.38.

19.4 Atticus had a granddaughter by Agrippa, to whom he gave his daughter in her first marriage. This granddaughter, when hardly a year old, Caesar betrothed to his stepson Tiberius Claudius Nero, son of (Livia) Drusilla, an alliance which formally strengthened their friendly relationship and ensured that they spent even more time together.

20.1 Even before this betrothal, whenever Caesar was away from the city he never sent letters to any of his other friends without writing to Atticus what he was doing, particularly what he was reading, where he was and how long he was going to stay there. **2** In fact, even when he was in the city, but because of his countless commitments was unable to enjoy Atticus' company as much as he wished, hardly a single day passed when he did not write to him, either asking him some query about olden times or requesting his opinion on some passage of poetry, as well as teasing him to get him to write longer letters. **3** It was on account of this rapport, when the temple of Jupiter Feretrius on the Capitol, which Romulus had erected, was roofless and falling into disrepair through age and lack of care, that Caesar had it restored on Atticus' advice. **4** Mark Antony also kept up a correspondence with Atticus, despite the distance, and took care to send him full details of what he was doing even from the ends of the earth. **5** What this involved will be more easily understood by someone able to judge how much wisdom it takes to retain the friendship and goodwill of men who were not only rivals in the most momentous undertakings, but also such adversaries as Caesar and Antony were bound to become when each of them wanted to be the princeps (chief man) not only of the city of Rome but of the entire world.

14.39 Dio *Roman History* 48.44.1–5: Livia's 'three-months child'

In 40 BC Octavian had married Scribonia, the sister of Pompeius' father-in-law; he divorced her the day she gave birth to Julia, his only child. The marriage to Livia apparently took place on 17 January 38. Livia's first husband, T. Claudius Nero, had supported Lucius Antonius, Mark Antony and, finally, Pompeius.

1 Besides these occurrences at this time, Caesar married Livia. She was the daughter of Livius Drusus, who had been one of those proscribed on the register and committed suicide after the defeat in Macedonia, and the wife of Nero, whom she accompanied in his flight, as told earlier: she was in her sixth month of pregnancy by him. **2** Caesar was hesitant, at any rate, and asked the pontifices if it would be permissible to marry her while she was pregnant. They replied that if there were any doubt as to whether conception had taken place they should put back the marriage, but if this was agreed there was nothing to prevent its taking place now. Perhaps they actually found this in the ancient rulings, but even if they had not found it, they would certainly have said so. **3** Her husband gave her away like any other father – and at the feast the following incident took place: a little boy, one of the chatterers which women keep for fun, naked as a rule, on seeing Livia on one side reclining with Caesar, and on another Nero with some other man, went up to her and said, 'What are you doing here, lady? Your husband', pointing him out, 'is reclining over there.' **4** This is what occurred, and when the woman was living with Caesar she gave birth to Claudius Drusus Nero. Caesar both acknowledged him and sent him to his father, writing in his memoranda that 'Caesar returned to his father Nero the baby born by Livia, his wife.' **5** Nero died not long afterwards and left Caesar himself as guardian to this child and Tiberius. The populace gossiped a great deal about this and among other things said that 'The lucky have children in three months', a remark which passed into a proverb.

14.40 Livy *Periochae* 127–29: The end of Sextus Pompeius

In 38 BC Octavian's fleet was twice defeated by Sextus, off Cumae and in the Straits of Messana. Antony returned to Italy early in 37 and met Octavian at Tarentum, where a further agreement was reached: the role of Octavia in reaching a compromise was said to be crucial, and she appears on coins in 37–36. The triumvirate, which had lapsed in 38, was renewed for a further five-year term. The decisive battle against Sextus was fought on 3 September 36 off Naulochus under Agrippa: due to Agrippa's tactics, only 17 of Sextus' 300 ships escaped, and some 30,000 slaves were returned to their owners (6,000 without owners were crucified). When Lepidus then tried to take command of the combined land force, the troops supported Octavian, and Lepidus lost his command and membership of the triumvirate.

127 When Mark Antony . . . to make war on Caesar . . . his wife Fulvia, so that nothing should hinder harmony between the leaders, he made peace with Caesar and married his sister Octavia. He revealed that Quintus Salvidenus, on his own evidence, had engaged in nefarious plots against Caesar, and he was condemned and committed suicide. . . . As Sextus Pompeius, an enemy on Italy's doorstep, controlled Sicily and was hampering the grain trade, Caesar and Antony made peace with him at his request, on the terms that he should hold Sicily as a province. The book also covers the insurgence in Africa and the wars conducted there. **128** When Sextus Pompeius again made the sea unsafe by acts of piracy and did not keep to the peace he had agreed, Caesar undertook the necessary war against him and fought two naval battles with no definite outcome (38 BC). . . . The book also covers the preparations for war in Sicily (37 BC). **129** Naval battles with disparate outcomes were fought against Sextus Pompeius, in that one of Caesar's two fleets, commanded by Agrippa, was successful, while the other, led by Caesar, was wiped out and the soldiers who had been disembarked on land were in serious danger. Afterwards Pompeius was defeated and fled to Sicily (36 BC). Marcus Lepidus crossed from Africa as if to join Caesar in waging war against Sextus Pompeius, but when he also attacked Caesar he was deserted by his army and lost his position on the Board of Three; however, he was successful in begging for his life. Marcus Agrippa was awarded a naval crown by Caesar, an honour which no one before him had held.

14.41 Appian *Civil Wars* 5.13.130, 132: Octavian pacifies Italy, 36 BC

Octavian celebrated an ovatio for the victory over Pompeius on 13 November 36 BC, and a golden statue of him was set up in the forum on a column decorated with ships' rams. Emergency and unpaid taxes could now be cancelled. Octavian did not receive the tribuneship for life in 36 (this was in 23) but only tribunician sacrosanctity (Dio 49.15.5), perhaps reflecting that given to Caesar in 44. Maecenas was made responsible for the government of Rome (Dio 49.16).

130 When he arrived at Rome the senate voted him countless honours, of which they made him the arbiter as to whether he should accept all or as many as he might choose. They and the people, crowned with garlands, went an exceptional distance to meet him and when he arrived escorted him to the temples and then from the temples to his house. The following day he delivered speeches to the senate and to the people, detailing his actions and his policy from the beginning to the present: he also wrote down these speeches and published them in written form. He proclaimed peace and harmony, stated that the civil wars had come to an end, and released from their obligations those who still had taxes owing, as well as both the tax-collectors and farmers of contracts. Of the honours voted him he accepted an ovation, annual supplications on the days of his victories, and a golden statue of himself, in the dress in which he entered the city, on a column in the forum surrounded by the beaks of ships. The portrait was erected there with the inscription: 'Peace which had long been disrupted he re-established by land and sea.' . . . **132** This now seemed to be the end of the civil conflicts. Caesar at that point was 28 years of age. Cities dedicated statues of him alongside their own gods. Rome itself and Italy were openly plagued with companies of robbers, whose activities seemed more like audacious looting than surreptitious robbery, and Sabinus, who was chosen by Caesar to deal with this, executed many of those he captured and in a year had brought everything into a state of total security, and it was from this, they say, that there today exists the practice and structure of the force of nightwatchmen. Caesar caused amazement at the unprecedented speed with which this was resolved, and he allowed the annual magistrates to administer public affairs, in most instances, according to tradition. He also burnt records which pertained to the civil conflict and said that he would restore the constitution in its entirety when Antony returned from the Parthian wars – as he was convinced that Antony would also be prepared to lay down his magistracy now the civil wars were over. Consequently the people acclaimed him and appointed him as tribune for life, encouraging him through this permanent magistracy to relinquish his former one. He accepted this and wrote of his own accord to Antony regarding the government. Antony instructed Bibulus, who was leaving him, to meet with Caesar. Like him, he dispatched governors to his provinces and considered joining in his campaign against the Illyrians.

ANTONY, CLEOPATRA AND PARTHIA

During Antony's absence in Italy, in 39 BC Ventidius had defeated Labienus and the Parthians were pushed back across the Euphrates, with Pacorus being killed at the battle of Cyrrestica in June 38. After wintering in Athens, Antony went east early in 38 and in a further reorganisation of the Eastern provinces appears to have given Cleopatra Cyprus and part of Cilicia, perhaps to provide timber to strengthen his fleet, to which he later added further domains, including Crete and Cyrene. As part of his religious policy Antony appears to have continued to emphasise his identification with Dionysus (Dio 48.39.2). While Antony had given the promised ships to Octavian after the agreement at Tarentum, Octavian had not handed over the legions to Antony as he had agreed. There was now a break between the two, and Antony did not return to Octavia. Some four years after their previous meeting, Cleopatra met Antony again in Syria in 37, and in 36 she bore him Ptolemy Philadelphus. After his defeats by the Parthians in 36, Antony conquered Armenia in 34 and celebrated a triumph at Alexandria (not Rome), after which he formally granted Roman territories to Cleopatra and their children and recognised the legitimacy of Caesar's son Caesarion.

14.42 Livy *Periochae* 127–30: Events in the East, 40–36 BC

Criticisms of Antony's conduct of the Parthian campaign in 36 are unfair, but he did lose one-third of his army, mainly as a result of the defection of Artavasdes of Armenia and the unfavourable conditions during their retreat, in which they covered 300 miles in 21 days.

127 The Parthians invaded Syria under the command of Labienus, who was one of the Pompeian side, defeated Decidius Saxa, the legate of Mark Antony, and overran that entire province (40 BC). . . . Publius Ventidius, Antony's legate, defeated the Parthians in a battle and expelled them from Syria after their leader Labienus was killed (39 BC). . . . **128** Publius Ventidius, Antony's legate, defeated the Parthians in a battle in Syria and killed their king. The Jews were also conquered by Antony's legates. . . . **130** While Mark Antony was living it up with Cleopatra, he finally invaded Media and made war on the Parthians with 18 legions and 16,000 cavalry. After two legions were lost he withdrew with no favourable outcomes at all. The Parthians then came after him, but after great panic and serious risk to his whole army he returned to Armenia, covering 300 miles in 21 days in his flight. He lost some 8,000 men to bad weather. He met with these violent storms, in addition to the ill-starred Parthian war he had undertaken, through his own fault, as he was averse to wintering in Armenia because of his haste to return to Cleopatra (36 BC).

14.43 Plutarch *Life of Antony* 54.1–55.4: The 'Donations of Alexandria', 34 BC

In line with Octavian's propaganda at the time, Plutarch here depicts Antony as an Eastern ruler and a threat to Rome and its standards. At this point the twins Alexander Helios and Cleopatra Selene were six and Ptolemy two years of age. Antony's 'donations' suggested in Rome dynastic ambitions, and there were concerns about coins which featured the heads of Antony and Cleopatra, including one celebrating the Armenian triumph (doc. 14.44). While it was quite acceptable in the East for Cleopatra to identify herself with Isis and Antony with Dionysus or Osiris, as Isis' consort, this was capable of serious misinterpretation in the West.

54.1 Octavia was thought to have been treated with ignominy, and Caesar instructed her on her return from Athens to reside in her own house. **2** But she refused to leave her husband's residence and begged Caesar, unless he intended to make war on Antony on other grounds, to ignore his behaviour to her, since it would be monstrous to have it reported that the Romans were forced into civil war by their two greatest commanders, one out of passionate love for, and the other out of resentment on behalf of, a woman. **3** Her words were supported by her actions – for she lived in his house, just as if her husband were there himself, and took care of his children, not only her own but those by Fulvia, considerately and generously; **4** she also welcomed those of Antony's friends who were sent to Rome in pursuit of magistracies or business and gave them assistance in obtaining what they wanted from Caesar. **5** Unintentionally, however, she was damaging Antony by her conduct, for he was detested for his ill-treatment of such a woman. He was detested too for the distribution of his property which he put into effect in Alexandria for his children, which was seen as theatrical and arrogant and showing a hatred of Rome. **6** For he had a crowd fill the gymnasium, where he set up on a silver dais two golden thrones, one for himself and the other for Cleopatra, with lower ones for his children, and first of all proclaimed Cleopatra queen of Egypt, Cyprus, Libya and Coele Syria, with Caesarion as her co-ruler (he was believed to be a son of the earlier Caesar, who had left Cleopatra pregnant). **7** Then he proclaimed his own sons by Cleopatra to be Kings of Kings and bestowed on Alexander Armenia, Media and Parthia, as soon as it was conquered, and on Ptolemy Phoenicia, Syria and Cilicia. **8** At the same time he presented his sons publicly, Alexander in Median dress with a tiara and upright headdress and Ptolemy in boots, short cloak, and a broad-brimmed hat crowned with a diadem. The latter was the attire of the kings who succeeded Alexander, while the former was that of the Medes and Armenians. **9** When the children had embraced their parents, the one was given a bodyguard of Armenians and the other of Macedonians. Cleopatra, then as always when she appeared in public, wore a robe sacred to Isis and was addressed as the New Isis. **55.1** By reporting this behaviour to the senate and by frequently denouncing Antony before the people, Caesar kept rousing the anger of the populace against Antony. **2** Antony for his part kept sending counter-accusations against him. The main ones he brought were that, first, when he captured Sicily from Sextus Pompeius, he had not given him any share of the island; next, that having had the use of some of Antony's ships for the war he hung onto them; **3** thirdly, that after depriving his colleague Lepidus of office and demoting him, he kept the army, territory and revenues assigned to Lepidus; and, finally, that he had distributed almost all of Italy in allotments to his own soldiers and left nothing for Antony's. **4** Caesar's response to these accusations was that he had deposed Lepidus from his position because he was misusing it, and with regard to his conquests in war he would share these with Antony as soon as Antony shared Armenia with him. Moreover Antony's soldiers had no claim on Italy as they had Media and Parthia, which they had added to Roman territory by their gallant campaigns under their general.

14.44 Crawford *RRC* 179: Coinage of Antony and Cleopatra

A silver denarius, 32–31 (East) with the legend in Latin. This was the first portrait of a non-Roman woman on an official coin with a Latin inscription.

Obverse: Head of Antony, bareheaded, alongside an Armenian tiara. *Legend*: Of Antony. Armenia defeated.

Reverse: Bust of Cleopatra, wearing diadem, with a ship's prow. *Legend*: Of Cleopatra, queen of kings and of her sons who are kings.

14.45 Plutarch *Life of Antony* 27.3–4: Cleopatra VII

Cleopatra VII Philopator ('father-loving'), born in 70/69 BC, had ruled Egypt with two of her brothers, Ptolemy XIII and XIV, in succession. As Caesar's mistress, she was in Rome at the time of his assassination, when she returned to Egypt with her son Caesarion, ruling with him as her co-regent. The Ptolemaic dynasty in general spoke Greek, but Cleopatra also spoke Egyptian and represented herself as the incarnation of the goddess Isis.

3 It is said that her beauty, in and of itself, was not incomparable, nor such as to astound those that saw her, but her conversation was alluring and her appearance, together with her eloquence in conversing and the way her personality captivated those with whom she associated, produced an animating stimulation. **4** The very tone of her speech was delightful, and she could turn her tongue skilfully like a many-stringed instrument to whatever language she wanted, needing an interpreter in meetings with only a few non-Greek speakers while giving her replies to most of them on her own, for instance Ethiopians, Troglodytes, Hebrews, Arabs, Syrians, Medes and Parthians. It is also said that she knew the languages of many others as well, although the kings of Egypt before her had not even made the effort to learn the Egyptian language, and some of them had even left off speaking Macedonian.

14.46 Livy *Periochae* 131–32: Events 36–31 BC

The first military victory which Octavian achieved in his own right (rather than relying on Antony or Agrippa) was in Illyria. In the East, Pompeius was then found to be intriguing with the Parthians and was killed by Titius, one of Antony's generals. In 33 BC Octavian continued to refuse to Antony the opportunity to raise troops in Italy and find lands for his veterans and spoke against the 'donations' to Cleopatra's children in the senate.

131 Although Sextus Pompeius had put himself under Mark Antony's protection, he started planning to make war on him in Asia, and was surprised by his legates and killed (36–35 BC). Caesar put down a devastating insurgence among the veterans and subdued the Iapydae, Dalmatians and Pannonians (35 BC). Antony successfully tricked Artavasdes, king of Armenia, by pledging his good faith, but then ordered him to be thrown in chains and gave the kingdom of Armenia to his son by Cleopatra, with whom he had long been passionately in love and whom he now began to treat as his wife (34 BC). **132** Caesar overcame the Dalmatians in Illyricum (34–33 BC). Mark Antony, because of his passion for Cleopatra, by whom he had two sons, Philadelphus and Alexander, was unwilling to return to the city or lay down his command when his term on the Board of Three was completed and made plans for a war against the city and Italy; he assembled huge forces by sea and on land for this purpose, as well as sending notice of divorce to Octavia, Caesar's sister. Caesar crossed to Epirus with his army. The naval battles and cavalry engagements which followed, in which Caesar was successful, are described in this book.

PROPAGANDA AND INVECTIVE

While Octavian and his supporters were careful to broadcast at Rome the degree to which Antony was 'going native' in Egypt and showing his lack of respect for Roman traditions and institutions, it is clear that his relationship with Cleopatra was not 'a marriage' *per se* and was to some degree based on his reliance on Egypt's resources and their value to Rome and his own armies. To counter these attacks over his passion for Cleopatra, as well as over his supposedly degenerate and drunken lifestyle, Antony produced counter-propaganda to damage Octavian's reputation, portraying him as a hypocrite whose morals were equally as questionable as his own. However, Octavian had the advantage of geography in that he could ensure the support of Italy, while Antony's power base was in the East and he had no chance to present his own case in person.

14.47 Pliny *Natural History* 14.147–48: Antony's 'drunkenness'

Antony's work on his own drunkenness, written shortly before Actium, was presumably intended to answer accusations about his intemperance, which date back at least to Cicero's *Philippics* (cf. doc. 14.1). The author Tergilla is not known. A congius is approximately 3.5 litres.

147 Tergilla rebukes Cicero, the son of Marcus, for being in the habit of gulping down two congii at a single go, and with having thrown a cup (scyphus) at Marcus Agrippa when intoxicated. These are the normal works of inebriation. But it is no wonder that Cicero wanted to surpass the fame of Mark Antony, his father's murderer. **148** Antony, before young Cicero's time, had grasped so eagerly at being champion in this line that he even published a book about his own drunkenness, and dared in his own defence to prove indubitably, in my view, how many evils he had brought upon the world by his intemperance. It was a short time before the battle of Actium that he vomited forth this book, from which it can be easily understood that, drunk as he already was with the blood of citizens, he thirsted for it all the more. For it is an inescapable consequence of this vice that habitual drinking increases the eagerness for it, which is why the Parthians crave it so much.

14.48 Propertius *Elegies* 3.11, 29–72: Cleopatra demonised

Cleopatra was a frequent theme of Roman poets, particularly after her defeat and death. Here Propertius was writing some ten years after Actium: cf. docs 15.11 (Vergil), 16.31 (Horace).

What of she who recently heaped disgrace on our soldiers –

30 A woman worn out by her own household slaves,
Who demanded as the price of her foul marriage
The walls of Rome and senators under her rule?
Pernicious Alexandria, land most adept at guile,
And Memphis, so often bloody from our woe,
Where the sand robbed Pompey of his three triumphs –
Rome, no day will blot out this stain for you!
Better for you, had your funeral taken place on the Phlegraean plain,
Or you had bowed your neck to your father-in-law (Julius Caesar).
Truly, that harlot queen of incestuous Canopus,

40 Our only stigma branded by Philip's blood,
Dared to oppose yapping Anubis to our Jove,
To compel Tiber to endure the threats of Nile,
To repulse the Roman trumpet with clattering sistrum,
To pursue Liburnian rams with punted barges,
To stretch odious mosquito-nets over the Tarpeian rock,
And give judgements among Marius' arms and statues!
What was the use of breaking Tarquin's axes,
Whose proud life brands him with like name,
If a woman must be endured? Sing triumph!, Rome,

50 And in your safety pray long life for Augustus!
You fled, then, to the wandering streams of cowardly Nile:
Your hands received Romulus' chains.
I saw your arms bitten by sacred serpents,
Your limbs draw in the secret path of sleep.
'I was not to be feared, Rome, with such a citizen as him!'
So spoke the tongue engulfed in constant wine.
The city high on its seven hills, which governs the whole world,
In terror feared the threats of a female Mars.
The gods founded these walls, the gods protect them:

60   With Caesar living, Rome hardly need fear Jove.
       Where now are Scipio's ships, where Camillus' standards,
       Or Bosphorus, lately captured by Pompey's hand?
       Hannibal's spoils and conquered Syphax's monuments,
       Pyrrhus' glory shattered at our feet?
       Curtius set up his monument when he filled the lake,
       Decius broke the line with charging horse,
       Cocles' path attests the broken bridge,
       And there's one to whom the raven (corvus) gave his name.
       Apollo of Leucas (Actium) will call to mind the shattered battle-line:

70   One day destroyed a battle-array so great.
       But you, sailor, whether seeking port or leaving it,
       Through all the Ionian Sea remember Caesar.

14.49 Suetonius *Life of the Deified Augustus* 10, 11, 15, 27, 68–70: Antony's propaganda

Antony was not the only one whose reputation was vilified (cf. doc. 14.1). His counter-propaganda against Octavian is demonstrated here, and, like Octavian in his attack on Fulvia (doc. 14.30), he is stressing his own masculinity and Roman plain speaking. At 70.2, Antony's letter can be dated to 32 BC: Terentilla was the wife of Maecenas; Antony is portraying Octavian as a hypocrite for attacking his relationship with Cleopatra.

10.3 On the advice of certain people Octavian hired assassins to kill Antony and then, fearing retaliation when the plot was uncovered, recruited veterans for the protection of himself and the state using all possible funds. He was put in command of the army he had raised with the rank of propraetor and dispatched along with Hirtius and Pansa, who had become consuls, to assist Decimus Brutus, ending the war he had been assigned in three months and two battles. **4** In the first of these, Antony writes, he ran away and reappeared only two days later without his cloak and horse; but in the following one it is agreed that he played the part not only of a commander but of a soldier too, and in the midst of the battle, when his legion's eagle-bearer was badly wounded, he raised the eagle on his shoulders and carried it for some time. **11** As Hirtius died in battle during this war and Pansa shortly afterwards from a wound, rumour spread that both deaths were his work, so that, with Antony put to flight and the state without consuls, he might have total control of the victorious armies. Pansa's death was so particularly suspicious that Glyko, the doctor, was imprisoned on the charge of administering poison to the wound. Aquilius Niger adds that he killed the other consul Hirtius in the confusion of the fray. . . .

13.1 Then in alliance with Antony and Lepidus he also completed the war of Philippi in two battles, although he was indisposed and unwell, in the first being driven from his camp and only just managing to escape by fleeing to Antony's wing. He did not behave with moderation in his victory but had Brutus' head sent to Rome to be thrown at the feet of Caesar's statue, and he raged violently even at the most distinguished prisoners, not without the most abusive language. **2** For example, to one man who humbly requested burial, he is said to have replied, 'That is for the birds to decide', and in another case, when a father and son begged for their lives, to have told them to draw lots or play toss-and-catch to see which would be spared, and then to have watched while both died, since the father was executed after he volunteered, and the son then took his own life. As a result the rest, when they were led out in chains, one of whom was Marcus Favonius, the well-known emulator of Cato, saluted Antony courteously with the title 'Imperator' but reviled Augustus to his face with the most violent abuse. . . . **15** After the capture of Perusia he took vengeance on a large number of persons, answering all those who attempted to beg for pardon or excuse their actions with the one rejoinder, 'You must die!' Some write that 300 men from both (the senatorial and equestrian) orders were selected from the prisoners of war and slaughtered on the Ides of March on the altar raised in honour of the Deified Julius, just like sacrificial victims. Some have recorded that he had a specific aim in going to war, that his secret adversaries, and those whom fear rather than goodwill kept on his side, might be unmasked by giving them the opportunity of imitating Lucius Antonius, and once they were defeated using their confiscated estates to pay the bounties promised to his veterans. . . .

27.3 While he was triumvir his acts brought him universal odium. For example, on one occasion he was addressing his soldiers at an assembly when a crowd of countrymen were admitted, and he noticed that the Roman knight Pinarius was taking notes and, thinking him to be a spy and snooper, ordered him to be run through on the spot. And when Tedius Afer, consul-elect, criticised some action of his in very savage language, he terrified him with such dreadful threats that he hurled himself to his death; **4** similarly, when the praetor Quintus Gallus was holding a two-leaved tablet under his robe when paying his respects (salutatio), he suspected that he had a sword concealed and, not daring to have him searched immediately, in case it might be found to be something different, shortly afterwards had him seized from his tribunal by centurions and soldiers, had him tortured like a slave and ordered his execution, even though he admitted nothing, first gouging out his eyes with his own hands. However, he records that, after requesting an audience with him, Gallus treacherously attacked him and that he had him sent to prison, after which he was banished from the city and either died in a shipwreck or was ambushed by brigands. . . .

68 In his early youth he was subjected to disrepute for various forms of depravity. Sextus Pompeius upbraided him for effeminacy; Mark Antony for having earned his adoption by debauching himself to his great-uncle; and similarly Mark Antony's brother Lucius that, after surrendering his chastity to Caesar, he had prostituted himself to Aulus Hirtius in Spain for 300,000 sesterces and that he used to singe his legs with red-hot nutshells so the hair grew back softer. Moreover, one day when plays were being performed, the whole people took the following line as targeting him, joining in with loud applause when it was delivered on stage with reference to a eunuch priest of the Magna Mater as he beat his drum: 'Do you see how a sodomite rules the world with his finger?'

69.1 Not even his friends deny that he was given to adultery, although they condoned it as committed not from passion but from calculation, so he could more easily find out his opponents' plans through their womenfolk. Mark Antony accused him not only of his hurried marriage to Livia but of taking the wife of a man of consular rank from her husband's dining-room in his very presence into a bedroom, and bringing her back to the dinner party with blushing ears and dishevelled hair; that Scribonia was divorced because she complained too freely of the inappropriate influence of a mistress of his; that paramours were sought by his friends, who stripped and inspected matrons and fully grown girls as if Toranius the slave-dealer was offering them for sale. **2** Antony also writes to him in this familiar way before he was openly in conflict and on bad terms with him: 'What has changed you? Because I'm sleeping with the queen? Is she my wife? Of course not! Have I only just started or been doing it for nine years now? And are you screwing only Drusilla? Good luck to you, if when you read this letter you have not been inside Tertulla or Terentilla or Rufilla or Salvia Titisenia — or all of them! Does it make any difference where or whom you are fucking?' . . . **70.2** He was also criticised for his passion for expensive furniture and Corinthian bronzes and for his love of gaming – in fact, even at the time of the proscriptions, there was inscribed on his statue: 'My father was a money-dealer, and I'm now a Corinthian-bronze-dealer', since it was thought that he had had some men listed among the proscribed on account of their Corinthian bronzes. And later, during the Sicilian war, the following epigram did the rounds:

> 'Now he's been beaten twice at sea and lost his ships
> To ensure one victory he spends all his time at dice.'

CIVIL WAR

While Octavian, with the aid of Agrippa and his other supporters, was cleaning up and beautifying Rome, Antony was again concerned with Parthia, as in 33 BC he was planning another campaign, though his army returned to Ionia without engaging in one. The triumvirate came to an end on 31 December 33 and the consuls for 32, C. Sosius and Cn. Domitius Ahenobarbus, were strong Antonians (Dio 50.2 dates the start of war to early in 32). When Octavian surrounded himself with an armed guard in the senate the consuls fled to Antony at Ephesus, along with many other senators, whom Antony organised into an alternative senate. Octavia's divorce mid-year was a consequence of the need for Cleopatra and her troops to remain with the army (which also depended on Egyptian resources), though this was unpopular with a number of his subordinates; 200 of Antony's 800 warships were Egyptian. War was declared on Cleopatra as the foreign enemy; Antony was merely deprived of his consulship for 31. Antony had more funds (Octavian had had to raise emergency taxes) and 100,000 troops, against Octavian's 80,000, plus more numerous and heavier ships.

14.50 Plutarch *Life of Antony* 58.1–8: Preparations for war, 32 BC

In the lead up to war, the new taxation was again very unpopular, and at this point Octavian had an oath of personal loyalty taken to himself throughout Italy and the West. He may well have fabricated some of the terms of Antony's will to ensure support in Rome and Italy.

1 When Caesar heard of the speed and extent of Antony's preparations, he was alarmed in case he might be forced to fight the decisive engagement that summer – **2** for he lacked many things he needed, and people were unhappy at the taxes exacted, as citizens were compelled to pay one-quarter of their income and freedmen one-eighth of their property, and there were loud protests against him and disturbances from these causes throughout the whole of Italy. **3** Consequently, it is seen as one of Antony's greatest mistakes that he postponed the outbreak of war, for he gave Caesar time to make his preparations and put an end to people's disturbances, as while they were being taxed they were angry but once it had been exacted and they had paid up they stayed quiet. **4** Titius and Plancus, Antony's friends among the consulars, who had been insulted by Cleopatra (for they had been violently opposed to her accompanying the expedition), ran away to Caesar and informed him about Antony's will, of which they knew the terms. **5** It was deposited with the Vestal Virgins, and they did not give it to him at his request but told him if he wanted to take it to come and do so. **6** So he went and took it and first read the terms through by himself and marked some discreditable passages. He then assembled the senate and read it to them, though most of them thought this disgraceful – **7** as they thought it strange and awful that someone should be charged while alive with what he wanted to have done after his death. **8** He especially laid emphasis on the clause to do with his burial: for it instructed that Antony's body, even if he died in Rome, should be carried in procession through the forum and then sent to Alexandria to Cleopatra.

14.51 Velleius Paterculus *Compendium of Roman History* 2.84.1–87.3: Actium, 31 BC

Antony took his stand on the west coast of Greece and waited for Octavian. The role of Agrippa was crucial for Octavian's victory, and Antony's naval contingent had been seriously weakened before the decisive sea battle, and he seems to have planned for the option of flight. The critical battle took place on 2 September. Once Cleopatra and Antony had fled, leaving most of the fleet and army, Antony's remaining troops went over to Octavian. Despite his 'clemency', Octavian did have Caesarion and Antony's eldest son, Antyllus, put to death. Plutarch recounts how Antony committed suicide on hearing that Cleopatra was dead and how she drew up his body into her mausoleum for a final farewell. Octavian wanted Cleopatra for his triumph, and foiled two suicide attempts, but after nine days she employed an asp to kill herself along with her maids Iras and Charmion.

84.1 Then, in the consulship of Caesar and Messala Corvinus, matters were fought out at Actium, where long before the battle took place the victory of the Julian side was a foregone conclusion. On the one side, the soldiery and general were at their peak, on the other everything languished; on the one the rowers were unwavering, on the other weakened by hardship; on the one side ships of moderate size but not unsuitable for speed, on the other ones only apparently menacing; no one was deserting from his side to Antony, while from Antony's there was someone deserting to Caesar on a daily basis . . . **2** The distinguished Gnaeus Domitius, who alone of Antony's side refused to greet the queen except by name, defected to Caesar at the risk of very real danger to himself. Finally, in view of Antony and his fleet, Leucas was conquered by Marcus Agrippa and Patrai captured, Corinth was seized, and the enemy fleet was defeated twice before the final confrontation.

85.1 Then the day of the great confrontation arrived, when, with their fleets in battle formation, Caesar and Antony contended, the one for the safety, the other for the destruction of the world. **2** The right wing of the Julian fleet was led by Marcus Lurius, the left by Arruntius, while Agrippa had entire command of the conflict at sea; Caesar focused on any section of the battle where the fortunes of war ensured his help was needed and was everywhere at hand. Leadership of Antony's fleet was entrusted to Publicola and Sosius. Taurus commanded Caesar's land army, Canidius Antony's. **3** When the engagement began, on the one side was everything – commander, rowers and soldiers; on the other nothing except soldiers. Cleopatra was the first to take to flight. Antony made the choice of accompanying his queen in her flight rather than his soldiers in their struggle, and the commander who should have had the responsibility for severely disciplining deserters now deserted his own army. **4** Even in Antony's absence his men continued to fight bravely and loyally for some time and, with all hope of victory abandoned, contended to the death. Caesar, wishing to win over by words those whom he could have killed with the sword, kept shouting and pointing out that Antony had run away and kept asking for whom and with whom were they fighting? **5** After battling it out over a long period in the absence of their commander, they reluctantly put down their arms and admitted defeat, as Caesar had promised to spare their lives and pardon them even before they could force themselves to make this request; it was plain to see that the soldiers had acted the part of an ideal commander and the commander that of a faint-hearted soldier – **6** in fact you could ask whether in the case of victory he would have been guided by Cleopatra's decision or his own, since it was by her choice that he had turned to flight. The army on land also gave in when Canidius rushed in headlong flight after Antony.

86.1 What benefits this day bestowed upon the world and how it impacted on the good fortunes of the state who would dare recount in the space of so short a work? The victory was truly a most merciful one, and no one was put to death and extremely few were exiled – those who could not bring themselves to sue for pardon. . . . **87.1** The next year (30 BC) Caesar followed the queen and Antony to Alexandria and put the finishing touches to the civil war. As for Antony, he was not slow to kill himself, in this way clearing himself by his death from the many accusations of his indolence. Cleopatra, however, eluded her guards by having an asp introduced to her chambers and ended her life by means of its poisonous bite, showing herself unaffected by womanly fears. **2** It was typical of Caesar's fortune and clemency that he had none of those who had borne arms against him put to death – it was Antony's cruelty that had Decimus Brutus executed. As for Sextus Pompeius, even though conquered by Caesar, it was Antony again who deprived him of his life, although he had given his oath that his rank would be protected. **3** Brutus and Cassius, without waiting to discover their victors' plans for them, had died voluntary deaths.

14.52 Horace *Epodes* 9: Actium and its outcome

Cleopatra was demonised by Roman authors: in *Odes* 1.37 Cleopatra is described as a 'doom-laden monster', though Horace gives a positive view of her suicide: doc. 16.31, cf. doc. 15.11.

The Caecuban wine, put by for merry feasts,
When shall I, joyful at Caesar's victory,
With you in your lofty home – should Jove allow –
Fortunate Maecenas, drink it,
While the lyre sounds its flute-accompanied melodies,
One Dorian, one Phrygian.
How recently, driven from the strait, Neptune's son (Pompeius)
(General!), his ships all burned took flight,
Who threatened the city with the chains he'd torn

10 From faithless slaves he'd befriended.
Roman soldiers, alas! – Posterity, this you will not believe! –
Relinquished into a woman's power,
Bear palisades and weapons and endure
To serve wrinkled eunuchs,
While among our military standards (shame!)
The sun discerns mosquito-curtains.
To him with neighing steeds two thousand Gauls desert
With cries of 'Caesar',
And concealed in harbour sterns

20 Of enemy ships lurk in swift retreat.
Hail, Triumph! Do you delay the golden
Chariots and oxen never broken to the yoke?
Hail, Triumph! Even from Jugurtha's
War has there returned a leader equivalent to him? –
Even Scipio, to whom above the ruins of Carthage
Valour built a monument.
Beaten by land and sea the enemy
Has changed his cloak to one of Punic mourning.
Either to noble Crete with its one hundred towns

30 He plans to journey on unfavourable winds,
Or seeks the African sandbanks which the south wind stirs
Or wanders on the unpredictable sea.
Slave! Bring here more generous cups
And Chian wines or Lesbian –
Or to calm our queasy stomachs
Serve us out Caecuban.
Our anxiety and fear for Caesar's success, it's good
To wash away in Bacchus' sweet relaxing wine.

14.53 Plutarch *Life of Antony* 75.4–6: 'The god abandons Antony'

Octavian now commanded nearly 70 legions, and with some 40,000 veterans demanding land he needed to appropriate Egypt and its wealth. Alexandria fell on 1 August 31 BC, and the previous evening Octavian may have performed an evocation to tempt Egypt's gods to the Roman side (cf. doc. 3.57). Antony's entire fleet deserted. Antony had long associated himself in the East with Dionysus and Herakles, and his 'god' now leaves him to his fate.

4 During this night, it is reported, around the middle, when the city was quiet and low-spirited through fear and apprehension of what was going to happen, some melodious sounds of all kinds of musical instruments were suddenly heard and the shouting of a crowd, with Dionysiac cries and satyric leapings, as if a thiasos was clamorously departing the city; **5** their direction seemed to lie rather through the middle of the city towards the outer gate facing the enemy, where the clamour grew loudest, and then rushed out. **6** And those who sought to interpret the sign believed that it signified that the god was abandoning Antony – the god to whom he particularly likened and with whom he associated himself.

14.54 *Palatine Anthology* 6.236: A dedication from Actium

Written by Philippos, possibly in the second century AD. Octavian dedicated rostra from Antony's ships both at Actium and at Rome (Dio 51.1.3, 19.2).

> Bronze-toothed beaks, voyage-loving naval weapons
> Standing here as witnesses to the battle at Actium,
> We preserve as in a hive the waxy gifts of bees,
> Laden all around by the humming swarm.
> Excellent gift of Caesar's righteous government: for the weapons of enemies
> He has taught instead to bear the fruits of peace.

GAIUS CORNELIUS GALLUS

As praefectus fabrum (prefect of the engineers), Gallus took an important part in Octavian's Egyptian campaign after Actium. An eques, he was appointed by Octavian as the first prefect of Egypt and constructed a new forum, the Forum Julium, in or near Alexandria. He put down a revolt in the Thebaid and marched beyond the Second Cataract. His trilingual inscription at Philae (dated 15 April 29 BC), as well as inscriptions on the pyramids (Dio 53.23) and statues erected through Egypt, caused him to be recalled, and he was indicted and committed suicide in 27/26. He was also a poet and wrote four books of love elegies to 'Lycoris', apparently Cytheris, a past mistress of Mark Antony. Egypt was not made into a province but governed by an equestrian prefect appointed by Octavian (senators were not even allowed to go to Egypt without his permission).

14.55 *EJ* 374: The Forum Julium in Alexandria

AE 1964 255. The inscription, dated to c. 30 BC, was affixed to an obelisk in Egypt which was brought to Rome and then reused by the emperor Gaius. It now stands in St Peter's Square.

By order of Imperator Caesar, son of a god, Gaius Cornelius Gallus, son of Gnaeus, prefect of engineers of Caesar, son of a god, built the Forum Julium.

14.56 *ILS* 8995: The settlement of Egypt, 29 BC

An inscription in Greek and Latin set up by Gallus at Philae in Upper Egypt. The Latin version is translated here.

Gaius Cornelius Gallus, son of Gnaeus, Roman eques, after the kings had been defeated by Caesar, son of a god, first prefect of Alexandria and Egypt, put down the uprising of the Thebaid in 15 days, in which he defeated the enemy, and was victor in two pitched battles and conqueror of five cities, Boresis, Coptus, Ceramice, Diopsolis Magna and Opheieion. The leaders of these rebel cities were captured **5** and the army led beyond the cataract of the Nile, where neither the arms of the Roman people nor those of the kings of Egypt had previously reached. The Thebaid, a source of fear to all the kings alike, was overcome and envoys of the king of the Ethiopians given audience at Philae, with that king being received into protection and a ruler of the Ethiopian Triacontaschoenundus established. He made this dedication to the gods of his native land and to Nile, his helper.

14.57 Anderson *et al.*, *JRS* 69 (1979) 125: Gallus as poet

The date of this poem, found in a fragmentary Latin papyrus in Egyptian Nubia in 1978, is uncertain, but it probably refers to Octavian's return to Italy in 29 BC. Ovid (*Am.* 1.15.29–30) says of Gallus that his literary fame will reach as far as his military commands and last longer. Vergil's tenth eclogue was written in his honour.

> My fate will then, Caesar, be sweet to me, when you
> Have become the most important part of Roman history,
> And when after your return I read of the temples of many gods
> Now richer for being decorated with your trophies.

OCTAVIAN'S RETURN

14.58 Velleius Paterculus *Compendium of Roman History* 2.89.1–6: 'Restorer of the Republic'

Velleius is reflecting the propaganda regarding the 'Restoration of the Republic', as well as the relief at the cessation of civil conflict. Octavian returned to Italy in August 29 BC, during his fifth consulship, and had the *Georgics* read to him by Vergil. On 13–15 August he celebrated three triumphs: for Dalmatia, Actium and Egypt. From the Egyptian booty 400 sesterces was given to every citizen and 1,000 to each veteran, and the rate of interest fell sharply (Suet. *Aug.* 41).

1 When Caesar returned to Italy and Rome, the acclaim and welcome he received from men of every class, age and rank, the magnificence of his triumphs and the public spectacles he hosted – none of this could be properly narrated even within the parameters of a formal history, and still less in a limited one such as this. There is nothing that men can desire of the gods, **2** nor the gods grant to men, no conceivable wish, no realisable happiness which Augustus on his return to the city did not bestow on the Republic, the Roman people and the world. **3** Civil wars were ended after 20 years, foreign wars were concluded, peace was re-established, the tumult of arms everywhere put to rest. All was restored – the ascendancy of the law, the authority of the law-courts, the eminence of the senate, the power of the magistrates to its former status (except that two additional praetors were added to the normal eight). And so the ancient and traditional form of the Republic was re-established. **4** Agriculture returned to the fields, religious observances were once again respected, men felt safe from danger, and each man's property was now safely his own. Laws were productively reformed and beneficial ones brought into effect; senatorial membership was revised, impersonally but not without censure. Eminent men, who had enjoyed triumphs and the highest state offices, were at the invitation of the princeps asked to adorn the city with their presence. Only with the consulship, which Caesar continued to hold until the eleventh time in succession, **5** was he not able to have his way, despite his frequent attempts to oppose this – for the dictatorship, which the people persistently offered him, he as consistently refused. As for the wars waged under him as commander, the pacification of the world by his victories, **6** and his numerous achievements both outside of Italy and at home, they would weary even a writer prepared to spend his whole life on this one opus. For myself, mindful of the scope of my work, I have restricted myself to setting a general picture of his principate before the eyes and minds of my readers.

14.59 *FIRA* 1.56: Privileges for Octavian's veterans

On his return Octavian was faced with the urgent necessity of settling veterans and paying their promised bounties. This edict appears to have been cited in 31 BC by a veteran who was being drafted as a collector of taxes against his will.

Imperator Caesar, son of the god, triumvir for the second time for restoring the state, declares: I have decided to decree that all veterans be given exemption from tribute . . . **5** to grant to them, their parents and their children, and the wives which they have or shall have, exemption of all their property from taxation, **10** and so that they may be Roman citizens with the most complete rights by law they shall be exempt from taxation, free from military service, and exempt from the performance of public duties. Likewise, those mentioned above shall have the right to vote and be enrolled in the census in any tribe, and if they wish to be enrolled in absentia it shall be permitted, both for those mentioned above and for their parents, **15** wives and children; likewise, in the same way as I desired the veterans to be exempt, I permit them also to hold, use and enjoy whatever priesthoods, offices, prerogatives, privileges and stipends they possessed. Further, against their will, neither other magistrates nor a legate, **20** nor a procurator, nor a tribute-farmer shall be in their homes for the purpose of lodging or wintering, and no one is to be dispossessed against their will.

14.60 Suetonius *Life of the Deified Augustus* 22: Closing of the temple of Janus

The temple of Janus remained open during a state of war. According to Livy, it had been closed only once since the reign of Numa, in 235 BC in the consulship of Titus Manlius (1.19.3; cf. *RG* 13: doc. 15.1). Octavian had it closed in January of 29 BC, symbolising the restoration of peace.

The temple of Janus Quirinus, which since the foundation of the city had been closed only twice before his time, he closed three times in a much shorter period after peace had been made by land and sea. He twice entered the city in an ovation – after Philippi and again after the Sicilian war. He celebrated three regular triumphs, for victories in Dalmatia, at Actium and at Alexandria, all on three successive days.

14.61 *ILS* 81: Triumphal arch in the forum at Rome, 29 BC

The senate and people of Rome to Imperator Caesar, son of the deified Julius, consul five times, consul designate for a sixth, imperator seven times, the state having been saved.

14.62 Crawford *RRC* 243: Coin celebrating Octavian's successes

A denarius from the East, 28 BC.

Obverse: Head of Octavian, behind a lituus. *Legend*: Caesar consul six times.

Reverse: Crocodile standing right. *Legend*: Egypt captured.

PRINCEPS AND AUGUSTUS

On the Ides of January (13 January) 27 BC, in a speech to the senate, Octavian 'gave the state back' into the hands of the senate and people (a claim he makes in *RG* 34.1: doc. 15.1). However, the 'settlement' was a gradually developing process. Agrippa and Octavian in 28, as consuls with censoria potestas ('censorial power'), carried out a revision of the senate and a full census for the first time since 70 BC. With all their special powers terminated, they were again consuls for 27. In response to his speech, Octavian was given the provinces of Spain, Gaul, Syria and Egypt for ten years and could continue to stand for the consulship or govern them as proconsul through deputies (though Egypt remained under his personal control). Important dates from his career now became part of religious calendars, and he was granted the name 'Augustus' in 27, as well as the civic crown, for saving not the life of a single citizen in battle but that of all the citizens by ending civil war: *RG* 34.2 (doc. 15.1).

14.63 *Inscr. Ital.* 13.2: Excerpts from the *Fasti*, 82–27 BC

Fasti (calendrical lists) exist for some 18 towns in Italy and are dated primarily to the first centuries BC and AD. They listed religious festivals and other important occasions and celebrations, including the days on which business could be transacted (cf. doc. 3.30). The most important calendar is the Fasti Praenestini (the calendar from the town of Praeneste), compiled by the antiquarian Verrius Flaccus, tutor to Augustus' grandsons (see doc. 6.58).

82 BC

14 January. Evil day by decree of the senate: the birthday of Antony. Unfavourable (Verulae, Oppianum).

63 BC

23–24 September. Festival by senatorial decree as on this day Augustus Caesar, pontifex maximus, was born. Sacrifice to Neptune in the Campus Martius and to Apollo by the theatre of Marcellus (Acts of the Arval Brethren).

c. 48 BC

18 or 19 October. On this day Caesar assumed the toga virilis. Thanksgiving to Hope and Youth (Cumae).

43 BC

7 January. Imperator Caesar Augustus first took office (the fasces) in the consulship of Hirtius and Pansa (Praeneste).

14 April. On this day Caesar was victorious for the first time. Thanksgiving for the victory of Augustus (Cumae).

16 April. On this day Caesar was first acclaimed imperator. Thanksgiving to the Good Fortune of his imperium (Cumae).

19 August. On this day Caesar entered upon his first consulship. Thanksgiving (Cumae).

42 BC

23 October. Imperator Caesar Augustus was victor at Philippi, Brutus being killed in the second battle (Praeneste).

38 BC

17 January. Festival by senatorial decree as on this day Augusta married the deified Augustus (Verulae).

36 BC

3 September. Festival and thanksgiving ceremonies at all the couches of the gods as on this day Caesar, son of a god, was victorious in Sicily in the consulship of Censorinus and Calvisius (Amiternum – wrong date).

31 BC

2 September. Festival by senatorial decree as on this day Imperator Caesar Augustus, son of a god, was victorious at Actium; he and Titius were the consuls (Amiternum).

30 BC

1 August. Egypt brought under the rule of the Roman people. To Victory the Virgin on the Palatine; to Hope in the Forum Holitorium (vegetable market). Holiday by decree of the senate, since on this day Imperator Caesar Augustus liberated the Republic from the most dreadful peril (Praeneste).

29 BC

11 January. Imperator Caesar Augustus put an end to war and closed the temple of Janus for the third time since Romulus, in his fifth consulship with Appuleius as colleague (Praeneste).

13–15 August. Augustus celebrated a triumph (Antium).

28 BC

9 October. To the public Genius; to fortunate Felicity; to Venus the Victorious on the Capitol; to Apollo on the Palatine, games (Amiternum).

9 October. Games. Augustus dedicated the temple of Apollo (Antium).

27 BC

13 January. The senate decreed that an oak-leaf garland be placed above the door of the house of Imperator Caesar Augustus because he restored the Republic to the people of Rome (Praeneste).

16 January. On this day Caesar was named Augustus. Thanksgiving to Augustus. Imperator Caesar was named Augustus in his seventh consulship with Agrippa, in his third, as colleague (Cumae, Praeneste).

14.64 Dio *Roman History* 53.2.5–17.1: The 'first settlement' of 27 BC

Clearly members of the senate had been primed as to what to expect in this speech, and their response was carefully stage-managed.

2.5 Since he had put into effect many undertakings illegally and unjustly during the civil conflicts and in the wars, especially during his joint rule with Antony and Lepidus, he abolished them all in a single edict, putting his sixth consulship as their date of termination. **6** And as he was applauded and praised on this account he wanted to display a further example of magnanimity, so that he would be honoured even more for this and have his autocracy validated by people willingly rather than appear to have coerced them unwillingly. **7** He therefore prepared his most intimate friends among the senators and entered the senate in his seventh consulship and read out this address:

3.1 'I am aware, fathers, that to some of you I will appear to have made an incredible choice . . . **4.2** My army is in the best possible condition in terms of both loyalty and strength, and there are funds and allies, and – most important of all – you and the people are so well disposed to me that you would obviously desire to be governed by me. **3** However, I shall lead you no longer and no one will say that all my earlier conduct was in order to achieve absolute power. In fact I resign my power completely and restore absolutely everything to you – the army, laws and provinces, and not only those that you entrusted to me **4** but also all those that I myself later acquired for you, so you can ascertain from these actions themselves that from the very beginning I desired no domination, but in truth wanted to avenge my cruelly murdered father and rescue the city from serious and unending crises.' . . .

11.1 While Caesar was reading his address, a variety of feelings engaged the senators. Some of them knew what he had in mind and consequently kept up enthusiastic applause; of the rest, some were suspicious of what he said and others believed it, and accordingly both groups marvelled equally, one at his deviousness the other at his resolution, **2** while both were annoyed, one at his duplicity the other at his change of mind. For there were already some who loathed the Republican system as a cause of civil unrest and were pleased at the change in government and rejoiced in having Caesar, and so, while they reacted differently, their opinions coincided. **3** Those who believed that he had spoken the truth could not show their delight, with those who wished to being constrained by fear and the others by their hopes, while those who disbelieved it did not dare to attack and expose him, some because they were afraid and others because they did not wish to do so. **4** As a result everyone was either compelled to believe him, or pretended that they did. As far as praise was concerned, some were not courageous enough and others did not want to – rather, even while he was still reading, and afterwards, they kept shouting out, begging for a monarchy and saying everything with that end in view, until they compelled him, as it appeared, to accept absolute power. **5** His first act was to have an edict passed giving to the men who were to make up his bodyguard double the pay of that of other soldiers, to ensure he was strictly guarded. After this he was truly in earnest about establishing the monarchy.

12.1 In this way he had his sovereignty ratified by both the senate and the people, but as he wished even so to appear actually to be a Republican at heart, he declared that, while he accepted all the responsibility for and superintendence of public business on the grounds that it needed particular attention, he would not personally govern all the provinces, **2** and that in the case of those he did govern he would not do so in perpetuity. In fact the weaker ones, on the grounds that they were peaceful and free from war, he gave back to the senate, while the more powerful he kept control of on the grounds that they were unstable and at risk and either had enemies on their frontiers or were able on their own account to cause a serious uprising. **3** His rationale for this was that the senate could fearlessly enjoy the very best of the empire, while he himself had the hardships and the dangers, but in reality through this pretext he intended that they should be unarmed and unfit for battle, while only he had weapons and maintained soldiers. **4** Consequently Africa, Numidia, Asia, Greece with Epirus, the Dalmatian and Macedonian regions, Crete and the part of Libya adjoining Cyrene, Bithynia with the neighbouring Pontus, Sardinia and Baetica were considered as belonging to the people and senate. **5** Caesar had the rest of Spain – the region of Tarraco and Lusitania – and all the Gauls – Gallia Narbonensis and Lugdunensis, the Aquitani and the Belgae, both themselves and any settlers among them: **6** as some of the Celts, whom we call Germans, had occupied all the Belgic territory along the Rhine which resulted in its being named Germany, the upper part of which reached to the sources of the river and the lower to the British Ocean. **7** So these, together with Coele Syria, as it is called, Phoenicia, Cilicia, Cyprus and Egypt became Caesar's share then at least – for later he returned Cyprus and Gallia around Narbo to the people and himself took Dalmatia instead. . . . . **13.1** So this was how the provinces were divided up, and as Caesar wished even then to divert them all well away from the impression that he was thinking in terms of monarchy, he undertook the government of those given him for ten years. He promised during this period to put them in order and made the boastful claim that, if they were pacified sooner, he would return them sooner to the senate. **2** Then he first of all appointed the senators themselves to govern both types of provinces except Egypt (to this one alone he assigned to an eques earlier named, for reasons there mentioned). He then laid down that the governors of senatorial provinces should have an annual term and be chosen by lot, unless they had the privilege accorded to those who had numerous children or by right of marriage, **3** and they were to be sent out by a public assembly of the senate, neither armed with a sword nor wearing military dress, while the title of proconsul was to be employed not only for the two ex-consuls but for the rest who had served as praetors or who had at least been ranked as ex-praetors; **4** each of these groups was to employ as many lictors as was customary in the city, and he ordered that they were to assume the insignia of their magistracy immediately once outside the pomerium and to wear these continuously until they returned. **5** The other governors were to be chosen by him and to be called his envoys and propraetors even if they were ex-consuls. . . . **6** He had the group he chose himself use the title of propraetor and govern for much longer than a year, at his pleasure, and they wore military dress and a sword with which they were empowered to punish soldiers. . . . **14.1** It was in this way and under these conditions that it became customary for ex-praetors and ex-consuls to be sent out as governors of both types of province. In the first case, the emperor sent out someone wherever and whenever he wished, and many praetors and consuls while in office obtained provincial commands, as sometimes happens even now. **2** With the senatorial provinces, he allocated on his own responsibility Africa and Asia to the ex-consuls and the others to the ex-praetors, but prohibited in all cases that a governor be chosen by lot until five years had passed since his holding office in the city. **3** For a while all these, even if they exceeded the number of provinces, received one of them – but afterwards, since some of them did not govern well, these too were put under the control of the emperor, and in this way he, in some manner, grants governorships to them as well; **4** for he orders the allocation of exactly the same number of governors as provinces, and the men he wishes . . .

15.1 This then is what happens in the case of the people's provinces; to the others, called the emperor's provinces and which have more than one citizen legion, are sent lieutenants selected by the emperor himself generally from the ex-praetors, though sometimes from the ex-quaestors or those who have held some other magistracy between the two. **2** As for the equites, the emperor himself chooses those to be sent out as military tribunes, both those who are possible future senators and the others (the difference between them I have already covered: cf. 52.25.6–7), dispatching some to the citizen legions and others to the foreign units, according to the custom laid down by (Julius) Caesar. **3** The procurators (for this is what we call those who collect the public revenues and spend in accordance with their instructions) he sends to all the provinces alike, both his own and those of the people, some of these from the knights and others even from freedmen, except that the proconsuls collect the taxes from the provinces they govern. **4** He gives instructions to the procurators, proconsuls and propraetors so that they go out (to their provinces) on explicit conditions, and both this practice and the giving of salaries to them and the other officials was established at this time. **5** Earlier certain contractors from the treasury provided everything they needed for this magistracy, but it was under Caesar for the first time that they themselves began to receive a fixed sum. This was not assigned to them all in equal amounts but as their needs approximately required, and the procurators in fact got the very title of their office from the amount of the funds given them. **6** These laws were laid down for them all alike, that they were not to raise troops nor levy money beyond the amount appointed unless the senate should vote or the emperor order it; and when their successor arrived they were to set out from their province immediately and not to delay on their return but be back within three months.

16.1 These regulations were established at that time, so to speak, but in reality Caesar himself was to have absolute control of all matters for all time, in as much as he was not only in charge of all the moneys (nominally the public funds were separated from his own, but in practice he spent these too as he chose) but also commanded the soldiers. **2** At any rate, when his ten-year period came to an end another five years were voted him, then five more, then ten, then another ten, and the same a fifth time, so that by a succession of ten-year periods he continued sole ruler for life . . . . **17.1** In this way the power of both the people and the senate passed entirely to Augustus, and beginning with him there was in real truth a monarchy in place – for a monarchy, even if two or three men did later hold the power at the same time, it should unquestionably be considered.

14.65 Suetonius *Life of the Deified Augustus* 7.2: An 'august' title

Plancus had been one of Antony's generals who joined Octavian in 32. The name Romulus being that of a king and fratricide, Augustus was considered more appropriate as stressing positive qualities with religious overtones (majestic, venerable, worthy of honour), while also connected with the terms 'augeo' and 'auctus' (growth, increase, abundance).

He took the name Gaius Caesar, and then the surname Augustus, the former by the will of his great-uncle and the latter on the motion of Munatius Plancus. When some suggested that he ought to be called Romulus, being like him the founder of the city, Plancus prevailed with the proposal that he should rather be named Augustus, as this was not only a new title but a more honourable one, since sacred places too, and those in which anything is consecrated by augury, are called 'august', from the increase (auctus) in dignity or from the behaviour and feeding habits of birds, as Ennius demonstrates, when he writes (*Annales* 155): 'by august augury (augusto augurio) illustrious Rome was founded'.

14.66 Tacitus *Annals* 1.1.1–2.2: The death of the Republic

Tacitus in this passage is arguing that periods of temporary 'rule', by Sulla and Caesar for example, were the logical prelude to the autocracy of the principate and Augustus' sole rule (cf. doc. 12.1).

1.1 At the beginning of Rome's existence as a city it was ruled by kings; Lucius Junius Brutus then instituted the consulship, together with political liberty. Dictatorships were assumed for short periods of time; the powers of decemvirs did not last more than two years, while the consular authority of military tribunes was short-lived. The autocracies of both Cinna and Sulla were brief; the predominance of Pompey and Crassus was quickly superseded by that of Caesar, and the armed might of Lepidus and Antony by that of Augustus, who took the whole state, exhausted by civil discord, into his dominion under the name of 'princeps'.... **2.1** After the state had been left unarmed, following the killing of Brutus and Cassius, Pompeius overpowered in Sicily, Lepidus cast aside, Antony slain, even the Julian party had no leader left but Caesar. Having set aside the title of triumvir, he paraded himself as consul and was quite satisfied with the tribunician power of protecting the people. He won the support of the soldiery with gratuities, the people with grain, and everyone with the delights of peace, and then edged forward little by little, absorbing into himself the functions of the senate, the magistracies and the laws. He was opposed by no one, since the fiercest had fallen in line of battle or through proscription, while the rest of the nobility found that, the more one welcomed slavery, the quicker one was raised to wealth and office, and, having flourished on revolution, preferred safety and the current state of things to the old system and instability. **2** Nor were the provinces unhappy with this state of affairs, where the rule of senate and people had been distrusted as a result of the conflicts between rivals for power and the greed of magistrates, with no assistance from the laws, which were overturned by violence, corruption – and above all money.

15

The Age of Augustus

Augustus had entrusted four documents to the Vestals to be read and actioned after his death, one of which was a record of his achievements (his *Res Gestae*), which was to be erected on bronze columns at the entrance to his mausoleum in the Campus Martius (doc. 15.113). These pillars are lost, but the text, together with a Greek translation, was inscribed on the temple of Roma and Augustus at Ancyra, modern Ankara, Turkey (partial copies have also been found in two other sites in Galatia). It appears to have been composed just before Augustus' death and stresses the constitutional nature of his position and the fact that any powers he acquired were assumed with the full concurrence of the senate and people, while he glosses over a number of events in his life before Actium. It promotes an ideology rather than a factual narrative of his reign and puts him forward as a moral example for posterity, while being very much a political document demonstrating that the empire was now in its best possible state on account of his management (doc. 15.1). Following the 'settlement' of January 27, Dio at least considers Augustus' position to have been monarchical, though Augustus always made a show at least of consultation, having an advisory body for all proposed legislation. The senate and assemblies continued to meet as before, and constitutional normality was apparently maintained, but Augustus' approval was an essential part of any decision (doc. 15.2). There is nothing intrinsically impossible in Augustus' having composed the *Res Gestae* himself: like his great-uncle Caesar (doc. 13.64), he tried his hand at a number of literary genres, including a response to Brutus' eulogy of his father-in-law Cato, an autobiography (now lost), poetic works (some written at the baths), and a tragedy on Ajax, which he 'expunged' because he was unhappy with its style (doc. 15.3). The fasti continued to record his achievements and high points in his career (such as becoming pontifex maximus) and events within his family (doc. 15.4).

From 27 BC, Augustus' constitutional position was one of great subtlety. It was further refined in 23, after he had been seriously ill, when in July he resigned the consulship he had held continuously since 31. This had the benefit of allowing more senators to reach the consulship and to be available for consular duties such as governorships. Instead of the consulship Augustus accepted tribunician potestas for life (this was now to be the denominator of status and right of succession), and from this point he used this to date events in his reign. He was also awarded the right to put matters before the senate and, though no longer consul as such, retained his provinces and their armies. During this illness in 23 he passed his ring to Agrippa, thus designating him rather than his young nephew and son-in-law Marcellus as 'successor'. At this point there was no thought of handing on 'rule' as if he were a monarch; rather, the state, to ensure stability, needed an experienced man at the helm. Augustus' proconsular imperium was apparently such that it was superior to that of the other governors in the senatorial provinces ('maius', or greater, imperium), and he was able to override decisions made there, though he was careful not to draw attention to this (docs 15.5–6). Certainly, whatever Augustus' actual position in relation to the senatorial provinces, the provincials saw him as the main decision-maker, and the 'Cyrene edicts' appear to prove that he possessed maius imperium overriding that of the governor (docs 15.7, 10). The people in 23 were unhappy at his resigning the consulship, and in 21 and 20, during Augustus' absence in the East, there were difficulties over consular elections, and only one consul was elected for 19. At around this time, too, in 23/22 and 19 BC, there had also been two conspiracies against Augustus. When he returned from the East in October 19 he was granted further honours, including consular power for life and the prefecture of morals and the right to enact any laws on his own authority. The senate also built an altar to Fortuna Redux ('Fortunate Return'). Less obviously, in 18 his imperium was renewed for another five years, while Agrippa was given tribunician potestas and presumably imperium for the same period (docs 15.8–9).

Meanwhile it was still important for Augustus to be able to show himself a great general expanding the frontiers of Rome. In January 29 he had been granted the right to use 'Imperator' as a first name, and the doors of the temple of Janus had been closed signifying worldwide peace. Poets such as Vergil celebrated his victories at Actium and elsewhere (docs 15.11, 94–95). The return of the captured standards by the Parthians, though achieved by diplomacy rather than by conquest, was heralded as a personal triumph of arms on his coinage (doc. 15.18), while his victories were shown as having a worldwide impact, as in the embassy sent to him from India, which included a Buddhist priest who immolated himself at Athens (doc. 15.15). Victories over foreign opponents were still lauded, though increasingly such honours as triumphs were to be restricted to members of the imperial family. In addition, in 21 BC Augustus took care that the general Crassus should not be allowed the honour of the spolia opima for killing an enemy leader in single combat, since he had not been fighting under his own auspices but those of Augustus (docs 15.12–14). Augustus' triumphs in warfare which established stability and constitutional government were also shown as bearing the fruits of peace in his conquest of foreign enemies. The Ara Pacis Augustae (altar of Augustan Peace) was commissioned in 13 and dedicated in 9 BC, its reliefs depicting the advantages now enjoyed by Rome, with members of the imperial family prominently depicted (docs 15.15–18).

While in some respects proud to announce himself as an innovator, on the question of religion Augustus was careful to show himself a traditionalist and restorer. He established a festival to celebrate his victory at Actium near the site of the battle, restored temples (82 in the year 28 BC alone; *RG* 20.4: doc 15.1), and constructed many additional shrines, such as the temples of Apollo and Mars Ultor (the 'Avenger', in honour of his father Julius Caesar); this temple also housed the standards returned from the Parthians (doc. 15.96). After Lepidus finally died, after many years under house arrest, in 13 BC, Augustus finally took on the position of pontifex maximus, and from that point he had a justification for overseeing religious rituals generally and ensuring that they conformed to traditional practices, as well as continuing to restore many that had fallen into disuse. In this, as in everything else, he was publicly supported by his wife, Livia (docs 15.19–22).

One of the issues that most concerned Augustus in his moral and social legislation was the birth rate among the higher classes, and in 18 BC he attempted to encourage marriage and reward marriage and childbearing while imposing penalties on the unmarried and childless. He also made adultery (and other forms of sexual misconduct) a public as well as a private crime. There were, however, advantages: citizens, though not senators, could now formally marry freedpersons, while couples with three or more children had testamentary advantages in the inheritance of property (docs 15.23–27). This legislation was unpopular, especially with the equites, and in AD 9 the *lex Papia Poppaea* was passed to relax some of the earlier stipulations (the fact that neither of these consuls was married was an indication of the seriousness of the issue). His laws also addressed the concerns of freedpersons, releasing them under certain conditions from the guardianship (and right to inheritance) of their patron (docs 15.28–30). As part of his celebration of the restoration of traditional religion and its values, Augustus celebrated the centennial games (ludi Saeculares) in 17 BC, marking a new age and time of rebirth in tune with his legislation to encourage marriage and childbearing (docs 15.32–34). It was unfortunate for Augustus that both his daughter and granddaughter were seen openly to transgress his moral legislation, even if in so doing they were also inspired by political motives (doc. 15.31).

As Julia was Augustus' only child, it was imperative that he seek out a possible 'successor', although as yet the concept of handing on a form of monarchy would have been anachronistic. In his illness in 23 BC he had turned to Agrippa rather than his son-in-law and nephew Marcellus. He had, however, clearly been grooming Marcellus for high honours, including allowing him to hold a spectacular aedileship, until the boy's death at the age of 19 years. In his *Aeneid*, Vergil presents the young Marcellus in the underworld as the greatest of a long succession of Roman heroes (docs 15.5, 35–37). With his death, however, Augustus needed a new father for any grandchildren, and Julia was therefore married to his friend Agrippa (who had to divorce his current wife, Augustus' niece and Marcellus' sister). Sources hint at differences between Marcellus and Agrippa, but Agrippa's role in the East between 23 and 21 was that of deputising for Augustus as governor of Syria, and their duties did not overlap (doc. 15.38). Quite apart from his role as Augustus' second-in-command and overseer of his military campaigns, Agrippa left a lasting mark on Rome with his building and engineering projects. He held the aedileship in 33 in order to improve Rome's infrastructure and constructions, even though this was a step down in the cursus honorum, as he had held the consulship in 37; he was to be consul again with Augustus in 28 and 27. He spent a fortune on beautifying Rome, repairing and improving the aqueducts and sewers, constructing baths and fountains, erecting a basilica in honour of Augustus' victories, and building a complex in the Campus Martius including gardens and the Pantheon. He was also known as an art-lover (docs 15.39–41). His edicts and achievements in the East were acknowledged and honoured by the provincials, who erected numerous statues in honour of Agrippa and his family members, including Julia and their daughters: they were to have five children, the first, Gaius, born in 20 BC, followed by Lucius in 17. The third son, Agrippa Postumus, was born after Agrippa's death (docs 15.42–46). While Agrippa's decisions were noted for their justice and sense, on one occasion he lost his temper when Julia was nearly drowned in a storm crossing the River Scamander near Troy. He fined the city 100,000 silver drachmas, which would have left it destitute: fortunately Nikolaos of Damascus was at hand to ask King Herod of Judaea to plead on their behalf (doc. 15.47).

From 18 BC Agrippa was Augustus' colleague in both tribunician power and proconsular imperium, renewed for a further five years in 13, and his funeral oration suggests that, like Augustus, he possessed maius imperium. After the birth of Lucius, Agrippa and Julia's second son, Augustus had adopted both boys, and was clearly intending that they be seen as his designated successors. Agrippa died unexpectedly in March 12 BC and was buried in Augustus' mausoleum, and Dio gives a eulogistic summary of his achievements and loyalty to Augustus (docs 15.48–50). Augustus completed some of Agrippa's more outstanding undertakings, such as the first ever map of the known world, while the responsibility for Rome's water supply, together with the 'household' of expert slaves Agrippa had maintained as workmen, were handed over to the senate (docs 15.51–52). Augustus' grandsons were as yet too young to be involved in public life, and for a colleague in the interim Augustus turned to Livia's elder son, Tiberius. In 11 BC Tiberius had to divorce his wife, Vipsania, a daughter of Agrippa, and marry Julia (doc. 15.50).

While Augustus did not allow divine honours to be paid to him in Rome, he promoted his status as 'son of the god' by such means as his coinage and his construction of the temple of Mars Ultor (Mars the Avenger) in honour of his assassinated 'father' (dedicated in 2 BC). In the East the goddess Roma had long possessed a cult, as had certain successful generals such as Flamininus, and after Actium shrines started to be erected to 'Roma and Augustus', as for example in Ancyra, where the text of the *Res Gestae* was displayed. The cult was important in major centres such as Pergamum and Athens (doc. 15.53), and in 9 BC Fabius, the proconsul of Asia, made not only Augustus' birthday a public holiday but also the start of the New Year throughout the province (as 'the beginning of all things' and 'the time for life'). For this innovation he won himself the crown designated for the person 'who formulated the highest honours for the god (Augustus)' (doc. 15.54). Oaths of loyalty were taken throughout the East to Augustus and his family on pain of total obliteration of oneself and all one's descendants, and one of the important duties of magistrates was to hold sacrifices to Imperator Caesar

Augustus and his two sons, as well as festivals in honour of the imperial family. Such games could be held in honour of the imperial family generally, Roma and Augustus, Julius Caesar, or even Agrippa. Similar honours took place in the West: an altar at Narbonne in honour of Augustus' divine power (numen) was set up to worship his divine spirit in perpetuity (docs 15.55–58).

One of the factors in Augustus' earlier marriage legislation had been to permit marriages with freedpersons (except for senators) and to enable freedpersons with an appropriate number of children to avoid nominating their patron as sole heir. Further legislation concerning slaves and freedmen was to follow. Probably in 17 BC Augustus settled the issue of 'Junian Latins', slaves who had been freed informally, to ensure that their patrons remained their heirs and that they were formally recognised as freedpersons with certain citizen rights. In 2 BC, in the *lex Fufia Caninia*, he dealt with the question of manumission by will, restricting the numbers of slaves who could be manumitted in this way (never more than 100), though this had no impact on other forms of manumission, while the *lex Aelia Sentia* in AD 4 laid down minimum age limits both for owners and for slaves who were to be manumitted (docs 15.59–61). Now that adultery was a public crime, with serious penalties for both parties, he also ensured that measures were put in place to ensure both that slaves of accused persons could be tortured for their evidence and that compensation should be granted should the slaves die under this treatment (doc. 15.62).

Following the death of Agrippa, Augustus had turned to Tiberius as a colleague and husband for Julia. His adopted grandsons were his heirs, and there seemed every chance that they would be suitable successors at the appropriate time. Julia had received an excellent education and inherited her father's quick wit, as well as his independence of character. Macrobius preserves some of her 'sayings' as evidence of her intelligence and outspokenness, and, while he was very fond of her, Augustus used to say that he had two spoilt daughters, Rome and Julia (docs 15.63–64, cf. 66). Family life at this period is shown as affectionate, with positive relationships between all family members, including Tiberius (doc. 15.65). It was unfortunate, however, that the marriage between Tiberius and Julia was not a happy one, and in 2 BC Julia's indiscretions were such that Augustus was forced to banish her after he had made a public outburst about her behaviour in the senate. There was possibly a political agenda, as a close member of the imperial family, Iullus Antonius, son of Mark Antony and husband of Augustus' niece Marcella, was implicated and committed suicide (doc. 15.67). Livia's relationship with Augustus stood the test of time, and, while she clearly had influence over her husband, she projected the image of a discreet and loyal wife. The island of Samos certainly felt that she could represent their interests with Augustus (he mentions 'his wife' in his reply), and Suetonius preserves a letter from Augustus to her detailing his concerns about their problem grandchild Claudius (docs 15.69–72). Some further insight into Livia's domestic life is seen by her possession of the smallest female dwarf in Rome, Andromeda, her recipes for medicaments, such as a cure for a sore throat, and her villa north of Rome, which provided laurel wreaths for Augustus and subsequent emperors after a chicken carrying a branch of laurel had fallen auspiciously into her lap when being carried off by a passing eagle (docs 15.68, 73–74; 6.68).

Augustus was a painstaking administrator, with his eye on issues both in the provinces and in Rome, and a letter of his is preserved giving judgement in a case on Knidos, which had been brought directly to him by the Knidians when one of their citizens had been killed accidentally by a falling chamber-pot (doc. 15.75). More importantly, it was vital to keep the supply of grain flowing into Rome, and he established a commission of ex-praetors to oversee the grain distribution. A *lex Julia* on the grain supply prevented trafficking in grain prices and hoarding, and the efficient transportation of grain from Egypt to Rome was ensured, while within Egypt ships transporting grain down the Nile were escorted by Roman legionaries (docs 15.76–77). Other laws passed by Augustus included ones on violence, embezzlement, bribery and extortion, and, like Caesar, he attempted in a sumptuary law to restrict excessive spending on private and public banquets (docs 15.79–80). Apart from the temples and sanctuaries he constructed and repaired in Rome, he had a secular building programme, including his mausoleum, the Curia Julia, and the Forum Augustum. Districts of Rome were supervised by annual magistrates, a fire service was introduced, the Tiber was cleaned and widened, and highways leading to Rome were improved (doc. 15.81).

Having resigned the consulship in 23 BC, Augustus accepted it again only to introduce his two eldest grandsons to public life in 5 and 2 BC. Many duties were open to ex-consuls, and there were often more than a single pair in a particular year: the substitute consuls were known as 'suffect'. This allowed more senators to reach the pre-eminent position and afterwards to take on governorships, administer the treasury, and oversee the grain and water supply. Augustus also formed an advisory group, consisting of certain magistrates and senators chosen by lot, for the purposes of consultation prior to proposals going before the senate. He was concerned to limit membership of the senate but was able to reduce it only to 600 members. Election to magistracies was still extremely competitive, but from AD 3 more senators from Italian towns appear, and there was scope for 'new men' to reach the highest political positions. Such positions were highly prized, as were other forms of service such as priesthoods, governorships and a variety of administrative positions (docs 15.83–87).

Like architecture and the fine arts, literature was to flourish in Augustus' time, and his reign was to be seen as a 'Golden Age' of poetry. Young writers were deliberately encouraged and supported by Augustus' childhood friend Maecenas, who had held many duties in Rome while deputising for Augustus in his absence, dealing with at least one conspiracy (docs 15.88–89), and who was a generous patron of literature, if a verbose and pretentious poet in his own right. Vergil, Horace and Propertius were all part of his literary circle and encouraged to write on Augustan themes and promote Augustan ideology (docs 15.90–97). Maecenas died in 8 BC, not long after Agrippa, and, as with Agrippa, Dio gives a eulogy for him, praising him for his moderating influence on Augustus and his unobtrusiveness in remaining an equestrian (he was never a senator), even though he bestowed such honours on others. He was also known for his love of luxurious living and was the first person in Rome to possess a heated swimming pool (doc. 15.98).

The last years of the first century BC were especially propitious for Augustus. In 8 BC the month Sextilis, in which his main triumphs and achievements had taken place, was named August in his honour. He was also in 2 BC named 'pater patriae', father of his country, which he presents in the *Res Gestae* (35.1) as the pinnacle of his career and the ultimate honour awarded him. His adopted sons were growing up, Gaius especially being popular with the people, and were allowed to attend senate meetings while taking on roles such as priesthoods and leadership of the equestrian order (as 'princeps iuventutis'). The boys received honours from across the empire, and it was agreed at Sardis in 5 BC that the day on which Gaius put on the toga virilis (adult toga) was to be a public holiday. Augustus took the consulship in 5 BC and 2 BC to introduce them to public life, and Gaius was designated consul for AD 1 and Lucius for AD 4. Augustus' letter on his 64th birthday to Gaius in the East, cited by Aulus Gellius, shows the affectionate joking relationship between them and reveals that Augustus definitely saw his two grandsons as his successors. Both boys were given the opportunity to gain the requisite military experience, and Gaius was sent to the East in 1 BC with proconsular powers. In AD 1, his consular year, he campaigned in or near Arabia. In AD 2 he made a treaty with the Parthian ruler Phraataces V after which he headed north to Armenia, which had revolted (docs 15.99–104).

In 2 BC the boys' mother, Julia, had been exiled to the island of Pandateria as a result of her scandalous behaviour. This was a blow both to the moral image Augustus wished to present and to the imperial family. Then, in AD 2, Lucius, the younger of Augustus' grandsons, died at Massalia on his way to Spain and, in January AD 4, Gaius, who had been wounded in a siege in Armenia, died on his way back to Italy. Cities across the empire, such as Pisa, awarded them full funerary honours. Julia's third son, Agrippa Postumus, was then adopted by Augustus, but proved unsatisfactory and was exiled in AD 7, and the following year his sister Julia was banished, like her mother, for adultery and possible treason. Militarily, the position of the empire seemed secure, and Tiberius, with his adopted son Germanicus, had been achieving some great victories in Illyricum since AD 6. Then, three days after their triumphal arrival in Rome in AD 9, news came of an unprecedented disaster in Germany, with three legions under the governor Varus lured into an ambush and wiped out. Augustus was devastated and there was panic in Rome; conscription was introduced in this emergency, with heavy penalties for those who did not comply (docs 15.105–10). Tiberius therefore returned to campaign in Germany for another three years, while, more importantly, Augustus had perforce to turn to him as a colleague and successor, as he had lost or exiled all the members of his own family (it was suggested that Livia may have had a hand in some of these deaths), and, whatever Augustus' own view of Tiberius, it was only in AD 13 that he was given imperium equal to that of Augustus. Tacitus comments that nothing was now left of 'the good, old way of life' and that equality had been abolished. At this point, as Augustus' life was drawing to a close, there was concern as to what would follow, whether freedom or further warfare (docs 15.111).

After a few days on the island of Capri, and attending the games at Naples, Augustus died on his way home to Rome, at Nola on 19 August AD 14. Livia was with him to the last, and typically he cracked a joke or two with his friends. He had left Tiberius as heir to two-thirds of his estate and Livia as heir to the rest, and made huge donatives to the military, as well as bequeathing 40,000,000 sesterces to the people of Rome. Apart from his will (one of the four documents left with the Vestals), he left directions for his funeral, his *Res Gestae*, which was to be set up in front of his mausoleum, and a summary of the troops and finances of the empire. He was buried in his mausoleum, alongside Marcellus, Agrippa, Octavia Minor, Gaius and Lucius (docs 15.112–13). It was inevitable that evidence of his divinity would appear, and when an ex-praetor called Numerius Atticus swore that he had seen Augustus ascending into heaven Livia presented him with a million sesterces. Full divine honours were paid him, and his birthday was to be honoured with the celebration of games known as the Augustalia (doc. 15.114).

Augustus' achievements were viewed from very different perspectives by writers and historians: Nikolaos of Damascus sees him as 'attaining the utmost power and wisdom', while Pliny the Elder lists in detail all the disappointments and failures he had to face and dwells particularly on the dubious morality of his early years, ending with the final disappointment of having to leave the empire to Tiberius. Tacitus presents him from two antithetical viewpoints, those of his supporters and those of his opponents. By giving the negative portrait last, the implication is that Tacitus saw Augustus' reign as one ending in failure and disillusionment – though he was still granted temples and divine rites and became a god (doc. 15.117).

THE RES GESTAE DIVI AUGUSTI

15.1 Augustus *Res Gestae*: Augustus' view of his achievements

In this document Augustus is particularly concerned to list the honours awarded him by the senate and people of Rome (culminating with the title pater patriae in 2 BC) and the monies which he expended as a benefactor of the people and army. Where the Greek version differs from the Latin, the Greek is given in square brackets.

Below is a copy of the achievements of the deified Augustus, through which he made the whole world subject to the rule of the Roman people, and of the monies which he expended on the state and people of Rome, as inscribed on two bronze columns set up at Rome [translated and inscribed below are the achievements and gifts of the god Augustus, which he left engraved at Rome on two bronze stelai].

The Ides of March and aftermath

1.1 At the age of 19 (44 BC), on my own decision and at my own expense, I raised an army with which I liberated the state, which had been oppressed by a tyrannical faction [from the slavery imposed by the conspirators]. **2** In acknowledgement of this, the senate passed honorific degrees admitting me to its order in the consulship of Gaius Pansa and Aulus Hirtius (43 BC), as well as granting me the right to state my opinion as a consular, and granted me imperium [as well as granting me the right to state my opinions with the status of an ex-consul, and gave me the rods (of office)]. **3** It ordered me as propraetor to take measures together with the consuls to ensure that the state come to no harm. **4** The people, moreover, in this same year, made me consul, both the consuls having fallen in battle, and triumvir for the settlement of public affairs.

2.1 Those who killed my father I drove into exile, punishing their crime through the proper law-courts, and afterwards, when they made war on the state, defeated them twice in battle [those who killed my father I exiled through legitimate trials, avenging their impiety, and afterwards defeated them twice in battle when they made war against the fatherland].

Warfare and triumphs

3.1 I often conducted wars, civil and foreign, by land and sea across the whole world, and as victor pardoned all citizens who asked for mercy. **2** Foreign peoples, whom it was safe to pardon, I preferred to spare rather than execute. **3** Some 500,000 Roman citizens have been under oath of allegiance to me [nearly 500,000 Romans came to serve in the army under my oath], of whom somewhat more than 300,000 I settled in colonies or sent back to their own towns after they had served their term, and to all of them I allocated land or gave them money as reward for their military service. **4** I captured 600 ships, excluding those smaller than triremes.

4.1 I twice celebrated an ovation and have driven triumphal chariots three times [I twice triumphed on horseback and three times in a chariot] and have been hailed as imperator on 21 occasions; though the senate decreed other triumphs for me I declined them all. I deposited the laurel from my fasces [rods] in the Capitoline temple after fulfilling the vows I had made in each war. **2** For successes by land and sea accomplished under my auspices by me or my legates, the senate on 55 occasions decreed thanksgivings to the immortal gods. Moreover, the days on which thanksgivings were held by senatorial decree came to 890. **3** In my triumphs nine kings or kings' children have been led before my chariot. **4** I have been consul 13 times at the time of writing and have held tribunician power 37 times.

Powers and magistracies

5.1 The dictatorship offered to me both in my absence and in my presence by both the people and the senate in the consulship of Marcus Marcellus and Lucius Arruntius (22 BC) I did not accept. **2** I did not refuse, in a time of severe grain shortage, responsibility for the grain supply [supervision of the market], which I administered in such a way that within a few days I freed the entire city from the fear and danger facing it through my own expenditure and management. **3** The consulship also offered to me at that time for a year and for life I did not accept.

6.1 In the consulship of Marcus Vinicius and Quintus Lucretius (19 BC) and then of Publius Lentulus and Gnaeus Lentulus [18 BC] and thirdly of Paullus Fabius Maximus and Quintus Tubero (11 BC), though the senate and people of

Rome agreed that I should be appointed as sole guardian of laws and customs with absolute power, I accepted no magistracy conferred contrary to the custom of our ancestors. **2** The measures which the senate at that time wished me to carry out I accomplished by virtue of my tribunician power, and on five occasions of my own accord requested and received from the senate a colleague to share that power. **7.1** For ten consecutive years I was a member of the triumvirate for the settlement of the state. **2** I have been princeps senatus [I held first place in rank in the senate], up until the day when I wrote this, for forty years. **3** I have been pontifex maximus [chief priest], augur, one of the Fifteen for conducting sacred rites, one of the Seven for religious feasts [one of the Seven in charge of sacred rites], Arval brother, member of the fraternity of Titius, and fetial.

Restructure of society

8.1 As consul for the fifth time (29 BC) I increased the number of patricians by order of the people and senate. **2** I revised the membership of the senate three times [I selected the senate three times], and in my sixth consulship (28 BC), with Marcus Agrippa as my colleague, I carried out a census of the people. I held a lustrum 42 years after the previous one (17 BC), and 4,063,000 [4,603,000] individual Romans were registered. **3** I then for a second time conducted a lustrum on my own with consular power in the consulship of Gaius Censorinus and Gaius Asinius (8 BC), at which lustrum 4,233,000 individual Romans were registered. **4** And I conducted a lustrum for a third time with consular power with my son Tiberius Caesar as colleague in the consulship of Sextus Pompeius and Sextus Appuleius (AD 14), in which 4,937,000 individual Roman citizens were registered. **5** Through new laws which I initiated I revived many patterns of ancestral practices that were dying out in our generation, and I myself handed down to posterity numerous models for them to imitate [I myself handed myself down to posterity as a model of many things].

Religious honours

9.1 The senate decreed that vows for my health be offered by consuls and priests every four years. In accordance with these vows, games have often been celebrated in my lifetime [in my lifetime omitted in Greek], sometimes by the four most prestigious colleges of priests [sometimes through the collaboration of the four priests] and sometimes by the consuls. **2** Furthermore, the whole citizen body, both privately and as municipalities, have with one accord continuously offered prayers for my good health at all the couches of the gods [sacrificed on behalf of my safety].

10.1 By decree of the senate my name was included in the hymn of the Salii, and it was enacted by law that I should be sacrosanct in perpetuity and should possess tribunician power as long as I lived. **2** I refused to become pontifex maximus [I refused to accept the chief priesthood] in place of my colleague (Lepidus) during his lifetime, though the people were offering me that priesthood, which my father had held. Some years later I did accept this priesthood, at the eventual death of that person who had used the opportunity of civil unrest to seize it, when from the whole of Italy such a huge crowd flooded into Rome for my election, in the consulship of Publius Sulpicius and Gaius Valgius (12 BC), as had never previously been recorded. **11** In thanks for my return the senate consecrated the altar of Fortune the Returner (Fortune the Saviour) in front of the temple of Honour and Virtue at the Capena gate, where it ordered the priests and Vestal virgins [priestesses] to perform an annual sacrifice on the anniversary of the day (12 October) on which I had returned to the city from Syria in the consulship of Quintus Lucretius and Marcus Vinicius (19 BC), and named the day *Augustalia* after my title [from our name].

12.1 In accordance with a resolution of the senate some of the praetors and tribunes of the plebs, with the consul Quintus Lucretius and leading senators, were sent to Campania to meet me, an honour up to this time accorded to no one except me. **2** When I returned from Spain and Gaul, after the successful conclusion of affairs in those provinces, in the consulship of Tiberius Nero and Publius Quinctilius (Varus) (13 BC), the senate decreed in honour of my return that an altar of Augustan Peace be consecrated on the Campus Martius, where it ordered the magistrates and priests and Vestal virgins [priestesses] to perform an annual sacrifice.

Closure of the temple of Janus

13 The temple of Janus Quirinus, which our ancestors resolved should be closed when peace had been achieved throughout the whole empire of the Roman people by victories by land and sea [when all land and sea was at peace under the Romans], and which before I was born is recorded as having been closed only ever twice since the foundation of the city, the senate decreed to be closed three times while I was princeps.

Honours for his sons

14.1 My sons, whom fortune snatched away from me as youths, Gaius and Lucius Caesar, the senate and the Roman people appointed in my honour as consuls (designate) when they were 14 years of age so that they could enter into the magistracy after a five-year period, and that, from that day when they were led into the forum, they were to participate in councils of state [be members of the senate]. **2** Moreover, the whole body of Roman equites named both of them as Leader of Youth ('princeps iuventutis') and presented them with silver shields and spears.

Expenditure on citizens and soldiery

15.1 To every member of the Roman plebs I paid 300 sesterces [75 denarii] in accordance with my father's will, and I gave in my own name 400 sesterces [100 denarii] from the spoils of war when I was consul for the fifth time (29 BC), and again in my tenth consulship (24 BC) I paid out a donative of 400 sesterces [100 denarii] per man from my own patrimony, and as consul for the eleventh time (23

BC] I bought up grain in a private capacity and made 12 grain distributions, and in my twelfth year of tribunician power (12 BC) I gave out 400 sesterces [100 denarii] per man for the third time. These handouts of mine never reached fewer than 250,000 people. **2** In my eighteenth year of tribunician power, as consul for the twelfth time (5 BC), I gave 60 denarii per man to 320,000 [330,000] members of the urban plebs. **3** And as consul for the fifth time [29 BC] I gave to the colonists who had been my soldiers 1,000 sesterces [250 denarii] each out of spoils; some 120,000 men in the colonies received this triumphal handout. **4** As consul for the thirteenth time (2 BC) I gave 60 denarii to each of the plebs at that time in receipt of public grain; these numbered slightly more than 200,000 men.

16.1 I paid money to municipalities in exchange for the land which I allocated to my soldiers in my fourth consulship (30 BC), and later in the consulship of Marcus Crassus and Gnaeus Lentulus Augur (14 BC); the total amount paid was about 600,000,000 sesterces [150,000,000] for Italian estates and about 260,000,000 [65,000,000] for land in the provinces. I was the first and only one to have done this of all who have founded colonies of soldiers in Italy or the provinces in living memory [until my generation]. **2** And afterwards, in the consulship of Tiberius Nero and Gnaeus Piso (7 BC), and, likewise, in the consulship of Gaius Antistius and Decimus Laelius (6 BC), and in the consulship of Gaius Calvisius and Lucius Pasienus (4 BC), and in the consulship of Lucius Lentulus and Marcus Messalla (3 BC), and in the consulship of Lucius Caninius and Quintus Fabricius (2 BC), I paid cash bounties in full to the soldiers whom I settled in their own municipalities when they had completed their period of service; for this undertaking I paid out about 400,000,000 sesterces [100,000,000].

17.1 On four occasions I assisted the treasury with my own money, transferring 150,000,000 sesterces [37,500,000] to those in charge of the treasury. **2** And in the consulship of Marcus Lepidus and Lucius Arruntius (AD 6) I transferred 170,000,000 sesterces [42,500,000] from my own patrimony into the military treasury, which had been established on my advice, from which bounties were given to soldiers who had completed 20 or more years of service. **18** From the year when Gnaeus and Publius Lentulus were consuls (18 BC), whenever the revenues were inadequate, I gave out distributions of grain and money from my own granary and patrimony [gave payments of grain and cash from my property], sometimes to 100,000 persons, sometimes to many more.

Augustus and Rome

19.1 I built the senate house and the Chalcidicum adjoining it, and the temple of Apollo on the Palatine with its porticoes, the temple of the deified Julius, the Lupercal, the portico at the Circus Flaminius, which I allowed to be called the Octavian after the name of the man who had erected an earlier one on the same site, the platform of the gods (pulvinar) at the Circus Maximus, **2** the temples on the Capitol of Jupiter Feretrius and Jupiter the Thunderer, the temple of Quirinus, the temples of Minerva and Queen Juno and Jupiter Libertas on the Aventine, the temple of the Lares at the top of the Via Sacra, the temple of the Penates on the

Velia, the temple of Youth, and the temple of the Great Mother on the Palatine [I built the council chamber and next to it the Chalcidicum, the temple of Apollo on the Palatine with its porticoes, the temple of the god Julius, the shrine of Pan, the portico at the Circus Flaminius, which I allowed to be called the Octavian after the name of the man who first set it up, the temple near the great hippodrome, **2** the temples on the Capitol of Zeus Trophy-Bearer and Zeus Thunderer, the temple of Quirinus, the temples of Athena and Queen Hera and Zeus Liberator on the Aventine, of the Heroes next to the Sacred Way, of the household gods on the Velia, the temple of Youth, and the temple of the Mother of the gods on the Palatine].

20.1 I restored the Capitoline temple and the theatre of Pompey, both at great expense, without any inscription of my name on them. **2** I repaired the conduits of the aqueducts which in numerous places were collapsing through old age, and I doubled the capacity of the aqueduct called the Marcian aqueduct by diverting a new source into it. **3** I completed the Forum Julium and the basilica which stood between the temple of Castor [the Dioscuri] and the temple of Saturn [Cronus], works began and nearly completed by my father, and I commenced the rebuilding on a more extensive site of the same basilica, when it had been destroyed by fire, under an inscription in the name of my sons, and ordered that if I had not completed it in my lifetime it should be completed by my heirs. **4** As consul for the sixth time (28 BC) I restored 82 temples of the gods in the city in accordance with a resolution of the senate, with not one omitted that was in need of repair at this time. **5** As consul for the seventh time (27 BC) I rebuilt the Via Flaminia from the city to Ariminum and all the bridges except the Mulvian and Minucian [except for two which were not in need of repair].

21.1 On my own land I built the temple of Mars the Avenger and the Forum of Augustus out of the spoils of war. Near the temple of Apollo, on a site purchased mainly from private individuals, I built the theatre, named for my son-in-law Marcus Marcellus. **2** From the spoils of war I consecrated gifts in the Capitoline temple and in the temple of the deified Julius [in the temple of Julius] and in the temple of Apollo and in the temple of Vesta [Hestia] and in the temple of Mars the Avenger [Ares], which cost me about 100,000,000 sesterces [nearly 2,500,000]. **3** As consul for the fifth time (29 BC) I returned 35,000 pounds of gold for crowns to the municipalities and Italian colonies which had contributed this towards my triumphs, and later, whenever I was hailed as imperator, I refused to accept crown gold [I did not accept the offers of a crown] though the municipalities and colonies decreed it just as generously as before [with the same eagerness as before].

22.1 On three occasions I put on a gladiatorial show in my own name and on five occasions in the name of my sons or grandsons; some 10,000 men fought it out in these shows. Twice in my own name and a third time in the name of my grandson I presented to the people a display of athletes summoned from far and wide. **2** I put on games in my own name on four occasions, as well as 23 times on behalf of other magistrates. On behalf of the College of Fifteen, as Master of the College with Marcus Agrippa as my colleague, I put on the Secular Games [on behalf of the Fifteen, with Marcus Agrippa as my colleague I put on the spectacles that take place after 100 years called Saeculares] in the consulship of Gaius Furnius and Gaius Silanus (17 BC). As consul for the thirteenth time (2 BC) I was the first to hold the Games of Mars [Ares], which from this time onwards the consuls have held in succeeding years by senatorial decree and by law. **3** I put on hunting spectacles of wild beasts from Africa for the people 26 times in my name or the name of my sons and grandsons in the circus or forum or amphitheatre, in which some 3,500 beasts were slaughtered.

23 I put on for the people the spectacle of a naval battle on the other side of the Tiber, at the place where the Grove of the Caesars now stands, after a site 1,800 feet in length and 1,200 in width had been excavated; here 30 beaked ships, triremes or biremes [on it 30 ships with rams, triremes or two-banked ships], as well as many smaller ships, met in battle. In these fleets some 3,000 men were engaged in the fighting apart from the rowers.

Offerings to the gods

24.1 As victor I replaced in the temples of all the cities in the province of Asia the ornaments [dedications] which the man against whom I had waged war had appropriated for himself after plundering the temples. **2** Silver statues which stood in the city of myself on foot, on horseback and in a four-horse chariot [in chariots] I personally removed and from the resulting funds placed offerings of gold in the temple of Apollo in my name and in the name of those who had honoured me with the statues.

Internal enemies

25.1 I brought peace to the sea, freeing it from the threat of pirates (i.e., Sextus Pompeius). In that war I handed back to their masters for punishment nearly 30,000 slaves who had run away from their masters and taken up arms against the state [I brought peace to the sea subjected to piracy by runaway slaves; of these I handed over some 30,000 to their masters for punishment]. **2** The whole of Italy of its own accord took an oath of allegiance to me and demanded that I be the leader in the war which I won at Actium. The provinces of Gaul and Spain, and Africa, Sicily, Sardinia [the provinces Gaul, Spain, Libya, Sicily, Sardinia] took the same oath. **3** Of those who served under my standards at that time, more than 700 were senators, of whom 83 either before or afterwards, up to the day of writing, have been made consuls and some 170 have been made priests.

World conquest

26.1 I extended the frontiers of all the provinces of the Roman people where the neighbouring peoples were not subject to our rule. **2** I pacified the Gallic and Spanish provinces [Gauls and Spains], and Germany likewise, the area bounded by Ocean from Cadiz to the mouth of the River Elbe. **3** I brought peace to the Alps from the region adjoining the Adriatic Sea as far as the Tuscan Sea [from the region near the Ionian Gulf as far as the Tyrrhenian Sea] without making war on any people unjustly. **4** My fleet navigated through Ocean from the mouth of the Rhine to the region of the rising sun as far as the territory of the Cimbri, which no Roman had ever reached either by land or by sea, and the Cimbri and the Charydes and the Semnones and other peoples of Germany of the same region through their envoys sought my friendship and that of the Roman people. **5** Under my command and under my auspices [under my command and with auspicious omens] two armies were led at almost the same time into Ethiopia and into that part of Arabia called Felix, and immense enemy forces of both peoples were killed in battle and numerous towns captured. They advanced into Ethiopia as far as the town Napata, very close to Meroe. The army penetrated into Arabia as far as the territory of the Sabaei to the town of Mariba [as far as the city Mariba].

27.1 I added Egypt to the empire of the Roman people. **2** Greater Armenia, which I could have made a province when its king, Artaxes, was murdered [after the king was killed], I preferred in accordance with the example of our ancestors to grant as a kingdom to Tigranes, the son of King Artavasdes and also grandson of King Tigranes, through the agency of Tiberius Nero, who at that point was my stepson. And when that same people later revolted and rebelled and were then reduced through the agency of my son Gaius, I handed them over to King Ariobarzanes, son of Artabazus, king of the Medes, for him to rule over, and after his death to his son Artavasdes; and when he was killed I sent to rule this kingdom Tigranes, who was descended from the Armenian royal family. **3** I won back all the provinces which lie towards the East and Cyrene across the Adriatic Sea [beyond the Ionian Gulf], which were at that point mostly in the possession of kings, and before that Sicily and Sardinia, which had been occupied in the slave war (i.e., under the control of Sextus Pompeius).

Colonial foundations

28.1 I established colonies of soldiers in Africa [Libya], Sicily, Macedonia, both Spains, Achaea, Syria, Gallia Narbonensis [Gaul around Narbo], Pisidia. **2** Moreover Italy has 28 colonies established under my authority, which in my own lifetime have become very populous and well inhabited [moreover Italy has 28 colonies established by me, which became very populous in my lifetime].

Military standards

29.1 After subduing the enemy I recovered numerous military standards, lost by other commanders, from Spain and Gaul and from the Dalmatians. **2** I compelled the Parthians to return to me the spoils and standards of three Roman armies and to request as suppliants the friendship of the Roman people. These standards, moreover, I placed in the sanctum of the temple of Mars [Ares] the Avenger.

The Danube

30.1 The peoples of Pannonia, whom no army of the Roman people had ever reached before my principate [before I was leader], I brought under the rule of the Roman people after they had been subdued by Tiberius Nero, at that time my stepson and legate, and I extended the frontiers of Illyricum to the bank of the River Danube [Ister]. **2** An army of Dacians which crossed over to this side was defeated and overwhelmed under my auspices [under my favourable omens], and afterwards my army was led across the Danube and compelled the peoples of Dacia to submit to the commands of the Roman people.

Diplomatic successes

31.1 Embassies of kings were frequently sent to me from India, such as had never been seen before that time in the presence of any Roman commander. **2** The Bastarnae sought our friendship though envoys, as did the Scythians, and kings of the Sarmatians on this side of the River Don and the further side [and the Sarmatians who are on this side of the River Don and the kings beyond], and the kings of the Albani and of the Hiberians and of the Medes.

32.1 Kings fled to me as suppliants, Tiridates, king of the Parthians, and later Phraates, son of King Phraates; Artavasdes, king of the Medes; Artaxares of the Adiabeni; Dumnobellaunus and Tincomarus of the Britons; Maelo of the Sygambri; and . . . rus of the Marcomannian Suebi. **2** Phraates, son of Orodes, king of the Parthians, sent into Italy to me all his sons and grandsons, not after defeat in war but in search of our friendship through the pledges of his children. **3** And a large number of other peoples have enjoyed the good faith of the Roman people during my principate [while I have been leader], with whom there had not previously been any exchange of embassies and friendship with the Roman people. **33** The peoples of Parthia and Media received kings they had requested using their leading men as envoys [kings, who were requested using leading men as envoys, received kingdoms from me]: the Parthians Vonones, son of King Phraates, grandson of King Orodes, the Medes Ariobarzanes, son of King Artavasdes, grandson of King Ariobarzanes.

Pre-eminence of Augustus

34.1 In my sixth and seventh consulships (28–27 BC), after I had put an end to the civil wars and acquired control of all affairs with everyone's consent [in accordance with the prayers of my fellow citizens], I transferred government from my own authority to the sovereignty of the senate and Roman people. **2** For this service of mine I received the name Augustus [Sebastos] by senatorial decree and the doorposts of my house were [my entranceway was] publicly arrayed in laurels, a civic crown was affixed above my door [the wreath of oak leaves which is granted for saving the lives of fellow citizens was fixed above the gateway of my house], and a golden shield was set up in the Julian senate house [in the council chamber]; through the inscription on this shield it is stated that the senate and people of Rome granted this to me in honour of my valour, clemency, justice and piety. **3** After that time I excelled everyone in auctoritas but had no more power than those who were also my colleagues in any magistracy [I excelled all in rank, but had no more power than those in office with me]. **35.1** While I was holding

677

my thirteenth consulship (2 BC), the senate and equestrian order and the entire
Roman people gave me the title of 'Father of his Country' (pater patriae) and
decreed that it should be inscribed in the vestibule [entranceway] of my house and
the Julian senate house [council chamber] and in the Forum of Augustus beneath
the chariot which was set up in my honour by senatorial decree. **2** When I wrote
this, I was in my seventy-sixth year (AD 13/14).

Appendix

1 The total amount of money that he gave either to the treasury or to the Roman
plebs or to discharged soldiers: 600,000,000 denarii. **2** The new works he completed: the temples of Mars, Jupiter the Thunderer and Feretrius, Apollo, the deified Julius, Quirinus, Minerva, Queen Juno, Jupiter Libertas, the Lares, the Penates
deities, Youth, the Great Mother; the Lupercal, platform of the gods (pulvinar) at
the Circus, senate house with the Chalcidicum, Forum of Augustus, basilica Julia,
theatre of Marcellus, Octavian portico, Grove of the Caesars across the Tiber
[the temples of Mars, Jupiter the Thunderer and Trophy-Bringer, Pan, Apollo,
god Julius, Quirinus, Athena, Queen Hera, Zeus the Liberator, Heroes, ancestral gods, Youth, Mother of Gods; council-chamber with Chalcidicum, Augustan
Forum, theatre of Marcellus, basilica Julia, Grove of Caesars, porticoes on the
Palatine, porticoes in the Flaminian hippodrome]. **3** He restored the Capitoline
temple and 82 sacred shrines, the theatre of Pompey, aqueducts, and Flaminian
Way [Flaminian Way, aqueducts]. **4** Expenses outlaid for theatrical shows and
gladiatorial games and for athletes and hunting spectacles and the sea battle, and
money given to colonies, municipalities, towns destroyed by earthquake or fire
[gifts to colonies and cities in Italy, and to cities in the provinces that had suffered
from earthquakes and fires], or individually to friends and senators, whose census
qualification he rounded up: immeasurable.

15.2 Dio *Roman History* 53.20.1, 21.1–22.1: Augustus' government

From 31 to 27 BC Octavian held the consulship every year, with his constitutional position
resting on the consulship and the oath taken to him by soldiers and citizens (*RG* 25.2; doc.
15.1). By the settlement of January 27 (doc. 14.64) he was to hold proconsular imperium
for ten years, governing a suite of provinces, including Egypt, through legates, as well as
controlling the greatest proportion of Rome's armed forces. Despite the pretence of the
restoration of the republic, Dio considers Augustus' power from 27 as monarchical.

20.1 Caesar, as I have said, was granted the name of Augustus (27 BC), and a sign
of no little importance to him took place that very night – for the Tiber flooded
and covered all the level areas of Rome which became navigable, and from this
the diviners prophesied that he would rise to great things and hold the whole city
in his power. . . . **21.1** Augustus conducted all the business of the empire with
even more commitment than before, as if he had received it spontaneously as a
present from everyone, and in particular enacted a considerable amount of legislation – however, I need not describe each piece in detail, but only those that are
relevant to my history. **2** And I shall do the same with regard to later events, so

that I shall not become tedious by dragging in all the sorts of things of which not even those dedicated to such studies have an intimate knowledge. **3** However, he did not enact all these laws just based on his own judgement, but some of them he first put before the public assembly, so that if they gave rise to discontent in any way he would know this in advance and make amendments – as he encouraged anybody whatever to give him their advice in case someone should think of a way to improve them – and granted people total freedom of speech, even redrafting some of them. **4** Most significantly, he took as advisors for six-month periods the consuls, or the other consul when he also held the consulship himself, one of each of the other types of magistrate, and 15 men chosen by lot from the remainder of the senatorial body, and in consequence the legislation proposed was in some way communicated through these to all the other senators. **5** For, while he brought some proposals before the whole senate, he generally followed this procedure, thinking it better to scrutinise most matters quietly in advance, especially the most important ones, in consultation with a few counsellors, and he even sometimes tried judicial cases with them. **6** The complete senate in its own right continued to sit in judgement as it had previously, and in some cases dealt with embassies and heralds from both assemblies and kings, while the people and plebs continued to meet for the elections – though nothing was ever done that did not meet with Augustus' approval. **7** At any rate it was he who chose and nominated for office some of the future magistrates, while in the case of others he maintained the old custom and left their selection in the hands of the people and plebs, while ensuring that none were elected who were unsuitable or appointed as the result of factional interests or bribery. **22.1** This then, in short, was how he governed the empire.

15.3 Suetonius *Life of the Deified Augustus* 85.1–2, 89.2–3: Augustus as author

Augustus, like Caesar (doc. 13.64), clearly tried his hand at a number of literary genres. In 46 BC Brutus published a eulogy of his father-in-law Cato, to which Augustus later wrote a response. His joke on his unsuccessful tragedy *Ajax* is typical of his sense of humour (see docs 15.65–66): in the Trojan war Ajax went mad and fell on his sword after failing to receive Achilles' weapons, which were given to the greatest Greek warrior. Augustus also wrote an autobiography in 13 books down until the Cantabrian war (27–26 BC). It is now lost, but Nikolaos of Damascus used material from it on Augustus' education in his (fragmentary) *Life of Augustus*, which is therefore a valuable source for his early life (cf. docs 14.7, 10).

85.1 He wrote numerous works of various kinds in prose, some of which he read aloud at a group of his close friends, as if in a lecture-room, for example his 'Response to Brutus' *Eulogy of Cato*'. In the case of this work, as he was now elderly, when he had nearly finished and was tired, he handed the rest over to Tiberius to read. He also wrote *Exhortations to Study Philosophy* and an *Autobiography* in 13 volumes which went up to the time of the Cantabrian war, but no further. **2** He also made light attempts at poetic works. One of these, written in hexameters, has come down to us, with the subject and title *Sicily*. There is another, equally short, of *Epigrams*, which he composed mainly at the baths. He also began a tragedy with great enthusiasm, but was unhappy with the style and destroyed it, telling his friends when they asked how *Ajax* was going that 'his *Ajax* had fallen on its sponge'. . . .

89.2 In reading authors in either Greek or Latin there was nothing to which he paid more attention than useful precepts and examples both to the public and to individuals, and he would often copy these word for word and send them to members of his household, or governors of armies and provinces, or city magistrates, whenever they needed counselling. He even read out entire volumes to the senate and made the people aware of them through proclamations, for example the speeches of Quintus Metellus (cos. 143) on 'Increasing the Birth-Rate' and Rutilius' (cos. 105) 'On the Size of Buildings', to convince them that he was not the first to pay attention to such matters, but that they had been of concern to their forefathers. **3** He encouraged the men of talent of his time in every way possible: he listened to their readings with goodwill and patience, not only poetry and history, but speeches and dialogues as well. But he was annoyed at being written about unless seriously and by the most distinguished writers, and used to warn the praetors not to allow his name to be devalued in prose declamations.

PRINCIPAL EVENTS

15.4 *Inscr. Ital.* **13.2: Excerpts from the *Fasti*, 19 BC–AD 14**

For the fasti, see the comment at doc. 14.63.

19 BC
12 October. Festival by senatorial decree, as on this day Imperator Caesar Augustus returned from the overseas provinces, entered the city and the altar of Fortuna Redux was set up (Amiternum).

13 BC
4 July. Festival by senatorial decree, as on this day the Altar of Augustan Peace in the Campus Martius was set up in the consulship of (Tiberius Claudius) Nero and (P. Quinctilius) Varus (Amiternum).

12 BC
6 March. Festival by senatorial decree, as on this day Imperator Caesar Augustus was made pontifex maximus in the consulship of (P. Sulpicius) Quirinius and (Gaius) Valgius (Rufus). The duoviri for this reason make sacrifice and the people wear garlands and abstain from work (Praeneste).
28 April. Festival by senatorial decree, as on this day buildings and the altar of Vesta were dedicated in the house of Imperator Caesar Augustus, pontifex maximus in the consulship of (P. Sulpicius) Quirinius and (Gaius) Valgius (Rufus) (Praeneste).

9 BC
30 January. Festival by senatorial decree, as on this day the Altar of Augustan Peace in the Campus Martius was dedicated in the consulship of (Nero Claudius) Drusus and (Titus Quinctius) Crispinus (Praeneste).

2 BC

5 February. Festival by senatorial decree, as on this day Imperator Caesar Augustus, pontifex maximus, holding tribunician power for the 21st time, consul for the 13th time, was named father of his country (pater patriae) by the senate and Roman people (Praeneste).

AD 2

20 August. Sacrifice in honour of the dead Lucius Caesar (Antium).

AD 4

21 or 22 February. Sacrifice in honour of the dead Gaius Caesar (Verulae).

26 June. Festival by senatorial decree, as on this day Imperator Caesar Augustus adopted as his son Tiberius Caesar, in the consulship of (Sextus) Aelius (Catus) and (Gaius) Sentius (Saturninus) (Amiternum).

AD 14

17 September. Festival by senatorial decree, as on this day divine honours to the deified Augustus were decreed by the senate in the consulship of Sextus Appuleius and Sextus Pompeius (Amiternum).

AUGUSTUS' CONSTITUTIONAL POSITION

In 23 BC, because of ill-health, and possibly also because of the conspiracy of Fannius Caepio and Varro Murena (which is not securely dated), Augustus resigned the consulship (on 1 July), which he had held continuously since 31. In its place he took tribunician potestas for life (he already had tribunician sacrosanctity), the right to bring matters to the senate, and the right to retain proconsular imperium in the city. He was to retain the office of tribune until his death in AD 14, and the tribunate was to be an identifying mark of the princeps, with Augustus dating his reign by it. From this point he designated potential successors by taking them as tribunician colleagues. Although no longer consul, he retained his provinces, and much scholarship has been spent on the question of whether from this period his proconsular imperium was 'greater' than that of senatorial governors (maius imperium), and whether he therefore could override the governors in the senatorial provinces. Pompey had possessed such imperium in his command in the 60s against the pirates, and the senate had granted it to Brutus and Cassius in 44. The sources below suggest that Augustus did possess maius imperium, but that he was careful not to draw attention to it and preferred to focus on his tribunician role as protector of the people. The funeral oration for Agrippa, who was Augustus' deputy in the East 23–21 BC, also suggests that he was granted maius imperium (doc. 15.48, cf. doc. 14.3 for Brutus and Cassius).

15.5 Dio *Roman History* 53.30.1–32.6: The 'second settlement', 23 BC

At this point Augustus passed over his young nephew Marcellus as his successor, instead nominating Agrippa; Agrippa was sent to the East in 23 BC not because of hostility between himself and Marcellus (cf. doc. 15.38) but to deal with issues in the East, perhaps including negotiation over the Parthian standards. This passage (53.32.5) is frequently cited as evidence for Augustus' maius imperium.

30.1 When Augustus was consul for the eleventh time, with (Gnaeus) Calpurnius Piso (23 BC), he again fell ill, and so seriously, that he had no hope of recovering. At any rate he arranged everything as if he were going to die and collected around him the magistrates and the most prominent senators and knights, though he did not appoint a successor, **2** despite the fact that they all expected that Marcellus would be nominated for this position. In fact, after talking a little with them about public affairs, he gave Piso a list of the armed forces and public revenues written in a book and his ring to Agrippa . . . **31.1** When restored to health he brought his will into the senate and wanted to read it, to show everyone that he had not appointed a successor – though in fact he didn't read it out as no one would let him. **2** Everyone was absolutely astonished at this, as he loved Marcellus as both son-in-law and nephew, and as well as the other honours he had given him had helped him make an outstanding success of the festival he put on as aedile, **3** by providing the forum with curtains overhead all summer and presenting on stage a dancer who was a knight and a woman of noble birth, and yet he had not entrusted the monarchy to him, but had actually preferred Agrippa. **4** It seems, therefore, that he did not yet have confidence in the youth's judgement but wanted either the people to regain their liberty or that Agrippa should receive the leadership from them – for he clearly realised that Agrippa was very highly regarded by them, and he didn't want to appear to be handing sovereignty over to him on his own initiative. **32.1** So when he recovered, and learnt that because of this Marcellus was not on good terms with Agrippa, he immediately sent Agrippa to Syria so there should be no chance of their falling out by having to associate with each other. Agrippa left the city straight away but did not get to Syria: with rather more than his usual self-restraint, he sent his legates there and remained on Lesbos.

2 Apart from doing all this, Augustus appointed ten praetors, as he no longer needed any more, and this happened for several more years. The rest were to perform the same duties as in previous years, but two of them were to be in charge of each year's financial administration. **3** After arranging all these details, he went to the Alban Mount and resigned the consulship. Since things had settled down, he and most of the other consuls had held office for the entire year, and he wanted to put an end to this now, so that as many people as possible might become consuls, and he did this outside the city so that no one would stop him. **4** He was praised for this and because he had selected to fill his place Lucius Sestius, who had always been a fervent supporter of Brutus and had served with him in all his wars, and even at this late date still kept his memory alive, had statues of him, and delivered panegyrics in his favour. Not only did Augustus not disapprove of such friendship and loyalty, he actually respected them. **5** Because of this the senate decreed that he should be tribune for life, granted him the right at each senate meeting to bring forward any matter he wished at any time, even if he were not consul, and allowed him to have the rank of proconsul once for all and in perpetuity so that he did not have to lay it down when entering the pomerium or have it renewed again, and to hold authority in subject territory superior to that of the governors in each case. **6** Consequently both he and the emperors after him had a certain legal right to use the tribunician power in addition to their other powers – for the actual title of tribune was not held by Augustus or any other emperor.

15.6 Strabo *Geography* 17.3.25: The division of the provinces

Strabo, writing not long after Augustus' death, states here that Augustus was given authority to make war or peace for his lifetime across all Roman territory (not merely restricted to 'his' provinces). Gallia Narbonensis and Cyprus became senatorial provinces in 23 BC.

The provinces have been divided up in different ways at different times, but at present they are as Caesar Augustus organised them. For when his country entrusted him with the government of the empire and he was granted authority to make war or peace for his lifetime, he divided all the territory into two parts and granted one to himself and the other to the people. To himself he allocated whatever had need of a military garrison – that is the barbarian territory close to the tribes that had not as yet been subjugated or where the land is poor and not adapted to agriculture, with the result that the people rebel and are disobedient because of its poverty and the abundance of strongholds. To the people he allocated the remaining territory, which is peaceful and easy to govern without an army. He divided each part into a number of provinces, some called *Caesar's*, the others *the people's*. Caesar sends out governors and administrators to Caesar's provinces, organising the territories differently at different periods and administering them according to the circumstances of the time, while the people send praetors and consuls to the public provinces; these too are organised into different groupings as expedience demands. To begin with he made two provinces consular – Libya, the region under Roman rule, excluding that area formerly ruled by Juba and now by his son Ptolemy, and Asia within the Halys and Taurus, excluding the Galatians and the tribes under Amyntas, as well as Bithynia and the Propontis – and ten provinces praetorian: in Europe and the neighbouring islands, the region called Further Spain, which reaches to the River Baetis, Narbonese Gaul, third Sardinia with Corsica, fourth Sicily, fifth and sixth the part of Illyricum next to Epirus and Macedonia, seventh Achaea (Greece), including Thessaly and the Aetolians and Acharnanians and some of the Epirote tribes which border Macedonia, eighth Crete and Cyrenaica, ninth Cyprus, tenth Bithynia with the Propontis and some areas of Pontus. Caesar has the other provinces, to which he sends consulars to supervise some of them, praetorians to some and equestrians to others: and kings and dynasts and decarchies are in his area and always were.

15.7 *RDGE* 61: Restoration of property in Asia, 27 BC

As consuls in 27 BC, Augustus and Agrippa pronounced that public places and properties then in the hands of individuals had to be restored to the city or to the gods. Interestingly the province of Asia, to which this applies, was under the control of the senate from 27, and technically, therefore, Augustus had no role in its governorship. It was presumably the case that the consuls had been instructed by the senate to investigate the situation following the end of the civil wars. There follows a letter in Latin by Vinicius (identity unknown), who was governor of Asia shortly after 27 and who had been approached by the people of Kyme to carry out the consuls' instructions. That Augustus alone is named in his letter and that he was to be seen as 'restorer' of the sanctuary of Dionysos (in Latin: Liber Pater) is significant for the understanding of attitudes towards his unique position at this point.

A. Imperator Caesar Augustus, son of the god, . . . and Marcus Agrippa, son of Lucius, consuls . . . If there are any public or sacred places in the cities (or in the territory) of each city of the province, and if there are or will be **5** any dedications at these places, no one is to remove or buy them or take them as security or gift. Whatever has been taken away from there or bought and given as a gift, whoever is in charge of the province is to ensure that it is restored to the public or **10** sacred account of the city, and whatever money may have been given as security, he is not to use this in administering justice.

B. . . . Vinicius, proconsul, sends greetings to the magistrates of Kyme. Apollonides, son of Lucius, the Noracean, your citizen, came to me and demonstrated that the temple of Liber Pater is, by title of sale, in the possession of Lysias, son of Diogenes, your citizen, **15** and when the worshippers (thiasitae) wished to restore the sacred property to the god, according to the order of Augustus Caesar, by paying the price which is inscribed on the temple, (it was withheld) by Lysias. I wish you to ensure that, if this is the case, Lysias accepts the price which has been put on the temple and restores the temple to the god and that there be inscribed on it, 'Imperator Caesar, son of the god, Augustus **20** restored it'. But if Lysias refuses what Apollonides demands, let him give adequate bail (to appear) where I will be. I approve more that Lysias promises (bail).

15.8 Dio *Roman History* 54.10.1–6: Further powers, 19 BC

Augustus was absent from Rome in the East for three years from September 22 BC. In 21 BC the people tried to insist on electing him consul, and in 20 they refused to elect more than one consul for 19, C. Sentius Saturninus, leaving the other position for Augustus. In 19 envoys were sent to try to persuade him to take the vacant office, but he selected one of the envoys instead. When he returned, in October that year, the senate constructed an altar to Fortuna Redux ('Fortunate Return': doc. 15.4), decreeing that on that date the priests and Vestals should offer a sacrifice, and wanted to offer him a triumph, which he refused though he accepted triumphal ornaments. On his return he was also granted the prefecture of morals, consular power for life, and the right to enact any laws that he wished, presumably without taking them to the assembly. These new powers were demonstrated by his sitting between the two consuls in the senate and having 12 lictors at all times. More importantly, but less obviously, in 18 his proconsular imperium was renewed for another five years, while Agrippa was also given tribunician potestas and presumably imperium for five years.

1 The consul that year was Gaius Sentius (19 BC). When it was found necessary to elect a colleague to serve with him (for on this occasion as well Augustus refused the magistracy which was being kept open for him), there was civil strife again in Rome and a number of murders, so that the senators voted Sentius a guard. **2** When he refused to make use of it, they sent envoys to Augustus, each with two lictors. When he learnt of what had been happening, realising that there would be no end to the evil, he did not deal with the matter as he had before but appointed as consul one of the envoys themselves, Quintus Lucretius, although he had been listed among the proscribed, and himself hurried to Rome. **3** For this and for other things he had achieved while absent, he was voted many honours of all kinds, none of which he would accept, except the establishment of an altar to Fortuna Redux (this was the name they gave her) and that the day on which he returned should be counted among the holidays and named Augustalia. **4** Since even then the magistrates and the others made preparations to go and meet him on the way, he entered the city at night, and on the next day gave Tiberius the rank of an ex-praetor and Drusus the right to stand for magistracies five years before the customary time. **5** In addition, as there was no similarity between the behaviour of the people in his absence, when they rioted, and when he was in Rome, when they were afraid, on their invitation he was elected supervisor of morals (praefectus moribus) for five years, and accepted the authority of the censors for the same period, and that of consul for life, and consequently was able to use the 12 fasces always and everywhere, and to sit on the curule chair between the consuls of each year. **6** After voting these privileges they begged him to set everything to rights, and that the laws proposed by him should be called 'leges Augustae', and they wanted to swear an oath that they would abide by them. He accepted all the other measures as he thought them necessary but absolved them from the oath.

15.9 *ILS* 244: Augustus' constitutional powers

This law of AD 70 appears to be a law of the people reflecting a senatorial decree outlining the constitutional powers possessed by the emperor Vespasian. It quotes as precedents earlier grants of imperium to Augustus, Tiberius and Claudius. The powers given to Augustus in the 'settlement' of 23 may have been embodied in a similar law passed by the assembly.

. . . that he (Vespasian) shall have the right to conclude treaties with whomever he wishes, just as the deified Augustus and Tiberius Julius Caesar Augustus and Tiberius Claudius Caesar Augustus Germanicus had; and that he shall have the right to convene the senate, to put and refer proposals to it, and to have decrees of the senate to be enacted by proposal and division of the senate, **5** just as the deified Augustus and Tiberius Julius Caesar Augustus and Tiberius Claudius Caesar Augustus Germanicus had; and that, when the senate is convened, in accordance with his wish, authority, order or command, or in his presence, everything transacted shall be considered and declared as fully irrevocable as if the meeting of the senate had been convoked and held as normal; **10** and that, at all elections, particular consideration shall be granted to candidates for a magistracy, office, imperium or any supervisory position whom he has recommended to the Roman senate and people or to whom he has given and promised his vote; . . . and that he shall have the right to transact and act upon whatever divine, human, private and public matters he considers to serve the advantage and paramount interest of the state, just as the deified Augustus and **20** Tiberius Julius Caesar Augustus and Tiberius Claudius Caesar Augustus Germanicus had; and that those laws and plebiscites which were declared not binding on the deified Augustus and Tiberius

Julius Caesar Augustus and Tiberius Claudius Caesar Augustus Germanicus shall not be binding on the Emperor Caesar **25** Vespasian, and the Emperor Caesar Vespasian Augustus shall have the right to do whatever was proper for the deified Augustus and Tiberius Julius Caesar Augustus and Tiberius Claudius Caesar Augustus Germanicus to do by virtue of any law or enactment; and that whatever was done, **30** executed, decreed or ordered before the enactment of this law by the Emperor Caesar Vespasian Augustus, or by anyone at his order or command, shall be as fully irrevocable and valid as if they had been done by order of the people or plebs.

15.10 *SEG* 9.8: Edicts relating to Cyrene, 7/6 BC

The five Cyrene edicts date from 7/6 and 4 BC and concern a number of issues, including revision of the judiciary system, a case of treason and liability for public services. The province of Crete and Cyrene was senatorial, but from the fact of his involvement these edicts appear to demonstrate that Augustus as princeps possessed maius imperium overriding that of the governor, and these edicts are often cited in that regard.

I The emperor Caesar Augustus, pontifex maximus, in the seventeenth year of tribunician potestas, acclaimed imperator 14 times, declares:

Since I find that all the Romans in the provincial territory of Cyrene **5** of all ages who have a census rating of 2,500 denarii or more, from whom the judges are taken, and since embassies from the cities of the province have complained that among these same Romans there are certain conspiracies to oppress the Greeks in law-suits with capital penalties, with the same people acting in turn as **10** accusers and witnesses for each other; and since I have myself ascertained that some innocent people have been maltreated in this way and carried off to pay the ultimate penalty, until the senate should make some decision on this, or I myself find a better solution, in my view it will be the right and appropriate thing for those governing the province of Crete and Cyrene to appoint in the provincial territory **15** of Cyrene the same number of Greek jurors from the highest census ratings as Romans, none, whether Roman or Greek, to be less than 25 years and none to have a census rating and property of less than 7,500 denarii, if there is a sufficient number of such men. If the number of those judges who need to be appointed cannot be filled up in this way, they shall appoint men **20** of half this census rating, but not less, to be jurors in the trials of Greeks on capital charges. . . .

II The emperor Caesar Augustus, pontifex maximus, in the seventeenth year of tribunician potestas, declares: Publius Sextius Scaeva does not merit reproach or blame in that he decided that Aulus Stlaccius Maximus son of Lucius, Lucius Stlaccius Macedo son of Lucius, and Publius Lacutanius Phileros freedman of Publius **45** should be sent on to me under guard from the province of Cyrene as they had stated that they knew and wished to declare something with regard to my safety and public affairs; in doing this Sextius acted conscientiously and properly. But since they have no information relating to me or to public affairs and have made it clear to me that they **50** fabricated and lied in what they said in the province, I have released them and set them free from custody. But as for Aulus Stlaccius Maximus, whom the Cyrenaean envoys accuse of having removed statues from public places, among them even the one on which the city engraved my name on the base, until I have investigated this matter **55** I order him not to depart without my permission.

III The emperor Caesar Augustus, pontifex maximus, in the seventeenth year of tribunician potestas, declares: If people from the province of Cyrene have been honoured with (Roman) citizenship, I order them nonetheless to perform in their turn the compulsory public services (liturgies) of the Greeks, apart from those to whom in accordance with a law or decree of the senate, or by the decree of my father or myself exemption was granted **60** along with citizenship. And even for these, to whom exemption was granted, it is my pleasure that they shall be exempt with regard to the property they possessed at the time, but that they should be charged for all property acquired subsequently.

AUGUSTUS 'IMPERATOR'

At its first meeting on 1 January 29 BC, when Octavian was still in the East, the senate granted him the right to use 'imperator' as a first name. It also decreed that the doors of the temple of Janus should now be closed (this took place on 11 January) as Octavian had 'put an end to all wars'; this did not of course refer to ongoing wars such as in Spain (doc. 14.60). Caesar had also been granted the name imperator as a title, as well as liberator (doc. 13.55). To celebrate his triple triumph Augustus gave 400 sesterces to every citizen and 1,000 to discharged soldiers, and Antony's birthday (14 January) became an unlucky day (nefastus; doc. 14.63)

15.11 Vergil *Aeneid* 8.675–90, 714–31: Augustus' triple triumph

In book 8 of Vergil's epic the *Aeneid*, Aeneas meets King Evander, who is ruling on the future site of Rome. He is given a shield that his mother Venus has had made by Vulcan, depicting Rome's future glories. The final scenes of Rome's triumphs that are shown include Augustus' victory at Actium and his triple triumph over Cleopatra (Actium), the Egyptians and Dalmatia, celebrated 13–15 August 29.

675 In the centre bronze ships, the battle of Actium,
    Could be discerned and you could see in warfare's preparation
    All Leucas afire, the waves gleaming with gold.
    On one side Augustus Caesar leads Italians into battle
    With senate, people, household and great gods,
680 Standing on the high stern; his forehead shoots twin flames,
    His father's star displayed upon his head.
    Elsewhere Agrippa, favoured by winds and gods
    Leads troops; the proud prize in war
    Shines on his brow, the naval crown with beaks.
    On the other side Antony, with barbarous wealth and foreign weapons,
    Conqueror of eastern peoples and oriental shores,

Leads behind him Egypt, and the Orient's might
And utmost Bactria, his Egyptian consort following him (abomination!).
All press on together, and the whole sea foams,
690   Churned by the circling oars and the three-pronged rams. . . .

714   Next Caesar, entering Rome's walls in triple triumph,
Dedicates immortal offerings to the Italian gods,
Three hundred massive shrines throughout the city.
The streets resound with happiness, games, applause:
Crowds of women in every temple, altars in each one.
Before the altars slaughtered bullocks strew the ground.
720   He, sitting at the snow-white threshold of shining Apollo,
Inspects the gifts of nations, and fixes them to proud doors.
Conquered peoples pass in a long line,
As diverse in language as in appearance, dress and arms.
Here Vulcan has formed the Nomad race and loose-robed Africans,
There the Leleges and Carians and arrow-bearing Gelonians;
Euphrates runs with gentler waves, and the Morini,
Remotest of mankind, the two-horned Rhine,
The untamed Dahae, and Araxes, resentful of its bridge.
Such things on Vulcan's shield, his mother's gift,
730   He wonders at, delighting in the images, ignorant of what will come,
Raising to his shoulder the glory and destinies of his descendants.

15.12 Suetonius *Life of the Deified Augustus* 21.1–3: Augustus' foreign policy

Augustus' contribution to the defeat of Brutus and Cassius had not been conspicuous, but he had increasingly gained ground against the experienced commander Antony when his successful Illyrian campaigns (35–33 BC) were compared with Antony's failure to achieve victories against the Parthians at the same period. This Illyrian campaign was one of the only two led personally by Augustus, and he was primarily responsible for its success; he was even wounded in battle. The standards lost in the campaigns of Crassus, Decidius Saxa and Mark Antony were returned by Phraates IV in 20 BC after negotiations relating to Phraates' kidnapped son, but their return was heralded as a great triumph of arms and a personal victory for Augustus (doc. 15.18).

21.1 Sometimes as general and sometimes under his own auspices he overcame Cantabria, Aquitania, Pannonia and Dalmatia together with all Illyricum, and like-wise Raetia and the Vindelici and Salassi, Alpine tribes. He brought to an end the invasions of the Dacians, with three of their leaders and huge numbers slain, and pushed the Germans back over the River Albis, except for the Suebi and Sigambri, who surrendered and whom he escorted into Gaul and settled in lands next to the Rhine. Similarly, he subjugated other unruly peoples. **2** He never made war on any nation without just and necessary cause, and he was so far from wishing to expand his empire or military reputation at all costs that he compelled the leaders of certain barbarians to swear an oath in the temple of Mars the Avenger that they would maintain the faith and peace which they requested, while in some cases he tried exacting a new kind of hostage – women – realising that they disregarded males as surety; he also gave everyone the power of reclaiming their hostages whenever they wished. On those who rebelled frequently and duplicitously, he never imposed any heavier punishment than that of selling the prisoners on condition that they should not be slaves in a neighbouring country, nor be freed within 30 years. **3** On account of this reputation for valour and moderation, he brought even the Indians and Scythians, known to us only by hearsay, to send envoys to request his friendship and that of the Roman people. The Parthians as well readily gave up Armenia at his command, and at his request returned the military standards which they had won from Marcus Crassus (52 BC) and Mark Antony (40, 36 BC), and furthermore offered him hostages, while, when there were on one occasion several people claiming the throne, they would only accept the person selected by him.

15.13 *ILS* 886: Triumph for Plancus, after 22 BC

A mausoleum near Caieta, Latium. Plancus (cos. 42 BC) had supported Antony but defected to Octavian in 32. It was on his proposal that Octavian was voted the name Augustus in 27 (doc. 14.65). While Plancus had been allowed a triumph, these became increasingly restricted to Augustus and his family. Victories won by governors in Augustus' provinces was seen as Augustus' own, as the governor was fighting under his auspices. The last triumph held by a non-member of the imperial family was that of Cornelius Balbus in 19 BC.

Lucius Munatius Plancus, son of Lucius, grandson of Lucius, great-grandson of Lucius, consul, censor, twice imperator, one of the Seven for feasts, triumphed over the Raetians, built the temple of Saturn from spoils, divided lands in Italy at Beneventum, settled two colonies in Gaul, Lugdunum and Raurica.

15.14 Livy *History of Rome* 4.20.7: The spolia opima

M. Licinius Crassus (cos. 30 BC), who was awarded a triumph for victories over the Thracians in 21 BC, claimed the right to dedicate the spolia opima for having killed the leader of the enemy. Only three Romans had previously been given this honour, one of whom, Cossus, was a military tribune when he killed the king of the Veientes in 437 BC, and so not fighting under his own auspices. Crassus claimed Cossus as a precedent, but the honour was refused by Octavian because he claimed that Cossus *had* been consul and therefore fighting under his own auspices, unlike Crassus, who was fighting under Octavian's auspices, not his own. An inscription 'found' during the restoration of the temple of Jupiter fortuitously proved that Cossus had actually been consul and fighting under his own auspices; Augustus therefore refused to award Crassus the spolia opima. Livy clearly doubts the veracity of this evidence.

I myself heard Augustus Caesar, the founder or restorer of all the temples, say that he entered the shrine of Jupiter Feretrius when it was collapsing from age, and restored it, and he actually read himself that inscription on the linen breastplate – so I considered it almost sacrilegious to rob Cossus of the evidence witnessed by Caesar, in his restoration of that actual temple, as to his plunder.

15.15 Nikolaos of Damascus *F* 100: An Indian embassy

Cf. Strabo 15.1.73, Dio 54.9.8–10, who adds the details that the gifts included tigers and that Augustus was in Athens at the time. The holy man was presumably a Buddhist priest. Plutarch comments that the tomb was well known in his day (*Alex.* 69.8); herms, sculptured pillars of Hermes with heads but no arms, stood outside houses in classical Athens.

To these may be added the account of Nikolaos of Damascus. He says that at Antioch, near Daphne, he met with envoys from the Indians who had been sent to Augustus Caesar. It seems from the letter that there were more, but only three had survived, whom he says he saw: the rest had died owing to the length of the journey. The letter was written in Greek on a skin and revealed that the writer was Porus, who, although he ruled 600 kings, put the highest value on the friendship of Caesar and was prepared to allow him access to his country, whichever part he wished, and would co-operate in anything that was fair. He says that this is what the letter said. Eight naked servants, wearing girdles and anointed with perfumes, presented the gifts they had brought. The presents were a 'Hermes', who from infancy had no arms from his shoulders, whom I have seen, huge snakes, a serpent 10 cubits in length, a river tortoise 3 cubits in length, and a partridge larger than a vulture. They were accompanied, it is said, by the person who burnt himself to death at Athens. This is what they do when they are in distress and want to escape their present adversity, while those in prosperity do the same like this man; for as everything till now had succeeded with him, he thought it necessary to depart this life, in case some unwished-for circumstance should fall on him while he was still alive – and so with a smile, naked and anointed, wearing a girdle, he leapt onto the pyre: on his tomb was inscribed: 'Here lies Zarmanochegas ("sramana teacher"), an Indian from Bargosa, who made himself immortal in accordance with the customs of the Indians.'

15.16 Ovid *Fasti* 1.709–22: The Ara Pacis Augustae

This altar ('the altar of Augustan Peace') was commissioned in honour of Augustus' return from Spain and Gaul in 13 BC and dedicated on 30 January 9 BC to celebrate the peace brought to Rome by Augustus. It stood in the north-east corner of the Campus Martius, and its surrounding walls depicted the advantages and security Rome now enjoyed and the importance of traditional piety. Many of the figures portrayed specific individuals such as members of the imperial family.

My song has led me to the Altar of Peace.
710 This will be one day from the month's end.
With your hair tied back and crowned with Actian laurel fronds,
Peace be present and gently remain throughout the whole world.
While we lack enemies, there is also no reason for a triumph:
You will be a greater glory to our leaders than war.
May the soldier take arms only to restrain arms,
And may the fierce trumpet sound only for ceremonies.

May all the ends of the earth dread Aeneas' line.
If any land fears Rome too little, then may it love her!
Priests, throw incense on the flames of peace,
720 And let a white victim stricken on its head fall down.
That the house that champions peace may last with peace for ever
Beseech the deities who favour pious prayers.

15.17 Pliny the Elder *Natural History* 3.136–37: Trophy in the Alps, 7–6 BC

This victory monument celebrated Augustus' victories (or, rather, those of his stepsons Tiberius and Drusus) over the Alpine tribes before 6 BC (*RG* 26.3: doc. 15.1). It stood on the highest point of the Roman road (the Via Julia Augusta) into Gaul (modern La Turbie, just north of Monaco).

To Imperator Caesar Augustus, son of the god, pontifex maximus, imperator 14 times, in the seventeenth year of tribunician power, the senate and people of Rome because under his leadership and auspices all the Alpine peoples, from the upper sea to the lower, have been brought under the power of the Roman people.

Alpine peoples conquered: Trumplini, Camunni, Venostes, Vennonetes, Isarci, Breuni, Genaunes, Focunates, four Vindelician peoples, Consuanetes, Rucinates, Licates, Catenates, Ambisontes, Rugusci, Sunaetes, Calucones, Brixenetes, Leponti, Uberi, Nantuates, Seduni, Varagri, Salassi, Acitavones, Medulli, Ucenni, Caturiges, Brigiani, Sogiontii, Brodiontii, Nemaloni, Edenates, Vesubiani, Veamini, barbarous Gauls, Ulatti, Ecdini, Vergunni, Egui, Turi, Nematuri, Oratelli, Nerusi, Velauni and Suetri.

15.18 Crawford *RRC* 4453: Triumph over Parthia

An aureus of 18–17 BC. The negotiations with Parthia were facilitated by the return of the kidnapped son of Phraates IV (taken to Rome as hostage by Tiridates, a pretender to the Parthian throne) in exchange for the lost legionary standards and any remaining prisoners of war in 20 BC. Augustus depicted this as a military victory linked with the subjugation of Armenia, which became a client state (see *RG* 29.2; doc. 15.1): a new temple was built to house the standards, that of Mars Ultor, and coins were minted with the legend below, while the victory was also featured on the breastplate of the Prima Porta statue of Augustus.

Obverse: Head of Augustus, bareheaded. Legend: The senate and people of Rome to Imperator Caesar Augustus, consul 11 times, in his sixth year of tribunician power.

Reverse: Triumphal arch with three portals; above the central portal a quadriga with figure of Augustus; over the left portal a Parthian soldier offering Augustus a standard; over the right portal another Parthian offering an eagle with the right hand and holding a bow in the left. Legend: Citizens and military standards recovered from the Parthians.

AUGUSTUS AND TRADITIONAL RELIGION

15.19 Dio *Roman History* 53.1.3–6: The Actian games, 27 BC

Augustus and Agrippa were consuls in 27, as in 28 BC. Octavian established the Actian games at Nicopolis, near the site of the battle of Actium, in commemoration of his victory over Antony and Cleopatra in 31 BC. The games had Olympic status and were celebrated every four years from 27 until the mid-third century AD. The Roman or Great Games featured a procession of Roman youths and were also noted for their chariot races (doc. 2.70).

3 At this particular time he not only attended to his normal duties but completed the taking of the census, and in connection with this was called 'princeps senatus', as had been customary when there really was a Republic. He also completed and dedicated the temple of Apollo on the Palatine, the precinct around it, and the libraries. **4** He held with Agrippa the festival decreed to celebrate the victory at Actium and as part of this put on the Circus games for youths and men of the nobility. **5** This was held for a time every four years and was in the charge of the four priesthoods in succession – I mean the pontiffs, augurs, the 'Seven' and the 'Fifteen', as they were called. On this occasion, a wooden stadium was constructed in the Campus Martius and an athletics competition held, as well as gladiatorial combats between prisoners. **6** These went on for several days and continued even when Caesar fell ill, as Agrippa discharged all Caesar's duties as well as his own.

15.20 Suetonius *Life of the Deified Augustus* 31.1–4: Religious reforms

Augustus prided himself on his restoration of temples (82 in 28 BC, according to *RG* 20.4) and construction of additional sacred monuments such as the temples of Apollo and Mars Ultor. In order to restore traditional religious practices and values, he revived priesthoods and ancient ceremonies, including the ludi Saeculares. Lepidus died in 13, but Augustus did not assume the role until March 12, as the pontifex maximus traditionally took office in March. From this point he had a justification for overseeing all religious practices and centred state religion around his own house, where he dedicated a shrine to Vesta rather than taking up residence in the domus publica, as would have been normal for the pontifex maximus.

1 After he had eventually taken on the position of pontifex maximus after Lepidus' death (as he could not bring himself to assume it while Lepidus was still alive), he collected all prophetic books, Greek or Latin in origin, which were in circulation anonymously or under the names of authors of poor reputation, and burnt them, retaining only the Sibylline Books, and these too only selectively, placing them in two gilded cases under the pedestal of the Palatine Apollo. **2** The calendar, which had been laid down by the divine Julius, but afterwards disordered and confused through negligence, he returned to its former regular system, and as part of this arrangement he called the month Sextilis (August) by his own cognomen (8 BC), rather than September in which he had been born, because it was in this month that his first consulship and most outstanding victories had occurred. **3** He increased both the number and the prominence of the priests, as well as their privileges, especially those of the Vestal Virgins. And when it was necessary for another to be selected in place of one who had died (when many people intrigued to ensure their daughters were not part of the selection by lot), he swore that if any of his granddaughters were of the right age he would have put her name forward. **4** He also resurrected some of the ancient rites that had gradually become neglected, such as the augury of Safety, the position of flamen dialis, the Lupercalia, the ludi Saeculares and the Compitalia. At the Lupercalia he forbade beardless boys from running, and similarly at the ludi Saeculares stopped young people of both sexes from attending any ceremony at night unless with an older relative. He arranged that the Lares of the crossroads (Lares Compitales) should be decorated twice a year with spring and summer flowers.

15.21 Ovid *Fasti* 2.617–34: Household cults

At the Caristia, on 22 February, families gathered to dine together and make offerings to their Lares. It followed the Parentalia, a nine-day festival where families visited their ancestral tombs and made offerings to the spirits of the dead.

> The following day is called the Caristia, from 'dear ones',
> When a crowd of relatives comes to see their kindred gods.
> After our family tombs and our departed it is, no doubt,
> 620 Pleasant to turn our faces on living family,
> After all those lost, to behold what remains of our blood,
> And reckon up the degrees of our kinship.
> Let the blameless come: stay far from here, far away
> Faithless brother, and mothers severe on their children,
> Those who think their father too much alive, who count up their mother's years,
> The unjust mother-in-law who treats her hated son's wife harshly . . .
>
> 631 Good people, offer incense to your family's gods
> (Concord will especially favour you on this day)
> Make food offerings, welcome tokens of respect,
> So the offering-dish will feed the ungirt Lares.
> And when cool night entices you to your peaceful sleep,
> Pour out wine with a lavish hand and pray,
> 'Lares, be well!, you too, country's father, best of men, O Caesar!'
> Hallowed words to utter as you pour the unmixed wine.

15.22 *CIL* 6.883: Livia and Fortuna Muliebris

Livia supported Augustus in all his religious reforms and was responsible for restoring the temple of the women-only cult of Bona Dea on the Aventine. She also restored the ancient shrine of Fortuna Muliebris ('Fortune of Women') at the fourth milestone along the Via Latina; for this cult, see doc. 7.84 (women who participated were expected to be univirae – having only one husband – which Livia, of course, was not). She identifies herself in this case by both her father and her husband, suggesting perhaps that this restoration was undertaken of her own volition.

Livia, daughter of Drusus, wife of Caesar Augustus . . . .

MARRIAGE, DIVORCE AND ADULTERY

Augustus instituted wide-ranging legislation, much of which targeted the morality and behaviour of the senatorial and equestrian classes, which he brought before the assembly in his position as tribune. He was particularly concerned with issues of marriage and the birth rate, and in 18 BC he promulgated the *lex Julia de maritandis ordinibus* (encouraging marriage in the upper-class orders and restricting whom they could marry) and the *lex Julia de adulteriis coercendis* (making adultery and other sexual misconduct such as pederasty with a citizen boy a public as well as a private crime). His laws offered inducements to marriage and childbearing and imposed penalties on the unmarried and childless. Adultery was now strictly punished by exile and confiscation of property, and celibacy by the inability to receive certain legacies. His legislation of 18 BC was not well received, and he updated it in AD 9 through the *lex Papia Poppaea*, named for the two (unmarried) consuls of that year, Papius and Poppaeus.

15.23 Suetonius *Life of the Deified Augustus* 34.1–2: New laws on marriage

Augustus' marriage legislation required all citizen males between 25 and 60 years, and women between 20 and 50, to marry or suffer penalties including those of restricted inheritance rights. The married but childless were also penalised. Targeting primarily the senatorial and equestrian orders, this caused an outcry and various forms of evasion, such as betrothal to infants so a marriage could be delayed. These laws were still arousing hostility two decades later and had to be revised in AD 9, to which this passage refers. Germanicus was the son of Livia's younger son, Drusus, who was married to Agrippina the Elder (Julia's daughter). They had nine children, including the future emperor Gaius (Caligula).

1 He revised existing laws and enacted new ones, such as on extravagance, adultery and chastity, bribery, and on encouraging marriage among members of the orders. The last, more rigorously formulated than the others, he was unable to carry through because of the outcry by objectors until he had removed or moderated part of the penalties, allowed three years' grace for widows and widowers, and increased the rewards. **2** When the equites still persistently demanded its repeal at a public festival, he sent for the children of Germanicus and showed them off, some on his lap and some on their father's, making the point both by gesture and expression that they should not refuse to follow that young man's example. And when he found that the force of the law was being evaded by betrothals to immature girls and frequent changes of spouse, he shortened the length allowed for betrothals and limited the number of divorces.

15.24 Dio *Roman History* 56.3.3–5: Augustus on married life

Augustus is talking here in AD 9 to the unmarried members of the equites, who had persistently sought the repeal of his marriage legislation, in an attempt to encourage them to marry and bring up children. Apart from Julia, banished for adultery in 2 BC, Augustus himself had no other child and none by Livia. For acknowledging an infant, see doc. 1.34.

3 What could be better than a wife who is decorous, a home-body, manager of the household, childrearer, who gives you joy when you are well and cares for you when you are sick, who shares your successes and comforts your ill-fortune, who restrains the wild nature of youth and softens the harsh austerity of old age? **4** How can it not be delightful to pick up and acknowledge a baby born from you both and to feed and educate it, a mirror of your body and of your soul, so that as it grows another self comes into being? **5** How can it not be the greatest of blessings that, when you depart this life, you leave behind your own successor and heir to both the family and property, born of yourself, so that, while the corporeal human body passes away, we live on in our successor, so that the family does not fall into the hands of strangers and be as obliterated as totally as in warfare?

15.25 Justinian: *Lex Julia* on adultery, 18 BC

This law was concerned not with liaisons with slaves, prostitutes and low-class professions but with adultery and stuprum (sexual misconduct) among the aristocracy. Adultery, for the wife and her citizen lover, was now an official crime. For the first time, men were also publicly targeted. Any citizen could bring a prosecution after 60 days, if the father and husband of the woman involved did not do so, and any husband who did not divorce his wife risked prosecution as a pimp. A convicted adulteress lost half her dowry and one-third of her other property and was banished to an island; she could not remarry. The adulterer could lose half his property and be banished to a different island or, if caught in the act in his or the husband's house, could be killed by the woman's father.

(i) Digest 4.4.37 (Tryphonus Disputations 371)

But let us turn to the provisions of the lex Julia for punishing adultery, where there is no lessening of the punishment if someone under age confesses that he has committed adultery. Nor, as I have said, is there if he commits any of those offences which the same law punishes as adultery, for instance if he knowingly marries a wife convicted of adultery, or does not divorce a wife caught in adultery, or where he makes a profit from his wife's adultery, or accepts a bribe to conceal any sexual misconduct (stuprum), or lends his house for the commission of sexual misconduct or adultery within it; age is no excuse against the provisions of the law for someone who, while he appeals to the law, himself transgresses it.

(ii) Digest 48.5.4.1 (Ulpian)

The power to bring the accusation after the husband and father is granted to strangers who have the right to do so; for after 60 days have elapsed, four months are granted to strangers.

(iii) Digest 48.5.5 (Julian)

There is no doubt that I am able to bring my wife to trial on a charge of adultery in a previous marriage, since it is clearly provided for in the *lex Julia de adulteriis coercendis*; if the woman accused of adultery is a widow, the accuser is free to choose to accuse either the adulterer or the adulteress first, whichever he chooses; but if she is married, he must first accuse the adulterer, then the woman.

(iv) Digest 48.5.23.2, 4 (Papinian)

2 The right to kill the adulterer is granted to the father in his own house, even though his daughter does not live there, or in the house of his son-in-law. **4** The father and not the husband is granted the right to kill the woman and every adulterer, because generally the sense of duty belonging to a father gives him wisdom towards his children, while the warmth and impetuosity of a husband who forms judgements too easily is to be restrained.

(v) Digest 48.5.26 (Ulpian)

In the fifth section of the lex Julia it is laid down that, when a man seizes an adulterer with his wife and does not wish or is not able to kill him, he is permitted by his own right to hold him for not more than 20 consecutive hours of the day or night for the sake of finding evidence of the crime without duplicity.

(vi) Justinian Institutes 4.18.3–4

3 Public cases are these: the lex Julia on treason, which applies its force to those who have organised some intrigue against the emperor or state – the penalty for this is loss of life and the memory of the defendant condemned after death. **4** Likewise the lex Julia on adultery, which punishes with the sword not only those who defile the marriages of others but also those who dare to exercise unspeakable lust against males. Under this same lex Julia the crime of stuprum is also punished, when anyone without force has debauched a girl or widow living virtuously. The same law lays down as the penalty for offenders confiscation of half their estate, if they are respectable, and corporal punishment and banishment if they are low-born.

15.26 Ulpian *Epitome* 13.1–2, 14, 16.1–2: *Lex Julia de maritandis ordinibus*

This law regulated the marriages of senators, who could not marry freedwomen, though marriages with freedwomen were otherwise encouraged by Augustus. Those who were unmarried or childless were able to inherit only from close relations, and even the amount that a husband or wife could leave the other was regulated by the number of their children. Widows and divorcees were penalised if not remarried within a certain time-frame.

13.1 By the lex Julia senators and their children are forbidden to marry wives who are freedwomen or who have themselves, or their father or mother, practised the dramatic art, likewise any that have made any profit from their body. **2** Other freeborn males are forbidden to marry a procuress, or a woman manumitted by a procuress, or one caught in adultery, or convicted in a public court or who has practised the dramatic art: Mauricius adds also a woman convicted by the senate . . . . **14** The lex Julia gives women a respite of a year after the death of their husband (before they have to remarry) and of six months after a divorce; the lex Papia, however, gives two years after the death of a husband and a year and six months after divorce.

16.1 Sometimes a husband and wife are able to receive from each other the entire inheritance: for instance, if both or either of them are not yet at the age at which the law insists on children – that is, if the husband is less than 25 years or the wife less than 20; also if both of them have during the marriage exceeded the ages laid down by the lex Papia – that is, 60 years for the husband and 50 for the wife; likewise if relations within the sixth degree have married, or if the husband is absent, both while he is away and within a year after he has ceased to be absent. They also have complete capacity to make a will in favour of each other if they have obtained the right of children from the princeps, or if they have a son or daughter in common, or have lost a son of 14 years or a daughter of 12, or have lost two children of three years, or three after their naming day, provided, however, that even one child lost under the age of puberty, whatever the age, grants the right of taking the entire inheritance within the period of a year and six months (from the death). Likewise, if the wife gives birth to a child by her husband within ten months of his death, she takes his entire property. **2** Sometimes they cannot take anything from each other – that is, if they have contracted a marriage against the lex Julia and lex Papia Poppaea, for instance marrying a notorious wife, or a senator marrying a freedwoman.

15.27 Augustus' marriage legislation, 18 BC

The legislation made provision for rewards for those who had three or more children, and in order for a betrothal to count as a marriage the marriage had to follow within two years. Augustus and Livia had no children between them, which increased the hostility to Augustus' laws. Livia had two sons by her previous marriage, but at the death of her younger son, Drusus, she was granted the privileges and status accorded to women with three children. For the Voconian law of 169 BC, see doc. 7.69.

(i) Dio Roman History 54.16.1–5, 7

1 He imposed heavier penalties on unmarried men and women and at the same time awarded privileges for marriage and the production of children. **2** And since among the nobility there were far more males than females, he permitted any who wished, apart from senators, to marry freedwomen and ruled that their offspring would be legitimate. **3** Meanwhile an outcry arose in the senate concerning the disorderly behaviour of women and young men, this being the reason, it was alleged, for their unwillingness to enter into marital relationships, and when they urged him to remedy this as well, with a sly allusion to his affairs with numerous women, **4** he at first replied to them that the most essential regulations had already been laid down and it was impossible to legislate on further issues in the same way. When he was finally coerced into answering, he replied that 'You all ought to counsel your wives and instruct them as to your wishes – that is what I do.' **5** On hearing this, they pressed him all the more in their desire to learn what were the pieces of advice that he professed to give to Livia, and he reluctantly made some comments about dress and other forms of adornment and visits outside the house and decorous behaviour, not in the least worried that his remarks were not borne out by his actions …

7 Furthermore, as some men were betrothing themselves to infant girls and through this enjoying the privileges granted to those who were married, though not performing their part of the bargain, he ordered that no betrothal would be valid unless the person married within two years of the engagement – that is, that the girl was in every case to be at least ten years at the time of betrothal, if the man was to benefit from it (for, as I have said, girls are thought to be ready for marriage after completing 12 full years).

(ii) Dio Roman History *55.2.5–7 (9 BC)*

5 The same festivities were being prepared for Drusus (as for Tiberius), and even the Feriae (the Latin festival) was to be held a second time because of him, so that he could celebrate his triumph at that time – but this was prevented by his death, and Livia was given statues as a consolation and she was registered among the mothers of three children. **6** For to those, both men and women, to whom the gods have not granted the possession of that many children, the law (formerly through the senate, but now through the emperor) awards them the privileges of those who have had three children, so that they are not liable for the penalties for childlessness and may enjoy all but a few of the rewards for large families – **7** and this applies not only to men but to gods as well, so that if anyone leaves them a bequest at his death they may receive it.

(iii) Dio Roman History *56.10.1–3 (AD 9)*

1 Afterwards he increased the privileges for those who had children, while he made a distinction in the penalties for the married and unmarried, allowing both groups a year in which to observe the requirements and avoid the penalties. **2** He permitted some women to receive inheritances contrary to the Voconian law, by which it was not permissible for any woman to inherit more than HS 100,000. He also granted the Vestal Virgins all the privileges possessed by mothers. **3** After this the lex Papia Poppaea was proposed by Marcus Papius Mutilus and Quintus Poppaeus Secundus, who were consuls for part of the year. It was the case that neither had children and not even a wife – from which the need for the law was indisputable.

THE *LEX PAPIA POPPAEA*, AD 9

15.28 Gaius *Institutes* 3.42–46, 49–50: *Lex Papia Poppaea* on inheritance

Augustus' legislation on marriage was revised in AD 9 to try to make it less unpopular. The *lex Papia Poppaea* addressed the concerns of freedpersons in particular. If a freedman had three children, his patron no longer received a share of the inheritance, while freedwomen with four children were released from their patron's guardianship.

3.42 Later on the rights of patrons were increased by the lex Papia as far as wealthier freedmen were concerned. For by this law, where a freedman leaves property worth 100,000 sesterces or more and has fewer than three children, whether he dies after making a will or intestate, an equal share of his estate is due to his patron. Accordingly, if a freedman leaves a single son or daughter as heir, then half the estate is due to the patron, just as if he had died without any son or daughter; if he leaves two male or female children as heirs, a third is due to him; if he leaves three, the patron is excluded. **43** Regarding the property of freedwomen, patrons suffered no injury by the ancient law. For since they were in the legal guardianship of their patron, they could not make a will without their patron's consent, so that if he consented to the making of a will he would be the heir, or if not it was his own fault. For if he did not consent to its being made and the freedwoman died intestate, he would inherit, because no one could exclude a patron from the estate of his freedwoman. **44** But later on by the lex Papia the birth of four children released freedwomen from the guardianship of her patron, so that they were allowed to make a will without the authority of a guardian, and it provided that a share equal to that of each of the children whom the freedwoman had at time of death should be due to the patron. Accordingly, if a freedwoman left four children, a fifth part of her property went to her patron, but if she survived all her children the property would pass to the patron. **45** What we have said of the patron, we understand to apply as well to the son of the patron; likewise to his grandson by a son, as well as to a great-grandson born to the grandson by a son. **46** Although a daughter of a patron, a granddaughter by a son and a great-granddaughter by a grandson by a son under the Law of the XII Tables have the same rights as the patron, only the children of the male sex are granted inheritance rights by the edict, but the daughter of a patron can demand half the property of the estate of a freedman contrary to the provisions of the will, or in the case of intestacy, against an adoptive son, wife or daughter-in-law in manus, by the lex Papia, by the right of being the mother of three children, otherwise she would not have that right. . . .

49 Previously, before the lex Papia, patronesses had only that right in the property of their freedman that was granted to patrons under the Law of the XII Tables. For they could not demand half the estate of an ungrateful freedman contrary to the will, or on the ground of intestacy, against an adopted son, wife or daughter-in-law, which right the praetor granted in the case of a freedman and his children. **50** But the lex Papia granted almost the same rights to a freeborn patroness with two children and to a freedwoman who had three which male patrons possess under the edict of the praetor; and it granted the same rights to a freeborn patroness who had three children as had been given by the same law to a patron, but did not award the same rights to a patroness who was a freedwoman.

15.29 Gaius *Institutes* 2.111: On celibacy and childlessness

The *lex Papia Poppaea* revised the legislation to allow those who were childless to receive one half of inheritances.

Celibates too, who are forbidden by the lex Julia from taking inheritances or legacies, and those who do not have children, whom the lex Papia prohibits from
taking more than half an inheritance or legacy, are exempt from these restrictions
under the will of a soldier.

15.30 Gaius *Institutes* 1.144–45, 194: On guardianship

Before the *lex Papia Poppaea*, only the Vestals had no need of guardians (doc. 1.35); from
AD 9, the right of children allowed freeborn women and freedwomen the same status.

144 Parents are permitted by will to appoint guardians for their children who are
in their potestas, for males under the age of puberty and for females whatever their
age may be, even if they are married; for the ancients desired that women, even if
of full age, on account of their levity of mind, should remain under guardianship.
145 Accordingly, if anyone appoints by will a guardian for a son and daughter,
and both reach the age of puberty, the son will cease to have a guardian but the
daughter will nonetheless remain under guardianship; for it is only under the lex
Julia and Papia Poppaea that by the right of children women are released from
guardianship – with the exception of the Vestal Virgins, that is, whom even the
ancients desired to be free in honour of their priesthood, and so it was laid down
by the Law of the XII Tables.
    194 Freeborn women are freed from guardianship by right of three children,
and freedwomen by the right of four, if they are in the statutory guardianship of
their patron or his freedmen; others who have different kinds of guardians, such as
Atilian or fiduciary, are freed from guardianship by right of three children.

15.31 Tacitus *Annals* 3.24.2: The Julias

Julia the elder, Augustus' only child, was banished to an island in 2 BC for adultery, though
there may also have been political connotations to her behaviour. She had been married to
Marcellus, Agrippa and then Tiberius and had five children by Agrippa. Her elder daughter,
Julia the younger, who was married to L. Aemilius Paullus, was banished in AD 8 for
adultery with D. Junius Silanus. Her husband was later executed for conspiracy, and it is
possible that her exile might also have had political undertones.

While fortune was very propitious towards Augustus in public life, it was disastrous in private because of the immoral conduct of his daughter and granddaughter, whom he banished from the city while he punished their adulterers with death
or exile. For, in labelling misconduct between men and women – an everyday
occurrence – by the heinous names of sacrilege and treason, he transcended not
only the tolerance of our ancestors but even his own laws.

THE LUDI SAECULARES

In 17 BC Augustus celebrated the ludi Saeculares (centennial games) to restore and purify
the state and usher in a time of rebirth. These games were held only once in the life of any

citizen, and so were on a cycle of 110 years; the previous games were held in 149 or 146 BC. This celebration was commanded by a Sibylline oracle (doc. 15.34) and took place beside the Tiber. Offerings of black victims were made at night to underworld deities, and the festival specifically invoked Phoebus Apollo, Diana, Jupiter and Juno, as well as the Greek deities of childbirth (the Ilithyiae) and the Fates (Moerae). Part of the festival involved a banquet for the gods, and choirs of girls and boys, and one of matrons, sang hymns; the centennial hymn itself was written for the occasion by the poet Horace (doc. 15.33).

15.32 *ILS* 5050: Official record of the secular games

The festival took place from 31 May to 3 June 17 with nocturnal sacrifices at the Campus Martius, and sacrifices to other deities on the Capitoline and Palatine hills, followed by theatrical performances. The senate decreed that a record of the games be set up on pillars of bronze and marble in the Campus Martius, but the beginning of the document is lost. The Fifteen are the quindecimvirs, the priestly college which guarded and consulted the Sibylline Books (both Augustus and Agrippa were members).

90 On the following night in the Campus by the Tiber, Imperator Caesar Augustus sacrificed to the divine Moerae nine she-lambs, offered whole in the Greek manner, and in the same way nine she-goats and prayed as follows: Moerae, as it is written regarding you in those books in order that each and everything may prosper for the Roman people, the Quirites, that a sacrifice of nine she-lambs and nine she-goats should be made to you, I beseech you and pray that you increase the empire and sovereignty of the Roman people, the Quirites, in war and at home, and that you always protect the Latin name, **95** that you grant the Roman people, the Quirites, eternal safety, victory and health, and that you favour the Roman people, the Quirites, and the legions of the Roman people, the Quirites, and keep safe the state of the Roman people, the Quirites, and that you be well disposed and propitious to the Roman people, the Quirites, the college of Fifteen, myself, my family and household, and that you accept this sacrifice of nine she-lambs and nine she-goats offered appropriately. For these reasons be honoured by this sacrificial she-lamb and now and in future be well disposed and propitious to the Roman people, the Quirites, the Fifteen for performing religious ceremonies, myself, my family and household.

100 With the sacrifice completed, the games began at night on stage, where no theatre had been constructed and no seats positioned, and 110 matrons, who had been instructed by the Fifteen, held sellisternia with two seats positioned for Juno and Diana.

1 June on the Capitol: Imperator Caesar Augustus duly sacrificed a bull to Jupiter Optimus Maximus, in the same place Marcus Agrippa sacrificed another and then they prayed as follows: **105** 'Jupiter Optimus Maximus, as it is written regarding you in those books in order that each and everything may prosper for the Roman people, the Quirites, that a sacrifice of a fine bull should be made to you, I beseech you and pray'; the rest as above.

Present at the sacred vessel (*atalla*) were Caesar, Agrippa, Scaevola, Sentius, Lollius, Asinius Gallus, Rebilus. Then Latin performances took place in the wooden theatre which was erected in the Campus next to the Tiber, and in the same way mothers of families held sellisternia, and the performances which began at night were not interrupted, **110** and an edict was proclaimed.

The Fifteen for performing religious ceremonies proclaim: 'Whereas it has seemed proper that the mourning of matrons should be restricted in accordance with a worthy custom, and has been adhered to by frequent precedents, whenever there has been a proper reason for public rejoicing, and since at a time of such solemn ceremonies and games it seems best that this shall be repeated and adhered to diligently and shall be appropriate to the honour of the gods and the memory of their worship, we have decided that it is our responsibility to announce officially to women by edict that they shall restrain their lamentations.'

115 At night by the Tiber Imperator Caesar Augustus made a sacrifice to the divine Ilithyiae with nine barley-cakes, nine round-cakes and nine tiny cakes (Greek: phthoïs), and prayed as follows: 'Ilithyiae, as it is written regarding you in those books in order that each and everything may prosper for the Roman people, the Quirites, the sacrifice of nine barley-cakes, nine round-cakes and nine tiny cakes should be made to you, I beseech you and pray'; the rest as above.

2 June on the Capitol: Imperator Caesar Augustus duly sacrificed a cow to Juno the queen, in the same place **120** Marcus Agrippa sacrificed another and then he prayed as follows: 'Juno the Queen, as it is written regarding you in those books in order that each and everything may prosper for the Roman people, the Quirites, that a sacrifice of a fine cow should be made to you, I beseech you and pray'; the rest as above.

Then 110 married mothers of households, who had been instructed by . . . spoke as follows: **125** 'Juno the Queen whatever may prosper for the Roman people, the Quirites . . . married mothers of households with bent knees . . . you that . . . you increase the sovereignty of the Roman people, the Quirites, in war and at home, and that you always protect the Latin name, that you grant the Roman people, the Quirites, eternal safety, victory and health, and that you favour the Roman people, the Quirites, and the legions of the Roman people, the Quirites, and keep safe the state of the Roman people, the Quirites, and that you be well disposed and propitious to the Roman people, **130** the Quirites, the Fifteen for performing religious ceremonies, myself . . . These things we 110 married mothers of households of the Roman people, the Quirites, with bent knees, beseech and pray.'

Present at the *atalla* were Marcus Agrippa . . . Performances were held as on the previous day . . .

At night by the Tiber **135** Imperator Caesar Augustus sacrificed a pregnant sow to Earth the Mother, and prayed as follows: 'Earth the Mother, as it is written regarding you in those books in order that each and everything may prosper for the Roman people, the Quirites, that the sacrifice of a pregnant sow should be made to you, I beseech you and pray'; the rest as above.

The matrons held sellisternia on this day in the same way as on the previous day.

3 June on the Palatine: Imperator Caesar Augustus and Marcus Agrippa made a sacrifice to Apollo and Diana with nine barley-cakes, **140** nine round-cakes

and nine tiny cakes, and they prayed as follows: 'Apollo, as it is written regarding you in those books in order that each and everything may prosper for the Roman people, the Quirites, that the sacrifice of nine round-cakes, nine barley-cakes, and nine tiny cakes should be made to you, I beseech you and pray'; the rest as above. 'Apollo, as I have prayed to you with offerings of round-cakes and a "good prayer", for this reason be honoured by these offered barley-cakes and be well-disposed and propitious.'

145 Similarly for the tiny cakes. In the same words to Diana.

With the sacrifice completed, 27 boys who had been instructed, who had fathers and mothers still living, and the same number of girls sang the hymn; and in the same way on the Capitol. Quintus Horatius Flaccus composed the hymn. **150** Present from the Fifteen were Imperator Caesar, Marcus Agrippa, Quintus Lepidus, Potitus Messalla, Gaius Stolo, Gaius Scaevola, Gaius Sosius, Gaius Norbanus, Marcus Cocceius, Marcus Lollius, Gaius Sentius, Marcus Strigo, Lucius Arruntius, Gaius Asinius, Marcus Marcellus, Decimus Laelius, Quintus Tubero, Gaius Rebilus, Messala Messallinus.

With the performances on stage concluded . . . next to the place where sacrifice had been made on the previous nights and a theatre and stage erected, turning-posts were put in place and four-horse chariots were started and Potitus Messalla presented acrobats on horseback.

155 And an edict was proclaimed in these words: The Fifteen for performing religious ceremonies proclaim: 'To the traditional games we have added seven days of games at our own expense: on 5 June Latin games in the wooden theatre, which is by the Tiber, at the second hour; Greek musicians in Pompey's theatre at the third hour; Greek actors in the theatre which is in the Circus Flaminius, at the fourth hour.'

Interval of a day: 4 June.

160 5 June performances took place . . . Latin games in the wooden theatre, Greek musicians in Pompey's theatre, Greek actors in the theatre, which is in the Circus Flaminius.

10 June an edict was proclaimed in these words: 'The Fifteen for performing religious ceremonies proclaim: On June 12 we shall give a wild-beast hunt in . . . and we shall put on games in the Circus . . .'

12 June a procession took place, boys . . . **165** Marcus Agrippa started the chariots . . .

All these things were conducted by the Fifteen for performing religious ceremonies: Imperator Caesar Augustus, Marcus Agrippa . . . . Gnaeus Pompeius, Gaius Stolo, Gaius . . . , Marcus Marcellus . . .

15.33 Horace *Carmen Saeculare*

While not considered one of Horace's best compositions, the 'centennial hymn' was the official hymn of the ludi Saeculares, to be chanted by a chorus of specially chosen girls and boys. Leading matrons also played an important role. It refers to Rome's prosperity and greatness while also highlighting Augustus' moral reforms and marriage legislation, which was to underpin the fertility and growth of the next cycle of 110 years.

Phoebus, and Diana queen of woodland,
Radiant glories of the sky, you to be worshipped
For ever and to be honoured, grant what we pray for
At this sacred time,

5   When the Sibylline verses counselled
Chosen girls and chaste boys
To the gods who protect the seven hills
To chant a song.

Kind sun, who in your shining chariot
10   Bring and hide the day, who are born different
And yet the same – may you never be able to behold a city
Greater than Rome!

You who duly bring forth ready offspring
Gently protect, Ilithyia, our mothers,
15   Whether you wish to be called Lucina
Or Genitalis:

Goddess, may you produce offspring
And help the decrees of the senate to thrive
For the joining of women and fruitful progeny
20   By the marriage law,

So that every 11 decades the fixed cycle
Brings back throngs to view the songs and games
For three bright days and as many
Pleasant nights.

25   You Fates, who have sung truthfully,
What was once foretold – may the immoveable
Divide keep it so, and to our past deeds
Join good fortune. . . .

61   Augur, splendid in shining bow,
Phoebus, beloved of the nine Muses,
Who with medical skill can raise
The body's tired limbs,

65   If you look favourably on the Palatine altars
Prolong the Roman state and prosperous Latium
Into future lustra and better ages
For ever,

And she who holds the Aventine and Algidus,
70   Diana, attend the prayers of the Fifteen priests
     And to the vows of the children, lend
     Your kindly ears.

     That Jove and all the gods hear this
     We carry homewards good and steadfast hope,
75   The trained chorus who to Phoebus and Diana
     Chant their praises.

15.34 Zosimus *New History* 2.5.1–6: The Sibyl on the secular games

Zosimus, a pagan author writing in the early sixth century AD, gives a detailed account of
the games. He considers that Rome's decline was due to the failure to uphold these ancient
traditions. Only the beginning of the 37-line Sibylline Oracle is given here.

1 This is the way the festival is described as being celebrated: heralds go around
summoning everyone to the festival as a sight which they had never seen before
and would never see again. In summer, a few days before the spectacle commences, the Fifteen sit on a tribunal on the Capitol and in the temple on the
Palatine and distribute objects of purification to the people: these are torches,
brimstone and pitch. Slaves do not participate, only free persons. **2** When all the
people have congregated in the above-mentioned places, and in the temple of
Diana situated on the Aventine, each bringing wheat, barley and beans, they hold
solemn all-night vigils to the Fates (Moerae) for . . . nights. When the time for
the festival arrives, which they celebrate for three days and an equal number of
nights in the Campus Martius, they dedicate the victims on the bank of the Tiber
at Tarentum: they sacrifice to the deities Jupiter, Juno, Apollo, Latona and Diana,
and also to the Moerae, Ilithyiae, Ceres, Hades and Proserpine.

3 On the first night of the spectacle at the second hour the emperor along with
the Fifteen sacrifices three lambs on three altars set up on the bank of the river,
and after sprinkling the altars with blood offers the victims burnt whole. After preparing a stage like that of a theatre, they light torches and fire, sing a hymn composed for the occasion, and present sacred spectacles. **4** Those who participate are
given the first fruits of the wheat, barley and beans, for these are distributed to all
the people, as I said. On the next day they go up to the Capitol, and there offer the
accustomed sacrifices, and from there on to the theatre which has been prepared,
where they celebrate games in honour of Apollo and Diana. On the following day
noble women assemble on the Capitol at the place which the oracle prescribed and
pray to and sing hymns in honour of the god, as is right. **5** On the third day in the
temple of Apollo on the Palatine, 27 outstanding boys and the same number of
girls, all 'flourishing on both sides' (that is, with both parents living), sing hymns
and victory songs in both Greek and Latin for the preservation of all cities under
Roman rule. There were other celebrations as well, held in accordance with the
god's instruction, and as long as these were observed the Roman empire remained

intact. To convince us that all this is really true, I will give the Sibyl's oracle, although it has already been referred to by others before me:

6   When the longest term of man's life has passed
       And travelled the circle of 110 years,
       Remember, Romans, and let this not be forgotten
       Remember all this, to the immortal gods
5   Sacrifice on the plain by the boundless stream of Tiber,
       Where it is narrowest, when night comes over the earth,
       And the sun has hidden its light. Then sacrifice
       To the all-generating Fates lambs and she-goats,
       Black ones, and conciliate the Ilithyiae,
10   Who bring forth children through sacrifices, as is proper; and to Earth
       Offer a black sow on the point of parturition.
       But let pure while bulls be led to the altar of Zeus,
       By day, not by night; for to the heavenly deities
       The way of sacrifice is in the daytime, and thus
       You should make offerings.

MARCELLUS AND AGRIPPA

M. Claudius Marcellus, born in 42 BC, was the son of Octavia Minor (Augustus' younger sister) and C. Claudius Marcellus (cos. 50). As Augustus' nephew, he took part in his triumph of 29 BC (along with Augustus' stepson Tiberius) and married his daughter Julia in 25. As both his nephew and his son-in-law, Marcellus was expected to be Augustus' heir and successor. The fact that during his illness in 23 Augustus passed his signet ring to Agrippa, signifying that he would take over government, was unexpected (doc. 15.5). Marcellus had been granted the right to sit among the ex-praetors, and Augustus helped him to put on a splendid spectacle as aedile in 23; he was clearly marked as his potential heir in the absence of grandchildren, though not adopted. However, he died in the autumn of 23 at the age of 19, apparently from the same epidemic that attacked Augustus. He was the first of the family to be buried in Augustus' mausoleum.

    M. Vipsanius Agrippa was one of Augustus' childhood friends and was responsible for the victories over Sextus Pompeius and Mark Antony. He was married to Caecilia Pomponia, Atticus' daughter, then to Marcella the elder (Augustus' niece) in 28, and after Marcellus' death to Julia in 21. His daughter Vipsania was married to Tiberius. He was consul in 37, 28 and 27 and aedile in 33, when he spent a fortune on beautifying Rome. He died in Campania in 12 BC and was buried in Augustus' mausoleum. Augustus in 17 BC had adopted Agrippa's two eldest sons by Julia, Gaius and Lucius, and made them his heirs.

15.35 *Palatine Anthology* 6.161: Marcus Claudius Marcellus

Written by Crinagoras of Mytilene, a poet of the Augustan age. Marcellus took part with Augustus in his campaign against the Cantabri in northern Spain (26–24 BC), returning before Augustus to marry Julia.

Marcellus, returning from the western war
Laden with plunder to the boundaries of rocky Italy
First shaved his ruddy beard; his country's desire
This was – to send him out a boy, and receive him back a man.

15.36 Vergil *Aeneid* 6.860–86: You shall be Marcellus!

In the underworld, Aeneas' father, Anchises, describes the future of the Trojan descendants in Italy. Marcellus closes the parade of great Romans seen there by Aeneas. Famously Octavia fainted when she heard Vergil recite this passage (doc. 15.90). Marcellus' ancestor, also M. Claudius Marcellus, who accompanied him in this procession, was five times consul, an outstanding general in the Second Punic War, and won the spolia opima for killing the Gallic king Viridomarus (cf. docs 4.46–47).

860   And now Aeneas asked – since he saw there come
        A youth of outstanding beauty and with shining arms,
        His face not joyful, and his eyes cast down –
        'Who is this, father, thus accompanying him on his way?
        His son? Or another of his long line of descendants?
        What murmuring round them! How impressive he appears!
        But dark night circles his head with its sad shadows.'
        Then father Anchises, eyes full of tears, replied:
        'My son, ask not about the great sorrow of your people.
        The Fates will only show him to the world, nor allow him
870   A longer stay. The Roman people would seem to you
        Too powerful, gods, were this gift permanent.
        What mourning from mankind will that great city
        Hear from the Field of Mars! And Tiber, you will see
        What funerary rites, as you flow past his recent tomb!
        No boy of Ilius' line will so raise up his Latin
        Forefathers by such hopeful promise, nor will Romulus'
        Land ever pride itself so much on one of its sons.
        Alas duty!, alas ancient honour, and right hands
        Invincible in war! No one would have attacked him safely
880   When in arms, whether he met the enemy on foot,
        Or dug spurs in the flanks of his foaming horse.
        Ah, poor boy!, if only you may break the dictates of harsh fate –
        You shall be Marcellus! Give me lilies with full hands,
        Let me scatter brilliant flowers, let me heap my descendant's spirit
        With these gifts at least, in performing that poor service.'

15.37 *ILS* 898: Marcellus as patron

Marcellus, clearly seen as an important member of the imperial family, was also a patron of Pompeii and of Tanagra in Boeotia.

The city of the Delphians honoured Claudius Marcellus, its patron.

15.38 Velleius Paterculus *Compendium of Roman History* 2.93.1–2: Marcellus and Agrippa, 23 BC

For Marcellus' aedileship, see doc. 15.5. Between 23 and 21, Agrippa was in the East as governor of Syria but based at the island of Lesbos, deputising for Augustus. In 21 he returned to Rome and remained in charge of affairs there while Augustus spent time in Greece and Samos. In 19 he was in Gaul and Spain, where he finished the Cantabrian war. In 18 Augustus made him his colleague in tribunician power for five years and gave him proconsular imperium. Egnatius stood in 19 for the consulship, but his candidature was refused. A subsequent plot was easily dealt with by the senate in Augustus' absence. Caepio and Murena were executed for treason in 22 BC.

1 About three years before the plot of Egnatius broke out, around the time of the conspiracy of Murena and Caepio, 50 years ago, Marcus Marcellus, the son of Augustus' sister Octavia, died, whom people thought would have succeeded to power should anything have happened to Caesar, though they considered, however, that this would not happen without some opposition from Marcus Agrippa. He died while still a youth, after presenting most magnificent games in his role as aedile. Indeed, as they say, he had noble qualities, was cheerful in mind and disposition, and equal to the destiny for which he was being brought up. **2** After his death Agrippa, who had gone to Asia on the pretext of imperial business, but who had really, as rumour reports, taken himself off for the time being because of his secret dislike of Marcellus, now returned and married Julia, Caesar's daughter, who had been Marcellus' wife, a woman whose children did no good either to herself or to the state.

15.39 Dio *Roman History* 53.26.5–27.5: Agrippa beautifies the city

This is the second closing of the temple of Janus in 25 BC, following Augustus' campaign in Spain (cf. doc. 14.60). Agrippa was responsible for numerous monuments in Rome, including the basilica of Neptune in honour of Augustus' victories and a new complex in the Campus Martius, with the Saepta Julia (a voting hall), baths, gardens and the Pantheon. Marcellus and Julia married while Augustus was ill in Spain in 25; Agrippa performed the ceremony.

26.5 After Augustus' successes in these wars, he closed the precinct of Janus, which had been opened because of them. **27.1** In the meantime Agrippa adorned the city at his own expense. He first constructed the basilica called 'Poseidon's' in honour of the victories at sea and made it splendid by decorating it with the painting of the Argonauts, and then built the Laconian steam bath (sudatorium) – he gave the gymnasium the name 'Laconian' because the Spartans were thought at that time to be particularly fond of stripping and exercising after anointing themselves with oil. **2** He also completed the building called the Pantheon, so named, perhaps, because its decorations included the statues of many gods among its images, such as Mars and Venus, but my view is that it was named for its domed roof, which resembles the heavens. **3** Agrippa wanted to place a statue of Augustus there as well and give his name to the building, but when Augustus would accept neither honour he placed a statue of the former Caesar in the temple, and in the anteroom figures of Augustus and himself. **4** He did this not out of any ambition or rivalry with Augustus but out of genuine goodwill towards him and continual eagerness for the common good, and Augustus, far from blaming him for this, honoured him the more. **5** For when Augustus was unable because of illness to be in Rome to celebrate the marriage of his daughter Julia and nephew Marcellus, he had Agrippa conduct this in his absence. And when the house on the Palatine, which had previously been Antony's and had been given to Agrippa and (M. Valerius) Messalla (Corvinus) burnt down, he gave Messalla money but made Agrippa share his own house.

15.40 Pliny the Elder *Natural History* 36.121: Agrippa's water works

From his own funds Agrippa made extensive repairs to Rome's water supply, including constructing baths and cleaning the Cloaca Maxima. His *Autobiography* is lost, as is his *Geography* and map of the known world (doc. 15.51). Although it was unusual to hold the aedileship after a consulship (he had been consul in 37), the agenda was clearly to gain support for Augustus (then Octavian) through providing amenities for the city of Rome. Augustus continued work on the water system after Agrippa's death (doc. 15.52). The Aqua Virgo is still operational today.

Quintus Marcius Rex, when ordered by the senate to repair the conduits of the Aqua Appia, Anio and Tepula, tunnelled passages through the mountains and brought Rome a new water supply, named for him (Aqua Marcia) and completed during the period of his praetorship (144–143 BC). Then Agrippa in his aedileship (33 BC) added to these the Aqua Virgo (19 BC), repaired and restored the channels of the others, and constructed 700 basins, as well as 500 fountains and 130 distribution reservoirs, many of these richly ornamented. On these works he added 300 statues of bronze or marble and 400 columns of marble – all these carried out in the space of a year. He himself, in his memoirs of his aedileship, added that games lasting 59 days were celebrated and all 170 public baths were opened free of charge, a number which has now been greatly increased at Rome.

15.41 Pliny the Elder *Natural History* 35.26: Agrippa as art-lover

Agrippa as governor of Syria was in Cyzicus at some time between 17 and 13 when he acquired these paintings, as well as Lysippus' *Dying Lion* from Lampsacus. At the time of his death, Agrippa was building a villa at Boscotrecase. The frescoes there are some of the finest examples of Roman wall painting.

It was the dictator Caesar who was responsible for making painting fashionable by dedicating pictures of Ajax and Medea in front of the temple of Venus Genetrix. After him, there was Marcus Agrippa, a man whose taste tended towards rustic simplicity rather than elegant refinement. There exists, however, a magnificent oration of his, worthy of the greatest of our citizens, on the subject of having all statues and painting publicly exhibited, which would have been far preferable to sending them off as exiles to country villas. Serious as he was in his tastes, he bought two pictures, an Ajax and a Venus, from the people of Cyzicus for 1,200,000 sesterces. Furthermore he ordered small painted panels to be set into the marble in even the hottest part of his baths; these remained there until they were removed a short time ago, when the building was being restored.

15.42 Josephus *Antiquities of the Jews* 16.6.172–73: Agrippa and the Jews

Iullus Antonius, son of Mark Antony and Fulvia and raised by Octavia, was consul in 10 and proconsul of Asia in 7 BC. When Agrippa divorced Marcella in 21 to marry Julia, Iullus then married Marcella, by whom he had three children. He was involved in the scandal surrounding Julia the Elder in 2 BC (he was named as her main lover, though there may rather have been political implications in the relationship) and committed suicide. High in Augustus' favour until then, he is depicted on the Ara Pacis. Josephus cites a number of such decrees and letters on Jewish rights (cf. doc. 14.33); what is interesting is that this one mentions Agrippa several years after his death. Horace mentions Iullus as a fellow poet in *Odes* 4.2.

172 Iullus Antonius, proconsul, to the magistrates, council and people of the Ephesians, greetings. While I was dispensing justice at Ephesus on the Ides of February (13 February 7 BC), the Jews resident in Asia pointed out to me that Caesar Augustus and Agrippa permitted them to follow their own laws and customs and to make without hindrance the donations (gift of first fruits) which each of them of his own choice makes for the sake of piety towards the divinity, which they collaborate in conveying. **173** And they requested that I should confirm my opinion in agreement with those given by Augustus and Agrippa. It is therefore my wish that you know that I coincide with the decisions of Augustus and Agrippa and allow them to behave and act without hindrance in accordance with their ancestral customs.

15.43 *IG* II² 4122: Athens honours Agrippa

An inscribed base that supported a statue of Agrippa in a four-horse chariot which stood in front of the propylaea to the acropolis.

The people (dedicated this statue of) Marcus Agrippa, son of Lucius, consul for the third time (27 BC), their benefactor.

15.44 *RDGE* 63: Agrippa's letter to the Argive Gerousia

A stele from Argos. The gerousia was probably an association of elder citizens concerned with the management of local cults and may have been the equivalent of the Augustales in Italy and thus associated with the imperial cult. This letter dates to 17–13, when Agrippa was in the Greek East, and probably to the winter of 17/16, when he was at Corinth. Danaos and his daughter Hypermestra were the ancestors of the Argive kings.

Of the Elder Citizens. Agrippa to the elder citizens of the Argives, descended from Danaos and Hypermestra, greetings. I am mindful of my own responsibility for providing for the continuance of your organisation **5** and the safeguarding of its ancient prestige, and for restoring to you many of your lost rights. For the future I intend to take thought for you and . . .

15.45 *IG* XII.2.204: Mytilene honours Julia

A marble base from Mytilene, Lesbos. This inscription may date from the period 23–21, when Agrippa and Julia were based on Lesbos, although they wintered there on subsequent occasions. Their daughter Agrippina may have been born there.

The people (dedicated this statue of) Julia, daughter of Imperator Caesar god Augustus, wife of Marcus Agrippa, our benefactress, because of her excellence in every way **5** and her goodwill towards our city.

15.46 *EJ* 76: Honours for the imperial family at Thespiae

Agrippa and his family, while in Greece, seem to have attended the festival of the Muses at Thespiae in Boeotia. The inscription dates to between 17 and 12.

(a)   The people honoured Agrippina, daughter of Marcus Agrippa.
      The people honoured Marcus Agrippa, son of Lucius. To the Muses.
(b)   The people honoured Lucius Caesar.
      The people honoured Gaius Caesar.
      The people honoured Julia, daughter of Imperator Caesar Augustus, wife of Marcus Agrippa. To the Muses.
      The people honoured Livia, wife of Imperator Caesar Augustus. To the Muses.

15.47 Nikolaos of Damascus *F*134: Julia and an unexpected storm

At this point Agrippa was in Paphlagonia returning from Sinope on the south coast of the Black Sea. This episode, in which Julia nearly drowned, took place in 14 BC when she was 25 years of age.

Nikolaos' act of philanthropy. The people of Ilium (Troy) were unaware that Julia, daughter of Caesar and wife of Agrippa, had arrived among them at night, and that the Scamander was running high as a result of numerous storms, and that she was in danger of being killed along with the household slaves who were accompanying her. In consequence of this Agrippa was enraged because the people of Ilium had not come to her assistance, and he fined them 100,000 silver drachmas. They were left destitute and, although they had not foreseen the storm or that the young lady was arriving in it, did not have the courage to say anything to Agrippa. When Nikolaos arrived, they begged him to get Herod to be their supporter and protector. Nikolaos enthusiastically gave them his assistance because of the city's renown and appealed to the king, explaining the circumstances to him, that it was unreasonable of Agrippa to be angry with them because he had not warned them that he was sending his wife to them, and they were totally unaware that she was arriving at night. In the end Herod assumed their protection and had them excused from the fine. Since they had already departed as they despaired of the possibility of deliverance, he gave Nikolaos, who was sailing to Chios and Rhodes, where his sons were, the letter announcing this, for Herod himself was continuing on to Paphlagonia with Agrippa. Nikolaos sailed from Amisos to Byzantium, and from there to the Troad, and went to Ilium, and when he handed over the letter of release from the debt, both he, and the king even more particularly, were paid great honour by the people of Ilium.

15.48 *P. Köln* 10: Funeral oration for Agrippa, 12 BC

A Greek papyrus fragment of the first century BC from the Fayum in Egypt, a translation of the Latin original delivered by Augustus. Varus (docs 15.107–8) was married to Vipsania Marcella Agrippina, the daughter of Agrippa and Claudia Marcella. This fragment appears to confirm that, like Augustus, Agrippa had maius imperium, at least from 13 BC.

. . . the tribunician power for five years in accordance with a decree of the senate was given to you when the Lentuli were consuls (18 BC), and again this was granted for another Olympiad (five-year period) **5** when Tiberius (Claudius) Nero and (Publius) Quinctilius Varus, your sons-in-law, were consuls (13 BC). And into whatever provinces the Romans' state should dispatch you, **10** it had been sanctioned by law that your power was to be not less than any other magistrate's in those. Considered worthy of the supreme (tribunician) authority and a colleague in our rule, by your own virtues and achievements you surpassed all men.

15.49 *SEG* 18.518: The 'friends of Agrippa'

A slab of blue marble from Smyrna commemorating one of the members of the association of the friends of Agrippa. Such associations were unofficial groups that met for social and religious purposes to honour benefactors or for cult purposes.

The members of the association of the friends of Agrippa erected this monument for their own associate, Marion, also known as Mares, citizen of Adana, in his memory.

15.50 Dio *Roman History* 54.28.1–29.8, 31.1–4: Agrippa's legacy

Clearly, despite the length of time during which Agrippa had supported Augustus' position, his naval victories, his three consulships and his beautification of Rome, he was still not accepted by the nobility (29.6). With Marcellus and Agrippa both dead, Julia now had to marry Augustus' stepson Tiberius, who was the logical replacement for Agrippa until Julia's children came of age.

28.1 Meanwhile, when Agrippa returned from Syria, Augustus increased his authority by giving him the tribunician power again for another five years and sent him to Pannonia, which was on the point of war, granting him greater authority than that possessed ordinarily by governors outside of Italy. **2** He went off on campaign, although the winter had already begun (this was the year in which Marcus Valerius and Publius Sulpicius were consuls, 12 BC), but when the Pannonians were frightened at his approach and abandoned their rebellion, he returned, falling ill when in Campania. **3** When Augustus learnt this (he was putting on contests for armed warriors at the Panathenaia in the name of his sons) he rushed back, and finding him dead brought his body back to the city and laid it in state in the forum. He also delivered the eulogy for him, after hanging up a curtain in front of the corpse. **4** I have no idea why he did this, but some have said it was because he was pontifex maximus, others because he was carrying out the duties of censor . . . **5** Augustus not only did this but had the funeral procession carried out in the same way in which his own was later conducted, and buried him in his own mausoleum, although Agrippa had taken one for himself in the Campus Martius.

29.1 This was how Agrippa died. He had in every respect clearly shown himself to be the best of the men of his time, and had made use of Augustus' friendship to the greatest advantage of both Augustus himself and the state. **2** For the more he surpassed others in excellence, the more he deliberately kept himself in a lesser position to that of Augustus, and, while he dedicated all his wisdom and valour to the best interests of Augustus, he handed over all the honour and power he received from him to benefit others. **3** It was for this reason in particular that he never became objectionable to Augustus himself or hated by the rest of the citizens, but rather established the monarchy for him as if he was genuinely committed to autocracy, while he won the support of the people through his philanthropy, as if he were the greatest advocate for popular government. **4** At any rate he left them gardens and the baths named for him so they could bathe for free, and to this end gave Augustus certain properties. Augustus not only made these over to the people, but distributed 400 sesterces each to the people, on the grounds that Agrippa had instructed this. **5** Augustus actually inherited most of his property, among others the Chersonese on the Hellespont, which had, I'm not sure how, come into Agrippa's possession. Augustus felt his loss for a considerable time and consequently made sure he was honoured by the people, and named the son born to him posthumously Agrippa. **6** However, he did not allow the others to omit any of the traditional observances, although none of the leading men wanted to attend the festivals, and he himself oversaw the gladiatorial contests, although they were often held in his absence. **7** This misfortune not only affected Agrippa's own household but had so great an impact on all the Romans that as many omens as customarily occur prior to the greatest disasters were observed on this occasion. Owls kept flying around the city, and a thunderbolt struck the house on the Alban Mount where the consuls stay during the sacred rites (the Feriae Latinae). **8** The star called the comet hovered for many days over the city and dispersed in flashes of flame. Numerous city buildings were destroyed by fire, including the hut of Romulus, which was set alight when crows dropped on it burning meat from some altar. . . .

31.1 Now that Agrippa was dead, whom he had loved because of his excellence, not because of their family relationship, Augustus needed a colleague to assist with public affairs, one who would far surpass the rest in rank and power, so that he could handle business promptly and without being the object of jealousy or intrigue. Reluctantly, he chose Tiberius, for his grandsons were still children at this time. **2** He made him divorce his wife, although she was the daughter of Agrippa by another wife, and was raising one child while pregnant with another, betrothed Julia to him, and dispatched him against the Pannonians. Out of fear for Agrippa, they had been quiet for some time, but after his death they revolted. **3** Tiberius conquered them, after ravaging a large part of their country and causing much distress to the people, making intensive use of his allies the Scordisci, who shared the same border and carried similar weaponry. He took away their weapons and had most of the men of military age sold into slavery and deported. **4** As a result the senate voted him a triumph; however, Augustus did not allow him to celebrate one but granted him triumphal honours instead.

15.51 Pliny the Elder *Natural History* 3.16–17: Agrippa's map

Agrippa's *Geography* influenced the works of Strabo and Pliny the Elder. He was also the author of a map (the first ever made of the known world), copies of which were later circulated to all major cities of the empire, though no copy survives today. The map was completed after his death and displayed in the Portico Vipsania, erected by his sister Polla (Dio 55.8.4). A Roman mile was 1,000 paces, each being 5 feet (equalling 1,618 yards).

16 Marcus Agrippa has also stated that the length (of Hispania Baetica) is 475 miles and its breadth 257, but this was when its boundaries extended to (New) Carthage, a fact that has often caused serious errors in calculations, which are usually the result of changes made in the boundaries of provinces or because, in the calculation of distances, the miles have been increased or diminished . . . . **17** Today, the length of Baetica, from the town of Castulo on its border, to Gades is 250 miles, and from Murci, on the coast, 25 miles more. The breadth measured from the coast of Carteia is 234 miles. When you consider the diligence of Agrippa and the care which he employed in this project, when he was about to display a map of the world to be gazed upon by that world, who could believe that he could make such a mistake, and the deified Augustus as well? For it was Augustus who completed the work when the portico containing the map had been begun by Agrippa's sister in accordance with Marcus Agrippa's plan and notes.

15.52 Frontinus *On Aqueducts* 2.98–106: Rome's water, 11 BC

After the death of Agrippa, the senate was given the responsibility for the water system. Augustus nominated the curator, but the senate defined the powers and duties. The number of fountains is actually given by Pliny (doc. 15.40).

98 First Marcus Agrippa, after his aedileship (33 BC), which he held after being consul, was a kind of perpetual curator of the works and services he had put into place. Now that the supply permitted it, he decided how much water should be allocated to the public structures, how much to the collection basins, and how much to private citizens. He possessed his own 'household' of slaves to maintain the aqueducts, reservoirs and basins. Augustus inherited this gang and gave it to the state.

99 After him, in the consulship of Quintus Aelius Tubero and Paulus Fabius Maximus (11 BC), decrees of the senate were passed and a law promulgated on the subject, which until that time had been managed by officials and lacked definite regulations. Augustus also laid down in an edict the rights possessed by those who were drawing water according to Agrippa's records, in this way making the whole matter subject to his own grants. The discharge pipes, which I spoke of above, were established by him, and he named Messalla Corvinus curator for the maintenance and operation of the system, giving him as assistants Postumius Sulpicius, an ex-praetor, and Lucius Cominius, a junior member of the senate. They were allowed to wear the insignia as if magistrates, and a resolution of the senate was passed concerning their duties, which is as follows:

100 Whereas Quintus Aelius Tubero and Paulus Fabius Maximus, consuls, reported concerning the appointment of the curators of the public water supply nominated by Caesar Augustus with the approval of the senate, and inquired of the senate what action it wished to approve in the said matter, the senators proposed as follows with regard to the said matter:

It is the pleasure of this body that those who are in charge of the public water supply, when they are outside the city engaged in their duties, are each to have two lictors, three public slaves and one architect, and the same number of clerks, copyists, aides and criers as those possessed by those in charge of the distribution of grain to the plebs. When they are in the city, engaged in some aspect of their position, they shall have the use of all these attendants, apart from the lictors. Furthermore the curators of the water supply are to report to the treasury, within the ten days following this decree of the senate, (the names of) the attendants approved for their use by this decree of the senate; to those reported in this way, the praetors of the treasury are to grant and assign the salary and yearly rations, which the prefects for the distribution of grain are accustomed to allocate; and they are permitted to expend these funds for that purpose without prejudice. Furthermore they shall provide to the curators tablets, paper and all other materials necessary for their duties and Quintus Aelius and Paulus Fabius, the consuls, either one or both, if it seems preferable to them, in consultation with the praetors of the treasury, shall place contracts (for these) . . . .

104 Whereas Quintus Aelius Tubero and Paulus Fabius Maximus, consuls, reported concerning the number of public fountains within the city and its suburbs, established by Marcus Agrippa, and inquired of the senate as to what action it wished to approve, the senators proposed as follows:

It is our pleasure that the number of public fountains should neither be increased nor decreased, from the number [of 500] currently in existence according to the report of those commissioned by the senate to inspect the public water supply and to determine the number of public fountains. Likewise it is our pleasure that the curators of the water supply, whom Caesar Augustus nominated with the approval of the senate, shall provide that the public fountains shall by day and night as unremittingly as possible provide water for the use of the public . . .

106 Whereas Quintus Aelius Tubero and Paulus Fabius Maximus, consuls, reported that certain private individuals were drawing water from the public mains, and inquired of the senate as to what action it wished to approve in the said matter, the senators proposed as follows:

That no private person shall be permitted to draw water from the public mains, and furthermore all those to whom the right of drawing water had been given should draw it from reservoirs; and the curators of the water supply should decide at what places within the city private persons might be able appropriately to make reservoirs from which they can draw water, which they all receive in common from a public reservoir with the agreement of the curators of the water supply. And no one of those granted the right to use public water, within 50 feet of the reservoir from which they draw water, shall have the right to lay a pipe wider than a *quinaria*.

AUGUSTUS AND IMPERIAL CULT

While Augustus refused divine honours at Rome in his lifetime, Roma (the goddess of Rome) and Roman commanders since Flamininus had been objects of cult in the East (doc 5.26), where ruler worship was normal. Following Actium, cults to Roma and Augustus jointly were set up at Pergamum and Nicomedia, and members of the imperial family other than Augustus quickly had cults set up in their honour. Roman citizens were not permitted to worship the living emperor but could pay honours to the goddess Roma and the divus Julius and the numen or genius of Augustus.

15.53 *IG* II² 3173: A temple at Athens

A temple on the Athenian acropolis was erected to Roma and Augustus. Areios was archon in one of the years between 27/6 and 18/17 BC.

The people (dedicated this temple) to the goddess Roma and Augustus Caesar, when the hoplite general was Pammenes, son of Zenon of Marathon, priest of the goddess Roma and Augustus the Saviour on the acropolis, when the priestess of Athena Polias was Megiste, daughter of Asklepiades of Halieus. In the archonship of Areios, son of Dorion of Paianieus.

15.54 *OGIS* 2.458: Imperial cult and the provincial calendar, 9 BC

Paulus Fabius Maximus (cos. 11 BC), proconsul of Asia, addressed this letter to the assembly of Asia, suggesting that Augustus' birthday be a public holiday and the beginning of the New Year in the province's cities. Most cities in the province of Asia were currently using the Macedonian calendar, which started close to Augustus' birthday, which made this a feasible proposition. The temple in which the stele is erected is that of Roma and Augustus in Pergamum.

I . . . from those we formerly received . . . goodwill of the gods and . . . whether the birthday of the most divine Caesar is of greater pleasure or benefit, **5** which we should consider rightly to be the beginning of all things, and he has restored, if not to its natural state, at least to a workable condition, all forms that had become imperfect and fallen into misfortune, and he has given another aspect to the whole world, which would have happily accepted its destruction if Caesar had not been born for the general good fortune of every person. Accordingly, anyone would justly suppose that his birth **10** was the beginning of life and existence for every person, as well as the end and termination of regret that one had been born. And since from no other day could any person receive more auspicious beginnings, either for the public or for private benefit, than from this one, which has been auspicious for everyone, and since it is the case that nearly all the cities of Asia employ the same date for entering upon office, **15** it is clear that this arrangement was preordained by the will of some god so that its beginning should contribute to the honour of Augustus; and since it is difficult to give adequate thanks for all his numerous benefactions, unless we were to create a new way of reciprocating each and every one, people should celebrate his birthday more joyfully as a holiday shared by everyone, **20** as if some specific source of happiness had accrued for them from his government.

I therefore lay down that, for all citizens, the birthday of the most divine Caesar should serve as the one and only New Year's Day, and that everyone should enter into office on that day, which is the ninth day before the Kalends of October (23 September), so that it may be more highly honoured by receiving a great religious significance from outside itself, **25** and that it may become more widely recognised by everyone, which I think will provide the greatest benefit to the province. There will be a need for a decree from the association (koinon) of Asia to be proposed comprising all his virtues so that our consideration for the honour of Augustus may remain in perpetuity. I shall give orders that the decree shall be engraved on the stele in the temple, with the requirement that **30** the edict be written in both languages.

II It has been decreed by the Greeks of Asia, on the motion of the high priest Apollonios, son of Menophilos, the Aizanian: since Providence, which has divinely ordered our lives, has employed zeal and ambition and arranged the most perfect consummation of life by producing Augustus, whom for the benefit of mankind she has filled **35** with excellence, as if granting us and our descendants a saviour who has ended war and brought about peace; and since at his appearance Caesar exceeded the hopes of all those who received good news previously, not only surpassing all those who had earlier been benefactors but not even leaving any hope of surpassing him for those to come in the future; **40** and since the birthday of the god was the beginning of the good news to come through him for the world, and since Asia decreed in Smyrna, when Lucius Volcacius Tullus was proconsul (cos. 33) and the secretary was Papion from Dios Hieron, that the person who formulated the highest honours for the god should have a crown, and Paulus Fabius Maximus the proconsul, benefactor of the province, **45** who has been sent from his right hand and mind along with the others through whom he has given benefits to the province, of which benefits no speech could compass the magnitude, has found for the honour of Augustus something as yet unknown to the Greeks, that from his birthday should begin the time for life. Accordingly by good fortune and for our salvation, **50** it has been decreed by the Greeks in Asia that the New Year shall begin for all cities on the ninth day before the Kalends of October (23 September), which is the birthday of Augustus. So that the day shall always correspond in each city, the Greek day shall be used as well as the Roman. The first month shall be 'Caesar', as previously decreed, beginning **55** with the ninth day before the Kalends of October, the birthday of Caesar, and the crown decreed for the person who devised the highest honours for Caesar shall be awarded to Maximus the proconsul, who will be publicly proclaimed on each occasion at the gymnastic festival at Pergamum in honour of Roma and Augustus, as follows: 'that Asia crowns Paulus Fabius Maximus for devising **60** most piously the honours for Caesar'. Likewise there shall be a proclamation at the festivals held for Caesar in each city. The rescript of the proconsul and the decree of Asia shall be inscribed on a white marble stele, which will be set up in the precinct of Roma and Augustus. And the 'advocates' of this year shall ensure that, **65** in the cities at the head of administrative districts, the rescript of the proconsul and the decree of Asia shall be inscribed on white marble steles, and that these steles are set up in the temples of Caesar.

The months shall be reckoned as follows: Caesar, 31 days; Apellaios, 30 days; Audnaios, 31 days; Peritios, 31 days; Dystros, 28; Xandikos, 31; **70** Artemision, 30 days; Daisios, 31; Panemos, 30; Loos, 31; Gorpiaios, 31; Hyperberetaios, 30; total of days, 365. For this year, because of the intercalated day, Xandikos shall be reckoned at 32 days. In order that from now there will be a correspondence of months and days, the current month of Peritios shall be reckoned up to the 14th, and on the ninth day before the Kalends of February (24 January) we shall reckon the first day of the month of **75** Dystros, and for each month the beginning of the new month shall be the ninth day before the Kalends. The intercalated day shall always be that of the intercalated Kalends of the month of Xandikos, at two-year intervals.

15.55 *ILS* 8781: Oath of loyalty to Augustus and his family

A stele from Gangra in Paphlagonia, dated to 6 March 3 BC; Paphlagonia had been attached to the province of Galatia in 6/5 BC. Similar oaths in the East are attested for Assos, Samos and Palaipaphos on Cyprus.

Of Imperator Caesar, son of the god, Augustus in his twelfth consulship, third year (of the province), on the day before the Nones of March, in Gangra in the agora, **5** the oath completed by the inhabitants of Paphlagonia and the Romans who are in business among them.

I swear by Zeus, Earth, Sun, all the gods and goddesses, and Augustus himself, that I will bear goodwill towards **10** Caesar Augustus and his children and descendants through my whole life in word and deed and thought, regarding as friends those whom they regard as friends and considering as enemies those whom they judge as enemies, and that with regard to their interests **15** I will spare neither my body nor my soul nor my life nor my children, but that in every way with regard to whatever affects them I will undergo all dangers; and whatever I might perceive or hear **20** being said or plotted or done against them I shall report it, and be the enemy of whoever says or plots or engages in any of these; and those whom they judge to be their enemies I shall pursue and repel by land and by sea with weapons and **25** sword.

If I do anything contrary to this oath or not in agreement with what I have sworn, I will call down upon myself and my body and soul and life and **30** upon my children and all my family and property destruction and total obliteration until the end of my bloodline and all of my descendants, and may neither land nor **35** sea receive the bodies of my family or my descendants, nor bear fruit for them.

In these same words the oath was sworn by all those in the land, in the (temples) of Augustus throughout the districts at the altars of Augustus; and likewise the Phazimonians, residing at what is now called **40** Neapolis, all of them swore the oath in the temple of Augustus at the altar of Augustus.

.

15.56 *SEG* 32.1243: A prytanis at Kyme, 2 BC–AD 2

This eulogistic record of the career of the prytanis (chief magistrate) Kleanax from Kyme in Asia Minor includes his making sacrifices at the games of the imperial family put on by the koinon of Asia in honour of Augustus and his grandsons Gaius and Lucius.

The strategoi proposed the motion and three chosen by lot wrote it down: Asklapon, son of Dionysios, Hegesandros, son of Herakleides, Athenagoras, son of Dionysos, as well as the secretary of the people Heraios, son of Antipatros.

Since Kleanax, son of Sarapion and natural son of Philodemos, our prytanis (magistrate), **5** who has well-born ancestors on both sides of his family and unsurpassable devotion to love of glory towards his country, has throughout his entire life achieved many great things for his city, surrendering at no time to a neglect of care for the people, and conducting himself in public life most advantageously for the city in both word and deed, and consequently, in the present circumstances of his **10** love of glory suitable for a prytanis, the praise of the people has at present born witness on his behalf, while the gratitude of the people has responded to his actions through earlier decrees, when as priest of Dionysios Pandemos he performed his duties for the Mysteries founded by the city, paying the expenses towards the fourth-yearly organisation of the Mysteries, when **15** the proportion of the expenditure showed his outstanding love of glory and piety, alone and first taking on the office and having invited by announcement the citizens and Romans and residents and foreigners to a banquet in the precinct of Dionysos and having entertained them sumptuously, organising the feast every year, and having given a banquet for the multitude at the marriage of his daughter; **20** for these reasons, the people, having the recollection and appreciation of these good deeds, forgot none of his other activities to which they had become accustomed.

For this reason also the prytanis Kleanax is to be praised and honoured because he became the father of handsome children, and took thought for his son's education in letters, and presented the people with Sarapion, a man worthy of his family, a protector and helper and who in many respects **25** has already demonstrated his zeal towards the city through his brave deeds, a father-loving man who deserves this name officially, who also bears witness to his affection towards his father by public decree in perpetuity; for all these reasons the people acknowledge Kleanax the prytanis and praises him for constantly preserving **30** his goodwill towards the people. He has performed all his duties as prytanis, on the one hand at the first day of the New Year with sacrifices to the gods according to ancestral custom, and has treated with sweet wine everyone in the city and hosted the spectacles luxuriously and made the sacrifices for prosperity according to ancestral custom and entertained in the town hall for several days many of the citizens and Romans, while on the other hand he has made sacrifices **35** for the departed on the accustomed day according to ancestral custom and distributed porridge to all the free and slaves in the city, and at the Lark festival was the first and only person to invite by proclamation the citizens and Romans and residents and foreigners to dinner in the town hall, and he performed the Throwing ceremony in the same way as other prytaneis, and made the processions of the Laurel, and to the priests and **40** triumphant athletes and magistrates and many of the citizens he gave a banquet; and in the games of the imperial family given by (the koinon) of Asia, as he announced, he performed the sacrifices and festivities, sacrificing oxen to Imperator Caesar Augustus and his two sons and the other gods, after which sacrifice he also entertained . . . in the agora, by proclamation, Greeks and Romans and residents and foreigners . . . **45** after performing this public service and completed the other rites . . . because of this the council and people have decreed to crown him at the Dionysia at the altar of Zeus after the sacrifice . . . .

15.57 Moretti *IAG* no. 60: A pentathlete from Kos, c. AD 5

Festivals were widely established in honour of members of the imperial family, including games in honour of Agrippa held at the Isthmus of Corinth; for the Actian games established by Augustus, see doc. 15.19. This stele commemorates the victories of a certain young athlete from Kos. The different festivals in honour of the imperial family clearly extended the annual athletic circuit for committed participants. 'Pythian' boys were between 12 and 14 years, 'Isthmian' from 14 to 17, youths from 17 to 20.

. . . victor at the Nemean games in the men's pentathlon; at the imperial family's Great Actian games in the young men's pentathlon, first of the Koans (to win this); **5** at the games of Roma and Augustus established by the Koinon of Asia in Pergamum at the Pythian boys' pentathlon; at the Great games of Asklepios in the Isthmian boys' pentathlon; at the imperial family's games **10** established for Julius Caesar in the Isthmian boys' stadion and pentathlon on the same day; at the games of Agrippa in the Isthmian (boys') pentathlon; at the games of Apollo at Myndos in the Isthmian boys' **15** stadion; at the Dorian games at Knidos in the Pythian boys' pankration; at the imperial family's games at Halikarnassos in the Isthmian boys' pentathlon; at the games of Herakles at Iasos **20** in the Isthmian boys' pentathlon; at the games of Dionysos at Teos in the Pythian (boys') pentathlon; at the imperial family's games at Sardis in the Isthmian boys' pentathlon.

15.58 *ILS* 112: An altar to Augustus at Narbonne, AD 12–13

Narbo, founded as a Roman colony in 118 BC, was under Augustus the capital of all the Gallic provinces, not merely of Gallia Narbonensis. This inscription is from a marble altar dedicated to the numen (divine power) of the emperor, re-engraved in the second century AD.

A In the consulship of Titus Statilius Taurus and Lucius Cassius Longinus (AD 11), on the tenth day before the Kalends of October (22 September), a vow **5** to the divine spirit of Augustus taken by the people of the Narbonensians in perpetuity:

May it be good, auspicious and fortunate for Imperator Caesar, son of the god, Augustus, father of the county, pontifex maximus, in the 34th year of his tribunician power, and for his wife, children and gens, and for the senate **10** and Roman people, and for the colonists and residents of the colony of Julia Paterna Narbo Martius who have bound themselves to worship his divine spirit in perpetuity.

The people of the Narbonensians have set up an altar at Narbo in the forum, at which each year on the ninth day before the Kalends of October (23 September), on which day **15** the Good Fortune of the age produced him as the ruler of the world, three Roman equites from the people and three freedmen shall each sacrifice a victim and shall provide on that day incense and wine **20** at their own expense for the colonists and residents for supplication of his divine spirit; and on the eighth day before the Kalends of October (24 September) they shall likewise provide incense and wine for the colonists and residents; and on the Kalends of January (1 January) they shall also provide incense and wine for the colonists and residents; and also on the seventh day before the Ides of January (7 January), on which day he first entered upon his command (imperium) **25** of the whole world, they shall make supplication with incense and wine and each sacrifice a victim and on that day provide incense and wine for the colonists and residents; and on the day before the Kalends of June (31 May), because on that day in the consulship of Titus Statilius **30** Taurus and Manius Aemilius Lepidus (AD 11) he reconciled the judgements of the people with the decurions, they shall each sacrifice a victim and shall provide incense and wine for the colonists and residents **35** for supplication of his divine spirit. And from these three Roman equites and three freedmen . . .

B The Narbonese people have dedicated this altar to the divine spirit of Augustus . . . by the laws which are written below. **5** Divine spirit of Caesar Augustus, father of the country, when to you on this day I will give and dedicate this altar, I will give and dedicate it with such laws and regulations which here today I will openly have declared to be the **10** foundation both of the altar and of its inscriptions; if anyone wishes to clean, decorate or repair it as a public service it shall be right and lawful; or if anyone makes the sacrifice of a victim, **15** but does not bring the additional offering, that however will be properly done; if anyone wishes to give a gift to this altar and enrich it, it shall be permitted and the same law that applies to the altar shall apply to the gift; **20** other laws for this altar and inscriptions shall be the same as for the altar of Diana on the Aventine. With these laws and these regulations, just as I have said, this altar on behalf of Imperator **25** Caesar Augustus, father of the county, pontifex maximus, in the 35th year of his tribunician power (AD 12), and on behalf of his wife, children and gens, and to the senate and Roman people, and to the colonists and residents of the colony of Julia Paterna Narbo Martius, who have bound themselves to worship his divine spirit in perpetuity, **30** I give and dedicate that you may be willingly propitious (towards us).

LEGISLATION ON SLAVES AND FREEDMEN

Out of a population of some 700,000 in Rome, there may have been 200,000 freedmen and their families at this period. There was a 5 per cent tax on manumissions, and freedmen who were set free informally could not make a will or receive legacies, as they were neither slave nor citizen. However, if they married a citizen woman they could request citizenship for themselves and their children. Through the *lex Junia*, probably in 17 BC, Augustus tried to address this issue. The peculium was the slave's personal fund which they could use to buy their freedom and which was transferable with the slave.

15.59 Gaius *Institutes* 3.55–57: The Junian Latins

By this law, Junian Latins were granted rights similar to those who were members of the Latin cities (hence the name). Slaves freed informally were now recognised and granted freedom and certain citizen rights.

3.55 Next we consider the estates of Latin freedmen. **56** So that this part of the law may become clearer we must remember what we stated elsewhere, that those who are now called Junian Latins were once slaves by the laws of the Quirites but placed in a form of freedom by the aid of the praetor, so that their property was accustomed to pass to their patrons by the right of peculium. More recently, through the Junian law, all of those whom the praetor had kept in freedom began to be free and were called Junian Latins: Latins, because the law intended them to be free just like those freeborn Roman citizens who left Rome and settled in Latin colonies and began to be Latin colonists; Junian, because they had been made free by the Junian law, even though they were not Roman citizens. Accordingly the author of the Junian law, as he realised that in future the property of deceased Latins would cease to pass to their patrons because they would not die as slaves, in which case their property would pass to their patrons by right of peculium, while the property of a Latin freedman would not pass to his patrons by right of manumission, thought it necessary, so that the benefit given to them should not become a loss to their patrons, to provide that their estates should pass to their manumitters, as if the law had not been enacted; accordingly, by the right, as it were, of peculium, the estates of Latins under this law pass to those who manumitted them. **57** Hence it happens that there is a considerable difference between the rights which pertain to the estates of Latins under the lex Junia and those observed with regard to inheritance from citizen Roman freedmen.

15.60 Gaius *Institutes* 1.42–44, 46: *Lex Fufia Caninia*, 2 BC

The *lex Fufia Caninia* restricted the number of slaves from a household that could be manumitted by will (never more than 100 at a time), though owners were still able to free as many as they wished in their lifetime.

1.42 Moreover, by the lex Fufia Caninia a certain limit is laid down with regard to slaves manumitted by will. **43** For a person who has more slaves than two and fewer than ten is permitted to manumit up to half that number; one who has more than ten and fewer than 30 is permitted to manumit up to a third of that number; authority is given to one who has more than 30 and fewer than 100 to manumit up to a quarter of that number. Finally one who has more than 100 and up to 500 is not permitted to manumit more than a fifth; and however many someone possesses he is not permitted to manumit more than this number, for the law lays down that no one is allowed to manumit more than 100. But if a person has only one slave or two, the law does not apply and he has unlimited power of manumission. **44** Nor does this law apply to any except those who manumit in some way by will. Therefore persons who manumit by the form of vindicta, or by the census registers, or in the presence of friends, are permitted to free their entire household, provided that no other cause prevents the grant of freedom. . . . **46** If freedom should be granted by will to more slaves, with their names in a circle so that no order of manumission can be discovered, none of them shall be free, because the lex Fufia Caninia has declared void any actions designed to evade the law.

15.61 Gaius *Institutes* 1.13, 18–20, 28–30, 36–41: *Lex Aelia Sentia*

The consuls under whom this legislation was passed in AD 4 were Sextus Aelia Catus and Gaius Sentius Saturninus. The law laid down minimum age limits both for the owners before they were able to manumit slaves (20 years) and for the slaves who were to be manumitted (30 years). There were also provisions for slaves who had been manumitted informally to become citizens.

13 It is laid down by the lex Aelia Sentia that slaves who have been put in chains by their masters, or have been branded, or have been examined with torture and convicted, or have been delivered up to fight with others or wild beasts or sent to a gladiatorial school or a public prison, if later manumitted by the same or another owner, shall acquire by manumission the status of enemies who have surrendered at discretion (peregrini dedicitii).

18 It was introduced by the lex Aelia Sentia that a certain age of the slave is requisite, for that law lays down that slaves less than 30 years of age cannot when manumitted become Roman citizens unless manumitted by the form vindicta, with the reasonable motive for the manumission previously approved before the council. **19** There is a reasonable motive for manumission if, for example, someone presents for manumission before the council a natural son or daughter or brother or sister, or foster child, or pedagogus, or a slave who is to be a steward, or female slave for the sake of matrimony. **20** The council in the city of Rome consists of five senators and five equites of the age of puberty, and in the provinces of 20 magistrates who are Roman citizens and who meet on the last day of the session. In Rome, however, manumissions take place before the council on fixed days. Slaves older than 30 years can be manumitted at any time, and can even be manumitted in the streets when the praetor or proconsul is on his way to the bath or theatre.

28 Latins have many ways of acquiring Roman citizenship. **29** For, by the lex Aelia Sentia, when slaves less than 30 years of age are manumitted and become Latins, if they marry wives who are either Roman citizens or Latin colonists, or someone of their own condition, and prove this by the testimony of not fewer than seven Roman citizens of the age of puberty, and they have a son: when that son reaches the age of one year, authority is permitted them by that law to go before the praetor, or in the provinces before the governor, and to prove that they have married a wife in accordance with the lex Aelia Sentia and have had by her a son who has reached the age of one year; and if the magistrate before whom the case is proved pronounces that this is true, then both the Latin and his wife, if she is of the same condition, and their son are declared to be Roman citizens.

36 Not every owner who wishes is permitted to manumit. **37** An owner who is manumitting to defraud his creditors or his patron does so in vain, because the lex Aelia Sentia prevents the granting of freedom. **38** Likewise, by the same law, an owner who is less than 20 years of age is not permitted to manumit except by the form vindicta, after a reasonable motive for manumission has been previously proved before the council. **39** Reasonable motives for manumission are, for example, if someone is manumitting his father or mother or pedagogus or foster brother. But those motives, which were specified above with regard to a slave of less than 30 years, may also be adduced in the case of which we speak. And, likewise, those motives which we stated in the case of an owner less than 20 years of age may be brought forward in the case of a slave under 30 years. **40** As, therefore, a certain restriction on the manumission of slaves is laid down for owners under the age of 20 years by the lex Aelia Sentia, it follows that, though anyone who has completed his 14th year is permitted to make a will and in that to nominate an heir and leave bequests, if, however, he is less than 20 years of age, he is not able to grant liberty to a slave. **41** And even though an owner under the age of 20 years may wish to make a slave a Latin, he must, however, prove his motive for doing so before the council and afterwards manumit him in the presence of friends.

15.62 Legislation on the torture of slaves in cases of adultery

Following the *lex Julia* (18 BC) adultery was a public crime, with serious penalties in place for both parties (doc. 15.25). As a result in such cases slaves could be tortured for their testimony, and Augustus ensured that such slaves could be sold either to him or the state so that they would be able to give evidence against their owner.

(i) Justinian Digest *48.1.6 (Papinian* On Adultery)

When a father or a husband brings an accusation of adultery and they demand that torture be used on the slaves of the accused party, if an acquittal should result after the case has been argued and the witnesses produced, an estimate must be made of the value of the slaves who have died; but in the case of a conviction the slaves that have survived shall be confiscated.

(ii) Justinian Digest *48.1.8 (Paulus* On Adultery*)*

Edict of the Divine Augustus, which he proposed in the consulship of Vibius Habitus and Lucius Apronius (AD 8), is as follows: 'I do not think that inquiry by torture should be used in every case and on every person; but, when capital and atrocious crimes cannot be detected and investigated except through the torture of slaves, I consider this to be the most effective way of determining the truth and I hold that it should be employed.'

(iii) Dio Roman History *55.5.3–4*

3 In the case of candidates for magistracies he demanded a sum of money from them in advance of the elections as a surety, which they would forfeit if they did anything illegal. **4** Everyone approved of this measure. But it was not so with another of his laws: as it was not possible for a slave to be tortured to give evidence against his owner, he commanded that, however often the need for this might arise, the slave should be sold either to the state or to himself, so that he might be examined as someone unconnected with the defendant. Some people criticised this on the grounds that the change of masters would invalidate the law, but others stated it to be essential, as many were using this to conspire both against Augustus and against the magistrates.

FAMILY LIFE

Augustus had no qualms about insisting that members of his family divorce and remarry according to his political agenda. He had been married to Clodia Pulchra (the daughter of Mark Antony and Fulvia) and Scribonia (Sextus Pompeius' closest female relative: Scribonia's brother was Pompeius' father-in-law) before his own marriage to Livia took place when she was six months' pregnant by her first husband. His daughter Julia was married to her cousin Marcellus, then to Augustus' friend and compeer Agrippa, and finally to Livia's son Tiberius, a relationship which was not altogether happy. The passage below, like Julia's conduct in her third marriage, suggests the problems which such dynastic divorces and marriages could cause.

15.63 Suetonius *Life of Tiberius* 7.2–3: Tiberius and Julia

Following the deaths of Marcellus and then Agrippa, Augustus turned in 12 BC to his stepson Tiberius to support his regime, although he considered Julia's sons, his adopted children, as his own successors. This involved a further marriage for Julia, this time with Tiberius, who had to divorce his existing wife, Vipsania Agrippina, by whom he already had a son, Drusus.

Tiberius married (Vipsania) Agrippina, daughter of Marcus Agrippa and granddaughter of Caecilius Atticus, a Roman knight, to whom Cicero wrote his letters. After he had acknowledged a son by her, Drusus, and despite the fact that the marriage was harmonious and she was again pregnant, he was compelled to divorce her and quickly marry Julia, Augustus' daughter – not without great mental distress, for he was living happily with Agrippina and disapproved of Julia's conduct, as he realised that she had a passion for him, even in her former husband's lifetime, as was certainly the general belief. **3** But even after the divorce he was unhappy at the separation, and on the only time that he happened to see Agrippina he followed her with such eager and tearful eyes that care was taken that she would never come into his sight again.

15.64 Macrobius *Saturnalia* 2.5.2–6, 8: 'Caesar's daughter'

Julia, Augustus' only child, had married her cousin Marcellus in 25 BC, when she was 14 years of age. After his death, in 21 BC she married Agrippa, who was nearly 25 years her senior, who died in 12 BC. By him she had five children: Gaius, Julia the Younger, Lucius, Agrippina and Agrippa Postumus. Augustus had adopted Gaius and Lucius as his sons and heirs in 17 BC. Julia was exiled for adultery and treachery in 2 BC: her mother, Scribonia, whom Augustus had divorced the day Julia was born, went into exile on the island of Pandateria with her. For Claudia, see docs 3.61, 7.30.

2 Julia was 38 years of age and was at that period of life which, if she had been sensible, she would have realised to be verging on old age, but she misused both the indulgence of her father and her own good fortune. She had a love of letters and considerable learning, an easy thing to come by in her home, and moreover had a gentle humanity and a warm-hearted nature, which won her high regard, though those who knew of her faults marvelled at such a great discrepancy in her character. **3** On many occasions her father had urged her, in words pitched between indulgence and gravity, to moderate her extravagant style of dress and the notoriety of her entourage. At the same time he noted the similarity of his crowd of grandchildren to Agrippa, and blushed that he should have doubts about his daughter's chastity. **4** And so Augustus flattered himself that his daughter's high spirits were harmless, even if they gave the impression of shamelessness, and dared to believe her to be a modern Claudia. Accordingly, among his friends he used to say that he had two spoilt daughters whom he had to put up with – the state and Julia!

5 On one occasion she came into her father's presence with a rather immodest dress which offended her father's eyes, though he said nothing. On the following day, she changed the style of her dress and embraced her delighted father with assumed gravity. Although he had repressed his disapproval on the day before, he was unable to contain his pleasure, making the remark, 'How much more appropriate this dress is for Augustus' daughter!' But Julia did not hesitate to come to her own defence with the words, 'Today I dressed myself for my father's eyes, yesterday for my husband's!' **6** Here is another well-known saying: at a gladiatorial spectacle, the dissimilarity between the attendants of Livia and of Julia caught the people's eye, with serious men surrounding Livia and a crowd of young and extremely elegant men seated round Julia. Her father sent to her in writing, that she should look at how marked a distinction there was between the two principal ladies of Rome. She neatly wrote back, 'These will be old when I am.' . . . **8**

Moreover, when Julia heard one of her serious-minded friends trying to persuade her that it would be better for her to conform to the pattern of her father's austere ways, she responded, 'He forgets that he is Caesar, but I remember that *I* am Caesar's daughter!'

15.65 Suetonius *Life of the Deified Augustus* 71.1–4, 75–76.2: Fun and games at dinner

December was the month associated particularly with gambling because of the games played at the Saturnalia; the Quinquatria was a five-day festival in honour of Minerva, 20–25 March. Criticism of Augustus focused on his love of gambling: doc. 14.49.

71.1 He did not concern himself with the gossip about his love of dice and played simply and openly for fun even as an old man, not only in the month of December but on other holidays and even on working days. **2** There is no doubt about this as, in a letter in his own handwriting, he says, 'I had dinner, my dear Tiberius, with the same people; we were joined by Vinicius and the older Silius as guests. We played like old men do during the dinner, both yesterday and today; for when the dice were thrown, whoever threw the "dog" (two aces) or a six put a denarius in the pool for each of the dice, and the person who threw Venus (different numbers) took the lot.' **3** And again, in another letter, 'My dear Tiberius, we spent the Quinquatria very pleasantly, for we played all day long and kept the gaming table red-hot. Your brother (Drusus) made a terrible row about his luck, but in the end did not lose much, for after heavy losses he unexpectedly clawed his way back little by little. I lost 20,000 sesterces for my part, but that's because, as usual, I was lavishly sportsmanlike in my play. If I had demanded that everyone paid me the stakes they owed, or not handed over all that I gave away, I would have won at least 50,000. But I'm happier that way – for my munificence will earn me immortal glory!' **4** To his daughter he writes, 'I've sent you 250 denarii, the amount I gave each of my guests, in case they wanted to play during dinner at dice or odds and evens.'

75 Festivals and holidays he usually celebrated lavishly, but sometimes only light-heartedly. At the Saturnalia, and at other times when he felt like it, he would sometimes give as gifts clothes or gold and silver, at others coins of every sort, even old ones from the time of the kings or from foreign parts, and sometimes nothing but goat's-hair cloth, sponges, pokers and tongs and similar items under misleading and mysterious names. At dinner he used to auction off tickets for items of very different values and paintings with their backs turned, thus by the whim of fate either frustrating or fulfilling the hopes of the purchasers, with all the guests having to take part in the bidding and share in the loss or profit. **76.1** As for food – for I would not even leave that out – he was a light eater and generally of plain food. He liked best coarse bread, little fishes, and moist cheese pressed by hand and twice-bearing green figs, and would eat even before dinner at any time or place that he felt hungry. These are his comments in some of his letters . . . : **2** 'While coming home from the Regia I devoured an ounce of bread and some firm-skinned eating grapes.' And again, 'No Jew, my dear Tiberius, keeps his fast so diligently on the Sabbaths as I have today, as it was only in the bath after the first hour of the night that I ate two mouthfuls before I began to be anointed.'

15.66 Macrobius *Saturnalia* 2.4.10–11, 13–14, 31: The last laugh

As he does for Julia, Macrobius records some well-known witticisms of Augustus to demonstrate his quick-wittedness in debate, though he emphasises that Augustus' humour was always decent and that he never resorted to buffoonery. Both father and daughter had a sharp wit. **11**: the joke was made in Greek with the play on words 'hus' (pig) and 'hyios' (son); from his experiences in the East, Augustus was obviously aware of Jewish dietary requirements (cf. doc. 15.65).

10 A certain Vettius had ploughed up a memorial to his father, at which Augustus remarked, 'That is certainly a good way of cultivating your father's memory.' **11** When he heard that Herod, king of the Jews, had ordered boys in Syria under the age of two to be put to death and that the king's son was among them, he said, 'Better to be Herod's pig than Herod's son.' **13** He seldom refused an invitation, and when he was once entertained to a very poor and so to say 'day-to-day' dinner, he whispered to his host as he was saying farewell after this miserable and ill-provisioned meal, 'I didn't think I was so intimate a friend of yours.' **14** When he had occasion to complain that some cloth of Tyrian purple which he had ordered was too dark, the vendor told him to hold it up higher to look at it. This inspired the witty comeback, 'Do I have to walk on my roof garden so that the Roman people can say that I am well-dressed?' **31** As he was going down from (his house on) the Palatine, a poor Greek frequently tried to offer him an honorific epigram with no success, so when Augustus saw him about to attempt it again he wrote a short epigram in Greek on paper with his own hand and sent it to the Greek as he came up to him. The Greek read it and praised it, showing his appreciation in both words and facial expression, and then, coming up to the imperial litter, he put his hand in a shabby purse and drew out a few denarii to give to the princeps, with the words (in Greek), 'I swear by your good fortune, Augustus, if I had more I would give you more.' Everyone around laughed, and Augustus summoned his steward and ordered him to pay the Greek 100,000 sesterces.

15.67 Dio *Roman History* 55.10.12–16: Julia's misbehaviour, 2 BC

Despite the ill-sorted match between Julia and Tiberius, there is the possibility that the episode covered up more than just adultery (which was a convenient excuse), and Julia's 'lovers', who were exiled, had political motivations. It may have been the case that there was a plot to replace Tiberius with Iullus Antonius (son of Mark Antony and husband of Augustus' niece Marcella: see doc. 15.42), who committed suicide. Scribonia was Augustus' second wife; she was older than he was and reported to be a shrew (he had divorced her on the day Julia was born). A few years earlier (8 BC), Julia had figured on Augustus' coinage as Diana, so the scandal was something of an embarrassment.

12 When Augustus finally discovered that his daughter Julia was so dissolute that she partied and revelled at night even in the forum and on the rostra itself, he was furious. **13** Even before this he had gathered that her lifestyle was not blameless, but however he had not believed it – for those in positions of power know everyone else's affairs better than their own and, while their own actions do not escape the notice of their intimate friends, they have no accurate knowledge of what these friends are doing. **14** So when at this point Augustus learnt what was going on, he was so enraged that he was unable to keep this to himself privately but actually published it to the senate. Consequently Julia was banished to the island of Pandateria off the coast of Campania, and her mother, Scribonia, volunteered to accompany her. **15** Of the men who had associated with her, Iullus Antonius (along with other distinguished men) was executed on the grounds that in so behaving he had designs on the monarchy, while the rest were banished to islands. Since one of them was a tribune he was not put on trial until he had completed his term of office. **16** As a result of this, many other women were accused on similar charges, but he would not accept all the law-suits, and instead laid down a specific date so that actions prior to that could not be looked into. Though he showed no moderation in his daughter's case, he showed leniency to the others, remarking that he wished he'd been Phoebe's father, not hers – Phoebe had been a freedwoman of Julia's and her accomplice and had voluntarily killed herself before she could be punished, hence Augustus' praise of her.

15.68 Pliny the Elder *Natural History* 7.75: Dwarfish rivalry

Dwarfs and other physically challenged persons were considered amusing not only within the household; they were also featured at entertainments: Suet. *Aug.* 43.3 mentions a dwarf only 2 feet high, weighing 17 pounds, whom Augustus exhibited at the games. He also put on show a rhinoceros, a tiger and a snake 50 cubits long. For the 'little naked prattlers' that matrons such as Livia had in their entourage, see doc. 14.39.

When the same man (Augustus) was ruling, the smallest person was 2 feet and a hand high, called Conopas, the pet of his granddaughter Julia, and the smallest female was Andromeda, a freedwoman of Julia Augusta (Livia).

15.69 Tacitus *Annals* 5.1.1–4: Livia and Augustus

Livia died on 28 September AD 29. She had been married to Augustus for more than 50 years. She was the daughter of M. Livius Drusus Claudianus (praetor 50 BC), who committed suicide at the battle of Philippi, and wife of Tiberius Claudius Nero, her cousin, who supported the liberators, Fulvia and Lucius Antonius, and then Sextus Pompeius. She divorced Tiberius in order to marry Octavian in 39, when six months' pregnant (doc. 14.39). She was mother of Tiberius, Augustus' successor, and through her second son, Drusus, grandmother of Claudius (who deified her in AD 42), great-grandmother of Gaius (Caligula) and great-great-grandmother of Nero.

1.1 In the consulship of Rubellius and Fufius, whose cognomens were both Geminus, Julia Augusta (Livia) died in extreme old age. She was of the highest nobility through her own Claudian family and through her adoption into the Livii and Julii. Her first marriage, by which she had children, was to Tiberius Nero, who went into exile during the Perusian war but returned to the city when peace was made between Sextus Pompeius and the triumvirs. **2** Caesar, captivated by her beauty, took her from her husband (it is unclear whether this was against her wishes) in such haste that he took her to his house even though she was pregnant, not allowing time for the birth. She had no other children, but, connected as she was to Augustus' bloodline through the marriage of Agrippina and Germanicus, they had great-grandchildren in common. **3** In the decency of her home she followed traditional values, though her graciousness exceeded that of women of earlier times, and she was a domineering mother, a compliant wife, and quite equal to coping with the cleverness of her husband and the dissimulation of her son. **4** Her funeral was simple and the execution of her will long delayed.

15.70 Dio *Roman History* 58.2.4–5: The decent thing to do

Mark Antony's propaganda against Augustus included a list of the women with whom he was having affairs, including Terentilla, the wife of Maecenas (doc. 14.49). As part of Augustus' return to traditional values, the imperial couple lived modestly. Livia made his clothes and avoided ostentatious dress or jewellery, though she had her own circle of clients and was an ambitious mother (docs 14.54, 15.117). Compare the behaviour of Aemilia, the discreet wife of Scipio Africanus (doc. 7.29).

4 Other reported sayings of Livia are as follows: once when some naked men met her and were about to be put to death as a result, she saved their lives by saying that, **5** to decent women, such men are no different from statues. When someone asked her how and by what actions she had gained her influence over Augustus, she replied that it was by being totally chaste herself and happily complying with whatever pleased him, by not interfering in any of his affairs, and by neither hearing nor seeing the objects of his passion.

15.71 Suetonius *Life of Claudius* 4.1–6: A problem grandchild

Augustus is writing to Livia about Claudius (the future emperor), Livia's grandson, the son of Drusus and Antonia Minor, who was born in 10 BC. He was the younger brother of the talented general Germanicus, and since he had a slight deafness and limped he was excluded from public life and spent much time with his grandmother Livia. This letter contains an extensive number of Greek terms, here rendered in italics. The ludi Martiales were connected with the dedication of the temple of Mars Ultor in 2 BC and held on 12 May.

4.1 'I have talked with Tiberius, as you told me, my dear Livia, about what is to be done about your grandson Tiberius (Claudius) at the ludi Martiales. Both of us were in agreement that we must decide once and for all what strategy we should follow with regard to him. For if he is, so to speak, totally normal, for what reason should we hesitate to bring him forward by the same stages as we did with his brother? **2** But if we feel that he is *deficient* and *damaged both in physique and in soundness of mind* we should not give those persons *accustomed to mock and sneer at such things* the opportunity of making fun of both him and us. We will always be vacillating if we have to debate on each separate occasion *without having first agreed in principle* whether we think he is able to hold down magistracies or not. **3** For the moment, however, regarding the matter on which you're asking my advice, I do not mind his presiding at the triclinium of the priests at the ludi Martiales, as long as he allows himself to be advised by Silanus' son, his relative, so that he doesn't behave in such a way as to cause himself to be stared or laughed at. But I don't think he should watch the games from the imperial box, as he will be exposed to view in the very front of the theatre. I don't think he ought to go to the Alban Mount or be in Rome during the Latin festival (Feriae Latinae). For if he is up to following his brother to the Mount, why should he not be made prefect of the city? **4** These, my dear Livia, are my thoughts on the matter. In my view we ought to settle the question once and for all, so as not to be always wavering between hope and fear. If you wish, you may give this part of my letter to our dear Antonia to read.' And in another letter: 'While you are away, I will invite young Tiberius (Claudius) to dinner every day, so that he does not dine alone with Sulpicius and Athenodorus. I do wish he would pick out for himself more carefully and less *casually* someone whose manners and appearance and way of walking he might copy. The poor lad *is unhappy*, as the *nobility of his mind* is quite apparent in his *serious studies* when his mind is not wandering. And in a third letter, 'May I perish!, my dear Livia, if I'm not amazed at how much the declaiming of your grandson Tiberius delighted me. For I can't see how he, who talks so *badly*, should be able to declaim so *clearly* what is to be spoken.'

15.72 Reynolds *Aphrodisias* no. 13: Livia and freedom for Samos

Other inscriptions on Samos honour Livia's family, and the temple of Hera on the island contained statues of her. This inscription cannot be precisely dated, but it makes clear that Livia could act as patron of a community and present its case to the emperor; Augustus here publicly apologises for being unable to accede to her request.

Imperator Caesar, son of the god Julius, Augustus wrote to the Samians underneath their petition: you yourselves can see that I have given the privilege of freedom to no people except that of the Aphrodisians, who supported me in the war and were taken prisoner because of their goodwill towards us. For it is not right to grant the greatest privilege of all without reason and cause. I have goodwill towards you and would be willing to do a service for my wife who is enthusiastic on your behalf, but not so far as to contravene my custom. For it is not the money I care about which you pay into our taxes, but I am not willing to have the most valued privileges given to anyone without cause.

15.73 Marcellus Burdigalensis *De medicamentis* 15.6: Recipe for a sore throat

Hostile historians, such as Suetonius and Tacitus, suggested that many of the deaths leading to the succession of her son Tiberius were the results of deliberate poisoning by Livia. Her recorded interest in compounding medicaments may have encouraged this rumour. The one reported here by Marcellus of Bordeaux in the early fifth century AD would have been very serviceable, not just to Augustus but to many other family members.

This medicine has proved beneficial to many. 2 denarii of each of the following: costus, opium, anis, aromatic rush; 1 denarius of coriander, 2 victoriati of amomum, 2 denarii of seed of hazelwort, 1 denarius of split alum, 5 grains (chick-pea size) from the centre of an oak apple, 2 denarii of saffron, 1 victoriatus of saffron residue, 1 victoriatus of myrrh, 4 denarii of Greek birthwort, 3 denarii of cinnamon, 5 denarii of the ash of baked chicks of wild swallows, 1 victoriatus of a grain of nard.

Grind all these thoroughly and mix with skimmed Attic honey. Livia always had this to hand, stored in a glass jar, for it is exceptionally effective against quinsy and inflammation of the throat.

15.74 Pliny the Elder *Natural History* 15.136: Livia and 'the white chickens'

Livia's villa 'ad Gallinas albas' ('to the white chickens'), north of Rome, which may have been part of her dowry, is under excavation. Its magnificent frescoes are on display at the National Museum of Rome, and the statue Augustus 'of Prima Porta' was discovered in the grounds. The laurel grove was the source of triumphal crowns until the trees died shortly before the death of Nero.

136 There are some remarkable incidents relating to the deified Augustus. For Livia Drusilla, who later took the name Augusta on her marriage, when she was betrothed to him was seated when an eagle dropped from on high a brilliantly white hen unharmed into her lap, and as she viewed it unalarmed, a further marvel occurred, as it held in its beak a laurel branch laden with berries. The haruspices ordered that the bird and her issue should be carefully looked after and the branch planted and tended religiously. **137** This was done at the Caesars' villa situated on the River Tiber near the ninth marker on the Flaminian Way, and consequently the road has since been called the 'ad gallinas' (to the chickens). Quite remarkably a grove has grown there from that branch, and later on, when Caesar was celebrating a triumph, he held a branch of it in his hand and wore a wreath of it on his head, and since then all succeeding emperors have done the same.

AUGUSTUS AS ADMINISTRATOR

15.75 *RDGE* 67: An appeal from Knidos, 6 BC

Knidos was a free city in south-west Asia Minor. The Knidians in this case brought their case directly to Augustus. C Asinius Gallus (cos. 8 BC), currently in Rome and here acting as 'Augustus' friend' and one of his council, was proconsul of Asia in 5 BC. He was married to Vipsania, first wife of Tiberius.

Kairogenes son of Leukatheos was demiourgos. Imperator Caesar Augustus, son of the god, pontifex maximus, consul-designate for the 12th time, holder of tribunician power for the 18th time, **5** to the magistrates, council and people of the Knidians, greetings.

Your envoys, Dionysios and Dionysios II, son of Dionysios, have appeared before me in Rome, and having presented your decree have accused Eubulus, son of Anaxandrides now deceased, and his wife Tryphera, who was present, **10** of the killing of Eubulus, son of Chrysippus. When I ordered Gallus Asinius, my friend, to examine with torture their slaves who were included in the charge, I learnt that Philinus, son of Chrysippus, had gone three nights running to the house of Eubulus **15** and Tryphera with insults and in the manner of a siege, and on the third night was accompanied by his brother Eubulus. Eubulus and Tryphera, the owners of the house, since they had no dealings with Philinus, and even though they barricaded themselves against the attacks, **20** were unable to find safety in their own home, ordered one of their slaves not to kill him, as perhaps one might be inclined to do through not unreasonable anger, but to drive them off by pouring faeces over them. But the slave – whether deliberately **25** or accidentally, for he persisted in denying this – along with the contents let go of the container, and Eubulus was killed, though it would have been more just if he had been saved instead of his brother. I have sent you their testimonies.

I might wonder why **30** the defendants so greatly feared your examination of their slaves, unless you appeared very harsh towards them, and hating, on the contrary, as rascals not those who deserved to suffer anything – who had three times at night attacked a private house with arrogance and violence, and in their rage endangered the common safety of you all – **35** but those who suffered misfortune when trying to defend themselves and who had committed no crime whatsoever. Accordingly you will act correctly in my judgement if you take notice of my opinion of this affair and acknowledge my letter in your public records. Be well.

15.76 Justinian *Digest* 48.12.2.1 (Ulpian): *Lex Julia* on the grain supply

This law, dating probably to 18 BC, prevents the raising of market prices or other unfair practices in the sale and transportation of grain. The grain supply was critical for the stability of Rome even under Augustus. Sextus Pompeius' blockade of Italy had caused serious grain shortages and famine in Rome in 40 BC, and Augustus' resignation of the consulship in 23 was highly unpopular because he was associated in the popular mind with the security of the grain supply (the cura annonae). In 22 he accepted formal responsibility for the cura annonae and in 18 established a commission of four ex-praetors to supervise the grain distribution. According to Augustus himself, in 23 BC he distributed 12 rations to at least 250,000 people, and in 2 BC grain was distributed to just over 200,000 citizens (*RG* 15.1, 4: doc. 15.1). One of the reasons why Augustus kept the control of Egypt in his own hands was its ability to feed Rome.

By the lex Julia about the annona a penalty is fixed against those who act or form an association by which grain shall become dearer. In the same law it is laid down that no one should delay a ship or sailor or act with malice aforethought to detain them longer; and the penalty is fixed at 20 gold coins.

15.77 Guérard 1950: Transport of grain to Alexandria, 2 BC

The grain supply was so important that the ships transporting grain down the Nile were officially escorted by Roman legionaries. This text is on a terracotta grain jar, found at

Oxyrhynchus, which carried a sample of the grain carried by two ships to Alexandria; the sample would be compared with the cargo when they reached their destination. The sitologos was the collector of the grain tax at the local granary. 433¼ artabae would be approximately 22,529 litres. The XXII legion was the Deiotariana, stationed at Alexandria. 1 Egyptian *artabe* = 4.5 *modii Italici* = 38.78 litres and would hold 30.28 kg of Egyptian wheat.

From the Oxyrhynchite nome. Ammonios, son of Ammonios, pilot of a public vessel, of which the emblem is A . . . through the agency of Lucius Oclatius, soldier on marine escort duty of the legion XXII, cohort II, century of Maximus Stoltius, and Hermias son of Petalos, pilot of another vessel of which the emblem is Egypt, through the agency of Lucius Castricius, soldier on marine escort duty of the legion XXII, cohort IV, century of **5** Titus Pompeius. This is a sample of what we have put on board from the harvest of the 28th year of Caesar (3 BC); Ammonios (loaded) up to the bulwarks with 433¼ arbatai of wheat, and Hermias similarly with 433¼ arbatai of wheat, all this loaded through the agency of Leonidas and Apollonias, the sitologoi of the eastern part of the lower toparchy (of the nome): 866½ arbatai of wheat, and we added for every hundred arbatai of wheat ½ of an arbate (as tax). We accomplished the loading from 2nd Hathyr to 4th of the same month, and we have sealed (this jar) with both our seals, that of Ammonios, whose image is Ammon, and of Hermias, whose image is Harpokrates. (Year) 29 of Caesar, 4 Hathyr.

10 (Another hand) We, Hermias and Ammonios, have sealed the samples. (Year) 29 of Caesar, 4 Hathyr.

15.78 *CIL* 3.6687: The census in Syria, AD 6

A marble stele from Syria, in Latin. P. Sulpicius Quirinius (cos. 12 BC) had served on the staff of Gaius Caesar and, after his death, on that of Tiberius. He was governor of Syria AD 6–12, when he carried out a census of Judaea for taxation purposes (cf. Luke 2.1–5).

Quintus Aemilius, son of Quintus, (of the tribe) Palatina, Secundus, in the camp of the deified Augustus under Publius Sulpicius Quirinius, legate **5** of Caesar in Syria: decorated with honours, prefect of Cohort I of Augustus, prefect of Cohort II Classica. Also by order of Quirinius I conducted the census **10** of the city of Apamea of 117,000 citizens; I was also sent by Quirinius against the Ityraeans on Mount Lebanon and I captured their fortress; and before **15** this service, I was prefect of the fabri and was transferred to the treasury. In my colony I was quaestor, twice aedile, twice duovir, and pontifex. **20** Here are placed Quintus Aemilius, son of Quintus, (of the tribe) Palatina, and Aemilia Chia, freedwoman. This monument will not pass any further in the possession of an heir.

15.79 Justinian *Institutes* 4.18.8–9, 11: Violence and embezzlement

Augustus also passed laws on violence, embezzlement, bribery and extortion; the dates of these are not known.

8 The lex Julia on violence, public or private, is directed against those who use violence either with or without weapons. If armed violence is proved, the penalty laid down by the lex Julia on public violence is deportation; if unarmed, confiscation of a third of the offender's property. But if, however, the rape of a girl or widow or religious, veiled or otherwise, is perpetrated, then both the offenders and those who assisted the crime suffer capital punishment as laid down in our constitution, from which the details may be learnt more clearly. **9** The lex Julia on embezzlement punishes those who appropriate money or other property of the state, or that intended for the purposes of religion. But if judges, in their period of office, embezzle public funds, they are punishable with death, and not only these but also those who are their accomplices in this or who receive such money knowing it to be stolen: others who contravene this law suffer deportation . . . **11** Moreover, other public prosecutions can be brought under the lex Julia on bribery and the lex Julia on extortion and the lex Julia on the grain supply and the lex Julia on arrears of public money, which deal with specific offences and do not involve loss of life, but subject to other punishments those who contravene their injunctions.

15.80 Aulus Gellius *Attic Nights* 2.24.14–15: Sumptuary laws

Like Caesar (doc. 13.66), Augustus legislated against luxury, particularly with regard to public and private banquets. C. Ateius Capito was a Roman jurist under Augustus and Tiberius and consul in AD 5.

14 Finally the lex Julia went to the people when Caesar Augustus was ruling, under which 200 sesterces was the limit for expenditure on ordinary days, 300 on the Kalends, Ides, Nones and other holidays, and at weddings and the subsequent banquets 1,000. **15** Ateius Capito also states that there was another edict – I cannot remember whether of the divine Augustus or Tiberius Caesar – under which on various sacred days expenditure on dinners was raised from 300 to 2,000 sesterces, so that the rising tide of luxury might be restrained at least by this limit.

15.81 Suetonius *Life of the Deified Augustus* 28.3–30.1: 'From brick to marble'

RG 20.4: Augustus boasted that in one year alone (28 BC) he had restored 82 temples, and temples and sanctuaries were his first priority. Many of the amenities of Rome were due to Agrippa (docs 15.39–40); Augustus' construction included the Curia Julia and the temple of divus Julius (dedicated 29), his mausoleum (28) the temple of Jupiter Tonans ('the Thunderer', dedicated 22), the Forum Augustum and the temple of Mars Ultor (dedicated 2 BC).

28.3 The city, which was not adorned to match the dignity of the empire and was at risk from floods and fires, he beautified to such an extent that he could justly boast that he had left it in marble, though he had found it in brick. Indeed he also made it safe for the future, in so far as this can be provided for by human foresight. **29.1** He constructed many public works, most notably the following: his forum with the temple of Mars the Avenger (2 BC), the shrine of Apollo on the Palatine (28 BC) and the temple of Jupiter the Thunderer on the Capitol (22 BC). His rationale for building the forum was the huge number of people and law-suits, which seemed to require a third, since two were no longer sufficient. So it was opened to the public in some haste, before the temple of Mars was completed, and it was arranged that the public trials be held there separately as well as the selection of jurors by lot. **2** He vowed the temple of Mars in the war at Philippi which he undertook to avenge his father (Julius Caesar); he therefore decreed that the senate should meet here to discuss wars and triumphs, that it was from here that those going off with imperium to their provinces should be escorted, and when victors returned it was to here that they should bring the tokens of their triumphs. **3** He erected the shrine of Apollo in that part of his house on the Palatine, which, after being struck by lightning, the soothsayers declared to be the choice of the god; he added colonnades with Latin and Greek libraries, and when he was getting old often held senate meetings there and revised the lists of jurors. He dedicated the temple to Jupiter the Thunderer after an escape from danger, when on his Cantabrian expedition during a night march a bolt of lightning grazed his litter and killed the slave who was lighting the way. **4** He also erected some works in the names of others, such as his grandsons and wife and sister, like the colonnade and basilica of Gaius and Lucius (12 BC), as well as the porticoes of Livia and Octavia (15 and 33 BC) and the theatre of Marcellus (13 BC). Moreover he often encouraged other leading men to adorn the city with new monuments or ones that were restored and embellished, according to what they could afford. **5** Many buildings were erected by numerous people, such as the temple of Hercules and the Muses by Marcius Philippus (cos. 38), the temple of Diana by Lucius Cornificius (cos. 35), the hall of Liberty by Asinius Pollio (cos. 40), the temple of Saturn by Munatius Plancus (cos. 42), a theatre by Cornelius Balbus (cos. 40), an amphitheatre by Statilius Taurus (cos. 37), and many spectacular edifices by Marcus Agrippa in particular.

    30.1 He divided the area of the city into districts and neighbourhoods and arranged that the former should be under the supervision of annual magistrates chosen by lot and the latter under 'masters' elected by the people of each neighbourhood. To combat fires he devised night-watches and watchmen; to keep the floods under control he widened and cleared the channel of the Tiber, which had for a while been filled with rubbish and narrowed by extensions to buildings. Moreover, to make it easier to approach the city from every direction, he himself undertook to restore the Flaminian Way as far as Ariminum and allocated the rest to those who had celebrated triumphs to pave from their money from spoils. **2** He restored sacred buildings that were either dilapidated through old age or had been destroyed by fire, and adorned these and others with the most magnificent gifts, as when for example in a single offering he deposited in the shrine of Jupiter Capitolinus 16,000 pounds of gold as well as gems and pearls worth 50,000,000 sesterces.

15.82 *ILS* 4966: Musicians at public rites

This funerary inscription from Rome for the guild of bandsmen who performed at religious ceremonies is evidence for the fact that Augustus laid down through a *lex Julia*, probably in

AD 7, that every club had to be sanctioned by the senate or emperor. In practice, these clubs met once a month to pay their funeral contributions, though they also engaged in social activities.

To the departed spirit. For the association of those who sing in choirs, who perform at public sacrifices, to whom **5** the senate has given permission to hold meetings, to be convened, to be gathered under the lex Julia by authority of Augustus for the sake of the games.

SENATORS AND NEW MEN

When Augustus resigned his consulship on 1 July 23, having held it for 11 years in succession, one of the motives was to give more senators the chance to reach high office and be available for proconsular duties such as provincial government. He held the consulship on only two more occasions, to introduce his grandsons to public life. There was often more than one set of consuls in a year, especially from AD 5, so that four men could reach the pre-eminent position (the second set were known as suffect consuls). Higher-ranking senators were given the roles of administering the military treasury and being in charge of the water supply, public buildings and roads. Augustus also formed a consilium, consisting of the consuls, one each of the other magistracies, and 15 others chosen by lot from the rest of the senators, to act as a personal consultative group before measures went before the senate. He revised the senatorial role three times, with the membership reduced to 600 in 18 BC, and by 13 BC he had fixed the minimum qualification for senators as 1 million sesterces. While there were more senators from Italian towns in Augustus' senate, the consulship still remained highly competitive, and before AD 3 very few consuls were 'new men' from non-senatorial families.

15.83 *ILS* 915: A new man in the senate

In this inscription, from Histonium on the Adriatic coast, Paquius displays his pride in his Italian lineage (he was married to his cousin). While he failed to reach the consulship, he held two provincial governorships in Cyprus and various administrative positions, as well as a priesthood as one of the fetials (cf. doc. 3.14). His second governorship was decided not by the lot, as normal, but by direct appointment by Augustus. Possibly this was a special appointment to organise Cyprus following the earthquake of 15 BC.

Publius Paquius Scaeva, son of Scaeva and Flavia, grandson of Consus and Didia, great-grandson of Barbus and Dirutia, quaestor, one of the Ten for the settling of disputes by senatorial decree after his quaestorship, one of the Four for executions by senatorial decree after his quaestorship, and member of the Ten for settling disputes, tribune of the plebs, curule aedile, court judge, praetor of the treasury, governed the province Cyprus as proconsul, curator of roads outside the city of Rome by senatorial decree for five years, proconsul for the second time outside the lot by authority of Augustus Caesar and decree of the senate, and sent to restore the state of the province of Cyprus for the future, fetial, cousin and also husband of Flavia, daughter of Consus, granddaughter of Scapula, great-granddaughter of Barbus, buried together with her.

Flavia, daughter of Consus and Sinnia, granddaughter of Scapula and Sinnia, great-granddaughter of Barbus and Dirutia, cousin and also wife of Publius

Paquius Scaeva, son of Scaeva, grandson of Consus, great-grandson of Barbus, buried together with him.

15.84 *ILS* 921: Triumphal ornaments for Plautius

The last triumph held by a non-member of the imperial family was that of Cornelius Balbus in 19. From this point it was normal instead, often even for members of the imperial family, to receive triumphal ornaments. Plautius' mother, Urgulania, was a friend of Livia and grandmother of Plautia Urgulanilla, first wife of the emperor Claudius, and responsible for her son's successful career. He was co-consul with Augustus in 2 BC and later proconsul of Asia, after which he served with Tiberius in Pannonia and Dalmatia.

Marcus Plautius Silvanus, son of Marcus, grandson of Aulus, consul (2 BC), one of the Seven for feasts. To him the senate decreed triumphal ornaments for successful achievements in Illyricum. Lartia, daughter of Gnaeus, his wife. Aulus Plautius Urgulanius, son of Marcus, lived nine years.

15.85 *ILS* 932: The 'first of his town'

Varius, from Superaequum of the Paeligni (now Castelvecchio Subequo) in central Italy, was very obviously a novus homo (new man), being the first of his town to enter the senate as well as holding a proconsulship. He was a patron of his home community, and this inscription was set up at public expense by his proud townsfolk.

To Quintus Varius Geminus, son of Quintus, legate of the god Augustus for two years, proconsul, praetor, tribune of the plebs, quaestor, court judge, prefect for the distribution of grain, one of the Ten for settling disputes, curator for the supervision of sacred buildings and public monuments. He was the first of all the Paeligni to become a senator and to hold these magistracies. The Superaequani at public expense to their patron.

15.86 *ILS* 938: A Titian sodalis

An inscription from Epidaurus in Dalmatia. The Titii sodales were a college of priests, supposedly established by the Sabine king Titus Tatius and revived by Augustus.

To Publius Cornelius Dolabella, consul (AD 10), one of the Seven for feasts, Titian sodalis, propraetorian legate of the god Augustus and Tiberius Caesar Augustus of the states of the upper province of Illyricum.

15.87 *ILS* 9483: Reviewer of the equites

From Ipsus in Asia. One of the new positions set up by Augustus was for reviewing the companies of the equites when necessary. The sodales Augustales were an order of priests whose duties were to attend to Augustus' cult.

To . . . Favonius, consul (date unknown), proconsul of Asia, one of the Fifteen for the performance of sacred rites, sodalis Augustalis, triumvir for the review of the centuries of equites with censorial powers, legate of the god Augustus and Tiberius Caesar Augustus . . .

MAECENAS AND AUGUSTAN LITERATURE

Gaius 'Cilnius' Maecenas was one of Octavian's closest friends and also one of the most committed supporters of his regime. He was of distinguished birth, being descended from two ancient Etruscan families: the name Cilnius, which he is sometimes given, appears to be a matronymic. In Octavian's absences, Agrippa and Maecenas acted as his deputies, and Maecenas' first recorded diplomatic undertaking was to negotiate the marriage to Scribonia in 40 BC. Maecenas' role, from the period of the triumvirate, had been to keep an eye on affairs at Rome in Octavian's interests and to act as an unofficial advisor and negotiator. He always refused official honours, even to not becoming a member of the senate. As well as an author in his own right (Augustus criticises his prose style: doc. 15.92) he was a generous patron of literature and encouraged poets such as Vergil and Horace towards themes that would reflect glory on the regime. Maecenas was fabulously wealthy, partly as a result of Augustus' generosity, and, according to Suetonius, Augustus, whose living conditions were deliberately frugal, would stay at Maecenas' splendid villa on the Esquiline when he was ill.

15.88 Velleius Paterculus *Compendium of Roman History* 2.88.1–3: Maecenas' efficiency

After Actium, or possibly after the fall of Alexandria in 30 BC, Lepidus' son appears to have stirred up a conspiracy against Augustus in his absence. Although there were consuls in office, it was Augustus' unofficial friend the eques Maecenas who dealt with the issue. Members of the equestrian order had a narrow purple stripe, as opposed to the broad senatorial one, on their toga.

1 While Caesar was putting the last touches to the war at Actium and Alexandria, Marcus Lepidus, a young man of better appearance than intelligence, son of that Lepidus who was a triumvir for restoring the state and of Junia, Brutus' sister, had made plans for assassinating Caesar as soon as he returned to the city. 2 Gaius Maecenas was at that point in charge of the city's guards, a man of equestrian rank but of splendid lineage, a man who was literally sleepless when matters required vigilance, and quick to see what needed doing, and knowing how to do it, though when it was possible to relax at all from business he would abandon himself to ease and luxury almost more than a woman would. He was no less dear to Caesar than Agrippa was but awarded fewer honours – since he was thoroughly satisfied to live with just the narrow stripe – not that he wasn't capable of achieving as much but had less desire for it. 3 He investigated the plans of the rash youth very quietly and cleverly, and by overcoming Lepidus with amazing speed and no disturbance either to affairs or men he extinguished the dread beginnings of a new and renascent civil war.

15.89 Pliny the Elder *Natural History* 37.10: A frog in the post

While deputising for Octavian, Maecenas had the right to use Octavian's seal and send dispatches in his name even to altering the contents as appropriate, and he was obviously skilled at extracting tax payments.

The deified Augustus at first used a seal engraved with a sphinx, as he had found two of them among his mother's rings that were remarkably similar. During the civil war, when he was absent, his friends used one of these to seal those letters and edicts which the circumstances of the times made it necessary to issue in his name – it was a pointed joke among those who received them that the sphinx had come with its riddles. And the frog as well on the seal of Maecenas was an object which brought great terror with it, because it meant that a monetary contribution was being demanded.

15.90 Aelius Donatus *Life of Vergil* 20–41: Vergil, Maecenas and Augustus

Maecenas may have played a role in helping Vergil to recover the family farm in the confiscations of 41–40, and it was he who commissioned Vergil to write his *Georgics*. He also procured a pardon for Horace, who fought on the liberators' side at Philippi, and gave him a farm from which he could acquire a livelihood and devote himself to poetry. Plotius Tucca and Varius Rufus were poets and the executors named to oversee the publication of Vergil's poetry. For Vergil's description of Marcellus, see doc. 15.36.

20 After that, Vergil published the *Georgics* in honour of Maecenas, who had assisted him (though only slightly acquainted with him) against the violence of a veteran, who all but killed him in an argument over his land . . . . **25** The *Eclogues* he finished in three years, the *Georgics* in seven, the *Aeneid* in eleven. The *Eclogues* were so successful on their first appearance that singers frequently recited them, even on stage. **27** When Augustus was returning after his victory at Actium and stayed at Atella to rest his throat, Vergil read the *Georgics* to him continuously for four days; Maecenas took over reading from him whenever his voice failed. **28** Nonetheless, Vergil's reading was sweet and strangely seductive . . . . **30** Even when the *Aeneid* was scarcely begun, its reputation was such that Sextus Propertius (*Odes* 2.34.65) did not hesitate to predict in these words:

> Give way, Roman authors; give way, Greeks:
> Something greater than the *Iliad* is being born.

31 Indeed, Augustus (for, as it happened, he was away on an expedition in Cantabria) jokingly demanded of him in his letters, with threats as well as prayers, that he should send him (to employ his own words) 'something from the *Aeneid*, either your first draft or any section, it does not matter which'. **32** But it was not until much later, when he had finally put the finishing touches to his subject matter, that Vergil read out to him three books in all: the second, fourth and sixth, this last from his well-known affection for Octavia, who was present at the recitation and at these verses about her son, ' . . . You shall be Marcellus!' [*Aen.* 6.884] is said to have fainted and been revived only with difficulty.

35 In his fifty-second year he decided to retire to Greece and Asia, to put the finishing touches to the *Aeneid*, and after doing nothing but revise it for three straight years to give the remainder of his life to philosophy. But, after setting out for Athens, he met up at Athens with Augustus, who was returning to Rome from the East. He then resolved not to leave him, and even to return with him, but while he was visiting the nearby town of Megara under a scorching sun he was taken with a fever and made this worse by not breaking his journey. As a result on his arrival at Brundisium his condition was more serious, and after a few days he died there, on the eleventh day before the Kalends of October (21 September 19 BC), in the consulship of Gnaeus Sentius and Quintus Lucretius. **36** His bones were taken to Naples, and buried on the Via Puteolana, only 2 miles from the city, in a tomb for which he composed the couplet:

Mantua gave birth to me, Calabria slew me, and now
Parthenope holds me. I have sung pastures, fields, generals.' . . .

39 Before leaving Italy, he had arranged with Varius that, if anything should happen to him, he would burn the *Aeneid*, but Varius had refused to do so. So, when he was very ill, he kept calling for his scroll-cases, intending to burn them up himself, but since no one came forward it did not happen, even though he gave precise directions about this. **40** He left his writings to the above-mentioned Varius and Tucca, on the condition that they publish nothing which he himself had not revised. **41** Nevertheless, Varius published them, acting under the authority of Augustus, after only minor revisions, even leaving the unfinished lines just as they were.

15.91 Seneca *Letters* 114.4–7: Maecenas' literary style

Seneca the Younger here makes a blistering attack on Maecenas' prose style, which he sees as reflecting his effeminate and pretentious lifestyle, though this criticism of his conduct is not entirely borne out by earlier contemporary accounts. He wrote a natural history, referred to by Pliny, apparently focusing on fish and gems, and may have written a biography of Augustus, as well as a *Symposium*, featuring Horace, Vergil and Messalla. For the 'king of the grove', see doc. 3.11.

4 How Maecenas lived is too well known for there to be any need to describe how he walked, how effeminate he was, and how he desired to be stared at, as well as how he did not want his vices to escape notice. What, then? Does not the looseness of his speech match his ungirt style of dress? Are not his words as remarkable as his habits, his retinue, his house, his wife? He would have been a man of great talent had he gone there by a straighter path, had he not avoided making himself understood, had he not been so diffuse in his style of speech as well. You will therefore see that his eloquence was that of an intoxicated man – intricate, wandering, full of licence.

5 What is more disagreeable than 'a stream and a bank with long-haired woods'? And see how 'men plough the channel with boats and in turning up the shallows leave behind gardens'; or 'he waves his love locks, and bills and coos with his lips, and begins to sigh, like a king of the grove who offers prayers with bent neck'; or 'an unregenerate crew, they rummage for food at feasts, and assail households with a flagon, and, by hope, exact death'; or 'a Genius can hardly be witness to his own festival'; or 'threads of fine wax tapers and creaking meal'; or 'mothers or wives clothe the hearth.'

6 When you read these, doesn't it immediately occur to you that this was the man who always paraded through the city with a flowing tunic? – for even when he was performing duties for the absent emperor, he was always ungirt when they asked him for the password. Or that this was the man who, on the judge's bench or the rostra, or at any public gathering, appeared with his head wrapped in his cloak, with only his ears exposed, like a rich man's runaway slave in a mime? Or that this was the man who, at the time when the state was riven with civil war, when the city was in a panic and under arms, was attended in public by two eunuchs – better men than he was? Or that this was the man who was married countless times but had one wife? **7** These words of his, badly arranged, thrown off so casually and set out in such contrast to the usual practice, show that the writer's character was equally unusual, debased and outlandish. Of course, we grant him praise for his humanity – he was sparing with the sword and refrained from bloodshed – and he made a show of his power in nothing other than his loose living; but he spoiled this praise by such convolutions of his quite unnatural style, for these show that he was not considerate, but effeminate.

15.92 Macrobius *Saturnalia* 2.4.12: Augustus and Maecenas

Augustus is here playing on Maecenas' Etruscan origins. His mother's family, the Cilnii, had been prominent at Arretium; Lars Porsena was the Etruscan king known for his war against Rome; Iguvium is modern Gubbio in Etruscan territory; and Medullia was one of the towns in Latium captured by Tarquinius Priscus.

Knowing that his friend Maecenas wrote in a loose, effeminate and decadent style, he would often write in the same way in the letters he sent to Maecenas and, in contrast to the restrained way of expressing himself which he used in writing other letters, an intimate letter to Maecenas would include as a joke an outpouring of phrases such as: 'Farewell, my ebony from Medullia, ivory from Etruria, silphium of Arretium, diamond of the Adriatic, pearl of Tiber, Cilnian emerald, jasper of the Iguvians, beryl of Porsenna, Adriatic carbuncle – or, in short, softener-up of adulterous wives!'

15.93 [Suetonius] *Life of Horace* 1–3: Horace and Augustus

Q. Horatius Flaccus was a leading Roman lyric poet during Augustus' reign. Initially a Republican, on returning to Italy after defeat at Philippi (where he depicts himself running away) he found that, like Vergil, he had lost his father's estate through the confiscations, but he gained employment in the treasury. Again like Vergil, he joined Maecenas' literary circle, and the two poets accompanied Maecenas in 37 when he travelled to Brundisium to arrange the treaty of Tarentum. Maecenas' gift of a farm allowed Horace to be independent, and in his poems he increasingly referred to public affairs, including wars and military victories, and was commissioned by Augustus to write the *Carmen Saeculare* for the ludi Saeculares in 17 BC (doc. 15.33). Ninnius is unknown.

1 Horace served as a military tribune in the war at Philippi under Marcus Brutus as general; when his side was conquered, he received pardon and obtained the position of a quaestor's clerk. He won the favour first of Maecenas, and shortly afterwards of Augustus, and held a central place among the friends of both. How much Maecenas loved him is shown in this well-known epigram:

'Unless more than life itself, my Horace,
I love you, then see your intimate friend
More thin and wasted than Ninnius!'

But he wrote far more strongly in his will with this comment to Augustus, 'Be as mindful of Horatius Flaccus, as of myself!' **2** Augustus offered him the position of secretary, as the remark in a letter to Maecenas shows: 'Previously I was able to write letters to my friends, but now I am so overwhelmed with work and in poor health that I would like to take our friend Horace from you. He will then come from your parasitical table to my imperial one and will help me write my letters.' Even when he refused, Augustus was not at all resentful and continued his attempts to win his friendship. There are letters from which I will add some extracts to prove it: 'Enjoy any rights at my house, as if you were living there with me; you will do so both rightly and reasonably, as that was the relationship I wished to have with you had your health permitted.' . . . **3** As regards his writings, Augustus valued them so highly and was so sure that they would be immortal that he chose him to compose not only the *Secular Hymn* but also the victory of his stepsons Tiberius and Drusus over the Vindelici, and so forced him to write a fourth book of *Odes* after a long period of silence. Also after reading several of his *Epistles* he queried why there was no mention of him at all, with the words: 'You should not fear that I am cross with you, since in your numerous writings of that kind you do not dialogue with me; are you afraid that your name will be disreputable to posterity, because you'll be seen to be my friend?' And he obliged him to write the collection which begins:

'Since you alone bear the weight of tasks so many and so great,
Protecting Italy's affairs with arms, improving it with morals,
Reforming it by laws: I would sin against the public good,
Were I to waste your time with long discourse, Caesar.' (= *Epistle* 2.1)

15.94 Horace *Epistle* 1.13: A package for Augustus

In this humorous epistle, Horace envisages his volume of poetry (perhaps *Odes* 1–3) delivered to Augustus by a clumsy and over-enthusiastic messenger.

As you were setting out I told you often and at length:
Deliver these volumes sealed to Augustus, Vinnius,
If he's well and if he's happy and if finally he asks for them;
Don't blunder in your zeal for me and have dislike for my books

5   Caused by the over-eagerness of an over-enthusiastic servant.
     If you find the heavy burden of my pages irksome,
     Toss them away, rather than go throwing down the pack-saddle
     Where told to take it, like a wild thing, making a joke
     Of your father's name *As*ina and a good story to be told of you.
10   Use your strength to conquer mountains, rivers, marshes,
     But when you've made it and arrive there,
     Don't hold your parcel so as to carry the book package
     Under your arm, like a countryman a lamb,
     Or tipsy Pyrria her stolen ball of wool,
15   Or a dinner guest of a fellow tribesman his cap and slippers.
     And don't tell everyone how much you've sweated,
     Carrying poems, that could engage the eyes and ears
     Of Caesar! Entreated by many prayers, press on,
     Go, farewell – and do not trip and damage your precious charge!

15.95 Propertius *Elegies* 3.4: Augustus conquers India

Sextus Propertius (died c. 15 BC), perhaps the greatest Roman elegiac poet, produced four books of elegies, the first of which was devoted to a lady known as Cynthia and which was published c. 28 BC. This brought Propertius to the attention of Maecenas, after which he joined his circle. In his first two volumes, love is his primary philosophy and the reason for existence, but from book 3, which appeared c. 23, he starts to handle wider themes relating to Augustus' regime, including a lament for Marcellus (3.18). In this poem, while he calls Augustus a god and incites him to war on Parthia and even to the ends of the earth, this enthusiasm cannot be taken seriously. The martial thrust of the poem is deftly undercut at line 15, where he explains that his only interest will be to view the victory procession while relaxing with his 'girl'. Others can win the booty – his only concern is to applaud it while safely at home.

     Caesar, our god, plans war on the rich Indes,
     Cleaving with his fleet the straits of the pearl-bearing sea.
     Romans, rewards are great: the ends of the earth prepare triumphs;
     Tigris and Euphrates will flow under your laws.
5   Too late, but the province will come under Italian fasces –
     Parthia's trophies will come to know Latin Jupiter.
     Go now!, experienced prows in warfare, set sail!,
     And armour-wearing horses do your usual service!
     I sing auspicious omens. Avenge the Crassi and disaster!
10   Go and be mindful of Rome's history!
     Father Mars, and fatal lights of holy Vesta,
     I pray that day will come before I die,
     That I may see Caesar's axles laden with spoils
     His horses halting often for the mob's cheers –
15   *Then* resting on the bosom of my girl I'll start
     To look and survey the captured cities' names,

The shafts of fleeing cavalry, the bows of trousered soldiers,
And captive leaders seated beneath their weapons.
Venus, preserve your own descendants; let it be immortal,
20   This head you see surviving from Aeneas' line.
Let booty go to those whose labours deserve it –
Enough for me that I can applaud them on the Sacred Way.

15.96 Ovid *Fasti* 5.545–98: The Temple of Mars Ultor

O. Ovidius Naso (43 BC–AD 17/18) was a prolific and popular poet who, for some
unknown reason, was exiled by Augustus to the Black Sea in AD 8 (perhaps because of
a connection with the scandal of Julia the Younger, though there is no evidence for this).
Much of his early poetry has erotic themes, such as his *Amores* and *Art Amatoria* (*The
Art of Love*), but he also eulogises Augustus' regime and buildings, sometimes tongue-in-
cheek, as when he describes the porticoes of Octavia and Livia as a good place to pick up
girls. More seriously, in this treatment of the temple of Mars Ultor (the 'Avenger'), built to
commemorate the defeat of Caesar's assassins and to mark the recovery of the standards
from Parthia, Ovid describes statues of the mythical ancestors of Augustus and ancient
heroes as being placed in the apses, including Aeneas and Romulus. The date of dedication
was 12 May 2 BC.

But why are Orion and the other stars
Hastening to leave the sky, and why is night shortening its course?
Why does bright day, from the liquid ocean, lift
Its radiance more swiftly, preceded by the Morning Star?
Do I mistake, or was there a sound of arms? I'm not, there was –
550   Mars comes and coming gives the sign for war!
The Avenger himself descends from heaven
To see his honours and his temple in Augustus' forum.
Both god and shrine are mighty: Mars ought
To dwell nowhere but in the city of his son.
555   The temple is worthy of trophies won from Giants;
From here Mars the 'Marcher' initiates fierce wars,
When an impious enemy attacks us from the East, or
Those from the setting sun who must be conquered.
Strong in his arms he views the summit of the building
560   And approves of unconquered gods dwelling on the heights.
He sees the doors arrayed with weapons of every kind
And arms from countries conquered by his soldiers.
Here he sees Aeneas weighed down with his dear burden,
And many forefathers of the Julian noble family;
565   There he sees Romulus bearing the weapons of a general on his shoulders,
And famous heroes' deeds named below their statues.
He sees Augustus' name on the temple's front,
And with reading 'Caesar', the work seems greater still.
He vowed it in his youth, when dutifully taking up his arms –

570 With such deeds a Princeps came into being.
     Stretching out his hand, loyal troops are here –
     There conspirators – and spoke these words,
     'If my father, priest of Vesta, is my cause for war,
     I prepare to avenge both godheads:
575 Mars, come!, and glut the sword with criminal blood
     And may your favour stand with the better side;
     You'll win a temple, and (if I am victor) be called Avenger.'
     He vowed, and joyfully returned from the routed enemy,
     Not satisfied to have earned Mars that name –
580 But seeks the signals kept in Parthian hands,
     That people guarded by plains, cavalry, archers,
     Inaccessible behind their encircling rivers . . . .
589 He removed that well-known, old disgrace:
     The regained standards knew their proper hands.
     What use the arrows fired customarily in retreat,
     Your deserts, and your swift horses,
     Parthians? You bring the eagles home, and offer unstrung bows;
     Now you no longer possess the pledges of our shame.
595 Rightly the god has his temple and twice title of Avenger,
     The honour earned has paid the vowed debt.
     Quirites, celebrate solemn festival in the Circus,
     The stage seems hardly fitting for a mighty god.

15.97 Ovid *Fasti* 2.127–44: Augustus versus Romulus

Earlier in his career Augustus had rejected the name Romulus for the less martial and more pious one of Augustus (doc. 14.65), though this did not mean that Romulus was not revered as son of Mars, ancestor of the Romans and founder of Rome. In this passage Ovid draws a witty contrast between Augustus as benign father and ruler of the whole world with the petty murderous rapist Romulus. While eulogising Augustus, Ovid at the same time is quietly undercutting the traditional values which were so important to Augustus in his social and religious reforms.

     Holy father of your country!, to you the plebs and senate gave the name
     And we the equites gave you this as well.
     Already granted by events, you received the title late.
130 The name, you – long since father of the world –
     Possess on earth, which Jupiter has in lofty heaven
     – You're father of men, he of the gods.
     Romulus, give way! Caesar by his care has made your walls
     Mighty, the ones *you* constructed Remus could jump over!
135 Tatius, and poverty-stricken Cures, and Caenina knew you –
     With him as leader both sides of the sun are Roman!
     You possessed some tiny piece of conquered land,
     Whatever lies under lofty Jupiter, Caesar holds.
     You raped married women, he as leader orders them be chaste.

746

140 You allowed impiety in your grove, he drives it off.
　　You welcomed violence, under Caesar our laws flourish.
　　Your name was 'Lord', his is 'Princeps'.
　　Remus accused you of murder, while *he* gives enemies pardon.
　　Your father deified you, *he* deified his own!

15.98 Dio *Roman History* 55.7.1–6: The death of Maecenas, 8 BC

Octavian's rise to power had greatly depended on the support of his old friends Agrippa and
Maecenas, both of whom deliberately renounced overt power in his favour. Now both of
them were gone. According to Plutarch (*Mor.* 207), Maecenas gave Augustus a drinking cup
for every birthday and in his will requested that he look after Horace. There may have been
an awkwardness between Augustus and Maecenas in 23 or 22, when there was a conspiracy
against Augustus headed by L. Licinius Varro Murena and Fannius Caepio (it was serious
enough for the conspirators to be put to death). It appears that Maecenas' wife, Terentia, was
Murena's adopted sister, and Suetonius records that Maecenas had leaked details to his wife.
It was also widely known that Augustus and Terentia had had or were having an affair; Mark
Antony criticises Augustus for this in the late 30s (doc. 14.49), so it would have been ancient
history by the time of Maecenas' death. As Augustus expected of his friends, Maecenas, who
was childless, left Augustus his vast estate, including the gardens on the Esquiline.

1 Augustus was distressed when Maecenas died. He had received many benefits
from him and, as a result, though he was only an eques, entrusted him with the
supervision of the city for a long period, and found him especially useful at those
times when his own temper was ungovernable, as Maecenas would always do
away with his anger and bring him to a milder state of mind. **2** One example is
when Maecenas was at hand when Augustus was holding court and, seeing that
he was on the point of condemning a number of people to death, tried to push his
way through the onlookers and get near to him, and when he was unable to do
this wrote on a tablet, 'Rise at last, executioner!' and threw this into his lap as if
concerning some other minor matter. As a result Augustus put no one to death but
stood up and left. **3** He was not only not annoyed at such actions but was actually
glad of them, since, whenever he became inappropriately irritated by his innate
disposition or by the pressure of affairs, these were corrected by the free speech
of his friends. **4** This was also the greatest proof of Maecenas' good qualities, that
he not only endeared himself to Augustus, even though he checked his outbreaks,
but made everyone else like him as well and, while he had the greatest degree of
influence with Augustus, to the extent that he gave honours and magistracies to
many people, did not lose his presence of mind but passed his life as a member of
the equestrian order. **5** So for these reasons Augustus missed him excessively and
also because Maecenas, although upset over Augustus' relationship with his wife,
had made him his heir and had left it in his power to dispose of the whole property,
with a very few exceptions, should he wish to give anything to any of his friends
or not. This was the sort of person Maecenas was and this was how he behaved to
Augustus. **6** He was the first person to construct a swimming pool of warm water
in the city and the first to invent a system of symbols to speed up writing, and he
had a number of people trained in this through a freedman, Aquila.

THE GOLDEN YEARS

15.99 Macrobius *Saturnalia* 1.12.35: Sextilis renamed, 8 BC

Although Augustus was born in September, Sextilis was the month particularly associated with his achievements and triumphs, and the name of Sextilis was changed to August by senatorial decree. For entries in the fasti, see docs 14.63, 15.4; the occasion on which he led out legions from the Janiculum hill is unknown.

Whereas Imperator Caesar Augustus in the month Sextilis entered on his first consulship (19 August 43), made three triumphal entries into the city (13–15 August 29), and led out his loyal legions from the Janiculum under his own auspices; and whereas Egypt in this month was brought into the power of the Roman people (1 August 30), and an end of civil war was made in this month; and whereas this month is and has been most propitious to this Empire for these reasons, it is the pleasure of the senate that this month shall be named August.

15.100 Dio *Roman History* 55.9.1–5, 9, 10.1: The young Gaius and Lucius

Gaius, eldest son of Julia and Agrippa, was born in 20 and adopted by Augustus, along with his brother Lucius, in 17 BC; in 5 BC he was designated for the consulship in AD 1 and made princeps iuventutis ('first of the youth'), an important new position which involved the leadership of the equestrian order (*RG* 14.1–2: doc. 15.1). In 6 BC Tiberius went into retirement on Rhodes for several years, despite the granting of tribunician power and the renewal of his imperium.

1 The next year, in which Gaius Antistius and Laelius Balbus were consuls (6 BC), Augustus noticed that both Gaius and Lucius, though brought up in the princeps' house, were by no means inclined to copy his conduct, for they not only pursued a luxurious lifestyle but also tended to be insolent – on one occasion Lucius entered the theatre without attendants. **2** They were being flattered by everyone in the city, sometimes genuinely, sometimes to butter them up, and so were becoming more and more spoilt (among other things, the people had elected Gaius consul before he was even of military age), and Augustus even prayed that no similar circumstances to his own might arise to make anyone less than 20 years a consul. **3** When they kept insisting, he said that no one should receive this magistracy until they were able not only to avoid committing any error themselves but also to oppose the passionate impulses of the people. **4** After this he gave Gaius a priesthood and the right of attending senate meetings and of viewing spectacles and banqueting with the senators. Because he wished for some way of sobering their behaviour, he granted Tiberius tribunician power for five years and allocated him Armenia, which was becoming alienated from Rome following the death of Tigranes. **5** What happened was that he needlessly upset both the boys and Tiberius, as they thought they had been overlooked, and he was afraid of their anger. At any rate Tiberius was sent to Rhodes on the grounds that he needed some education, and he did not even take with him his whole retinue, the idea being that he and his activities should be out of their way . . . . **9** The following year (5 BC), in his twelfth consulship, Augustus put Gaius among the youths of military age and at the same time introduced him into the senate, declared him princeps iuventutis, and allowed him to become commander of a division of cavalry. **10.1** After another year Lucius too received all the honours that had been given to his brother Gaius.

15.101 *RDGE* 68: Honours for Gaius at Sardis, 5 BC

A stele of blueish marble found at Sardis with 12 documents relating to the notable citizen Menogenes. The koinon of Asia and the citizens of Sardis decreed that the day on which Gaius put on the toga virilis was to be a public holiday; in a letter Augustus replies to give his thanks. The strategoi were annually elected civil magistrates at Sardis. In this year Gaius was made princeps iuventutis and allowed to give his opinion in the senate.

I The association (koinon) of the Greeks in Asia and the people of the Sardians and the Elder Citizens (gerousia) honoured **5** Menogenes, son of Isidoros and grandson of Menogenes, by what is written below:

Metrodoros, son of Konon, Kleinias, Mousaios and Dionysios, the strategoi, put the motion: since Gaius Julius Caesar, the eldest of the sons of Augustus, has put on the toga most diligently prayed for and bright with every decoration in place of the one with the purple border (toga praetexta), all men rejoice seeing the prayers which have arisen on all sides to Augustus on behalf of his sons, and **10** our city on the occasion of such great good fortune has decided that the day which completed his transition from child to man shall be holy, and on this day each year everyone in their brightest clothes shall wear garlands, and the strategoi of that year shall present sacrifices to the gods and prayers be offered by the sacred heralds for his safety, and on it they shall join in dedicating his statue and shall set it up in the temple of his father; on that day too, on which the city received the good news and this decree was ratified, **15** garlands shall be worn and magnificent sacrifices offered to the gods; and (as it has been decided) that an embassy regarding this be sent to arrive at Rome and to congratulate both him and Augustus, it has been decreed by the council and people to dispatch envoys from the foremost men to bring salutations from the city and to give him the copy of this decree sealed with the public seal, and to speak **20** with Augustus concerning affairs of common interest to Asia and the city. Chosen as envoys were Iollas, son of Metrodoros, and Menogenes, son of Isidoros and grandson of Menogenes.

II Imperator Caesar, son of the god, Augustus, pontifex maximus, holding tribunician power for the nineteenth time (5 BC), to the magistrates, council and people of the Sardians, greetings. Your envoys, Iollas, son of Metrodoros, and Menogenes, son of Isidoros and grandson of Menogenes, met me in Rome and **25** gave me the decree from you through which you revealed what had been decreed by you concerning yourselves and rejoiced (with me) at the attainment of manhood by the elder of my sons. Accordingly I praise your eagerness in demonstrating your gratitude to me and all my family in return for the benefits given by me. Farewell.

15.102 Suetonius *Life of the Deified Augustus* 57.2–58.2: 'Pater patriae'

On 5 February 2 BC the senate granted Augustus, now aged 60 years, the title 'pater patriae', father of his country, an honour which he specifically emphasised in the *Res Gestae* as the pinnacle of his career (*RG* 35.1), as it completes his account of his life and achievements. The title had earlier been given to Cicero and Caesar. The title also appears frequently on his coinage. M. Valerius Messalla (cos. 31) had celebrated a triumph in 27 and, like Maecenas, was a noted patron of literature.

57.2 To restore his house on the Palatine which had been destroyed by fire, the veterans, guilds of minor officials (decuriae) and the tribes, and even individuals of all kinds, willingly contributed money according to their means, though he, to show his gratitude, took only a little from each pile, and not more than a denarius from any of them. When he returned from the provinces, he was greeted not only with auspicious salutations but even with songs of joy, and it was the custom too that whenever he entered the city all punishments were cancelled. **58.1** In a spontaneous unanimous movement everyone offered him the title of pater patriae, first the plebs through a deputation sent to Antium, and then, because he declined it, by a huge crowd wearing laurel wreaths as he entered the theatre at Rome, and finally, in the senate house, by the senate, not through a decree or acclamation but through Valerius Messala. **2** He spoke for the whole body: 'May good fortune and divine favour attend you and your family, Caesar Augustus! – for in this way we believe we are praying that our state be eternally prosperous and our city fortunate. The senate, in agreement with the people of Rome, salutes you as Father of your Country.' With tears in his eyes, Augustus in these words – and I have given them verbatim as I did for Messalla – replied, 'Having attained my highest ambitions, Fathers, what have I left to ask from the immortal gods than that I may be permitted to retain the same unanimous approval of yours to the very end of my life?'

15.103 *SEG* 23.206: Gaius' successes, AD 2

A stele from Messene in Greece. Gaius set out in 1 BC for the East, where he had imperium over the whole region. In the same year he had married his step-relative Livilla, daughter of Drusus and Antonia Minor. While in the East he entered on his consulship for AD 1, with L. Aemilius Paullus as his colleague. After a short campaign in Arabia, he had a diplomatic meeting with the new Parthian king, Phraataces V, on an island in the Euphrates, then marched to Armenia to set a Roman nominee on the Armenian throne.

Philoxenidas was secretary of the council members in the magistracy of Theodoros.

Decree: since Publius Cornelius Scipio, quaestor with pro-praetorian power, with extraordinary goodwill towards Augustus and all his family **5** has made the greatest and most honourable vow to protect him against all harm, as shown by all his actions, and has organised the games of the imperial family and has omitted no expense or effort, nor on behalf of the sacrifices for Augustus spared his thanks-givings to the gods, at the same time instructing most of the cities in the province **10** to do the same along with himself; and when he learnt that Gaius, son of

Caesar, who took part in battle with the barbarians for the good of everyone, was in good health and had escaped danger, and had taken vengeance on the enemy, exceedingly joyful at this excellent news he instructed everyone to wear garlands and sacrifice in uninterrupted holiday, and he personally sacrificed oxen for **15** the preservation of Gaius and put on a variety of performances, being anxious both to ensure that they rivalled those given in the past and to preserve (Gaius') honoured position. He removed two days from the days of Augustus, and made the beginning of the sacrifices for Gaius from the day on which he was designated consul for the first time and ordered us to celebrate this day every year with **20** sacrifices and the wearing of wreaths as graciously as possible, and the council members decreed on the fifteenth day before the Kalends of . . .

15.104 Aulus Gellius *Attic Nights* 15.7.1–3: A letter to Gaius

Suetonius here reveals that he had access to a volume of letters written by Augustus to Gaius, of which this is one. It was written in September AD 2 to Gaius in Syria. Here, in a chatty and light-hearted message to his 'son', Augustus shows how much he missed his company and reveals his intention that Gaius and Lucius should be his successors, formally continuing the principate into a new generation.

1 It has been noted of most old men, throughout much of human memory, and found to be correct, that the sixty-third year of their life is generally marked by danger or some disaster involving either serious bodily illness or loss of life, or mental incapacity. **2** Accordingly, those who are engaged in the study of matters and terms of that kind call that year of life the 'climacteric'. **3** The night before last, too, when I was reading the volume of letters which the deified Augustus wrote to his grandson Gaius, and was led on by the elegance of the style, which was neither over-elaborate nor punctilious, but, by Hercules!, easy and simple, in one of these letters I came across a reference to this actual belief about the same year:

The ninth day before the Kalends of October (23 September): 'Greetings my Gaius, my dearest little donkey, whom I constantly miss, Heaven knows!, when you're away from me. But on days like today my eyes are particularly eager to see my Gaius, and, wherever you may happen to have been today, I hope that you are in good spirits and well enough to celebrate my 64th birthday. For, as you see, I've passed the "climacteric" common to all old men, the sixty-third year. And I pray to the gods that whatever time is left me I may to spend it with you safe and well, and with our country prospering, while you two boys do deeds of valour and get ready to succeed to my position.'

DISAPPOINTMENT AND DISASTER

It was unfortunate that in 2 BC, the year of the awarding of the title 'pater patriae' of which Augustus was so proud, the imperial family had to withstand the blow of Julia the Elder's exile on grounds that struck at the heart of Augustus' moral and social legislation. Whether or not there were political implications as well as moral ones is unclear, but her main lover, Iullus, committed suicide, and Julia was sent to Pandateria. The scandal must have impacted on her two sons, who were being groomed for the succession, and accounted for Augustus' hard-line reaction to the daughter who was defying his own legislation on the dignity of family life. The younger of the brothers, Lucius, died in AD 2, to be followed by Gaius in January of AD 4. Augustus had perforce to turn to Tiberius and Julia's youngest son, Agrippa Postumus, both of whom he adopted in June AD 4. Tiberius was also made to adopt his nephew Germanicus, Drusus' elder son, who was married to Agrippina, Julia's daughter. Tiberius again achieved some great victories in Germany from AD 4 to 6, when the news came that Illyricum was in revolt. He spent the next three years coping with this rebellion against a background of rationing and rioting. In AD 7 the young Agrippa was exiled to Planasia, and in AD 8 his sister Julia the Younger, like her mother, was banished for adultery (with D. Junius Silanus). In AD 9 the stage was set for the triumphal return of Tiberius and his adopted son Germanicus from Illyricum, when five days after their arrival the news came of the disaster of Varus in Germany: three legions massacred and everything beyond the Rhine lost. This was the most serious of all military disasters in Augustus' reign (that of Lollius was more a matter of disgrace). Tiberius spent another three years consolidating the region, but without regaining the province of Germany. In AD 13 Augustus' and Tiberius' powers were renewed, with Tiberius having equal imperium to Augustus. It is unclear to what extent Augustus turned to Tiberius reluctantly: his will, which Tiberius had read out in the senate, stated: 'Since cruel fate has snatched my sons, Gaius and Lucius, from me, let Tiberius Caesar be heir to two-thirds of my estate' (Suet. *Tib.* 23.1). This was hardly an acknowledgement of Tiberius' indispensability.

15.105 *ILS* 139: Rites for Lucius Caesar, Pisa AD 2–3

Lucius died at Massalia in Gaul on 21 or 22 February AD 2, before reaching Spain. The Gabinian cincture ('belting'), derived from the Etruscans, was a way of wearing a toga so that both hands were free, as was necessary for the performance of many religious rites. The inscription outlines the correct offerings to the spirits of the dead (dark-coloured togas (the toga pulla), black animals, libations of milk, honey and oil).

19 September, at Pisa in the Augusteum in the forum; present when this was drafted were: Quintus Petillius, son of Quintus, Publius Rasinius Bassus, son of Lucius, Marcus Puppius, son of Marcus, Quintus Sertorius Pica, son of Quintus, Gnaeus Octavius Rufus, son of Gnaeus, Aulus Albius Gutta, son of Aulus.

5 Since Gaius Canius Saturninus, son of Gaius, duumvir, proposed a resolution to offer increased (funerary) honours to Lucius Caesar, son of Augustus Caesar, father of the country, pontifex maximus, in the twenty-fifth year of his tribunician power, (Lucius being) augur, consul designate, princeps iuventutis, patron of our colony, the town council decreed as follows:

As the senate of the people of Rome among all the other numerous and greatest honours **10** to Lucius Caesar, augur and consul designate, son of Augustus Caesar, father of the country, pontifex maximus, in the twenty-fifth year of his tribunician power, with the agreement of all the classes, zealously . . . the responsibility has been given to Gaius Caninius Saturninus, duumvir, and the decemviri of selecting **15** and seeing which of their two sites seems more appropriate, and of buying with public funds from the owners the place which they have approved as the better one. (It was also decided) that every year on 20 August sacrifices in honour of the dead be offered at that altar to his departed spirit at public expense by the magistrates, or those in charge of the administration of justice, clothed in dark togas, those among them who have the right to wear such clothing on that day; **20** a black ox and ram decorated with dark fillets are to be sacrificed to his departed spirit, and these victims are to be burnt on that spot, and over them are to be poured libations, a urn each of milk, honey and oil, and when that has been done (by the city), other persons, who wish as individuals to make sacrifices to his spirit, may do so, provided that they do not offer more than one taper or torch or wreath, while those **25** who have made the sacrifice, girt in the Gabinian manner, kindle the pile of logs and attend to it. (It was also decided) that the ground in front of the altar, on which the pile of wood is collected and constructed, shall be 40 feet square and be fenced with oak stakes, and that every year a heap of wood shall be constructed there for that purpose, and that this decree, together with the earlier decrees concerning the honours paid to him, shall be inscribed or carved on a large gravestone **30** set up alongside the altar. Regarding other ceremonies, which they had resolved and now resolve to abstain from and avoid on that day, the procedure should be followed as decreed by the senate and people of Rome. (It was also decided) that at the first opportunity envoys from our order should approach Imperator Caesar Augustus, **35** father of the country, pontifex maximus, in the twenty-fifth year of his tribunician power, and request that he allow the Julian colonists of the colony of Obsequens Julia Pisa to carry out and perform all the provisions of this decree.

15.106 *ILS* 140: Mourning for Gaius Caesar, Pisa AD 4

In AD 3, while in Armenia, at an unknown place named Artagera, Gaius was wounded. While he appeared to recover, his health was not good, and he died at Lycia on his journey back to Italy. Members of his entourage were executed in Rome (doc. 6.27). The Gauls had defeated the Romans at the battle of Allia in 390 BC. Sources hint that Livia may have been involved in the death of both boys.

. . . at Pisa, in the Augusteum in the forum; present when this was drafted were: Quintus Sertorius Atilius Tacitus, son of Quintus, Publius Rasinius Bassus, son of Lucius, Lucius Lappius Gallus, son of Lucius, Quintus Sertorius Alpius Pica, son of Quintus, Gaius Vettius Virgula, son of Lucius, Marcus Herius Priscus, son of Marcus, Aulus Albius Gutta, son of Aulus, Tiberius Petronius Pollio, son of Tiberius, Lucius Fabius Bassus, son of Lucius, Sextus Aponius Creticus, son of Sextus, Gaius Canius Saturninus, son of Gaius, and Lucius Otacilius Panthera, son of Quintus.

5 Whereas it was stated that, since there were no magistrates in our colony because of the campaigns of candidates for election, the actions recorded below were taken:

Since on 2 April it was reported to us that Gaius Caesar, son of Augustus (father of the country, pontifex maximus, guardian of the Roman empire and protector of the whole world), grandson of the god, after the consulship, which he had auspiciously concluded by waging war beyond the furthermost boundaries **10** of the Roman people, and after administering the state well with most bellicose and powerful nations conquered or received into our good faith, had been seized by cruel fates from the Roman people as a result of wounds received on behalf of the state as a result of this misfortune, at a time when he had already been designated as princeps most just and most like his father in excellence and the only protection of our colony, and since this event, which took place when the mourning was not yet concluded, which our entire colony had engaged in on the death **15** of his brother Lucius Caesar, consul designate, augur, our patron, princeps iuventutis, has renewed and intensified the grief of everyone, individually and collectively:

For these reasons the decurions and colonists, since at the time of this misfortune there were neither duoviri or prefects nor anyone in charge of the administration of justice, agreed among themselves, **20** because of the magnitude of so great and unexpected a catastrophe, that from that day on which his death was reported to that when his bones are brought back and buried and appropriate rites performed to his departed spirit, everyone, dressed in mourning, with the temples of the immortal gods, public baths and all shops closed, should abstain from dinner parties, and the matrons in our colony should make lamentation; and **25** that the day on which Gaius Caesar died, 21 February, should go down in memory as a day of mourning like that of the Allia and be observed at the present time by the order and wish of all, and that it shall be prohibited for the future to hold, plan or announce for that day or on that day, 21 February, any public sacrifices, thanksgivings, weddings or public banquets, **30** or to hold or attend on that day any theatrical performances or circus games; that every year on that day offerings to his departed spirit are to be made publicly by the magistrates, or by those who are in charge of the administration of justice at Pisa, in the same place and in the same manner as the offerings established for Lucius Caesar; that there be erected in the most frequented place in our colony an arch **35** decorated with the spoils of the nations conquered or received into our good faith by him, and that upon it be set up a statue of him on foot in triumphal attire, and on each side of this two gilded equestrian statues of Gaius and Lucius Caesar; that as soon as we shall have been able to elect legally and have in place duovirs for the colony, the first duoviri elected shall put this decision of the decurions **40** and the whole colony to the decurions to ensure it is legally enacted through their public authority and entered into the public records on their authorisation; and that meanwhile Titus Statulenus Juncus, flamen of Augustus, pontifex minor of the public rites of the Roman people, shall be requested to go with envoys to explain the present unavoidable state of the colony and report **45** this public service, which is desired of everyone, by delivering notification to Imperator Caesar Augustus, pontifex maximus, in the twenty-sixth year of his tribunician power; and that Titus Statulenus Juncus, princeps of our colony, flamen of Augustus, pontifex minor of the public rites of the Roman people, has done this, delivering the notification as stated above, to Imperator Caesar Augustus, pontifex maximus, in the twenty-sixth year of his tribunician power, **50** father of the country.

It is hereby decreed by the decurions that all that was done, enacted and decided with the agreement of all classes on 2 April in the consulship of Sextus

Aelius Catus and Gaius Sentius Saturninus shall be so done, performed, kept and observed by Lucius Titius, son of Aulus, and by Titus Allius Rufus, son of Titus, the duovirs, and **55** by whoever for the future shall be duovirs, prefects, or any other magistrates in our colony, and that all these things shall be done, performed, kept and observed in perpetuity; and that Lucius Titius, son of Aulus, and Titus Allius Rufus, son of Titus, the duoviri, shall ensure that everything recorded above is in accordance with the decree to be entered at the first possible occasion in the public records by the public scribe in the presence of the proquaestors. **60** Passed.

15.107 Suetonius *Life of the Deified Augustus* 23.1–2: Lollius and Varus

Marcus Lollius (cos. 21 BC) was governor of Macedonia in 19/18 and then of Gaul in 17/16. In the 'Lollian disaster' Lollius failed to guard the Rhine against Germanic tribes, who defeated his legions and captured the standard of the Legion V Macedonica. Lollius was, however, to remain in favour with Augustus until he accompanied Gaius to the East in 1 BC: the two fell out and Lollius, accused of taking Parthian bribes, possibly committed suicide. Augustus himself went to Gaul in 16 and remained in the West for three years, with his stepson Drusus taking over in 13 BC when he returned to Rome. To intimidate the Germans and ensure that such a defeat was not repeated, more legions were assigned to the area and forts positioned at key places along the Rhine. The defeat of Varus in AD 9 was far more serious, with three legions annihilated in Germany.

23.1 He encountered only two serious and ignominious defeats, both in Germany, those of Lollius and Varus, but that of Lollius (16 BC) was more a matter of disgrace than dangerous, while that of Varus was nearly catastrophic, as three entire legions, their general, legates and auxiliary troops were totally slaughtered. When this was reported, he ordered that watch be kept throughout the city in case of any unrest and prolonged the commands of provincial governors so the allies might be kept to their loyalty by experienced men with whom they were familiar. **2** He also vowed great games to Jupiter Optimus Maximus should the condition of the state improve, as had been done in the wars with the Cimbri and Marsi. In fact they say that he was so distraught that for months on end he cut neither his beard nor his hair, while occasionally dashing his head against the door, crying out, 'Quinctilius Varus, give me back my legions!'

15.108 Velleius Paterculus *Compendium of Roman History* 2.117.1–19.5: The Teutoberg Forest

Varus was a member of Augustus' inner circle, married firstly to Vipsania Marcella, Augustus' great-niece and the daughter of Agrippa and Claudia Marcella the Elder, and then to Claudia Pulchra, daughter of Claudia Marcella the Younger, another of Augustus' great-nieces. Varus was consul in 13 BC, with Tiberius as his colleague, after which he governed Africa (8/7 BC) and then Syria (7/6 BC), when he put down a revolt in Judaea. After long campaigns in Germany waged by Tiberius, Drusus and Germanicus, Germany was considered pacified, and in AD 6 Varus was appointed governor with a view to organising the area as subject territory. Arminius, a Germanic prince and Roman citizen, lured the Romans into an ambush near the Teutoberg Forest: this was the worst disaster of Augustus' reign, and the numbers XVII, XVIII and XIX were never used again.

117.1 Caesar had only just put the final touches to the Pannonian and Dalmatian war when, within five days of this task being finished, awful letters from Germany brought the news of the slaughter of Varus and the annihilation of three legions, the same number of cavalry divisions, and six cohorts – as if fortune was at least granting this favour, that so great a calamity should fall upon us when our leader was not otherwise occupied. **2** Varus Quinctilius, who was descended from a family which was rather famous than noble, was a man of easy-going character, quiet in his manners, as slow in mind as he was in body, and more used to the leisure of the camp than active military service, and that he did not despise money is shown by Syria, which he governed, which was a rich province when he entered it as a poor man and poor when he left it rich. **3** When put in charge of the army in Germany, he believed that they were a people who were men only in limbs and voice and that they, who could not be conquered by swords, could be appeased by law. **4** With this preconception in mind, he entered the heart of Germany as if he were going among a people in enjoyment of the pleasures of peace and wasted summer campaigning time in court cases and legal matters. . . . **118.2** There then appeared a young man of noble birth, brave in action, swift in mind, possessing intelligence far beyond barbarians in general, called Arminius, son of Sigimer, a leader of that race, who displayed his mind's ardour in his countenance and expression, and who had constantly accompanied our army on previous campaigns, been granted Roman citizenship and even acquired the honour of equestrian rank. He made use of the idleness of the general as an opportunity for duplicity, cleverly discerning that no one could be more swiftly overpowered than the man who feared nothing, and that a sense of security was the most frequent introduction to calamity . . .

119.1 The detailed facts of this most awful calamity, the most serious the Romans had suffered in foreign territory after the disaster of Crassus in Parthia, I shall endeavour to expound, like others, in my larger history: here I can merely lament over the larger picture. **2** The bravest of all armies, the best of Roman forces in discipline, valour and experience of warfare, through the indolence of its general, the perfidiousness of the enemy, and the cruelty of fate, was surrounded, without the opportunity which they wished for being given them of either fighting or retreating, unless at impossible odds, with some of them even heavily punished for bringing to bear the weapons and spirit of Romans – encompassed by woods, marshes and ambushes, it was annihilated to the point of extermination by the very enemy it had always before slaughtered like cattle and whose life or death had depended on the Romans' anger or clemency. **3** The leader had more courage in dying than in fighting: following the example of his father and grandfather, he ran himself through. Of the two prefects of the camp, **4** Lucius Eggius presented an example that was as splendid as Ceionius was cowardly, who, after the greater part of the army had fallen, proposed surrender, preferring to die by torture than in battle. Vala Numonius, Varus' legate, who had until then been retiring and upright, set a frightful precedent in that he left the infantry deserted by the cavalry and tried in flight to reach the Rhine with his cavalry squadrons. However, fate avenged his action – he did not survive those he deserted but was killed while deserting them. **5** The enemy's ferocity tore apart Varus' half-burnt corpse; his head was cut off and taken to Maroboduus, who sent it to Caesar, and despite the circumstances it was honoured by burial in the family tomb.

15.109 *ILS* 2244: Epitaph for a centurion, AD 9

The stone cenotaph, found at Castra Vetera in Germany, depicts the relief of a centurion with cuirass and military decorations, between the busts of two freedmen, Marcus Caelius Privatus and Marcus Caelius Thiaminus, who may have died with him in the attack. Bononia is in Cisalpine Gaul.

Marcus Caelius, son of Titus, (of the tribe) Lemonia, from Bononia, centurion of the Eighteenth Legion. At 53 years he fell in the Varian War. As to the bones of his freedmen, it will be allowed to bury them here. Publius Caelius, son of Titus, **5** (of the tribe) Lemonia, his brother, made this.

15.110 Dio *Roman History* 56.23.1–24.1: Panic in Rome

Manpower in Rome had already been stretched thin for the campaign in Illyricum, and in this crisis conscription was introduced, with serious penalties for those who tried to avoid involvement. The German threat appeared so real that Augustus even sent his German bodyguard out of Rome.

23.1 When Augustus learned of what had happened to Varus, he tore his clothes, as some report, and lamented excessively, not only because of the soldiers who had been lost but also because of his fear of the Germans and Gauls, and most particularly because he expected that they would march on Italy and Rome itself. For there were no citizens of military age left, and the allied forces that were of any use had been badly hit. **2** Nevertheless, he made the preparations he could in view of the situation, and when no one of military age was willing to be enlisted he made them draw lots, confiscating the property and disenfranchising every fifth man of those not yet 35 and every tenth man of those older than that age. **3** In the end, as a great many people paid no attention to him even then, he had some of them killed. He chose by lot as many as possible of those who had completed their term of service and freedmen, and after enlisting them sent them with all speed with Tiberius into Germany. **4** Since there were a large number of Gauls and Germans, some of them living in Rome for various reasons and others being in the praetorian guard, he was afraid they might start an insurrection, and so he sent away the guard to certain islands and ordered those who were unarmed to leave the city. **24.1** This was the way he dealt with the situation, and none of the usual business was carried on, nor were the festivals celebrated.

15.111 Tacitus *Annals* 1.3.1–4.2: The succession

Having lost Marcellus, Agrippa and his two eldest grandsons, Augustus had in AD 4 to turn to his stepson Tiberius, who had been in retirement on Rhodes for some years. He also adopted Agrippa Postumus, Julia's youngest son; the reason why he was later exiled to the island of Planasia in AD 7 is unclear. At the same time Tiberius was made to adopt his nephew Germanicus, the elder son of his dead brother Drusus. With Postumus banished, Tiberius was the only choice as Augustus' heir in the short term, and it was only in AD 13 that he received imperium equal to that of Augustus.

3.1 Meanwhile Augustus, to bolster his power, elevated Claudius Marcellus, his sister's son and still an adolescent, to the pontificate and curule aedileship, and Marcus Agrippa, of humble birth but skilful in warfare and his associate in victory, to two successive consulships, and shortly afterwards, on the death of Marcellus, to the position of his son-in-law. He gave the title of Imperator to his two stepsons, Tiberius Nero and Claudius Drusus, though his own family was still intact – **2** for he had included Agrippa's children, Gaius and Lucius, in the Caesarian family, and even while they still wore the youthful toga (praetexta) had them named the principes iuventutis and had a burning desire to have them consuls designate, though he pretended otherwise. **3** At Agrippa's demise, premature death – or the guile of their stepmother Livia – carried off Lucius Caesar, while on his way to the Spanish armies, and then Gaius, returning from Armenia while sick with a wound. Drusus had long been dead, and Nero (Tiberius) was the sole surviving stepson, with all focusing on him: adopted as son, colleague in the empire and co-sharer of the tribunician power, he was exhibited through all the armies, not as before by the hidden artifice of his mother but openly at her urging – **4** for so tightly had she fettered Augustus in his old age that he exiled to the island of Planasia his only remaining grandson, Agrippa Postumus, who, though untouched by any good qualities and doggedly violent in his bodily strength, had not been convicted of any wrongdoing. **5** But strangely he placed Germanicus, Drusus' son, at the head of the eight legions on the Rhine and ordered that he be adopted by Tiberius, although Tiberius had a youthful son in his home, as an additional safeguard. **6** No war was being waged at that time, except for the ongoing one against the Germans, more to expunge the disgrace of the army annihilated with Quinctilius Varus than from any desire to extend the empire or for any worthy profit.

7 All was peaceful at home, titles of magistrates remained the same; younger men had been born after the victory at Actium, and even most of the older men during the civil wars: was there anyone still alive who had actually seen the Republic? **4.1** Consequently it was a very different state, with no trace left of the good, old way of life: equality had been abolished, and everyone looked to the commands of the princeps, with no fears for the present, while Augustus in the vigour of life upheld himself, his house and peace. **2** But afterwards, when with the advance of old age he was worn by physical illness and an end and new hopes were at hand, some few began to talk vainly of the good of freedom, more were fearful of war – and others desired it.

THE END OF AN AGE

15.112 Suetonius *Life of the Deified Augustus* 99.1, 100–1.1–4: Augustus' farewell

Augustus died at Nola on 19 August AD 14. Both Tacitus and Dio suggest that Livia may have had a hand in his death. In AD 13 Tiberius had finally been granted imperium equal to that of Augustus. He was travelling to Illyricum, and Augustus accompanied him as far as Beneventum. Augustus then spent a few days on Capri and attended the games at Naples. While returning to Rome, he died at Nola. His donatives reflected how important the support of the military had been to the success of his regime.

99.1 On the final day of his life he inquired now and again whether there was any disturbance outside on his account, then called for a mirror and had his hair combed and his sagging jaw set straight. When his friends were admitted he asked whether he'd seemed to them to have played life's charade appropriately, and added the couplet:

'Since my part has been played well, give me applause
and all of you joyfully send me on my way.'

After dismissing them all, while he was asking some recent arrivals from the city about Drusus' daughter, who was sick, he suddenly died as he was kissing Livia, uttering the words, 'Live mindful of our marriage, Livia, and farewell!', thus lucky in his easy death just as he had always wanted. . . . **100** He died in the same bedroom as his father Octavius, in the consulship of two Sextuses, Pompeius and Appuleius, on the 14th day before the Kalends of September (19 August) at the ninth hour, just 35 days before his 76th birthday. . . . **101.1** He had made a will in the consulship of Lucius Plancus and Gaius Silius (AD 13), on the third day before the Nones of April (3 April), a year and four months before he died, in two notebooks written partly in his hand and partly in those of his freedmen Polybius and Hilarion, which had been deposited with the Vestals, who now produced it together with three volumes sealed in the same way. All these were opened and read out in the senate. **2** He named as his main heirs Tiberius, to take two-thirds of the estate, and Livia, one-third, and instructed that they should also take his name. The heirs in the second degree were Drusus, son of Tiberius, to take one-third, while the remainder would go to Germanicus and his three male children. In the third degree he named many of his relations and friends. To the Roman people he left 40,000,000 sesterces; to the tribes 3,500,000; to the soldiers of the praetorian guard 1,000 each; to the city cohorts 500; and to the legionaries 300. This money he ordered to be paid at once, as he had always kept the money ready and at hand. **3** He made other bequests to various people, some as large as 20,000 sesterces, which were not to be paid until a year after his death, giving the reason for this as the small size of his property, and stating that not more than 150,000,000 would go to his heirs, for though he had received 14 hundred millions over the last 20 years from the wills of his friends, he had spent nearly all of it, as well as the patrimonies of his two fathers and those of others, for the good of the state. He gave instructions that the Julias, his daughter and granddaughter, should anything happen to them, were not to be placed in his mausoleum. **4** Of the three volumes, in one he included directions for his funeral, in the second there was a record of his achievements which he wished to have engraved on bronze tablets to stand in front of his mausoleum, and in the third a summary of the whole empire: how many soldiers were in service and where, and how much money there was in the treasury and privy-purse and what revenues needed to be collected. He added as well the names of the freedmen and slaves from whom the details could be demanded.

15.113 Strabo *Geography* 5.3.8: Augustus' mausoleum

His mausoleum was one of the first projects that Augustus began after his victory at Actium. Located on the Campus Martius, the mausoleum was circular, planted with cypresses on the summit of the building, and measured 90 metres in diameter and 42 metres in height. Before those of Augustus himself, the ashes of Marcellus (the first, in 23 BC), Agrippa, Drusus, Octavia Minor, and Gaius and Lucius were interred there. Both Julias were specifically refused burial there by Augustus.

Considering this to be the holiest spot of all, they have erected there the tombs of their most distinguished men and women. Most noteworthy is the one called the mausoleum, a huge mound near the river on an elevated foundation of white marble, covered with evergreen trees right up to the summit; at the top stands a bronze statue of Augustus Caesar; beneath the mound are the tombs of himself and his family and intimates; behind is a vast grove with wondrous promenades; and in the centre of the Campus (Martius) is the wall of his crematorium, also of white marble.

15.114 Dio *Roman History* 56.46.1–47.1: Augustus' apotheosis

Julius Caesar had officially become the divus Julius (divine Julius) in 42 BC following the comet in July 44 which was claimed by Octavian to be Caesar's soul ascending to heaven. From that time Octavian styled himself 'son of the god', and in 40 Antony took up his position as flamen of the cult. During his lifetime Augustus has been worshipped in the provinces, in association with the goddess Roma, though citizens were allowed to worship his numen or genius. As there was a witness to his apotheosis, this junior senator rewarded for his input by Livia, the senate had sufficient evidence to acclaim Augustus as a god.

46.1 These rumours began to circulate later on. At the time they declared him to be immortal, gave him priests and sacred rites, and made Livia, already called Julia **2** and Augusta, his priestess. They also allowed her to make use of a lictor when engaged in her religious duties. She herself made a present of a million sesterces to a certain senator and ex-praetor called Numerius Atticus because he swore that he saw Augustus ascending into heaven, as is said to have happened to Proculus and Romulus. **3** A shrine voted by the senate was built to him in Rome by Livia and Tiberius, and many others in different places, some erected by communities willingly and others unwillingly. The house at Nola, where he died, was also dedicated as a shrine. **4** While his temple at Rome was being set up, they placed a golden image of him on a couch in the temple of Mars and paid all the honours to this that they were going to give to his statue. They also decreed that no image of him should be carried in procession at anyone's funeral, and that the consuls should celebrate his birthday with games like those at the ludi Martiales, and that the tribunes, being sacrosanct, were to be in charge of the Augustalia. **5** These conducted everything in the customary manner, even to wearing triumphal dress at the chariot race, except that they did not ride in the chariot. Apart from all this, Livia held a private three-day festival in the palace in his honour, which has been continued up to the present day by the current emperor.

47.1 Such were the decrees passed regarding Augustus, theoretically by the senate, but in reality by Tiberius and Livia: for when various proposals were made, the senate decreed that Tiberius should receive them in writing and choose the ones he preferred. I have added Livia's name, because she was fully involved, as if she were herself ruler.

VIEWS OF AUGUSTUS AND HIS REGIME

15.115 Nikolaos of Damascus *Life of Augustus* 1–2

Nikolaos' *Life* seems to have been completed after AD 14. An intimate of Herod of Judaea and tutor of the children of Antony and Cleopatra in Italy after their parents' death, Nikolaos was also a personal friend of Augustus and travelled with him to Syria in 20 BC. His account is clearly eulogistic and politically correct.

1 Men gave him this name because of his claim to honour and worshipped him with temples and sacrifices, distributing these over islands and continents and through cities and nations, in this way recompensing him for the greatness of his virtue and his benefactions towards themselves. For this man, after attaining the utmost power and wisdom, ruled over the greatest number of people within human memory, established the most distant boundaries for the Romans' empire, and settled not only the tribes of Greeks and barbarians but also their dispositions, at first with arms but afterwards even without arms, by attracting them of their own free will and by persuading them to obey him by making himself known through benevolence. Some of their names men had never heard before, nor had they been subject to anyone within living memory, but he pacified all of them that live as far as the Rhine and beyond the Ionian Sea and the Illyrian peoples. These are called Pannonians and Dacians. **2** To demonstrate the full extent of this man's wisdom and pre-eminence, both in the government which he exercised in his own country and in his direction of great wars both civil and foreign, is a subject for competition in speech and writing, that men may become famous through their excellent presentations. I myself shall relate his achievements, so that everyone may know the truth.

15.116 Pliny the Elder *Natural History* 7.147–50: Augustus' chequered fortunes

Pliny, in his discussion of the workings of fate, is here presenting all the difficulties, disappointments and dangers that Augustus had to face. Apart from Tacitus (doc. 15.117), Pliny gives the most negative appraisal of Augustus' reign. He focuses primarily on Augustus' early years and his ambition, though every episode is deliberately presented to give the worst possible slant on his motives.

147 In the case of the deified Augustus, too, whom all of humanity ranks in this [fortunate] category, immense revolutions of the wheel of human destiny would be revealed if all facts were rigorously appraised: his disappointment with his uncle regarding the position of magister equitum when the opposing candidate Lepidus was chosen, the ill-will caused by the proscriptions, his association in the triumvirate with the worst of citizens – and that not even as an equal member, but with Antony as the foremost – **148** his flight at the battle of Philippi, when he was sick and spent three days lying low in a marsh (as Agrippa and Maecenas admitted) though ill and in a swollen dropsical state, his shipwreck off Sicily and another period there of hiding in a cave, his prayers to Proculeius to kill him in the naval defeat when an enemy troop was close at hand, the anxiety of the conflict at Perusia, the trepidation of the battle at Actium, his fall from a tower in the Pannonian wars, **149** all the mutinies of his soldiers, his serious illnesses, the doubtful loyalty of Marcellus, the ignominious exile of Agrippa, the many conspiracies against his life, the accusations of causing the death of his children; and the griefs that were not due to bereavement – the adultery of his daughter, the revelation of her plans for parricide, the disrespectful withdrawal of his stepson Tiberius, the further adultery of his granddaughter, then a long series of disasters – lack of funds for the army, rebellion in Illyricum, enlistment of slaves, shortage of young men, plague in the city, famine in Italy, decision to commit suicide with death over half achieved by four days' hunger-strike; **150** then that disaster of Varus' and disgraceful affront to his dignity, the disowning of Postumus Agrippa after his adoption, the yearning for him after his banishment, then his suspicion with regard to Fabius and the betrayal of secrets, and afterwards the plots of his wife and Tiberius, which caused him unease in his final days. In short, this god – whether divine through effort or merit, I am unsure – expired leaving his enemy's son his heir.

15.117 Tacitus *Annals* 1.9.3–10.8: Tacitus' judgement

Tacitus is giving the reactions of two factions to Augustus' death and his reign. By leaving the damning critique of Augustus' motives and failures until last, the impression that remains is one of overall failure and despondency. Like Pliny (doc. 15.116), Tacitus focuses his attention on events during the lawless period of the triumvirate, while he sees Augustus' last years overall as ones of disappointment. For Vedius Pollio, see doc. 6.26.

9.3 Among men of intelligence, his life was praised or criticised from various points of view. Some considered that 'duty (pietas) towards a father and the needs of the state, which at that point had no place for laws, had driven him into civil war – which can never be planned or carried on by honourable methods. **4** He had had to make many concessions to Antony and many to Lepidus in order to take revenge on his father's assassins. After Lepidus grew old and inactive and Antony had succumbed to debauchery, there was no other cure for the dysfunctional state than rule by one man. **5** However, he instituted neither a monarchy nor dictatorship but rule under the name of a princeps; the empire was protected by the Ocean and distant rivers; legions, provinces, fleets were all part of the same organisational structure; there was law for the citizens, respectful treatment of allied communities; the city of Rome was marvellously beautified; little had been dealt with by violence and then only to ensure peace and quiet for everyone else.' **10.1** Against this it was said that 'duty towards his father and the state crisis had been put forward as a pretext; it was his desire for power which led to mobilising the veterans through hand-outs, raising an army while still a youth and private citizen, enticing away a consul's legions, and pretending support for the Pompeian side. **2** Soon afterwards by a senatorial decree he assumed the fasces and powers of a praetor; with Hirtius and Pansa killed, whether by the enemy or, in Pansa's case, through poison being administered to his wound, and in Hirtius' murder by his own soldiers, with Caesar stage-managing the treachery and taking over the armies of both; a consulship was extorted from an unwilling senate, and the weapons which he had received to deal with Antony turned against the state; while the proscriptions of citizens and allocations of land had not been approved even by those who carried them out. **3** Even if Cassius and the Brutuses had met their deaths because of enmities inherited from his father – although properly private hatreds should give way to the needs of the state – Pompey was deceived by the pretence of a peace, Lepidus by the appearance of friendship; then Antony was entrapped by the treaties of Tarentum and Brundisium and marriage with his sister and paid with his life the penalty of that treacherous relationship. Certainly that was followed by peace, but a bloody one – **4** the disasters of Lollius and Varus, the executions at Rome of a Varro, Egnatius, Iullus.' **5** Nor was his private life spared: the theft of Nero's wife (Livia) and the charade of the query to the pontiffs as to whether, with a child already conceived, a legal marriage could take place; the extravagance of Vedius Pollio; finally Livia – as a mother a disaster for the state, as a stepmother a disaster to the house of Caesar. **6** 'There was no scope left for the worship of the gods, while he wished to be venerated by flamens and priests in temples and statues. **7** Even the choice of Tiberius as his successor was not motivated by affection or concern for the state, but when he had appreciated Tiberius' arrogance and cruelty he had sought to add to his own glory by this atrocious contrast.' For Augustus, a few years earlier, when requesting an extension of Tiberius' tribunician potestas, had in his speech, though complimentary, made comments on his dress, demeanour and lifestyle which, while apparently excuses, were actually criticisms. **8** However, his funeral was according to tradition and he was decreed a temple and divine rites.

16

The Ancient Sources

There are various ancient sources of evidence for the history of the Roman Republic. This collection has, for obvious reasons, concentrated on literary sources, whether the works of historical writers, such as Polybius, Livy, Sallust and Appian, or of biographers, notably Suetonius and Plutarch. There are also valuable excerpts from works now lost given in the writings of antiquarians and scholars (Varro, Dionysius of Halicarnassus, Pliny the Elder, Aulus Gellius and Macrobius), while useful light on issues in political and social history can be cast by poets: Ennius, Lucilius, Catullus and the comic dramatists. There are, of course, in addition, speeches delivered in the law-courts, notably by one of the most prolific of Roman writers and orators, Cicero, although it is important to be aware that Cicero's speeches give only one side of the case, and that a very biased one. Similarly, the reader should be aware that his *Letters* are private communications which convey much contemporary gossip information on family matters and often contradict his public statements. However, this collection has also attempted to provide access to other sources, most importantly information recorded on stone (epigraphy), as well as to historians whose work survives only in 'fragments', phrases, sentences or paragraphs quoted or paraphrased by other ancient historians or commentators. Relevant archaeological and numismatic evidence (evidence from artefacts, excavations and coins) has been referred to wherever possible. The notes below are intended as a general introduction to Roman historiography (historical writing), whether in Latin or Greek, and are aimed at helping the reader to understand the aims and methodology of the ancient authors.

EPIGRAPHY

Epigraphy is the study of texts which have been inscribed, generally on stone or bronze or on some less durable material such as pottery. There are often problems of dating with inscriptions, and many are partially damaged and hence difficult to read or interpret. Such texts are often 'impersonal', such as state decrees, treaties or laws (docs 3.66, 5.22, 15.32, for example), but inscriptions can be personal, as when they record a funerary epitaph (the largest group of

Latin inscriptions, in which the deceased or their relatives reveal important information about the family and about the members' perceptions of each other and their domestic role); they can also record a dedication or personal gift: see docs 7.23–25, 31–33, 37, 66. Inscriptions may detail the achievements of individuals, particularly generals or public benefactors, whether commissioned by themselves or by communities in their honour: in either case the account is not necessarily objective (docs 4.10, 5.33, 5.42–43, 12.18, 14.25, 14.56, 15.43–46, 83–87). Epigraphy can act as a valuable supplement to literary sources: inscribed slingshots reveal the insults that were being traded during the Social War and in the siege of Perusia in 41 BC (docs 10.16, 14.31). Inscriptions are essential evidence for Augustus' constitutional position, for the question of whether or not he possessed maius imperium (docs 15.9, 15.10) and for the development of imperial cult during his reign (docs 15.53–58), as well as for the details of the organisation and government of colonies and of municipalites in Italy as laid down in Julius Caesar's legislation as dictator (docs. 2.80, 13.59–60). Augustus' *Res Gestae* (doc. 15.1), the lengthy document which enshrined his imperial ideology and recorded what he chose to see as his greatest triumphs, including his massive expenditure on behalf of Rome, was inscribed on bronze pillars in front of his mausoleum. This version is lost, but the account survives in three copies, all from Galatia in Asia Minor, one of which preserves the full text of the Latin alongside a Greek translation, and which was set up at the temple of Roma and Augustus in Ancyra (modern Ankara).

THE ROMAN ANNALISTIC TRADITION

The pontifex maximus used to keep an annual record called the *annales maximi*, which was posted on a whitened board outside the Regia, his official residence; it contained the names of magistrates and of important events such as triumphs, treaties, wars, the building of temples, eclipses, plagues, earthquakes and portents. It was continued until the pontificate of P. Mucius Scaevola (pontifex maximus 130–115 BC) and was a valuable source for historians of early Rome, when it comprised some 80 books. While some of the earlier books were reflections of legendary characters and themes, the records from 400 BC (an eclipse of the sun on 21 June 400: Cic. *Rep.* 1.25) seem to have been genuine, though their content was of course limited. Cato the Elder, in his *Origines* (*HRR* I² 77), stated: 'I do not choose to copy out what is on the pontifex maximus' tablet: how many times grain became dear, how many times the sun and moon were obscured or eclipsed.' The pontiffs also kept the *libri pontificales*, which contained instructions for cult formulae and rituals and recorded the dedication dates of temples, while the *libri lintei* ('Linen Books') were preserved in the temple of Juno Moneta and apparently contained lists of magistrates and other historical information. Early historians also had access to lists of Republican consuls (or other chief magistrates) called *fasti*, which were kept as records for chronological purposes, since these magistrates gave their name to the year (see docs 3.30, 14.63, 15.4).

THE ANCIENT SOURCES

HISTORIANS AND ANNALISTS

16.1 Fabius Pictor and the early historians

Quintus Fabius Pictor, who wrote in Greek, was the first Roman historian and went on an embassy to Delphi during the Second Punic War in 216 BC. He makes use of the history of Timaeus of Tauromenium (c. 350–260), whom Polybius criticises in book 12 of his *Histories* for factual errors and inappropriate methodology. Polybius makes use of Fabius, though aware of his pro-Roman bias (as in his belief that the Barcid family was responsible for the outbreak of the Second Punic War): see docs 4.5, 4.25, 4.36 for Polybius' comments on Fabius Pictor and Philinus of Acragas in Sicily. It is not clear whether Livy knew Fabius' work at first-hand.

Fabius dwelt at length on the legendary foundation of Rome: *SEG* 26.1123, F2, col. A (from Taormina, second century BC), 'Quintus Fabius, called Pictorinus, a Roman son of Gaius, who related the arrival of Heracles in Italy and the return of Lanoeus, an ally of Aeneas and Ascanius; much later there were Romulus and Remus and the foundation of Rome by Romulus, who was the first to be king.'

L. Cincius Alimentus, another pioneer historian, was a contemporary of Fabius Pictor and was at one stage Hannibal's prisoner; praetor in 210, he also wrote in Greek, as did the philhellene A. Postumius Albinus, whose history was published before Cato's death in 149. Among Latin writers were M. Porcius Cato (cos. 195), L. Cassius Hemina (first half of the 2nd century BC), L. Calpurnius Piso Frugi (cos. 133 BC), C. Sempronius Tuditanus (cos. 129), L. Coelius Antipater (c. 120 BC), Q. Claudius Quadrigarius (a contemporary of Sulla), C. Licinius Macer (tr. pl. 73 BC) and Valerius Antias (first century BC). The documentary sources from which they drew their information could include the *annales maximi* and pontifical records, the *libri lintei*, public records from the state archives, and private family records and oral traditions, as well as the writings of earlier annalists.

16.2 Cato the Elder (234–149 BC)

Cato was consul in 195 BC (when he served in Spain: doc. 5.46) and censor in 184 (doc. 1.17). His *Origines* (*Beginnings*), which he started in 168, was the first full-scale history in Latin dealing with the origins of various peoples in Italy (from Aeneas to 149 BC). He claimed Greek descent for the settlers of Italy and drew heavily on Fabius Pictor. He was also the pre-eminent orator of his time, with more than 150 speeches known to Cicero: for his style, see Cicero *Brutus* 65–69; Sallust *Histories* 1 F1 calls him 'disertissimus', 'most eloquent'. Cato was also the author of a work on morals, one of advice to his son, a book of sayings, one on priestly law, and a manual on soldiering.

With regard to his history, Dionysius of Halicarnassus 1.11.1 classes Cato among the most learned of Roman historians and (1.74.2) praises his care in the collection of data. Cornelius Nepos (*Cato* 3.2–4) relates that the first of the seven books of the *Origines* contained the deeds of the kings of the Roman people, the second and third the origin of each of the Italian states, the fourth book the narrative of the First Punic War and the fifth that of the second. He dealt 'with the other wars' in the same way down to the praetorship of Servius Sulpicius Galba, who

766

robbed the Lusitanians (doc. 5.48). His comment on Cato as an historian is that 'He displays great industry and diligence, but no learning' (3.4).

In his *Origines*, Cato stressed the collective role of the Roman people rather than individual 'heroes'. Pliny *Nat. Hist.* 8.5 states that Cato removed the names of military commanders but recorded that the elephant in the Carthaginian army which was the bravest in battle was called the Syrian and that it had one broken tusk. Aulus Gellius *Attic Nights* 3.7.18–19 (*HRR* I² 80–1) cites Cato on the military tribune Caedicius in the First Punic War in Sicily, who engaged the Carthaginians with 400 men, allowing the rest of the army to retreat. Cato compared him with the Spartan king Leonidas, who 'was honoured by all Greece with especial glory and gratitude through monuments of the most illustrious renown', whereas Cato in contrast makes clear that this military tribune acted simply as a normal Roman.

Docs 2.15–17, 6.34–36 come from Cato's *De agri cultura* (*On Farming*) of c. 160 BC, which gives detailed, practical advice on the running of a villa estate and on the treatment of slaves on such a property; docs 3.23, 3.28, 3.34–35 refer to religious rites appropriate on such a farm, while docs 2.17 and 3.70 prescribe medical treatments. At doc. 5.62 Cato gives advice 'to his son' or to a more general readership; at docs 5.57–58 he is cited by Diodorus Siculus and Polybius regarding his criticism of 'modern' luxurious tastes. Gellius cites Cato's speeches on several occasions: doc. 5.37 (in support of the Rhodians), 7.11 (in support of the Voconian law) and 7.18 (on the relationship between adultery and alcohol in women). Livy puts a speech into his mouth against the repeal of the Oppian law (doc. 7.67), but this should not be taken as reflecting anything actually said on the occasion by Cato.

16.3 Polybius of Megalopolis (c. 200–c. 118 BC)

Polybius, a prominent Achaean from the region in the north-east of the Peloponnese, served as hipparch of the Achaean confederacy in 170/69. Following Rome's victory at Pydna in 168 he was deported to Italy with 1,000 other Achaeans and released only in 150. After being lucky enough to become a close friend of Scipio Aemilianus (Polyb. 31.23.1–25.1) he was allowed to stay in Rome during this period and went to Spain and Africa with Scipio. He assisted after 146 in the Roman settlement of Greece, where many statues were erected in his honour: Pausanias *Description of Greece* 8.37.2 quotes an inscription at Lycosoura: 'Greece would never have come to grief had she obeyed Polybius in all things, and, having come to grief, she found succour through him alone.'

The greater part of his history, which was in 40 books, is lost; only books 1–5 are complete. The work was concerned with events from 220 to 167 BC in particular: later Polybius continued the history in a further ten books down to 146 (*Hist.* 3.4); unfortunately the Penguin translation is not complete and omits many significant passages. Polybius wrote what he titled 'pragmatike historia', pragmatic history, or military and political history with a practical, didactic bias. His work is a systematic historical treatise ('pragmateia') covering world history, not just isolated events or geographical areas (1.4.1–7), and he stresses the importance of accurate research and information rather than history's use as entertainment.

As an Achaean, Polybius has certain pro-Achaean and anti-Aeolian biases, and he idealises the character of his friend Scipio Aemilianus and the rest of his family (such as Scipio's father, L. Aemilius Paullus). He has an intimate knowledge of the Scipiones and Aemilii and discusses the character of Scipio Africanus at doc. 4.51 (cf. doc 6.8; *Hist.* 10.2.2–13) and that of Scipio Aemilianus at docs 5.58, 7.70. As a Greek living in aristocratic circles in Rome, he gives a detailed view as an outsider of Roman institutions and customs, providing information so central to Roman life that the Roman accounts do not mention them; especially important are docs 1.59 on the Roman constitution; 3.76–77 on Roman religious and funerary practices; and 7.70 on women's festival paraphernalia.

Polybius is given to cite treaties verbatim, or at least to paraphrase them closely: for treaties in the Punic Wars, see docs 4.1–3, 17, 45, 58; for those relevant to the conquest of the Mediterranean: docs 5.23, 28, 30–31, 38; at doc. 4.19 he shows that he has used official figures for troop numbers before the Second Punic War. At *Hist.* 1.1.5–6 he gives his reasons for writing:

> for who is there so indifferent or frivolous that he does not wish to know by what means and under what system of government nearly the whole inhabited world has in less than 53 years been subjugated and fallen under a single rule, that of the Romans – an entirely unprecedented state of affairs – or who is so dedicated to other spectacles or studies as to consider anything more important than this knowledge?

He is concerned to explicate his use of sources and methodology: docs 4.1–5, 21, 31; gives his reasons for concentrating on the First Punic War: doc. 4.5; uses logic to back up his statements: doc. 4.8; shows an interest in underlying causation: docs 4.21, 23–24 (the Second Punic War); is fair in assigning responsibility: doc. 4.27; and personally tests the truth of statements (crossing the Alps in Hannibal's footsteps): doc. 4.31. At *Hist.* 31.22.8–11 he makes it clear that he expects his most interested readers to be Romans, who can check most of his facts.

On the importance of truth Polybius states, *Hist.* 12.11a, that the greatest fault in history is falsehood and that (12.12.3), just as a living creature when deprived of its eyes is totally incapacitated, so, when history is deprived of truth, nothing is left but an unprofitable tale (cf. doc. 4.5). He sees dramatisation of history as a serious fault; *Hist.* 2.56:

> it is not a historian's business to startle his readers with sensational descriptions, nor should he try, as the tragic poets do, to represent speeches which might have been delivered . . . it is his task first and foremost to record with fidelity what actually happened and was said, however commonplace this might be.

16.4 Julius Caesar (100–44 BC)

Caesar's *Gallic War* is an account of his campaigns in Gaul in seven books; an eighth continuing the account is by Aulus Hirtius (cos. 43), one of Caesar's officers. Caesar's narrative is impersonal (written in the third person) and dispassionate, while intended to keep him before the eyes of the Roman world during his absence in Gaul, and he provides information on Gallic and British customs as well as military campaigns (see docs 3.46, 12.90). The title *Commentarii* (*Notebooks*) which he gave to his work on the *Gallic War* implies that they were later to be written up in a more sophisticated style. Caesar also wrote three books on the *Civil War* which give his perspective on events. Needless to say, they are not entirely objective, particularly with regard to his motive for invading Italy (see esp. docs 13.24, 13.27, 13.42, 13.44), and his justification of events differs from the account in Cicero's letters and Asinius Pollio's quotation of Caesar's words after the battle of Pharsalus: 'They wanted it like this; with all my great achievements, I, Gaius Caesar, would have been condemned if I had not looked to my army for help' (Suet. *Jul.* 30.4: doc. 13.28). The *Alexandrian War*, *Spanish War* and *African War* dealing with the campaigns in 48–45 are not by Caesar (Hirtius may have written the *Alexandrian War*: Suet. *Jul.* 56.1).

Caesar was also the author of light-hearted poetry (Pliny *Letters* 5.3.5), and Plutarch *Caes.* 2 records that, while a captive of the Cilician pirates (cf. doc. 6.13), he wrote and recited poetry. In oratory Caesar believed in the use of analogy (on which he wrote a treatise) and ordinary, not high-flown, words: Gell. 1.10.4. His oratory was highly praised by Cicero (doc. 2.68). His brief letters to Oppius and Cornelius Balbus and to Cicero (docs 13.37, 13.39) show his command of terse, lucid expression while in action. For his literary talents, see doc. 13.64, where Suetonius cites Asinius Pollio as believing that Caesar intended to revise and correct his work.

16.5 Sallust (86–c. 35 BC)

Gaius Sallustius Crispus was tribune in 52 and expelled from the senate in 50; as tribune he opposed Cicero and Milo and was supposed to have had an affair with Milo's wife. He commanded a legion for Caesar in 49 and was praetor in 46 and governor of Africa. After being accused of extortion he withdrew from politics to write history. He was very wealthy: the *horti Sallustiani* (Sallustian gardens) belonged to him. He was said to have married Cicero's divorced wife, Terentia (Jerome *adversus Jovinianum* 1). His *Bellum Catilinae* (*Catiline's War*, or *Catilinarian Conspiracy*), written c. 42, deals with the career of Catiline and events in Cicero's consulship (63 BC) and afterwards (docs 12.14–16, 19–23, 2.44). In this work he stresses Rome's moral decline and polarises the figures of Caesar and Cato the Younger, his 'heroes', as *exempla* of moral excellence (doc. 13.62). Cicero must have been one of his main sources, but he also spoke directly to participants: at *Cat.* 48.9 he personally overheard Crassus blaming Cicero for trying to implicate him in the conspiracy. His reasons for writing on Catiline he gives as follows (*Cat.* 3.2, 4.3–4):

Although the narrator and doer of deeds win by no means equal renown, I myself still consider the writing of history as one of the most difficult of undertakings; in the first place, because your words have to be equal to the deeds narrated; and in the second place because most people will think your criticisms of misdeeds to be inspired by malice and jealousy; when you commemorate the great merit and reputation of good men, people will happily accept the things they think they could easily do themselves, but dismiss anything beyond this as fictitious – if not untrue . . . So I shall give a brief account of the conspiracy of Catiline as truthfully as I can; for I consider that villainy to have been especially memorable on account of the unprecedented nature of the crime itself and the danger to which it gave rise.

Sallust's second work, the *Jugurthine War*, was written c. 41/40 and concerns Jugurtha's war with Rome under the command of Metellus Numidicus and Marius (docs 9.2, 6–7, 9–10); Sulla is also given considerable space (doc. 9.12). The author is here emphasising again the decline of Rome, particularly within the nobility and its values, and the war is a good subject through which to show a brilliant novus homo (Marius) contrasted with the corrupt and incompetent nobility. Sallust's rationale for writing is as follows (*BJ* 4.1, 5.1–2):

But among intellectual pursuits, one of the most important is the recording of historical events . . . I am going to write of the war which the Roman people waged with Jugurtha, king of the Numidians, first because it was a long and bloody conflict, with victory alternating between the two sides, and second because it was then for the first time that resistance was made to the arrogance of the nobles – a struggle which was to throw everything, divine and human, into confusion and reach such a frenzied pitch that civil strife was ended only by a war and the devastation of Italy.

Sallust comments (*BJ* 17.7) that, regarding the original inhabitants of Africa, his account varies from tradition but was translated for him from the Punic books said to have been written by King Hiempsal. His main sources were probably the autobiographies of Aemilius Scaurus (cos. 115), Rutilius Rufus (cos. 105) and Sulla.

Sallust also wrote a history beginning in 78, the death of Sulla, which is extant only in fragments: one important fragment from this work is Pompey's dispatch from Spain to the senate (doc. 12.3). The *Histories* were perhaps a continuation of the work of L. Cornelius Sisenna, praetor in 78. Sallust criticises him for speaking of Sulla with 'insufficient frankness': *BJ* 95.2 (doc. 9.12); Cicero speaks of him highly (*Brut.* 228). An invective against Cicero and two letters to Caesar attributed to Sallust appear not to be genuine. Sallust was a Caesarian, and Suetonius (*Gram.* 15) records that he was satirised for his criticisms of Pompey; his *Histories* tend to be censorious where Pompey is concerned. He was a popularis earlier in his career, and his sympathies tend that way: his view of the Gracchi (doc. 8.40) is very positive and in marked contrast to Cicero's negative portrayals. While, however, his criticisms are reserved primarily for the corrupt nobility (docs 9.3, 9.7), he is also disparaging about irresponsible tribunes in 110 BC (*BJ* 37.1).

16.6 Diodorus Siculus (c. 80–c. 29 BC)

Diodorus of Agyrium in Sicily (hence 'Siculus', the Sicilian) wrote a *Bibliotheke* (*Library of History*), in 40 books, covering universal history from the earliest times down to 60 BC. It was probably completed in Rome in 30 BC. At 40.8 he states that 'The subject matter is contained in 40 books, and in the first six I have recorded the events and legends before the Trojan War; I have not given dates in these with any precision since no chronological record for them was at hand . . . ' Only books 1–5 and 11–20 (covering the period 480–302 BC) survive, with others preserved in fragments. For the Roman period Diodorus follows the narrative of Polybius and then Posidonius (from 146 BC). His account of the second-century Sicilian slave rebellions, which depends greatly on Posidonius (c. 135–51 BC), is the main source for these revolts (see doc. 6.48, and 6.30 for conditions in the Spanish silver mines, for which he cites Posidonius). His narrative also helps to shed light on the events leading up to the Social War, in particular the tribunate of M. Livius Drusus and the oath supposedly taken in his name by the Italians (docs 10.7–8, cf. 10.12). In addition he records the divine vengeance taken on a mocker of the Great Mother's priest (doc. 3.63).

16.7 Livy (59 BC–AD 17)

Titus Livius came from the city of Patavium (Padua) and was criticised for his Patavinitas (Paduanism) by Asinius Pollio. He wrote an annalistic history, his *Ad urbe condita* (*From the Foundation of the City*), which dealt with the period from the foundation of the city to 9 BC. The work consisted of 142 books, of which only books 1–10 and 21–45 survive (with some additional fragments), though there is an *Epitome* (summary) for books 37–40 and 48–55 and a series of fourth-century AD summaries (the *Periochae*) for all books except 136 and 137. Some of these summaries do not entirely reflect the contents of the extant books, and they may have been made from an earlier *précis*, not directly from Livy's work. Livy's history is based on literary sources, particularly in books 31–145 on the work of Polybius, with some additions from later writers such as Valerius Antias and Claudius Quadrigarius, now lost. While he cites other authors, it appears that often, though not always, his references to second-century writers such as Calpurnius Piso and Fabius Pictor may have been derived at second-hand from first-century authors. His use of Polybius is so close that gaps in the latter's narrative can be supplied from Livy's account (as in doc. 5.28: the peace treaty with the Aetolian League, 189 BC). At doc. 4.42 he prefers not to refer there to an early Latin demand for one of the magistracies because 'Coelius and other writers' have with some reason omitted it. He therefore does not set it down as certain. Similarly, in doc. 7.42 he affects to disbelieve the account of aristocratic women as mass poisoners in 331 BC as not all accounts mention it, though he still proceeds to give a narrative of events. However, he can show some critical awareness, as with the false genealogies created for the aggrandisement of various families, which have falsified the historical record (doc. 2.28).

Livy had access to earlier histories, the researches of antiquarians (such as Varro) and original records (inscriptions, paintings, documents, lists of consuls, and records of priesthoods). He made little use of non-literary sources and has been criticised for not directly consulting the 'linen rolls' (*libri lintei*), which contained the lists of magistrates, when his sources were at variance (4.23.1–3):

> I find in Licinius Macer that the same consuls were re-elected the following year (434 BC) . . . Valerius Antias and Quintus Tubero state that Marcus Manlius and Quintus Sulpicius were the consuls for that year. But, despite such a great discrepancy, both Tubero and Macer give the Linen Rolls as their authority; neither conceals the fact that older writers had recorded that there were military tribunes in office for that year. Licinius prefers to follow the Linen Rolls without hesitation; Tubero is uncertain of the truth. Along with all the other matters buried in antiquity, this also should remain undecided.

At 6.1.1–3, Livy explains that, for the history of early Rome (books 1–5), sources were few and far between, with only the commentaries of the pontiffs and other public and private records available – and that these were nearly all lost when the city was fired by the Gauls (c. 390 BC), while he admits (pref. 6) that 'events belonging to the time before the city was founded or was about to be founded, with their adornment of poetic legends rather than irrefutable historical record, it is my intention neither to affirm nor to deny.' On the other hand, his recording of Augustus' statement that he had personally seen the linen breastplate from 437 BC which incontrovertibly provided the evidence that M. Licinius Crassus could not be awarded the spolia opima in 30 BC by its very nature leads the reader to question the evidence that supported Augustus' wish to restrict triumphs to within the imperial family (doc. 15.14).

Livy shows awareness of alternative versions, as on casualty numbers at Cynoscephalae in 197 (33.10.7–10); similarly, Cornell 1995: 356 points out that, at 10.17.11–12, he is aware of four different accounts of a campaign in 296 BC. He is, however, often inclined to let the reader decide on the truth of variant versions. In his account of events in 362, when Marcus Curtius devoted himself to death after an earthquake in Rome (cf. doc. 3.18), Livy states that the Lacus Curtius could have been named for him, or for Mettius Curtius, a soldier of Titus Tatius in the time of Romulus (7.6.5–6). Here he seems to suggest that the Lacus Curtius was named after M. Curtius (though in 1.13.5 he seems to accept that it was named after Mettius Curtius). He states, 'I would have spared no effort had there been any way a researcher could reach the truth; as it is, tradition must be adhered to where antiquity makes certainty impossible, and the name of the pool is better known from this more recent legend.' In contrast, Varro (*On the Latin Language* 5.148–50) shows himself aware of three different versions of the story and cites four authors as his authorities: Procilius (tr. pl. 56 BC?), L. Calpurnius Piso Frugi (cos. 133), Q. Lutatius Catulus (cos. 102) and an unknown Cornelius.

Livy's objectivity is praised in Tacitus (*Ann.* 4.34): Aulus Cremutius Cordus, who was prosecuted in AD 25 for praising Brutus and calling Cassius 'last of the Romans' in his *History*, mentions Livy as an exemplum; foreseeing condemnation, Cremutius starved himself to death, stating, 'I am charged with having praised Brutus and Cassius, of whose deeds many have written and no one without respect. Titus Livius, outstanding for eloquence and objectivity, praised Pompey to such a degree that Augustus called him a Pompeian: but their friendship did not suffer.' Livy sees a grave moral decline in his own time compared with the virtues that enabled Rome to defeat Hannibal, and his aim in his writing is ostensibly a moral one (pref. 9–10):

> These are the points to which I would like all my readers to direct their attention – the lifestyle and behaviour of our ancestors, the men and the means by which in both politics and war the empire was first acquired and then increased; then let him see how, as the old teaching gradually lapsed, morals at first declined and then sank lower and lower and finally began the headlong plunge, bringing us to the present day, when we can tolerate neither our vices nor their remedies. What makes the study of history especially salutary and profitable is that you behold instances of all kinds of human experiences set forth on a conspicuous monument; from this you may find for yourself and your state things to imitate, as well as things – rotten in the conception and outcome – to avoid.

He is above all a conservative and is uniformly hostile to all popular politicians, depicting a unified senate responding to provocation.

Livy is an invaluable source on early Rome: see doc. 1.11 on the first consuls; 1.15 on the censorship; 1.25 on the first secession; 1.30 on the decemvirate; 1.46–56, 2.46 on the conflict of the orders; 1.61–68, 70–72, 2.33, 5.2–3, 5.8, 6.7 on the struggle for Italy; 2.9 on public works; 5.11 on the early Roman army; and 7.15 on magisterial duty vis-à-vis family life. For religious rituals and practices in early Rome, see docs 3.6, 3.14–16, 3.18, 3.33, 3.56–57, 3.72, 7.77 and 7.85; he is especially detailed on augury and portents: 3.41, 3.50, 3.52; for the importation of foreign cults, see docs 3.59, 3.61, 3.38. At doc. 3.25 he gives the formula for the declaration of war established by the fourth king of Rome, Ancus Marcius, in a form which, though it may be an antiquarian reconstruction, he seems to consider an accurate transcription of an ancient formula. Livy (books 21–30) is an essential source for the Second Punic War, especially doc. 4.20 on Roman manpower in 217 BC. He is a patriotic writer, and his account is intended to put Roman actions in the best possible light – and Hannibal's in the worst: see docs 4.22, 4.25, 4.28–29, though at doc. 4.54 he admits to praise for Hannibal at Zama. He gives useful information on war loans by businessmen: docs 4.40, 4.60. Books 31–45 of his *History* deal with Rome's conquest of the Greek East down to 167 BC (see docs 5.34, 5.55–56), and doc. 5.9 on the centurion Spurius Ligustinus gives valuable information regarding the number of campaigns in which a centurion in 171 could have been engaged. His speeches are rhetorical additions to his *History*, often intended to drive home his message of moral decline: the call for the repeal of the Oppian law is, for example, a good chance for him to put a suitably moralising speech into the mouth of Cato the Elder (doc. 7.67).

Livy's fame was certainly well established by AD 79: Pliny the Younger, luckily for himself, preferred not to accompany his uncle to observe the eruption of Vesuvius, staying behind to read a volume of Livy, and he records the anecdote of the 'man from Cadiz' who 'was so excited by the famous name of Livy that he came from his far corner of the earth to have a look at him and then went home again' (*Letters* 6.20, 2.3).

16.8 Flavius Josephus (AD 37–c. AD 100)

A Jewish priest and Pharisee who, despite his pro-Roman leanings, was involved in the Jewish revolt of AD 66–70, Josephus became the translator and advisor of Titus (eldest son of the emperor Vespasian) and was granted Roman citizenship and given a residence in Rome. Once there, he dedicated himself to writing history, in particular his *Antiquities of the Jews*, which, in 20 books, covered the period from the creation of the world to AD 65; it was published in AD 93 and was directed towards a wide Greco-Roman readership. In this work he makes considerable use of the writings of Nikolaos of Damascus. Though Josephus is an able apologist for Judaism and its culture, his work on the *Jewish War*, written between 75 and 79, was intended to discourage rebellion against the Romans, and in writing this he may have had access to the diaries of Vespasian and Titus. His *Autobiography*, written c. AD 99, also defended his own less than committed conduct during the revolt: he considered that God was at that moment on the Romans' side. While his works flatter the Romans and their empire, he is a valuable source for Jewish affairs and the Romans' administration of subject peoples, and he cites numerous edicts and letters relating to the Jews in the Roman empire. He cites at length Antony's letter to the high priest Hyrcanus after the battle of Philippi, outlining his plans for the East and ensuring that any Jews who had been reduced to slavery under the administration of Cassius should be freed; a letter and edict to Tyre (a similar letter went to other cities such as Antioch) makes clear that all confiscated Jewish possessions and property should also be returned to their owners. Josephus comments that this is a good example of the consideration shown the Jews by the Romans (doc. 14.33). A further document, a letter of Iullus Antonius as governor of Asia in 7 BC to the Ephesians, confirms that Augustus and Agrippa protected Jewish laws and customs (doc. 15.41). There has been considerable debate about the authenticity of references to Jesus, John the Baptist and early Christianity in the *Antiquities*: 'about this time there lived Jesus, a wise man, if indeed one ought to call him a man': 18.3.3). Current scholarship believes this reference to be an interpolation, but that other references to John the Baptist and James, the brother of Jesus, are authentic.

16.9 Tacitus (AD c. 55–120)

Publius(?) Cornelius Tacitus is one of the most outstanding of Roman historiographers. He was a lawyer by training, and one of his many works, *Dialogue on Oratory*, written perhaps in AD 101, discusses the decline of public speaking during the imperial period. It owes much to Cicero's *De oratore*. Tacitus engaged in a political career under Vespasian, Titus and Domitian and reached the praetorship in AD 88, when he was also a member of the priesthood of Fifteen (the quindecemviri). He was suffect consul in 97 and in 112 held the governorship of the province of Asia.

His first work in AD 98 was a biography of his father-in-law, Gnaeus Julius Agricola, governor of Britain for seven years from 77 or 78, which both eulogises Agricola and reflects hostility to the regime during which he was writing, that of Domitian (he speaks of the latter 'draining the life-blood of the state': *Agricola* 44). Written in the same year, his *Germania* discusses the institutions and customs of the Germanic tribes in comparison to those of Rome and describes in detail individual tribes and their practices. These were followed by his two major works: the *Annals* and the *Histories*. The *Annals* comprise 18 books covering the period AD 14–68, while his *Histories*, perhaps in 12 volumes, continued the *Annals* and dealt with the years AD 69–96. These works have suffered in transmission, with only four volumes of the *Histories* and ten complete volumes of the *Annals* extant.

However, Tacitus is also critical of prominent figures in the Republican period. In his *Histories* he blames the tribunes generally (doubtless referring to the Gracchi, Saturninus and Livius Drusus), as well as consulars such as Marius and Sulla, for the demise of the Republic. From the time of Pompey ('who was no better, though cleverer in concealing his aims') every prominent politician aimed at autocracy, and Roman armies had no scruples about fighting each other (doc. 12.1).

Tacitus accurately records facts while interweaving them with innuendo and rumour for entertainment value, as in his portrayal of Livia: her marriage to Octavian when six months' pregnant and the deliberate gaffe made by her 'little chatterer'; he hints at the suspicion that she had been responsible for the deaths of Gaius and Lucius Caesar, and he considers her 'as a mother a disaster for the state, as a stepmother a disaster to the house of Caesar' (docs 14.39, 15.69, 111, 117). Philosophically opposed to monarchy, and in favour of an aristocratically controlled republic, he views the imperial court with a satirical eye and an underlying pessimism. In his *Annals* he depicts Augustus as appropriating the functions of the senate, magistrates and laws. Following this, once wars and proscriptions had taken their toll, the remaining aristocrats 'found that, the more one welcomed slavery, the quicker one was raised to wealth and office, and, having flourished on revolution, preferred safety and the current state of things to the old system and instability' (doc. 14.66). In the preface to his *Histories* he expands on this, stating that policy was known only to the emperor, while the former 'ruling class' had now polarised into those who flattered and those who (silently) hated autocracy (*Histories* 1.1). In summing up Augustus' reign, it is significant that Tacitus gives the hostile viewpoint last, so that the impression left with the reader is of an ambitious, dissembling, treacherous, incompetent ruler. Even so, while at the end of Augustus' reign 'equality had been abolished', and the good old way of life gone forever, there were still fears (and hopes) that the current stability might not last and that his death might usher in either freedom or further wars as his legacy to Rome (doc. 15.117). This reflects his tendency to give both good and critical accounts of Rome's rulers and prominent men without conclusively stating his own opinion, thus leaving it to his readership to draw their own conclusions.

Tacitus' view of history is generally pessimistic, writing as he was during the reign of an emperor who was corrupt and tyrannical, and he deplores the fact that the balance of power was shifting continually towards the emperor as opposed to the senate as the empire grew in wealth and autocracy. His pessimism stems from his realisation that the senatorial order is condemned to insignificance and apathy, with freedom of speech a lost cause, although he hopes that history will record and remember the evil deeds of which mankind is capable.

16.10 Velleius Paterculus (c. 20 BC–after AD 30)

Following a successful military career, Velleius was a candidate for the praetorship of AD 15. At doc. 10.18 he relates that his great-grandfather, Minatius Magius of Aeculanum, served in the Social War; the Roman people granted him citizenship as a reward and made his sons praetors. In his brief *Compendium of Roman History*, in two books, he covers the period from mythological times down to AD 29 (the death of Livia); most of book 1 is lost. As a senator and an official (quaestor in AD 8 and praetor in AD 15), he took part in or witnessed many events that he described, being present at the meeting between Augustus' grandson Gaius and the Parthian king Phraataces and serving for eight years in Germany and Pannonia under Tiberius. Despite his summary treatment of a lengthy period and his relentlessly flattering portraits of the emperors Augustus and Tiberius (see docs 14.51, 58), he is still the only source for certain important historical details (such as for the Social War, in which he had a family interest, and the Teutoberg Forest defeat in AD 9: docs 10.13, 18, 20; 15.108) and is the only Latin historical writer on Roman affairs between Livy and Tacitus whose work has survived.

16.11 Appian of Alexandria (AD c. 95–c. 165)

Appian was an Egyptian Greek who lived in the mid-second century AD (he died in the 160s) and wrote a history of Rome to the conquest of Egypt in 30 BC. At *BC* pref. 15 he describes himself as 'having reached the highest place in my own country and acted as advocate at Rome in front of the emperors, until they considered me worthy of being made a procurator'. Appian was a friend of the orator M. Cornelius Fronto, whose letter to Antoninus Pius, requesting the appointment of Appian as procurator, survives (Fronto *Letter to Antoninus* 9). He comments at *BC* 1.6: 'I have written and compiled this work, which is valuable for those who wish to see men's immeasurable ambition, their terrible love of power, their untiring perseverance, and the forms taken by innumerable evils.' In his preface, Appian states that he will deal with the Romans' history in terms of their dealings with various peoples and regions. The first three books will cover Rome's expansion into Italy, and the following books will cover Rome's enemies arranged chronologically. He will end with the civil wars, the annexation of Egypt and the establishment of the monarchy. Of his 24 books, only the preface and books 6–9 (*Spanish, Hannibalic, Punic* and *Macedonian Wars*) and 11–17 (*Syrian, Mithridatic* and *Civil Wars*) survive intact.

Appian uses reliable sources, such as Polybius, Asinius Pollio, Caesar, and the work of Hieronymus of Cardia (323–c. 272). He may also be following the narrative of Posidonius, who continued the history of Polybius. He often conflates events when summarising in his attempt to cover 1,000 years of history but provides a useful chronological framework within which to fit other sources. His work is especially valuable as many of the sources he employed are now lost.

Appian begins his *Civil Wars*, books 13–17 of his history, where Romans are fighting Romans, with the tribunate of Tiberius Gracchus. His *Celtica* 13, now only fragmentary, presumably dealt with Marius' campaigns; see also 9.28, 9.31–33 on Saturninus and Glaucia and events late in Marius' career. The five books entitled the *Civil Wars* cover the period of Sulla (book 13), Caesar (14), the war of Mutina (15), the war against Brutus and Cassius (16) and the war against Sextus Pompeius (17). His work is an important narrative for Drusus and the Social War, as well as for Sulla, and he provides an invaluable framework for the fall of the Republic in chapters 12 and 13. He is one of the few historical sources for the period of the Second Triumvirate down to Octavian and Agrippa's defeat of Sextus Pompeius in 36 and Pompeius' death in the East at the hands of Antony's legate in 35. The four succeeding volumes on the Egyptian war, against Cleopatra and Antony, are lost. At docs 4.13, 4.15, 4.63 Appian provides crucial information on the Punic Wars, especially on the sack of Carthage; docs 5.46, 48, 52–53 are essential for the Roman conquest of Spain; doc. 6.48 is a valuable source on the revolt of Spartacus (cf. 6.50 on the plebs at Rome).

16.12 Cassius Dio (AD 164–after 229)

Cassius Dio, a Greek from Bithynia, was prominent in Roman politics in the early third century AD and was suffect consul c. AD 204 and consul again in 229 with the emperor Severus Alexander. His father had been governor of Cilicia and Dalmatia. Dio's history of Rome in 80 books, from its beginnings to AD 229, is generally well preserved for the period 69 BC to AD 46, though the first 36 books, beginning with the arrival of Aeneas in Italy, are only fragmentary, and large sections of his work are known only through Byzantine summaries and excerpts. His history took 22 years of research and writing and was inspired, he tells the reader, by a dream of the goddess Fortune, which came to him after the emperor Severus had approved a short book concerning the dreams and omens relating to his accession (73.23.3–5):

I then felt the wish to compose an account of everything else that concerned the Romans; consequently I resolved not to leave the first account separate but to include it in the current history, in order that I might compose and leave behind me in a single treatise a narrative of everything from the beginning down to a point to be determined by Fortune . . . She, it appears, is fated to be the guardian of the course of my life, and in consequence I have dedicated myself to her. I took ten years to collect the material for all Roman history from its beginning down to the death of Severus, and I spent 12 more years in the composition of the work; as for later events, they shall be recorded down to whatever point may be possible.

As a senator under Commodus and governor of Asia, Africa and Dalmatia and Upper Pannonia, as well as consul on two occasions, Dio was able to observe events and personalities at first-hand, though in the last third of his account he is very circumspect in his judgements, stating that, with the accession of Commodus, the golden age of his history has to give way to one of iron. His narrative is analystic, dealing with one year at a time.

Dio's stylistic model was Thucydides, and, except for his own time, he uses literary sources which are often impossible to identify, but he does comment at 53.19 that it is easier to find sources for the period before 27 BC because everything was reported to the senate and people and historians generally had access to material. He is a very valuable source for the period following Pompey and Crassus' first consulship – though, as a monarchist, he sees all participants in the conflicts of the first century BC as aiming at autocracy – and is one of the most important sources for the reign of Augustus, since Appian's account of the period after 35 BC is lost. He does refer to the memoirs of Augustus, Hadrian and Severus and appears to have consulted them. Inaccuracies (as at doc. 12.76) may be due to the fact that he was working from notes which he made during his initial ten years of study. Like Thucydides, Dio puts speeches into the mouths of his protagonists, which are often lengthy and heavily rhetorical and take up a considerable portion of the narrative. The most extensive of these are the speeches to Augustus put in the mouths of Agrippa and Maecenas regarding the relative merits of republic and monarchy, which take up the whole of book 52. In the following book, he presents a version of the address that Augustus made to the senate which resulted in the 'first settlement' of January 27 BC, when Augustus offered in his seventh consulship to resign his powers and restore authority to the senate but was 'compelled' by the senators to accept absolute power (doc. 14.64).

CICERO

Marcus Tullius Cicero (106–43 BC) is one of the most important sources for Roman history of the first century BC. He was not, of course, an historian, but as consul in 63 he was responsible for dealing with the Catilinarian conspiracy, and from that point he was deeply involved in politics down to the period of the Second Triumvirate and his own death in 43 BC. His speeches and letters provide very important information on the society and politics of the period. In his voluminous letters, to friends (16 books), to Atticus (16 books), to his brother Quintus and to Brutus, Cicero expresses privately his personal feelings and doubts on politics and society at Rome, often on a daily basis, alongside more official letters of business and patronage. Much of what he reports in his personal letters is often trivial gossip, with news on trials and politics mixed up with reports on his personal health and current literary pursuits (see, for example, doc. 12.86). While he may have considered publishing a small selection of these letters (*Att.* 16.5.5), the *Letters to his Friends* were not published (by his freedman Tiro) until after his death (see doc. 6.52), and the others considerably later, and because of their private and personal nature they often present Cicero in a very 'unheroic' light; he is very much aware of his own status and importance (see, for example, docs 2.49, 12.32, 12.34, 12.61, 12.66) and can be beset by indecision as to the political course to take (docs 12.40, 12.70, 13.35), while in some letters he gives his real views on a situation, which contradict the stance he has maintained in public (docs 12.35, 12.37, 12.74, 12.77, 13.54).

Some 58 speeches of Cicero survive, his first major trial being the defence of Roscius of Ameria for parricide in 80 BC (docs 2.56, 11.25). In his 'courtroom' speeches (generally for the defence, except for the prosecution of Verres: doc. 5.68) he is of course giving a partisan viewpoint intended to convince a jury of his client's innocence. In addition, the speeches, often delivered mostly *ex tempore*, were actually polished up after the event for publication, although the actual content (as opposed to the style) presumably could not be altered to any great extent from what was actually delivered. Asconius states that Cicero's speech on behalf of Milo in 52 was extremely weak and hesitant, due to the threat of violence, and so the speech that is extant bears no relation to that actually given at the trial (doc. 13.5); similarly, the second series of speeches against Verres, though they were prepared, were not delivered in court, because Verres went into exile after the first. Cicero discusses his forensic training and early experience in doc. 2.67 and gives general advice in his *On Duties* on the rationale for undertaking prosecution or defence (doc. 2.65). His attack on Catiline before the people (*In Catilinam II*: doc. 12.18), delivered on 9 November 63, is a grand set-piece of insult and abuse which bears little relation to the actual past deeds of Catiline and his supporters – nor was it meant to; Cicero was drumming up opposition to the revolt in any way possible and using every conceivable form of vilification to achieve his aim. Furthermore, his views, as on the Gracchi, can vary depending on his audience (docs 8.37–39). Without his letters to Atticus and friends, little detail would be known about the 18 months following the assassination of Caesar. He considered himself to be a statesman advising and mentoring the young Octavian and was unaware that the young man had agendas of his own which were very different to Cicero's. Cicero sent Atticus bulletins, often daily, of his conversations and encounters with the protagonists (docs 14.4, 14.9, 14.12), as well as writing what he considered to be good advice to his friends such as Decimus Brutus, M. Iunius Brutus and Trebonius (docs 14.9, 14.14, 14.16–17). The letter collections also contain correspondence from his friends (docs 14.11, 14.18), but, despite their clearer view of events, Cicero continued to rely on the goodwill of Octavian.

Cicero was also a philosopher, and particularly relevant to the study of the history of this period is his *Republic*, a dialogue between Scipio Aemilianus and his friends on the ideal state (cf. doc. 1.4). At *On Divination* 2.6–7 he explains why he turned to the study of philosophy:

The state's serious crisis was the cause of my expounding philosophy, since during the civil war I was able neither to protect the state as I was accustomed to do, nor to remain inactive, nor to find anything that I preferred to do that was worthy of me. Therefore my fellow citizens will pardon me – rather they will be grateful to me – because, when the state was in the power of one man, I neither hid myself, deserted my post, was cast down, nor behaved like one enraged at the man or the times . . . Accordingly it was in my books that I delivered my opinion to the senate or harangued the people, believing that I had exchanged care of the state for philosophy.

Cicero's contribution to the theory of Latin rhetoric comprises his *De oratore*, *Orator* and *Brutus* (see docs 2.67, 7.22, 8.12, 26, 34), while his *De inventione* is a treatise expounding certain rhetorical techniques. He was also a poet, writing, among other things, a poem on his consulship (doc. 12.26, cf. 12.33, 12.86).

STRABO

The Greek scholar Strabo (c. 64 BC–c. AD 21), from Amaseia in Pontus, near the Black Sea, wrote his *Geography*, in 17 books, under the Roman emperors Augustus and Tiberius. He studied philosophy in Rome, having moved there in 44 BC. He travelled extensively and is the most important source for ancient geography, with useful material too on political and economic history. Aelius Gallus, prefect of Egypt, was his patron, and Strabo spent some time in Egypt during his governorship. The whole of Strabo's first book (1.1.1–4.9) is worth reading for an account of his methodology and the work of his predecessors, such as the third-century geographer Eratosthenes. He also wrote *Historical Sketches* in 47 books, which took Polybius' work down to the end of the Republic, but this is now almost entirely lost. In his writing he demonstrates that an awareness of geography is essential to an understanding of the demands of empire:

> The usefulness (of geography) is of various kinds, in respect both of the actions of politicians and commanders and of the knowledge of the heavens and the things on land and sea, animals and plants and fruits and everything else that can be seen in each, and indicates that the geographer is a philosopher, one who is concerned with the art of life and happiness. (1.1.1)

At 1.1.16 Strabo emphasises why his work is of especial use to statesmen and generals – 'those who unite cities and peoples into a single empire and political government' – and he comments that the audience he is addressing consists of 'those in high positions'. He compares his work to a colossal construction or statue, more important in its overall effect than in small details: 'explaining the facts relating to large things, and wholes, unless some petty detail too is able to stir the interest of the man who is fond of learning or the man of affairs' (1.1.23). He provides useful accounts of Rome's site, amenities and early fortifications, engineering projects, and Augustus' mausoleum (docs 1.2, 2.1, 15.2), as well as of ritual practices at specific sites, such as the priest at Diana's grove at Aricia, who was a fugitive slave who had killed the previous priest and succeeded to his position.

BIOGRAPHERS

16.13 Cornelius Nepos (c. 110–24 BC)

Nepos is the first Latin biographer whose work survives. Originally from Cisalpine Gaul, he lived in Rome from about 65 BC and was a correspondent of

Cicero and a personal friend of Atticus. His biography of Atticus (doc. 12.27, cf. 14.38) is of immense value for the importance and interests of wealthy equites, as well as providing useful material on Cicero and other personalities with whom he was intimate. Catullus dedicated a book of his poems to Nepos (poem 1). He wrote some 16 books *On Famous Men*, grouped according to categories (such as generals, kings and historians), and, like Plutarch later, he compared Greeks with Romans. His *Lives of Famous Foreign Generals*, which is extant, includes Hamilcar and Hannibal, though they were apparently not in the first edition, which appeared c. 34 BC, only in the second (c. 27 BC). Of the lives of historians, only those of M. Porcius Cato and Atticus (doc. 12.27) are extant. Nepos also wrote a universal history, a geography, and several books of anecdotes, plus a life of Cicero (Gell. 15.28.2). The *Lives* are not intended for a scholarly readership and are both entertaining and moralising, though the author does not always use first-hand sources, especially for his Greek subjects. He provides an interesting comparison of Roman and Athenian women (doc. 7.28) and, in one of the fragments of his work on Latin historians, quotes a letter purporting to be from Cornelia to her son Gaius Gracchus (doc. 8.25).

16.14 Suetonius (AD c.69–c. 150)

Gaius Suetonius Tranquillus was of equestrian rank. He was known by Pliny the Younger, who mentions him in his *Letters*, and probably accompanied Pliny to Bithynia (c. 110) when Pliny governed that province. A high-ranking bureaucrat, he wrote numerous categories of biographies of literary figures (grammarians, rhetoricians, poets, historians, and so on), of which those on grammarians and rhetoricians are extant (see docs 2.66, 6.18, 6.58 and 6.59 for his *Life of Terence*). A biography of the poet Horace is also attributed to him (doc. 15.93). His best-known work is the *Lives of the Caesars*, the biographies of the 12 emperors from Julius Caesar to Domitian; these survive except for the first few chapters of the *Life of the Deified Julius*. Suetonius avoids a chronological structure, instead presenting the achievements and characters of these emperors under a series of topics, illustrated with anecdotes from their lives. He obviously had access to archival material in his *Life* of Julius Caesar, which is one of the longest and most detailed, and he frequently quotes from documents or cites earlier authors. Passages from Suetonius' *Life of the Deified Julius* have been extensively used in chapters 12 and 13. In his *Life of Augustus* he gives information about Augustus' private life, sometimes citing archived letters for this purpose, giving details of his subject's literary efforts (doc. 15.3), family life and background (docs 14.2, 15.65, 67, 71, 107) and the scene at his death-bed (doc. 15.112). One of the most sensational sections is where he repeats the propaganda circulated by Antony about Octavian, particularly the gossip about Octavian's love affairs and passion for gambling (doc. 14.49). He also provides corroborative details of Augustus' religious reforms (doc. 15.20), his building programme (doc. 15.81), and some valuable information on the battle of Teutoberg and the defeat of Varus in Germany (doc. 15.107).

16.15 Plutarch (AD c. 46–c. 126)

Plutarch of Chaeronea is best known as a biographer, despite his many works on rhetoric and moral philosophy. He was also the author of antiquarian works, 'Greek Questions' and 'Roman Questions' (see docs. 2.36, 5.64), concerned primarily with traditional religious practices. He travelled widely, to Egypt as well as to Italy and Rome, and was a priest at Delphi for 30 years. For the study of Roman history, his most important work is his 23 pairs of *Parallel Lives*, 19 of which have comparisons. The comparisons (omitted in the Penguin translation) are an important part of the text, though Plutarch's deliberate pairing of *Lives* can lead to distortion in focus and misleading overviews and generalisations. Often he leaves his final conclusion and summing-up of the biography until the comparison, as in doc. 8.41 (the Gracchi compared to Agis IV and Cleomenes III of Sparta).

Plutarch is unashamedly a biographer, not an historian, and in his study of great political and military figures he is concerned primarily with the revelation of character through action and with demonstrating exempla of virtues and vices. In his work he conflates information from different sources and concentrates on anecdote rather than 'fact'. For Plutarch's source methodology, see Plutarch *Life of Numa* 1.1–7, where he admits that there is a 'vigorous debate about the time at which King Numa lived' and proceeds to cite various views on the subject. After noting that the chronological problems are insurmountable, he then proceeds anyway with Numa's life (1.6–7):

> So it is difficult to be accurate about the chronology, and especially that based on the names of Olympic victors, the list of which is said to have been published at a late date by Hippias of Elis, who had no authoritative basis for his work; I shall, therefore, start from a suitable point and recount the facts which I have found most worthy of mention in Numa's life.

Plutarch sees character as determining destiny; for him characters are an unchanging constant in any biography, determining vice or virtue and not swayed by or developing through events. This leads to sweeping statements and judgements of earlier motives extrapolated from later actions. Plutarch, for example, sees Caesar as unnaturally ambitious and as planning world domination from his earliest youth, not driven to it by the opposition of the optimates (*Life of Caesar* 58.2):

> As Caesar was naturally possessed of ambition and the ability to succeed, his numerous achievements did not make him stop and enjoy what he had laboured for, but instead inspired him with confidence for future deeds and gave rise to plans for greater successes and a passion for new glory, as though he had used up his earlier stock. What he felt was exactly like competitive rivalry with himself, as if he were someone else, and a desire that his future achievements should surpass his old ones . . .

The same methodology can be seen in other descriptions, such as that of Marius (doc. 9.1), Crassus (doc. 2.21) or the young Pompey (doc. 11.17), where he presents his 'heroes' as stereotypes of their most marked characteristics. Similarly, rather than seeing rivalry as gradually developing between colleagues, he tends to predate hostility to an early point in their careers: see especially doc. 9.13 (Marius and Sulla), 12.5, 12.42, 12.82 (Pompey and Crassus) and 12.79 (Pompey and Caesar).

Plutarch has a great love of anecdote, believing it to reveal character ('Those who are sketching, as it were, a portrait of a soul ought not to leave out even tiny marks of character': *Life of Cato the Younger* 24.1). On these grounds he leaves Caesar and Cato squared off in the senate house over the Catilinarian issue to give the history of Caesar's love affair with Cato's sister Servilia, the immorality of Cato's womenfolk, and Cato's own divorce and remarriage to Marcia (who in the meantime he had permitted to marry Hortensius, his best friend, on the latter's request: *Life of Cato the Younger* 24.1–25.4, 25.8–13). For some of his most memorable anecdotes, see docs 2.14, 2.63, 4.61, 5.61, 6.38, 7.20–21, 7.58 (Cato the Elder), 2.22, 2.64, 7.64 (Lucullus), 9.1, 7.59 (Marius), 11.1 (Sulla), 2.21, 12.82 (Crassus), 10.4 (Cato the Younger) and 8.33 (the death of Gaius Gracchus).

Plutarch provides detailed descriptions of incidents, which flesh out the more prosaic accounts in other sources: note particularly the *Lives* of Fabius Maximus and Marcellus for the Second Punic War (docs 4.47–48, 4.52) and his *Life* of the Gracchi (especially docs 8.1, 8.3, 8.9, 8.29, 8.33), as well as his account of the death of Pompey (doc. 13.46). As a Greek, and because of his interest in Roman religious practices, he gives valuable information on the lifestyle and punishments of the Vestal Virgins and on the Bona Dea cult (docs 7.86–87, 7.90). He sees Fortune as playing an important role in men's lives and makes moralising judgements on that basis. On Crassus' death in Parthia, he states (*Life of Pompey* 53.9–10):

> How small a thing is Fortune when compared with human nature! For she cannot satisfy its desires, since the entire extent of the empire and huge immensity of space was not enough for two men, who had heard and read that the gods 'divided everything in existence into three parts and each received his share' yet did not consider Rome's dominion sufficient for themselves, though there were only two of them.

16.16 Nikolaos of Damascus (b. c. 64)

A scholar, historian, statesman, philosopher and dramatist from Damascus in Syria, Nikolaos was one of the best-educated men of his time. He was the tutor of the children of Antony and Cleopatra after their deaths, when they were raised by Augustus' sister Octavia, and, as the friend, advisor and historian of Herod the Great from 14 BC, he went on diplomatic missions for Herod and represented his interests in Rome. His literary output was voluminous: he wrote a *Universal History* in 144 books, from the beginnings of history (the Assyrians, Medes and Persians) to the death of Herod; some of this material on the latter is preserved in the works of Josephus, in particular the description of his rule and kingdom in *The Jewish War* (book 1) and *Antiquities of the Jews* (books 15–17). As well as an ethnographic work on the customs of various races, he wrote a *Life of Augustus*, based on Augustus' own autobiography, which covered the period down to c. 23 BC (see doc. 14.7): two lengthy sections of Nikolaos' work are extant, on Caesar's assassination and Octavian's youth, and his account of Octavian's education and early life are invaluable in reconstructing sections of his subject's lost *Autobiography*. He provides detailed information on events during 44 BC which help to flesh out the accounts of other writers – for example, his information on Octavian's access to state assets on arrival in Italy and his relations with Antony during 44 BC (doc. 14.10). Nikolaos also wrote his own autobiography, works of philosophy (especially commentaries on Aristotle), and a series of tragic and comic dramatic works. He acted as Herod's representative to Marcus Agrippa in 14 BC, when the Jews of Asia Minor submitted their complaints against the inhabitants of the Greek cities. His close connection with Herod allows him to record intimate details of events in the East, as when Julia and her entourage were nearly drowned crossing the River Scamander near Troy, Agrippa's reaction to this danger of his wife's, and Herod's role in ameliorating Agrippa's anger against the inhabitants of the city (doc. 15.47). He also recounts the episode involving the envoys sent from India to Augustus and the immolation of one of the party, an Indian priest, in Athens (doc. 15.15)

ANTIQUARIANS AND SCHOLARS

16.17 M. Terentius Varro (116–27 BC)

Varro studied firstly at Rome with L. Aelius 'Stilo', the great Roman scholar born c. 150 BC who was responsible for a commentary on the XII Tables, and then at Athens. Although a Pompeian, who served with Pompey in Spain and against the pirates, as well as on Caesar's 20-person land commission in 59, Caesar commissioned him in 45 to organise Rome's first public library (Suet. *Jul.* 44.2). His 41 books of *Human and Divine Antiquities* no longer survive, but books 5–10 of his 25-book *De lingua Latina* (*On the Latin Language*) are partly extant; books 5–25 were dedicated to Cicero and probably published in 43 BC. They parenthetically provide valuable information on customs and traditions in their discussion of grammar and language: see, for example, doc. 3.17, which, in providing the etymology of 'pomerium', also describes the Etruscan ritual for founding a town (cf. doc. 3.19 on priesthoods; 1.13 on the magistracies; 3.2 on early deities). At docs 3.24 and 3.49 he quotes from the *Censors' Records* and the augural books to illustrate his analysis of the terms *inlicium* and *templum*. His *De re rustica* (*On Farming*), written for his wife in 37 BC, is also extant: see doc. 6.39. He was Rome's greatest scholar and a prolific writer: Gellius records that he had written 490 books by the age of 78 (Gell. 3.10.17).

16.18 Dionysius of Halicarnassus (c. 60–after 7 BC)

Dionysius of Halicarnassus came to Rome in 30 BC, after the end of the civil wars, where he taught rhetoric and published his 20 books of *Roman Antiquities* (which covered the period from Rome's origins down to the beginning of the First Punic War). At 1.3.7 he states that he began his work in 30 BC and completed it in 7 BC. Most of the first 11 books (down to 441 BC) survive, presenting, along with Livy's history, a coherent account of Rome's early history, and his material was used extensively by Plutarch in his *Lives* of Camillus and Coriolanus. His descriptions of Rome's political development provide valuable information about early Roman institutions (for example, docs 1.20, 23, 25), as well as of the XII Tables and decemvirates and the city's relationships with its Italian neighbours (1.26–28, 30, 43). As a Greek, Dionysius describes much in Roman society of which we would otherwise know little, and his work is a very useful source for the constitution and customs of early Rome. Particularly important are his descriptions and criticism of manumission procedures and his discussion of non-Greek religious practices, such as the Aegei thrown into the Tiber by the Vestals on 14 May, the celebration of the Feriae Latinae, the consultation of the Sibylline Books, the Vestals, and the nature of Roman worship generally (docs 3.7–9, 32, 38, 48, 67, 88–89). While writing for a Roman as well as a Greek readership, one of his main aims was to assist the Greeks in accepting Roman rule, and he attempts to prove that Rome was essentially in origin a Greek city, as at 7.70.1–71.1:

> I promised at the end of my first book, which I wrote and published concerning the Romans' background, that I would confirm this theory with innumerable proofs by bringing in ancient customs, laws and practices, which they preserve down to my own time, just as they received them from their forefathers; for I do not believe that it is sufficient for those who write the ancient history of other countries to recount it in a trustworthy fashion as they received it from the country's inhabitants, but consider that it also needs numerous and indisputable pieces of supporting evidence if it is going to appear reliable . . . I shall use Quintus Fabius as my authority, without needing any further confirmation; for he is the most ancient of all Roman historians, and provides proof not only from what he has heard from others but also from his own knowledge.

His work has been extensively employed in chapters 1 and 2. He was also the author of a number of works on the theory of rhetoric and the Attic orators, including Demosthenes.

While his work is full of lengthy rhetorical and moralising speeches, Dionysius is, however, concerned with questions of accuracy and authenticity and attempts to make sense of the quasi-legendary material with which he is working, as with the family relationships of the Tarquinii (4.6.1): 'These children were not his sons but his grandsons. Due to their total lack of thought and laziness, the authors have published this historical account of them without having examined any of the impossibilities and irrationalities which undermine it, each of which I will try to make clear in a few words . . . '. At 1.7.2–3 he lists as his sources 'men of the greatest learning' with whom he associated and histories written by the approved Roman authorities: Cato, Fabius Maximus, Valerius Antias, Licinius Macer, the 'Aelii, Gellii and Calpurnii' and 'many other renowned writers'.

16.19 Valerius Maximus (fl. AD 30)

Valerius Maximus composed his anecdotal compilation *Memorable Deeds and Sayings* in the reign of the emperor Tiberius (AD 14–37), and it was probably published shortly after AD 31. It comprises various series of short anecdotes, with both Roman and foreign examples, under a series of moral headings. Valerius uses his sources uncritically, borrowing from Livy and Cicero in particular. Though entertaining on issues such as imperious fathers, women who represented themselves in court, punishments dealt out to adulterers, and wife-beating (e.g., docs. 7.14, 17, 29, 41, 43, 76), his work is valuable mainly when he borrows from authors now lost.

16.20 Pliny the Elder (AD 23–79)

The antiquarian and miscellanist Pliny the Elder, who died at the eruption of Vesuvius on 24 August 79, is best known for his 37-book encyclopaedia the *Natural History*, which aimed at including all the knowledge of his time – astronomical, geographical, physiological, biological, botanical, metallurgical, and so on. In his preface (17), Pliny states that he has collected 20,000 important facts through reading approximately 2,000 volumes written by 100 authors. Few of these works had ever been handled by scholars, he tells us, because of the recondite nature of their contents. The value of these 'facts' is considerably enhanced because he usually cites his source for each. Much of the information he imparts helps to add new dimensions to our knowledge of Roman life and customs: see especially docs 3.26, 7.92 (for religious rites), 1.28 (colossal art), 6.3, 6.12, 6.16 (the treatment of slaves), 7.65 (life expectancies) and 7.71 (for the price of lampstands and a very lucky hunchback slave). The *Natural History* is a rich source for enhancing the detail of what is known more generally from other sources, and Pliny provides valuable snippets of information from Augustus' time, such as Antony's work 'On his own drunkenness', Agrippa's public benefactions and art collection, his map of the known world, dwarfs belonging to imperial women, Livia's laurel grove, and some of the embarrassing vicissitudes encountered by Augustus himself (docs 14.47, 15.40–41, 51, 74, 116).

16.21 Aulus Gellius (AD c. 123–c. 169)

Gellius was born in the early second century AD and apparently spent much of his life at Rome. The 20 books of his *Attic Nights*, which were probably published c. AD 180, are concerned particularly with matters of Latin grammar and expression; the work is arranged in short chapters based on notes which Gellius had made on various texts, referring to philosophy, history, religion, grammar and literary and textual criticism, and the depth of his reading, especially in Latin, enables him to comment on numerous erudite works that are now lost. His preface states that he decided to write up these notes into a readable form while in Attica (hence the title) and completed them later for the instruction and entertainment of his children (pref. 1): this needs be no more than a literary device, as is the frequent dialogue-setting between Gellius and his teachers and friends. His discussion of literary usages often includes valuable citations, often quite lengthy, of passages of texts no longer extant. Some of the most notable of these are extracts from speeches of well-known political figures and orators, such as Gaius Gracchus (tr. pl. 123, 122; docs 8.22–24, 8.27), Cato's *On the Voconian Law* and *On the Dowry* (docs 7.11, 18) and his support for the Rhodians in 167, taken from Tiro's criticism of this speech (doc. 5.37), and Scipio Aemilianus' attack as censor on P. Sulpicius Gallus and other effeminate men (doc. 7.57). Gellius also gives definitions of ancient terms, such as pomerium, plebiscite, capite censi and the various assemblies (docs 1.3, 1.21, 1.58, 9.11), and cites the exact wording of military oaths dating from 190 BC, taken from Cincius' *On Military Science* (doc. 5.21), and the details of sumptuary legislation in 161 and 81 BC (docs 5.59, 11.37). One of his most important and lengthy citations is from Fabius Pictor *On the Pontifical Law*, where he informs the reader of the taboos which hedged the flamen dialis (doc 3.21).

Gellius' love of reading shines through the fragmented structure of his miscellany (pref. 22–23):

To this day I have already made 20 volumes of notes. Whatever longer life remains to me by the gods' will and leisure from managing my affairs and seeing to the education of my children, I shall spend all that remaining spare time in gathering brief and amusing memoranda of the same type. And so the number of books, with the help of the gods, will keep pace with the years of life itself, however few or many there may be, nor do I wish to be granted a life which will outlast my capacity to write and take notes.

16.22 Macrobius (c. 400)

Ambrosius Theodosius Macrobius was a high-ranking senator in the fifth century AD. His *Saturnalia* is set in the form of a series of dialogues at the Saturnalia of (perhaps) AD 383, beginning the night before the festival (which commenced on 17 December) and lasting through the holiday. The guests include great pagan literary and political figures of the time, whose discussion ranges through various topics both serious (a great deal of space is given to the poet Vergil) and more trivial, such as facts about types of food and drink. Like Gellius' *Attic Nights*, Macrobius' main value for the Roman Republic is in his citation of works no longer extant: these include a speech of Scipio Aemilianus against Tiberius Gracchus' judiciary law (doc. 8.20), Sulla's sumptuary laws (doc. 11.37), the formula for an evocatio in 146 BC, calling the gods from Carthage (doc. 3.58), numerous witticisms of Cicero (doc. 12.25) and the menu of a pontifical banquet c. 69 BC (doc. 2.23). He also records numerous witty comments, puns and jokes made by Augustus and his daughter Julia (doc. 15.64, 66)

POETS

16.23 Quintus Ennius (239–169 BC)

Born in southern Italy, Q. Ennius was brought by Cato the Elder to Rome in 204 from Sardinia, where he was serving with a Calabrian regiment (Nepos *Cato* 1.4). He was thus trilingual, in Oscan, Greek and Latin, and Gellius describes him as having three hearts: Gell. 17.17.1. He naturalised various Greek metres and considered himself a 'poeta', writing poemata (poems), not carmina (songs). At Rome he was on friendly terms with the Cornelii Scipiones, Sulpicii, Fulvii and Caecilii, and Fulvius Nobilior took him to the East with him in 189 (for which he was criticised by Cato: Cicero *Tusc. Disp.* 1.3). Ennius chronicled the campaign and wrote a play, the *Ambracia*, on the capture of that town in Aetolia. He was given Roman citizenship in 184 by Nobilior's son. According to L. Aelius Stilo (Gell. 12.4.4), the friend portrayed in Ennius' portrait of Servilius Geminus (doc. 2.51) was Ennius himself.

Ennius wrote at least 20 tragedies, many freely adapted from Greek works, three comedies, some four or more books of satires (saturae), a gastronomic poem, an account of the gods (the *Epicharmus*), epigrams, and a prose work, the *Euhemerus*, on the gods as men of olden times. His best-known work was, however, his *Annals*, originally in 15 books, to which three more were later added, in which he attempted to improve on Naevius' *Song of the First Punic War* (doc. 4.18, cf. 4.57). Homer, seen by Ennius in a dream on Mount Helicon, was supposedly the source of the poetic inspiration for his *Annals*, and in it Homer tells how his soul migrated into Ennius' body (1.4–15; Skutsch 1985: 70–1, as lines 2–11).

Ennius provides some useful maxims on Roman customs and tradition, all the more valuable because they are cited as significant in other later works: doc. 1.9 (on custom); 1.10 (on kingship); 2.51 (on friendship and the values of the *nobiles*); 5.63 (on Roman views of nudity). He also records details of traditional religious practices and beliefs: doc. 3.1 (the 12 Olympians in council), 3.5 (Numa and religious institutions) and 3.47 (Romulus and divination). He was frequently cited on Hannibal and the Second Punic War (docs 4.30, 4.34, 4.37), while his epigram on Scipio Africanus (d. 184) accorded the latter semi-divine status (doc. 4.58).

On his own satires, Ennius wrote:

Greetings, poet Ennius, you who pledge mortal men
In flaming verses from your inmost marrow. (*Sat.* 6–7)

On himself (*Epigrams* 7–10), he wrote (for his imago, funerary mask):

Look, O citizens, on the portrait of Ennius in his old age.
It was he who depicted the greatest deeds of your ancestors.

And for his tomb:

Let no one grace me with tears or make a funeral with weeping.
Why? Because I wing my way alive from one man's mouth to another's.

16.24 Gaius Lucilius (c. 180–102/1 BC)

Lucilius was of equestrian rank and the great-uncle of Pompey the Great (Vell. 2.29.2). He served with Scipio Aemilianus at Numantia (docs 5.52–53), and there are many allusions in his poetry to this campaign. He was on friendly terms with Scipio and C. Laelius. Some 1,400 lines of his satires are extant, and his work contains many personal attacks, perhaps modelled on the Greek poet Archilochus, on noted political figures and on moral decline generally. At *Satires* 26.1.632–4 he writes:

> . . . (I don't want) that by the very uneducated
> Or the extremely learned, I should be read; Manius Manilius
> Or Persius I don't want to read these lines, I want Junius Congus to.

Manilius was consul in 149, Persius a well-born orator; Congus clearly is the ideal reader – not overly well informed but sufficiently educated to appreciate the work. Cicero *De orat.* 2.25, who gives Laelius Decumus, not Congus, explains as the reason for this that the one would understand nothing and the other understand perhaps more than Lucilius did himself.

Lucilius presents a satirical view of life in the second century: doc. 1.7 (on life in the forum); 4.55 (on Hannibal); 5.4 (on Rome's invincibility); 5.59 (on sumptuary legislation). He is particularly enlightening on social issues: 6.4–5 (the slaves owned (or not owned) by rich and poor in Rome); 6.19 (his own favourite slave); 6.34 (a prominent gladiatorial match); 6.45 (the runaway slave's dog-collar); 7.38 (a 'good' wife); 7.56 (on the ways noble women are idealised as beautiful); and 7.62 (the charges for an aging prostitute).

16.25 Gaius Valerius Catullus (c. 84–c. 54 BC)

Catullus came from a wealthy family in Verona and as a young man served on the staff of C. Memmius, who was governor of Bithynia in 57–56 BC. He seems to have died in 54 BC at the age of only 30: at least there is no mention of events after 55 in his writing. He was the author of numerous works of invective against Caesar and his engineer Mamurra (docs 7.49, 12.89, 13.63; Caesar refused to take offence) and was part of a cultivated literary circle which modelled itself on Hellenistic culture. Much of what he produced (some 114 poems) is taken up with the theme of a love affair with 'Lesbia', perhaps a poetic construct rather than Clodia, the sister of the tribune Clodius, with whom she has been identified (docs 7.47–49, 51), and he does address himself to other loves as well (see especially doc. 7.61). In doc. 7.46 he satirises conventional morals in Roman aristocratic society.

16.26 Publius Vergilius Maro (70–19 BC)

Vergil was arguably the greatest poet of the Augustan Age, rivalling the best works of archaic and classical Greek poetry in his output. He came from Mantua in Cisalpine Gaul, and it was later thought that his family had been dispossessed from its estate as part of the settlement of the triumvirate's veterans, and that this was rescinded after Vergil appealed to Octavian. This event and Octavian's involvement is immortalised in Vergil's *First Eclogue* (doc. 14.28), written perhaps in 41 BC, which refers to 'that youth . . . in whose praise twelve days a year my altars will give smoke'. Vergil's *Life* is found in a commentary to his works by the grammarian Aelius Donatus but may well have originally been part of Suetonius' *Lives of Famous Men*, which included a number of poets such as Horace (doc. 15.93). Wealthy and talented patrons, such as Asinius Pollio and Cornelius Gallus, recommended Vergil to Octavian, and one of his earliest patrons was Gaius Maecenas, Octavian's friend and cultural arm. The *Georgics* were written in honour of Maecenas, and Vergil himself recited them to Octavian over a four-day period in 29 BC on his return from Actium (doc. 15.90).

Vergil's works comprise the *Eclogues*, pastoral poems idealising the rural life-style (heavily dependent on the Greek pastoral poet Theocritus), the *Georgics*, which celebrate agriculture in Italy, and his epic in 12 books, the *Aeneid*, which competes with the Homeric poems in terms of subject and scope. While Vergil's poems do on occasion reflect the unpleasant political realities of life at Rome under the principate, the *Aeneid* in particular also disseminates the values and ideals promoted by Augustus, including the realisation of national unity, the importance of ancestral values, and the world empire destined for Rome. Similarly, the *Eclogues*, though praising the simple rustic lifestyle, also highlight the impact of political turmoil and civil strife in Italy when farmers were evicted to make way for veterans being settled on the land:

> Some godless soldier will now possess my well-tilled fallow,
> A foreigner these crops! What misery civil strife
> Has brought us! For these we have sown our fields! (doc. 14.28)

The *Georgics*, too, which appeared in 29 BC, speak of Octavian restoring peace and stability to a 'shipwrecked era', that of the triumvirate, when:

> So many wars abound,
> And crimes have many faces: the plough
> Is given little honour, with farmers removed, the neglected fields rot,
> And curved sickles are beaten into unyielding swords.
> There the Euphrates rises, here Germany's at war;
> Neighbouring cities, treaties broken, against each other
> Bear arms; wicked Ares rages through the entire world. (*Georg.* 1.505–11)

While Vergil clearly had some reservations about the principate, he flattered Augustus and the imperial family in fulsomely praising Marcellus, Augustus' nephew, heir and son-in-law, who died in 23 BC at the age of 19. Immortalised in the *Aeneid*, Marcellus is shown at the summit of Rome's future power and dignity. His mother, Octavia, was present when Vergil read book 6 of the *Aeneid* to Octavian, and famously she fainted at the culminating line of the passage describing this 'youth of outstanding beauty and with shining arms' at the end of a long procession of great Romans, with the 'prophetic' words 'You shall be Marcellus!' (doc. 15.34). The *Aeneid* also has set-pieces glorifying Octavian and Rome's future under his government. The shield made by Vulcan for Aeneas features the defeat of Antony and his Eastern consort (Cleopatra) and depicts Octavian's triple triumph of August 29 BC as the epitome of Rome's future successes (doc. 15.11). Furthermore, at the start of the epic, Jupiter prophesies to Venus (the ancestor of Julius Caesar and Augustus) the future military success of Rome, an empire limited by no boundaries or time which wields a worldwide dominion without end (doc. 5.6). According to Donatus' *Life* (doc. 15.90), Vergil died in 19 BC after meeting Augustus at Brundisium. At the age of 52, he had decided to retire to the East for three years to complete the *Aeneid*, but, on meeting Augustus in Athens, returned to Italy with him. He was suffering at this point from an illness contracted at Megara and died after arriving at Brundisium.

16.27 Quintus Horatius Flaccus (65–8 BC)

Horace, born at Venusia in southern Italy, was of relatively lowly birth, being the son of a freedman, but became the leading lyric poet of Augustus' age. His father ensured that he was well educated, taking him to Rome for that purpose, and Horace later continued his studies at Athens at the Academy. It was in Athens that he met Brutus, whom he joined as a military tribune, and as a 'Republican' he served under Brutus at Philippi, later humorously recounting the fact that he ran away without his shield. Following the victory of Octavian and Antony he accepted the amnesty offered by Octavian and from that point eschewed politics and devoted himself to literature. His family estate, like that of Vergil's, was confiscated for the settlement of veterans, and it was Vergil who introduced him to Maecenas in 38 BC. Like Vergil he became an integral part of the literary circle which Maecenas orchestrated and Octavian encouraged. To ensure him a livelihood he was given the position of quaestor's clerk in Rome, while later Maecenas made him a gift of a Sabine farm which features markedly in his poetry. His poems deal with love, philosophy and politics, as well as the nature of poetry itself (the *Ars Poetica*) and many are autobiographical, or purport to be so. Much of the anecdotal information about his life is found in the Suetonian biography of him (doc. 15.93), which details the background to many of the incidents and personalities that are reflected in his poetry.

His first works, the *Satires* (or 'Sermons') and *Epodes* (c. 35–30), are relatively apolitical, although in *Sat.* 1.5 Horace gives a lengthy description of his journey to Brundisium with Maecenas, who was organising the treaty of Tarentum between Octavian and Antony (doc. 14.40). He may also have been with Maecenas at Actium, and in *Epodes* 9 (doc. 14.52), which is addressed to Maecenas, he celebrates Octavian's triumph over the effeminate Egyptians (with their eunuchs and mosquito nets). He increasingly became a spokesperson for Augustus' regime, and his works, which are heavily autobiographical, or at least purport to be so, give a valuable picture of the social and intellectual life of the first half of the Augustan period. From 30 BC his writing begins to show political sensitivity to the regime's developing ideology (e.g., *Odes* 1.2), and from 27 to 24 he alludes to foreign wars in Arabia, Britain, Parthia and Spain (1.29, 1.35, 2.2, 3.8). The first three books of the *Odes* were apparently published together in 23 BC, the earliest dateable poem in the collection being 1.37, which deals with the defeat of Cleopatra at Actium. In Horace's depiction Cleopatra is not so much demonised, as in the works of Propertius and Vergil (docs 14.48, 15.11), as honoured for her courageous suicide:

> But boldly gazing on her desolate palace,
> Calm of countenance, unflinchingly
> She handled the murderous serpents
> So her body could drink down the deadly venom,
>
> More savage than ever, in her chosen death;
> By cruel Liburnians, was *she* to be paraded
> Dethroned, in an arrogant triumph? –
> Too proud a woman she! (*Odes* 1.37)

Horace was disappointed with the reception of the *Odes*, and a fourth book followed only at Augustus' instigation (c. 11 BC), in which the poet overtly promotes the values of the Augustan age and includes odes commissioned by Augustus celebrating the victories of his stepsons Tiberius and Drusus (*Odes* 4.4, 4.14). The eulogising tone of *Odes* book 4 resembles that of the *Carmen Saeculare*, which Horace was commissioned to write for the ludi Saeculares celebrated in 17 BC, and which portrays the regime as a period of peace and moral reform and as a golden age (doc. 15.33). This official hymn of the festival, sung by chorus of girls and boys, highlights Rome's greatness and praises Augustus' moral and social legislation which will underpin the next 110-year cycle. Before producing the *Carmen Saeculare*, Horace had returned to the more relaxed approach of his early satires in a collection entitled the *Epistles*, letters in verse presenting philosophical reflections on the ideal lifestyle, which appeared in 20 or 19 BC. This collection was perhaps his most innovative work, and in 1.13 he describes the presentation of his volume of *Odes* to Augustus by a clumsy messenger (doc. 15.97). Though a friend of Augustus, he declined the position of secretary when Augustus offered it to him, preferring to remain independent. He died in November 8 BC, leaving Augustus as his heir, and his work greatly influenced that of his younger contemporaries Propertius and Ovid.

16.28 Sextus Propertius (c. 50–before 2 BC)

Propertius was born between 54 and 47 BC at Asisium in Umbria. Like Vergil and Horace, his family property was affected by Octavian's confiscations for his veterans in 41–40, and in two poems in book 1 of his *Elegies* he identifies with those affected by Octavian's defeat of Fulvia and Lucius Antonius at the siege of Perusia (docs 14.29–31). Little, however, is known of his life except what can be deduced from his works. His poems are best known for their love interest and are addressed to a mistress called Cynthia, portrayed as an educated courtesan, perhaps a poet herself, who dominates the poems in book 1 in particular, with the first line stating the poet's obsession with this relationship ('Cynthia first captured me – poor me! – with her eyes, I who had never before been touched by romantic love'). While he addresses poems to Maecenas (the opening poem of book 2 refuses to comply with his request for a poem on a specific theme), a tone of political independence persists throughout his work, and apparent eulogies of Augustan triumphs are often undercut by an irreverent aside at the conclusion of the poem. *Elegies* 3.4 (doc. 15.95), which incites Augustus to war against Parthia and even 'India', enthuses about avenging Crassus and his son, the conquest of the Tigris and Euphrates, and the booty and prisoners to be paraded in Augustus' triumph but ends with the poet's declaration that his only interest in these is in viewing the triumph on the Via Sacra while relaxing with his 'girl'. Similarly, in 2.14 he compares himself to Agamemnon, seeing himself as having achieved even more than the conquest of Troy, or in contemporary terms a triumph over Parthia, in having his 'girl' accept him for the entire night as a lover:

Agamemnon did not so rejoice at his Trojan triumph! . . .
The girl, at her ease, laid her head next to mine.
This victory means more than defeating the Parthians,
She is my plunder, my kings, my chariot!
I will place great gifts, Cytherea, on your columns
And this will be the verse under my name:
Goddess, I, Propertius, place before your temple
These spoils, for being accepted as a lover for a whole night.

The focus of much of Propertius' poetry is on his position as slave of his mistress, and his love affairs are depicted as of greater importance to him than contemporary politics. His celebration of passionate love suggests that he would not have been in tune with Augustus' moral and social legislation, with its emphasis on the importance of the marriage tie and the procreation of children (docs 15.23–27). He did, however, compose a lament on the death of Augustus' nephew Marcellus (*Elegies* 3.18), as well as a celebration of Cleopatra's defeat, written some ten years after the event, in which she is satisfactorily demonised as an embodiment of all Eastern luxury and self-indulgence, 'that harlot queen of incestuous Canopus' (doc. 14.48, cf. 14.52, 15.11).

16.29 Publius Ovidius Naso (43 BC–AD 17)

Born at Sulmo into an equestrian family of long standing, Ovid was educated at Rome. A younger contemporary of Vergil and Horace, from an early period in his career he devoted himself to poetry and became, like Tibullus, one of the circle of M. Valerius Messalla Corvinus, a rival patron to Maecenas who supported his own group of young poets. His early poetry includes the *Amores*, 'Loves', three books detailing the tribulations of a young poet with his mistress Corinna; the *Heroides*,

'Heroines', letters or monologues written from the point of view of tragic heroines such as Phaedra and Ariadne; the *Ars Amatoria*, 'Art of Love', which deals with courtship and intrigue, advising men, and women, how to approach the opposite sex; and the *Remedia amoris*, 'Remedies for love', counselling the reader how to extricate himself from a relationship. While focusing on erotic themes and frequently eulogising the princeps, Ovid subtly undercuts the tone of the Augustan regime with its imposing constructions by describing the porticoes of Octavia and Livia as a good place to pick up girls.

His *Metamorphoses*, 'Transformations', ostensibly an epic in 15 books, deals with more than 250 myths from the classical and Near Eastern past which feature the transformations of humans, animals and inanimate objects into new entities, often under the power of love. By AD 8 Ovid was one of the leading poets in Rome, but in that same year he was banished by Augustus to Tomis (modern Constanta), a backwoods town on the western coast of the Black Sea. In an autobiographical poem in his five-book *Tristia*, 'Lamentations', written in exile, Ovid refers to a mistake ('error') which led to his banishment, and elsewhere to a poem which was viewed with disapproval (presumably the *Ars Amatoria*, or 'Art of Love', books 1–2 of which appeared c. 1 BC). He was obviously implicated in some kind of scandal which involved the imperial family, and significance has been attached to the fact that his exile in AD 8 occurred in the same year as the banishment of the younger Julia, Augustus' granddaughter, for adultery and possible treason (doc. 15.31). His own account of his exile is given in the *Tristia* (4.10.85–90, 95–102):

> But if anything other than our names survive for those of us deceased,
> If some slight shade escapes the funeral pyre,
> If news of me, my parental ghosts, has reached you
> And my crimes are being judged in the Stygian court,
> Know, I beg you, that the reason (for I should not deceive you)
> For my banishment was for a mistake and not a crime . . .
> Since my birth the victorious Olympian charioteer crowned with olive
> Had ten times taken the Olympian prizes
> When – to Tomis on the west of the Black Sea –
> The wrath of the princeps banished me.
> The reason for my ruin is known to all –
> No need for words of mine.
> Why talk of the duplicity of comrades and deceitful servants?
> I had much to bear as bad as exile!

Ovid remained at Tomis until his death, probably in AD 17, despite many pleas to Augustus for his recall, suggesting that Augustus was firmly opposed to his presence in Rome. It was at Tomis that Ovid revised his *Fasti*, 'Calendar', an antiquarian work on religious rites and folklore, which discusses the months of the calendar year and the festivals celebrated in each: only the first six books survive. Augustus features throughout as the embodiment of traditional Roman religion, not always without subtle irony (see doc. 15.97 for the comparison of Augustus with Romulus), and the anniversaries of his foundations such as the Ara Pacis and the temple of Mars Ultor feature prominently in Ovid's work (docs 15.16, 96). A valuable source for Roman festivals, Ovid describes the role of both matrons and prostitutes on occasions such as the Matronalia (1 March), Veneralia (1 April), Vinalia (23 April) and Matralia (11 June) (docs 7.79, 81–83), while among other celebrations he gives the details of the Caristia, held in honour of the household deities, and the Robigalia, when a dog sacrifice was made to propriate the deity of Mildew and protect the crops (docs 15.21, 3.74).

His *Tristia*, like his *Letters from Pontus*, were addressed from exile to his wife and other recipients detailing the miseries of his situation, but Ovid was unable to effect a reconsideration of his banishment. In *Tristia* 3.3 he presents his own epitaph:

I who lie here, the poet Naso, skilled virtuoso of the tender passions,
Was undone by my own wit.
You who pass by, if you have ever been in love, be kind enough
To say, 'May Naso's bones lie softly'. (*Tristia* 3.3.73–76)

Abbreviations of Personal Names and Magistracies

A.	Aulus
App.	Appius
C.	Gaius
Cn.	Gnaeus
D.	Decimus
L.	Lucius
M.	Marcus
M'	Manius
P.	Publius
Q.	Quintus
Ser.	Servius
Sex.	Sextus
Sp.	Spurius
T.	Titus
Ti.	Tiberius
Aed.	aedile
Cos.	Consul
Cos. suff.	Suffect (or substitute) consul
Procos.	Proconsul
Tr. pl.	tribune of the plebs

Abbreviations of Journals, Editions of Inscriptions, Commentaries and Frequently Cited Works

AC	*Antiquité Classique*
AE	*L'Année Epigraphique*
AHB	*Ancient History Bulletin*
AHR	*American Historical Review*
AJAH	*American Journal of Ancient History*
AJPh	*American Journal of Philology*
AncSoc	*Ancient Society*
ANRW	*Aufstieg und Niedergang der Römischen Welt*, Berlin.
BGU	*Berliner griechische Urkunden*
BICS	*Bulletin of the Institute of Classical Studies*
Bruns *FIRA*	Bruns, C.G. 1919, *Fontes iuris Romani antiqui*, seventh edition, Tübingen.
Brunt 1988	Brunt, P.A. 1988, *The Fall of the Roman Republic and Related Essays*, Oxford.
CAH	*The Cambridge Ancient History*
C&M	*Classica et Mediaevalia*
CIL	*Corpus Inscriptionum Latinarum*, Berlin.
ClAnt	*Californian Studies in Classical Antiquity*
CPh	*Classical Philology*
CQ	*Classical Quarterly*
Crawford *RRC*	Crawford, M.H. 1974, *Roman Republican Coinage*, vols I–II, Cambridge.
Crawford *Statutes*	Crawford, M.H. (ed.) 1996, *Roman Statutes*, vols I–II, London.
EJ	Ehrenberg, V. and Jones, A.H.M. (eds) 1976, *Documents Illustrating the Reigns of Augustus and Tiberius*, second edition, Oxford.
EMC/CV	*Echos du Monde Classique/Classical Views*
FGrH	Jacoby, F. 1954–64, *Die Fragmente der griechischen Historiker*, with *Supplements*, Leiden.
FIRA	Riccobono, S. 1941, *Fontes iuris Romani antejustiniani*, part 1, second edition, Florence.
G&R	*Greece and Rome*

ABBREVIATIONS

Grueber	Grueber, H.A. 1910, *Coins of the Roman Republic in the British Museum*, vols I–III, London.
Guérard 1950	Guérard, O. 1950, *Journal of Juristic Papyrology* 4: 106–111.
HRR	Peter, H. 1906, 1914, *Historicorum Romanorum Reliquiae*, vol. 1, second edition (1914), vol. 2, first edition (1906), Stuttgart.
HSCPh	*Harvard Studies in Classical Philology*
IG	*Inscriptiones Graecae*
IGRR	Cagnat, R. 1927, *Inscriptiones Graecae ad Res Romanas Pertinentes*, vol. 4, Paris.
ILLRP	Degrassi, A. 1963–65, *Inscriptiones Latinae Liberae Rei Publicae*, vol. 1, second edition, 1965, vol 2, first edition, 1963, Florence.
ILS	Dessau, H. 1892–1916, *Inscriptiones Latinae Selectae*, Berlin, vols I–III.
Inscr. Ital.	Degrassi, A. 1937–63, *Inscriptiones Italiae*, Rome.
JRA	*Journal of Roman Archaeology*
JRMES	*Journal of Roman Military Equipment Studies*
JRS	*Journal of Roman Studies*
LSAG²	Jeffrey, I. 1990, *Local Scripts of Archaic Greece*, second edition, Oxford.
MH	*Museum Helveticum*
Moretti *IAG*	Moretti, L. 1953, *Iscrizione agonistiche greche*, Rome.
MRR	Broughton, T.R.S. 1951–60, *The Magistrates of the Roman Republic*, vols 1–3, New York.
OGIS	Dittenberger, W. 1903–5, *Orientis Graeci Inscriptiones Selectae*, vols 1–2, Leipzig.
ORF⁴	Malcovati, H. 1976, *Oratorum Romanorum Fragmenta. Liberae Rei Publicae*, fourth edition, Turin.
P&P	*Past and Present*
PBSR	*Papers of the British School at Rome*
PCPhS	*Proceedings of the Cambridge Philological Society*
P. Köln	Gronewald, M. et al. 2001, *Kölner Papyri*, Cologne.
Raubitschek	Raubitschek, A.E. with Jeffrey, L.H. 1949, *Dedications from the Athenian Acropolis. A Catalogue of the Inscriptions of the Sixth and Fifth Centuries BC*, Cambridge, MA.
RDGE	Sherk, R.E. 1969, *Roman Documents from the Greek East*, Baltimore.
Reynolds *Aphrodisias*	Reynolds, J. 1982, *Aphrodisias and Rome. Documents from the Excavation of the Theatre at Aphrodisias*, London.
RG	Cooley, A.E. 2009, *Res Gestae Divi Augusti*, Cambridge.
RhM	*Rheinisches Museum*
RIDA	*Revue internationale des droits de l'antiquité*
Scullard *GN*	Scullard, H.H. 2010, *From the Gracchi to Nero. A History of Rome from 133 BC to AD 68*, sixth edition, London.
SEG	*Supplementum Epigraphicum Graecum*
SIG³	Dittenberger, W. 1915–24, *Sylloge Inscriptionum Graecarum*, vols I–IV, Leipzig.
TAPhA	*Transactions of the American Philological Association*
WS	*Wiener Studien*
ZSS	*Zeitschrift der Savigny-Stiftung für Rechtsgeschichte romanistische Abteilung*

Bibliography

GENERAL BIBLIOGRAPHY AND
BACKGROUND READING

Listed immediately below are works which serve as a useful introduction to Roman history. The books in this list generally do not appear in the chapter bibliographies which follow.

Adkins, L. & Adkins, R.A. 1994, *A Handbook to Life in Ancient Rome*, New York.

Alföldy, G. 1988, *The Social History of Rome*, Baltimore.

Beard, M. & Crawford, M.H. 1999, *Rome in the Late Republic*, second edition, London.

Blois, L. de & Spek, R.J. van der 1997, *An Introduction to the Ancient World*, London.

Boardman, J., Green, J. & Murray, O. 1986, *The Oxford History of the Classical World*, Oxford = 2001, *The Oxford History of the Roman World.*

Boatwright, M.T., Gargola, D.J., Lenski, N. & Talbert, R. 2012, *The Romans. From Village to Empire*, second edition, Oxford.

Boatwright, M.T., Gargola, D.J., Lenski, N. & Talbert, R. 2014, *A Brief History of the Romans*, second edition, Oxford.

Boren, H.C. 1977, *Roman Society. A Social, Economic, and Cultural History*, Lexington.

Christiansen, E. 1995, *A History of Rome*, Cambridge.

Cornell, T. & Matthews, J. 1982, *Atlas of the Roman World*, revised edition, Oxford.

Crawford, M. 1992, *The Roman Republic*, second edition, London.

Dupont, F. 1992, *Daily Life in Ancient Rome*, Oxford.

Grant, M. 1978, *A History of Rome*, New York.

Grant, M. 1992, *Greeks and Romans. A Social History*, London.

Hornblower, S. & Spawforth, A. (eds) 1996, *The Oxford Classical Dictionary*, third edition, Oxford.

Jones, P. & Sidwell, K. 1997, *The World of Rome. An Introduction to Roman Culture*, Cambridge.

Kamm, A. 1995, *The Romans. An Introduction*, London.

Lintott, A. 2000, *The Roman Republic*, Stroud.

Ogilvie, R.M. 1976, *Early Rome and the Etruscans*, London.

Rosenstein, N. & Morstein-Marx, R. (eds) 2006, *A Companion to the Roman Republic*, Malden & Oxford.

Scarre, C. 1995, *The Penguin Historical Atlas of Ancient Rome*, Harmondsworth.

Scullard, H.H. 1980, *A History of the Roman World 753–146 BC*, fourth edition, London.

Scullard, H.H. 2010, *From the Gracchi to Nero*, sixth edition, London.

Starr, C. 1990, *A History of the Ancient World*, Oxford.

BIBLIOGRAPHY

Swain, H. & Davies, M.E. 2010, *Aspects of Roman History 82 BC–AD 14. A Source-Based Approach*, London.

Ward, A.M, Heichelheim, F.M. & Yeo, C.A. 1998, *A History of the Roman People*, third edition, Upper Saddle River.

SOURCE BOOKS AND ANTHOLOGIES

Aicher, P.J. 2004, *Rome Alive. A Source-Guide to the Ancient City*, Wauconda, IL.

Beard, M., North, J. & Price, S. 1998, *Religions of Rome*, vol. 2. *A Sourcebook*, Cambridge.

Braund, D. 1985, *Augustus to Nero. A Source Book on Roman History 31 BC–AD 68*, London.

Carter, J.M. 1970, *Sallust. Fragments of the Histories and Pseudo-Sallust. Letters to Caesar*, Lactor 6, London.

Cherry, D. 2001, *The Roman World. A Sourcebook*, Malden, MA.

Chisholm, K. & Ferguson, J. 1981, *Rome. The Augustan Age*, Oxford.

Cooley, M.G.L. 2003, *The Age of Augustus*, Lactor 17, London.

Dudley, D.R. 1967, *Urbs Roma. A Source Book of Classical Texts on the City and its Monuments*, London.

Ferguson, J. 1980, *Greek and Roman Religion. A Source Book*, Park Ridge.

Gardner, J.F. & Wiedemann, T.E.J. 1991, *The Roman Household. A Sourcebook*, London.

Grant, F.C. 1957, *Ancient Roman Religion*, New York.

Humphrey, J.W., Oleson, J.P. & Sherwood, A.N. 1998, *Greek and Roman Technology. A Sourcebook*, London.

Lacey, W.K. & Wilson, B.W.J.G. 1970, *Res Publica. Roman Politics and Society According to Cicero*, Oxford.

Lefkowitz, M.R. & Fant, M.B. 1992, *Women's Life in Greece and Rome. A Source Book in Translation*, second edition, Baltimore.

Levick, B. 2000, *The Government of the Roman Empire. A Sourcebook*, second edition, London.

Lewis, N. & Reinhold, M. (eds) 1990, *Roman Civilization. Selected Readings*, vol. I. *The Republic and the Augustan Age*, third edition, New York.

Lomas, K. 1996, *Roman Italy, 338 BC–AD 200. A Sourcebook*, London.

Luck, G. 1985, *Arcana Mundi. Magic and the Occult in the Greek and Roman World. A Collection of Ancient Texts*, Baltimore.

McDermott, W.C. & Caldwell, W.E. 1970, *Readings in the History of the Ancient World*, second edition, New York.

Meijer, F. & Nijf, O. van 1992, *Trade, Transport and Society in the Ancient World*, London.

Mellor, R. 1998, *The Historians of Ancient Rome. An Anthology of the Major Writings*, London.

Plant, I.M. 2004, *Women Writers of Ancient Greece and Rome. An Anthology*, London.

Rawson, B. 1978, *The Politics of Friendship. Pompey and Cicero*, Sydney.

Ridley, R.T. 1987, *History of Rome. A Documented Analysis*, Rome.

Sabben-Clare, J. 1971, *Caesar and Roman Politics 60–50 BC. Source Material in Translation*, Oxford.

Shaw, B.D. 2001, *Spartacus and the Slave Wars. A Brief History with Documents*, Boston.

Shelton, J. 1988, *As the Romans Did. A Sourcebook in Roman Social History*, New York.

Sherk, R.K. 1984, *Rome and the Greek East to the Death of Augustus*, Cambridge.

Sherk, R.K. 1988, *The Roman Empire. Augustus to Hadrian*, Cambridge.

Stockton, D.L. 1981, *From the Gracchi to Sulla. Sources for Roman History, 133–80 BC*, Lactor 13, London.

Thorpe, M.A. 1970, *Roman Politics, 80–44 BC*, Lactor 7, London.

Treggiari, S. 1996, *Cicero's Cilician Letters*, Lactor 10, second edition, London.

BIBLIOGRAPHY

Wiedemann. T.E.J. 1981, *Greek and Roman Slavery*, London.
Wilkinson, L.P. 1966, *Letters of Cicero. A Selection in Translation*, revised edition, London.
Yavetz, Z. 1988, *Slaves and Slavery in Ancient Rome*, New Brunswick.

CHAPTER ONE: EARLY REPUBLICAN ROME: 507–264 BC

Alföldi, A. 1965, *Early Rome and the Latins*, Ann Arbor.
Aubet, M.E. 2001, *The Phoenicians and the West. Politics, Colonies and Trade*, second edition, Cambridge.
Brunt, P.A. 1971, *Social Conflicts in the Roman Republic*, London.
Cornell, T.J. 1995, *The Beginnings of Rome. Italy and Rome from the Bronze Age to the Punic Wars (c. 1000–264 BC)*, London.
Develin, R. 1985, *The Practice of Politics at Rome, 366–167 BC*, Brussels.
Drummond, A. 1989, 'Rome in the fifth century I: the social and economic framework' in *CAH* VII.2²: 113–71.
Drummond, A. 1989a, 'Rome in the fifth century II: the citizen community' in *CAH* VII.2²: 172–242.
Eckstein, A.M. 2006, *Mediterranean Anarchy, Interstate War, and the Rise of Rome*, Berkeley.
Gabba, E. 1991, *Dionysius and 'The History of Archaic Rome'*, Berkeley.
Grandazzi, A. 1997, *The Foundations of Rome. Myth and History*, Ithaca and London.
Gruen, E.S. 1992, *Culture and National Identity in Republican Rome*, London.
Kunkel, W. 1973, *An Introduction to Roman Legal and Constitutional History*, second edition, Oxford.
Lintott, A.W. 1999, *The Constitution of the Roman Republic*, Oxford.
Lomas, K. 1993, *Rome and the Western Greeks 350 BC–AD 200*, London.
Miles, G.B. 1995, *Livy. Reconstructing Early Rome*, Ithaca and London.
Mitchell, R.E. 1990, *Patricians and Plebeians. The Origin of the Roman State*, Ithaca.
Momigliano, A. 1989, 'The origins of Rome' in *CAH* VII.2²: 52–112.
Mouritsen, H. 2001, *Plebs and Politics in the Late Roman Republic*, Cambridge.
Ogilvie, R.M. & Drummond, A. 1989, 'The sources for early Roman history' in *CAH* VII.2²: 1–29.
Palmer, R.E.A. 1970, *The Archaic Community of the Romans*, Cambridge.
Patterson, J.R. 2000, *Political Life in the City of Rome*, Bristol.
Raaflaub, K.A. (ed.) 1986, *Social Struggles in Archaic Rome. New Perspectives on the Conflict of the Orders*, Berkeley.
Salmon, E.T. 1967, *Samnium and the Samnites*, Cambridge.
Salmon, E.T. 1982, *The Making of Roman Italy*, London.
Sandberg, K.A.J. 2001, *Magistrates and Assemblies. A Study of Legislative Practice in Republican Rome*, Rome.
Scullard, H.H. 1973, *Roman Politics, 220–150 BC*, second edition, Oxford.
Seager, R. 1977, '*Populares* in Livy and the Livian tradition' *CQ* 27: 377–90.
Smith, C.J. 1996, *Early Rome and Latium: Economy and Society c. 1000–500 BC*, Oxford.
Staveley, E.S. 1972, *Greek and Roman Voting and Elections*, London.
Staveley, E.S. 1989, 'Rome and Italy in the early third century' in *CAH* VII.2²: 420–55.
Stewart, R. 1998, *Public Office in Early Rome. Ritual Procedure and Political Practice*, Ann Arbor.
Taylor, L.R. 1966, *Roman Voting Assemblies from the Hannibalic Wars to the Dictatorship of Caesar*, Ann Arbor.
Watson, A. 1975, *Rome of the XII Tables*, Princeton.
Westbrook, R. 1988, 'The nature and origins of the Twelve Tables' *ZSS* 105: 74–121.

BIBLIOGRAPHY

CHAPTER TWO: THE PUBLIC FACE OF ROME

Astin, A.E. 1978, *Cato the Censor*, Oxford.

Beacham, R.C. 1999, *Spectacle Entertainments of Early Imperial Rome*, New Haven.

Beard, M. 2007, *The Roman Triumph*, Cambridge, MA.

Brunt, P.A. 1966, 'The Roman mob' *P&P* 35: 3–27.

Brunt, P.A. 1982, 'Nobilitas and Novitas' *JRS* 72: 1–17.

Brunt, P.A. 1988, 'Amicitia in the Roman Republic' in Brunt 1988: 351–81.

Brunt, P.A. 1988a, 'Clientela' in Brunt 1988: 382–442.

Brunt, P.A. 1988b, 'Factions' in Brunt 1988: 443–502.

Crook, J.A. 1967, *Law and Life of Rome*, London.

Develin, R. 1985, *The Practice of Politics at Rome, 366–167 BC*, Brussels.

Drummond, A. 1989, 'Early Roman clientes' in Wallace-Hadrill, A. (ed.) *Patronage in the Ancient World*, London: 89–116.

Eisenstadt, S.N. & Roniger, L. 1984, *Patrons, Clients and Friends*, Cambridge.

Epstein, D.F. 1987, *Personal Enmity in Roman Politics 218–43 BC*, London.

Flower, H.I. 1996, *Ancestor Masks and Aristocratic Power in Roman Culture*, Oxford.

Flower, H.I. 2004, 'Spectacle and political culture in the Roman Republic' in Flower, H.I. (ed.) *The Cambridge Companion to the Roman Republic*, Cambridge: 322–43.

Gelzer, M. 1969, *The Roman Nobility*, Oxford.

Gruen, E.S. 1968, *Roman Politics and the Criminal Courts, 149–78 BC*, Cambridge, MA.

Gruen, E.S. 1992, *Culture and National Identity in Republican Rome*, London.

Hall, U. 1964, 'Voting procedure in Roman assemblies' *Historia* 13: 267–306.

Higginbotham, J. 1997, *Piscinae. Artificial Fishponds in Roman Italy*, Chapel Hill.

Keaveney, A. 1992, *Lucullus, a Life*, London.

Kleijn, G. de 2001, *The Water Supply of Ancient Rome*, Amsterdam.

Kyle, D.G. 1998, *Spectacles of Death in Ancient Rome*, London.

Laurence, R. 1999, *The Roads of Roman Italy*, London.

Lintott, A. 1990, 'Electoral bribery in the Roman republic' *JRS* 80: 1–16.

Lintott, A. 1999, *Violence in Republican Rome*, revised edition, Oxford.

Mackie, N. 1992, '*Popularis* ideology and popular politics at Rome' *RhM* 135: 49–73.

Mouritsen, H. 2001, *Plebs and Politics in the Late Roman Republic*, Cambridge.

Nippel, W. 1995, *Public Order in Ancient Rome*, Cambridge.

Patterson, J.R. 2000, *Political Life in the City of Rome*, Bristol.

Plass, P.C. 1995, *The Game of Death in Ancient Rome*, Madison.

Rosenstein, N. 1992, '*Nobilitas* and the political implications of military defeat' *AHB* 6: 117–26.

Rosenstein, N. 1993, 'Competition and crisis in mid-Republican Rome' *Phoenix* 47: 313–38.

Seager, R. 1972, 'Factio: some observations' *JRS* 62: 53–8.

Seager, R. 1972a, 'Cicero and the word *popularis*' *CQ* 22: 328–38.

Shackleton Bailey, D.R. 1986, '*Nobiles* and *novi* reconsidered' *AJPh* 107: 255–60.

Stone, S. 1994, 'The toga: from national to ceremonial costume' in Sebesta, J.L. & Bonfante, L. (eds) *The World of Roman Costume*, Wisconsin: 13–45.

Taylor, L.R. 1960, *The Voting Districts of the Roman Republic*, Ann Arbor.

Toner, J.P. 1995, *Leisure and Ancient Rome*, Cambridge.

Ulrichs, R.B. 1994, *The Roman Orator and the Sacred Stage*, Brussels.

van Sickle, J. 1987, 'The elogia of the Cornelii Scipiones and the origin of epigram at Rome' *AJPh* 108: 41–55.

Vanderbroeck, P.J.J. 1986, 'Homo novus again' *Chiron* 16: 239–42.

Veyne, P. 1990, *Bread and Circuses*, Harmondsworth.

Vishnia, R.F. 1996, *State, Society and Popular Leaders in Mid-Republican Rome 241–167 BC*, London.

Wallace-Hadrill, A. 1989, 'Patronage in Roman society: from republic to empire' in Wallace-Hadrill, A. (ed.) *Patronage in the Ancient World*, London: 63–87.

Wallinga, T. 1994, 'Ambitus in the Roman world' *RIDA* 41: 411–42.

Wiseman, T.P. 1971, *New Men in the Roman Senate, 139 BC–AD 14*, Oxford.

Wiseman, T.P. 1985, *Roman Political Life 90 BC to AD 69*, Exeter.

Yacobsen, A. 1992, '*Petitio et largitio*: popular participation in the centuriate assembly of the late republic' *JRS* 82: 32–52.

Yacobsen, A. 1995, 'Secret ballot and its effects in the late Roman Republic' *Hermes* 123: 426–42.

Yacobsen, A. 1999, *Elections and Electioneering in Rome. A Study in the Political System of the Late Republic*, Stuttgart.

CHAPTER THREE: RELIGION IN THE ROMAN REPUBLIC

Beard, M. 1988, 'Roman priesthoods' in Grant, M. & Kitzinger, R. (eds) *Civilization of the Ancient Mediterranean*, vol. II, New York: 933–9.

Beard, M. 1990, 'Priesthood in the Roman Republic' in Beard, M. & North, J. (eds) *Pagan Priests. Religion and Power in the Ancient World*, London: 19–48.

Beard, M. 1994, 'Religion' in *CAH* IX²: 729–68.

Beard, M. 1994a, 'The Roman and the foreign: the cult of the "Great Mother" in imperial Rome' in Thomas, N. & Humphrey, C. (eds) *Shamanism. History and the State*, Ann Arbor: 164–90.

Bispham, E. & Smith, C. 2000, *Religion in Archaic and Republican Rome and Italy*, Edinburgh.

Burkert, W. 1987, *Ancient Mystery Cults*, Cambridge, MA.

Burton, P.J. 1996, 'The summoning of the Magna Mater to Rome' *Historia* 45: 36–63.

Feeney, D. 1998, *Literature and Religion at Rome. Cultures, Contexts, and Beliefs*, Cambridge.

Flower, H.I. 1996, *Ancestor Masks and Aristocratic Power in Roman Culture*, Oxford.

Gabba, E. 1991, *Dionysius and 'The History of Archaic Rome'*, Berkeley.

Goar, R.J. 1972, *Cicero and the State Religion*, Amsterdam.

Goodman, M.D. & Holladay, A.J. 1986, 'Religious scruples in ancient warfare' *CQ* 36: 151–71.

Gordon, R. 1999, '"What's in a list?" Listing in Greek and Graeco-Roman malign magical texts' in Jordan, D.R., Montgomery, H. & Thomassen, E. (eds) *The World of Ancient Magic*, Bergen.

Graf, F. 2000, 'The rite of the Argei – once again' *MH* 57: 94–103.

Harmon, D.P. 1978, 'The public festivals of Rome' *ANRW* II.16.2: 1440–68.

Kragelund, P. 2001, 'Dreams, religion and politics in Republican Rome' *Historia* 50: 53–95.

Liebeschuetz, J.H.W.G. 1979, *Continuity and Change in Roman Religion*, Oxford.

Linderski, J. 1986, 'The augural law' *ANRW* II.16.3: 2146–312.

Lindsay, H. 2000, 'Death-pollution and funerals in the city of Rome' in Hope, V.M. & Marshall, E. (eds) *Death and Disease in the Ancient City*, London: 152–73.

North, J.A. 1976, 'Conservatism and change in Roman religion' *PBSR* 44: 1–12.

North, J.A. 1979, 'Religious toleration in Republican Rome' *PCPhS* 205: 85–103.

North, J.A. 1980, 'Novelty and choice in Roman religion' *JRS* 70: 186–91.

North, J.A. 1989, 'Religion in Republican Rome' in *CAH* VII.2²: 573–624.

North, J.A. 1990, 'Diviners and divination at Rome' in Beard, M. & North, J. (eds) *Pagan Priests. Religion and Power in the Ancient World*, London: 51–71.

North, J.A. 1995, 'Religion and rusticity' in Cornell, T.J. & Lomas, K. (eds) *Urban Society in Roman Italy*, London: 135–50.

North, J.A. 2000, *Roman Religion*, Oxford.

Orlin, E.M. 1997, *Temples, Religion and Politics in the Roman Republic*, Leiden.

Parke, H.W. 1988, *Sibyls and Sibylline Prophecy in Classical Antiquity*, London.

Rawson, E. 1991, 'Religion and politics in the late second century BC at Rome' in Rawson, E. *Roman Culture and Society*, Oxford: 149–68 = 1974, *Phoenix* 28: 193–212.

Rüpke, J. 2004, 'Roman religion' in Flower, H.I. (ed.) *The Cambridge Companion to the Roman Republic*, Cambridge: 179–95.

Scheid, J. 1992, 'The religious roles of Roman women' in Schmitt Pantel, P. (ed.) *A History of Women*, vol. I. *From Ancient Goddesses to Christian Saints*, Cambridge, MA: 377–408.

Scheid, J. 2003, *An Introduction to Roman Religion*, Edinburgh.

Stambaugh, J.E. 1978, 'The functions of Roman temples' *ANRW* II.16.1: 554–608.

Takács, S.A. 2000, 'Politics and religion in the Bacchanalian affair of 186 BCE' *HSCPh* 100: 301–10.

Turcan, R. 1996, *The Cults of the Roman Empire*, Oxford.

Turcan, R. 2000, *The Gods of Ancient Rome*, Edinburgh.

Walsh, P.G. 1996, 'Making a drama out of a crisis: Livy on the Bacchanalia' *G&R* 43: 188–203.

Wiedemann, T. 1986, 'The *fetiales*: a reconsideration' *CQ* 36: 478–90.

Wildfang, R.L. 2001, 'The Vestals and annual public rites' *C&M* 52: 223–55.

Witt, R.E. 1997, *Isis in the Ancient World*, London (a republication of 1971, *Isis in the Greco-Roman World*, London).

CHAPTER FOUR: THE PUNIC WARS: ROME AGAINST CARTHAGE

Astin, A.E. 1967, 'Saguntum and the origins of the Second Punic War' *Latomus* 26: 577–96.

Astin, A.E. 1978, *Cato the Censor*, Oxford.

Bagnall, N. 1990, *The Punic Wars. Rome, Carthage and the Struggle for the Mediterranean*, London.

Bagnall, N. 2002, *The Punic Wars 264–146 BC*, Oxford.

Bernstein, A.H. 1994, 'The strategy of a warrior-state: Rome and the wars against Carthage, 264–201 BC' in Murray, W., Knox, M. & Bernstein, A. (eds) *The Making of Strategy. Rulers, States, and War*, Cambridge: 56–84.

Briscoe, J. 1989, 'The Second Punic War' in *CAH* VII.2²: 44–80.

Caven, B. 1980, *The Punic Wars*, London.

Cornell, T.J., Rankov, B. & Sabin, P. (eds) 1996, *The Second Punic War. A Reappraisal*, London.

Daly, G. 2002, *Cannae. The Experience of Battle in the Second Punic War*, London.

Dorey, T.A. & Dudley, D.R. 1971, *Rome Against Carthage*, London.

Eckstein, A.M. 1982, 'Human sacrifice and fear of military disaster in Republican Rome' *AJAH* 7: 69–95.

Eckstein, A.M. 1987, *Senate and General. Individual Decision Making and Roman Foreign Relations 264–194*, Berkeley.

Edwards, J. 2001, 'The irony of Hannibal's elephants' *Latomus* 60: 900–5.

Erdkamp, P. 1992, 'Polybius, Livy and the "Fabian Strategy"' *AncSoc* 23: 127–47.

Erskine, A. 1993, 'Hannibal and the freedom of the Italians' *Hermes* 121: 58–62.

Goldsworthy, A. 2000, *The Punic Wars*, London.

Goldsworthy, A. 2001, *Cannae*, London.

Harris, W.V. 1979, *War and Imperialism in Republican Rome, 327–70 BC*, Oxford.

Hoyos, B.D. 1983, 'Hannibal: what kind of genius?' *G&R* 30: 171–80.

Hoyos, D. 1994, 'Barcid "proconsuls" and Punic politics, 237–218 BC' *RhM* 137: 246–74.

Hoyos, D. 2003, *Hannibal's Dynasty. Power and Politics in the Western Mediterranean*, London.

Hoyos, D. (ed.) 2011, *A Companion to the Punic Wars*, Malden, MA.

Khader, A. & Soren, D. (eds) 1987, *Carthage: A Mosaic of Ancient Tunisia*, New York.

Lancell, S. 1995, *Carthage. A History*, Oxford.

Lancell, S. 1998, *Hannibal*, Oxford.

Lazenby, J.F. 1978, *Hannibal's War. A Military History of the Second Punic War*, London.

Lazenby, J.F. 1996, *The First Punic War. A Military History*, London.

Lazenby, J.F. 2004, 'Rome and Carthage' in Flower, H.I. (ed.) *The Cambridge Companion to the Roman Republic*, Cambridge: 225–41.

Palmer, R.E.A. 1997, *Rome and Carthage at Peace*, Stuttgart.

Peddie, J. 1997, *Hannibal's War*, Stroud.

Picard, G.C. & Picard, C. 1987, *Carthage*, second edition, London.

Rich, J. 1996, 'The origins of the Second Punic War' in Cornell, Rankov & Sabin 1996: 1–37.

Richardson, J.S. 1986, *Hispaniae. Spain and the Development of Roman Imperialism, 218–82 BC*, Cambridge.

Ridley, R.T. 1986, 'To be taken with a pinch of salt: the destruction of Carthage' *CPh* 81: 140–46.

Ridley, R.T. 2000, 'Livy and the Hannibalic war' in Bruun, C. (ed.) *The Roman Middle Republic. Politics, Religion, and Historiography c. 400–133 BC*, Rome: 13–40.

Samuels, M. 1990, 'The reality of Cannae' *Militärgeschichtliche Mitteilungen* 47: 7–29.

Scullard, H.H. 1970, *Scipio Africanus, Soldier and Politician*, London.

Scullard, H.H. 1989, 'Carthage and Rome' in *CAH* VII.2²: 486–569.

Scullard, H.H. 1989a, 'The Carthaginians in Spain' in *CAH* VIII²: 17–43.

Shean, J.F. 1996, 'Hannibal's mules: the logistical limitations of Hannibal's army and the Battle of Cannae, 216 BC' *Historia* 45: 141–87.

Smith, P.J. 1993, *Scipio Africanus and Rome's Invasion of Africa. A Historical Commentary on Titus Livius, Book XXIX*, Amsterdam.

Steinby, C. 2000, 'The Roman boarding-bridge in the First Punic War: a study of Roman tactics and strategy' *Arctos* 34: 193–210.

Walbank, F.W. 1967–79, *A Historical Commentary on Polybius*, vol. I, Oxford.

Wise, T. & Healy, M. 1999, *Hannibal's War with Rome. The Armies and Campaigns, 216 BC*, Oxford.

CHAPTER FIVE: ROME'S MEDITERRANEAN EMPIRE

Adams, C.E.P. 2001, 'Feeding the wolf: logistics and the Roman army' *JRA* 14: 465–72.

Astin, A.E. 1967, *Scipio Aemilianus*, Oxford.

Astin, A.E. 1989, 'Roman government and politics, 200–134 BC' in *CAH* VIII²: 163–96.

Astin, A.E. 1989a, 'Sources' in *CAH* VIII²: 1–16.

BIBLIOGRAPHY

Badian, E. 1968, *Roman Imperialism in the Late Republic*, second edition, Ithaca.

Badian, E. 1970, *Titus Quinctius Flamininus. Philhellenism and Realpolitik*, Cincinnati.

Balsdon, J.P.V.D. 1967, 'T. Quinctius Flamininus' *Phoenix* 21: 177–90.

Bishop, M.C. & Coulston, J.C.N. 1993, *Roman Military Equipment from the Punic Wars to the Fall of Rome*, London.

Carrié, J.-M. 1993, 'The Soldier' in Giardina, A. (ed.) *The Romans*, Chicago: 100–37.

Connolly, P. 1989, 'The early Roman army' in Hackett, J. (ed.) *Warfare in the Ancient World*, London: 136–48.

Connolly, P. 1989a, 'The Roman army in the age of Polybius' in Hackett, J. (ed.) *Warfare in the Ancient World*, London: 149–68.

Connolly, P. 1997, 'Pilum, gladius and pugio in the late Republic' *JRMES* 8: 41–57.

Couston, J.C.N. 1998, 'How to arm a Roman soldier' in Austin, M., Harries, J. & Smith, C. (eds) *Modus Operandi. Essays in Honour of Geoffrey Rickman*, London: 167–90.

Crawford, M.H. 1978, 'Greek intellectuals and the Roman aristocracy in the first century BC' in Garnsey, P.D.A. & Whittaker, C.R. (eds) *Imperialism in the Ancient World*, Cambridge: 193–207, 330–38.

Curchin, L.A. 1991, *Roman Spain: Conquest and Assimilation*, Routledge.

Derow, P.S. 1979, 'Polybius, Rome and the East' *JRS* 69: 1–15.

Derow, P.S. 1989, 'Rome, the fall of Macedon and the sack of Corinth' in *CAH* VIII²: 290–323.

Eckstein, A.M. 1987, *Senate and General. Individual Decision Making and Roman Foreign Relations 264–194*, Berkeley.

Eckstein, A.M. 2006, *Mediterranean Anarchy, Interstate War, and the Rise of Rome*, Berkeley.

Erdkamp, P. 1998, *Hunger and the Sword. Warfare and Food Supply in Roman Republican Wars (264–30 BC)*, Amsterdam.

Errington, R.M. 1989, 'Rome against Philip and Antiochus' in *CAH* VIII²: 244–89.

Erskine, A. 2010, *Roman Imperialism*, Edinburgh.

Gabba, E. 1976, *Republican Rome, the Army and the Allies*, Oxford.

Gilliver, C.M. 1999, *The Roman Art of War*, Stroud.

Goldsworthy, A.K. 1996, *The Roman Army at War, 100 BC–AD 200*, Oxford.

Goldsworthy, A.K. 2000, *Roman Warfare*, London.

Gruen, E.S. 1984, 'Material rewards and the drive for empire' in Harris, W.V. (ed.) *The Imperialism of Mid-Republican Rome*, Rome: 59–82.

Gruen, E.S. 1986, *The Hellenistic World and the Coming of Rome*, Berkeley.

Habicht, C. 1989, 'The Seleucids and their rivals' in *CAH* VIII²: 324–87.

Hanson, V.D. 1995, 'From phalanx to legion 350–250 BC' in Parker, G. (ed.) *The Cambridge Illustrated History of Warfare. The Triumph of the West*, Cambridge: 32–49.

Harris, W.V. 1979, *War and Imperialism in Republican Rome 327–70 BC*, Oxford.

Harris, W.V. 1989, 'Roman expansion in the West' in *CAH* VIII²: 107–62.

Keay, S. 2001, 'Romanization and the Hispaniae' in Keay, S. & Terrenato, N. (eds) *Italy and the West. Comparative Issues in Romanization*, Oxford: 115–44.

Keppie, L. 1989, 'The Roman army of the later Republic' in Hackett, J. (ed.) *Warfare in the Ancient World*, London: 169–91.

Lintott, A.W. 1993, *Imperium Romanum. Politics and Administration*, London & New York.

MacMullen, R. 1991, 'Hellenizing the Romans (2nd Century BC)' *Historia* 40: 419–38.

McColl, J.B. 2002, *The Cavalry of the Roman Republic*, London.

North, J.A. 1981, 'The development of Roman imperialism' *JRS* 71: 1–9.

Pollitt, J.J. 1978, 'The impact of Greek art on Rome' *TAPhA* 108: 155–74.

Potter, D. 2004, 'The Roman army and navy' in Flower, H.I. (ed.) *The Cambridge Companion to the Roman Republic*, Cambridge: 66–88.

Richardson, J.S. 1976, *Roman Provincial Administration*, Basingstoke.

Richardson, J.S. 1986, *Hispaniae. Spain and the Development of Roman Imperialism, 218–82 BC*, Cambridge.

Richardson, J.S. 2000, *Appian. Wars of the Romans in Iberia*, Warminster.

Rosenstein, N. 2004, *Rome and War. Farms, Families and Death in the Middle Republic*, Chapel Hill and London.

Roth, J.P. 1999, *The Logistics of the Roman Army at War (264 BC–AD 235)*, Leiden.

Roth, J.P. 2009, *Roman Warfare*, Cambridge.

Sabin, P. 2000, 'The face of Roman battle' *JRS* 90: 1–17.

Sabin, P.,van Wees, H. & Whitby, M. (eds) 2007, *The Cambridge History of Greek and Roman Warfare*, 2 vols, Cambridge.

Saunders, C. 1944, 'The nature of Rome's early appraisal of Greek culture' *CPh* 39: 209–17.

Scullard, H.H. 1973, *Roman Politics, 220–150 BC*, second edition, Oxford.

Sherwin-White, A.N. 1984, *Roman Foreign Policy in the East 168 BC to AD 1*, London.

Stephenson, I.P. 1997, 'Roman Republican training equipment: form, function and the mock battle' *JRMES* 8: 311–15.

Vishnia, R.F. 1996, *State, Society and Popular Leaders in Mid-Republican Rome 214–167 BC*, London.

Wallace-Hadrill, A. 1998, 'To be Roman, go Greek: thoughts on Hellenization at Rome' in Austin, M., Harries, J. & Smith, C. (eds) *Modus Operandi. Essays in Honour of Geoffrey Rickman*, London: 79–91.

Walsh, J.J. 1996, 'Flamininus and the propaganda of liberation' *Historia* 45: 344–63.

Zhmodikov, A. 2000, 'Roman Republican heavy infantrymen in battle (IV–II centuries BC)' *Historia* 49: 67–78.

CHAPTER SIX: SLAVES AND FREEDMEN

Astin, A.E. 1978, *Cato the Censor*, Oxford.

Balsdon, J.P.V.D. 1979, *Romans and Aliens*, London.

Bradley, K.R. 1979, 'Holidays for slaves' *SO* 54: 111–18.

Bradley, K.R. 1985, 'The early development of slavery at Rome' *Historical Reflections/ Réflexions Historiques* 12: 1–8.

Bradley, K.R. 1987, *Slaves and Masters in the Roman Empire. A Study in Social Control*, New York.

Bradley, K.R. 1989, *Slavery and Rebellion in the Roman World, 140 BC–70 BC*, Indiana.

Bradley, K. 1992, '"The regular, daily traffic in slaves": Roman history and contemporary history' *CJ* 87: 125–38.

Bradley, K.R. 1994, *Slavery and Society at Rome*, Cambridge.

Dalby, A. 1998, *Cato. On Farming. De Agricultura*, Devon.

Finley, M.I. 1980, *Ancient Slavery and Modern Ideology*, Harmondsworth.

Finley, M.I. 1987, *Classical Slavery*, London.

Forrest, W.G. & Stinton 1962, 'The First Sicilian Slave War' *P&P* 22: 87–92.

Green, P. 1961, 'The First Sicilian Slave War' *P&P* 20: 10–29.

Harris, W.V. 1980, 'Towards a study of the Roman slave trade' *MAAR* 36: 117–40.

Hopkins, K. 1978, *Conquerors and Slaves*, Cambridge.

Jones, A.H.M. 1960, 'Slavery in the Ancient World' in Finley, M.I. (ed.) *Slavery in Classical Antiquity. Views and Controversies*, Cambridge: 1–15 = 1956, *The Economic History Review* 9: 185–99.

Jongman, W. 2003, 'Slavery and the growth of Rome: the transformation of Italy in the second and first centuries BCE' in Edwards, C. & Woolf, G. (eds) *Rome the Cosmopolis*, Cambridge: 100–22.

Konstan, D. 1975, 'Marxism and Roman slavery' *Arethusa* 8: 145–69.

Libourel, J.M. 1973, 'Galley slaves in the Second Punic War' *CPh* 68: 116–19.

Lintott, A. 1999, *Violence in Republican Rome*, second edition, Oxford.

McCarthy, K. 2000, *Slaves, Masters, and the Art of Authority in Plautine Comedy*, Princeton.

McDermott, W.C. 1972, 'M. Cicero and M. Tiro' *Historia* 21: 259–86.

Millar, F. 1995, 'The Roman *libertus* and civic freedom' *Arethusa* 28: 99–105.

Parker, H. 1998, 'Loyal slaves and loyal wives; the crisis of the outsider-within and Roman *exemplum* literature' in Joshel, S.R. & Murnaghan, S. (eds) *Women and Slaves in Greco-Roman Culture*, London: 152–73.

Rathbone, D.W. 1983, 'The slave mode of production in Italy' *JRS* 73: 160–68.

Raymer, A.J. 1940/1, 'Slavery – the Graeco-Roman defence' *G&R* 10: 17–21.

Rei, A. 1998, 'Villains, wives and slaves in the comedies of Plautus' in Joshel, S.R. & Murnaghan, S. (eds) *Women and Slaves in Greco-Roman Culture*, London: 92–108.

Rubinsohn, Z.W. 1982, 'Some remarks on the causes and repercussions of the so-called "Second Slave Revolt" in Sicily' *Athenaeum* 60: 436–51.

Shaw, B.D. 2001, *Spartacus and the Slave Wars. A Brief History with Documents*, Boston.

Taylor, L.R. 1961, 'Freedmen and freeborn in the epitaphs of imperial Rome' *AJPh* 82: 113–32.

Thalmann, W.G. 1996, 'Versions of slavery in the *Captivi* of Plautus' *Ramus* 25: 112–49.

Thébert, Y. 1993, 'The slave' in Giardina, A. (ed.) *The Romans*, Chicago: 138–74.

Thompson, F.H. 2003, *The Archaeology of Greek and Roman Slavery*, London.

Treggiari, S.M. 1969, *Roman Freedmen during the Late Republic*, Oxford.

Vogt, J. 1974, *Ancient Slavery and the Ideal of Man*, Oxford.

Watson, A. 1987, *Roman Slave Law*, Baltimore.

Wiedemann, T.E.J. 1981, *Greek and Roman Slavery*, London.

Wiedemann, T.E.J. 1985, 'The regularity of manumission at Rome' *CQ* 35: 162–75.

Wiedemann, T.E.J. 1997, *Slavery: Greece and Rome*, revised edition, Oxford.

Yavetz, Z. 1988, *Slaves and Slavery in Ancient Rome*, New Brunswick.

Ziolkowski, A. 1986, 'The plundering of Epirus in 167 BC: economic considerations' *PBSR* 54: 69–80.

CHAPTER SEVEN: WOMEN, SEXUALITY AND THE FAMILY

Bauman, R.A. 1992, *Women and Politics in Ancient Rome*, London.

Beard, M. 1980, 'The sexual status of vestal virgins' *JRS* 70: 12–27.

Beard, M. 1990, 'Priesthood in the Roman Republic' in Beard, M. & North, J. (eds) *Pagan Priests. Religion and Power in the Ancient World*, London: 19–48.

Beard, M. 1995, 'Re-reading (Vestal) virginity' in Hawley, R. & Levick, B. (eds) *Women in Antiquity. New Assessments*, London: 166–77.

Champlin, E. 1991, *Final Judgements. Duty and Emotion in Roman Wills 200 BC–AD 250*, Berkeley.

Clark, G. 1981, 'Roman women' *G&R* 28: 193–212.

Clarke, J.R. 1998, *Looking at Lovemaking. Constructions of Sexuality in Roman Art 100 BC–AD 250*, Berkeley.

BIBLIOGRAPHY

Crook, J.A. 1967, 'Patria potestas' *CQ* 17: 113–22.

Crook, J.A. 1986, 'Women in Roman succession' in Rawson, B. (ed.) *The Family in Ancient Rome. New Perspectives*, London: 59–82.

Dixon, S. 1983, 'A family business: women's role in patronage and politics at Rome 80–44 BC' *C&M* 34: 91–112.

Dixon, S. 1985, 'Polybius on Roman women and property' *AJPh* 196: 147–70.

Dixon, S. 1985a, 'The marriage alliance in the Roman elite' *Journal of Family History* 10: 353–78.

Dixon, S. 1988, *The Roman Mother*, London.

Dixon, S. 1992, *The Roman Family*, Baltimore.

Dixon, S. 2001, *Reading Roman Women. Sources, Genres and Real Life*, London.

Dixon, S. (ed.) 2001a, *Childhood, Class and Kin in the Roman World*, London.

Fantham, E. 1991, '*Stuprum*: public attitudes and penalties for sexual offences in Republican Rome' *EMC/CV* 10: 267–91.

Fantham, E. et al. (eds) 1994, *Women in the Classical World. Image and Text*, Oxford.

Gardner, J.F. 1986, *Women in Roman Law and Society*, London.

Gardner, J.F. 1998, *Family and Familia in Roman Law and Life*, Oxford.

Gardner, J.F. 1999, 'Status, sentiment and strategy in Roman adoption' in Corbier, M. (ed.) *Adoption et fosterage*, Paris: 63–80.

Golden, M. 1992, 'Continuity, change and the study of ancient childhood' *EMC/CV* 11: 7–18.

Hales, S. 2000, 'At home with Cicero' *G&R* 47: 44–55.

Hallett, J.P. 1984, *Fathers and Daughters in Roman Society. Women and the Elite Family*, Princeton.

Hallett, J.P. & Skinner, M.B. (eds) 1997, *Roman Sexualities*, Princeton.

Harlow, M. & Laurence, R. 2002, *Growing Up and Growing Old in Ancient Rome. A Life Course Approach*, London.

Harris, W.V. 1986, 'The Roman father's power of life and death' in Bagnall, R.S. & Harris, W.V. (eds) *Studies in Roman Law*, Leiden: 81–95.

Harris, W.V. 1994, 'Child-exposure in the Roman Empire' *JRS* 84: 1–22.

Hemelrijk, E.A. 1999, *Matrona Docta. Educated Women in the Roman Elite from Cornelia to Julia Domna*, London.

Hillard, T.W. 1993, 'On the stage, behind the curtain: images of politically active women in the Late Roman Republic' in Garlick, B., Dixon, S. & Allen, P. (eds) *Stereotypes of Women in Power. Historical Perspectives and Revisionist Views*, New York: 37–64.

James, S.L. 2003, *Learned Girls and Male Persuasion. Gender and Reading in Roman Love Elegy*, Berkeley.

Joshel, S.R. & Murnaghan, S. (eds) 1998, *Women and Slaves in Greco-Roman Culture. Differential Equations*, London.

Kertzer, D.I. & Saller, R.P. 1991, *The Family in Italy from Antiquity to the Present*, New Haven.

Kleiner, D.E.E. & Matheson, S.B. 1996, *I Claudia. Women in Ancient Rome*, New Haven.

Lefkowitz, M.R. & Fant, M.B. 1992, *Women's Life in Greece and Rome*, second edition, Baltimore.

McGinn, T.A.J. 1998, *Prostitution, Sexuality and the Law in Ancient Rome*, Oxford.

Plant, I.M. 2004, *Women Writers of Ancient Greece and Rome. An Anthology*, London.

Pomeroy, S.B. 1975, *Goddesses, Whores, Wives, and Slaves. Women in Classical Antiquity*, London.

Ramage, E.S. 1994, 'The so-called Laudatio Turiae as panegyric' *Athenaeum* 82: 341–70.

Rawson, B. (ed.) 1986, *The Family in Ancient Rome. New Perspectives*, London.

BIBLIOGRAPHY

Rawson, B. (ed.) 1991, *Marriage, Divorce and Children in Ancient Rome*, Oxford.

Rawson, B. 2003, *Children and Childhood in Roman Italy*, Oxford.

Rawson, B. & Weaver, P. (eds) 1997, *The Roman Family in Italy. Status, Sentiment, Space*, Canberra.

Richlin, A. 1993, 'Not before homosexuality: the materiality of the *cinaedus* and the Roman law against love between men' *Journal of the History of Sexuality* 3: 523–73.

Saller, R.P. 1986, '*Patria potestas* and the stereotype of the Roman family' *Continuity and Change* 1: 7–22.

Saller, R.P. 1999, 'Pater familias, mater familias and the gendered semantics of the Roman household' *CPh* 94: 182–97.

Scheid, J. 1992, 'The religious roles of Roman women' in Schmitt Pantel, P. (ed.) *A History of Women*, vol. I. *From Ancient Goddesses to Christian Saints*, Cambridge, MA: 377–408.

Sebesta, J.L. 1994, 'Symbolism in the costume of the Roman woman' in Sebesta, J.L. & Bonfante, L. (eds) *The World of Roman Costume*, Wisconsin: 46–53.

Shaw, B.D. 1987, 'The age of Roman girls at marriage: some reconsiderations' *JRS* 77: 30–46.

Shaw, B.D. 2001, 'Raising and killing children: two Roman myths' *Mnemosyne* 54: 33–77.

Staples, A. 1998, *From Good Goddess to Vestal Virgin. Sex and Category in Roman Religion*, London.

Tatum, W.J. 1990, 'Cicero and the *Bona Dea* scandal' *CPh* 85: 202–8.

Treggiari, S. 1991, *Roman Marriage. Iusti Coniuges from the time of Cicero to the Time of Ulpian*, Oxford.

Treggiari, S. 1999, 'The upper-class house as a symbol and focus of emotion in Cicero' *JRA* 12: 33–56.

Treggiari, S. 2002, *Roman Social History*, London.

Wildfang, R.L. 2001, 'The Vestals and annual public rites' *C&M* 52: 223–55.

Williams, C.A. 1999, *Roman Homosexuality. Ideologies of Masculinity in Classical Antiquity*, Oxford.

CHAPTER EIGHT: TIBERIUS AND GAIUS GRACCHUS

Adshead, K. 1981, 'Further inspiration for Tiberius Gracchus?' *Antichthon* 15: 118–28.

Astin, A.E. 1967, *Scipio Aemilianus*, Oxford.

Badian, E. 1969, 'From the Gracchi to Sulla (1940–1959)' in Seager 1969: 3–51 = 1962, *Historia* 11: 197–245.

Badian, E. 1972, 'Tiberius Gracchus and the beginning of the Roman Revolution' *ANRW* I.1: 668–731.

Balsdon, J.P.V.D. 1969, 'The history of the extortion court at Rome, 123–70 BC' in Seager 1969: 132–48 = 1938, *PBSR* 14: 98–114.

Bernstein, A.H. 1978, *Tiberius Sempronius Gracchus. Tradition and Apostasy*, Ithaca.

Boren, H.C. 1958, 'Numismatic light on the Gracchan crisis' *AJPh* 79: 14–55.

Boren, H.C. 1961, 'Tiberius Gracchus: the opposition view' *AJPh* 82: 140–55.

Boren, H.C. 1968, *The Gracchi*, New York.

Boren, H.C. 1969, 'The urban side of the Gracchan economic crisis' in Seager 1969: 54–68 = 1957/8, *AHR* 6: 890–902.

Briscoe, J. 1974, 'Supporters and opponents of Tiberius Gracchus' *JRS* 64: 125–35.

Brunt, P.A. 1971, *Social Conflicts in the Roman Republic*, London.

Brunt, P.A. 1988, 'The army and the land in the Roman Revolution' in Brunt, P.A. *The Fall of the Roman Republic and Related Essays*, Oxford: 240–75; revision of 1962, *JRS* 52: 69–86.

Brunt, P.A. 1988a, 'The equites in the Late Republic' in Brunt, P.A. *The Fall of the Roman Republic and Related Essays*, Oxford: 144–93, revision of 1962, *Trade and Politics in the Ancient World* 1: 117–49 = in Seager 1969: 83–115.

Earl, D.C. 1963, *Tiberius Gracchus. A Study in Politics*, Brussels.

Garnsey, P. & Rathbone, D. 1985, 'The background to the grain law of Gaius Gracchus' *JRS* 75: 20–25.

Gruen, E.S. 1968, *Roman Politics and the Criminal Courts, 149–78 BC*, Cambridge, MA.

Hall, U. 1977, 'Notes on M. Fulvius Flaccus' *Athenaeum* 55: 280–88.

Henderson, M.I. 1951, 'The process "de repetundis"' *JRS* 41: 71–88.

Henderson, M.I. 1969, 'The establishment of the *equester ordo*' in Seager 1969: 69–80 = 1963, *JRS* 53: 61–72.

Horsfall, N. 1987, 'The "letter of Cornelia": yet more problems' *Athenaeum* 65: 231–4.

Keaveney, A. 2003, 'The tragedy of Caius Gracchus: ancient melodrama or modern farce?' *Klio* 85: 322–32.

Linderski, J. 2002, 'The pontiff and the tribune: the death of Tiberius Gracchus' *Athenaeum* 80: 339–66.

Lintott, A.W. 1981, 'The *leges de repetundis* and associate measures under the Republic' *ZSS* 98: 162–212.

Lintott, A.W. 1992, *Judicial Reform and Land Reform in the Roman Republic*, Cambridge.

Lintott, A.W. 1994, 'Political history, 146–95 BC' in *CAH* IX^2: 40–77.

Lintott, A.W. 1999, *Violence in Republican Rome*, second edition, Oxford.

Morley, N. 2001, 'The transformation of Italy, 225–28 BC' *JRS* 91: 50–62.

Rich, J.W. 1983, 'The supposed Roman manpower shortage of the later second century BC' *Historia* 32: 287–331.

Richardson, J.S. 1980, 'The ownership of Roman land: Tiberius Gracchus and the Italians' *JRS* 70: 1–11.

Riddle, J.M. 1970, *Tiberius Gracchus. Destroyer or Reformer of the Republic?*, Lexington, MA.

Scullard, H.H. 1960, 'Scipio Aemilianus and Roman politics' *JRS* 50: 59–74.

Seager, R. (ed.) 1969, *The Crisis of the Roman Republic*, Cambridge.

Sherwin-White, A.N. 1972, 'The date of the lex repetundarum and its consequences' *JRS* 62: 83–99.

Sherwin-White, A.N. 1973, *The Roman Citizenship*, second edition, Oxford.

Sherwin-White, A.N. 1982, 'The lex repetundarum and the political ideas of Gaius Gracchus' *JRS* 72: 18–31.

Shotter, D. 1994, *The Fall of the Roman Republic*, London.

Stockton, D. 1979, *The Gracchi*, Oxford.

Taylor, L.R. 1962 'The forerunners of the Gracchi' *JRS* 52: 19–27.

White, K.D. 1967, 'Latifundia: a critical review of the evidence on large estates in Italy and Sicily up to the end of the first century AD' *BICS* 14: 62–79.

Williams, P. 2004, 'The Roman tribunate in the "Era of Quiescence" 287–133 BC' *Latomus* 63: 281–94.

CHAPTER NINE: MARIUS AND CHAPTER TEN: THE SOCIAL WAR

Astin, A.E. 1967, *Scipio Aemilianus*, Oxford.

Badian, E. 1969, 'From the Gracchi to Sulla (1940–1959)' in Seager 1969: 3–51 = 1962, *Historia* 11: 197–245.

Badian, E. 1984, 'The death of Saturninus: studies in chronology and prosopography' *Chiron* 14: 101–47.

BIBLIOGRAPHY

Bell, M.J.V. 1965, 'Tactical reform in the Roman Republican army' *Historia* 14: 404–22.

Bishop, M.C. & Coulston, J.C. 1993, *Roman Military Equipment*, London.

Brunt, P.A. 1971, *Social Conflicts in the Roman Republic*, London.

Brunt, P.A. 1988, *The Fall of the Roman Republic and Related Essays*, Oxford.

Brunt, P.A. 1988a, 'Italian aims at the time of the Social War' in Brunt 1988: 93–143; revision of 1965, *JRS* 55: 90–109.

Brunt, P.A. 1988b, 'The army and the land in the Roman Revolution' in Brunt 1988: 240–80; revision of 1962, *JRS* 52: 69–86.

Burns, T.S. 2003, *Rome and the Barbarians, 100 BC–AD 400*, Baltimore.

Cagniart, P.F. 1989, 'L. Cornelius Sulla's quarrel with C. Marius at the time of the Germanic invasions' *Athenaeum* 67: 139–49.

Carney, T.F. 1960, 'Cicero's picture of Marius' *WS* 73: 83–122.

Carney, T.F. 1961, *A Biography of C. Marius*, Assen.

Dench, E. 1995, *From Barbarians to New Men*, Oxford.

Evans, R.J. 1994, *Gaius Marius. A Political Biography*, Pretoria.

Fantham, E. 1987, 'Lucan, his scholia, and the victims of Marius' *AHB* 1: 89–96.

Gabba, E. 1976, *Republican Rome, the Army and the Allies*, Oxford.

Gabba, E. 1994, 'Rome and Italy: the Social War' in *CAH* IX^2: 104–28.

Goldsworthy, A.K. 2000, *Roman Warfare*, London.

Gruen, E.S. 1968, *Roman Politics and the Criminal Courts, 149–78 BC*, Cambridge, MA.

Hands, A.R. 1972, 'Livius Drusus and the courts' *Phoenix* 26: 268–74.

Kallet-Marx, R. 1990, 'The trial of Rutilius Rufus' *Phoenix* 44: 122–39.

Keaveney, A. 1983, 'What happened in 88?' *Eirene* 20: 53–86.

Keaveney, A. 2005, *Sulla. The Last Republican*, second edition, London.

Keaveney, A. 2005a, *Rome and the Unification of Italy*, second edition, Liverpool.

Last, H. 1932, 'The wars of the age of Marius' in *CAH* IX^1: 102–57.

Lintott, A.W. 1971, 'The tribunate of P. Sulpicius Rufus' *CQ* 21: 442–53.

Lintott, A.W. 1994, 'The Roman empire and its problems in the late second century' in *CAH* IX^2: 16–39.

Lintott, A.W. 1994a, 'Political history, 146–95 BC' in *CAH* IX^2: 40–103.

Luce, T.J. 1970, 'Marius and the Mithridatic command' *Historia* 19: 161–94.

Morley, N. 1996, *Metropolis and Hinterland. The City of Rome and the Italian Economy, 200 BC–AD 200*, Cambridge.

Mouritsen, H. 1998, *Italian Unification. A Study in Ancient and Modern Historiography*, London.

Raven, S. 1993, *Rome in Africa*, third edition, London.

Salmon, E.T. 1962, 'The cause of the Social War' *Phoenix* 16: 107–19.

Salmon, E.T. 1967, *Samnium and the Samnites*, Cambridge.

Seager, R. (ed.) 1969, *The Crisis of the Roman Republic. Studies in Political and Social History*, Cambridge.

Sherwin-White, A.N. 1969, 'Violence in Roman politics' in Seager 1969: 151–9 = 1956, *JRS* 46: 1–9.

Sherwin-White, A.N. 1973, *The Roman Citizenship*, second edition, Oxford.

Shotter, D. 1994, *The Fall of the Roman Republic*, London.

Syme, R. 1964, *Sallust*, Berkeley.

Weinrib, E.J. 1970, 'The judiciary law of M. Livius Drusus (tr. pl. 91 BC)' *Historia* 19: 414–43.

BIBLIOGRAPHY

CHAPTER ELEVEN: LUCIUS CORNELIUS SULLA 'FELIX'

Badian, E. 1964, 'Waiting for Sulla' in Badian, E. (ed.) *Studies in Greek and Roman History*, Oxford: 206–34 = 1962, *JRS* 52: 47–61.

Badian, E. 1969, 'From the Gracchi to Sulla' in Seager 1969: 34–9 = 1962, *Historia* 11: 197–245.

Badian, E. 1972, *Publicans and Sinners. Private Enterprise in the Service of the Roman Republic*, Oxford.

Badian, E. 1976, 'Lucius Sulla: the deadly reformer' in Dunstan, A.J. (ed.) *Essays on Roman Culture. The Todd Memorial Lectures*, Toronto: 35–74 = 1970, *Lucius Sulla: the Deadly Reformer*, Sydney.

Baker, G.P. 1967, *Sulla the Fortunate, the Great Dictator*, Rome.

Balsdon, J.P.V.D. 1951, 'Sulla Felix' *JRS* 41: 1–10.

Brennan, T.C. 1992, 'Sulla's career in the nineties: some reconsiderations' *Chiron* 22: 103–58.

Brunt, P.A. 1971, *Social Conflicts in the Roman Republic*, London.

Brunt, P.A. 1990, 'Sulla and the Asian publicans' in Brunt, P.A. (ed.) *Roman Imperial Themes*, Oxford: 1–8 = 1956, *Latomus* 19: 17–25.

Cloud, D. 1994, 'The constitution and public criminal law' in *CAH* IX²: 491–530.

Dowling, M.B. 2000, 'The clemency of Sulla' *Historia* 49: 303–40.

Frier, B.W. 1971, 'Sulla's propaganda: the collapse of the Cinnan Republic' *AJPh* 92: 585–604.

Garton, C. 1964, 'Sulla and the theatre' *Phoenix* 18: 137–56.

Gruen, E.S. 1968, *Roman Politics and the Criminal Courts, 149–78 BC*, Cambridge, MA.

Hill, H. 1932, 'Sulla's new senators in 81 BC' *CQ* 26: 170–77.

Hillard, T.W. 1991, 'Sulla's early fortunes and his reputation' *Antichthon* 25: 63–71.

Hillman, T.P. 1997, 'Pompeius in Africa and Sulla's order to demobilize (Plutarch, *Pompeius* 13, 1–4)' *Latomus* 56: 94–106.

Hind, J. 1994, 'Mithridates' in *CAH* IX²: 129–64.

Katz, B.R. 1975, 'The first fruits of Sulla's march' *AC* 44: 100–25.

Katz, B.R. 1976, 'Studies on the period of Cinna and Sulla' *AC* 45: 497–549.

Katz, B.R. 1976a, 'The siege of Rome in 87 BC' *CPh* 71: 328–36.

Keaveney, A. 1982, 'Sulla augur: coins and the curiate law' *AJAH* 7: 150–71.

Keaveney, A. 1982a, 'Sulla and Italy' *Critica Storica* 19: 499–544.

Keaveney, A. 1982b, 'Young Pompey: 106–79 BC' *AC* 51: 111–39.

Keaveney, A. 1983, 'Studies in the *dominatio Sullae*' *Klio* 65: 185–208.

Keaveney, A. 1983a, 'What happened in 88?' *Eirene* 20: 53–86.

Keaveney, A. 1983b, 'Sulla and the gods' in Deroux, C. (ed.) *Studies in Latin Literature and Roman History*, Brussels: 44–79.

Keaveney, A. 1984, 'Who were the Sullani?' *Klio* 66: 114–50.

Keaveney, A. 1992, *Lucullus. A Life*, London.

Keaveney, A. 2005, *Sulla: the Last Republican*, second edition, London.

Levick, B.M. 1982, 'Sulla's march on Rome in 88 BC' *Historia* 31: 503–8.

Lintott, A.W. 1999, *Violence in Republican Rome*, second edition, Oxford.

Lovano, M. 2002, *The Age of Cinna. Crucible of Late Republican Rome*, Stuttgart.

Mackay, C.S. 2000, 'Sulla and the monuments: studies in his public persona' *Historia* 49: 161–210.

Ramage, E.S. 1991, 'Sulla's propaganda' *Klio* 73: 93–121.

Seager, R. (ed.) 1969, *The Crisis of the Roman Republic. Studies in Political and Social History*, Cambridge.

BIBLIOGRAPHY

Seager, R. 1994, 'Sulla' in *CAH* IX²: 165–207.

Shotter, D. 1994, *The Fall of the Roman Republic*, London.

Stockton, D. 1966, 'Sulla, le monarque malgré lui' in Kagan, D. (ed.) *Problems in Ancient History*, vol. 2. *The Roman World*, first edition, London: 259–66.

Sumi, G.S. 2002, 'Spectacles and Sulla's public image' *Historia* 51: 414–32.

Twyman, B.L. 1976, 'The date of Sulla's abdication and the chronology of the first book of Appian's Civil Wars' *Athenaeum* 54: 271–95.

CHAPTER TWELVE: THE COLLAPSE OF THE REPUBLIC
AND CHAPTER THIRTEEN: CIVIL WAR AND DICTATORSHIP

Astin, A.E. 1968, *Politics and Policies in the Roman Republic*, Belfast.

Balsdon, J.P.V.D. 1967, *Julius Caesar. A Political Biography* (= *Julius Caesar and Rome*), London.

Billows, R.A. 2009, *Julius Caesar. The Colossus of Rome*, London & New York.

Brunt, P.A. 1988, 'The fall of the Roman Republic' in Brunt, P.A. *The Fall of the Roman Republic and Related Essays*, Oxford: 1–92.

Butler, S. 2002, *The Hand of Cicero*, London.

Chauveau, M. 2002, *Cleopatra: Beyond the Myth*, Ithaca.

Clarke, M.L. 1981, *The Noblest Roman. Marcus Brutus and his Reputation*, London.

Collins, J.H. 1972, 'Caesar as political propagandist' *ANRW* I.1: 922–66.

Corbeill, A. 1996, *Controlling Laughter. Political Humour in the Late Roman Republic*, Princeton.

Crawford, M.H. 1989, 'The lex Iulia Agraria' *Athenaeum* 67: 179–90.

Crook, J.A., Lintott, A. & Rawson, E. 1994, 'The fall of the Roman Republic' in *CAH* IX²: 769–76.

Drummond, A. 1999, 'Tribunes and tribunician programmes in 63 BC' *Athenaeum* 87: 121–67.

Ehrhardt, C.T.H.R. 1995, 'Crossing the Rubicon' *Antichthon* 29: 30–41.

Everitt, A. 2001, *Cicero. A Turbulent Life*, London.

Fantham, E. 1975, 'The trials of Gabinius in 54 BC' *Historia* 24: 425–43.

Fuhrmann, M. 1992, *Cicero and the Roman Republic*, Oxford.

Gelzer, M. 1968, *Caesar. Politician and Statesman*, Oxford.

Goldsworthy, A. 2006, *Caesar*, London.

Greenhalgh, P. 1980, *Pompey. The Roman Alexander*, London.

Greenhalgh, P. 1981, *Pompey. The Republican Prince*, London.

Griffin, M. (ed.) 2009, *A Companion to Julius Caesar*, Malden & Oxford.

Gruen, E.S. 1969, 'Notes on the "First Catilinarian Conspiracy"' *CPh* 64: 20–24.

Gruen, E.S. 1995, *The Last Generation of the Roman Republic*, second edition, Berkeley.

Habicht, C. 1990, *Cicero the Politician*, Baltimore.

Hillman, T.P. 1990, 'Pompeius and the senate: 77–71' *Hermes* 118: 444–54.

Hillman, T.P. 1998, 'Notes on the trial of Pompeius at Plutarch, *Pomp.* 4.1–6' *RhM* 141: 176–93.

Holland, T. 2003, *Rubicon. The Triumph and Tragedy of the Roman Republic*, London.

Hoyos, D. 1979, 'Imperial Caesar?' *Ancient Society* 9: 134–57.

Huzar, E.G. 1978, *Mark Antony. A Biography*, Minneapolis.

Jimenez, R.L. 2000, *Caesar against Rome*, Westport, CT.

Kamm, A. 2006, *Julius Caesar. A Life*, London.

Keaveney, A. 2007, *The Army in the Roman Revolution*, London & New York.

Lacey, W.K. 1961, 'The tribunate of Curio' *Historia* 10: 318–29.

Lacey, W.K. 1978, *Cicero and the End of the Roman Republic*, London.

Last, H. & Gardner, R. 1932, 'The breakdown of the Sullan system and the rise of Pompey' in *CAH* IX[1]: 313–49.

Leach, J. 1978, *Pompey the Great*, London.

Levene, D.S. 2000, 'Sallust's Catiline and Cato the Censor' *CQ* 50: 170–91.

Lintott, A.W. 1999, *Violence in Republican Rome*, second edition, Oxford.

Marshall, B.A. 1976, *Crassus. A Political Biography*, Amsterdam.

Meier, C. 1995, *Caesar. A Biography*, New York.

Millar, F. 1995, 'The last century of the Republic: whose history?' *JRS* 85: 236–43.

Millar, F. 1998, *The Crowd in Rome in the Late Republic*, Michigan.

Mitchell, T.N. 1979, *Cicero. The Ascending Years*, New Haven.

Mitchell, T.N. 1991, *Cicero. The Senior Statesman*, New Haven.

Morgan, L. 1997, '"Levi quidem de re . . . ": Julius Caesar as tyrant and pedant' *JRS* 87: 23–40.

Mouritsen, H. 2001, *Plebs and Politics in the Late Roman Republic*, Cambridge.

Murphy, J. 1993, 'Pompey's eastern acta' *AHB* 7: 136–42.

Patterson, J.R. 2000, *Political Life in the City of Rome*, Bristol.

Powell, A. 1998, 'Julius Caesar and the presentation of massacre' in Welch, K. & Powell, A. (eds) *Julius Caesar as Artful Reporter. The War Commentaries as Political Instruments*, London: 111–38.

Raditsa, L. 1973, 'Julius Caesar and his writings' *ANRW* I.3: 417–56.

Ramage, E.S. 2001, 'The *bellum iustum* in Caesar's *de Bello Gallico*' *Athenaeum* 89: 145–70.

Ramage, E.S. 2002, 'The *Populus Romanus*, imperium, and Caesar's presence in the *De Bello Gallico*' *Athenaeum* 90: 125–46.

Rawson, E. 1983, *Cicero. A Portrait*, London.

Rawson, E. 1994, 'Caesar: civil war and dictatorship' in *CAH* IX[2]: 424–67.

Ridley, R.T. 1999, 'What's in the name: the so-called First Triumvirate' *Arctos* 33: 133–44.

Seager, R. 1964, 'The First Catilinarian Conspiracy' *Historia* 13: 338–47.

Seager, R. 1965, 'Clodius, Pompeius and the exile of Cicero' *Latomus* 24: 519–31.

Seager, R. (ed.) 1969, *The Crisis of the Roman Republic*, Cambridge.

Seager, R. 1994, 'The rise of Pompey' in *CAH* IX[2]: 208–28.

Seager, R. 2002, *Pompey the Great. A Political Biography*, second edition, Oxford.

Sherwin-White, A.N. 1969, 'Violence in Roman politics' in Seager 1969: 151–9.

Sherwin-White, A.N. 1994, 'Lucullus, Pompey and the East' in *CAH* IX[2]: 229–73.

Shotter, D. 1994, *The Fall of the Roman Republic*, London.

Southern, P. 2001, *Julius Caesar*, Stroud.

Southern, P. 2002, *Pompey*, Stroud.

Stockton, D. 1971, *Cicero. A Political Biography*, Oxford.

Syme, R. 1939, *The Roman Revolution*, Oxford.

Syme, R. 1979, 'A Roman post-mortem: an inquest on the fall of the Roman Republic' in Badian, E. (ed.) *Ronald Syme. Roman Papers*, Oxford, vol. I: 205–17.

Tatum, W.J. 1999, *The Patrician Tribune. Publius Clodius Pulcher*, Chapel Hill.

Tatum, W.J. 2008, *Always I am Caesar*, Oxford & Maldon, MA.

Taylor, L.R. 1949, *Party Politics in the Age of Caesar*, Berkeley.

Townend, G.B. 1983, 'A clue to Caesar's unfulfilled intentions' *Latomus* 42: 601–6.

Ward, A.M. 1972, 'Cicero's fight against Crassus and Caesar in 65 and 63 BC' *Historia* 21: 244–58.

Ward, A.M. 1977, *Marcus Crassus and the Late Roman Republic*, Columbia.

Weinstock, S. 1971, *Divus Julius*, Oxford.

White, P. 1997, 'Julius Caesar and the publication of *acta* in late Republican Rome' *Chiron* 27: 73–84.

Wiseman, T.P. (ed.) 1985, *Roman Political Life 90 BC–AD 69*, Exeter.

Wiseman, T.P. 1994, 'The senate and the *populares*, 69–60 BC' in *CAH* IX²: 327–67.

Wiseman, T.P. 1994a, 'Caesar, Pompey and Rome, 59–50 BC' in *CAH* IX²: 368–423.

Wyke, M. 2006, *Julius Caesar in Western Culture*, Malden, MA.

Yavetz, Z. 1983, *Julius Caesar and his Public Image*, London.

CHAPTER FOURTEEN: OCTAVIAN'S RISE TO POWER AND CHAPTER FIFTEEN: THE AGE OF AUGUSTUS

Anderson, R.D., Parsons, P.J. & Nisbet, R.G.M. 1979, 'Elegiacs by Gallus from Qasr Ibrim', *JRS* 69: 125–55.

Barrett, A.A. 2004, *Livia. First Lady of Imperial Rome*, New Haven.

Breed, B., Damon, C. & Rossi, A. (eds) 2010, *Citizens of Discord. Rome and its Civil Wars*, Amherst.

Brenk, F.E. 1992, 'Antony–Osiris, Cleopatra–Isis, the end of Plutarch's Antony' in Stadter, P.A. (ed.) *Plutarch and the Historical Tradition*, London & New York: 159–82.

Brunt, P.A. 1984, 'The role of the senate in the Augustan regime' *CQ* 34.2: 423–44.

Carter, J.M. 1970, *The Battle of Actium. The Rise and Triumph of Augustus Caesar*, New York.

Carter, J. 1982, *Suetonius' Life of Augustus*, London.

Charlesworth, M. 1933, 'Some fragments of the propaganda of Mark Antony' *CQ* 27: 172–7.

Chauveau, M. 2002, *Cleopatra. Beyond the Myth*, Ithaca.

Clarke, M.L. 1981, *The Noblest Roman. Marcus Brutus and his Reputation*, London.

Cooley, A.E. 2000, 'Inscribing history at Rome' in Cooley, A.E. (ed.) *The Afterlife of Inscriptions. Reusing, Rediscovering, Reinventing and Revitalising Ancient Inscriptions*, London: 7–20.

Cooley, A.E. 2006, 'Beyond Rome and Latium: Roman religion in the age of Augustus' in Schultz, C. & Harvey, P.B. (eds) *Religion in Republican Italy*, Cambridge: 228–52.

De Ruggiero, P. 2014, *Mark Antony. A Plain Blunt Man*, Barnsley.

Eck, W. 2007, *The Age of Augustus*, second edition, Oxford.

Edmonson, J. 2009, *Augustus*, Edinburgh.

Etman, A. 1992, 'Cleopatra and Egypt in the Augustan poetry' in *Roma e l'Egitto nell'antichità classica, Cairo 6–9, Febbraio 1989. Atti del I Congresso Internazionale Italo-Egiziano*, Rome: 161–75.

Everitt, A. 2006, *The First Emperor. Caesar Augustus and the Triumph of Rome*, Ann Arbor.

Fantham, E. 2006, *Julia Augusti, the Emperor's Daughter*, London & New York.

Favro, D. 1996, *The Urban Image of Augustan Rome*, Cambridge.

Flower, H.I. 2000, 'The tradition of the *spolia opima*: M. Claudius Marcellus and Augustus' *ClAnt* 19: 34–59.

Galinsky, K. 1996, *Augustan Culture. An Interpretative Introduction*, Princeton.

Galinsky, K. (ed.) 2007, *The Cambridge Companion to the Age of Augustus*, Cambridge.

Galinsky, K. 2012, *Augustus. Introduction to the Life of an Emperor*, Cambridge.

Garnsey, P. 1982, *The Early Principate. Augustus to Trajan*, Oxford.

Goldsworthy, A. 2010, *Antony and Cleopatra*, New Haven.

Goldsworthy, A. 2014, *Augustus. First Emperor of Rome*, New Haven.

BIBLIOGRAPHY

Gradel, I. 2002, *Emperor Worship and Roman Religion*, Oxford.

Gruen, E.S. 1995, *The Last Generation of the Roman Republic*, second edition, Berkeley.

Gurval, R.A. 1995, *Actium and Augustus. The Politics and Emotions of Civil War*, Ann Arbor.

Harrison, S.J. 2006, 'The epic and the monuments: interactions between Virgil's Aeneid and the Augustan building programme' in Clarke, M.J., Curries, B.G.F. & Lyne, R.O.A.M. (eds) *Epic Interactions. Perspectives on Homer, Virgil, and on the Epic Tradition*, Oxford: 159–83.

Hjort Lange, C. 2009, *Res Publica Constituta. Actium, Apollo and the Accomplishment of the Triumviral Assignment*, Leiden.

Keaveney, A. 2007, *The Army in the Roman Revolution*, London & New York.

Keppie, L. 1983, *Colonisation and Veteran Settlement in Italy, 47–14 BC*, London.

Kleiner, D.E.E. 2005, *Cleopatra and Rome*, Cambridge, MA.

Lacey, W.K. 1996, *Augustus and the Principate. The Evolution of the System*, Leeds.

Levick, B. 1967, 'Imperial control of the elections under the early principate: commendatio, suffragatio and nominatio' *Historia* 16: 207–23.

Levick, B. 2014, *Augustus. Image and Substance*, London & New York.

Lowrie, M. 2009, *Writing, Performance and Authority in Augustan Rome*, Oxford.

McGinn, T.A.J. 2004, 'Missing females? Augustus' encouragement of marriage between freeborn males and freedwomen' *Historia* 53.2: 200–8.

Mellor, R. 1975, *Thea Rome. The Worship of the Goddess Roma in the Greek World*, Göttingen.

Millar, F.G.B. 1966, 'The emperor, the senate and the provinces' *JRS* 56: 156–66.

Millar, F.G.B. 1992, *The Emperor in the Roman World, 31 BC–AD 337*, second edition, London.

Millar, F.G.B. 2000, 'The first revolution: imperator Caesar, 36–28 BC' in *La révolution romaine après Ronald Syme. Bilans et perspectives*, Rome: 1–30.

Millar, F.G.B. & Segal, E. (eds) 1984, *Caesar Augustus. Seven Aspects*, Oxford.

North, J. 1986, 'Religion and politics, from Republic to principate' *JRS* 76: 251–8.

Osgood, J. 2006, *Caesar's Legacy. Civil War and the Emergence of the Roman Empire*, Cambridge.

Pandey, N.B. 2013, 'Caesar's comet, the Julian star, and the invention of Augustus' *TAPhA* 143.2: 405–49.

Pelling, C.B.R. 1996, 'The triumviral period' in *CAH* X[2]: 1–69.

Phillips, D.A. 1997, 'The conspiracy of Egnatius Rufus and the election of suffect consuls under Augustus' *Historia* 46.1: 103–12.

Powell, A. (ed.) 1992, *Roman Poetry and Propaganda in the Age of Augustus*, London.

Powell, A. & Welch, K. (eds) 2002, *Sextus Pompeius*, London.

Powell, L. 2014, *Marcus Agrippa. Right-Hand Man of Augustus*, Barnsley.

Raaflaub, K.A. & Toher, M. (eds) 1993, *Between Republic and Empire. Interpretations of Augustus and his Principate*, Berkeley.

Ramage, E.S. 1987, *The Nature and Purpose of Augustus' Res Gestae*, Stuttgart.

Rawson, E. 1994, 'The aftermath of the Ides' in *CAH* IX[2]: 468–90.

Reinhold, M. 1988, *From Republic to Principate. An Historical Commentary on Cassius Dio's Roman History Books 49–52 (36–29 BC)*, Atlanta.

Rich, J.W. 1989, 'Dio on Augustus' in Cameron, A. (ed.) *History as Text. The Writing of Ancient History*, London: 86–110.

Rich, J.W. 1990, *The Augustan Settlement (Cassius Dio, Roman History 53–55.9)*, Warminster.

Rich, J.W. 1996, 'Augustus and the spolia opima' *Chiron* 26: 85–127.

Rich, J.W. 1998, 'Augustus' Parthian honours, the temple of Mars Ultor and the arch in the Forum Romanum' *PBSR* 66: 71–128.

BIBLIOGRAPHY

Ridley, R.T. 2003, *The Emperor's Retrospect: Augustus' Res gestae in Epigraphy, Historiography and Commentary*, Leuven.

Roller, D.W. 2010, *Cleopatra. A Biography*, Oxford.

Sedley, D. 1997, 'The ethics of Brutus and Cassius' *JRS* 87: 41–53.

Sherwin-White, A. 1984, *Roman Foreign Policy in the East, 168 BC to AD 1*, London.

Shotter, D., 2005, *Augustus Caesar*, second edition, London.

Smith, C., and Powell, A. (eds) 2009, *The Lost Memoirs of Augustus and the Development of Roman Autobiography*, Swansea.

Stahl, H.-P. 1985, *Propertius, 'Love' and War. Individual and State under Augustus*, Berkeley.

Stockton, D. 1965, 'Primus and Murena' *Historia* 14: 18–40.

Swan, P.M. 2004, *The Augustan Succession. An Historical Commentary on Cassius Dio's Roman History Books 55–56 (9 BC–AD 14)*, Oxford.

Syme, R. 1979, *History in Ovid*, Oxford.

Syme, R. 1986, *The Augustan Aristocracy*, Oxford.

Syme, R. 2002, *The Roman Revolution*, Oxford.

Talbert, R.A. 1984, *The Senate of Imperial Rome*, Princeton.

Tarn, W.W. 1931, 'The battle of Actium' *JRS* 21: 173–9.

Thomas, R.F. 2001, *Virgil and the Augustan Reception*, Cambridge.

Walker, S. 2000, 'The moral museum: Augustus and the city of Rome' in Coulston, J. & Dodge, H. (eds) *Ancient Rome. The Archaeology of the Eternal City*, Oxford: 61–75.

Wallace-Hadrill, A. 1981, 'Family and inheritance in the Augustan marriage-laws' *PCPhS* 207: 250–74.

Wallace-Hadrill, A. 1982, '*Civilis princeps*: between citizen and king' *JRS* 72: 32–48.

Wallace-Hadrill, A. (ed.) 1989, *Patronage in Ancient Society*, London.

Wallace-Hadrill, A. 1993, *Augustan Rome*, London.

Wallace-Hadrill, A. 2008, *Rome's Cultural Revolution*, Cambridge.

Wardle, D. 2012, 'Suetonius on Augustus as god and man' *CQ* 62.1: 307–26.

Weigel, R.D. 1992, *Lepidus. The Tarnished Triumvir*, London & New York.

Wells, C.M. 1972, *The German Policy of Augustus*, London.

Whitehorne, J. 1994, *Cleopatras*, London.

Wiedemann, T. 1992, *Emperors and Gladiators*, London & New York.

Williams, G.W. 1962, 'Poetry and the moral climate of Augustan Rome' *JRS* 52: 28–46.

Woodman, A.J. & West, D.A. (eds) 1984, *Poetry and Politics in the Age of Augustus*, Cambridge.

Zanker, P. 2002, *The Power of Images in the Age of Augustus*, Ann Arbor.

CHAPTER SIXTEEN: THE ANCIENT SOURCES

Bodel, J. (ed.) 2001, *Epigraphic Evidence. Ancient History from Inscriptions*, London.

Bucher, G.S. 1995, 'The annales maximi in the light of Roman methods of keeping records' *AJAH* 12: 2–61.

Bucher, G.S. 2002, 'The origins, program, and composition of Appian's *Roman History*' *TAPhA* 130: 411–58.

Cairns, F. 1989, *Virgil's Augustan Epic*, Cambridge.

Chaplin, J.D. 2000, *Livy's Exemplary History*, Oxford.

Clarke, K. 1999, *Between Geography and History: Hellenistic Constructions of the Roman World*, Oxford.

Coffey, M. 1995, *Roman Satire*, second edition, London.

Collins, J.H. 1972, 'Caesar as a political propagandist' *ANRW* I.1: 922–66.

Comber, M. 1997, 'Re-reading the Roman historians' in Bentley, M. (ed.) *Companion to Historiography*, London: 43–56.

Cooley, A.E. 2000, 'Inscribing history at Rome' in Cooley, A.E. (ed.) *The Afterlife of Inscriptions*, London.

Cooley, A.E. 2000a, *The Epigraphic Landscape of Roman Italy*, London: 7–20.

Cooley, A.E. 2009, *Res Gestae Divi Augusti: Text, Translation and Commentary*, Cambridge.

Cooley, A. 2012, *The Cambridge Manual of Latin Epigraphy*, Cambridge.

Cornell, T.J. 1986, 'The value of the literary tradition concerning archaic Rome' in Raaflaub, K.A. (ed.) *Social Struggles in Archaic Rome. New Perspectives on the Conflict of the Orders*, Berkeley: 52–76.

Cornell, T.J. 1995, *The Beginnings of Rome. Italy and Rome from the Bronze Age to the Punic Wars (c. 1000–264 BC)*, London.

Crawford, M. 1983, 'Numismatics' in Crawford, M. (ed.) *Sources for Ancient History*, Cambridge: 183–233.

Derow, P.S. 1994, 'Polybius and his predecessors' in Hornblower, S. (ed.) *Greek Historiography*, Oxford: 73–90.

Dorey, T.A. (ed) 1965, *Cicero*, London.

Dorey, T.A. (ed.) 1966, *Latin Historians*, London.

Dorey, T.A. (ed.) 1967, *Latin Biography*, London.

Dorey, T.A. 1971, *Livy*, London.

Edwards, M.J. 1991, *Plutarch. The Lives of Pompey, Caesar and Cicero*, Bristol.

Feldherr, A. 1998, *Spectacle and Society in Livy's History*, Berkeley.

Forsythe, G. 1999, *Livy and Early Rome. A Study in Historical Method and Judgment*, Stuttgart.

Fox, M. 1993, 'History and rhetoric in Dionysius of Halicarnassus' *JRS* 83: 31–47.

Gabba, E. 1991, *Dionysius and 'The History of Archaic Rome'*, Berkeley.

Geiger, J. 1985, *Cornelius Nepos and Ancient Political Biography*, Stuttgart.

Ginsberg, J. 1981, *Tradition and Theme in the Annals of Tacitus*, New York.

Gowing, A.M. 1992, *The Triumviral Narratives of Appian and Cassius Dio*, Ann Arbor.

Grant, M. 1995, *Greek and Roman Historians. Information and Misinformation*, London.

Griffin, J. 1984, 'Augustus and the poets: "Caesar qui cogere posset"' in Millar, F. & Segal, E. (eds) *Caesar Augustus: Seven Aspects*, Oxford: 189–218.

Hardie, P. 1998, *Virgil*, Oxford.

Henderson, J. 1989, 'Livy and the invention of History' in Cameron, A. (ed.) *History as Text: the Writing of Ancient History*, London: 64–85.

Herbert-Brown, G. 1994, *Ovid and the Fasti: An Historical Study*, Oxford.

Hill, H. 1961, 'Dionysius and the origins of Rome' *JRS* 51: 88–93.

Hubbard, M. 2001, *Propertius*, second edition, London.

Jaeger, M. 1997, *Livy's Written Rome*, Ann Arbor.

Jocelyn, H.D. 1972, 'The poems of Quintus Ennius' *ANRW* I.2: 987–1026.

Keppie, L. 1991, *Understanding Roman Inscriptions*, Baltimore.

Kirby, J.T. 1997, 'Ciceronian rhetoric: theory and practice' in Dominik, W.J. (ed.) *Roman Eloquence. Rhetoric in Society and Literature*, London: 13–31.

Kraus, C.S. (ed.) 1999, *The Limits of Historiography. Genre and Narrative in Ancient Historical Texts*, Leiden.

Kraus, C.S. & Woodman, A.J. 1997, *Latin Historians*, Oxford.

Lamberton, R. 2002, *Plutarch*, Yale.

Lintott, A. 1994, 'The crisis of the Republic: sources and source-problems' in *CAH* IX^2: 1–15.

BIBLIOGRAPHY

Lyne, R.O.A.M. 1995, *Horace. Behind the Public Poetry*, New Haven.

MacKendrick, P. 1995, *The Speeches of Cicero. Context, Law, Rhetoric*, London.

Mellor, R. 1999, *The Roman Historians*, London.

Miles, G. 1995, *Livy. Reconstructing Early Rome*, Ithaca.

Millar, F. 1983, 'Epigraphy' in Crawford, M. (ed.) *Sources for Ancient History*, Cambridge: 80–136.

Mitchell, T.N. 1991, *Cicero, the Senior Statesman*, New Haven.

Moxon, I.S. et al. (eds) *Past Perspectives. Studies in Greek and Roman Historical Writing*, Cambridge.

Newlands, C. 1995, *Playing with Time. Ovid and the Fasti*, Ithaca.

Ogilvie, R.M. & Drummond, A. 1989, 'The sources for early Roman history' in *CAH* VII.2^2: 1–29.

Pelling, C.B.R. 1988, *Plutarch. Life of Antony*, Cambridge.

Powell, A. (ed.) 1992, *Roman Poetry and Propaganda in the Age of Augustus*, London.

Powell, J. & Patterson, J. (eds) 2004, *Cicero, the Advocate*, Oxford.

Rawson, E. 1991, *Roman Culture and Society*, Oxford.

Richardson, J.S. 1979, 'Polybius' view of the Roman empire' *PBSR* 34: 1–11.

Rudd, N. (ed.) 1993, *Horace 2000. A Celebration*, Ann Arbor.

Sachs, K.S. 1994, 'Diodorus and his sources' in Hornblower, S. (ed.) *Greek Historiography*, Oxford: 213–32.

Sacks, K.S. 1981, *Polybius on the Writing of History*, Berkeley.

Skidmore, C. 1996, *Practical Ethics for Roman Gentlemen. The Work of Valerius Maximus*, Exeter.

Skutsch, O. 1985, *The Annals of Q. Ennius*, Oxford.

Stadter, P.A. (ed.) 1992, *Plutarch and the Historical Tradition*, London.

Starr, R.J. 1981, 'The scope and genre of Velleius' *History*' *CQ* 31: 162–74.

Swain, S. 1990, 'Plutarch's *Lives* of Cicero, Cato, and Brutus' *Hermes* 118: 192–203.

Syme, R. 1958, *Tacitus*, 2 vols., Oxford.

Syme, R. 1964, *Sallust*, Berkeley.

Syme, R. 1979, *History in Ovid*, Oxford.

Syme, R. 1984, 'Velleius Paterculus' in Badian, E. (ed.) *Ronald Syme. Roman Papers*, Oxford, vol. 3: 1090–1104.

Titchener, F. 2003, 'Cornelius Nepos and the biographical tradition' *G&R* 50: 85–99.

Walbank, F.W. 1972, *Polybius*, Berkeley.

Walbank, F.W. 2002, *Polybius, Rome and the Hellenistic World. Essays and Reflections*, Cambridge.

Wallace-Hadrill, A. (ed.) 1989, *Patronage in Ancient Society*, London.

Wallace-Hadrill, A. 1990, 'Pliny the Elder and Man's Unnatural History' *G&R* 37: 80–96.

Wallace-Hadrill, A. 1995, *Suetonius*, second edition, London.

Walsh, P.G. 1961, *Livy, his Historical Aims and Methods*, Cambridge.

Welch, K. & Powell, A. (eds) 1998, *Julius Caesar as Artful Reporter. The War Commentaries as Political Instruments*, London.

White, P. 1993, *Promised Verse. Poets in the Society of Augustan Rome*, Cambridge MA.

Wiseman, T.P. 1985, *Catullus and his World*, Cambridge.

Wray, D. 2001, *Catullus and the Poetics of Roman Manhood*, Cambridge.

Index of Ancient Sources

Numbers here refer to documents. Abbreviations used for authors and titles are given in square brackets: Appian [App.] *Civil Wars* [*BC*].

General Index

Numbers refer to documents and their introductions. For ancient authors, see also the index of ancient sources.

Claudius Crassinus Inregillensis Sabinus, App. (cos. 471, decemvir 451/450), 1.31

Claudius Drusus Germanicus, Nero (second son of Livia), 14.39, 15.8, 15.17, 15.23, 15.27, 15.65, 15.71, 15.93, 15.103, 15.107–8, 15.113

Claudius Drusus, Nero (son of Tiberius), 15.63, 15.112

Claudius Marcellus, C. (cos. 50), 2.49, 12.80, 13.9–10, 13.12, 13.15, 13.19, 13.21–3, 13.51, 14.9

Claudius Marcellus, C. (cos. 49), 13.24, 13.43

Claudius Marcellus, M. (cos. 222, 214, 210, 208, suff. cos. 215), 4.46, 4.47, 4.60, 13.65, 15.36, 16.26

Claudius Marcellus, M. (cos. 166, 155, 152), 5.48

Claudius Marcellus, M. (cos. 51), 13.5, 13.7–9, 13.11–13, 13.24, 13.32, 13.52–3

Claudius Marcellus, M. (nephew of Augustus), 5.6, 6.66, 14.37, 15.5, 15.31, 15.35–9, 15.50, 15.63–4, 15.90, 15.95, 15.111, 15.113, 15.116, 16.26, 16.28; 14.63, 15.1, 15.81 (theatre of)

Claudius Nero, Ti. (praet. 42, first husband of Livia), 14.39, 15.69, 15.117

Claudius Pulcher, App. (cos. 143), 8.11, 8.13, 8.16–17, 8.19

Claudius Pulcher, App. (cos. 54), 5.71, 6.58, 12.60, 12.63, 12.71

Claudius Pulcher, P. (cos. 249), 3.53, 6.54

Claudius Quadrigarius, Q. (historian), 16.1, 16.7

Cleomenes III of Sparta, 8.1, 8.41

Cleopatra VII Philopator (queen of Egypt, 69–30), 13.48, 14.34, 14.42–6, 14.48–52, 15.11, 15.19, 15.115, 16.11, 16.16, 16.26, 16.27, 16.28

Cleopatra Selene, daughter of Cleopatra and Antony, 14.43, 15.115

Clesippus Geganius (hunchback), 7.71

clientela, 2.38, 2.54–62, 12.11, 12.70–1, 12.74, 12.88; see also freedmen, freedwomen

Clodia (wife of L. Licinius Lucullus, sister of Clodius), 12.10

Clodia Metelli (wife of Q. Metellus Celer, cos. 60; sister of Clodius), 7.51–2, 12.69, 16.25

Clodia Pulchra (first wife of Octavian), 14.20, 14.30

Clodius Pulcher, P. (tr. pl. 58), 2.3, 7.87, 12.10, 12.37, 12.48–50, 12.54–64, 12.69, 12.71, 12.91, 13.1–2, 13.5, 13.32, 14.1, 16.25

Coelius Antipater, L. (historian), 16.1, 16.7

Coelius Caldus, C. (tr. pl. 107), 2.42

coinage, 82, 6.49, 7.93–4, 9.36–8, 10.12, 10.29–31, 11.1, 11.45–50, 13.71–4, 14.14, 15.18, 15.102

collegia, 2.38, 6.57, 7.73, 11.6, 11.38, 12.54, 13.56, 15.82

colonies, 1.56, 1.65–6, 1.68, 2.40, 2.80, 8.5, 8.28–30, 9.18, 9.27, 10.6, 10.9, 11.49, 12.13, 13.59–60, 14.5–8, 14.14, 14.19–20, 14.17–28, 15.1, 15.13, 15.58, 15.59, 15.61, 15.78, 15.105–6

comitia centuriata, 1.20–21, 1.31, 11.5, 12.60–1, 12.72, 13.54; see also elections

comitia curiata, 1.21, 12.49

comitia tributa, 1.21–2, 8.13–14, 9.36, 10.17, 10.26, 11.12, 12.45, 13.54

Compitalia, the, 6.36, 15.20

concordia ordinum, the, 12.35, 12.38

confarreatio, 3.21, 7.10; see also marriage

Conflict of the Orders, the, 1.25–6, 1.29–58, 3.52, 7.77; see also decemvirate, Twelve Tables

consuls, duties of, 1.11, 1.13, 1.18, 1.47–50, 1.59, 2.49, 2.50, 3.40, 12.44–5, 13.3–4, 13.6, 15.5–6, 15.8

Corinth, 1.4, 5.41–3

Coriolanus, see Marcius Coriolanus

Cornelia ('mother of the Gracchi'), 5.39, 7.8, 7.22, 7.29, 7.70, 8.1–2, 8.9, 8.12, 8.15, 8.21, 8.25, 8.29, 8.33, 16.13

Cornelia (daughter of Cinna, wife of Julius Caesar), 7.35

Cornelia (wife of P. Licinius Crassus and Pompey the Great), 12.80, 13.46

Cornelius Balbus, L. (suff. cos. 40), 3.43, 9.27, 10.21, 12.40, 13.20, 13.34, 13.50, 13.55, 14.9, 15.13, 15.81, 15.84, 16.4

Cornelius Cethegus, P., 7.64

Munatius Plancus, L. (cos. 42), 14.10,
14.13, 14.18, 14.23, 14.50, 14.65, 15.13,
15.81, 15.112
Munatius Plancus Byrsa, T. (tr. pl. 52),
13.1
Munda, battle of, 13.55, 13.64
Murdia (epitaph of), 7.23
Murena, *see* Licinius Murena
Musa, freedman doctor, 6.66
Mutina, siege of, 14.17–8, 14.23

Naevius (poet), 16.23; *and see Index of
Sources*
naval power, Roman, 4.6, 4.8–10, 4.16,
10.25
nemus, *see* rex Nemorensis
Nepos, *see* Cornelius Nepos
Nervii, the, 2.31, 12.68; *see also* Gallic War
nexum, *see* debt-slavery
Nicias of Athens, 6.2
Nicomedes IV of Bithynia (c.94–75/4),
7.60, 11.3, 11.8
Nicopolis (mistress of Sulla), 11.1
Nikolaos of Damascus, 15.3, 15.47,
15.115, 16.8, 16.16; *and see Index of
Sources*
nobiles, 1.55, 2.40–44, 2.51, 3.76, 9.2–3,
9.6, 9.24–5, 11.14, 11.16, 12.3, 12.45,
16.5; *see also* optimates
nomenclator, 12.61
Norbanus, C. (cos. 83), 11.12, 11.14,
11.20, 11.23
novus homo, the, 1.55, 2.38, 2.44–45,
4.32, 4.35, 9.2–4, 9.6–9, 10.1, 15.83,
15.85, 16.5
Numa Pompilius (second king of Rome,
715–673), 3.5–6, 3.13–14, 3.48, 14.60,
16.15
Numantia (Spain), 4.62, 5.50–3, 8.7–8,
9.3, 9.22, 16.24
Numerius Atticus, senator, 15.114
Nymphe (epitaph of), 7.25

obnuntiatio, 3.75–6, 12.43, 12.45, 12.47,
12.54, 12.62, 12.78; *see also* augurs,
auspices, magistracies
Octavia Major (sister of Octavian), 14.2
Octavia Minor (sister of Octavian), 12.80,
14.2, 14.9, 14.40, 14.43, 14.46, 15.36,

15.38, 15.90, 15.113, 16.16, 16.26;
15.81, 15.90, 15.96, 15.113, 16.29
(portico of)
Octavian (*and see also* Augustus), 14.2
(family and upbringing), 14.2 (eulogy
of his grandmother Julia), 13.57, 13.68,
14.2 (and Julius Caesar), 14.5–6, 14.8,
14.10–15, 14.36–7, 14.40–1 (relations
with Antony), 14.6–7, 14.9 (takes the
name Caesar), 13.68, 14.2, 14.6, 14.8
(Caesar's will), 14.8–9, 14.11–12,
14.14–18 (and Cicero), 14.13, 14.19,
14.21 (bounties to veterans), 7.37,
7.75, 14.19–23, 15.116–17 (and
the triumvirate), 14.20 (marriage to
Clodia), 14.23, 14.25–7 (campaign
against the liberators), 14.28–31,
14.59, 15.1, 15.90, 15.93 (settlement
of veterans), 14.30 (abuse of Fulvia),
14.38 (and Atticus), 14.39 (marriage to
Scribonia), 14.39, 14.63, 16.9 (marriage
to Livia), 14.41 (granted tribunician
sacrosanctity), 14.40, 15.117, 16.11
(defeat of Sextus Pompeius), 14.41,
14.61, 14.63, 15.4 (honours awarded),
14.49 15.98 (propaganda against),14.49
(love affairs), 14.50–4, 14.60 (battle
of Actium), 14.58–62 (restorer of the
republic), 14.64 ('first settlement' of),
14.63 (triumph), 14.60, 14.63 (closing
of temple of Janus), 16.26 (and Vergil),
16.27 (and Horace), 14.62 (coinage),
14.63, 14.65, 15.97 (named Augustus),
14.66 (assessment by Tacitus)
Octavius, C. (father of Octavian), 14.2
Octavius, Cn. (cos. 87), 10.26
Octavius, M. (tr. pl. 133), 8.9, 8.13,
8.29
October horse, the, 3.73
Ogulnius Gallus, Q. (tr. pl. 300, cos. 269),
1.56
omens, *see* augurs, divination, Delphi,
haruspices
Opimia (Vestal), 7.89
Opimius, L. (cos. 121), 1.60, 8.28, 8.32–3,
8.34, 9.7
Oppius, C. (tr. pl. 215), 7.67
Oppius, C. (eques, friend of Julius Caesar),
13.34, 13.64, 14.12, 16.4